An Exegetical
Bibliography
of the
New Testament

LUKE AND ACTS

MERCER UNIVERSITY PRESS • MACON, GEORGIA

An
Exegetical
Bibliography
of the
New Testament

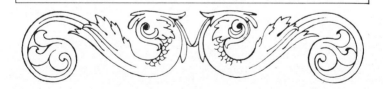

EDITED BY

GÜNTER WAGNER

ISBN 0-86554-140-X

All books published by Mercer University Press are produced
on acid-free paper that exceeds the minimum standards set by the
National Historical Publications and Records Commission.

Library of Congress Cataloging in Publication Data
Main entry under title:
An Exegetical bibliography of the New Testament.
    5 vols., 1983–

    1. Bible, N.T.—Bibliography. I. Wagner, Günter, 1928–
Z7772.L1E93   1985   [BS2361.2]   016.225   83-969
ISBN 0-86554-013-6 [vol. 1, Matthew–Mark]
ISBN 0-86554-140-X [vol. 2, Luke–Acts]

Preface

This bibliography is an "unwanted child," but it may well deserve its place. When I started teaching in 1958, I devised a detailed system for the collection of bibliographical information relevant to New Testament studies, ranging from the Old Testament background to the theology of the Early Church. Year after year I used—or misused—all available student help and secretarial assistance to work through our library holdings and current additions to glean references to all sorts of materials and to type each individual reference that was considered useful on a separate card. The card was then filed under its proper heading, so that it would take me—or any student who wished to use the file—no more than a minute to pick up a sizable pile of cards representing a basic bibliography on any topic in the entire New Testament field. The purpose of the whole undertaking was to enable the student as quickly as possible to get down to research without wasting days, even weeks, on the search for literature.

The students who helped me represented more than a dozen nationalities and spoke as many different mother tongues. Knowing or not knowing French, German, Spanish, Danish, Italian, Polish, etc., naturally proved to be both an asset and a liability, in regard to accuracy and consistency; however, as the whole collection was intended to be nothing but a tool for our research, perfectionism in matters of form did not plague us. Postgraduate students who majored in the field of New Testament and later started teaching in various parts of the world got "homesick" for that monstrous steel cabinet in my office and wondered how they could still have access to it. We decided to type up the data of the exegetical section and to photocopy a reduced size of the condensed text, again on separate cards—so that everyone could add further references to his own card file.

Between 1973 and 1979 we made available "Bibliographical Aids" on all New Testament writings. Since 1981 I am editing the Second Series, copied by offset printing, again in a postcard size, looseleaf edition; upon request we are adding the place of publication from the Second Series onward and hope that our customers will not mind the inconsistency. We are most grateful to Mercer University Press for publishing at this time Series One and Two together in book form in one text. Updates/supplements for the card editions (Series Three) will continue to be available from Rüschlikon in the future.

The first volume of *An Exegetical Bibliography of the New Testament (Matthew and Mark)* was published in 1983. Here we present volume two with a bibliography on Luke and Acts. A third volume (the Gospel of John and the Epistles of John) is in the press. I am grateful to all who have assisted in the production of these bibliographies, especially to Martin Scott, Dietmar Wowra, and my wife Doris, who have helped with the editing, typing, and proofreading of the manuscripts for the Second Series and of this volume. I want to express my appreciation also to the administration of the Baptist Theological Seminary, Rüschlikon, for the support given to this project, to my friends Margaret and Floyd Patterson (Washington DC), whose encouragement and help have been invaluable throughout the years, and to Sally and Ben Fisher (Raleigh NC), who took the initiative for the publication of the bibliography in book form.

Baptist Theological Seminary   Günter Wagner
Rüschlikon-Zürich
28 May 1985

List of Abbreviations

BiRe Bible Revue (Ravenna)
BJRL Bulletin of the John Rylands Library (Manchester)
BLE Bulletin de Littérature Ecclésiastique (Toulouse)
BR Biblical Research (Chicago)
BTh Biblical Theology (Belfast)
BThB Biblical Theology Bulletin (Rome)
BTr Bible Translator (London)
BTS Bible et Terre Sainte (Paris)
BuK Bibel und Kirche (Stuttgart)
BuL Bibel und Liturgie (Klosterneuburg)
BVieC Bible et Vie Chrétienne (Bruges)
BZ Biblische Zietschrift (Paderborn)

CahCER Cahiers du Cercle Ernest-Renan (Paris)
CahJos Cahiers de Joséphologie (Montreal)
CBQ Catholic Biblical Quarterly (Washington)
ChrC Christian Century (Chicago)
ChrTo Christianity Today (Washington)
ChSt Chicago Studies (Mundelein, Illinois)
CiCa Civiltà Cattolica (Rome)
CiDi Ciudad de Dios (Madrid)
ClM Clergy Monthly (Ranchi)
ClR Clergy Review (London)
CoTh Collectanea Theologica (Warsaw)
CrCu Cross Currents (West Nyack, New Jersey)
CrQ Crozer Quarterly (Chester, Pennsylvania)
CSR Christian Scholar's Review (St. Paul, Minnesota)
CThJ Calvin Theological Journal (Grand Rapids, Michigan)
CThM Concordia Theological Monthly (St. Louis, Missouri)
CV Communio Viatorum (Prague)

DBM Deltion Biblikon Meleton (Athens)
DDSR Duke Divinity School Review (Durham, North Carolina)
DiThom Divus Thomas (Poscenza)
DoLi Doctrine and Life (Dublin)
DRev Downside Review (Bath)
DTT Dansk Teologisk Tidsskrift (Copenhagen)
DuRev Dunwoodie Review (New York)

EFr Estudios Fransiscanos (Madrid)
EphC Ephemerides Carmeliticae (Rome)
EphL Ephemerides Liturgicae (Rome)
EphM Ephemerides Mariologicae (Madrid)

EphT Ephemerides Theologicae Lovanienses (Louvain)
EQ Evangelical Quarterly (London)
ER Ecumenical Review (Geneva)
EstBi Estudios Biblicos (Madrid)
EstEc Estudios Eclesiásticos (Madrid)
EsVe Escritos del Vedat (Torrente)
EsVie Espirit et Vie (Langres)
ET Expository Times (Birmingham)
ETh Église et Théologie (Ottawa)
EThR Études Théologiques et Religieuses (Montpelliar)
EuA Erbe und Auftrag (Beuren)
EuD Euntes Docete (Rome)
EvKomm Evangelische Theologie (München)
Exp The Expositor (London)
FrR Frieburger Rundbrief (Frieburg)
FSt Franziskanische Studien (Münster)
FZPhTh Freiburger Zeitschrift für Philosphie und Theologie (Fribourg)

GOThR Greek Orthodox Theological Review (Brookline, Massachusetts)
GPM Göttinger Predigtmeditationen (Göttingen)
GRBS Greek, Roman and Byzantine Studies (Durham, North Carolina)
GThT Gereformeerd Theologisch Tijdschrift (Amsterdam)
GuL Geist und Leben (München)

HerKor Herder Korrespondenz (Freiburg)
Herm Hermathena (Dublin)
HeyJ Heythrop Journal (London)
HPR Homiletic and Pastoral Review (New York)
HR History of Religion (Chicago)
HThR Harvard Theological Review (Cambridge, Massachusetts)
HUCA Hebrew Union College Annual (Cincinnati)

IEJ Israel Exploration Journal (Jerusalem)
IES Indian Ecclesiastical Studies (Bangalore)
IJTh Indian Journal of Theology (Serampore)
IKiZ Internationale Kirchliche Zeitschrift (Bern)
IKZ Internationale Katholische Zeitschrift (Rodenkirchen)
IndTheolStu Indian Theological Studies (Bangalore)
Interp Interpretation (Richmond, Virginia)
IThQ Irish Theological Quarterly (Marynooth)

JAAR Journal of the American Academy of Religion (Atlanta, Georgia)
JAC Jahrbuch für Antike und Christentum (Münster)
JAOS Journal of the American Oriental Society (Baltimore)

JBL Journal of Biblical Literature (Atlanta, Georgia)
JEH Journal of Ecclesiastical History (London)
JES Journal of Ecumenical Studies (Philadelphia)
JEThS Journal of the Evangelical Theological Society (Wheaton)
JHebS Journal of Hebraic Studies (New York)
JHS Journal of Hellenic Studies (London)
JJS Journal of Jewish Studies (London)
JR Journal of Religion (Chicago)
JRomS Journal of Roman Studies (London)
JRTh Journal of Religious Thought (Washington)
JSJ Journal for the Study of Judaism (Leiden)
JSS Journal of Semitic Studies (Manchester)
JThS Journal of Theological Studies (Oxford)

KG Katholische Gedanke (Bonn)
KuD Kerygma und Dogma (Göttingen)

LiBi Linguistica Biblica (Bonn)
LM Lutherische Monatshefte (Hamburg)
LQ Lutheran Quarterly (Gettysburg)
LR Lutherische Rundschau (Geneva)
LSt Louvian Studies (Louvain)
LThPh Laval Théologique et Philosophique (Quebec)
LThQ Lexington Theological Quarterly (Lexington, Kentucky)
LuVie Lumière et Vie (Lyons)
LuVit Lumen Vitae (Brussels)
LW Lutheran World (Geneva)

MCh Modern Churchman (Ludlow)
MisC Miscelánea Comillas (Madrid)
MSR Mélanges de Science Religieuse (Lille)
MTh Melita Theologica (La Valetta)
MThZ Münchener Theologische Zeitschrift (München)

NEAJTh North East Asia Journal of Theology (Tokyo)
NedThT Nederlands Theologisch Tijdschrift (The Hague)
NGTT Nederuits Gereformeerde Teologiese Tydskrif (Stellenbosch)
NKZ Neue kirchliche Zeitschrift (Erlangen)
NovT Novum Testamentum (Leiden)
NRTh Nouvelle Revue Théologique (Louvain)
NTS New Testament Studies (Cambridge)
NTT Norsk Teologisk Tidsskrift (Oslo)
NV Nova et Vetera (Geneva)
NW Neue Weg (Zürich)

OCP Orientalia Christiana Periodica (Rome)
OKS Ostkirchliche Studien (Würzburg)
OLZ Orientalistische Literaturzeitung (Berlin)

PaCl Palestra del Clero (Rovigo)
PEQ Palestine Exploration Quarterly (London)
PSThJ Perkins School of Theology Journal (Dallas)
PThR Princeton Theological Review (Princeton)

RAM Rassegna di Ascetica y Mistica (Florence)
RB Revue Biblique (Jerusalem)
RBen Revue Bénédictine (Maredsous)
RBL Ruch Biblijny i Liturgiczny (Cracow)
RBR Ricerche Bibliche e Religiose (Milan)
RCB Revista de Cultura Biblica (São Paulo)
RCIA Revue de Clerge Africian (Inkisi, Zaire)
RCT Revista de Cultura Teologica (São Paulo)
REA Revue des Études Augustiniennes (Paris)
REB Revista Eclesiástica Brasileira (Petropolis)
RechSR Recherches de Science Religieuse (Paris)
ReL Religion in Life (Nashville)
REsp Revista de Espiritualidad (Madrid)
RestQ Restoration Quarterly (Abilene, Texas)
RET Revista Española de Teología (Madrid)
RevBi Revista Biblica (Buenos Aires)
RevEx Review and Expositor (Louisville)
RevQ Revue de Qumran (Paris)
RevR Revue Réformée (Saint-German-en-Laye)
RevSR Revue des Science Religieuses (Strasbourg)
RHE Revue d'Histoire Ecclésiastique (Strasbourg)
RHPR Revue d'Histoire et de Philosophie Religieuses (Strasbourg)
RHR Revue de l'Histoire des Religions (Paris)
RHSp Revue d'Histoire de la Spiritualité (Paris)
RivAC Rivista di Archeologia Cristiana (Rome)
RivB Rivista Biblica (Brescia)
RQ Römische Quartalschrift (Freiburg)
RSLR Rivista di Storia e Letteratura Religiosa (Turin)
RSPhTh Revue des Sciences Philosophiques et Théologiques (Paris)
RSt Religious Studies (London)
RT Rassegna di Teologia (Naples)
RThAM Recherches de Théologie Ancienne et Médiévale (Louvain)
RThL Revue Théologique de Louvain (Louvain)

RThom Revue Thomiste (Toulouse)
RThPh Revue de Théologie et de Philosophie (Lausanne)
RThR Reformed Theological Review (Hawthorn, Victoria)
RTK Roczniki Teologiczno-Kanoniczne (Lublin)
RUO Revue de l'Université d'Ottawa (Ottawa)

SaDo Sacra Dottrina (Bologna)
SaDoBB Sacra Dottrina Bolletino Bibliografico (Bologna)
SBFLA Studii Biblici Franciscani Liber Annuus (Jerusalem)
SciE Science et Esprit (Montreal)
ScrB Scripture Bulletin (London)
ScrTh Scripta Theologica (Pamplona)
ScuC Scuola Cattolica (Milan)
SEA Svensk Exegetisk Arsbok (Uppsala)
SEAJTh South East Asia Journal of Theology (Singapore)
SJTh Scottish Journal of Theology (Edinburgh)
SouJTh Southwestern Journal of Theology (Fort Worth)
SThV Studia Theologica Varsaviensia (Warsaw)
StLit Studia Liturgica (Rotterdam)
StPa Studia Patavina (Padua)
StPh Studia Philonica (Chicago)
StR/SciR Studies in Religion/Sciences Religieuses (Toronto)
StTh Studia Theologica (Lund)
StZ Stimmen der Zeit (München)
SVThQ St. Vladimir's Theological Quarterly (Crestwood, New York)
SvTK Svensk Teologisk Kvartalskrift (Lund)

TAik Teologinen Aikakauskirja (Helsinki)
TB Tyndale Bulletin (Cambridge)
Th Theology: A Journal of Historic Christianity (London)
ThG Theologie und Glaube (Paderborn)
ThLZ Theologische Literaturzeitung (Leipzig)
ThPh Theologie und Philosophie (Frankfurt)
ThQ Theologische Quartalschrift (Tübingen)
ThR Theologische Rundschau (Tübingen)
ThRv Theologische Revue (Münster)
ThSK Theologische Studien und Kritiken (Hamburg)
ThSt Theological Studies (New York)
ThT Theology Today (Princeton)
ThZ Theologische Zeitschrift (Basel)
TRE Theologische Realenzyklopädie
     (Berlin/New York: Walter de Gruyter)

TsTK Tidsskrift for Teologi og Kirke (Oslo)
TT Theologisch Tidschrift (Amsterdam)
TThZ Trierer Theologische Zeitschrift (Trier)
TvTh Tijdschrift voor Theologie (Nijmegen)

US Una Sancta (Niederaltaich)
USQR Union Seminary Quarterly Review (New York)

VChr Vetera Christianorum (Bari)
VD Verbum Domini (Rome)
VE Vox Evangelica (London)
VF Verkündigung und Forschung (München)
VieS Vie Spirituelle (Paris)
VigChr Vigiliae Christianae (Amsterdam)
VR Vox Reformata (Geelong, Victoria)
VT Vetus Testamentum (Leiden)

WThJ Westminster Theological Journal (Philadelphia)
WuW Wissenschaft und Weisheit (Düsseldorf)

ZAW Zeitschrift für die Alttestamentliche Wissenschaft (Berlin)
ZDMG Zeitschrift der Deutschen Morgenländischen Gesellschaft
(Wiesbaden)
ZKG Zeitschrift für Kirchengeschichte (Stuttgart)
ZKTh Zeitschrift für Katholische Theologie (Innsbruck)
ZNW Zeitschrift für die Neutestamentliche Wissenschaft (Berlin)
ZRGG Zeitschrift für Religions und Geistesgeschichte (Erlangen)
ZThK Zeitschrift für Theologie und Kirche (Tübingen)
ZyMy Zycie i Mysl (Warsaw)

Notations

ET English Translation
GT German Translation
n Footnote or note

In case of doubt consult S. Schwertner, IATC: *Internationales Abkür-zungsverzeichnis für Theologie und Grenzgebiete* (1974) 3-343. This is identical to TRE: *Theologische Realenzyklopädie: Abkürzungsverzeichnis* (1976) 3-343, with supplements.

To Sally and Ben Fisher

Luke

ΚΑΤΑ ΛΟΥΚΑΝ

1:1-9:50 DANKER, F. W., CThM 44 (1,1973) 53-56.

1ff. EHRHARDT, A.,The Acts of the Apostles (1969) 1f., 6, 12, 15, 17f., 22, 41f., 44.

1-4 SUMMERS, R., The Secret Sayings of the Living Jesus (1968) 15, 54.

1:1-4:30 GOULDER, M. D., Type and History in Acts (1964) 119-25, 143. JEREMIAS, J., New Testament Theology I (1971).

1:1-4:22 BRODIE, L. T., "A New Temple and a New Law. The Unity and Chronicler-based Nature of Luke 1:1-4:22a" JSNT 5 (1979) 21-45.

1:1-4:15 SELBY, D. I., Introduction to the New Testament (New York 1971) 162-68.

1-3 BORNHÄUSER, K., Die Geburts- und Kindheitsgeschichte Jesu (1930).

1:1-3:38 "Anna" in TRE 2 (1978) 752.

1-2 EWALD, H., Die drei ersten Evangelien (1850) 177ff. CONY-BEARE, F. C., "Ein Zeugnis Ephräms über das Fehlen von c. 1 und 2 im Texte des Lucas." ZNW 3 (1902) 192-97.
ROBERTSON, A. T., Luke the Historian in the Light of Research (1920) 18, 57, 64, 65, 86, 103, 107, 161, 219, 221, 222. KLOS-TERMANN, E., Das Lukasevangelium (1929) 4f. HARNACK, A. von, Studien zur Geschichte des Neuen Testaments und der Alten Kirche (1931) 62ff. KERN, H., Der lebendige Christus (1937) 11-44. BURROWS, E., "The Form of Luke Chapters 1 and 2," in: The Gospel of the Infancy (1940), E. F. Sutcliffe (ed.) 1-39. RENGSTORF, K. H., Das Evangelium nach Lukas (1949) 51ff. STREETER, B. H., The Four Gospels (1951) 208f. MUNOZ, I. S., "Géneros literarios en los Evangelios," EstEc XIII (1954) 289-318. WINTER, P., "Some Observations on the Language in the Birth and Infancy Stories of the Third Gospel." NTS 1/2 (1954) 111-21. WINTER, P., "The Cultural Background of the Narrative in Luke I and II," JQR XLV/2 (1954) 159-67; XLV/3 (1955) 120-242. SCHMID, J., Das Evangelium nach Lukas (1955) 84-91. TURNER, N., "The Relation of Luke I and II to Hebraic Sources and to the Rest of Luke-Acts." NTS 2 (1955-1956) 100ff. AU-DET, J.-P., "Traces d'allusions étymologiques en Luc 1-2 (I)," Biblica 37 (1956) 435-56. WINTER, P., "On Luke and Lukan Sources," ZNW 47 (1956) 217-42. GOULDER, M. D., and SANDERSON, M. L., "St. Luke's Genesis," JThS 8 (1, 1957) 12-30. GRANT, F. C., The Gospels (1957) 46f. GUY, H. A., "The Virgin in St. Luke." ET 68/5 (1957) 157-58. LAURENTIN, R., Structure et théologie de Luc 1 à 2 (1957). LAURENTIN, R., "Traces d'allusions étymologiques en Luc 1-2 (II)," Biblica 38 (1, 1957) 1-23. WINTER, P., " 'Nazareth' and 'Jerusalem' in Luke

chs i and ii,'' NTS 3 (2, 1957) 136-42. WINTER, P., ''The Main Literary Problem of the Lucan Infancy Story,'' VoxTheol 28 (1957-1958) 117-22. IGLESIAS, S. M., ''El Evangelio de la Infancia en San Lucas y las infancias de los héroes biblicos,'' EstBi 17 (3-4, 1958) 329-82. DE ROOVER, A., ''De Evangelii Infantie (Lc I-II) Chronologia,'' VerbDom 36 (2, 1958) 65-82. SALAZAR, A. M., ''Questions about St. Luke's Sources,'' NovTest 2 (3-4, 1958) 316-17. WINTER, P., ''Lukanische Miszellen,'' ZNW 49 (1-2, 1958) 65-77. WINTER, P., ''The Main Literary Problems of the Lucan Infancy Story,'' AThR 40 (4, 1958) 257-64. WINTER, P., ''On the Margin of Luke I,II,'' StTh 12 (1, 1958) 103-107. AUDET, J.-P., ''Autour de la théologie de Luc I-II,'' SciE 11 (3, 1959) 409-18. BOUWMAN, G., ''Het kindsheidsevangelie van Lucas'' [The Lukan Infancy Gospel], NedThT 55 (10, 1959) 289-98. PEINA-DOR, M., ''Conocimiento que de Jesus tuvo la Virgen,'' EphM 9 (2-3, 1959) 283-304. SALAZAR, A. M., ''The Nativity in Luke,'' Faith and Freedom 13 (1, 1959) 39-40. NEIRYNCK, F., ''Structuur en theologie van Lc 1-2,'' CollBrugGand 6 (2, 1960) 222-27. PERETTO, L. M., ''La 'Natività' di Maria,'' Marianum 22 (1, 1960) 176-96. MALY, E. H., '' 'Now it Came to Pass in those Days . . .','' Bible Today 1 (3, 1962) 172-78. STRECKER, G., Der Weg der Gerechtigkeit (1962) 91[1]. WEATHERHEAD, B., ''Our Lady in Scripture-IV: Daughter of Zion,'' LifeSpir 17 (195, 1962) 183-90. HAHN, F., Christologische Hoheitstitel (1963) 73. STÖGER, A., ''Spiritualität der lukanischen Kindheitsgeschichte,'' GuL 36 (6, 1963) 404-17. OLIVER, H. H., ''The Lucan Birth Stories and the Purpose of Luke-Acts,'' NTS 10 (1963-1964) 202-26. DU-PONT, J., The Sources of Acts (1964) 29, 84, 88. GOULDER, M. D., Type and History in Acts (1964) 10, 54, 61, 72, 74, 164, 172. KING, P. J., ''Elizabeth, Zachary and the Messiah,'' Bible Today 1 (15, 1964) 992-97. KRAFFT, E., ''Die Vorgeschichten des Lukas. Eine Frage nach ihrer sachgemässen Interpretation,'' in Zeit und Geschichte (1964), Dinkler, E. (ed.), 217-23. QUINN, J. D., ''Mary, Seat of Wisdom,'' Bible Today 1 (12, 1964) 787-92. RIEDL, J., Die Vorgeschichte Jesu (1964) 46-77. MARTIN, R. A., ''Syntactical Evidence of Aramaic Sources in Acts 1-14'', NTS 11 (1964-1965) 52f., 54f. FUCHS, D. E., ''Adventsansprache 1963 (unveröffentlicht),'' in Glaube und Erfahrung (1965) 480-86. SCHÜRMANN, H., ''Aufbau, Eigenart und Geschichtswert der Vorgeschichte von Lukas 1-2,'' BuK 21 (4, 1966) 106-11. VOSS, G., ''Die Christusverkündigung der Kindheitsgeschichte im Rahmen des Lukasevangeliums,'' BuK 21 (4, 1966) 112-15. van GOUDOEVER, J., ''The Place of Israel in Luke's Gospel,'' NovT 8 (1966) 111-23. HEISING, A., ''The Epoch of Israel,'' NTS 13

(1966-1967) 184-95. MINEAR, P. S., "Luke's Use of Birth Stories" in: L. E. Keck, J. L. Martyn (eds), Studies in Luke-Acts. FS. P. Schubert (Nashville, 1966) 111-30. LAURENTIN, R., Struktur und Theologie der lukanischen Kindheitsgeschichte (1967). SONGER, H. S., "Luke's Portrayal of the Origins of Jesus," RevEx 64 (4, 1967) 453-63. TATUM, W. B., "The Epoch of Israel: Luke i-ii and the Theological Plan of Luke-Acts," NTS 13 (2, 1967) 184-95. JONES, D., "The Background and Character of the Lukan Psalms," JThS 19 (1, 1968) 19-50. NEWMAN, B. M., "Something New for Something Old," BTr 20 (2, 1969) 62-74. RUDDICK, C. T., "Birth Narratives in Genesis and Luke," NovTest 12 (4, 1970) 343-48. VÖGTLE, A., "Offene Fragen zur lukanischen Geburts- und Kindheitsgeschichte," BuL 11 (1, 1970) 51-67. KERSCHENSTEINER, J., Die Kindheitsgeschichte bei Matthaeus und Lukas (1971) 7-33. SCHNACKENBURG, R., Schriften zum Neuen Testament (1971) 201-19. VÖGTLE, A. Das Evangelium und die Evangelien (1971) 65-67. KÜMMEL, W. G., Einleitung in das Neue Testament (1973) 100f., 105f. ZEDDA, S., "Un aspetto della cristologia di Luca: il titolo Kyrios in Lc 1-2 e nel resto del III Vangelo," RT 13 (5, 1972) 305-15. GT:"Die Funktion der Kindheitsgeschichten im Werk des Lukas" in: G. Braumann (ed.) Das Lukas-Evangelium (Darmstadt 1974) 204-235. GEORGE, A., "Le parallèle entre Jean-Baptiste et Jésus en Luc 1-2" in: A. Descamps/A. de Halleux (eds.), Méllanges Bibliques en hommage au R. P. Béda Rigaux (Gembloux 1970) 147-171. ZMIJEWSKI, J., Die Eschatologiereden des Lukas-Evangeliums (Bonn 1972) 10, 44, 184, 185, 229, 233, 254, 323, 330. SCHUBERT, K.,Jesus im Lichte der Religionsgeschichte des Judentums (Wien/ München 1973) 33-37. LAURINI, H. C., "Esquemas Exegético-Litúrgicos de Luc 1-2" RCB 11 (1974) 12-33. TALBERT, C. H., Literary Patterns, Theological Themes, and the Genre of Luke-Acts (Missoula 1974) 2, 44, 45, 80, 103, 104, 106, 112, 117, 143. TATUM, W. B., "Die Zeit Israels: Lukas 1-2 und die theologische Intention der lukanischen Schriften" (orig: "The Epoch of Israel: Luke 1-2 and the Theological Plan of Luke-Acts" NTS 13 (1967) 184-195) in: G. Braumann (ed.), Das Lukas-Evangelium (Darmstadt 1974) 317-336. VICENT CERNUDA, A., "El paralelismo de *gennō y tiktō* en LC 1-2" Biblica 55 (1974) 260-64. DERRETT, J. D. M., "Further Light on the Narratives of the Nativity" NovT 17 (1975) 81-108. FRANKLIN, E., Christ the Lord: A Study in the Purpose and Theology of Luke Acts (London 1975) 80-87. GASQUE, W., A History of the Criticism of the Acts of the Apostles (Tübingen 1975) 133, 268, 294. GRYGLEWICZ, F., "Die Herkunft der Hymnen des Kindheitsevangeliums des Lukas" NTS 21

(1975) 265-73. LEONARDI, G., L'infanzia de Gesu nei vangeli di Matteo e di Luca (Padova 1975). LOHFINK, G., Die Sammlung Israels (München 1975) 17-32. RESENHÖFFT, W., Die Apostelgeschichte im Wortlaut ihrer beiden Urquellen (Bern 1975). STEINMUELLER, J. E., "The Infancy Gospels" HPR 76 (1975) 25-28. TSUCHIYA, H., "The History and the Fiction in the Birth Stories of Jesus—An Observation on the Thought of Luke the Evangelist" AJBI 1 (1975) 73-90. DRURY, J., Tradition and Design in Luke's Gospel (Atlanta 1976) 46-66, 122-28, 185-89. FORD, J. M., "Zealotism and the Lukan Infancy Narratives" NovT (1976) 280-92. BROWN, R. E., The Birth of the Messiah. A Commentary on the Infancy Narratives in Matthew and Luke (New York 1977); *Recensions*: McHUGH, J., "A New Approach to the Infancy Narratives" Marianum 40 (1978) 277-87; LAURENTIN, R., "Exégèses réductrices des Evangiles de l'enfance" Marianum 41 (1979) 76-100; MEDISCH, R., "Ein neuer Kommentar zu den Kindheitsgeschichten" Theologie der Gegenwart 22 (Frankfurt 1979) 242-47; MIGUENS, M., "The Infancy Narratives and Critical Biblical Method" Communio 7 (1980) 24-54. DÖMER, M., Das Heil Gottes: Studien zur Theologie des lukanischen Doppelwerkes (Köln/Bonn 1978) 18-25. ESCUDERO FREIRE, C., Devolver el evangelio a los pobres. A propósito de Lc 1-2 (Salamanca 1978). LACH, J., "Egzegetyczne problemy Lukaszowej ewangelii dzieciectwa Jezusa (Exegetische Probleme der lukanischen Kindheitsgeschichte Jesu)" SThV 16 (1978) 3-15. LAURENTIN, R., "Les charismes de Marie. Écriture, Tradition et Sitz im Leben" EphM 28 (1978) 309-21. MAILLOT, A., "Quelques remarques sur la Naissance Virginale du Christ" FV 77 (1978) 30-44. MUNOZ IGLESIAS, S., "La concepción virginal de Cristo en los Evangelios de la infancia" EstBi 37 (1978) 5-28, 213-41. RAYAN, S., The Holy Spirit: Heart of the Gospel and Christian Hope (New York 1978) 18-29. MATTILL, A. J., Luke and the Last Things: a Perspective for the Understanding of Lukan Thought (Dillsboro 1979) 17, 19. SALAS, A., "La figura de Maria en los evangelios de la infancia" CiDi 192 (1979) 337-354. SWIDLER, L., Biblical Affirmations of Woman (Philadelphia 1979) 261, 272.

1:1-2:20 BECKWITH, R. T., "St. Luke, the Date of Christmas and the Priestly Courses at Qumran" RevQ 9 (1977) 73-94.

1 LEIVESTAD, R., Christ the Conqueror (1954) 37ff. BENOIT, P., "L'Enfance de Jean Baptiste Selon Luc 1.", NTS 3 (1956-1957) 169ff. BARTH, K., Die Verheissung. Lukas 1 (1960). RUDOLPH, K., Die Mandäer I (1960) 78. STEMPVOORT, P. A. van, "Maria in Lukas I," HomBib 20 (6, 1961) 166-76. BARTH, K., The Great Promise. Luke I (1963). BRAUN, H., Qumran und NT

II (1966) 15, 19, 24, 242, 246. BLACK, M., An Aramaic Approach to the Gospels and Acts (1967) 62f. GREENLEE, J. H., Nine Uncial Palimpsests of the Greek New Testament (1968) 62-65. HEISING, A., "Der Verkündigungsengel" Wort and Antwort 8 (1967) 161-66. BROWN, R. E., "Luke's Description of the Virginal Conception" ThSt 35 (1974) 360-62. DAVIES, W. D., The Gospel and the Land (London 1974) 261-65. GESE, H., Vom Sinai zum Zion (München 1974) 130ff. BROWN, R. E., "Luke's Method in the Annunciation Narrative of Chapter One" in; C. H. Talbert (ed.) Perspectives on Luke-Acts (Danville 1978) 126-38. PERETTO, E., "Zaccaria Elisabetta Giovanni visti dal primo lettore di Luca (Cap 1)" Marianum 40 (1978) 350-70. SWIDLER, L., Biblical Affirmations of Woman (Philadelphia 1979) 262. GERSENBERGER, E. S. und SCHRAGE, W., Frau und Mann (Stuttgart 1980) 113-14.

1:1ff. FEINE, D. P. & Behm, D. J. Einleitung in das Neue Testament (1950) 296f. STAEHELIN, E. Die Verkündigung des Reiches Gottes in der Kirche Jesu Christi I (1951) 65.

1:1-56 STONEHOUSE, N. B. The Witness of Matthew and Mark to Christ (1944) 94.

1:1-8 BROWN, S., "The Role of the Prologues in Determining the Purpose of Luke-Acts" in: C. H. Talbert (ed.) Perspectives on Luke-Acts (Danville 1978) 99-111.

1:1-4 ROBERTSON, A. T. Luke the Historian in the Light of Research (1920) 5, 18, 21, 42, 57, 86, 103, 136. KLOSTERMANN, E. Das Lukasevangelium (1929) 1f. SAHLIN, H. Der Messias und das Gottesvolk (1945) 39-47. TAYLOR, V. The Formation of the Gospel Tradition (1949) 185f., 195, 198, 200. DIBELIUS, M. Aufsätze zur Apostelgeschichte (1951) 108f., 127f. STONEHOUSE, N. B. The Witness of Luke to Christ (1951) 12f., 24ff. DOEVE, J. W. "L'évangile de Luc; un moyan de prédication de la mission Chrétienne primitive," NedThT 9/6 (1954-1955) 332-37. VAN UNNIK, W. C. "Opmerkingen over het doel van Lucas' geschiedwerk (Luc 1, 4)," NedThT 9/6 (1954-1955) 323-31. DIBELIUS, M. Studies in the Acts of the Apostles (1956) 123f., 146f. GRANT, F. C. The Gospels (1957) 120ff. BLAIR, E. P. Jesus in the Gospel of Matthew (1960) 16. GRANT, F. C. "Religio licita," in: Studia Patristica IV (1961), F. L. Cross (ed.), 84-89. BULTMANN, R., The History of the Synoptic Tradition (1963) 355-56. BARTSCH, H. W., Wachet aber zu jeder Zeit (Hamburg-Bergstedt 1963) 12-14. MULDER, H., "Vele Evangelienverhlen" 1965) 42-78. FLENDER, H. St. Luke Theologian of Redemptive History (1967) 62ff. KLEIN, G. "Lukas I, 1-4 als theologisches Programm," in: Zeit und Geschichte (1964), E. Dinkler (ed.), 193-216. FLEN-

DER, H. Heil und Geschichte in der Theologie des Lukas (1965) 61-64. WIJNGAARDS, J. "Saint Luke's Prologue in the Light of Modern Research," ClM 31 (5, 1967) 172-79; (7, 1967) 251-58. GÜTTGEMANNS, E. Offene Fragen zur Formgeschichte des Evangeliums (1970) 191, 192, 193. HIGGINS, A. J. B., "The Preface to Luke and the Kerygma in Acts," in: Apostolic History and the Gospels (1970) W. W. Gasque/R. P. Martin (eds.) 78-91. SNEEN, D. J. "An Exegesis of Luke 1:1-4 with Special Regard to Luke's Purpose as a Historian," ET 83 (2, 1971) 40-43. VÖGTLE, A., Das Evangelium und die Evangelien (1971) 31-42. KÜMMEL, W. G. Einleitung in das Neue Testament (1973) 97f. GOULDER, M. D. Midrash and Lection in Matthew (1974) 456f, 466. S. Björck et al. (eds.) Valda Texter ur Nya Testamentet (Stockholm 1972) 14-15. LOHSE, E., Die Einheit des Neuen Testaments (Göttingen 1973) 145-64. SAMAIN, E., "L'Évangile de Luc: un témoignage ecclésial et missionnaire. Lc 1, 1-4; 4, 14-15" AssS 34 (1973) 60-73. van UNNIK, W. C., "Once More St. Luke's Prologue" Neo-testamentica 7 (1973) 7-26. van UNNIK, W. C., Sparsa Collecta I (Leiden 1973) 6-15. KLEIN, G., "Lukas 1, 1-4 als theologisches Programm" (orig: Zeit und Geschichte (Tübingen 1964) in: G. Braumann (ed.) Das Lukas-Evangelium (Darmstadt 1974) 170-203. du PLESSIS, I. J., "Once More: The Purpose of Luke's Prologue" NovT 16 (1974) 259-71. SCHÜRMANN, H., "Evangelienschrift und kirchliche Unterweisung" in: G. Braumann (ed.) Das Lukas-Evangelium (Darmstadt 1974) 135-69. TALBERT, C. H., Literary Patterns, Theological Themes, and the Genre of Luke-Acts (Missoula 1974) 16, 18, 80. WILCKENS, U., Die Missionsreden der Apostelgeschichte (Neukirchen 1974 [3]) 14, 68-69, 227. CONZELMANN, H. und LINDEMANN, A., Arbeitsbuch zum Neuen Testament (Tübingen 1975) 18, 31, 52, 54, 328, 383, 427. DRURY, G., " 'Who's in, Who's Out' " in: M. Hooker/C. Hickling (eds.) What About the New Testament? FS. C. Evans (London 1975) 231-32. GLÖCKNER, R., Die Verkündigung des Heils beim Evangelisten Lukas (Mainz 1975) 3-41. MUSSNER, F., "Καθεξῆς im Lukasprolog" in: E. E. Ellis/E. Grässer (eds.) Jesus und Paulus. FS. W. G. Kümmel (Göttingen 1975) 253-55. GOPPELT, L., Theologie des Neuen Testaments II (Göttingen 1976) 604-05. SCHNEIDER, G., Das Evangelium nach Lukas (Gütersloh/Würzburg 1977) 37 (lit!). TRITES, A. A., The New Testament Concept of Witness (London 1977) 136, 198. "Apostelgeschichte" in: TRE 3 (1978) 501, 518. BROWN, S., "The Role of the Prologues in Determining the Purpose of Luke-Acts" in: C. H. Talbert (ed.) Perspectives on Luke-Acts (Danville 1978) 99-111. DÖMER, M., Das Heil Gottes: Studien zur Theologie des lukanischen Doppel-

werkes (Köln/Bonn 1978) 5-14, 203. PRAST, F., Presbyter und
Evangelium in nachapostolischer Zeit (Stuttgart 1979) 16, 170,
189f, 318. ROBBINS, V. K., "Prefaces in Greco-Roman Biography and Luke-Acts" PRSt 6 (1979) 94-108. PALLIS, A., Notes
on St. Luke and the Acts (London 1928) 1-3. GOODMAN, F. W.,
"A Proposed Emendation" StEv 4 (1968) 205-08. BAUER, J. B.,
Scholia Biblica et Patristica (Graz 1972) 75-78. SAMAIN, E., "La
Notion de APXH" in: F. Neirynck (ed.) L'Evangile de Luc (Gembloux 1973) 316-24. GASQUE, W., A History of the Criticism of
the Acts of the Apostles (Tübingen 1975) 25, 32n, 33, 60, 102, 112,
143, 144, 159, 216, 262, 301, 303. GLÖCKNER, R., Die Verkündigung des Heils beim Evangelisten Lukas (Mainz 1975) 11-17,
19, 27. PÉTRIN, J., Le sens de l'oeuvre de saint Luc et le mystère
marial (Ottawa 1979). PRAST, F., Presbyter und Evangelium in
nachapostolischer Zeit (Stuttgart 1979) 1n.1, 272.

1:1-3 PETZKE, G. Die Traditionen über Apollonius von Tyana und das
Neue Testament (1970) 66f.

1:1-2 BULTMANN, R. The History of the Synoptic Tradition (1963) 294-
97.

1:1 ROBERTSON, A. T. Luke the Historian in the Light of Research
(1920) 44, 47, 49f., 55, 72. FLEW, R. N., Jesus and His Church
(1956) 182n. BAUER, J. "POLLOI Luk i 1," Nov Test 4 (4, 1960)
263-66.

1:2 BLAIR, E. P. Jesus in the Gospel of Matthew (1960) 39. DU-
PONT, J. The Sources of Acts (1964) 103, 106, 107, 110, 111.
PALLIS, A., Notes on St. Luke and the Acts (London 1928) 3.
FEUILLET, A., " 'Témoins oculaites et serviteurs de la parole' (Lc
i 2b)" NovT 15 (1973) 241-59. SAMAIN, E., "La Notion de
APXH" in: F. Neirynck (ed.) L'Evangile de Luc (Gembloux 1973)
316-24. WANKE, J., Die Emmauserzählung. Eine Redaktions-
geschichtliche Untersuchung zu Lk 24, 13-35 (Leipzig 1973) 117.
CONZELMANN, H., und LINDEMANN, A., Arbeitsbuch zum
Neuen Testament (Tübingen 1975) 31, 92, 119, 263, 337ff.
GLÖCKNER, R., Die Verkündigung des Heils beim Evangelisten
Lukas (Mainz 1975) 18-26, 46. NELLESSEN, E., Zeugnis für Jesus und das Wort (Köln 1976) 231-35. "Apostel" in: TRE 3 (1978)
442.

1:3-4 GLÖCKNER, R., Die Verkündigung des Heils beim Evangelisten
Lukas (Mainz 1975) 26-31, 38f.

1:3 PALLIS, A., Notes on St. Luke and the Acts (London 1928) 3.
SAMAIN, E., "La Notion de APXH" in: F. Neirynck (ed.) l'E-
vangile de Luc (Gembloux 1973) 316-24. TALBERT, C. H., Literary Patterns, Theological Themes, and the Genre of Luke-Acts

(Missoula 1974) 18. VÖLKEL, M., "Exegetische Erwägungen zum Verständnis des Begriffs *kathexēs* im Lukanischen Prolog" NTS 20 (1974) 289-99. SCHNEIDER, G., "Zur Bedeutung von *kathexēs* im lukanischen Doppelwerk" ZNW 68 (1977) 128-31. MARX, W. G., "A New Theophilus" EQ 52 (1980) 17-26. CADBURY, H. J. " 'WE' and 'I' Passages in Luke and Acts", NTS 3 (1956-1957) 130ff. DUPONT, J. The Sources of Acts (1964) 82, 104, 197 (bis), 110. RINALDI, G. " 'Risalendo alle più lontane origini della tradizione' (Luca 1, 3)," BiblOr 7 (6, 1965) 252-58.

1:4 GASQUE, W., A History of the Criticism of the Acts of the Apostles (Tübingen 1975) 24, 32n, 33, 60, 102, 112, 143, 144, 159, 186, 216, 262, 301, 303. GLÖCKNER, R., Die Verkündigung des Heils beim Evangelisten Lukas (Mainz 1975) 3-4, 10-11, 31-34. METZGER, B. M., The Early Versions of the New Testament (Oxford 1977) 176-77. QUINN, J. D., "The Last Volume of Luke: The Relations of Luke-Acts to the Pastoral Epistles" in: C. H. Talbert (ed.) Perspectives on Luke-Acts (Danville 1978) 70.

1:5-9:50 DÖMER, M., Das Heil Gottes: Studien zur Theologie des lukanischen Doppelwerkes (Köln/Bonn 1978) 79-83.

1:5-4:15 TALBERT, C. H., Literary Patterns, Theological Themes, and the Genre of Luke-Acts (Missoula 1974) 47, 48, 105.

1:5-3:38 O'NEILL, J. C. The Theology of Acts in its Historical Setting (1970) 69-71.

1:5-3:20 DÖMER, M., Das Heil Gottes: Studien zur Theologie des lukanischen Doppelwerkes (Köln/Bonn 1978) 15-42.

1:5-2:52 HIRSCH, E. Frühgeschichte des Evangeliums (1941) 171-92. TAYLOR, V., The Formation of the Gospel Tradition (1949) 159-64. TALBERT, C. H., Literary Patterns, Theological Themes, and the Genre of Luke-Acts (Missoula 1974) 47, 89. GLÖCKNER, R., Die Verkündigung des Heils beim Evangelisten Lukas (Mainz 1975) 25, 68-72, 74-79, 89, 93, 114-24, 142ff. SCHNEIDER, G., Das Evangelium nach Lukas (Gütersloh/Würzburg 1977) 42-43 (Lit!).

1:5-2:40 LAURENTIN, R., "Traces d'allusions étymologiques en Luc 1-2," Biblica 37 (1956) 435-56.

1:5-2:7 SCHUBERT, K., Jesus im Lichte der Religionsgeschichte des Judentums (Wien/München 1973) 35-37.

1:5ff. RENGSTORF, K. H. Das Evangelium nach Lukas (1949) 15-17. HAHN, F. Christologische Hoheitstitel (1963) 304.

1:5-80 ANON, "Ain-Karim source de la joie," BibTerreSainte 61 (1964) 7. BRUNOT, A. "Le sanctuaire du Magnificat," BibTerreSainte 61 (1964) 9-10, 15. "Le sanctuaire du Benedictus," BibTerreSainte 61 (1964) 16-19. FENASSE, J.-M. "La visitation et la naissance de Jean-Baptiste," BibTerreSainte 61 (1964) 20-21. PO-

TIN, J., "Zacharie était de race sacerdotale," BibTerreSainte 61 (1964)3. MINEAR, P., To Heal and to Reveal (New York 1976) 81-101. BAGATTI, B., "Antiche leggende sull'infanzia di S. Giovanni Battista" EuD 30 (1977) 260-69.

1:5-56 KLAIBER, W., "Eine lukanische Fassung des sola gratia. Beobachtungen zu Lk 1:5-56" in: J. Friedrich et al. (eds.) Rechtfertigung. FS. E. Käsemann (Tübingen/Göttingen 1976) 211-28.

1:5-45 SAHLIN, H. Der Messias und das Gottesvolk (1955) 63-65, 70-151.

1:5-38 DIGNATH,W., Die lukanische Vorgeschichte (1971) 11-23. TALBERT, C. H., Literary Patterns, Theological Themes, and the Genre of Luke-Acts (Missoula 1974) 44.

1:5-25 BENOIT, P. "L'Enfance de Jean-Baptiste selon Luc I," NTS 3 (3, 1957) 169-94. HAHN, F. Christologische Hoheitstitel (1963) 371, 173f. STECK, K. GPM 21/1 (1966-1967) 28-35. WINK, W. John the Baptist in the Gospel Tradition (1968) 68-70. DESCAMPS, A. and DE HALLEUX, A. Mélanges Bibliques en hommage au R. P. Béda Rigaux (1970) 149-51. VÖGTLE, A. Das Evangelium und die Evangelien (1971) 52-54. BARTSCH, H. W., Wachet aber zu jeder Zeit! (Hamburg-Bergstedt 1963) 28. HUBBARD, B. J., "Commissioning Stories in Luke-Acts: A Study of their Antecedents, Form and Content" in: Semeia 8 (1977) 103-26. SCHNEIDER, G., Das Evangelium nach Lukas (Gütersoh/Würzburg 1977) 44 (lit!). HUBBARD, B. J., "The Role of the Commissioning Accounts in Acts" in: C. H. Talbert (ed.) Perspectives on Luke-Acts (Danville 1978) 190. SWIDLER, L., Biblical Affirmations of Woman (Philadelphia 1979) 263.

1:5-21 ZINGG, P., Das Wachsen der Kirche. Beiträge zur Frage der lukanischen Redaktion und Theologie (Freiburg 1974) 137.

1:5-7 TALBERT, C. H., Literary Patterns, Theological Themes, and the Genre of Luke-Acts (Missoula 1974) 44.

1:5 TALBERT, C. H., Literary Patterns, Theological Themes, and the Genre of Luke-Acts (Missoula 1974) 36. METZGER, B. M., The Early Versions of the New Testament (Oxford 1977) 179, 200, 201. JEREMIAS, J., Die Sprache des Lukasevangeliums (Göttingen 1980) 15-22.

1:6 PALLIS, A., Notes on St. Luke and the Acts (London 1928) 3. KNOX, W. L. The Sources of the Synoptic Gospels II (1957) 40. ZIESLER, J. A. The Meaning of Righteousness in Paul (1972) 138f, 145, 209. ADINOLFI, M., "La giustizia nel terzo vangelo" RivB 27 (1979) 233-60. BERGMEIER, R., Glaube als Gabe nach Johannes (Stuttgart 1980) 201. JEREMIAS, J., Die Sprache des Lukasevangeliums (Göttingen 1980) 22-24.

1:7 SAHLIN. H. Der Messias und das Gottesvolk (1945) 324f. BÖCHER, O., "Johannes der Täufer in der Neutestamentlichen Überlieferung" in: G. Müller (ed.) Rechtfertigung Realismus. FS. A. Köberle (Darmstadt 1978) 47-52. JEREMIAS, J., Die Sprache des Lukasevangeliums (Göttingen 1980) 24-25.

1:8-62 SWIDLER, L., Biblical Affirmations of Woman (Philadelphia 1979) 263.

1:8-11 TALBERT, C. H., Literary Patterns, Theological Themes, and the Genre of Luke-Acts (Missoula 1974) 44.

1:8-9 JEREMIAS, J., Die Sprache des Lukasevangeliums (Göttingen 1980) 25-29.

1:8 KNOX, W. L. The Sources of the Synoptic Gospels II (1957) 84, 106. AVI-YONAH, M., "L'Inscription 'Nazareth' à Césarée," BibTerreSaint 61 (1964) 2-5. BRAUN, H. Qumran und NT II (1966) 15, 107. NEIRYNCK, F., "La Matière Marcienne dans Luc" in: F. NEIRYNCK (ed.) L'Evangile de Luc (Gembloux 1973) 184-91. METZGER, B. M., Early Versions of the New Testament (Oxford 1977) 179. JEREMIAS, J., Die Sprache des Lukasevangeliums (Göttingen 1980) 29.

1:9 KNOX, W. L. The Sources of the Synoptic Gospels II (1957) 40. JEREMIAS, J., Die Sprache des Lukasevangeliums (Göttingen 1980) 29-30.

1:10 NICKELS, P. Targum and New Testament (1967) 27. METZGER, B. M., The Early Versions of the New Testament (Oxford 1977) 176. JEREMIAS, J., Die Sprache des Lukasevangeliums (Göttingen 1980) 30-31.

1:11-20 DORMEYER, D., Die Passion Jesu als Verhaltensmodell (Münster 1974) 229f.

1:11 Knox, W. L. The Sources of the Synoptic Gospels II (1957) 40. JEREMIAS, J., Die Sprache des Lukasevangeliums (Göttingen 1980) 31-32.

1:12 TALBERT, C. H., Literary Patterns, Theological Themes, and the Genre of Luke-Acts (Missoula 1974) 44. JEREMIAS, J., Die Sprache des Lukasevangeliums (Göttingen 1980) 32-33.

1:13-17 TALBERT, C. H., Literary Patterns, TheologicalThemes, and the Genre of Luke-Acts (Missoula 1974) 44, 104. BROWN, R. E., "Luke's Method in the Annunciation Narrative of Chapter One" in: C. H. Talbert (ed.) Perspectives on Luke-Acts (Danville 1978) 136-38.

1:13-14 STRECKER, G. Der Weg der Gerechtigkeit (1962) 531.

1:13 HENNECKE, W./SCHNEEMELCHER, W. Neutestamentliche Apokryphen (1964) I 281. LAURENTIN, R. Struktur and Theologie der Lukanischen Kindheitsgeschichte (1967) 18, 40, 50, 53, 81, 116, 119, 138, 142, 154, 204. SCHÜTZ, R. Johannes der Täufer (1967). METZGER, B. M., The Early Versions of the New Testament (Oxford 1977) 202. JEREMIAS, J., Die Sprache des Lukasevangeliums (Göttingen 1980) 33-35.

1:14-17 HAHN, F. Christologische Hoheitstitel (1963) 371f., 373. GASTON, L. No Stone on Another (1970) 262, 268-69.

1:14 HAHN, F. Christologische Hoheitstitel (1963) 377. NICKELS, P. Targum and New Testament (1967) 28.

1:15-17 GILLIÈRON, B., Le Saint-Esprit, actualité du Christ. Ce qu'en ont dit Paul, Luc et Jean (Geneva 1978).

1:15 RUDOLPH, K. Die Mandäer I (1960) 78. HAHN, F. Christologische Hoheitstitel (1963) 307, 318. LAURENTIN, R. Struktur und Theologie der lukanischen Kindheitsgeschichte (1967) 18, 42f., 50f., 64, 70, 80, 90, 92, 112, 170. "Aramäisch" in: TRE 3 (1978) 609. JEREMIAS, J., Die Sprache des Lukasevangeliums (Göttingen 1980) 35-36.

1:16 PALLIS, A., Notes on St. Luke and the Acts (London 1928) 4.

1:17 PALLIS, A., Notes on St. Luke and the Acts (London 1928) 4. NÖTSCHER, F., Altorientalischer und alttestamentlicher Auferstehungsglaube (Darmstadt 1970 = 1926) 127. LOHFINK, G., Die Sammlung Israels (München 1975) 20, 22-23, 28. JEREMIAS, J., Die Sprache des Lukasevangeliums (Göttingen 1980) 37-38. SNODGRASS, K. R., "Streams of Tradition Emerging from Isaiah 40:1-5 and their Adaptation in the New Testament" JSNT 8 (1980) 24-45. KNOX, W. L. The Sources of the Synoptic Gospels II (1957) 41. STRECKER, G. Der Weg der Gerechtigkeit (1962) 91₁. FRIEDRICHSEN, G. W. S. "The Gothic Text of Luke in its Relation to the Codex Brixianus (f) and the Codex Palatinus (e)", NTS 11 (1964-1965) 282f. THEYSSEN, G. W. "Unbelief" in the New Testament (1965) 7ff. LAURENTIN, R. Struktur und Theologie der Lukanischen Kindheitsgeschichte (1967) 45, 57f., 49f., 90, 116, 126f., 138, 145, 204. KRÄNKEL, E. Jesus der Knecht Gottes (1972) 95f. ZIESLER, J. A. The Meaning of Righteousness in Paul (1972) 138ff., 145.

1:18-35 LENTZEN-DEIS, F. Die Taufe Jesu nach den Synoptikern (1970) 82ff.

1:18-26 SWIDLER, L., Biblical Affirmations of Woman (Philadelphia 1979) 241.

1:18 TALBERT, C. H., Literary Patterns, Theological Themes, and the Genre of Luke-Acts (Missoula 1974) 44. JANSSEN, E., "Testament Abrahams" in: W. G. Kümmel (ed.) Jüdische Schriften aus hellenistisch-römischer Zeit III (Gütersloh 1975) 222. JE-

REMIAS, J., Die Sprache des Lukasevangeliums (Göttingen 1980) 39.

1:19-23 Talbert, C. H., Literary Patterns, Theological Themes, and the Genre of Luke-Acts (Missoula 1974) 44.

1:19 STAEHELIN, E. Die Verkündigung des Reiches Gottes in der Kirche Jesu Christi I (1951) 303. HAHN, F., Christologische Hoheitstitel (1963) 270, JEREMIAS, J., Die Sprache des Lukasevangeliums (Göttingen 1980) 39-41.

1:20 THEYSSEN, G. W. "Unbelief" in the New Testament (1965) 69f. LAURENTIN, R. Struktur und Theologie der Lukanischen Kindheitsgeschichte (1967) 41, 51f., 54, 64, 204. NICKELS, P. Targum and New Testament (1967) 28. ANDERSON, J. G., "A New Translation of Luke 1:20" BTr 20 (1969) 21-24. JEREMIAS, J., Die Sprache des Lukasevangeliums (Göttingen 1980) 41-44.

1:21 METZGER, B. M., Early Versions of the New Testament (Oxford 1977) 200. JEREMIAS, J., Die Sprache des Lukasevangeliums (Göttingen 1980) 44.

1:23 NEIRYNCK, F., "La Matière Marcienne dans Luc" in: F. Neirynck (ed.) L'Evangile de Luc (Gembloux 1973) 184-91. FRIEDRICH, G., "Das Amt im Neuen Testament" in: Auf das Wort kommt es an (Göttingen 1978) 421. JEREMIAS, J., Die Sprache des Lukasevangeliums (Göttingen 1980) 45.

1:24-25 TALBERT, C. H., Literary Patterns, Theological Themes, and the Genre of Luke-Acts (Missoula 1974) 44.

1:24 PALLIS, A., Notes on St. Luke and the Acts (London 1928) 4-5. JEREMIAS, J., Die Sprache des Lukasevangeliums (Göttingen 1980) 46. SAHLIN, H. Der Messias und das Gottesvolk (1945) 110-13.

1:25 WINTER, P. "Hoti 'recitativum' in Lc 1, 25, 61; 2, 23" ZNW 46 (1955) 261-63. WINTER, P., "Zu Lukas 1:25, 61, 2:23" ZNW 46 (1955) 261. LAURENTIN, R. Struktur und Theologie der Lukanischen Kindheitsgeschichte (1967) 18, 41, 48, 62, 87, 123.

1:26-2:20 RUETHER, R. R., Mary—The Feminine Face of the Church (London 1979) 25-30.

1:26ff. STAEHELIN, E. Die Verkündigung des Reiches Gottes in der Kirche Jesu Christi I (1951) 135. FAHY, T., "The Marriage of Our Lady and St. Joseph," IThQ 24 (3, 1957) 261-67. DEL PARAMO, S. "La Anunciacion de la Virgen," EstBi 16 (2, 1957) 161-85. LAURENTIN, R. Struktur und Theologie der Lukanischen Kindheitsgeschichte (1967) 55, 204-07. PETZKE, G. Die Traditionen über Apollonius von Tyana und das Neue Testament (1970) 138, 162, 202. RUDOLPH, K., Die Gnosis (Göttingen 1978) 180.

1:26-56 KNOX, W. L. The Sources of the Synoptic Gospels II (1957) 42.

1:26-45 MUSSNER, F. "Der Glaube Mariens im Lichte des Römerbriefs," Catholica 18 (4, 1964) 258-68. BALAGUE, M. "LaGruta
de la Anunciacion," CultBib 23 (210, 1966) 272-81. MUSSNER,
F. "Der Glaube Mariens im Lichte des Römerbriefs," Prasentia
Salutis (1967) 284.

1:26-38 RENGSTORF, K. H. Das Evangelium nach Lukas (1949) 26f.
SCHMID, J. Das Evangelium nach Lukas (1955) 44-50. DE TUYA,
M. "en el Relato de la Anunciacion (Luc., I.26-38) esta Expresada
la Divinidad del Mesias?" CiTom 82 (1955) 383-420. AUDET, J.-
P. "L'annonce à Marie", RB 63/3 (1956) 346-74. DONNELLY,
P. J. "Our Lady's Virginity ante partum," Scripture 10 (12, 1958)
116-21. GOTHARD, D. "The Annunciation," Scripture 10 (1958)
116-121. JONES, A. "Background of the Annunciation," Scripture 11 (15, 1959) 65-81. KUGELMAN, R., "The Object of Mar-
y's Consent in the Annunciation," MarStud 11 (1960) 60-84.
IWAND, GPM (1960-1961) 18ff. GRUNDMANN, W. Das Evangelium nach Lukas (1961) 50-61. COCHRAN, R. T. "The Liturgy's Use of the Annunciation Scene," AER 146 (2, 1962) 89-93.
STRECKER, G. Der Weg der Gerechtigkeit (1962) 52. BULT-
MANN, R. The History of the Synoptic Tradition (1963) 295f.
HAHN, F. Christologische Hoheitstitel (1963) 259, 268f., 274, 275-
77, 304-08, 314-18. HARRINGTON, W., "The Annunciation,"
DoLi 13 (6, 1963) 306-15. IWAND, H.-J. Predigt-Meditationen
(1964) 202-07. FLENDER, H. Heil und Geschichte in der Theologie des Lukas (1965) 44. LANGKAMMER, H. "The Soterio-
logical Character of Mary's Fiat," SBFLA 15 (1964-1965) 293-301.
KAMPHAUS, F. Von der Exegese zur Predigt (1968) 216-22, 249-
59. GAECHTER, P. "Der Verkündigungsbericht Lk 1, 26-38,"
ZKTh 91 (2, 1969) 322-63; (4, 1969) 567-86. LORENZ, F. Streit
um Jesus (1969) 30-35. BURGER, C. Jesus als Davidssohn (1970)
132-35. DESCAMPS, A. and DE HALLEUX, A. Mélanges Bibliques en hommage au R. P. Béda Rigaux (1970) 149-51. LANGE,
E. (ed.) Predigtstudien für das Kirchenjahr 1970-1971. Perikopenreihe V. (1970) 42-48. MÖLLER, C. Von der Predigt zum Text
(1970) 93-101. PRETE, B., "Il racconto dell'Annunziazione di
Luca 1, 26-38 nella nuova traduzione della Bibbia a cura della
C.E.I.," BiblOr 15 (2, 1973) 75-88. BENOIT, P., "L'Annonciation" AssS 6 (1965) 40-57. DORMEYER, D., Die Passion Jesu
als Verhaltensmodell (Münster 1974) 229. HUNTER, A. M., Gospel and Apostle (London 1975) 30-32. ORBE, Z., Annunciación.
Meditaciones sobre Lucas 1, 26-38 (Madrid 1976). HUBBARD,
B. J., "Commissioning Stories in Luke-Acts: A Study of their Antecedents, Form and Content" in: Semeia 8 (1977) 103-26. KLEIN,
G., in: GPM 31 (1976-1977) 22-29. SCHNEIDER, G., Das Evan-

1:30-40 BÜCHSEL, D. F. Der Geist Gottes in Neuen Testament (1926) 196-201.

1:30-38 HENNECKE, E./SCHNEEMELCHER, W. Neutestamentliche Apokryphen (1964) I 284.

1:30-35 GRISPINO, J. A. "When Did Mary Learn that Her Son Was Divine?" EphM 15 (1, 1965) 126-30. BUSSE, U., Das Nazareth-Manifest Jesu. Eine Einführung in das lukanische Jesusbild nach Lk 4,16-30 (Stuttgart 1978) 71.

1:30-33 GESE, H., Vom Sinai zum Zion (München 1974) 131-32. JEREMIAS, J., Die Sprache des Lukasevangeliums (Göttingen 1980) 48-49.

1:30 STRECKER, G. Der Weg der Gerechtigkeit (1962) 54$_2$. JEREMIAS, J., Die Sprache des Lukasevangeliums (Göttingen 1980) 49-50.

1:31-35 STRECKER, G. Der Weg der Gerechtigkeit (1962) 54.

1:31-33 HOYOS, F. "Daras a luz un hijo y le pondras por nombre Jesus," RevBi 28 (4, 1966) 239-46. REHM, M. Der königliche Messias (1968) 58f. LEVIN, S., The Father of Joshua/Jesus (New York 1978).

1:31 STRECKER, G. Der Weg der Gerechtigkeit (1962) 53. BAUER, J. B. "Philologische Bemerkungen zu Lk 1,34," Biblica 45 (1964) 536-37. QUECKE, H. "Lukas 1,31 in den alten Übersetzungen," Biblica 46 (3, 1965) 333-48. LAURENTIN, R. Struktur und Theologie der Lukanischen Kindheitsgeschichte (1967) 52, 78f., 80f., 96, 98, 144, 168, 196, 204. TALBERT, C. H., Literary Patterns, Theological Themes, and the Genre of Luke-Acts (Missoula 1974) 117. van der MEULEN, F., "Zum jüdischen und hellenistischen Hintergrund von Lukas 1:31" in: W. Haubeck/M. Bachmann (eds.) Wort in der Zeit. FS. K. H. Rengstorf (Leiden 1980) 108-122.

1:32-33 LÖVESTAM, E. Son and Saviour (1961) 13, 73, 81, 93f. HAHN, F. Christologische Hoheitstitel (1963) 247f., 288. RESE, M. Alttestamentliche Motive in der Christologie des Lukas (1969) 185. GASTON, L. No Stone on Another (1970) 256, 270-271, 276, 336. LAURENTIN, R. Struktur und Theologie der Lukanischen Kindheitsgeschichte (1967) 44, 82f., 119, 204. SOBOSAN, J. G., "Completion of Prophecy. Jesus in Lk 1:32-33" BThB 4 (1974) 317-23.

1:32 STONEHOUSE, N. B. The Witness of Matthew and Mark to Christ (1944) 223. STAEHELIN, E. Die Verkündigung des Reiches Gottes in der Kiche Jesu Christi I (1951) 290. BLAIR, E. P. Jesus in the Gospel of Matthew (1960) 62. ROBINSON, J. M. Kerygma und historischer Jesus (1960) 69. HAHN, F. Christologische Hoheitstitel (1963) 254, 281, 287. FLENDER, H. St Luke Theologian of Redemptive History (1967) 21, 22, 43, 44n. LAURENTIN, R. Struktur and Theologie der Lukanischen Kindheitsgeschichte (1967) 17, 42f., 48f., 51, 82, 96, 116, 127, 129, 142, 147, 159ff., 164, 166. NICKELS, P. Targum and New Testament (1967) 28. KRÄNKL, E. Jesus der Knecht Gottes (1972) 86, 92, 138, 157f. JEREMIAS, J., Die Sprache des Lukasevangeliums (Göttingen 1980) 51.

1:33 STAEHELIN, E. Die Verkündigung des Reiches Gottes in der Kirche Jesu Christi I (1951) 247, 266. HAHN, F. Christologische Hoheitstitel (1963) 187. McNAMARA, M. The New Testament and the Palestinian Targum to the Pentateuch (1966) 149. LAUREN-TIN, R. Struktur und Theologie der Lukanischen Kindheitsge-schichte (1967) 19, 22, 55, 78, 116, 128,138ff. CLARK, K. W., "The Israel of God" in: The Gentile Bias and Other Essays (Leiden 1980) 23.

1:34ff. VOGELS, H., "Zur Textgeschichte von Lk 1:34ff" ZNW 43 (1950-1951) 256-60.

1:34-38 GALOT, J. "Vierge entre les vierges," NRTh 79 (5, 1957) 463-77.

1:34-35 HARNACK, A. "Zu Luk 1:34-35" ZNW (1901) 53. GILLI-ÈRON, B., Le Saint-Esprit, actualité du Christ. Ce qu'en ont dit Paul, Luc et Jean (Geneva 1978). FLANAGAN, N. M., "Our La-dy's Vow of Virginity," MarSt 7 (1956) 103-21. SCHNEIDER, G. "Lk 1,34. 35 als redaktionelle Einheit," BZ 15 (2, 1971) 255-59. TALBERT, C. H., Literary Patterns, Theological Themes, and the Genre of Luke-Acts (Missoula 1974) 117.

1:34 BRINKMANN, B. "Die Jungfrauengeburt und das Lukasevan-gelium," Biblica 34 (1953) 327-32. BRODMANN, B. "Mariens Jungfräulichkeit nach Lk 1,34 in der Auseinandersetzung von heute," Antonianum /A.XXX/1 (1955) 27-44. ROETS, A. "Mar-ia's voornemen tot Magdelijkheid", ColBG 1 (1955) 448-77. SCHWANK, B. "Lk 1,34 im Lichte von I Kor 7,36-38," Ober-rheinisches Pastoral- Blatt 57 (1956) 317-23. BAUER, J. B. "Die Antwort der Jungfrau (Lk 1,34)," Oesterreichisches Klerusblatt 90 (1:25, 1957) 244-45. CEROKE, C. P. "Luke 1,34 and Mary's Vir-ginity," CBQ 19 (3, 1957) 329-42. GROEGER, Erwägungen zu: "Wie soll das geschehen. . . ?" BuK 12/2 (1957) 55-57. GUY, H. "The Virgin Birth in St. Luke," ET 68 (1957) 157. VILLANU-EVA, M. "Nueva controversia en torno al voto de virginidad de Nuestra Señora," EstBi 16 (3-4, 1957) 307-28. BAUER, J. B. "Monstra te esse matrem, Virgo singularis!" MThZ 9 (2, 1958) 124-35. GRABER, O. "Wollte Maria eine normale Ehe einge-hen?" Marianum 20 (1, 1958) 1-9. JELLOUSCHEK, C. J. "Mariä Verkündigung in neuer Sicht,"MThZ 10 (2, 1959) 102-13. ZER-

WICK, M., " '. . . quoniam virum non cognosco' (Lc 1,34)," VerbDom 37 (4, 1959) 276-88. DIEKHANS, M. "Lc 1,34 e a Virgindade de Maria Ssma.," REB 20 (1, 1960) 29-35. GRABER, O. "Marias Jungfräulichkeitswille vor der Engelsbotschaft," Marianum 22 (2-3, 1960) 290-304. GEWIESS, J. "Die Marienfrage, Lk 1,34," BZ 5 (2, 1961) 221-54. SCHURR, V., "Die Marienfrage" in: Theologie der Gegenwart 4 (1961) 249-52. DEVAULT, J. "The Concept of Virginity in Judaism," MarSt 13 (1962) 23-40. QUECKE, H. "Lk 1,34 in den alten Übersetzungen und im Protevangelium des Jakobus," Biblica 44 (4, 1963) 499-520. BAUER, J. B. "Philologische Bemerkungen zu Lk 1,34," Biblica 45 (4, 1964) 535-540. QUECKE, H. "Lk 1,34 im Diatessaron," Biblica 45 (1,1964) 85-88. QUECKE, H. "Zur Auslegungsgeschichte von Lk 1,34," Biblica 47 (1,1966) 113-14. LAURENTIN, R. Struktur und Theologie der Lukanischen Kindheitsgeschichte (1967) 86, 89f., 120, 129, 137, 186, 190f., 196, 198, 201-06, 210, 215. RO-MANO, C. "Il voto di verginità di Maria Santissima," PaCl 46 (Feb. 1, 1967) 148-53. IGLESIAS, S. M. "A proposito de Lucas 1,34," EstBi 28 (1-2, 1969) 143-49. CARROLL, E. R. CBQ 32 (3, 1970) 451-53. PRETE, B. "A Proposito di Luca I, 34," RivB 18 (4, 1970) 379-93. PHIPPS, W. E. Was Jesus Married? (1970) 40-42. CZEKALA, T. "Lk 1,34 w egzegezie katolickiej XX wieku", CoTh 41 (3, 1971) 29-40. GRAYSTONE, G. "Virgin of all Virgins. The Interpretation of Luke 1,34," EphM 21 (1, 1971) 5-20. BLINZLER, J., Die Brüder und Schwestern Jesu (Stuttgart 1967) 61-62. IGLESIAS, M. S., "A propósito de Lucas 1:34" EstBi 28 (1969) 143-49. WANKE, J., Die Emmauserzählung. Eine redaktionsgeschichtliche Untersuchung zu Lk 24, 13-35 (Leipzig 1973) 57. TALBERT, C. H., Literary Patterns, Theological Themes, and the Genre of Luke-Acts (Missoula 1974) 44. OB-ERLINNER, L., Historische Überlieferung und christologische Aussage (Stuttgart 1975) 62-65. KLAIBER, W., "Eine lukanische Fassung des sola gratia. Beobachtungen zu Lk 1:5-56" in: J. Friedrich et al. (eds.) Rechtfertigung. FS. E. Käsemann (Tübingen/Göttingen 1976) 214-15. PRETE, B., "Il significato di Luca 1,34 nella struttura del racconto dell'annunziazione" Marianum 40 (1978) 248-76.

1:35-37 TALBERT, C. H., Literary Patterns, Theological Themes, and the Genre of Luke-Acts (Missoula 1974) 44.

1:35 CLARKE, W. K. L. New Testament Problems (1929) 75ff. SALIN, H. Der Messias und das Gottesvolk (1945) 186-89. DAUBE, D. "The Gospels and the Rabbis," Listener 56 (1956) 342-46. BAARDA, T. J. "Dionysios Bar Salibi and the Text of Luke I.35," VigChr 17 (4, 1963) 225-29. HAHN, F. Christologische Ho-

heitstitel (1963) 248. LEGRAND, L. "L'arrière-plan néotesta-
mentaire de Lc. I,35," RevBi 70 (2, 1963) 161-92. HOYOS, P. "
'Espiritu Santo descendera sobre ti'. Reflexiones sobre la Anunciacion," RevBi 28 (2, 1966) 105-10. FLENDER, H. St Luke
Theologian of Redemptive History (1967) 21, 22, 43, 44n, 136 &
n,137. LAURENTIN, R. Struktur und Theologie der Lukanischen
Kindheitsgeschichte (1967) 17f., 21., 41, 49f., 52, 59f., 71, 85ff.,
89ff., 96, 120, 122, 129, 132, 138f., 150, 154f., 158, 161, 164,
166, 168, 180, 216. IGLESIAS, S. M. "Lucas 1,35b," EstBi 27
(4, 1968) 275-99. JOURJON, M. et BOUHOT, J., "Luc 1:35 dans
la patristique grecque" Bulletin de la Française Societè d'Mariales
25 (1968) 65-76. MUNOZ, S., "Auslegung über Lk 1:35b" EstBi
27 (1968) 275-99. La Idea de Dios en la Biblia (Madrid 1971).
RESE, M. Alttestamentliche Motive in der Christologie des Lukas
(1969) 185-188. SCHNEIDER, G., Anfragen an das Neue Testament (Essen 1971) 103, 104, 107, 108, 109, 110, 111, 112, 113.
VICENT, A., "La presunta sustantivación *to gennōmenon* en Lc
1,35b" EstBi 33 (1974) 265-73. ESCUDERO FREIRE, C., "Alcance Cristológico de Lc 1,35 y 2,49" Communio 8 (1975) 5-77.
BUSSE, U., Das Nazareth-Manifest Jesu. Eine Einführung in das
lukanische Jesusbild nach Lk 4,16-30 (Stuttgart 1978) 15-17. PI-
KAZA, X., "El Espíritu Santo y María en la obra de San Lucas"
EphM 28 (1978) 151-68. RAYAN, S., The Holy Spirit: Heart of
the Gospel and Christian Hope (New York 1978) 6,32.
SCHWEIZER, E., Heiliger Geist (Stuttgart 1978) 77-79. SWID-
LER, L., Biblical Affirmations of Woman (Philadelphia 1979) 56.
JEREMIAS, J., Die Sprache des Lukasevangeliums (Göttingen
1980) 51-52.

1:36 DEISSMANN, A. Licht vom Osten (1923) 309f. LAURENTIN,
R. Struktur und Theologie der Lukanischen Kindheitsgeschichte
(1967) 52, 57, 62, 69, 80, 90, 116, 124, 130, 204. TALBERT, C.
H., Literary Patterns, Theological Themes, and the Genre of Luke-
Acts (Missoula 1974) 104. JEREMIAS, J., Die Sprache des
Lukasevangeliums (Göttingen 1980) 52-53.

1:37 METZGER, B. M., Early Versions of the New Testament (Oxford
1977) 178, 391. JEREMIAS, J., Die Sprache des Lukasevangeliums (Göttingen 1980) 54.

1:38 STRECKER, G. Der Weg der Gerechtigkeit (1962) 53₂. DE CRE,
D. "Le Fiat de l'Annonciation," EFr 13 (29, 1963) 129-62; (31,
1963) 113-142. ROYAL, E. P. "The Fullness of Time and the
Consent of the Holy Virgin to the Incarnation," EphM 15 (2-3,
1965) 287-99. LAURENTIN, R. Struktur und Theologie der Lukanischen Kindheitsgeschichte (1967) 41, 48, 50, 52, 96, 120, 168,
173. TALBERT, C. H., Literary Patterns, Theological Themes, and

the Genre of Luke-Acts (Missoula 1974) 44. "Anna" in: TRE 2 (1978) 752. GALOT, J., "Riflessioni sul primo atto di fede cristiana, Maria, la prima credente" CiCa 129 (1978) 27-39. JEREMIAS, J., Die Sprache des Lukasevangeliums (Göttingen 1980) 54-55.

1:39ff. HAHN, F. Christologische Hoheitstitel (1963) 272.

1:39-56 NEIRYNCK, F., "Visitation B.M.V.—Bijdrage tot de Quellenkritik van Luc. 1-2", CollBrugGand 6 (3, 1960) 387-404. HARRINGTON, W. "The Visitation," DoLi 14 (7, 1964) 411-15. DIGNATH, W. Die lukanische Vorgeschichte (1971) 23-30. TALBERT, C. H., Literary Patterns, Theological Themes, and the Genre of Luke-Acts (Missoula 1974) 44, 45, 104, 105. SCHNEIDER, G., Das Evangelium nach Lukas (Gütersloh/Würzburg 1977) 54-55 (lit!).

1:39-50 LUZ, U. und WINTZER, F., in: P. Krusche et al. (eds) Predigtstudien für das Kirchenjahr 1976/1977, I/5 (Stuttgart 1976) 32-39.

1:39-55 BULTMANN, R. The History of the Synoptic Tradition (1963) 296f. WEBER, GPM (1964-1965) 21f. WEBER, O. Predigtmeditationen (1967) 303-07.

1:39-50 WEBER, O. GPM 19 (4, 1964) 21-26.

1:39-49 SCHMIDT, L. "Mein Geist freuet sich Gottes," in: Kleine Predigt-Typologie III (1965) Schmidt, L. (ed.) 228-32.

1:39-47 STECK, K. G. in: Hören und Fragen Bd. 5,2 (1967) G. Eichholz und A. Falkenroth (eds.) 29ff.

1;39-45 HAHN, F. Christologische Hoheitstitel (1963) 271₆. SCHÖRER, H. GPM 25 (4, 1970) 30-35. JACQUEMIN, P.-E. "La Visitation. Lc 1,39-45," AssS 8 (1972) 65-75. SWIDLER, L., Biblical Affirmations of Woman (Philadelphia 1979) 265.

1:39.65 SCHALIT, A. König Herodes (1969) 209.

1:39 HOSPODAR, B. "Meta Spoudes in Lk 1,39", CBQ 18 (1956) 14-18. PLASSMANN, T. "Cum Festinatione in Luke 1:39," AER 137 (4, 1957) 230-34. PALLIS, A., Notes on St. Luke and the Acts (London 1928) 5. METZGER, B. M., Early Versions of the New Testament (Oxford 1977) 92, JEREMIAS, J., Die Sprache des Lukasevangeliums (Göttingen 1980) 55-56.

1:40 DATTLER, F. "A Casa de Zacarias (Lc 1,40)," RCB 5 (10-11, 1968) 112-14.

1:41-50 SINT, J. A., "Mutter des Herrn" Am Tische des Wortes 4 (1965) 33-42.

1:41-48 HENNECKE, E./SCHNEEMELCHER, W. Neutestamentliche Apokryphen (1964) I 284f., 298.

1:41-45 SWIDLER, L., Biblical Affirmations of Woman (Philadelphia 1979) 300.

1:41-43 SWIDLER, L., Biblical Affirmations of Woman (Philadelphia 1979) 265.

1:41-42 GILLIÈRON, B., Le Saint-Esprit, actualitè du Christ. Ce qu'en ont dit Paul, Luc et Jean (Geneva 1978).

1:41 LAURENTIN, R. Struktur und Theologie der Lukanischen Kindheitsgeschichte (1967) 18, 43, 50f., 64, 70, 90, 92, 169f. NEIRYNCK, F., "La Matière Marcienne dans Luc" in; F. Neirynck (ed.) L'Evangile de Luc (Gembloux 1973) 184-91. TALBERT, C. H., Literary Patterns, Theological Themes, and the Genre of Luke-Acts (Missoula 1974) 105.

1:42-55 CREED, J. M. The Gospel According to St. Luke (1953) 303-07.

1:42 DAUBE, D. "Tria mystēria kraugēs: Ignatius, Ephesians, XIX. 1," JThS 16 (1, 1965) 128-29. LAURENTIN, R. Struktur und Theologie der Lukanischen Kindheitsgeschichte (1967) 41, 92, 94f, 98, 194. SCHENK, W. Der Segen im Neuen Testament (1967) 113-15. JEREMIAS, J., Die Sprache des Lukasevangeliums (Göttingen 1980) 57.

1:43 STANLEY, D. M. "The Mother of My Lord," Worship 34 (6, 1960) 330-32. HAHN, F. Christologische Hoheitstitel (1963) 88. LOHFINK, G., Die Sammlung Israels (München 1975) 19-20, 23. JEREMIAS, J., Die Sprache des Lukasevangeliums (Göttingen 1980) 57-58.

1:44 LAURENTIN, R. Struktur und Theologie der Lukanischen Kindheitsgeschichte (1967) 43, 51, 68, 70, 80, 92, 138, 170. JEREMIAS, J., Die Sprache des Lukasevangeliums (Göttingen 1980) 58-59.

1:45 PALLIS, A., Notes on St. Luke and the Acts (London 1928) 5-6. LAURENTIN, R. Struktur und Theologie der Lukanischen Kindheitsgeschichte (1967) 41, 51, 64, 96, 98, 168, 173. KLAIBER, W., "Eine lukanische Fassung des sola gratia. Beobachtungen zu Lk 1:5-56" in: J. Friedrich et al. (eds.) Rechfertigung. FS. E. Käsemann (Tübingen/Göttingen 1976) 218-19. JEREMIAS, J., Die Sprache des Lukasevangeliums (Göttingen 1980) 59.

1:46-2:32 SMITMANS, A. "Die Hymnen der Kindheitsgeschichte nach Lukas," BuK 21 (4, 1966) 115-18.

1:46ff. RENGSTORF, K. H. Das Evangelium nach Lukas (1949) 34f. KÜMMEL, W. G. Einleitung in das Neue Testament (1973) 105f. ROETS, A. "Het geloofsfiat van Maria" Mary's fiat of faith, CollBrugGand 3 (1957) 289-307.

1:46-79 FLOOD, E. "The Magnificat and Benedictus," C1R 51 (3, 1966) 205-10.

1:46-55, 68-79 WINTER, P. "Magnificat and Benedictus-Maccabaean Psalms?"
BJRL 37/1 (1954) 328-47.

1:46-56 MARTINDALE, C. C. "The Magnificat", Worship 20 (1956) 140-
42.

1:46-55 KÖSTLIN, H. A., "Das Magnifikat Lk 1:46-55, Lobesang der
Maria oder der Elisabeth?" ZNW 3 (1902) 142. HARNACK, A.
von, Studien zur Geschichte des Neuen Testaments und der Alten
Kirche (1931) 62ff. SAHLIN, H. Der Messias und das Gottesvolk
(1945) 159-75. HEIM, K. Der unerschütterliche Grund (1946) 12.
LOEWENICH, W. von, Luther als Ausleger der Synoptiker (1954)
256f. KOONTZ, J. V. G. "Mary's Magnificat," BiblSA 116 (464,
1959) 336-49. LEUENBERGER, E. Das Magnificat. Eine evan-
gelische Betrachtung des Lobgesanges der Maria (1960). FORES-
TELL, J. T. "Old Testament Background of the Magnificat,"
MarSt 12 (1961) 205-44. SULLIVAN, K. "His Lowly Maid,"
Worship 36 (6, 1962) 374-79. Verkündigt das angenehme Jahr des
Herrn. Predigtgedanken aus Vergangenheit und Gegenwart, Reihe
C, Bd. 1 (1962) 54ff. KRUSCHE, GPM (1962/1963) 25ff.
SQUILLACI, D. "I cantici del Nuovo Testamento," P1C1 42
(Aug. 1-15, 1963) 805-13. WILDER, A. N. The Language of the
Gospel (1964) 112f. FENASSE, J.-M. "La force et las faiblesse
dans la Bible. Comment la Bible chemine vers le Magnificat,"
BibTerreSainte 71 (1965) 6-7. SCHNACKENBURG, R. "Das
Magnificat, seine Spiritualität und Theologie," GuL 38 (5, 1965)
342-57. BRAUN, H. Qumran und NT II (1966) 242, 246, 291.
BENKO, S. "The Magnificat: A History of the Controversy," JBL
86 (3, 1967) 263-75. NICKELS, P. Targum and New Testament
(1967) 28. LUTHER, M., Das Magnifikat. Vorlesung über den 1.
Johannesbrief (München/Hamburg 1968) 22-107. RAMARO-
SON, L. "Ad structuram cantici 'Magnificat' ", VerbDom 46 (1,
1968) 30-46. WINK, W. John the Baptist in the Gospel Tradition
(1968) 62-65. ROSCHINI, G. "Il 'Magnificat' cantico della Ver-
gine," Marianum 31 (2-4, 1969) 360-323. ANDRESEN, D. "Gott
übt Gewalt," in: Weihnachten heute gesagt (1970) H. Nitschke (ed.)
14-20. GASTON, L. No Stone on Another (1970) 255, 258, 260,
269-70. OTTO, G. Denken-um zu glauben (1970) 118-23.
SCHRÖER, H. "Weihnachten zwischen Depression und Repres-
sion," in: Weihnachten heute gesagt (1970) H. Nitsche (ed.) 132-
37. BJÖRK, S. et al., Valda Texter ur Nya Tstamentet (Stockholm
1972) 16-17. BONHOEFFER, D., Gesammelte Schriften 5
(München 1972) 489ff. JACQUEMIN, P.-E. "Le Magnificat. Lc
1,46-55," AssS 66 (1973) 28-40. SCHMIDT, P., "Maria in der
Sicht des Magnifikat" GuL 46 (1973) 417-30. MEZGER, M., in:
GPM 29 (1974) 26-30. TANNEHILL, R. C., "The Magnificat as

Poem" JBL 93 (1974) 263-75. CONZELMANN, H. und LIN-DEMANN, A., Arbeitsbuch zum Neuen Testament (Tübingen 1975) 109. GLÖCKNER, R., Die Verkündigung des Heils beim Evangelisten Lukas (Mainz 1975) 122ff, 211. SCHMIDT, P., "Maria und das Magnifikat. Maria im Heilshandeln Gottes im Alten und Neuen Gottesvolk" Catholica 29 (1975) 230-46. VOGELS, W., "Le Magnificat, Marie et Israël" ETh 6 (1975) 279-96. MONLOUBOU, L., La prière selon saint Luc. Recherche d'une Structure (Paris 1976). HAMEL, E., "La donna e la promozione della giustizia nel 'Magnificat' "RT (1977) 417-33. MÜLLER, H.-M. und WIESE, W., in: P. Krusche et al. (eds.) Predigtstudien für das Kirchenjahr 1978/1979. I/2 (Stuttgart 1978) 49-55. SCHOTTROFF, L., "Das Magnificat und die älteste Tradition über Jesus von Nazareth" EvTh 38 (1978) 289-313. "Armut" in: TRE 4 (1979) 78. BAILEY, K. E., "The Song of Mary: Vision of a New Exodus (Luke 1:46-55)" NESTThR 2 (1979) 29-35. SWIDLER, L, Biblical Affirmations of Woman (Philadelphia 1979) 266, 300. TRÈVES, M., "Le Magnificat et le Benedictur" CahCER 27 (1979) 105-10. DUPONT, J., "Le Magnificat comme discours sur Dieu" NRTh 102 (1980) 321-43. MALY, E. H., "Women and the Gospel of Luke" BThB 10 (1980) 99-104. MÍNGUEZ, D., "Poética generativa del Magnificat" Biblica 61 (1980) 55-77.

1:46-47 BARTINA, S. "Fuerza hifilica de la palabra 'Yahweh', en el Magnificat (Lc 1,46-47; Hab 3,18; Miq 7,7)" EstBi 22 (3-4, 1963) 363-66.

1:46 STROBEL, A. Untersuchungen zum Eschatologischen Verzögerungsproblem (1961) 284f. DAVIES, J. G. "The Ascription of the Magnificat to Mary," JThS 15 (2, 1964) 307-08. BLACK, M. An Aramaic Approach to the Gospels and Acts (1967) 129f. METZGER, B. M. "Explicit references in the works of Origen to variant readings in New Testament manuscripts," in: Historical and Literary Studies (1968) 95.

1:47 LAURENTIN, R. Struktur und Theologie der Lukanischen Kindheitsgeschichte (1967) 96f., 138, 143.

1:48f. MUSSNER, F. "Lk. 1,48f; 11,27f und die Anfänge der Marienverehrung in der Urkirche," Catholica 21 (4, 1967) 187-94.

1:48 LAURENTIN, R. Struktur und Theologie der Lukanischen Kindheitsgeschichte (1967) 17, 52, 96f., 111, 120f., 168, 176.

1:49-50 SEMMELROTH, O. " 'Grosses hat an mir getan der Mächtige. Sein Embarmen währt von Geschlecht zu Geschlecht'. Um die rechte Perspektive in der Marienverehrung," GuL 35 (2, 1962) 86-95.

1:49 SERRA, A. M., " 'Fecit mihi magna' (Lc 1,49a). Una formula comunitaria?" Marianum 40 (1978) 305-343.

1:50 STONEHOUSE, N. B. The Witness of Matthew and Mark to Christ (1944) 197. "Barmherzigkeit" in: TRE 5 (1980) 226. JEREMIAS, J., Die Sprache des Lukasevangeliums (Göttingen 1980) 60.

1:51-53 HAMEL, E., "Le Magnificat et le Renversement des Situations. Réflexion théologico-biblique" Gregorianum 60 (1979) 55-84.

1:51 SCHOONHEIM, P. L., "Der alttestamentliche Boden der Vokabel ὑπερήφανος Lukas I 51" NovT 8 (1966) 235-46. JEREMIAS, J., Die Sprache des Lukasevangeliums (Göttingen 1980) 60-61.

1:52-53 JEREMIAS, J., Die Sprache des Lukasevangeliums (Göttingen 1980) 61-62.

1:52 KÄSEMANN, E. Exegetische Versuche und Besinnungen (1964) I 78. LAURENTIN, R. Struktur und Theologie der Lukanischen Kindheitsgeschichte (1967) 17, 55, 97, 121f. RAYAN, S. The Holy Spirit; Heart of the Gospel and Christian Hope (New York 1978) 124-25.

1:53 MÖLLER, C. Von der Predigt zum Text (1970) 167-77. JEREMIAS, J. Die Sprache des Lukasevangeliums (Göttingen 1980) 62.

1:54-55 "Abraham" in; TRE 1 (1977) 376.

1:54 FRIEDRICHSEN, G. S. S. The Gothic Text of Luke in its Relation to the Codex Brixianus (f) and the Codex Palatinus (e). NTS 11 (1964-1965) 282f. LOHFINK, G., Die Sammlung Israels (München 1975) 25-27, 85, 91. "Barmherzigkeit" in: TRE 5 (1980) 226. JEREMIAS, J., Die Sprache des Lukasevangeliums (Göttingen 1980) 62.

1:55 JEREMIAS, J., Die Sprache des Lukasevangeliums (Göttingen 1980) 62.

1:56-64 SAHLIN, H. Der Messias und das Gottesvolk (1945) 65f., 152-158.

1:56 HENNECKE,E./SCHNEEMELCHER, W. Neutestamentliche Apokryphen (1964) I 285. JEREMIAS, J., Die Sprache des Lukasevangeliums (Göttingen 1980) 63-64.

1:57-2:52 TALBERT, C. H., Literary Patterns, Theological Themes, and the Genre of Luke-Acts (Missoula 1974) 44, 77.

1:57-80 TALBERT, C. H., Literary Patterns, Theological Themes, and the Genre of Luke-Acts (Missoula 1974) 78. SCHNEIDER, G., Das Evangelium nach Lukas (Gütersloh/Würzburg 1977) 59 (lit!). JEREMIAS, J., Die Sprache des Lukasevangeliums (Göttingen 1980) 77.

1:57-66 HAHN, F., Christologische Hoheitstitel (1963) 371. WINK, W.

John the Baptist in the Gospel Tradition (1968) 68-70. DES-
CAMPS, A. & DE HALLEUX, A. Mélanges Bibliques en hommage au R. P. Béda Rigaux (1970) 151-53, 166-67.

1:57-64 SWIDLER, L., Biblical Affirmations of Women (Philadelphia
1979) 268.

1:57, 58 DIGNATH, W. Die lukanische Vorgeschichte (1971) 30-41.

1:57 TALBERT, C. H., Literary Patterns, Theological Themes, and the
Genre of Luke-Acts (Missoula 1974) 44. JEREMIAS, J., Die
Sprache des Lukasevangeliums (Göttingen (1980) 64.

1:58 TALBERT, C. H., Literary Patterns, Theological Themes, and the
Genre of Luke-Acts (Missoula 1974) 44. "Barmherzigkeit" in: TRE
5 (1980) 226, 227. JEREMIAS, J., Die Sprache des Lukasevangeliums (Göttingen 1980) 64-65.

1:59-80 DIGNATH, W. Die lukanische Vorgeschichte (1971) 41-50.

1:59-64 TALBERT, C. H., Literary Patterns, Theological Themes, and the
Genre of Luke-Acts (Missoula 1974) 44, 78.

1:59 DELLING, G. Die Taufe im Neuen Testament (1963) 138. NEI-
RYNCK, F., "La Matière dans Luc" in: F. Neirynck (ed.) L'E-
vangile de Luc (Gembloux 1973) 184-91. METZGER, B. M., Early
Versions of the New Testament (Oxford 1977) 392. "Beschnei-
dung" in: TRE 5 (1980) 723. JEREMIAS, J., Die Sprache des
Lukasevangeliums (Göttingen 1980) 65.

1:60 SWIDLER, L., Biblical Affirmations of Woman (Philadelphia
1979) 265. JEREMIAS, J., Die Sprache des Lukasevangeliums
(Göttingen 1980) 65-67.

1:61 WINTER, P., "Zu Lukas 1:25, 61; 2:23" ZNW 46 (1955) 261.

1:62 FRIEDRICHSEN, G. W. S. "The Gothic Text of Luke in its Relation to the Codex Brixianus (f) and the Codex Palatinus (e)", NTS
11 (1964-1965) 282f. JEREMIAS, J., Die Sprache des Lukasevangeliums (Göttingen 1980) 67.

1:63 FRIEDRICHSEN, G. W. S. "The Gothic Text of Luke in its Relation to the Codex Brixianus (f) and the Codex Palatinus (e)", NTS
11 (1964-1965) 286f. NICKELS, P. Targum and New Testament
(1967) 28. JEREMIAS, J., Die Sprache des Lukasevangeliums
(Göttingen 1980) 67-70.

1:64 NICKELS, P. Targum and New Testament (1967) 28. SCHENK,
W. Der Segen im Neuen Testament (1967) 118f. JEREMIAS, J.,
Die Sprache des Lukasevangeliums (Göttingen 1980) 70.

1:65-66 SAHLIN, H. Der Messias und das Gottesvolk (1945) 175-77.
TALBERT, C. H., Literary Patterns, Theological Themes, and the
Genre of Luke Acts (Missoula 1974) 44.

1:65 JEREMIAS, J., Die Sprache des Lukasevangeliums (Göttingen 1980) 70-71.

1:66 KNOX, W. L. The Sources of the Synoptic Gospels II (1957) 40. LAURENTIN, R. Struktur und Theologie der Lukanischen Kindheitsgeschichte (1967) 34ff., 48, 50f., 111, 113. NICKELS, P. Targum and New Testament (1967) 28. FISCHER, U., Eschatologie und Jenseitserwartung im hellenistischen Diasporajudentum (Berlin 1978) 94. JEREMIAS, J., Die Sprache des Lukasevangeliums (Göttingen 1980) 71-72.

1:67-80 HAHN, F. Christologische Hoheitstitel (1963) 371.

1:67-79 GERTNER, M. "Midrashim in the New Testament," JSS 7 (1962) 267-92. Verkündigt das angenehme Jahr des Herrn, in: Predigtgedanken aus Vergangenheit und Gegenwart, Reihe C, Bd. 1 (1962) 9-24. HAHN, F. GPM (1962-1963) 6ff. MAURER, C. GPM 23/1 (1968-1969) 5-11. THYEN, H. Studien zur Sündenvergebung (1970) 143f. LINK, H.-G., in; GPM 29 (1974) 2-11.

1:67 GILLIÈRON, B., Le Saint-Esprit, actualité du Christ ce qu'en ont dit Paul, Luc et Jean (Geneva 1978).

1:68ff. KÜMMEL, W. G. Einleitung in das Neue Testament (1973) 105f.

1:68-80 BRAUN, H. Qumran und NT II (1966) 12, 20f., 39, 70, 76, 82, 90, 127, 162, 213, 311.

1:68-79 HARNACK, A. von, Studien zur Geschichte des Neuen Testaments und der Alten Kirche (1931) 80ff. SAHLIN, H. Der Messias und das Gottesvolk (1945) 286-306. GNILKA, J., "Der Hymnus des Zacharias," BZ 6 (2, 1962) 215-38. IWAND, H.J., in: Herr, tue meine Lippen auf, Bd. 3 (1964). G. Eichholz (ed.) 1ff. VIELHAUER, Ph. "Das Benedictus des Zacharias (Lk 1,68-79)," Aufsätze zum Neuen Testament (1965) 28-46. VANHOYE, A. NTS 12 (1965-1966) 382f. HAGGENMUELLER, O. "Der Lobgesang des Zacharias (Lk 1,68-79)," BuL 9 (1968) 249-60. WINK, W. John the Baptist in the Gospel Tradition (1968) 65-68. BURGER, C. Jesus als Davidssohn (1970) 128-32. WANKE, J., Die Emmauserzählung. Eine redaktionsgeschichtliche Untersuchung zu Lk 24, 13-35 (Leipzig 1973) 68. TALBERT, C. H., Literary Patterns, Theological Themes, and the Genre of Luke-Acts (Missoula 1974) 44, 80. CONZELMANN, H. und LINDEMANN, A., Arbeitsbuch zum Neuen Testament (Tübingen 1975) 109. GLÖCKNER, R., Die Verkündigung des Heils beim Evangelisten Lukas (Mainz 1975) 114, 122ff, 165, 211. DUNN, J. D. G., Unity and Diversity in the New Testament (London 1977) 132-33. AUFFRET, P., "Note sur la structure littéraire de Lc i.68-79" NTS 24 (1978) 248-58. SWIDLER, L., Biblical Affirmations of Woman (Philadelphia 1979) 165.

1:68-72 HAHN, F. Christologische Hoheitstitel (1963) 246f. KELLER-
MANN, U. Messias und Gesetz (1971) 102f.

1:68 LAURENTIN, R. Struktur und Theologie der Lukanischen Kindheitsgeschichte (1967) 35f., 48, 116. SCHENK, W. Der Segen im
Neuen Testament (1967) 102-107. MIKALSEN, T. "The Traditio-Historical Place of the Christology of 1 Peter in Light of 1:18-
21," (Rüschlikon 1971) 17ff. ZMIJEWSKI, J., Die Eschatologiereden des Lukas-Evangeliums (Bonn 1972) 117, 229, 232, 254.
GERLACH, W., in; P. Krusche et al. (eds.) Predigtstudien für das
Kirchenjahr 1976-1977, I/5 (Stuttgart 1976) 40-46. JEREMIAS, J.,
Die Sprache des Lukasevangeliums (Göttingen 1980) 73.

1:69 STONEHOUSE, N. B. The Witness of Matthew and Mark to Christ
(1944) 223. WILCKENS, U. Die Missionsreden der Apostelgeschichte (1961) 142, 161, 163, 167, 175, 184. LAURENTIN, R.
Struktur und Theologie der Lukanischen Kindheitsgeschichte (1967)
17, 19, 127ff., 143. RESE, M. Alttestamentliche Motive in der
Christologie des Lukas (1969) 179-80. WILCKENS, U., Die Missionsreden der Apostelgeschichte (Neukirchen 1974($_3$)) 143, 162,
164, 167, 176, 185. LOHFINK, G., Die Sammlung Israels
(München 1975) 17, 21, 27-28. JEREMIAS, J., Die Sprache des
Lukasevangeliums (Göttingen 1980) 73.

1:70 KNOX, W. L. The Sources of the Synoptic Gospels II (1957) 44.
FRIEDRICHSEN, G. W. S. "The Gothic Text of Luke in its Re-
lation to the Codex Brixianus (f) and the Codex Palatinus (e)", NTS
11 (1964-1965) 286f. LAURENTIN, R. Struktur und Theologie der
Lukanischen Kindheitsgeschichte (1967) 55, 86, 113, 134, 139.
NICKELS, P. Targum and New Testament (1967) 29. JE-
REMIAS, J., Die Sprache des Lukasevangeliums (Göttingen 1980)
73-74.

1:71 FRIEDRICHSEN, G. W. S. "The Gothic Text of Luke in its Relation to the Codex Brixianus (f) and the Codex Palatinus (e)", NTS
11, 1964-1965) 282f. JEREMIAS, J., Die Sprache des Lukasevangeliums (Göttingen 1980) 74.

1 72-73 "Abraham" in TRE 1 (1977) 379.

1:72 PALLIS, A., Notes on St. Luke and the Acts (London 1928) 6.
"Barmherzigkeit" in: TRE 5 (1980) 226.

1:73-79 VANHOYE, A. "Structure du 'Benedictus', " NTS 12 (4, 1966)
386-87.

1:73 METZGER, B. M., Early Versions of the New Testament (Oxford
1977) 202. JEREMIAS, J., Die Sprache des Lukasevangeliums
(Göttingen 1980) 74-75.

1:74-77 JEREMIAS, J., Die Sprache des Lukasevangeliums (Göttingen
1980) 75-76.

1:74 PALLIS, A., Notes on St. Luke and the Acts (London 1928) 6.

1:75 FRIEDRICHSEN, G. W. S. "The Gothic Text of Luke in its Relation to the Codex Brixianus (f) and the Codex Palatinus (e)'', NTS 11 (1964-1965) 286f. "Abraham" in: TRE 1 (1977) 379.

1:76-79 HAHN, F. Christologische Hoheitstitel (1963) 372-74. WINTER, P. NTS 10 (1963-1964) 524f. SNODGRASS, K. R., "Streams of Tradition emerging from Isaiah 40:1-5 and their adaptation in the New Testament" JSNT 8 (1980) 24-45.

1:76 LAURENTIN, R. Struktur und Theologie der Lukanischen Kindheitsgeschichte (1967) 36, 44f., 47ff., 66f., 99, 126f., 138, 145, 150, 154. RESE, M. Alttestamentliche Motive in der Christologie des Lukas (1969) 180-181. KRÄNKEL, E. Jesus der Knecht Gottes (1972) 92, 94f. SCHNIDER, F., Jesus der Prophet (Freiburg 1973) 39, 41, 42, 53. TALBERT, C. H. Literary Patterns, Theological Themes, and the Genre of Luke-Acts (Missoula 1974) 104.

1:77 PALLIS, A. Notes on St. Luke and the Acts (London 1928) 6-7. SAHLIN, H. Der Messias und das Gottesvolk (1945) 385f. FLEW, R. N. Jesus and His Church (1956) 95. LAURENTIN, R. Struktur und Theologie der Lukanischen Kindheitsgeschichte (1967) 36, 55, 67, 116, 143, 155. STROBEL, A. Erkenntnis und Bekenntnis der Sünde in neutestamentlicher Zeit (1968) 41. 6-7. BERGMEIER, R. Glaube als Gabe nach Johannes (Stuttgart 1980) 120.

1:78f. RESE, M. Alttestamentlich Motive in der Christologie des Lukas (1969) 181-83.

1:78 VOLZ, P, Die Eschatologie der Jüdischen Gemeinde (1934) 165, 210. BOUSSET, W. Die Religion des Judentums in Späthellenistischen Zeitalter (1966 = 1926) 265. "Barmherzigkeit" in: TRE 5 (1980) 226. JEREMIAS, J., Die Sprache des Lukasevangeliums (Göttingen 1980) 76.

1:78b LAMBERTZ, M. "Sprachliches aus Septuaginta und Neuen Testament," Wissenschaftliche Zeitschrift der Karl-Marx-Universität 1/3 (1952-1953) 79-87.

1:79 JEREMIAS, J., Die Sprache des Lukasevangeliums (Göttingen 1980) 76.

1:80 SAHLIN, H. Der Messias und das Gottesvolk (1945) 177-82. GEYSER, A. S. "The youth of John the Baptist; a deduction from the break in the parallel account of the Lucan infancy story," NovTest 1 (1956) 70-75. DELLING, G. Die Taufe im Neuen Testament (1963) 52. HAHN, F. Christologische Hoheitstitel (1963) 318. LAURENTIN, R. Struktur und Theologie der Lukanischen Kindheitsgeschichte (1967) 33, 35, 50f., 112, 116, 161, 186. PETZKE, G. Die Traditionen über Apollonius von Tyana und das Neue Testament (1970) 78, 168. TALBERT, C. H., Literary Patterns, Theological Themes, and the Genre of Luke-Acts (Missoula 1974) 44. ZINGG, P., Das Wachsen der Kirche (Freiburg 1974) 40-59. JEREMIAS, J., Die Sprache des Lukasevangeliums (Göttingen 1980) 76-77.

—————————

2 NESTLE, E., "Die Schätzung in Lukas 2 und Psalm 87 (86), 6" ZNW 11 (1910) 87. NUGENT, E. P. "The Closed Womb of the Blessed Mother of God," EphM 8 (1958) 249-70. FLENDER, H. Heil und Geschichte in der Theologie des Lukas (1965) 56-58. BRAUN, H. Qumran und NT II (1966) 19, 24, 107, 242, 246. BLACK, M. An Aramaic Approach to the Gospels and Acts (1967) 62f. KELLERMANN, U. Messias und Gesetz (1971) 55. DAVIES, W. D., The Gospel and the Land (London 1974) 261-65. TALBERT, C. H., Literary Patterns, Theological Themes, and the Genre of Luke-Acts (Missoula 1974) 78. CONZELMANN, H. und LINDEMANN, A., Arbeitsbuch zum Neuen Testament (Tübingen 1975) 42. BROWN, R. E., An Adult Christ at Christmas. Essays on the Three Biblical Christmas Stories (Collegeville 1978). SWIDLER, L., Biblical Affirmations of Woman (Philadelphia 1979) 262. GERSTENBERGER, E. S. und SCHRAGE, W. Frau and Mann (Stuttgart 1980) 161-62. GLOBE, A., "Some Doctrinal Variants in Matthew 1 and Luke 2, and the Authority of the Neutral Text" CBQ 42 (1980) 52-72.

2:1ff. HAHN, F. Christologische Hoheitstitel (1963) 275. PETZKE, G. Die Traditionen über Apollonius von Tyana und das Neue Testament (1970) 138, 162, 164.

2:1-52 HIRSCH, E. Frühgeschichte des Evangeliums (1941) 171-92.

2:1-38 SAHLIN, H. Der Messias und das Gottesvolk (1945) 66-68, 190-286. BISHOP, E. F. F. "Bethlehem and the Nativity: Some Travesties of Christmas," AThR 46 (4, 1964) 401-13.

2:1-25 STREETER, B. H. The Four Gospels (1951) 582f.

2:1-21 HARRINGTON, W. "The Nativity in St. Luke," DoLi 13 (12, 1963) 618-22.

2:1-20 DIBELIUS, M. Botschaft und Geschichte I (1953) 1-78. VOGEL, H. in: Herr, tue meine Lippen auf Bd. 1 (1957) Eichholz, G. (ed.) 20-34. RENGSTORF, K. H. "Die Weihnachtserzählung des Evangeslisten Lukas," in: Stat Crux Dum Volvitur Orbis. Festschrift D. H. Lilje (1959) 15-30. FUCHS, E. "Das Weihnachtsevangelium," Zur Frage nach dem historischen Jesus. Gesammelte Aufsätze II (1960) 431-35. GRUNDMANN, W. Das Evangelium nach Lukas (1961) 76-79. HASPECKER, J., "Is 9,1-6 -ein prophetisches Weihnachtslied?" BuL 3 (4, 1962) 249-57. BRINKMAN, B. R. "The First-Born of all Creation," The Way 2 (4, 1962) 261-71. HOWELL, C. "The Mystery of Advent," The Way 2 (4, 1962) 243-53. McCarthy, D. J. "The Fulfillment of the Promise," The Way 2 (4, 1962) 254-60. REIDY, G. "You Will Find a Child," The Way 2 (4, 1962) 289-300. WALSH, J. "A Virgin Shall Conceive," The Way 2 (4, 1962) 282-88. YEOMANS, W. "Sharers of the Divine Nature," The Way 2 (4, 1962) 272-81. BAILY, M. "The Crib and Exegesis of Luke 2,1-20," IrEccRec 100 (6, 1963) 359-76. BULTMANN, R. The History of the Synoptic Tradition (1963) 297-99. GEORGE, A., "La naissance du Christ Seigneur," AssS 10 (1963) 44-57. HAHN, F. Christologische Hoheitstitel (1963) 268, 269-73. BAILY, M. "The Shepherds and the Sign of a Child in a Manger," IThQ 31 (1, 1964) 1-23. McKENZIE, J. L. "Exegete at the Manger," Commonweal 81 (1964) 439-42. MERTON, T. "The Good News of the Nativity. A Monastic Reading of the Christmas Gospels," Bible Today 1 (21, 1965) 1367-75. VÖGTLE, A. "Die Geburt der Erlösers," BuL 7 (4, 1966) 235-42. GIBLIN, C. H. "Reflections on the Sign of the Manger," CBQ (1, 1967) 87-101. OTTO, G. Handbuch des Religions-Unterrichts (1967) 230-55. KAMPHAUS, F. Von der Exegese zur Predigt (1968) 222-26, 259-79. AHNE, L. "Vom Anbruch des Menschheitsfrühlings," in: Weihnachten heute gesagt (1970) H. Nitschke (ed.) 9-13. BURGER, C. Jesus als Davidssohn (1970) 135-37. MARTI, K. "Wir können uns nicht mehr auf Engel verlassen," in: Weihnachten heute gesagt (1970) H. Nitschke (ed.) 96-98. OTTO, G. Denken-um zu glauben (1970) 102-06. DIGNATH, W. Die lukanische Vorgeschichte (1971) 30-41, 94-101. WESTERMANN, C. "Alttestamentliche Elemente in Lukas 2,1-20," in: Tradition und Glaube (1971) G. Jeremias (ed.) 317-27. ACHTEMEIER, E. The Old Testament and the Proclamation of the Gospel (1973) 165ff. SCHMITHALS, W., "Die Weihnachtsgeschichte Lukas 2,1-20" in: G. Ebeling et al. (eds.) Festschrift für E. Fuchs (Tübingen 1973) 281-97. WESTERMANN, C., "Alttestamentliche Elemente in Lukas 2:1-20 [orig: Tradition und Glaube (Göttingen 1971) 317-27] in: R. Albertz/E. Ruprecht (eds.) Forschung am Alten Testament II (München 1974). BROWN, R. E., "The Meaning of the Manger; the Significance of the Shepherds" Worship 50 (1976) 528-38. CHEVALLIER, M.-A., "L'Analyse litéraire des textes du Nouveau Testament (Conseils aux étudiants)" RHPR 57 (1977) 367-78. SCHNEIDER, G., Das Evangelium nach Lukas (Gütersloh/Würzburg 1977) 64 (lit!). VÖGTLE, A., Was Weihnachten bedeutet. Meditation zu Lukas 2,1-20 (Freiburg/Basel/Wien 1977). SCHRAGE, W., "Was fällt dem Exegeten zu Weihnachten ein?" Der Evangelische Erzieher 31 (Frankfurt 1979) 338-44. JEREMIAS, J., Die Sprache des Lukasevangeliums (Göttingen 1980) 88-99.

2:1-14 HAMEL, GPM (1960-1961) 24ff. Verkündigt das angeneme Jahr des Herrn. Predigtgedanken aus Vergangenheit und Gegenwart, Reihe C,Bd. 1 (1962) 74ff. FUCHS, GPM (1962-1963) 32ff. LUTHER, M. Predigten über die Christus-Botschaft (1966) 55-62. RIEDL, J. "Gottes Herrlichkeit-Des Menschen Glück. Biblische Gedanken zur lukanischen Weihnachtsbotschaft," BuLit 38 (6, 1966) 341-50. RIEDL, J. "La gloria de Dios-y la dicha sin fin del hombre. Pensamientos Biblicos en torno al Mensaje de Navidad segun San Lucas," RevBi 29 (5, 1967) 103-205. FÜRST, W. in: Hören und Fragen Bd. 5,3 (1967) G. Eichholz & A. Falkenroth (eds.) 42ff. WEBER, O. Predigtmeditationen (1967) 218-22. KOCH, G. GPM 23/1 (1968-1969) 31-37. PESCH, W. Den Menschen helfen (1969) 12-18. FISCHER, K. M. GPM 25 (4, 1970) 35-45. LANGE, E. (ed.) Predigtstudien für das Kirchenjahr 1970-1971. Perikopenreihe V (1970) 49-55. REVENTLOW, H. G. GPM 27/1 (1972-1973) 32-38. CASALIS, G., in: GPM 29 (1974) 30-36. SEIM, J., in: GPM 31 (1976-1977) 32-36.

2:1-8 McGrath, B. " 'He Came All So Still'," Bible Today 1, (9, 1963) 580-85.

2:1-7 ROBERTSON, A. T. Luke the Historian in the Light of Research (1920) 118, 120, 124, 126, 127, 129, 132. LEE, G. M. "The Census in Luke," ChurchQuartRev 167 (365, 1966) 431-36. EVANS, C. F. "Tertullian's References to Sentius Saturninus and the Lukan Census," JThS 24 (1, 1973) 24-39. TALBERT, C. H., Literary Patterns, Theological Themes, and the Genre of Luke-Acts (Missoula 1974) 44. CLARK, K. W., "The Theological Relevance of Textual Variation in Current Criticism of the Greek New Testament" in: The Gentile Bias and Other Essays (Leiden 1980) 116.

2:1-5 STAUFFER, E. "Die Dauer des Census Augusti-Neue Beiträge zum lukanischen Schatzbericht," in: Studien zum Neuen Testament und zur Patristik. Festschrift für E. Klostermann (1961) Kommission für spätantike Religionsgeschichte (eds.) 9-35. HAYLES, D. J. "The Roman Census & Jesus' Birth. Was Luke Correct? Part 1: The Roman Census System," Buried History 9 (4, 1973) 113-32. BARNETT, P. W., "*apographē* and *apographesthai* in Luke 2:1-5" ET 85 (1974) 377-80. HAYLES, D. J., "The Roman Census and Jesus' Birth. Was Luke Correct? Part II: Quirinius' Career and a Census in Herod's Day'' Buried History 10 (1974) 16-31.

2:1-3 DRURY, J., Tradition and Design in Luke's Gospel (Atlanta 1976) 189-90.

2:1-2 SCHALIT, A. König Herodes (1969) 276, 281. MOEHRING, H. R. ''The Census in Luke as an Apologetic Device,'' in: Studies in New Testament and Early Christian Literature (1972) D. E. Aune (ed.) 144-60. SHERWIN-WHITE, A. N., Roman Society and Roman Law in the New Testament (Grand Rapids 1978) 163-64, 167. THORLEY, J., ''The Nativity Census: What Does Luke Actually Say?'' Greece and Rome 26 (Oxford 1979) 81-84. SCHRECK-ENBERG, H., ''Flavius Josephus und die lukanischen Schriften'' in: W. Haubeck/M. Bachmann (eds.) Wort in der Zeit. FS K. H. Rengstorf (Leiden 1980) 182-86.

2:1 HENNECKE, E./SCHNEEMELCHER, W. Neutestamentliche Apokryphen (1964) I 285. NEIRYNCK, F., ''La Matière Marcienne dans Luc'' in: F. Neirynck (ed.) L'Evangile de Luc (Gembloux 1973) 184-91. CONZELMANN, H. und LINDEMANN, A., Arbeitsbuch zum Neuen Testament (Tübingen 1975) 141, 331. HORTON, F. L., ''Reflections on the Semitisms of Luke-Acts'' in: C. H. Talbert (ed.) Perspectives on Luke-Acts (Danville 1978) 9-10, 22. JEREMIAS, J., Die Sprache des Lukasevangeliums (Göttingen 1980) 77-78.

2:2-4 BARTINA, S. ''Orden censal de Gayo Vibio Maximo,'' CultBib 17 (171, 1960) 96-101.

2:2 KLOSTERMANN, E. Das Lukasevangelium (1929) 32-34. RENGSTORF, K. H. Das Evangelium nach Lukas (1949) 38f. SCHMID, J., Das Evangelium nach Lukas (1955) 66-70. FRIEDRICHSEN, G. W. S. NTS 11 (1964-1965) 282f. OGG, G. ''The Quirinius Question Today,'' ET 79 (8, 1968) 231-36. CONZELMANN, H. und LINDEMANN, A., Arbeitsbuch zum Neuen Testament (Tübingen 1975) 145.

2:3 JEREMIAS, J., Die Sprache des Lukasevangeliums (Göttingen 1980) 78.

2:4 STONEHOUSE, N. B. The Witness of Matthew and Mark to Christ (1944) 223. LUSSIER, E. ''Bethlehem,'' Bible Today 1, (3, 1962) 158-63. LAURENTIN, R. Struktur und Theologie der Lukanischen Kindheitsgeschichte (1967) 17f., 40, 93, 100f., 116. JEREMIAS, J., Die Sprache des Lukasevangeliums (Göttingen 1980) 78-79. KRAFT, H., Die Entstehung des Christentums (Darmstadt 1981) 76-86.

2:5 BRINKMANN, B. ''Die Jungfrauengeburt und das Lukasevangelium,'' Biblica 34 (1953) 327-32.

2:6 NICKELS, P. Targum and New Testament (1967) 29. NEI-
RYNCK, F., "La Matière Marcienne dans Luc" in: F. Neirynck
(ed.) L'Evangile de Luc (Gembloux 1973) 184-191. METZGER,
B. M., Early Versions of the New Testament (Oxford 1977) 249.

2:7.12.16 DERRETT, J. D. M. "The Manger: Ritual Law and Soteriology,"
Theology 74 (618, 1971) 566-71.

2:7 BLASS, F. Philosophy of the Gospels (1898) 165ff. MIGUENS,
M. " 'In una mangiatoia, perchè non c' era posto . . . '," BiblOr
2 (6, 1960) 193-98. MULDER, H. "Geen plaats in de herberg, Luc.
2:7", HomBib 21 (11, 1962) 246-48. SIEBENECK, R. "Her First-
Born Son," Bible Today 1 (3, 1962) 194-200. HENNECKE, E./
SCHNEEMELCHER, W. Neutestamentliche Apokryphen (1964)
I 128, 289. PAX, E. " 'Denn sie fanden keinen Platz in der Her-
berge.' Jüdisches and frühchristliches Herbergswesen," BuL 6 (4,
1965) 285-98. DALMAN, G. Orte und Wege Jesu (1967) 44f., 47f.
LAURENTIN, R. Struktur und Theologie der Lukanischen Kind-
heitsgeschichte (1967) 17, 70, 118, 120, 128, 179. BLINZLER,
J., Die Brüder und Schwestern Jesu (Stuttgart 1967) 55-61. BE-
NOIT, P., "Non erat eis locus in diversoiro (Luc 2,7)" in: A. Des-
camps/A. de Halleux (eds.) Mélanges Bibliques en hommage au R.
P. Béda Rigaux (Gembloux 1970) 173-86. OBERLINNER, L.,
Historische Überlieferung und christologische Aussage (Stuttgart
1975) 57-61. BAILEY, K. E., "The Manger and the Inn: The Cul-
tural Background of Luke 2:7" NESTThR 2 (1979) 33-44. JE-
REMIAS, J., Die Sprache des Lukasevangeliums (Göttingen 1980)
79-80.

2:8-20 MERCURIO, R. "The Shepherds at the Crib—A Lucan Vi-
gnette," Bible Today 1 (3, 1962) 140-45. MURPHY, R. T. A. "On
Shepherds," Bible Today 1 (15, 1964) 986-91. SCHILLE, G.
Frühchristliche Hymnen (1965) 138f. LEGRAND, L. "L'Evan-
gile aux Bergers. Essai sur le genre littéraire de Luc, II,8-20,"
RevBi 75 (2, 1968) 161-87. TALBERT, C. H., Literary Patterns,
Theological Themes, and the Genre of Luke-Acts (Missoula 1974)
44. HUBBARD, B. J., "Commissioning Stories in Luke-Acts: A
Study of their Antecedents, Form and Content" Semeia 8 (1977)
103-26. HUBBARD, B. J., "The Role of Commissioning Ac-
counts in Acts" in: C. H. Talbert (ed.) Perspectives on Luke-Acts
(Danville 1978) 190.

2:8-15 RENGSTORF, K.H. Das Evangelium nach Lukas (1949) 42-44.

2:8-14 FLENDER, H. St Luke Theologian of Redemptive History (1967)
57ff.

2:8-9 HORTON, F. L., "Reflections on the Semitisms of Luke-Acts"
in: C. H. Talbert (ed.) Perspectives on Luke-Acts (Danville 1978)
3-4.

2:8 LAURENTIN, R. Struktur und Theologie der Lukanischen Kind-
heitsgeschichte (1967) 22, 99ff., 121, 124, 194. METZGER, B.
M., Early Versions of the New Testament (Oxford 1977) 179.
"Bethlehem" in: TRE 5 (1980) 759.

2:9-10 BETZ, H. D. Lukian von Samosata und das Neue Testament (1961)
55, 57, 105.

2:9 HAHN, F. Christologische Hoheitstitel (1963) 271. LAUREN-
TIN, R. Struktur und Theologie der Lukanischen Kindheitsgeschichte (1967) 48, 122, 124, 154, 158. NICKELS, P. Targum and
New Testament (1967) 29. METZGER, B. M., Early Versions of
the New Testament (Oxford 1977) 143. JEREMIAS, J., Die Sprache
des Lukasevangeliums (Göttingen 1980) 80-81.

2:10-11 GASTON, L. No Stone on Another (1970) 271-73, 276, 297.

2:10 NICKELS, P. Targum and New Testament (1967) 29. STROBEL,
A. Erkenntnis und Bekenntnis der Sünde in neutestamentlicher Zeit
(1968) 41. OTTO, G. Denken-um zu glauben (1970) 64-68. WIL-
SON, S. G., The Gentiles and the Gentile Mission in Luke-Acts
(Cambridge 1973) 34-35, 48, 51, 53, 61. JEREMIAS, J., Die
Sprache des Lukasevangeliums (Göttingen 1980) 81.

2:11-12 REHN, M. Der Königliche Messias (1968) 36f.

2:11 STONEHOUSE, N. B. The Witness of Matthew and Mark to Christ
(1944) 223. SAHLIN, H. Der Messias und das Gottesvolk (1945)
383-85. BARRETT, C. K. The New Testament Background: Selected Documents (1956) 250. WILCKENS, U. Die Missionsreden
der Apostelgeschichte (1961) 151, 172, 176-76. HAHN, F. Christologische Hoheitstitel (1963) 88, 208, 224. LAURENTIN, R.
Struktur und Theologie der Lukanischen Kindheitsgeschichte (1967)
17, 48, 55, 60, 67, 71, 78, 100f., 121, 123, 127, 144-48, 154. VAN
DEN HUEVEL, A. "Heiliger Abend: Lukas 2,11," in: Predigtstudien Perikopenreihe I (1972-1973) Lange, E. (ed.) 44-49. PAL-
LIS, A., Notes on St. Luke and the Acts (London 1928) 7.
GLÖCKNER, R., Die Verkündigung des Heils beim Evangelisten
Lukas (Mainz 1975) 118ff, 201, 218. DRURY, J., Tradition and
Design in Luke's Gospel (Atlanta 1976) 70-71. BUSSE, U., Das
Nazareth-Manifest Jesu. Eine Einführung in das lukanische Jesus-
bild nach Lk 4,16-30 (Stuttgart 1978) 70. JEREMIAS, J., Die
Sprache des Lukasevangeliums (Göttingen 1980) 81.

2:12 DALMAN, G. Orte und Wege Jesu (1967) 44f. LOEWENICH, v.
"Zeichen des Friedens," in: Weihnachten heute gesagt (1970) H.
Nitschke (ed.) 74-77. METZGER, B. M., Early Versions of the
New Testament (Oxford 1977) 177. JEREMIAS, J., Die Sprache
des Lukasevangeliums (Göttingen 1980) 81-83.

2:13-22 HAAR, GPM (1960-1961) 305ff.

2:13-14 STAEHELIN, E. Die Verkündigung des Reiches Gottes in der Kirche Jesu Christi I (1951) 66. WESTERMANN, C., "Alttestamentliche Elemente in Lukas 2:1-20" [orig: Tradition und Glaube (Göttingen 1971) 317-27] in: R. Albertz/E. Ruprecht (eds.) Forschung am Alten Testament II München 1974) 274-78.

2:13 NICKELS, P. Targum and New Testament (1967) 29. METZGER, B. M., Early Versions of the New Testament (Oxford 1977) 84. TRITES, A. A., The New Testament Concept of Witness (London 1977) 128-29. JEREMIAS, J., Die Sprache des Lukasevangeliums (Göttingen 1980) 83.

2:14 JEREMIAS, J. ZNW 28 (1929) 13-20. VON RAD, G. ZNW 29 (1930) 111-15. HARNACK, A. von, Studien zur Geschichte des Neuen Testaments und der Alten Kirche (1931) 153ff. VOLZ, P. Die Eschatologie der jüdischen Gemeinde (1934) 394. STAEHELIN, E. Die Verkündigung des Reiches Gottes in der Kirche Jesu Christi I (1951) 258. HUNZINGER, C.-H. "Neues Licht auf Lk 2:14," ZNW 44 (1952-1953) 85-90. VOGT, E. "Pax hominibus bonae voluntatis Lc 2,14," Biblica 34 (1953) 427-29. KRAGERUD, A. "Einzugshymnus und Engelgesang," NTT (1956) 218-34. FITZMYER, J. A. " 'Peace upon Earth among Men of His Good Will' (Lk. 2:14)," ThSt 19 (2, 1958) 225-227. HUNZINGER, C.-H. "Ein Weiterer Beleg zu Lc 2:14 anthropoi eudokias," ZNW 49 (1-2, 1958) 129-30. KAHMANN, J. "De 'mensen van goaden wil' in Lucas 2,14",NedKathStem 65 (12, 1959) 353-57. F. V., "Pax hominibus bonae voluntatis," RivB 7 (4, 1959) 369-70. DEICHGRAEBER, R. "Lc 2:14: anthrōpoi eudokias," ZNW 51 (1-2, 1960) 132. DOEVE, J. W. "De 'ere Gods' in de engelenzang (Luc 2:14)", HomBib 20 (6, 1961) 177-83. KÖRBET, R. "Sabrâ tabâ im syrischen Tatian Luc. 2,14," Biblica 42 (1, 1961) 90-91. FLUSSER, D. "Sanktus und Gloria," in: Abraham unser Vater. Festschrift f. O. Michel (1963) 129-52. BISHOP, E. F. F. "Men of God's Good Pleasure," AThR 48 (1, 1966) 63-69. BRAUN, H. Qumran und NT II (1966) 104. McNAMARA, M. The New Testament and the Palestinian Targum to the Pentateuch (1966) 136 fn.35, 204 fn.45a. KARAVIDOPULOS, J., "Eine Auslegung der Stelle Luk 2:14" GregPa 50 (1967) 470-75. LAURENTIN, R. Struktur und theologie der Lukanischen Kindheitsgeschichte (1967) 18, 59, 118, 138. NICKELS, P. Targum and New Testament (1967) 29. GASTON, L. No Stone on Another (1970) 246, 258, 272-73, 276, 336. KLAWEK, A., "Der Hymnus der Engel" RBL 22 (1970) 65-72. FITZMYER, J. A. Essays on the Semitic Background of the New Testament (1971) 101-04. SCHWARZ, G. "Der Lobgesang der Engel (Lukas, 2,14)," BZ 15 (2, 1971) 260-64. FEUILLET, A., "Les hommes de bonne volonté ou les hommes que Dieu aime. Note sur la traduction de Luc 2,14b'' Bulletin de l'association Guilllaume Budé 4 (1974) 91-92. MINEAR, P., To Heal and To Reveal (New York 1976) 50. DUNN, J. D. G., Unity and Diversity in the New Testament (London 1977) 133. HANSACK, E., ''Luk 2,14: 'Friede den Menschen auf Erden, die guten Willens sind? Ein Beitrag zur Übersetzungstechnik der Vulgata'' BZ 21 (1977) 117-18. METZGER, B. M., Early Versions of the New Testament (Oxford 1977) 41, 208, 330. MUELLER, T., ''An Application of Case Grammar to Two New Testament Passages'' CThQ 43 (1979) 320-25. SWIDLER, L., Biblical Affirmations of Women (Philadelphia 1979) 284. JEREMIAS, J., Die Sprache des Lukasevangeliums (Göttingen 1980) 83-84.

2:15-20 TRILLHAAS, GPM 4 (1949-1950) 32ff. Predigtgedanken aus Vergangenheit und Gegenwart, Reihe A, Bd. 1 (1960) 153-72. TRAUB, GPM 15 (1960-1961) 29ff. DOERNE, M. Er kommt auch noch heute (1961) 22-24. KRUSE, M. GPM 27/1 (1972/73) 38-42. NEDDEN-AMSLER, B. T. und SKRIVER, J., in: P Krusche et al. (eds.) Predigtstudien für das Kirchenjahr 1978-1979. I/2 (Stuttgart 1978) 63-71. SWIDLER, L., Biblical Affirmations of Woman (Philadelphia 1979) 269.

2:15 ADLER, N. Das erste christliche Pfingstfest (1938) 33f. HAHN, F. Christologische Hoheitstitel (1963) 271. LAURENTIN, R. Struktur und Theologie der Lukanischen Kindheitsgeschichte (1967) 48, 51, 108, 118. NICKELS, P. Targum and New Testament (1967) 29. PALLIS, A., Notes on St. Luke and the Acts (London 1928) 7. NEIRYNCK, F., ''La Matière Marcienne dans Luc'' in: F. Neirynck (ed.) L'Evangile de Luc (Gembloux 1973) 184-91. METZGER, B. M., Early Versions of the New Testament (Oxford 1977) 212. JEREMIAS, J., Die Sprache des Lukasevangeliums (Güttingen 1980) 84-85.

2:16-22 STREETER, B. H. The Four Gospels (1951) 205f. CLARK, K. W., ''The Theological Relevance of Textual Variants in Current Criticsm of the Greek New Testament'' in: The Gentile Bias and Other Essays (Leiden 1980) 116.

2:16 WULF, F. '' 'Sie fanden Maria und Josef und das Kind, das in der Krippe lag' (Lk 2,16),'' GuL 31 (6, 1958) 401-03. LOHFINK, G. ''Weihnachten und die Armut,'' GuL 35 (6, 1962) 401-05. TRILLHAAS, W. ''Die heilige Familie,'' in: Kleine Predigt-Typologie III (1965) L. Schmidt (ed.) 70-83. LAURENTIN, R. Struktur und Theologie der Lukanischen Kindheitsgeschichte (1967) 17, 23, 40, 51, 121, 138, 170. NICKELS, P. Targum und New Testament (1967) 29. JEREMIAS, J., Die Sprache des Lukasevangeliums (Göttingen 1980) 85.

2:17-18 TALBERT, C. H., Literary Patterns, Theological Themes, and the Genre of Luke-Acts (Missoula 1974) 44.

2:17 JEREMIAS, J., Die Sprache des Lukasevangeliums (Göttingen 1980) 86.

2:18 JAENICKE, T. "Sehet dies Wunder," in: Weihnachten heute gesagt (1970) H. Nitschke (ed.) 55-58. JEREMIAS, J., Die Sprache des Lukasevangeliums (Göttingen 1980) 86.

2:19.51 NEIRYNCK, F. " 'Maria bewaarde al de woorden in haar hart.' Lk. 2,19.51 in hun context verklaard",CollBrugGand 5 (4, 1959) 433-66. MEYER, B. F., " 'But Mary Kept All These Things . . . ' (Lk 2,19.51)," CBQ 26 (1, 1964) 31-49. SERRA, A. "Motivi sapienziali in Lc. 2,19.51," Marianum 31 (2-4, 1969) 248-59.

2:19 PALLIS, A. Notes on St. Luke and the Acts (London 1928) 7-8. LAURENTIN, R. Struktur und Theologie der Lukanischen Kindheitsgeschichte (1967) 22, 33, 37, 108, 113, 118. NICKELS, P. Targum and New Testament (1967) 29. van UNNIK, W. C., Sparsa Collecta. The Collected Essays of W. C. van Unnik, I (Leiden 1973) 72-91. METZGER, B. M., Early Versions of the New Testament (Oxford 1977) 176. SWIDLER, L., Biblical Affirmations of Woman (Philadelphia 1979) 271. JEREMIAS, J., Die Sprache des Lukasevangeliums (Göttingen 1980) 86-88.

2:20-24 GEIGER, R., Die lukanischen Endzeitreden (Bern 1973) 193-210.

2:20 CLEMEN, C. Primitive Christianity and Its Non-Jewish Sources (1912) 239f. LAURENTIN, R. Struktur und Theologie der Lukanischen Kindheitsgeschichte (1967) 35, 111, 118, 138. NICKELS, P. Targum and New Testament (1967) 29. HORTON, F. L., "Reflections on the Semitism of Luke-Acts" in: C. H. Talbert (ed.) Perspectives on Luke-Acts (Danville 1978) 22. JEREMIAS, J., Die Sprache des Lukasevangeliums (Göttingen 1980) 88.

2:21-41 SCHNEIDER, G., Das Evangelium nach Lukas (Gütersloh/Würzburg 1977) 70 (lit!).

2:21-40 KAMPHAUS, F. Von der Exegese zur Predigt (1963) 226-28. DIGNATH, W. Die lukanische Vorgeschichte (1971) 41-51.

2:21 ADLER, N. Das erste christliche Pfingstfest (1938) 33, 120f. WEBER, O. GPM 4 (1949-1950) 38ff. TRAUB, GPM 9 (1954-1955) 34ff. GOLLWITZER, H. in: Herr, tue meine Lippen auf Bd.1 (1957) G. Eichholz (ed.) 40-44. Predigtgedanken aus Vergangenheit und Gegenwart Reihe A, Bd.1 (1960) 205-26. DOERNE, M. Er kommt auch noch heute (1961) 27-29. DEVILLE, R., Jésus unique Sauveur du monde" AssS 12 (1964) 28-43. GALBIATI, E., "La circoncisine de Gesù (Luca 2,21)" BiOr 8 (1966) 37-45. GALBIATI, E. "La circoncisione de Gesù (Luca 2,21)," BiblOr 8 (1, 1966) 37-45. LAURENTIN, R. Struktur und Theologie der

Lukanischen Kindheitsgeschichte (1967) 32, 36, 51f., 62ff., 80f., 114, 118, 183. NICKELS, P. Targum and New Testament (1967) 30. WEBER, O. Predigtmeditationen (1967) 126-130. MARXSEN, W. Predigten (1968) 89-95. JERVELL, J., "Den omskàrne Messias", SEA 37-38 (1972-1973) 145-55. TALBERT, C. H., Literary Patterns, Theological Themes, and the Genre of Luke-Acts (Missoula 1974) 44,78. METZGER, B. M., Early Versions of the New Testament (Oxford 1977) 249. "Beschneidung" in: TRE 5 (1980) 723. JEREMIAS, J., Die Sprache des Lukasevangeliums (Göttingen 1980) 89-90.

2:22ff. LAURENTIN, R. Struktur und Theologie der Lukanischen Kindheitsgeschichte (1967) 48, 59f., 116, 131f., 194.

2:22-52 HARRINGTON, W. "The Presentation," DoLi 15 (6, 1964) 366-72.

2:22-40 TRAUB, GPM 6 (1951-1952) 28ff. SURKAU, H.W., GPM 12 (1957-1958) 33ff. GALBIATI, E., "La presentazione al tempio (Luca 2,22-40)," BiblOr 6 (1, 1964) 28-37. BROWN, R. E., "The Presentation of Jesus (Luke 2:22-40)" Worship 51 (1977) 2-11.

2:22-39 DESCAMPS, A./DE HALLEUX, A. Mélanges Bibliques en hommage au R. P. Béda Rigaux (1970) 153-54, 167-68, 170.

2:22-38 TALBERT, C. H., Literary Patterns, Theological Themes, and the Genre of Luke-Acts (Missoula 1974) 44, 47. ZINGG, P., Das Wachsen der Kirche (Freiburg 1974) 137. FIGUERAS, P., "Syméon et Anne, ou le témoignage de la loi et des prophètes" NovT 20 (1978) 84-99. MIYOSHI, M., "Jesu Darstellung oder Reinigung im Tempel unter Berücksichtigung von 'Nunc Dimittis' Lk II 22-38" AJBI 4 (1978) 85-115.

2:22-35 LOEWENICH, W. von, Luther als Ausleger der Synoptiker (1954) 86f.

2:22-32 SURKAU, H. W. GPM 12/1, (1957-1958) 33-38.

2:22-24 KNOX, W. L. The Sources of the Synoptic Gospels II (1957) 40.

2:22-23 CLEMEN, C. Primitive Christianity and Its Non-Jewish Sources (1912) 310ff. BLINZLER, J., Die Brüder und Schwestern Jesu (Stuttgart 1967) 59-60.

2:22 KNOX, W. L. The Sources of the Synoptic Gospels II (1957) 40. FRIEDRICHSEN, G. W. S. "The Gothic Text of Luke in its Relation to the Codex Brixianus (f) and the Codex Palatinus (e)," NTS 11 (1964-1965) 282f. BAUMERT, N., Täglich Sterben und Auferstehen. Der Literalsinn von 2 Kor 4,12 - 5,10 (München 1973) 287ff, 298-99. JEREMIAS, J., Die Sprache des Lukasevangeliums (Göttingen 1980) 90.

2:23-24 HOLTZ, T. Untersuchungen über die Alttestamentlichen Zitate bei Lukas (1968) 82.

2:23 DE ALDAMA, J. A. "La virginidad 'in partu' en la exégesis patristica," Salmanticensis 9 (1-2, 1962) 113-53. RESE, M. Alttestamentliche Motive in der Christologie des Lukas (1969) 140-42. WINTER, P., "Zu Lukas 1:25,61; 2:23" ZNW 46 (1955) 261.

2:24 LAURENTIN, R. Struktur und Theologie der Lukanischen Kindheitsgeschichte (1967) 17, 58, 61, 69, 117, 139.

2:25-43 CUTLER, A. "Does the Simeon of Luke 2 Refer to Simeon the son of Hillel?" JournBibRel 34 (1, 1966) 29-35.

2:25-38 HOLZE, H. und AZBEL, H., in: P. Krusche et al. (eds.) Predigtstudien für das Kirchenjahr 1978-1979. I/2)Stuttgart 1978) 81-87.

2:25-35 MEYER, B. F. "A Word of Simeon," Bible Today 1 (16, 1964) 998-1002. OCKENGA, H., "Simeon and the Child Jesus" ChrTo 15 (1970) 260-62. TRITES, A. A., The New Testament Concept of Witness (London 1977) 197-98.

2:25-32 GOLLWITZER, H. in: Herr, tue meine Lippen auf Bd. 1 (1957) G. Eichholz (ed.) 37-40. TILLICH, P. Das Neue Sein (1959) 93-96. WILCKENS, U. Die Missionsreden der Apostelgeschichte (1961) 97, 160f., 202.

2:25-28 GILLIÈRON, B., Le Saint-Esprit, acutalité du Christ ce qu'en ont dit Paul, Luc et Jean (Geneva 1978).

2:25 VOLZ, P. Die Eschatologie der jüdischen Gemeinde (1934) 340. BARRETT, C. K. The New Testament Background: Selected Documents (1956) 241. HENNECKE, E./SCHNEEMELCHER, W. Neutestamentliche Apokryphen (1964) I 290. McNAMARA, M. The New Testament and the Palestinian Targum to the Pentateuch (1966) 241, 243. LAURENTIN, R. Struktur und Theologie der Lukanischen Kindheitsgeschichte (1967) 50f., 64, 67f., 116, 121, 138. NICKELS, P. Targum and New Testament (1967) 30. ZIESLER, J. A. The Meaning of Righteousness in Paul (1972) 138f., 146. JEREMIAS, J., Die Sprache des Lukasevangeliums (Göttingen 1980) 91-93.

2:26 ROBERTSON, A. T. Luke the Historian in the Light of Research (1920) 33, 157f. DELLING, G. Die Taufe im Neuen Testament (1963) 90. HAHN, F. Christologische Hoheitstitel (1963) 224, 271. LAURENTIN, R. Struktur und Theologie der Lukanischen Kindheitsgeschichte (1967) 48, 73, 116, 123, 137, 145, 170. NICKELS, P. Targum and New Testament (1967) 30. DÖMER, M., Das Heil Gottes: Studien zur Theologie des lukanischen Doppelwerkes (Köln/Bonn 1978) 44. JEREMIAS, J., Die Sprache des Lukasevangeliums (Göttingen 1980) 93-94.

2:27ff. STAEHELIN, E. Die Verkündigung des Reiches Gottes in der Kirche Jesu Christi I (1951) 66.

2:27-43 VAWTER, B. This Man Jesus (1973) 186ff.

2:27 LAURENTIN, R. Struktur und Theologie der Lukanischen Kindheitsgeschichte (1967) 23, 51, 60, 64, 68, 117f., 145f. NICKELS, P. Targum and New Testament (1967) 30. GUNKEL, H., The Influence of the Holy Spirit (Philadelphia 1979) 24. JEREMIAS, J., Die Sprache des Lukasevangeliums (Göttingen 1980) 94-95.

2:28-35 HENNECKE, E./SCHNEEMELCHER, W. Neutestamentliche Apokryphen (1964) I 346f.

2:28 SCHENK, W. Der Segen im Neuen Testament (1967) 119.

2:29-35 GRYGLEWICZ, F. "Theologizne aspekty blogoslawienstwa Symeona (Lk 2,29-35)," RTK 19 (1, 1972) 73-82.

2:29-32 MARTINDALE, C. C. "Simeon's Canticle," Worship 30 (1956) 199-201. McNAMARA, M. The New Testament and the Palestinian Targum to the Pentateuch (1966) 243. GASTON, L. No Stone on Another (1970) 258, 273-74. DAVIES, W. D., The Gospel and the Land (London 1974) 261. DUNN, J. D. G., Unity and Diversity in the New Testament (London 1977) 133.

2:29 STAEHELIN, E. Die Verkündigung des Reiches Gottes in der Kirche Jesu Christi I (1951) 256, 286. HAHN, F. Christologische Hoheitstitel (1963) 92. METZGER, B. M., Early Versions of the New Testament (Oxford 1977) 211. JEREMIAS, J., Die Sprache des Lukasevangeliums (Göttingen 1980)95.

2:30ff. STROBEL, A. Erkenntnis und Bekenntnis der Sünde in neutestamentlicher Zeit (1968) 41.

2:30-32 WILSON, S. G., The Gentiles and the Gentile Mission in Luke-Acts (Cambridge 1973) 36-39, 51, 53, 55, 243. LOHFINK, G., Die Sammlung Israels (München 1975) 28-30. PRAST, F., Presbyter und Evangelium in nachapostolischer Zeit (Stuttgart 1979) 274, 283.

2:30-31 SNODGRASS, K. R., "Streams of Tradition emerging from Isaiah 40:1-4 and their adaptation in the New Testament" JSNT 8 (1980) 24-45.

2:30 HAHN, F. Das Verständnis der Mission im Neuen Testament (²1965) 119. BRAUN, H. Qumran und NT II (1966) 79. LAURENTIN, R. Struktur und Theologie der Lukanischen Kindheitsgeschichte (1967) 36, 69, 73, 122, 138, 143, 200. RESE, M. Alttestamentliche Motive in der Christologie des Lukas (1969) 184.

2:31 KILPATRICK, G. D. "Laoi at Luke II.31 and Acts IV.25, 27,"JThS 16 (1, 1965) 127. JEREMIAS, J., Die Sprache des Lukasevangeliums (Göttingen (1980) 96.

2:32 HAHN, F. Das Verständnis der Mission im Neuen Testament (²1965) 117. BRAUN, H. Qumran und NT II (1966) 63. LAURENTIN, R. Struktur und Theologie der Lukanischen Kindheitsgeschichte (1967) 36, 38, 72f., 116, 118, 122, 132, 140f., 154, 158, 163, 183. NICKELS, P. Targum and New Testament (1967) 30.

RESE, M. Alttestamentliche Motive in der Christologie des Lukas (1969) 184-85. PALLIS, A., Notes on St. Luke and the Acts (London 1928) 8. RADL, W., Paulus und Jesus im lukanischen Doppelwerk. Untersuchungen zu Parallelmotiven im Lukasevangelium und der Apostelgeschichte (Bern/Frankfurt 1975) 69-81. PRAST, F. Presbyter und Evangelium in nachapostolischer Zeit (Stuttgart 1979) 323, 327-28.

2:33-40 GOLLWITZER, H. in: Herr, tue meine Lippen auf (1957) G. Eichholz (ed.) 34-37. "Tochter Zion, freue dich," Predigtgedanken aus Vergangenheit und Gegenwart, Reihe A, Bd. 1 (1960) 173-87. DOERNE, M. Er kommt auch noch heute (1961) 24-27.

2:33-35 SWIDLER, L., Biblical Affirmations of Woman (Philadelphia 1979) 269, 271. CLARK, K. W., "The Theological Relevance of Textual Variations in Current Criticsm of the Greek New Testament" in: The Gentile Bias and Other Essays (Leiden 1980) 116.

2:33 JEREMIAS, J., Die Sprache des Lukasevangeliums (Göttingen 1980) 96-97.

2:34-35 WINANDY, J. "La prophétie de Syméon (Lc, ii, 34-35)," RevBi 72 (3, 1965) 321-51. LAURENTIN, R. Struktur und Theologie der Lukanischen Kindheitsgeschichte (1967) 36, 50f., 64. GASTON, L. No Stone on Another (1970) 258, 273-74, 290, 313, 340.

2:34 PALLIS, A., Notes on St. Luke and the Acts (London 1928) 8. WINTER, P. "Some Observations on the Language in the Birth and Infancy Stories of the Third Gospel," NTS 1 (1954-1955) 118ff. LAURENTIN, R. Struktur und Theologie der Lukanischen Kindheitsgeschichte (1967) 17, 69, 104, 116, 138. NICKELS, P. Targum and New Testament (1967) 30. SCHENK, W. Der Segen im Neuen Testament (1967) 120f. RADL, W., Paulus und Jesus im lukanischen Doppelwerk. Untersuchungen zu Parallelmotiven im Lukasevangelium und in der Apostelgeschichte (Bern/Frankfurt 1975) 69-81. PRAST, F., Presbyter und Evangelium in nachapostolischer Zeit (Stuttgart 1979) 171. JEREMIAS, J., Die Sprache des Lukasevangeliums (Göttingen 1980) 97.

2:35 PALLIS, A., Notes on St. Luke and the Acts (London 1928) 8-9. GALLUS, T. "De snesu verborum Lc 2,35 eorumque momento mariologico," Biblica 29 (1948) 22-39. ANDRIESSEN, P. "Simeon's profetie aangaande Maria", NedKathStem 55 (1959) 179-89. BENOIT, P. " 'Et toi-même,' (Luc 2,35)," CBQ 25 (3, 1963) 251-61. OLES, M. "Maryjne znaczenie slow Lk 2,35 w patrologii od poczatku az do VIII wieku," RBL 17 (1, 1964) 4-19. LAURENTIN, R. Struktur und Theologie der Lukanischen Kindheitsgeschichte (1967) 36f., 52, 68, 102, 104, 138, 168, 171. KELLY, N. J. "The Hidden Years of Jesus: A Personal View," MCh 11 (3,

1968) 144-47. STROBEL, A. Erkenntnis und Bekenntnis der Sünde in neutestamentlicher Zeit (1968) 41. JEREMIAS, J., Die Sprache des Lukasevangeliums (Göttingen 1980) 97.

2:36-38 GIRONÉS, GUILLEM G., "Maria, comparada con Eva en el Nuevo Testamento" EphM 29 (1979) 279-84. SWIDLER, L., Biblical Affirmations of Woman (Philadelphia 1979) 183, 185, 194, 270, 300, 304.

2:36f. BOUSSET, W. Die Religion des Judentums im Späthellenistischen Zeitalter (1966 = 1926) 180, 428.

2:36 NICKELS, P. Targum and New Testament (1967) 30. METZGER, B. M., Early Versions of the New Testament (Oxford 1977) 34, 277.

2:37 METZGER, B. M., Early Versions of the New Testament (Oxford 1977) 391. JEREMIAS, J., Die Sprache des Lukasevangeliums (Göttingen 1980) 98.

2:38 PALLIS, A., Notes on St. Luke and the Acts (London 1928) 9. McNAMARA, M. The New Testament and the Palestinian Targum to the Pentateuch (1966) 242. BLACK, M. An Aramaic Approach to the Gospels and Acts (1967) 111f. LAURENTIN, R. Struktur und Theologie der Lukanischen Kindheitsgeschichte (1967) 18, 36, 50f., 62, 111, 116, 118, 121, 138. WANKE, J., Die Emmauserzählung. Eine redaktionsgeschichtliche Untersuchung zu Lk 24, 13-35 (Leipzig 1973) 68. JEREMIAS, J., Die Sprache des Lukasevangeliums (Göttingen 1980) 98.

2:39-40 SAHLIN, H. Der Messias und das Gottesvolk (1945) 306-08. TALBERT, C. H., Literary Patterns, Theological Themes, and the Genre of Luke-Acts (Missoula 1974) 44.

2:39 HENNECKE, E./SCHNEEMELCHER, W. Neutestamentliche Apokryphen (1964) II 467. LAURENTIN, R. Struktur und Theologie der Lukanischen Kindheitsgeschichte (1967) 22, 36, 48, 51, 64, 69, 111, 116ff. METZGER, B. M., Early Versions of the New Testament (Oxford 1977) 212. JEREMIAS, J., Die Sprache des Lukasevangeliums (Göttingen 1980) 99.

2:40-52 GLOMBITZA, O. "Der zwölfjährige Jesus. Luk. ii 40-52. Ein Beitrag zur Exegese der lukanischen Vorgeschichte," NovTest 5 (1, 1962) 1-4. BULTMANN, R. The History of the Synoptic Tradition (1963) 302-05.

2:40 HAHN, F. Christologische Hoheitstitel (1963) 318, 373. LAURENTIN, R. Struktur und Theologie der Lukanischen Kindheitsgeschichte (1967) 33, 35f., 61, 117, 155, 161. PETZKE, G. Die Traditionen über Apollonius von Tyana und das Neue Testament (1970) 78, 167f. ZINGG, P. Das Wachsen der Kirche (Freiburg

1974) 40-59. JEREMIAS, J. Die Sprache des Lukasevangeliums (Göttingen 1980) 99.

2:41-52 HARNACK, A. von, Studien zur Geschichte des Neuen Testament und der Alten Kiche (1931) 77ff. SAHLIN, H. Der Messias und das Gottesvolk (1945) 308-11. BARTH, K. GPM 4 (1949-1950) 46ff. KRAUS, H., GPM 9 (1954-1955) 45ff. OBENDIET, H. in: Herr, tue meine Lippen auf Bd. 1 (1957) G. Eichholz (ed.) 47-52. ''Zu Suchen Seine Herrlichkeit,'' Predigtgedanken aus Vergangeheit und Gegenwart, Reihe A, Bd. 1 (1960) 24-49. SCHMAUCH, GPM 15 (1960-1961) 56ff. DOERNE, M. Er kommt auch noch heute ;(1961) 33-35. GRUNDMANN, W. Das Evangelium nach Lukas (1961) 97f. VAN STEMPVOORT, P. A. ''De Twaalfjarige Jesus in de tempel'', HomBib 20 (6, 1961) 187-88. BARTSCH, H. W., Wachet aber zu jeder Zeit (Hamburg-Bergstedt 1963) 32-43. HENNECKE, E./SCHNEEMELCHER, W. Neutestamentliche Apokryphen (1964) I 298. BRAUN, H. Qumran und Nt II (1966) 21, 25, 106. KAMPHAUS, F. Von der Exegese zur Predigt (1968) 228-230, 296-306. DIGNATH, W. Die lukanische Vorgeschichte (1971) 51-68. DESCAMPS, A./DE HALLEUX, A. Mélanges Bibliques en hommage au R. P. Béda Rigaux (1970) 154-44. ELLIOTT, J. K. ''Does Luke 2:41-52 Anticipate the Resurrection?'' ET 83 (3, 1971) 87-89. KOCH, E. GPM 27/1 (1972-1973) 70-75. MÜLLER, H. M. ''Erster Sonntag nach Epiphanias: Lukas 3, 41-52,'' in: Predigtstudien (1972-1973) E. Lange (ed.) 78-84. BERGMAN, J., ''Zum Zwei-Wege Motiv. Religionsgeschichtliche und exegetische Bemerkungen'' SEA 41-42. (1977) 27-56. SCHNEIDER, G., Das Evangelium nach Lukas (Gütersloh/Würzburg 1977) 74 (lit!). van der HORST, P. W., ''Notes on the Aramaic Background of Luke II 41-52'' JSNT 7 (1980) 61-66.

2:41-51 IERSEL, B. van, ''The Finding of Jesus in the Temple. Some Observations on the original form of Luke ii 41-51a,'' NovTest 4 (3, 1960) 161-73. MANNS, F., ''Luc 2,41-50 témoin de la bar Mitswa de Jésus'' Marianum 40 (1978) 344-49. GILL, J. H., ''Jesus, Irony, and the 'New Quest' '' Encounter (1980) 139-51.

2:41 NICKELS, P. Targum and New Testament (1967) 30.

2:42-52 PHIPPS, W. E. Was Jesus Married? (1970) 36, 47-48, 56. LOHFINK, G., ''Die Unbedingtheit und die Faszination im Leben Jesu'' EuA (1980) 89-98.

2:42 LAURENTIN, R. Struktur und Theologie der Lukanischen Kindheitsgeschichte (1967) 36, 58, 93, 116f., 121. PRAST, F., Presbyter und Evangelium in nachapostolischer Zeit (Stuttgart 1979) 73, 167, 319.

2:43-46 GRAY, J. R. ''Was our Lord an Only Child?—Luke ii.43-46,'' ET

71 (2, 1959) 53. EDITOR, "Was our Lord an Only Child—Luke ii.43-46," ET 71 (6, 1960) 187.

2:44 NICKELS, P. Targum and New Testament (1967) 30.

2:46-47 SCHRECKENBERG, H., "Flavius Josephus und die lukanischen Schriften" in W. Haubeck/M. Bachmann (eds.) Wort in der Zeit. FS. K. H. Rengstorf (Leiden 1980) 186-87. BOUSSET, W. Die Religion des Judentums in Späthellenistischen Zeitalter (1966 = 1926) 167.

2:46 NEIRYNCK, F., "La Matière dans Luc" in: F. Neirynck (ed.) L'Evangile de Luc (Gembloux 1973) 184-91.

2:47-48 PETZKE, G. Die Traditionen über Apollonius von Tyana und das Neue Testament (1970) 166, 168, 190-91.

2:47 STONEHOUSE, N. B. The Witness of Matthew and Mark to Christ (1944) 106.

2:48-50 MICHEL, A. "La divinité de Jésus fut-elle connue par Marie?" AmiCler 74 (Oct. 29, 1964) 654-56. LAURENTIN, R. Jésu au temple (1966). RASCO, E. Gregorianum 48 (2, 1967) 354-58. GNILKA, J. ThRv 65 (2, 1969) 111. LAURENTIN, R. Struktur und Theologie der Lukanischen Kindheitsgeschichte (1967) 23, 37, 40, 52, 138, 162.

2:48 PESCH, R., " 'Kind warum hast du so an uns getan?' (Lk 2,48)," BZ 12 (2, 1968) 245-48.

2:49-50 CORTES, J. B. and GATTI, F. M. "Jesus' first recorded words (Lk. 2:49-50)," Marianum 32 (3, 1970) 404-18.

2:49 TEMPLE, P. J. "Origen and the Ellipsis in Lk 2,49," IThQ XXI (1954) 367-75. WINTER, P., "Lc 2,49 and Targum Yerushalmi," ZNW 45 (1954) 145-79. HAHN, F. Christologische Hoheitstitel (1963) 321. SCHRAGE, W. Das Verhältnis des Thomas-Evangeliums zur Synoptischen Tradition und zu den Koptischen Evangelienübersetzungen (1964) 128. LAURENTIN, R. Struktur und Theologie der Lukanischen Kindheitsgeschichte (1967) 1, 23, 37, 64, 118, 128, 161, 164, 166. NICKELS, P. Targum and New Testament (1967) 30. ESCUDERIO FREIER, C., "Alcance Cristológico de Lc.1,35 y 2,49" Communio 8 (1975) 5-77."

2:50 SPADAFORA, F., " 'Et ipsi non intellexerunt' (Lc. 2,50)," Divinitas 11 (1, 1967) 55-70. BERGMEIER, R., Glaube als Gabe nach Johannes (Stuttgart 1980) 225.

2:51 ARGYLE, A. W. "A Parallel between Luke II,51 and Genesis XXXVII,11," ET 65/1 (1953) 29. MEYER, B. F., "But Mary kept all these things. . . . " CBQ 26 (1964) 31-49. LAURENTIN, R. Struktur und Theologie der Lukanischen Kindheitsgeschichte (1967) 20, 22, 33-36, 111, 116, 121.

2:51b HAHN, F. Christologische Hoheitstitel (1963) 270.

2:52 HAHN, F. Christologische Hoheitstitel (1963) 318, 373. LAU-
RENTIN, R. Struktur und Theologie der Lukanischen Kindheitsgeschichte (1967) 33, 37, 111, 117, 155, 162. PETZKE, G. Die
Traditionen über Apollonius von Tyana und das Neue Testament
(1970) 78, 167f. COUROYER, B., "A propos de Luc, II,52" RB
86 (1979) 92-101.

———————

3-24 MARTIN, V. and KASSER, R. (eds.) Papyrus Bodmer XIV
(1961). LAURENTIN, R. Jésus au Temple (1966). KÜMMEL, W.
G. Einleitung in das Neue Testament (1973) 106f.

3:1-21:38 BOUHOURS, J. F. "Une étude de l'ordonnance de la triple tradition," RechSR 60 (4, 1972) 595-614.

3:1-9:50 FRANSEN, I. "Cahier de Bible: Ce que Jésus a fait et enseigné
(Luc 3,1-9,50)," BVieC 22 (1958) 58-72. SANDMEL, S., We
Jews and Jesus (New York 1977) 19.

3-4 DELOBEL, J., "La Rédaction de Lc. IV 14-16a" in: F. Neirynck
(ed.) L'Evangile de Luc (Gembloux 1973) 209, 222-23. NEI-
RYNCK, F. "La Matière Marcienne dans Luc" in F. Neirynck,
(ed.) L'Evangile de Luc (Gembloux 1973) 199-201. TALBERT,
C. H., Literary Patterns, Theological Themes, and the Genre of
Luke-Acts (Missoula 1974) 44, 45-50, 99, 103-06, 112, 143.

3:1-4:30 TAYLOR, V. Behind the Third Gospel (1926) 145ff., 172ff.
KECK, L. E. "Jesus' Entrance Upon His Mission. Luke 3:1-4:30,"
RevEx 64 (4, 1967) 465-83.

3:1-4:15 EWALD, H. Die drei ersten Evangelien (1850) 154ff. SCHRAMM,
T. Der Markus-Stoff bei Lukas (1971) 34-36.

3 NESTLE, E., "Zur Genealogie in Lukas 3" ZNW 4 (1903) 188.
NESTLE, E., "Salomo und Nathan" ZNW 8 (1907) 72. SAHLIN,
H. Studien zum Dritten Kapitel Des Lukasevangeliums (1949).

3:1ff. STRECKER, G. Der Weg der Gerechtigkeit (1962) 91₁.

3:1-22 CRIBBS, F. L. in: SBL Seminar Papers Vol. 2 (1973) MacRae, G.
(ed.) 20-23.

3:1-20 HIRSCH, E. Frühgeschichte des Evangeliums (1941) 27-35.
BARTSCH, H. W., Wachet aber zu jeder Zeit! (Hamburg-Bergstedt 1963) 43-50. SCHNIDER, F., Jesus der Prophet (Freiburg
1973) 46-47. TALBERT, C. H., Literary Patterns, Theological

Themes, and the Genre of Luke-Acts (Missoula 1974) 50. SCHNEIDER, G., Das Evangelium nach Lukas (Gütersloh/Würzburg 1977) 81-82 (lit!). DÖMER, M., Das Heil Gottes: Studien zur Theologie des lukanischen Doppelwerkes (Köln/Bonn 1978) 25-35. FUCHS, A., "Die Überschneidungen von Mk und 'Q' nach B. H. Streeter und E. P. Sanders und ihre wahre Bedeutung (Mk 1,1-8 par)" in: W. Haubeck/M. Bachmann (eds.) Wort in der Zeit. FS. K. H. Rengstorf (Leiden 1980) 57-81.

3:1-19 BIEDER, W., Die Verheissung der Taufe im Neuen Testament (Zürich 1966) 43-44.

3:1-18 BORNHÄUSSER, K. Studien zum Sondergut des Lukas (1934) 1-20. CREED, J. M. The Gospel According to St. Luke (1953) 309-13. REICKE, B. "Döparens förkunnelse enligt Lukas", SEA 37-38 (1972-1973) 156-66. CONZELMANN, H. und LINDEMANN, A., Arbeitsbuch zum Neuen Testament (Tübingen 1975) 61.

3:1-8 (9-15) GOLLWITZER, H. GPM 5 (1960-1961) 179ff.

3:1-14 HEINRICH, G. und ROSENBOOM, E., in: P. Krusche et al. (eds.) Predigtstudien für das Kirchenjahr 1980-1981, I/3 (Stuttgart 1980) 23-29. SURKAU, H.-W., in: GPM 35 (1980) 18-25.

3:1-9 Verkündigt das angenehme Jahr des Herrn. Predigtgedanken aus Vergangenheit und Gegenwart Reihe C, Bd.1 (1962) 40-53. BOHREN, GPM 7 (1962-1963) 19ff. HOLTZ, T. GPM 23/1 (1968-1969) 18-23. NIEBERGALL, A., in: GPM 29 (1974) 18-25.

3:1-6 DUPONT, J. "Le Salut des Gentils et la Signification Theologique du Livre des Acts," NTS 6 (1959-1970) 137f. SUHL, A. Die Funktion der alttestamentlichen Zitate und Anspielungen im Markusevangelium (1965) 133ff. NICKELS, Targum and New Testament (1967) 31. RAHNER, K., Was sollen wir jetzt tun? Vier Meditationen (Freiburg/Wien 1974). TALBERT, C. H., Literary Patterns, Theological Themes, and the Genre of Luke-Acts (Missoula 1974) 45, 46, 105. KRAFT, H., Die Entstehung des Christentums (Darmstadt 1981) 16-18.

3:1-3 EWALD, H. Die drei ersten Evangelien (1850) 189f. ROBINSON, J. M. Kerygma und historischer Jesus (1960) 146. FLENDER, H. Heil und Geschichte in der Theologie des Lukas (1965) 105, 111-112. HAHN, F. Das Verständnis der Mission im Neuen Testament (^{2}1965) 74-76. WINK, W. John the Baptist in the Gospel Tradition (1968) 55-58. SHERWIN-WHITE, A. N., Roman Society and Roman Law in the New Testament (Grand Rapids 1978) 166.

3:1-2 TALBERT, C. H., Literary Patterns, Theological Themes, and the Genre of Luke-Acts (Missoula 1974) 46. CONZELMANN, H. und LINDEMANN, A., Arbeitsbuch zum Neuen Testament (Tübingen

1975) 332. SCHRECKENBERG, H., "Flavius Josephus und die lukanischen Schriften" in: W. Haubeck/M. Bachmann (eds.) Wort in der Zeit. FS. K. H. Rengstorf (Leiden 1980) 187-90.

3:1 CREED, J. M. The Gospel According to St. Luke (1953) 307-09. SCHMID, J. Das Evangelium nach Lukas (1955) 94-98. BARRETT, C. K. The New Testament Background: Selected Documents (1956) 197. STRECKER, G. Der Weg der Gerechtigkeit (1962) 47;7. WILSON, S. F., The Gentiles and the Gentile Mission in Luke-Acts (Cambridge 1973) 38-39, 62. MEYER, B. F., The Aims of Jesus (London 1979) 115. SCHRECKENBERG, H., "Flavius Josephus und die lukanischen Schriften" in: W. Haubeck/M. Bachmann (eds.) Wort in der Zeit. FS. K. H. Rengstorf (Leiden 1980) 190-91. KRAFT, H., Die Entstehung des Christentums (Darmstadt 1981) 10.

3:2-22 BÖCHER, O., "Johannes der Täufer in der neutestamentlichen Überlieferung" in: G. Müller (ed.) Rechtfertigung Realismus. FS. A. Köberle (Darmstadt 1978) 45-52.

3:2 DELLING, G. Die Taufe im Neuen Testament (1963) 52, 54. METZGER, B. M., Early Versions of the New Testament (Oxford 1977) 172, 368. DÖMER, M., Das Heil Gottes: Studien zur Theologie des lukanischen Doppelwerkes (Köln/Bonn 1978) 28f. JEREMIAS, J., Die Sprache des Lukasevangeliums (Göttingen 1980) 103.

3:3ff. KNOX, W. L. The Sources of the Synoptic Gospels II (1957) 4f. HAHN, F. Das Verständnis der Mission im Neuen Testament (²1965) 112, 114.

3:3-20 CONZELMANN, H. Die Mitte der Zeit (1964) 12ff. SCHNIEWIND, J., Die Parallelperikopen bei Lukas und Johannes (Darmstadt (1958 = 1914) 7-11.

3:3-18 TALBERT, C. H., Literary Patterns, Theological Themes, and the Genre of Luke-Acts (Missoula 1974) 117. MATTILL, A. J., Luke and the Last Things: a Perspective for the Understanding of Lukan Thought (Dillsboro 1979) 6-7.

3:3-14 GOLLWITZER, H. EvTh 11 (1951-1952) 141-51.

3:3-6 SNODGRASS, K. R., "Streams of Tradition emerging from Isaiah 40:1-5 and their adaptation in the New Testament" JSNT (1980) 24-45.

3:3-4 SCHRAMM, T. Der Markus-Stoff bei Lukas (1971) 34f.

3:3 MASSAUX, E. Influence de l'Evangile de saint Matthieu sur la littérature chrétienne avant saint Irénée (1950) 348-50, 355-56. RUDOLPH, K. Die Mandäer I (1960) 62. DELLING, G. Die Taufe im Neuen Testament (1963) 42f.,62. KÄSEMANN, E. Exegetische Versuche und Besinnungen (1964) I 45. JÜNGEL, E. Paulus und Jesus (1966) 174. SMITH, M. Tannaitic Parallels to the Gospels (1968) 7.21. STROBEL, A. Erkenntnis und Bekenntnis der Sünde in neutestamentlicher Zeit (1968) 42. O'NEILL, J. C. The Theology of Acts in its historical setting (1970) 151-52. CRIBBS, F. L. in: SBL Seminar Papers Vol. 2 (1973) MacRae, G. (ed.) 3. LEROY, H., Zur Vergebung der Sünden (Stuttgart 1974) 64-66. METZGER, B. M., Early Versions of the New Testament (Oxford 1977) 248. MEYER, B. F., The Aims of Jesus (London 1979) 119. JEREMIAS, J., Die Sprache des Lukasevangeliums (Göttingen 1980) 103.

3:4-6 LOCKYER, H. All the Parables of the Bible (1963) 136ff. HOLTZ, T. Untersuchungen über die Alttestamentlichen Zitate bei Lukas (1968) 37-39. RESE, M. Alttestamentliche Motive in der Christologie des Lukas (1969) 168-71. TALBERT, C. H., Literary Patterns, Theological Themes, and the Genre of Luke-Acts (Missoula 1974) 46.

3:4-5 WANKE, J., Die Emmauserzählung. Eine redaktionsgeschichtliche Untersuchung zu Lk 24,13-35 (Leipzig 1973) 118.

3:4 TALBERT, C. H., Literary Patterns, Theological Themes, and the Genre of Luke-Acts (Missoula 1974) 105. JEREMIAS, J., Die Sprache des Lukasevangeliums (Göttingen 1980) 103-04. KRAFT, H., Die Entstehung des Christentums (Darmstadt 1981) 10-15.

3:5 DERRETT, J. D. M. " 'Every valley shall be exalted': Borrowings from Isaiah in ancient India?" ZRGG 24 (2, 1972) 153-55.

3:6 HAHN, F. Das Verständnis der Mission im Neuen Testament (²1965) 114, 119. WILSON, S. G., The Gentiles and the Gentile Mission in Luke-Acts (Cambridge 1973) 38-39, 48, 51, 53, 123, 243. "Apokalyptik" in: TRE 3 (1978) 254. RAYAN, S., The Holy Spirit: Heart of the Gospel and Christian Hope (New York 1978) 2. PRAST, F., Presbyter und Evangelium in nachapostolischer Zeit (Stuttgart 1979) 274, 283, 332.

3:7-4:13 DRURY, J. Tradition and Design in Luke's Gospel (Atlanta 1976) 128-31.

3:7-9 HOFFMANN, P. Studien zur Theologie der Logienquelle (1972) 4, 14, 15-33, 34, 307f., 239. LÜHRMANN, D. Die Redaktion der Logienquelle (1969) 24-31.

3:7ff. BOUSSET, W. Die Religion des Judentums in Späthellenistischen Zeitalter (1966 = 1926) 291.

3:7-20 MICHALKO, GPM 19 (1964-1965) 14-21. BAUER, K. A. in: Hören und Fragen Bd. 5, 3 (1967) G. Eichholz & A. Falkenroth (eds.) 19ff. LANGE, E. (ed.) Predigtstudien für das Kirchenjahr 1970-1971 (1970) 35-41. STECK, K. G. GPM 24 (1970) 21-30. GRÄSSER, E., in: GPM 31 (1977) 15-21.

3:7-18 SCHULZ, S., Q Die Spruchquelle der Evangelisten (1972) 366-78. STADTLAND, T. und JÖRNS, K.-P., in: P. Krusche et al. (eds.) Predigtstudien für das Kirchenjahr 1976/1977. V (Stuttgart 1976) 26-31.

3:7-17 BRAUN, H. GPM 13 (1958-1959) 9-13. TALBERT, C. H., Literary Patterns, Theological Themes, and the Genre of Luke-Acts (Missoula 1974) 45, 46, 47.

3:7-14 BARRETT, C. K. The New Testament Background: Selected Documents (1956) 198. RIST, J. M., On the Independence of Matthew and Mark (Cambridge 1978) 17-22.

3:7-9 DELOBEL, J., "La Rédaction de Lc., IV 14-16a" in: F. Neirynck (ed.) L'Evangile de Luc (Gembloux 1973) 219-20. TALBERT, C. H., Literary Patterns, Theological Themes, and the Genre of Luke-Acts (Missoula 1974) 46. EDWARDS, R. A., A Theology of Q (Philadelphia 1976) 80-82. POLAG, A., Die Christologie der Logienquelle (Neukirchen-Vluyn 1977) 154-56. DÖMER, M., Das Heil Gottes: Studien zur Theologie des lukanischen Doppelwerkes (Köln/Bonn 1978) 29. McDONALD, J. I. H., Kerygma and Didache (Cambridge 1980) 17-18.

3:7-8 MOORE, G. F. Judaism (1946) I 544.

3:7 MASSAUX, E. Influence de l'Evangile de saint Matthieu sur la littérature chrétienne avant saint Irénée (1950) 348-50, 355-56. SCHLATTER, A. Johannes der Täufer (1956) 99ff. DELLING, G. Die Taufe im Neuen Testament (1963) 49. TALBERT, C. H., Literary Patterns, Theological Themes, and the Genre of Luke-Acts (Missoula 1974) 46. HOLTZ, T., " 'Euer Glaube an Gott'. Zu Form und Inhalt von 1 Thess, 1:9f." in: R. Schnackenburg et al. (eds.) Die Kirche des Anfangs. FS. H. Schürmann (Freiburg/Basel/Wien 1978) 466, 479-80. JEREMIAS, J., Dis Sprache des Lukasevangeliums (Göttingen 1980) 104. McDONALD, J. I. H., Kerygma and Didache (Cambridge 1980) 80. RICE, G. E., "The Anti-Judaic Bias of the Western Text in the Gospel of Luke" AUSS 18 (1980) 54.

3:8 DELLING, G. Die Taufe im Neuen Testament (1963) 43. FRIEDRICHSEN, G. W. S. The Gothic Text of Luke in its Relation to the Codex Brixianus (f) and the Codex Palatinus (e). NTS 11 (1964-1965) 285f. JÜNGEL, E. Paulus und Jesus (1966) 175. STROBEL, A. Erkenntnis und Bekenntnis der Sünde in neutestamentlicher Zeit (1968) 42. HASLER, V. Amen (1969) 55. DAVALLIN, H. C. C., Life after Death. I (Lund 1974) 5.2.4., 7.2.3.6. METZGER, B. M., Early Versions of the New Testament (Oxford 1977) 249. BRUCE, F. F., The Time is Fulfilled (Exeter 1978) 62. MEYER, B. F., The Aims of Jesus (London 1979) 116,

121. JEREMIAS, J., Die Sprache des Lukasevangeliums (Göttingen 1980) 105-06.

3:9-10 RUDOLPH, K. Die Mandäer II (1961) 257,3.

3:9 TALBERT, C. H., Literary Patterns, Theological Themes, and the Genre of Luke-Acts (Missoula 1974) 46. SCHNEIDER, G., Parusiegleichnisse im Lukas-Evangelium (Stuttgart 1975) 47-49. McDONALD, J. I. H., Kerygma and Didache (Cambrige 1980) 80.

3:10-18 FRIEDRICH, G. GPM 11 (1956-1957) 14-17. RAHNER, K., Was sollen wir jetzt tun? Vier Meditationen (Frieburg/Wien 1974).

3:10-14 SCHLATTER, A. Johannes der Täufer (1956) 136ff. CONZELMANN, H. Die Mitte der Zeit (1964) 21, 93f. DEGENHARDT, H.-J. Lukas, Evangelist der Armen (1964) 59-60. HOLTZ, T. "Die Standespredigt Johannes des Täufers," in: Ruf und Antwort, Festgabe für wo Fuchs (1964) 461-74. TALBERT, C. H., Literary Patterns, Theological Themes, and the Genre of Luke-Acts (Missoula 1974) 46. BETZ, O., "Rechtfertigung und Heiligung" in: G. Müller (ed.) Rechtfertigung Realismus. FS. A. Köberle (Darmstadt 1978) 36. DÖMER, M., Das Heil Gottes: Studien zur Theologie des lukanischen Doppelwerkes (Köln/Bonn 1978) 29-30. MATTILL, A. J., Luke and the Last Things: a Perspective for the Understanding of Lukan Thought (Dillsboro 1979) 15. McDONALD, J. I. H., Kerygma and Didache (Cambridge 1980) 79-80.

3:10 TALBERT, C. H., Literary Patterns, Theological Themes, and the Genre of Luke-Acts (Missoula 1974) 47. METZGER, B. M., Early Versions of the New Testament (Oxford 1977) 245, 390. RICE, G. E., "The Anti-Judaic Bias of the Western Text in the Gospel of Luke" AUSS 18 (1980) 55.

3:11 BRAUN, H. Qumran und NT II (1966) 18, 288, 291. JEREMIAS, J., Die Sprache des Lukasevangeliums (Göttingen 1980) 107-08.

3:12-14 FRIEDRICH, G., "Das Problem der Autorität in Neuen Testament" in: Auf das Wort kommt es an (Göttingen 1978) 406.

3:12 HAHN, F. Christologische Hoheitstitel (1963) 77. METZGER, B. M., Early Versions of the New Testament (Oxford 1977) 390. FRICKEL, J., "Die Zöllner, Vorbild der Demut und wahrer Gottesverehrung" in: E. Dassmann/K. S. Frank (eds.) Pietas. FS. B. Kötting (Münster 1980) 369. RICE, G. E., "The Anti-Judaic Bias of the Western Text in the Gospel of Luke" AUSS 18 (1980) 55.

3:13 JEREMIAS, J., Die Sprache des Lukasevangeliums (Göttingen 1980) 108-09.

3:14 RICE, G. E., "The Anti-Judaic Bias of the Western Text in the Gospel of Luke" AUSS 18 (1980) 55.

3:15-18 EDWARDS, R. A., A Theology of Q (Philadelphia 1976) 81-82.

3:15-17 TALBERT, C. H., Literary Patterns, Theological Themes, and the Genre of Luke-Acts (Missoula 1974) 46, 105.

3:15-16 CRIBBS, F. L. in: SBL Seminar Papers Vol. 2 (1973) MacRae, G. (ed.) 25-27.

3:15 PALLIS, A., Notes on St. Luke and the Acts (London 1928) 9. RUDOLPH, K. Die Mandäer I (1960) 77. BAILEY, J. A. The Traditions Common to the Gospels of Luke and John (1963) 9-11. HAHN, F. Christologische Hoheitstitel (1963) 224, 374, 380. CRIBBS, F. L. SBL Seminar Papers Vol. 2 (1973) MacRae, G. (ed.) 3. TALBERT, C. H., Literary Patterns, Theological Themes, and the Genre of Luke-Acts (Missoula 1974) 47. DÖMER, M., Das Heil Gottes: Studien zur Theologie des lukanischen Doppelwerkes (Köln/Bonn 1978) 33-34. FRIEDRICH, G., (ed.), "Beobachtungen zur messianischen Hohepriestererwartung in den Synoptikern" in: Auf das Wort kommt es an (Göttingen 1978) 93. MATTILL, A. J., Luke and the Last Things: a Perspective for the Understanding of Lukan Thought (Dillsboro 1979) 22-23. JEREMIAS, J., Die Sprache des Lukasevangeliums (Göttingen 1980) 109.

3:16-21 MERKEL/GEORGI/BALTZER, GPM (1960-1961) 172ff.

3:16-17 POLAG, A., Die Christologie der Logienquelle (Nerkirchen-Vluyn 1977) 155. McDONALD, J. I. H., Kerygma and Didache (Cambridge 1980) 17. KRAFT, H., Die Entstehung des Christentums (Darmstadt 1981) 18-27.

3:16, 17, 21b HOFFMANN, P. Studien zur Theologie der Logienquelle (1972) 4, 31, 36, 152f., 155, 177, 190, 201, 214f., 223f., 232, 290, 292.

3:16 ADLER, N. Das erste christliche Pfingstfest (1938) SCHWEIZER, E. "With the Holy Ghost and Fire (Lk. 3,16)," ET 65/1 (1953) 29. SCHLATTER, A. Johannes der Täufer (1956) 103ff. GLASSON, T. F. "Water, Wind and Fire (Lk. 3:16) and Orphic Initiation," NTS 3 (1956-1957) 69ff. DELLING, G. Die Taufe im Neuen Testament (1963) 46, 62. ELLIS, E. E. NTS 12 (1965-1966) 29f. SIMPSON, R. T. NTS 12 (1965-1966) 277f. NICKELS, P. Targum and New Testament (1967) 31. WILSON, S. G. NTS 16 (1969-1970) 330f. DUNN, J. D. G. Baptism in the Holy Spirit (1970) 8-14, 18-21. SCHRAMM, T. Der Markus-Stoff bei Lukas (1971) 35f. GOPPELT, L., Theologie des Neuen Testaments. I (Göttingen 1975) 90-91. SANDMEL, S., We Jews and Jesus (New York 1977) 120. DÖMER, M., Das Heil Gottes: Studien zur Theologie des lukanischen Doppelwerkes (Köln/Bonn 1978) 34. KIEFFER, R., "Me-än'-kristologin hos synoptikerna" SEA 44 (1979) 134-47. JEREMIAS, J., Die Sprache des Lukasevangeliums (Göttingen 1980) 109-10.

3:17-18 REICKE, B., "Die Verkündigung des Täufers nach Lukas" in: A. Fuchs (ed.) Jesus in der Verkündigung der Kirche (Freistadt 1976) 50-61.

3:17 MANSON, T. W. The Teaching of Jesus (1945) 322ff. FLEW, R. N. Jesus and His Church (1956) 67. SIMPSON, R. T. NTS 12 (1965-1966) 277f. WILSON, S. G., The Gentiles and the Gentile Mission in Luke-Acts (Cambridge 1973) 60-61. SCHNEIDER, G., Parusiegleichnisse im Lukas-Evangelium (Stuttgart 1975) 47-49. HOLM-NIELSEN, S., "Die Psalmen Salomos" in: W. G. Kümmel (ed.) Jüdische Schriften aus hellenistisch-römischer Zeit. IV/2 (Gütersloh 1977) 87.

3:18-20 TALBERT, C. H., Literary Patterns, Theological Themes, and the Genre of Luke-Acts (Missoula 1974) 45, 47, 105.

3:18 MARXSEN, W. Mark the Evangelist (1969) 119, 143f. SAMAIN, E., "La Notion de APXH" in: F. Neirynck (ed.) L'Evangile de Luc (Gembloux 1973) 310-11. DÖMER, M., Das Heil Gottes: Studien zur Theologie des lukanischen Doppelwerkes (Köln/Bonn 1978) 31-33. JEREMIAS, J., Die Sprache des Lukasevangeliums (Göttingen 1980) 110-11.

3:19-20 KNOX, W. L. The Sources of the Synoptic Gospels II (1957) 4. GNILKA, J., "Das Martyrium Johannes des Täufers (Mk 6,17-29)" in: P. Hoffmann (ed.) Orientierung an Jesus. FS. J. Schmid (Freiburg 1973) 79, 89-90. SWIDLER, L., Biblical Affirmations of Woman (Philadelphia 1979) 229, 238. BACHMANN, M., "Johannes der Täufer bei Lukas: Nachzügler oder Vorläufer?" in: W. Haubeck/M. Bachmann (eds.) Wort in der Zeit. FS. K. H. Rengstorf (Leiden 1980) 139-54. KRAFT, H., Die Entstehung des Christentums (Darmstadt 1981) 34-37.

3:19 BAUMBACH, G. Das Verständnis des Bösen in den synoptischen Evangelien (1963) 123ff. BERGMEIER, R., Glaube als Gabe nach Johannes (Stuttgart 1980) 270n.558. JEREMIAS, J., Die Sprache des Lukasevangeliums (Göttingen 1980) 111-12.

3:20 JEREMIAS, J., Die Sprache des Lukasevangeliums (Göttingen 1980) 112.

3:21-4:44 BUSSE, U., Das Nazareth-Manifest Jesu. Eine Einführung in das lukanische Jesusbild nack Lk 4,16-30 (Stuttgart 1978).

3:21-38 FLENDER, H. Heil und Geschichte in der Theologie des Lukas (1965) 50-51. TALBERT, C. H., Literary Patterns, Theological Themes, and the Genre of Luke-Acts (Missoula 1974) 45, 46, 47. BUSSE, U., Das Nazareth-Manifest Jesu. Eine Einführung in das lukanische Jesusbild nach Lk 4,16-30 (Stuttgart 1978) 12-25.

3:21-23 TALBERT, C. H. NTS 14 (1967-1968) 266f.

3:21-22 HIRSCH, E. Frühgeschichte des Evangeliums (1941) 35-37, 195f.

RENGSTORF, K. H. Das Evangelium nach Lukas (1949) 59. MASSAUX, E. Influence de l'Evangile de saint Matthieu sur la litterature chrétienne avant saint Irénée (1950) 224-25, 350-52, 552-53. DENNEY, J. The Death of Christ (1956) 18f. GILS, F. Jésus Prophète D'Après Les Evangiles Synoptiques (1957) 49-73. KNOX, W. L. The Sources of the Synoptic Gospels II (1957) 4. GRUND-MANN, W. Das Evangelium nach Lukas (1961) 108-110. CON-ZELMANN, H. Die Mitte der Zeit (1964) 15. SUHL, A. Die Funktion der alttestamentlichen Zitate und Anspielungen in Markusevangelium (1965) 92, 97ff. WILSON, S. G. NTS 16 (1969-1970) 331f. DUNN, J. D. G. Baptism in the Holy Spirit (1970) 26f., 33f. LENTZEN-DEIS, F. Die Taufe Jesu nach den Synoptikern (1970) 284-86. JEREMIAS, J. Neutestamentliche Theologie I (1971) 57f., 183. BEUTLER, J. Martyria (1972) 254, 285f. CRIBBS, F. L. in: SBL Seminar Papers Vol. 2 (1973) MacRae, G. (ed.) 27-28. BARTH, M., Die Taufe - ein Sakrament? (Zürich 1951) 59ff.BARTSCH, H. W., Wachet aber zu jeder Zeit (Hamburg-Bergstedt 1963) 50-53. BIEDER, W., Die Verheissung der Taufe im Neuen Testament (Zürich 1966) 84-86. NEIRYNCK, F., "La Matière Marcienne dans Luc" in: F. Neirynck (ed.) L'Evangile de Luc (Gembloux 1973) 184-91, 199-200. TALBERT, C. H., Literary Patterns, Theological Themes, and the Genre of Luke-Acts (Missoula 1974) 18, 117. COLLINS, R. F., "Luke 3:21-22, Baptism or Anointing" Bible Today 84 (1976) 821-31. MINEAR, P., To Heal and to Reveal (New York 1976) 45. CHEVALLIER, M.-A., "L'analyse littéraire des textes du Nouveau Testament (Conseils aux édudiants)" RHPR 57 (1977) 367-78. POLAG, A., Die Christologie der Logienquelle (Neukirchen-Vluyn 1977) 151-54. SCHNEIDER, G., Das Evangelium nach Lukas (Gütersloh/Würzburg 1977) 91 (lit!). BUSSE, U., Das Nazareth-Manifest Jesu. Eine Einführung in das lukanische Jesusbild nach Lk 4,16-30 (Stuttgart 1978) 14-17, 20, 70, 72. DÖMER, M., Das Heil Gottes: Studien zur Theologie des lukanischen Doppelwerkes (Köln/Bonn 1978) 45-49, 61-62. GILLIÈRON, B., Le Saint-Esprit, actualité du Christ ce qu'en ont dit Paul, Luc et Jean (Geneva 1978). MEDIAVILLA, R., "La Oraciòn de Jesus en el tercer evangelio" Mayeutica (1978) 5-34. "Berufung" in: TRE 5 (1980) 684. JEREMIAS, J., Die Sprache des Lukasevangeliums (Göttingen 1980) 113-14.

3:21 CONZELMANN, H. Die Mitte der Zeit (1964) 13ff. TALBERT, C. H., Literary Patterns, Theological Themes, and the Genre of Luke-Acts (Missoula 1974) 16. JEREMIAS, J., Die Sprache des Lukasevangeliums (Göttingen 1980) 112-13.

3:22ff. BLASS, F. Philosophy of the Gospels (1898) 167ff., 171ff.

3:22-38 HENNECKE, E./SCHNEEMELCHER, W. Neutestamentliche Apokryphen (1964) I 103, 320.

3:22-28 RICE, G. E., "Luke 3:22-28 in Codex Bezae: The Messianic King" AUSS 17 (1979) 203-08.

3:22-23 BERTRAND, D. A., Le Baptême de Jésus (Tübingen 1973) 8, 13, 34, 35, 44, 45, 96, 101, 111, 112, 119, 125.

3:22 ARVEDSON, T. Das Mysterium Christi (1937) 124f. HOOKER, M. D. Jesus and the Servant (1959) 68-73. WAINWRIGHT, A. W. The Trinity in the New Testament (1962) 183-83. HAHN, F. Christologische Hoheitstitel (1963) 302, 318, 345. CZAJ-KOWSKI, M. "De lectione 'occidentali' in Lc. 3,22," RTK 12 (1, 1965) 35-44. JEREMIAS, J. Abba; Studien zur neutestamentlichen Theologie und Zeitgeschichte (1966) 192-94. LENTZEN-DEIS, F. "Ps. 2, 7, ein Motiv früher 'hellenistischer' Christologie. Der Psalmvers in der Lectio varians von Lk 3,22, im Ebionäerevangelium und bei Justus Martyr," ThPh 44 (2, 1969) 342-62. RESE, M. Alttestamentliche Motive in der Christologie des Lukas (1969) 191-95. KECK, L. E. "The Spirit and the Dove", NTS 17 (1970-1971) 41-67. JEREMIAS, J. Neutestamentliche Theologie I (1971) 58-61. KRÄNKL, E. Jesus der Knecht Gottes (1972) 91, 125, 137f. TALBERT, C. H., Literary Patterns, Theological Themes, and the Genre of Luke-Acts (Missoula 1974) 16, 46, 47, 116, 117, 118. Dunn, J. D. G., Jesus and the Spirit (London 1975) 63, 65, 122, 147, 336. DRURY, J., Tradition and design in Luke's Gospel (Atlanta 1976) 70-71. SWIDLER, L., Biblical Affirmations of Woman (Philadelphia 1979) 60.

3:23-4:13 SANDELIN, K.-G., Die Auseinandersetzung mit der Weisheit in 1 Korinther 15 (Abo 1976) 110-11.

3:23ff. HAHN, F. Christologische Hoheitstitel (1963) 273. GOULDER, M. D. Type and History in Acts (1964) 206ff.

3:23-38 EWALD, H. Die drei ersten Evangelien (1850) 170f. KLOSTER-MANN, E. Das Lukasevangelium (1929) 57. Evangelium nach Lukas (1949) 61f. HAHN, F. Christologische Hoheitstitel (1963) 243-45. FRIEDRICHSEN, G. W. S. "The Gothic Text of Luke in its Relation to the Codex Brixianus (f) and the Codex Platinus (e)," NTS 11 (1964-1965) 288f. NELLESSEN, E. Das Kind und seine Mutter (1969) 17f. BURGER, C. Jesus als Davidssohn (1970) 116-27. BYSKOV, M. "Verus Deus-verus homo, Luc 3.23-38," StTh 26 (1, 1972) 25-32. BARTSCH, H. W., Wachet aber zu jeder Zeit (Hamburg-Bergstedt 1963) 53-55. da SPINETOLLI, O., "Les généalogies de Jésus et leur signification. Mt. 1,1-25; Lc 3,23-38" AssS 9 (1974) 6-19. TALBERT, C. H., Literary Patterns, Theological Themes, and the Genre of Luke-Acts (Missoula 1974) 46,

117. GLÖCKNER, R., Die Verkündigung des Heils beim Evangelisten Lukas (Mainz 1975) 144-45. SCHNEIDER, G., Das Evangelium nach Lukas (Gütersloh/Würzburg 1977) 93 (lit!). DÖMER, M., Das Heil Gottes: Studien zur Theologie des lukanischen Doppelwerkes (Köln/Bonn 1978) 27-28, 49. SWIDLER, L., Biblical Affirmations of Woman (Philadelphia 1979) 246, 278. KRAFT, H., Die Entstehung des Christentums (Darmstadt 1981) 68-76.

3:23 SPITTA, F., "Zu Lk 3:23" ZNW 8 (1907) 66. LEAL, J. "Et ipse Jesus erat incipiens quasi annorum triginta, ut putabatur, filius Joseph (Lc 3,23)," CultBib 20 (193, 1963) 331-34. LEE, G. M. "Luke iii.23," ET 79 (10, 1968) 310. PETZKE, G. Die Traditionen über Apollonius von Tyana und das Neue Testament (1970) 163, 185. TALBERT, C. H., Literary Patterns, Theological Themes, and the Genre of Luke-Acts (Missoula 1974) 117, 123, 127. SANDMEL, S., We Jews and Jesus (New York 1977) 20. JEREMIAS, J., Die Sprache des Lukasevangeliums (Göttingen 1980) 114.

3:24-38 NESTLE, E. ZNW 4 (1903) 188f.

3:31ff. STAEHELIN, E. Die Verkündigung des Reiches Gottes in der Kirche Jesus Christi I (1951) 109.

3:31 STONEHOUSE, N. B. The Witness of Matthew and Mark to Christ (1944) 223. TALBERT, C. H., Literary Patterns, Theological Themes, and the Genre of Luke-Acts (Missoula 1974) 104.

3:32 METZGER, B. M., Early Versions of the New Testament (Oxford 1977) 201, 202.

3:33 METZGER, B. M., Early Versions of the New Testament (Oxford 1977) 201.

3:35-36 "Agende" in: TRE 2 (1978) 3.

3:35 METZGER, B. M., Early Versions of the New Testament (Oxford 1977) 201.

3:36 METZGER, B. M., Early Versions of the New Testament (Oxford 1977) 202.

3:38 NICKELS, P. Targum and New Testament (1967) 31. TALBERT, C. H., Literary Patterns, Theological Themes, and the Genre of Luke-Acts (Missoula 1974) 47, 118.

_____

4:1-24:53 GRYGLEWICZ, F. "The St. Adalbert Codex of the Gospels," NTS 11 (1964-1965) 259f.

4:1-9:50 O'NEILL, J. C. The Theology of Acts in its historical setting (1970) 69-71.

4-8 TALBERT, C. H., Literary Patterns, Theological Themes, and the Genre of Luke-Acts (Missoula 1974) 2, 39, 43,76, 120, 143.

4:1-5:16 DRURY, J., Tradition and Design in Luke's Gospel (Atlanta 1976) 85-89.

4:1-5:2 FARRER, A. St Matthew and St. Mark (1954) 166.

4 RUDOLPH, K. Die Mandäer II (1961) 234, KLAWEK, A. "Jezus naucza w synagogach," RBL 19 (4-5, 1966) 255-60. GREEN-LEE, J. H. Nine Uncial Palimpsests of the Greek New Testament (1968) 66-67. HOLTZ, T. Untersuchungen über die Alttestamentlichen Zitate bei Lukas (1968) 61-64. STANTON, G. N., Jesus of Nazareth in New Testament Preaching (Cambridge 1974) 57-58. MERK, O., "Das Reich Gottes in den lukanischen Schriften" in: E. E. Ellis/E. Grässer (eds.) Jesus und Paulus. FS. W. G. Kümmel (Götingen 1975) 207ff. SANDERS, J. A., "From Isaiah 61 to Luke 4" in: J. Neusner, (ed.) Christianity, Judaism, and Other Graeco-Roman Cults. I. FS. M. Smith (Leiden 1975) 75-107.

4:1ff. LENTZEN-DEIS, F. Die Taufe Jesu nach den Synoptikern (1970) 285.

4:1-13 Böklen, E., "Zu der Versuchung Jesu" ZNW 18 (1917-1918) 244. HIRSCH, E. Frühgeschichte des Evangeliums (1941) 73-77. BARRETT, C. K. The Holy Spirit and the Gospel Tradition (1947) 46-53. MASSAUX, E. Influence de l'Evangile de saint Matthieu sur la littérature chrétienne avant saint Irénée (1950) 543-45. AR-GYLE, A. W. "The Accounts of the Temptations of Jesus in Relation to the Q Hypothesis," ET 64 (1952-1953) 382. LEIVESTAD, R. Christ the Conqueror (1954) 51ff. LOEWENICH, W. von, Luther als Ausleger der Synoptiker (1954) 67f., 80f. DENNEY, J. The Death of Christ (1956) 20. DUPONT, J. "L'Arrierefond Biblique du Recit des Tentations de Jésus," NTS 3 (1956-1957) 287f. GILS, F. Jésus Prophète D'Après Les Evangiles Synoptiques (1957) 83-85. FEUILLET, A. "Le récit lucanien de la tentation (Lc 4,1-13)," Biblica 40 (3, 1959) 613-31. TAYLOR, A. B. "Decision in the Desert. The Temptation of Jesus in the Light of Deuteronomy," Interpretation 14 (3, 1960) 300-09. DUPONT, J. "Les tentations de Jésus dans le récit de Luc (Luc, 4,1-13)," SciEccl 14 (1, 1962) 7-29. BARTSCH, H. W., Wachet aber zu jeder Zeit (Hamburg-Bergstedt 1963) 55-59. BAUMBACH, G. Das Verständnis des Bösen in den Synoptischen Evangelien (1963) 169ff. HAHN, F. Christologische Hoheitstitel (1963) 72. CONZELMANN, H. Die Mitte der Zeit (1964) 21ff. SWANSTON, H. "The Lukan Temptation Narrative," JTHS 17 (1, 1966) 71. DUPONT, J. Les Ten-

tations de Jésus au Désert (1968) 45-72. NAVONE, J. "The
Temptation Account in St. Luke (4,1-13)," Scripture 20 (51, 1968)
65-72. BLANK, J. Schriftauslegung in Theorie und Praxis (1969)
117-21. DUPONT, J. Die Versuchungen Jesu in der Wüste (1969).
JEREMIAS, J. Neutestamentliche Theologie I (1971) 74ff.
SCHNACKENBURG , R. Schriften zum Neuen Testament; Ex-
egese in Fortschritt und Wandel (1971) 108-128. SCHULZ, S. Q
Die Spruchquelle der Evangelisten (1972) 177-90. STANTON, G.
N., "On the Christology of Q" in: B. Lindars/S. S. Smalley (eds.)
Christ and the Spirit in the New Testament. FS. C. F. D. Moule
(Cambridge 1973) 34-35. COLLINS, R. F., "The Temptation of
Jesus" MTh 26 (1974) 32-45. TALBERT, C. H., Literary Pat-
terns, Theological Themes, and the Genre of Luke-Acts (Missoula
1974) 45, 46, 47, 117. WILKENS, W., "Die Versuchungsges-
chichte Luk. 4, 1-13 und die Komposition des Evangeliums" ThZ
30 (1974) 262-72. GLÖCKNER, R., Die Verkündigung des Heils
beim Evangelisten Lukas (Mainz 1975) 72-73, 145, 174ff. KUR-
ICHIANIL, J., "The Temptations of Christ, Their Meaning" Biblebhashyam 1 (1975) 106-25. LAFON, C., "La genèse de
l'homme. Lecture de Luc 4,1-13" Christus 22 (1975) 443-44.
CALLOUD, J., Structural Analysis of Narrative (Philadelphia 1976)
47-108. EDWARDS, R. A., A Theology of Q (Philadelphia 1976)
82-84. BERGMAN, J., "Zum Zwei-Wege-Motiv. Religionsgeschichtliche und exegetische Bemerkungen" SEA 41-42 (1977) 27-
56. POLAG, A., Die Christologie der Logienquelle (Neukirchen-
Vluyn 1977) 146-51. SCHNEIDER, G., Das Evangelium nach Lukas (Gütersloh/Würzburg 1977) 98-99 (lit!). BUSSE, U., Das Nazareth-Manifest Jesu. Eine Einführung in das lukanische Jesusbild
nach Lk 4,16-30 (Stuttgart 1978) 17-19, 22, 25. RIST, J. M., On
the Independence of Matthew and Mark (Cambridge 1978) 22-24.
QUERDRAY, G., "La tentation de Jésus au désert. Prélude de la
Passion" EsVie 90 (1980) 184-89. ZELLER, D., "Die Versuchungen Jesu in der Logienquelle" TThZ 89 (1980) 61-73.
KRAFT,H., Die Entstehung des Christentums (Darmstadt 1981) 96-
103.

4:1-4, 9-12 HAHN, F., Christologische Hoheitstitel (1963) 303.

4:1-2 STREETER, B. H. The Four Gospels (1951) 205f. Text von Papyrus p[7] bietet Aland, NTS 3 (1957) 261-86. HAHN, F. Christologische Hoheitstitel (1963) 401.

4:1 HAHN, F. Christologische Hoheitstitel (1963) 318. STÄHLIN, G.,
"Τὸ πνεῦμα 'Ιησοῦ (Apostelgeschichte 16:7)" in: B. Lindars/
S. S. Smalley (eds.) Christ and the Spirit in the New Testament.
FS. C. F. D. Moule (Cambridge 1973) 243-44, 246. RAYAN, S.,
The Holy Spirit: Heart of the Gospel and Christian Hope (New York

1978) 99-100. JEREMIAS, J., Die Sprache des Lukasevangeliums (Göttingen 1980) 114-15.

4:2 FRIEDRICHSEN, G. W. S. "The Gothic Text of Luke in its Relation to the Codex Brixianus (f) and the Codex Palatinus (e)," NTS 11 (1964-1965) 282f. BOUSSET, W. Die Religion des Judentums im Späthellenistischen Zeitalter (1966 = 1926) 180. METZGER, G. M., Early Versions of the New Testament (Oxford 1977) 88. BÖHLIG, A., Die Gnosis III: Der Manichäismus (Zürich/München 1980) 338n.93.

4:3ff. Parker, P. The Gospel Before Mark (1953) 61ff.

4:3.9 ROBERTSON, A. T. Luke the Historian in the Light of Research (1920) 158f.

4:3 TALBERT, C. H., Literary Patterns, Theological Themes, and the Genre of Luke-Acts (Missoula 1974) 46, 47, 118. FRIEDRICH, G., "Beobachtungen zur messianischen Hohepriestererwartung in den Synoptiker" in: Auf das Wort kommt es an (Göttingen 1978) 91-92. JEREMIAS, J., Die Sprache des Lukasevangeliums (Göttingen 1980) 115.

4:4ff. STONEHOUSE, N. B. The Witness of Matthew and Mark to Christ (1944) 195.

4:5-15 HAMEL, GPM 7 (1962-1963) 83ff.

4:5-8 HAHN, F. Christologische Hoheitstitel (1963) 175f.

4:5.6 SCHÜRMANN, H. "Sprachliche Reminiszenzen an abgeänderte oder ausgelassene Bestandteile der Spruchsammlung im Lukas- und Matthäusevangelium," NTS 6 (1959-1960) 209f.

4:5 NICKELS, P. Targum and New Testament (1967) 31. METZGER, B. M., Early Versions of the New Testament (Oxford 1977) 88, 179. JEREMIAS, J., Die Sprache des Lukasevangeliums (Göttingen 1980) 116-17.

4:6 LANGE, J., Das Erscheinen des Auferstandenen im Evangelium nach Mattäus (Würzburg 1973) 25, 91-94, 150, 293. JEREMIAS, J., Die Sprache des Lukasevangeliums (Göttingen 1980) 117.

4:7-8 HAHN, F. Christologische Hoheitstitel (1963) 86.

4:8-11 McNAMARA, M. The New Testament and the Palestinian Targum to the Pentateuch (1966) 250.

4:8 WAINWWRIGHT, A. W. The Trinity in the New Testament (1962) 103-104. HAHN, F. Christologische Hoheitstitel (1963) 72. "Bibel" in: TRE 6 (1980) 62.

4:9-12 HYLDAHL, N. "Die Versuchung auf der Zinne des Tempels (Matth 4,5-7 = Luk 4,9-12)," StTh 15 (2, 1961) 113-27. HAHN, F. Christologische Hoheitstitel (1963) 240.

4:9 BETZ, H. D. Lukian von Samosata und das Neue Testament (1961)

40, 168. NICKELS, P. Targum and New Testament (1967) 31. TALBERT, C. H., Literary Patterns, Theological Themes, and the Genre of Luke-Acts (Missoula 1974) 46, 47, 118. METZGER, B. M., Early Versions of the New Testament (Oxford 1977) 206.

4:10-11 HOLTZ, T. Untersuchungen über die Alttestamentlichen Zitate bei Lukas (1968) 57f.

4:10 JEREMIAS, J., Die Sprache des Lukasevangeliums (Göttingen 1980) 117.

4:13 HAHN, F. Christologische Hoheitstitel (1963) 167. BOUSSET, W. Die Religion des Judentums im Späthellenistischen Zeitalter (1966 = 1926). BROWN, S. Apostasy and Perseverance in the Theology of Luke (1969) 1, 5f., 12, 16f., 19. SCHNEIDER, G. Verleugnung, Verspottung und Verhör Jesu nach Lukas 22,54-71 (1969) 170, 181, 182, 201. ZMIJEWSKI, J., Die Eschatologiereden des Lukasevangeliums (Bonn 1972) 51, 189, 308, 434. JEREMIAS, J., Die Sprache des Lukasevangeliums (Göttingen 1980) 110.

4:14-9:50 KUDASIEWICZ, J., "Znaczenie Jerusalem w czasie dzalanósci. . . . " RTK 17 (1970) 43-59. PERRIN, N., The New Testament: An Introduction (New York 1974) 207-09.

4:14ff. KNOX, W. L. The Sources of the Synoptic Gospels II (1957) 4.

4:14-44 ESCUDERO FREIRE, C., "Jesús profeta, libertador del hombre. Vision lucana de su ministerio terrestre" EstEc 51 (1976) 463-95. KENIK, H. A., "Messianic Fulfillment in Luke" Bible Today 18 (1980) 236-41.

4:14-30 PREVALLET, E. M. "The Rejection at Nazareth: Luke 4:14-30," Scripture 20 (49, 1968) 5-9. SCHREINER, J. Gestalt und Anspruch des Neuen Testaments (1969) 215-20. DESCAMPS, A./DE HALLEUX, A. Mélanges Bibliques en hommage au R. P. Béda Rigaux (1970) 201-03, 205. PIDWELL, H. J. Blessed are the Poor (1972) 66-72. BARTSCH, W. H., Wachet aber zu jeder Zeit! (Hamburg-Bergstedt 1963) 59-63. LOHSE, E., Die Einheit des Neuen Testaments (Göttingen 1973) 155-56. REICKE, B., "Jesus in Nazareth - Lk 4,14-30" in: H. Balz/S. Schulz (eds.) Das Wort und die Wörter (Stuttgart 1973) 47-55.

4:14-21 BENCHERT, GPM 19 (1964-1965) 53ff. TRAUB, H. in: Hören und Fragen Bd. 5,3 (1967) G. Eichholz & A. Falkenroth (eds.) 84ff. WEBER, O. Predigtmeditationen (1967) 271-74. FRICK, R. GPM 25 (4, 1970) 72-76. LANGE, E. (ed.) Predigtstudien für das Kirchenjahr 1970-1971 (1970) 91-96. DOMAY, E., in: P. Krusche et al. (eds.) Predigtstudien für das Kirchenjahr 1976-1977, V/1 (Stuttgart 1976) 68-72.

4:14-16 SCHÜRMANN, H. "Der 'Bericht vom Anfang.' Ein Rekonstruktionsversuch auf Grund von Lk. 4,14-16," in: Studia Evangelica II (1964) F. L. Cross (ed.) 242-58. CRIBBS, F. L. in: SBL Seminar Papers Vol. 2 (1973) MacRae, G. (ed.) 3. DELOBEL, J., "La Rédaction de Lc., IV 14-16a" in: F. Neirynck (ed.) L'Evangile de Luc (Gembloux 1973) 203-23. BUSSE, U., Das Nazareth-Manifest Jesu. Eine Einführung in das lukanische Jesusbild nach Lk 4,16-30 (Stuttgart 1978) 23-24.

4:14-15 CONZELMANN, H. Die Mitte der Zeit (1964) 23ff. SAMAIN, E., "L'Evangile de Luc: un témoignage ecclésial et missionnaire. Lc 1,1-14; 4,14-15" AssS 34 (1973) 60-73. TALBERT, C. H., Literary Patterns, Theological Themes, and the Genre of Luke-Acts (Missoula 1974) 45, 47, 48. EGGER, W., Frohbotschaft und Lehre (Frankfurt 1976) 37, 45-46, 54-55, 77-78. SOARES PRABHU, G. M., The Formula Quotations in the Infancy Narrative of Matthew (Rome 1976) 115-19. SCHNEIDER, G., Das Evangelium nach Lukas (Gütersloh/Würzburg 1977) 104 (lit!). BUSSE,U., Das Nazareth-Manifest Jesu. Eine Einführung in das lukanische Jesusbild nach Lk 4,16-30 (Stuttgart 1978) 19-21, 23-25.

4:14 HAHN, F. Christologische Hoheitstitel (1963) 224, 318. CONZELMANN, H. Die Mitte der Zeit (1964) 168f. MARXSEN, W. Mark the Evangelist (1969) 51, 60, 99, 146. SCHNIDER, F. Jesus der Prophet (Freiburg 1973) 108, 189, 238. STÄHLIN, G. "Tò πνεῦμα 'Iησοῦ (Apostelgeschichte 16:7)" in B. Lindars/S. S. Smalley (eds.) Christ and the Spirit in the New Testament. FS. C. F. D. Moule (Cambridge 1973) 243-44, 246-47. RAYAN, S. The Holy Spirit: Heart of the Gospel and Christian Hope (New York 1978) 99-100. JEREMIAS, J. Die Sprache des Lukasevangeliums (Göttingen 1980) 11-19.

4:15.31 FLEW, R. N. Jesus and His Church (1956) 112.

4:15 JEREMIAS, J., Die Sprache des Lukasevangeliums (Göttingen 1980) 119.

4:16-7:17 TALBERT, C. H., Literary Patterns, Theological Themes, and the Genre of Luke-Acts (Missoula 1974) 39-44.

4:16ff. LIGHTFOOT, R. H. History and Interpretation in the Gospels (1934) 184ff. MOORE, G. F. Judaism (1946) I 300f. HAHN, F. Christologische Hoheitstitel (1963) 239, 318. CONZELMANN, H. Die Mitte der Zeit (1964) 25ff., 94. HAHN, F. Das Verständinis der Mission im Neuen Testament (²1965) 112. FLENDER, H. St Luke Theologian of Redemptive History (1967) 49, 146ff. STROBEL, A. Kerygma und Apokalyptik (1967) 105-11.

4:16-44 SELBY, D. J., Introduction to the New Testament (New York 1971) 168-70.

4:16-32 TROCME, A. Jésus et la révolution non violente (1961).

4:16-30 EWALD, H., Die drei ersten Evangelien (1850) 243ff. JÜ-
LICHER, D. A. Die Gleichnisreden Jesu (1910) 171-73. BORN-
HÄUSSER, K. Studien zum Sondergut des Lukas (1934) 20-35.
VIOLET, B., "Zum rechten Verständnis der Nazareth-Perikope Lk
4,16-30" ZNW 37 (1938) 251-71. HIRSCH, E. Frühgeschichte des
Evangeliums (1941) 38-41. STONEHOUSE, N. B. The Witness of
Luke to Christ (1951) 68ff., 152f. FARRER, A. St Matthew and
St Mark (1954). DUPONT, D. J. "Le Salut des Gentils et la Sig-
nification Théologique du Livre des Actes," NTS 6 (1959-1960)
142f. GUILDING, A., The Fourth Gospel and Jewish Worship
(Oxford 1960) 125-26. MASSON, C. Vers les Sources D'eau Vive
(1961) 38ff. SCHULZ, A. Nachfolge und Nachahmen (1962) 36-
39. STRECKER, G. Der Weg der Gerechtigkeit (1962) 64. FIN-
KEL, A. "Jesus' Sermon at Nazareth (Luk. 4,16-30)," in: Abraham unser Vater, Festschrift für O. Michel (1963) 106-15. HAHN,
F. Christologische Hoheitstitel (1963) 394-96. ANDERSON, H.
"Broadening Horizons. The Rejection at Nazareth. Pericope of
Luke 4:16-30 in Light of Recent Critical Trends," Interpretation
18 (3, 1964) 259-75. CAVE, C. H. "The Sermon at Nazareth and
the Beatitudes in the Light of the Synagogue Lectionary," in: Studia Evangelica III (1964) F. L. Cross (ed.) 231-35. GEORGE, A.
"La Prédication inaugurale de Jésus dans la synagogue de Nazareth. Luc 4,16-30," BVieC 59 (1964) 17-29. CROCKETT, L.
"Luke iv. 16-30 and the Jewish Lectionary Cycle: A Word of Cau-
tion," JJS 17 (1-2, 1966) 13-45. STUHLMACHER, P. Das Paulinische Evangelium (1968) 225. BAJARD, J. "La structure de la
péricope de Nazareth en Lc., IV,16-30. Propositions pour une lecture plus cohérente," EphT 45 (1, 1969) 165-71. GASTON, L. No
Stone on Another (1970) 252, 255, 283-85, 286, 312-13, 317.
SCHÜRMANN, H., "Zur Traditionsgeschichte der Nazareth-Perikope Lk 4,16-30," in: A Descamps/A. de Halleux (eds.) Mélanges Bibliques en hommage au R. P. Béda Rigaux (Gembloux
1970) 187-205. HILL, D. "The Rejection of Jesus at Nazareth
(Luke iv 16-30)," NovTest 13 (3, 1971) 161-80. JEREMIAS, J.
Neutestamentliche Theologie I (1971) 107f., 200, 235. SELBY, D.
J., Introduction to the New Testament (New York 1971) 28-29, 154,
229, 246, 313. ELTESTER, W. "Israel im lukanischen Werk und
die Nazarethperikope," in: Jesus in Nazareth (1972) Grässer, Erich
et al (eds.) 76-147. ENSLIN, M. S. Reapproaching Paul (1972) 44f.
STROBEL, A. "Die Ausrufung des Jubeljahres in der Nazareth-
predigt Jesu; zur apokalyptischen Tradition Lc 4:16-30," in: Jesus
in Nazreth (1972) Grässer, Erich, et al. (eds.) 38-50. STROBEL,
A. "Das apokalyptische Terminproblem in der sogenannten An-
trittspredigt Jesu (Lk 4,16-30)," ThLZ 92 (1972) 251-54. TAN-

NEHILL, R. C. "The Mission of Jesus according to Luke iv 16-30," in: Jesus in Nazareth (1972) Grässer, Erich, et al (eds.) 51-75. COMBRINK, H. J. B., "The Structure and Significance of Luke 4,16-30" Neotestamentica 7 (1973) 27-47. DELOBEL, J., "La Rédaction de Lc., IV 14-16a" in: F. Neirynck (ed.) L'Evangile de Luc (Gembloux 1973) 217-18. PERROT, C. "Luc 4,16-30 et la Lecture Biblique de L'Ancienne Synagogue," in: Exegese Biblique et Judaism (1973) J. E. Ménard (ed.) 170-86. PERROT, C. "Luc 4,16-30 et la lecture biblique de l'ancienne Synagogue," RevSR 47 (2-4, 1973) 324-340. SAMAIN, E., "La Notion de APXH" in: F. Neirynck (ed.) L'Evangile de Luc (Gembloux 1973) 309-10. SCHNIDER, F., Jesus der Prophet (Freiburg 1973) 163ff. STANTON, G. N., "On the Christology of Q" in: B. Lindars/S. S. Smalley (eds.) Christ and the Spirit in the New Testament. FS. C. F. D. Moule (Cambridge 1973) 32-33. WANKE, J., Die Emmauserzählung. Eine redaktionsgeschichtliche Untersuchung zu Lk 24,13-35 (Leipzig 1973) 61. WILSON, S. G., The Gentiles and the Gentile Misson in Luke-Acts (Cambridge 1973) 40-41, 130, 241. STANTON, G. N., Jesus of Nazareth in New Testament Preaching (Cambridge 1974) 58, 65, 130, 138. TALBERT, C. H., Literary Patterns, Theological Themes, and the Genre of Luke-Acts (Missoula 1974) 16, 18, 19, 39, 40, 41, 97, 117. CONZELMANN, H. und LINDEMANN, A., Arbeitsbuch zum Neuen Testament (Tübingen 1975) 41. GLÖCKNER, R., Die Verkündigung des Heils beim Evangelisten Lukas (Mainz 1975) 126ff, 145ff, 164. LOHFINK, G., Die Sammlung Israels (München 1975) 44-46. RADL, W., Paulus und Jesus im lukanischen Doppelwerk. Untersuchungen zu Parallelmotiven im Lukasevangelium und in der Apostelgeschichte (Bern/Frankfurt 1975) 94-100. DRURY, J., Tradition and Design in Luke's Gospel (Atlanta 1976) 66. EGGER, W., Frohbotschaft und Lehre (Frankfurt 1976) 46. SCHMEICHEL, W., "Christian Prophecy in Lukan Thought. Luke 4:16-30 as a Point of Departure" in: G. MacRae (ed.) SBL Seminar Papers 1976 (Missoula 1976) 293-304. SOARES PRABHU, G. M., The Formula Quotations in the Infancy Narrative of Matthew (Rome 1976) 116-19. REUMANN, J., "A History of Lectionaries: From the Synagogue at Nazareth to Post-Vatican II" Interp 31 (1977) 116-30. SCHNEIDER, G., Das Evangelium nach Lukas (Gütersloh/Würzburg 1977) 106 (lit!). BUSSE, U., Das Nazareth-Manifest Jesu. Eine Einführung in das lukanische Jesusbild nach Lk 4,16-30 (Stuttgart 1978). RIST, J. M., On the Independence of Matthew and Mark (Cambridge 1978) 60-61. JEWETT, R., Jesus against the Rapture. Seven Unexpected Prophecies (Philadelphia 1979) 51-65. PRAST, F., Presbyter und Evangelium in nachapostolischer Zeit

(Stuttgart 1979) 265-75, 351. SWIDLER, L., Biblical Affirmations of Woman (Philadelphia 1979) 178. McDONALD, J. I. H., Kerygma and Didache (Cambridge 1980) 48.

4:16-24 GOODSPEED, E. J. A Life of Jesus (1950) 95-99.

4:16-22 FALCKE, H., in: GPM 31 (1976-1977) 56-64.

4:16-21 FITZMYER, J. A. "A Qumran parallel for the same exegetical method used in Lk 4,16-21," NTS 7 (1960-1961) 316. BRÜCK-MANN, O. in: Herr, tue meine Lippen auf Bd. 3 (1964) G. Eichholz (ed.) 63ff. BRAUN, H. Qumran und NT II (1966) 78, 106. SAMAIN, E. "Le discours-programme de Nazareth. Lc 4,16-21," AssS 20 (1973) 17-27. WIGGERMANN, K.-F. und KRÜGER, U., in: P. Krusche et al. (eds.) Predigtstudien für das Kirchenjahr 1978-1979. I/2 (Stuttgart 1978) 96-102. SAMAIN, E., "Manifesto de Libertação: o Discurso-programa de Nazaré (Lc 4,16-21)" REB 34 (1974) 261-87.

4:16-20 MÄRZ, C.-P., Das Wort Gottes bei Lukas (Leipzig 1973) 41-44.

4:16-18 WILCKENS, U., Die Missionsreden der Apostelgeschichte (1961) 102, 107, 132, 160, 167, 202.

4:16-17 McNAMARA, M. The New Testament and the Palestinian Targum to the Pentateuch (1966) 43. DÖMER, M., Das Heil Gottes: Studien zur Theologie des lukanischen Doppelwerkes (Köln/Bonn 1978) 53-55. PRAST, F., Presbyter und Evangelium in nachapostolischer Zeit (Stuttgart 1979) 266.

4:16 SCHMID, J. Das Evangelium nach Lukas (1955) 114-16. TALBERT, C. H., Literary Patterns, Theological Themes, and the Genre of Luke-Acts (Missoula 1974) 95. BUSSE, U., Das Nazareth-Manifest Jesu. Eine Einführung in das lukanische Jesusbild nach Lk 4,16-30 (Stuttgart 1978) 31-32. JEREMIAS, J., Die Sprache des Lukasevangeliums (Göttingen 1980) 119-21.

4:17ff. LENTZEN-DEIS, F. Die Taufe Jesus nach den Synoptikern (1970) 146ff.

4:17-24 DESCAMPS, A./DE HALLEUX, A. Mélanges Bibliques en hommage au R. P. Béda Rigaux (1970) 188-89.

4:17-21 DESCAMPS, A./De HALLEUX, A. Mélanges Bibliques en hommage au R. P. Béda Riaux (1970) 190, 191-93, 203-04. TALBERT, C. H., Literary Patterns, Theological Themes, and the Genre of Luke-Acts (Missoula 1974) 19.

4:17-19 GERSTENBERGER, G. und SCHRAGE, W., Leiden (Stuttgart 1977) 129; ET: J. E. Steely (trans.) Suffering (Nashville 1980) 150-51. "Armut" in: TRE 4 (1979) 78.

4:17 BUSSE, U., Das Nazareth-Manifest Jesu. Eine Einführung in das lukanische Jesusbild nach Lk 4,16-30 (Stuttgart 1978) 32-33. JE-

REMIAS, J., Die Sprache des Lukasevangeliums (Göttingen 1980) 121.

4:18ff. EDGAR, S. L. NTS 5 (1958-1959) 50ff. CONZELMANN, H. Die Mitte der Zeit (1964) 98f., 177ff. STROBEL, A. Erkenntnis und Bekenntnis der Sünde in neutestamentlicher Zeit (1968) 41. GLÖCKNER, R., Die Verkündigung des Heils beim Evangelisten Lukas (Mainz 1975) 129, 132ff, 184, 191ff, 200-01.

4:18-21 FLEW, R. N. Jesus and His Church (1956) 60. EUGSTER, W. A., The Healing Ministry of Jesus in the Gospel of Luke (Th.M. thesis, Rüschlikon/Switzerland, Baptist Theological Seminary 1978).

4:18-19 NESTLE, E. ZNW 2 (1901) 153-57. NESTLE, E., "Zu Lk 4:18,19" ZNW 8 (1907) 77-78. HAHN, F. Christologische Hoheitstitel (1963) 72. HOLTZ, T. Untersuchungen über die Alttestamentlichen Zitate bei Lukas (1968) 39-41. RESE, M. Alttestamentliche Motive in der Christologie des Lukas (1969) 143-54. DUNN, J. D. G., Jesus and the Spirit (London 1975) 54-55. MAILLOT, A., "Réparer les coeurs brisés. Réunifier les vies en miettes" RevR 27 (1976) 97-103. DUNN, J. D. G., Unity and Diversity in the New Testament (London 1977) 189. BUSSE, U., Das Nazareth-Manifest Jesu. Eine Einführung in das lukanische Jesusbild nach Lk 4,16-30 (Stuttgart 1978) 27, 33-36, 69, 70, 76, 77-84. DÖMER, M., Das Heil Gottes: Studien zur Theologie des lukanischen Doppelwerkes (Köln/Bonn 1978) 55-56. RAYAN, S., The Holy Spirit: Heart of the Gospel and Christian Hope (New York 1978) 95. MEYER, B. F., The Aims of Jesus (London 1979) 157-58. PRAST, F., Presbyter und Evangelium in nachapostolischer Zeit (Stuttgart 1979) 267-69, 287-88.

4:18 PALLIS, A., Notes on St. Luke and the Acts (London 1928) 9-10. MESSINA, G. "Parallelismi semitismi leziono tendenziose nell'armonia Persiana," Biblica 30 (1949) 374-75. FLEW, R. N. Jesus and His Church (1956) 50. DELLING, G. Die Taufe im Neuen Testament (1963) 107. HAHN, F. Christologische Hoheitstitel (1963) 224, 319. MICHL, J., "Der Geist der Herrn ruht auf mir" BuK 21 (1967) 42-45. JEREMIAS, J. Neutestamentliche Theologie I (1971) 20, 114, 116, 198, 200. MINEAR, P., To Heal and to Reveal (New York 1976) 64. RINALDI, B., "Proclamare ai prigionieri la liberazione (Lc. 4,18)" BiOr 18 (1976) 241-45. METZGER, B. M., Early Versions of the New Testament (Oxford 1977) 41. BEST, E., From Text to Sermon (Atlanta 1978) 24. FRIEDRICH, G., "Beobachtungen zur messianischen Hohepriestererwartung in den Synoptikern" in: Auf das Wort kommt es an (Göttingen 1978) 76-77. KARRIS, R. J., "Poor and Rich: The Lukan Sitz im Leben" in: C. H. Talbert (ed.) Perspectives on Luke-Acts (Danville 1978) 117-18. RAYAN, S., The Holy Spirit: Heart

of the Gospel and Christian Hope (New York 1978) 7-8, 99-100/
PRAST, F., Presbyter und Evangelium in nachapostolischer Zeit
(Stuttgart 1979) 104n.283, 271. JEREMIAS, J., Die Sprache des
Lukasevangeliums (Göttingen 1980) 122.

4:19-30, 39-42 SOUCEK, GPM 7 (1962-1963) 224ff.

4:20-22 DÖMER, M., Das Heil Gottes: Studien zur Theologie des lukanischen Doppelwerkes (Köln/Bonn 1978) 54-55.

4:20 BUSSE, U., Das Nazareth-Manifest Jesu. Eine Einführung in das
lukanische Jesusbild nach Lk 4,16-30 (Stuttgart 1978) 36. JE-
REMIAS,J., Die Sprache des Lukasevangeliums (Göttingen 1980)
122.

4:21-30 SAMAIN, E. "Aucun prophète n'est bien reçu dans sa patrie. Lc
4,21-30," AssS 35 (1973) 63-72.

4:21-22 PRAST, F., Presbyter und Evangelium in nachapostolischer Zeit
(Stuttgart 1979) 106, 210, 269-71.

4:21 STRECKER, G. Der Weg der Gerechtigkeit (1962) 851. HAHN,
F. Christologische Hoheitstitel (1963) 364. FLENDER, H. St Luke
Theologian of Redemptive History (1967) 147, 151, 152, 154, 156.
KIRK, A. "La conciencia mesianica de Jesus en el sermon de Na-
zaret: Lc 4,16ss," RevBi 33 (2, 1971) 127-37. ZMIJEWSKI, J.,
Die Eschatologiereden des Lukasevangeliums (Bonn 1972) 11, 35,
185, 190, 212, 517. WILSON, S. G., The Gentiles and the Gentile
Mission in Luke-Acts (Cambridge 1973) 53, 55, 63, 67, 87. TAL-
BERT, C. H., Literary Patterns, Theological Themes, and the Genre
of Luke-Acts (Missoula 1974) 117. BANKS, R., Jesus and the Law
in the Synoptic Tradition (London 1975) 211-212. DRURY, J.,
Tradition and Design in Luke's Gospel (Atlanta 1976) 70-71.
METZGER, B. M., Early Versions of the New Testament (Oxford
1977) 249. BUSSE, U., Das Nazareth-Manifest Jesu. Eine Einführung in das lukanische Jesusbild nach Lk 4,16-30 (Stuttgart 1978)
36-37, 75. JEREMIAS, J., Die Sprache des Lukasevangeliums
(Göttingen 1980) 122-23.

4:22-30 TANNEHILL, R. C. "The Mission of Jesus," in: Jesus in Nazareth (1972) Grässer, Erich, et al (eds.) 53-63. PRAST, F., Presbyter und Evangelium in nachapostolischer Zeit (Stuttgart 1979)
271-73.

4:22 PALLIS, A., Notes on St. Luke and the Acts (London 1928) 10.
GILS, F. Jésus Prophète D'Après Les Evangiles Synoptiques (1957)
12-19. FLENDER, H. St Luke Theologian of Redemptive History
(1967) 26n, 51n, 152, 153 & n, 154, 156, 161n. GRAESSER, E.
NTS 16 (1969-1970) 15f. DESCAMPS, A./DE HALLEUX, A.
Mélanges Bibliques en hommage au R. P. Béda Rigaux (1970) 190,
196-97. PETZKE, G. Die Traditionen über Apollonius von Tyana

und das Neue Testament (1970) 163, 168, 190. BEUTLER, J. Martyria (1972) 172, 181, 221. NELLESSEN, E., Zeugnis für Jesus und das Wort (Köln 1976) 65-69. TRITES, A. A., The New Testament Concept of Witness (Cambridge 1977) 128-129. BUSSE, U., Das Nazareth-Manifest Jesu. Eine Einführung in das lukanische Jesusbild nach Lk 4,16-30 (Stuttgart 1978) 24-26, 37-38. NOLLAND, J., "Impressed Unbelievers as Witnesses to Christ (Luke 4:22a)" JBL 98 (1979) 219-29. SWIDLER, L., Biblical Affirmations of Woman (Philadelphia 1979) 278. JEREMIAS, J., Die Sprache des Lukasevangeliums (Göttingen 1980) 123.

4:23-24 SUMMERS, R. The Secret Sayings of the Living Jesus (1968) 36. DESCAMPS, A./DE HALLEUX, A. Mélanges Bibliques en hommage au R. P. Béda Rigaux (1970) 197-99.

4:23 JÜLICHER, D. A. Die Gleichnisreden Jesu (1910) 171-74. BONHOEFFER, A. Epiktet und das Neue Testament (1911) 95ff., 304. STONEHOUSE, N. B. The Witness of Luke to Christ (1951) 72ff. METZGER, B. M., Early Versions of the New Testament (Oxford 1977) 201, 244. BUSSE, U., Das Nazareth-Manifest Jesu. Eine Einführung in das lukanische Jesusbild nach Lk 4,16-30 (Stuttgart 1978) 26-27, 28, 38-40. NOLLAND, J., "Classical and Rabbinic Parallels to 'Physician, heal yourself' (Lk. iv 23)," NovT 21 (1979) 193-209. JEREMIAS, J., Die Sprache des Lukasevangeliums (Göttingen 1980) 124-125. McDonald, J. I. H., Kerygma and Didache (Cambridge 1980) 81. KRAFT, H., Die Entstehung des Christentums (Darmstadt 1981) 85.

4:24-27 BUSSE, U., Das Nazareth-Manifest Jesu. Eine Einführung in das lukanische Jesusbild nach Lk 4,16-29 (Stuttgart 1978) 27-28. SWIDLER, L., Biblical Affirmations of Woman (Philadelphia 1979) 167, 253.

4:24-25 HASLER, V. Amen (1969) 99.

4:24 GILS, F. Jésus Prophète D'Après Les Evangiles Synoptiques (1957) 9-10. KNOX, W. L. The Sources of the Synoptic Gospels II (1957) 154. HAHN, F. Christologische Hoheitstitel (1963) 92. HENNECKE, E./SCHNEEMELCHER, W. Neutestamentliche Apokryphen (1964) I 69. SCHRAGE, W. Das Verhältnis des Thomas-Evangeliums zur Synoptischen Tradition und zu den Koptischen Evangelienübersetzungen (1964) 75. BERGER, K. Die Amen-Worte Jesus (1970) 88-89. JEREMIAS, J., Die Sprache des Lukasevangeliums (Göttingen 1980) 125-26.

4:25-27 STONEHOUSE, N. B. The Witness of Luke to Christ (1951) 90ff. CROCKETT, L. C. "Luke 4:25-27 and Jewish-Gentile Relations in Luke-Acts," JBL 88 (1, 1969) 177-83. DESCAMPS, A./DE HALLEUX, A. Mélanges Bibliques en hommage au R. P. Béda

Rigaux (1970) 189-90, 191-95, 204, 205. TRUDINGER, L. P. "Subtle Symbols of Sacramentarianism? A Note on Luke 4:25-27," RThR 31 (3, 1972) 95-96. WILSON, S. G., The Gentiles and the Gentile Mission in Luke-Acts (Cambridge 1973) 40-41, 51, 53, 55, 243-44. TALBERT, C. H., Literary Patterns, Theological Themes, and the Genre of Luke-Acts (Missoula 1974) 98. BUSSE, U., Das Nazareth-Manifest Jesu. Eine Einführung in das lukanische Jesus-bild nach Lk 4,16-30 (Stuttgart 1978) 29, 41-45. DÖMER, M., Das Heil Gottes: Studien zur Theologie des lukanischen Doppelwerkes (Köln/Bonn 1978) 51-52. SWIDLER, L., Biblical Affirmations of Woman (Philadelphia 1979) 184, 272.

4:25 STONEHOUSE, N. B. The Witness of Matthew and Mark to Christ (1944) 210. KNOX, W. L. The Sources of the Synoptic Gospels II (1957) 115. NICKELS, P. Targum and New Testament (1967) 31. JEREMIAS, J. Neutestamentliche Theologie I (1971) 21f. METZ-GER, B. M., Early Versions of the New Testament (Oxford 1977) 89. JEREMIAS, J., Die Sprache des Lukasevangeliums (Göttin-gen 1980) 126-27.JEREMIAS, J., Die Sprache des Lukasevangel-iums (Göttingen 1980) 127.

4:27 FARRER, A. St Matthew and St Mark (1954) 45n. METZGER, B. M., Early Versions of the New Testament (Oxford 1977) 368.

4:28-30 DÖMER, M., Das Heil Gottes: Studien zur Theologie des luka-nischen Doppelwerkes (Köln/Bonn 1978) 57. SWIDLER, L., Bib-lical Affirmations of Woman (Philadelphia 1979) 283.

4:28-29 BUSSE, U., Das Nazareth-Manifest Jesu. Eine Einführung in das lukanische Jesusbild nach Lk 4,16-30 (Stuttgart 1978) 45-46.

4:28 NICKELS, P. Targum and New Testament (1967) 31. METZ-GER, B. M., Early Versions of the New Testament (Oxford 1977) 89. BUSSE,U., Das Nazareth-Manifest Jesu. Eine Einführung in das lukanische Jesusbild nach Lk 4,16-30 (Stuttgart 1978) 28-29.

4:29-43 BUSSE, U., Das Nazareth-Manifest Jesu. Eine Einführung in das lukaniche Jesusbild nach Lk 4,16-30 (Stuttgart 1978) 25.

4:29 BETZ, H. D. Lukian von Samosata und das Neue Testament (1961) 115, 178. DALMAN, G. Orte und Wege Jesu (1967) 83f. BUSSE, U., Das Nazareth-Manifest Jesu. Eine Einführung in das lukan-ische Jesusbild nach Lk 4,16-30 (Stuttgart 1978) 40-44. VIEL-HAUER, Ph., "Oikodome. Das Bild vom Bau in der christlichen Literatur vom Neuen Testament bis Clemens Alexandrinus" in: G. Klein (ed.) Oikodome (München 1979) 54. JEREMIAS, J., Die Sprache des Lukasevangeliums (Göttingen 1980) 127-28.

4:30 KÜNZI, M. Das Naherwartungslogion Matthäus 10,23 (1970) 14, 61, 69, 81, 108, 113, 155. BUSSE, U., Das Nazareth-Manifest Jesu. Eine Einführung in das lukanische Jesusbild nach Lk 4,16-30

(Stuttgart 1978) 29, 46. JEREMIAS, J., Die Sprache des Lukas-evangeliums (Göttingen 1980) 128.

4:31-9:50 TALBERT, C. H., "The Lukan Presentation of Jesus' Ministry in Galilee. Luke 4:31-9:50," RevEx 64 (4, 1967) 485-97. NEI-RYNCK, F., "La Matière dans Luc" in: F. Neirynck (ed.) L'E-vangile de Luc (Gembloux 1973) 162-67.

4:31-8:56 TALBERT, C. H., Literary Patterns, Theological Themes, and the Genre of Luke-Acts (Missoula 1974) 16, 19, 20.

4:31ff. BRUNNER, E. Dogmatik II (1950) 322.

4:31-44 EWALD, H. Die drei ersten Evangelien (1850) 193ff. HEINRICI, G. Neutestamentliche Studien (1914) 101ff. TAYLOR, V. Behind the Third Gospel (1926) 78-80. STONEHOUSE, N. B. The Witness of Luke to Christ (1951) 94, 95f. CONZELMANN, H. Die Mitte der Zeit (1964) 32ff. SCHRAMM, T. Der Markus-Stoff bei Lukas (1971) 85-91.

4:31-41 TALBERT, C. H., Literary Patterns, Theological Themes, and the Genre of Luke-Acts (Missoula 1974) 40, 41, 42. BUSSE, U., Das Nazareth-Manifest Jesu. Eine Einführung in das lukanische Jesus-bild nach Lk 4, 16-30 (Stuttgart 1978) 25.

4:31-39 SWIDLER, L., Biblical Affirmations of Woman (Philadelphia 1979) 225.

4:31-38 MERKEL/BRANDENBURGER, GPM 19 (1964-1965) 329ff.

4:31-37 GOULDER, M. D. Type and History in Acts (1964) 125-37. MÄRZ, C.-P., Das Wort Gottes bei Lukas (Leipzig 1973) 38-41. SCHNEIDER, G., Das Evangelium nach Lukas (Gütersloh/Würz-burg 1977) 113 (lit!). ACHTEMEIER, P. J. "The Lukan Perspec-tive on the Miracles of Jesus: a Preliminary Sketch" in: C. H. Talbert (ed.) Perspectives on Luke-Acts (Danville 1978) 156-57. RIST, J. M., On the Independence of Matthew and Mark (Cambridge 1978) 26-28. MEYER, B. F., The Aims of Jesus (London 1979) 162-68.

4:31-34 NEIRYNCK, F., "La Matière dans Luc" in: F. Neirynck (ed.) L'Evangile de Luc (Gembloux 1973) 162-64, 166.

4:31-32 EGGER, W., Frohbotschaft und Lehre (Frankfurt 1976) 36.

4:31 FLEW, R. N. Jesus and His Church (1956) 112. KNOX, W. L. The Sources of the Synoptic Gospels II (1957) 78. WANKE, J., Die Emmauserzählung. Eine redaktionsgeschichtliche Untersu-chung zu Lk 24,13-35 (Leipzig 1973) 34. TALBERT, C. H., Lit-erary Patterns, Theological Themes, and the Genre of Luke-Acts (Missoula 1974) 95. METZGER, B. M., Early Versions of the New Testament (Oxford 1977) 200, 201.

4:32 STONEHOUSE, N. B. The Witness of Matthew and Mark to Christ (1944) 135.

4:33-39 SWIDLER, L., Biblical Affirmations of Woman (Philadelphia 1979) 258.

4:33 TALBERT, C. H., Literary Patterns, Theological Themes, and the Genre of Luke-Acts (Missoula 1974) 41.

4:34 LOVESTAM, E. Son and Saviour (1961) 101f. HAHN, F. Christologische Hoheitstitel (1963) 386. GLÖCKNER, R., Die Verkündigung des Heils beim Evangelisten Lukas (Mainz 1975) 190-91. ARENS, E. The HΛΘON-Sayings in the Synoptic Tradition (Fribourg 1976) 210-12, 216-21.

4:35 FARRER, A. St Matthew and St Mark (1954) 56. BARRETT, C. K. The New Testament Background: Selected Documents (1956) 34. TALBERT, C. H., Literary Patterns, Theological Themes, and the Genre of Luke-Acts (Missoula 1974) 41.

4:36 HAHN, F. Christologische Hoheitstitel (1963) 319.PALLIS, A., Notes on St. Luke and the Acts (London 1928) 10-11. METZGER, B. M., Early Versions of the New Testament (Oxford 1977) 435.

4:38-39 PESCH, R. Neuere Exegese - Verlust oder Gewinn? (1968) 169-75. DIETRICH, W. Das Petrusbild der lukanischen Schriften (1972) 18-81. SCHNEIDER, G., Das Evangelium nach Lukas (Gütersloh/Würzburg (1977) 115 (lit!). RIST, J. M., On the Independence of Matthew and Mark (Cambridge 1978) 29. STAGG, E./F., Woman in the World of Jesus (Philadelphia 1978) 220. SWIDLER, L., Biblical Affirmations of Woman (Philadelphia 1979) 180, 184, 236.

4:38 STRECKER, G. Der Weg der Gerechtigkeit (1962) 206₄.

4:39 KNOX, W. L. The Sources of the Synoptic Gospels II (1957) 124. BETZ, H. D. Lukian von Samosata und das Neue Testament (1961) 149, 157. FRIEDRICHSEN, G. W. S. "The Gothic Text of Luke in its Relation to the Codex Brixianus (f) and the Codex Palatinus (e)," NTS 11 (1964-1965) 288f. BOUSSET, W. Die Religion des Judentums im Späthellenistischen Zeitalter (1966 = 1926) 339f. TALBERT, C. H., Literary Patterns, Theological Themes, and the Genre of Luke-Acts (Missoula 1974) 41.

4:40-41 EGGER, W., Frohbotschaft und Lehre (Frankfurt 1976) 37, 70-71. SCHNEIDER, G., Das Evangelium nach Lukas (Gütersloh/Würzburg 1977) 116 (lit!).

4:40 HARTMAN, L. Testimonium Linguae (1963) 22f.

4:41 BLAIR, E. P. Jesus in the Gospel of Matthew (1960) 52. de KRUIJF, Th., Der Sohn des lebendigen Gottes (Rome 1962) 50, 61, 96, 99. HAHN, F., Christologische Hoheitstitel (1963) 219. TALBERT, C. H., Literary Patterns, Theological Themes, and the Genre of Luke-Acts (Missoula 1974) 41. METZGER, B. M., Early Versions of the New Testament (Oxford 1977) 391. BUSSE,U., Das Nazareth-Manifest Jesu. Eine Einführung in das lukanische Jesus-

bild nach (Lk 4,16-30) (Stuttgart 1978) 69. FRIEDRICH, G.,
"Beobachtungen zur messianischen Hohepriestererwartung in den
Synoptikern" in: Auf das Wort kommt es an (Göttingen 1978) 67-
69, 84. SWIDLER, L., Biblical Affirmations of Woman (Philadelphia 1979) 217.

4:42-44 SCHNEIDER, G., Das Evangelium nach Lukas Gütersloh/Würz-
burg 1977) 117 (lit!).

4:42-43 BORSCH, F. H., "Jesus the Wandering Preacher?" in: M. Hooker/
C. Hickling (eds.) What about the New Testament? FS. C. Evans
(London 1975) 48. ARENS, E., The HΛΘON-Sayings in the Synoptic Tradition (Fribourg 1976) 193-209. BUSSE,U., Das Nazareth-Manifest Jesu. Eine Einführung in das lukanische Jesusbild
nach Lk 4,16-30 (Stuttgart 1978) 77-84.

4:42 METZGER, B. M., Early Versions of the New Testament (Oxford
1977) 391.

4:43 NICKELS, P. Targum and New Testament (1967) 32. JE-
REMIAS, J. Neutestamentliche Theologie I (1971) 23, 40, 42f.,
100. SCHWARZ, G., " 'Auch den anderen Städten'? (Lukas
iv.43a)" NTS 23 (1977) 344. PRAST, F., Presbyter und Evangelium in nachapostolischer Zeit (Stuttgart 1979) 265, 275-77, 280-
81, 287-88, 311, 314, 333, 339, 351-52.

4:44 TALBERT, C. H., Literary Patterns,Theological Themes, and the
Genre of Luke-Acts (Missoula 1974) 95. EGGER, W., Frohbotschaft und Lehre (Frankfurt 1976) 77-78. BUSSE, U., Das Nazareth-Manifest Jesu. Eine Einführung in das lukanische Jesusbild
nach Lk 4,16-30 (Stuttgart 1978) 20-21, 23-25. RIST, J. M., On
the Independence of Matthew and Mark (Cambridge 1978) 29.

5:1-9:50 SELBY, D. J., Introduction to the New Testament (New York 1971)
170-74.

5 KNOX, W. L. The Sources of the Synoptic Gospels II (1967) 4.
STANTON, G. N., Jesus of Nazareth in New Testament Preaching
(Cambridge 1974) 57-58.

5:1ff. HAHN, F. Das Verständnis der Mission im Neuen Testament
(²1965) 37. PETZKE, G. Die Traditionen über Apollonius von
Tyana und das Neue Testament (1970) 144, 177, 183.

5:1-16 EWALD, H. Die drei ersten Evangelien (1850) 192f.

5:1-14 STECK, GPM 19 (1964-1965) 346ff.

5:1-11 TAYLOR, V. Behind the Third Gospel (1926) 172ff. BORN-HÄUSSER, K. Studien zum Sondergut des Lukas (1934) 34-41. RICHARDSON, A. The Miracle-Stories of the Gospels (1948) 109f. WEBER, O., GPM 4 (1949-1950) 200ff. LEANEY, R. "Jesus and Peter: the Call and Postresurrection Appearance (Lk 5,1-11 and 24,34)," ET 65/12 (1954) 381-82. IWAND, H. -J., GPM 9 (1954-1955) 177ff. IWAND, H.-J. in: Herr, tue meine Lippen auf Bd.1 (1957) G. Eichholz (ed.) 228-33. SCHNIEWIND, J., Die Parallelperikopen bei Lukas und Johannes (Darmstadt 1958 = 1914) 11-16. KLEIN, G., GPM 15 (1960-1961) 201ff. DOERNE, M. Er kommt auch noch heute (1961) 10-12. STRECKER, G. Der Weg der Gerechtigkeit (1962) 206. BAILEY, J. A. The Traditions Common to the Gospels of Luke and John (1963) 12-17. BARTSCH, W. H., Wachet aber zu jeder Zeit (Hamburg-Bergstedt 1963) 63-66. FULLER, R. H. Interpreting the Miracles (1963) 120ff. HAHN, F. Christologische Hoheitstitel (1963) 85, 394. CONZELMANN, H. Die Mitte der Zeit (1964) 35ff. SCHÜRMANN, H. "Die Verheissung an Simon Petrus. Auslegung von Lk 5,1-11," BuL 5 (1, 1964) 18-24. FISCHER, C. "Der Fischzug des Petrus," in: Kleine Predigt-Typologie III (1965) L. Schmidt (ed.) 171-75. HEPHATA, Predigtgedanken aus Vergangenheit und Gegenwart, Reihe A, Bd. 5 (1966) 104-33. SCHULZ, A., "Das kirchliche Amt als Diener von Menschenfischer" in: Am Tisch des Wortes 11 (1966) 30-35. VOOBUS, A. The Gospels in Study and Preaching (1966) 145-72. ZILLESSEN, K. "Das Schiff des Petrus und die Gefährten vom andern Schiff. (Zur Exegese Luc 5:1-11)," ZNW 57 (1-2, 1966) 137-39. KLEIN, G. "Die Berufung des Petrus," ZNW 58 (1-2, 1967) 1-44. WEBER, O. Predigtmediatationen (1967) 143-45. WUELLNER, W. H. The Meaning of "Fishers of Men" (1967) 232f., 236-38. HAENCHEN, E. "Historie und Verkündigung bei Markus und Lukas," in: Die Bibel und Wir (1968) 156-81. BROWN, S. Apostasy and Perseverance in the Theology of Luke (1969) 57f. KASTING, H. Die Anfänge der Urchristlichen Mission (1969) 49-52, 84, 86. KLEIN, G. "Die Berufung des Petrus", Rekonstruktion und Interpretation, Gesammelte Aufsätze zum Neuen Testament (1969) 11-48. PESCH, R., Der reiche Fischfang Lk 5,1-11/Jo 21,1-14 (Düsseldorf 1969), (lit!).GRASS, H. Ostergeschehen und Osterberichte (1970) 79ff. ITTEL, G. W. Jesus und die Jünger (1970) 18-23. LEHMANN, M. Synoptische Quellenanalyse und die Frage nach dem historischen Jesus (1970) 60-61.MÖLLER, C. Von der Predigt zum Text (1970) 110-17. OTOMO, Y. Nachfolge Jesu und Anfänge der Kirche im Neuen Testament (1970) 122-26. SCHÜRMANN, H.

Ursprung und Gestalt (1970) 268-73. JEREMIAS, J., Neutestamentliche Theologie I (1971) 48, 90-92. SCHRAMM, T. Der Markus-Stoff bei Lukas (1971) 37-40. DELORME, J., "Luc v.1-11:
Analyse Structurale et Histoire de la Rédaction," NTS 18 (2, 1972)
331-50. DIETRICH, W. Das Petrusbild der lukanischen Schriften
(1972) 23-81. ERNST, J., Anfänge der Christologie (Stuttgart 1972)
127-28. GHIBERTI, G. RivB 20 (2, 1972) 201-06. BROWN, R.
E. et al. (eds.) Peter in the New Testament (Minneapolis 1973) 114-
19. CRIBBS, F. L. in: SBL Seminar Papers 2 (1973) G. MacRae
(ed.) 28-31. SCHÜRMANN, H. "La promesse à Simon-Pierre. Lc
5,1-11," AssS 36 (1974) 63-70. PESCH, R., "Le Logion des Pêcheurs" in: F. Neirynck (ed.) L'Evangile de Luc (Gembloux 1973)
225-44. WANKE, J., Die Emmauserzählung. Eine redaktionsgeschichtliche Untersuchung zu Lk 24,13-35 (Leipzig 1973) 103ff,
n.118. SCHÜRMANN, H., "La promesse à Simon-Pierre. Lc 5,1-
11" AssS 36 (1974) 63-70. TALBERT, C. H., Literary Patterns,
Theological Themes, and the Genre of Luke-Acts (Missoula 1974)
40, 41, 42. DRURY, J., Tradition and Design in Luke's Gospel
(Atlanta 1976) 66-67. MUSSNER, F., Petrus und Paulus (Frei-
burg/Basel/Wien 1976) 22-23. SCHNEIDER, G., Das Evangelium nach Lukas (Gütersloh/Würzburg 1977) 122-27. (lit!). Signes
et paraboles. Sémiotique et texte évangélique (Paris 1977). "Amt"
in: TRE 2 (1978) 511. HUBBARD, B. J., "The Role of the Commissioning Accounts in Acts" in: C. H. Talbert (ed.) Perspectives
on Luke-Acts (Danville 1978) 190. LOSADA, D. A., "El relato
de la pesca milagrosa" RevBi 40 (1978) 17-26. McKNIGHT, E.
V., Meaning in Texts. The Historical Shaping of a Narrative Her-
meneutics (Philadelphia 1978) 275-95. PRAST, F., Presbyter und
Evangelium in nachapostolischer Zeit (Stuttgart 1979) 293-97, 209-
11. RUHBACH, G., in: GPM 33 (1979) 303-09. DERRETT, J. D.
M., "*Esan gar haleeis* (Mk 1.16). Jesus's Fishermen and the Parable of the Net" NovT 22 (1980) 103-37. KUHN, H.-W., "Nachfolge nach Ostern" in: D. Lührmann/G. Strecker (eds.) Kiche. FS
G. Bornkamm (Tübingen 1980) 107-10.

5:1-10 IWAND, H.-J. Predigt-Meditationen (1964) 447-54.

5:1-3 LEHMANN, M. Synoptische Quellenanalyse und die Frage nach
dem historischen Jesus (1970) 59.

5:1-2 JEREMIAS, J., Die Sprache des Lukasevangeliums (Göttingen
1980) 129-30.

5:1 KILPATRICK, G. D., "Three Problems of New Testament Text"
NovT 21 (1979) 289-92. PRAST, F., Presbyter und Evangelium in
nachapostolischer Zeit (Stuttgart 1979) 292-97. JEREMIAS, J., Die
Sprache des Lukasevangeliums (Göttingen 1980) 129.

5:2,3 FRIEDRICHSEN, G. W. S. "The Gothic Text of Luke in its Relation to the Codex Brixianus (f) and the Codex Palatinus (e),'' NTS 11 (1964-1965) 282f.

5:2 NICKELS, P. Targum and New Testament (1967) 32. PALLIS, A., Notes on St. Luke and the Acts (London 1928) 11.

5:3 NICKELS, P. Targum and New Testament (1967) 32. JE-REMIAS, J., Die Sprache des Lukasevangeliums (Göttingen 1980) 130-31.

5:4ff. STAEHELIN, E. Die Verkündigung des Reiches Gottes in der Kirche Jesu Christi I (1951) 354.

5:4-7 SANFORD, J. A., The Kingdom Within (New York 1970) 199-200.

5:4 JEREMIAS, J., Die Sprache des Lukasevangeliums (Göttingen 1980) 131.

5:5 HAHN, F. Christologische Hoheitstitel (1963) 77. JEREMIAS, J., Die Sprache des Lukasevangeliums (Göttingen 1980) 132.

5:6 JEREMIAS, J., Die Sprache des Lukasevangeliums (Göttingen 1980) 132.

5:7 JEREMIAS, J., Die Sprache des Lukasevangeliums (Göttingen 1980) 132-34. METZGER, B. M., Early Versions of the New Testament (Oxford 1977) 435.

5:8-10 LINNEMANN, E. Gleichnisse Jesu (1969) 70ff., 150ff.

5:8 HAHN, F. Christologische Hoheitstitel (1963) 84, 85. WULF, F. '' ' . . . denn ich bin ein sündiger Mensch' (Lk 5,8),'' GuL 36 (1, 1963) 1-4. DAVIES, D. P. ''Luke v.8 Simon Petros,'' ET 79 (12, 1968) 382. STROBEL, A. Erkenntnis und Bekenntnis der Sünde in neutestamentlicher Zeit (1968) 42. JEREMIAS, J., Die Sprache des Lukasevangeliums (Göttingen 1980) 134-36.

5:9 JEREMIAS, J., Die Sprache des Lukasevangeliums (Göttingen 1980) 136.

5:10 GROLLENBEG, L. ''Mensen 'vangen' (Lk. 5,10): hen redden van de dood,''NvTh 5, (3, 1965) 330-36. NICKELS, P. Targum and New Testament (1967) 32. PESCH, R. ''La rédaction lucanienne du logion des pêcheurs d'homme (Lc. V,10C),'' EphT 46 (3-4, 1970) 413-32. PESCH, R., ''Luke's Formulation of the Saying on the Fishers of Men (Lc 5:10c)'' Biblehashyam 2 (1976) 44-59. JE-REMIAS, J., Die Sprache des Lukasevangeliums (Göttingen 1980) 136-27.

5:11 KARRIS, R. J., ''Poor and Rich: The Lukan Sitz im Leben'' in: C. H. Talbert (ed.) Perspectives on Luke-Acts (Danville 1978) 118.

5:12-6:19 TAYLOR, V. Behind the Third Gospel (1926) 80-81. DRURY, J., Tradition and Design in Luke's Gospel (Atlanta 1976) 89-91.

5:12-6:16 STONEHOUSE, N. B. The Witness of Luke to Christ (1951) 94,

97, 98f. NEIRYNCK, F., "La Matière dans Luc" in: F. Neirynck, (ed.) L'Evangile de Luc (Gembloux 1973) 180-84. SCHNEIDER, G., Das Evangelium nach Lukas (Gütersloh/Würzburg 1977) 129 (lit!). ACHTEMEIER, P. J., "The Lukan Perspective on the Miracles of Jesus: a Preliminary Sketch" in: C. H. Talbert (ed). Perspectives on Luke-Acts (Danville 1978) 157. RIST, J. M., On the Independence of Matthew and Mark (Cambridge 1978) 29-30.

5:12-26 CONZELMANN, H. Die Mitte der Zeit (1964) 37.

5:12-16 SUHL, A. Die Funktion der Alttestamentlichen Zitate und Anspielungen im Markusevangelium (1965) 120ff. ZIMMERMANN, H. Neutestamentliche Methodenlehre (1967) 237-43. SCHRAMM, T. Der Markus-Stoff bei Lukas (1971) 91-99.

5:12-14 HENNECKE, E./SCHNEEMELCHER, W. Neutestamentliche Apokryphen (1964) I. 60. CRIBBS, F. L. in: SBL Seminar Papers 2 (1973) MacRae, G. (ed.) 12-13.

5:12 ADLER, N. Das erste christliche Pfingstfest (1938) 33f. STONEHOUSE, N. B. The Witness of Matthew and Mark to Christ (1944) 135. HAHN, F. Christologische Hoheitstitel (1963) 84, 85. PESCH, R. Jesu ureigene Taten? in: Quaestiones Disputatae Bd. 52 (1970) K. Rahner und H. Schlier (eds.) 101-03.TALBERT, C. H., Literary Patterns, Theological Themes, and the Genre of Luke-Acts (Missoula 1974) 95. METZGER, B. M., Early Versions of the New Testament (Oxford 1977) 248.

5:13 FARRER, A. St Matthew and St Mark (1954) 56. PESCH, R. Jesu ureigene Taten? in: Quaestiones Disputatae Bd. 52 (1970) K. Rahner und H. Schlier (eds.) 103-04. WESTERHOLM, S., Jesus and Scribal Authority (Lund 1978) 68.

5:14 MOORE, G. F. Judaism (1946) II 9. BROX, N. Zeuge und Märtyrer (1961) 26f. FRIEDRICHSEN, G. W. S. "The Gothic Text of Luke in its Relation to the Codex Brixianus (f) and the Codex Palatinus (e)," NTS 11 (1964-1965) 288f. NELLESSEN, E., Zeugnis für Jesus und das Wort (Köln 1976) 71-73. TRITES, A. A., The New Testament Concept of Witness (Cambridge) 128-29, 178.

5:15-16 EGGER, W., Frohbotschaft und Lehre (Frankfurt 1976) 37, 83.

5:16 MEDIAVILLA, R., "La Oraciòn de Jesus en el tercer evangelio" Mayeutica (1978) 5-34.

5:17-6:11 EWALD, H. Die drei ersten Evangelien (1850) 196ff. SCHÜTZ, F. Der leidende Christus (1969) 52ff., 62, 79.

5:17-26 BOSCH, D. Die Heidenmission in der Zukunftsschau Jesu (1959) 60-64. FULLER, R. H. Interpreting the Miracles (1963) 50ff. BECKER,U./WIBBING, S. Wundergeschichten (1965) 12ff. KAMPHAUS, F. Von der Exegese zur Predigt (1968) 125-26. SCHRAMM, T. Der Markus-Stoff bei Lukas (1971) 99-103. NEI-

RYNCK, F., "La Matière Marcienne dans Luc" in: F. Neirynck (ed.) L'Evangile de Luc (Gembloux 1973) 184-91. NEIRYNCK, F., "Les accords mineurs et la rédaction des évangiles. L'épisode du paralytique (Mt., IX,1-8/Lc., V,17-26, par. Mc., II,1-2)" EphT 50 (1974) 251-320. TALBERT, C. H., Literary Patterns, Theological Themes, and the Genre of Luke-Acts (Missoula 1974) 16, 19, 40, 42. CONZELMANN,H. und LINDEMANN, A., Arbeitsbuch zum Neuen Testament (Tübingen 1975) 54-55. REICKE, B., "The Synoptic Reports of the Healings of the Paralytic" in: J. K. Elliott (ed.) Studies in New Testament Language and Text. FS. G. D. Kilpatrick (Leiden 1976) 319-29. SCHNEIDER, G., Das Evangelium nach Lukas (Gütersloh/Würzburg 1977) 132 (lit!). RIST, J. M., On the Independence of Matthew and Mark (Cambridge 1978) 30. RIVKIN, E., A Hidden Revolution (Nashville 1978) 115-17. KRAFT, H., Die Entstehung des Christentums (Darmstadt 1981) 164-66.

5:17 ADLER, N. Das erste christliche Pfingstfest (1939) 33f. HAHN, F. Christologische Hoheitstitel (1963) 73, 319. BOUSSET, W. Die Religion des Judentums im Späthellenistischen Zeitalter (1966 = 1926) 166. SCHALIT, A. König Herodes (1969) 737. TALBERT, C. H., Literary Patterns, Theological Themes, and the Genre of Luke-Acts (Missoula 1974) 19, 42. METZGER, B. M., Early Versions of the New Testament (Oxford 1977) 437.

5:18 NICKELS, P. Targum and New Testament (1967) 32

5:19 JAHNOW, H., "Das Abdecken des Daches" ZNW 24 (1925) 155. KRAUSS, S., "Das Abdecken des Daches" ZNW 25 (1926) 307. KLOSTERMANN, E. Das Lukasevangelium (1929) 72f.

5:20-30 GOPPELT, L., Theologie des Neuen Testaments. II (Göttingen 1976) 640.

5:20-26 KARRIS, R. J., "Poor and Rich: The Lukan Sitz im Leben" in: C. H. Talbert (ed.) Perspectives on Luke-Acts (1978) 17-18.

5:20 STROBEL, A. Erkenntnis und Bekenntnis der Sünde in neutestamentlicher Zeit (1968) 42, 59.

5:21 NICKELS, P. Targum and New Testament (1967) 32. RICE, G. E., "The Anti-Judaic Bias of the Western Text in the Gospel of Luke" AUSS 18 (1980) 53-54.

5:22 NICKELS, P. Targum and New Testament (1957) 32. EPP, E. J., The Theological Tendency of Codex Bezae Cantabrigiensis in Acts (Cambridge 1966) 44-45. METZGER, B. M., Early Versions of the New Testament (Oxford 1977) 212. RICE, G. E., "The Anti-Judaic Bias of the Western Text in the Gospel of Luke" AUSS 18 (1980) 51-57.

5:25-26 STONEHOUSE, N. B. The Witness of Matthew and Mark to Christ (1944) 71.

  5:26 STONEHOUSE, N. B. The Witness of Matthew and Mark to Christ (1944) 106. FRIEDRICHSEN, G. W. S. "The Gothic Text of Luke in its Relation to the Codex Brixianus (f) and the Codex Palatinus (e)," NTS 11 (1965-1965) 286f. PETZKE, G. Die Traditionen über Apollonius von Tyana und das Neue Testament (1970) 190f. ZMI-JEWSKI, J., Die Eschatologiereden des Lukasevangeliums (Bonn 1972) 137, 184, 228, 429. GLÖCKNER, R., Die Verkündigung des Heils beim Evangelisten Lukas (Mainz 1975) 132-33. DRURY, J., Tradition and Design in Luke's Gospel (Atlanta 1976) 70-71. GERHARDSON, B., "Jesu maktgärningar Om de urkristna ber-ättarnas val av termer" SEA (1979) 122-33.

5:27-6:5 TALBERT, C. H., Literary Patterns, Theological Themes, and the Genre of Luke-Acts (Missoula 1974) 40, 42.

  5:27ff. FRICKEL, J., "Die Zöllner, Vorbild der Demut und wahrer Got-tesverehrung" in: E. Dassmann/K. S. Frank (eds.) Pietas. FS. B. Kötting (Münster 1980) 377.

5:27-32 WANKE, J., Die Emmauserzählung. Eine redaktionsge-schichtliche Untersuchung zu Lk 24,13-35. (Leipzig 1973) 106-07. SCHNEIDER, G., Das Evangelium nach Lukas (Gütersloh/Würz-burg 1977) 135-36. RIST, J. M., On the Independence of Matthew and Mark (Cambridge 1978) 30-32.

5:27-28 ERNST, J., Anfänge der Christologie (Stuttgart 1972) 128-30.

  5:27 BÖHLIG, A., Die Gnosis III: Der Manichäismus (Zürich/München 1980) 344 n.51.

  5:28 METZGER, B. M., The Early Versions of the New Testament (Oxford 1977) 390. KARRIS, R. J., "Poor and Rich: The Lukan Sitz im Leben" in: C. H. Talbert (ed.) Perspectives on Luke-Acts (Danville 1978) 118.

5:29-6:11 TALBERT, C. H., Literary Patterns, Theological Themes, and the Genre of Luke-Acts (Missoula 1974) 16. ARENS, E., The HΛΘON-Sayings in the Synoptic Tradition (Freiburg 1976) 28-36. MEYER, B. F., The Aims of Jesus (London 1979) 158-62, 166.

  5:29 WANKE, J., Die Emmauserzählung. Eine redaktionsge-schichtliche Untersuchung zu Lk 24,13-35 (Leipzig 1975) 101. TALBERT, C. H., Literary Patterns, Theological Themes, and the Genre of Luke-Acts (Missoula 1974) 42.

  5:30 TALBERT, C. H., Literary Patterns, Theological Themes, and the Genre of Luke-Acts (Missoula 1974) 42. WESTERHOLMS, S., Jesus and Scribal Authority (Lund 1978)70-71.

5:31-32 CARLSTON, C. E., The Parables of the Triple Tradition (Phila-delphia 1975) 10-13, 58-60, 110-16. FRICKEL, J., "Die Zöllner,

Vorbild der Demut und wahrer Gottesverehrung" in: Pietas. FS. B. Kötting (Münster 1980) 375.

5:31 KLAUCK, H.-J., Allegorie and Allegorese in Synoptischen Gleichnistexten (Münster 1978) 148-60.

5:32 "Berufung" in: TRE 5 (1980) 686.

5:33-39 SCHLATTER, A. Johannes der Täufer (1956) 87ff. FERNANDEZ, J., "La cuestion del ayuno (Mt 9,14-17; Mc 2,18-22; Lc 5,33-39)," CultBib 19 (184, 1962) 162-69. CREMER, F. G. "Lukanisches Sondergut zum Fastenstreitgespräch. Lk 5,33-39 im Urteil der patristischen und scholastischen Exegese," TThZ 76 (3, 1967) 129-54. SCHÜTZ, F. Der leidende Christus (1969) 49ff. OTOMO, Y. Nachfolge Jesu und Anfänge der Kiche im Neuen Testament (1970) 179-81. SCHRAMM, T. Der Markus-Stoff bei Lukas (1971) 105-11. PATSCH, H. Abendmahl und historischer Jesus (1972) 109f. REICKE, B., "Die Fastenfrage nach Lk. 5,33-39" ThZ 30 (1974) 321-28. SCHNEIDER, G., Das Evangelium nach Lukas (Gütersloh/Würzburg 1977) 139. WESTERHOLM, S., Jesus and Scribal Authority (Lund 1978) 96-100.

5:33-35 JÜLICHER, D. A. Die Gleichnisreden Jesu (1910) 178-88. CARLSTON, C. E., The Parables of the Triple Tradition (Philadelphia 1975) 13-14, 60-62, 116-25. KRAFT, H., Die Entstehung des Christentums (Darmstadt 1981) 38-39.

5:33 SCHRAGE, W. Das Verhältnis des Thomas-Evangeliums zur synoptischen Tradition und zu den Koptischen Evangelienübersetzungen (1964) 193. TALBERT, C. H., Literary Patterns, Theological Themes, and the Genre of Luke-Acts (Missoula 1974) 42.

5:34-35 KLAUCK, H.-J., Allegorie und Allegorese in Synoptischen Gleichnistexten (Münster 1978) 160-69. BÖHLIG, A., Die Gnosis III: Der Manichäismus (Zürich/München 1980) 343 n.31.

5:34 PALLIS, A. Notes on St. Luke and the Acts (London 1928) 11. JÜNGEL, E. Paulus und Jesus (1966) 97, 211. ERNST, J., Anfänge der Christologie (Stuttgart 1972) 154-58.

5:35 CREMER, F. G. Die Fastenansage Jesu Mk 2,20 und Parallelen (1965). STROBEL, A. Erkenntnis und Bekenntnis der Sünde in neutestamentlicher Zeit (1968) 41.

5:36-39 JÜLICHER, D. A. Die Gleichnisreden Jesu (1910) 188-202. SUMMERS, R. The Secret Sayings of the Living Jesus (1968) 38. SANFORD, J. A., The Kingdom Within (New York 1970) 74-75. CARLSTON, C. E., The Parables of the Triple Tradition (Philadelphia 1975) 14-16, 62-66, 125-29. KLAUCK, H.-J., Allegorie und Allegorese in Synoptischen Gleichnistexten (Münster 1978) 169-74. FLUSSER, D., "Do You Prefer New Wine?" Immanuel 8 (1979) 26-31.

5:36-37 SCHRAGE, W. Das Verhältnis des Thomas-Evangeliums zur Synoptischen Tradition und zu den Koptischen Evangelienübersetzungen (1964) 113.

5:38 NICKELS, P. Targum and New Testament (1967) 32.

5:39 KNOX, W. L. The Sources of the Synoptic Gospels II (1957) 114. DUPONT, J. "Vin vieux, vin nouveau (Luc 5,39)," CBQ 25 (3, 1963) 286-304. SCHRAGE, W. Das Verhältnis des Thomas-Evangeliums zur Synoptischen Tradition und zu den Koptischen Evangelienübersetzungen (1964) 112. ALAND, K. NTS 12 (1965-1966) 197f. METZGER, B. M., The Early Versions of the New Testament (Oxford 1977) 134.

———————————

6:1-7:50 CONZELMANN, H. Die Mitte der Zeit (1964) 37ff.

6-7 CERFAUX, L., "L'Utilisation de la Source Q par Luc" in: F. Neirynck (ed.) L'Evangile de Luc (Gembloux 1973) 61-69.

6 McARTHUR, H. K. Understanding the Sermon on the Mount (1960) 15, 23, 173. GREENLEE, J. H. Nine Uncial Palimpsests of the Greek New Testament (1968) 68-69.

6:1-15 FRIEDRICH, T. G., GPM 15 (1960-1961) 99ff.

6:1-5 SUHL, A. Die Funktion der alttestamentlichen Zitate und Anspielungen im Markusevangelium (1965) 82ff. SCHRAMM, T. Der Markus-Stoff bei Lukas (1971) 111f. HÜBNER, H., Das Gesetz in der Synoptischen Tradition (Witten 1973) 113ff. BANKS. R., Jesus and the Law in the Synoptic Tradition (London 1975) 247-48. AICHINGER, H., "Quellenkritische Untersuchung der Perikope vom Ährenraufen am Sabbat Mk. 2:23-28 par Mt. 12;1-8 par Lk. 6;1-5" in: A. Fuchs (ed.) Jesus in der Verkündigung der Kirche (Freistadt (1976) 110-53. SANDMEL, S., We Jews and Jesus (New York 1977) 1977) 136. SCHNEIDER, G., Das Evangelium nach Lukas (Gütersloh/Würzburg 1977) 141. KRAFT, H., Die Entstehung des Christentums (Darmstadt 1981) 165-67.

6:1-2 KNOX, W. L. The Sources of the Synoptic Gospels II (1957) 78.

6:1 MOORE, G. F. Judaism (1946) II 29n. AUDET, J.-P. "Jésus et le 'Calendrier sacerdotal ancien.' Autour d'une variante de Luc 6,1," SciEccl 10 (3, 1958) 361-83. VOGT, E. "Sabbatum 'deuteropröton' in Lc 6,1 et antiquum kalendarium saerdotale," Biblica 40 (1, 1959) 102-05. NICKELS, P. Targum and New Testament (1967)

32. NEIRYNCK, F., "La Matière Marcienne dans Luc" in: F. Neirynck (ed.) L'Evangile de Luc (Gembloux 1973) 184-92. DELEBEQUE, É., "Sur un certain sabbat, en Luc 6,1" Revue de Philologie 38 (1974) 26-29. TALBERT, C. H., Literary Patterns, Theological Themes, and the Genre of Luke-Acts (Missoula 1974) 42. MEZGER, E., "Le sabbat 'second-premier' de Luc" ThZ 32 (1976) 138-43. BUCHANAN, G. W., and WOLFE, C., "The 'Second-First Sabbath' (Luke 6:1)" JBL 97 (1978) 259-62.

6:2-4 SCHWARZ, G., "Emmendation und Rückübersetzung" NTS 15 (1968-1969) 233-47.

6:2 NICKELS, P. Targum and New Testament (1967) 32.

6:4 HENNECKE, E./SCHNEEMELCHER, W. Neutestamentliche Apokryphen (1964) I 55. SUMMERS, R. The Secret Sayings of the Living Jesus (1968) 54. MORGAN, C. S., " 'When Abiatar was High Priest' (Mark 2:26)" JBL 98 (1979) 409-10.

6:5 STONEHOUSE, N. B. The Witness of Matthew and Mark to Christ (1944) 255. KÄSER, W. "Exegetische Erwägungen zur Seligpreisung des Sabbatarbeiters Lk 6,5 D," ZThK 65 (4, 1968) 414-30. SANFORD, J. A., The Kingdom Within (New York 1970) 93. ERNST, J., Anfänge der Christologie (Stuttgart 1972) 152f. BANKS, R., Jesus and the Law in the Synoptic Tradition (London 1975) 121f. "Agrapha" in: TRE 2 (1978) 104.

6:6ff. KNOX, W. L. The Sources of the Synoptic Gospels II (1957) 84.

6:6-11 CRIBBS, F. L. in: SBL Seminar Papers 2 (1973) MacRae, G. (ed.) 14-15. SCHNEIDER, G., Das Evangelium nach Lukas (Gütersloh 1977) 143. WESTERHOLM, S., Jesus and Scribal Authority (Lund 1979) 162-68. SWIDLER, L., Biblical Affirmations of Woman (Philadelphia 1979) 182.

6:6 FARRER, A. St Matthew and St Mark (1954) 56. KNOX, W. L. The Sources of the Synoptic Gospels II (1957) 59.

6:7 KNOX, W. L. The Sources of the Synoptic Gospels II (1957) 78. FRIEDRICHSEN, G. W. S. "The Gothic Text of Luke in its Relation to the Codex Brixianus (f) and the Codex Platinus (e)," NTS 11 (1964-1965) 282f. METZGER, B. M., The Early Versions of the New Testament (Oxford 1977) 176.

6:8 KNOX, W. L. The Sources of the Synoptic Gospels II (1957) 94.

6:9-11 RICE, G. E., "The Anti-Judaic Bias of the Western Text in the Gospel of Luke" AUSS 18 (1980) 55-57.

6:9-10 SANFORD, J. A., The Kingdom Within (New York 1970) 92f.

6:9 KNOX, W. L. The Sources of the Synoptic Gospels II (1957) 78, 94. JÜNGEL, E. Paulus und Jesus (1966) 209. METZGER, B. M., The Early Versions of the New Testament (Oxford 1977) 177.

6:11 PALLIS, A., Notes on St. Luke and the Acts (London 1928) 11. WANKE, J., Die Emmauserzählung. Eine redaktionsge-schichtliche Untersuchung zu Lk 24, 13-35 (Leipzig 1973) 94.

6:12-8:3 TAYLOR, V. Behind the Third Gospel (1926) 149f, 172ff.

6:12-49 EWALD, H. Die drei ersten Evangelien (1850) 204ff.

6:12-20 LOHFINK, G., Die Sammlung Israels (München 1975) 63-65, 72.

6:12-19 HIRSCH, E. Frühgeschichte des Evangeliums (1941) 44-46. SCHRAMM, T. Der Markus-Stoff bei Lukas (1971) 113f.

6:12-16 BECQ, J., "Il en choisit douze" BTS 6 (1965). 18f. ROLOFF, J. Apostolat-Verkündigung-Kirche (1965) 178ff. FREYNE, S. The Twelve: Disciples and Apostles (1968) 90ff., 228. ITTEL, G. W. Jesus und die Jünger (1970) 28-41. OTOMO, Y. Nachfolge Jesu und Anfänge der Kirche im Neuen Testament (1970) 62-68. DIE-TRICH, W. Das Petrusbild der lukanischen Schriften (1972) 82-94. TALBERT, C. H., Literary Patterns, Theological Themes, and the Genre of Luke-Acts (Missoula 1974) 40, 42, 113, 116. SCHNEIDER, G., Das Evangelium nach Lukas (Gütersloh 1977) 145. DÖMER, M., Das Heil Gottes: Studien zur Theologie des lukanischen Doppelwerkes (Köln/Bonn 1978) 128f. MEDIA-VILLA, R., "La Oraciòn de Jesus en el tercer evangelio" May-eutica (1978) 5-34. STAGG, E., and F., Woman in the World of Jesus (Philadelphia 1978) 123-25. PRAST, F., Presbyter und Evangelium in nachapostolischer Zeit (Stuttgart 1979) 380f. KRAFT, H., Die Entstehung des Chrisentums (Darmstadt 1981) 139-45.

6:12-13 KLEIN, G. Die Zwölf Apostel (1961) 34f., 203f.

6:12 GOULDER, M. D. Type and History in Acts (1964) 125, 127, 129, 167. NEIRYNCK, F., "La Matière Marciènne dans Luc" in: F. Neirynck, (ed.) L'Evangile de Luc (Gembloux 1973) 184-92. TALBERT, C. H., Literary Patterns, Theological Themes, and the Genre of Luke-Acts (Missoula 1974) 95. METZGER, B. M., The Early Versions of the New Testament (Oxford 1977) 92.

6:13-16 RIST, J. M., On the Independence of Matthew and Mark (Cambridge 1978) 47.BÖHLIG, A., Die Gnosis III: Der Manichäismus (Zürich/München 1980) 344 n.63.

6:13-14 BROWN, S. Apostacy and Perseverance in the Theology of Luke (1969) 54.BÖHLIG, A., Die Gnosis III: Der Maichäismus (Zürich/ München 1978) 343 n.39, 41, 42, 43.

6:13 FLEW, R. N. Jesus and His Church (1956) 85. ROLOFF, J. Apo-stolat-Verkündigung-Kirche (1965) 140-69. NICKELS, P. Tar-gum and New Testament (1967) 32. BROWN, S. Apostasy and Perseverance in the Theology of Luke (1969) 87f., 91, 95. "Apos-tel" in: TRE 3 (1978) 430, 442. BÖHLIG, A., Die Gnosis III: Der

Manichäismus (Zürich/München 1980) 343 n.36. McDONALD,
J. I. H., Kerygma and Didache (Cambridge 1980) 109. KRAFT,
H., Die Entstehung des Christentums (Darmstadt 1981) 145ff.

6:14ff. STAEHELIN, E. Die Verkündigung des Reiches Gottes in der
Kirche Jesu Christi I (1951) 55.

6:14-16 TALBERT, C. H., Literary Patterns, Theological Themes, and the
Genre of Luke-Acts (Missoula 1974) 113. ''Apostel'' in: TRE 3
(1978) 434.

6:14-15 BÖHLIG, A., Die Gnosis III: Der Manichäismus (Zürich/München
1980) 343 n.44, 45, 46, 48.

6:14 NICKELS, P. Targum and New Testament (1967) 33. METZ-
GER, B. M., The Early Versions of the New Testament (Oxford
1977) FITZMYER, J. A., ''Aramaic Kepha' and Peter's name in
the New Testament'' in: E. Best/R. McL. Wilson (eds.) Text and
Interpretation. FS. M. Black (Cambridge 1979) 122-24.

6:15-16 BÖHLIG, A. Die Gnosis III: Der Manichäismus (Zürich/München
1980) 343 n.49.

6:15 HAHN, F. Christologische Hoheitstitel (1963) 164. METZGER,
B. M., The Early Versions of the New Testament (Oxford 1977)
201.

6:16 NICKELS, P. Targum and New Testament (1967) 33.

6:17ff. BARTSCH, H.-W. ''Feldrede und Bergpredigt. Redaktionsarbeit
in Luk. 6,'' ThZ 16 (1, 1960) 5-18.

6:17-49 RENGSTORF, K. H. Das Evangelium nach Lukas (1949) 83f.
BARTSCH, H. W., Wachet aber zu jeder Zeit! (Hamburg-Berg-
stedt 1963) 66-76. BROWN, R. E. ''The Beatitudes According to
Luke,'' in: New Testament Essays (1965) 265-71. REUMANN, J.
Jesus in the Church's Gospels (1968) 228-41. TALBERT, C. H.,
Literary Patterns, Theological Themes, and the Genre of Luke-Acts
(Missoula 1974) 40, 41. FRANKLIN, E., Christ the Lord (London
1979) 168-70.

6:17-20 SCHÜTZ, F. Der leidende Christus (1969) 119-22.

6:17-19 STONEHOUSE, N. B. The Witness of Luke to Christ (1951) 98,
99f. JEREMIAS, J. ''Perikopen-Umstellung bei Lukas?'' NTS 4
(1957-1958) 115ff. JEREMIAS, J. Abba; Studien zur neutestamentlichen Theologie und Zeitgeschichte (1966) 94-96. MÄRZ, C.-
P., Das Wort Gottes bei Lukas (Leipzig 1973) 59f. TALBERT, C.
H., Literary Patterns, Theological Themes, and the Genre of Luke-
Acts (Missoula 1974) 42f. EGGER, W., Frohbotschaft und Lehre
(Frankfurt 1976) 37, 77f, 100. SCHNEIDER, G., Das Evangelium
nach Lukas (Gütersloh 1977) 148. PRAST, F. Presbyter und Evangelium in nachapostolischer Zeit (Stuttgart 1979) 309.

6:17-18 DALMAN, G. Orte und Wege Jesu (1967) 166f.

6:17 NESTLE, E., "Eine kleine Korrektur zur Vulgata" in: ZNW 8 (1907).KNOX, W. L. The Sources of the Synoptic Gospels II (1957) 7. BLAIR, E. P. Jesus in the Gospel of Matthew (1960) 134. TAL-BERT, C. H., Literary Patterns, Theological Themes, and the Genre of Luke-Acts (Missoula 1974) 42f, 95.

6:19 METZGER, B. M., The Early Versions of the New Testament (Oxford 1977) 245.

6:20-8:3 STREETER, B. H. The Four Gospels (1951) 203f.

6:20ff. FIEBIG, P. Jesu Bergpredigt (1924). MOORE, G. F. Juda-ism(1946) II 157n. STAEHELIN, E. Die Verkündigung des Reiches Gottes in der Kirche Jesu Christi I (1951) 284. KNOX, W. L. The Sources of the Synoptic Gospels II (1957) 9ff. YATES, J. E. The Spirit and the Kingdom (1963) 66ff. KÜMMEL, W. G. Einleitung in das Neue Testament (1973) 31ff., 41f.

6:20-49 HIRSCH, E. Frühgeschichte des Evangeliums (1949) 77-88, 300f, 304f. BUTLER, B. C. The Originality of St Matthew (1951) 37ff. STONEHOUSE, N. B. The Witness of Luke to Christ (1951) 99f. DUPONT, D. J. Les Béatitudes (1958) 196-200. KAHLEFELD, H. Der Jünger (1962). JEREMIAS, J. Abba; Studien zur neutes-tamentlichen Theologie und Zeitgeschichte (1966) 171-89. SCHÜRMANN, H., "Die Warnung des Lukas vor der Falschlehre in der 'Predigt am Berg' Lk 6,20-49," BZ 10 (1, 1966) 57-81. REUMANN, J. Jesus in the Church's Gospels (1968) 232-33. SMITH, M. Tannaitic Parallels to the Gospels (1968) 4 B; C. LÜHRMANN, D. Die Redaktion der Logienquelle (1969) 53-56. SEITZ, O. J. F. NTS 16 (1969-1970) 40f. GASTON, L. No Stone on Another (1970) 255, 313-14. SCHNACKENBURG, R., Auf-sätze und Studien zum Neuen Testament (Leipzig 1973) 51ff., 187. TALBERT, C. H., Literary Patterns, Theological Themes, and the Genre of Luke-Acts (Missoula 1974) 42. BLIGH, J., The Sermon on the Mount (Slough 1975) 24-38. CONZELMANN, H./LIN-DEMANN, A., Arbeitsbuch zum Neuen Testament (Tübingen 1975) 61f., 66. DRURY, J., Tradition and Design in Luke's Gos-pel (Atlanta 1976) 131-138. GRUNDMANN, W., "Weisheit im Horizont des Reiches Gottes. Eine Studie zur Verkündigung Jesu nach der Spruchüberlieferung Q" in: R. Schnackenburg et al. (eds.) Die Kirche des Anfangs. FS H. Schürmann (Leipzig 1977) 188-93. SCHNEIDER, G., Das Evangelium nach Lukas (Gütersloh 1977) 149. ZIMMERLI, W., Die Seligpreisungen der Bergpredigt und das Alte Testament" in: E. Bammel et al. (eds.) Donum Gentilicium. FS. D. Daube (Oxford 1978) 8-26. "Berpredigt" in: TRE 5 (1980) 605.

6:20-31 DIEM, H. EvTh 14 (1954) 241-46.

6:20-30 STRECKER, G. "Die Makarismen der Bergpredigt," NTS 17 (1970-1971) 255-75.

6:20-26 DUPONT, D. J. Les Béatitudes (1958) 338-41. CAVE, C. H. "The Sermon at Nazareth and the Beatitudes in the Light of the Synagogue Lectionary," in: Studia Evangelica III (1964) F. L. Cross (ed.) 231-25. BROWN, R. E. "Le 'Beatitudini' secondo San Luca," BiblOr 7 (1, 1965) 3-8. BROWN, R. E. "The Beatitudes according to St. Luke," Bible Today 1, (18, 1965) 1176-80. PIDWELL, H. Blessed are the Poor (1972) 71-77. AGOURIDÈS, S., "La tradition des Béatutides chez Matthieu et Luc" in: A. Descamps/A. de Halleux (eds.) Mélanges Bibliques en hommage au R. P. Béda Rigaux (Gembloux 1970) 9-27. HENGEL, M., Was Jesus a Revolutionist? (Philadelphia 1971) 9. DUPONT, J., Les Béatitudes, III: Les Evangèlistes (Paris 1973). FRANKLIN, E. Christ the Lord: A Study in the Purpose and Theology of Luke-Acts (London 1975) 168-72, 190. SCHNEIDER, G., Das Evangelium nach Lukas (Gütersloh/Würzburg 1977) 150-51 (lit!). FLUSSER, D., "Some Notes to the Beatitudes (Matthew 5:3-12, Luke 6:20-26)" Immanuel 8 (1978) 37-47.

6:20-23 FIEBIG. P. "Die mündliche Ueberlieferung als Quelle der Synoptiker," in: Neutestamentliche Studien, Festschrift für G. Heinrici (1914) A. Deissmann & H. Windisch (eds.) 85ff. DEGENHARDT, H.-J. Lukas, Evangelist der Armen (1964) 45-51.HOFFMANN, P. Studien zur Theologie der Logienquelle (1972) Passim.HOFFMANN, P. und EID, V., Jesus von Nazareth und eine christliche Moral (Freiburg/Basel/Wien 1975) 29-35. LOHFINK, G. "Zur Möglichkeit christlicher Naherwartung" in: G. Greshake/ G. Lohfink, Naherwartung - Auferstehung - Unsterblichkeit (Freiburg 1975) 43-44. EDWARDS, R. A., A Theology of Q (Philadelphia 1976) 84-85. POLAG, A., Die Christologie der Logienquelle (Neukirchen 1977) 10. KARRIS, R. J., "Poor and Rich: The Lukan Sitz im Leben" in: C. H. Talbert (ed.) Perspectives on Luke-Acts (Danville 1970) 118. "Armenfürsorge" in: TRE 4 (1979) 16. STRECKER, G., "Die Makarismen der Bergpredigt" [orig,: NTS 17, (1971) 255-75] in: Eschaton und Historie (Göttingen 1979) 108-31. JEREMIAS, J., Die Sprache des Lukasevangeliums (Göttingen 1980) 138.

6:20-22 MINEAR, P., To Heal and to Reveal (New York 1976) 64.

6:20-21 MARRIOTT, H. The Sermon on the Mount (1925).DUPONT, D. J. Les Béatutudes (1958) 280-82. ROBINSON, J. M. Kerygma und historischer Jesus (1960) 163. JÜNGEL, E. Paulus und Jesus (1966) 186, 188, 190. SCHWEIZER, E. "Formgeschichtliches zu den Seligpreisungen Jesu," NTS 19 (2, 1973) 121-26. DUNN, J. D.

G., Jesus and the Spirit (London 1975) 54,55. SCHÜRMANN, H., "Beobachtungen zum Menschensohn-titel in der Redequelle" in: R. Pesch/R. Schnackenburg (eds.) Jesus und der Menschensohn (Freiburg/Basel/Wien 1975) 130-31. BEISSER, F., Das Reich Gottes (Göttingen 1976) 45-48. EDWARDS, R. A., A Theology of Q (Philadelphia 1976) 62-63. POLAG, A., Die Christologie der Logienquelle (Neukirchen 1977) 41-42. GRIMM, W., "Die Hoffnung der Armen. Zu den Seligpreisungen Jesu" ThB 11 (1980) 100-13.

6:20b-21 MANEK, J. "Vier Bibelstudien zur Problematik der sozialen Umwandlung," CommViat 10 (1, 1967) 61-70; (2-3, 1967) 179-82. SCHULZ, S. Q Die Spruchquelle der Evangelisten (1972) 76-84.

6:20-24 KOCH, R. "Die Wertung des Besitzes im Lukasevangelium, Biblica 38 (1957) 151-69. WREGE, H.-T. Die Ueberlieferungsgeschichte der Berpredigt (1968) 6ff.

6:20 KNOX, W. L. The Sources of the Synoptic Gospels II (1957) 125. DUPONT, D. J. Les Béatitudes (1958) 209f., 212-14, 282f. SCHRAGE, W. Das Verhältnis des Thomas-Evangeliums zur Synoptischen Tradition und zu den Koptischen Evangelienübersetzungen (1964) 118. SUMMERS, R. The Secret Sayings of the Living Jesus (1968) 23. JEREMIAS, J. Neutestamentliche Theologie I (1971) 33, 40, 83, 111, 114f., 118, 213. SANFORD, J. A., The Kingdom Within (New York 1970) 189-90. TALBERT, C. H., Literary Patterns, Theological Themes, and the Genre of Luke-Acts (Missoula 1974) 43. GRUNDMANN, W., "Weisheit im Horizont des Reiches Gottes. Eine Studie zur Verkündigung Jesu nach der Spruchüberlieferung Q" in: R. Schnackenburg et al. (eds.) Die Kirche des Anfangs. FS. H. Schürmann (Leipzig 1977) 182. SCHLOSSER, J., "La règne de Dieu dans les dits de Jésus" RevSR 53 (1979) 164-76.

6:21-25 WREGE, H.-T. Die Ueberlieferungsgeschichte der Bergpredigt (1968), 16-19.

6:21 HUNTER, A. M. Design for Life (1953) 32f. STAUDINGER, J. Die Bergpredigt (1957) 45-48, 48-49. DUPONT, D. J. Les Béatitudes (1958) 218-23, 265-72. ROBINSON, J. M. Kerygma und historischer Jesus (1960) 181. SCHRAGE, W. Das Verhältnis des Thomas-Evangeliums zur Synoptischen Tradition und zu den Koptischen Evangelienübersetzungen (1964) 149. FRIEDRICHSEN, G. W. S. "The Gothic Text of Luke in its Relation to the Codix Brixianus (f) and the Codex Palatinus (e)," NTS 11 (1964-1965) 283f. BOERMA, C., Rich Man, Poor Man - and the Bible (London 1979) 46-48.

6:22-30 SCHÜRMANN, H. "Sprachliche Reminiszenzen an abgeänderte oder ausgelassene Bestandteile der Spruchsammlung im Lukas- und Matthäusevangelium," NTS 6 (1959-1960) 209f.

6:22-29 SCHMAUCH, GPM 17 (1962-1963) 142ff.

6:22-26 WREGE, H.-T. Die Ueberlieferungsgeschichte der Bergpredigt (1968) 20. "Armut" in TRE 4 (1979) 78.

6:22-23 HAHN, F. Christologische Hoheitstitel (1963) 43.BROWN, J. P. NTS 10 (1963-1964) 30f. SATAKE, A. Die Gemeindeordnung in der Johannesapokalypse (1966) 177-79. SMITH, M. Tannaitic Parallels to the Gospels (1968). A. WREGE, H.-T. Die Ueberlieferungsgeschichte der Bergpredigt (1968) 20-24. SCHÜTZ, F. Der leidende Christus (1969) 11-13, 108f. JEREMIAS, J. Neutestamentliche Theologie I (1971) 114, 248, 250. PATSCH, H. Abendmahl und historischer Jesus (1972) 204ff. SCHNIDER, F., Jesus der Prophet (Freiburg 1972) 130, 133ff. SCHULZ, S. Q Die Spruchquelle der Evangelisten (1972) 452-57. GOULDER, M. D. Midrash and Lection in Matthew (1974) 279-81. EDWARDS, R. A., A Theology of Q(Philadelphia 1976) 63. POLAG, A., Die Christologie der Logienquelle (Neukirchen 1977) 97. GERSTEN-BERGER, G. und SCHRAGE, W., Leiden (Stuttgart 1977) 126-27; ET: J. E. Steely, Suffering (Nashville 1980) 147-48. GNILKA, J., "Martyriumsparänese und Sühnetod in synoptischen und jüdischen Traditionen" in: R. Schnackenburg (ed.) Die Kirche des Anfangs. FS. H. Schürmann (Freiburg/Basel/Wien 1978) 234-35. KRAFT, H., Die Entstehung des Christentums (Darmstadt 1981) 170ff.

6:22 PALLIS, A. Notes on St. Luke and the Acts (London 1928) 11-12. STAUDINGER, J. Die Bergpredigt (1957) 50-53. DUPONT, D. J. Les Béatutides (1958) 227-43. STRECKER, G. Der Weg der Gerechtigkeit (1962) 30. HAHN, F. Christologische Hoheitstitel (1963) 43. KÄSEMANN, E. Exegetische Versuche und Besinnungen (1964) I 170. SCHRAGE, W. Das Verhältnis des Thomas-Evangeliums zur Synoptischen Tradition und zu den Koptischen Evangelienübersetzunge (1964) 147. JÜNGEL, E. Paulus und Jesus (1966) 243. BLACK, M. An Aramaic Approach to the Gospels and Acts (1967) 135f. BORSCH, H. The Christian & Gnostic Son of Man (1970) 22-23. GOULDER, M. D. Midrash and Lection in Matthew (1974) 91, 152, 350f. SCHWARZ, G., "Lukas 6:22a. 23c. 26. Emendation, Rückübersetzung, Interpretation" ZNW 66 (1975) 169-74. SATAKE, A., "Das Leiden der Jünger 'um meinetwillen' " ZNW 67 (1976) 4-19. WILLIAMS, J. A., A Conceptual History of Deuteronomism in the Old Testament, Judaism, and the New Testament (Ph. D. Diss., Louisville 1976) 310. JEREMIAS, J. Die Sprache des Lukasevangeliums (Göttingen 1980) 138.

6:23 STAUDINGER, J. Die Bergpredigt (1957) 50-53. FRIEDRICH-
SEN, G. W. S. "The Gothic Text of Luke in its Relation to the
Codex Brixianus (f) and the Codex Palatinus (e)," NTS 11 (1964-
1965) 288f. BLACK, M. An Aramaic Approach to the Gospels and
Acts (1967) 191f. JEREMIAS, J. Neutestamentliche Theologie I
(1971) 20, 83, 179, 230. SCHWARZ, G., "Lukas 6:22a. 23c. 26.
Emendation, Rückübersetzung, Interpretation" ZNW 66 (1975)
269-74. JEREMIAS, J., Die Sprache des Lukasevangeliums (Göttingen 1980) 138-39.

6:24-26 DUPONT, D. J. Les Béatitudes (1958) 299-43. DEGENHARDT,
H.-J. Lukas, Evangelist der Armen (1964) 51-53. LINTON, O.,
"Coordinated Sayings and Parables in the Synoptic Gospels: Anal-
ysis versus Theories" NTS 26 (1980) 139-63.

6:24-25 ROBINSON, J. M. Kerygma und historischer Jesus (1960) 163,
181. JÜNGEL, E. Paulus und Jesus (1966) 186. MANEK, J. "Vier
Bibelstudien zur Problematik der sozialen Umwandlung,"
CommViat 10 (1, 1967) 61-70; (2-3, 1967) 179-82.DORMEYER,
D., Die Passion Jesu als Verhaltensmodell (Münster 1974) 98A,
234. THEISSEN, G., Soziologie der Jesusbewegung (München
1977) 18.

6:24 STAUDINGER, J. Die Bergpredigt (1957) 53-55. GOPPELT, L.,
Theologie des Neuen Testaments. I (Göttingen 1975) 130-31, 137.
GERSTENBERGER, G. und SCHRAGE, W., Leiden (Stuttgart
1977) 227; ET: J. E. Steely, Suffering (Nashville 1980) 261-62.
BOERMA, C., Rich Man, Poor Man - and the Bible (London 1979)
46-48. JEREMIAS, J., Die Sprache des Lukasevangeliums (Göttingen 1980) 139-40.

6:25 STAUDINGER, J. Die Bergpredigt (1957) 55-57. DUPONT, D.
J. Les Béatitudes (1958) 266-72.

6:25b STAUDINGER, J. Die Bergpredigt (1957) 57-59.

6:26 STAUDINGER, J. Die Bergpredigt (1957) 59-62. SCHWARZ, G.,
"Lukas 6:22a. 23c. 36. Emendation, Rückübersetzung, Interpretation" ZNW 66 (1975) 269-74.

6:27ff. HAHN, F. Christologische Hoheitstitel (1963) 34. GUNDRY, R.
H., NTS 13 (1966-1967) 341ff. CONZELMANN, H. und LIN-
DEMANN, A., Arbeitsbuch zum Neuen Testament (Tübingen
1975) 62.

6:27-38 DEGENHARDT, H.-J. Lukas, Evangelist der Armen (1964) 53-
57.

6:27-36 KNOX, W. L. The Sources of the Synoptic Gospels II (1957) 34.
DUPONT, D. J. Les Béatitudes (1958) 151-56, 191-93, 201f.
BLACK, M. An Aramaic Approach to the Gospels and Acts (1967)
179f. FURNISH, V. P. The Love Command in the New Testament

(1972) 54-59. LÜHRMANN, D. "Liebet eure Feinde (Lk 6,27-36/ Mt 5,39-48)," ZThK 69 (4, 1972) 412-38. DESCAMPS, A./De HALLEUX, A. Melanges Bibliques en hommage au R. P. Béda Rigaux (1970) 17, 18, 20. SANFORD, J. A., The Kingdom Within (New York 1970) 124-25. SAND, A., Das Gesetz und die Propheten (Regensburg 1974) 49-51. EDWARDS, R. A., A Theology of Q (Philadelphia 1976) 85-87. SCHNEIDER, G., Das Evangelium nach Lukas (Gütersloh/Würzburg 1977) 154 (lit!). MOULDER, J., "Who are my Enemies? An Exploration of the Semantic Background of Christ's Command" Journal of Theology for South Africa 25 (1978) 41-49. SCHOTTROFF, L., "Non-Violence and the Love of One's Enemy" in: L. Schottroff et al. (eds.) Essays in the Love Commandment (Philadelphia 1978) 9-39.

6:27-30 GOULDER, M. D. Midrash and Lecture in Matthew (1974) 294f.

6:27f. 32-36 WREGE, H.-T. Die Ueberlieferungsgeschichte der Bergpredigt (1968) 82-94. SCHULZ, S. Q Die Spruchquelle der Evangelisten (1972) 127-39.

6:27, 32-34 O'NEILL, J. C. The Theology of Acts in its historical setting (1970) 32-33, I.

6:27-28 MASSAUX, E. Influence de L'Evangile de saint Matthieu sur la littérature chrétienne avant saint Irénée (1950) 44-15, 580-82, 596-97, 608-11. SEITZ, O. F. J. "Love Your enemies. The Historical Setting of Matthew v. 43f.; Luke vi. 27f.," NTS XVI (1969) 39-54. HENGEL, M., Was Jesus a Revolutionist? (Philadelphia 1971) 26f. JEREMIAS, J. Neutestamentliche Theologie I (1971) 31, 187, 206, 240. JEREMIAS, J., Die Sprache des Lukasevangeliums. Redaktion und Tradition im Nicht-Markusstoff des dritten Evangeliums (Göttingen 1980) 141f.

6:27 DUPONT, D. J. Les Béatitudes (1958) 189-91, 313-16. HENNECKE, E./SCHNEEMELCHER, W. Neutestamentliche Apokryphen (1964) I 135. HASLER, V. Amen (1969) 59. SCHÜTZ, F. Der leidende Christus (1969) 13. SANFORD, J. A., The Kingdom Within (New York 1970) 148f. SUGGS, M. J., "The Antitheses as Redactional Products" in: L. Schottroff et al. (eds.) Essays in the Love Commandment (Philadelphia 1978) 99-101. JEREMIAS, J., Die Sprache des Lukasevangeliums. Redaktion und Tradition im Nicht-Markusstoff des dritten Evangeliums (Göttingen 1980) 140f.

6:28-29 HOFFMANN, P. and EID, V., Jesus von Nazareth und eine christliche Moral (Freiburg 1975) 157-64.

6:28 SCHENK, W. Der Segen im Neuen Testament (1967) 78-80. BEST, E. NTS 16 (1969-1970) 105f., 111f. WESTERMANN, C.,

Blessing. In the Bible and the Life of the Church (Philadelphia 1978) 91-93, 98-101.

6:29-36 PIROT, J. Paraboles et Allégories Evangeliques (1949) 42-49.

6:29-31 STAUDINGER, J. Die Bergpredigt (1957) 11-20.

6:29-30 WREGE, H.-T. Die Ueberlieferungsgeschichte der Bergpredigt (1968) 75-82. ERNST, J., Anfänge der Christologie (Stuttgart 1972) 154-58. SCHULZ, S. Q Die Spruchquelle der Evangelisten (1972) 120-27. SCHÜRMANN, H., "Wie hat Jesus seinen Tod bestanden und verstanden?" in: P. Hoffmann (ed.) Orientierung an Jesus. FS. J. Schmid (Freiburg 1973) 347f.

6:29 KITTEL, G. Die Probleme des Palästinischen Spätjudentums und das Urchristentum (1926) 33. MANSON, W. Jesus the Messiah (1948) 30-32. MASSAUX, E. Influence de L'Evangile de saint Matthieu sur la littérature chrétienne avant saint Irénée (1950) 44-46, 482-84, 611-12. GLOVER, R. NTS 5 (1958-1959) 14ff. GERSTENBERGER, G. and SCHRAGE, W., Leiden (Stuttgart 1977) 227; ET: J. E. Steeley, Suffering (Nashville 1980) 261f. SWIDLER, L. Biblical Affirmations of Woman (Philadelphia 1979) 284. JEREMIAS, J., Die Sprache des Lukasevangeliums. Redaktion und Tradition im Nicht-Markusstoff des dritten Evangeliums (Göttingen 1980) 142f.

6:30-38 MOORE, G. F. Judaism (1946) II 165.

6:30-31 BARRETT, C. K. The New Testament Background: Selected Documents (1956) 223.

6:30 MASSAUX, E. Influence de L'Evangile de saint Matthieu sur la littérature chrétienne avant saint Irénée (1950) 473-74, 611-13. METZGER, B. M., The Early Versions of the New Testament (Oxford 1977) 207. JEREMIAS, J., Die Sprache des Lukasevangeliums. Redaktion und Tradition im Nicht-Markusstoff des dritten Evangeliums (Göttingen 1980) 144.

6:31-35 HENNECKE, E./SCHNEEMELCHER, W. Neutestamentliche Apokryphen (1964) I 115, 135, II 393.

6:31 MASSAUX, E. Influence de l'Evangile de saint Matthieu sur la littérature chrétienne avant saint Irénée (1950) 9-13, 594-95, 607-08. KNOX, W. L. The Sources of the Synoptic Gospels II (1957) 125. DUPONT, D. J. Les Béatitudes (1958) 173-75. BOUSSET, W. Die Religion des Judentums im Späthellenistischen Zeitalter (1966 = 1926) 139. BEST, E. NTS 16 (1969-1970) 112f. BORNKAMM, G. Geschichte und Glaube II (1971) 94-96. SCHULZ, S. Q Die Spruchquelle der Evangelisten (1972) 139-41. CONZELMANN, H. and LINDEMANN, A., Arbeitsbuch zum Neuen Testament (Tübingen 1975) 259f. HOFFMAN, P. and EID, V., Jesus von Nazareth und eine christliche Moral Freiburg 1975) 148-50.

POLAG, A., Die Christologie der Logienquelle (Neukirchen-Vluyn 1977) 77. BÖHLIG, A., Die Gnosis III: Der Manichäismus (Zürich/München 1980) 328 n. 156. JEREMIAS, J., Die Sprache des Lukasevangeliums. Redaktion und Tradition im Nicht-Markusstoff des dritten Evangeliums (Göttingen 1980) 144.

6:32ff. KNOX, W. L. The Sources of the Synoptic Gospels II (1957) 15, 24. STROBEL, A. Erkenntnis und Bekenntnis der Sünde in neutestamentlicher Zeit (1968) 43.

6:32-44 SCHÜRMANN, H. "Sprachliche Reminiszenzen an abgeänderte oder ausgelassene Bestandteile der Spruchsammlung im Lukas- und Matthäusevangelium," NTS 6 (1959-1960) 190f.

6:32-36 POLAG, A., Die Christologie der Logienquelle (Neukirchen-Vluyn 1977) 77.

6:32-35 VAN UNNIK, W. C. "Die Motivierung der Feindesliebe in Lukas vi 32-35," NovTest 8 (2-4, 1966) 284-300. SMITH, M. Tannaitic Parallels to the Gospels (1968) A; B 30. VAN UNNIK, W. C. Sparsa Collecta. The Collected Essays of W. C. van Unnik (Leiden 1973) 111-126.

6:32 MASSAUX, E. Influence de l'Evangile de saint Matthieu sur la littérature chrétienne avant saint Irénée (1950) 471-72, 596-97, 608-11. STRECKER, G. Der Weg der Gerechtigkeit (1962) 1644. SCHÜRMANN, H. Ursprung und Gestalt (1970) 33-55, 57, 285, 286, 292. JEREMIAS, J. Die Sprache des Lukasevangeliums. Redaktion und Tradition im Nicht-Markusstoff des dritten Evangeliums (Göttingen 1980) 144f.

6:33 JEREMIAS, J., Die Sprache des Lukasevangeliums. Redaktion und Tradition im Nicht-Markusstoff des dritten Evangeliums (Göttingen 1980) 145.

6:34-36 KNOX, W. L. The Sources of the Synoptic Gospels II (1957) 9.

6:34-35 JEREMIAS, J. Neutestamentliche Theologie I (1971) 21, 176f., 208, 215.

6:34 METZGER, B. M., The Early Versions of the New Testament (Oxford 1977) 390. JEREMIAS, J., Die Sprache des Lukasevangeliums. Redaktion und Tradition im Nicht-Markusstoff des dritten Evangeliums (Göttingen 1980) 145.

6:35 KNOX, W. L. The Sources of the Synoptic Gospels II (1957) 9, 15, 17, 24, 41. BLAIR, E. P. Jesus in the Gospel of Matthew (1960) 91. STRECKER, G. Der Weg der Gerechtigkeit (1962) 182. BAUMBACH, C. Das Verständnis des Bösen in den synoptischen Evangelien (1963) 125ff. JÜNGEL, E. Paulus und Jesus (1966) 213f. McNAMARA, M. The New Testament and the Palestinian Targum to the Pentateuch (1966) 135, 135 fn.35.

6:36-50 "Jesus et las prostituées" in: RThL 7 (1976) 237-54.

6:36-42 IWAND, H.-J., GPM 3 (1948-1950) 195ff. KRECK, GPM 9 (1954-1955) 174ff. BRUNNER, P. in: Herr, tue meine Lippen auf Bd. 1 (1957) G. Eichholz (ed.) 223-27. TRAUB, GPM 15 (1960-1961) 198ff. DOERNE, M. Er Kommt auch noch heute (1961) 107-10. IWAND, H.-J. Predigt-Meditationen (1964) 234-39. Hephata (Predigtgedanken aus Vergangenheit und Gegenwart, Reihe A, Bd. 5 1966) 86-103. VOOBUS, A. The Gospels in Study and Preaching (1966) 110-144. FÜRST, W. GPM 27 (1973) 334-40. MAURER, C., in: GPM 33 (1979) 296-302.

6:36-39 MASSAUX, E. Influence de L'Evangile de saint Matthieu sur la littérature chrétienne avant saint Irénée (1950) 9-13.

6:36-38 BEST, E. NTS 165 (1969-1970) 112f.

6:36-37 SWIDLER, L., Biblical Affirmations of Woman (Philadelphia 1979) 286.

6:36 MASSAUX, E. Influence de L'Evangile de saint Matthieu sur la littérature chrétienne avant saint Irénée (1950) 477-79. KNOX, W. L. The Sources of the Synoptic Gospels II 1957) 15. SCHULZ, A. Nachfolge und Nachahmen (1962) 231f., 234-37. STRECKER, G. Der Weg der Gerechtigkeit (1962) 141$_2$. McNAMARA, M. The New Testament and the Palestinian Targum to the Pentateuch (1966) 56, 133ff., 136. NICKELS, P. Targum and New Testament (1967) 33. POLAG, A., Die Christologie der Logienquelle (Neukirchen-Vluyn 1977) 61f. "Barmherzigkeit" in: TRE 5 (1980) 227, 237.

6:37-42 VAGANAY, L. "Existe-t-il chez Marc quelques Traces du Sermon sur la Montague?" NTS 1 (1954-1955) 193ff. DUPONT, D. J. Les Béatitudes (1958) 163-167. EDWARDS, R. A., A Theology of Q (Philadelphia 1976) 87-90. SCHNEIDER, G., Das Evangelium nach Lukas (Gütersloh/Würzburg 1977) 157.

6:37-40 HAAR, GPM 17 (1962-1963) 59ff.

6:37f., 41f. SCHULZ, S. Q Die Spruchquelle der Evangelisten (1972) 146-49.

6:37-38 KÄSEMANN, E. Exegetische Versuche und Besinnungen (1964) II 97. McNAMARA, M. The New Testament and the Palestinian Targum to the Pentateuch (1966) 139, 142. WREGE, H.-T. Die Ueberlieferungsgeschichte der Bergpredigt (1968) 124-29. KÄSEMANN, E. New Testament Questions of Today (1969) 99.

6:37-38 MASSAUX, E. Influence de L'Evangile de saint Matthieu sur la littérature chrétienne avant saint Irénée (1950) 166-68. DESCAMPS, A./DE HALLEUX, A. (eds.) Mélanges Bibliques en hommage au R. P. Béda Rigaux (1970) 502-03. TANNEHILL, R. C., The Sword of His Mouth (Philadelphia/Missoula 1975) 107-14.

6:37 KNOX, W. L. The Sources of the Synoptic Gospels II (1957) 30. STAUDINGER, J. Die Bergpredigt (1957) 124, 212, 215. DUPONT, D. J. Les Béatitudes (1958) 51-53. SCHRAGE, W. Die

konkreten Einzelgebote in der paulinischen Paränese (1961) 243.
SANFORD, J. A., The Kingdom Within (New York 1970) 122f.
METZGER, B. M., The Early Versions of the New Testament
(Oxford 1977) 207.

6:37b STROBEL, A. Erkenntnis und Bekenntnis der Sünde in
neutestamentlicher Zeit (1968) 60.

6:38 PALLIS, A., Notes on St. Luke and the Acts (London 1928) 12.
DUPONT, D. J. Les Béatitudes (1958) 50-54. FRIEDRICHSEN,
G. W. S. NTS 11 (1964-1965) 286f. McNAMARA, M. The New
Testament and the Palestinian Targum to the Pentateuch (1966)
138f., 142. NICKELS, P. Targum and New Testament (1967) 33.
SMITH, M. Tannaitic Parallels to the Gospels (1968) 6 b n 1, b n
5. JEREMIAS, J. Neutestamentliche Theologie I (1971) 20, 22, 31,
35. JEREMIAS, J., Die Sprache des Lukasevangeliums. Redak-
tion und Tradition im Nicht-Markusstoff des dritten Evangeliums
(Göttingen 1980) 146.

6:39-45 GEORGE, A. "Le disciple fraternel et efficace. Lc 6,39-45," AssS
39 (1972) 68-77.

6:39-40 DUPONT, D. J. Les Béatitudes (1958) 53-58.

6:39 Jülicher, D. A. Die Gleichnisreden Jesu (1910) 50-54. BLAIR, E.
P. Jesus in the Gospel of Matthew (1960) 100, 115. HENNECKE,
E./SCHNEEMELCHER, W. Neutestamentliche Apokryphen I
(1964) 153. SCHRAGE, W. Das Verhältnis des Thomas-Evangeliums zur synoptischen Tradition und zu den koptischen Evangelien
übersetzungen (1964) 85. SCHULZ, S. Q Die Spruchquelle der
Evangelisten (1972) 472-74.JEREMIAS, J., Die Sprache des
Lukasevangeliums. Redaktion und Tradition im Nicht-Markusstoff
des dritten Evangeliums (Göttingen 1980) 146.

6:40 JÜLICHER, D. A. Die Gleichnisreden Jesu (1910) 44-50. HAHN,
F. Christologische Hoheitstitel (1963) 77, 78f. BRAUN, H. Qum-
ran und NT II (1966) 102. SCHULZ, S. Q Die Spruchquelle der
Evangelisten (1972) 449-51. POLAG, A., Die Christologie der
Logienquelle (Neukirchen-Vluyn 1977) 82.

6:41-42 SCHRAGE, W. Das Verhältnis des Thomas-Evangeliums zur Synoptischen Tradition und zu den Koptischen Evangelienübersetzungen (1964) 71. FRIEDRICHSEN, G. W. S. NTS 11 (1964-1965)
283f. WREGE, H.-T., Die Ueberlieferungsgeschichte der Bergpredigt (1968) 129-31. SANFORD, J. A., The Kingdom Within
(New York 1970) 148. TANNEHILL, R. C., The Sword of His
Mouth (Philadelphia/Missoula 1975) 114-18.

6:41 JEREMIAS, J., Die Sprache des Lukasevangeliums. Redaktion und
Tradition in Nicht-Markusstoff des dritten Evangeliums (Göttingen
1980) 147.

6:42 KNOX, W. L. The Sources of the Synoptic Gospels II (1957) 154. HENNECKE, E./SCHNEEMELCHER, W. Neutestamentliche Apokryphen (1964) I 67. NICKELS, P. Targum and New Testament (1967) 33. JEREMIAS, J., Die Sprache des Lukasevangeliums. Redaktion und Tradition im Nicht-Markusstoff des dritten Evangeliums (Göttingen 1980) 147f.

6:43-46 JÜLICHER, D. A. Die Gleichnisreden Jesu (1910) 116-28. KRÄMER, M., "Hütet euch von den falschen Propheten. Eine überlieferungsgeschichtliche Untersuchung zu Mt 7,15-23/Lk 6,43-36/Mt 12,33-37" in: Biblica 57 (1976) 349-77.

6:43-45 KNOX, W. L. The Sources of the Synoptic Gospels II (1957) 11. HAHN, F. Christologische Hoheitstitel (1963) 96. SUMMERS, R. The Secret Sayings of the Living Jesus (1968) 37. WREGE, H.-T. Die Ueberlieferungsgeschichte der Bergpredigt (1968) 137-46. SCHULZ, S. Q Die Spruchquelle der Evangelisten (1972) 316-20. EDWARDS, R. A., A Theology of Q (Philadelphia 1976) 90f. SCHNEIDER, G., Das Evangelium nach Lukas (Gütersloh 1977) 159.

6:43-44 DUPONT, D. J. Les Béatitudes (1958) 46-50. MONTEFIORE, H. NTS 7 (1960-1961) 238f. SANFORD, J. A., The Kingdom Within (New York 1970) 110f. GOULDER, M. D. Midrash and Lection in Matthew (1974) 243, 307f.

6:43 BLACK, M. An Aramaic Approach to the Gospels and Acts (1967) 202f. NICKELS, P. Targum and New Testament (1967) 33. JEREMIAS, J. Neutestamentliche Theologie I (1971) 25f. BÖHLIG, A., Die Gnosis III: Der Manichäismus (Zürich/München 1980) 328 n.1. JEREMIAS, J., Die Sprache des Lukasevangeliums. Redaktion and Tradition im Nicht-Markusstoff des dritten Evangeliums (Göttingen 1980) 148.

6:44-45 SCHÜRMANN, H. Sprachliche Reminiszenzen an abgeäanderte oder ausgelassene Bestandteile der Spruchsammlung im Lukas- und Matthäusevangelium. NTS 6 (1959-1960) 209f., 253f. SCHRAGE, W. Das Vertnhältnis des Thomas-Evangeliums zur Synoptischen Tradition und zu den Koptischen Evangelienübersetzungen (1964) 100.

6:44 FRIEDRICHSEN, F. W. S. NTS 11 (1964-1965) 286f. JEREMIAS, J., Die Sprache des Lukasevangeliums. Redaktion und Tradition im Nicht-Markusstoff des dritten Evangeliums (Göttingen 1980) 148f.

6:45 DUPONT, D. J. Les Béatitudes (1958) 43-50. BAUMBACH, G. Das Verständnis des Bösen in den synoptischen Evangelien (1963) 128ff. JEREMIAS, J. Neutestamentliche Theologie I (1971) 25, 27,

32. McDONALD, J. I. H., Kerygma and Didache (Cambridge 1980). 81.

6:46-49 BARCLAY, W. And Jesus Said (1970) 217-22. ACHTEMEIER, E. The Old Testament and the Proclamation of the Gospel (1973) 182ff. BLANK, J., Verändert Interpretation den Glauben? (Freiburg1972) 102-12. EDWARDS, R. A., A Theology of Q (Philadelphia 1976) 91-93. SCHNEIDER, G., Das Evangelium nach Lukas (Gütersloh 1977) 151.

6:46 KNOX, W. L. The Sources of the Synoptic Gospels II (1957) 31. HAHN, F. Christologische Hoheitstitel (1963) 83, 85, 97f., 321. HENNECKE, E./SCHNEEMELCHER, W. Neutestamentliche Apokryphen (1964) I. 60. KÄSEMANN, E. Exegetische Versuche und Besinnungen (1964) II 84. NICKELS, P. Targum and New Testament (1967) 33. KÄSEMANN, E. New Testament Questions of Today (1968) 84. O'NEILL, J. C. The Theology of Acts in its historical setting (1970) 38-40, IX. SCHULZ, S. Q Die Spruch-quelle der Evangelisten (1972) 427-30. LANGE, J., Das Erschei-nen des Auferstandenen im Evangelium nach Mattäus (Würzburg 1973) 39, 45-47, 53f., 89, 108, 219-22. MEES, M., "Ausserka-nonische Parallelstellen zu den Gerichtsworten Mt. 7,32-23; Lk. 6,46; 13, 26-28 und ihre Bedeutung für die Formung der Jesus-worte" in: VChr 10 (1973) 79-102. SCHNEIDER, G., "Christus-bekenntnis und christliches Handeln. Lk 6,46 und Mt 7,32 im Kontext der Evangelien" in: R. Schnackenburg et al. (eds.) Die Kirche des Anfangs. FS. H. Schürmann (Leipzig 1977) 9-24.

6:47ff. FINDLAY, J. A. Jesus and His Parables (1951) 95ff. KNOX, W. L. The Sources of the Synoptic Gospels II (1957) 32. BISER, E. Die Gleichnisse Jesu (1965) 71ff., 157.

6:47-57 HAAR, GPM 19 (1964-1965) 129ff.

6:47-49 JÜLICHER, D. A. Die Gleichnisreden Jesu (1910) 259-68. PI-ROT, J. Paraboles et Allégories Evangeliques (1949) 57-61. HAHN, F. Christologische Hoheitstitel (1963) 96. WREGE, H.-T. Die Ueberlieferungsgeschichte der Bergpredigt (1968) 152-55. SANFORD, J. A., The Kingdom Within (New York 1979) 202f. SCHULZ, S. Q Die Spruchquelle der Evangelisten (1972) 312-16. MANEK, J., . . . und brachte Frucht. Die Gleichnisse Jesu (Berlin 1977) 37-39. VIELHAUER, P., "Oikodome. Das Bild vom Bau in der christlichen Literatur vom Neuen Testament bis Clemens Al-exandrinus" in: G. Klein (ed.) Oikodome (München 1979) 55.

6:47-48 SANFORD, J. A., The Kingdom Within (New York 1970) 77.

6:47 JÜNGEL, E. Paulus und Jesus (1966) 104. JEREMIAS, J., Die Sprache des Lukasevangeliums. Redaktion und Tradition im Nicht-Markusstoff des dritten Evangeliums (Göttingen 1980) 149.

6:48-7:5, 11-13 MASSAUX, E. "Deux fragments d'un manuscrit oncial de la vulgate (Lc., VI,48-VII,5, 11-13; Jo., XII,39-49; XIII,6-15)," EphT 37 (1,1971) 112-27.

    6:48 FRIEDRICHSEN, G. W. S. *NTS* 11 (1964-1965), 286f. PALLIS, A., Notes on St. Luke and the Acts (London 1928) 12. JEREMIAS, J., Die Sprache des Lukasevangeliums. Redaktion und Tradition im Nicht-Markusstoff des dritten Evangeliums (Göttingen 1980) 150.

    6:49 JEREMIAS, J., Die Sprache des Lukasevangeliums. Redaktion und Tradition im Nicht-Markusstoff des dritten Evangeliums (Göttingen 1980) 150f.

---

    7 CERFAUX, L., "L'Utilisation de la Source Q par Luc" in: F. Neirynck (ed.) L'Evangile de Luc (Gembloux 1973) 66-68.

    7:1ff. PARKER, P. The Gospel Before Mark (1953) 63ff.

    7:1-23 BORNKAMM-BARTH-HELD, Ueberlieferung und Auslegung im Matthäus-Evangelium ([2]1961) 239.

    7:1-17 CERFAUX, L., "L'Utilisation de la Source Q par Luc" in: F. Neirynck (ed.) L'Evangile de Luc (Gembloux 1973) 64f. NEIRYNCK, F., "La Matière Marcienne dans Luc" in: F. Neirynck (ed.) L'Evangile de Luc (Gembloux 1973) 184-92.

    7:1-10 EWALD, H. Die drei ersten Evangelien (1850) 224ff. HIRSCH, E. Frühgeschichte des Evangeliums (1941) 88-90. STONEHOUSE, N. B. The Witness of Matthew and Mark to Christ (1944) 230. RENGSTORF, K. H. Das Evangelium nach Lukas (1949) 94f. STONEHOUSE, N. B. The Witness of Luke to Christ (1951) 100f. KNOX, W. L. The Sources of the Synoptic Gospels II (1957) 47. SCHNIEWIND, J., Die Parallelperikopen bei Lukas und Johannes (Darmstadt 1958 = 1914) 16-21. BARTSCH, H. W., Wachet aber zu jeder Zeit! (Hamburg-Bergstedt (1963) 76-79. HAHN, F. Christologische Hoheitstitel (1963) 218. BLANK, J. Schriftauslegung in Theorie und Praxis (1969) 107, 112-17. LÜHRMANN, D. Die Redaktion der Logienquelle (1969) 57f. WEISER, A. Glaube und Wunder (1969). GEORGE, A. "Guérison de l'esclave d'un centurion. Lc 7,1-10," AssS 40 (1972) 66-77. SCHNIDER, F./ STENGER, W. Johannes und die Synoptiker (1971) 54-88. SCHRAMM, T. Der Markus-Stoff bei Lukas (1971) 40-43.

HOFFMANN, P. Studien zur Theologie der Logienquelle (1972) 4, 39, 208, 299. SCHULZ, S. Q Die Spruchquelle der Evangelisten (1972) 236-46. HAHN, F. Das Verständnis der Mission im Neuen Testament (²1965) 24f., 112. WILSON, S. G., The Gentile and the Gentile Mission in Luke-Acts (Cambridge 1973) 11, 31, 52, 176, 217. TALBERT, C. H., Literary Patterns, Theological Themes, and the Genre of Luke-Acts (Missoula 1974) 16, 19, 39, 43. ZINGG, P., Das Wachsen der Kirche (Freiburg 1974) 251. HOWARD, V. P., Das Ego in den Synoptischen Evangelien (Marburg 1975) 168-74. EDWARDS, R. A., A Theology of Q (Philadelphia 1976) 93f. POLAG, A., Die Christologie der Logienquelle (Neukirchen-Vluyn 1977) 158. SCHNEIDER, G., Das Evangelium nach Lukas (Gütersloh 1977) 165. ACHTEMEIER, P. J., "The Lukan Perspective on the Miracles of Jesus: A Preliminary Sketch" in: C. H. Talbert (ed.) Perspectives on Luke-Acts (Danville 1978) 154-56. MARTIN, R. P., "The Pericope of the Healing of the 'Centurion's' servant/son (Matt 8:5-13 par Luke 7:1-10); some exegetical notes" in: R. A. Guelich (ed.) Unity and Diversity in New Testament Theology. FS. G. E. Ladd (Grand Rapids 1978) 14-22.

7:1-5 SCHÜRMANN, H. Sprachliche Reminiszenzen an abgeänderte oder ausgelassene Bestandteile der Spruchsammlung im Lukas- und Matthäusevangelium. NTS 6 (1959-1960) 209f.

7:1 LJUNGMAN, H. Das Gesetz Erfüllen (1954) 58-60. NICKELS, P. Targum and New Testament (1967) 33. TALBERT, C. H., Literary Patterns, Theological Themes, and the Genre of Luke-Acts (Missoula 1974) 43, 95. SOARES PRABHU, G. M., The Formula Quotations in the Infancy Narrative of Matthew (Rome 1976) 60. JEREMIAS, J., Die Sprache des Lukasevangeliums (Göttingen 1980) 151.

7:2ff. KNOX, W. L. the Sources of the Synoptic Gospels II (1957) 7.

7:2 KNOX, W. L. The Sources of the Synoptic Gospels II (1957) 68, 81. JEREMIAS, J., Die Sprache des Lukasevangeliums (Göttingen 1980) 151-52.

7:3-5 STRECKER, G. Der Weg der Gerechtigkeit (1962) 99₂. TALBERT, C. H., Literary Patterns, Theological Themes, and the Genre of Luke-Acts (Missoula 1974) 19.

7:3 HAHN, F. Christologische Hoheitstitel (1963) 86. JEREMIAS, J., Die Sprache des Lukasevangeliums (Göttingen 1980) 152.

7:4 NICKELS, P. Targum and New Testament (1967) 33. JEREMIAS, J., Die Sprache des Lukasevangeliums (Göttingen 1980) 152-53.

7:5 VIELHAUER, P., "Oikodome. Das Bild vom Bau in der christ-

lichen Literatur vom Neuen Testament bis Clemens Alexandrinus''
in: G. Klein (ed.) Oikodome (München 1979) 54.

7:6 HAHN, F. Christologische Hoheitstitel (1963) 82f., 85. JE-
REMIAS, J. Neutestamentliche Theologie I (1971) 161f. TAL-
BERT, C. H., Literary Patterns, Theological Themes, and the Genre
of Luke-Acts (Missoula 1974) 19. JEREMIAS, J., Die Sprache des
Lukasevangeliums (Göttingen 1980) 153-54.

7:7 METZGER, B. M., The Early Versions of the New Testament
(Oxford 1977) 206. JEREMIAS, J., Die Sprache des Lukasevangeliums (Göttingen 1980) 154-55.

7:8-9 DUNN, J. D. G., Jesus and the Spirit (London 1975) 77.

7:8 PALLIS, A., Notes on St. Luke and the Acts (London 1928) 12-
13. BAUER, J. B., Scholia Biblica et Patristica (Graz 1972) 12-13.
MINEAR, P., To Heal and to Reveal (New York 1976) 16-18.

7:9 KNOX, W. L. The Sources of the Synoptic Gospels II (1957) 87.
HASLER, V. Amen (1969) 60. JEREMIAS, J., Die Sprache des
Lukasevangeliums (Göttingen 1980) 155-56.

7:10-18 KRECK, GPM 19 (1964-1965) 95ff.

7:10 NICKELS, P. Targum and New Testament (1967) 33. JE-
REMIAS, J., Die Sprache des Lukasevangeliums (Göttingen 1980)
156.

7:11ff. KNOX, W. L. The Sources of the Synoptic Gospels II (1957) 5, 8,
45. NÖTSCHER, F., Altorientalischer und alttestamentlicher Auferstehungsglaube (Darmstadt 1970 = 1926) 303.

7:11-17 BORNHÄUSSER, K. Studien zum Sondergut des Lukas (1934) 52-
64. FARRER, A. St Matthew and St Mark (1954) 120n. SCHLIER,
H. in: Herr, tue meine Lippen auf Bd 1 (1957), G. Eichholz, ed.,
280-83. JETTER, GPM 15 (1960-1961) 264ff. BORNKAMM-
BARTH-HELD, Ueberlieferung und Auslegung im Matthäus
evangelium (^{2}1961) 259, 270. JANKOWSKI, A. "Znak spod Nain.
De signo ad oppidum Nain facto (Lc 7,11-17)," CoTh 32 (1-4,
1962) 1-180. HAHN, F. Christologische Hoheitstitel (1963) 392.
BARTSCH, H. W., Wachet aber zu jeder Zeit! (Hamburg-Bergstedt 1963) 78-81. IWAND, H.-J. Predigt-Meditationen (1964) 239-
44. LUTHER, M. Predigten über die Christus-Botschaft (1966) 84-
87. JEREMIAS, J. Neutestamentliche Theologie I (1971) 92f.
KRAUSE, G. GPM 27 (1973) 414-23. SCHÜTZ, H.-G. Wie pre-
digen wir Wundergeschichte? (1971). SCHNIDER, F., Jesus der
Prophet (Freiburg 1973) 108ff, 237. WANKE, J. , Die Emmauserzählung. Eine redaktionsgeschichtliche Untersuchung zu Lk
24,13-35 (Leipzig 1973) 31-32, 51. TALBERT, C. H., Literary
Patterns, Theological Themes, and the Genre of Luke-Acts (Missoula 1974) 16, 19, 39, 43. DRURY, J., Tradition and Design in

Luke's Gospel (Atlanta 1976) 71-72. BERGER, K., Exegese des Neuen Testaments (Heidelberg 1977) 200. SCHNEIDER, G., Das Evangelium nach Lukas (Gütersloh/Wurzburg 1977) 167 (lit!). SWIDLER, L., Biblical Affirmations of Woman (Philadelphia 1979) 185, 216, 272.

7:11-16 IQAND, H.-J. GPM 4 (1949-1950) 247ff. TRAUB, GPM 9 (1954-1955) 224ff. JETTER, GPM 15 (1960-1961) 264ff. DOERNE, M. Er kommt auch noch heute (1961) 136-38. TERNANT, P., "La résurrection du fils de la veuve de Nain" AssS 69 (1964) 29-40. Wir wissen weder Tag noch Stunde, Predigtgedanken aus Vergangenheit und Gegenwart, Reihe A, Band 6 (1966) 38-55. PETZKE, G. Die Traditionen über Apollonius von Tyana und das Neue Testament (1970) 130, 137, 171, 179, 190. VAWTER, B. This Man Jesus (1973) 129ff.

7:11-15 SWIDLER, L., Biblical Affirmations of Woman (Philadelphia 1979) 283.

7:11 ADLER, N. Das erste christliche Pfingstfest (1938) 33f. TALBERT, C. H., Literary Patterns, Theological Themes, and the Genre of Luke-Acts (Missoula 1974) 95. METZGER, B. M., The Early Versions of the New Testament (Oxford 1977) 391. JEREMIAS, J., Die Sprache des Lukasevangeliums. Redaktion und Tradition im Nicht-Markusstoff des dritten Evangeliums (Göttingen 1980) 156f.

7:12-15 "Barmherzigkeit" in: TRE 5 (1980) 233.

7:12 ZINGG, P., Das Wachsen der Kirche (Freiburg 1974) 62f. JEREMIAS, J., Die Sprache des Lukasevangeliums. Redaktion und Tradition im Nicht-Markusstoff des dritten Evangeliums (Göttingen 1980) 157f.

7:13 HAHN, F. Christologische Hoheitstitel (1963) 89. "Barmherzigkeit" in: TRE (1980) 227, 234. JEREMIAS, J., Die Sprache des Lukasevangeliums. Redaktion und Tradition im Nicht-Markusstoff des dritten Evangeliums (Göttingen 1980) 158.

7:14ff. STROBEL, A. Erkenntnis und Bekenntnis der Sünde in neutestamentlicher Zeit (1968) 58.

7:14-15 HENNECKE, E./SCHNEEMELCHER, W. Neutestamentliche Apokryphen (1963) I 128, II 213.

7:15 FARRER, A. St Matthew and St Mark (1954) 56. KNOX, W. L. The Sources of the Synoptic Gospels II (1957) 90. JEREMIAS, J., Die Sprache des Lukasevangeliums. Redaktion und Tradition im Nicht-Markusstoff des dritten Evangeliums (Göttingen 1980) 159.

7:16 BORNKAMM-BARTH-HELD, Ueberlieferung und Auslegung im Matthäus-Evangelium (²1961) 265. HAHN, F. Christologische Hoheitstitel (1963) 390, 392. FLENDER, H. St Luke Theologian of Redemptive History (1967) 42, 46, 47, 49, 81, 158n. ZMI-JEWSKI, J., Die Eschatologiereden des Lukas-Evangeliums (Bonn 1972) 117, 136, 228, 429. JEREMIAS, J., Die Sprache des Lukasevangeliums. Redaktion und Tradition im Nicht-Markustoff des dritten Evangeliums (Göttingen 1980) 159.

7:17 KNOX, W. L. The Sources of the Synoptic Gospels II (1957) 8. NICKELS, P. Targum and New Testament (1967) 34. METZGER, B. M., The Early Versions of the New Testament (Oxford 1977) 179. JEREMIAS, J., Die Sprache des Lukasevangeliums. Redaktion und Tradition im Nicht-Markusstoff des dritten Evangeliums (Göttingen 1980) 159f.

7:18ff. KNOX, W. L. The Sources of the Synoptic Gospels II (1957) 45, 145.

7:18-8:56 TALBERT, C. H., Literary Patterns, Theological Themes, and the Genre of Luke-Acts (Missoula 1974) 39-44.

7:18-57 CERFAUX, L., "L'Utilisation de la Source Q par Luc" in: F. Neirynck (ed.) L'Evangile de Luc (Gembloux 1973) 65f. DENAUX, A., "L'Hypocrisie de Pharisiens" in: F. Neirynck (ed.) L'Evangile de Luc (Gembloux 1973) 258f.

7:18-35 EWALD, H. Die drei ersten Evangelien (1850) 251ff. HIRSCH, E. Frühgeschichte des Evangeliums (1941) 90-94. STROBEL, A. Untersuchungen zum Eschatologischen Verzögerungsproblem (1961) 267-73. LÜHRMANN, D. Die Redaktion der Logienquelle (1969) 24-31. GASTON, L. No Stone on Another (1970) 286-87. SUGGS, M. J. Wisdom, Christology, and Law in Matthew's Gospel (1970) 36ff. BARTSCH, H. W., Wachet aber zu jeder Zeit! (Hamburg-Bergstedt 1963) 81-83. DRURY, J., Tradition and Design in Luke's Gospel (Atlanta 1976) 167. JEREMIAS, J., Die Sprache des Lukasevangeliums. Redaktion und Tradition im Nicht-Markusstoff des dritten Evangeliums (Göttingen 1980) 160, 167.

7:18-34 HOFFMANN, P. Studien zur Theologie der Logienquelle (1972) passim.

7:18-30 TALBERT, C. H., Literary Patterns, Theological Themes, and the Genre of Luke-Acts (Missoula 1974) 39, 40, 41.

7:18-23 MANSON, W. Jesus the Messiah (1948) 36f., 38f., 64f. BLANK, J. Schriftauslegung in Theorie und Praxis (1969) 121, 124-28. VÖGTLE, A. Das Evangelium und die Evangelien (1971) 219-42. PIDWELL, H. J. Blessed are the Poor (1972) 77-80. SCHULZ, S. Q Die Spruchquelle der Evangelisten (1972) 190-203. SABUGAL, S. "La embajada mesianica del Bautista (Mt 11,2-6 = Lc 7,18-23). Análisis histórico-traditional," Augustinianum 13 (2, 1973) 215-78. STANTON, G. N., "On the Christology of Q" in: B. Lindars/S. S. Smalley (eds.) Christ and the Spirit in the New Testament. FS. C. F. D. Moule (Cambridge 1973) 33f. SABUGAL, S., "La embajada mesiánica del Bautista (Mt 11,2-6 = Lc 7,18-23)" Augustinianum 14 (1974) 5-39. DUNN, J. D. G., Jesus and the Spirit (London, 1975) 54, 55-60. GLÖCKNER, R., Die Verkündigung des Heils beim Evangelisten Lukas (Mainz 1975) 131f. EDWARDS, R. A., A Theology of Q (Philadelphia 1976) 64, 94-96. POLAG, A. Die Christologie der Logienquelle (Neukirchen-Vluyn 1977) 35-38. SABUGAL, S., "La embajada mesianica del Bautista (Mt 11,2-6 par.). V: Hacia el evento historico" Augustinianum 17 (1977) 511-39. SCHNEIDER, G., Das Evangelium nach Lukas (Gütersloh 1977) 169. TRITES, A. A., The New Testament Concept of Witness (Cambridge 1977) 179) BÖCHER, O., "Johannes der Täufer in der Neutestamentlichen Überlieferung" in: G. Müller (ed.) Rechtfertigung Realismus. FS. A Köberle (Darmstadt 1978) 46-52.

7:18-19 HAHN, F. Christologische Hoheitstitel (1963) 393f.

7:18 KNOX, W. L. The Sources of the Synoptic Gospels II (1957) 4. JEREMIAS, J., Die Sprache des Lukasevangeliums. Redaktion und Tradition im Nicht-Markusstoff des dritten Evangeliums (Göttingen 1980) 160f.

7:19-22 SCHNIDER, F., Jesus der Prophet (Freiburg 1973) 112ff, 237, 259.

7:19-20 KRAFT, H., Die Entstehung des Christentums (Darmstadt 1981) 27-29.

7:19 STROBEL, A. Untersuchungen zum Eschatologischen Verzögerungsproblem (1961) 265-77. HAHN, F. Christologische Hoheitstitel (1963) 88. DESCAMPS, A./DE HALLEUX, A. Mélanges Bibliques en hommage au R. P. Béda Rigaux (1970) 125-26, 145.

7:20 JEREMIAS, J., Die Sprache des Lukasevangeliums. Redaktion und Tradition im Nicht-Markusstoff des dritten Evangeliums (Göttingen 1980) 161.

7:21 STAEHELIN, E. Die Verkündigung des Reiches Gottes in der Kirche Jesu Christi I (1951) 184. BLACK, M. An Aramaic Approach to the Gospels and Acts (1967) 109f. CRAGHAN, J. F., "A Redactional Study of Lk 7,21 in the Light of Dt 19,15" CBQ 29 (1967) 353-67. JEREMIAS, J., Die Sprache des Lukasevangeliums. Redaktion und Tradition im Nicht-Markusstoff des dritten Evangeliums (Göttingen 1980) 161f.

7:22-23 STONEHOUSE, N. B. The Witness of Matthew and Mark to Christ (1944) 194. STONEHOUSE, N. B. The Witness of Luke to Christ (1951) 121f. HAHN, F., Christologische Hoheitstitel (1963) 393f. JÜNGEL, E. Paulus und Jesus (1966) 190. JEREMIAS, J. Neutestamentliche Theologie I (1971) 31, 83, 91, 106f., 111, 114. EUGSTER, W. A., The Healing Ministry of Jesus in the Gospel of

Luke (Th.M. thesis, Rüschlikon/Switzerland, Baptist Theological Seminary (1978).

7:22 FLEW, R. N. Jesus and His Church (1956) 60. KNOX, W. L. The Sources of the Synoptic Gospels II (1957) 8. NICKELS, P. Targum and New Testament (1967) 34. PESCH, R. Jesu ureigene Taten? in: Quaestiones Disputatae Bd. 52 (1970), Rahner, K. und Schlier, H. (eds.), 36-44. TALBERT, C. H., Literary Patterns, Theological Themes, and the Genre of Luke-Acts (Missoula 1974) 41. MINEAR, P., To Heal and to Reveal (New York 1976) 64. KARRIS, R. J., ''Poor and Rich: The Lukan Sitz im Leben'' in: C. H. Talbert (ed.) Perspectives on Luke-Acts (Danville 1978) 117f. MEYER, B. F., The Aims of Jesus (London 1979) 240. BÖHLIG, A., Die Gnosis III: Der Manichäismus (Zürich 1980) 344 n.60. JEREMIAS, J., Die Sprache des Lukasevangeliums. Redaktion und Tradition im Nicht-Markusstoff des dritten Evangeliums (Göttingen 1980) 162.

7:23 FLEW, R. N. Jesus and His Church (1956) 66. TALBERT, C. H., Literary Patterns, Theological Themes, and the Genre of Luke-Acts (Missoula 1974) 41. BOERMA, C., Rich Man, Poor Man - and the Bible (London 1979) 50f. SCHILLEBEECKX, E., Die Auferstehung Jesu als Grund der Erlösung (Basel 1979) 80.

7:24ff. STONEHOUSE, N. B. The Witness of Matthew and Mark to Christ (1944) 245.

7:24-35 HAHN, F. Christologische Hoheitstitel (1963) 374-77. SCHNIDER, F., Jesus der Prophet (Freiburg 1973) 40f, 50. EDWARDS, R. A., A Theology of Q (Philadelphia 1976) 96-99. SCHNEIDER, G., Das Evangelium nach Lukas (Gütersloh 1977) 172.

7:24-30 BIEDER, W., Die Verheissung der Taufe im Neuen Testament (Zürich 1966) 44f. KIEFFER, R., ''Mer-än' -kristologin hos synoptikerna'' in: SEA (1979) 134-47.

7:24-28 FLEW, R. N. Jesus and His Church (1956) 22. SCHULZ, S. Q Die Spruchquelle der Evangelisten (1972) 229-36.

7:24-27 MEYER, B. F., The Aims of Jesus (London 1979) 125f.

7:24-26 POLAG, A., Die Christologie der Logienquelle (Neukirchen-Vluyn 1977) 47.

7:24-25 SCHRAGE, W. Das Verhältnis des Thomas-Evangeliums zur Synoptischen Tradition und zu den Koptischen Evangelienübersetzungen (1964) 160.

7:24 STRECKER, G. Der Weg der Gerechtigkeit (1962) 63. METZGER, B. M., The Early Versions of the New Testament (Oxford 1977) 391.

7:25 JEREMIAS, J., Die Sprache des Lukasevangeliums. Redaktion und

Tradition im Nicht-Markusstoff des dritten Evangeliums (Göttingen 1980) 163f.

7:26 HASLER, V. Amen (1969) 64. JEREMIAS, J. Neutestamentliche Theologie I (1971) 25, 53f., 86, 280.

7:27-28 POLAG, A., Die Christologie der Logienquelle (Neukirchen-Vluyn 1977) 158.

7:27 STONEHOUSE, N. B. The Witness of Matthew and Mark to Christ (1944) 194. RESE, M., Alttestamentliche Motive in der Christologie der Lukas (1969) 165-68. TALBERT, C. H., Literary Patterns, Theological Themes, and the Genre of Luke-Acts (Missoula 1974) 97. BÖCHER, O., "Johannes der Täufer in der Neutestamentlichen Überlieferung" in: G. Müller (ed.) Rechtfertigung Realismus. FS. A. Köberle (Darmstadt 1978) 47-52. JEREMIAS, J., Die Sprache des Lukasevangeliums. Redaktion und Tradition im Nicht-Markusstoff des dritten Evangeliums (Göttingen 1980) 164.

7:28 LEANEY, R. "Jesus and the Symbol of the Child," ET 66 (3, 1954) 91-92. SCHNACKENBURG, R. Gottes Herrschaft und Reich (1959) 90-92, 111, 153. SCHRAGE, W. Das Verhältnis des Thomas-Evangeliums zur Synoptischen Tradition und zu den Koptischen Evangelienübersetzungen (1964) 107. JÜNGEL, E. Paulus und Jesus (1966) 176. NICKELS, P. Targum and New Testament (1967) 34. HASLER, V. Amen (1969) 64. JEREMIAS, J. Neutestamentliche Theologie I (1971) 25, 40, 53, 56, 87. "Aramäisch" in: TRE 3 (1978) 609. DÖMER, M., Das Heil Gottes: Studien zur Theologie des lukanischen Doppelwerkes (Köln/Bonn 1978) 37. MATTILL, A. J., Luke and the Last Things (Dillsboro 1979) 159-64. SCHLOSSER, J., "Le Règne de Dieu dans les dits de Jésus" RevSR 53 (2, 1979) 164-76. KRAFT, H., Die Entstehung des Christentums (Darmstadt 1981) 32.

7:29-35 PIROT, J. Parables et Allégories Evangeliques (1948) 63-70.

7:29-30 JÜLICHER, D. A. Die Gleichnisreden Jesu (1910) 365-85. SCHLATTER, A. Johannes der Täufer (1956) 76ff. STRECKER, G. Der Weg der Gerechtigkeit (1962) 153. HAHN, F. Christologische Hoheitstitel (1963) 376. JÜNGEL, E. Paulus und Jesus (1966) 175. WINK, W. John the Baptist in the Gospel Tradition (1968) 18-20, 83-84. CHRIST, F. Jesus Sophia (1970) 75, 77, 78. HOFFMANN, P. Studien zur Theologie der Logienquelle (1972) 192, 194-96, 286. GOULDER, M. D. Midrash and Lection in Matthew (1974) 358f. DÖMER, M., Das Heil Gottes: Studien zur Theologie der lukanischen Doppelwerkes (Köln/Bonn 1978) 15-18. RIVKIN, E., A Hidden Revolution (Nashville 1978) 117. FRICKEL, J., "Die Zöllner, Vorbild der Demut und wahrer Gottesverehrung" in: E. Dassmann/K. S. Frank (eds.) Peitas. FS. B. Kötting (Münster 1980) 369.

7:29 KNOX, W. L. The Sources of the Synoptic Gospels II (1957) 115. RUDOLPH, K. Die Mandäer II (1961) 76, 1. DELLING, G. Die Taufe im Neuen Testament (1963) 42. CHRIST, F. Jesus Sophia (1970) 64, 66, 77, 79. PALLIS, A., Notes on St. Luke and the Acts (London 1928) 13. TALBERT, C. H., Literary Patterns, Theological Themes, and the Genre of Luke-Acts (Missoula 1974) 41. JEREMIAS, J., Die Sprache des Lukasevangeliums. Redaktion und Tradition im Nicht-Markusstoff des dritten Evangeliums (Göttingen 1980) 165. RICE, G. E., "The Anti-Judaic Bias of the Western Text in the Gospel of Luke" AUSS 18 (1980) 55.

7:30 BOUSSET, W. Die Religion des Judentums im Späthellenistischen Zeitalter (1960 = 1926) 166. PALLIS, A., Notes on St. Luke and the Acts (London 1928) 13f. BLACK, M. An Aramaic Approach to the Gospels and Acts (1967) 103f. NICKELS, P. Targum and New Testament (1967) 34. WANKE, J. Die Emmauserzählung (Leipzig 1973) 94. JEREMIAS, J., Die Sprache des Lukasevangeliums. Redaktion und Tradition im Nicht-Markusstoff des dritten Evangeliums (Göttingen 1980) 165f.

7:31-35 JÜLICHER, D. A. Die Gleichnisreden Jesu (1910) 23-36. MUSSNER, F. "Der Nicht erkannte Kairos" Biblica 40 (3-4, 1959) 599-612. CHRIST, F. Jesus Sophia (1970) 63-80. SCHULZ, S. Q Die Spruchquelle der Evangelisten (1972) 379-88. TALBERT, C. H., Literary Patterns, Theological Themes, and the Genre of Luke-Acts (Missoula 1974) 40, 42. ARENS, E., The HΛΘON-SAYINGS in the Synoptic Tradition (Fribourg 1976) 221-43. LINTON, O., "The Parable of the Children's Game. Baptist and Son of Man (Matt. xi.16-10 = Luke vii 31-5): A Synoptic Text-Critical, Structural and Exegetical Investigation" in: NTS 22 (1976) 159-79. GRUNDMANN, W., "Weisheit im Horizont des Reiches Gottes. Eine Studie zur Verkündigung Jesu nach der Spruchüberlieferung Q" in: R. Schnackenburg et al. (eds.) Die Kirche des Anfangs. FS. H. Schürmann (Leipzig 1977) 180f. MANEK, J., . . . und brachte Frucht. Die Gleichnisse Jesu (Berlin 1977) 39-41. WEBER, H.-R., Jesus and the Children (Atlanta 1979). KRAFT, H., Die Entstehung des Christentums (Darmstadt 1981) 167-68.

7:31-34 POLAG, A. Die Christologie der Logienquelle (Neukirchen 1977) 47, 89. MEYER, B. F., The Aims of Jesus (London 1979) 224.

7:31-32 HAHN, F. Christologische Hoheitstitel (1963) 376. ZELLER, D., "Die Bildlogik des Gleichnisses Mt 11:16f/Lk 7:31f" ZNW 68 (1977) 252-57.

7:32-34 JEREMIAS, J., Die Sprache des Lukasevangeliums (Göttingen 1980) 166.

7:32 NICKELS, P. Targum and New Testament (1967) 34. JE-
REMIAS, J., Die Sprache des Lukasevangeliums (Göttingen 1980)
166.

7:33-35 SCHENKE, H. M., "Die Tendenz der Weisheit zur Gnosis" in: B.
Aland et al. (eds.) Gnosis. FS. H. Jonas (Göttingen 1978) 359-65.

7:33-34 HAHN, F. Christologische Hoheitstitel (1963) 44.SCHÜRMANN,
H., "Beobachtungen zum Menschensohn-Titel in der Redequelle"
in: R. Pesch/R. Schnackenburg (eds.) Jesus und der Menschensohn
(Freiburg/Basel/Wien 1975) 131-32.

7:33 BÖCHER, O., "Ass Johannes der Täufer kein Brot (Luk. viii.33)?"
NTS 18 (1, 1971) 90-92. PALLIS, A., Notes on St. Luke and the
Acts (London 1928) 14.

7:34-35 ROBINSON, J. M. Kerygma und historischer Jesus (1960) 34.

7:34 ROBINSON, J. M. Kerygma und historischer Jesus (1960) 148.
SCHWEIZER, E. Erniedrigung und Erhöhung bei Jesus und seinen
Nachfolgern (1962) § 3 1. STROBEL, A. Erkenntnis und Bekennt-
nis der Sünde in neutestamentlicher Zeit (1968) 42, 60. JE-
REMIAS, J. Neutestamentliche Theologie I (1971) 25, 111, 117,
120, 123, 142, 248, 249. HOFFMANN, P., "Mk 8,31. Zur Herkunft und markinischen Rezeption einer alten Überlieferung" in:
P. Hoffmann (ed.) Orientierung an Jesus. FS. J. Schmid (Freiburg
1973) 180-81. STANTON, G. N., Jesus of Nazareth in New Testament Preaching (Cambridge 1974) 142, 143, 156, 158, 159.
TALBERT, C. H., Literary Patterns, Theological Themes, and the
Genre of Luke-Acts (Missoula 1974) 42. ORBE, A., "El Hijo del
hombre come y bebe (Mt 11,19; Lc 7,34)" Gregorianum (1977)
523-55.

7:35-50 NAVONE, J. "The Lucan Banquet Community," Bible Today 51
(1970) 155-61.

7:35 KLEIN, G., "Kinder oder Werke" ZNW 2 (1901) 346. PALLIS,
A., Notes on St. Luke and the Acts (London 1928) 14.KNOX, W.
L. The Sources of the Synoptic Gospels II (1957) 115. LÖVES-
TAM, E. "Till förstaelse av Luk. 7:35" /A Contribution to the Un-
derstanding of Lk 7:35/ , SEA 22-23 (1957-1958) 47-63.
BOUSSET, W. Die Religion des Judentums im Späthellenisti-
schen Zeitalter (1966 = 1926) 346. JEREMIAS, J., Die Sprache des
Lukasevangeliums (Göttingen 1980) 167.

7:36-9:50 PIDWELL, H. J. Blessed are the Poor (1972) 80-86.

7:36-9:17 DRURY, J., Tradition and Design in Luke's Gospel (Atlanta 1976)
91-96.

7:36-8:3 EWALD, H. Die drei ersten Evangelien (1850) 342f.

7:36ff. FEINE, D. P. & BEHM, D. J. Einleitung in das Neue Testament
(1950) 71f. KNOX, W. L. The Sources of the Synoptic Gospels II

(1957) 45. STROBEL, A. Erkenntnis und Bekenntnis der Sünde in neutestamentlicher Zeit (1968) 60.

7:36-50 JÜLICHER, D. A. Die Gleichnisreden Jesu (1910) 290-302. HIRSCH, E. Frühgeschichte des Evangeliums (1941) 6f., 199-205. RIESENFELD, H., Jésus Transfiguré (Copenhagen 1947) 327. PIROT, J. Paraboles et Allégories Evangeliques (1949) 71-78. RENGSTORF, K. H. Das Evangelium nach Lukas (1949) 102. TAYLOR, V. The Formation of the Gospel Tradition (1949) 153f. MICHAELIS, D. W. Die Gleichnisse Jesu (1956) 196-202. SCHNIEWIND, J., Die Parallelperikopen bei Lukas und Johannes (Darmstadt 1958 = 1914) 21-26. DONOHUE, J. J. "The Penitent Woman and the Pharisee: Luke 7:36-50," AER 142 (6, 1960) 414-21. WINANDY, J. "Simon et la Pécheresse (Luc 7,36-50)," BVie 47 (1962) 38-46. HAHN, F. GPM 17 (1962-1963) 285-91. BAILEY, J. A. The Traditions Common to the Gospels of Luke and John (1963) 1-8. Erhaltet euch in der Liebe Gottes, Predigtgedanken aus Vergangenheit und Gegenwart, Reihe C, Bd. 3-4 (1963) 164-83. BARTSCH, H. W., Wachet aber zu jeder Zeit! (Hamburg-Bergstedt 1963) 84. BRAUMANN, G. "Die Schuldner und die Sünderin Luk. vii. 36-50," NTS 10 (4, 1964) 487-93. IWAND, H.-J. Predigt-Meditationen (1964) 312-16. STECK, K. G., in: Herr, tue meine Lippen auf Bd. 3 (1964), G. Eichholz ed., 368ff. HAHN, F. Das Verständnis der Mission im Neuen Testament (²1965) 101. BRAUN, H. Qumran und NT II (1966) 288, 295. DELOBEL, J. "L'onction par la pécheresse. La composition littéraire de Lc., VII, 36-50," EphT 42 (3, 1966) 415-75. BLACK, M. An Aramaic Approach to the Gospels and Acts (1967) 181f. GUTBROD, K. Ein Weg zu den Gleichnissen Jesu (1967) 22-24. HENSS, W. Das Verhältnis zwischen Diatessaron, christlicher Gnosis und "Western Text" (1967) DREXLER, H. "Die grosse Sünderin Lucas 7:36-50," ZNW 59 (3-4, 1968) 159-73. SURKAU, H.-W. GPM 23 (3, 1968-1969) 305-13. DELOBEL, J. "Encore la pécheresse Quelque réflexions critiques," EphT 45 (1, 1969) 180-83. BOUWMAN, G. "La pécheresse hospitalière (Lc., VIII, 36-50)," EphT 45 (1, 1969) 172-79. SCHÜTZ, F. Der leidende Christus (1969) 54f. BARCLAY, W. And Jesus Said (1970) 188-92. GASTON, L. No Stone on Another (1970) 252, 255, 315-16. LEHMANN, M. Synoptische Quellenanalyse und die Frage nach dem historischen Jesus (1970) 145, 146. PHIPPS, W. E. Was Jesus Married? (1970) 63-66. EICHHOLZ, G. Gleichnisse der Evangelien (1971) 55-64. JEREMIAS, J. New Testament Theology I (1971) 114, 119, 151, 156, 217, 226. JEREMIAS, J. Neutestamentliche Theologie I (1971) 115, 121, 150, 155, 210, 218. LÖNING, K. "Ein Platz für die Verlorenen. Zur Formkritik zweier neutestamentlicher Legen-

den (Lk 7,36-50; 19,1-10)," BuL 12 (2, 1971) 198-208.
SCHRAMM, T. Der Markus-Stoff bei Lukas (1971) 43-45. RA-
MAROSON, L. "Simon et la pécheresse anonyme (lc 7,36-50),"
SciE 24 (3, 1972) 379-83. PESCH, R., "Die Salbung Jesu in Be-
hanien (Mk 14, 3-9)" in: P. Hoffmann (ed.) Orientierung an Jesus.
FS. J. Schmid (Freiburg 1973) 269-70. SCHNIDER, F., Jesus der
Prophet (Freiburg 1973) 116ff, 237. WANKE, J., Die Emmaus-
erzählung. Eine redaktionsgeschichtliche Untersuchung zu Lk
24,13-35 (Leipzig 1973) 71A 517. WILCKENS, U., "Vergebung
für die Sünderin (Lk 7,36-50)" in: P. Hoffmann (ed.) Orientierung
an Jesus. FS. J. Schmid (Freiburg 1973) 394-424. LEROY, H., Zur
Vergebung der Sünden (Stuttgart 1974) 71-78. TALBERT, C. H.,
Literary Patterns, Theological Themes, and the Genre of Luke-Acts
(Missoula 1974) 16, 20, 40, 42. FEUILLET, A., "Les deux onc-
tions faites sur Jésus, et Marie-Madeleine. Contribution à l'étude
des rapports entre les Synoptiques et le quatrième évangile" RThom
75 (1975) 357-94. GEENSE, A., in: GPM 29 (1975) 365-70.
GERBER, H. und BÜHLER, K.-W., in: P. Krusche et al. (eds.)
Predigtstudien für das Kirchenjahr 1974-1975. III/2 Stuttgart 1975)
173-78. GLÖCKNER, R., Die Verkündigung des Heils beim
Evangelisten Lukas (Mainz 1975) 149ff. HOLST, R., "The One
Annointing of Jesus: Another Application of the Form-Critical
Method" JBL 95 (1976) 435-46. AHERN, B. M., "By the Grace
of God" Way 17 (1977) 3-11. SANFORD, J. A., Healing and
Wholeness (New York 1977) 119. SCHNEIDER, G., Das Evan-
gelium nach Lukas (Gütersloh/Würzburg 1977) 176 (lit!). MOULE,
C. F. D., " '. . . As we forgive . . .' - A Note on the Distinction
between Deserts and Capacity in the Understanding of Forgive-
ness" in: E. Bammel et al. (eds.) Donum Gentilicium. FS. D. Daube
(Oxford 1978) 72-74. RIST, J. M., On the Independence of Matthew and Mark (Cambridge 1978) 83-84. SWIDLER, L., Biblical
Affirmations of Woman (Philadelphia 1979) 187, 188, 224, 272,
275, 289. "Barmherzigkeit" in: TRE 5 (1980) 233. FRICKEL, J.,
"Die Zöllner, Vorbild der Demut und wahrer Gottesverehrung" in:
E. Dassmann/K. S. Frank (eds.) Pietas. FS. B. Kötting (Münster
1980) 375. GERSTENBERGER, E. S. und SCHRAGE, W., Frau
und Mann (Stuttgart 1980) 117-18. JEREMIAS, J., Die Sprache
des Lukasevangeliums (Göttingen 1980) 174. KRAFT, H., Die
Entstehung des Christentums (Darmstadt 1981) 119.

7:36 JEREMIAS, J., Die Sprache des Lukasevangeliums (Göttingen
1980) 167-68.

7:37-50 SWIDLER, L., Biblical Affirmations of Woman (Philadelphia
1979) 208, 250, 274.

7:36-47 TILLICH, P. Das Neue Sein (1959) 13-22.

7:36-40 STROBEL, A. Erkenntnis und Bekenntnis der Sünde in neutestamentlicher Zeit (1968) 59.

7:36-38 DERRETT, J./Duncan, M. Law in the New Testament (1970) 266-68. CRIBBS, F. L. in: SBL Seminar Papers 2 (1973), G. MacRae ed., 32-38.

7:36 NICKELS, P. Targum and New Testament (1967) 34.

7:37-39 SCHWEIZER, E. GPM 17 (1962-1963) 210ff.

7:37 NICKELS, P. Targum and New Testament (1967) 34. STROBEL, A. Erkenntnis und Bekenntnis der Sünde in neutestamentlicher Zeit (1968) 42. PALLIS, A., Notes on St. Luke and the Acts (London 1928) 15. JEREMIAS, J., Die Sprache des Lukasevangeliums (Göttingen 1980) 168.

7:38ff. SANDERS, J. N. Those Whom Jesus Loved. NTS 1 (1954-1955) 36ff.

7:38.44 Jüdische Schriften aus hellenistisch-römischer Zeit I/1 (1973), W. G. Kümmel, ed., 40, 42.

7:38 PALLIS, A., Notes on St. Luke and the Acts (London 1928) 15-16. JANSSEN, E., "Testament Abrahams" in: W. G. Kümmel (ed.) Jüdische Schriften aus hellenistisch-römischer Zeit III (Gütersloh 1975) 211n.76. JEREMIAS, J., Die Sprache des Lukasevangeliums (Göttingen 1980) 168-69.

7:39-50 URRUTIA, J. D. de, "La parabola de los dos deudores Lc 7,39-50," EstEc 38 (147, 1963) 459-82. SANFORD, J. A., The Kingdom Within (New York 1970) 129-30.

7:39-40 DERRETT, J./DUNCAN, M. Law in the New Testament (1970) 268-70.

7:39 HAHN, F. Christologische Hoheitstitel (1963) 398. HENSS, W. Das Verhältnis zwischen Diatessaron, Christlicher Gnosis und "Western Text" (1967) 35-38, 51, 53. STROBEL, A. Erkenntnis und Bekenntnis der Sünde in neutestamentlicher Zeit (1968) 42.

7:40ff. HENSS, W. Das Verhältnis zwischen Diatessaron, Christlicher Gnosis und "Western Text" (1967) 19, 29f.

7:40 HAHN, F. Christologische Hoheitstitel (1963) 76, 77. JEREMIAS, J., Die Sprache des Lukasevangeliums. Redaktion und Tradition im Nicht-Markusstoff des dritten Evangeliums (Göttingen 1980) 169f.

7:41-43 MORGAN, G. C. The Parables and Metaphors of Our Lord (1943) 171ff. LOCKYER, H. All the Parables of the Bible (1963) 256ff. STROBEL, A. Erkenntnis und Bekenntnis der Sünde in neutestamentlicher Zeit (1968) 59. MANEK, J., . . . und brachte Frucht. Die Gleichnisse Jesu (Berlin 1977) 80-82. MEYER, B. F., The Aims of Jesus (London 1979) 158-62.

7:41-42 MICHAELIS, D. W. Die Gleichnisse Jesu (1956) 199-202.

7:41 JEREMIAS, J., Die Sprache des Lukasevangeliums. Redaktion und Tradition im Nicht-Markusstoff des dritten Evangeliums (Göttingen 1980) 170.

7:42.47 WOOD, H. G. "The Use of ἀγαπάω in Luke VII, 42, 47," ET 66 (10, 1955) 312-20.

7:42 FRIEDRICHSEN, G. W. S. NTS 11 (1964-1965) 283f. HENSS, W. Das Verhältnis zwischen Diatessaron, Christlicher Gnosis und "Western Text" (1967) 3-8. JEREMIAS, J., Die Sprache des Lukasevangeliums. Redaktion und Tradition im Nicht-Markusstoff des dritten Evangeliums (Göttingen 1980) 170.

7:43 HENSS, W., Das Verhältnis zwischen Diatessaron, Christlicher Gnosis und "Western Text" (1967) 3-5, 10f. JEREMIAS, J., Die Sprache des Lukasevangeliums. Redaktion und Tradition im Nicht-Markusstoff des dritten Evangeliums (Göttingen 1980) 170f.

7:44-50 STROBEL, A. Erkenntnis und Bekenntnis der Sünde in neutestamentlicher Zeit (1968) 59.

7:44 KNOX, W. L. The Sources of the Synoptic Gospels II (1957) 87. JANSSEN, E., "Testament Abrahams" in: W. G. Kümmel (ed.) Jüdische Schriften aus hellenistisch-römischer Zeit III (Gütersloh 1975) 211 n.75. METZGER, B. M., The Early Versions of the New Testament (Oxford 1977) 391. JEREMIAS, J., Die Sprache des Lukasevangeliums. Redaktion und Tradition im Nicht-Markusstoff des dritten Evangeliums (Göttingen 1980) 171f.

7:45 PALLIS, A. Notes on St. Luke and the Acts (London 1928) 16. JEREMIAS, J. "Lukas 7:45: eisēlthon," ZNW 51 (1-2, 1960) 131. JEREMIAS, J., Die Sprache des Lukasevangeliums. Redaktion und Tradition im Nicht-Markusstoff des dritten Evangeliums (Göttingen 1980) 172.

7:46 WEISS, K. "Der westliche Text von Lc 7,46 und sein Wert," ZNW 46 (3-5, 1955) 241-45.

7:47-48 JEREMIAS, J. Neutestamentlich Theologie I (1971) 22, 26, 116, 121, 210. DELLING, G. Die Taufe im Neuen Testament (1963) 57.

7:47 BLACK, M. An Aramaic Approach to the Gospels and Acts (1967) 129f. HENSS, W. Das Verhältnis zwischen Diatessaron, Christlicher Gnosis und "Western Text" (1967) 24-31. STROBEL, A. Erkenntnis und Bekenntnis der Sünde in neutestamentlicher Zeit (1968) 42, 59. JEREMIAS, J. Die Sprache des Lukasevangeliums. Redaktion und Tradition im Nicht-Markusstoff des dritten Evangeliums (Göttingen 1980) 172f.

7:48-50 HENSS, W. Das Verhältnis zwischen Diatessaron, Christlicher Gnosis und "Western Text" (1967) 22f. MANKE, J., Die

Emmauserzählung (Leipzig 1973) 427. JEREMIAS, J., Die Sprache des Lukasevangeliums. Redaktion und Tradition im Nicht-Markusstoff des dritten Evangeliums (Göttingen 1980) 173.

7:48 HAHN, F. Das Verständnis des Mission im Neuen Testament (²1965) 41. STROBEL, A. Erkenntnis und Bekenntnis der Sünde in neutestamentlicher Zeit (1968) 59. LADD, G. E., A Theology of the New Testament (Grand Rapids 1974) 77, 79, 134.

7:49 STROBEL, A. Erkenntnis und Bekenntnis der Sünde in neutestamentlicher Zeit (1968) 47, 59. JEREMIAS, J., Die Sprache des Lukasevangeliums. Redaktion und Tradition im Nicht-Markusstoff des dritten Evangeliums (Göttingen 1980) 173f.

7:50 ROBINSON, J. M. Kerygma und historischer Jesus (1960) 30. BORNKAMM-BARTH-HELD, Ueberlieferung und Auslegung im Matthäus-Evangelium (²1961) 253. BRAUMANN, G. NTS 10 (1963-1964) 489f. FRIEDRICHSEN, G. W. S. NTS 11 (1964-1965) 283f. HENSS, W. Das Verhältnis zwischen Diatessaron, Christlicher Gnosis und "Western Text" (1967) 18, 35f. SWIDLER, L., Biblical Affirmations of Woman (Philadelphia 1979) 264. JEREMIAS, J., Die Sprache des Lukasevangeliums. Redaktion und Tradition im Nicht-Markusstoff des dritten Evangeliums (Göttingen 1980) 174.

8:1-9:50 GOULDER, M. D. Type and History in Acts (1964) 131-33.

8:1-9:27 BARTSCH, H. W., Wachet aber zu jeder Zeit! (Hamburg-Bergstedt 1963) 84-87.

8:1-9:9 CONZELMANN, H. Die Mitte der Zeit (1964) 40ff.

8 FEINE, D. P./BEHM, D. J. Einleitung in das Neue Testament (1950) 28f. GREENLEE, J. H. Nine Uncial Palimpsests of the Greek New Testament (1968) 70-71. SWIDLER, L., Biblical Affirmations of Woman (Philadelphia 1979) 165.

8:1-3 HIRSCH, E. Frühgeschichte des Evangeliums (1941) 5f., 205-07. HENGEL, M. "Maria Magdalena und die Frauen als Zeugen", in: Abraham unser Vater. Festschrift f. Otto Michel (1963) 243-56. SCHÜTZ, F. Der leidende Christus (1969) 113, 116ff. LEHMANN, M. Synoptische Quellenanalyse und die Frage nach dem historischen Jesus (1970) 140. DENAUX, A., "L'Hypocrisie des Pharisiens" in: F. Neirynck (ed.) L'Evangile de Luc (Gembloux 1973) 247f. NEIRYNCK, F., "La Matière Marcienne dans Luc"

in: F. Neirynck (ed.) L'Evangile de Luc (Gembloux 1973) 184-92.
WANKE, J., Die Emmauserzählung (Leipzig 1973) 75. TAL-
BERT, C. H., Literary Patterns, Theological Themes, and the Genre
of Luke-Acts (Missoula 1974) 40, 42, 43. SCHNEIDER, G., Das
Evangelium nach Lukas (Gütersloh 1977) 179. STAGG, E. and F.,
Woman in the World of Jesus (Philadelphia 1978) 121-25, 225.
"Armut" in: TRE 4 (1979) 78. CHILTON, B., "The Gospel of
Jesus and the Ministry of Women" MCh 22 (1978-1979) 18-21.
PRAST, F., Presbyter und Evangelium in nachapostolischer Zeit
(Stuttgart 1979) 311f. SWIDLER, L., Biblical Affirmations of
Woman (Philadelphia 1979) 194, 208, 209, 272, 305. WITHER-
INGTON, B., "On the Road with Mary Magdalene, Joanna, Su-
sanna, and Other Disciples—Luke 8:1-3" ZNW 70 (1979) 243-48.
GERSTENBERGER, E. S. and SCHRAGE, W., Frau und Mann
(Stuttgart 1980) 118. MALY, E. H., "Women and the Gospel of
Luke" BThB 10 (1980) 99-104.

8:1-2 PRAST, F., Presbyter und Evangelium in nachapostolischer Zeit
(Stuttgart 1979) 277.

8:1 ADLER, N. Das erste christliche Pfingstfest (1938) 33f. DAL-
TON, W. J., Christ's Proclamation to the Spirits (Rome 1965) 152.
TALBERT, C. H., Literary Patterns, Theological Themes, and the
Genre of Luke-Acts (Missoula 1974) 43, 95. EGGER, W., Fo-
rhbotschaft und Lehre (Frankfurt a. M. 1976) 31. METZGER, B.
M., The Early Versions of the New Testament (Oxford 1977) 91f,
212. HORTON, F. L., "Reflections on the Semitisms of Luke-
Acts" in: C. H. Talbert (ed.) Perspectives on Luke-Acts (Danville
1978) 4. PRAST, F., Presbyter und Evangelium in nachaposto-
lischer Zeit (Stuttgart 1979) 115f, 280f, 314f, 333, 338f. JE-
REMIAS, J., Die Sprache des Lukasevangeliums (Göttingen 1980)
174-76.

8:2 RUDOLPH, K. Die Mandäer I (1960) 96. BOUSSET, W. Die Religion des Judentums im späthellenistischen Zeitalter (1966⸗1926)
339. HENSS, W. Das Verhältnis zwischen Diatessaron, Christlicher Gnosis und "Western Text" (1967) 12n. 17, 41f., 44f., 56.
METZGER, B. M., The Early Versions of the New Testament
(Oxford 1977) 245. JEREMIAS, J., Die Sprache des Lukasevangeliums (Göttingen 1980) 176-78.

8:3 NICKELS, P. Targum and New Testament (1967) 34. BAUER, J.
B., Scholia Biblica et Patristica (Graz 1972) 102. METZGER, B.
M., The Early Versions of the New Testament (Oxford 1977) 202.
JEREMIAS, J., Die Sprache des Lukasevangeliums (Göttingen
1980) 178. KRAFT, H., Die Entstehung des Christentums (Darm-
stadt 1981) 123.

8:4-9:50 TAYLOR, V. Behind the Third Gospel (1926) 84ff. JEREMIAS, J. Neutestamentliche Theologie I (1971) 48f.

8:4-9:17 STONEHOUSE, N. B. The Witness of Luke to Christ (1951) 94, 102f.

8:4ff. KNOX, W. L. The Sources of the Synoptic Gospels II (1957) 45-47. Au service de la Parole de Dieu. Mélanges offerts à Monseigneur André-Marie Charue, Evêque de Namur (1969). GOULDER, M. D. Midrash and Lection in Matthew (1974) 50, 59f.

8:4-21 SCHÜRMANN, H. Ursprung und Gestalt (1970) 29-41. ROBINSON, W. C., "On Preaching the Word of God" in: L. E. Keck/J. L. Martyn (eds.) Studies in Luke-Acts. FS. P. Schubert (Nashville 1966) 131-38. SCHÜRMANN, H., "Lukanische Reflexionen über die Wortverkündigung" in: L. Scheffczyk et al. (eds.) Wahrheit und Verkündigung. FS. M. Schmaus (München 1967) 213-28. SCHÜRMANN, H., "Lukanische Reflexionen über die Wortverkündigung" Theologisches Jahrbuch 11 (Leipzig 1968) 91-99. HAHN, F., "Die Worte vom Licht, Lk 11,33-36" in: P. Hoffmann (ed.) Orientierung an Jesus. FS. J. Schmid (Freiburg 1973) 121-24, 133. MÄRZ, C.-P., Das Wort Gottes bei Lukas (Leipzig 1973) 57-59. PRAST, F. Presbyter und Evangelium in nachapostolischer Zeit (Stuttgart 1979) 197-301, 312.

8:4-18 EWALD, H. Die drei ersten Evangelien (1850) 230ff. GERHARDSSON, B. NTS 14 (1967-1968) 182f. WEDER, H., Die Gleichnisse Jesu als Metaphern (Göttingen 1980) 99-108.

8:4-15 PIROT, J. Paraboles et Allégories Evangeliques (1949) 91-103. VIELHAUER, GPM 4 (1949-1950) 73ff. LOEWENICH, W. von. Luther als Ausleger der Synoptiker (1954) 31ff., 36. SURKAU, GPM 9 (1954-1955) 62ff. STECK, K. G. in: Herr, tue meine Lippen auf Bd. 1 (1957), G. Eichholz, ed., 83-88. Zu Suchen Seine Herrlichkeit, Predigtgedanken aus Vergangenheit und Gegenwart, Reihe A, Bd. 2 (1960) 206-35. VARGA, GPM 15 (1960-1961) 72ff. DOERNE, M. Er kommt auch noch heute (1961) 49-52. DUPONT, J., "Le semeur" AssS 23 (1965) 37-54. SCHRAMM, T. Der Markus-Stoff bei Lukas (1971) 114-23. SOBLE, W. W. Preparation for 'The Way' (1972). HAMEL, J. GPM 27/1 (1972-1973) 115-20. HUBEL, U./LANGENBACH, U. "Sexagesimae: Lukas 8,4-15", in: Predigtstudien (1972-1973), E. Lange, ed., 125-30. ZINGG, P., Das Wachsen der Kiche (Freiburg 1974) 76-100. SCHNEIDER, G., Das Evangelium nach Lukas (Gütersloh 1977) 182.

8:4-8.11-15 HARRINGTON, W. J. A Key to the Parables (1964) 71-78. LINNEMANN, E. Gleichnisse Jesu (1969) 17, 18, 19, 24, 52, 120ff., 179ff.

8:4-8 MICHAELIS, D., Die Gleichnisse Jesu (1956) 17-35. DUPONT, J. "La parabole du semeur dans la version du Luc," in: Apophoreta (1964) 97-108. BARCLAY, W. And Jesus Said (1970) 18-24. SCHÜRMANN, H. Ursprung und Gestalt (1970) 31-33. KOKOT, M. "Znaczenie nasienia w Lukaszowej przypowiesci o seiwcy (The significance of the seed in Luke's parable of the sower)," CoTh 43 (2, 1973) 77-83. TALBERT, C. H., Literary Patterns, Theological Themes, and the Genre of Luke-Acts (Missoula 1974) 40, 42, 43. CARLSTON, C. E. The Parables of the Triple Tradition (Philadelphia 1974) 21-26, 70-76, 137-49. SWIDLER, L., Biblical Affirmations of Woman (Philadelphia 1979) 166, 226.

8:4 KNOX, W. L. The Sources of the Synoptic Gospels II (1957) 47. WALKER, M. B. "Luke viii.4," ET 75 (5, 1964) 151. LEHMANN, M. Synoptische Quellenanalyse und die Frage nach dem historischen Jesus (1970) 59f., 77, 79. TALBERT, C. H., Literary Patterns, Theological Themes, and the Genre of Luke-Acts (Missoula 1974) 43. ZINGG, P., Das Wachsen der Kirche (Freiburg 1974) 79. KLAUCK, H.-J., Allegorie und Allegorese in Synoptischen Gleichnistexten (Münster 1978) 240f.

8:5ff. JEREMIAS, J. NTS 13 (1966-1967) 48ff.

8:5-15 COURTHIAL, P. "Du texte au sermon (17). La parabole du semeur en Luc 8/5-15," EThR 47 (4, 1972) 397-420. MARSHALL, I., "Tradition and Theology in Luke" TB 20 (1969) 56-75. MANEK, J., . . . und brachte Frucht. Die Gleichnisse Jesu (Berlin 1977) 20-25.

8:5-8 JÜLICHER, D. A. Die Gleichnisreden Jesu (1910) 514-38. SCHRAGE, W. Das Verhältnis des Thomas-Evangeliums zur synoptischen Tradition und zu den Koptischen Evangelienübersetzungen (1964) 42. BISER, E. Die Gleichnisse Jesu (1965) 51ff., 129. PERRIN, N., Jesus and the Language of the Kingdom (London 1976) 8, 39, 96, 101, 129, 130, 143, 160, 162, 203. KLAUCK, H.-J., Allegorie und Allegorese in Synoptischen Gleichnistexten (Münster 1978) 186-200. HORMAN, J., "The Source of the Version of the Parable of the Sower in the Gospel of Thomas" NovT 21 (1979) 326-43. WEDER,H., Die Gleichnisse Jesu als Metaphern (Göttingen 1980) 108-17.

8:5 ZINGG, P., Das Wachsen der Kirche (Freiburg 1974) 80. METZGER, B. M., The Early Versions of the New Testament (Oxford 1977) 391, 438.

8:6 ZINGG, P., Das Wachsen der Kirche (Freiburg 1974) 81.

8:7 MASSAUX, E. Influence de l'Evangile de saint Matthieu sur la littérature chrétienne avant saint Irénée (1950) 267-71. ZINGG, P., Das Wachsen der Kirche (Freiburg 1974) 81f.

8:8 KNOX, W. L. The Sources of the Synoptic Gospels II (1957) 88. SCHRAGE, W. Das Verhältnis des Thomas-Evangeliums zur Synoptischen Tradition und zu den Koptischen Evangelienübersetzungen (1964) 40. ZINGG, P., Das Wachsen der Kirche (Freiburg 1974) 82-84. KLAUCK, H.-J., Allegorie und Allegorese in Synoptischen Gleichnistexten (Münster 1978) 241f.

8:9-18 SCHÜRMANN, H. Ursprung und Gestalt (1970) 33-40.

8:9-10 SUHL, A. Die Funktion der alttestamentlichen Zitate und Anspielungen im Markusevangelium (1965) 145ff. BROWN, R. E. "The Semitic Background of the New Testament Mysterion (I)", Biblica 39 (1958) 427-31. SCHÜRMANN, H. Ursprung und Gestalt (1970) 34-36, 38. CARLSTON, C. E. The Parables of the Triple Tradition (Philadelphia 1975) 3-9, 55-57, 97-109. EGGER, W., Frohbotschaft und Lehre (Frankfurt a. M. 1976) 114.

8:9 HARTMAN, L. Testimonium Linguae (1963) 28ff. ZINGG, P., Das Wachsen der Kirche (Freiburg 1974) 86f. METZGER, B. M., The Early Versions of the New Testament (Oxford 1977) 91. KLAUCK, H.-J., Allegorie und Allegorese in Synoptischen Gleichnistexten (Münster 1978) 141-45.

8:10 GUY, H. A. New Testament Prophecy Its Origin and Significance (1947) 79ff. HESSE, F. Das Verstockungsproblem im Alten Testament (1955) 4, 64f. CERFAUX, L. La connaissance des secrets du Royaume d'après Matt. 13:11 et parallèles. NTS 2 (1955-1956) 238ff. GNILKA, J. Die Verstockung Israels (1961) 122-25. CONZELMANN, H. die Mitte der Zeit (1964) 94f. SANFORD, J. A., The Kingdom Within (New York 1970) 43f. ZINGG, P., Das Wachsen der Kirche (Freiburg 1974) 87-89. KLAUCK, H.-J., Allegorie und Allegorese in Synoptischen Gleichnistexten (Münster 1978) 245-53. PRAST, F., Presbyter und Evangelium in nachapostolischer Zeit (Stuttgart 1979) 312, 314, 338f. SWIDLER, L., Biblical Affirmations of Woman (Philadelphia 1979) 165. BERGMEIER, R., Glaube als Gabe nach Johannes (Stuttgart 1980) 264 n.483, 266 n.492.

8:11-15 JÜLICHER, D. A. Die Gleichnisreden Jesu (1910) 514-38. GERHARDSSON, B. "The Parable of the Sower and its Interpretation," NTS 14 (1968) 165-93. SCHÜRMANN, H. Ursprung und Gestalt (1970) 33, 34, 35, 36-38. CARLSTON, C. E., The Parables of the Triple Tradition (Philadelphia 1975) 21-26, 70-76, 137-49. KLAUCK, H.-J., Allegorie und Allegorese in Synoptischen Gleichnistexten (Münster 1978) 200-09. PRAST, F., Presbyter und Evangelium in nachapostolischer Zeit (Stuttgart 1979) 338.

8:11 ZINGG, P., Das Wachsen der Kirche (Freiburg (1974) 89-91. HOFRICHTER, P., Nichts aus Blut sondern monogen aus Gott geboren (Würzburg 1978) 65-67. KLAUCK, H.-J., Allegorie und Allegorese in Synoptischen Gleichnistexten (Münster 1978) 253-55. PRAST, F., Presbyter und Evangelium in nachapostolischer Zeit (Stuttgart 1979) 292f., 297-300.

8:12-16 HROMADKA, GPM 17 (1962-1963) 41ff.

8:12-13 GOPPELT, L., Theologie des Neuen Testaments. I (Göttingen 1975) 199f.

8:12 THEYSSEN, G. W. "Unbelief" in the New Testament (1965) 34ff. NICKELS, P. Targum and New Testament (1967) 34. ZINGG, P., Das Wachsen der Kirche (Freiburg 1974) 91f. METZGER, B. M., The Early Versions of the New Testament (Oxford 1977) 88.

8:13.15 SCHÜTZ, F. Der leidende Christus (1969) 13f.

8:13 HENNECKE, E./SCHNEEMELCHER, W. Neutestamentliche Apokryphen (1964) I 258. BROWN, S. Apostasy and Perseverance in the Theology of Luke (1969) 14, 16, 21, 24, 29, 31, 40, 47, 50, 85, 87, 113, 116, 119. ZINGG, P., Das Wachsen der Kirche (Freiburg 1974) 92f. PRAST, F., Presbyter und Evangelium in nachapostolischer Zeit (Stuttgart 1979) 67f.

8:14-15 GERVAIS, J. "Les épines étouffantes. Luc 8,14-15," ETh 4 (1, 1973) 5-39.

8:14 PALLIS, A., Notes on St. Luke and the Acts (London 1928) 16. HARTMANN, L. Testimonium Linguae (1963) 15ff. ZEDDA, S., "*Poreuomenoi sympnigontai* (Lc 8,14) EuD 27 (1974) 92-108. ZINGG, P. Das Wachsen der Kirche (Freiburg 1974) 93. METZGER, B. M., The Early Versions of the New Testament (Oxford 1977) 179.

8:15ff. STROBEL, A. Erkenntnis und Bekenntnis der Sünde in neutestamentlicher Zeit (1968) 43.

8:15 CERFAUX, L. "Fructifier en supportant (l'épreuve), à propos de Luc, VIII,15," RevBi 64 (4, 1957) 481-91. BROWN, S. Apostasy and Perseverance in the Theology of Luke (1969) 45, 47, 50, 114, 119, 121. ZINGG, P., Das Wachsen der Kirche (Freiburg 1974) 93-97. PRAST, F., Presbyter und Evangelium in nachapostolischer Zeit (Stuttgart 1979) 64.

8:16ff. CONZELMANN, H. and LINDEMANN, A., Arbeitsbuch zum Neuen Testament (Tübingen 1975) 63.

8:16-21 TALBERT, C. H., Literary Patterns, Theological Themes, and the Genre of Luke-Acts (Missoula 1974) 40, 42, 43.

8:16-18 GNILKA, J. Die Verstockung Israels (1961) 125f. SCHÜRMANN, H. Ursprung und Gestalt (1970) 31, 35, 38-40. SCHNEIDER, G., Das Evangelium nach Lukas (Gütersloh 1977) 186. PRAST, F., Presbyter und Evangelium in nachapostolischer Zeit

(Stuttgart 1979) 336-38. SWIDLER, L., Biblical Affirmations of Woman (Philadelphia 1979) 258.

8:16-17 KNOX, W. L. The Sources of the Synoptic Gospels II (1957) 65. SCHRAMM, T. Der Markus-Stoff bei Lukas (1971) 23ff. SWID-LER, L., Biblical Affirmations of Woman (Philadelphia 1979) 166, 226, 253.

8:16 JÜLICHER, D. A. Die Gleichnisreden Jesu (1910) 79-88. KNOX, W. L. The Sources of the Synoptic Gospels II (1957) 18. MON-TEFIORE, H. NTS 7 (1960-1961) 241f. SCHRAGE, W. Das Ver-hältnis des Thomas-Evangeliums zur Synoptischen Tradition und zu den Koptischen Evangelienübersetzungen (1964) 81. JE-REMIAS, J. Abba; Studien zur neutestamentlichen Theologie und Zeitgeschichte (1966) 99-102. SUMMERS, R. The Secret Sayings of the Living Jesus (1968) 29. CARLSTON, C. E., The Parables of the Triple Tradition (Philadelphia 1975) 48-49, 89-92, 149-53. KLAUCK, H.-J., Allegorie und Allegorese in Synoptischen Gleichnistexten (Münster 1978) 227-35.

8:17 JÜLICHER, D. A. Die Gleichnisreden Jesu (1910) 91-97. KNOX, W. L. The Sources of the Synoptic Gospels II (1957) 88. SCHRAGE, W. Das Verhältnis des Thomas-Evangeliums zur Syn-optischen Tradition und zu den Koptischen Evangelienübersetzun-gen (1964) 34. CARLSTON, C. E., The Parables of the Triple Tradition (Philadelphia 1975) 49-51, 92-94, 153-55. KLAUCK, H.-J., Allegorie und Allegorese in Synoptischen Gleichnistexten (Münster 1978) 235-38.

8:18-21 TALBERT, C. H., Literary Patterns, Theological Themes, and the Genre of Luke-Acts (Missoula 1974) 43.

8:18 PALLIS, A., Notes on St. Luke and the Acts (London 1928) 16-17. KNOX, W. L. The Sources of the Synoptic Gospels II (1957) 30. KAESEMANN, E. Exegetische Versuch und Besinnungen (1964) II 97. SCHRAGE, W. Das Verhältnis des Thomas-Evan-geliums zur Synoptischen Tradition und zu den Koptischen Evan-gelienübersetzungen (1964) 96. NICKELS, P. Targum and New Testament (1967) 34. KAESEMANN, E. New Testament Ques-tions of Today (1969) 98. KLAUCK, H.-J., Allegorie und Alle-gorese in Synoptischen Gleichnistexten (Münster 1978) 239-42, 245-53.

8:19ff. KNOX, W. L. The Sources of the Synoptic Gospels II (1957) 63. KAESEMANN, E. Exegetische Versuche und Besinnungen (1964) I 246.

8:19-21 EWALD, H. Die drei ersten Evangelien (1850) 224ff. JE-REMIAS, J. "Perikopen-Umstellung bei Lukas?" NTS 4 (1957-1958) 115ff. CONZELMANN, H. Die Mitte der Zeit (1964) 28f.,

41f. SCHRAGE, W. Das Verhältnis des Thomas-Evangeliums zur Synoptischen Tradition und zu den Koptischen Evangelienübersetzungen (1964) 185. JEREMIAS, J. Abba; Studien zur neutestamentlichen Theologie und Zeitgeschichte (1966) 94-96. SCHÜRMANN, H. Ursprung und Gestalt (1970) 29, 31, 33, 40-41. SCHRAMM, T. Der Markus-Stoff bei Lukas (1971) 123f. SANFORD, J. A., The Kingdom Within (New York 1970) 86-87. MÄRZ, C.-P., Das Wort Gottes bei Lukas (Gütersloh 1973) 67-69. SCHNEIDER, G., Das Evangelium nach Lukas (Gütersloh 1977) 188. THEISSEN, G., Soziologie der Jesusbewegung (München 1977) 18. BROWN, R. E., "Luke's Method in the Annunciation Narrative of Chapter One" in: C. H. Talbert (ed.) Perspectives on Luke-Acts (Danville 1978) 135. STAGG, E. and F., Woman in the World of Jesus (Philadelphia (1978) 138-39. RUETHER, R. R., Mary - The Feminine Face of the Church (London 1979) 31-35. SWIDLER, L., Biblical Affirmations of Woman (Philadelphia 1979) 178, 193, 225, 237, 258, 278. MALY, E. H., "Women and the Gospel of Luke" BThB 10 (1980) 99-104.

8:19 TALBERT, C. H., Literary Patterns, Theological Themes, and the Genre of Luke-Acts (Missoula 1974) 43.

8:20 HENNECKE, E./SCHNEEMELCHER, W. Neutestamentliche Apokryphen (1964) I 260.

8:21 STONEHOUSE, N. B. The Witness of Matthew and Mark to Christ (1944) 176. FLEW, R. N. Jesus and His Church (1956) 59. PRAST, F., Presbyter und Evangelium in nachapostolischer Zeit (Stuttgart 1979) 292-93, 300-01.

8:22-56 EWALD, H. Die drei ersten Evangelien (1850) 237ff.

8:22-39 CONZELMANN, H. Die Mitte der Zeit (1964) 42f.

8:22-25 KAMPHAUS, F. Von der Exegese zur Predigt (1968) 131-33. BROWN, S. Apostasy and Perseverance in the Theology of Luke (1969) 58f. ITTEL, G. W. Jesus und die Jünger (1970) 46-48. SCHRAMM, T. Der Markus-Stoff bei Lukas (1971) 124f. SANFORD, J. A., The Kingdom Within (New York 1970) 75-77. NEIRYNCK, F., "La Matière Marcienne dans Luc" in: F. Neirynck (ed.) L'Evangile de Luc (Gembloux 1973) 180-84, 184-92. TALBERT, C. H., Literary Patterns, Theological Themes, and the Genre of Luke-Acts (Missoula 1974) 40, 41, 42. SCHNEIDER, G., Das Evangelium nach Lukas (Gütersloh 1977) 189. KLAUCK, H.-J., Allegorie und Allegorese in Synoptischen Gleichnistexten (Münster 1978) 340-48. RIST, J. M., On the Independence of Matthew and Mark (Cambridge 1978) 56-57.

8:22-23 LEHMANN, M. Synoptische Quellenanalyse und die Frage nach dem historischen Jesus (1970) 59f. HAHN, F. Christologische Hoheitstitel (1963) 77.

8:24 PALLIS, A., Notes on St. Luke and the Acts (London 1928) 17-18.

8:25 KNOX, W. L. The Sources of the Synoptic Gospels II (1957) 59. THEYSSEN, G. W. "Unbelief" in the New Testament (1965) 22f. METZGER, B. M., The Early Versions of the New Testament (Oxford 1977) 173.

8:26-39 MUSSNER, F. Die Wunder Jesu (1967) 50f. LAMARCHE, P. "Le Possédé de Gérasa (Mt 8,28-34; Mc 5,1-20; Lc 8,26-39)", NRTh 90 (1968) 581-97. PESCH, R., Der Besessene von Gerasa (Stuttgart 1972). TALBERT, C. H., Literary Patterns, Theological Themes, and the Genre of Luke-Acts (Missoula 1974) 40, 41. SCHNEIDER, G., Das Evangelium nach Lukas (Gütersloh 1977) 193. TRITES, A. A., The New Testament Concept of Witness (Cambridge 1977) 178. SWIDLER, L., Biblical Affirmations of Woman (Philadelphia 1979) 228.

8:26-29 ZINGG, P., Das Wachsen der Kirche (Freiburg 1974) 249-50.

8:26-37 BAARDA, Tj. "Gadarenes, Gerasenes, Gergesenes and the 'Diatessaron' Traditions," in: Neotestamentica et Semitica (1969), E. E. Ellis/M. Wilcox ed., 181-97.

8:26 HAHN, F. Christologische Hoheitstitel (1963) 33, 34. KAESEMANN, E. Exegetische Versuche und Besinnungen (1964) I 246. WANKE, J., Die Emmauserzählung (Leipzig 1973) 34. TALBERT, C. H., Literary Patterns, Theological Themes, and the Genre of Luke-Acts (Missoula 1974) 95. METZGER, B. M., The Early Versions of the New Testament (Oxford 1977) 179.

8:27 TALBERT, C. H., Literary Patterns, Theological Themes, and the Genre of Luke-Acts (Missoula 1974) 41.

8:28 KNOX, W. L. The Sources of the Synoptic Gospels II (1957) 41. TALBERT, C. H., Literary Patterns, Theological Themes, and the Genre of Luke-Acts (Missoula 1974) 41. ARENS, E., The HΛΦON-Sayings in the Synoptic Tradition (Fribourg 1976) 212-15, 216-21.

8:29 PALLIS, A., Notes on St. Luke and the Acts (London 1928) 18. NICKELS, P. Targum and New Testament (1967) 34. METZGER, B. M., The Early Versions of the New Testament (Oxford 1977) 245.

8:32 FARRER, A. St Matthew and St Mark (1954) 56.

8:34 METZGER, B. M., The Early Versions of the New Testament (Oxford 1977) 391.

8:39 HARTMAN, L. Testimonium Linguae (1963) 37ff.

8:40-56 FULLER, R. H. Interpreting the Miracles (1963) 55ff.
SCHRAMM, T. Der Markus-Stoff bei Lukas (1971) 126f. TAL-
BERT, C. H., Literary Patterns, Theological Themes, and the Genre
of Luke-Acts (Missoula 1974) 41. SCHNEIDER, G., Das Evan-
gelium nach Lukas (Gütersloh 1977) 196. TRITES, A. A., The New
Testament Concept of the Witness (Cambridge 1977) 179. RIST,
J. M., On the Independence of Matthew and Mark (Cambridge
1978) 58-60. SWIDLER, L., Biblical Affirmations of Woman
(Philadelphia 1979) 181, 215, 228, 237, 259.

8:40-42 TALBERT, C. H., Literary Patterns, Theological Themes, and the
Genre of Luke-Acts (Missoula 1974) 43.

8:40 TALBERT, C. H., Literary Patterns, Theological Themes, and the
Genre of Luke-Acts (Missoula 1974) 95.

8:41 KNOX, W. L. The Sources of the Synoptic Gospels II (1957) 59.
NICKELS, P. Targum and New Testament (1967) 35.

8:42 NICKELS, P. Targum and New Testament (1967) 35.

8:43-48 HULL, J. M., Hellenistic Magic and the Synoptic Tradition (London 1974) 106, 107, 109ff. TALBERT, C. H., Literary Patterns,
Theological Themes, and the Genre of Luke-Acts (Missoula 1974)
39, 43.

8:43 ROBERTSON, A. T. Luke the Historian in the Light of Research
(1920) 10, 92f. WANKE, J. Die Emmauserzählung (Leipzig 1973)
93. METZGER, B. M., The Early Versions of the New Testament
(Oxford 1977) 433. HENNECKE, E./SCHNEEMELCHER, W.
Neutestamentliche Apokryphen (1964) I 129.

8:44 BORNKAMM-BARTH-HELD, Ueberlieferung und Auslegung im
Matthäus-Evangelium (²1961) 222. BOUSSET, W. Die Religion
des Judentums im Späthellenistischen Zeitalter (1966 = 1926) 179.

8:45-56 ZAMORA, H., "Un interesante fragmento del Evangelio Griego
de Lucas en el Monasterio de Guadalupe" EstBi 32 (1973) 271-82.

8:45 HAHN, F. Christologische Hoheitstitel (1963) 77. MUSSNER, F.,
Petrus und Paulus (Freiburg 1976) 24. METZGER, B. M., The
Early Versions of the New Testament (Oxford 1977) 435.

8:46 NICKELS, P. Targum and New Testament (1967) 35. HOWARD,
V. P., Das Ego in den Synoptischen Evangelien (Marburg 1975)
213-15. METZGER, B. M., The Early Versions of the New Testament (Oxford 1977) 214.

8:47 STONEHOUSE, N. B. The Witness of Matthew and Mark to Christ
(1944) 108. FRIEDRICHSEN, G. W. S. NTS 11 (1964-1965) 285f.

8:48 BORNKAMM-BARTH-HELD, Ueberlieferung und Auslegung im
Matthäus-Evangelium (²1961) 205, 207.

8:49ff. HENNECKE, E./SCHNEEMELCHER, W. Neutestamentliche Apokryphen (1964) I 128.

8:49-56 TALBERT, C. H., Literary Patterns, Theological Themes, and the Genre of Luke-Acts (Missoula 1974) 43.

8:49 HAHN, F. Christologische Hoheitstitel (1963) 79. NICKELS, P. Targum and New Testament (1967) 35.

8:52-56 WESTERHOLM, S. Jesus and Scribal Authority (Lund 1978) 68.

8:52 BORNKAMM-BARTH-HELD, Ueberlieferung und Auslegung im Matthäus-Evangelium (²1961) 252.

8:53ff. STONEHOUSE, N. B. The Witness of Matthew and Mark to Christ (1944) 78.

8:54-55 NÖTSCHER, F., Altorientalischer und alttestamentlicher Auferstehungsglaube (Darmstadt (1970 = 1926) 303.

8:54 METZGER, B. M., The Early Versions of the New Testament (Oxford 1977) 177.

8:55 FARRER, A. St Matthew and St Mark (1954) 56. SCHWEIZER, E., Heiliger Geist (Stuttgart 1978) 153.

8:56 STONEHOUSE, N. B. The Witness of Matthew and Mark to Christ (1944) 108.

9-18 BLIGH, J. Christian Deuteronomy (Luke 9-18) (1970). GIRARD, L. "L'Evangile des Voyages de Jésus," BLE 56 (1955) 169. TALBERT, C. H., Literary Patterns, Theological Themes, and the Genre of Luke-Acts (Missoula 1974) 120.

9-10 SCHOTT, E., "Die Aussendungsrede Mt 19. Mc 6. Lc 8.10" ZNW 7 (1906) 140-40. GOULDER, M. D. Type and History in Acts (1964) 56, 142, 170, 173. KÜNZI, M. Das Naherwartungslogion Matthäus 10,23 (1970) 127, 139, 144.

9 DAVIES, W. D., The Sermon on the Mount (Cambridge 1966) 4. GREENLEE, J. H. Nine Uncial Palimpsests of the Greek New Testament (1968) 72-73. HIERS, R. H., The Historical Jesus and the Kingdom of God (Gainesville 1973) 61-62. WANKE, J., Die Emmauserzählung (Leipzig 1973) 10. MIYOSHI, M., Der Anfang des Reiseberichts Lk 9,51 - 10,24. Eine redaktionsgeschichtliche Untersuchung (Rome 1974) 74-75, 141-42. TALBERT, C. H., Literary Patterns, Theological Themes, and the Genre of Luke-Acts (Missoula 1974) 2, 26, 27, 61-66, 111, 120, 142, 143. ELLIS, E.

E., "The Composition of Luke 9 and the Sources of its Christology" in: G. F. Hawthorne (ed.) Current Issues in Biblical and Patristic Interpretation. FS. M. C. Tenney (Grand Rapids 1975) 121-27. FITZMYER, J. A., "The Composition of Luke, Chapter 9" in: C. H. Talbert (ed.) Perspectives on Luke-Acts (Danville 1978) 139-52.

9:1ff. KNOX, W. L. The Sources of the Synoptic Gospels II (1957) 48. HAHN, F. Christologische Hoheitstitel (1963) 168.

9:1-50 WILKENS, W., "Die Auslassung von Mark. 6,45—8,26 bei Lukas im Licht der Komposition Luk, 9,1-25" ThZ 32 (1976) 193-200.

9:1-48 TALBERT, C. H., Literary Patterns, Theological Themes, and the Genre of Luke-Acts (Missoula 1974) 26-34.

9:1-34 TALBERT, C. H., Literary Patterns, Theological Themes, and the Genre of Luke-Acts (Missoula 1974) 61.

9:1-6 EWALD, H. Die drei ersten Evangelien (1850) 246ff. RICHARDSON, A. The Miracle-Stories of the Gospels (1948) 41f. CONZELMANN, H. Die Mitte der Zeit (1964) 43f. DEGENHARDT, H.-J. Lukas, Evangelist der Armen (1964) 60-63. FREYNE, S. The Twelve: Disciple and Apostles (1968) 94. ITTEL, G. W. Jesus und die Jünger (1970) 53. OTOMO, Y. Nachfolge Jesu und Anfänge der Kirche im Neuen Testament (1970) 68-70. HOFFMANN, P. Studien zur Theologie der Logienquelle (1972) 243f., 245-48. MUSSNER, F., "Gab es eine 'galiläische Krise?' " in: P. Hoffmann (ed.) Orientierung an Jesus (Freiburg 1973) 224-48. TALBERT, C. H., Literary Patterns, Theological Themes, and the Genre of Luke-Acts (Missoula 1974) 26, 27, 61, 62. EDWARDS, R. A., A Theology of Q (Philadelphia 1976) 99-100. SCHNEIDER, G., Das Evangelium nach Lukas (Gütersloh 1977) 200. KARRIS, R. J., "Poor and Rich: The Lukan Sitz im Leben" in: C. H. Talbert (ed.) Perspectives on Luke-Acts (Danville 1978) 118-19. KERTELGE, K., "Offene Fragen zum Thema 'Geistliches Amt' und das neutestamentliche Verständnis von der 'repraesentatio Christi' " in: R. Schnackenburg et al. (eds.) Die Kiche des Anfangs. FS. H. Schürmann (Freiburg 1978) 588-90. PRAST, F., Presbyter und Evangelium in nachapostolischer Zeit (Stuttgart 1979) 312-15. TESTA, E., "I 'Discorsi de Missione' di Gesu" SBFLA 29 (1979) 7-41. MCDONALD, J. I. H., Kerygma and Didache (Cambridge 1980) 118.

9:1-5 BARRETT, C. K. The Holy Spirit and the Gospels Tradition (1947) 127-30. HAHN, F. Das Verständnis der Mission im Neuen Testament (²1965) 32, 33-36, 114. DUNGAN, D. L. The Sayings of Jesus in the Churches of Paul. (1971) 48-51, 71-74. BORSCH, F.

H., "Jesus the Wandering Preacher?" in: M. Hooker/C. Hickling (eds.) What about the New Testament? FS. C. Evans (London 1975) 48-49.

9:1-2 MCDONALD, J. I. H., Kerygma and Didache (Cambridge 1980) 109.

9:1 CONZELMANN, H. Die Mitte der Zeit (1964) 169ff. TALBERT, C. H., Literary Patterns, Theological Themes, and the Genre of Luke-Acts (Missoula 1974) 62.

9:2 FRIEDRICHSEN, G. W. S. NTS 11 (1964-1965) 283f. JEREMIAS, J. Neutestamentliche Theologie I (1971) 43, 100, 132, 227. "Abendmahl" in: TRE 1 (1977) 216. PRAST, F., Presbyter und Evangelium in nachapostolischer Zeit (Stuttgart 1979) 280-81, 333, 339. KRAFT, H., Die Entstehung des Christentums (Darmstadt 1981) 145ff.

9:3-4 LEGRAND, L., "Bare foot Apostles? The Shoes of St Mark (Mk 6:8-9 and parallels)" IndTheolStud 16 (1979) 201-19.

9:3 PALLIS, A., Notes on St. Luke and the Acts (London 1928) 18. KNOX, W. L. The Sources of the Synoptic Gospels II 1957) 49. NICKELS, P. Targum and New Testament (1967) 35. HOFFMANN, P. Studien zur Theologie der Logienquelle (1972) 244, 264-67, 269, 322. DERRETT, J. D. M., Jesus's Audience (London 1973) 181ff. TALBERT, C. H., Literary Patterns, Theological Themes, and the Genre of Luke-Acts (Missoula 1974) 27.

9:4-5 JEREMIAS, J. Neutestamentliche Theologie I (1971) 30, 228f.

9:4 PALLIS, A., Notes on St. Luke and the Acts (London 1928) 18-19.

9:5 NICKELS, P. Targum and New Testament (1967) 35. HOFFMANN, P. Studien zur Theologie der Logienquelle (1972) 268-72, 278. WANKE, J., Die Emmauserzählung (Leipzig 1973) 101. NELLESSEN, E., Zeugnis für Jesus und das Wort (Köln 1976) 89f. METZGER, B. M., The Early Versions of the New Testament (Oxford 1977) 209. TRITES, A. A.,, The New Testament Concept of Witness (Cambridge 1977) 128f.

9:6 NICKELS, P. Targum and New Testament (1967) 35.

9:7ff. SCHÜTZ, F. Der leidende Christus (1969) 62ff., 66f., 80, 86.

9:7-17 RIST, J. M., On the Independence of Matthew and Mark (Cambridge 1978) 63-67.

9:7-9 EWALD, H. Die drei ersten Evangelien (1850) 257ff. CONZELMANN, H. Die Mitte der Zeit (1964) 44. SCHRAMM, T. Der Markus-Stoff bei Lukas (1971) 128f. TALBERT, C. H., Literary Patterns, Theological Themes, and the Genre of Luke-Acts (Missoula 1974) 26, 27. SCHNEIDER, G., Das Evangelium nach Lukas (Gütersloh 1977) 203. BÖCHER, O., "Johannes der Täufer in der Neutestamentlichen Überlieferung" in: G. Müller (ed.) Rechtfertigung Realismus. FS. A. Köberle (Darmstadt 1978) 46-52. FITZMYER, J. A., "The Composition of Luke, Chapter 9" in: C. H. Talbert (ed.) Perspectives on Luke-Acts (Danville 1978) 141-43. SWIDLER, L., Biblical Affirmations of Woman (Philadelphia 1979) 229, 238. SCHRECKENBERG, H., "Flavius Josephus und die lukanischen Schriften" in: W. Haubeck/M. Bachmann (eds.) Wort in der Zeit. FS. K. H. Rengstorf (Leiden 1980) 187-90.

9:7 TYSON, J. B., "Source Criticism of the Gospel of Luke" in: C. H. Talbert (ed.) Perspectives on Luke-Acts (Danville 1978) 31.

9:8 VOLZ, P. Die Eschatologie der jüdischen Gemeinde (1934) 269. BACHMANN, M., "Johannes der Täufer bei Lukas: Nachzügler oder Vorläufer?" in: W. Haubeck/M. Bachmann (eds.) Wort in der Zeit. FS. K. H. Rengstorf (Leiden 1980) 133.

9:9 GREEVEN, "H. Erwägungen zur Synoptischen Textkritik," NTS 6 (1959-1960) 292f. TALBERT, C. H., Literary Patterns, Theological Themes, and the Genre of Luke-Acts (Missoula 1974) 27. BACHMANN, M., "Johannes der Täufer bei Lukas: Nachzügler oder Vorläufer?" in: W. Haubeck/M. Bachmann (eds.) Wort in der Zeit. FS. K. H. Rengstorf (Leiden 1980) 136-37.

9:10-17 EWALD, H. Die drei ersten Evangelien (1850) 259ff. CONZELMANN, H. Die Mitte der Zeit (1964) 45. HEISING, A. Die Botschaft der Brotvermehrung (1967 = 1966). KAMPHAUS, F. Von der Exegese zur Predigt (1968) 142-44. BROWN, S. Apostasy and Perseverance in the Theology of Luke (1969) 59f. CRIBBS, F. L. in: SBL Seminar Papers 2 (1973) 38-45. WANKE, J., Die Emmauserzählung (Leipzig 1973) 36, 101, 106f, A.724. TALBERT, C. H., Literary Patterns, Theological Themes, and the Genre of Luke-Acts (Missoula 1974) 26, 27, 28, 61, 62. CANGH, J.-M. van, La multiplication des pains et l'Eucharistie (Paris 1975). STEGNER, W. R., "Lucan Priority in the Feeding of the Five Thousand" BR 21 (1976) 19-28. SCHNEIDER, G., Das Evangelium nach Lukas (Gütersloh 1977) 204-25. FITZMYER, J. A., "The Composition of Luke, Chapter 9" in: C. H. Talbert (ed.) Perspectives on Luke-Acts (Danville 1978) 144-45. SWIDLER, L., Biblical Affirmations of Woman (Philadelphia 1979) 249, 279.

9:10-11 BOISMARD, M.-E., "The Two Source Theory at an Impasse" NTS 26 (1979) 1-17. EGGER, W., Frohbotschaft und Lehre (Frankfurt a. M. 1976) 132-33.

9:10 SCHOTT, E., "Die Aussendungsrede" ZNW 7 (1906). STONEHOUSE, N. B. The Witness of Luke to Christ (1951) 104ff., 197. STREETER, B. H. The Four Gospels (1951) 176f. NEPPER-

CHRISTSENSEN, P. Das Matthäusevangelium (1958) 182, 187, 189, 190. KLEIN, G. Die Zwölf Apostel (1961) 33f. GOULDER, M. D. Type and History in Acts (1964) 56, 61, 131, 170. WANKE, J., Die Emmauserzählung (Leipzig 1973) 34. TALBERT, C. H., Literary Patterns, Theological Themes, and the Genre of Luke-Acts (Missoula 1974) 95. CONZELMANN, H. and LINDEMANN, A., Arbeitsbuch zum Neuen Testament (Tübingen 1975) 64. "Aramäisch" in: TRE 3 (1978) 604. PRAST, F., Presbyter und Evangelium in nachapostolischer Zeit (Stuttgart 1979) 312-15. TESTA, E., "I 'Discorsi di Missione' di Gesu" SBFLA 29 (1979) 7-41.

9:11-17 BECKER, U. & WIBBING, S. Wundergeschichten (1965) 55f.

9:11 TALBERT, C. H., Literary Patterns, Theological Themes, and the Genre of Luke-Acts (Missoula 1974) 27, 62. PRAST, F., Presbyter und Evangelium in nachapostolischer Zeit (Stuttgart 1979) 227, 280-81, 315, 333, 339.

9:12-13 KNACKSTEDT, J. NTS 10 (1963-1964) 310f.

9:12 STREETER, B. H. The Four Gospels (1951) 569f. FRIEDRICH-SEN, G. W. S. NTS 11 (1964-1965) 283f. WANKE, J., Die Emmauserzählung (Leipzig 1973) 97-98, 101-02. PRAST, F., Presbyter und Evangelium in nachapostolischer Zeit (Stuttgart 1979) 315.

9:13 NICKELS, P. Targum and New Testament (1967) 35. PALLIS, A. Notes on St. Luke and the Acts (London 1928) 19. GRASSI, J. A., " 'You yourselves give them to eat.' An easily forgotten command of Jesus (Mk. 6:37; Mt. 14:16; Lk. 9:13)" Bible Today 97 (1979) 1704-09.

9:16 BROCK, S. P. "A Note on Luke IX.16 (D)," JThS 14 (2, 1963) 391-93. WANKE, J., Die Emmauserzählung (Leipzig 1973) 98. MINEAR, P., To Heal and to Reveal (New York 1976) 49. WESTERMANN, C., Blessing. In the Bible and the Life of the Church (Philadelphia 1978) 83, 86, 98-101.

9:17 METZGER, B. M., The Early Versions of the New Testament (Oxford 1977) 213.

9:18ff. VÖGTLE, A. Das Evangelium und die Evangelien (1971) 146-48.

9:18-50 EWALD, H. Die drei ersten Evangelien (1850) 169ff. STONE-HOUSE, N. B. The Witness of Luke to Christ (1951) 112f, 126.

9:18-45 ROLOFF, J. Apostolat-Verkündigung-Kirche (1965) 182f.

9:18-27 CONZELMANN, H. Die Mitte der Zeit (1964) 48ff. HAENCHEN, E. "Die Komposition von Mk vii 27 - ix 1 und Par.", in: ΧΑΡΙΣ ΚΑΙ ΣΟΦΙΑ. Festschrift K. H. Rengstorf (1964) 81-109. HAENCHEN, E. "Leidensnachfolge," Die Bibel und Wir (1968) 102-34. PERRIN, N. What is Redaction Criticism? (1969) 62f.

CORBIN, M., "Le Christ de Dieu. Méditation théologique sur *Lc* 9, 18-27" NRTh 99 (1977) 641-80.

9:18-26 BÜCKMANN, O. in: Herr, tue meine Lippen auf Bd. 3 (1964), G. Eichholz ed., 322ff. WEBER, O. Predigtmeditationen (1967) 252-55.

9:18-23 CLARK, K. W., "The Theological Relevance of Textual Variation in Current Criticism of the Greek New Testament" in: The Gentile Bias and other Essays (Leiden 1980) 116-17.

9:18-22 FLENDER, H. Heil und Geschichte in der Theologie des Lukas (1965) 46-50. ITTEL, G. W. Jesus und die Jünger (1970) 75-76. SCHRAMM, T. Der Markus-Stoff bei Lukas (1971) 130-36. DIETRICH, W. Das Petrusbild der lukanischen Schriften (1972) 94-104. NEIRYNCK, F., "La Matière dans Luc" in: F. Neirynck (ed.) L'Evangile de Luc (Gembloux 1973) 180-84. SCHNEIDER, G., Das Evangelium nach Lukas (Gütersloh 1977) 207. MEDIAVILLA, R., "La Oraciòn de Jesus en el tercer evangelio" (Mayeutica 1978) 5-34. MEYER, B. F., The Aims of Jesus (London 1979) 215-16.

9:18-21 MOORE, G. F. Judaism (1946) II 309, 326n. SUMMERS, R. The Secret Sayings of the Living Jesus (1968) 31. BROWN, S. Apostasy and Perseverance in the Theology of Luke (1969) 60-62. FITZMYER, J. A., "The Composition of Luke, Chapter 9" in: C. H. Talbert (ed.) Perspectives on Luke-Acts (Danville 1978) 145-46. SWIDLER, L. Biblical Affirmations of Woman (Philadelphia 1979) 217.

9:18.22 LÜTGERT, W. "Die Juden im Johannesevangelium," in: Neutestamentliche Studien Georg Heinrici zu seinem 70. Geburtstag (1914) A. Deissmann/H. Windisch eds., 148-50.

9:18-19 BULTMANN, R., "Die Frage nach dem Messianischen Bewusstsein . . ." ZNW 19 (1919-1920) 165.

9:18 HIRSCH, E. Frühgeschichte des Evangeliums (1941) 52-55. HAHN, F. Christologische Hoheitstitel (1963) 403. OTT, W. Gebet und Heil (1965) 95, 96, 99, 130.

9:19 STONEHOUSE, N. B. The Witness of Matthew and Mark to Christ (1944) 180f. GILS, F. Jésus Prophète D'Après Les Evangiles Synoptiques (1957) 20-23. FLENDER, H. St Luke Theologian of Redemptive History (1967) 46f., 48, 49f.

9:20-22 TALBERT, C. H., Literary Patterns, Theological Themes, and the Genre of Luke-Acts (Missoula 1974) 26, 27.

9:20 HAHN, F. Christologische Hoheitstitel (1963) 224. FRIEDRICHSEN, G. W. S. NTS 11 (1964-1965) 283f. WANKE, J., Die Emmauserzählung (Leipzig 1973) 93. DÖMER, M., Das Heil

Gottes (Köln-Bonn 1978) 43. MEYER, B. F., The Aims of Jesus (London1979) 175-80.

9:22 STONEHOUSE, N. B. The Witness of Matthew and Mark to Christ (1944) 237. DENNEY, J. The Death of Christ (1956) 24f., 28. HOOKER, M. D. Jesus and the Servant (1959) 92-97. DUPONT, J. "Ressuscité 'le troisième jour' ", Biblica 40 (1959) 753-55. BORNKAMM-BARTH-HELD, Ueberlieferung und Auslegung im Matthäus-Evangelium (²1961) 113. WILCKENS, U. Die Missionsreden der Apostelgeschichte (1961) 117, 137-38, 143. SCHNEIDER, G. Verleugnung, Verspottung und Verhör Jesu nach Lukas 22, 54-71 (1969) 37, 109, 171, 174, 175, 176, 177, 187. BAMMEL, E. The Trial of Jesus (1970) 56ff. GÜTTGEMANNS, E. Offene Frage zur Formgeschichte des Evangeliums (1970) 218,222. O'NEILL, J. C. The Theology of Acts in its historical setting (1970) 43, 43-4n, XIII. PATSCH, H. Abendmahl und historischer Jesus (1972) 185ff.

9:22 ZMIJEWSKI, J., Die Eschatologiereden des Lukas-Evangeliums (Bonn 1972) 282, 347, 406-08, 419. STÄHLIN, G., "Tὸ πνεῦμα Ἰησοῦ (Apostelgeschichte 16:7)" in: B. Lindars/S. Smalley (eds.) Christ and the Spirit in the New Testament. FS. C. F. D. Moule (Cambridge 1973) 240-41. WANKE, J., Die Emmauserzählung (Leipzig 1973) 88, 93, 118. TALBERT, C. H., Literary Patterns, Theological Themes, and the Genre of Luke-Acts (Missoula 1974) 97, 115. WILCKENS, U., Die Missionsreden der Apostelgeschichte (Neukirchen 1974 (3)) 118, 137, 139, 143. RADL, W., Paulus und Jesus im lukanischen Doppelwerk. (Frankfurt 1975) 149-58. THEUNISSEN, M., "ὁαίπῶν λαμβάνει. Der Gebetsglaube Jesu und die Zeitlichkeit des Christseins" in: B. Casper et al. (eds.) Jesus, Ort der Erfahrung Gottes (Basel 1976) 28-29. BÖHLIG, A., Die Gnosis III: Der Manichäismus (Zürich 1980) 338 n.93. KRAFT, H., Die Entstehung des Christentums (Darmstadt 1981) 169.

9:23-27 SCHRAMM, T. Der Markus-Stoff bei Lukas (1971) 29f. TALBERT, C. H., Literary Patterns, Theological Themes, and the Genre of Luke-Acts (Missoula 1974) 26, 28. SCHNEIDER, G., Das Evangelium nach Lukas (Gütersloh 1977) 210-11.

9:23-24 LOHSE, E. et al., eds., Der Ruf Jesu und die Antwort der Gemeinde (1970) 262-67.

9:23 KNOX, W. L. The Sources of the Synoptic Gospels II (1957) 86, 87. GREEVEN, H. "Erwägungen zur Synoptischen Textkritik," NTS 6 (1959-1960) 290f. BROWN, S. Apostasy and Perseverance in the Theology of Luke (1969) 56, 69, 122f. SCHÜTZ, F. Der leidende Christus (1969) 15-20, 197. OTOMO, Y. Nachfolge Jesu und Anfänge der Kirche im Neuen Testament (1970) 122-26. TALBERT, C. H., Literary Patterns, Theological Themes, and the Genre of Luke-Acts (Missoula 1974) 28. MATTILL, A. J., Luke and the Last Things (Dillsboro 1979) 114-16. BÖHLIG, A., Die Gnosis III: Der Manichäismus (Zürich 1980) 344 n.62. GERSTENBERGER, G. and SCHRAGE, W., Leiden (Stuttgart 1977) 156; ET: J. E. Steely, Suffering (Nashville 1980) 180f. KUHN, H.-W., "Nachfolge nach Ostern" in: D. Lührmann/G. Strecker (eds.) Kirche. FS. G. Bornkamm (Tübingen 1980) 130.

9:24 KAESEMANN, E. Exegetische Versuche und Besinnungen (1964) II 97. KAESEMANN, E. New Testament Questions of Today (1969) 98. SANFORD, J. A., The Kingdom Within (New York 1970) 188-89. ZMIJEWSKI, J., Die Eschatologiereden des Lukas-Evangeliums (Bonn 1972) 159, 341, 349, 350, 471, 473, 479, 480. HOFFMANN, P. and EID, V., Jesus von Nazareth und eine christliche Moral (Freiburg 1975) 212-14. GNILKA, J., "Martyriumsparänese und Sühnetod in synoptischen und jüdischen Traditionen" in: H. Schürmann (ed.) Die Kirche des Anfangs (Freiburg 1978) 235. LEROY, H., " 'Wer sein Leben gewinnen will . . .' Erlöste Existenz heute" FZPhTh 25 (1978) 171-86.

9:25 SANFORD, J. A., The Kingdom Within (New York 1970) 160-61.

9:26.28 HENNECKE, E./SCHNEEMELCHER, W. Neutestamentliche Apokryphen (1964) II 472, 475, 481.

9:26-27 MATTILL, A. J., Luke and the Last Things (Dillsboro 1979) 58-70.

9:26 KNOX, W. L. The Sources of the Synoptic Gospels II (1957) 17, 66. KAESEMANN, E. Exegetische Versuche und Besinnungen (1964) II 97. JÜNGEL, E. Paulus und Jesus (1966) 242, 244, 258f. BORNKAMM, G. "Das Wort Jesu vom Bekennen", Geschichte und Glaube I (1968) 25-36. CARLSTON, C. E. "The Things that Defile (Mark 7:14), and the Law in Matthew and Mark," NTS 15 (1968-1969) 79-80. KAESEMANN, E. New Testament Questions of Today (1969) 99. PALLIS, A., Notes on St. Luke and the Acts (London 1928) 19. METZGER, B. M., The Early Versions of the New Testament (Oxford 1977) 251. PESCH, R., "Über die Autorität Jesu. Eine Rückfrage anhand des Bekenner- und Verleugnerspruchs Lk. 12:8f. par." in: R. Schnackenburg et al. (eds.) Die Kirche des Anfangs. FS. H. Schürmann (Leipzig 1977) 25-55. TRITES, A. A., The New Testament Concept of Witness (Cambridge 1977) 181.

9:27 STONEHOUSE, N. B. The Witness of Matthew and Mark to Christ (1944) 210, 239. CONZELMANN, H. Die Mitte der Zeit (1964) 95f., 105f. ELLIS, E. E. NTS 12 (1965-1966) 30f., 33f. HASLER, V. Amen (1969) 32. KÜMMEL, W. G. Einleitung in das

Neue Testament (1973) 111f. WILSON, S. G., The Gentiles and the Gentile Mission in Luke-Acts (Cambridge 1973) 69-70, 77, 82. SCHILDENBERGER, J., "Die Vertauschung der Aussagen über Zeichen und Bezeichnetes. Eine hermeneutisch bedeutsame biblische Redeweise" in: Kirche und Bibel. FS. E. Schick (Paderdorn 1979) 402-03. BERGMEIER, R., Glaube als Gabe nach Johannes (Stuttgart 1980) 250 n. 242. CLARK, K. W., "Realized Eschatology" in: The Gentile Bias and other Essays (Leiden 1980) 53-55. HARRINGTON, D. J., God's People in Christ (Philadelphia 1980) 25.

9:28ff. STAEHELEN, E. Die Verkündigung des Reiches Gottes in der Kirche Jesu Christi I (1951) 400. SUHL, A. Die Funktion der alttestamentlichen Zitate und Anspielungen im Markusevangelium (1965) 97, 104ff. DALMAN, G. Orte und Wege Jesu (1967) 215f.

9:28-44 MIYOSHI, M., Der Anfang des Reiseberichts Lk 9,51 - 10, 24 (Rome 1974) 21-22, 148-51.

9:28-43 TALBERT, C. H., Literary Patterns, Theological Themes, and the Genre of Luke-Acts (Missoula 1974) 28.

9:28-36 HIRSCH, E. Frühgeschichte des Evangeliums (1941) 94-96. RIESENFELD, H. Jésus Transfiguré (Copenhagen 1947). GOODSPEED, E. J. a Life of Jesus (1950) 127-29. GILS, F. Jésus Prophète D'Après Les Evangiles Synoptiques (1957) 73-78. MANEK, J. "The New Exodus of the Books of Luke," NovTest 2 (1, 1957) 8-23. FEUILLET, A. "Les Perspectives propres à chaque Evangéliste dans les Récits de la Transfiguration", Biblica 39 (1958) 289-92. BALTENSWEILER, H. Die Verklärung Jesu (1959). CONZELMANN, H. Die Mitte der Zeit (1964) 50ff. RIVERA, L. F. "El relato de la transfiguracion de Jesus en Lucas (9,28-36)," RevBi 28 (2, 1966) 148-64. BROWN, S. Apostasy and Perseverance in the Theology of Luke (1969) 61. ITTEL, G. W. Jesus und die Jünger (1970) 88-90. SCHRAMM, T. Der Markus-Stoff bei Lukas (1971) 136-39. DIETRICH, W. Das Petrusbild der lukanischen Schriften (1972) 104-16. COUNE, M. "Radieuse Transfiguration. Mt. 17:1-9; Mc 9:2-10; Lc 8:28-36," AssS 15 (1973) 44-84. BARTSCH, H. W., Wachet aber zu jeder Zeit! (Hamburg-Bergstedt 1963) 87-89. DAVIES, W. D., The Sermon on the Mount (Cambridge 1966) 20-26. NEIRYNCK, F., "La Matière Marcienne dans Luc" in: F. Neirynck (ed.) L'Evangile de Luc (Gembloux 1973) 173-74, 180-84. NÜTZEL, J. M., Die Verklärungserzählung im Markusevangelium (Würzburg 1973) 289-99. TALBERT, C. H., Literary Patterns, Theological Themes, and the Genre of Luke-Acts (Missoula 1974) 26, 28, 61. MINEAR, P., To Heal and to Reveal (New York 1976) 127ff. SAITO, T., Die Mosevorstellungen im Neuen Testament, Europäische Hochschulschriften, Reihe XXIII—Theologie 10 (Bern 1977) 73-77, 142-43, 147. SCHNEIDER, G., Das Evangelium nach Lukas (Gütersloh 1977) 214. TRITES, A. A., The New Testament Concept of Witness (Cambridge 1977) 180-81. FITZMYER, J. A., "The Composition of Luke, Chapter 9" in: C. H. Talbert (ed.) Perspectives on Luke-Acts (Danville 1978) 146-47. FRIEDRICH, G., "Beobachtungen zur messianischen Hohepriestererwartung in den Synoptikern" in: Auf das Wort kommt es an (Göttingen 1978) 98-101. RUDOLPH, K., Die Gnosis (Göttingen 1978) 165. MATTILL, A. J., Luke and the Last Things (Dillsboro 1979) 59. KRAFT, H., Die Entstehung des Christentums (Darmstadt 1981) 134-39.

9:28-29 SCHEP, J. A., The Nature of the Resurrection Body (Grand Rapids 1976) 165f.

9:29 NEIRYNCK, F., "La Matière Marcienne dans Luc" in: F. Neirynck (ed.) L'Evangile de Luc (Gembloux 1973) 180, 181, 184-92. NEIRYNCK, F., "Minor Agreements Matthew-Luke in the Transfiguration Story" in: P. Hoffman (ed.) Orientierung an Jesus. FS. J. Schmid (Freiburg 1973) 256-60.TALBERT, C. H., Literary Patterns, Theological Themes, and the Genre of Luke-Acts (Missoula 1974) 61, 95. MEDIAVILLA, R., La Oraciòn de Jesus en el tercer evangelio (Mayeutica 1978) 5-34.

9:30-31 PRAST, F., Presbyter und Evangelium in nachapostolischer Zeit (Stuttgart 1979) 229.

9:30 TALBERT, C. H., Literary Patterns, Theological Themes, and the Genre of Luke-Acts (Missoula 1974) 61, 62.

9:31-32 SCHELKLE, K. H. Die Passion Jesu in der Verkündigung des Neuen Testament (1949) 81f.WANKE, J., Die Emmauserzählung (Leipzig 1973) 35, 89-90, 94.

9:31 ADLER, N. Das erste christliche Pfingstfest (1938) 33, 77f. SCHOONENBERG, P. "Woestijn en Tabor" Verbum 24 (1957) 50-55. HAHN, F. Christologische Hoheitstitel (1963) 198, 336, 397, 403. BLACK, M. An Aramaic Approach to the Gospels and Acts (1967) 53f. TALBERT, C. H., Literary Patterns, Theological Themes, and the Genre of Luke-Acts (Missoula 1974) 16, 61, 62, 115. ZINGG, P., Das Wachsen der Kirche (Freiburg 1974) 138. WILLIAMS, J. A., A Conceptual History of Deuteronomism in the Old Testament, Judaism, and the New Testament (Ph.D. Diss. Southern Baptist Theological Seminary; Louisville 1976) 300.

9:32 TALBERT, C. H., Literary Patterns, Theological Themes, and the Genre of Luke-Acts (Missoula 1974) 61, 62.

9:33 HAHN, F. Christologische Hoheitstitel (1963) 77. NICKELS, P.

Targum and New Testament (1967) 35. PALLIS, A., Notes on St. Luke and the Acts (London 1928) 20.

9:34-35 TALBERT, C. H., Literary Patterns, Theological Themes, and the Genre of Luke-Acts (Missoula 1974) 61.

9:34 NEIRYNCK, F., "Minor Agreements Matthew-Luke in the Transfiguration Story" in: P. Hoffmann (ed.) Orientierung an Jesus. FS. J. Schmid (Freiburg 1973) 260-64.

9:35 HOOKER, M. D. Jesus and the Servant (1959) 68-73. DELLING, G. Die Taufe im Neuen Testament (1963) 56. MARSHALL, I. H. "The Son of Man or Servant of Yahweh? - A Reconsideration of Mark 1:11," NTS 15 (1968-1969) 327ff. RESE, M. Alttestamentliche Motive in der Christologie des Lukas (1969) 195-96. WANKE, J., Die Emmauserzählung (Leipzig 1973) 63.

9:37-50 BARTSCH, H. W., Wachet aber zu jeder Zeit! (Hamburg-Bergstedt 1963) 89-92.

9:37-43 SCHRAMM, T. Der Markus-Stoff bei Lukas (1971) 239f. NEIRYNCK, F., "La Matière Marcienne dans Luc" in: F. Neirynck (ed.) L'Evangile de Luc (Gembloux 1973) 180-84. TALBERT, C. H., Literary Patterns, Theological Themes, and the Genre of Luke-Acts (Missoula 1974) 26, 28. HOWARD, V. P., Das Ego in den Synoptischen Evangelien (Marburg 1975) 86-97. SCHNEIDER, G., Das Evangelium nach Lukas (Gütersloh 1977) 218. FITZMYER, J. A., "The Composition of Luke, Chapter 9" in: C. H. Talbert (ed.) Perspectives on Luke-Acts (Danville 1978) 147-48. RIST, J. M., On the Independence of Matthew and Mark (Cambridge 1978) 61-62.

9:37 STONEHOUSE, N. B. The Witness of Matthew and Mark to Christ (1944) 78.

9:38 HAHN, F. Christologische Hoheitstitel (1963) 76, 77.

9:39 PALLIS, A., Notes on St. Luke and the Acts (London 1928) 20.

9:41 THEYSSEN, G. W. "Unbelief" in the New Testament (1965) 27ff.

9:42 FARRER, A. St Matthew and St Mark (1954) 56. PALLIS, A., Notes on St. Luke and the Acts (London 1928) 20.

9:43-45 SCHARMM, T. Der Markus-Stoff bei Lukas (1971) 130-36. DAVIES, W. D., The Sermon on the Mount (Cambridge 1966) 24. NEIRYNCK, F., "La Matière Marcienne dans Luc" in: F. Neirynck (ed.) L'Evangile de Luc (Gembloux 1973) 174-75, 180-84. WANKE, J., Die Emmauserzählung (Leipzig 1973) 66, 88-89, 118. TALBERT, C. H., Literary Patterns, Theological Themes, and the Genre of Luke-Acts (Missoula 1974) 27, 29. FITZMYER, J. A., "The Composition of Luke, Chapter 9" in: C. H. Talbert (ed.) Perspectives on Luke-Acts (Danville 1978) 148.

9:43b-45 GAMBA, G. "Senso e significato funzionale di Luca, 9, 43b-45," Il Messianismo, 233-67.

9:44-45 RADL, W., Paulus und Jesus in Lukanischen Doppelwerk (Bern 1975). KRAFT, H., Die Entstehung des Christentums (Darmstadt 1981) 169.

9:44 STONEHOUSE, N. B. The Witness of Matthew and Mark to Christ (1944) 237. HOOKER, M. D. Jesus and the Servant (1959) 92-97. SCHWEIZER, E. Erniedrigung und Erhöhung bei Jesus und seinen Nachfolgern (1962) § 3k. HAHN, F. Christologische Hoheitstitel (1963) 26, 46. POPKES, W. Christus Traditus (1967) 147f., 153ff., 167, 184f., 280. SCHNEIDER, G. Verleugnung, Verspottung und Verhör Jesu nach Lukas 22,54-57 (1969) 171, 176, 177, 178. PATSCH, H. Abendmahl und historischer Jesus (1972) 185ff. TALBERT, C. H., Literary Patterns, Theological Themes, and the Genre of Luke-Acts (Missoula 1974) 97, 115. BASTIN, M., "L'annonce de la passion et les critères de l'historicité" RevSR 59 (1976) 289-329. BASTIN, M., "L'annonce de las Passion et les critères de l'historicité (suite)" RevSr. 51 (1977) 187-213.

9:45 HAHN, F. Christologische Hoheitstitel (1963) 77. TALBERT, C. H., Literary Patterns, Theological Themes, and the Genre of Luke-Acts (Missoula 1974) 16. BERGMEIER, R., Glaube als Gabe nach Johannes (Stuttgart 1980) 225.

9:46-50 SCHRAMM, T. Der Markus-Stoff bei Lukas (1971) 140f.

9:46-48 BRAUN, H. Qumran und NT (1966) 102. SANFORD, J. A., The Kingdom Within (New York 1970) 191-92. TALBERT, C. H., Literary Patterns, Theological Themes, and the Genre of Luke-Acts (Missoula 1974) 27, 29. HOFFMANN, P. and EID, V., Jesus von Nazareth und eine christliche Moral (Freiburg 1975) 188-89, 190-200. SCHNEIDER, G., Das Evangelium nach Lukas (Gütersloh 1977) 222. FITZMYER, J. A., "The Composition of Luke, Chapter 9" in: C. H. Talbert (ed.) Perspectives on Luke-Acts (Danville 1978) 148. SWIDLER, L., Biblical Affirmations of Woman (Philadelphia 1979) 276. WEBER, H.-R., Jesus and the Children (Atlanta 1979).

9:46 SCHRAGE, W. Das Verhältnis des Thomas-Evangeliums zur Synoptischen Tradition und zu den Koptischen Evangelienübersetzungen (1964) 51. METZGER, B. M., The Early Versions of the New Testament (Oxford 1977) 254.

9:47-48 SANFORD, J. A. The Kingdom Within (New York 1970) 54.

9:48 METZGER, B. M. "Explicit references in the works of Origen to variant readings in New Testament mauscripts," Historical and Literary Studies (1968) 95.

9:49.51-56 BOUSSET, W. Die Religion des Judentums im Späthellenistischen Zeitalter (1966 = 1926) 87, 340.

9:49-50 SCHNEIDER, G., Das Evangelium nach Lukas (Gütersloh 1977) 223. FITZMYER, J. A., "The Composition of Luke, Chapter 9" in; C. H. Talbert (ed.) Perspectives on Luke-Acts (Danville 1978) 148-49.

9:50 KNOX, W. L. The Sources of the Synoptic Gospels II (1957) 101. KAESEMANN, E. Exegetische Versuche und Besinnungen (1964) I 245. NICKELS, P. Targum and New Testament (1967) 36. "-Agrapha" in: TRE 2 (1978) 108.

9:51-19:48 BAILEY, K. E., Poet and Peasant (Grand Rapids 1976) 79-85.

9:51-19:46 DAVIES, J. H. "The Purpose of the Central Section of St. Luke's Gospel," in: Studia Evangelica II (1964) F. L. Cross ed., 164-69. GOULDER, M. D. "The Chiastic Structure of the Lucan Journey", Studia Evangelica II (1964) F. L. Cross, ed., 195-202. TALBERT, C. H., Literary Patterns, Theological Themes, and the Genre of Luke-Acts (Missoula 1974) 51, 95, 112, 114. KARIA-MADAM, P., "Discipleship in the Lucan Journey Narrative" Jeevadhara 10 (1980) 111-30.

9:51-19:44 DEANUX, A. "Het lucaanese reisverhaal (Lc 9:51-19:44)" /The Lukan Travel Account (Lk 9:51-19:44)/, CollBrugGand 14 (2, 1968) 214-42; 15 (4, 1969) 464-501. GILL, D. "Observations on the Lukan Travel Narrative and Some Related Passages," HThR 63 (2, 1970) 199-221. DÖMER, M., Das Heil Gottes (Köln-Bonn 1978) 83-89. MIESNER, D. R., "The Missionary Journeys Narrative: Patterns and Implications" in: C. H. Talbert (ed.) Perspectives on Luke-Acts (Danville 1978) 199-202.

9:51-19:40 OSTEN-SACKEN, P. von der, "Zur Christologie des lukanischen Reiseberichts," EvTh 33 (5, 1973) 476-96.

9:51-19:28 OGG, G. "The Central Section of the Gospel according to St. Luke," NTS 18 (1, 1971) 39-53. TALBERT, C. H., Literary Patterns, Theological Themes, and the Genre of Luke-Acts (Missoula 1974) 16, 20. SELLIN, G., "Komposition, Quellen und Funktion des Lukanischen Reiseberichtes (Lk. ix 51-xix 28)" NovT 20 (1978) 100-35. PRAST, F., Presbyter und Evangelium in nachapostolischer Zeit (Stuttgart 1979) 85, 109, 228-33.

9:51-19:27 GRUNDMANN, W. "Fragen der Komposition des lukanischen 'Reiseberichts', ZNW 50 (3-4, 1959) 252-70. CONZELMANN, H. Die Mitte der Zeit (1964) 53ff. STAGG, F. "The Journey Toward Jerusalem in Luke's Gospels. Luke 9:51-19:27," RevEx 64 (4, 1967) 499-512. STÖGER, A. "Armut und Ehelosigkeit-Besitz und Ehe der Jünger nach dem Lukasevangelium," GuL 40 (1, 1967) 43-59. KUDASIEWICZ, J. "Rola Jeruzalem w Lukaszowej sekcji podrozy (9,51-19,27) (De vi et ponere Iersolymae in Lucae sectione Jesu iter tractante 9,51-19,27)," RKT 16 (1, 1969) 17-40. BERNADICOU, P. J. "Self-Fulfillment according to Luke," Bible Today 56 (1971) 505-12. LAPOINTE, R. "L'espace-temps de Lc 9,51-19,27," ETh 1, (3, 1970) 275-90. KÜMMEL, W. G. Einleitung in das Neue Testament (1973) 110f. TROMPF, G. W. "La section médiane de l'ēvangile de Luc: l'organisation des documents," RHPhR 53 (2, 1973) 141-54. SELBY, D. J., Introduction to the New Testament (New York 1971) 174-87. ZMIJEWSKI, J., Die Eschatologiereden des Lukas-Evangeliums (Bonn 1972) 45, 46, 105, 328. SCHNEIDER, G., Das Evangelium nach Lukas (Gütersloh 1977) 226.

9:51-18:30 FARRER, A. St Matthew and St Mark (1954) 53, 54. GOULDER, M. D. Type and History in Acts (1964) 131-42, 222.

9:51-18:14 EWALD, H. Die drei ersten Evangelien (1850) 282ff. TAYLOR, V. Behind the Third Gospel (1926) 151ff., 172ff. GIRARD, L. L'Evangile des Voyages de Jésus (1951). STONEHOUSE, N. B. The Witness of Luke to Christ (1951) 111f., 114ff. BLINZLER, J. "Die literarische Eigenart des sogenannten Reiseberichts im Lukasevangelium". Synoptische Studien (1953) 20-52. SCHNEIDER, J. "Zur Analyse des lukanischen Reiseberichts". Synoptische Studien (1953) 207-29. EVANS, C. F. "The Central Section of St. Luke's Gospel" in: Studies in the Gospels (1955) D. E. Nineham ed., 37-53. REICKE, B. "Instruktion och diskussion i reseberättelsen hos Lukas" Instruction and Discussion in the Lukan Narrative of the journey/, SvTK 33 (1957) 224-33. Also in: The Gospels Reconsidered (1960) 107-17. BLINZLER, J. "Der 'Reisebericht' in Lukasevangelium", Aus der Welt und Umwelt des Neuen Testaments (1969) 62-93. JEREMIAS, J. Neutestamentliche Theologie I (1971) 48f. JEREMIAS, J. New Testament Theology I (1971) 40, 41. WILSON, S. G., The Gentiles and the Gentile Mission in Luke-Acts (Cambridge 1973) 41-45. TALBERT, C. H., Literary Patterns, Theological Themes, and the Genre of Luke-Acts (Missoula 1974) 52. DRURY, J., Tradition and Design in Luke's Gospel (Atlanta 1976) 138-64. SANDMEL, S., We Jews and Jesus (New York 1977) 19. SWIDLER, L., Biblical Affirmations of Woman (Philadelphia 1979) 261, 271, 272.

9:51-13:35 O'NEILL, J. C. The Theology of Acts in its historical setting (1970) 69-71.

9:51-11:13 BERNADICOU, P. J., "The Spirituality of Luke's Travel Narrative" RR 36 (1977) 455-66.

9:51-10:24 MIYOSHI, M., Der Anfang des Reiseberichts, Lk 9,51 - 10,24 (Rome 1974).

9:51ff. KNOX, W. L. The Sources of the Synoptic Gospels II (1957) 45, 58. ROBINSON, W. C. "The Theological Context for Interpreting Luke's Travel Narratives (9:51ff.)," JBL 79 (1, 1960) 20-31. CONZELMANN, H. Die Mitte der Zeit (1964) 53ff. HAHN, F. Das Verständnis der Mission im Neuen Testament (²1965) 23, 112f. STROBEL, a. Erkenntnis und Bekenntnis der Sünde in neutestamentlicher Zeit (1968) 43. BARTSCH, H. W., Wachet aber zu jeder Zeit! (Hamburg-Bergstedt 1963) 92ff. DRURY, J., Tradition and Design in Luke's Gospel (Atlanta 1976) 67-68.

9:51-57 SCHÖNHERR, GPM 21/1 (1966-1967) 131.

9:51-56 HIRSCH, E. Frühgeschichte des Evangeliums (1941) 205-08. FARRER, A. St Matthew and St Mark (1954) 53. BOSCH, D. Die Heidenmission in der Zukunftsschau Jesu (1959) 104-08. KLAAS, W. in: Herr, tue meine Lippen auf Bd 3. (1964) G. Eichholz ed., 147ff. ROLOFF, J. Apostolat-Verkündigung-Kirche (1965) 156f. LEHMANN, M. Synoptische Quellenanalyse und die Frage nach dem historischen Jesus (1970) 142-44. MIYOSHI, M., Der Anfang des Reiseberichts Lk 9,51 - 10,24 (Rome 1974) 6-32. SCHNEIDER, G., Das Evangelium nach Lukas (Gütersloh 1977) 228. FITZMYER, J. A., "The Composition of Luke, Chapter 9" in: C. H. Talbert (ed.) Perspectives on Luke-Acts (Danville 1978) 149. HEUTGER, N., "Die lukanischen Samaritanererzählungen in religionspädagogischer Sicht" in: W. Haubeck/M. Bachmann (eds.) Wort in der Zeit. FS. K. H. Rengstorf (Leiden 1980) 286-87.

9:51-53 ZINGG, P., Das Wachsen der Kirche (Freiburg 1974) 138. WILLIAMS, J. A., A Conceptual History of Deuteronomism in the Old Testament, Judaism, and the New Testament (Ph.D. Diss. Southern Baptist Theological Seminary: Louisville 1976) 300.

9:51-52 HAHN, F. Christologische Hoheitstitel (1963) 403. LOHFINK, G. Die Himmelfahrt Jesu (1971) 212-17.

9:51 ADLER, N. Das erste christliche Pfingstfest (1938) 33f., 120. ROBINSON, J. M. Kerygma und historischer Jesus (1960) 146. FLENDER, H. St Luke Theologian of Redemptive History (1967) 32, 33, 76n, 95, 96n, 125, 139. ZEHNLE, R. F. Peter's Pentecost Discourse (1971) 88, 101-02, 104, 122, 124, 128n, 129.KRÄNKL, E. Jesus der Knecht Gottes (1972) 165f., 209. ZMIJEWSKI, J., Die Eschatologiereden des Lukas-Evangeliums (Bonn 1972) 45, 205, 282, 315, 328, 402, 418, 495, 505. DENAUX, A., "L'hypocrisie des Pharisiens et le dessein de Dieu. Analyse de Lc., xiii, 31-33" in: F. Neirynck (ed.) L'Evangile de Luc (Gembloux 1973) 248, 266. FRIEDRICH, G., "Lk 9,51 und die Entrückungschristologie des Lukas" in: P. Hoffmann (ed.) Orientierung an Jesus. FS. J. Schmid (Freiburg 1973) 70-74. LOHSE, E., Die Einheit des Neuen Testaments (Göttingen 1973) 151-52, 166, 170-71, 174, 186-87. NEIRYNCK, F., "La Matière Marcienne dans Luc" in: F. Neirynck (ed.) L'Evangile de Luc (Gembloux 1973) 184-92. VAN UNNIK, W. C., "Eléments atistiques dans l'évangile de Luc" in: F. Neirynck (ed.) L'Evangile de Luc (Gembloux 1973) 138. MIYOSHI, M., Der Anfang des Reiseberichts Lk 9,51 - 10,24 (Rome 1974) 6-10. TALBERT, C. H., Literary Patterns, Theological Themes, and the Genre of Luke-Acts (Missoula 1974) 16,17, 20, 121, 112, 114, 115, 122. RADL, W., Paulus und Jesus im lukanischen Doppelwerk (Bern/Frankfurt 1975) 117-26. GOPPELT, L., Theologie des Neuen Testaments. II (Göttingen 1976) 611. FRIEDRICH, G., "Lukas 9,51 und die Entrückungschristologie des Lukas" in: Auf das Wort kommt es an (Göttingen 1978) 26-55. PRAST, F., Presbyter und Evangelium in nachapostolischer Zeit (Stuttgart 1979) 85, 228f. JEREMIAS, J., Die Sprache des Lukasevangeliums (Göttingen 1980) 179.

9:52-56 TAYLOR, V. The Formation of the Gospel Tradition (1949) 69f. DELLING, G. Die Taufe im Neuen Testament (1963) 65. JERVELL, J., "The Lost Sheep of the House of Israel" in: Luke and the People of God (Minneapolis 1972) 113-32.

9:52-53 ZINGG, P., Das Wachsen der Kirche (Freiburg 1974) 250-51.

9:52 MIYOSHI, M., Der Anfang des Reiseberichts Lk 9,51 - 10,24 (Rome 1974) 10-11. METZGER, B. M., The Early Versions of the New Testament (Oxford 1977) 391. JEREMIAS, J., Die Sprache des Lukasevangeliums (Göttingen 1980) 179-80. SNODGRASS, K. R., "Streams of Tradition emerging from Isaiah 40:1-5 and their adaptation in the New Testament" JSNT 8 (1980) 24-45.

9:53 MIYOSHI, M., Der Anfang des Reiseberichts Lk 9,51 - 10,24 (Rome 1974) 12. TALBERT, C. H., Literary Patterns, Theological Themes, and the Genre of Luke-Acts (Missoula 1974) 17, 20, 114. JEREMIAS, J., Die Sprache des Lukasevangeliums (Göttingen 1980) 180.

9:54-56 ROSS, J. M. "The Rejected Wirds in Luke 9:54-56," ET 84 (3, 1972) 85-86. COLOMER I CARLES, O., "Lc 9,54-56: Un estudi sobre la critica textual" RevCt 1 (1976) 375-91.

9:54 BORNKAMM-BARTH-HELD, Ueberlieferung und Auslegung im Matthäus-Evangelium (²1961) 113. HAHN, F. Christologische Hoheitstitel (1963) 84, 85, 164, 403. MIYOSHI, M., Der Anfang des Reiseberichts Lk 9, 51 - 10,24 (Rome 1974) 12-13. METZGER, B. M., The Early Versions of the New Testament (Oxford 1977) 391. JEREMIAS, J., Die Sprache des Lukasevangeliums (Göttingen 1980) 180.

9:55 KNOX, W. L. The Sources of the Synoptic Gospels II (1957) 87.

FRIEDRICHSEN, G. W. S. NTS 11 (1964-1965) 288f. MI-
YOSHI, M., Der Anfang des Reiseberichts Lk 9,51 - 10,24 (Rome
1974) 14. METZGER, B. M., The Early Versions of the New Testament (Oxford 1977) 42. "Agrapha" in: TRE 2 (1978) 104.

9:56 MIYOSHI, M., "Der Anfang des Reiseberichts Lk 9,51 - 10,24
(Rome 1974) 14-15. ARENS, E., The HΛΘON-Sayings in the
Synoptic Tradition (Fribourg 1976) 180-91. "Agrapha" in: TRE 2
(1978) 104.

9:57ff. KNOX, W. L. The Sources of the Synoptic Gospels II (1957) 46f.
BORNKAMM-BARTH-HELD, Ueberlieferung und Auslegung im
Matthäus-Evangelium (²1961) 27, 190f. SCHWEIZER, E. Erniedrigung und Erhöhung bei Jesus und seinen Nachfolgern (1962) §§
lg. 31.

9:57-62 TAYLOR, V. The Formation of the Gospel Tradition (1949) 72f.
SCHULZ, A. Nachfolgen und Nachahmen (1962) 105-08. FUCHS,
GPM 17 (1962-1963) 285ff. BULTMANN, R. The History of the
Synoptic Tradition (1963) 28f., 56-67, 61f. Erhaltet euch in der
Liebe Gottes, Predigtgedanken aus Vergangenheit und Gegenwart,
Reihe C, Bd. 3-4 (1963) 58. FUCHS, E. GPM 17 (1963) 255-58.
HAHN, F. Christologische Hoheitstitel (1963) 83f. NIESEL, W.,
in: Herr, tue meine Lippen aud Bd. 3 (1964) G. Eichholz ed., 445ff.
ZIMMERMANN,H. Neutestamentliche Methodenlehre (1967) 116-
19. SCHNEIDER, G., Anfragen an das Neue Testament (Essen
1971) 40, 134-35, 140. DRESCHER, H.-G., Nachfolge und Be-
gegnung (Gütersloh 1972) 94-121. ERNST, J. Anfänge der Chri-
stologie (Stuttgart 1972) 130-33. HAHN, F., "Die Jüngerberufung
Joh 1,35-51" in: J. Gnilka (ed.) Neues Testament und Kirche. FS.
R. Schnackenburg (Freiburg 1974) 179-80. MIYOSHI, M., Der
Anfang des Reiseberichts Lk 9,51 - 10,24 (Rome 1974) 33-58.
HAAR, J., in: GPM 29 (1975) 324-29. SCHÜRMANN, M.,
"Beobachtungen zum Menschensohn-Titel in der Redequelle" in:
R. Pesch/R. Schnackenburg (eds.) Jesus und der Menschensohn
(Freiburg 1975) 132-33. SCHMIDT, E. R. and SEILER, D., in: P.
Krusche et al. (eds.) Predigtstudien für das Kirchenjahr 1974-1975.
III/2 (Stuttgart 1975) 132-40. TANNEHILL, R. C., The Sword of
his Mouth (Philadelphia 1975) 157-65. EDWARDS, R. A., A
Theology of Q (Philadelphia 1976) 100-01. WILLIAMS, J. A., A
Conceptual History of Deuteronomism in the Old Testament, Ju-
daism, and the New Testament (Ph.D. Diss. Southern Baptist
Theological Seminary; Louisville 1976) 309. FURST, W., in: GPM
33 (1979) 147-51. POLAG, A., Die Christologie der Logienquelle
(Neukirchen-Vluyn 1977) 84-85. PRAST, F., Presbyter und Evan-
gelium in nachapostolischer Zeit (Stuttgart 1979) 338-40.
SCHNEIDER, G., Das Evangelium nach Lukas (Gütersloh 1977)

230-31, 233. KUHN, W.-W., "Nachfolge nach Ostern" in: D. Lührmann/G. Strecker (eds.) Kirche. FS. G. Bornkamm (Tübingen 1980) 107-10, 113ff.

9:57-60 (61f) LÜHRMANN, D. Die Redaktion der Logienquelle (1969) 58.

9:57-60 HOFFMANN, P. Studien zur Theologie der Logienquelle (1972) 5, 72f., 90f., 93, 96, 142, 149f., 158, 181-87. SCHULZ, S. Q Die Spruchquelle der Evangelisten (1972) 434-42. BORSCH, F. H., "Jesus the Wandering Preacher?" in: M. Hooker/C. Hickling (eds.) What about the New Testament? FS. C. Evans (London 1975) 50-52. LOHFINK, G., "Die Unbedingtheit und die Faszination im Leben Jesu" EuA (1980) 89-98.

9:57-58 SANFORD, J. A., The Kingdom Within (New York 1970) 88-89. SCHÜRMANN, H. Ursprung und Gestalt (1970) 49, 52, 53, 54. MIYOSHI, M., Der Anfang des Reiseberichts Lk 9,51 - 10,24 (Rome 1974) 36-38, 44-45.

9:57 BONHOEFFER, D. Nachfolge (1950) 15ff., 69. KNOX, W. L. The Sources of the Synoptic Gospels II (1957) 59. NICKELS, P. Targum and New Testament (1967) 46. MIYOSHI, M., Der Anfang des Reiseberichts Lk 9,51 - 10,24 (Rome 1974) 34-36. TALBERT, C. H., Literary Patterns, Theological Themes, and the Genre of Luke-Acts (Missoula 1974) 114. JEREMIAS, J., Die Sprache des Lukasevangeliums (Göttingen 1980) 180-81.

9:58 BLAIR, E. P. Jesus in the Gospel of Matthew (1960) 72. HAHN, F. Christologische Hoheitstitel (1963) 44. SCHRAGE, W. Das Verhältnis des Thomas-Evangeliums zur Synoptischen Traditon und zu den Koptischen Evangelienübersetzungen (1964) 168. GÄRTNER, B. The Temple and the Community in Qumran and the New Testament (1965) 125. JEREMIAS, J. Neutestamentliche Theologie I (1971) 25, 33, 35, 248, 250. STANTON, G. N., Jesus of Nazareth in New Testament Preaching (Cambridge 1974) 132-33, 156, 158, 159. DUNN, J. D. G., Unity and Diversity in the New Testament (London 1977) 38-40. GRUNDMANN, W., "Weisheit im Horizont des Reiches Gottes. Eine Studie zur Verkündigung Jesu nach der Spruchüberlieferung Q" in: R. Schnackenburg et al. (eds.) Die Kirche des Anfangs. FS. H. Schürmann (Leipzig 1977) SWIDLER, L., Biblical Affirmations of Woman (Philadelphia 1979) 289. JEREMIAS, J., Die Sprache des Lukasevangeliums (Göttingen 1980) 181. KELBER, W. H., "Mark and Oral Tradition" in: N. R. Petersen (Ed.) Perspectives on Mark's Gospel. Semeia 16 (Missoula 1980) 25-27. KRAFT, H., Die Entstehung des Christentums (Darmstadt 1981) 161-54.

9:59-62 BRAUN, H. Qumran und NT II (1966) 299.

9:59-61 SCHÜRMANN, H. Sprachliche Reminiszenzen an abgeänderte oder ausgelassene Bestandteile der Spruchsammlung im Lukas- und Matthäusevangelium. NTS 6 (1959-1960) 209f.

9:59-60 STAEHELIN, E. Die Verkündigung des Reiches Gottes in der Kirche Jesu Christi I (1951) 67. HENGEL, M. Nachfolge und Charisma (1968) 21. SANFORD, J. A., The Kingdom Within (New York 1970) 87-88. MIYOSHI, M., Der Anfang des Reiseberichts Lk 9,51 - 10,24 (Rome 1974) 38-41, 46-52

9:59 BARRETT, C. K. The New Testament Background (1956) 222. KLEMM, H. G. NTS 16 (1969-1970) 61f. METZGER, B. M., The Early Versions of the New Testament (Oxford 1977) 249. POLAG, A., Die Christologie der Logienquelle (Neukirchen-Vluyn 1977) 85. JEREMIAS, J., Die Sprache des Lukasevangeliums (Göttingen 1980) 181.

9:60 PERLES, F., "Zwei Übersetzungsfehler im Text der Evangelien" ZNW 19 (1919-1920) 96. PERLES, F., "Noch einmal Lk 9:60" ZNW 25 (1926) 286. KERN, H. Der lebendige Christus (1937) 88-94. JÜNGEL, E. Paulus und Jesus (1966) 182, 269. BLACK, M. An Aramaic Approach to the Gospels and Acts (1967) 207f. KLEMM, H. G. NTS 16 (1969-1970) 60-75. JEREMIAS, J. Neutestamentliche Theologie I (1971) 32, 40, 43, 100, 132, 133, 175. SCHROEDER, H.-M., Eltern und Kinder in der Verkündigung Jesu (Hamburg-Bergstadt 1972) 82-85. PERRIN, N., Jesus and the Language of the Kingdom (London 1976) 41, 48, 51-52. FRIED-RICH, G., "Das Problem der Autorität im Neuen Testament" in: Auf das Wort kommt es an (Göttingen 1978) 383"-85. PRAST, F., Presbyter und Evangelium in nachapostolischer Zeit (Stuttgart 1979) 280-81. JEREMIAS, J., Die Sprache des Lukasevangeliums (Göttingen 1980) 181-82. KELBER, W. H., "Mark and Oral Tradition" in: Semeia 16 (Missoula 1980) 25-27. MCDONALD, J. I. H., Kerygma and Didache (Cambridge 1980) 81.

9:61-62 STAEHELIN, E. Die Verkündigung des Reiches Gottes in der Kirche Jesu Christ I (1951) 67. SCHÜRMANN, H. Ursprung und Gestalt (1970) 51, 52, 53, 55. JEREMIAS, J. Neutestamentliche Theologie I (1971) 35, 40, 42, 100, 133. MIYOSHI, M. Der Anfang des Reiseberichts Lk 9,51 - 10,24 (Rome 1974) 41-43, 52-57. POLAG, A., Die Christologie der Logienquelle (Neukirchen-Vluyn 1977) 85. SCHROEDER, H.-H., " 'Oikos' y justicia en los evangelios sinópticos" RevB 41 (1979) 249-59.

9:61 HAHN, F. Christologische Hoheitstitel (1963) 85. NICKELS, P. Targum and New Testament (1967) 36. JEREMIAS, J., Die Sprache des Lukasevangeliums (Göttingen 1980) 182.

9:62 ROBINSON, J. M. Kerygma und historischer Jesus (1960) 161. HAHN, F. Christologische Hoheitstitel (1963) 403. JÜNGEL, E.

Paulus und Jesus (1966) 181f. NICKELS, P. Targum and New
Testament (1967) 36. BLAIR, H. J. "Putting One's Hand to the
Plough. Luke ix. 62 in the light of 1 Kings xix. 19-21," 342-43.
SANFORD, J. A., The Kingdom Within (New York 1970) 52-53.
PERRIN, N., Jesus and the Language of the Kingdom (London
1976) 41, 48, 53-54. FRIEDRICH, G., "Das Problem der Auto-
rität im Neuen Testament" in: Auf das Wort kommt es an (Göttin-
gen 1978) 288. JEREMIAS, J., Die Sprache des Lukasevangeliums
(Göttingen 1980) 182-83. MCDONALD, J. I. H., Kerygma and
Didache (Cambridge 1980) 81.

———————————

10-13 GOULDER, M. D. Type and History in Acts (1964) 59ff.

10 ARVEDSON, T. Das Mysterium Christi (1937) 112f. HIERS, R.
H., The Historical Jesus and the Kingdom of God (Gainesville 1973)
61-62, 63. WANKE, J. Die Emmauserzählung (Leipzig 1973) 10-
11. PERRIN, N. Jesus and the Language of the Kingdom (London
1976) 84. RICHARDS, W. L., "Manuscript Grouping in Luke 10
by Quantitive Analysis" JBL 98 (1979) 379-91.

10:1ff. STAEHELIN, E. Die Verkündigung des Reiches Gottes in der
Kirche Jesu Christi I (1951) 67, KNOX, W. L. The Sources of the
Synoptic Gospels II (1957) 46-48. HAHN, F. Christologische Hoheitstitel (1963) 46-48. SCHRAMM, T. Der Markus-Stoff bei Lukas (1971) 26ff.

10:1-24 ARVEDSON, T. Das Mysterium Christi (1937) 129f. GASTON,
L. No Stone on Another (1970) 255, 318-19. LOHFINK, G., Die
Sammlung Israels (München 1975) 67, 68-80. MINEAR, P. S., To
Heal and to Reveal (New York 1976). MATTILL, A. J., Luke and
the Last Things (Dillsboro 1979) 7. TESTA, E., "I 'Discorsi de
Missione' de Gesu" SBFLA 29 (1979) 7-41.

10:1-20 RICHARDSON, A. The Miracle-Stories of the Gospels (1948) 41f.
ITTEL, G. W. Jesus und die Jünger (1970) 53-56. BORSCH, F.
H., "Jesus the Wandering Preacher?" in: M. Hooker/C. Hickling
(eds.) What about the New Testament? FS. C. Evans (London 1975)
48-49. PRAST, F., Presbyter und Evangelium in nachapostolischer Zeit (Stuttgart 1979) 312, 340-44.

10:1-18 HANSON, S. The Unity of the Church in the New Testament (1946)
39f.

10:1-12, 16-20 HIRSCH, E. Frühgeschichte des Evangeliums (1941) 51-56, 208-
11.

10:1-16 BARRETT, C. K. The Holy Spirit in the Gospel Tradition (1947) 127-30. GEORGI, D., Die Gegner des Paulus im 2. Korinther-Brief (Neukirchen 1964) 206ff. MUSSNER, F., "Gab es eine 'galiläische Krise'?" in: P. Hoffmann (ed.) Orientierung an Jesus. FS. J. Schmid (Freiburg 1973) 244-48. MIYOSHI, M., Der Anfang des Reiseberichts Lk 9,51 - 10,24 (Rome 1974) 59-94. MINEAR, P., To Heal and to Reveal (New York 1976) 8-11. POLAG, A., Die Christologie der Logienquelle (Neukirchen-Vluyn 1977) 67-72. MATTILL, A. J., Luke and the Last Things (Dillsboro 1979) 77-79.

10:1-12 DEGENHARDT, H.-J. Lukas, Evangelist der Armen (1964) 63-66. HAHN, F. Das Verständnis der Mission im Neuen Testament (²1965) 32, 33-36, 113. LEHMANN, M. Synoptische Quellenanalyse und die Frage nach dem historischen Jesus (1970) 149f. OTOMO, Y. Nachfolge Jesu und Anfänge der Kiche im Neuen Testament (1970) 68-70. DUNGAN, D. L. The Sayings of Jesus in the Churches of Paul. LIGNÉE, H., "La mission des soixantedouze. Lc 10,1-12. 17-20" AssS 45 (1975) 64-74. TALBERT, C. H., Literary Patterns, Theological Themes, and the Genre of Luke-Acts (Missoula 1974) 16, 20, 78. EDWARDS, R. A., A Theology of Q (Philadelphia 1976) 101-104. SCHNEIDER, G., Das Evangelium nach Lukas (Gütersloh 1977) 235. "Apostel" in: TRE 3 (1978) 433. KARRIS, R. J., "Poor and Rich: The Lukan Sitz im Leben" in: C. H. Talbert (ed.) Perspectives on Luke-Acts (Danville 1978) 118-19. KRAFT, H. Die Entstehung des Christentums (Darmstadt 1981) 146-50.

10:1-10 VOIGT, M. GPM 28 (1973) 329-34.

10:1-8 HUBBARD, B. J., "Commissioning Stories in Luke-Acts: A Study of their Antecedents, Form and Content" in: Semeia 8 (1977) 103-26.

10:1-2 WILSON, S. G., The Gentiles and the Gentile Mission in Luke-Acts (Cambridge 1973) 42-43, 45-47, 89. MIYOSHI, M., Der Anfang des Reiseberichts Lk 9,51 - 10,24 (Rome 1974) 59-62.

10:1.17 METZGER, B. M. "Seventy or seventy-two disciples?", Historical and Literary Studies (1968) 67-76.

10:1 FLEW, R. N. Jesus and His Church (1956) 77-78, 131n. KNOX, W. L. The Sources of the Synoptic Gospels (1957) II 49, 103. METZGER, B. M. "Seventy or Seventy-two Diciples?" NTS 5 (4, 1959) 299-306. JELLICOE, S. "St Luke and the Seventy Two," NTS 6 (4, 1960) 319-21. HAHN, F. Christologische Hoheitstitel (1963) 85, 88. GOULDER, M. D. Type and History in Acts (1964) 56, 61, 134, 163. DESCAMPS, A./DE HALLEUX, A. Mélanges Bibliques en hommage au R. P. Béda Rigaux (1970) 126-28, 145.

KÜNZI, M. Das Naherwartungslogion Matthäus 10,23 (1970) 82, 104, 109. JEREMIAS, J. Neutestamentliche Theologie I (1971) 225f. MIYOSHI, M. Der Anfang des Reiseberichts Lk 9, 51 - 10, 24 (Rome 1974) 26-27. TALBERT, C. H., Literary Patterns, Theological Themes, and the Genre of Luke-Acts (Missoula 1974) 20. 114. SWIDLER, L., Biblical Affirmations of Woman (Philadelphia 1979) 289, 298. JEREMIAS, J., Die Sprache des Lukasevangeliums (Göttingen 1980) 183.

10:2ff. HAHN, F. Christologische Hoheitstitel (1963) 88.

10:2-16 SMITH, M. Tannaitic Parallels to the Gospels (1968) 4 E. HOFFMANN, P. Studien zur Theologie der Logienquelle (1972) Passim.

10:2-12 LÜHRMANN, D. Die Redaktion der Logienquelle (1969) 59f. SCHULZ, S. Q Die Spruchquelle der Evangelisten (1972) 404-19. "Apostel" in: TRE 3 (1978) 435. KUHN, H.-W. "Nachfolge nach Ostern" in: D. Lührmann/G. Strecker (eds.) Kirche. FS. G. Bornkamm (Tügingen 1980) 126-27. VENETZ, H.-J., "Bittet den Herrn der Ernte. Ueberlegungen zu Lk. 10:2/Mt. 9:37: Diakonia 11 (1980) 148-61.

10:2-11 MIYOSHI, M., Der Anfang des Reiseberichts Lk 9,51 - 10,24 (Rome 1974) 75-76.

10:2-4 SEEBERG, A. "Vaterunser und Abendmahl" in: Neutestamentliche Studien Georg Heinrici zu seinem 70. Geburtstag (1914) A. Deissmann & H. Windisch eds., 108-14. MIYOSHI, M., Der Anfang des Reiseberichts Lk 9,51 - 10,24 (Rome 1974) 63.

10:2-3 NICKELS, P. Targum and New Testament (1967) 36.

10:2 KNOX, W. L. The Sources of the Synoptic Gospels II (1957) 51, 56. YATES, J. E. The Spirit and the Kingdom (1963) 74ff. SCHRAGE, W. Das Verhältnis des Thomas-Evangeliums zur Synoptischen Tradition und zu den Koptischen Evangelienübersetzungen (1964) 153. POLAG, A., Die Christologie der Logienquelle (Nerkirchen-Vluyn 1977) 71. JEREMIAS, J., Die Sprache des Lukasevangeliums (Göttingen 1980) 184. VENETZ, H.-J., "Bittet den Herrn der Ernte. Ueberlegungen zu Lk 10,2/Mt 9,37" Diakonia 11 (1980) 148-61.

10:3-4 SCHÜRMANN, H. "Sprachliche Reminiszenzen an abgeänderte oder ausgelassene Bestandteile der Spruchsammlung im Lukas- und Matthäusevangelium," NTS 6 (1959-1960) 209f.

10:3 MASSAUX, E. Influence de l'Evangile de saint Matthieu sur la littérature chrétienne avant saint Irénée (1950) 150-52. KNOX, W. L. The Sources of the Synoptic Gospels II (1957) 51. HAHN, F. Christologische Hoheitstitel (1963) 168. HOWARD, V. P., Das Ego in den Synoptischen Evangelien (Marburg 1975) 149-52. POLAG, A., Die Christologie der Logienquelle (Neukirchen-Vluyn 1977)

99. JEREMIAS, J., Die Sprache des Lukasevangeliums (Göttingen 1980) 184.

10:4-12 BUTLER, B. C. The Originality of St. Matthew (1951) 14ff.

10:4-7 POLAG, A., Die Christologie der Logienquelle (Neukirchen-Vluyn 1977) 67.

10:4 PALLIS, A., Notes on St. Luke and the Acts (London 1928) 20-21. KNOX, W. L. The Sources of the Synoptic Gospels II (1957) 48, 59. HAHN, F. Christologische Hoheitstitel (1963) 169. O'-HAGAN, A. " 'Greet no one on the way' (Lk 10:4b)," SBFLA 16 (1965-1966) 69-84. SCHÜRMANN, H. Ursprung und Gestalt (1970) 55, 132, 133, 134. JEREMIAS, J. Neutestamentliche Theologie I (1957) 133f., 226, 227. HOFFMANN, P. Studien zur Theologie der Logienquelle (1972) 264-67, 269. HENGEL, M., Was Jesus a Revolutionist? (Philadelphia 1971) 21. DERRETT, J. D. M., Jesus's Audience (London 1973) 183ff., 1886. BOSOLD, I., Pazifismus und prophetische Provokation. Das Grussverbot Lk 10,4b und sein historischer Kontext (Stuttgart 1978). LEGRAND, L., "Bare foot Apostles? The shoes of St. Mark (Mk 6:8-9 and parallels)" IndTheolStud 16 (1979) 201-19. MATTILL, A. J., Luke and the Last Things (Dillsboro 1979) 225-26. SWIDLER, L., Biblical Affirmations of Woman (Philadelphia 1979) 289. JEREMIAS, J., Die Sprache des Lukasevangeliums (Göttingen 1980) 184.

10:5ff. THEISSEN, G., Soziologie der Jesusbewegung (München 1977) 19.

10:5-11 HOFFMANN, P. "Lk 10:5-11 in der Instruktionsrede der Logienquelle", in Evangelisch-Katholischer Kommentar zum Neuen Testament, Vorarbeiten Heft 3 (1971) 37-53.

10:5-7 KNOX, W. L. The Sources of the Synoptic Gospels II (1957) 52. HOFFMANN, P. Studien zur Theologie der Logienquelle (1972) 272-74.MIYOSHI, M., Der Anfang des Reiseberichts Lk 9,51 - 10,24 (Rome 1974) 64.

10:5-6 SCHENK, W. Der Segen im Neuent Testament (1967) 92f. JEREMIAS, J. Neutestamentliche Theologie I (1971) 25, 27, 134, 222.WESTERMANN, C., Blessing. In the Bible and the Life of the Church (Philadelphia 1978) 91, 93-98, 98-101. SWIDLER, L., Biblical Affirmations of Woman (Philadelphia 1979) 284.

10:5 KNOX, W. L. The Sources of the Synoptic Gospels II (1957) 51.

10:6 BÖHLIG, A., Die Gnosis III: Der Manichäismus (Zürich 1980) 339 n.103. JEREMIAS, J., Die Sprache des Lukasevangeliums (Göttingen 1980) 185.

10:7 PALLIS, A., Notes on St. Luke and the Acts (London 1928) 21. BEST, E. One Body in Christ (1955) 99. HAHN, F. Christologi-

sche Hoheitstitel (1963) 92. HENNECKE, E./SCHNEE-
MELCHER, W. Neutestamentliche Apokryphen (1964) II 390.
SMITH, M. Tannaitic Parallels to the Gospels (1968) 3 b n
36.MCDONALD, J. I. H., Kerygma and Didache (Cambridge
1980) 81.

10:8ff. KNOX, W. L. The Sources of the Synoptic Gospels II (1957) 52.

10:8-12 JEREMIAS, J. Neutestamentliche Theologie I (1971) 29f. PO-
LAG, A., Die Christologie der Logienquelle (Neukirchen-Vluyn
1977) 68-70.

10:8-11 ROLOFF, J. Das Kerygma und der irdische Jesus (1970) 186-87.
MIYOSHI, M., Der Anfang des Reiseberichts Lk 9,51 - 10,24
(Rome 1974) 64-67.

10:8-9 SCHRAGE, W. Das Verhältnis des Thomas-Evangeliums zur Synoptischen Tradition und zu den Koptischen Evangelienübersetzungen (1964) 52. SUMMERS, R. The Secret Sayings of the Living
Jesus (1968) 31.

10:8 NESTLE, E., "Zu Band 7,278; 8,241 (Mt 10,32; Lk 10,8)" ZNW
9 (1908) 253. PALLIS, A., Notes on St. Luke and the Acts (London 1928) 21. KNOX, W. L. The Sources of the Synoptic Gospels
II (1957) 142.HOFFMANN, P. Studien zur Theologie der Logienquelle (1972) 276-81.

10:9-23 HUBBARD, B. J., "Commissioning Stories in Luke-Acts: A Study
of Their Antecedents, Form and Content" in: Semeia 8 (1977) 103-
26.

10:9-11 RICHARDSON, A. The Miracle-Stories of the Gospels (1948).
JEREMIAS, J. Neutestamentliche Theologie I (1971) 40, 100, 103,
195, 132, 227. PERRIN, N., Jesus and the Language of the Kingdom (London 1976) 37. PRAST, F., Presbyter und Evangelium in
nachapostolischer Zeit (Stuttgart 1979) 280-81.

10:9 HOFFMANN, P. Studien zur Theologie der Logienquelle (1972)
274-76. SCHULZ, S., "Die Gottesherrschaft ist nahe herbeige-
kommen (Mt 10,7/Lk 10,9). Der Kerygmatische Entwurf der Q-
Gemeinde Syriens" in: H. Balz/ S. Schulz (eds.) Das Wort und die
Wörter (Stuttgart 1973) 57-67. WILSON, S. G., The Gentiles and
the Gentile Mission in Luke-Acts (Cambridge 1973) 73-74, 82, 85.
LADD, G. E., A Theology of the New Testament (Grand Rapids
1974) 67, 76, 103. MIYOSHI, M., Der Anfang des Reiseberichts
Lk 9,51 - 10,24 (Rome 1974) 80-82, 90-91. SCHNEIDER, G., Pa-
rusiegleichnisse im Lukas-Evangelium (Stuttgart 1975) 49-54.
"Abendmahl" in: TRE 1 (1977) 216. SEYBOLD, K. and
MÜLLER, U., Krankheit und Heilung (Stuttgart 1978) 158-59.
MATTILL, A. J., Luke and the Last Things (Dillsboro 1979) 70-
79.

10:10-16 MIYOSHI, M., Der Anfang des Reiseberichts Lk 9,51 - 10, 24 (Rome 1974) 91.

10:10-12 SANFORD, J. A., The Kingdom Within (New York 1970) 72-73.

10:10-11 HOFFMANN, P. Studien zur Theologie der Logienquelle (1972) 267-72.

10:11 JEREMIAS, J. Neutestamentliche Theologie I (1971) 40f., 100, 103, 105, 132, 228. WILSON, S. C., The Gentiles and the Gentile Mission in Luke-Acts (Cambridge 1973) 73-74, 82, 85. MIYOSHI, M., Der Anfang des Reiseberichts Lk 9,51 - 10,24 (Rome 1974) 80-82, 90-91. CONZELMANN, H. and LINDEMANN, A., Arbeitsbuch zum Neuen Testament (Tübingen 1975) 81-19. SCHNEIDER, G., Parusiegleichnisse im Lukas-Evangelium (Stuttgart 1975) 49-54. MATTILL, A. J., Luke and the Last Things (Dillsboro 1979) 70-79. JEREMIAS, J., Die Sprache des Lukasevangeliums (Göttingen 1980) 186.

10:12-15 EDWARDS, R. A., A Theology of Q (Philadelphia 1976) 68-69, 104-05.

10:12-14 CAIRD, G. B., "Eschatology and Politics: Some Misconceptions" in: J. R. McKay/M. R. Miller (eds.) Biblical Studies. FS. W. Barclay (London 1976) 75f.

10:12ff. KNOX, W. L. The Sources of the Synoptic Gospels II (1957) 53f.

10:12 HASLER, V. Amen (1969) 62. PATSCH, H. Abendmahl und historischer Jesus (1972) 109f. ZMIJEWSKI, J., Die Eschatologiereden des Lukas-Evangeliums (Bonn 1972) 289, 437, 466, 491. MIYOSHI, M., Der Anfang des Reiseberichts Lk 9,51 - 10,24 (Rome 1974) 67-69. POLAG, A., Die Christologie der Logienquelle (Neukirchen-Vluyn 1977) 74, 89. FURNISH, V. P., The Moral Teaching of Paul (Nashville 1979) 56. JEREMIAS, J., Die Sprache des Lukasevangeliums (Göttingen 1980) 186.

10:13ff. MCDONALD, J. I. H., Kerygma and Didache (Cambridge 1980) 21.

10:13-15, HIRSCH, E. Frühgeschichte des Evangeliums (1941) 51f., 97-100.
21-24 LÜHRMANN, D. Die Redaktion der Logienquelle (1969) 60-68.

10:13-16 SCHNEIDER, G., Das Evangelium nach Lukas (Gütersloh 1977) 238.

10:13-15 MUSSNER, F. Die Wunder Jesu (1967) 25-28. SCHULZ, S. Q Die Spruchquelle des Evangelisten (1972) 360-66. MIYOSHI, M., Der Anfang des Reiseberichts Lk 9,51 - 10,24 (Rome 1974) 69. BORSCH, F. H., "Jesus the Wandering Preacher?" in: M. Hooker/ C. Hickling (eds.) What about the New Testament? FS. C. Evans (London 1975) 52. TANNEHILL, R. C., The Sword of His Mouth

(Missoula 1975) 122-28. POLAG, A., Die Christologie der Logienquelle (Neukirchen-Vluyn 1977) 74, 89.

10:13 STONEHOUSE, N. B. The Witness of Luke to Christ (1951) 104f. STREETER, B. H. The Four Gospels (1951) 569f. STROBEL, A. Erkenntnis und Bekenntnis der Sünde in neutestamentlicher Zeit (1968) 42. DORMEYER, D., Die Passion Jesu als Verhaltensmodell (Münster 1974) 98, 234. SAND, A., Das Gesetz und die Propheten (Regensburg 1974) 86-87. DUNN, J. D. G., Jesus and the Spirit (London 1975) 70-71.

10:14 JEREMIAS, J., Die Sprache des Lukasevangeliums (Göttingen 1980) 186.

10:15 MÜLLER, U. B., "Die Griechische Esra-Apokalypse" in: W. G. Kümmel (ed.) Jüdische Schriften aus hellenistisch-römischer Zeit." V. (Gütersloh 1976) 96 n.32a.

10:16 FLEW, R. N. Jesus and His Church (1956) 48. KLEIN, G. Die Zwölf Apostel (1961) 30f. ESTEBAN, J., "Un texto de San Lucas sobre la obediencia," Manresa 34 (130, 1962) 29-34. TÖDT, H. E. Der Menschensohn in der synoptischen Ueberlieferung (1963) 234-36. STEIDLE, B., "Wer euch hört, hört mich" EuA 40 (1964) 179-96. NICKELS, P. Targum and New Testament (1967) 36. O'-NEILL, J. C. The Theology of Acts in its historical setting (1970) 38-40, IX. JEREMIAS, J. Neutestamentliche Theologie I (1971) 26, 33, 229, 242. KERTELGE, K. Gemeinde und Amt im Neuen Testament (1972) 159f. SCHULZ, S. Q Die Spruchquelle der Evangelisten (1972) 467-59. MIYOSHI, M., Der Anfang des Reiseberichts Lk 9,51 - 10,24 (Rome 1974) 70-73. EDWARDS, R. A., A Theology of Q (Philadelphia 1976) 105-06. POLAG, A., Die Christologie der Logienquelle (Neukirchen-Vluyn 1977) 70. "Agrapha" in: TRE 2 (1978) 104. "Amt" in: TRE 2 (1978) 570. KERTELGE, K., "Offene Fragen zum Thema 'Geistliches Amt' und das neutestamentliche Verständnis von der 'repraesentatio Christi' " in: R. Schnackenburg et al. (eds.) Die Kirche des Anfanges. FS. H. Schürmann (Freiburg 1978) 588-90. "Autorität" in: TRE 5 (1980) 32, 35. JEREMIAS, J., Die Sprache des Lukasevangeliums (Göttingen 1980) 187.

10:17ff. STAEHELIN, E. Die Verkündigung des Reiches Gottes in der Kirche Jesu Christi I (1951) 68.

10:17-24 CHARLIER, C. "L'Action de grâces de Jésus (Luc 10,17-24 et Matth. 11,25-30)," BVieC 17 (1957) 87-99. MINEAR, P., To Heal and to Reveal (New York 1976) 11-13.

10:17-20 BARRETT, C. K. The Holy Spirit and the Gospel Tradition (1947) 63ff. LEIVESTAD, R. Christ the Conqueror (1954) 48ff. FLEW, R. N. Jesus and His Church (1956) 47-48, 77-78, 131n. BAUM-

BACH, G. Das Verständnis des Bösen in den synoptischen Evangelien (1963) 178ff. IWAND, H.-J. Predigt-Meditationen (1964) 99-104. OBENDIEK, H., in: Herr, tue meine Lippen auf Bd. 3 (1964) G. Eichholz ed., 138f. KRUSCHE, GPM 19 (1964-1965) 186ff. HAHN, F. Das Verständnis der Mission im Neuen Testament (²1965) 33. HARDER, G. in: Hören und Fragen Bd. 5,3 (1967) G. Eichholz & A. Falkenroth eds., 284ff. EISINGER, W. GPM 25 (1971) 211-17. LANGE, E. ed., Predigstudien für das Kirchenjahr 1970-1971 (1970) 67-71. HOFFMANN, P. Studien zur Theologie der Logienquelle (1972) 24f., 252-54, 259. LIGNÉE, M., "La mission des soixante-doize. Lc 10,1-12. 17-20" AssS 45 (1974) 64-74. MIYOSHI, M., Der Anfang des Reiseberichts Lk 9,51 - 10,24 (Rome 1974) 95-119. LUDOLF, U. and KOPPE, R., in: P.Krusche et al. (eds.) Predigtstudien für das Kirchenjahr 1976-1977. II (Stuttgart 1977) 40-46. SCHNEIDER, G., Das Evangelium nach Lukas (Gütersloh 1977) 240-41. STECK, K. G., in: GPM 31 (1976-1977) 204-11. JEWETT, R., Jesus against the Rapture (Philadelphia 1979) 34-50.

10:17-19 BETZ, H. D. Lukian von Samosata und das Neue Testament (1961) 29, 155, 175. MUSSNER, F. Die Wunder Jesu 1967) 49f.

10:17-18 BOUSSET, W. Die Religion des Judentums im Späthellenistischen Zeitalter (1966 = 1926) 341.

10:17 METZGER, B. M. "Seventy or Seventy-two Disciples?" NTS 6 (4, 1959) 299-306. JELLICOE, S. "St Luke and the Seventy-Two," (4, 1960) 319-21. DELLING, G. Die Zueignung des Heils in der Taufe (1961) 46. HAHN, F. Christologische Hoheitstitel (1963) 84, 85. KÜNZI, M. Das Naherwartungslogion Matthäus 10,23 (1970) 69, 72, 103f., 140. MIYOSHI, M., Der Anfang des Reiseberichts Lk 9,51 - 10,24 (Rome 1974) 96-99, 110-111. TALBERT, C. H., Literary Patterns, Theological Themes, and the Genre of Luke-Acts (Missoula 1974) 114. HOFFMANN, P. and EID, V., Jesus von Nazareth und eine christliche Moral (Freiburg 1975) 38. KRAFT, H., Die Entstehung des Christentums (Darmstadt 1981) 150.

10:18-19 MINEAR, P., To Heal and to Reveal (New York 1976) 35-37.

10:18 STAEHELIN, E. Die Verkündigung des Reiches Gottes in der Kirche Jesu Christi I (1951) 257. ROBINSON, J. M. Kerygma und historischer Jesus (1960) 143. FLENDER,H. Heil und Geschichte in der Theologie des Lukas (1965) 95. OTT, W. Gebet und Heil (1965) 76-78. JÜNGEL, E. Paulus und Jesus (1966) 189, 240. FLENDER, H. St Luke Theologian of Redemptive History (1967) 22, 83n., 103, 148, 149. ALDEN, R. L. "Lucifer, Who or What?" BullEvangTheolSoc 11 (1, 1968) 35-39. PERRIN, H., The Kingdom of God in the Teaching of Jesus (Philadelphia 1963) 76, 89,

114, 171, 186. ZMIJEWSKI, J., Die Eschatologiereden des Lukas-Evangeliums (Bonn 1972) 76, 387, 389, 404. LADD, G. E.,
A Theology of the New Testament (Grand Rapids 1974) 67, 297,
625. MIYOSHI, M., Der Anfang des Reiseberichts Lk 9,51 - 10,24
(Rome 1974) 99-101, 117-19. DUNN, J. D. G., Jesus and the Spirit
(London 1975) 33, 48, 65, 85. DUNN, J. D. G., Unity and Di-
versity in the New Testament (London 1977) 184-85. TRITES, A.
A., The New Testament Concept of Witness (Cambridge 1977) 195-
96. TÀRRECH, A. P., "Lc 10,18: La visió de la caiguda de Sa-
tanàs" RevCT 3 (1978) 217-43. SEYBOLD, K. and MÜLLER, U.,
Krankheit und Heilung (Stuttgart 1978) 97-98. MATTILL, A. J.,
Luke and the Last Things (Dillsboro 1979) 164-67. JEREMIAS,
J., Die Sprache des Lukasevangeliums (Göttingen 1980) 187-88.
KRAFT, H., Die Entstehung des Christentums (Darmstadt 1981)
151ff.

10:19-22 TREU, K. "Ein neues neutestamentliches Unzialfragment aus Damaskus (= 0253)," ZNW 55 (3-4, 1964) 274-77.

10:19-20 VOLZ, P. Die Eschatologie der Jüdischen Gemeinde (1934) 392,
400. JEREMIAS, J. Neutestamentliche Theologie I (1971) 74, 97-
99, 228, 242.

10:19 STAEHELIN, E. Die Verkündigung des Reiches Gottes in der
Kiche Jesu Christi I (1951) 136, 257. BULTMANN, R. Theologie
des Neuen Testaments (1965) 50f. OTT, W. Gebet und Heil (1965)
110-12. MIYOSHI, M., Der Anfang des Reiseberichts Lk 9,51 -
10,24 (Rome 1974) 101-07, 111-17. DUNN, J. D. G., Jesus and
the Spirit (London 1975) 72, 78, 81, 90. METZGER, B. M., The
Early Versions of the New Testament (Oxford 1977) 390.

10:20 FLEW, R. N. Jesus and His Church (1956) 52. GÄRTNER, B. The
Temple and the Community in Qumran and the New Testament
(1965) 98. DUNN, J. D. G. Baptism in the Holy Spirit (1970) 39,
53. JEREMIAS, J. Neutestamentliche Theologie I (1971) 20, 22,
26, 96, 99. DALTON, W. J., Christ's Proclamation to the Spirits
(Rome 1965) 147-48. MIYOSHI, M., Der Anfang des Reiseberichts Lk 9,51 - 10,54 (Rome 1974) 107-09, 117-19. KLIJN, A. F.
T., "Die syrische Baruch-Apokalyspe" in: W. G. Kümmel (ed.)
Jüdische Schriften aus hellenistisch-römischer Zeit. V. (Gütersloh
1976) 139 nla BERGMEIER, R., Glaube als Gabe nach Johannes
(Stuttgart 1980) 59. JEREMIAS, J., Die Sprache des Lukasevangeliums (Göttingen 1980) 188-89.

10:21-18:30 TALBERT, C. H., Literary Patterns, Theological Themes, and the
Genre of Luke-Acts (Missoula 1974) 51-55.

10:21ff. BLAIR, E. P. Jesus in the Gospel of Matthew (1960) 65.

10:21-24 KRECK, GPM 19 (1964-1965) 230ff. BRUNNER, P. in: Hören

und Fragen Bd. 5,3 (1967) G. Eichholz & A. Falkenroth eds., 342ff.
LEHMANN, M. Synoptische Quellenanalyse und die Frage nach
dem historischen Jesus (1970) 126-28. STECK, K. G. GPM 25
(1971) 260-70. MIYOSHI, M., Der Anfang des Reiseberichts Lk
9,51 - 10,24 (Rome 1974) 120-52. TALBERT, C. H., Literary
Patterns, Theological Themes, and the Genre of Luke-Acts (Missoula 1974) 51, 53. EDWARDS, R. A., A Theology of Q (Philadelphia 1976) 106-07. MINEAR, P., To Heal and to Reveal (New
York 1976) 41-45. BÖHMIG, W. and SIMPFENDÖRFER, G., in:
P. Krusche et al. (eds.) Predigtstudien für das Kirchenjahr 1976/
1977. II (Stuttgart 1977) 86-93. JOSUTTIS, M., in: GPM 31 (1976-
1977) 265-71. SCHNEIDER, G., Das Evangelium nach Lukas
(Gütersloh 1977) 242.

10:21-22 STONEHOUSE, N. B. The Witness of Matthew and Mark to Christ
(1944) 17. MANSON, T. W. The Teaching of Jesus (1945) 32, 95f.,
109-12. GUY, H. A. New Testament Prophecy (1947) 75ff. GILS,
F. Jésus Prophète d'Apres Les Evangiles Synoptiques (1957) 78-
82. KNOX, W. L. The Sources of the Synoptic Gospels II (1957)
140. WAINWRIGHT, A. W. The Trinity in the New Testament
(1962) 137-38, 177-78. CHRIST, F. Jesus Sophia (1970) 91-99.
JEREMIAS, J. Neutestamentliche Theologie I (1971) 21, 25, 33,
68, 70, 118f. HOFFMANN, P. Studien zur Theologie der Logienquelle (1972) 98-100, 101f., 104-42, 153f, 286ff., 305-07, 325f.
SCHULZ, S. Q Die Spruchquelle der Evangelisten (1972) 213-28.

10:21-22 HOFFMANN, P., ''Mk 8,31. Zur Herkunft und markinischen Re-
zeption einer alten Ueberlieferung'' in: P. Hoffmann (ed.)
Orientierung an Jesus. FS. J. Schmid (Freiburg 1973) 182-83. MI-
YOSHI, M., Der Anfang des Reisebeichts (Lk 9,51 - 10,24 (Rome
1974) 122-31. GRUNDMANN, W., ''Weisheit im Horizont des
Reiches Gottes. Eine Studie zur Verkündigung Jesu nach der
Spruchüberlieferung Q'' in: R. Schnackenburg et al. (eds.) Die
Kirche des Anfangs. FS. H. Schürmann (Leipzig 1977) 182-87.
POLAG, Die Christologie der Logienquelle (Neukirchen-Vluyn
1977) 160-62. SCHENKE, H. M., ''Die Tendenz der Weisheit zur
Gnosis'' in: B. Aland et al. (eds.) Gnosis. FS. H. Jonas (Göttingen
1978) 360-65. ''Auferstehung'' in TRE 4 (1979) 495. JEREMIAS,
J. Die Sprache des Lukasevangeliums (Göttingen 1980) 189.

10:21 FLEW, R. N. Jesus and His Church (1956) 62-65. GRUND-
MANN, W. NTS 5 (1958-1959) 201ff. SCHRAGE, W. Die kon-
kreten Einzelgebote in der paulinischen Paränese (1961) 243.
HAHN, F. Christologische Hoheitstitel (1963) 319. MARCHEL,
W. Abba, Père! Prière du Christ et des Chrétiens (1963) 149-65.
HENNECKE, E./SCHNEEMELCHER, W. Neutestamentliche
Apokryphen (1964) II 394. BOUSSET, W. Die Religion des Ju-

dentums im Späthellenistischen Zeitalter (1966 = 1926) 165, 187. JEREMIAS, J. Abba; Studien zur neutestamentlichen Theologie und Zeitgeschichte (1966) 56-59. BLACK, M. An Aramaic Approach to the Gospels and Acts (1967) 111f. NICKELS, P. Targum and New Testament (1967) 36. LANGE, J., Das Erscheinen des Auferstandenen im Evangelium nach Mattäus (Würzburg 1973) 158-61. MIYOSHI, M., Der Anfang des Reiseberichts Lk 9,52-10,24. Eine redaktionsgeschichtliche Untersuchung (Rome 1974) 134-37, 120-22, 125-26. METZGER, B. M. The Early Versions of the New Testament (Oxford 1977) 145. MEYER, B. F. The Aims of Jesus (London 1979) 169-70.

10:22 PALLIS, A., Notes on St. Luke and the Acts (London 1928) 22.MANSON, W. Jesus the Messiah (1948) 71-73, 107-09. BARRETT, C. K. The New Testament Background: Selected Documents (1956) 90. DELLING, G. Die Zueignung des Heils in der Taufe (1961) 95. HAHN, F. Christologische Hoheitstitel (1963) 321-26. SCHRAGE, W. Das Verhältnis des Thomas-Evangeliums zur Synoptischen Tradition und zu den Koptischen Evangelienübersetzungen (1964) 128. GRUNDMANN, W. NTS 12 (1965-1966) 42f. JEREMIAS, J. Abba; Studien zur neutestamentlichen Theologie und Zeitgeschichte (1966) 47-54. SCHREINER, J. Gestalt und Anspruch des neuen Testaments (1969) 14ff., 147. O'-NEILL, J. C. The Theology of Acts in its historical setting (1970) 20n, 34-35,IV. JEREMIAS, J. Neutestamentliche Theologie I (1971) 62-57, 246. JEREMIAS, J. New Testament Theology I (1971) 56-61, 258. DEHANDSCHUTTER, B., "L'Evangile selon Thomas" in: F. Neirynck (ed.) L'Evangile de Luc (Gembloux 1973) 291-92. LANGE, J., Das Erscheinen des Auferstandenen im Evangelium nach Mattäus (Würzburg 1973) 152, 155, 158-59, 161, 165-67, 172, 200-201, 208-13, 215, 230-32, 243-46, 314-15, 488, 495-97, 499-500, 504. ROBINSON, J. A. T., "The Use of the Fourth Gospel for Christology Today" in: B. Lindars/S. S. Smalley (eds.) Christ and the Spirit in the New Testament. FS. C. F. D. Moule (Cambridge 1973) 69-70, 73. MIYOSHI, M., Der Anfang des Reiseberichts Lk 9,51 - 10,24 (Rome 1974) 126-31.

10:23-37 BARTH, GPM 4 (1949-1950) 234ff. GOLLWITZER, GPM 9 (1954-1955) 213ff. DEHN, G. in: Herr, tue meine Lippen auf Bd. 1 (1957) G. Eichholz ed., 266-70. MERKEL/GEORGI/BALTZER, GPM 15 (1960-61) 245ff, DOERNE, M. Er kommt auch noch heute (1961) 129-32. Hephata, Predigtgedanken aus Vergangenheit und Gegenwart Reihe A, Bd. 5 (1966) 263-89. DREYFUS, F., "Que est mon prochain" AssS 66 (1966) 32-49.

10:23-26 PERRIN, N., Jesus and the Language of the Kingdom (London 1976) 37.

10:23-24 TILLICH, P. Das Neue Sein (1959) 93-96. BLAIR, E. P. Jesus in the Gospel of Matthew (1960) 103.KAESEMANN, E. Exegetische Versuche und Besinnungen (1964) I 246. ROLOFF. J. Apostolat-Verkündigung-Kirche (1965) 183f. JÜNGEL, E. Paulus und Jesus (1966) 112, 188. McNAMARA, M. The New Testament and the Palestinian Targum to the Pentateuch (1966) 145. SATAKE, A. Die Gemeindeordnung in der Johanesapokalypse (1966) 177. CHRIST, F. Jesus Sophia (1970) 81, 93, 98, 99. GRIMM, W., "Selige Augenzeugen, Luk. 10, 23f. Alttestamentlicher Hintergrund und ursprünglicher Sinn," ThZ 26 (3, 1970) 172-83. VÖGTLE, A. Das Evangelium und die Evangelien (1971) 240-42. HOFFMANN, P. Studien zur Theologie der Logienquelle (1972) 70f., 210-12. SCHULZ, S. Q Die Spruchquelle der Evangelisten (1972) 419-21.SCHNIDER, F., Jesus der Prophet (Freiburg 1973) 75, 176ff., 259. MIYOSHI, M. Der Anfang des Reiseberichts Lk 9,51 - 10,24 (Rome 1974) 131-34. HOFFMANN, P. and EID, V., Jesus von Nazareth und eine christliche Moral (Freiburg 1975) 35-36. EDWARDS, R. A., A Theology of Q (Philadelphia 1976) 64-65. POLAG, A., Die Christologie der Logienquelle (Neukirchen-Vluyn 1977) 162.

10:23 WANKE, J., Die Emmauserzählung (Leipzig 1973) 15.

10:24 SCHÜRMANN, H. "Sprachliche Reminiszenzen an abgeänderte oder ausgelassene Bestandteilt der Spruchsammlung im Lukas- und Matthäusevangelium," NTS 6 (1959-1960) 209f. KAESEMANN, E. Exegetische Versuche und Besinnungen (1964) II 91. McNAMARA, M. The New Testament and the Palestinian Targum to the Pentateuch (1966) 240-242, 244f. NICKELS, P. Targum and New Testament (1967) 36. HASLER, V. Amen (1969) 66. KAESEMANN, E. New Testament Questions of Today (1969) 92.

10:25ff. HAHN, F. Das Verständnis der Mission im Neuen Testament (²1965) 113. KNOW, W, L. The Sources of the Synoptic Gospels II (1957) 57f. GOULDER, M. D. Midrash and Lection in Matthew (1974) 55f., 60. DAVIES, W. D., The Sermon on the Mount (Cambridge 1966) 146-47. GERSTENBERGER, G., und SCHRAGE, W., Leiden (Stuttgart 1977) 220-21; ET: J. E. Steeley, Suffering (Nashville 1980) 254-55.

10:25-37 BORNHÄUSSER, K. Studien zum Sondergut des Lukas (1934) 65-80. MORGAN, G. C. The Parables and Metaphors of Our Lord (1943) 176ff. BRUNNER, E. Saat und Frucht (1946) 73-86. MOORE, G. F. Judaism (1946) II 174n. RENGSTORF, K. H. Das Evangelium nach Lukas (1949) 138f. CRANFIELD, C. E. B., "The Good Samaritan (Luke 10, 25-37)," ThT XI (1954) 368-72. LOEWENICH, W. von, Luther als Ausleger der Synoptiker (1954) 44ff., 187f. MICHAELIS, D. W. Die Gleichnisse Jesu (1956) 203-12.

MERKEL/GEORGI/BALTZER, GPM 15 (1960-1961) 245ff.
GOLLWITZER, H. Die Gleichnis vom Barmberzigen Samariter
(1962). JEREMIAS, J. Das Gleichnisse Jesu (1962) 200-03.
BARTSCH, H. W., Wachet aber zu jeder Zeit! (Hamburg-Bergstedt 1963) 96-100. LOCKYER, H. All the Parables of the Bible
(1963) 259ff. SPICQ, C. "The Charity of the Good Samaritan—
Luke 10:25-37," Bible Today 1 (6, 1963) 360-66. DERRETT, J.
D. M. "Law in the New Testament: Fresh Light on the Parable of
the Good Samaritan," NTS 11 (1, 1964) 22-37. GIAVINI, G. "Il
'prossimo' nella parabola del buon samaritano," RivB 12 (4, 1964)
419-21. BOLEWSKI, H. in: Kleine Predigt-Typologie III (1965)
L. Schmidt ed., 143-50. CASTELLINO, G. R. "Il Sacerdote e il
Levita nella parabola del buon samaritano," Divinitas 9 (1, 1965)
134-40. FUNK, R. W. "The Old Testament in Parable. A Study
of Luke 10:25-37," Encounter 26 (1, 1965) 251-67. DE DIEGO,
J. R. "Quién es mi projimo?" EstEc 41 (156, 1966) 93-109. JÜN-
GEL, E. Paulus und Jesus (1966) 160, 169. MONSELEWSKI, W.
Der barmherzige Samariter (1967). FURNESS, J. M. "Fresh Light
on Luke 10:25-37," ET 80 (6, 1969) 182. LINNEMANN, E.
Gleichnisse Jesu (1969) 57ff., 143ff. SMART, J. D. The Quiet
Revolution (1969) 56-70. BARCLAY, W. And Jesus Said (1970)
79-85. BURCHARD, C., "Das doppelte Liebesgebot" in: E. Lohse
(ed.) Der Ruf Jesus und die Antword der Gemeinde. FS. J. Je-
remias (Göttingen 1970) 39-62. DERRETT, J. D. M. Law in the
New Testament (1970) 208-27, 223 n.7. ZIMMERMANN, H. in:
Die Zeit Jesu. Festschrift für H. Schlier (1970) G. Bornkamm & K.
Rahner eds., 58-69. EICHHOLZ, G. Gleichnisse der Evangelien
(1971) 148-78. JERVELL, J. "The Lost Sheep of the House of Israel" in: Luke and the People of God (Minneapolis 1972) 113-132.
CRESPY, G. "La parabole dite: 'Le bon Samaritain.' Recherches
structurales," EThR 48 (1, 1973) 61-79. JENS, W. (ed.) Der
barmherzigen Samariter (Stuttgart 1973). LAMBRECHT, J., "The
Message of the Good Samaritan (Lk 10:25-37) LSt 5 (1974) 121-
25. SELLIN, G. "Lukas als Gleichniserzähler: Die Erzählung vom
barmherzigen Samariter (Lk 10,35-37)" ZNW 65 (1974) 166-89.
TALBERT, C. H., Literary Patterns, Theological Themes, and the
Genre of Luke-Acts (Missoula 1974) 51, 53. TERNANT, P., "Le
bon Samaritain. Lc 10, 25-37" AssS 46 (1974) 66-77. GOPPELT,
L., Theologie des Neuen Testaments. I (Göttingen 1975) 149-50.
SELLIN, G., "Lukas als Gleichniserzähler: Die Erzählung vom
barmherzigen Samariter (Lk 10:25-37)" ZNW 66 (1975) 19-60.
PERRIN, N., Jesus and the Language of the Kingdom (London
1976) 84. EULENSTEIN, R., " 'Und wer ist mein Nächster?'. Lk
10,25-37 in der Sicht eines klassischen Philologen" ThG 67 (1977)

127-45. MANEK, J., . . . und brachte Frucht (Berlin 1977) 82-90. SCHNEIDER, G., Das Evangelium nach Lukas (Gütersloh 1977) 246, 260. YOUNG, N. H., " 'Once again, Now, "Who is my Neighbour?" ' A Comment" EQ 49 (1977) 178-79. GEWALT, D., "Der 'Barmherzige Samariter'. Zu Lukas 10,25-37" EvTh 38 (1978) 403-17. KIEFFER, R., "Om Jesu under och liknelser. Semiotiska analyser" SEA 43 (1978) 98-106. BUKOWSKI, P., in: GPM 33 (1979) 350-57. KIEFFER, R., "Analyse sémiotique et commentaire. Quelques réflexions à propos d'études de Luc 10.25-37." NTS 25 (1979) 454-68. MATTILL, A. J., "The Anonymous Victim (Luke 10:25-37). A new look at the Story of the Good Samaritan" Unitarian Universalist Christian (Boston 1979) 38-54. WINK, W., "The Parable of the Compassionate Samaritan: A Communal Exegesis Approach" RevEx 76 (1979) 199-217. FEUILLET, A., "Le bon Samaritain (Luc 10,25-37). Sa signification christologique et l'universalisme de Jésus" EsVie 90 (1980) 337-51. HEUTGER, N., "Die lukanischen Samaritanererzählungen in religionspädagogischer Sicht" in: W. Haubeck/M. Bachmann (eds.) Wort in der Zeit FS. K. H. Rengstorf (Leiden 1980) 280-83.

10:25-35 TOLBERT, M. A., Perspectives on the Parables (Philadelphia 1979) 59.

10:25-32 FURNISH, V. P. The Love Command in the New Testament (1972) 34-45.

10:25-29 BERGER, K. Die Gesetzesauslegung Jesu (1940) 182, 232-42, 257.

10:25-28 HIRSCH, E. Frühgeschichte des Evangeliums (1941) 56-58. MANSON, T. W. The Teaching of Jesus (1945) 302-05. BUTLER, B. C. The Originality of St Matthew (1951) 19ff. SUHL, A. Die Funktion der alttestamentlichen Zitate und Anspielungen im Markusevangelium (1965) 10,87ff. JÜNGEL, E. Paulus und Jesus (1966) 169f., 172. BORNKAMM, G. "Das Doppelgebot der Liebe", Geschichte und Glauben I (1968) 37-45. BLANK, J. Schriftauslegung in Theorie und Praxis (1969) 221, 222-27. LOHSE, E. et al., eds., Der Ruf Jesu und die Antwort der Gemeinde (1970) 39-62. BORNKAMM, G. Geschichte und Glaube II (1971) 92-94. SCHRAMM, G. Der Markus-Stoff bei Lukas (1971) 47-49. NISSEN, A., Gott und der Nächste im antiken Judentum (Tübingen 1974). TALBERT, C. H., Literary Patterns, Theological Themes, and the Genre of Luke-Acts (Missoula 1974) 52-53. STRECKER, G., (ed.) Jesus Christus in Historie und Theologie. FS. H. Conzelmann (Tübingen 1975) 311, 317ff. FULLER, R. H., "The Double Commandment of Love - A Test Case for the Criteria of Authenticity" in: L. Schottroff et al. (eds.) Essays in the

Love Commandment (Philadelphia 1978) 41-56. RIVKIN, E., A Hidden Revolution (Nashville 1978) 117.

10:25-27 PIROT, J. Paraboles et Allégories Evangeliques (1949) 163-77. LINDIJER, C. H. "Oude en nieuwe visies op de gelijkenis van de barmhartige Samaritaan" NedThT 15 (I, 1960) 11-23. KLEIN, G. GPM 28 (1973) 393-401.

10:25 HAHN, F. Christologische Hoheitstitel (1963) 76. GOULDER, M. D. Type and History in Acts (1964) 58, 275f. BOUSSET, W. Die Religion des Judentums im Späthellenistischen Zeitalter (1966 = 1926) 166. NICKELS, P. Targum and New Testament (1967) 36. METZGER, B. M., The Early Versions of the New Testament (Oxford 1977) 89. JEREMIAS, J., Die Sprache des Lukasevangeliums (Göttingen 1980) 190.

10:27ff. STONEHOUSE, N. B. The Witness of Matthew and Mark to Christ (1944) 200.

10:27 BEST, E. One Body in Christ (1955) 220. SCHRAGE, W. Das Verhältnis des Thomas-Evangeliums zur Synoptischen Tradition und zu den Koptischen Evangelienübersetzungen (1964) 70. HOLTZ, T. Untersuchungen über die Alttestamentlichen Zitate bei Lukas (1968) 64-68. PIPER, J., "Is Self-Love Biblical?" ChrTo 21 (1977) 1150-53.

10:28 JÜNGEL, E. Paulus und Jesus (1966) 211.

10:29ff. BORNKAMM, G. Jesus von Nazareth (1956) 101ff.

10:29-37 JÜLICHER, D. A. Die Gleichnisreden Jesu (1910) 585-98. HIRSCH, E. Frühgeschichte des Evangeliums (1941) 58-60, 211f. LEENHARDT, F. "La parabole due Samaritain. Schema d'une exegese existentialiste," in: Aux Sources de la Tradition Chrétienne (1950) M. M. Goguel ed., 132-38. LILLIE, W. Studies in New Testament Ethics (1961) 167f. SANCHIS, D. "Samaritanus ille. L'éxègese augustinienne de la parabole du bon Samaritain," RechSR 49 (3, 1961) 406-25. DOWNEY, G. "Who is My Neighbor? The Greek and Roman Answer," AThR 47 (1, 1965) 3-65. MUSSNER, F. "Der Begriff des 'Nächsten' in der Verkündigung Jesu. Dargelegt am Gleichnis vom barmberzigen Samariter," Praesentia Salutis (1967) 125. KAHLEFELD, H. " 'Wer ist mein Nächster?' Das Lehrstück vom barmherzigen Samariter und die heutige Situation," BuK 24 (3, 1969) 74-77. LEHMANN, M. Synoptische Quellenanalyse und die Frage nach dem historischen Jesus (1970) 153. REICKE, B. "Der barmherzige Samariter," in Verborum Veritas, Festschrift für Gustav Stählin (1970) O. Böcher & K. Haacker eds., 103-09. RAMAROSON, L., "Comme 'Le Bon Samaritain', ne chercher qu'à aimer (Lc 10,29-37)" Biblica 56 (1975) 533-36. SANDERS, J. T. Ethics in the New Testament

(Philadelphia 1975) 38. DRURY, J., Tradition and Design in Luke's Gospel (Atlanta 1976) 77-78. PERRIN, N., Jesus and the Language of the Kingdom (London 1976) 6, 8, 55, 96-97, 102, 120, 128,143, 160, 203. TRUDINGER, L. P. "Once Again, Now, 'Who is my Neighbour?' " EQ 48 (1976) 160-63.

10:29 KNOX, W. L. The Sources of the Synoptic Gospels (1957) 115. SCHWANK, B. " 'Wer ist mein Nächster?' (Lk 19,29), Eine Erklärung des Evangeliums des 12. Sonntags nach Pfingsten," BenMon 33 (7-8, 1957) 292-95. SCHRAGE, W. Die konkreten Einzelgebote in der paulinischen Paränese (1961) 209. JÜNGEL, E. Paulus und Jesus (1966) 169f. AALEN, S. NTS 13 (1966-1967)1ff. STROBEL, A. Erkenntnis und Bekenntnis der Sünde in neutestamentlicher Zeit (1968) 43. PALLIS, A., Notes on St. Luke and the Acts (London (1951) 22. JEREMIAS, J., Die Sprache des Lukasevangeliums (Göttingen 1980) 190.

10:30ff. FINDLAY, J. A. Jesus and His Parables (1951) 62ff. KLEMM, H. G. "Schillers ethisch-ästhetische Variationen zum Thema Lk 10,30ff.," KuD 17 (2, 1971) 127-40.

10:30-37 WILKINSON, F. H. "Oded: Proto-Type of the Good Samaritan," ET 69 (3, 1957) 94. GERHARDSSON, B. The Good Samaritan - The Good Shepherd? Coniectanea Neotestamentica XVI (1958). BINDER, H. "Das Gleichnis vom barmherzigen Samariter," ThZ 15 (3, 1959) 176-94. HARRINGTON, W. J. A Key to the Parables (1964) 149-54. HAHN, F. Das Verständnis der Mission im Neuen Testament (²1965) 23. JÜNGEL, E. Paulus und Jesus (1966) 99, 170. DANIEL, C. Les Esseniens et l'arrière-fond historique de la parabole du Bon Samaritain," NovTest 11 (1-2, 1969) 71-104. SEITZ, D. J. F. NTS 16 (1969-1970) 47f. SANDERS, J. T. Ethics in the New Testament (Philadelphia 1975) 6-9, 17, 25, 26, 38, 39, 100.

10:30-35 BISER, E. Die Gleichnisse Jesu (1965) 93ff., 116. JÜNGEL, E. Paulus und Jesus (1966) 169-73. VAN DEN EYNDE, P. "Le Bon Samaritain," BVieC 70 (1966) 22-35. KLEMM, H. G., Das Gleichnis vom Barmherzigen Samariter. Grundzüge der Auslegung im 16./17. Jahrhundert (Stuttgart 1973). SEVEN, F. "Hermeneutische Erwägungen zur poetischen Realisation eines neutestamentlichen Textes ('Sprachereignis' bei Eberhard Jüngel und Erhardt Güttgemanns), LiBi 29-30 (1973) 52-55. CROSSAN, J. D., "The Good Samaritan: Towards a Generic Definition of Parable" Semeia 2 (1974) 82-112. FUNK, R. W., "The good Samaritan as Metaphor" Semeia 2 (1974) 74-81. PATTE, D., "An Analysis of Narrative Structure and the Good Samaritan" Semeia 2 (1974) 1-26. CONZELMANN, H. and LINDEMANN, A., Arbeitsbuch zum Neuen Testament (Tübingen 1975) 85-86. PATTE,

D., "Structural Network in Narrative: The Good Samaritan" Soundings 58 (1975) 221-42. FUNK, R. W., "The Narrative Parables: The Birth of a Language Tradition" in: J. Jervell/W. A. Meeks (eds.) God's Christ and His People. FS. N. A. Dahl (New York 1977) 43-50.

10:30.36 SCHALIT, A. König Herodes (1969) 721.

10:30 BISHOP, E. F. F. " 'Down from Jerusalem to Jericho', " EQ 35 (2, 1963) 97-102. JEREMIAS, J., Die Sprache des Lukasevangeliums (Göttingen 1980) 191.

10:31-32 ZMIJEWSKI, J. Die Eschatologiereden des Lukas-Evangeliums (Bonn 1972) 360, 456, 458, 524.

10:31 NICKELS, P. Targum and New Testament (1967) 36.

10:32 NICKELS, P. Targum and New Testament (1967) 37. "Barmherzigkeit" in: TRE 5 (1980) 227, 234. JEREMIAS, J., Die Sprache des Lukasevangeliums (Göttingen 1980) 191.

10:34 METZGER, B. M., The Early Versions of the New Testament (Oxford 1977) 207. SCHOLZ, G., "Ästhetische Beobachtungen am Gleichnis vom Reichen Mann und Armen Lazarus und an drei anderen Gleichnissen" LiBi 43 (1978) 67-74. JEREMIAS, J., Die Sprache des Lukasevangeliums (Göttingen 1980) 192.

10:35 KNOX, W. L. The Sources of the Synoptic Gospels II (1957) 116. BLACK, M. An Aramaic Approach to the Gospels and Acts (1967) 135f. JEREMIAS, J., Die Sprache des Lukasevangeliums (Göttingen 1980) 192.

10:36-41 SMART, J. D. The Quiet Revolution (1969) 29-42.

10:36-37 JÜNGEL, E. Paulus und Jesus (1966) 169f.

10:36 JEREMIAS, J., Die Sprache des Lukasevangeliums (Göttingen 1980) 192-93.

10:37 EGGER, W., Frohbotschaft und Lehre (Frankfurt a. M. 1976) 54, 78. "Barmherzigkeit" in: TRE 5 (1980) 225,235.

10:38ff. STAEHELIN, E. Die Verkündigung des Reiches Gottes in der Kirche Jesu Christi I (1951) 375. KNOX, W. L. The Sources of the Synoptic Gospels II (1957) 57, 59. KEMMER, A. "Maria and Martha. Zur Deutungsgeschichte von Lk 10,38ff. im alten Mönchtum," EuA 40 (5, 1964) 355-67.

10:38-42 VAN STOCKUM, TH. C. "Lucas 10, 38-42 Catholice, Calvinisticae, Mystice," NedThT 12 (1957-1958) 32-37. PUZO, F. "Marta y Maria. Nota exegética a Lc 10,38-42 y 1 Cor 7,29-35," EstEc 34 (134-35, 1960) 851-57. BRUNNER, P. in: Herr, tue meine Lippen auf Bd. 3 (1964) G. Eichholz ed., 115ff. IWAND, H.-J. Predigt-Meditationen (1964) 628-32. BOHREN, R. GPM 19 (1964-1965) 105-10. QUERVAIN, A., de, in: Hören und Fragen Bd. 5,3

(1967) G. Eicholz & A. Falkenroth eds., 171ff. BRANDENBUR-GER, E./BALTZER, K./MERKEL, F. GPM 25 (1970) 119-24. LANGE, E. ed., Predigtstudien für das Kirchenjahr 1970-1971 (1970) 133-37. SCHILLE, G. Das vorsynoptische Judenchristentum (1970) 76-79. MAGASS, W. "Maria und Martha-Kirche und Haus. Thesen zu einer institutionellen Konkurrenz (Lk 10,38-42)," LiBi 27-28 (1973) 2-5. TALBERT, C. H., Literary Patterns, Theological Themes, and the Genre of Luke-Acts (Missoula 1974) 51, 54. SANDERS, J. T., Ethics in the New Testament (Philadelphia 1975) 38. SCHMIDT, E. R. and KIRCHGÄSSNER, A., in: P. Krusche et al. (eds.) Predigtstudien für das Kirchenjahr 1976-1977. I (Stuttgart 1976) 118-24. GEENSE, A., in: GPM 31 (1976-1977) 111-16. SCHNEIDER, G., Das Evangelium nach Lukas (Gütersloh 1977) 252. KNOCKAERT, A., "Structural Analysis of the Biblical Text" LuVit 33 (1978) 471-81. CHILTON, B., "The Gospel of Jesus and the Ministry of Women" ModCh 22 (1978-1979) 18-21. SWIDLER, L., Biblical Affirmations of Woman (Philadelphia 1979) 192, 196, 216, 273, 311. "Beruf" in: TRE 5 (1980) 660. MALY, E. H., "Women and the Gospel of Luke" BThB 10 (1980) 99-104. HINZ, C., in: GPM 35 (1981) 142-50. KRAFT, H., Die Entstehung des Christentums (Darmstadt 1981) 120, 133. PIETRON, J. and BARTELS, C., "Sonntag vor der Passionszeit (Estomihi) Lukas 10:38-42: Wie gelingt christliches Leben?" in: P. Krusche et al. (eds.) Predigtstudien für das Kirchenjahr 1980-1981. I (Stuttgart 1980) 127-134.

10:38 NICKELS, P. Targum and New Testament (1967) 37. WANKE, J., Die Emmauserzählung (Leipzig 1973) 101. TALBERT, C. H., Literary Patterns, Theological Themes, and the Genre of Luke-Acts (Missoula 1974) 114. "Aramäisch" in: TRE 3 (1978) 608. GERSTENBERGER, E. S. and SCHRAGE, W., Frau und Mann (Stuttgart 1980) 116. JEREMIAS, J., Die Sprache des Lukasevangeliums (Göttingen 1980) 193.

10:39 HAHN, F. Christologische Hoheitstitel (1963) 85. NICKELS, P. Targum and New Testament (1967) 37. JEREMIAS, J., Die Sprache des Lukasevangeliums (Göttingen 1980) 193-94.

10:40 HAHN, F. Christologische Hoheitstitel (1963) 84, 85. NICKELS, P. Targum and New Testament (1967) 37.

10:40-41 "Aramäisch" in: TRE 3 (1978) 608. JEREMIAS, J., Die Sprache des Lukasevangeliums (Göttingen 1980) 194.

10:41-42 ALAND, K. NTS 12 (1965-1966) 197f.

10:41 HAHN, F. Christologische Hoheitstitel (1963) 85. METZGER, B. M., The Early Versions of the New Testament (Oxford 1977) 41. JEREMIAS, J., Die Sprache des Lukasevangeliums (Göttingen 1980) 194.

10:42 SUDBRACK, J. " 'Nur eines ist notwendig' (Lk 10,42)," CuL 37 (3, 1964) 161-64. BAKER, A. "One Thing Necessary," CBQ 27 (2, 1965) 127-37. AUGUSTEN, M. NTS 14 (1967-1968) 581f. SANFORD, J. A., The Kingdom Within (New York 1970) 159-60. THEUNISSEN, M., "Ὁ αἰτῶν λαμβάνει. Der Gebetsglaube Jesu und die Zeitlichkeit des Christseins" in: Jesus, Ort der Erfahrung Gottes (Basel 1976) 22. DUPONT, J., "De quoi est-il besoin (Lk. 10:42)?" in: E. Best/R. McL. Wilson (eds.) Text and Interpretation. FS. M. Black (Cambridge 1979) 115-20. JEREMIAS, J., Die Sprache des Lukasevangeliums (Göttingen 1980) 194-95.

———————————

11 DAVIES, W. D., The Sermon on the Mount (Cambridge 1966) 4.

11:1ff. BLASS, F. Philosophy of the Gospels (1898) 174ff.

11:1-14 SCHNEIDER, G. Der Herr unser Gott (1965) 137-41.

11:1-13 RENGSTORF, K. H. Das Evangelium nach Lukas (1949) 142f. KNOX, W. L. The Sources of the Synoptic Gospels II (1957) 30, 45, 60. IWAND, H.-J. Predigt-Meditationen (1964) 71-76. OTT, W. Gebet und Heil (1965) 92-123. TALBERT, C. H., Literary Patterns, Theological Themes, and the Genre of Luke-Acts (Missoula 1974) 52, 54. VELLANICKAL, M., "Prayer-Experience in the Gospel of Luke" Biblebhashyam 2 (1976) 23-43.

11:1-10 LOCKYER, H. All the Parables of the Bible (1963) 264ff.

11:1-4 LOHMEYER, E. Das Vater-unser (1946). SCOTT, E. F. The Lord's Prayer (1951). OTOMO, Y. Nachfolge Jesu und Anfänge der Kirche im Neuen Testament (1970) 70-80. SCHULZ, S. Q Die Spruchquelle der Evangelisten (1972) 84-93. ELLIOTT, J. K. "Did the Lord's Prayer Originate With John the Baptist?" ThZ 29 (3, 1973) 215. EDWARDS, R. A., A Theology of Q (Philadelphia 1976) 107-08. SCHNEIDER, G. Das Evangelium nach Lukas (Gütersloh 1977) 255.

11:1-2 OTT, W. Gebet und Heil (1965) 92-94. BOUSSET, W. Die Religion des Judentums im Späthellenistischen Zeitalter (1966 = 1926) 178.

11:1 KNOX, W. L. The Sources of the Synoptic Gospels II (1957) 26, 60. HAHN, F. Christologische Hoheitstitel (1963) 84, 85. OTT, W. Gebet und Heil (1965) 85, 91, 94, 96f., 99, 114. JÜNGEL, E. Paulus und Jesus (1966) 155. JEREMIAS, J. Neutestamentliche

Theologie I (1971) 167, 191f. NEIRYNCK, F., "La Matière Marcienne dans Luc" in: F. Neirynck (ed.) L'Evangile de Luc (Gembloux 1973) 184-92. TALBERT, C. H., Literary Patterns, Theological Themes, and the Genre of Luke-Acts (Missoula 1974) 114. MEDIAVILLA, R., "La Oraciòn de Jesus en el tercer evangelio" (Mayeutica 1978) 5-34. JEREMIAS, J., Die Sprache des Lukasevangeliums (Göttingen 1980) 195.

11:2ff. STAEHELIN, E. Die Verkündigung des Reiches Gottes in der Kirche Jesus Christi I (1951) 68. KNOX, W. L. The Sources of the Synoptic Gospels II (1957) 26.

11:2-4 THIELICKE, H. Das Gebet das die Welt umspannt (1945). LEANEY,R. "The Lucan Text of the Lord's Prayer (Lk. xi 2-4)," NovTest 1 (1956) 103-11. LÜTHI, W. The Lord's Prayer (1961 = 1946). BAUMBACH, G. Das Verständnis des Bösen in den synoptischen Evangelien (1963) 156ff. EBELING, G. Vom Gebet (1963). OTT, W. Gebet und Heil (1965) 91, 112-23. STUHLMACHER, P. Gerechtigkeit Gottes bei Paulus (1965) 252-54. VICEDOM, G. F. Gebet für die Welt (1965). JEREMIAS, J. Abba; Studien zur neutestamentlichen Theologie und Zeitgeschichte (1966) 152-71. JÜNGEL, E. Paulus und Jesus (1966) 155. REUMANN, J. Jesus in the Church's Gospels (1968) 92-108. FREUDENBERGER, R. "Zum Text der zweiten Vaterunserbitte," NTS 15 (1968-1969) 430ff. SCHWARZ, G. "Matthäus VI:91-13/Lukas XI;2-4," NTS 15 (1968-1969) 233ff. KNÖRZER, W. Vater Unser (1969). JEREMIAS, J. in: New Testament Issues (1970) R. Batey Ed., 88-101. JEREMIAS, J. Neutestamentliche Theologie I (1971) 188-96. JEREMIAS, J. New Testament Theology I (1971) 193ff. HOFFMANN, P. Studien zur Theologie der Logienquelle (1972) 4, 39f. CONZELMANN, H. and LINDEMANN, A., Arbeitsbuch zum Neuen Testament (Tübingen 1975) 27. HARNER, P. B., Understanding the Lord's Prayer (Philadelphia 1975). SIMON, L., "La prière non religieuse chez Luc" FY 74 (1975) 8-22. VÖGTLE, A., "Der 'eschatologische' Bezug der Wir-Bitten des Vaterunsers" in: E. E. Ellis/E. Grässer (eds.) Jesus und Paulus. FS. W. G. Kümmel (Göttingen 1975) 344-63. PERRIN, N., Jesus and the Language of the Kingdom (London 1976) 41, 47-48. BIGUZZI, G., "Mc 11,23-25 e il Pater" RivB 27 (1979) 57-68. MEYER, B. F., The Aims of Jesus (London 1979) 208. "Bergpredigt" in: TRE 5 (1980) 607. EDMONDS, P., "The Lucan Our Father: A Summary of Luke's Teaching on Prayer?" ET 91 (1980) 140-43.

11:2.5-8 SCHÜRMANN, H. "Sprachliche Reminiszenzen an abgeänderte oder ausgelassene Bestandteile der Spruchsammlung im Lukas- und Matthäusevangelium," NTS 6 (1959-1960) 209f.

11:2-3 HUNTER, A. M. Design for Life (1953) 64-74.

11:2.4 MOORE, G. F. Judaism (1946) II 94n, 205n, 208n.

11:2 ROBINSON, J. M. Kergyma und historischer Jesus (1960) 143.
GRUNDMANN, W. Das Evangelium nach Lukas (1961) 229-31.
MARCHEL, W. Abba, Père! La Prière du Christ et des Chrétiens
(1963) 191-202. YATES, J. E. The Spirit and the Kingdom (1963)
195ff. WURZINGER, A. "Es komme Dein Königreich. Zum Ge-
betsanliegen nach Lukas," BuL 38 (2, 1964-1965) 89-94. BRAUN,
H. Qumran und NT II (1966) 162, 189, 213, 252. NICKELS, P.
Targum and New Testament (1967) 37. FREUDENBERGER, R.
"Zum Text der zweiten Vaterunserbitte." NTS 15 (4, 1969) 419-
32. JEREMIAS, J. Neutestamentliche Theologie I (1971) 21f., 40f.,
68, 70, 100, 103. DUNN, J. D. G., Jesus and the Spirit (London
1975) 21, 24-25, 41, 240. GOPPELT, L., Theologie des Neuen
Testaments. I (Göttingen 1975) 250-51. POLAG, A., Die Christologie der Logienquelle (Neukirchen-Vluyn 1977) 49. THÜS-
ING, W., "Die Bitten des johanneischen Jesus in dem Gebet Joh.
17 und die Intentionen Jesu von Nazaret" in: R. Schnackenburg et
al. (eds.) Die Kirche des Anfangs. FS. H. Schürmann (Freiburg
1978) 316-19. SCHLOSSER, J., "Le règne de Dieu dans les dits
de Jésus" RevSR 53 (1979) 164-76. HARRINGTON, D. J., God's
People in Christ (Philadelphia 1980) 25.

11:3 VOGT, E. "De initiis urbis Jericho," Biblica 35 (1954) 136-37.
NICKELS, P. Targum and New Testament (1967) 37. OR-
CHARD, B. "The Meaning of ton epiousion (Mt 6:11 = Lk 11:3),"
BThB 3 (3, 1973) 274-82. BRAUN, F.-M., "Le pain dont nous
avons besoin. Mt. 6, 11; Lc 11, 3" NRTh 100 (1978) 559-68.
MATTILL, A. J., Luke and the Last Things (Dillsboro 1979)
115:21.

11:4 JEREMIAS, J. Neutestamentliche Theologie I (1971) 25, 27, 196,
234. SANFORD, J. A., The Kingdom Within (New York 1970)
134-36. BAUER, J. B., Scholia Biblica et Patristica (Graz 1972)
228. MOULE, C. F. D., "An Unsolved Problem in the Tempta-
tion-Clause in the Lord's Prayer" RThR 33 (1974) 65-75. WIL-
LIS, G. G., "Lead Us Not Into Temptation" DRev 93 (1975) 281-
88. POLAG, A., Die Christologie der Logienquelle (Neukirchen-
Vluyn 1977) 77. MOULE, C. F. D., " '. . . As we forgive. . . ' -
A Note on the Distinction between Deserts and Capacity in the Understanding of Forgiveness" in: E. Bammel et al. (eds.) Donum
Gentilicium. FS. D. Daube (Oxford 1978) 68-77. PRAST, F.,
Presbyter und Evangelium in nachapostolischer Zeit (Stuttgart 1979)
67-68. JEREMIAS, J., Die Sprache des Lukasevangeliums (Göttingen 1980) 195-96.

11:5ff. FINDLAY, J. A. Jesus and His Parables (1951) 65ff. STAE-
HELIN, E. Die Verkündigung des Reiches Gottes in der Kirche Jesu

Christi I (1951) 328. GERSTENBERGER, G. and SCHRAGE, W., Leiden (Stuttgart 1977) 234; ET: J. E. Steeley, Suffering (Nashville 1980) 269-70.

11:5-13 BRUNNER, E. Saat und Frucht (1946) 127-39. BORNKAMM, G. "Bittet, suchet, klopfet an". EvTh 13 (1953) 1-5. Glaubet an den Gottgesandten, Predigtgedanken aus Vergangenheit und Gegenwart Reihe C, Bd. 2 (1962) 240ff. GEORGI/MERKEL, GPM 17 (1963) 201-206. STECK, K. G., in: Herr, tue meine Lippen auf Bd. 3 (1964) G. Eichholz ed., 242ff. MÜLLER-SCHWEFE, H. R. GPM 23/2 (1968-1969) 199-204. OTTO, G. Denken-um zu glauben (1970) 129-33. GABRIS, K., in: GPM 29 (1975) 238-44. LUZ, U. and WINTZER, F., in: P. Krusche et al. (eds.) Predigtstudien für das Kirchenjahr 1975-1976. III/2 (Stuttgart 1975) 51-59. BAILEY, K. E., Poet and Peasant (Grand Rapids 1976). RICKARDS, R. R., "The Translation of Luke 11.5-13" BTr 28 (1977) 239-43.

11:5-9 SWIDLER, L., Biblical Affirmations of Woman (Philadelphia 1979) 166.

11:5-8 JÜLICHER, D. A. Die Gleichnisreden Jesu (1910) 268-76, 286ff. MICHAELIS, D. W. Die Gleichnisse Jesu (1956) 230-36. KNOX, W. L. The Sources of the Synoptic Gospels II (1957) 30. DUPONT, D. J. Les Béatitudes (1958) 71-73. JEREMIAS, J. Die Gleichnisse Jesu (1962) 85f., 96, 105, 155, 157-59. OTT, W. Gebet und Heil (1965) 99-102, 103. BOUSSET, W. Die Religion des Judentums im Späthellenistischen Zeitalter (1966 = 1926) 411. JÜNGEL, E. Paulus und Jesus (1966) 155-57. BARCLAY, W. And Jesus Said (1970) 113-19. DELLING, G. Studien zum Neuen Testament und zum hellenistischen Judentum (1970) 204-06. O'-NEILL, J. C. The Theology of Acts in its historical setting (1970) 70-71. GÜTTGEMANNS, E., "Struktural-generative Analyse der Parabel" LiBi 2 (1970) 7-11. BAILEY, K. K., Poet and Peasant (Grand Rapids 1976) 119-33. PERRIN, N., Jesus and the Language of the Kingdom (London 1976) 96, 196. MANEK, J., . . . und brachte Frucht. Die Gleichnisse Jesu (Berlin 1977) 90. SCHNEIDER, G., Das Evangelium nach Lukas (Gütersloh 1977) 259. DERRETT, J. D. M., "The Friend at Midnight - Asian Ideas in the Gospel of St. Luke" in: E. Bammel et al. (eds.) Donum Gentilicium. FS. D. Daube (Oxford 1978) 78-87. HUFFARD, E. W., "The Parable of the Friend at Midnight: God's Honor or Man's Persistence?" RestQ 21 (1978) 154-60. JOHNSON, A. F., "Assurance for Man: the Fallacy of Translating Anaideia by 'Persistence' in Luke 11:5-8" JEThS 22 (1979) 123-31.

11:5 KNOX, W. L. The Sources of the Synoptic Gospels II (1957) 60. JEREMIAS, J., Die Sprache des Lukasevangeliums (Göttingen 1980) 196-97.

11:8-9 HASLER, V. Amen (1969) 100.

11:8 OTT, W. Gebet und Heil (1965) 24f., 25-31, 41f., 56-63, 71, 92, 142. PALLIS, A. Notes on St. Luke and the Acts (London 1928) 22-23. JEREMIAS, J., Die Sprache des Lukasevangeliums (Göttingen 1980) 197-98.

11:9ff. "Anfechtung" in: TRE 2 (1978) 698.

11:9-13 HUNTER, A. M. Design for Life (1953) 84f. FLEW, R. N. Jesus and His Church (1956) 47, 50. KNOX, W. L. The Sources of the Synoptic Gospels II (1957) 30. OTT, W. Gebet und Heil (1965) 15, 91f., 93, 94, 99-101. SMITH, M. Tannaitic Parallels to the Gospels (1968) 4.31, 6 b n 5. SCHULZ, S. Q Die Spruchquelle der Evangelisten (1972) 161-64. BAILEY, K. E., Poet and Peasant (Grand Rapids 1976) 134-41. EDWARDS, R. A., A Theology of Q (Philadelphia 1976) 108-09. SCHNEIDER, G., Das Evangelium nach Lukas (Gütersloh 1977) 260, 262. MCDONALD, J. I. H., Kerygma and Didache (Cambridge 1980) 82.

11:9-11 GRUNDMANN, W., "Weisheit im Horizont des Reiches Gottes. Eine Studie zur Verkündigung Jesu nach der Spruchüberlieferung Q" in: R. Schnackenburg et al. (eds.) Die Kirche des Anfangs. FS. H. Schürmann (Leipzig 1977) 187-88.

11:9-10 BLAIR, E. P. Jesus in the Gospel of Matthew (1960) 91. JÜNGEL, E. Paulus und Jesus (1966) 155. JEREMIAS, J. Neutestamentliche Theologie I (1971) 22, 33, 186, 289.THEUNISSEN, M., " 'Ο αἰτῶν λαμβάνει. Der Gebetsglaube Jesu und die Zeitlichkeit des Christseins" in: Jesus, Ort der Erfahrung Gottes (Basel 1976) 21-22.

11:9 KNOX, W. L. The Sources of the Synoptic Gospels II (1957) 60. RUDOLPH, K. Die Mandäer II (1961) 232, 5. SCHRAGE, W. Das Verhältnis des Thomas-Evangeliums zur Synoptischen Tradition und zu den Koptischen Evangelienübersetzungen (1964) 177. BROX, N., "Suchen und Finden" in: P. Hoffmann (ed.) Orientierung an Jesus. FS. J. Schmid (Freiburg 1973) 17-36. HOWARD, V. P., Das Ego in den synoptischen Evangelien (Marburg 1975) 174-76.

11:10 SCHRAGE, W. Das Verhältnis des Thomas-Evangeliums zur Synoptischen Tradition und zu den Koptischen Evangelienübersetzungen (1964) 181.

11:11-13 JÜLICHER, D. A. Die Gleichnisreden Jesu (1910) 36-44. OTT, W. Gebet und Heil (1965) 101, 102-04, 107-09, 111.

11:11 BLAIR, E. P. Jesus in the Gospel of Matthew (1960) 91. NICKELS, P. Targum and New Testament (1967) 37.

11:12-13 MATTILL, A. J., Luke and the Last Things (Dillsboro 1979) 182-84.

11:13 MOORE, G. F. Judaism (1946) II 205n. STAUDINGER, J. Die Bergpredigt (1957) 149, 167, 168, 174, 299, 300. STRECKER, G. Der Weg der Gerechtigkeit (1962) 18$_2$. HAHN, F. Christologische Hoheitstitel (1963) 107. YATES, J. E. The Spirit and the Kingdom (1963) 191f., 196ff. OTT, W. Gebet und Heil (1965) 25, 114f., 123, 131, 138. McNAMARA, M. The New Testament and the Palestinian Targum to the Pentateuch (1966) 136. DUNN,, J. D. G., Baptism in the Holy Spirit (1970) 33n, 53, 56n. POLAG, A., Die Christologie der Logienquelle (Neukirchen-Vluyn 1977) 62. JE-REMIAS, J., Die Sprache des Lukasevangeliums (Göttingen 1980) 198.

11:14-36 TALBERT, C. H., Literary Patterns, Theological Themes, and the Genre of Luke-Acts (Missoula 1974) 52, 54. MATTILL, A. J., Luke and the Last Things (Dillsboro 1979) 79-85.

11:14-32 HAHN, F., "Die Worte vom Licht Lk 11,33-36" in: P. Hoffmann (ed.) Orientierung an Jesus. FS. J. Schmid (Freiburg 1973) 131-33, 134.

11:14-26, LÜHRMANN, D. Die Redaktion der Logienquelle (1969) 32-43.
29-32 HOFFMANN, P. Studien zur Theologie der Logienquelle (1972) 4, 37f., 50, 63, 70f.

11:14-28 STECK, GPM 4 (1949-1950) 96ff. KAESEMANN, E. GPM 9 (1954-1955) 83ff. IWAND, H.-J. in: Herr, tue meine Lippen auf Bd. 1 (1957) G. Eichholz ed., 102-06. KNOX, W. L. The Sources of the Synoptic Gospels II (1957) 62. LOCHMANN, GPM 15 (1960-1961) 93ff. DOERNE, M. Er kommt auch noch heute (1961) 59-63. Sehet, welch ein Mensch, Predigtgedanken aus Vergangenheit und Gegenwart, Reihe A, Bd. 3 (1961) 57-79. KAESE-MANN, E. Exegetische Versuche und Besinnungen (1964) I 242-48. BEAUVERY, R., "Jésus et Béelzéboul" AssS 30 (1964) 26-36.

11;14-26 JÜLICHER, D. A. Die Gleichnisreden Jesu (1910) 214-40. CARLSTON, C. E., The Parables of the Triple Tradition (Philadelphia 1975) 16-21, 66-70, 129-37.

11:14-23 BARRETT, C. K. The Holy Spirit and the Gospel Tradition (1947) 59-63. BUTLER, B. C. The Originality of St Matthew (1951) 25ff. HAHN, F. Christologische Hoheitstitel (1963) 298[1]. BLANK, J. "Zur Christologie ausgewählter Wunderberichte", EvangErz 20 (1968) 470-83. SCHÜTZ, F. Der leidende Christus (1969) 56f. LOCHMAN, J. M. Das Radikale Erbe (1972) 287-96. SCHULZ, S. Q Die Spruchquelle der Evangelisten (1972) 203-13. SCHRÖRER, H./BÖHMIG, W. "Okuli: Lukas 11,14-23," in Predigtstudien (1972) Lange, E. ed., 156-63. MIYOSHI, M., Der

Anfang des Reiseberichts Lk 9,51 - 10,24 (Rome 1974) 83-84. ED-WARDS, R. A., A Theology of Q (Philadelphia 1976) 110-12. SCHNEIDER, G., Das Evangelium nach Lukas (Gütersloh 1977) 264-65. TRITES, A. A., The New Testament Concept of Witness (Cambridge 1977) 191-92. MARXSEN, W., Christologie praktisch (Gütersloh 1978) 41.

11:14-20 POLAG, A., Die Christologie der Logienquelle (Neukirchen-Vluyn 1977) 39-41.

11:14-16 TALBERT, C. H., Literary Patterns, Theological Themes, and the Genre of Luke-Acts (Missoula 1974) 40.

11:14 FARRER, A. St Matthew and St Mark (1954) 55, 56, KNOX, W. L. The Sources of the Synoptic Gospels II (1957) 125. BLAIR, E. P. Jesus in the Gospel of Matthew (1960) 191. GIBBS, J.M. NTS 10 (1963-1964) 455f. BLANK, J. Schriftauslegung in Theorie und Praxis (1969) 107, 110f. NEIRYNCK, F., "La Matière Marcienne dans Luc" in: F. Neirynck (ed.) L'Evangile de Luc (Gembloux 1973) 184-92. JEREMIAS, J., Die Sprache des Lukasevangeliums (Göttingen 1980) 199.

11:15-23 SCHRAMM, T. Der Markus-Stoff bei Lukas (1971) 46f.

11:15 METZGER, B. M., The Early Versions of the New Testament (Oxford 1977) 102.

11:16-17 KNOX, W. L. The Sources of the Synoptic Gospels II 1957) 62, 64.

11:16 NICKELS, P. Targum and New Testament (1967) 37. ED-WARDS, R. A., A Theology of Q (Philadelphia 1976) 113-15. JEREMIAS, J., Die Sprache des Lukasevangeliums (Göttingen 1980) 199.

11:17-23 BUTLER, B. C. The Originality of St Matthew (1951) 9ff. LEI-VESTAD, R. Christ the Conqueror (1954) 44ff. MUSSNER, F. Die Wunder Jesu (1967) 28-31. BROWN, S. Apostasy and Perseverance in the Theology of Luke (1969) 6.

11:17 NICKELS, P. Targum and New Testament (1967) 37. SANFORD, J. A., The Kingdom Within (New York 1970) 109. POLAG, A., Die Christologie der Logienquelle (Neukirchen-Vluyn 1977) 39. KLAUCK, H.-J., Allegorie und Allegorese in synoptischen Gleichnistexten (Münster 1978) 174-79. BÖHLIG, A., Die Gnosis III: Der Manichäismus (Zürich 1980) 310 n. 108, 325 n.115. JE-REMIAS, J., Die Sprache des Lukasevangeliums (Göttingen 1980) 200.

11:18-19 "Aramäisch" in: TRE 3 (1978) 604.

11:18 POLAG, A. Die Christologie der Logienquelle (Neukirchen-Vluyn 1977). JEREMIAS, J., Die Sprache des Lukasevangeliums (Göttingen 1980) 200.

11:19ff. DAVIES, W. D., The Sermon on the Mount (Cambridge 1966) 12-20.

11:19-20 BLANK, J. Schriftauslegung in Theorie und Praxis (1969) 121-23. HOWARD, V. P., Das Ego in den Synoptischen Evangelien (Marburg 1975) 156-63. POLAG, A. Die Christologie der Logienquelle (Neukirchen-Vluyn 1977) 40-41. MEYER, B. F., The Aims of Jesus (London 1979) 155-56.

11:19 PALLIS, A., Notes on St. Luke and the Acts (London 1928) 23-24. BARRETT, C. K. The New Testament Background (1956) 31. NICKELS, P. Targum and New Testament (1967) 37. HENGEL, M. Judentum und Hellenismus (Tübingen 1969) 442; ET: Judaism and Hellenism. I (London 1974) 241. ZINGG, P., Das Wachsen der Kirche (Freiburg 1974) 199-204, 225. HOWARD, V. P., Das Ego in den Synoptischen Evangelien (Marburg 1975) 162-63. JEREMIAS, J., Die Sprache des Lukasevangeliums (Göttingen 1980) 200-01.

11:20-31 HOFFMANN, P. Studien zur Theologie der Logienquelle (1972) 42-43, 46.

11:20-21 PERRIN, N., Jesus and the Languge of the Kingdom (London 1976) 37, 41, 42-43, 46.

11:20 STONEHOUSE, N. B. The Witness of Matthew and Mark to Christ (1944) 244. KÜMMEL, W. G. Verheissung und Erfüllung (1953) 98-100. FLEW, R. N. Jesus and His Church (1956) 23, 50, 51. KNOX, W. L. The Sources of the Synoptic Gospels II (1957) 62. ROBINSON, J. M. Kerygma und historischer Jesus (1960) 87, 137, 163, 143. HAHN, F. Christologische Hoheitstitel (1963) 220, 236, 238, 298f. PERRIN, N., The Kingdom of God in the Teaching of Jesus (Philadelphia 1963) 20, 42, 59, 60, 64, 76, 86, 110, 170, 171. TÖDT, H. E. Der Menschensohn in der synoptischen Ueberlieferung (1963) 237ff. YATES, J. E. The Spirit and the Kingdom (1963) 90-94. YATES, J. E. "Luke's Pneumatology and Lk 11,20", in: Studia Evangelica II (1964) F. L. Cross ed., 295-99. HAMERTON-KELLY, R. G. NTS 11 (1964-1965) 167f, HAHN, F. Das Verständnis der Mission im Neuen Testament (²1965) 25f. BOUSSET, W. Die Religion des Judentums im Späthellenistischen Zeitalter (1966 = 1926) 253. GEORGE, A. "Note sur quelques traits lucaniens de l'expression 'Par le doigt de Dieu' (Luc XI,20)," SciEccl 18 (3, 1966) 461-66. JÜNGEL, E. Paulus und Jesus (1966) 112, 185-87. NICKELS, P. Targum and New Testament (1967) 38. DESCAMPS, A. & DE HALLEUX, A. Mélanges Bibliques en hommage au R. P. Béda Rigaux (1970) 471-72. SANFORD, J. A. The Kingdom Within (New York 1970) 57. JEREMIAS, J. Neutestamentliche Theologie I (1971) 25, 40, 42. RAHNER, K. and THÜSING, W., Christologie-systematisch und exegetisch (Freiburg 1972) 197-98, 208-09. LORENZMEIER, T., "Zum Logion Mt 12,28; Lk 11,20" in: M. D. Betz/L. Schottroff (eds.) Neues Testament und Christliche Existenz. FS. H. Braun (Tübingen 1973) 289-304. SCHUBERT, K., Jesus im Lichte der Religionsgeschichte des Judentums (München 1973) 128-29. MIYOSHI, M., Der Anfang des Reiseberichts (Lk 9,51 - 20,24 (Rome 1974) 82-84. PERRIN, N., The New Testament. An Introduction. Proclamation and Parenesis, Myth and History (New York 1974) 288-90, 298. ZINGG, P., Das Wachsen der Kirche (Freiburg 1974) 204-07, 225-26. CONZELMANN, H. and LINDEMANN, A., Arbeitsbuch zum Neuen Testament (Tübingen 1975) 18-19, 353, 355. DUNN, J. D. G., Jesus and the Spirit (London 1975) 44-49, 52, 60, 78, 90. HOFFMANN, P. and EID, V., Jesus von Nazareth und eine christliche Moral (Freiburg 1975) 36-38. HOWARD, V. P., Das Ego in den Synoptischen Evangelien (Marburg 1975) 158-62. KOCH, D.-A., Die Bedeutung der Wundererzählungen für die Christologie des Markusevangeliums (Berlin 1975) 173-75. BEIS-SER, F., Das Reich Gottes (Göttingen 1976) 36-43. METZGER, B. M., The Early Versions of the New Testament (Oxford 1977) 255. BRUCE, F. F., The Time is Fulfilled (Exeter 1978) 21. SEY-BOLD, K. and MÜLLER, U., Krankheit und Heilung (Stuttgart 1978) 97-98. MATTILL, A. J., Luke and the Last Things (Dillsboro 1979) 168-77. PRAST, F., Presbyter und Evangelium in nachapostolischer Zeit (Stuttgart 1979) 277. SCHLOSSER, J., "Le règn de Dieu dans les dits de Jésus" RevSR 53 (1979) 164-76. CLARK, K. W., "Realized Eschatology" in: The Gentile Bias and other Essays (Leiden 1980) 48, 55-62. HARRINGTON, D. J., God's People in Christ (Philadelphia 1980) 24, 25. JEREMIAS, J., Die Sprache des Lukasevangeliums (Göttingen 1980) 201. MCDONALD, J. I. H., Kerygma and Didache (Cambridge 1980) 22.

11:21-22 LEGASSE, S. " 'L'homme fort' de Luc. xi 21-22," NovTest 6 (1, 1962) 5-9. DUNN, J. D. G., Jesus and the Spirit (London 1975) 44, 48. POLAG, A., Die Christologie der Logienquelle (Neukirchen-Vluyn 1977) 42-43. KLAUCK, H.-J., Allegorie und Allegorese in Synoptischen Gleichnistexten (Münster 1978) 179-84. MEYER, B. F., The Aims of Jesus (London 1979) 156-57.

11:21 ZINGG, P., Das Wachsen der Kirche (Freiburg 1974) 207-08, 226. JEREMIAS, J., Die Sprache des Lukasevangeliums (Göttingen 1980) 201.

11:22 PALLIS, A., Notes on St. Luke and the Acts (London 1928) 24. ZINGG, P., Das Wachsen der Kirche (Freiburg 1974) 208-09, 226. METZGER, B. M., The Early Versions of the New Testament

(Oxford 1977) 214. JEREMIAS, J., Die Sprache des Lukas-evangeliums (Göttingen 1980) 201.

11:23 SIMPSON, R. T. NTS 12 (1965-1966) 281f. ZINGG, P. Das Wachsen der Kirche (Freiburg 1974) 210-12, 226. POLAG, A., Die Christologie der Logienquelle (Neukirchen-Vluyn 1977) 44.

11:24-26 STRECKER, G. Der Weg der Gerechtigkeit (1962) 103. SCHULZ, S. Q Die Spruchquelle der Evangelisten (1972) 476-80. ED-WARDS, R. A., A Theology of Q (Philadelphia 1976) 112. MA-NEK, J., . . . und brachte Frucht. Die Gleichnisse Jesu (Berlin 1977) 42-43. POLAG, A. Die Christologie der Logienquelle (Neu-kirchen-Vluyn 1977) 76. SCHNEIDER, G., Das Evangelium nach Lukas (Gütersoh 1977) 267.

11:24 ZINGG, P., Das Wachsen der Kirche (Freiburg 1974) 212-13, 226. JEREMIAS, J., Die Sprache des Lukasevangeliums (Göttingen 1980) 202.

11:25 ZINGG, P., Das Wachsen der Kirche (Freiburg 1974) 213-17, 226-27.

11:26 NICKELS, P. Targum and New Testament (1967) 38. DALTON, W. J., Christ's Proclamation to the Spirits (Rome 1965) 147-48.

11:27-28 BULTMANN, R. The History of the Synoptic Tradition (1963) 30f., 60-62. SCHRAGE, W. Das Verhältnis des Thomas-Evan-geliums zur Synoptischen Tradition und zu den Koptischen Evan-gelienübersetzungen (1964) 164. JACQUEMIN, P.-E. "L'accueil de la parole de Dieu. Lc 11,27-28," AssS 66 (1973) 10-19. ZIM-MERMANN, H., " 'Selig, die das Wort Gottes hören und es be-wahren.' Eine exegetische Studie zu Lk 11,27f" Catholica 29 (1975) 114-19. DRURY, J., Tradition and Design in Luke's Gospel (At-lanta 1976) 151. SCHNEIDER, G., Das Evangelium nach Lukas (Gütersloh 1977) 268. STAGG, E. and F., Woman in the World of Jesus (Philadelphia 1978) 141-42. SWIDLER, L., Biblical Affir-mations of Woman (Philadelphia 1979) 178, 193, 273.

11:27 KNOX, W. L. The Sources of the Synoptic Gospels II (1957) 64. McNAMARA, M. The New Testament and the Palestinian Tar-gum to the Pentateuch (1966) 131f., 256. NICKELS, P. Targum and New Testament (1967) 38. NEIRYNCK, F., "La Matière Marcienne dans Luc" in: F. Neirynck (ed.) L'Evangile de Luc (Gembloux 1973) 184-92. KLIJN, A. F. J., "Die syrische Baruch-Apokalypse" in: W. G. Kümmel (ed.) Jüdische Schriften aus hellenistisch-römischer Zeit. V. (Gütersloh 1976) 159n 10a. JE-REMIAS, J., Die Sprache des Lukasevangeliums (Göttingen 1980) 203.

11:28ff. THEISSEN, G., Soziologie der Jesusbewegung (München 1977) 18.

11:28 RIEDL, J., "Selig sind die das Wort Gottes hören und befolgen" BiLe 4 (1963) 252-60. SCOTT, M. P., "A Note on the Meaning and Translation of Luke 11:28" IThQ 41 (1974) 235-50. ZINGG, P., Das Wachsen der Kieche (Freiburg 1974) 71-72. MEYER, B. F., The Aims of Jesus (London 1979) 210-11. PRAST, F., Presbyter und Evangelium in nachapostolischer Zeit (Stuttgart 1979) 292-93, 301. JEREMIAS, J., Die Sprache des Lukasevangeliums (Göttingen 1980) 203.

11:29ff. SCHWEIZER, E. Erniedrigung und Erhöhung bei Jesus und seinen Nachfolgern (1962) §30. BAUMBACH, G. Das Verständnis des Bösen in den synoptischen Evangelien (1963) 131ff. STROBEL, A. Erkenntnis und Bekenntnis der Sünde in neutestamentlicher Zeit (1968) 42.

11:29-32 HIRSCH, E. Frühgeschichte des Evangeliums (1941) 102-04. KNOX, W. L. The Sources of the Synoptic Gospels II (1957) 62-63. GNILKA, J. Die Verstockung Israels (1961) 133f. STRECKER, G. Der Weg der Gerechtigkeit (1962) 104. NICKELS, P. Targum and New Testament (1967) 38. EDWARDS, R. A. The Sign of Jonah in the Theology of the Evangelists and Q (1971). SCHULZ, S. Q. Die Spruchquelle der Evangelisten (1972) 250-57. HAMERTON-KELLY, R. G. Pre-Existence, Wisdom, and The Son of Man (1973) 23, 33, 36, 43, 93, 95. MIYOSHI, M., Der Anfang des Reiseberichts Lk 9,51 - 10,24 (Rome 1974) 82-83. PERRIN, N., Jesus and the Language of the Kingdom (London 1976) 45-46. SCHNEIDER, G., Das Evangelium nach Lukas (Gütersloh 1977) 270. SCHMITT, G., "Das Zeichen des Jona" ZNW 69 (1978) 123-29. KIEFFER, R., "Mer-än -kristologin hos synoptikerna" SEA (1979) 134-47. SWIDLER, L., Biblical Affirmations of Woman (Philadelphia 1979) 168, 243, 253, 257.

11:29-30 PATSCH, H. Abendmahl und historischer Jesus (1972) 202ff.

11:29 KNOX, W. L. The Sources of the Synoptic Gospels II (1957) 8, 64. HAHN, F. Christologische Hoheitstitel (1963) 76, 390f. JÜNGEL, E. Paulus und Jesus (1966) 257f. McNAMARA, M. The New Testament and the Palestinian Targum to the Pentateuch (1966) 77 fn. 21. STROBEL, A. Erkenntnis und Bekenntnis der Sünde in neutestamentlicher Zeit (1968) 41. EDWARDS, R. A. The Sign of Jonah (1971). VÖGTLE, A. Das Evangelium und die Evangelien (1971) 103-05, 111-15. SCHÜRMANN, H., "Beobachtungen zum Menschensohn-Titel in der Redequelle" in: R. Pesch/R. Schnackenburg (eds.) Jesus und der Menschensohn (Freiburg 1975) 133-34. POLAG, A., Die Christologie der Logienquelle (Neukirchen-Vluyn 1977) 74, 89-90. JEREMIAS, J., Die Sprache des Lukasevangeliums (Göttingen 1980) 203-04.

11:30-32 GLOMBITZA, O. "Das Zeichen des Jona," NTS 8 (1961-1962) 360f.

11:30-31 KNOX, W. L. The Sources of the Synoptic Gospels II (1957) 64.

11:30 SCHWEIZER, E. Erniedrigung und Erhöhung bei Jesus uns seinen Nachfolgern (1962) §3gl. HAHN, F. Christologische Hoheitstitel (1963) 37, 41, 46. GÄRTNER, B. The Temple and the Community in Qumran and the New Testament (1965) 113. JÜNGEL, E. Paulus und Jesus (1966) 242, 244, 257f. NICKELS, P. Targum and New Testament (1967) 38. VÖGTLE, A. Das Evangelium und die Evangelien (1971) 107-09, 127-35. DRURY, J., Tradition and Design in Luke's Gospel (Atlanta 1976) 151-52. POLAG, A., Die Christologie der Logienquelle (Neukirchen-Vluyn 1977) 90, 95, 133. MERRILL, E. H., "The Sign of Jonah" JEThS 23 (1980) 23-30.

11:31-32 HENNECKE, E./SCHNEEMELCHER, W. Neutestamentliche Apokryphen (1964) II 80.STRECKER, G. Der Weg der Gerechtigkeit (1962) 103. JÜNGEL, E. Paulus und Jesus (1966) 189f. VÖGTLE, A. Das Evangelium und die Evangelien (1971) 117-19. SCHNIDER, F., Jesus der Prophet (Freiburg 1973) 174ff., 259. CAIRD, G. B., "Eschatology and Politics: Some Misconceptions" in: J. R. McKay/J. F. Miller (eds.) Biblical Studies. FS. W. Barclay (London 1976) 77-79. PERRIN, N., Jesus and the Language of the Kingdom (London 1976) 37. POLAG, A. Die Christologie der Logienquelle (Neukirchen-Vluyn 1977) 90. TRITES, A. A., The New Testament Concept of Witness (Cambridge 1977) 192. CORRENS, D., "Jona und Salomo" in: W. Haubeck/M. Bachmann (eds.) Wort in der Zeit. FS. K. H. Rengstorf (Leiden 1980) 85-94.

11:31 NICKELS, P. Targum and New Testament (1967) 38. POLAG, A., Die Christologie der Logienquelle (Neukirchen-Vluyn 1977) 74. JEREMIAS, J., Die Sprache des Lukasevangeliums (Göttingen 1980) 204.

11:32 BRAUN, H. Qumran und NT II (1966) 89, 249. JÜNGEL, E. Paulus und Jesus (1966) 258. JEREMIAS, J. Neutestamentliche Theologie I (1971) 86f.

11:33ff. 39-52 HOFFMANN, P. Studien zur Theologie der Logienquelle (1972) passim.

11:33-36 KNOX, W. L. The Sources of the Synoptic Gospels II (1957) 25, 65. SANFORD, J. A., The Kingdom Within (New York 1970) 146-48. HAHN, F., "Die Worte vom Licht Lk 11,33-36" in: P. Hoffmann (ed.) Orientierung an Jesus. FS. J. Schmid (Freiburg 1973) 107-38, esp. 127-34. SCHNEIDER, G. Das Evangelium nach Lukas (Gütersloh 1977) 272. SWIDLER, L., Biblical Affirmations of Woman (Philadelphia 1979) 165, 166, 258.

11:33 JÜLICHER, D. A. Die Gleichnisreden Jesu (1910) 79-88. DODD, C. H. The Parables of the Kingdom (1948) 143ff. KNOX, W. L. The Sources of the Synoptic Gospels II (1957) 18. MONTEF-IORE, H. NTS 7 (1960-1961) 241f. SCHRAGE, W. Das Verhält-nis des Thomas-Evangeliums zur Synoptischen Tradition und zu den Koptischen Evangelienübersetzungen (1964) 81. JEREMIAS, J. Abba; Studien zur neutestamentlichen Theologie und Zeitge-schichte (1966) 99-102. SUMMERS, R. The Secret Sayings of the Living Jesus (1968) 29. DERRETT, J. D. M. Law in the New Tes-tament (1970) 194, 202, 203, 204. SCHULZ, S. Q Die Spruch-quelle der Evangelisten (1972) 474-76. CARLSTON, C. E., The Parables of the Triple Tradition (Philadelphia 1975) 48-49, 89-92, 149-53. CONZELMANN, H. and LINDEMANN, A., Arbeits-buch zum Neuen Testament (Tübingen 1975) 63. JEREMIAS, J., Die Sprache des Lukasevangeliums (Göttingen 1980) 204-05.

11:34ff. KNOX, W. L. The Sources of the Synoptic Gospels II (1957) 65.

11:34-36 JÜLICHER, D. A. Die Gleichnisreden Jesu (1910) 98-108. HELD, H. J., GPM 17 (1962-1963) 262ff. Erhaltet euch in der Liebe Gottes, Predigtgedanken aus Vergangenheit und Gegenwart, Reihe C, Bd. 3-4 (1963) 118-22. SMITH, M. Tannaitic Parallels to the Gospels (1968) 7 end. WREGE, H.-T. Die Ueberlieferungsgeschichte der Bergpredigt (1968) 113-15. NIEBERGALL, A. GPM 23/3 (1968-1969) 283-90. BALTENSWEILER, H. and NEIDHART, W., in: P. Krusche et al. (eds.) Predigtstudien für das Kirchenjahr 1974-1975. III/2 (Stuttgart 1975) 147-53. WALTER, N., in: GPM 29 (1975) 341-47.

11:34-35 EDLUND, C. Das Auge der Einfalt. Eine Untersuchung zu Matth. 6,22-23 und Luk. 11,34-35. Acta Seminarii Neotestamentici Up-saliensis, 19 (1952). SCHULZ, S. Q Die Spruchquelle der Evan-gelisten (1972) 468-70.

11:34 KNOX, W. L. The Sources of the Synoptic Gospels II (1957) 28. BOUSSET, W. Die Religion des Judentums im Späthellenisti-schen Zeitalter (1966 = 1926) 419.

11:35 PALLIS, A., Notes on St. Luke and the Acts (London 1928) 24-25.

11:36 KNOX, W. L. The Sources of the Synoptic Gospels II (1957) 28.

11:37ff. KNOX, W. L. The Sources of the Synoptic Gospels I (1953) 94ff. HAHN, F. Christologische Hoheitstitel (1963) 88.

11:37-54 HIRSCH, E. Frühgeschichte des Evangeliums (1941) 106-14. TALBERT, C. H., Literary Patterns, Theological Themes, and the Genre of Luke-Acts (Missoula 1974) 52, 54. GIRARD, R., ''Les malédictions contre les Pharisiens et la révélation évangélique''

Bulletin de Centre Protestant d'Etudes 27 (1975) 5-29. SCHNEI-DER, G., Das Evangelium nach Lukas (Gütersloh 1977) 274.

11:37-52 STREETER, B. H. The Four Gospels (1951) 253f. KNOX, W. L. The Sources of the Synoptic Gospels II (1957) 10, 65. OTOMO, Y. Nachfolge Jesu und Anfänge der Kirche im Neuen Testament (1970) 104-06.

11:37-47 LIGHTSTONE, J. N., "Sadoq the Yavnean" in: W. S. Green (ed.) Persons and Institutions in Early Rabbinic Judaism (Missoula 1977) 63.

11:37-44 RIVKIN, E., A Hidden Revolution (Nashville 1978) 118.

11:37-41 HÜBNER, H., Das Gesetz in der synoptischen Tradition (Witten 1973) 142-43. WESTERHOLM, S., Jesus and Scribal Authority (Lund 1978) 71-85.

11:37-38 SCHÜRMANN, H. "Sprachliche Reminiszensen an abgeänderte oder ausgelassene Bestandteile der Spruchsammlung im Lukas- und Matthäusevangelium," NTS 6 (1959-1960) 209f. HAHN, F. Christologische Hoheitstitel (1963) 88.

11:37 KLEIN, G., "Rein oder unrein - Mt 23,25. Lc 11,37.42" ZNW (1906) 252-54. JEREMIAS, J., Die Sprache des Lukasevangeliums (Göttingen 1980) 205-206.

11:38 DELLING, G. Die Zueignung des Heils in der Taufe (1961) 69. RUDOLPH, K. Die Mandäer II (1961) 404. NICKELS, P. Targum and New Testament (1967) 38. JEREMIAS, J., Die Sprache des Lukasevangeliums (Göttingen 1980) 206.

11:39ff. DORMEYER, D., Die Passion Jesu als Verhaltensmodell (Münster 1974) 98a, 234.

11:39-52 LÜHRMANN, D. Die Redaktion der Logienquelle (1969) 43-48.SCHULZ, S. Q Die Spruchquelle der Evangelisten (1972) 94-114.

11:39-48 SANDMEL, S., We Jews and Jesus (New York 1977) 137.

11:39-41 STRECKER, G. Der Weg der Gerechtigkeit (1962) 31. DEGEN-HARDT, H.-J. Lukas, Evangelist der Armen (1964) 57-59. PO-LAG, A., Die Christologie der Logienquelle (Neukirchen-Vluyn 1977) 81. WESTERHOLM, S., Jesus and Scribal Authority (Lund 1978) 85-90.

11:39-40 HAHN, F. Christologische Hoheitstitel (1963) 88, 89. SCHRAGE, W. Das Verhältnis des Thomas-Evangeliums zur Synoptischen Tradition und zu den Koptischen Evangelienübersetzungen (1964) 170. SANFORD, J. A., The Kingdom Within (New York 1970) 97-98.

11:39 HAHN, F. Christologische Hoheitstitel (1963) 88. STROBEL, A.

Erkenntnis und Bekenntnis der Sünde in neutestamentlicher Zeit (1968) 43.

11:41 PALLIS, A., Notes on St. Luke and the Acts (London 1928) 25. DUPONT, D. J. Les Béatitudes (1958) 318-20. HAHN, F. Christologische Hoheitstitel (1963) 88, 89. MASINI, M. " 'quod superest . . . ,' " Servitium 1 (4, 1967) 448-53. NICKELS, P. Targum and New Testament (1967) 38.KARRIS, F. J., "Poor and Rich: The Lukan Sitz im Leben" in: C. H. Talbert (ed.) Perspectives on Luke-Acts (Danville 1978) 119-20. JEREMIAS, J., Die Sprache des Lukasevangeliums (Göttingen 1980) 206.

11:42-52 LUND, N. W. Chiasmus in the New Testament (1942) 293f.

11:42-47 MCDONALD, J. I. H., Kerygma and Didache (Cambridge 1980) 21-22.

11:42 KLEIN, G. "Rein oder unrein Mt 23,25. Lc 11,37.52" ZNW 7 (1906) 252-54. PALLIS, A., Notes on St. Luke and the Acts (London 1928) 25. CORRENS, D. "Die Verzehntung der Raute. Lk xi 42 und M Schebi ix 1," NovTest 6 (2-3, 1963) 11-12. O'NEILL, J. C. The Theology of Acts in its historical setting (1970) 36-37. VI. EDWARDS, R. A., A Theology of Q (Philadelphia 1976) 69. METZGER, B. M., The Early Versions of the New Testament (Oxford 1977) 92. POLAG, A., Die Christologie der Logienquelle (Neukirchen-Vluyn 1977) 80-81. WESTERHOLM, S., Jesus and Scribal Authority (Lund 1978) 57-61. JEREMIAS, J., Die Sprache des Lukasevangeliums (Göttingen 1980) 206-07.

11:44 NICKELS, P. Targum and New Testament (1967) 38. SMITH, M. Tannaitic Parallels to the Gospels (1968) 7 b n 17.. EDWARDS, R. A. A Theology of Q (Philadelphia 1976) 69-70. POLAG, A., Die Christologie der Logienquelle (Neukirchen-Vluyn 1977) 82. SCHWARZ, G., " 'Unkenntliche Gräber'? (Lukas xi. 44)" NTS (1977) 345-46. JEREMIAS, J., Die Sprache des Lukasevangeliums (Göttingen 1980) 207.

11:45-50 RIVKIN, E., A Hidden Revolution (Nasvhille 1978) 118-19.

11:45-46 BOUSSET, W. Die Religion des Judentums im Späthellenistischen Zeitalter (1966 = 1926) 166.

11:45 HAHN, F. Christologische Hoheitstitel (1963) 76, 77.

11:46 GERSTENBERGER, G. and SCHRAGE, W., Leiden (Stuttgart 1977) 139; ET: J. E. Steeley, Suffering (Nashville 1980) 161-62. POLAG, A., Die Christologie der Logienquelle (Neukirchen-Vluyn 1977) 82. JEREMIAS, J., Die Sprache des Lukasevangeliums (Göttingen 1980) 207-08.

11:47-51 DERRETT, M., "You build the Tombs of the Prophets" StEv 4 (1968) 187-93. WILLIAMS, J. A., A Conceptual History of Deuteronomism in the Old Testament, Judaism, and the New Testament (Ph.D. Diss. Southern Baptist Theological Seminary; Louisville 1976) 289-93, 310. TRITES, A. A., The New Testament Concept of Witness (Cambridge 1977) 194.

11:47-48 SATAKE, A. Die Gemeindeordnung in der Johannesapokalypse (1966) 179f. WREGE, H.-T. Die Ueberlieferungsgeschichte der Bergpredigt (1968) 22, 54, 173. CHRIST, F. Jesus Sophia (1970) 120, 122, 133, 134. WILLIAMS, J. A., A Conceptual History of Deuteronomism in the Old Testament, Judaism, and the New Testament (Ph.D. Diss. Southern Baptist Theological Seminary; Louisville 1976) 290-93. VIELHAUER, P., "Oikodome. Das Bild vom Bau in der christlichen Literatur vom Neuen Testament bis Clemens Alexandrinus" in: G. Klein (ed.) Oikodome (München 1979) 54.

11:47 PALLIS, A., Notes on St. Luke and the Acts (London 1928) 25-26. EDWARDS, R. A., A Theology of Q (Philadelphia 1976) 70.

11:48 NELLESSEN, E., Zeugnis für Jesus und das Wort (Köln 1976) 69-71. TRITES, A. A., The New Testament Concept of Witness (Cambridge 1977) 128-29.

11:49ff. WREGE, H.-T. Die Ueberlieferungsgeschichte der Bergpredigt (1968) 22, 54, 173.

11:49-52 BOUSSET, W. Die Religion des Judentums im Späthellenistischen Zeitalter (1966 = 1926) 166, 346. SCHREINER, J. Gestalt und Anspruch des Neuen Testaments (1969) 137f., 145.

11:49-51 MANSON, W. Jesus the Messiah (1948) 64-66. ELLIS, E. E. "Luke xi. 49-52: An Oracle of a Christian Prophet?" ET 74 (5, 1963) 157-58. SATAKE, A. Die Gemeindeordnung in der Johannesapokalypse (1966) 180-85. CHRIST, F. Jesus Sophia (1970) 120-35. GASTON, L. No Stone on Another (1970) 321-22, 344. SUGGS, M. J. Wisdom, Christology, and Law in Matthew's Gospel (1970) 13ff. HOFFMANN, P. Studien zur Theologie der Logienquelle (1972) 70., 164-71, 182-87. SCHULZ, S. Q Die Spruchquelle der Evangelisten (1972) 236-45. HAMERTON-KELLY, R. G. Pre-Existence, Wisdom, and the Son of Man (1973) 23, 24, 31, 35, 67, 83. SCHNIDER, F., Jesus der Prophet (Freiburg 1973) 74, 76, 139ff. LANG, B., Frau Weisheit (Düsseldorf 1975) 180. MINEAR, P., To Heal and to Reveal (New York 1976) 124ff. GRUNDMANN, W., "Weisheit im Horizont des Reiches Gottes. Eine Studie zur Verkündigung Jesu nach der Spruchüberlieferung Q" in: R. Schnackenburg et al. (eds.) Die Kirche des Anfangs. FS. H. Schürmann (Leipzig 1977) 180. POLAG, A., Die Christologie der Logienquelle (Neukirchen-Vluyn 1977) 90. SCHENKE, H. M., "Die Tendenz der Weisheit zur Gnosis" in: B. Aland et al. (eds.) Gnosis. FS. H. Jonas (Göttingen 1978) 359-65. MEYER, B. F., The Aims of Jesus (London 1979) 207.

11:49-50 WILLIAMS, J. A., A Conceptual History of Deuteronomism in the Old Testament, Judaism, and the New Testament (Ph.D. Diss. Southern Baptist Theological Seminary; Louisville (1976) 315.

11:49 ARVEDSON, T. Das Mysterium Christi (1937) 209f. SCHÜRMANN, H. "Sprachliche Reminiszenzen an abgeänderte oder ausgelassenen Bestandteile der Spruchsammlung im Lukas- und Matthäusevangelium," NTS 6 (1959-1960) 209f. KLEIN, G. Die Zwölf Apostel (1961) 33f. BRAUN, H. Qumran und NT II (1966) 303. SEITZ, O. J. F., "The Commission of Prophets and Apostles" StEv 4 (1968) 236-40. JEREMIAS, J. Neutestamentliche Theologie I (1971) 21, 39, 129, 269. KLEIN, G. "Die Verfolgung der Apostel. Lukas 11, 49," in: Neues Testament und Geschichte (1972) H. Baltensweiler/B. Reicke eds., 113-24. SEITZ, O. J. F., "The Commission of Prophets and Apostles" StEv 4 (1968) 236-40. SCHNIDER, F., Jesus der Prophet (Freiburg 1973) 130, 136ff. HOWARD, V. P., Das Ego in den Synoptischen Evangelien (Marburg 1975) 163-67. SWIDLER, L., Biblical Affirmations of Woman (Philadelphia 1979) 49, 64. JEREMIAS, J., Die Sprache des Lukasevangeliums (Göttingen 1980) 208-09. KRAFT, H., Die Entstehung des Christentums (Darmstadt 1981) 174.

11:50 STRECKER, G. Der Weg der Gerechtigkeit (1962) 71₁. JEREMIAS, J. Neutestamentliche Theologie I (1971) 209-10.

11:51 McNAMARA, M. The New Testament and the Palestinian Targum to the Pentateuch (1966) 160. NICKELS, P. Targum and New Testament (1967) 38. STROBEL, A. Erkenntnis und Bekenntnis der Sünde in neutestamentlicher Zeit (1968) 41. HASLER, V. Amen (1969) 61. JEREMIAS, J., Die Sprache des Lukasevangeliums (Göttingen 1980) 210.

11:52-53 SUMMERS, R. The Secret Sayings of the Living Jesus (1968) 30, 72.

11:52 MANSON, T. W. The Teaching of Jesus (1945) 121ff. FLEW, R. N. Jesus and His Church (1956) 95. SCHRAGE, W. Das Verhältnis des Thomas-Evangeliums zur Synoptischen Tradition und zu den Koptischen Evangelienübersetzungen (1964) 91. BLACK, M. An Aramaic Approach to the Gospels and Acts (1967) 129f. NICKELS, P. Targum and New Testament (1967) 38. HENGEL, M., Judentum und Hellenismus (Tübingen 1969) 313ff.; ET: Judaism and Hellenism II (London 1974) 113. EDWARDS, R. A., A Theology of Q (Philadelphia 1976) 70.

11:53-54 KNOX, W. L. The Sources of the Synoptic Gospels II (1957) 66ff. RIVKIN, E., A Hidden Revolution (Nashville 1978) 119.

11:53 PALLIS, A., Notes on St. Luke and the Acts (London 1928) 26-

27. JEREMIAS, J., Die Sprache des Lukasevangeliums (Göttingen 1980) 210.

———————————

12:1-13:35 MATTILL, A. J., Luke and the Last Things (Dillsboro 1979) 7-8, 87-89.

12 IWAND, H.-J. Die Gegenwart des Kommenden (1966). BERTRAND, D., "Hypocrites selon Luc 12, 1-59" Christus 21 (1974) 323-33. AVANZO, M., Jesús y la Conducción de la Comunidad" RevBi 37 (1975) 16-22.

12:1-48 TALBERT, C. H., Literary Patterns, Theological Themes, and the Genre of Luke-Acts (Missoula 1974) 52, 55.

12:1-46 GOULDER, M. D. Type and History in Acts (1964) 136-40.

12:1-12, 22-59 HIRSCH, E. Frühgeschichte des Evangeliums (1941) 114-27.

12:1-12 TALBERT, C. H., Literary Patterns, Theological Themes, and the Genre of Luke-Acts (Missoula 1974) 52, 55. SCHNEIDER, G., Das Evangelium nach Lukas (Gütersoh 1977) 277.

12:1-8 HÜBNER, H., Das Gesetz in der synoptischen Tradition (Witten 1973) 113ff.

12:1, 4f. SCHÜRMANN, H. "Sprachliche Reminiszenzen an abgëanderte oder ausgelassene Bestandteile der Spruchsammlung im Lukas- und Matthäusevangelium," NTS 6 (1959-1960) 209f.

12:1-3 SANFORD, J. A., The Kingdom Within (New York 1970) 110-11.

12:1 KNOX, W. L. The Sources of the Synoptic Gospels II (1957) 68. STROBEL, A. Erkenntnis und Bekenntnis der Sünde in neutestamentlicher Zeit (1968) 43. DENAUX, A., "L'Hypocrisie des Pharisiens" in: F. Neirynck (ed.) L'Evangile de Luc (Gembloux 1973) 262-63. RIVKIN, E., A Hidden Revolution (Nashville 1978) 119, 123. JEREMIAS, J., Die Sprache des Lukasevangeliums (Göttingen 1980) 211.

12:2ff. KNOX, W. L. The Sources of the Synoptic Gospels II (1957) 54, 66, 68, 72, 73.

12:2-53 No Stone on Another (1970) 256, 323-36.

12:2-10 HOFFMANN, P. Studien zur Theologie der Logienquelle (1972) Passim.

12:2-9 LÜHRMANN, D. Die Redaktion der Logienquelle (1969) 49-52.

GOULDER, M. D. Midrash and Lection in Matthew (1974) 350ff.
TRITES, A. A., The New Testament Concept of Witness (Cambridge 1977) 181-83. EDWARDS, R. A., A Theology of Q (Philadelphia 1976) 120-21.

12:2-4 CARLSTON, C. E., The Parables of the Triple Tradition (Philadelphia 1975) 49-51, 92-94, 153-55.

12:2-3 JÜLICHER, D. A. Die Gleichnisreden Jesu (1910) 91-97. SCHULZ, S. Q. Die Spruchquelle der Evangelisten (1972) 461-65. HAHN, F., "Die Worte vom Licht Lk 11,33-36" in: P. Hoffman (ed.) Orientierung an Jesus. FS. J. Schmid (Freiburg 1973) 113, 120-21. POLAG, A., Die Christologie der Logienquelle (Neukirchen-Vluyn 1973) 96.

12:2 SCHRAGE, W. Das Verhältnis des Thomas-Evangeliums zur Synoptischen Tradition und zu den Koptischen Evangelienübersetzungen (1964) 34. CLARK, K. W., "Realized Eschatology" in: The Gentile Bias and other Essays (Leiden 1980) 53. JEREMIAS, J., Die Sprache des Lukasevangeliums (Göttingen 1980) 211.

12:3-4 KÜMMEL, W. G., "Das Verhalten Jesus gegenüber und das Verhalten des Menschensohns" in: R. Pesch/R. Schnackenburg (eds.) Jesus und der Menschensohn (Freiburg 1975) 210-24.

12:3 PALLIS, A., Notes on St. Luke and the Acts (London 1928) 27. STRECKER, G. Der Weg der Gerechtigkeit (1962) 190. SCHRAGE, W. Das Verhältnis des Thomas-Evangeliums zur Synoptischen Tradition und zu den Koptischen Evangelienübersetzungen (1964) 79. DALTON, W. J., Christ's Proclamation to the Spirits (Rome 1965) 152-53. SUMMERS, R. The Secret Sayings of the Living Jesus (1968) 29. JANSSEN, E., "Testament Abrahams" in: W. G. Kümmel (ed.) Jüdische Schriften aus hellenistisch-römischer Zeit. III (Gütersloh 1975) 215 n97.

12:4-7 SCHULZ, S. Q Die Spruchquelle der Evangelisten (1972) 157-61.

12:4, 5, 8 HASLER, V. Amen (1969) 73.

12:4-5 KÖHLER, K., "Zu Lk 12:4-5" ZNW 18 (1917-1918) 140-41. MASSAUX, E. Influence de l'Evangile de saint Matthieu sur la littérature chrétienne avant saint Irénée (1950) 150-52. O'NEILL, J. C. The Theology in Acts in its historical setting (1970) 37-38, VIII. GNILKA, J., "Martyriumsparänese und Sühnetod in synoptischen und jüdischen Traditionen" in: R. Schnackenburg et al. (eds.) Die Kirche des Anfangs. FS. H. Schürmann (Freiburg 1978) 232. MATTILL, A., Luke and the Last Things (Dillsboro 1979) 34-35.

12:4 BEST, E. One Body in Christ (1955) 216. JEREMIAS, J., Die Sprache des Lukasevangeliums (Göttingen 1980) 212.

12:5 STAEHELIN, E. Die Verkündigung des Reiches Gottes in der Kirche Jesu Christi I (1951) 179. METZGER, B. M., The Early

Versions of the New Testament (Oxford 1977) 102, 253. JE-REMIAS, J., Die Sprache des Lukasevangeliums (Göttingen 1980) 212.

12:6 DESCAMPS, A. & DE HALLEUX, A. Mélanges Bibliques en hommage au R. P. Béda Rigaux (1970) 506-07. JEREMIAS, J., Die Sprache des Lukasevangeliums (Göttingen 1980) 212-13.

12:7 JEREMIAS, J., Die Sprache des Lukasevangeliums (Göttingen 1980) 213.

12:8ff. WAINWRIGHT, A. W. The Trinity in the New Testament (1962) 118-19, 207-08, 209-10. CARLSTON, C. E. "The Things that Defile (Mark VIII.14) and the Law in Matthew and Mark," NTS 15 (1968-1969) 79-80.

12:8-10. 11f. HAHN, F. Das Verständnis der Mission im Neuen Testament (²1965) 44.

12:8-10 KAESEMANN, E. Exegetische Versuche und Besinnungen (1964) II 97. KAESEMANN, E. New Testament Questions of Today (1969) 99.

12:8-9 KNOX, W. L. The Sources of the Synoptic Gospels II (1957) 66. BLAIR, E. P. Jesus in the Gospel of Matthew (1960) 91. ROB-INSON, J. M. Kerygma und historischer Jesus (1960) 34, 148. SCHWEIZER, E. Erniedrigung und Erhöhung bei Jesus und seinen Nachfolgern (1962) § 3fgil. HAHN, F. Christologische Hoheitstitel (1963) 24, 30, 33-36, 40-42, 321. FULLER, R. H. The Foundation of New Testament Christology (1965) 121ff. HAHN, F. Das Verständnis der Mission im Neuen Testament (²1965) 27. MARSHALL, I. H. NTS 12 (1965-1966) 330f., 346f. JÜNGEL, E. Paulus und Jesus (1966) 242f., 244, 258-60. BORNKAMM, G. "Das Wort Jesu vom Bekennen", Geschichte und Glaube I (1968) 25-36. BORSCH, F. H. The Christian & Gnostic Son of Man (1970) 16-20. BERGER, K. "Zu den Sogenannten Sätzen Heiligen Rechts," NTS 17 (1970-1971) 19f. JEREMIAS, J. Neutestamentliche Theologie I (1971) 21, 25, 248, 262. SCHULZ, S. Q Die Spruchquelle der Evangelisten (1972) 66-76. ZMIJEWSKI, J., Die Eschatologiereden des Lukas-Evangeliums (Bonn 1972) 166-68, 249, 250, 323. LANGE, J., Das Erscheinen des Auferstandenen im Evangelium nach Mattäus (Würzburg 1973) 104, 156, 189-91, 195, 200, 208, 296, 490, 499. LOHSE, E., Die Einheit des Neuen Testaments (Göttingen 1973) 15, 42-44. SCHUBERT, K., Jesus im Lichte der Religionsgeschichte des Judentums (München/Wien 1973) 129. LOHSE, E., Grundriss der neutestamentlichen Theologie (Stuttgart 1974) 47-49, 115. HIGGINS, A. J. B., " 'Menschensohn' oder 'ich' in Q: Lk 12,8-9/Mt 10,32-33?" in: R. Pesch/ R. Schnackenburg (eds.) Jesus und der Menschensohn (Freiburg

1975) 117-23. HOWARD, V. P., Das Ego in den Synoptischen Evangelien (Marburg 1975) 152-56. MCDERMOTT, J. M., "Luke, XII,8-9: Stone of Scandal" RB 84 (1977) 523-37. PESCH, R., "Ueber die Autorität Jesu. Eine Rückfrage anhand des Bekenne und Verleugnerspruchs Lk 12:8f par." in: R. Schnackenburg et al. (eds.) Die Kirche des Anfangs. FS. H. Schürmann (Leipzig 1977) 25-55. POLAG, A. Die Christologie der Logienquelle (Neukirchen-Vluyn 1977) 98, 114, 133. "Apokalyptik" in: TRE 3 (1978) 253. MCDERMOTT, J. M., "Luc, XII,8-9: Pierre angularie" RB 85 (1978) 381-401. SCHILLEBEECKX, E., Die Auferstehung Jesu als Grund der Erlösung" in: K. Rahner/H. Schlier (eds.) Quaestiones Disputatae (Basel 1979) 80. JEREMIAS, J., Die Sprache des Lukasevangeliums (Göttingen 1980) 213-14.

12:8 KNOX, W. L. The Sources of the Synoptic Gospels II (1957) 142. ROBINSON, J. M. Kerygma und historischer Jesus (1960) 143. HENNECKE, E./SCHNEEMELCHER, W. Neutestamentliche Apokryphen (1964) I 113. JÜNGEL, E. Paulus und Jesus (1966) 230. PESCH R., Die Vision des Stephanus (1966) 18, 19, 34, 63. JEREMIAS, J. Neutestamentliche Theologie I (1971) 10, 15, 135, 260, 257f. HAMERTON-KELLY, R. G. Pre-Existence, Wisdom, and The Son of Man (1973) 26, 42, 46, 61, 83, 86, 93, 95. VAWTER, B. This Man Jesus (1973) 115ff. RUPPERT, L., Jesus der leidende Gerechte? (Stuttgart 1972) 61, 62, A67, A69, 66, 69, 70, 71, A98. GOPPELT, L., Theologie des Neuen Testaments. I (Göttingen 1975) 172, 208, 228, 241ff. HOLTZ, T., " 'Euer Glaube an Gott' Zu Form und Inhalt von 1 Thess. 1.9f" in: R. Schnackenburg et al. (eds.) Die Kirche des Anfangs. FS. H. Schürmann (Freiburg 1978) 465-66. HORTON, F. L., "Reflections on the Semitisms of Luke-Acts" in: C. H. Talbert (ed.) Perspectives on Luke-Acts (Danville 1978) 9.

12:9 PERSCH, R. Die Vision des Stephanus (1966) 35, 55, 56, 63.

12:10 MANSON, T. W. The Teaching of Jesus (1945) 215ff. BARRETT, C. K. The Holy Spirit and the Gospel Tradition (1947) 103-07. 133f. BUTLER, B. C. The Originality of St Matthew (1951) 8ff. KNOX, W. L. The Sources of the Synoptic Gospels II (1957) 66, 72. SCHWEIZER, E. Erniedrigung und Erhöhung bei Jesus und seinen Nachfolgern (1962) §30. HAHN, F. Christologische Hoheitstitel (1963) 43, 107. YATES, J. E. The Spirit and the Kingdom (1963) 90-94. KAESEMANN, E. Exegetische Versuche und Besinnungen (1964) I 246. MARSHALL, I. H. "Hard Sayings-VII. Luke 12.10," Theology 67 (524, 1964) 65-67. SCHRAGE, W. Das Verhältnis des Thomas-Evangeliums zur Synoptischen Tradition und zu den Koptischen Evangelienübersetzungen (1964) 98. WILLIAMS, J. C. NTS 12 (1965-1966) 75f. SATAKE, A. Die Ge-

meindeordnung in der Johannesapokalypse (1966) 172-75. BLACK,
M. An Aramaic Approach to the Gospels and Acts (1967) 194f.
NICKELS, P. Targum and New Testament (1967) 39. LÖVES-
TAM, E. Spiritus Blasphemia (1968) 69ff. WREGE, H.-T. Die
Ueberlieferungsgeschichte der Bergpredigt (1968) 156-80.
BROWN, S. Apostasy and Perseverance in the Theology of Luke
(1969) 107f., 112. HOLST, R. "Reexamining Mk 3:28 and Its
Parallels," ZNW 63 (1972) 122-24. LOHSE, E. et al., eds., Der
Ruf Jesu und die Antwort der Gemeinde (1970) 63-79. JE-
REMIAS, J. Neutestamentliche Theologie I (1971) 22, 25, 47, 248f.
SCHULZ, S. Q Die Spruchquelle der Evangelisten (1972) 246-50.
LÖVESTAM, E., "Logiet om hädelse mot den helige Ande" SEA
XXXIII (1968) 101-17. DUNN, J. D. G., Jesus and the Spirit
(London 1975) 44, 49-53. BORING, M. E., "The Unforgivable
Sin Logion Mark III 22-29/Matt XII 31-32/Luke XII 10: Formal
Analysis and History of Tradition" NovT 18 (1976) 258-79. ED-
WARDS, R. A., A Theology of Q (Philadelphia 1976) 121-22.
POLAG, A., Die Christologie der Logienquelle (Neukirchen-Vluyn
1977) 162. BÖHLIG, A., Die Gnosis III: Der Manichäismus (Zü-
rich 1980) 330 n.44. JEREMIAS, J., Die Sprache des Lukas-
evangeliums (Göttingen 1980) 214. KRAFT, H., Die Entstehung
des Christentums (Darmstadt 1981) 168-69.

12:11-12 BÜCHSEL, D. F. Der Geist Gottes im Neuen Testament (1926)
184ff. BARRETT, C. K. The Holy Spirit and the Gospel Tradition
(1947) 130-32. HAHN, F. Christologische Hoheitstitel (1963) 107.
KÜNZI, M. Das Naherwartungslogion Matthäus 10,23 (1970) 7,
158ff. PATSCH, II. Abendmahl und historischer Jesus (1972) 124f.
SCHULZ, S. Q Die Spruchquelle der Evangelisten (1972) 442-
44.DUPONT, J., "La persécution comme situation missionaire
(Marc 13:9-11)" in: R. Schnackenburg et al. (eds.) Die Kirche des
Anfangs. FS. H. Schürmann (Leipzig 1977) 102-04, 107-11. PO-
LAG, A., Die Christologie der Logienquelle (Neukirchen-Vluyn
1977) 98. KREMER, J., "Jesu Verheissung des Geistes. Zur Verankerung der Aussage von Joh 16:13 im Leben Jesu" in: R.
Schnackenburg et al. (eds.) Die Kirche des Anfangs. FS. H. Schürmann (Freiburg 1978) 262-67. PRAST, F., Presbyter und Evangelium in nachapostolischer Zeit (Stuttgart 1979) 66.

12:11 SCHÜRMANN, H. "Sprachliche Reminiszenzen an abgeänderte
oder ausgelassene Bestandteile der Spruchsammlung im Lukas- und
Matthäusevangelium," NTS 6 (1959-1960) 209f. MORRISON, C.
The Power that be (1960) 25, 42f. JEREMIAS, J., Die Sprache des
Lukasevangeliums (Göttingen 1980) 214.

12:12-32 SCHÜRMANN, H. "Sprachliche Reminiszenzen an abgeänderte oder ausgelassene Bestandteile der Spruchsammlung im Lukas- und Matthäusevangelium,'' NTS 6 (1959-1960) 209f.

12:12 HAHN, F. Christologische Hoheitstitel (1963) 107. BLACK, M. An Aramaic Approach to the Gospels and Acts (1967) 108f., 111f. SCHWEIZER, E., Heiliger Geist (Stuttgart 1978) 144.

12:13-34 BORNHÄUSSER, K. Studien zum Sondergut des Lukas (1934) 81-93. TALBERT, C. H., Literary Patterns, Theological Themes, and the Genre of Luke-Acts (Missoula 1974) 52. ''Armut'' in: TRE 4 (1979) 78.

12:13-31 MATTILL, A. J. Luke and the Last Things (Dillsboro 1979) 35-36.

12:13-21 HIRSCH, E. Frühgeschichte des Evangeliums (1941) 114f, 213-15. MORGAN, G. C. The Parables and Metaphors of Our Lord (1943) 187ff. STECK, GPM 4 (1949-1950) 252ff. FÜRST, GPM 9 (1954-1955) 227ff. MICHAELIS, D. W. Die Gleichnisse Jesu (1956) 221-24. SCHWEIZER, E. GPM 15 (1960-1961) 280ff. BARTSCH, H. W., Wachet aber zu jeder Zeit! (Hamburg-Bergstedt 1963) 101-102. LOCKYER, H. All the Parables of the Bible (1963) 266 ff. SCHWEIZER, E. Neues Testament und heutige Verkündigung (1969) 61-65. BARCLAY, W. And Jesus Said (1970) 120-26. LEHMANN, M. Synoptische Quellenanalyse und die Frage nach dem historischen Jesus (1970) 157-59. EICHHOLZ, G. Gleichnisse der Evangelien (1971) 179-91. PIDWELL, H. Blessed are the Poor (Rüschlikon 1972) 87-93. TALBERT, C. H., Literary Patterns, Theological Themes, and the Genre of Luke-Acts (Missoula 1974) 55. DERRETT, J. D. M., ''The Rich Fool: A Parable of Jesus Concerning Inheritance'' HeyJ 18 (1977) 131-51. MANEK, J., . . . und brachte Frucht. Die Gleichnisse Jesu (Berlin 1977) 97-98. SCHNEIDER, G., Das Evangelium nach Lukas (Gütersloh 1977) 281. KARRIS, R. J., ''Poor and Rich: The Lukan Sitz im Leben'' in: C. H. Talbert (ed.) Perspectives on Luke-Acts (Danville 1978) 120.

12:13-15 TAYLOR, V. The Formation of the Gospel Tradition (1949) 23f. MAIER, G., ''Verteilt Jesus die Güter dieser Erde? Eine Untersuchung zu Luk. 12,13-15'' ThB 5 (1974) 149-58. EIBACH, U., ''Jesus und die Güter dieser Erde!—Oder 'Von der Pflicht eines biblischen Exegeten'! Einige Anfragen zu einer höchst bedenklichen Art, biblische Exegese zu 'verwerten' '' ThB 6 (1975) 27-30. NEUSNER, J., (ed.) Christianity, Judaism, and other Greco-Roman Cults. I. FS. M. Smith (Leiden 1975) 107-62. WEISSKOPF, R., 'Lächeln reicht nicht'' ThB 6 (1975) 23-27. TRITES, A. A., The New Testament Concept of Witness (Cambridge 1977) 183.

12:13-14 KNOX, W. L. The Sources of the Synoptic Gospels II (1957) 69.
DEGENHARDT, H.-J. Lukas, Evangelist der Armen (1964) 69-
73. SCHRAGE, W. Das Verhältnis des Thomas-Evangeliums zur
Synoptischen Tradition und zu den Koptischen Evangelienübersetzungen (1964) 151.

12:13 HAHN, F. Christologische Hoheitstitel (1963) 76, 77. NICKELS,
P. Targum and New Testament (1967) 39.

12:14 JEREMIAS, J., Die Sprache des Lukasevangeliums (Göttingen
1980) 215.

12:15-40 SMITH, M. Tannaitic Parallels to the Gospels (1968) 4 C.

12:15-21 BÜCKMANN, O. in: Herr, tue meine Lippen auf Bd. 1 (1957) G.
Eichholz ed., 342-47. GLÖCKNER, R., Die Verkündigung des
Heils beim Evangelisten Lukas (Mainz 1975) 139ff., 152. DEMKE,
C., in: GPM 33 (1979) 374-80.

12:15.19 AALEN, S. NTS 13 (1966-1967) 4ff.

12:15 DEGENHARDT, H.-J., Lukas, Evangelist der Armen (1964) 73-
76. PALLIS, A., Notes on St. Luke and the Acts (London 1928)
27.

12:16ff. BIRDSALL, J. N. "Luke XII.16ff. and the Gospel of Thomas,"
JThS 13 (3, 1962) 332-36. GOULDER, M. D. Midrash and Lection in Matthew (1974) 50, 55f., 60.

12:16-34 PIROT, J. Paraboles et Allégories Evangeliques (1949) 300-05.

12:16-21 JÜLICHER, D. A. Die Gleichnisreden Jesu (1910) 608-17. KNOX,
W. L. The Sources of the Synoptic Gospels II (1957) 29.
BARTSCH, H.-W. "Gib acht! Es ist später, als du denkst!", in:
Kleine Predigt-Typologie III (1965) L. Schmidt, ed., 112-17.
SUMMERS, R. The Secret Sayings of the Living Jesus (1968) 27,
46. GENSICHEN, H.-W. "Gerechtigkeit im Kampf gegen Hun-
ger und Armut", Zuwendung und Gerechtigkeit (1969) 60-64.
DUPONT, J., "Die individuelle Eschatologie im Lukas-Evangelium und in der Apostelgeschichte" in: P. Hoffmann (ed.) Orientierung an Jesus. FS. J. Schmid (Freiburg 1973) 38-39, 41, 42.
GOPPELT, L., Theologie des Neuen Testaments. I (Göttingen
1975) 131. SANDERS, J. T., Ethics in the New Testament (Philadelphia 1975) 37. PERRIN, N., Jesus and the Language of the
Kingdom (London 1976) 128, 196. SENG, E. W., "Der reiche Tor:
Eine Untersuchung von Lk. xii 16-21 unter besonderer Berücksichtigung form- und motivgeschichtlicher Aspekte" NovT 20
(1978) 236-55. VIELHAUER, P., "Oikodome. Das Bild vom Bau
in der christlichen Literatur vom Neuen Testament bis Clemens Alexandrinus" in: G. Klein (ed.) Oikodome (München 1979) 56.

12:16-20 DEGENHARDT, H.-J. Lukas, Evangelist der Armen (1964) 76-
78. SCHRAGE, W. Das Verhältnis des Thomas-Evangeliums zur

Synoptischen Tradition und zu den koptischen Evangelien übersetzungen (1964) 131. JÜNGEL, E. Paulus und Jesus (1966) 99.

12:16 NICKELS, P. Targum and New Testament (1967) 39. METZ-
GER, B. M., The Early Versions of the New Testament (Oxford
1977) 179. JEREMIAS, J., Die Sprache des Lukasevangeliums
(Göttingen 1980) 215.

12:17-18 JEREMIAS, J., Die Sprache des Lukasevangeliums (Göttingen
1980) 215-16.

12:17 MASSAUX, E. Influence de l'Evangile de saint Matthieu sur la littérature chrétienne avant saint Irénée (1950) 267-71. METZGER,
B. M., The Early Versions of the New Testament (Oxford 1977)
244.

12:19.21 ALAND, K. NTS 12 (1965-1966) 198f.

12:19 BAUER, J. B., Scholia Biblica et Patristica (Graz 1972) 105-06.
JEREMIAS, J., Die Sprache des Lukasevangeliums (Göttingen
1980) 216.

12:20 FISCHER, U., Eschatologie und Jenseitserwartung im hellenistischen Diasporajudentum (Berlin 1978) 142, 145.

12:21 DEGENHARDT, H.-J. Lukas, Evangelist der Armen (1964) 78-
80. STROBEL, A. Erkenntnis und Bekenntnis der Sünde in
neutestamentlicher Zeit (1968) 43. LOHSE, E., Die Einheit des
Neuen Testaments (Göttingen 1973) 58-59. HOLM-NIELSEN, S.,
"Die Psalmen Salomos" in: W. G. Kümmel (ed.) Jüdische Schriften aus hellenistisch-römischer Zeit. IV (Gütersloh 1977) 83.
METZGER, B. M., The Early Versions of the New Testament
(Oxford 1977) 134. JEREMIAS, J., Die Sprache des Lukasevangeliums (Göttingen 1980) 216.

12:22ff. BLAIR, E. P. Jesus in the Gospel of Matthew (1960) 91.

12:22-59 HIRSCH, E. Frühgeschichte des Evangeliums (1941) 114-27. RO-
LOFF, J. Apostolat-Verkündigung-Kirche (1965) 211-17. "Apostel" in: TRE 3 (1978) 443.

12:22-46, 51- HOFFMANN, P. Studien zur Theologie der Logienquelle (1972)
53, 57-59 passim.

12:22-34 STAUDINGER, J. Die Bergpredigt (1957) 64, 256, 257. TAL-
BERT, C. H., Literary Patterns, Theological Themes, and the Genre
of Luke-Acts (Missoula 1974) 55.

12:22-32 WREGE, H.-T. Die Ueberlieferungsgeschichte der Bergpredigt
(1968) 116-24. AGRELL, G., Work, Toil and Sustenance (Hägersten 1976). EDWARDS, R. A., A Theology of Q (Philadelphia
1976) 123-24. SCHNEIDER, G., Das Evangelium nach Lukas
(Gütersloh 1977) 284.

12:22-31 DEGENHARDT, H.-J. Lukas, Evangelist der Armen (1964) 80-85. BLACK, M. An Aramaic Approach to the Gospels and Acts (1967) 178f. SCHULZ, S. Q Die Spruchquelle der Evangelisten (1972) 149-57. BORSCH, F. H., "Jesus the Wandering Preacher?" in: M. Hooker/C. Hickling (eds.) What about the New Testament? FS. C. Evans (London 1975) 50. OLSTHOORN, M. F., The Jewish Background and the Synoptic Setting of Mt. 6:25-33 and Lk. 12:22-31 (Jerusalem 1975). TANNEHILL, R. C., The Sword of His Mouth (Missoula 1975) 60-67.

12:22-24 MASSAUX, E. Influence de l'Evangile de saint Matthieu sur la littérature chrétienne avant saint Irénée (1950) 479-81.

12:22 PALLIS, A., Notes on St. Luke and the Acts (London 1928) 28. SCHRAGE, W. Das Verhältnis des Thomas-Evangeliums zur Synoptischen Tradition und zu den Koptischen Evangelienübersetzungen (1964) 90. HASLER, V. Amen (1969) 59. SWIDLER, L., Biblical Affirmations of Woman (Philadelphia 1979) 289.

12:24 BLAIR, E. P. Jesus in the Gospel of Matthew (1960) 91. NICKELS, P. Targum and New Testament (1967) 39. JEREMIAS, J., Die Sprache des Lukasevangeliums (Göttingen 1980) 217.

12:25-28 MANEK, J., . . . und brachte Frucht. Die Gleichnisse Jesu (Berlin 1977) 35-36.

12:25 JEREMIAS, J., Die Sprache des Lukasevangeliums (Göttingen 1980) 217.

12:26 HAHN, F. Christologische Hoheitstitel (1963) 24.

12:27 HASLER, V. Amen (1969) 59. "Arbeit" in: TRE 3 (1978) 627.

12:28-32 GRUNDMANN, W., "Weisheit im Horizont des Reiches Gottes. Eine Studie zur Verkündigung Jesu nach der Spruchüberlieferung Q" in: R. Schnackenburg et al. (eds.) Die Kirche des Anfangs. FS. H. Schürmann (Leipzig 1977) 195-96.

12:29-31 MASSAUX, E. Influence de l'Evangile de saint Matthieu sur la littérature chrétienne avant saint Irénée (1950) 479-81. OTT, W. Gebet und Heil (1965) 108f., 139, 142.

12:29 PALLIS, A., Notes on St. Luke and the Acts (London 1928) 28-29. MOLITOR, J., "Zur Uebersetzung von Lk 12:29" BZ 10 (1966) 461-66.

12:30-33 ROTTENBERG, I. C., The Promise and the Presence (Grand Rapids 1980) 17.

12:30 HAUBST, R. "Eschatologie. 'Der Wetterwinkel' - 'Theologie der Hoffnung', " TThZ 77 (1968) 35-65. LADD, G. E., A Theology of the New Testament (Grand Rapids 1974) 54, 85, 225.

12:31 NÖTSCHER, F. "Das Reich (Gottes) und seine Gerechtigkeit (Mt 6,33 vgl. Lc 12,31)", Biblica 31 (1950) 237-41. OTT, W., Gebet und Heil (1965) 33f, 104, 116, 119, 142. SCHÜRMANN, H. Ursprung und Gestalt (1970) 48, 50, 55, 56, 133, 280. JEREMIAS, J. Neutestamentliche Theologie I (1971) 22, 25, 40, 42, 234. SANFORD, J. A., The Kingdom Within (New York 1970) 57-58. LADD, G. E., A Theology of the New Testament (Grand Rapids 1974) 73, 103, 134.

12:32ff. STAEHELIN, E. Die Verkündigung des Reiches Gottes in der Kirche Jesu Christ I (1951) 388.

12:32-48 GEORGE, A., "L'attente du maître qui vient. Lc 12,32-48" AssS 50 (1974) 66-76.

12:32-33 DEGENHARDT, H.-J, Lukas, Evangelist der Armen (1964) 85-88.

12:32 GRILL, J., Untersuchungen über die Entstehung des vierten Evangeliums. II (Leipzig 1923) 154-55. VOLZ, P. Die Eschatologie der jüdischen Gemeinde (1934) 380. FLEW, R. N. Jesus and his Church (1956) 38-39. BLAIR, E. P. Jesus in the Gospel of Matthew (1960) 84. PESCH, W. "Zur Formgeschichte und Exegese von Lk 12,32'', Biblica 41 (1960) 25-40. MINEAR, P. S. Images of the Church in the New Testament (1960) 84f. BRUCE, F. F. "The Book of Zechariah and the Passion Narrative'', BJRL 43 (1960-1961) 346. LINDARS, B. New Testament Apologetic (1961) 128, 183-85, 280. FISCHER, GPM 17 (1962-1963) 51ff. NICKELS, P. Targum and New Testament (1967) 39. HAMEL, J. GPM 23 (1968-1969) 55-60. JEREMIAS, J. Neutestamentliche Theologie I (1971) 40, 100, 105, 163, 165, 176f., 199, 234, 253, 261. PESCH, R. Die Kleine Herde (1973). FORCK, G., in: GPM 29 (1974) 69-73. FÜRST, W., in: GPM 29 (1974) 63-69. LADD. G. E., A Theology of the New Testament (Grand Rapids 1974) 72, 85, 103, 108, 134. POLAG, A., Die Christologie der Logienquelle (Neukirchen-Vluyn 1977) 97. PRAST, F., Presbyter und Evangelium in nachapostolischer Zeit (Stuttgart 1979) 242. SCHLOSSER, J., "Le Règne de Dieu dans les dits de Jésus'' RevSR 53 (1979) 164-76.

12:33-48 EDWARDS, R. A., A Theology of Q (Philadelphia 1976) 125-27.

12:33-34 MOORE, G. F. Judaism (1946) II 91. BARRETT, C. K. The New Testament Background (1956) 223. DUPONT, D. J. Les Béatitudes (1958) 79-81. SCHÜRMANN, H. "Sprachliche Reminiszenzen an abgeänderte oder ausgelassene Bestandteile der Spruchsammlung im Lukas- und Matthäusevangelium.'' NTS 6 (1959-1960) 209f. PESCH, W. "Zur Exegese von Mt 6,19-21 und Lk 12,33-34," Biblica 41 (4, 1960) 356-78. DEGENHARDT, H.-J., Lukas, Evangelist der Armen (1964) 88-93. WREGE, E.-T. Die Ueberlieferungsgeschichte der Bergpredigt (1968) 109. SANFORD, J. A., The Kingdom Within (New York 1970) 200-01.

SCHULZ, S. Q Die Spruchquelle der Evangelisten (1972) 142-45. DUPONT, J., "Die individuelle Eschatologie im Lukas-Evangelium und in der Apostelgeschichte" in: P. Hoffmann (ed.) Orientierung an Jesus. FS. J. Schmid (Freiburg 1973) 38-39. BORSCH, F. H., "Jesus the Wandering Preacher?" in: M. Hooker/ C. Hickling (eds.) What about the New Testament? FS. C. Evans (London 1975) 50. EDWARDS, R. A., A Theology of Q (Philadelphia 1976) 124-25. SCHNEIDER, G., Das Evangelium nach Lukas (Gütersloh 1977) 286. KARRIS, R. J., "Poor and Rich: The Lukan Sitz im Leben" in: C. H. Talbert (ed.) Perspectives on Luke-Acts (Danville 1978) 120. MATTILL, A. J., Luke and the Last Things (Dillsboro 1979) 36-37. MEYER, B. F., The Aims of Jesus (London 1979) 145.

12:33 SCHRAGE, W. Das Verhältnis des Thomas-Evangeliums zur Synoptischen Tradition und zu den Koptischen Evangelienübersetzungen (1964) 159. SUMMERS, R. The Secret Sayings of the Living Jesus (1968) 30. BEST, E. NTS 16 (1969-1970) 103f. JEREMIAS, J. Neutestamentliche Theologie I (1971) 20, 25, 213f. JEREMIAS, J., Die Sprache des Lukasevangeliums (Göttingen 1980) 218.

12:34-35 KNOX, W. L. The Sources of the Synoptic Gospels II (1957) 150.

12:34 NICKELS, P. Targum and New Testament (1967) 39. BERGMEIER, R., Glaube als Gabe nach Johannes (Stuttgart 1980) 163 n.303.

12:35ff. STAEHELIN, E. Die Verkündigung des Reiches Gottes in der Kirche Jesu Christi I (1951) 199.

12:35-48 TALBERT, C. H., Literary Patterns, Theological Themes, and the Genre of Luke-Acts (Missoula 1974) 52, 54. SCHNEIDER, G., Das Evangelium nach Lukas (Gütersloh 1977) 288. MATTILL, A. J., Luke and the Last Things (Dillsboro 1979) 85-89. PRAST, F., Presbyter und Evangelium in nachapostolischer Zeit (Stuttgart 1979) 59, 98-99, 136, 233-48.

12:35-46 REICKE, B. Diakonie, Festfreude und Zelos (1951) 234ff. LAMBRECHT, J. "Die Logia-Quellen von Markus 13", Biblica 57 (1966) 350-54. WEBER, O. Predigtmeditationen (1967) 61-65.

12:35-40 FISCHER, GPM 15 (1960-1961) 37ff. BOURBECK, GPM 17 (1962-1963) 370ff. Erhaltet euch in der Liebe Gottes, Predigtgedanken aus Vergangenheit und Gegenwart Reihe C, Bd. 3-4 (1963) 406-18. KRECK, W. in: Herr, tue meine Lippen auf Bd. 3 (1964) G. Eichholz ed., 58ff. HAAR, J. GPM 23 (1968-1969) 416-22. FISCHER, K. M. GPM 27 (1972-1973) 50-55. WEISSGERBER, H. & STAMMLER, E. "Silvester: Lukas 12,35-40," in: Predigtstudien 1972-1973 (1972) E. Lange ed., 66-71. SCHIERSE, F. J.

and KÖKE, H.-H., in: P. Krusche et al. (eds.) Predigtstudien für das Kirchenjahr 1974-1975. II (Stuttgart 1975) 279ff. STEIGER, L., in: GPM 29 (1975) 491-99. LÜWE, H. and ZIPPERT, C., in: P. Krusche et al. (eds.) Predigtstudien für das Kirchenjahr 1978-1979. I (Stuttgart 1978) 88-95. DETERDING, P. E., "Eschatological and Eucharistic Motifs in Luke 12.35-40" Concordia Journal 5 (1979) 85-94. SWIDLER, L., Biblical Affirmations of Woman (Philadelphia 1979) 169, 279.

12:35-39 KÜVEN, C. "Advent in der Entscheidung nach Lukas 12,35-39," BuK 16 (4, 1961) 109-11.

12:35-38 JÜLICHER, D. A. Die Gleichnisreden Jesu (1910) 161-71. DODD, C. H. The Parables of the Kingdom (1948) 160ff. MICHAELIS, D. W. Die Gleichnisse Jesu (1956) 81-86. SCHÜRMANN, H. "Sprachliche Reminiszenzen an abgeänderte oder ausgelassene Bestandteile der Spruchsammlung im Lukas- und Matthäusevangelium." NTS 6 (1959-1960) 209f. JEREMIAS, J. Die Gleichnisse Jesu (1962) 50-52, 67, 85. WEISER, A. Die Knechtsgleichnisse der synoptischen Evangelien (1971) 161-77. LÖVESTAM, E. Spiritual Wakefulness in the New Testament (1963) 92f. CARLSTON, C. E., The Parables of the Triple Tradition (Philadelphia 1975) 84-87, 197-202. SANDERS, J. T., Ethics in the New Testament (Philadelphia 1975) 34-35. SCHNEIDER, G. Parusiegleichnisse im Lukas-Evangelium (Stuttgart 1975) 30-37. POLAG, A., Die Christologie der Logienquelle (Neukirchen-Vluyn 1977) 81-100. KLAUCK, H.-J., Allegorie und Allegorese in Synoptischen Gleichnistexten (Münster 1978) 329-31. LOSADA, D. A., "La venida imprevista del Senor" RevBi 40 (1978) 201-16. WEDER, H., Die Gleichnisse Jesu als Metaphern (Göttingen 1980(2) 162-68.

12:35-37 MINEAR, P. To Heal and to Reveal (New York 1976) 23-24.

12:35.37 SCHRAGE, W. Das Verhältnis des Thomas-Evangeliums zur Synoptischen Tradition und zu den Koptischen Evangelienübersetzungen (1964) 193.

12:35 STREETER, B. H. The Four Gospels (1951) 510f. NICKELS, P. Targum and New Testament (1967) 39. JEREMIAS, J., Die Sprache des Lukasevangeliums (Göttingen 1980) 219.

12:36-38 DESCAMPS, A. & DE HALLEUX, A. Mélanges Bibliques en hommage au R. P. Béda Rigaux (1970) 102-07.

12:36 PALLIS, A., Notes on St. Luke and the Acts (London 1928) 29. JEREMIAS, J., Die Sprache des Lukasevangeliums (Göttingen 1980) 219.

12:37ff. FINDLAY, J. A. Jesus and His Parables (1951) 8ff.

12:37 PALLIS, A., Notes on St. Luke and the Acts (London 1928) 215.

HASLER, V. Amen (1969) 101. "Abendmahl" in: TRE 1 (1977) 215. METZGER, B. M., The Early Versions of the New Testament (Oxford 1977) 115, 176. JEREMIAS, J., Die Sprache des Lukasevangeliums (Göttingen 1980) 220.

12:38-40 WILSON, S. G., The Gentiles and the Gentile Mission in Luke-Acts (Cambridge 1973) 74, 75, 82, 83, 85.

12:38 STAEHELIN, E. Die Verkündigung des Reiches Gottes in der Kirche Jesu Christi I (1951) 389.

12:39-13:9 FARRER, A. St. Matthew and St. Mark (1954) 140n.

12:39-46 KNOX, W. L. The Sources of the Synoptic Gospels II (1957) 135. SCHÜRMANN, H. "Sprachliche Reminiszenzen an abgeänderte oder ausgelassene Bestandteile der Spruchsammlung im Lukas- und Matthäusevangelium." NTS 6 (1959-1960) 209f.

12:39-46 LÜHRMANN, D. Die Redaktion der Logienquelle (1969) 69-70.

12:39-40 JÜLICHER, D. A. Die Gleichnisreden Jesu (1910) 137-45. JEREMIAS, J. Die Gleichnisse Jesu (1962) 38, 45-48. SANFORD, J. A., The Kingdom Within (New York 1970) 206. PATSCH, H. Abendmahl und historischer Jesus (1972) 114f. SCHULZ, S. Q Die Spruchquelle der Evangelisten (1972) 268-71.HARNISCH, W., Eschatologische Existenz (Göttingen 1973) 10, 13, 62, 76, 84-85, 87, 87A, 90, 93, 93A, 94-95, 98, 110. SCHNEIDER, G., Parusiegleichnisse im Lukas-Evangelium (Stuttgart 1975) 20-23. MANEK, J., . . . und brachte Frucht. Die Gleichnisse Jesu (Berlin 1977) 66-67. POLAG, A. Die Christologie der Logienquelle (Neukirchen-Vluyn 1977) 95, 133. LOSADA, D. A., "La venida imprevista del Senor" RevBi 40 (1978) 201-16. PRAST, F., Presbyter und Evangelium in nachapostolischer Zeit (Stuttgart 1979) 239.

12:39 HAHN, F. Christologische Hoheitstitel (1963) 92. SCHRAGE, W. Das Verhältnis des Thomas-Evangeliums zur Synoptischen Tradition und zu den Koptischen Evangelienübersetzungen (1964) 67. ALAND, K. NTS 12 (1965-1966) 198f. DESCAMPS, A. & DE HALLEUX, A. Mélanges Bibliques en hommage au R. P. Béda Rigaux (1970) 108-15. HARNISCH, W., Eschatologische Existenz (Göttingen 1973) 85, 87A, 89, 92A, 93A, 94, 94A, 95, 95A, 96-98.

12:40ff. STONEHOUSE, N. B. The Witness of Matthew and Mark to Christ (1944) 254ff.

12:40 BLAIR, E. P. Jesus in the Gospel of Matthew (1960) 74. JÜNGEL, E. Paulus und Jesus (1966) 240f. NICKELS, P. Targum and New Testament (1967) 39. HARNISCH, W., Eschatologische Existenz (Göttingen 1973) 88, 90, 93A, 95, 95A, 97. PERRIN, N., The New Testament (New York 1974) 75-77.

12:41-48 JÜLICHER, D. A. Die Gleichnisreden Jesu (1910) 145-61. MOR-

GAN, G. C. The Parables and Metaphors of Our Lord (1943) 191ff.
WILSON, S. G., The Gentiles and the Gentile Mission in Luke-Acts (Cambridge 1973) 74, 75, 82, 83, 85. "Amt" in: TRE 2 (1978) 525. PRAST, F., Presbyter und Evangelium in nachapostolischer Zeit (Stuttgart 1979) 197, 227, 260-52, 349, 435. "Autorität" in TRE 5 (1980) 42.

12:41-46 MICHAELIS, D. W. Die Gleichnisse Jesu (1956) 71-80. JEREMIAS, J. Die Gleichnisse Jesu (1962) 38, 53-55, 64f., 85, 89. SCHNEIDER, G., Parusiegleichnisse im Lukas-Evangelium (Stuttgart 1975) 23-29. MANEK, J., . . . und brachte Frucht. Die Gleichnisse Jesu (Berlin 1977) 67-69.

12:41-43 MUSSNER, F., Petrus und Paulus—Pole der Einheit (Freiburg 1976) 24.

  12:41 STRECKER, G. Der Weg der Gerechtigkeit (1962) 198₃. HAHN, F. Christologische Hoheitstitel (1963) 84, 85, 88. LOHFINK, G. Die Himmelfahrt Jesu (1971) 155f. PRAST, F., Presbyter und Evangelium in nachapostolischer Zeit (Stuttgart 1979) 234-38. JEREMIAS, J., Die Sprache des Lukasevangeliums (Göttingen 1980) 220.

12:42-48 WEISER, A. Die Knechtsgleichnisse der synoptischen Evangelien (1971) 178-225. PRAST, F., Prebyter und Evangelium in nachapostolischer Zeit (Stuttgart 1979) 238-48.

12:42-46 DODD, C. H. The Parables of the Kingdom (1948) 158ff. PIROT, J. Paraboles et Allégories Evangeliques (1949) 422-28. SCHULZ, S. Q Die Spruchquelle der Evangelisten (1972) 271-77. POLAG, A., Die Christologie der Logienquelle (Neukirchen-Vluyn 1977) 81, 100. SWIDLER, L., Biblical Affirmations of Woman (Philadelphia 1979) 169.

12:42-44 MINEAR, P., To Heal and to Reveal (New York 1976) 24. EDWARDS, R. A., A Theology of Q (Philadelphia 1976) 65-66.

  12:42 HAHN, F. Christologische Hoheitstitel (1963) 85, 88. HENNECKE, E./SCHNEEMELCHER, W. Neutestamentliche Apokryphen (1964) II 387. BEST, E. NTS 16 (1969-1970) 111f. DESCAMPS, A. & DE HALLEUX, A. Mélanges Bibliques en hommage au R. P. Béda Rigaux (1970) 141-43, 146. PRAST, F., Presbyter und Evangelium in nachapostolischer Zeit (Stuttgart 1979) 194-95. JEREMIAS, J., Die Sprache des Lukasevangeliums (Göttingen 1980) 221.

  12:43 NICKELS, P. Targum and New Testament (1967) 39.

  12:44 STONEHOUSE, N. B. The Witness of Matthew and Mark to Christ (1944) 210. HASLER, V. Amen (1969) 72. JEREMIAS, J., Die Sprache des Lukasevangeliums (Göttingen 1980) 221-22.

  12:45 PALLIS, A., Notes on St. Luke and the Acts (London 1928) 29-

30. JEREMIAS, J. Die Gleichnisse Jesu (1962) 53-55, 154. HEN-NECKE, E./SCHNEEMELCHER, W. Neutestamentliche Apo-kryphen (1964) II 387. NICKELS, P. Targum and New Testament (1967) 39. JEREMIAS, J., Die Sprache des Lukasevangeliums (Göttingen 1980) 222.

12:46 THEYSSEN, G. W. "Unbelief" in the New Testament (1965) 34ff. NICKELS, P. Targum and New Testament (1967) 39. ELLING-WORTH, P., "Luke 12.46—Is there an anti-climax here?" BTr 31 (1980) 242-43. JEREMIAS, J., Die Sprache des Lukasevangel-iums (Göttingen 1980) 222.

12:47-48 MOORE, G. F. Judaism (1946) I 464. STAEHELIN, E. Die Ver-kündigung des Reiches Gottes in der Kirche Jesu Christi I (1951) 353. POLAG, A., Die Christologie der Logienqelle (Neukirchen-Vluyn 1977) 163. PRAST, F., Presbyter und Evangelium in nachapostolischer Zeit (Stuttgart 1979) 245-57.

12:48 KAESEMANN, E. Exegetische Versuche und Besinnungen (1964) II 97. NICKELS, P. Targum and New Testament (1967) 40. KAE-SEMANN, E. New Testament Questions of Today (1969) 98. JE-REMIAS, J. Neutestamentliche Theologie I (1971) 20, 22, 26, 35.

12:49-13:9 TALBERT, C. H., Literary Patterns, Theological Themes, and the Genre of Luke-Acts (Missoula 1974) 52, 55.

12:49-56 FRICK, R. GPM 11/4 (1956-57) 188-93. MATTILL, A. J., Luke and the Last Things (Dillsboro 1979) 208-11.

12:49-53 KNOX, W. L. The Sources of the Synoptic Gospels II (1957) 74. GASTON, L. No Stone on Another (1970) 289-90. TALBERT, C. H., Literary Patterns, Theological Themes, and the Genre of Luke-Acts (Missoula 1974) 52, 55. TANNEHILL, R. C., The Sword of His Mouth (Missoula 1975) 144-47. ARENS, E., The HΛΘON-Sayings in the Synoptic Tradition (Fribourg 1976) 63-90. ED-WARDS, R. A., A Theology of Q (Philadelphia 1976) 127-28. POLAG, A., Die Christologie der Logienquelle (Neukirchen-Vluyn 1977) 164-65. SCHNEIDER, G., Das Evangelium nach Lukas (Gütersloh 1977) 292.

12:49-50 VOLZ, P. Die Eschatologie der jüdischen Gemeinde (1934) 159. ROBINSON, J. A. T. "The One Baptism", Twelve New Testa-ment Studies (1962) 158-75. BULTMANN, R. The History of the Synoptic Tradition (1963) 152-55. HAHN, F. Christologische Ho-heitstitel (1963) 20, 167. BIEDER, W., Die Verheissung der Taufe im Neuen Testament (Zürich 1966) 99-101. DELLING, G. Studien zum Neuen Testament und zum hellenistischen Judentum (1970) 244-53.GERSTENBERGER, G. and SCHRAGE, W., Leiden (Stuttgart 1977) 149-50; ET: J. E. Steeley, Suffering (Nashville

1980) 173-74. MEYER, B. F. The Aims of Jesus (London 1979) 213.

12:49 PALLIS, A., Notes on St. Luke and the Acts (London 1928) 30. SEPER, F. H. "Kai ti thelō ei ēdē anēphthē (Lk 12:49b)," Verb Dom 36 (3, 1958) 147-53. KAESEMANN, E. Exegetische Versuche und Besinnungen (1964) II 96. SCHRAGE, W. Das Verhältnis des Thomas-Evangeliums zur Synoptischen Tradition und zu den Koptischen Evangelienübersetzungen (1964) 49. SUMMERS, R. The Secret Sayings of the Living Jesus (1968) 75. KAESEMANN, E. New Testament Questions of Today (1969) 97. SANFORD, J. A., The Kingdom Within (New York 1970) 81. ZEHNLE, R. F. Peter's Pentecost Discourse (1971) 116-17. MATTILL, A. J., Luke and the Last Things (Dillsboro 1979) 208-35. SWIDLER, L., Biblical Affirmations of Woman (Philadelphia 1979) 283. JEREMIAS, J., Die Sprache des Lukasevangeliums (Göttingen 1980) 223.

12:50 BARTH, M., Die Taufe—Ein Sakrament? (Zürich 1951). STAEHELIN, E. Die Verkündigung des Reiches Gottes in der Kirche Jesu Christi I (1951) 389. BEST, E. One body in Christ (1955) 48. BEASLEY-MURRAY, G. R. Baptism in the New Testament (1962) 53f., 72ff. WAGNER, G. Das religionsgeschichtliche Problem von Römer 6,1-11 (1962) 301f. DELLING, G. Die Taufe im Neuen Testament (1963) 81. DELLING, G. "βάπτισμα βαπτισθῆναι" in: Studien zum Neuen Testament und zum hellenistischen Judentum (1970) 236-56. TALBERT, C. H., Literary Patterns, Theological Themes, and the Genre of Luke-Acts (Missoula 1974) 16, 115. RADL, W., Paulus und Jesus im lukanischen Doppelwerk (Bern 1975) 149-58. MATTILL, A. J., Luke and the Last Things (Dillsboro 1979) 212-13. JEREMIAS, J. Die Sprache des Lukasevangeliums (Göttingen 1980) 223.

12:51-53 ROBERTS, T. A. "Some Comments on Matthew X,34-36 and Luke XII,51-53," ET LXIX/10 (1958) 304-06. SCHRAGE, W. Das Verhältnis des Thomas-Evangeliums zur Synoptischen Tradition und zu den Koptischen Evangelienübersetzungen (1964) 57. SCHULZ, S. Q Die Spruchquelle der Evangelisten (1972) 258-60. SCHENKE, H. M., "Die Tendenz der Weisheit zur Gnosis" in: B. Aland et al. (eds.) Gnosis. FS. H. Jonas (Göttingen 1979) 214-15. MATTILL, A. J., Luke and the Last Things (Dillsboro 1979) 214-15. SWIDLER, L., Biblical Affirmations of Woman (Philadelphia 1979) 179, 242, 257, 259, 274. KUHN, H.-W., "Nachfolge nach Ostern" in: D. Lührmann/G. Strecker (eds.) Kiche. FS. G. Bornkamm (Tübingen 1980) 126.

12:51 HAHN, F. Christologische Hoheitstitel (1963) 167. NICKELS, P. Targum and New Testament (1967) 40. HASLER, V. Amen (1969)

75. JEREMIAS, J. Neutestamentliche Theologie I (1971) 25f.
SANFORD, J. A., The Kingdom Within (New York 1970) 80-81.
HENGEL, M., Was Jesus a Revolutionist? (Phildelphia 1971) 23.
POLAG, A., Die Christologie der Logienquelle (Neukirchen-Vluyn 1977) 164. JEREMIAS, J. Die Sprache des Lukasevangeliums (Göttingen 1980) 223.

12:52-53 DELLING, G. Die Taufe im Neuen Testament (1963) 74. PO-LAG, A. Die Christologie der Logienquelle (Neukirchen-Vluyn 1977) 165. THEISSEN, G., Soziologie der Jesusbewegung (München 1977) 18.

12:52 JEREMIAS, J. Die Sprache des Lukasevangeliums (Göttingen 1980) 224.

12:53 WILLIAMS, J. A., A Conceptual History of Deuteronomism in the Old Testament, Judaism, and the New Testament (Ph.D. Diss. Southern Baptist Theological Seminary; Louisville 1976) 309. JE-REMIAS, J. Die Sprache des Lukasevangeliums (Göttingen 1980) 224.

12:54-13:35 GASTON, L. No Stone on Another (1970) 256, 327.

12:54-13:9 GASTON, L. No Stone on Another (1970) 339-43, 347. WIL-SON, S. G., The Gentiles and the Gentile Mission in Luke-Acts (Cambridge 1973) 75, 76, 82, 85.

12:54ff. KNOX, W. L. The Sources of the Synoptic Gospels II (1957) 74ff.

12:54-59 TALBERT, C. H., Literary Patterns, Theological Themes, and the Genre of Luke-Acts (Missoula 1974) 52, 55.

12:54-58 SCHÜRMANN, H. "Sprachliche Reminiszenzen an abgeänderte oder ausgelassene Bestandteile der Spruchsammlung im Lukas- und Matthäusevangelium." NTS 6 (1959-1960) 209f.

12:54-56 KNOX, W. L. The Sources of the Synoptic Gospels II (1957) 21. ROBINSON, J. M. Kerygma und historischer Jesus (1960) 143. KLEIN, G. "Die Prüfung der Zeit (Lukas 12,54-56)," ZThK 61 (1964) 373-90. BOURBECK, C. "Erkennen wir die Zeichen der Zeit?" in: Kleine Predigt-Typologie III (1965) L. Schmidt ed., 130-36. ZMIJEWSKI, J., Die Eschatologiereden des Lukas-Evangeliums (Bonn 1972) 258-60. TANNEHILL, R. C., The Sword of His Mouth (Philadelphia 1975) 128-34. SCHNEIDER, G., Das Evangelium nach Lukas (Gütersloh 1977) 293. MATTILL, A. J., Luke and the Last Things (Dillsboro 1979) 215-17.

12:54-55 JÜNGEL, E. Paulus und Jesus (1966) 131.

12:56 BLAIR, E. P. Jesus in the Gospel of Matthew (1960) 100. SCHRAGE, W. Das Verhältnis des Thomas-Evangeliums zur Synoptischen Tradition und zu den Koptischen Evangelienübersetzungen (1964) 175. JÜNGEL, E. Paulus und Jesus (1966) 188.

12:57-59 JÜLICHER, D. A. Die Gleichnisreden Jesu (1910) 240-46. DODD, C. H. The Parables of the Kingdom (1948) 136ff. WOOD, M. G. "Interpreting This Time," NTS II/4 (1956) 262-66. DUPONT, D. J. Les Béatitudes (1958) 103-06. SCHÜRMANN, H. Ursprung und Gestalt (1970) 279, 281-83, 284, 285, 286, 289, 290, 291, 295. SCHULZ, S. Q Die Spruchquelle der Evangelisten (1972) 421-24. SANFORD, J. A., The Kingdom Within (New York 1970) 116-18. CONZELMANN, H. and LINDEMANN, A., Arbeitsbuch zum Neuen Testament (Tübingen 1975) 62. SCHNEIDER, G., Das Evangelium nach Lukas (Gütersloh 1977) 295.

12:57 PALLIS, A. Notes on St. Luke and the Acts (London 1928) 30-31.

12:58-59 FLEW, R. N. Jesus and His Church (1956) 44. KNOX, W. L. The Sources of the Synoptic Gospels II (1957) 20. JEREMIAS, J. Die Gleichnisse Jesu (1962) 39-41, 95, 179. MOWRY, L. "Parable", IDB III (1962) 652a.b. GOULDER, M. D. Midrash and Lection in Matthew (1974) 25, 288f. MANEK, J., . . . und brachte Frucht. Die Gleichnisse Jesu (Berlin 1977) 36-37.

12:58 NICKELS, P. Targum and New Testament (1967) 40. JEREMIAS, J. Die Sprache des Lukasevangeliums (Göttingen 1980) 225.

12:59 KNOX, W. L. The Sources of the Synoptic Gospels II (1957) 67. HANHART, K. The Intermediate State in the New Testament (1966) 189-90. HASLER, V. Amen (1969) 57. JEREMIAS, J. Die Sprache des Lukasevangeliums (Göttingen 1980) 225.

———————

13 FLENDER, H. Heil und Geschichte in der Theologie des Lukas (1965) 101-02. GERSTENBERGER, G. und SCHRAGE, W., Leiden (Stuttgart 1980) 197-98. ET: Suffering (Nashville 1980).

13:1ff. KNOX, W. L. The Sources of the Synoptic Gospels II (1957) 75. PETZKE, G. Die Traditionen über Apollonius von Tyana und das Neue Testament (1970) 175, 207.

13:1-9 BORNHÄUSSER, K. Studien zum Sondergut des Lukas (1934) 94-102. HIRSCH, E. Frühgeschichte des Evangeliums (1941) 216-18. PIROT, J. Paraboles et Allégories Evangeliques (1949) 243-49. WEBER, GPM 4 (1949-1950) 301ff. FRICK, GPM 9 (1954-1955) 261ff. BÜCKMANN, O. in: Herr, tue meine Lippen auf Bd. 1 (1957) G. Eichholz ed., 355-59. MERKEL/GEORGI/BALTZER, GPM 16 (1960-1961) 320ff. FARMER, W. R. "Notes on a Literary and Form-Critical Analysis of Some of the Synoptic Material Peculiar to Luke,'' NTS 8 (4, 1962) 301-16. Wir wissen weder Tag noch Stunde, Predigtgedanken aus Vergangenheit und Gegenwart, Reihe A, Bd. 6 (1966) 267-88. WEBER, O., Predigtmeditationen (1967) 150-54. GOLLWITZER, H. GPM 27 (1973) 482-88. WILSON, S. G., The Gentiles and the Gentile Mission in Luke-Acts (Cambridge 1973) 42, 75, 76. SCHNEIDER, G., Das Evangelium nach Lukas (Gütersloh/Würzburg 1977) 296 (lit!).

13:1-8 WILSON, S. G. NTS 16 (1969-1970) 346f.

13:1-5 VOLZ, P. Die Eschatologie der Jüdischen Gemeinde (1934) 132. MOOEW, G. F. Judaism (1946) II 249n, 322. BLINZLER, J. ''Eine Bemerkung zum Geschichtsrahmen des Johannesevangeliums,'' Biblica 36 (1955) 23-35. BOUSSET, W. Die Religion des Judentums im Späthellenistischen Zeitalter (1966 = 1926) 210, 391. BLINZLER, J. Aus der Welt und Umwelt des Neuen Testaments (1969) 70f., 95-98, 105f. SCHWARZ, G. ''Lukas xiii 1-5, Eine Emendation,'' NovTest 11 (1-2, 1969) 121-26. JEREMIAS, J. Neutestamentliche Theologie I (1971) 129, 135, 155, 179, 220. BONHOEFFER, D., Gesammelte Schriften, V. (München 1972) 521ff. TALBERT, C. H., Literary Patterns, Theological Themes, and the Genre of Luke-Acts (Missoula 1974) 52, 55. SEYBOLD, K. und MÜLLER, U., Krankheit und Heilung (Stuttgart 1978) 105-07, 142.

13:1-3 HAHN, F. Christologische Hoheitstitel (1963) 164. ZEITLIN, S., ''Who Were the Galileans? New Light on Josephus' Activities in Galilee'' JQR (1974) 189-203.

13:1 KNOX, W. L. The Sources of the Synoptic Gospels II (1957) 70, 76. HAHN, F. Christologische Hoheitstitel (1963) 164. BLINZLER, J. Aus der Welt und Umwelt des Neuen Testaments (1969) 70, 96-99, 102, 104. SANDMEL, S., We Jews and Jesus (New York 1977) 36. JEREMIAS, J. Die Sprache des Lukasevangeliums (Göttingen 1980) 226.

13:2-5 JÜLICHER, D. A. Die Gleichnisreden Jesu (1910) 441-44.

13:2 STROBEL, A., Erkenntnis und Bekenntnis der Sünde in neutestamentlicher Zeit (1968) 42. JEREMIAS, J., Die Sprache des Lukasevangeliums (Göttingen 1980) 226.

13:3-5 HASLER, V. Amen (1969) 104.

13:3 MEYER, B. F., The Aims of Jesus (London 1979) 210-11.

13:4-12 ZINGG, P., Das Wachsen der Kirche (Freiburg 1974) 229-30.

13:4 STROBEL, A. Erkenntnis und Bekenntnis der Sünde in neutestamentlicher Zeit (1968) 42. METZGER, B. M., The Early Versions of the New Testament (Oxford 1977) 202. JEREMIAS, J. Die Sprache des Lukasevangeliums (Göttingen 1980) 226-27.

13:6ff. FINDLAY, J. A. Jesus and His Church (1951) 30ff. HENNECKE,
E./SCHNEEMELCHER, W. Neutestamentliche Apokryphen
(1964) II 472. GÄRTNER, B. The Temple and the Community in
Qumran and the New Testament (1965) 106.

13:6-9 JÜLICHER, D. A. Die Gleichnisreden Jesu (1910) 433-48. MOR-
GAN, G. C. The Parables and Metaphors of Our Lord (1943) 196ff.
RICHARDSSON, A. The Miracle-Stories of the Gospels (1948)
55f. FLEW, R. N. Jesus and His Church (1956) 38. MICHAELIS,
D. W. Die Gleichnisse Jesu (1956) 95-99. GNILKA, J. Die Ver-
stockung Israels (1961) 136f. ROBIN, A. "The Cursing of the Fig
Tree in Mark XI. A Hypothesis." NTS 8 (1961-1962) 272f.
LOCKYER, H. All the Parables of the Bible (1963) 270ff. BLINZ-
LER, J., "Die letzte Gnadenfrist" BiLe 37 (1963-1964) 155-69.
VAN DER LOOS, H. The Miracles of Jesus (1965) 694-96. BAR-
CLAY, W. And Jesus Said (1970) 127-32. DERRETT, J. D. M.,
"Figtrees in the New Testament" HeyJ 14 (1973) 249-65. DAV-
IES, W. D., The Gospel and the Land (London 1974) 260n.51, 355,
355n.54, 357. TALBERT, C. H., Literary Patterns, Theological
Themes, and the Genre of Luke-Acts (Missoula 1974) 52,55. HEIN,
K., Eucharist and Excommunication. A Study in Early Christian
Doctrine and Discipline (Bern/Frankfurt 1975) 15-17. MANEK, J.,
. . . und brachte Frucht. Die Gleichnisse Jesu (Berlin 1977) 92-94.
HEMPEL, J., in: GPM (1979) 207. JEREMIAS, J. Die Sprache
des Lukasevangeliums (Göttingen 1980) 227.

13:7-8 METZGER, B. M., The Early Version of the New Testament (Oxford 1977) 324.

13:7 BLAIR, E. P. Jesus in the Gospel of Matthew (1960) 115. JE-
REMIAS, J. Die Sprache des Lukasevangeliums (Göttingen 1980)
227.

13:9 SCHOLZ, G., "Ästhetische Beobachtungen am Gleichnis vom
reichen Mann und armen Lazarus und an drei anderen Gleichnissen" LiBi 43 (1978) 67-74.

13:10-35. KNOX, W. L. The Sources of the Synoptic Gospels II (1957) 78ff.,
83.

13:10-17 RICHARDSON, A. The Miracle-Stories of the Gospels (1948) 110-
12. KNOX, W. L. The Sources of the Synoptic Gospels II (1957)
78. ROLOFF, J. Das Kerygma und der irdische Jesus (1970) 66-
69. LOHSE, E., Die Einheit des Neuen Testaments (Göttingen
1973) 63-64. TALBERT, C. H., Literary Patterns, Theological
Themes, and the Genre of Luke-Acts (Missoula 1974) 52, 56.
SCHNEIDER, G., Das Evangelium nach Lukas (Gütersloh/Würz-
burg 1977) 299 (lit!). WILKINSON, J., "The Case of the Bent
Woman in Luke 13:10-17" EQ 49 (1977) 195-205. SWIDLER, L.,

Biblical Affirmations of Woman (Philadelphia 1979) 182, 273. McDONALD, J. I. H., Kerygma and Didache (Cambridge 1980) 50.

13:10 TALBERT, C. H., Literary Patterns, Theological Themes, and the Genre of Luke-Acts (Missoula 1974) 114. JEREMIAS, J. Die Sprache des Lukasevangeliums (Göttingen 1980) 228.

13:11-17 FARRER, A. St Matthew and St Mark (1954) 130n.

13:11-13 BRAUN, H. Qumran und NT II (1966) 97, 106.

13:11 BOUSSET, W. Die Religion des Judentums im Späthellenistischen Zeitalter (1966 = 1926) 339. METZGER, B. M., The Early Versions of the New Testament (Oxford 2977) 213. JEREMIAS, J. Die Sprache des Lukasevangeliums (Göttingen 1980) 228-29.

13:12 JEREMIAS, J. Die Sprache des Lukasevangeliums (Göttingen 1980) 229.

13:12.13 BETZ, H. D. Lukian von Samosata und das Neue Testament (1961) 150, 155, 157.

13:13-16 ZINGG, P., Das Wachsen der Kirche (Freiburg 1974) 230-31.

13:13 FARRER, A. St Matthew and St Mark (1954) 56.

13:14-17 BOUSSET, W. Die Religion des Judentums im Späthellenistischen Zeitalter (1966 = 1926) 125. RIVKIN, E., A Hidden Revolution (Nashville 1978) 122-23. MEYER, B. F., The Aims of Jesus (London 1979) 162-68.

13:14 METZGER, B. M., The Early Versions of the New Testament (Oxford 1977) 211. JEREMIAS, J. Die Sprache des Lukasevangeliums (Göttingen 1980) 229.

13:15-16 SANFORD, J. A., The Kingdom Within (New York (1970) 96-97. WESTERHOLM, S., Jesus and Scribal Authority (Lund 1978) 102.

13:15 STRECKER, G. Der Weg der Gerechtigkeit (1962) 19_3. HAHN, F. Christologische Hoheitstitel (1963) 89. STROBEL, A. Erkenntnis und Bekenntnis der Sünde in neutestamentlicher Zeit (1968) 43. DESCAMPS, A. & DE HALLEUX, A. Mélanges Bibliques en hommage au R. P. Béda Rigaux (1970) 132-34.

13:16 BAUMBACH, G. Das Verständnis des Bösen in den synoptischen Evangelien (1963) 185ff. BRUCE, F. F., The Time is fulfilled (Exeter 1978) 62. JEREMIAS, J. Die Sprache des Lukasevangeliums (Göttingen 1980) 230.

13:17 GERHARDSON, B., "Jesu maktgärningar. Om de urkristna berättarnas val av termer" SEA (1979) 122-33. JEREMIAS, J. Die Sprache des Lukasevangeliums (Göttingen 1980) 230.

13:18-21, 23-35 HIRSCH, E. Frühgeschichte des Evangeliums (1941) 127-34.

13:18-30 TALBERT, C. H., Literary Patterns, Theological Themes, and the Genre of Luke-Acts (Missoula 1974) 56.

13:18-21 JÜLICHER, D. A. Die Gleichnisreden Jesu (1910) 569-81. BUTLER, B. C. The Originality of St Matthew (1951) 22ff. MICHAELIS, D. W. Die Gleichnisse Jesu (1956) 54-60. KUSS, O. "Zum Sinnegehalt des Doppelgleichnisses vom Senfkorn und Sauerteig," Biblica 40 (1959) 641-53. HARRINGTON, W. J. A Key to the Parables (1964) 78-81. ZIMMERMANN, H. Neutestamentliche Methodenlehre (1967) 123-25. TALBERT, C. H., Literary Patterns, Theological Themes, and the Genre of Luke-Acts (Missoula 1974) 56. ZINGG, P., Das Wachsen der Kirche (Freiburg 1974) 100-09, 114. DUPONT, J., "Le couple parabolique du sénevé et du levain; Mt 13,31-33; Lc 13,18-21" in: G. Strecker (ed.) Jesus Christus in Historie und Theologie. FS. H. Conzelmann (Tübingen 1975) 331-45. SCHNEIDER, G., Das Evangelium nach Lukas (Gütersloh/Würzburg 1977) 301 (lit!) MATTILL, A. J., Luke and the Last Things: a Perspective for the Understanding of Lukan Thought (Dillsboro 1979) 177-82. SWIDLER, L., Biblical Affirmations of Woman (Philadelphia 1979) 170. WEDER, H., Die Gleichnisse Jesu als Metaphern (Göttingen 1980) 99-108.

13:18-19 PIROT, J. Paraboles et Allégories Evangeliques (1949) 125-31. STAEHELIN, E. Die Verkündigung des Reiches Gottes in der Kirche Jesu Christi I (1951) 392. SCHRAGE, W. Das Verhältnis des Thomas-Evangeliums zur Synoptischen Tradition und zu den Koptischen Evangelienübersetzungen (1964) 61. BISER, E. Die Gleichnisse Jesu (1965) 79ff. JÜNGEL, E. Paulus und Jesus (1966) 151-54. BARCLAY, W. And Jesus Said (1970) 52-59. SANFORD, J. A., The Kingdom Within (New York 1970) 44-45. SCHULZ, S. Q Die Spruchquelle der Evangelisten (1972) 298-307. TALBERT, C. H., Literary Patterns, Theological Themes, and the Genre of Luke-Acts (Missoula 1974) 40. PERRIN, N., Jesus and the Language of the Kingdom (London 1976) 39, 111, 119, 126, 129, 160. MANEK, J., . . . und brachte Frucht. Die Gleichnisse Jesu (Berlin 1977) 27-29. MEYER, B. F., The Aims of Jesus (London 1979) 163-64. LAUFEN, R., "ΒΑΣΙΛΕΙΑ und EKΚΛΗΣΙΑ. Eine traditions- und redaktionsgeschichtliche Untersuchung des Gleichnisses vom Senfkorn" in: J. Zmijewski/ E. Nellessen (eds.) Begegnung mit dem Wort. FS. H. Zimmermann (Bonn 1980) 105-40. WEDER, H., Die Gleichnisse Jesus als Metaphern (Göttingen 1980(^{2}) 128-38.

13:18 CONZELMANN, H. und LINDEMANN, A., Arbeitsbuch zum Neuen Testament (Tübingen 1975) 55-56.

13:19 SCHÜRMANN, H. "Sprachliche Reminiszenzen an abgeänderte oder ausgelassene Bestandteile der Spruchsammlung im Lukas- und

Matthäusevangelium.'' NTS 6 (1959-1960) 209f. JEREMIAS, J.,
Die Sprache des Lukasevangeliums (Göttingen 1980) 230.

13:20-21 PIROT, J. Paraboles et Allégories Evangeliques (1949) 139-43.
SCHRAGE, W. Das Verhältnis des Thomas-Evangeliums zur Synoptischen Tradition und zu den Koptischen Evangelienübersetzun-
gen (1964) 183. BISER, E. Die Gleichnisse Jesu (1965) 79ff.
BARCLAY, W. And Jesus Said (1970) 60-66. SANFORD, J. A.,
The Kingdom Within (New York 1970) 44-45. SCHULZ, S. Q Die
Spruchquelle der Evangelisten (1972) 307-09. FUNK, R. W., Je-
sus as Precursor (Philadelphia/Missoula 1975) 51-72. MANEK, J.,
. . . und brachte Frucht. Die Gleichnisse Jesu (Berlin 1977) 46-48.
SWIDLER, L., Biblical Affirmations of Woman (Philadelphia
1979) 242, 253, 257. HARRINGTON, D. J., God's People in Christ
(Philadelphia 1980) 23. WALLER, E., ''The Parable of the Leaven:
A Sectarian Teaching and the Inclusion of Women'' USQR (1979-
1980) 99-109. WEDER, H., Die Gleichnisse Jesu als Metaphern
(Göttingen 1980[²]) 128-38.

13:20 KNOX, W. L. The Sources of the Synoptic Gospels II (1957) 130.
DUPONT, J., ''Le Couple Parabolique de Sénevé et du Levain: Mt
13,31-33; Lc 13,18-21'' in: G. Strecker (ed.) Jesus Christus in Historie und Theologie. FS. H. Conzelmann (Tübingen 1975) 333-35.

13:22ff. KNOX, W. L. The Sources of the Synoptic Gospels II (1957) 31.

13:22-35 HAHN, F. Das Verständnis der Mission im Neuen Testament
(²1965) 113.

13:22-30 MUSSNER, F. ''Das 'Gleichnis' vom Gestrengen Mahlherrn. Ein
Beitrag zum Redaktionsverfahren und zur Theologie des Lukas (Lk
13:22-30),'' TThZ 65 (1956) 129-43. KNOX, W. L. The Sources
of the Synoptic Gospels II (1957) 78. DUPONT, D. J. Les Béatitudes (1958) 94-98. Verkündigt das angenehme Jahr des Herrn.
Predigtgedanken aus Vergangenheit und Gegenwart Reihe C, Bd.
1 (1962) 236-50. TRAUB, GPM 17 (1962-1963) 94ff. HARRING-
TON, W. J. A Key to the Parables (1964) 113-16. HOFFMANN,
P. ''Pantes ergatai adikias. Redaktion und Tradition in Lc 13:22-
30,'' ZNW 58 (3-4, 1967) 188-214. MUSSNER, F. ''Das
'Gleichnis' vom gestrengen Mahlherrn (Lk 13,22-30). Ein Beitrag
zum Redaktionsverfahren und zur Theologie des Lukas,'' in: Pre-
sentia Salutis (1967) 113. SEYNAEVE, J., ''La parabole de la porte
étroite: l'acceptation 'pratique' du Christ. Lc 13, 22-30'' AssS 52
(1974) 68-77. TALBERT, C. H., Literary Patterns, Theological
Themes, and the Genre of Luke-Acts (Missoula 1974) 56. ED-
WARDS, R. A., A Theology of Q (Philadelphia 1976) 130-32.
SCHNEIDER, G., Das Evangelium nach Lukas (Gütersloh/Würz-
burg 1977) 304 (lit!).

13:22-37 THIELICKE, H. Das Leben kann noch einmal beginnen (1956) 224-39.

13:22-23 JEREMIAS, J. "Die Drei-Tage-Worte der Evangelien," in: Tradition und Glaube (1971) G. Jeremias ed., 221-29.

13:22.31-35 HIRSCH, E. Frühgeschichte des Evangeliums (1941) 130-32, 219f., 227f.

13:22 STONEHOUSE, N. B. The Witness of Luke to Christ (1951) 116f. SCHURR, V., "Herr, sind es wenige die gerettet werden?" Theologie der Gegenwart 9 (1966) 49-51. DENAUX, A., "L'hypocrisie des Pharisiens et le dessein de Dieu. Analyse de Lc. XIII,31-33" in: F. Neirynck (ed.) L'Evangile de Luc (Gembloux 1973) 247-48, 265-67. MIYOSHI, M., Der Anfang des Reiseberichts Lk 9,51 - 10,24. Eine redaktionsgeschichtliche Untersuchung (Rome 1974) 24-25. TALBERT, C. H., Literary Patterns, Theological Themes, and the Genre of Luke-Acts (Missoula 1974) 17, 20, 114. ZINGG, P., Das Wachsen der Kirche (Freiburg 1974) 138. WILLIAMS, J. A., A Conceptual History of Deuteronomism in the Old Testament, Judaism, and the New Testament (Ph. D. Diss., Louisville 1976) 300. JEREMIAS, J., Die Sprache des Lukasevangeliums (Göttingen 1980) 231.

13:33ff. WREGE, H.-T. Die Ueberlieferungsgeschichte der Bergpredigt (1968) 149ff., 178.

13:23-34 CAVALLIN, H. C. C., Life After Death (Lund 1974) 2, 12, I.

13:23-30 EHRENBERG, G. GPM 6/1, (1951-52) 56-59.

13:23-24 MOORE, G. F. Judaism (1946) II 322n. JÜNGEL, E. Paulus und Jesus (1966) 184. WREGE, H.-T. Die Ueberlieferungsgeschichte der Bergpredigt (1968) 132. SCHULZ, S. Q Die Spruchquelle der Evangelisten (1972) 309-12.

13:23 HAHN, F. Christologische Hoheitstitel (1963) 84, 85. BROWN, S. Apostasy and Perseverance in the Theology of Luke (1969) 140f. MEYER, B. F., The Aims of Jesus (London 1979) 210-11. BERGMEIER, R., Glaube als Gabe nach Johannes (Stuttgart 1980) 60. JEREMIAS, J., Die Sprache des Lukasevangeliums (Göttingen 1980) 231-32.

13:24-30 HAHN, F. Christologische Hoheitstitel (1963) 96. MANEK, J., . . . und brachte Frucht. Die Gleichnisse Jesu (Berlin 1977) 94-95.

13:24 HAHN, F. Christologische Hoheitstitel (1963) 92. NICKELS, P. Targum and New Testament (1967) 40. JEREMIAS, J. Neutestamentliche Theologie I (1971) 25, 28, 100, 131. SANFORD, J. A., The Kingdom Within (New York 1970) 65-66. ROSZA, M., "Passer sur l'autre rive" Christus 26 (Paris 1979) 323-32. JEREMIAS, J., Die Sprache des Lukasevangeliums (Göttingen 1980) 232.

13:25ff. STONEHOUSE, N. B. The Witness of Matthew and Mark to Christ (1944) 225. FEUILLET, A. Essai d'Interprétation de Chapitre xi de l'Apocalypse. NTS 4 (1957-1958) 186ff.

13:25-27 POLAG, A., Die Christologie der Logienquelle (Neukirchen-Vluyn 1977) 79-91.

13:25 PACKETT, E. B. "Lk XIII,25", ET 67 (6, 1956) 178. HAHN, F. Christologische Hoheitstitel (1963) 85, 96, 98.

13:26-30 STONEHOUSE, N. B. The Witness of Matthew and Mark to Christ (1944) 231.

13:26-28 MEES, M., "Ausserkanonische Parallelstellen zu den Gerichtworten Mt. 7,21-23; Lk. 6,46; 13,26-28 und ihre Bedeutung für die Formung der Jesusworte" VChr 10 (1973) 79-102.

13:26-27 DUPONT, D. J. Les Béatitudes (1958) 101-03. HAHN, F. Christologische Hoheitstitel (1963) 96f. KAESEMANN, E. Exegetische Versuche und Besinnungen (1964) II 84. KAESEMANN, E. New Testament Questions of Today (1969) 84. O'NEILL, J. C. The Theology of Acts in its historical setting (1970) 39-40. BLANK, J., Verändert Interpretation den Glauben? (Freiburg 1972) 102-12. SCHULZ, S. Q Die Spruchquelle der Evangelisten (1972) 424-27.

13:26 NICKELS, P. Targum and New Testament (1967) 40.

13:27-29 HENNECKE, E./SCHNEEMELCHER, W., Neutestamentliche Apokryphen (1964) I 113, II 394.

13:27 KNOX, W. L. The Sources of the Synoptic Gospels II (1957) 94. HOLTZ, T. Untersuchungen über die Alttestamentlichen Zitate bei Lukas (1968) 158f. STROBEL, A. Erkenntnis und Bekenntnis der Sünde in neutestamentlicher Zeit (1968) 43. JEREMIAS, J., Die Sprache des Lukasevangeliums (Göttingen 1980) 232-33.

13:28-29 FLEW, R. N. Jesus and His Church (1956) 26, 62. STRECKER, G. Der Weg der Gerechtigkeit (1962) 100. HAHN, F. Das Verständnis der Mission im Neuen Testament (²1965) 26f., 113. WREGE, H.-T. Die Ueberlieferungsgeschichte der Bergpredigt (1968) 57, 150, 178. NÖTSCHER, F., Altorientalischer und alttestamentlicher Auferstehungsglaube (Darmstadt 1970 = 1926) 191, 314. JEREMIAS, J. Neutestamentliche Theologie I (1971) 22, 25, 40, 103, 131, 134, 161, 236. SCHULZ, S. Q Die Spruchquelle der Evangelisten (1972) 330ff. ZINGG, P., Das Wachsen der Kirche (Freiburg 1974) 253. "Abraham" in: TRE I (1977) 278. POLAG, A., Die Christologie der Logienquelle (Neukirchen-Vluyn 1977) 92. BRUCE, F. F., The Time is Fulfilled (Exeter 1978) 62. SCHLOSSER, J., "Le règne de Dieu dans les dits de Jésus" RevSR 53 (1979) 164-76. CLARK, K. W., "The Israel of God" in: J. L. Sharpe (ed.) The Gentile Bias and other Essays (Leiden 1980) 23.

13:28 SMITH, M. Tannaitic Parallels to the Gospels (1968) 3.10. WIL-

SON, S. G., The Gentiles and the Gentile Mission in Luke-Acts (Cambridge 1973) 3, 33, 52, 53,70. CAVALLIN, H. C. C., Life After Death I (Lund 1974) 7, 2n23. MÜLLER, U. B., "Die griechische Esra-Apokalypse" in: W. G. Kümmel (ed.) Jüdische Schriften aus hellenistisch-römischer Zeit V/2 (Gütersloh 1976) 91n9a. METZGER, B. M., The Early Versions of the New Testament (Oxford 1977) 145. JEREMIAS, J., Die Sprache des Lukasevangeliums (Göttingen 1980) 233.

13:29 MOORE, G. F. Judaism (1946) II 365n. SANFORD, J. A., The Kingdom Within (New York 1970) 49-50, 196-97. JEREMIAS, J., Die Sprache des Lukasevangeliums (Göttingen 1980) 233.

13:30 ROBINSON, J. M. Kerygma und historischer Jesus (1960) 166. SCHRAGE, W. Das Verhältnis des Thomas-Evangeliums zur synoptischen Tradition und zu den Koptischen Evangelienübersetzungen (1964) 32. JÜNGEL, E. Paulus und Jesus (1966) 163. OTOMO, Y. Nachfolge Jesu und Anfänge der Kirche im Neuen Tesament (1970) 57-60. JEREMIAS, J. Neutestamentliche Theologie I (1971) 25f., 28. HOFFMANN, P. und EID, V., Jesus von Nazareth und eine christliche Moral (Freiburg/Basel/Wien 1975) 201-08. POLAG, A., Die Christologie der Logienquelle (Neukirchen-Vluyn 1977) 96.

13:31ff. GRIMM, W. "Eschatologischer Saul wider eschatologischen David. Eine Deutung von Lc. xiii 31ff.," NovTest 15 (2, 1973) 114-33.

13:31-35 ZERWICK, M. "Vivamos la palabra de Dios. Id y decid a esa raposa . . . (Lc 13,31-35)," RevBi 25 (107-108, 1963) 59-61. CASALIS, G. GPM 19 (1964) 111-13. QUERVAIN, A. de in: Hören und Fragen Bd. 5,3 (1967) G. Eichholz & A. Falkenroth eds., 177ff. ENGELHARDT, K. GPM 25 (1970) 124-29. LANGE, E., ed., Predigtstudien für das Kirchenjahr 1970-1971 (1970) 138-42. TER-NEDDEN-AMSLER, B. und SKRIVER, J., in: P. Krusche et al. (eds.) Predigtstudien für das Kirchenjahr 1976-1977, I/5 (Stuttgart 1976) 125-32. HÜBNER, F., in: GPM 31/2 (1976-1977) 120-25. SCHNEIDER, G., Das Evangelium nach Lukas (Gütersloh/Würzburg 1977) 308 (lit!).

13:31-33 STONEHOUSE, N. B. The Witness of Luke to Christ (1951) 119ff., 123. LEHMANN, K. Auferweckt am Dritten Tag nach der Schrift (1968) 231-41. BLINZLER, J. Der Prozess Jesu (1969) 76, 288, 293, 294, 300. DERRETT, J. D. M. Law in the New Testament (1970) 256-57. LEHMANN, M. Synoptische Quellenanalyse und die Frage nach dem historischen Jesus (1970) 146-48. HOEHNER, H. W. Herod Antipas (1972) 214-24, 243-47. DENAUX, A., "L'hypocrisie des Pharisiens et le dessein le Dieu. Analyse de Lc. XIII,31-33" in: F. Neirynck (ed.) L'Evangile de Luc (Gembloux

1973) 245-85. SCHNIDER, F., Jesus der Prophet (Freiburg 1973) 52, 167ff. WANKE, J., Die Emmauserzählung. Eine redaktions-geschichtliche Untersuchung zu Lk 24,13-35 (Leipzig 1973) 61-62. MIYOSHI, M., Der Anfang des Reiseberichts Lk 9,51 - 10,24. Eine redaktionsgeschichtliche Untersuchung (Rome 1974) 22-24. TAL-BERT, C. H., Literary Patterns, Theological Themes, and the Genre of Luke-Acts (Missoula 1974) 52, 56. GOPPELT, L., Theologie des Neuen Testaments. I (Göttingen 1975) 77, 239-40.

13:31-32 NÖTSCHER, F., Altorientalischer und alttestamentlicher Auf-erstehungsglaube (Darmstadt 1970 = 1926) 144.

13:31 GOULDER, M. D. Type and History in Acts (1964) 58f., 61. BLACK, M. An Aramaic Approach to the Gospels and Acts (1967) 111f. NICKELS, P. Targum and New Testament (1967) 40. JE-REMIAS, J., Die Sprache des Lukasevangeliums (Göttingen 1980) 233-34.

13:32-35 TALBERT, C. H., Literary Patterns, Theological Themes, and the Genre of Luke-Acts (Missoula 1974) 115.

13:32-33 TAYLOR, V. Jesus and His Sacrifice (1948) 89, 167-71, 258. HAHN, F. Christologische Hoheitstitel (1963) 20, 65. FER-RARO, G. " 'Oggi e domani e il terzo giorno' (osservazioni su Luca 13,32,33)," RivB 16 (4, 1968) 297-407. BLINZLER, J. Aus der Welt und Umwelt des Neuen Testaments (1969) 72, 83-87. JE-REMIAS, J. Neutestamentliche Theologie I (1971) 22, 40, 96, 220, 260, 271. JEREMIAS, J. "Die Drei-Tage-Worte der Evange-lien," in: Tradition und Glaube (1971) G. Jeremias ed., 221-29.RADL, W., Paulus und Jesus im lukanischen Doppelwerk (Bern 1975) 149-58. DRURY, J., Tradition and Design in Luke's Gospel (Atlanta 1976) 70-71.

13:32 HAHN, F. Das Verständnis der Mission im Neuen Testament (²1965) 54. PALLIS, A., Notes on St. Luke and the Acts (London 1928) 31. SEYBOLD, K. und MÜLLER, U., Krankheit und Hei-lung (Stuttgart 1978) 103-04. MEYER, B. F., The Aims of Jesus (London1979) 154-55. JEREMIAS, J., Die Sprache des Lukas-evangeliums (Göttingen 1980) 234.

13:33-34 ZINGG, P., Das Wachsen der Kirche (Freiburg 1974) 138-39.

13:33 GNILKA, J. Die Verstockung Israels (1961) 138f. NICKELS, P. Targum and New Testament (1967) 40. SCHNEIDER, G. Ver-leugnung, Verspottung und Verhör Jesu nach Lukas 22,54-71 (1969) 171, 174, 175, 199, 202, 203. JEREMIAS, J. Neutestamentliche Theologie I (1971) 83, 267, 269, 271. RUPPERT, L., Jesus als der leidende Gerechte? (Stuttgart 1972) 57, 60, 64, 74. DAVIES, W. D., The Gospel and the Land (London 1974) 247, 351, 254, 260n51. TALBERT, C. H., Literary Patterns, Theological Themes, and the

Genre of Luke-Acts (Missoula 1974) 16, 17, 20, 97, 114. WIL-LIAMS, J. A., A Conceptual History of Deuteronomism in the Old Testament, Judaism and the New Testament (Ph. D. Diss., Louisville 1976) 300, 310. JEREMIAS, J., Die Sprache des Lukasevangeliums (Göttingen 1980) 234.

13:34-35 ROBINSON, W. C., The Way of the Lord (Diss., Basel 1960) 87-90. ROBINSON, W. C. Der Weg des Herrn (1964) 54f. SATAKE, A. Die Gemeindeordnung in der Johannesapokalypse (1966) 185-87. CHRIST, F. Jesus Sophia (1970) 136-52. GASTON, L. No Stone on Another (1970) 244, 290, 322, 344-47, 455. HOFFMANN, P. Studien zur Theologie der Logienquelle (1972) 171-73. SCHULZ, S. Q Die Spruchquelle der Evangelisten (1972) 346-60. HAMERTON-KELLY, R. G. Pre-Existence, Wisdom, and The Son of Man (1973) 32, 33, 35, 67, 211, 265.HOFFMANN, P., ''Mk 8,31. Zur Herkunft und markinischen Rezeption einer alten Überlieferung'' in: P. Hoffmann (ed.) Orientierung an Jesus. FS. J. Schmid (Freiburg 1973) 180-81, 182, 184. SCHNIDER, F., Jesus der Prophet (Freiburg 1973) 74ff, 142ff. TALBERT, C. H., Literary Patterns, Theological Themes, and the Genre of Luke-Acts (Missoula 1974) 52-56. WILCKENS, U., Die Missionsreden der Apostelgeschichte (Neukirchen 1974($_3$)) 201-04, 218. GOPPELT, L., Theologie des Neuen Testaments. I (Göttingen 1975) 235, 239-40. EDWARDS, R. A., A Theology of Q (Philadelphia 1976) 66-68, 132-33. WILLIAMS, J. A., A Conceptual History of Deuteronomism in the Old Testament, Judaism, and the New Testament (Ph. D. Diss., Louisville 1976) 294-97. GRUNDMANN, W., ''Weisheit im Horizont des Reiches Gottes. Eine Studie zur Verkündigung Jesu nach der Spruchüberlieferung Q'' in: R. Schnackenburg et al. (eds.) Die Kirche des Anfangs. FS. H. Schürmann (Leipzig 1977) 180. POLAG, A., Die Christologie der Logienquelle (Neukirchen-Vluyn 1977) 93-95.

13:34 HAHN, F. Christologische Hoheitstitel (1963) 382. JEREMIAS, J., Neutestamentliche Theologie I (1971) 22, 150, 174, 270. SANFORD, J. A., The Kingdom Within (New York 1970) 190-91. WILLIAMS, J. A., A Conceptual History of Deuteronomism in the Old Testament, Judaism, and the New Testament (Ph. D. Diss., Louisville 1976) 306, 310. SCHENKE, H. M., ''Die Tendenz der Weisheit zur Gnosis'' in: B. Aland et al (eds.) Gnosis. FS. H. Jonas (Göttingen 1978) 359-65. MEYER, B. F., The Aims of Jesus (London 1979) 210-11. SWIDLER, L. Biblical Affirmations of Woman (Philadelphia 1979) 173, 242, 257, 284. BERGMEIER, R., Glaube als Gabe nach Johannes (Stuttgart 1980) 215. JEREMIAS, J., Die Sprache des Lukasevangeliums (Göttingen 1980) 235.

13:35 KÜMMEL, W. G. Verheissung und Erfüllung (1953) 73-75. HOLTZ, T. Untersuchungen über die Alttestamentlichen Zitate bei Lukas (1968) 160. HASLER, V. Amen (1969) 71. RESE, M. Alttestamentliche Motive in der Christologie des Lukas (1969) 188-91. PALLIS, A., Notes on St. Luke and the Acts (London 1928) 31. "Auferstehung" in: TRE 4 (1979) 490. JEREMIAS, J., Die Sprache des Lukasevangeliums (Göttingen 1980) 235.

14:1-19:27 O'NEILL, J. C. The Theology of Acts in its historical setting (1970) 69-71.

14:1-18:30 TALBERT, C. H., Literary Patterns, Theological Themes, and the Genre of Luke-Acts (Missoula 1974) 51.

14-18 GOULDER, M. D. Type and History in Acts (1964) 60f.

14:1-24 KNOX, W. L. The Sources of the Synoptic Gospels II (1957) 78, 84ff. SQUILLACI, D. "Gesù invitato a cena. Luca 14,1-24," PaCl 44 (Sept. 15, 1965) 992-97. GASTON, L. No Stone on Another (1970) 256, 327-28. ERNST, J. "Gastmahlgespräche: Luke 14:1-24" in: R. Schnackenburg et al. (eds.) Die Kirche des Anfangs. FS. H. Schürmann (Leipzig 1977) 57-78.

14:1-11 KLAAS, W. in: Herr, tue meine Lippen auf Bd. 1 (1957) G. Eichholz ed., 283-88. ZERWICK, M. "Vivamos la palabra de Dios. Los primeros puestos (Lc 14,1-11)," RevBi 26 (111-112, 1964) 87-90. SIMSON, P., "Le code de bienséance de l'assemblée chrétienne" AssS 71 (1965) 31-41.

14:1-7 ZINGG, P., Das Wachsen der Kirche (Freiburg 1974) 237-40.

14:1-6 HIRSCH, E. Frühgeschichte des Evangeliums (1941) 134-36. RICHARDSON, A. The Miracle-Stories of the Gospels (1948) 110-12. BORNKAMM, G. GPM 4 (1949-1950) 257ff. FARRER, A. St Matthew and St Mark (1954) 130n. BENCKERT, GPM 15 (1960-1961) 237ff. DOERNE, M. Er kommt auch noch heute (1961) 138-40. STRECKER, G. Der Weg der Gerechtigkeit (1962) 19_3. Wir wissen weder Tag noch Stunde, Predigtgedanken aus Vergangenheit und Gegenwart Reihe A, Bd. 6 (1966) 56-65. ROLOFF, J. Das Kerygma und der irdische Jesus (1970) 56-69. JEREMIAS, J. Neutestamentliche Theologie I (1971) 90, 93f., 202, 265. FALCKE, H. GPM 27 (1973) 424-43. TALBERT, C. H., Literary Patterns, Theological Themes, and the Genre of Luke-Acts (Missoula 1974) 52, 56. BANKS, R., Jesus and the Law in the Synoptic Tradition

(London 1975) 247-48. SCHNEIDER, G., Das Evangelium nach Lukas (Gütersloh/Würzburg 1977) 311 (lit!). RIVKIN, E., A Hidden Revolution (Nashville 1978) 117-18, 122-23. SWIDLER, L., Biblical Affirmations of Woman (Philadelphia 1979) 182.

14:1-5 BOUSSET, W. Die Religion des Judentums im Späthellenistischen Zeitalter (1966 = 1926) 126, 166.

14:1, 7-11 HERBERT, GPM 21/1 (1966-1967) 96-103.

14:1-2 JEREMIAS, J., Die Sprache des Lukasevangeliums (Göttingen 1980) 235-36.

14:1 NEIRYNCK, F., "La Matiére dans Luc" in: F. Neirynck (ed.) L'Evangile de Luc (Gembloux 1973) 184-92. TALBERT, C. H., Literary Patterns, Theological Themes, and the Genre of Luke-Acts (Missoula 1974) 20, 114. METZGER, B. M., The Early Versions of the New Testament (Oxford 1977) 176.

14:3-6 MEYER, B. F., The Aims of Jesus (London 1979) 162-68.

14:3 SCHALIT, A. König Herodes (1969) 737.

14:4 FARRER, A. St Matthew and St Mark (1954) 56. NICKELS, P. Targum and New Testament (1967) 40. "Apostel" in: TRE 3 (1978) 443. JEREMIAS, J., Die Sprache des Lukasevangeliums (Göttingen 1980) 236.

14:5-7 ZINGG, P., Das Wachsen der Kirche (Freiburg 1974) 240.

14:5 SCHÜRMANN, H. "Sprachliche Reminiszenzen an abgeänderte oder ausgelassene Bestandteile der Spruchsammlung im Lukas- und Matthäusevangelium." NTS 6 (1959-1960) 209f. BLACK, M. An Aramaic Approach to the Gospels and Acts (1967) 168f. NICKELS, P. Targum and New Testament (1967) 40. LOHSE, E., Die Einheit des Neuen Testaments (Göttingen 1973) 40, 69-72. POLAG, A., Die Christologie der Logienquelle (Neukirchen-Vluyn 1977) 80, 43. WESTERHOLM, S., Jesus and Scribal Authority (Lund 1978) 101.

14:6 NICKELS, P. Targum and New Testament (1967) 40.

14:7ff. FINDLAY, J. A. Jesus and His Parables (1951) 15ff.

14:7-24 TALBERT, C. H., Literary Patterns, Theological Themes, and the Genre of Luke-Acts (Missoula 1974) 52, 56.

14:7-14 MICHAELIS, D. W. Die Gleichnisse Jesu (1956) 164-70. FLENDER, H. St Luke Theologian of Redemptive History (1967) 81ff. PIDWELL, J. J. Blessed are the Poor (1972) 92-97. MAGASS, W. "Semiotik einer Tischordnung (Lk 14,7-14)," LiBi 25-26 (1973) 2-8. SCHNEIDER, G., Das Evangelium nach Lukas (Gütersloh Würzburg 1977) 314 (lit!).

14:7-11 JÜLICHER, D. A. Die Gleichnisreden Jesu (1910) 246-54. DEGENHARDT, H.-J. Lukas, Evangelist der Armen (1964) 98-100.

BRAUN, H. Qumran und NT II (1966) 102. BARCLAY, W. And Jesus Said (1970) 213-16. GUILDING, A., The Fourth Gospel and Jewish Worship (Oxford 1960) 137-39. MANEK, J., . . . und brachte Frucht. Die Gleichnisse Jesu (Berlin 1977) 95-96. SWIDLER, L., Biblical Affirmations of Woman (Philadelphia 1979) 288.

14:7 KNOX, W. L. The Sources of the Synoptic Gospels II (1957) 110. JEREMIAS, J., Die Sprache des Lukasevangeliums (Göttingen 1980) 237.

14:8-19 ZINGG, P., Das Wachsen der Kirche (Freiburg 1974) 240-42.

14:8 PALLIS, Notes on St. Luke and the Acts (London 1928) 32.

14:9 NICKELS, P. Targum and New Testament (1967) 40. JEREMIAS, J., Die Sprache des Lukasevangeliums (Göttingen 1980) 237-38.

14:10 METZGER, B. M., The Early Versions of the New Testament (Oxford 1977) 208. JEREMIAS, J., Die Sprache des Lukasevangeliums (Göttingen 1980) 238.

14:11 ROBINSON, J. M. Kerygma und historischer Jesus (1960) 165. SCHRAGE, W. Die konkreten Einzelgebote in der paulinischen Paränese (1961) 243. BERGER, K. "Zu den Sogenannten Sätzen Heiligen Rechts." NTS 17 (1970-1971) 19f. JEREMIAS, J. Neutestamentliche Theologie I (1971) 22, 25f. SCHULZ, S. Q Die Spruchquelle der Evangelisten (1972) 451-52. SANFORD, J. A., The Kingdom Within (New York 1970) 188-89. HOFFMANN, P. und EID, V., Jesus von Nazareth und eine christliche Moral (Freiburg/Basel/Wien 1975) 208-11. PERRIN, N., Jesus and the Language of the Kingdom (London 1976) 41, 48, 52. POLAG, A., Die Christologie der Logienquelle (Neukirchen-Vluyn 1977) 163. JEREMIAS, J., Die Sprache des Lukasevangeliums (Göttingen 1980) 238.

14:12ff. STROBEL, A. Erkenntnis und Bekenntnis der Sünde in neutestamentlicher Zeit (1968) 43.

14:12-24 HIRSCH, E. Frühgeschichte des Evangeliums (1941) 136-43. GLOMBITZA, O. "Das Grosse Abendmahl. Luk. xiv 12-24," NovTest 5 (1, 1962) 10-16. NAVONE, J. "The Parable of the Banquet," Bible Today 1 (14, 1964) 923-29. ZERWICK, M. "Vivamos la Palabra de Dios. El gran banquete (Lc. 14,12-24). Aborrecer a su propia alma (Lc 14,25-35)," RevBi 26 (113-114, 1964) 188-95. GUILDING, A., The Fourth Gospel and Jewish Worship (Oxford 1960) 137-39. SANFORD, J. A., The Kingdom Within (New York 1970) 176. "Agape" in: TRE 1 (1977) 752. KARRIS, R. J., "Poor and Rich: The Lukan Sitz im Leben" in: C. H. Talbert (ed.) Perspectives on Luke-Acts (Danville 1978) 120-21.

14:12-15 SURKAU, H. W. GPM 11/4, (1956-57) 260-64.

14:12-14 JÜLICHER, D. A. Die Gleichnisreden Jesu (1910) 146-54. DE-
GENHARDT, H.-J. Lukas, Evangelist der Armen (1964) 100-01.
FLENDER, H. Heil und Geschichte in der Theologie des Lukas
(1965) 77-78.

14:12-13 STAEHELIN, E. Die Verkündigung des Reiches Gottes in der
Kirche Jesu Christi I (1951) 139.

14:12 NICKELS, P. Targum and New Testament (1967) 41.

14:13 GERSTENBERGER, G. und SCHRAGE, W., Leiden (Stuttgart
1977) 220; ET: J. E. Steely, Suffering (Nashville 1980) 253-54.

14:14-24 LOEWENICH, W. VON, Luther als Ausleger der Synoptiker
(1954) 47f.

14:14 VOLZ, P. Die Eschatologie der jüdischen Gemeinde (1934) 269.
BOUSSET, W. Die Religion des Judentums im Späthellenistischen Zeitalter (1966 = 1926) 272. NÖTSCHER, F., Altorientalischer und alttestamentlicher Auferstehungsglaube (Darmstadt
1970 = 1926) 305-06. "Apostel" in: TRE 3 (1978) 443.

14:15-24 JÜLICHER, D. A. Die Gleichnisreden Jesu (1910) 407-33. MOR-
GAN, G. C. The Parables and Metaphors of Our Lord (1943) 201ff.
PIROT, J. Paraboles et Allégories Evangeliques (1949) 354-60.
FRIEDRICH, GPM 4 (1949-1950) 185ff. STECK, GPM 9 (1954-
1955) 164ff. MICHAELIS, D. W. Die Gleichnisse Jesu (1956) 145-
63. BOSCH, D. Die Heidenmission in der Zukunftsschau Jesu
(1959) 124-31. HUNTER, A. M. Interpreting the Parables (1960)
55ff. FUCHS, GPM 15 (1960-1961) 190ff. DOERNE, M. Er
kommt auch noch heute (1961) 103-05. GNILKA, J. Die Verstockung Israels (1961) 132f. LOCKYER, H. All the Parables of
the Bible (1963) 257ff. d'A. S. J. "Heureux les inutiles," VieS 110
(506, 1964) 718-31. DEGENHARDT, H.-J. Lukas, Evangelist der
Armen (1964) 101-05. BISER, E. Die Gleichnisse Jesu (1965) 87ff.,
126. BRAUN, H. Qumran und NT II (1966) 93, 95, 106.
VOOBUS, A. The Gospels in Study and Preaching (1966) 63-92.
Hephata, Predigtgedanken aus Vergangenheit und Gegenwart,
Reihe A., Bd. 5 (1966) 52-69. HAENCHEN, E. "Das Gleichnis
vom grossen Mahl," Die Bibel und Wir (1968) 135-55. LINNE-
MANN, E. Die Gleichnisse Jesu (1970) 151-57. OTTO, G. Den-
ken-um zu glauben (1970) 87-91. DERRETT, J. D. M. Law in the
New Testament (1970) 126-55. SANFORD, J. A., The Kingdom
Within (New York 1970) 193-94. PIDWELL, H. Blessed are the
Poor (1972) 97-100. SURKAU, H. W. GPM 27 (1973) 319-29.
WANKE, J., Die Emmauserzählungen. Eine redaktionsge-
schichtliche Untersuchung zu Lk 24, 14-35 (Leipzig 1973) 106-07.
DORMEYER, D., "Literarische und theologische Analyse der
Parabel Lukas 15,15-24" BiLe 15 (1974) 206-19. FUNK, R. W.,

"The Narrative Parables: The Birth of a Language Tradition" in: J. Jervell/W. A. Meeks (eds.) God's Christ and His People. FS. N. A. Dahl (New York 1977) 43-50. SCHNEIDER, G., Das Evangelium nach Lukas (Gütersloh/Würzburg 1977) 316 (Lit!). "Arbeit" in: TRE 3 (1978) 623. DUPONT, J. et al., La parabola degli invitati al banchetto. Dagli evangelisti a Gesù (Brescia 1978). OSTEN-SACKEN, P. van d., in: GPM 33 (1979) 281-89. SWIDLER, L., Biblical Affirmations of Woman (Philadelphia 1979) 244, 279. WEDER, H., Die Gleichnisse Jesu als Metaphern (Göttingen ²1978) 177-93.

14:15-17 "Abendmahl" in: TRE 1 (1977) 49.

14:15 MOORE, G. F. Judaism (1946) II 365. TALBERT, C. H., Literary Patterns, Theological Themes, and the Genre of Luke-Acts (Missoula (1974) 56.

14:16ff. FINDLAY, J. A. Jesus and His Parables (1951) 67ff.

14:16-26 HOFFMANN, P. Studien zur Theologie der Logienquelle (1972) 5, 41, 72f.

14:16-24 DODD, C. H. The Parables of the Kingdom (1948) 121ff. PARKER, P. The Gospel Before Mark (1953) 65ff. BRUNNER, P. in: Herr, tue meine Lippen auf Bd. 1 (1957) 210-15. BLAIR, E. P. Jesus in the Gospel of Matthew (1960) 60. MONTEFIORE, H. NTS 7 (1960-1961) 235f. JEREMIAS, J. Die Gleichnisse Jesu (1962) 41, 61-63, 65-67, 175-77. MOWRY, L. "Parable", IDB III (1962) 652a. SCHRAGE, W. Das Verhältnis des Thomas-Evangeliums zur Synoptischen Tradition und zu den Koptischen Evangelienübersetzungen (1964) 133. GALBIATI, E. "Gli invitati al convito (Luca 14,16-24)," BiOr 7 (3, 1965)129-35. HAHN, F. Das Verständnis der Mission im Neuen Testament (²1965) 28, 113. SUMMERS, R. The Secret Sayings of the Living Jesus (1968) 47. GRABNER-HAIDER, A. Verkündigung als Einladung (1969) 79-81. SCHÜTZ, F. Der leidende Christus (1969) 59ff., 107. HAHN, F. "Das Gleichnis von der Einladung zum Festmahl", in: Verborum Veritas (1970) O. Böcher & K. Haacker eds., 51-82. EICHHOLZ, G. Gleichnisse der Evangelien (1971) 126-47. VÖGTLE, A. Das Evangelium und die Evangelien (1971) 171-218. WEISER, A. Die Knechtsgleichnisse der synoptischen Evangelien (1972) 58-63. SCHULZ, S. Q Die Spruchquelle der Evangelisten (1972) 391-403. GOULDER, M. D. Midrash and Lection in Matthew (1974) 56, 69, 62. WILSON, S. G., The Gentiles and the Gentile Mission in Luke-Acts (Cambridge 1973) 6, 34, 52-54, 57. CONZELMANN, H. und LINDEMANN, A., Arbeitsbuch zum Neuen Testament (Tübingen 1975) 87-88. PERRIN, N., Jesus and the Language of the Kingdom (London 1976) 96, 102, 116, 138, 161, 189. MANEK, J. . . . und brachte Frucht. Die Gleichnisse Jesu (Berlin 1977) 60-64.

POLAG, A., Die Christologie der Logienquelle (Neukirchen-Vluyn 1977) 75, 92. SANFORD, J. A., Healing and Wholeness (New York 1977) 32-33. RUDOLPH, K., Die Gnosis (Göttingen 1978) 287. "Armut" in: TRE 4 (1979) 78. RESENHOFFT, W., "Jesu Gleichnis von den Talenten, ergänzt durch die Lukas-Fassung" NTS 26 (1980) 318-31.

14:17.21 SCHÜRMANN, H. "Sprachliche Reminiszenzen an abgeänderte oder ausgelassene Bestandteile der Spruchsammlung im Lukas- und Matthäusevangelium." NTS 6 (1959-1960) 209f.

14:17 JEREMIAS, J., Die Sprache des Lukasevangeliums (Göttingen 1980) 239.

14:18-20 JEREMIAS, J., Die Sprache des Lukasevangeliums (Göttingen 1980) 239.

14:18 STAEHELIN, E. Die Verkündigung des Reiches Gottes in der Kirche Jesu Christi I (1951) 257. BLACK, M. An Aramaic Approach to the Gospels and Acts (1967) 129f. JEREMIAS, J., Die Sprache des Lukasevangeliums (Göttingen 1980) 239-40.

14:19 METZGER, B. M. "Explicit references in the works of Origen to variant readings in New Testament manuscripts", Historical and Literary Studies (1968) 95.

14:20 BLACK, M. An Aramaic Approach to the Gospels and Acts (1967) 129f. NICKELS, P. Targum and New Testament (1967) 41.

14:21-24 SCHRECKENBERG, H., "Flavius Josephus und die lukanischen Schriften" in: W.Haubeck/M. Bachmann (eds.) Wort in der Zeit. FS. K. H. Rengstorf (Leiden 1980) 191.

14:21-23 VÖGTLE, A. Das Evangelium und die Evangelien (1971) 183-88, 200-04. SANFORD, J. A., The Kingdom Within (New York 1970) 69-71.

14:21 HAHN, F. Christologische Hoheitstitel (1963) 92. NICKELS, P. Targum and New Testament (1967) 41. VÖGTLE, A. Das Evangelium und die Evangelien (1971) 199-204. MINEAR, P., To Heal and to Reveal (New York 1976) 64. METZGER, B. M., The Early Versions of the New Testament (Oxford 1977) 391. JEREMIAS, J., Die Sprache des Lukasevangeliums (Göttingen 1980) 240.

14:23 PALLIS, A., Notes on St. Luke and the Acts (London 1928) 32. SANFORD, J. A., The Kingdom Within (New York 1970) 49-50. "Bekehrung" in: TRE 5 (1980) 450. JEREMIAS, J., Die Sprache des Lukasevangeliums (Göttingen 1980) 240-41.

14:24 BROWN, S. Apostasy and Perseverance in the Theology of Luke (1969) 90. HASLER, V. Amen (1969) 105. VÖGTLE, A. Das Evangelium und die Evangelien (1971) 188-90. METZGER, B. M., The Early Versions of the New Testament (Oxford 1977) 92. JE-

REMIAS, J., Die Sprache des Lukasevangeliums (Göttingen 1980) 241.

14:25-17:10 HIRSCH, E. Frühgeschichte des Evangeliums (1941) 143-49.

14:25ff. KNOX, W. L. The Sources of the Synoptic Gospels II (1957) 54, 87f.

14:25-35 MORGAN, G. C. The Parables and Metaphors of Our Lord (1943) 106ff. DEGENHARDT, H.-J. Lukas, Evangelist der Armen (1964) 105. ZERWICK, M. "Vivamos la Palabra de Dios. El gran banquete (Lc 14,12-24). Aborrecer a su propia alma (Lc 14,25-35)," RevBi 26 (113-114, 1964) 188-95. ERNST, J. Anfänge der Christologie (Stuttgart 1972) 136-41. MIYOSHI, M., Der Anfang des Reiseberichts Lk 9,51 - 10,24. Eine redaktionsgeschichtliche Untersuchung (Rome 1974) 54-55. TALBERT, C. H., Literary Patterns, Theological Themes, and the Genre of Luke-Acts (Missoula (1974) 52. SCHNEIDER, G., Das Evangelium nach Lukas (Gütersloh/Würzburg 1977) 320 (lit!).

14:25-34 FLENDER, H. Heil und Geschichte in der Theologie des Lukas (1965) 71-72. FLENDER, H. St Luke Theologian of Redemptive History (1967) 75f.

14:25-33 JÜLICHER, D. A. Die Gleichnisreden Jesu (1910) 202-14. PIROT, J. Paraboles et Allégories Evangeliques (1949) 152-56. DUPONT, D. J. Les Béatitudes (1958) 89-91. BOURBECK, GPM 19 (1964-1965) 261ff. EICHHOLZ, G. in: Hören und Fragen Bd. 5,3 (1967) G. Eichholz & A. Falkenroth eds., 385ff. BARCLAY, W. And Jesus Said (1970) 204-08. LANGE, E. ed., Predigtstudien für das Kirchenjahr 1970-1971 (1970) 135-39. SCHELLONG, D. GPM 25 (1971) 298-307. PIDWELL, H. J. Blessed are the Poor (1972) 100-102. FEREL, M. und de HASS, P., in: P. Krusche et al. (eds.) Predigtstudien für das Kirchenjahr 1976-1977 II/5 (Stuttgart 1977) 121-28. SURKAU, H.-W., in: GPM 31 (1976-1977) 201-08. KARRIS, R. J., "Poor and Rich: The Lukan Sitz im Leben" in: C. H. Talbert (ed.) Perspectives on Luke-Acts (Danville 1978) 120-21.

14:25-30 LOCKYER, H. All the Parables of the Bible (1963) 278ff.

14:25-27 TALBERT, C. H., Literary Patterns, Theological Themes, and the Genre of Luke-Acts (Missoula (1974) 52, 55.

14:25-26 SANFORD, J. A., The Kingdom Within (New York 1970) 83-84. SWIDLER, L., Biblical Affirmations of Woman (Philadelphia 1979) 274.

14:25 KNOX, W. L. The Sources of the Synoptic Gospels II (1957) 64. TALBERT, C. H., Literary Patterns, Theological Themes, and the Genre of Luke-Acts (Missoula (1974) 114.

14:26-33 OTOMO, Y. Nachfolge Jesu und Anfänge der Kirche im Neuen Testament (1970) 122-26.

14:26-28 GNILKA, J., "Martyriumsparänese und Sühnetod in synoptischen und jüdischen Traditionen" in: H. Schürmann (ed.) Die Kirche des Anfangs (Freiburg/Wien/Basel 1978) 232-34.

14:26-27 FLEW, R. N. Jesus and His Church (1956) 56-57. BARTSCH, H.-W. "Das Thomas-Evangelium und die Synoptischen Evangelien," NTS 6 (1959-1960) 256f. SCHULZ, A. Nachfolge und Nachahmen (1962) 80ff., 94f. SCHRAGE, W. Das Verhältnis des Thomas-Evangeliums zur Synoptischen Tradition und zu den Koptischen Evangelienübersetzungen (1964) 120. SCHÜTZ, F., Der leidende Christus (1969) 15-20. DESCAMPS, A. & DE HALLEUX, A. Mélanges Bibliques en hommage au R. P. Béda Rigaux (1970) 498-501. POLAG, A. Die Christologie der Logienquelle (Neukirchen-Vluyn 1977) 85. SWIDLER, L., Biblical Affirmations of Woman (Philadelphia 1979) 259.

14:26 GREEVEN, D. H. "KAI Frequency in Greek Letters," NTS 15 (1968-1969) 374ff. HARRISVILLE, R. A. "Jesus and the Family", Interpretation 23 (1969) 425-38. PHIPPS, W. E. Was Jesus Married? (1970) 75-77. JEREMIAS, J. Neutestamentliche Theologie I (1971) 215f., 242. SCHULZ, S. Q Die Spruchquelle der Evangelisten (1972) 446-49. BAUER, J. B., Scholia Biblica et Patristica (Graz 1972) 112. SCHROEDER, H.-H., Eltern und Kinder in der Verkündigung Jesu (Hamburg-Bergstedt 1972) 78-109. LADD, G. E., A Theology of the New Testament (Grand Rapids 1974) 71, 131, 132, METZGER, B. M., The Early Versions of the New Testament (Oxford 1977) 206. SWIDLER, L., Biblical Affirmations of Woman (Philadelphia 1979) 179, 279, 354. JEREMIAS, J., Die Sprache des Lukasevangeliums (Göttingen 1980) 241. KELBER, W. H., "Mark and Oral Tradition" in: Semeia 16 (1980) 25-27. McDONALD, J. I. H., Kerygma and Didache (Cambridge 1980) 86.

14:27 SCHULZ, A. Nachfolge und Nachahmen (1962) 82-90, 163f., 195ff., 265ff. STRECKER, G. Der Weg der Gerechtigkeit (1962) 192. RESE, M. Alttestamentliche Motive in der Christologie des Lukas (1969) 174-77. LOHSE, E. et al., eds., Der Ruf Jesu und die Antwort der Gemeinde (1970) 262-67. SCHULZ, S. Q Die Spruchquelle der Evangelisten (1972) 430-33. METZGER, B. M., The Early Versions of the New Testament (Oxford 1977) 392. METZGER, B. M., "St. Jerome's explicit references to the variant readings in manuscripts of the New Testament" in: E. Best/R. McL. Wilson (eds.) Text and Interpretation. FS. M. Black (Cambridge 1979) 183. KUHN, H.-W., "Nachfolge nach Ostern" in D.

Lührmann/G. Strecker (eds.) Kirche. FS. G. Bornkamm (Tübingen 1980) 117, 121.

14:28ff. FINDLAY, J. A. Jesus and His Parables (1951) 98ff. SCHROEDER, H.-H., Eltern und Kinder in der Verkündigung Jesu (Hamburg-Bergstedt 1972) 94-96.

14:28-33 BULTMANN, R. The History of the Synoptic Tradition (1963) 170f., 199f. TALBERT, C. H., Literary Patterns, Theological Themes, and the Genre of Luke-Acts (Missoula 1974) 52, 55. MANEK, J., . . . und brachte Frucht. Die Gleichnisse Jesu (Berlin 1977) 97-98.

14:28-32 FARMER, W. R., "Form-Critical Analysis of Some Synoptic Material," NTS 8 (1961-1962) 313f. EICHHOLZ, G. Gleichnisse der Evangelien (1972) 192-99. DERRETT, J. D. M., "Nisi dominus aedificaverit donum: Towers and Wars (Lk xiv 28-32)" NovT 19 (1977) 241-61. POLAG, A., Die Christologie der Logienquelle (Neukirchen-Vluyn 1977) 85-86. "Agrapha" in: TRE 2 (1978) 106.

14:28-30 SANDERS, J. T., Ethics in the New Testament (Philadelphia 1975) 37. VIELHAUER, P., "Oikodome. Das Bild vom Bau in der christlichen Literatur vom Neuen Testament bis Clemens Alexandrinus" in: G. Klein (ed.) Oikodome (München 1979) 55-56.

14:28 JEREMIAS, J., Die Sprache des Lukasevangeliums (Göttingen 1980) 242.

14:29 JEREMIAS, J., Die Sprache des Lukasevangeliums (Göttingen 1980) 242.

14:31 NICKELS, P. Targum and New Testament (1967) 41. SUMMERS, R. The Secret Sayings of the Living Jesus (1968) 70. METZGER, B. M., The Early Versions of the New Testament (Oxford 1977) 254. JEREMIAS, J., Die Sprache des Lukasevangeliums (Göttingen 1980) 242.

14:33-34 KNOX, W. L. The Sources of the Synoptic Gospels II (1957) 17. STAUDINGER, J. Die Bergpredigt (1957) 44, 64, 68.

14:33 BROWN, S. Apostasy and Perseverance in the Theology of Luke (1969) 104f. METZGER, B. M., The Early Versions of the New Testament (Oxford 1977) 392. FRIEDRICH, G., "Das Problem der Autorität im Neuen Testament" in: Auf das Wort kommt es an (Göttingen 1978) 288.

14:34-35 JÜLICHER, D. A. Die Gleichnisreden Jesu (1910) 57-79. DODD, C. H. The Parables of the Kingdom (1948) 139ff. DUPONT, D. J. Les Béatitudes (1958) 89-91. LOCKYER, H. All the Parables of the Bible (1963) 135ff. LAMBRECHT, J. "Die Logia-Quellen von Markus 13", Biblica 47 (1966) 334-35. KARAVIDOPULOS, J., "Der Sinn des 'Salzes' in den Worten Jesu" Th 39 (1968) 386-93. JEREMIAS, J. Neutestamentliche Theologie I (1971) 18, 37f.

SCHULZ, S. Q Die Spruchquelle der Evangelisten (1972) 468-72. TALBERT, C. H., Literary Patterns, Theological Themes, and the Genre of Luke-Acts (Missoula (1974) 52, 55. CARLSTON, C. E., The Parables of the Triple Tradition (Philadelphia 1975) 46-48, 87-89, 174-78. KLAUCK, H.-J., Allegorie und Allegorese in Synoptischen Gleichnistexten (Münster 1978) 281.

14:34 BLACK, M. An Aramaic Approach to the Gospels and Acts (1967) 166f. PALLIS, A., Notes on St. Luke and the Acts (London 1928) 32-33.

14:35 PERLES, F., ''Zwei Übersetzungsfehler im Text der Evangelien'' ZNW 19 (1919-1920) 96.

15-18 SOLTAU, W., ''Die Anordnung der Logia in Lukas 15 - 18'' ZNW 10 (1909) 230-38.

15:1-16:13 HARRINGTON, W. ''The Setting of the Parables,'' DoLi 13 (4, 1963) 165-73.

15-16 HICKLING, C. J. A., ''A Tract on Jesus and the Pharisees? A Conjecture on the Redaction of Luke 15 and 16'' HeyJ 16 (1975) 253-65.

15 MORGAN, G. C. The Parables and Metaphors of Our Lord (1943) 211ff. DODD, C. H. The Parables of the Kingdom (1948) 119ff. FEINE, D. P. & BEHM, D. J. Einleitung in das Neue Testament (1950) 35f. KOSSEN, H. B. ''Quelques remarques sur l'ordre des paraboles dans Luc xv et sur la structure de Matthieu xviii 8-14,'' NovTest (1956) 75-80. GUILDING, A., The Fourth Gospel and Jewish Worship (Oxford 1960) 132-37. ROBINSON, J. M. Kerygma und historischer Jesus (1960) 20. GIBLIN, C. H. ''Structural and Theological Considerations on Luke 15,'' CBQ 24 (1, 1962) 15-31. LOCKYER, H. All the Parables of the Bible (1963) 281ff. ADAM, A. ''Gnostische Züge in der patristischen Exegese von Luk. 15'', in: Studia Evangelica III (1964) F. L. Cross, ed., 299-305. MORRIS, L., Glory in the Cross (London 1966) 52-54. RASCO, E. ''Les paraboles de Luc, XV'', in: De Jésus aux Evangiles (1967) I. de la Potterie ed., 165-83. GIBLIN, C. H. ''Why Jesus Spoke in Parables—an Answer from Luke 15,'' ChSt 7 (2, 1968) 213-20. STROBEL, A. Erkenntnis und Bekenntnis der Sünde in neutestamentlicher Zeit (1968) 60. JEREMIAS, J. ''Tradition und Redaktion in Lukas 15,'' ZNW 62 (3-4, 1971) 172-89. BAILEY, K. E., The Cross and the Prodigal. The 15th Chapter of Luke, seen through the eyes of Middle Eastern peasants (St. Louis 1973). DUPONT, J., ''Réjouissez-vous avec moi! Lc 15,1-32'' AssS 55 (1974) 70-79. TALBERT, C. H., Literary Patterns, Theological Themes, and the Genre of Luke-Acts Missoula 1974) 52. BOVON, F. et ROUILLER, G., (eds.) Exegesis. Problèmes de méthode et exercices de lecture (Genèse 22 et Luc 15) (Neuchâtel/Paris 1975).

GOPPELT, L., Theologie des Neuen Testaments. I (Göttingen 1975) 179ff. LAMBRECHT, J., "Parabels over 'het volorene' (Lc,15)" Collationes 22 (1976) 449-79. SCHNIDER, F., Die verlorenen Söhne (Freiburg/Göttingen 1977). WAELKENS, R., "L'analyse structurale des paraboles. Deux essais: Luc 15,1-32 et Matthieu 13,44-46" RThL 8 (1977) 160-78. STOCK, A., Textentfaltungen. Semiotische Experimente mit einer biblischen Geschichte (Düsseldorf 1978). RAMAROSON, L., "Le coeur du Troisième Evangile: Lc 15" Biblica 60 (1979) 248-60. FRICKEL, J., "Die Zöllner, Vorbild der Demut und wahrer Gottesverehrung" in: E. Dassmann/K. S. Frank (eds.) Pietas. FS. B. Kötting (Münster 1980) 373.

15:1ff. KNOX, W. L. The Sources of the Synoptic Gospels II (1957) 89ff. BULTMANN, R. Theologie des Neuen Testaments (1965) 21, 24f. STROBEL, A. Erkenntnis und Bekenntnis der Sünde in neutestamentlicher Zeit (1968) 42.

15:1-32 CANTINAT, J. CM. "Les Paraboles de la Miséricorde (Luc 15,1-32)" NRTh 77 (1955) 246-64. FARMER, W. F. "Form-Critical Analysis of some Synoptic Material," NTS 8 (1961-1962) 301f.

15:1-29 "APOSTEL" in: TRE 3 (1978) 443.

15:1-10 JÜLICHER, D. A. Die Gleichnisreden Jesu (1910) 314-33. IWAND, H.-J. GPM 4 (1949-1950) 190ff. LOEWENICH, W. von, Luther als Ausleger der Synoptiker (1954) 170ff. MICHAELIS, D. W. Die Gleichnisse Jesu (1956) 130-36. DUPONT, J. "La Brebis Perdue et la Drachme Perdue," LuVieSupp 34 (June, 1957) 15-23. BRUNNER, P. in: Herr, tue meine Lippen auf Bd. 1 (1957) G. Eichholz ed., 216-23. KNOX, W. L. The Sources of the Synoptic Gospels II (1957) 102. SURKAU, GPM 15 (1960-1961) 192ff. DOERNE, M. Er kommt auch noch heute (1961) 105-07. GALBIATI, E. "La parabole della pocora e della dramma ritrovate (Luca 15,1-10)," BiOr 6 (3, 1964) 129-33. IWAND, H.-J. Predigt-Meditationen (1964) 229-34. Hephata, Predigtgedanken aus Vergangenheit und Gegenwart (1966) 70-85. VOOBUS, A. The Gospels in Study and Preaching (1966) 93-118. TRILLING, W. "Gottes Erbarmen" in: Christusverkündigung in den Synoptischen Evangelien (1969) 108. SCHNEIDER, G., Das Evangelium nach Lukas (Gütersloh/Würzburg 1977) 323 (lit!). "Amt" in: TRE 2 (1978) 512.

15:1-7 PIROT, J. Paraboles et Allégories Evangeliques (1949) 251-72. LOEWENICH, W. von, Luther als Ausleger der Synoptiker (1954) 118f., 211f. SCHMIDT, W. "Der gute Hirte. Biblische Besinnung über Lukas 15,1-5," EvTh 24 (4, 1964) 173-77. BARCLAY, W. And Jesus Said (1970) 177-79. ARAI, S., "Das Gleichnis vom verlorenen Schaf - Eine traditionsgeschichtliche Untersuchung"

AJBI 2 (1976) 111-37. PERRIN, N. Jesus and the Language of the Kingdom (London 1976) 38, 115, 128, 143, 160, 203. LOHSE, E., in: GPM 33 (1979) 289-95.

15:1-5 SWIDLER, L., Biblical Affirmations of Woman (Philadelphia 1979) 172.

15:1-3 BAILEY, K. E., Poet and Peasant: A Literary Cultural Approach to the Parables in Luke (Grand Rapids 1976) 142-44. SWIDLER, L., Biblical Affirmations of Woman (Philadelphia 1979) 253.

15:1-2 JEREMIAS, J. Neutestamentliche Theologie I (1971) 111, 116, 120, 166. LADD, G. E., A Theology of the New Testament (Grand Rapids 1974) 54,75, 349. TALBERT, C. H., Literary Patterns, Theological Themes, and the Genre of Luke-Acts Missoula 1974) 20. SCHNIDER, F., Die verlorenen Söhne (Freiburg/Göttingen 1977) 24-28, 85. MEYER, B. F., The Aims of Jesus (London 1979) 158-62. JEREMIAS, J. Die Sprache des Lukasevangeliums (Göttingen 1980) 243.

15:1 BEST, E. One Body in Christ (1955) 99. KNOX, W. L. The Sources of the Synoptic Gospels II (1957) 79. METZGER, B. M., The Early Versions of the New Testament (Oxford 1977) 244. JEREMIAS, J., Die Sprache des Lukasevangeliums (Göttingen 1980) 244.

15:2 MICHAELIS, D. W. Die Gleichnisse Jesu (1956) 130-35. KNOX, W. L. The Sources of the Synoptic Gospels II (1957) 112. STROBEL, A. Erkenntnis und Bekenntnis der Sünde in neutestamentlicher Zeit (1968) 60. ''Abendmahl'' in: TRE 1 (1977) 49. FRIEDRICH, G., ''Das Problem des Autorität im Neuen Testament'' in: Auf das Wort kommt es an (Göttingen 1978) 285-87. WESTERHOLM, S., Jesus and Scribal Authority (Lund 1978) 70-71. SWIDLER, L., Biblical Affirmations of Woman (Philadelphia 1979) 274. JEREMIAS, J., Die Sprache des Lukasevangeliums (Göttingen 1980) 244.

15:3-32 BRAUN, H. Qumran und NT II (1966) 87, 89, 93, 95, 109, 115.

15:3-10 KNOX, W. L. The Sources of the Synoptic Gospels II (1957) 92. DERRETT, J. D. M., ''Fresh Light on the Lost Sheep and the Lost Coin'' NTS 26 (1979) 36-60.

15:3-7 JEREMIAS, J. Die Gleichnisse Jesu (1962) 35-37, 67, 102, 132-35. BISER, E. Die Gleichnisse Jesu (1965) 109ff., 139. HENSS, W. Das Verhältnis zwischen Diatessaron, Christlicher Gnosis und ''Western Text'' (1967) 35, 39. SUMMERS, R. The Secret Sayings of the Living Jesus (1968) 25. GOULDER, M. D. Midrash and Lection in Matthew (1974) 59f., 303. TALBERT, C. H., Literary Patterns, Theological Themes, and the Genre of Luke-Acts (Missoula 1974) 55. MANEK, J., . . . und brachte Frucht. Die Gleichnisse Jesu (Berlin 1977) 51-53. SCHNIDER, F., Die verlorenen Söhne (Freiburg/Göttingen 1977) 28-42, 85-87.

15:3-6 KNOX, W. L. The Sources of the Synoptic Gospels II (1957) 100.

15:3 JEREMIAS, J., Die Sprache des Lukasevangeliums (Göttingen 1980) 245.

15:4-32 SCHÜRMANN, H., "Wie hat Jesus seinen Tod bestanden und verstanden?" in: P. Hoffmann (ed.) Orientierung an Jesus. FS. J. Schmid (Freiburg 1973) 336-37. BEYSCHLAG, K., Simon Magus und die christliche Gnosis (Tübingen 1974) 36, 103n.4, 133. MEYER, B. F., The Aims of Jesus (London 1979) 158-62.

15:4-10 HIRSCH, E. Frühgeschichte des Evangeliums (1941) 146-49. JEREMIAS, J., Die Sprache des Lukasevangeliums (Göttingen 1980) 248.

15:4-7 MICHAELIS, D. W. Die Gleichnisse Jesu (1956) 130-35. DUPONT, J. "La parabole de la Brebis perdue (Matthieu 18,12-14; Luc 15:4-7)", Gregorianum 49 (1968) 265-87. LINNEMANN, E. Gleichnisse Jesu (1969) 13, 15, 23, 24, 26, 34, 47, 50, 70ff., 150ff. HOFFMANN, P. Studien zur Theologie der Logienquelle (1972) 387-91. SCHULZ, S., Q Die Spruchquelle der Evangelisten (Zürich 1972) 387-91. SANFORD, J. A., The Kingdom Within (New York 1970) 178-79. BAILEY, K. E., Poet and Peasant: A Literary Cultural Approach to the Parables in Luke (Grand Rapids 1976) 144-56. POLAG, A., Die Christologie der Logienquelle (Neukirchen-Vluyn 1977) 43. SCHNIDER, E., "Das Gleichnis vom verlorenen Schaf und seine Redaktoren. Ein intertextueller Vergleich" Kairos 19 (1977) 146-54. WEDER, H., Die Gleichnisse Jesu als Metaphern (Göttingen ²1980) 168-77.

15:4-6 TOLBERT, M. A., Perspectives on the Parables (Philadelphia 1979) 55-57.

15:4 BUSSBY, F. "Did a Shepherd Leave Sheep upon the Mountains or in the Desert? A Note on Matthew 18.12 and Luke 15.4," AThR 45 (1, 1963) 93-94. SCHRAGE, W. Das Verhältnis des Thomas-Evangeliums zur Synoptischen Tradition und zu den Koptischen Evangelienübersetzungen (1964) 193. NICKELS, P. Targum and New Testament (1967) 41. BERGMEIER, G., Glaube als Gabe nach Johannes (Stuttgart 1980) 132. BÖHLIG, A., Die Gnosis III: Der Manichäismus (Zürich/München 1980) 243n.32. JEREMIAS, J., Die Sprache des Lukasevangeliums (Göttingen 1980) 245-46.

15:5 JEREMIAS, J., Die Sprache des Lukasevangeliums (Göttingen 1980) 246.

15:6 JEREMIAS, J., Die Sprache des Lukasevangeliums (Göttingen 1980) 246.

15:7 VOLZ, P. Die Eschatologie der jüdischen Gemeinde (1934) 277.

MOORE, G. F. Judaism (1946) I 516n. STAEHELIN, E., Die Verkündigung des Reiches Gottes in der Kirche Jesu Christi I (1951) 287. JÜNGEL, E. Paulus und Jesus (1966) 175. STROBEL, A. Erkenntnis und Bekenntnis der Sünde in neutestamentlicher Zeit (1968) 42. HASLER, V. Amen (1969) 68. JEREMIAS, J. Neutestamentliche Theologie I (1971) 20, 37, 119, 146, 151, 156, 174, 177. ZIESLER, J. A. The Meaning of Righteousness in Paul (1972) 140f., 144f. KÜMMEL, W. G., Römer 7 und das Bild des Menschen im Neuen Testament (München 1974) 167-68. TALBERT, C. H., Literary Patterns, Theological Themes, and the Genre of Luke-Acts (Missoula 1974) 55. JEREMIAS, J., Die Sprache des Lukasevangeliums (Göttingen 1980) 246-67.

15:8ff. FINDLAY, J. A. Jesus and His Parables (1951) 70ff.

15:8-12 SWIDLER, L., Biblical Affirmations of Woman (Philadelphia 1979) 172.

15:8-10 PIROT, J. Paraboles et Allégories Evangeliques (1949) 273-79. MICHAELIS, D. W. Die Gleichnisse Jesu (1956) 135f. JEREMIAS, J. Die Gleichnisse Jesu (1962) 85, 132-35, 195. BARCLAY, W. And Jesus Said (1970) 179-80. TALBERT, C. H., Literary Patterns, Theological Themes, and the Genre of Luke-Acts (Missoula 1974) 55. BAILEY, K. E., Poet and Peasant: A Literary Cultural Approach to the Parables in Luke (Grand Rapids 1976) 156-58. PERRIN, N., Jesus and the Language of the Kingdom (London 1976) 38, 115, 141, 160. MANEK, J., . . . und brachte Frucht. Die Gleichnisse Jesu (Berlin 1977) 98-99. POLAG, A., Die Christologie der Logienquelle (Neukirchen-Vluyn 1977) 43. SCHNIDER, F., Die verlorenen Söhne (Freiburg/Göttingen 1977) 42, 87. SWIDLER, L., Biblical Affirmations of Woman (Philadelphia 1979) 275. WEDER, H., Die Gleichnisse Jesu als Metaphern (Göttingen ²1980) 249-52.

15:8-9 SANFORD, J. A., The Kingdom Within (New York 1970) 180-87.

15:8 SCHÜRMANN, H. ''Sprachliche Reminiszenzen an abgeänderte oder ausgelassene Bestandteile der Spruchsammlung im Lukas- und Matthäusevangelium,'' NTS 6 (1959-1960) 209f. JEREMIAS, J., Die Sprache des Lukasevangeliums (Göttingen 1980) 247.

15:10 VOLZ, P. Die Eschatologie der jüdischen Gemeinde (1923) 277. WALLS, A. F. '' 'In the Presence of the Angels' (Luke xv 10),'' NovTest 3 (4, 1959) 314-16. JÜNGEL, E. Paulus und Jesus (1966) 175, 260. STROBEL, A. Erkenntnis und Bekenntnis der Sünde in neutestamentlicher Zeit (1968) 42. HASLER, V. Amen (1969) 104. JEREMIAS, J. Neutestamentliche Theologie I (1971) 21, 119, 156, 174.

15:10 JEREMIAS, J., Die Sprache des Lukasevangeliums (Göttingen 1980) 247-28.

15:11ff. FINDLAY, J. A. Jesus and His Parables (1951) 72ff. ROSEN-KRANZ, D. G. "Das Gleichnis vom verlorenen Sohn im Lotus-Sûtra und im Lukasevangelium," in: Theologie als Glaubenswagnis. Festschrift für Karl Heim (1954) 176-93. BORNKAMM, G. Jesus von Nazareth (1956) 116ff. FUCHS, D. E. "Das Fest der Verlorenen", in: Glaube und Erfahrung (1965) 402-15. BEY-SCHLAG, K. Clemens Romanus und der Frühkatholizismus (1966) 64. GOULDER, M. D. Midrash and Lection in Matthew (1974) 56, 59f.

15:11-32 JÜLICHER, D. A. Die Gleichnisreden Jesu (1910) 333-65. SCHLATTER, A., "Jesu Gleichnis von den beiden Söhnen" Jahrbuch der Theologischen Schule Bethel 2 (1931) 35-63. BORN-HÄUSSER, K. Studien zum Sondergut des Lukas (1934) 103-37. HIRSCH, E. Frühgeschichte des Evangeliums (1941) 22-23. BRUNNER, E. Saat und Frucht (1946) 48-60. RENGSTORF, K. H. Das Evangelium nach Lukas (1949) 183. SCHMID, J. "Das textgeschichtliche Problem der Parabel von den zwei Söhnen", in: N. Adler (ed.), Vom Wort des Lebens (1951), 68-84. NYGREN, A., Agape and Eros (1953) 82ff. MICHAELIS, D. W. Die Gleichnisse Jesu (1956) 136-44. GIOANINA, L. "Amore e interesse nella parabola del Figliuol prodigo," PaCl 37 (24, 1958) 1280-82. DIAS, J. A. "Paralelos entre la Narracion del Libro de Jonas y la Parabola del Hijo Prodigo", Biblica 49 (1959) 632-40. HUNTER, A. M. Interpreting the Parables (1960) 60ff. GIBLET, J. "La parabole de l'accueil messianique (Luc 15,11-32)," BVieC 47 (1962) 17-28. LOCHMANN, GPM 17 (1962-1963) 241ff. Erhaltet euch in der Liebe Gottes, Predigtgedanken aus Vergangenheit und Gegenwart Reihe C, Bd. 3-4 (1963) 50-73. LOCKYER, H. All the Parables of the Bible (1963) 285ff. BARTSCH, H. W., Wachet aber zu jeder Zeit! (Hamburg-Bergstedt 1963) 102-06. BLINZLER, J., "Gottes grosse Freude über die Umkehr des Sünders" BiLi 37 (1963-1964) 21-28. EICHHOLZ, C. in: Herr, tue meine Lippen auf Bd. 3 (1964) G. Eichholz ed., 306ff. HARRINGTON, W. J. A Key to the Parables (1964) 128-34. IWAND, H.-J. Predigt-Meditationen (1964) 35-38. BISER, E. Die Gleichnisse Jesu (1965) 115ff., 163ff. FALEY, R. J. " 'There was once a man who had two sons . . .'," Bible Today 1 (18, 1965) 1181-86. STUHLMACHER, P. Gerechtigkeit Gottes bei Paulus (1965) 248f. DUPONT, J., "L'enfant prodigue" AssS 29 (1966) 52-68. JÜNGEL, E. Paulus und Jesus (1966) 98, 131, 160-64. LINDIJER, C. H. "Kerk en Israel in de gelijkenis van de verloren zon?" NedThT 20 (2, 1966) 161-70. SILVA, R. "La parabola del hijo prodigo," CultBib 23 (210,

1966) 259-63. DERRETT, J. D. M. "Law in the New Testament: The Parable of the Prodigal Son," NTS 15 (1, 1967) 56-74. RENGSTORF, K. H. Die Re-Investitur des Verlorenen Sohnes in der Gleichniserzählung Jesu Luk. 15,11-32 (1967). HAAR, J. GPM 23 (1968-1969) 256-63. BRAUN, H. Jesus (1969) 68. LINNE-MANN, E. Gleichnisse Jesu (1969) 79ff., 163ff. SANDERS, J. T. "Tradition and Redaction in Luke xv. 11-32," NTS 15 (4, 1969) 433-38. DERRETT, J. D. M. Law in the New Testament (1970) 100-25, 402 n.5. LEHMANN, M. Synoptische Quellenanalyse und die Frage nach dem historischen Jesus (1970) 156-57. LOHSE, E. et al., eds., Der Ruf Jesu und die Antwort der Gemeinde (1970) 157-78. SANFORD, J. A., The Kingdom Within (New York 1970) 52, 118-19. EICHHOLZ, G. Gleichnisse der Evangelien (1971) 200-20. JEREMIAS, J. Neutestamentliche Theologie I (1971) 67, 115f., 118, 150, 155. SCHOTTROFF, L. "Das Gleichnis vom verlorenen Sohn," ZThK 68 (1, 1971) 27-52. BJÖRK, S. et al. (eds.) Valda Texter ur Nya Testamentet (Stockholm 1972) 18-20. O'ROURKE, J. J. "Some Notes on Luke xv.11-32," NTS 18 (4, 1972) 431-33. LOCHMAN, J. M. Das Radikale Erbe (1972) 257-86. PATSCH, H. Abendmahl und historischer Jesus (1972) 216ff. RAD, G. von, Predigten (1972) 120-26. BROER, I., "Das Gleichnis vom verlorenen Sohn und die Theologie des Lukas" NTS 20 (1974) 435-62. HARRINGTON, W., "The Prodigal Son" Furrow 25 (1974) 432-37. TALBERT, C. H., Literary Patterns, Theological Themes, and the Genre of Luke-Acts (Missoula 1974) 55. CARLSTON, C. E., "Reminiscence and Redaction in Luke 15:11-32" JBL 94 (1975) 368-90. CONZELMANN, H. und LINDE-MANN, A., Arbeitsbuch zum Neuen Testament (Tübingen 1975) 85. SCHWEIZER, E. Gott Versöhnt: 6 Reden in Nairobi (1975) 69-79. SURKAU, H.-W., in: GPM 29 (1975) 309-20. BAILEY, K. E., Poet and Peasant: A Literary Cultural Approach to the Parables in Luke (Grand Rapids 1976) 158-206. DRURY, J. Tradition and Design in Luke's Gospel (Atlanta 1976) 75-77. MAGASS, W., "Geben, Nehmen, Teilen als Tischsequenz in Lk 15,11-32" LiBi 37 (1976) 31-48. PERRIN, N., Jesus and the Language of the Kingdom (London 1976) 38, 55, 100, 105, 115-16, 119, 120, 129, 150, 161. PESCH, R., "Zur Exegese Gottes durch Jesus von Nazaret. Eine Auslegung des Gleichnisses vom Vater und den beiden Söhnen (Lk 15:11-32)" in: Jesus, Ort der Erfahrung Gottes. FS. B. Welte (Basel 1976) 140-89. CROSSAN, J. D., "A Metamodel for Polyvalent Narration" in: Semeia 9 (1977) 105-47. Le DU,J. et al., Wie is eigenlijk de verloren zoon? Dieptepsychologische lezing en exegetische studie van Lucas 15,11-32 (Antwerp/Amsterdam 1977). FUNK, R. W., "The Narrative Parables: The Birth of a Language

Tradition" in: J. Jervell/W. A. Meeks (eds.) God's Christ and His People. FS. N. A. Dahl (New York 1977) 43-50. GRELOT, P., "Le père et ses deux fils: Luc XV, 11-32. Essai d'analyse structurale" RB 84 (1977) 321-38; "De l'analyse structurale a l'herméneutique" RB 84 (1977) 538-65. van den HOOGEN, T., "Omgaan met een neit-vanzelfsprekend Evangelie. Een theologische bezinning op het traditie-begrip" TvTh 17 (1977) 225-49. MANEK, J., . . . und brachte Frucht. Die Gleichnisse Jesu (Berlin 1977) 99-104. SCHNEIDER, G., Das Evangelium nach Lukas (Gütersloh/Würzburg 1977) 327 (lit!). SCHNIDER, F., Die verlorenen Söhne (Freiburg/Göttingen 1977) 42-66, 87-89. SCOTT, B. B., "The Prodigal Son: A Structuralist Interpretation" Semeia 9 (1977) 45-73. TOLBERT, M. A., "The Prodigal Son: An Essay in Literary Criticism from a Psychoanalytical Perspective" Semeia 9 (1977) 1-20. VIA, D. O., "The Prodigal Son: A Jungian Reading" Semeia 9 (1977) 21-43. BOVON, F. and ROUILLER, G. (eds.) Exegesis. Problems of Method and Exercises in Reading (Genesis 22 and Luke 15) (Pittsburgh 1978). CRAWFORD, R. G., "A Parable of the Atonement" EQ 50 (1978) 2-7. HOFIUS, O., "Alttestamentliche Motive im Gleichnis vom verlorenen Sohn" NTS 24 (1978) 240-48. KRUSE, H., "The Return of the Prodigal. Fortunes of a Parable on its Way to the Far East" Orientalia 47 (1978) 163-214. RUSTON, R., "A Christian View of Justice" NBL 59 (1978) 344-58. SCHOLZ, G., "Ästhetische Beobachtungen am Gleichnis vom Reichen Mann und Armen Lazarus und an drei anderen Gleichnissen" LiBi 43 (1978) 67-74. VAZQUEZ MEDEL, M. A., "El perdón libera del odio. Lectura estructural de Lc 15,11-32" Communio II (1978) 271-312. TOLBERT, M. A., Perspectives on the Parables (Philadelphia 1979) 57, 75, 93-114. OSBORN, R. T., "The Father and His Two Sons: A Parable of Liberation" Dialog 19 (1980) 204-09. RICKARDS, R. R., "Some Points to consider in translating the parable of the prodigal son (Luke 15.11-32)" BTr 31 (1980) 243-45. WEDER, H., Die Gleichnisse Jesu als Metaphern (Göttingen ²1980) 252-63.

15:11-24 BRAUN, H. Jesus (1969) 137, 168.

15:11-23 BARCLAY, W. And Jesus Said (1970) 180-87.

15:11-12 BAILEY, K. E., Poet and Peasant: A Literary Cultural Approach to the Parables in Luke (Grand Rapids 1976) 161-69.

15:11 KNOX, W. L. The Sources of the Synoptic Gospels II (1957) 92, 97. JEREMIAS, J., Die Sprache des Lukasevangeliums (Göttingen 1980) 248-49.

15:12-32 PIROT, J. Paraboles et Allégories Evangeliques (1949) 279-98. ROSENKRANZ, G. ThLZ 79 (1954) 281f. WILCKENS, U.,

"Vergebung für die Sünderin (Lk 7,36-50)" in: P. Hoffmann (ed.) Orientierung an Jesus. FS. J. Schmid (Freiburg 1973) 403-04.

15:12-13 BRUCE, F. F., "The Gospel Text of Marius Victorinus" in: E. Best/R. McL. Wilson (eds.) Text and Interpretation. FS. M. Black (Cambridge 1979) 71. PÖHLMANN, W., "Die Abschichtung des Verlorenen Sohnes (Lk 15:12f) und die erzählte Welt der Parabel" ZNW 70 (1979) 194-213.

15:12 NICKELS, P. Targum and New Testament (1967) 41. JEREMIAS, J., Die Sprache des Lukasevangeliums (Göttingen 1980) 249.

15:13-17 BAILEY, K. E., Poet and Peasant: A Literary Cultural Approach to the Parables in Luke (Grand Rapids 1976) 169-90.

15:13 JEREMIAS, J., Die Sprache des Lukasevangeliums (Göttingen 1980) 249.

15:14 JEREMIAS, J., Die Sprache des Lukasevangeliums (Göttingen 1980) 249-50.

15:15 JEREMIAS, J., Die Sprache des Lukasevangeliums (Göttingen 1980) 250.

15:16 JEREMIAS, J., Die Sprache des Lukasevangeliums (Göttingen 1980) 250.

15:17-19 SMITH, M. Tannaitic Parallels to the Gospels (1968) 3 b n 36.

15:17 METZGER, B. M., The Early Versions of the New Testament (Oxford 1977) 206. JEREMIAS, J., Die Sprache des Lukasevangeliums (Göttingen 1980) 250-51.

15:18.21 BOUSSET, W. Die Religion des Judentums im Späthellenistischen Zeitalter (1966 = 1926) 314.

15:18 BEST, E. One Body in Christ (1955) 132. STROBEL, A. Erkenntnis und Bekenntnis der Sünde in neutestamentlicher Zeit (1968) 42. JEREMIAS, J. Neutestamentliche Theologie I (1971) 20, 151f. HENGEL, M., Judentum und Hellenismus (Tübingen 1969) 544; ET: Judaism and Hellenism (London 1974) 199. LOHFINK, G., "'Ich habe gesündigt gegen den Himmel und gegen dich.' Eine Exegese von Lk 15,18.21" ThQ 155 (1975) 51-52. JEREMIAS, J., Die Sprache des Lukasevangeliums (Göttingen 1980) 251.

15:20-32 WOLFF, H. W., "Von der Mitfreude" in: . . . Wie eine Fackel. Predigten aus drei Jahrzehnten (Neukirchen-Vluyn 1980) 172-83.

15:20-24 SWIDLER, L., Biblical Affirmations of Woman (Philadelphia 1979) 286.

15:20 METZGER, B. M., The Early Versions of the New Testament (Oxford 1977) 211. "Barmherzigkeit" in: TRE 5 (1980) 227, 234. JEREMIAS, J., Die Sprache des Lukasevangeliums (Göttingen 1980) 251.

15:21 STROBEL, A. Erkenntnis und Bekenntnis der Sünde in neutestamentlicher Zeit (1968) 42. HENGEL, M., Judentum und Hellenismus (Tübingen 1969) 544; ET: Judaism and Hellenism II (London 1974) 199. LOHFINK, G., " 'Ich habe gesündigt gegen den Himmel und gegen dich.' Eine Exegese von Lk 15, 18.21" ThQ 155 (1975) 51-52. METZGER, B. M., The Early Versions of the New Testament (Oxford 1977) 392.

15:22-23 RUDOLPH, K. Die Mandäer II (1961) 184,3. NICKELS, P. Targum and New Testament (1967) 41."Abendmahl" in: TRE 1 (1977) 49.

15:22 METZGER, B. M., The Early Versions of the New Testament (Oxford 1977) 210.

15:24-32 BAILEY, K. E., Poet and Peasant: A Literary Cultural Approach to the Parables in Luke (Grand Rapids 1976) 190-206.

15:24 "Auferstehung" in: TRE 4 (1979) 484. BRAUMANN, G., "Tot - lebendig, verloren - gefunden (Lk 15,24 & 32)" in: W. Haubeck/ M. Bachmann (eds.) Wort in der Zeit. FS. K. H. Rengstorf (Leiden 1980) 156-64. JEREMIAS, J., Die Sprache des Lukasevangeliums (Göttingen 1980) 252.

15:25ff. KNOX, W. L. The Sources of the Synoptic Gospels II (1957) 90-91.

15:25-32 BRAUN, H. Jesus (1969) 139f. GOPPELT, L., Theologie des Neuen Testaments. I (Göttingen 1975) 185ff.

15:26.28-30 NICKELS, P. Targum and New Testament (1967) 41.

15:25 JEREMIAS, J., Die Sprache des Lukasevangeliums (Göttingen 1980) 252.

15:26 JEREMIAS, J., Die Sprache des Lukasevangeliums (Göttingen 1980) 253.

15:27 JEREMIAS, J., Die Sprache des Lukasevangeliums (Göttingen 1980) 253.

15:28 METZGER, B. M., The Early Versions of the New Testament (Oxford 1977) 391. "Barmherzigkeit" in: TRE 5 (1980) 227. JEREMIAS, J., Die Sprache des Lukasevangeliums (Göttingen 1980) 253.

15:29 JEREMIAS, J., Die Sprache des Lukasevangeliums (Göttingen 1980) 253.

15:30 METZGER, B. M., The Early Versions of the New Testament (Oxford 1977) 436.

15:31 JEREMIAS, J., Die Sprache des Lukasevangeliums (Göttingen 1980) 254.

15:32 "Auferstehung" in: TRE 4 (1979) 484. BRAUMANN, G., "Tot - lebendig, verloren - gefunden (Lk 15,24 & 32)" in: W. Haubeck/

M. Bachmann (eds.) Wort in der Zeit. FS. K. H. Rengstorf (Leiden 1980) 156-64. JEREMIAS, J., Die Sprache des Lukasevangeliums (Göttingen 1980) 254.

———————

16 RODENBUSCH, E., "Die Komposition von Lukas 16" ZNW 4 (1903) 243. DERRETT, J. D. M. "Fresh Light on St Luke xvi. I. The Parable of the Unjust Steward," NTS 7 (3, 1961) 198-219. "Fresh Light on St. Luke xvi: II. Dives and Lazarus and the preceding Sayings," NTS 7 (4, 1961) 364-80. REUMANN, J. NTS 13 (1966-1967) 166ff. DERRETT, J. D. M. Law in the New Testament (1970) 48-77, 92-99, 95 n. 5. TALBERT, C. H., Literary Patterns, Theological Themes, and the Genre of Luke-Acts (Missoula 1974) 52, 55. KARRIS, R. J., "Poor and Rich: The Lukan Stiz im Leben" in: C. H. Talbert (ed.) Perspectives on Luke-Acts (Danville 1978) 121-23. FEUILLET, A., "Les Paraboles de Luc: Chap. 16. Recherches sur la conception chrétienne du droit de propriété et sur les fondements scriptuaires de la doctrine sociale de l'Eglise" EsVie 89 (1979) 241-50, 257-71.

16:1ff. KNOX, W. L. The Sources of the Synoptic Gospels II (1957) 45, 93ff. KAMLAH, E. "Die Parabel vom ungerechten Verwalter (Luk. 16,1ff.) im Rahmen der Knechtsgleichnisse", in: Abraham unser Vater. Festschrift f. Otto Michel (1963) 276-94. BOUSSET, W. Die Religion des Judentums im Späthellenistischen Zeitalter (1966 = 1926) 411. REUMANN, J. Jesus in the Church's Gospels (1968) 189-98.

16:1-15 PIROT, J. Paraboles et Allégories Evangeliques (1949) 306-23. LILLIE, W. Studies in New Testament Ethics (1961) 100f. LUNT, R. G. "Expounding the Parables: III. The Parable of the Unjust Steward (Luke 16:1-15)," ET 77 (5, 1966) 132-26.

16:1-13 MORGAN, G. C. The Parables and Metaphors of Our Lord (1943) 216ff. MOWRY, L. "Parable", IDB III (1962) 652b f. CAEMMERER, R. R. "Investment for Eternity. A Study of Luke 16:1-13," CThM 34 (2, 1963) 69-76. FLETCHER, D. R. "The Riddle of the Unjust Steward: Is Irony the Key?" JBL 82 (1, 1963) 15-30. LOCKYER, H. All the Parables of the Bible (1963) 289ff. FITZMYER, J. A. "The Story of the Dishonest Manager (Lk 16:1-13)," ThS 25 (1, 1964) 23-42. WILLIAMS, F. E., "Is Almsgiving the Point of the 'Unjust Steward'?" JBL 83 (2, 1964) 293-97. CAMPS,

G. M. & UBACH, B. M. "Un sentido biblico de adikos, adikia, y la interpretacion de Lc 16,1-13," EstBi 25 (1, 1966) 75-82. KRAMER, M. "Aenigma parabolae de villico iniquo Lc 16,1-13," VerbDom 46 (6, 1968) 370-75. FITZMYER, J. A. Essays on the Semitic Background of the New Testament (1971) 161-84. PIDWELL, H. J. Blessed are the Poor (1972) 102-08. GOULDER, M. D. Midrash and Lection in Matthew (1974) 50, 56, 59, 62, 302, 437, 469. SCHUBERT, K. Jesus im Lichte der Religionsgeschichte des Judentums (Wien/München 1973) 125-26. DUPONT, J., "L'exemple de l'intendant débrouillard. Lc 16, 1-13" AssS 56 (1974) 67-78. TOPEL, L. J., "On the Injustice of the Unjust Steward: Lk 16:1-13" CBQ 37 (1975) 216-27. BAILEY, K. E., Poet and Peasant: A Literary Cultural Approach to the Parables in Luke (Grand Rapids 1976) 86-118. FUCHS, E., "L'Evangile et l'argent: la parabole de l'intendant intelligent" Bulletin du Centre Protestant d'Etudes (Geneva 1978) 3-14. MERKELBACH, R., "Über das Gleichnis vom ungerechten Haushalter (Lucas 16,1-13)" VigChr 33 (1979) 180-81. TOLBERT, M. A., Perspectives on the Parables (Philadelphia 1979) 61. WEDER,H., Die Gleichnisse Jesu als Metaphern (Göttingen 1980($_2$)) 262-67.

16:1-12 JÜLICHER, D. A. Die Gleichnisreden Jesu (1910) 495-514. LOEWENICH, W. von, Luther als Ausleger der Synoptiker (1954) 50ff., 184f. Hephata, Predigtgedanken aus Vergangenheit und Gegenwart, Reihe A,Bd. 5 (1966) 180-96. BARCLAY, W. And Jesus Said (1970) 146-50. LUNT, R., "Expounding the Parables" ET 77 (1966) 132-36.

16:1-9 KRECK, GPM 4 (1949-1950) 216ff. DAVIDSON, J. A. "A 'Conjecture' About the Parable of the Unjust Steward (Lk 16,1-9)", ET 66 (1, 1954) 31. DINKLER, GPM 9 (1954-1955) 200ff. DIEM, H. in: Herr, tue meine Lippen auf Bd. 1 (1957) 246-52. HOOLEY, B. A. & MASON, A. J. "Some Thoughts on the Parable of the Unjust Steward (Luke 16:1-9)," AusBR 6 (1-4, 1958) 47-59. BRAUN, GPM 15 (1960-1961) 223ff. DOERNE, M. Er kommt auch noch heute (1961) 120-22. WILLIAMS, F. E. "Is almsgiving the point of the 'unjust steward'?" JBS 83 (1964) 298-97. BIGO, P. "La richesse comme intendance, dans l'Evangile. A propos de Luc 16,1-9," NRTh 87 (3, 1965) 267-71. VOOBUS, A. The Gospels in Study and Preaching (1966) 259-88. KANNENGIESSER, C. "L'intendant malhonnête," Christus 18 (70, 1971) 213-18. DRURY, J., Tradition and Design in Luke's Gospel (Atlanta 1976) 78-79. PERRIN, N., Jesus and the Language of the Kingdom (London 1976) 112, 119, 150, 161. MANEK, J., . . . und brachte Frucht. Die Gleichnisse Jesu (Berlin 1977) 104-05. FEUILLET, A., "La parabole du mauvais riche et du pauvre Lazare (Lc 16,19-31) antithèse de la parabole de l'intendant astucieux (Lc 16,1-9)'' NRTh 101 (1979) 212-23. MATTILL, A. J., Luke and the Last Things: a Perspective for the Understanding of Lukan Thought (Dillsboro 1979) 37-39.

16:1-8 MICHAELIS, D. W. Die Gleichnisse Jesu (1956) 225-29. FYOT, J.-L. ''Sur la parabole de l'Intendant infidèle,'' Christus 6 (24, 1959) 500-04. JEREMIAS, J. Die Gleichnisse Jesu (1962) 30-33, 130f. MAASS, F., ''Das Gleichnis vom ungerechten Haushalter'' ThViat 8 (1962) 173-84. BLINZLER, J., ''Kluge Ausnützung der Gegenwart . . . '' BiLi 37 (1963-1964) 357-68. GAECHTER, P. ''Die Parabel vom ungetreuen Verwalter (Lk 16,1-8),'' Orientierung 27 (July 31, 1963) 149-50. DEGENHARDT, H.-J. Lukas, Evangelist der Armen (1964) 114-20. HARRINGTON, W. J. A Key to the Parables (1964) 101-06. BISER, E. Die Gleichnisse Jesu (1965) 41f., 105ff. MOORE, F. J. ''The Parable of the Unjust Steward,'' AThR 47 (1, 1965) 103-05. DERRETT, J. D. M. Law in the New Testament (1970) 79-80. BOHREN, R., Predigtlehre (München 1972) 150-51. FORCK, G. GPM 27 (1973) 367-72. TALBERT, C. H., Literary Patterns, Theological Themes, and the Genre of Luke-Acts (Missoula 1974) 52. CONZELMANN, H. und LINDEMANN, A., Arbeitsbuch zum Neuen Testament (Tübingen 1975) 85. SCHNEIDER, G., Das Evangelium nach Lukas (Gütersloh/Würzburg 1977) 331 (lit!). LINDARS, B., ''Jesus and the Pharisees'' in: E. Bammel et al. (eds.) Donum Gentilicium. FS. D. Daube (Oxford 1978) 553-56. RAYAN, S., The Holy Spirit: Heart of the Gospel and Christian Hope (New York 1978) 58-59. TOLBERT, M. A., Perspectives on the Parables (Philadelphia 1979) 83-89.

16:1-7 JÜNGEL, E. Paulus und Jesus (1966) 157-60. DREXLER, H. ''Zu Lukas 16:1-7,'' ZNW 58 (3-4, 1967) 286-88. CROSSAN, J. D. In: SBL Seminar Papers 2 (1973) G. MacRae ed., 101-02. DUPONT, J., ''Die individuelle Eschatologie im Lukas-Evangelium und in der Apostelgeschichte'' in: P. Hoffmann (ed.) Orientierung an Jesus. FS. J. Schmid (Freiburg 1973) 41-43.

16:1-2 FINDLAY, J. A. Jesus and His Parables (1951) 77ff.

16:1 TRITES, A. A., The New Testament Concept of Witness (Cambridge 1977) 196. JEREMIAS, J., Die Sprache des Lukasevangeliums (Göttingen 1980) 255.

16:2.4 BEST, E. One Body in Christ (1955) 132.

16:2 DERRETT, J. D., ''Fresh Light on Lk 16:2'' NTS 7 (1961) 364-380. JEREMIAS, J., Die Sprache des Lukasevangeliums (Göttingen 1980) 255.

16:3 FRIEDRICH, G., ''Das Amt im Neuen Testament'' in: Auf das

Wort kommt es an (Göttingen 1978) 422. JEREMIAS, J., Die Sprache des Lukasevangeliums (Göttingen 1980) 256.

16:5 METZGER, B. M., The Early Versions of the New Testament (Oxford 1977) 210. JEREMIAS, J., Die Sprache des Lukasevangeliums (Göttingen 1980) 256.

16:6-8 HAHN, F. Christologische Hoheitstitel (1963) 89.

16:6 DERRETT, J. D. M. " 'Take thy Bond . . . and Write Fifty' (Luke xvi.6). The Nature of the Bond," JThS 23 (2, 1972) 438-40.

16:7 NICKELS, P. Targum and New Testament (1967) 42. COLELLA, S. P. "Zu Lk 16,7," ZNW 64 (1973) 124-26.

16:8-13 JÜNGEL, E. Paulus und Jesus (1966) 158. REUMANN, J. Jesus in the Church's Gospels (1968) 194-98. FITZMYER, J. A. Essays on the Semitic Background of the New Testament (1971) 179-80, 180-81.

16:8-9 KRAMER, M. "Ad parabolam de villico iniquo: Lc, 16,8.9," VerbDom 38 (5-6, 1960) 278-91. BRAUN, H. Qumran und NT II (1966) 96f., 288, 291. MAILLOT, A. "Notules sur Luc 16/8b-9," EThR 44 (2, 1966) 127-30.

16:8 STAEHELIN, E. Die Verkündigung des Reiches Gottes in der Kirche Jesu Christi I (1951) 185. HAHN, F. Christologische Hoheitstitel (1963) 89, 90. BOUSSET, W. Die Religion des Judentums im Späthellenistischen Zeitalter (1966 = 1926) 245. JÜNGEL, E. Paulus und Jesus (1966) 157, 159. MARSHALL, I. H. "Luke xvi.8—Who Commended the Unjust Steward?" JThS 19 (2, 1968) 617-19. EHRHARDT, A. "Greek Proverbs in the Gospel", The Framework of the New Testament Stories (1964) 44-63. PALLIS, A. Notes on St. Luke and the Acts (London 1928) 33-34. SANFORD, J. A., The Kingdom Within (New York 1970) 129. SCHWARZ, G., " ' . . . lobte den betrügerischen Verwalter'? (Lukas 16,8a)" BZ 18 (1974) 94-95. NOONAN, J. T., Jr., "The Devious Employees" Commonweal 104 (1977) 681-83. THEISSEN, G., Soziologie der Jesusbewegung (München 1977) 18. BERGMEIER, R., Glaube als Gabe nach Johannes (Stuttgart 1980) 223, 257, 371-72.

16:9ff. STAEHELIN, E. Die Verkündigung des Reiches Gottes in der Kirche Jesu Christi I (1951) 69. HAHN, F. Christologische Hoheitstitel (1963) 89.

16:9-15 TALBERT, C. H., Literary Patterns, Theological Themes, and the Genre of Luke-Acts (Missoula 1974) 52.

16:9-13 DESCAMPS, A. "La composition littéraire de Luc XVI,9-13," NovTest 1 (1956) 49-53. JEREMIAS, J. Die Gleichnisse Jesu (1962) 42-45, 181. HAHN, F. Christologische Hoheitstitel

(1963)89. SCHNEIDER, G., Das Evangelium nach Lukas (Gütersloh 1977) 334.

16:9-11 GOPPELT, L., Theologie des Neuen Testaments. I (Göttingen 1975) 131-32.

16:9-10 OTT, W. Gebet und Heil (1965) 38-40, 100.

16:9, 11, 13 RÜGER, H. P. "Μαμῶνας," ZNW 64 (1973) 127-31.

16:9 STAEHELIN, E. Die Verkündigung des Reiches Gottes in der Kirche Jesu Christi I (1951) 179. LOEWENICH, W. von, Luther als Ausleger der Synoptiker (1954) 50ff., 193f. DEGENHARDT, H.-J. Lukas, Evangelist der Armen (1964) 120-25. JÜNGEL, E. Paulus und Jesus (1966) 157f. NICKELS, P. Targum and New Testament (1967) 42. FRIEDLANDER, G. The Jewish Sources of the Sermon on the Mount (1969) 169f. HASLER, V. Amen (1969) 108. HIERS, R. H. "Friends by Unrighteous Mammon: The Eschatological Proletariat (Luke 16:9)," JAAR 38 (2, 1970) 30-36. COLELLA, P. "De mamona iniquitatis," RivB 19 (4, 1971) 427-28. JEREMIAS, J. Neutestamentliche Theologie I (1971) 17, 20, 214, 238, 248. COLELLA, P. "Zu Lk 16:9," ZNW 64 (1-2, 1973) 124-26. GOULDER, M. D. Midrash and Lection in Matthew (1974) 301f. DUPONT, J., "Die individuelle Eschatologie im Lukas-Evangelium und in der Apostelgeschichte" in: P. Hoffmann (ed.) Orientierung an Jesus. FS. J. Schmid (Freiburg 1973) 42-43. HOWARD, V. P., Das Ego in den Synoptischen Evangelien (Marburg 1975) 215-23. METZGER, B. M., The Early Versions of the New Testament (Oxford 1977) 209. JEREMIAS, J., Die Sprache des Lukasevangeliums (Göttingen 1980) 257.

16:10-13 HIRSCH, E. Frühgeschichte des Evangeliums (1941) 151-53.

16:10-12 ENGELHARDT, K. GPM 17 (1963) 307-10. Erhaltet euch in der Liebe Gottes, Predigtgedanken aus Vergangenheit und Gegenwart Reihe C,Bd. 3-4 (1963) 232-41. DEGENHARDT, H.-J. Lukas, Evangelist der Armen (1964) 125-27. JÜNGEL, E. Paulus und Jesus (1966) 157. LÖWE, H. GPM 23 (1969-1970) 335-40. HENNECKE, E./SCHNEEMELCHER, W. Neutestamentliche Apokryphen (1964) I 114. NICKELS, P. Targum and New Testament (1967) 42. HEUE, R. and WITTRAM, H., in: P. Krusche et al. (eds.) Predigtstudien für das Kirchenjahr 1974-1975. III/2 (Stuttgart 1975) 198-205. LAHR, H., in: GPM 29 (1975) 392-98.

16:10 JEREMIAS, J. Neutestamentliche Theologie I (1971) 26, 29, 35, 215.

16:11 JEREMIAS, J. Neutestamentliche Theologie I (1971) 17, 158, 214f. PALLIS, A., Notes on St. Luke and the Acts (London 1928) 34.

16:12 SMITH, M. Tannaitic Parallels to the Gospels (1968) 6 b n 5. PALLIS, A. Notes on St. Luke and the Acts (London 1928) 34-35.

16:13.16-18 HOFFMANN, P. Studien zur Theologie der Logienquelle (1972) 5, 42, 50-79, 121f., 190, 194, 222, 295, 326, 332.

16:13 JÜLICHER, D. A. Die Gleichnisreden Jesu (1910) 108-15. KNOX, W. L. The Sources of the Synoptic Gospels II (1957) 29, 69, 95. DEGENHARDT, H.-J. Lukas, Evangelist der Armen (1964) 127-31. HENNECKE, E./SCHNEEMELCHER, W. Neutestamentliche Apokryphen (1964) I 113. SCHRAGE, W. Das Verhältnis des Thomas-Evangeliums zur Synoptischen Tradition und zu den Koptischen Evangelienübersetzungen (1964) 109. JÜNGEL, E. Paulus und Jesus (1966) 157f. SMITH, M. Tannaitic Parallels to the Gospels (1968) 6 b n 6. SUMMERS, R. The Secret Sayings of the Living Jesus (1968) 38. WREGE, H.-T. Ueberlieferungsgeschichte der Bergpredigt (1968) 115-16. JEREMIAS, J. Neutestamentliche Theologie I (1971) 17, 25f., 175. SCHULZ, S. Q Die Spruchquelle der Evangelisten (1972) 459-61. "Aramäisch" in: TRE 3 (1978) 607. JEREMIAS, J., Die Sprache des Lukasevangeliums (Göttingen 1980) 258.

16:14-31 BUSSE, U., Das Nazareth-Manifest Jesu (Stuttgart 1978) 88-90.

16:14-18 JÜLICHER, D. A. Die Gleichnisreden Jesu (1910) 632-34. DE-GENHARDT, H.-J. Lukas, Evangelist der Armen (1964) 131-33. HOFFMANN, P. Studien zur Theologie der Logienquelle (1972) 53-56. SCHNEIDER, G., Das Evangelium nach Lukas (Gütersloh 1977) 336.

16:14-16 SCHÜRMANN, H. "Sprachliche Reminiszenzen an abgeänderte oder ausgelassene Bestandteile der Spruchsammlung im Lukas- und Matthäusevangelium," NTS 6 (1959-1960) 209f.

16:14-15 "Armut" in: TRE 4 (1979) 78.

16:14 KNOX, W. L. The Sources of the Synoptic Gospels II (1957) 81. FRIEDLANDER, G. The Jewish Sources of the Sermon on the Mount (1969) 198f. TALBERT, C. H., Literary Patterns, Theological Themes, and the Genre of Luke-Acts (Missoula 1974) 20. KARRIS, R. J., "Poor and Rich: The Lukan Sitz im Leben" in: C. H. Talbert (ed.) Perspectives on Luke-Acts (Danville 1978) 122. JEREMIAS, J., Die Sprache des Lukasevangeliums (Göttingen 1980) 248.

16:15 KNOX, W. L. The Sources of the Synoptic Gospels II (1957) 96, 115. ROBINSON, J. M. Kerygma und historischer Jesus (1960) 165. JÜNGEL, E. Paulus und Jesus (1966) 208. AALEN, S. NTS 13 (1966-1967) 1ff. SANFORD, J. A., The Kingdom Within (New York 1970) 99. JEREMIAS, J., Die Sprache des Lukasevangeliums (Göttingen 1980) 258-59.

16:16-31 MATTILL, A. J., Luke and the Last Things (Dillsboro 1979) 8.

16:16-18 RODENBUSCH, E. ZNW 4 (1903) 243-54. HIRSCH, E. Frühge-

schichte des Evangeliums (1941) 65-68. BAMMEL, E. "Is Luke
16,16-18 of Baptist's Provenience?" HThR 51 (2, 1958) 101-06.
DUPONT, D. J. Les Béatitudes (1958) 113-17. BORNKAMM-
BARTH-HELD, Ueberlieferung und Auslegung im Matthäus-
Evangelium (²1961) 13, 58f. LAMBRECHT, J. "Die Logia-Quelle
von Markus 13," Biblica 47 (1966) 346-49.

16:16-17 BOUSSET, W. Die Religion des Judentums im Späthellenisti-
schen Zeitalter (1966 = 1926) 120, 144. HÜBNER, H., Das Gesetz
in der synoptischen Tradition (Witten 1973) 28ff. TALBERT, C.
H., Literary Patterns, Theological Themes, and the Genre of Luke-
Acts (Missoula 1974) 103. BANKS, R., Jesus and the Law in the
Synoptic Tradition (London 1975) 246-47. GLÖCKNER, R., Die
Verkündigung des Heils beim Evangelisten Lukas (Mainz 1975) 88-
89.

16:16 PALLIS, A., Notes on St. Luke and the Acts (London 1928) 35.
STONEHOUSE, N. B. The Witness of Matthew and Mark to Christ
(1944) 245ff. KÜMMEL, W. G. Verheissung und Erfüllung (1953)
114-17, 122. SCHLATTER, A. Johannes der Täufer (1956) 72-75.
DANKER, F. W. "Luke 16:16—An Opposition Logion," JBL 77
(3, 1958) 231-43. BERKHOF, H. Der Sinn der Geschichte: Christus (1959) 68f. BLAIR, E. P. Jesus in the Gospel of Matthew (1960)
88. ROBINSON, J. M. Kerygma und historischer Jesus (1960) 155.
STRECKER, G. Der Weg der Gerechtigkeit (1962) 91, 167.
HAHN, F. Christologische Hoheitstitel (1963) 165, 375, 380.
PERRIN, N., The Kingdom of God in the Teaching of Jesus (Phil-
adelphia 1963) 43, 60, 170, 171-74. FLENDER, H. Heil und Ge-
schichte in der Theologie des Lukas (1965) 112-14. JÜNGEL, E.
Paulus und Jesus (1966) 175, 190, 193. FLENDER, H. St Luke
Theologian of Redemptive History (1967) 22 & n, 49n, 101, 123ff.
WINK, W. John the Baptist in the Gospel Tradition (1968) 20-22,
46-48. WILSON, S. G. NTS 16 (1969-1970) 333-35. DES-
CAMPS, A. & DE HALLEUX, A. Mélanges Bibliques en hommage au R. P. Béda Rigaux (1970) 207, 209-12. KÜMMEL, W.
G. "Das Gesetz und die Propheten gehen bis Johannes - Lukas 16,16
im Zusammenhang der heilsgeschichtlichen Theologie der Lukas-
schriften", in: Verborum Veritas (1970) O. Böcher & K. Haacker
eds., 89-102. JEREMIAS, J. Neutestamentliche Theologie I (1971)
40, 43, 53f., 113f., 119. HOFFMANN, P. Studien zur Theologie
der Logienquelle (1972) 51-56, 59f. KRÄNKEL, E. Jesus der
Knecht Gottes (1972) 57, 90, 93f, 96, 211. SCHULZ, S. Q Die
Spruchquelle der Evangelisten (1972) 261-67. KÜMMEL, W. G.
Einleitung in das Neue Testament (1973) 113f. GOULDER, M. D.
Midrash and Lection in Matthew (1974) 285, 307, 359. KÜM-
MEL, W. G. "Das Gesetz und die Propheten gehen bis Johannes"

- Lukas 16,16 im Zusammenhang der heilsgeschichtlichen Theologie der Lukasschriften (1970) in: Das Lukas-Evangelium (1974) G. Braumann ed., 398-415. SANFORD, J. A., The Kingdom Within (New York 1970) 66-68. BERGER, K. Die Gesetzesauslegung Jesu (1972) 209-27. KRÄNKEL, E., Jesus der Knecht Gottes. (Rengsburg 1972) 57, 90, 93-94, 96, 211. ZMIJEWSKI, J., Die Eschatologiereden des Lukas-Evangeliums (Bonn 1972) 10, 12, 13, 15, 282, 283, 284, 409, 422, 511. DERRETT, J. D. M., Jesus's Audience (London 1973) 188-90. HIERS, R. H., The Historical Jesus and the Kingdom of God (Gainesville 1973) 49-50. KÜMMEL, W. G., "Luc en accusation dans la Théologie contemporaine" in: F. Neirynck (ed.) L'Evangile de Luc (Gembloux 1973) 102-03. SAMAIN, E., "La notion de APXH dans l'oeuvre lucanienne" in: F. Neirynck (ed.) L'Evangile de Luc (Gembloux 1973) 310-12. SCHNIDER, F., Jesus der Prophet (Freiburg 1973) 39, 179ff. WANKE, J., Die Emmauserzählung (Leipzig 1973) 754. WILSON, S. G., The Gentiles and the Gentile Mission in Luke-Acts (Cambridge 1973) 61, 63, 64, 65, 66, 70. DAVIES, W. D., The Gospel and the Land (London 1974) 245 n.7, 249, 338, 339 n.12. SAND, A. Das Gesetz und die Propheten (Regensburg 1974) 178-82. TALBERT, C. H., Literary Patterns, Theological Themes, and the Genre of Luke-Acts (Missoula 1974) 48, 103, 104. WILCKENS, U., Die Missionsreden der Apostelgeschichte (Neukirchen-Vluyn 1974(3)) 102, 104, 105, 229. GOPPELT, L., Theologie des Neuen Testaments. I (Göttingen 1975) 114-15. MENOUD, P. M., "Le sens du verbe BIAZETAI dans Luc 16:16" in: Jésus-Christ et la foi (Paris 1975) 125-130. MINEAR, P., To Heal and to Reveal (New York 1976) 112ff. POLAG, A., Die Christologie der Logienquelle (Neukirchen-Vluyn 1977) 48, 79. "Apostelgeschichte" in: TRE (1978) 516. BUSSE, U., Das Nazareth-Manifest Jesu (Stuttgart 1978) 84-90. CATCHPOLE, D. R., "On doing Violence to the Kingdom" Journal of Theology for Southern Africa 25 (1978) 50-61. DÖMER, M., Das Heil Gottes (Köln-Bonn 1978) 37-40. MATTILL, A. J., Luke and the Last Aims of Jesus (London 1979) 147-48. PRAST, F., Presbyter und Evangelium in nachapostolischer Zeit (Stuttgart 1979) 115, 278-81, 312, 314, 317, 333, 351-52. SCHLOSSER, J., "Le règne du Dieu dans les dits de Jésus" RevSR 53 (1979) 164-76. THIERING, B. E., "Are the 'Violent Men' False Teachers?" NovT 21 (1979) 293-97. BACHMANN, M., "Johannes der Täufer bei Lukas: Nachzügler oder Vorläufer?" in: W. Haubeck/M. Bachmann (eds.) Wort in der Zeit. FS. K. H. Rengstorf (Leiden 1980) 139-54. "Bergpredigt" in: TRE 5 (1980) 609, 610. HARRINGTON, D.J., God's People in Christ (Philadelphia 1980) 24. JEREMIAS, J., Die Sprache des

Lukasevangeliums (Göttingen 1980) 259. MCDONALD, J. I. H., Kerygma and Didache (Cambridge 1980) 19. KRAFT,H., Die Entstehung des Christentums (Darmstadt 1981) 33.

16:17 KNOX, W. L. The Sources of the Synoptic Gospels II (1957) 19, 27. BLAIR, E. P. Jesus in the Gospel of Matthew (1960) 121. STRECKER, G. Der Weg der Gerechtigkeit (1962) 13;1). KAESEMANN, E. Exegetische Versuche und Besinnungen (1964) II 85. LOHSE, E. et al., eds., Der Ruf Jesu und die Antwort der Gemeinde (1970) 195f. VÖGTLE, A. Das Neue Testament und die Zukunft des Kosmos (1970) 28, 99, 101f., 106f. SCHULZ, S. Q Die Spruchquelle der Evangelisten (1972) 114-16. SANFORD, J. A., The Kingdom Within (New York 1970) 50-51. POLAG, A., Die Christologie der Logienquelle (Neukirchen-Vluyn 1977) 79. "Bergpredigt" in: TRE 5 (1980) 606.

16:18 MOORE, G. F. Judaism (1946) II 124. KNOX, W. L. The Sources of the Synoptic Gospels II (1957) 22. STAUDINGER, J. Die Bergpredigt (1957) 100, 101, 260. SCHRAGE, W. Die konkreten Einzelgebote in der paulinischen Paränese (1961) 244. STRECKER, G. Der Weg der Gerechtigkeit (1962) 17, 131. BORNKAMM, G. "Ehescheidung und Wiederverheiratung im Neuen Testament," Geschichte und Glaube I (1968) 56-59. SHANER, D. W. A Christian View of Divorce (1969) 50ff. LOHSE, E. et al., eds., Der Ruf Jesu and die Antwort der Gemeinde (1970) 226-46. BERGER, K. "Zu den Sogenannten Sätzen Heiligen Rechts," NTS 17 (1970-1971) 15f. OLSEN, N. V. The New Testament Logia on Divorce (1971). SCHULZ, S. Q Die Spruchquelle der Evangelisten (1972) 116-20. ERNST, J., Anfänge der Christologie (Stuttgart 1972) 150-52. SAND, A. Das Gesetz und die Propheten (Regensburg 1974) 48-49. BANKS, R., Jesus and the Law in the Synoptic Tradition (London 1975) 182-83, 192-93. HOFFMANN, P. and EID, V., Jesus von Nazareth und eine christliche Moral (Freiburg 1975) 109-13, 121-22. WIJNGARDS, J. N. M., "Do Jesus' Words on Divorce (Lk 16:18) Admit of no Exception?" Jeevadhara 6 (1975) 399-411. METZGER, B. M., The Early Versions of the New Testament (Oxford 1977) 179. SANDMEL, S., We Jews and Jesus (New York 1977) 136. FRIEDRICH, G., "Das Problem der Autorität im Neuen Testament" in: Auf das Wort kommt es an (Göttingen 1978) 385. STAGG, E. and F., Woman in the World of Jesus (Philadelphia 1978) 133-35. WESTERHOLM, S., Jesus and Scribal Authority (Lund 1978) 117-20, 123-25. FURNISH, V. P., The Moral Teaching of Paul (Nashville 1979) 40. SCHÜRMANN, H., "Neutestamentliche Marginalien zur Frage nach der Institutionalität, Unauflösbarkeit und Sakramentalität der Ehe" in: Kirche und Bibel. FS. E. Schick (Paderborn 1979) 415-23. SWIDLER, L., Biblical Affirmations of Woman (Philadelphia 1979) 174, 175, 231, 239, 259. CONDON, K., "Apropos of the Divorce Sayings" IBS 2 (1980) 40-51. DESCAMPS, A.-L., "Les textes évangéliques sur le mariage (suite)" RThL 11 (1980) 5-50. JEREMIAS, J., Die Sprache des Lukasevangeliums (Göttingen 1980) 259-60.

16:19ff. VOLZ, P. Die Eschatologie der jüdischen Gemeinde (1934) 295. FINDLAY, J. A. Jesus and His Parables (1951) 86ff. STAE-HELIN, E. Die Verkündigung des Reiches Gottes in der Kirche Jesu Christi I (1951) 24, 155, 310. KNOX, W. L. The Sources of the Synoptic Gospels II (1957) 96. HAHN, F. Christologische Hoheitstitel (1963) 130. AALEN, S. NTS 13 (1966-1967) 5ff. GOULDER, M. D. Midrash and Lection in Matthew (1974) 50, 56, 60, 253.

16:19-31 JÜLICHER, D. A. Die Gleichnisreden Jesu (1910) 617-41. GRESSMANN, H. Vom Reichen Mann and Armen Lazarus (1918). BORNHÄUSSER, K. Studien zum Sondergut des Lukas (1934) 138-60. HIRSCH, E. Frühgeschichte des Evangeliums (1941) 224-27. MORGAN, G. C. The Parables and Metaphors of Our Lord (1943) 222-27; PIROT, J., Paraboles et Allégories Evangeliques (1949) 324-37. BORNKAMM, G. GPM 4 (1949-1950) 181ff. BARTSCH, H. W. "Vom reichen Mann and armen Lazarus", Deutsches Pfarrerblatt LII (1952) 141ff. (Abgedruckt in: Entmythologisierende Auslegung. Aufsätze aus den Jahren 1940 bis 1960 (1962) 183-87.) LOEWENICH, W. von, Luther als Ausleger der Synoptiker (1954) 85f. FUCHS, GPM 9 (1954-1955) 160ff. RIMMER, N. "Parable of Dives and Lazarus (Lk 16,19-31)", ET 66 (7, 1955) 215-16. MICHAELIS, D. W. Die Gleichnisse Jesu (1956) 213-20. EICHHOLZ, G. in: Herr, tue meine Lippen auf Bd. 1 (1957) G. Eichholz ed., 203, 209. STAUDINGER, J. Die Bergpredigt (1957) 53, 55, 56. DUNKERLEY, R. "Lazarus," NTS 5 (4, 1959) 321-27. HAAR, GPM 15 (1960-1961) 184ff. DOERNE, M. Er kommt auch noch heute (1961) 101-03. CADBURY, H. J. " A Proper Name for Dives. (Lexical Notes on Luke-Acts VI)," JBL 81 (4, 1962) 399-402. CANTINAT, J. "Le mauvais riche et Lazare (Luc 16,19-31)," BVieC 48 (1962) 19-26. JEREMIAS, J. Die Gleichnisse Jesus (1962) 181-86, 205. BAUMBACH, G. Das Verständnis des Bösen in den synoptischen Evangelien (1963) 139ff. BULTMANN, R. The History of the Synoptic Tradition (1963) 196f., 203f. LOCKYER, H. All the Parables of the Bible (1963) 292ff. GROEBEL, K. NTS 10 (1963-1964) 274ff. DEGENHARDT, H.-J Lukas, Evangelist der Armen (1964) 133-36. GROBEL, K. " ' . . . Whose Name was Neves'," NTS 10 (3, 1964) 373-82. HARRINGTON, W. J. A Key to the Parables (1964) 87-92. HENNECKE, E./SCHNEEMELCHER, W. Neutestament-

liche Apokryphen (1964) I 258. HANHART, K. The Intermediate
State in the New Testament (1966) 190-99. Hephata, Predigtgedanken aus Vergangenheit und Gegenwart, Reihe A,Bd. 5 (1966)
38-51. JÜNGEL, E. Paulus und Jesus (1966) 99. VOOBUS, A. The
Gospels in Study and Preaching (1966) 31-62. NICKELS, P. Tar-
gum and New Testament (1967) 42. HUIE, Jr., W. P. "The Pov-
erty of Abundance. From Text to Sermon on Luke 16:19-31,"
Interpretation 22 (4, 1968) 403-20. SUMMERS, R. The Secret
Sayings of the Living Jesus (1968) 24. CAVE, C. H. "Lazarus and
the Lukan Deuteronomy," NTS 15 (3, 1969) 319-25. BARCLAY,
W. And Jesus Said (1970) 92-98. DERRETT, J. D. M. Law in the
New Testament (1970) 78, 79, 85-99, 402 n.5. GLOMBITZA, O.
"Der reiche Mann und der arme Lazarus. Luk. xvi 19-31. Zur Frage
nach der Botschaft des Textes," NovTest 12 (2, 1970) 166-80.
EICHHOLZ, G. Gleichnisse der Evangelien (1971) 221-28. PE-
TERS, G. W. A Biblical Theology of Missions (1972) 18, 333-34.
PIDWELL, H. J. Blessed are the Poor (1972) 108-12. BISHOP, E.
F. F. "A Yawning Chasm," EQ 45 (1, 1973) 3-5. SAHLIN, H.
"Lasarus-gestalten i Luk 16 och Joh 11," SEA 37-38. (1972-1973)
167-74. STECK, K. G. GPM 27 (1973) 308-18. NÖTSCHER, F.,
Altorientalischer und alttestamentlicher Auferstehungsglaube
(Darmstadt 1970 = 1926) 184, 213, 313. SANFORD, J. A., The
Kingdom Within (New York 1970) 176-78. BJÖRCK, S. et al.,
Valda Texter ur Nya Testamentet (Stockholm 1972) 21-22. DU-
PONT, J., "Die individuelle Eschatologie im Lukas-Evangelium
und in der Apostelgeschichte" in: P. Hoffmann (ed.) Orientierung
an Jesus. FS. J. Schmid (Freiburg 1973) 43-44. TALBERT, C. H.,
Literary Patterns, Theological Themes, and the Genre of Luke-Acts
(Missoula 1974) 52. GOPPELT, L., Theologie des Neuen Testa-
ments. I (Göttingen 1974) 130-31. PAX, E., "Der reiche und der
arme Lazarus. Eine Milieustudie" SBFLA 25 (1975) 254-68.
LORENZEN, T., "A Biblical Meditation on Luke 16:19-31. From
the Text toward a Sermon" ET 87 (1975) 39-43. MANEK, J., . .
. und brachte Frucht (Berlin 1977) 105-08. SCHNEIDER, G., Das
Evangelium nach Lukas (Gütersloh 1977) 340, 342-43. THEIS-
SEN, G., Soziologie der Jesusbewegung (München 1977) 18.
TRITES, A. A., The New Testament Concept of Witness (Cambridge 1977) 196. MANRIQUE, A., "La Parábola del rico epulón
y de Lázaro y la justicia social en la época de Jesús (Lc 16,19-31)"
CiDi 191 (1978) 207-15. RAYAN, S., The Holy Spirit (New York
1978) 58. SCHOLZ, G., "Ästhetische Beobachtungen am Gleichnis
vom Reichen Mann und Armen Lazarus und an drei anderen
Gleichnissen (Lk 16,19-25 (16-31); 10,34; 13,19; 15,11-32)" LiBi
43 (1978) 67-74. "Armut" in: TRE 4 (1979) 78. MATTILL, A.

J., Luke and the Last Things (Dillsboro 1979) 26-40. MÖLLER, C., in: GPM 33 (1979) 273-80. SCHNIDER, F. and STENGER, W., "Die offene Tür und die unüberschreitbare Kluft. Struktur-analytische Überlegungen zum Gleichnis vom reichen Mann und armen Lazarus (Lk 16,19-31)" NTS 25 (1979) 273-83. JENSEN, H. J. L., "Dieseits und Jenseits des Raumes eines Textes. Textse-miotische Bemerkungen zur Erzählung 'Vom reichen Mann und ar-men Lazarus' (Lk 16,19-31)" LingBib 47 (1980) 39-60.

16:19 NICKELS, P. Targum and New Testament (1967) 42. LEFORT, T., Le nom due mauvais riche" ZNW 37 (1938) 65. METZGER, B. M., The Early Versions of the New Testament (Oxford 1977) 136, 243.

16:20 FRIEDRICHSEN, G. W. S. NTS 11 (1964-1965) 286f.

16:21.22.23 BEST, E. One Body in Christ (1955) 132.

16:21 GALE, H. M. The Use of Analogy in the Letters of Paul (1964) 268f. CADBURY, H. J. "The Name for Dives," JBL 84 (1, 1965) 73.

16:22ff. STAEHELIN, E. Die Verkündigung des Reiches Gottes in der Kirche Jesu Christi I (1951) 290.

16:22-31 CAVALLIN, H. C. C., Life After Death. I (Lund 1974) 4, 3, 7, 2n29. "Abraham" in: TRE I (1977) 279.

16:22-26 BOUSSET, W. Die Religion des Judentums im Späthellenisti-schen Zeitalter (1966-1926) 286, 294, 296, 385.

16:22-24 VOLZ, P. Die Eschatologie der Jüdischen Gemeinde (1934) 269, 271, 406, 416.

16:22 STAEHELIN, E. Die Verkündigung des Reiches Gottes in der Kirche Jesu Christi I (1951) 154, 312. BARRETT, C. K. The New Testament Background: Selected Documents (1956) 222. PLANAS, F., "En el seno de Abraham," CultBib 15 (160, 1958) 148-52. HAUBST, R. "Eschatologie. 'Der Wetterwinkel' - 'Theologie der Hoffnung'." TThZ 77 (1968) 35-65. NEIRYNCK, F., "La Ma-tière Marcienne dans Luc" in: F. Neirynck (ed.) L'Evangile de Luc (Gembloux 1973) 184-92. "Abraham" in: TRE I (1977) 380. JE-REMIAS, J., Die Sprache des Lukasevangeliums (Göttingen 1980) 260.

16:23ff. STAEHELIN, E. Die Verkündigung des Reiches Gottes in der Kirche Jesu Christ L (1951) 312.

16:23 NICKELS, P. Targum and New Testament (1967) 42. JE-REMIAS, J., Die Sprache des Lukasevangeliums (Göttingen 1980) 260.

16:24, 26f. BETZ, H. D. Lukian von Samosata und das Neue Testament (1961) 82, 89, 97, 195.

16:24 HAHN, F. Christologische Hoheitstitel (1963) 264. "Barmherzigkeit" in: TRE 5 (1980) 226.

16:25 MOORE, G. F. Judaism (1946) II 254n. STAEHELIN, E. Die Verkündigung des Reiches Gottes in der Kirche Jesu Christi I (1951) 208. CAVALLIN, H. C. C., Life After Death. I (Lund 1974) 6 n15.

16:26 JEREMIAS, J., Die Sprache des Lukasevangeliums (Göttingen 1980) 261.

16:27-31 NÖTSCHER, F., Altorientalischer und alttestamentlicher Auferstehungsglaube (Darmstadt (1970 = 1926) 299.

16:27-28 SOARES PRABHU, G. M., The Formula Quotations in the Infancy Narrative of Matthew (Rome 1976) 51.

16:27 JEREMIAS, J., Die Sprache des Lukasevangeliums (Göttingen 1980) 261.

16:28 BEUTLER, J. Martyria (1972) 201f. NELLESSEN, E., Zeugnis für Jesus und das Wort (Köln 1976) 73-75. TRITES, A. A., The New Testament Concept of Witness (Cambridge 1977) 128-29. JEREMIAS, J., Die Sprache des Lukasevangeliums (Göttingen 1980) 261.

16:29.31 BOUSSET, W. Die Religion des Judentums in Späthellenistischen Zeitalter (1966 = 1926) 144.

16:29 BRAUN, H. Qumran und NT II (1966) 303.

16:30 NICKELS, P. Targum and New Testament (1967) 42. STROBEL, A. Erkenntnis und Bekenntnis der Sünde in neutestamentlicher Zeit (1968) 42. JEREMIAS, J., Die Sprache des Lukasevangeliums (Göttingen 1980) 261-62

16:31 VOLZ, P. Die Eschatologie der jüdischen Gemeinde (1934) 269. THEYSSEN, G. W. "Unbelief" in the New Testament (1965) 34ff. EVANS, C. V. "Uncomfortable Words-V," ET 81 (8, 1970) 228-31.

—————————

17:1-18:8 FRANKLIN, E., Christ the Lord (London 1975) 16-21.

17 DOWNING, F. G. NTS 11 (1964-1965) 177f. GREENLEE, J. H. Nine Uncila Palimpsests of the Greek New Testament (1968) 74-75. RAYAN, S., The Holy Spirit (New York 1978) 55-56.

17:1 KNOX, W. L. The Sources of the Synoptic Gospels II (1957) 100ff.

17:1-10 KNOX, W. L. The Sources of the Synoptic Gospels II (1957) 45, 92. LOCKYER, H. All the Parables of the Bible (1963) 295ff.

TALBERT, C. H., Literary Patterns, Theological Themes, and the Genre of Luke-Acts (Missoula 1974) 52, 54.

17:1-6 HOFFMANN, P. Studien zur Theologie der Logienquelle (1972) 5, 42, 208, 299.

17:1-4 HEMPEL, J. GPM 21 (1966-1967) 378-83. SCHNEIDER, G., Das Evangelium nach Lukas (Gütersloh 1977) 345.

17:1-3 EDWARDS, R. A., A Theology of Q (Philadelphia 1976) 71.

17:1-2 BUTLER, B. C. The Originality of St Matthew (1951) 7ff. SCHRAGE, W. Die konkreten Einzelgebote in der paulinischen Paränese (1961) 243. RIST, J. M., On the Independence of Matthew and Mark (Cambridge 1978) 75-76.

17:1 FLEW, R. N. Jesus and His Church (1956) 67n. NICKELS, P. Targum and New Testament (1967) 42. DORMEYER, D., Die Passion Jesu als Verhaltensmodell (Münster 1974) 98. POLAG, A. Die Christologie der Logienquelle (Neukirchen-Vluyn 1977) 99. JEREMIAS, J., Die Sprache des Lukasevangeliums (Göttingen 1980) 262.

17:2 BOUSSET, W. Die Religion des Judentums im Spähellenistischen Zeitalter (1966 = 1926) 187.

17:3-4 MOORE, G. F. Judaism II (1946) 163f. STRECKER, G. Der Weg der Gerechtigkeit (1962) 12_2, 203, 222, 224_1. SCHULZ, S. Q Die Spruchquelle der Evangelisten (1972) 320-22. "Bann" in: TRE (1980) 165.

17:3 BORNKAMM-BARTH-HELD, Ueberlieferung und Auslegung im Matthäus-Evangelium (1961) 78. METZGER, B. M., The Early Versions of the New Testament Oxford 1977) 392.

17:4 JÜLICHER, D. A. Die Gleichnisreden Jesu (1910) 302-04. KNOX, W. L. The Sources of the Synoptic Gospels II (1957) 234. HAHN, F. Christologische Hoheitstitel (1963) 83, 86. NICKELS, P. Targum and New Testament (1967) 42. STROBEL, A. Erkenntnis und Bekenntnis der Sünde in neutestamentlicher Zeit (1968) 43, 60. METZGER, B. M., The Early Versions of the New Testament (Oxford 1977) 390.

17:5-10 MORGAN, C. G. The Parables and Metaphors of Our Lord (1943) 227ff. IWAND, H.-J. Predigt-Meditationen (1964) 56-59. WEBER, O. Predigt-Meditationen (1967) 178-81. GEORGE, A., "La foi des Apôtres. Efficacité et gratuité. Lc 17,5-10" AssS 58 (1974) 68-77.

17:5-6 HAHN, F. Christologische Hoheitstitel (1963) 88. HAMPEL, GPM 21 (1966-1967) 70-76. SCHULZ, S. Q Die Spruchquelle der Evangelisten (1972) 465-68. SCHNEIDER, G., Das Evangelium nach Lukas (Gütersloh 1977) 347.

17:5 PALLIS, A., Notes on St. Luke and the Acts (London 1928) 36.
BORNKAMM-BARTH-HELD, Ueberlieferung und Auslegung im
Matthäus-Evangelium (1961) 113. KLEIN, G. Die Zwölf Apostel
(1961) 33f. JEREMIAS, J., Die Sprache des Lukasevangeliums
(Göttingen 1980) 262-63.

17:6 FINDLAY, J. A. Jesus and His Parables (1951) 31ff.
FRIEDRICHSEN, G. W. S. NTS (1964-1965) 386f. THEYSSEN,
G. W. "Unbelief" in the New Testament (1965) 19ff. NICKELS,
P. Targum and New Testament (1967) 43. SANFORD, J. A., The
Kingdom Within (New York 1970) 157-58. DUNN, J. D. G., Je-
sus and the Spirit (London 1975) 72, 74,75. ZMIJEWSKI, J., "Der
Glaube und seine Macht. Eine traditionsgeschichtliche Untersu-
chung zu Mt 17,20; 21,21; Mk 11,23; Lk 17,16" in: J. Zmijewski/
E. Nellessen (eds.) Begegnung mit dem Wort. FS. H. Zimmer-
mann (Bonn 1980) 81-103.

17:7-10 PIROT, J. Paraboles et Allégories Evangeliques (1949) 216-20.
MICHAELIS, D. W. Die Gleichnisse Jesu (1956) 182-88. KNOX,
W. L. The Sources of the Synoptic Gospels II (1957) 106. FUCHS,
E. "Bemerkungen zur Gleichnisauslegung", Zur Frage nach dem
Historischen Jesus (Ges. Aufs. II 1960) 136-42. Verkündigt das
angenehme Jahr des Herrn, Predigtgedanken aus Vergangenheit und
Gegenwart Reihe C, Bd. 1 (1962) 272-82. FÜRST, GPM 17 (1962-
1963) 104ff. BOUSSET, W. Die Religion des Judentums im Spät-
hellenistischen Zeitalter (1966 = 1926) 387. MERKEL, F. GPM 23
(1968-1969) 91-94. BARCLAY, W. And Jesus Said (1970) 209-
12. WEISER, A. Die Knechtsgleichnisse der synoptischen Evangelien (1971) 105-20. CROSSAN, J. D. in: SBL Seminar Papers 2
(1973) 100-01. BACH, U., in: GPM 29 (1974) 121-32. MINEAR,
P. S., "A Note on Luke 17:7-10" JBL 93 (1974) 82-87. MANEK,
J., . . . und brachte Frucht (Berlin 1977) 108-10. SCHNEIDER,
G., Das Evangelium nach Lukas (Gütersloh 1977) 348. PRAST,
F., Presbyter und Evangelium in nachapostolischer Zeit (Stuttgart
1979) 58, 227, 249-53, 260, 349, 435. TRAUB, H., in: GPM 35
(1980) 126-32. BERBERS, C. A. P. and WIEDEMANN, H.-G.,
in: P. Krusche et al. (eds.) Predigtstudien für das Kirchenjahr 1980-
1981. I (Stuttgart 1981) 113-19.

17:7 NICKELS, P. Targum and New Testament (1967) 43. JE-
REMIAS, J., Die Sprache des Lukasevangeliums (Göttingen 1980)
263.

17:8 METZGER, B. M., The Early Versions of the New Testament
(Oxford 1977) 207. JEREMIAS, J., Die Sprache des Lukasevangeliums (Göttingen 1980) 263.

17:9-10 MINEAR, P., To Heal and to Reveal (New York 1976) 25.

17:10 HOLSTEIN, H. "Serviteurs inutiles? (Luc 17,10)," BVieC 48 (1962) 39-45. KAESEMANN, E. Exegetische Versuche und Besinnungen (1964) II 225. JÜNGEL, E. Paulus und Jesus (1966) 214. NICKELS, P. Targum and New Testament (1967) 43. STROBEL, A. Erkenntnis und Bekenntnis der Sünde in neutestamentlicher Zeit (1968) 43. KAESEMANN, E. New Testament Questions of Today (1969) 220. WARD, A. M. "Uncomfortable Words IV. Unprofitable Servants," ET 81 (7, 1970) 200-03. JEREMIAS, J., Die Sprache des Lukasevangeliums (Göttingen 1980) 264.

17:11ff. KNOX, W. L. The Sources of the Synoptic Gospels II (1957) 58, 106.

17:11-37 TALBERT, C. H., Literary Patterns, Theological Themes, and the Genre of Luke-Acts (Missoula 1974) 52, 54. HEUTGER, N., "Die lukanischen Samaritanererzählungen in religionspädagogischer Sicht" in: W. Haubeck/M. Bachmann (eds.) Wort in der Zeit. FS. K. H. Rengstorf (Leiden 1980) 283-86.

17:11-19 Ehrenberg, GPM 4 (1949-1950) 241ff. FARRER, A. St Matthew and St Mark (1954) 53. LOEWENICH, W. von, Luther als Ausleger der Synoptiker (1954) 25ff. BRAUN, GPM 9 (1954-1955) 217ff. DEHN, G. in: Herr, tue meine Lippen auf Bd. 1 (1957) G. Eichholz ed., 271-75. KLEIN, GPM 15 (1960-1961) 255ff. BORNKAMM-BARTH-HELD, Ueberlieferung und Auslegung im Matthäus-Evangelium (1961) 266. DOERNE, M. Er kommt auch noch heute (1961) 132-33. BULTMANN, R. The History of the Synoptic Tradition (1963) 56f., 60f. HAHN, F. Das Verständnis der Mission im Neuen Testament (^{2}1965) 23, 113. Hephata, Predigtgedanken aus Vergangenheit und Gegenwart, Reihe A, Bd. 5 (1966) 290-314. MARXSEN, W. Predigten (1968) 17-23. GLOMBITZA, O. "Der dankbare Samariter. Luk. XVII 11-20," NovTest 11 (4, 1969) 241-46. OTTO, G. Denken-um zu glauben (1970) 78-81. PESCH, R. Jesu ureigene Taten? (1970) 114-23. BETZ, H. D. "The Cleansing of the Ten Lepers (Luke 17:11-19)," JBL 90 (3, 1971) 3214-3328. JERVELL, J., "The Lost Sheep of the House of Israel" in: Luke and the People of God (Minneapolis 1972) 113-32. ZMIJEWSKI, J., Die Eschatologiereden des Lukas-Evangeliums (Bonn 1972) 48, 329, 330, 389, 394. BAUER, K. A. GPM 27 (1973) 401-08. CHARPENTIER, É., "L'étranger appelé au salut. Lc 17,11-19" AssS 59 (1974) 68-79. BRUNERS, W., Die Reinigung der zehn Aussätzigen und die Heilung des Samariters Lk 17,11-19 (Stuttgart 1977). SCHNEIDER, G., Das Evangelium nach Lukas (Gütersloh 1977) 350. MARXSEN, W., Christologie-praktisch (Gütersloh 1978) 51-52, 78-74. SEYBOLD, K. and MÜLLER, U., Krankheit und Heilung (Stuttgart 1978) 120-21. STECK, K. G., in: GPM 33 (1979) 357-63.

17:11 STONEHOUSE, N. B. The Witness of Luke to Christ (1951) 116f., 118, 120, 125, 127. BOSCH, D. Die Heidenmission in der Zukunftsschau Jesu (1959) 105-08. CONZELMANN, H. Die Mitte der Zeit (1964) 60ff. ZMIJEWSKI, J., Die Eschatologiereden des Lukas-Evangeliums (Bonn 1972) 45, 205, 328, 329, 383. LOHSE, E., Die Einheit des Neuen Testaments (Göttingen 1973) 166-68, 171. NEIRYNCK, F., "La Matière Marcienne dans Luc" in: F. Neirynck (ed.) L'Evangile de Luc (Gembloux 1973) 184-92. WANKE, J., Die Emmauserzählung (Leipzig 1973) 34. WILSON, S. G., The Gentiles and the Gentile Mission in Luke-Acts (Cambridge 1973) 42, 43, 44. DAVIES, W. D., The Gospel and the Land (London 1974) 244, 248, 251, 254. TALBERT, C. H., Literary Patterns, Theological Themes, and the Genre of Luke-Acts (Missoula 1974) 17, 20, 114. ZINGG, P., Das Wachsen der Kirche (Freiburg 1974) 138. WILLIAMS, J. A., A Conceptual History of Deuteronomism in the Old Testament, Judaism, and the New Testament (Ph.D. Diss. Southern Baptist Theological Seminary: Louisville 1976) 300. METZGER, B. M., The Early Versions of the New Testament (Oxford 1977) 95. JEREMIAS, J., Die Sprache des Lukasevangeliums (Göttingen 1980) 264.

17:12 NICKELS, P. Targum and New Testament (1967) 43. JEREMIAS, J., Die Sprache des Lukasevangeliums (Göttingen 1980) 264.

17:13-14 RUPPERT, L., Jesus als der leidende Gerechte? (Stuttgart 1972) 61.

17:13 KNOX, W. L. The Sources of the Synoptic Gospels II (1957) 86, 107. HAHN, F. Christologische Hoheitstitel (1963) 77, 263. "Barmherzigkeit" in: TRE 5 (1980) 225.

17:14 MOORE, G. F. Judaism II (1946) 9. BETZ, H. D. Lukian von Samosata und das Neue Testament (1961) 155f. NICKELS, P. Targum and New Testament (1967) 43. NEIRYNCK, F., "La Matière Marcienne dans Luc" in: F. Neirynck (ed.) L'Evangile de Luc (Gembloux 1973) 184-92. METZGER, B. M., The Early Versions of the New Testament Oxford 1977) 95, 206.

17:15 JEREMIAS, J., Die Sprache des Lukasevangeliums (Göttingen 1980) 265.

17:16 FARRER, A. St Matthew and St Mark (1954) 54.

17:18 JEREMIAS, J., Die Sprache des Lukasevangeliums (Göttingen 1980) 265-66.

17:19 ROBINSON, J. M. Kerygma und historischer Jesus (1960) 30. BORNKAMM-BARTH-HELD, Ueberlieferung und Auslegung im Matthäus-Evangelium (1961) 253. GOPPELT, L., Theologie des Neuen Testaments. I (Göttingen 1975) 199-200.

17:20-18:8 BARTSCH, H. W., Wachet aber zu jeder Zeit! (Hamburg-Bergstedt 1963) 106-09. MATTILL, A. J., Luke and the Last Things (Dillsboro 1979) 8.

17:20ff. KNOX, W. L. The Sources of the Synoptic Gospels II (1957) 106ff., 110, 142. CONZELMANN, H. Die Mitte der Zeit (1964) 111ff.

17:20-37 KNOX, W. L. The Sources of the Synoptic Gospels II (1957) 112ff. SCHOONHEIM, P. L. Een Semasiologisch Onderzoek van Parousia (1953) 29-32. STROBEL, A. "In dieser Nacht (Luk 17,34). Zu einer älteren Form der Erwartung in Luk 17,20-37," ZThK 58 (1, 1961) 16-29. GASTON, L. No Stone on Another (1970) 347-53. JEREMIAS, J. Neutestamentliche Theologie I (1972) 125-28, 255. JEREMIAS, J. New Testament Theology I (1971) 123f. SCHNACKENBURG, R. Schriften zum Neuen Testament (1971) 220-43. SCHNACKENBURG, R., "Der eschatologische Abschnitt Lk 17,20-37" in: A. Descamps/A. de Halleux (eds.) Mélanges Bibliques en hommage au R. P. Béda Rigaux (Gembloux 1970) 213-34. ZMIJEWSKI, J., Die Eschatologiereden des Lukas-Evangeliums (Bonn 1972) 326-571. GEIGER, R., Die Lukanischen Endzeitreden(Bern 1973). SCHNACKENBURG, R., Aufsätze und Studien zum Neuen Testament (Leipzig 1973) 230, 326-48. CONZELMANN,H., Theologie als Schriftauslegung (München 1974) 66a.23. PERRIN, N., Jesus and the Language of the Kingdom (London 1976) 57-60. SCHNEIDER, G., Das Evangelium nach Lukas (Gütersloh/Würzburg 1977) 353-54, 358 (lit!). "Apokalyptik" in: TRE 3 (1978) 254.

17:20-30 IWAND, H.-J. in: Herr, tue meine Lippen auf Bd. 3 (1964) G. Eichholz ed., 13ff.

17:20-24 (30) DANTINE, W. GPM 27 (1973) 469-74.

17:20-24 FISCHER, M., in: GPM 33 (1979) 422-27.

17:20-23 LAMBRECHT, J. "Die Logia-Quellen von Markus 13," Biblica 47 (1966) 338-41.

17:20-21 MANSON, T. W. The Teaching of Jesus (1945) 123ff. STAEHELIN, E. Die Verkündigung des Reiches Gottes in der Kirche Jesu Christi I (1951) 68, 192, 376. STROBEL, A., "Die Passa-Erwartung als urchristliches Problem in Lc 17:20f.," ZNW 49 (3-4, 1958) 157-96. SCHNACKENBURG, R. Gottes Herrschaft und Reich (1959) 54, 65, 92-94. BARTSCH, H.-W. "Das Thomas-Evangelium und die Synoptischen Evangelien," NTS 6 (1959-1960) 257f. RUSTOW, A. "Entos hymōn estin. Zur Deutung von Lukas 17:20-21," ZNW 51 (1960) 197-224. STROBEL, A. "A. Merx über Lc 17:20f.," ZNW 51 (1-2, 1960) 133-34. BULTMANN, R. The History of the Synoptic Tradition (1963) 53-55, 121f. HAW-

THORNE, G. F. "The Essential Nature of the Kingdom of God," WThJ 25 (1, 1963) 35-47. STROBEL, A., "Zu Lukas 17:20f" BZ 7 (1963) 111-13. TÖDT, H. E. Der Menschensohn in der synoptischen Ueberlieferung (1963) 97-99. YATES, J. E. The Spirit and the Kingdom (1963) 78-84. CONZELMANN, H. Die Mitte der Zeit (1964) 114ff. SCHRAGE, W. Das Verhältnis des Thomas-Evangeliums zur Synoptischen Tradition und zu den Koptischen Evangelienübersetzungen (1964) 199. JÜNGEL, E. Paulus und Jesus (1966) 193-96, 240. JEREMIAS, J. Neutestamentliche Theologie I (1971) 26, 40-42, 100, 193f., 125, 132, 255. GOLLWITZER, H., Veränderung im Diesseits (München 1973) 59. HIERS, R. H., The Historical Jesus and the Kingdom of God (Gainesville 1973) 29, 81-82. FRANKLIN, E., Christ the Lord: A Study in the Purpose and Theology of Luke-Acts (London 1975) 16-18. GOPPELT, L., Theologie des Neuen Testaments. I (Göttingen 1975) 101-02, 108, 113-14. PERRIN, N., Jesus and the Language of the Kingdom (London 1976) 41, 43-46, 57-58, 83. MATTILL, A. J., Luke and the Last Things: a Perspective for the Understanding of Lukan Thought (Dillsboro 1979) 190-203. SCHLOSSER, J., "Le règne de Dieu dans les dits de Jésus" RevSR 53 (1979) 164-76.

17:20 KNOX, W. L. The Sources of the Synoptic Gospels II (1957) 81. BORNKAMM, G. Die Frage nach dem historischen Jesus (1962) 65. MUSSNER, F. " 'Wann kommt das Reich Gottes?' Die Antwort Jesu nach Lk 17,20b,21," BZ 6 (1, 1962) 107-11. HENNECKE, E./SCHNEEMELCHER, W. Neutestamentliche Apokryphen (1964) II 472. JÜNGEL, E. Paulus und Jesus (1966) 252. PERRIN, N., The Kingdom of God in the Teaching of Jesus (Philadelphia 1963) 114, 170, 171-74.

17:21 STAEHELIN, E. Die Verkündigung des Reiches Gotte in der Kirche Jesu Christ: I (1951) 382, 391. KÜMMEL, W. G., Verheissung und Erfüllung (1953) 26-29. MUSSNER, F. ' 'Wann kommt das Reich Gottes?' Die Antwort Jesu nach Lk 17, 20b, 21," BZ 6 (1, 1962) 107-11. SNEED, R. "The Kingdom of God is Within You (Lk 17,21)," CBQ 24 (4, 1962) 363-82. TURNER, N. Grammatical Insights into the New Testament (1965) 61ff. BOUSSET, W. Die Religion des Judentums im Späthellenistischen Zeitalter (1966 = 1926) 217. JÜNGEL, E. Paulus und Jesus (1966) 253. HIERS, R. H. "Why Will They Not Say, 'Lo, here!' Or 'There!'?" JAAR 35 (4, 1967) 279-84. JEREMIAS, J. Neutestamentliche Theologie I (1971) 16, 31, 33, 96, 100f., 123, 131, 132, 163, 267. SANFORD, J. A., The Kingdom Within (New York 1970) 47-48. MIYOSHI, M., Der Anfang des Reiseberichts Lk 9,51 - 10,24. Eine redaktionsgeschichtliche Untersuchung (Rome 1974) 84-89. SANDMEL, S., We Jews and Jesus (New York 1977) 84. "Bergpredigt'' in: TRE 5 (1980) 619. HARRINGTON, D. J., God's People in Christ (Philadelphia 1980) 24, 25. ROTTENBERG, I. C., The Promise and the Presence: Toward a Theology of the Kingdom of God (Grand Rapids 1980) 82.

17:22ff. FLENDER, H. Heil und Geschichte in der Theologie des Lukas (1965) 89-91. FLENDER, H. St Luke Theologian of Redemptive History (1967) 13ff., 31, 33, 79, 94ff.

17:22-37 LAMBRECHT, J. ''Die Logia-Quellen von Markus 13,'' Biblica 47 (1966) 342-45.

17:22-31 JÜNGEL, E. Paulus und Jesus (1966) 253.

17:22-30 BLAIR, E. P. Jesus in the Gospel of Matthew (1960) 74.

17:22-26 DE SOUZA, B. ''The Coming of the Lord,'' SBFLA 20 (1970) 166-203.

17:22-23 PERRIN, N., Jesus and the Language of the Kingdom (London 1976) 58.

17:22 LEANEY, R./ASBY, E./POWELL, W. ''The Days of the Son of Man: Luke XVII,22,'' ET 67/1 (1955) 28-29; 4 (1956) 124-25; 7 (1956) 219. DELLING, G. Die Taufe im Neuen Testament (1963) 90. HAHN, F. Christologische Hoheitstitel (1963) 37. JÜNGEL, E. Paulus und Jesus (1966) 239. SMITH, M. Tannaitic Parallels to the Gospels (1968) 8 b n 9. DESCAMPS, A./DE HALLEUX, A. Mélanges Bibliques en hommage au R. P. Béda Rigaux (1970) 227-28. JEREMIAS, J. Neutestamentliche Theologie I (1971) 248, 251, 254, 261f., 268. RUPPERT, L., Jesus als der leidende Gerechte? (Stuttgart 1972) 62a.65. JEREMIAS, J., Die Sprache des Lukasevangeliums (Göttingen 1980) 266-67.

17:23-37 GEIGER, R., Die Lukanischen Endzeitreden (Bern 1973) 58-86. POLAG, A. Die Christologie der Logienquelle (Neukirchen-Vluyn 1977) 11. LÜHRMANN, D. Die Redaktion der Logienquelle (1969) 71-75. SCHULZ, S. Q Die Spruchquelle der Evangelisten (1972) 277-287. HOFFMANN, P. Studien zur Theologie der Logienquelle (1972) 5, 42-44, 93, 95-97, 131, 177, 284, 308.

17:23-24 JÜNGEL, E. Paulus und Jesus (1966) 194, 240. SANFORD, J. A., The Kingdom Within (New York 1970) 203-04.

17:23 POLAG, A. Die Christologie der Logienquelle (Neukirchen-Vluyn 1977) 99.

17:24.26.30 SCHWEIZER, E. Erniedrigung und Erhöhung bei Jesus und seinen Nachfolgern (1962) § 3 gio.

17:24 KÜMMEL, W. G. Verheissung und Erfüllung (1953) 31-33, 39f. KNOX, W. L. The Sources of the Synoptic Gospels II (1957) 107. HAHN, F. Christologische Hoheitstitel (1963) 26f., 41. BOUSSET, W. Die Religion des Judentums im Späthellenistischen Zeitalter (1966 = 1926) 265. JÜNGEL, E. Paulus und Jesus (1966) 240f., 244, 252-254. LEHMANN, M. Synoptische Quellenana- lyse und die Frage nach dem historischen Jesus (1970) 122f., 130, 155. JEREMIAS, J. Neutestamentliche Theologie I (1971) 26, 104, 125, 248, 151, 255, 259, 262. PERRIN, N., The New Testament. An Introduction (New York 1974) 75-77. POLAG, A. Die Chri- stologie der Logienquelle (Neukirchen-Vluyn 1977) 96. JE- REMIAS, J., Die Sprache des Lukasevangeliums (Göttingen 1980) 267.

17:25 TAYLOR, V. Jesus and His Sacrifice (1948) 29, 87, 91, 172-175, 255. SCHELKLE, K. H. Die Passion Jesu in der Verkündigung des Neuen Testaments (1949) 64f., 73f. WILCKENS, U. Die Mis- sionsreden der Apostelgeschichte (1961) 116-17, 162, 184. HAHN, F. Christologische Hoheitstitel (1963) 46, 51. FLENDER, H. St. Luke Theologian of Redemptive History (1967) 14, 31, 94, 144, 158n, 159n. GOPPELT, L. Christologie und Ethik (1968) 68f. STROBEL, A. Erkenntnis und Bekenntnis der Sünde in neutestamentlicher Zeit (1968) 41. DESCAMPS, A./DE HAL- LEUX, A. Mélanges Bibliques en hommage au R. P. Béda Rigaux (1970) 222-23, 230. GÜTTGEMANNS, E. Offene Fragen zur Formgeschichte des Evangeliums (1970) 214n, 206, 220, 222, 246. JEREMIAS, J. Neutestamentliche Theologie I (1971) 135, 250, 267f. PATSCH, H. Abendmahl und historischer Jesus (1972) 188f. WANKE, J., Die Emmauserzählung. Eine redaktionsge- schichtliche Untersuchung zu Lk 24,13-55. CONZELMANN, H., Theologie als Schriftauslegung (München 1974) 89-90. TAL- BERT, C. H., Literary Patterns, Theological Themes, and the Genre of Luke-Acts (Missoula 1974) 97. WILCKENS, U., Die Missions- reden der Apostelgeschichte (Neukirchen 1974($_3$)) 116, 117, 118, 162, 184. RADL, W., Paulus und Jesus im lukanischen Doppel- werk (Bern/Frankfurt 1975) 149-58. WILLIAMS, J. A., A Con- ceptual History of Deuteronomism in the Old Testament, Judaism, and the New Testament (Ph.D. Diss., Louisville 1976) 301, 303. METZGER, B. M., The Early Versions of the New Testament (Oxford 1977) 392. JEREMIAS, J., Die Sprache des Lukas- evangeliums (Göttingen 1980) 267-68.

17:26ff. HAHN, F. Christologische Hoheitstitel (1963) 36, 37, 41.

17:26-35 SANFORD, J. A., The Kingdom Within (New York 1970) 205- 06.

17:26-30 SCHLOSSER, J. ''Les jours de Noé et de Lot. A propos de Luc, XVII,26-30,'' RevBi 80 (1, 1973) 13-36. GEIGER, R., Die Luka- nischen Endzeitreden (Bern 1973) 87-108. SCHNEIDER, G., The New Testament. An Introduction (New York 1974) 75-77. TAN-

NEHILL, R. C., The Sword of His Mouth (Philadelphia/Missoula 1975) 118-22.

17:26-29 LÜHRMANN, D. Die Redaktion der Logienquelle (1969) 75-83. LÜHRMANN, D. "Noah and Lot (Lk 17:26-29)—ein Nachtrag," ZNW 63 (1-2, 1972) 130-32.

17:26-27 HAHN, F. Christologische Hoheitstitel (1963) 37f. JÜNGEL, E. Paulus und Jesus (1966) 241f., 254-56. JEREMIAS, J. Neutestamentliche Theologie I (1971) 125, 142, 248, 251, 259, 262. POLAG, A., Die Christologie der Logienquelle (Neukirchen-Vluyn 1977) 95. FRIEDRICH, G., "I Thessalonicher 5,1-11, der apologetische Einschub eines Späteren" in: Auf das Wort kommt es an (Göttingen 1978) 265.

17:26 VOLZ, P. Die Eschatologie der Jüdischen Gemeinde (1934) 337. JÜNGEL, E. Paulus und Jesus (1966) 240, 244. RUPPERT, L., Jesus als der leidende Gerechte? (Stuttgart 1972) 62a.65.

17:27 KNOX, W. L. The Sources of the Synoptic Gospels II (1957) 68, 109.

17:28-30 JUNGEL, E. Paulus und Jesus (1966) 241. POLAG, A., Die Christologie der Logienquelle (Neukirchen-Vluyn 1977) 94, 133.

17:28-29 HAHN, F. Christologische Hoheitstitel (1963) 36f.

17:28 METZGER, B. M., The Early Versions of the New Testament (Oxford 1977) 200. VIELHAUER, P., "Oikodome. Das Bild vom Bau in der christlichen Literatur vom Neuen Testament bis Clemens Alexandrinus" in: G. Klein (ed.) Oikodome (München 1979) 54.

17:29 MÜLLER, U. B., "Die griechische Esra-Apokalypse" in: W. G. Kümmel (ed.) Jüdische Schriften aus hellenistisch-römischer Zeit V/2 (Gütersloh 1976) 93n.19a.

17:30 HAHN, F. Christologische Hoheitstitel (1963) 37. JÜNGEL, E. Paulus und Jesus (1966) 240, 244, 254-56. NICKELS, P. Targum and New Testament (1967) 43. JEREMIAS, J. Neutestamentliche Theologie I (1971) 22, 248, 251, 259, 262.

17:31-37 GEIGER, R., Die Lukanischen Endzeitreden (Bern 1973) 109-31.

17:31-32 POLAG, A., Die Christologie der Logienquelle (Neukirchen-Vluyn 1977) 99-100.

17:31 MIYOSHI, M., Der Anfang des Reiseberichts Lk 9,51 - 10,24. Eine redaktionsgeschichtliche Untersuchung (Rome 1974) 52-54. MATTILL, A. J., Luke and the Last Things: A Perspective for the Understanding of Lukan Thought (Dillsboro 1979) 45-47. JEREMIAS, J., Die Sprache des Lukasevangeliums (Göttingen 1980) 269.

17:33 ROBINSON, J. M. Kerygma und historischer Jesus (1960) 165. NICKELS, P. Targum and New Testament (1967) 43. DES-

CAMPS, A./DE HALLEUX, A. Mélanges Bibliques en hommage au R. P. Béda Rigaux (1970) 224-25. OTOMO, Y., Nachfolge Jesu und Aufänge der Kirche im Neuen Testament (1970) 44-52. JE-REMIAS, J. Neutestamentliche Theologie I (1971) 25-27, 30, 36. SCHULZ, S. Q Die Spruchquelle der Evangelisten (1972) 444-46. BONHOEFFER, D., Gesammelte Schriften. V. (München 1972) 468 ff. LADD, G. E., A Theology of the New Testament (Grand Rapids 1974) 73,74, 257. HOFFMANN, P. und EID, V., Jesus von Nazareth und eine christliche Moral (Freiburg/Basel/Wien 1975) 212-14. POLAG, A., Die Christologie der Logienquelle (Neu-kirchen-Vluyn 1977) 100. GNILKA, J., "Martyriumsparänese und Sühnetod in synoptischen und jüdischen Traditionen" in: H. Schürmann (ed.), Die Kirche des Anfangs (Freiburg/Basel/Wien 1978) 235. LEROY, H., " 'Wer sein Leben gewinnen will . . . ' Erlöste Existenz heute' FZPhTh 25 (1978) 171-86.

17:34-37 GEIGER, R., Die Lukanischen Endzeitreden (Bern 1973) 132-41. SWIDLER, L., Biblical Affirmations of Woman (Philadelphia 1979) 242, 253, 257.

17:34-36 SWIDLER, L., Biblical Affirmations of Woman (Philadelphia 1979) 167.

17:34-35 JEREMIAS, J. Neutestamentliche Theologie I (1971) 22, 25, 125, 130.

17:34 SCHRAGE, W. Das Verhältnis des Thomas-Evangeliums zur Synoptischen Tradition und zu den Koptischen Evangelienübersetzungen (1964) 126. HASLER, V. Amen (1969) 109. POLAG, A., Die Christologie der Logienquelle (Neukirchen-Vluyn 1977) 95-96. JEREMIAS, J., Die Sprache des Lukasevangeliums (Göttingen 1980) 270.

17:35 JEREMIAS, J., Die Sprache des Lukasevangeliums (Göttingen 1980) 270.

17:37 JÜLICHER, D. A. Die Gleichnisreden Jesu (1910) 133-37. BEST, E. One Body in Christ (1955) 216. HAHN, F. Christologische Hoheitstitel (1963) 84, 85. JÜNGEL, E. Paulus und Jesus (1966) 252, 254. DESCAMPS, A./DE HALLEUX, A. Mélanges Bibliques en hommage au R. P. Béda Rigaux (1970) 225-26. POLAG, A., Die Christologie der Logienquelle (Neukirchen-Vluyn 1977) 95. JE-REMIAS, J., Die Sprache des Lukasevangeliums (Göttingen 1980) 270.

18 GREENLEE, J. H. Nine Uncial Palimpsests of the Greek New Testament (1968) 76-77.

18:1ff. KNOX, W. L. The Sources of the Synoptic Gospels II (1957) 110ff.

18:1-14 KNOX, W. L. The Sources of the Synoptic Gospels II (1957) 45. DUPONT, J. Le Discours de Milet (1962) 360-62. PESCH, W. Den Menschen helfen (1969) 70-76.

18:1-8 JÜLICHER, D. A. Die Gleichnisreden Jesu (1910) 176-90. BORNHÄUSSER, K. Studien zum Sondergut des Lukas (1934) 161ff. HIRSCH, E. Frühgeschichte des Evangeliums (1941) 228-30. MORGAN, G. C. The Parables and Metaphors of Our Lord (1943) 232ff. PIROT, J. Paraboles et Allégories Evangeliques (1949) 185-94. SARBE, M. "Das eschatologische Gebet in Lk 18,1-8" (flämisch,) Collationes I/2 (1955) 361-69. MICHAELIS, D. W. Die Gleichnisse Jesu (1956) 234-36. SPICQ, C. "La parabole de la venoe obstinke et du juge inerte, aux décisions impromptues (Lc. XVIII,1-8)," RevBi 68 (1961) 68-90. DELLING, G. "Das Gleichnis vom gottlosen Richter," ZNW 53 (1-2, 1962) 1-25. JEREMIAS, J. Die Gleichnisse Jesu (1962) 85f., 92, 153-57. HERBERT, GPM 17 (1962-1963) 355ff. CRANFIELD, C. E. B. "The Parables of the Unjust Judge and the Eschatology of Luke-Acts," SJTh 16 (3, 1963) 297-301. Erhaltet euch in der Liebe Gottes, Predigtgedanken aus Vergangenheit und Gegenwart Reihe C, Bd. 3-4 (1963) 362-75. LOCKYER, H. All the Parables of the Bible (1963) 298ff. IWAND, H.-J. Predigt-Meditationen (1964) 316-320. OTT, W. Gebet und Heil (1965) 19-72. BOUSSET, W. Die Religion des Judentums im Späthellenistischen Zeitalter (1966 = 1926) 180, 248, 411. DESCHRYVER, R. "La parabole du juge malveillant (Luc 18,1-8)," RHPhR 48 (4, 1968) 355-66. GRÄSSER, E. GPM 23 (1968-1969) 397-404. LINNEMANN, E. Gleichnisse Jesu (1969) 125ff., 183ff. DELLING, G. "Das Gleichnis vom gottlosen Richter" in: Studien zum Neuen Testament und zum hellenistischen Judentum (1970) 203-25. O'NEILL, J. C. The Theology of Acts in its historical setting (1970) 70-71. JEREMIAS, J. Neutestamentliche Theologie I (1971) 121, 137, 186, 234. DE RU,G. "De gelijkenis van de onrechtvaardige rechter (Lucas 18:1-8)," NedThT 25 (4, 1971) 279-92. DERRETT, J. D. M. "Law in the New Testament: The Parable of the Unjust Judge," NTS 18 (2, 1972) 178-91. ZMIJEWSKI, J. Die Eschatologiereden des Lukas-Evangeliums (Bonn 1972) 45, 331, 337, 352, 355, 539, 561. WILSON, S. G., The Gentiles and the Gentile Mission in Luke-Acts (Cambridge 1973) 42, 73, 85, 86. STÄHLIN, G., "Das Bild der Witwe. Ein Beitrag zur Bildersprache der Bibel und zum Phänomen der Personifikation in der Antike" JAC 17 (1974) 5-20. TALBERT, C. H., Literary Patterns, Theological Themes, and the Genre of Luke-Acts (Missoula 1974) 52, 54. GEORGE, A., "La parabole du juge qui fait attendre le jugement.

Lc 18,1-8'' AssS 60 (1975) 68-79. GEYER, H. G., in: GPM 29 (1975) 456-69. PODSWINNA, R. und GERLACH, W., in: P. Krusche et al. (eds.) Predigtstudien für das Kirchenjahr 1974-1975. III/2 (Stuttgart 1975) 262-67. SCHNEIDER, C., Parusiegleichnisse im Lukas-Evangelium (Stuttgart 1975) 71-78. SIMON, L., "La prière non religieuse chez Luc'' FV 74 (1975) 8-22. MANEK, J., . . . und brachte Frucht. Die Gleichnisse Jesu (Berlin 1977) 110-12. SCHNEIDER, G., Das Evangelium nach Lukas (Gütersloh/ Würzburg 1977) 360 (lit!). TRITES, A. A., The New Testament Concept of Witness (Cambridge 1977) 196-97. ZIMMERMANN, H., "Das Gleichnis vom Richter und der Witwe (Luke 18:1-8)'' in: R. Schnackenburg et al (eds.) Die Kirche des Anfangs. FS. H. Schürmann (Leipzig 1977) 79-95. MATTILL, A. J., Luke and the Last Things: A Perspective for the Understanding of Lukan Thought (Dillsboro 1979) 89-96. SWIDLER, L., Biblical Affirmations of Woman (Philadelphia 1979) 167, 184, 253, 272. WEDER, H., Die Gleichnisse Jesu als Metaphern (Göttingen 1980(2)) 267-73.

18:1-7 BARCLAY, W. And Jesus Said (1970) 113-19. TOLBERT, M. A., Perspectives on the Parables (Philadelphia 1979) 58.

18:1-2 FINDLAY, J. A. Jesus and His Parables (1951) 38ff.

18:1 OTT, W. Gebet und Heil (1965) 19-21, 66-68, 68-71, 73f. ZMIJEWSKI, J., Die Eschatologiereden des Lukas-Evangeliums (Bonn 1972) 289, 307, 331, 406, 333, 552. BAUMERT, N., Täglich Sterben und Auferstehen (München 1973) 320-21. "Agrapha'' in: TRE 2 (1978) 107. "Akoimeten'' in: TRE 2 (1978) 152.

18:2-8 BRAUN, H. Qumran und NT II (1966) 93.

18:2-5 TOLBERT, M. A., Perspectives on the Parables (Philadelphia 1979) 81-83.

18:2 STONEHOUSE, N. B. The Witness of Matthew and Mark to Christ (1944) 107. METZGER, B. M., The Early Versions of the New Testament (Oxford 1977) 177.

18:3 WILLIAMS, J. A., A Conceptual History of Deuteronomism in the Old Testament (Ph.D. Diss., Louisville 1976) 303-04.

18:4-5 NICKELS, P. Targum and New Testament (1967) 43.

18:6-8 MÜLLER, U. B., Zur frühchristlichen Theologiegeschichte (Gütersloh 1976) 41-42.

18:6 KNOX, W. L. The Sources of the Synoptic Gospels II (1957) 94, 112, 116. HAHN, F. Christologische Hoheitstitel (1963) 89, 90. DESCAMPS, A./DE HALLEUX, A. Mélanges Bibliques en hommage au R. P. Béda Rigaux (1970) 144-45, 146.

18:7-8 KÜMMEL, W. G. Einleitung in das Neue Testament (1973) 112f.

18:7 STRECKER, G. Der Weg der Gerechtigkeit (1962) 217$_6$. RIE-

SENFELD, H. "Zu μαϰϱοθυμεῖν Lk 18,7)" in: Neutestament-
liche Aufsätze. Festschrift für Josef Schmid (1963) J. Blinzler, O.
Kuss, F. Mussner, eds., 214-17. LJUNGVIN,H. "Zur Erklärung
einer Lukas-Stelle (Luk. xviii. 7)," NTS 10 (2, 1964) 289-94.
WIFSTRAND, A. "Lukas xviii. 7," NTS 11 (1, 1964) 72-74.
METZGER, B. M., The Early Versions of the New Testament
(Oxford 1977) 249, 390.

18:8 HAHN, F. Christologische Hoheitstitel (1963) 45. OTT, W. Gebet
und Heil (1965) 32-34, 63-68. JÜNGEL, E. Paulus und Jesus (1966)
239. FLENDER, H. St Luke Theologian of Redemptive History
(1967) 60n, 79, 79n, 80 & n,101. LEAL, J. "La oracion y la crisis
de fe," Manresa 39 (152, 1967) 213-20. NICKELS, P. Targum and
New Testament (1967) 44. BROWN, S. Apostasy and Perseverance in the Theology of Luke (1969) 39, 45f. HASLER, V. Amen
(1969) 110. JEREMIAS, J. Neutestamentliche Theologie I (1971)
137, 159, 248, 251f., 262. WILSON, S. G., The Gentiles and the
Gentile Mission in Luke-Acts (Cambridge 1973) 72, 73, 82, 83.
CATCHPOLE, D. R., "The Son of Man's Search for Faith (Luke
xviii 8b)" NovT 19 (1977) 81-104. JEREMIAS, J., Die Sprache
des Lukasevangeliums (Göttingen 1980) 272.

18:9ff. STROBEL, A. Erkenntnis und Bekenntnis der Sünde in
neutestamentlicher Zeit (1968) 42.

18:9-14 JÜLICHER, D. A. Die Gleichnisreden Jesu (1910) 598-608.
MORGAN, G. C. The Parables and Metaphors of Our Lord (1943)
238ff. BRUNNER, E. Saat und Frucht (1946) 22-33. PIROT, J.
Paraboles et Allégories Evangeliques (1949) 205-15. BORN-
KAMM, G.. GPM 4 (1949-1950) 226ff. LOEWENICH, W. von,
Luther als Ausleger der Synoptiker (1954) 52ff. SURKAU, GPM
9 (1954-1955) 206ff. MICHAELIS, D. W. Die Gleichnisse Jesu
(1956) 237-44. DIEM, H. in: Herr, tue meine Lippen auf Bd. 1
(1957) G. Eichholz ed., 256-60. BENCKERT, GPM 15 (1960-
1961) 233ff. DOERNE, M. Er kommt auch noch heute (1961) 124-
26. JEREMIAS, J. Die Gleichnisse Jesu (1962) 85f., 92, 139-43.
BAUMBACH, G. Das Verständnis des Bösen in den synoptischen
Evangelien (1963) 147ff. LOCKYER, H. All the Parables of the
Bible (1963) 301ff. STUHLMACHER, P. Gerechtigkeit Gottes bei
Paulus (1965) 244-46. Hephata, Predigtgedanken aus Vergangen-
heit und Gegenwart, Reihe A,Bd. 5 (1966) 209-36. JÜNGEL, E.
Paulus und Jesus (1966) 99, 208. BLANK, J. Schriftauslegung in
Theorie und Praxis (1969) 151. BRAUN, H. Jesus (1969) 67, 169.
LINNEMANN, E. Gleichnisse Jesu (1969) 64ff., 147ff. BAR-
CLAY, W. And Jesus Said (1970) 99-105. LEHMANN, M. Syn-
optische Quellenanalyse und die Frage nach dem historischen Jesus
(1970) 154. LOHSE, E. et al., eds., Der Ruf Jesu und die Antwort

der Gemeinde (1970) 168f. JEREMIAS, J. Neutestamentliche Theologie I (1971) 121, 150, 182, 242. CHARPENTIER, E. "Le chrétien: un homme 'juste' ou 'justifié'? Lc 18,9-14," AssS 61 (1972) 66-78. GOULDER, M. D. Midrash and Lection in Matthew (1974) 55, 60, 470. ZMIJEWSKI, J., Die Eschatologiereden des Lukas-Evangeliums (Bonn 1972) 45, 331, 337, 355, 392. WILCK-ENS, U., "Vergebung für die Sünderin (Lk 7,36-50)" in: P. Hoffmann (ed.) Orientierung an Jesus. FS. J.Schmid (Freiburg 1973) 403-04. WIEBERING, J. GPM 28 (1973) 378-83. GOULDER, M. D. Midrash and Lection in Matthew (1974) 55, 60, 470. MOTTU, H., "The Pharisee and the Tax Collector: Sartrian Notions as Applied to the Reading of Scripture" USQR 29 (1974) 195-213. TALBERT, C. H., Literary Patterns, Theological Themes, and the Genre of Luke-Acts (Missoula 1974) 20, 51, 54. SIMON, L., "La prière non religieuse chez Luc" FV 74 (1975) 8-22. PERRIN, N., Jesus and the Language of the Kingdom (London 1976) 115, 121, 160. MANEK, J., . . . und brachte Frucht (Berlin 1977) 112-15. MERKLEIN, H., " 'Dieser ging als Gerechter nach Hause . . .' Das Gottesbild Jesu und die Haltung der Menschen nach Lk 18,9-14" BuK 32 (1977) 34-42. SCHNEIDER, G., Das Evangelium nach Lukas (Gütersloh 1977) 363. WESTERHOLM, S., Jesus and Scribal Authority (Lund 1978) 55-57, 59-61. FÜRST, W., in: GPM 33 (1979) 341-45. SWIDLER, L., Biblical Affirmations of Woman (Philadelphia 1979) 288.

18:9 JEREMIAS, J., Die Sprache des Lukasevangeliums (Göttingen 1980) 272-73.

18:10-14 TOLBERT, M. A., Perspectives on the Parables (Philadelphia 1979) 75-78. FRICKEL, J., "Die Zöllner, Vorbild der Demut und wahrer Gottesverehrung" in: E. Dassmann/K. S. Frank (eds.) Pietas. FS. B. Kötting (Münster/Westfalen 1980) 372, 376. SCHNIDER, F., "Ausschliessen und ausgeschlossen werden. Beobachtungen zur Struktur des Gleichnisses vom Pharisäer und Zöllner Lk 18,10-14a" BZ 24 (1980) 42-56.

18:10-13 TOLBERT, M. A., Perspectives on the Parables (Philadelphia 1979) 59.

18:10 NICKELS, P. Targum and New Testament (1967) 44.

18:11-43 CAVALLIN, H. C. C., Life After Death. I (Lund 1974) 5 n41.

18:11.13 BETZ, H. D. Lukian von Samosata und das Neue Testament (1961) 71, 187, 193, 199.

18:11 BLACK, M. An Aramaic Approach to the Gospels and Acts (1967) 103f. NICKELS, P. Targum and New Testament (1967) 44. METZGER, B. M., The Early Versions of the New Testament

(Oxford 1977) 177. JEREMIAS, J., Die Sprache des Lukasevangeliums (Göttingen 1980) 273.

18:12 STROBEL, A. Erkenntnis und Bekenntnis der Sünde in
neutestamentlicher Zeit (1968) 29, 33, 97.

18:13 HOERBER, R. G. " 'God Be Merciful to Me a Sinner'. A Note on
Luke 18:13," CThM 33 (5, 1962) 283-86.

18:14 LOEWENICH, W. von. Luther als Ausleger der Synoptiker (1954)
229f. ROBINSON, J. M. Kerygma und historischer Jesus (1960)
165. SCHRAGE, W. Die konkreten Einzelgebote in der paulinischen Paränese (1961) 243. KAESEMANN, E. Exegetische Versuche und Besinnungen (1964) II 97. BOUSSET, W. Die Religion
des Judentums im Späthellenistischen Zeitalter (1966 = 1926) 393.
BRAUN, H. Qumran und NT II (1966) 168. BLANK, J.
Schriftauslegung in Theorie und Praxis (1969) 97, 151. HASLER,
V. Amen (1969) 111. KAESEMANN, E. New Testament Questions of Today (1969) 98. JEREMIAS, J. Neutestamentliche Theologie I (1971) 22, 25f., 116, 118f. SCHULZ, S. Q Die Spruchquelle
der Evangelisten (1972) 451-52. HOFFMANN, P. and EID, V.,
Jesus von Nazareth und eine christliche Moral (Freiburg 1975) 208-
22. JEREMIAS, J., Die Sprache des Lukasevangeliums (Göttingen 1980) 273-74.

18:15-21 DRURY, J., Tradition and Design in Luke's Gospel (Atlanta 1976)
103-09.

18:15-43 TAYLOR, V. Behind the Third Gospel (1926) 92f. JEREMIAS, J.
Neutestamentliche Theologie I (1971) 48f.

18:15-17 DELLING, G. Die Taufe im Neuen Testament (1963) 134.
BLINZLER, J. "Kind und Königreich Gottes (Mk 10,14)," in: Aus
der Welt und Umwelt des Neuen Testaments (1969) 41-53.
SCHRAMM, T. Der Markus-Stoff bei Lukas (1971) 141f. CRIBBS,
F. L. in: SBL Seminar Papers 2 (1973) 14-15. KRAUSE, G. (ed.),
Die Kinder im Evangelium (Stuttgart 1973). TALBERT, C. H.,
Literary Patterns, Theological Themes, and the Genre of Luke-Acts
(Missoula 1974) 51, 52, 53. SCHNEIDER, G., Das Evangelium
nach Lukas (Gütersloh 1977) 366. WESTERMANN, C., Blessing:
In the Bible and the Life of the Church (Philadelphia 1978) 83-85,
98-101. SWIDLER, L., Biblical Affirmations of Woman (Phila-
delphia 1979) 276.

18:15 NICKELS, P. Targum and New Testament (1967) 44. TALBERT,
C. H., Literary Patterns, Theological Themes, and the Genre of
Luke-Acts (Missoula 1974) 52.

18:16-17 TALBERT, C. H., Literary Patterns, Theological Themes, and the
Genre of Luke-Acts (Missoula 1974) 53.

18:16 SANFORD, J. A., The Kingdom Within (New York 1970) 107-08.

18:17 BOUSSET, W. Die Religion der Judentums im Späthellenistischen Zeitalter (1966 = 1926) 214. JÜNGEL, E. Paulus und Jesus (1966) 183. HASLER, V. Amen (1969) 38. WEBER, H.-R., Jesus and the Children (Atlanta 1979) BERGMEIER, R., Glaube als Gabe nach Johannes (Stuttgart 1980) 216.

18:18-31 KARRIS, R. J., "Poor and Rich: The Lukan Sitz im Leben" in: C. H. Talbert, Perspectives on Luke-Acts (Danville 1978) 123.

18:18-30 ZIMMERLI, W. Gottes Offenbarung (1963) 316-24. CELADA, B., "Distribuciòn de los bienes y seguimiento de Jesùs" Cultura Bibilica 25 (1969) 377-40. TRILLING, W. "Besitzverzicht und Nachfolge" in: Christusverkündigung in den Synoptischen Evangelien (1969) 123. PIDWELL, H. J. Blessed are the Poor (1972) 115-18. TALBERT, C. H., Literary Patterns, Theological Themes, and the Genre of Luke-Acts (Missoula 1974) 51, 52, 53. SCHNEIDER, G. Das Evangelium nach Lukas (Gütersloh 1977) 368-69. RIST, J. M., On The Independence of Matthew and Mark (Cambridge 1978) 57-58.

18:18-27 "Beruf" in: TRE 5 (1980) 660.

18:18-23 BERGER, K. Die Gesetzesauslegung Jesu (1972) 454-58. DEGENHARDT, H.-J. Lukas, Evangelist der Armen (1964) 136-49. OTOMO, Y. Nachfolge Jesu und Anfänge der Kirche in Neuen Testament (1970) 37-42. CRIBBS, F. L. in: SBL Seminar Papers 2 (1973) 15-20. SANFORD, J. A., The Kingdom Within (New York 1970) 102-05.

18:18-19 O'NEILL, J. C. The Theology of Acts in its Historical Setting (1970) 20n, 40-41, X.

18:18 MOORE, G. F. Judaism II (1946) 321. HAHN, F. Christologische Hoheitstitel (1963) 76.

18:19 PALLIS, A. Notes on St. Luke and the Acts (London 1928) 36.

18:20 STRECKER, G. Der Weg der Gerechtigkeit (1962) 22₅. HOLTZ, T. Untersuchungen über die Alttestamentlichen Zitate bei Lukas (1968) 81f. NELLESSEN, E., Zeugnis für Jesus und das Wort (Köln 1976) 59-60. TRITES, A. A., The New Testament Concept of Witness (Cambridge 1977) 128-29.

18:21-35 THOMPSON, W. G. Matthew's Advice to a Divided Community Mt. 17,22-18,35 (1970) 203-37.

18:21 METZGER, B. M., The Early Versions of the New Testament (Oxford 1977) 144.

18:22 STAUDINGER, J. Die Bergpredigt (1957) 44, 139, 190. BROWN, S. Apostasy and Perseverance in the Theology of Luke (1969) 34,

56, 101f., 106. ERNST, J., Anfänge der Christologie (Stuttgart 1972) 135-36. METZGER, B. M., The Early Versions of the New Testament (Oxford 1977) 438.

18:23-24 HARTMAN, L. Testimonium Linguae (1963) 24ff.

18:24ff. DEGENHARDT, H.-J. Lukas, Evangelist der Armen (1964) 149-53.

18:25 CELADA, B., "Más acerca del camello y la aguja" Cultura Bíblica 26 (1969) 157-58. SANFORD, J. A., The Kingdom Within (New York 1970) 54-55. KELBER, W. H., "Mark and Oral Tradition" in: Semeia 16 (1980) 25-27.

18:27 JÜNGEL, E. Paulus und Jesus (1966) 184.

18:28-30 DEGENHARDT, H.-J. Lukas, Evangelist der Armen (1964) 153-60. ERNEST, J., Anfänge der Christologie (Stuttgart 1972) 134-35. SWIDLER, L., Biblical Affirmations of Woman (Philadelphia 1979) 179, 232, 239, 257, 259, 274, 279.

18:29-30 STAEHELIN, E. Die Verkündigung des Reiches Gottes in der Kirche Jesu Christi I (1951) 139. NICKELS, P. Targum and New Testament (1967) 44. OTOMO, Y. Nachfolge Jesu und Anfänge der Kirche im Neuen Testament (1970) 57-60.SANFORD, J. A., The Kingdom Within (New York 1970) 58-59. GARCIA BUR-ILLO, J., "El ciento por uno (Mc 10,29-30par). Historia des las interpretaciones y exégesis" EstBi 37 (1978) 29-55.

18:29 STONEHOUSE, N. B. The Witness of Matthew and Mark to Christ (1944) 229. DELLING, G. Die Zueignung des Heils in der Taufe (1961) 43. HASLER, V. Amen (1969) 40. PRAST, F., Presbyter und Evangelium in nachapostolischer Zeit (Stuttgart 1979) 280-81.

18:31ff. PATSCH, H. Abendmal und historischer Jesus (1972) 185ff.

18:31-43 IWAND, H.-J. GPM 4 (1949-1950) 77ff. STAEMMLER, GPM 9 (1954-1955) 67ff. STECK, K. G. in: Herr, tue meine Lippen auf Bd. 1 (1957) G. Eichholz, ed., 88-92. Zu Suchen Seine Herrlichkeit, Predigtgedanken aus Vergangenheit und Gegenwart Reihe A,Bd. 2 (1960) 236-53. STECK, K. G. GPM 15 (1960-1961) 77ff. DOERNE, M. Er kommt auch noch heute (1961) 52-58. IWAND, H.-J. GPM 19 (1964) 207-11. HABERER, E. "Jesus verstösst nicht", in: Kleine Predigt-Typologie III (1965) L. Schmidt, ed., 158-63. VOSS, G., "Herr, dass ich sehe" Am Tisch des Wortes 15 (1967) 20-27. JOSUTTIS, M. GPM 26 (1972) 120-25. DIENST, K./RAISS, H. "Estomihi: Lukas 18, 31-43", in: Predigtstudien (1972) E. Lange, ed., 131-36. WILCKENS, U., Die Missionsreden der Apostelgeschichte (Neukirchen 1974 (3)) 102, 115, 118, 125, 131, 135, 140, 159.

18:31-34 SCHRAMM, T. Der Markus-Stoff bei Lukas (1971) 130-36. NEIRYNCK, F., "La Matière dans Luc" in: F. Neirynck (ed.) L'Evangile de Luc (Gembloux 1973) 174-75, 180-93. TALBERT, C. H., Literary Patterns, Theological Themes, and the Genre of Luke-Acts (Missoula 1974) 16, 97. RADL, W., Paulus und Jesus im lukanischen Doppelwerk (Bern 1975) 149-58. SCHNEIDER, G., Das Evangelium nach Lukas (Gütersloh 1977) 372. KRAFT, H., Die Entstehung des Christentums (Darmstadt 1981) 169.

18:31-33 HOOKER, M. D. Jesus and the Servant (1959) 92-97. WILCKENS, U. Die Missionsreden der Apostelgeschichte (1961) 102, 114, 117, 124, 130, 134, 138, 140, 143, 158. WELLS, G. The Jesus of the Early Christians (1971) 104-05. CAVALLIN, H. C. C., Life After Death. I (Lund 1974) 5,8n17.

18:31-32 SCHWEIZER, E. Erniedrigung und Erhöhung bei Jesus und seinen Nachfolgern (1962) § 3k.

18:31 WANKE, J., Die Emmauserzählung (Leipzig 1973) 33, 89, 92. TALBERT, C. H., Literary Patterns, Theological Themes, and the Genre of Luke-Acts (Missoula 1974) 17, 20, 114.

18:32 NICKELS, P. Targum and New Testament (1967) 44.

18:33 O'NEILL, J. C. The Theology of Acts in Its Historical Setting (1970) 43-44n.

18:34 BLAIR, E. P. Jesus in the Gospel of Matthew (1960) 106. WANKE, J. Die Emmauserzählung (Leipzig 1973) A. 640. TALBERT, C. H., Literary Patterns, Theological Themes, and the Genre of Luke-Acts (Missoula 1974) 16. BERGMEIER, R., Glaube als Gabe nach Johannes (Stuttgart 1980) 225.

18:35-43 BURGER, C. Jesus als Davidssohn (1970) 107-12. ROLOFF, J. Da Kerygma und der irdische Jesus (1970) 135. FUCHS, A. Sprachliche Untersuchungen zu Matthäus und Lukas (1971) 45-170. SCHRAMM, T. Der Markus-Stoff bei Lukas (1971) 143-45. MIYOSHI, M., Der Anfang des Reiseberichts (Lk 9,51-10,24) (Rome 1974) 142-45. SCHNEIDER, G., Das Evangelium nach Lukas (Gütersloh 1977) 374. RIST, J. M., On the Independence of Matthew and Mark (Cambridge (1978) 76-77.

18:35 TALBERT, C. H., Literary Patterns, Theological Themes, and the Genre of Luke-Acts (Missoula 1974) 44. METZGER, B. M., The Early Versions of the New Testament (Oxford 1977) 438.

18:36-37 BORNKAMM-BARTH-HELD, Ueberlieferung und Auslegung im Matthäus-Evangelium (1961) 211.

18:36 NICKELS, P. Targum and New Testament (1967) 44. KÜMMEL, W. G., Römer 7 und das Bild des Menschen im Neuen Testament (München 1974) 201-02.

18:37 RUDOLPH, K. Die Mandäer I (1960) 115. STRECKER, G. Der Weg der Gerechtigkeit (1962) $51_{1.2}$.

18:38-39 STONEHOUSE, N. B. The Witness of Matthew and Mark to Christ (1944) 223. HAHN, F. Christologische Hoheitstitel (1963) 245, 263."Barmherzigkeit" in: TRE 5 (1980) 225.

18:38 NICKELS, P. Targum and New Testament (1967) 45.

18:40 BORNKAMM-BARTH-HELD, Ueberlieferung und Auslegung im Matthäus-Evangelium (1961) 210f.

18:41 HAHN, F. Christologische Hoheitstitel (1963) 81, 84, 85.

18:42-43 BORNKAMM-BARTH-HELD, Ueberlieferung und Auslegung im Matthäus-Evangelium (1961) 211, 265. METZGER, B. M., The Early Versions of the New Testament (Oxford 1977) 207.

18:42 ROBINSON, J. M. Kerygma und historischer Jesus (1960) 30. NICKELS, P. Targum and New Testament (1967) 45.

18:43 FARRER, A. St Matthew and St Mark (1954) 56.

19:1ff. KNOX, W. L. The Sources of the Synoptic Gospels II (1957) 45, 112ff. HAHN, F. Christologische Hoheitstitel (1963) 47, 275. STROBEL, A. Erkenntnis und Bekenntnis der Sünde in neutestamentlicher Zeit (1968) 42.

19:1-48 TALBERT, C. H., Literary Patterns, Theological Themes, and the Genre of Luke-Acts (Missoula 1974) 26.

19:1-28 TAYLOR, V. Behind the Third Gospel (1926) 159f., 172ff. JEREMIAS, J. Neutestamentliche Theologie I (1971) 48f.

19:1-27 STREETER, B. H. The Four Gospels (1951) 214f.

19:1-10 HIRSCH, E. Frühgeschichte des Evangeliums (1941) 231-33. BULTMANN, R. The History of the Synoptic Tradition (1963) 33f., 56f., 64f. LOCHMAN, J., GPM 19 (1964-1965) 248ff. LINZ, M. in: Hören und Fragen Bd. 5,3 (1967) G. Eichholz & A. Falkenroth, eds., 370ff. DERRETT, J. D. M. Law in the New Testament (1970) 279-85. LEHMANN, M. Synoptische Quellenanalyse und die Frage nach dem historischen Jesus (1970) 140-41. JEREMIAS, J. Neutestamentliche Theologie I (1971) 55, 155, 173, 210f. LANGE, E. ed., Predigtstudien für das Kirchenjahr 1970-1971 (1970) 123-28. SCHMITHALS, W. GPM 25 (2, 1971) 285-91. LOCHMAN, J. M. Das Radikale Erbe (1972) 297-306. PIDWELL, H. J. Blessed are the Poor (1972) 119. COCAGNAC, A. M., "Zachée, L'Eglise et la maison des pécheurs" AssS 91 (1964) 39-51. SANFORD, J. A., The Kingdom Within (New

York 1970) 105-107. DRESCHER, H.-G., Nachfolge und Behgegnung (Gütersloh 1972) 38-58. WANKE, J., Die Emmauserzählung (Leipzig 1973) 106-07. LOEWE, W. P., "Towards an Interpretation of Lk 19:1-10" CBQ 36 (1974) 321-31. MIYOSHI, M., Der Anfang des Reiseberichts Lk 9,51-10,24 (Rome 1974) 145-48. DRURY, J., Tradition and Design in Luke's Gospel (Atlanta 1976) 72-75. "Abraham" in: TRE 1 (1977) 379. BACH, U. et al., in: GPM 31 (1976-1977) 282-95. SCHNEIDER, G., Das Evangelium nach Lukas (Gütersloh 1977) 376. TER-NEDDEN, B. and SKRIVER, J., in: P. Krusche et al. (eds.) Predigtstudien für das Kirchenjahr 1976/77 (Stuttgart 1977) 107-114. KARRIS, R. J., "Poor and Rich: The Lukan Sitz im Leben" in: C. H. Talbert (ed.) Perspectives on Luke-Acts (Danville 1978) 123-24. VOGELS, W., "Structural Analysis and Pastoral Work. The Story of Zacchaeus (Luke 19,1-10)" LuVit 33 (1978) 482-92. WALKER, W. O., Jr., "Jesus and the Tax Collectors" JBL (1978) 221-38. WHITE, R. C., "A Good Word for Zacchaeus? Exegetical Comment on Luke 19:1-10" LThQ 14 (1979) 89-96. WHITE, R. C., "Vindication for Zacchaeus?" ET 91 (1979) 21.

19:1-9 SCHILLE, G. Anfänge der Kirche (1966) 168ff.

19:1-6 SWIDLER, L., Biblical Affirmations of Woman (Philadelphia 1979) 289.

19:1-2 SCHALIT, A., König Herodes (1969) 296. SCHRAMM, T. Der Markus-Stoff bei Lukas (1971) 143f.

19:1 TALBERT, C. H., Literary Patterns, Theological Themes, and the Genre of Luke-Acts (Missoula 1974) 114.

19:2-3 JEREMIAS, J., Die Sprache des Lukasevangeliums (Göttingen 1980) 275.

19:3 HENSS, W. Das Verhältnis zwischen Diatessaron, Christlicher Gnosis und "Western Text" (1967) 7f., 17. PALLIS, A. Notes on St. Luke and the Acts (1928) 37. METZGER, B. M., The Early Versions of the New Testament (Oxford 1977) 210. SCHWARZ, G., "ὅτι τῇ ἡλικίᾳ μικρός ἦν" in: M. Görg (ed.) Biblische Notizen. 8 (Bamberg 1979) 23-24.

19:4 NICKELS, P. Targum and New Testament (1967) 45. JEREMIAS, J., Die Sprache des Lukasevangeliums (Göttingen 1980) 275-76.

19:5-10 ARENS, E., The ΗΛΘΟΝ-Sayings in the Synoptic Tradition (Fribourg 1976) 161-80.

19:5 DRURY, J., Tradition and Design in Luke's Gospel (Atlanta 1976) 70-71. FRICKEL, J., "Die Zöllner, Vorbild der Demut und wahrer Gottesverehrung" in: E. Dassmann/K. S. Frank (eds.) Pietas.

FS. B. Kötting (Münster/Westfalen 1980) 279. JEREMIAS, J., Die Sprache des Lukasevangeliums (Göttingen 1980) 276.

19:7 STROBEL, A. Erkenntnis und Bekenntnis der Sünde in neutestamentlicher Zeit (1968) 42, 60. WESTERHOLM, S., Jesus and Scribal Authority (Lund 1978) 70-71. JEREMIAS, J., Die Sprache des Lukasevangeliums (Göttingen 1980) 277.

19:8 HAHN, F. Christologische Hoheitstitel (1963) 85, 89. SALOM, A. P. "Was Zacchaeus Really Reforming?" ET 78 (3, 1966) 87. WATSON, N. M. "Was Zacchaeus Really Reforming?" ET 77 (9, 1966) 282-85. DESCAMPS, A./De HALLEUX, A. Mélanges Bibliques en hommage au R. P. Béda Rigaux (1970) 140-41. JEREMIAS, J. Neutestamentliche Theologie I (1971) 113, 152, 144, 213f. MEYER, B. F., The Aims of Jesus (London 1979) 158-62. JEREMIAS, J., Die Sprache des Lukasevangeliums (Göttingen 1980) 277.

19:9 FLENDER, H. St Luke Theologian of Redemptive History (1967) 28, 60, 81, 151n, 152. DRURY, J., Tradition and Design in Luke's Gospel (Atlanta 1976) 70-71. SWIDLER, L., Biblical Affirmations of Woman (Philadelphia 1979) 182.

19:10 MANSON, T. W. The Teaching of Jesus (1945) 223-26. BARRETT, C. K. The New Testament Background: Selected Documents (1956) 254. HAHN, F. Christologische Hoheitstitel (1963) 45, 51, 240, 270. STROBEL, A. Erkenntnis und Bekenntnis der Sünde in neutestamentlicher Zeit (1968) 42. SANFORD, J. A., The Kingdom Within (New York 1970) 175-76. BEYSCHLAG, K., Simon Magus und die christliche Gnosis (Tübingen 1974) 129, 130, 179n.98. LADD, G. E., A Theology of the New Testament (Grand Rapids 1974) 56, 75, 108. MEYER, B. F., The Aims of Jesus (London 1979) 166.

19:11ff. RUDOLPH, K. Die Mandäer II (1961) 23, 7. LEHMANN, M. Synoptische Quellenanalyse und die Frage nach dem historischen Jesus (1970) 130f. KÜMMEL, W. G. Einleitung in das Neue Testament (1973) 41f.

19:11-48 MIYOSHI, M., Der Anfang des Reiseberichts Lk 9,51 - 10,24. Eine redaktionsgeschichtliche Untersuchung (Rome 1974) 24-25.

19:11-44 FLENDER, H. St Luke Theologian of Redemptive History (1967) 57, 59ff.

19:11-28 MORGAN, G. C. The Parables and Metaphors of Our Lord (1943) 243ff. GOULDER, M. D. Midrash and Lection in Matthew (1974) 50, 59, 62, 289, 348, 470.

19:11-27 JÜLICHER, D. A. Die Gleichnisreden Jesu (1910) 472-95. HIRSCH, E. Frühgeschichte des Evangeliums (1941) 161-70. PIROT, J. Paraboles et Allégories Evangeliques (1949) 361-69. MI-

CHAELIS, D. W. Die Gleichnisse Jesu (1956) 100-12. ZERWICK, M. "Die Parabel vom Thronanwärter," Biblica 40 (3, 1959) 654-74. ROBINSON, W. C., The Way of the Lord (Diss., Basel 1960) 92-93. BARTSCH, H. W., Wachet aber zu jeder Zeit! (Hamburg-Bergstedt 1963) 106-18. HAHN, F. Christologische Hoheitstitel (1963) 110. HARRINGTON, W. J. A Key to the Parables (1964) 94-99. IWAND, H.-J. Predigt-Meditationen (1964) 584-89. NIE-SEL, W. in: Herr, tue meine Lippen auf Bd. 3 (1964) G. Eichholz, ed., 464ff. ROBINSON, W. C. Der Weg des Herrn (1964) 56f. BISER, E. Die Gleichnisse Jesu (1965) 65ff., 163f. FLENDER, H. Heil und Geschichte in der Theologie des Lukas (1965) 72-74. ROLOFF, J. Apostolat-Verkündigung-Kirche (1965) 215f. KAH-LEFELD, H. Parables and Instructions in the Gospels (1966) 132ff. FLENDER, H. St Luke Theologian of Redemptive History (1967) 12,76ff. LOHSE, E. Das Aergernis des Kreuzes (1969) 66-71. BARCLAY, W. And Jesus Said (1970) 174-76. GASTON, L. No Stone on Another (1970) 256, 329, 354-55. ZINGG, P., Das Wachsen der Kirche (Freiburg 1974) 138-39. MANEK, J., . . . und brachte Frucht. Die Gleichnisse Jesu (Berlin 1977) 71-74. SCHNEIDER, G., Das Evangelium nach Lukas (Gütersloh/Würzburg 1977) 379 (lit!). TRITES, A. A., The New Testament Concept of Witness (Cambridge 1977) 197. MATTILL, A. J., Luke and the Last Things: a Perspective for the Understanding of Lukan Thought (Dillsboro 1979) 121-30. RESENHÖFFT, W., "Jesu Gleichnis von den Talenten, ergänzt ducrh die Lukas-Fassung" NTS 26 (1980) 318-31. WEDER, H. Die Gleichnisse Jesu als Metaphern (Göttingen 1980 *(2)*) 193-210.

19:11-17 LOCKYER, H. All the Parables of the Bible (1963) 205ff.

19:11-12 DERRETT, J. D. M. Law in the New Testament (1970) 278-79.

19:11 HAHN, F. Christologische Hoheitstitel (1963) 168, 169. FLENDER, H. Heil und Geschichte in der Theologie des Lukas (1965) 58-60. McNAMARA, M. The New Testament and the Palestinian Targum to the Pentateuch (1966) 151f. FLENDER, H. St Luke Theologian of Redemptive History (1967) 28, 45n, 59, 60, 76n, 91, 150n. NICKELS, P. Targum and New Testament (1967) 45. SCHNEIDER, G. Verleugnung, Verspottung und Verhör Jesu nach Lukas 22,54-71 (1969) 196, 198, 199, 200. KRÄNKL, E. Jesus der Knecht Gottes (1972) 204f. KÜMMEL, W. G. Einleitung in das Neue Testament (1973) 111f. WILSON, S. G., The Gentiles and the Gentile Mission in Luke-Acts (Cambridge 1973), 68, 69, 70, 82, 84. DAVIES, W. D., The Gospel and the Land (London 1974) 251, 254, 256, 256n.44. LADD, G. E, A Theology of the New Testament (Grand Rapids 1974) 63, 103, 207, 319. TAL-BERT, C. H., Literary Patterns, Theological Themes, and the Genre

of Luke-Acts (Missoula 1974) 17, 20, 114. ZINGG, P., Das
Wachsen der Kirche (Freiburg 1974) 138-39. WILLIAMS, J. A.,
A Conceptual History of Deuteronomism in the Old Testament, Ju-
daism, and the New Testament (Ph.D. Diss., Louisville 1976) 300.
"Apokalyptik" in: TRE 3 (1978) 255. JEREMIAS, J., Die Sprache
des Lukasevangeliums (Göttingen 1980) 277-78.

19:12ff. KAMLAH, E., "Kritik und Interpretation der Parabel von den an-
vertrauten Geldern" KuD 15 (1968) 28-38.

19:12-27 MASSAUX, E. Influence de l'Evangile de saint Matthieu sur la litterature chrétienne avant saint Irénée (1950) 267-71. JEREMIAS,
J. Die Gleichnisse Jesu (1962) 55-60, 65, 85, 94. LAMBRECHT,
J. "Die Logia-Quellen von Markus 13," Biblica 47 (1966) 350-
54. LÜHRMANN, D. Die Redaktion der Logienquelle (1969) 70f.
DERRETT, J. D. M. Law in the New Testament (1970) 17-31.
WEISER, A. Die Knechtsgleichnisse der synoptischen Evangelien
(1971) 226-75. HOFFMANN, P. Studien zur Theologie der Logienquelle (1972) 5, 42f., 48-50. SCHULZ, S. Q Die Spruchquelle
der Evangelisten (1972) 288-98. SCHNEIDER, G., Parusiegleichnisse im Lukas-Evangelium (Stuttgart 1975) 38-42. PER-
RIN, N., Jesus and the Language of the Kingdom (London 1976)
149, 150-51, 154, 161, 196. POLAG, A., Die Christologie der Logienquelle (Neukirchen-Vluyn 1977) 165-66. SHERWIN-WHITE,
A. N., Roman Society and Roman Law in the New Testament
(Grand Rapids 1978) 134.

19:12-25 PARKER, P. The Gospel Before Mark (1953) 67ff.

19:12-17 CROSSAN, F. L. in: SBL Seminar Papers 2, (1973) 96-98.

19:12-15 SCHRECKENBERG, H., "Flavius Josephus und die lukanischen
Schriften" in: W. Haubeck/H. Bachmann (eds.) Wort in der Zeit.
FS. K. H. Rengstorf (Leiden 1980) 192.

19:12 WEINERT, F. D., "The Parable of the Throne Claimant (Luke
19:12, 14-15a, 27) Reconsidered" CBQ 39 (1977) 505-14.

19:14-15 WEINERT, F. D., "The Parable of the Throne Claimant (Luke
19:12, 14-15a, 27) Reconsidered" CBQ 39 (1977) 505-14.

19:14 HAHN, F. Christologische Hoheitstitel (1963) 187.

19:15 NICKELS, P. Targum and New Testament (1967) 45. NEI-
RYNCK, F., "La Matière Marcienne dans Luc" in: F. Neirynck
(ed.) L'Evangile de Luc (Gembloux 1973) 180-81, 184-93.
METZGER, B. M., The Early Versions of the New Testament
(Oxford 1977) 92. JEREMIAS, J. Die Sprache des Lukasevangel-
iums (Göttingen 1980) 278-79.

19:16ff. STAEHELIN, E. Die Verkündigung des Reiches Gottes in der
Kirche Jesu Christi I (1951) 238, 277.

19:16 JEREMIAS, J., Die Sprache des Lukasevangeliums (Göttingen 1980) 279.

19:17 JEREMIAS, J. Die Sprache des Lukasevangeliums (Göttingen 1980) 279.

19:18-19 NICKELS, P. Targum and New Testament (1967) 45.

19:19-27 DUPONT, J., "La Parable des talents" RThPh 4 (1969) 276-91.

19:22 FRIEDRICHSEN, G. W. S. NTS 11 (1964-1965) 285f. METZGER, B. M., The Early Versions of the New Testament (Oxford 1977) 391.

19:23 HENNECKE, E./SCHNEEMELCHER, W., Neutestamentliche Aprokryphen (1964) II 387. FRIEDRICHSEN, G. W. S. NTS 11 (1964-1965) 288f. METZGER, B. M., The Early Versions of the New Testament (Oxford 1977) 210. SHERWIN-WHITE, A. N., Roman Society and Roman Law in the New Testament (Grand Rapids 1978) 142. JEREMIAS, J., Die Sprache des Lukasevangeliums (Göttingen (1980) 280.

19:25-26 KNOX, W. L. The Sources of the Synoptic Gospels II (1957) 30.

19:25 PALLIS, A., Notes on St. Luke and the Acts (London 1928) 37. METZGER, B. M., The Early Versions of the New Testament (Oxford 1977) 134.

19:26 KAESEMANN, E. Exegetische Versuche und Besinnungen (1964) II 97. SCHRAGE, W. Das Verhältnis des Thomas-Evangeliums zur Synoptischen Tradition und zu den Koptischen Evangelienübersetzungen (1964) 96. HASLER, V. Amen (1969) 75. KAESEMANN, E. New Testament Questions of Today (1969) 98. KLAUCK, H.-J., Allegorie und Allegorese in Synoptischen Gleichnistexten (Münster 1978) 239-40.

19:27 HAHN, F. Christologische Hoheitstitel (1969) 187. KAHLEFELD, H. Parables and Instructions in the Gospel (1966) 135f. WEINERT, F. D., "The Parable of the Throne Claimant (Luke 19:12, 14-15a, 27) Reconsidered" CBQ 39 (1977) 505-14. JEREMIAS, J., Die Sprache des Lukasevangeliums (Göttingen (1980) 280. SCHRECKENBERG, M., "Flavius Josephus und die lukanischen Schriften" in: W. Haubeck/M. Bachmann (eds.) Wort in der Zeit. FS. K. H. Rengstorf (Leiden 1980) 192.

19:28-24:53 BLEVINS, J. L. "The Passion Narrative. Luke 19:28-24:53," RevEx 64 (4, 1967) 513-22. O'NEILL, J. C. The Theology of Acts in Its Historical Setting (1970) 69-71. SELBY, D. J., Introduction to the New Testament (New York 1971) 187-94.

19:28-21:38 MCDONALD, J. I. H., Kerygma and Didache (Cambridge 1980) 109.

19:28-20:19 DOEVE, J. W. Purification du Temple et Desséchement du Figuier. NTS 1 (1954-1955) 297ff.

. 19:28-44 LEIVESTAD, R. Christ the Conqueror (1954) 34ff.

19:28-40 BURGER, C. Jesus als Davidssohn (1970) 112-14. CRIBBS, F. L. in: SBL Seminar Papers 2 (1973) 43-46. SCHNIEWIND, J., Die Parallelperikopen bei Lukas und Johannes (Darmstadt (1958 = 1914) 26-28. SCHNEIDER, G., Das Evangelium nach Lukas(Gütersloh 1927) 384.

19:28-38 GROSCH, H. "Andere hat er gerettet . . . Exegetische und didaktische Besinnung über zwei lukanische Passionstexte," EvangErz 22 (6, 1970) 233-47. SCHRAMM, T. Der Markus-Stoff bei Lukas (1971) 145-49. SOARES PRABHU, G. M., The Formula Quotations in the Infancy Narrative of Matthew (Rome 1976) 144-46. KRAFT, H., Die Entstehung des Christentums (Darmstadt 1981) 183-87.

19:28-36 SOARES PRABHU, G. M., The Formula Quotations in the Infancy Narrative of Matthew (Rome 1976) 144.

19:28-35 RIST, J. M., On the Independence of Matthew and Mark (Cambridge 1978) 77-81.

19:28-29 TALBERT, C. H., Literary Patterns, Theological Themes, and the Genre of Luke-Acts (Missoula 1974) 114.

19:28 TALBERT, C. H., Literary Patterns, Theological Themes, and the Genre of Luke-Acts (Missoula 1974) 17, 20. WILLIAMS, J. A., A Conceptual History of Deuteronomism in the Old Testament, Judaism, and the New Testament (Ph.D. Diss., Louisville 1976) 300. PRAST, F., Presbyter und Evangelium in nachapostolischer Zeit (Stuttgart 1979) 288-29.

19:29-21:38 GUILDING, A., The Fourth Gospel and Jewish Worship (Oxford 1960) 192-97.

19:29-40 TAYLOR, V. Behind the Third Gospel (1926) 94f. WEBER, O. Predigtmeditationen (1967) 32-35.

19:29-38 JEREMIAS, J. Neutestamentliche Theologie I (1971) 48f. MEYER, B. F., The Aims of Jesus (London 1979) 168-170.

19:29-31 GOODSPEED, E. J. A Life of Jesus (1950) 160-64.

19:29 NEIRYNCK, F., "La Matière Marcienne dans Luc" in: F. Neirynck (ed.) L'Evangile de Luc (Gembloux 1973) 180-81, 184-93. MIYOSHI, M., Der Anfang des Reiseberichts Lk 9,51-10,24. Eine redaktionsgeschichtliche Untersuchung (Rome 1974) 27-28. METZGER, B. M., The Early Versions of the New Testament (Oxford 1977) 201.

19:30 HAHN, F. Christologische Hoheitstitel (1963) 110.

19:31-33 TALBERT, C. H., Literary Patterns, Theological Themes, and the Genre of Luke-Acts (Missoula 1974) 115.

19:31 STONEHOUSE, N. B. The Witness of Matthew and Mark to Christ (1944) 225. HAHN, F. Christologische Hoheitstitel (1963) 88.

19:37-48 GASTON, L. No Stone on Another (1970) 256, 355-64.

19:37-44 TAYLOR, V. Behind the Third Gospel (1926) 172ff. HIRSCH, E. Frühgeschichte der Evangeliums (1941) 69-72. ROBINSON, W. C. Der Weg der Herrn (1964) 55f. ROBINSON, W. C., Jr., The Way of the Lord (Diss. Basel 1960) 90-91.

19:37-40 BAILEY, J. A. The Traditions Common to the Gospels of Luke and John (1963) 22-28.

19:37-38 SOARES PRABHU, G. M., The Formula Quotations in the Infancy Narrative of Matthew (Rome 1976) 144-45.

19:37 CONZELMANN, H. Die Mitte der Zeit (1964) 66ff., 170f. WANKE, J., Die Emmauserzählung (Leipzig 1973) 34. TALBERT, C. H., Literary Patterns, Theological Themes, and the Genre of Luke-Acts (Missoula 1974) 17, 20, 114. METZGER, B. M., The Early Versions of the New Testament (Oxford 1977) 370.

19:38 STONEHOUSE, N. B. The Witness of Matthew and Mark to Christ (1944) 224, 229. STAEHELIN, E. Die Verkündigung des Reiches Gottes in der Kirche Jesu Christi I (1951) 258. KNOX, W. L. The Sources of the Synoptic Gospels II (1957) 82. ROBINSON, J. M. Kerygma und historischer Jesus (1960) 146. DELLING, G. Die Zueignung des Heils in der Taufe (1961) 45. HAHN, F. Christologische Hoheitstitel (1963) 187, 266. FLENDER, H. Heil und Geschichte in der Theologie der Lukas (1965) 95-96. FLENDER, H. St Luke Theologian of Redemptive History (1967) 8n, 61 & n, 78, 92, 93 & n, 97, 103f., 108. RESE, M. Alttestamentliche Motive in der Christologie des Lukas (1969) 196-99. CRIBBS, F. L. in: SBL Seminar Papers 2 (1973) 4. PALLIS, A., Notes on St. Luke and the Acts (London 1928) 38.

19:39-44 JEREMIAS, J. Neutestamentliche Theologie I (1971) 48f.

19:39-40 SWIDLER, L., Biblical Affirmations of Woman (Philadelphia 1979) 287.

19:39 HAHN, F. Christologische Hoheitstitel (1963) 76, 77.

19:40 STROBEL, A. Untersuchungen zum Eschatologischen Verzögerungsproblem (1961) 284. FRIEDRICHSEN, G. W. S. NTS 11 (1964-1965) 288f. HASLER, V. Amen (1969) 104.

19:41-48 FRICK, GPM 4 (1949-1950) 221ff. STAEMMLER, GPM 9 (1954-1955) 203ff. DIEM, H. in: Herr, tue meine Lippen auf Bd. 2 (1957) 252-56. STECK, K. G. GPM 15 (1960-1961) 227ff. DOERNE, M. Er kommt auch noch heute (1961) 122-24. UHSADEL, W. ''Predigt zum Gedächtnistage der Zerstörung Jerusalems, 10. Sonntag nach Trinitatis, gehalten am 6. August 1961 in der Stiftskirche zu Tübingen'', in: Abraham unser Vater. FS O. Michel (1963) 459-

66. Hephata, Predigtgedanken aus Vergangenheit und Gegenwart, Reihe A, Bd. 5 (1966) 197-208. GROO, G. GPM 27 (1973) 372-78. DANTINE, W., in: GPM 33 (1979) 336-41. WOLFF, H. W., "Was zu deinem Frieden dient" in: . . . Wie eine Fackel (Neukirchen-Vluyn 1980) 184-92.

19:41-47 GALBIATI, E. "Il pianto di Gesu per Gerusalemme (Luca 19,41-47a), BiOr 7 (4-5, 1965) 196-204.

19:41-46 WILSON, S. G., The Gentiles and the Gentile Mission in Luke-Acts (Cambridge 1973) 70, 71, 72, 83, 132, 233, 244.

19:41-44 GNILKA, J. Die Verstockung Israels (1961) 137f. ZMIJEWSKI, J., Die Eschatologiereden des Lukas-Evangeliums (Bonn 1972) 49, 89, 96, 117, 118, 126, 128, 181, 206, 207, 218, 220, 222, 224, 324. SCHNEIDER, G., Das Evangelium nach Lukas (Gütersloh 1977) 387-88, 389.

19:41 TALBERT, C. H., Literary Patterns, Theological Themes, and the Genre of Luke-Acts (Missoula 1974) 17, 114. ZINGG, P., Das Wachsen der Kirche (Freiburg 1974) 138. METZGER, B. M., The Early Versions of the New Testament (Oxford 1977) 391. JEREMIAS, J., Die Sprache des Lukasevangeliums (Göttingen (1980) 281.

19:43-44 REICKE, B. "Synoptic Prophecies on the Destruction of Jerusalem" in: Studies in New Testament and Early Christian Literature (1972), D. E. Aune, ed., 121-23. VIELHAUER, P., "Oikodome. Das Bild vom Bau in der christlichen Literatur vom Neuen Testament bis Clemens Alexandrinus" in: G. Klein (ed.) Oikodome (München 1979) 59, 64-66.

19:43 FRIEDRICHSEN, G. W. S. NTS 11 (1964-1965) 286f. NICKELS, P. Targum and New Testament (1967) 45. JEREMIAS, J., Die Sprache des Lukasevangeliums (Göttingen (1980) 282.

19:44 WOOD, H. G. Interpreting this Time. NTS 2 (1955-1956) 264ff. BRAUN, H. Qumran und NT II (1966) 105, 270, 278. DALMAN, G. Orte und Wege Jesu (1967) 323f. ZMIJEWSKI, J., Die Eschatologiereden des Lukas-Evangeliums (Bonn 1972) 49, 100, 117, 118, 206-08, 212, 315, 460. JEREMIAS, J., Die Sprache des Lukasevangeliums (Göttingen (1980) 282.

19:45-22:13 JEREMIAS, J. Neutestamentliche Theologie I (1971) 48f.

19:45-48 TAYLOR, V. Behind the Third Gospel (1926) 95ff. PATSCH, H. Abendmahl und historischer Jesus (1972) 43f. TALBERT, C. H., Literary Patterns, Theological Themes, and the Genre of Luke-Acts (Missoula 1974) 17, 21. SCHNEIDER, G., Das Evangelium nach Lukas (Gütersloh 1977) 391-92. MEYER, B. F., The Aims of Jesus (London 1979) 168-70.

19:45-47 KRAFT, H., Die Entstehung des Christentums (Darmstadt 1981) 187-91.

19:45-46 MASSAUX, E. Influence de l'Evangile de saint Matthieu sur la littérature de chrétienne avant saint Irénée (1950) 510-12. LEIVES-TAD, R. Christ the Conqueror (1954) 34ff. LOEWENICH, W. von, Luther als Ausleger der Synoptiker (1954) 214f. SCHNIDER, F./ STENGER, W. Johannes und die Synoptiker (1971) 26-53. MEYER, B. F., The Aims of Jesus (London 1979) 197-202.

19:45 SCHNEIDER, G. Verleugnung, Verspottung und Verhör Jesu nach Lukas 22,54-71 (1969) 51, 98, 201. DAVIES, W. D., The Gospel and the Land (London 1974) 257. TALBERT, C. H., Literary Patterns, Theological Themes, and the Genre of Luke-Acts (Missoula 1974) 20.

19:46 HOLTZ, T. Untersuchungen über die Alttestamentlichen Zitate bei Lukas (1968) 163-65. DAVIES, W. D., The Gospel and the Land (London 1974) 257.

19:47-48 TAYLOR, V. Behind the Third Gospel (1926) 172ff. KRAFT, H., Die Entstehung der Christentums (Darmstadt 1981) 191-93.

19:47 DAVIES, W. D., The Gospel and the Land (London 1974) 257.

19:48 NICKELS, P. Targum and New Testament (1967) 45. METZGER, B. M., The Early Versions of the New Testament (Oxford 1977) 213. SANDMEL, S., We Jews and Jesus (New York 1977) 138.

———————————

20:1-21:4 TAYLOR, V. Behind the Third Gospel (1926) 98f.

20-21 PERRIN, N., Jesus and the Language of the Kingdom (London 1976) 39, 111, 129, 160.

20:1-9 MICHAELIS, D. W. Die Gleichnisse Jesu (1956) 113-25.

20:1-8 GOODSPEED, E. J. A Life of Jesus (1950) 168-72. TILLICH, P. Das Neue Sein (1959) 82-92. SCHNIDER, F./STENGER, W. Johannes und die Synoptiker (1971) 26-53. SCHRAMM, T. Der Markus-Stoff bei Lukas (1971) 149f. HOWARD, V. P., Das Ego in den Synoptischen Evangelien (Marburg 1975) 107-16. MINEAR, P., To Heal and to Reveal (New York 1976) 37. SCHNEIDER, G., Das Evangelium nach Lukas (Gütersloh 1977) 394. MEYER, B. F., The Aims of Jesus (London 1979) 168-70.

20:1-6 ALAND, K. NTS 12 (1965-1966) 177f.

20:1 GREEVEN, H. "Erwägungen zur Synoptischen Textkritik," NTS 6 (1959-1960) 295f. BOUSSET, W. Die Religion des Judentums im Späthellenistischen Zeitalter (1966 = 1926) 167. KILPA-TRICK, G. D. "Some Problems in New Testament Text and Language", in: Neotestamentica et Semitica (1969) E. E. Ellis & M. Wilcox, eds. 203-08. SCHNEIDER, G. Verleugnung, Verspottung und Verhör Jesu nach Lukas 22,54-71 (1969) 107, 109, 117, 200. NEIRYNCK, F., "La Matière Marcienne dans Luc" in: F. Neirynck (ed.) L'Evangile de Luc (Gembloux 1973) 180-81, 184-93.

20:3-4 MEYER, B. F., The Aims of Jesus (London 1979) 125.

20:5 METZGER, B. M., The Early Versions of the New Testament (Oxford 1977) 392. NEIRYNCK, F., "PARAKYPSAS BLEPEI. Lc 24,12 et Jn 20,5" EphT 53 (1977) 113-52.

20:6 NICKELS, P. Targum and New Testament (1967) 45.

20:7 "Abendmahl" in: TRE I (1977) 56.

20:9ff. GOULDER, M. D. Midrash and Lection in Matthew (1974) 56, 59f.

20:9-19 JÜLICHER, D. A. Die Gleichnisreden Jesu (1910) 385-406. PI-ROT, J. Paraboles et Allégories Evangeliques (1949) 376-90. SWAELES, R. "L'Arriére-fond Scripturaire de Matt. XXI. 43 et son Lien Avec. Matt. XXI," 44. NTS 6 (1959-1960) 310f. SCHRAGE, W. Das Verhältnis des Thomas-Evangeliums zur Synoptischen Tradition und zu den Koptischen Evangelienübersetzungen (1964) 137. SUHL, A. Die Funktion der alttestamentlichen Zitate und Anspielungen im Markusevangelium (1965) 148ff. DILLON, R. J. "Towards a Tradition-History of the Parables of the True Israel (Matthew 21,33-22,14)", Biblica 47 (1966) 12-20. SUMMERS, R. The Secret Sayings of the Living Jesus (1968) 49. DASSONVILLE, A. E. The Parable of the Wicked Husbandmen in Luke (1970). DERRETT, J. D. M. Law in the New Testament (1970) 150-67. SCHRAMM, T. Der Markus-Stoff bei Lukas (1971) 150-67. PATSCH, H. Abendmahl und historischer Jesus (1972) 200ff. KLAUCK, H. J., "Das Gleichnis vom Mord im Weinberg" BiLe 2, (1970) 118-45. HUBAUT, M., "La parabole des vignerons homicides: son authenticité, sa visée permière" RThL 6 (1975) 51-61. ROBINSON, J. A. T., "The Parable of the Wicked Husbandmen: A Test of Synoptic Relationships" NTS 21 (1975) 443-61. PERRIN, N., Jesus and the Language of the Kingdom (London 1976) 8, 150, 161. WILLIAMS, J. A., A Conceptual History of Deuteronomism in the Old Testament, Judaism, and the New Testament (Ph.D. Diss. Louisville 1976) 284-89. SCHNEIDER, G., Das Evangelium nach Lukas (Gütersloh 1977) 397. KLAUCK, H.-J., Allegorie und Allegorese in Synoptischen Gleichnistexten

(Münster 1978) 286-316. VIELHAUER, P., "Oikodome. Bild vom Bau in der christlichen Literatur vom Neuen Testament bis Clemens Alexandrinus" in: G. Klein (ed.) Oikodome (München 1979) 56-58. WEDER, H., Die Gleichnisse Jesu als Metaphern (Göttingen 1980) 147-62. KRAFT, H., Die Entstehung des Christentums (Darmstadt 1981) 170-72.

20:9-18 BARCLAY, W. And Jesus Said (1970) 139-45. BÖHLIG, A., "Vom 'Knecht' zum 'Sohn' " in: Mysterion und Wahrheit (Leiden 1968) 60-61. CARLSTON, C. E., The Parables of the Triple Tradition (Philadelphia 1975) 40-45, 76-81, 178-90. MANEK, J., . . . und brachte Frucht (Berlin 1977) 29-33.

20:9-16 HARRINGTON, W. J. A Key to the Parables (1964) 108-12. BISER, E. Die Gleichnisse Jesu (1965) 137ff. WEISER, A. Die Knechtsgleichnisse der synoptischen Evangelien (1971) 49-57. TOLBERT, M. A., Perspectives on the Parables (Philadelphia 1979) 75, 83-89.

20:9-10 MASSAUX, E. Influence de l'Evangile de saint Matthieu sur la littérature chrétienne avant saint Irénée (1950) 267-71. MONTEFIORE, H. NTS 7 (1960-1961) 236f.

20:9 SCHRAMM, T. Der Markus-Stoff bei Lukas (1971) 154-56.

20:10-14 NICKELS, P. Targum and New Testament (1967) 46.

20:11 "Abendmahl" in: TRE 1 (1977) 56.

20:16 MASSAUX, E. Influence de l'Evangile de saint Matthieu sur la littérature chrétienne avant saint Irénée (1950) 328-29. METZGER, B. M., The Early Versions of the New Testament (Oxford 1977) 92.

20:17-38 "Apostel" in: TRE 3 (1978) 443.

20:17-18 TALBERT, C. H., Literary Patterns, Theological Themes, and the Genre of Luke-Acts (Missoula 1974) 98.

20:17 STONEHOUSE, N. B. The Witness of Matthew and Mark to Christ (1944) 193. SCHRAGE, W. Das Verhältnis des Thomas-Evangeliums zur Synoptischen Tradition und zu den Koptischen Evangelienübersetzungen (1964) 145. HOLTZ, T. Untersuchungen über die Alttestamentlichen Zitate bei Lukas (1968) 160-63. RESE, M. Alttestamentliche Motive in der Christologie des Lukas (1969) 171-73. TALBERT, C. H., Literary Patterns, Theological Themes, and the Genre of Luke-Acts (Missoula 1974) 97. BLOCK, R., "Midrash" in: W. S. Green (ed.) Approaches to Ancient Judaism: Theory and Practice (Missoula 1978) 49.

20:18 KAESEMANN, E. Exegetische Versuche und Besinnungen (1964) II 97. GAERTNER, B. The Temple and the Community in Qumran and the New Testament (1965) 133. KAESEMANN, E. New

Testament Questions of Today (1969) 98. NESTLE, E., "Zu Lk 20:18" ZNW 8 (1907).

20:19 BLACK, M., An Aramaic Approach to the Gospels and Acts (1967) 111f.

20:20-26 SCHALIT, A. König Herodes (1969) 272. DERRETT, J. D. M. Law in the New Testament (1970) 313-37. SCHRAMM, T. Der Markus-Stoff bei Lukas (1971) 168-70. HENNECKE, E./ SCHNEEMELCHER, W. Neutestamentliche Apokryphen (1964) I 60. SCHNEIDER, G., Das Evangelium nach Lukas (Gütersloh 1977) 401. SWIDLER, L., Biblical Affirmations of Woman (Philadelphia 1979) 282. ANON., "L'impôt à César (Luc, 20,20-26)" SeB 18 (1980) 8-15. KRAFT, H., Die Entstehung des Christentums (Darmstadt 1981) 121.

20:20 FARRER, A. St Matthew and St Mark (1954) 141n. WILCKENS, U. Die Missionsreden der Apostelgeschichte (1961) 115, 124, 169, 183. POPKES, W. Christus Traditus (1967) 147, 149, 183ff., 217. PALLIS, A., Notes on St. Luke and the Acts (London 1928) 39. WILCKENS, U. Die Missionsreden der Apostelgeschichte (Neukirchen 1974 ($_3$)) 115, 125, 169, 184.

20:21 HAHN, F. Christologische Hoheitstitel (1963) 76.

20:22-25 SCHRAGE, W. Das Verhältnis des Thomas-Evangeliums zur Synoptischen Tradition und zu den Koptischen Evangelienübersetzungen (1964) 189.

20:23 RICE, G. E., "The Anti-Judaic Bias of the Western Text in the Gospel of Luke" AUSS 18 (1980) 54.

20:24 NICKELS, P. Targum and New Testament (1967) 46.

20:25 SCHRAGE, W. Die konkreten Einzelgebote in der paulinischen Paränese (1961) 243. GIBLIN, C. H. " 'The Things of God' in the Question Concerning Tribute to Caesar (Lk 20:25; Mk 12:17; Mt. 22:21)," CBQ 33 (4, 1971) 510-27. BROER, I. Die Urgemeinde und das Grab Jesu (1972) 205f.

20:26 PALLIS, A., Notes on St. Luke and the Acts (London 1928) 39-40.

20:27ff. STAEHELIN, E. Die Verkündigung des Reiches Gottes in der Kirche Jesu Christi (1951) 383.

20:27-40 BARTINA, S. "Jesus y los saduceos. "El Dios de Abraham, de Isac y de Jacob es 'El que hace existir'. (Mt. 22,23-33; Hebr. 11,13-16)," EstBi (1962) 151-60. STECK, K. G. GPM 19 (1964-1965) 174ff. SUHL, A. Die Funktion der alttestamentlichen Zitate und Anspielungen im Markusevangelium (1965) 67ff. TRAUB, H. in: Hören und Fragen Bd. 5,3 (1967) G. Eichholz & A. Falkenroth, eds. 269ff. LANGE, E. ed., Predigtstudien für das Kirchenjahr 1970-1971 (1970) 54-59. SCHOTT, E. GPM 25 (2, 1971) 200-05.

SCHRAMM, T. Der Markus-Stoff bei Lukas (1971) 170. FISCHER, K. M., in: GPM 31 (1976-1977) 189-96. KLAUS, B. and OEFFNER, E., in: P. Krusche et al. (eds.) Predigtstudien für das Kirchenjahr 1976-1977. II (Stuttgart 1977) 24-33. SCHNEI-DER, G., Das Evangelium nach Lukas (Gütersloh 1977) 404. STAGG, E. and F., Woman in the World of Jesus (Philadelphia 1978) 137-38. SWIDLER, L., Biblical Affirmations of Woman (Philadelphia 1979) 232, 239.

20:27-39 TALBERT, C. H., Literary Patterns, Theological Themes, and the Genre of Luke-Acts (Missoula 1974) 17, 21.

20:27-38 STONEHOUSE, N. B. The Witness of Matthew and Mark to Christ (1944) 196. SWIDLER, L., Biblical Affirmations of Woman (Philadelphia 1979) 176, 260.

20:27 KNOX, W. L. The Sources of the Synoptic Gospels II (1957) 59. NÖTSCHER, F. Altorientalischer und alttestamentlicher Auferstehungsglaube (Darmstadt 1970 = 1926) 189, 271.

20:28 HAHN, F. Christologische Hoheitstitel (1963) 76. HOLTZ, T. Untersuchungen über die Alttestamentlichen Zitate bei Lukas (1968) 68-70.

20:29 BLACK, M. An Aramaic Approach to the Gospels and Acts (1967) 58f. NICKELS, P. Targum and New Testament (1967) 46.

20:30 STAEHELIN, E. Die Verkündigung des Reiches Gottes in der Kirche Jesu Christi I (1951) 177, 237, 390.

20:34ff. STAEHELIN, E. Die Verkündigung des Reiches Gottes in der Kirche Jesus Christi I (1951) 198.

20:34-38 NEIYRNCK, F., "La Matière Marcienne dans Luc" in: F. Neirynck (ed.) L'Evangile de Luc (Gembloux 1973) 176-77. "Auferstehung" in: TRE 4 (1979) 462.

20:34-36 MOORE, G. F. Judaism II (1946) 304, 392n. BAUMBACH, G., Das Verständnis des Bösen in den Synoptischen Evangelien (1963) 199ff. PHIPPS, W. E. Was Jesus Married? (1970) 92-98. SANFORD, J. A., The Kingdom Within (New York 1970) 209-10. HIERS, R. H., The Historical Jesus and the Kingdom of God (Gainesville 1973) 33-34. BERGMEIER, R., Glaube als Gabe nach Johannes (Stuttgart 1980) 144.

20:34 BLACK, M. An Aramaic Approach to the Gospels and Acts (1967) 366f. NICKELS, P. Targum and New Testament (1967) 46. "Askese" in: TRE 4 (1979) 206. BERGMEIER, R., Glaube als Gabe nach Johannes (Stuttgart 1980) 255 n.321; 257 n.371-72.

20:35-47 NÖTSCHER, F., Altorientalischer und alttestamentlicher Auferstehungsglaube (Darmstadt 1970 = 1926) 306-14.

20:35-36 STAEHELIN, E. Die Verkündigung des Reiches Gottes in der

Kirche Jesu Christ I (1951) 123. BERGMEIER, R., Glaube als Gabe nach Johannes (Stuttgart 1980) 255 n.323.

20:35 LADD, G. E., A Theology of the New Testament (Grand Rapids 1974) 47, 74, 76, 127.

20:36 NESTLE, E. ZNW 2 (1901) 262f. STAEHELIN, E. Die Verkündigung des Reiches Gottes in der Kirche Jesus Christi I (1951) 179, 185, 360. BOUSSET, W. Die Religion des Judentums im Späthellenistischen Zeitalter (1966 = 1926) 272. CAVALLIN, H. C. C., Life After Death. I (Lund 1974) 4, 4n17, 7, 2n13. KLIJN, A. F. J., "Die syrische Baruch-Apokalypse" in: W. G. Kümmel (ed.) Jüdische Schriften aus hellenistisch-römischer Zeit. V. (Gütersloh 1976) 156 n.10a. SCHEP, J. A., The Nature of the Resurrection Body (Grand Rapids 1976) 210-11. DELLING, G., "Die 'Söhne (Kinder) Gottes' im Neuen Testament" in: R. Schnackenburg et al. (eds.) Die Kirche des Anfangs. FS. H. Schürmann (Freiburg 1978) 622. FISCHER, U., Eschatologie und Jenseitserwartung im hellenistischen Diasporajudentum (Berlin 1978) 260.

20:37-38 NÖTSCHER, F., Altorientalischer und alttestamentlicher Auferstehungsglaube (Darmstadt 1970 = 1926) 299. CAVALLIN, H. C. C., Life After Death. I (Lund 1974) 4, 3, I.

20:37 HAHN, F. Christologische Hoheitstitel (1963) 73. PALLIS, A., Notes on St. Luke and the Acts (London 1928) 40. TALBERT, C. H., Literary Patterns, Theological Themes, and the Genre of Luke-Acts (Missoula 1974) 98. CLARK, K. W., "The Israel of God" in: The Gentile Bias and other Essays (Leiden 1980) 23.

20:38 AALEN, S. NTS 13 (1966-1967) 10ff. FISCHER, U., Eschatologie und Jenseitserwartung im hellenistischen Diasporajudentum (Berlin 1978) 96.

20:39-40 HIRSCH, E. Frühgeschichte des Evangeliums (1941) 56-58.

20:39 HAHN, F. Christologische Hoheitstitel (1963) 76, 77. TALBERT, C. H., Literary Patterns, Theological Themes, and the Genre of Luke-Acts (Missoula 1974) 21.

20:41ff. STONEHOUSE, N. B. The Witness of Matthew and Mark to Christ (1944) 223.

20:41-44 RENGSTORF, K. H. Das Evangelium nach Lukas (1949) 221f. HAHN, F. Christologische Hoheitstitel (1963) 88. FLENDER, H. Heil und Geschichte in der Theologie der Lukas (1965) 43. SUHL, A. Die Funktion der alttestamentlichen Zitate und Anspielungen im Markusevangelium (1965) 89ff. BLANK, J. Schriftauslegung in Theorie und Praxis (1969) 221, 227-31. BURGER, C. Jesus als Davidssohn (1970) 114-16. FITZMYER, J. A. Essays on the Semitic Background of the New Testament (1971) 113-26. SCHRAMM, T. Der Markus-Stoff bei Lukas (1971) 171f. SAND,

A., Das Gesetz und die Propheten (Regensburg 1974) 147-49. KRAFT, H., Die Entstehung des Christentums (Darmstadt 1981) 68-76.

20:41 STONEHOUSE, N. B. The Witness of Matthew and Mark to Christ (1944) 194. HAHN, F. Christologische Hoheitstitel (1963) 245.

20:42-43 STONEHOUSE, N. B. The Witness of Matthew and Mark to Christ (1944) 256. HOLTZ, T. Untersuchungen über die Alttestamentlichen Zitate bei Lukas (1968) 51-53. RESE, M. Alttestamentliche Motive in der Christologie des Lukas (1969) 173-74. HORTON, F. L., The Melchizedek Tradition (London 1976) 23-24.

20:42 BARRETT, C. K. The Holy Spirit and the Gospel Tradition (1947) 107-12.

20:43 BÖHLIG, A., Die Gnosis III: Der Manichäismus (Zürich 1980) 339 n.101.

20:44 SEEBERG, A. Der Katechismus der Urchristenheit (1966) 72f.

20:45-21:36 KECK, F., Die öffentliche Abschiedsrede Jesu in Lk 20,45-21,36. Eine redaktions- und motivgeschichtliche Untersuchung (Stuttgart 1976).

20:45-47 GOODSPEED, E. J. A Life of Jesus (1950) 182-84. KNOX, W. L. The Sources of the Synoptic Gospels II (1957) 10. SCHNEIDER, G., Das Evangelium nach Lukas (Gütersloh 1977) 409-10. SWIDLER, L., Biblical Affirmations of Woman (Philadelphia 1979) 184, 232, 256.

———

21-24 WINTER, P. & TAYLOR, V. "Sources of the Lucan Passion Narrative," ET 68 (1956) 95.

21:1-23:25 WILSON, W. R. The Execution of Jesus (1970) 53-62.

21 GASTON, L. "Sondergut und Markusstoff in Luk. 21," ThZ 16 (3, 1960) 161-72. CONZELMANN, H. Die Mitte der Zeit (1964) 112ff., 116ff. GOULDER, M. D. Type and History in Acts (1964) 140f. BURCHARD, C. Der dreizehnte Zeuge (1970) 176f., 181. DESCAMPS, A./DE HALLEUX, A. Mélanges Bibliques en hommage au R. P. Béda Rigaux (1970) 232-33. GEIGER, R., Die Lukanischen Endzeitreden (Bern 1973) 149-258, 259-68. FRANKLIN, E., Christ the Lord (London 1975) 12-16. DUNN, J. D. G., Unity and Diversity in the New Testament (London 1977) 347. COURT, J. M., Myth and History in the Book of Revelation (London 1979) 49-54.

21:1-4 DEGENHARDT, H.-J. Lukas, Evangelist der Armen (1964) 93-97. WEST, H. P. Jr. NTS 14 (1967-1968) 80f. SANDMEL, S., We Jews and Jesus (New York 1977) 134. SCHNEIDER, G., Das Evangelium nach Lukas (Gütersloh 1977) 412. RAYAN, S., The Holy Spirit (New York 1978) 62-63. SWIDLER, L., Biblical Affirmations of Woman (Philadelphia 1979) 180, 183, 232, 256.

21:2 WILDER, A. N. The Language of the Gospel (1964) 57f.

21:3 STONEHOUSE, N. B. The Witness of Matthew and Mark to Christ (1944) 210. HASLER, V. Amen (1969) 44.

21:5ff. STAEHELIN, E. Die Verkündigung des Reiches Gottes in der Kirche Jesu Christi I (1951) 358. FLENDER, H. Heil und Geschichte in der Theologie des Lukas (1965) 102-04. HAHN, F. Das Verständnis der Mission im Neuen Testament (:s21965)111.

21:5-38 GASTON, L. No Stone on Another (1970) 10, 19, 21, 22, 355-64, 368. SCHRAMM, T. Der Markus-Stoff bei Lukas (1971) 171-82.

21:5-36 HENNECKE, E./SCHNEEMELCHER, W. Neutestamentliche Apokryphen (1964) II 324, 437. JEREMIAS, J. Neutestamentliche Theologie I (1971) 124, 127f. JEREMIAS, J. New Testament Theology I (1971) 123, 126f. BARTSCH, H. W., Wachet aber zu jeder Zeit! (Hamburg-Bergstedt 1963) 118-23. ZMIJEWSKI, J., Die Eschatologiereden des Lukas-Evangeliums (Bonn 1972). NICOL, W., "Tradition and Redaction in Luke 21" Neotestamentica 7 (1973) 61-71. SCHNEIDER, G., Das Evangelium nach Lukas (Gütersloh 1977) 414. MATTILL, A. J., Luke and the Last Things (Dillsboro 1979) 8.

21:5-7 SCHRAMM, T. Der Markus-Stoff bei Lukas (1971) 173f.

21:5-6 GEIGER, R., Die Lukanischen Endzeitreden (Basel 1973) 161-65. SCHNEIDER, G., Das Evangelium nach Lukas (Gütersloh 1977) 416.

21:5 SMITH, M. Tannaitic Parallels to the Gospels (1968) 2 b n 115.

21:6-28 GOULDER, M. D. Type and History in Acts (1964) 112-19, 139, 175.

21:7-36 GOODSPEED, E. J. A Life of Jesus (1959) 186-88.

21:7-13 MATTILL, A. J., Luke and the Last Things (Dillsboro 1979) 130-33.

21:7-11 GEIGER, R., Die Lukanischen Endzeitreden (Bern 1973) 165-72.

21:7 HAHN, F. Christologische Hoheitstitel (1963) 76, 77. CONZELMANN, H. Die Mitte der Zeit (1964) 117ff. ROBINSON, W. C. Der Weg der Herrn (1964) 46f. MARXSEN, W. Mark the Evangelist (1969) 191, 193, 197. ROBINSON, W. C., Jr., The Way of the Lord (Diss. Basel 1960) 73. KLIJN, A. F. J., "Die syrische

Baruch-Apokalypse" in: W. G. Kümmel (ed.) Jüdische Schriften aus hellenistisch-römischer Zeit. V.(Gütersloh 1976) 139 n.XXV2a.

21:8-36 SMITH, M. Tannaitic Parallels to the Gospels (1968) 4 I. NEI-RYNCK, F., "La Matière Marcienne dans Luc" in: F. Neirynck (ed.) L'Evangile de Luc (Gembloux 1973) 177-79.

21:8-31 BARTSCH, H. W., Wachet aber zu jeder Zeit! (Hamburg-Bergstedt 1963) 106-09.

21:8-11 ROBINSON, W. C. Der Weg des Herrn (1964) 47f. SCHRAMM, T. Der Markus-Stoff bei Lukas (1971) 174f. ROBINSON, W. C., Jr., The Way of the Lord (Diss. Basel 1960) 73-76.

21:8 STRECKER, G. Der Weg der Gerechtigkeit (1962) 88. CONZELMANN, H. Die Mitte des Zeit (1964) 117ff. HENGEL, M. Nachfolge und Charisma (1968) 24f. HOWARD, V. P., Das Ego in den Synoptischen Evangelien (Marburg 1975) 116-23.

21:9ff. BEYSCHLAG, K. Clemens Romanus und der Frühkatholizismus (1966) 161.

21:9 STAEHELIN, E. Die Verkündigung des Reiches Gottes in der Kirche Jesu Christi I (1951) 162. NICKELS, P. Targum and New Testament (1967) 46.

21:11-12 GEIGER, R., Die Lukanischen Endzeitreden (Bern 1973) 173-80.

21:11 KÜMMEL, W. G. (ed.), Jüdische Schriften aus hellenistisch-römischer Zeit. V. (Gütersloh 1976) 139 n.XXV2a, 140 n.6a. MATTILL, A. J., Luke and the Last Things (Dillsboro 1979) 1-77.

21:12ff. HAHN, F. Christologische Hoheitstitel (1963) 168. KÜMMEL, W. G. Einleitung in das Neue Testament (1973) 113f.

21:12-19 SCHRAMM, T. Der Markus-Stoff bei Lukas (1971) 175-78. GEIGER, R., Die Lukanischen Endzeitreden (Bern 1973) 172-79. DUPONT, J., "La persécution comme situation missionaire (Marc 13:9-11)" in: R. Schnackenburg et al. (eds.) Die Kirche des Anfangs. FS. H. Schürmann (Leipzig 1977) 99-100. PRAST, F., Presbyter und Evangelium in nachapostolischer Zeit (Stuttgart 1979) 66. BUCK, E., "The Function of the Pericope 'Jesus before Herod' in the Passion narrative of Luke" in: W. Haubeck/M. Bachmann (eds.) Wort in der Zeit. FS. K. H. Rengstorf (Leiden 1980) 177.

21:12-17.19 SCHÜTZ, F. Der leidende Christus (1969) 14.

21:12 DELLING, G. Die Zueignung des Heils in der Taufe (1961) 40. ROBINSON, W. C. Der Weg des Herrn (1964) 48f. MARXSEN, W. Mark the Evangelist (1969) 122, 154, 193. ROBINSON, W. C., Jr., The Way of the Lord (Diss. Basel 1960) 76-77.

21:13 MASSAUX, E. Influence de l'Evangile des saint Matthieu sur la littérature chrétienne avant saint Irénée (1950) 633-35. BROX, N. Zeuge und Märtyrer (1961) 28ff. HARTMAN, L. Testimonium

Linguae (1963) 57-75. NELLESSEN, E., Zeugnis für Jesus und das Wort (Köln 1976) 100-04. GERSTENBERGER, G. und SCHRAGE, W., Leiden (Stuttgart 1977) 194; ET: J. E. Steely (trans.) Suffering (Nashville 1980) 224.

21:14-15 BARRETT, C. K. The Holy Spirit and the Gospel Tradition (1947) 130-32. KNOX, W. L. The Sources of the Synoptic Gospels II (1957) 16. HAHN, F. Christologische Hoheitstitel (1963) 107.FUCHS, A. Sprachliche Untersuchungen zu Matthäus und Lukas (1971) 37-44, 171-91. GEIGER, R., Die lukanischen End-zeitreden (Bern 1973) 179-80. SCHNEIDER, G., Das Evangelium nach Lukas (Gütersloh/Würzburg 1977) 419 (lit!). TRITES, A. A., The New Testament Concept of Witness (Cambridge 1977) 185. KREMER, J., "Jesu Verheissung des Geistes. Zur Verankerung der Aussage von Joh 16:13 im Leben Jesu" in: R. Schnackenburg et al. (eds.) Die Kirche des Anfangs. FS. H. Schürman (Freiburg/Basel/Wien 1978) 262-67.

21:15 WAINWRIGHT, A. W. The Trinity in the New Testament (1962) 209-10. YATES, J. E. The Spirit and the Kingdom (1963) 94-98. HOWARD, V. P., Das Ego in den synoptischen Evangelien (Marburg 1975) 223-30.

21:16 MASSAUX, E. Influence de l'Evangile de saint Matthieu sur la lit-tératre chrétienne avant saint Irénée (1950) 633-35. KNOX, W. L. The Sources of the Synoptic Gospels II (1957) 125.

21:18 JEREMIAS, J. Neutestamentliche Theologie I (1971) 127f.

21:19 PRAST, F., Presbyter und Evangelium in nachapostolischer Zeit (Stuttgart 1979) 64.

21:20ff. KNOX, W. L. The Sources of the Synoptic Gospels II (1957) 109. BRAUMANN, G. "Die lukanische Interpretation der Zerstörung Jerusalems", in: ΧΑΡΙΣ ΚΑΙ ΣΟΦΙΑ. Festschrift K. H. Rengstorf (1964) 120-27. CONZELMANN, H. Die Mitte der Zeit (1964) 120ff., 126. WREGE, H.-T. Die Ueberlieferungsge-schichte (1968) 151f., 174f.

21:20-36 TAYLOR, V. Behind the Third Gospel (1926) 110ff. LAM-BRECHT, J. Biblica 50 (1, 1969) 123-25.

21:20-30 SALAS, A. Discurso Eschatologico Pretucano. Estudio de Lc. xxi, 20-30 (1967).

21:20-28 BRAUMANN, G. "Die lukanische Interpretation der Zerstörung Jerusalems," NovTest 6 (2-3, 1963) 120-27.

21:20-26 JEREMIAS, J. Neutestamentliche Theologie I (1971) 127f.

21:20-24 GILS, F. Jésus Prophète D'Après Les Evangiles Synoptiques (1957) 128-30. ROBINSON, W. C. Der Weg des Herrn (1963) 49f. HAHN, F. Das Verständnis der Mission im Neuen Testament (^{2}1965) 111. SALAS, A. "Origen y estructura de Lc. XXI,20-24,"

CiDi 178 (3, 1965) 405-17. FLENDER, H. St Luke Theologian of Redemptive History (1967) 108, 109, 111ff. DODD, C. H. "The Fall of Jerusalem and the 'Abomination of Desolation' ", More New Testament Studies (1968) 69-83. O'NEILL, J. C. The Theology of Acts in Its Historical Setting (1970) 1-3. SCHRAMM, T. Der Markus-Stoff bei Lukas (1971) 178-80. FLUECKIGER, F. "Luk. 21,20-24 und die Zerstörung Jerusalems," ThZ 28 (6, 1972) 285-90. KUDASIEWICZ, J. " 'Jerusalem deptana bedzie przez pogan . . . ' (Lk 21, 20-24)"RTK 19 (1, 1972) 83-92. ROBINSON, W. C., The Way of the Lord (Diss., Basel 1960) 78-80. WILSON, S. G., The Gentiles and the Gentile Mission in Luke-Acts (Cambridge 1973) 50, 70-72, 82-84, 132. DUNN, J. D. G., Jesus and the Spirit (London 1975) 172. SCHNEIDER, G., Das Evangelium nach Lukas (Gütersloh/Würzburg 1977) 422, 424-25 (lit!). "Apostelgeschichte" in: TRE 3 (1978) 521. RIST, J. M., On the Independence of Matthew and Mark (Cambridge 1978) 81-82. MATTILL, A. J., Luke and the Last Things: A Perspective for the Study of Lukan thought (Dillsboro 1979) 63-64. SWIDLER, L., Biblical Affirmations of Woman (Philadelphia 1979) 233, 240, 260.

21:20-21 STAEHELIN, E. Die Verkündigung des Reiches Gottes in der Kirche Jesu Christ I (1951) 285.

21:20 ROBERTSON, A. T. Luke the Historian in the Light of Research (1920) 33f. VAN UNNIK, W. C., "Luke-Acts, A Storm Center in Contemporary Scholarship" in: L. E. Keck/J. L. Martyn (eds.) Studies in Luke-Acts. FS. P. Schubert (Nashville 1966) 24.

21:22 KNOX, W. L. The Sources of the Synoptic Gospels II (1957) 115.

21:23 SCHRAGE, W. Die konkreten Einzelgebote in der paulinischen Paränese (1961) 25. SAND, A., Das Gesetz und die Propheten (Regensburg 1974) 84-86. KLIJN, A. F. J., "Die syrische Baruch-Apokalypse" in: W. G. Kümmel (ed.) Jüdische Schriften aus hellenistisch-römischer Zeit V/2 (Gütersloh 1976) 140n.SSVI, la.

21:24 KNOX, W. L. The Sources of the Synoptic Gospels II (1957) 117. BURCHARD, C. Der dreizehnte Zeuge (1970) 177, 181f. WILSON, S. G., The Gentiles and the Gentile Mission in Luke-Acts (Cambridge 1973) 71, 72, 201, 203. "Apokalyptik" in: TRE 3 (1978) 254. MATTILL, A. J., Luke and the Last Things: a Perspective for the Understanding of Lukan Thought (Dillsboro 1979) 133-34.

21:25-36 SCHLIER, H. in: Herr, tue meine Lippen auf Bd. 1 (1957) G. Eichholz, ed., 7-12. NICKELS, P. Targum and New Testament (1967) 46. WEBER, O. Predigtmeditationen (1967) 122-26. TRAUB, H. GPM 27 (1972) 16-21. PREUSS, H. R./GERLACH, W. "Zweiter Advent: Lukas 21,25-36", in: Predigtstudien (1972), E. Lange ed., 23-28.

21:25-33 WEBER, GPM 4 (1949-1950) 11ff. GOLLWITZER, GPM 9 (1954-1955) 5ff. Tochter Zion, freue dich, Predigtgedanken aus Vergangenheit und Gegenwart Reihe A, Bd. 1 (1960) 34-52. GOLLWITZER, GPM 15 (1960-1961) 8ff. DOERNE, M. Er kommt auch noch heute (1961) 12-15. MARXSEN, W. Predigten (1968) 123-30. HAGGENMÜLLER, O., "Das Kommen des Menschensohnes" Am Tisch des Wortes 6 (1965) 27-39. BOHREN, R., Predigtlehre (München 1971) 235ff. SCHNEIDER, G., Parusiegleichnisse im Lukas-Evangelium (Stuttgart 1975) 55-61. MUTIUS, A. und KÖSTER, R., in: P. Krusche et al. (eds.) Predigtstudien für das Kirchenjahr 1978-1979, 1/2 (Stuttgart 1978) 20-26.

21:25-28 SALAS, A. "Los signos cosmicos de Lc. XXI,25-28, a la luz del concepto biblico 'dia de Yahvé'," CiDi 180 (1, 1967) 43-85. SCHRAMM, T. Der Markus-Stoff bei Lukas (1971) 180f. GEIGER, R., Die lukanischen Endzeitreden (Bern 1973) 212-15. RAHNER, K., Was sollen wir jetzt tun? Vier Meditationen (Freiburg/Wien 1974).

21:25-27 SANFORD, J. A., The Kingdom Within (New York 1970) 206-07.

21:25-26 ROBINSON, W. C., The Way of the Lord (Diss, Basel 1960) 106-11. ROBINSON, W. C. Der Weg des Herrn (1964) 64. KLIJN, A. F. J., "Die syrische Baruch-Apokalypse" in: W. G. Kümmel (ed.) Jüdische Schriften aus hellenistisch-römischer Zeit. V/2 (Gütersloh 1976) 140n.41.

21:25 MARXSEN, W. Mark the Evangelist (1969) 190, 194, 197. WILSON, S. G., The Gentiles and the Gentile Mission in Luke-Acts (Cambridge 1973) 71, 72, 201, 203. KLIJN, A. F. J., "Die syrische Baruch-Apokalypse" in: W. G. Kümmel (ed.) Jüdische Schriften aus hellenistisch-römischer Zeit. V/2 (Gütersloh 1976) 129n.XXV,2a.

21:27 JÜNGEL, E. Paulus und Jesus (1966) 243.

21:28-31 ROBINSON, W. C. Der Weg des Herrn (1964) 64f.

21:28 FLENDER, H. St Luke Theologian of Redemptive History (1967) 61n, 72, 94n, 98n, 114. JEREMIAS, J. Neutestamentliche Theologie I (1971) 127f. KLIJN, A. F. J., "Die syrische Baruch-Apokalypse" in: W. G. Kümmel (ed.) Jüdische Schriften aus hellenistisch-römischer Zeit. V/2 (Gütersloh 1976) 129n.7a. SALAS, A., "'Vuestra liberación está cerca' (Lc 21,28). Dimension liberacionista del acto redentor" CiDi 189 (1976) 3-22.

21:29-36 GEIGER, R., Die Lukanischen Endzeitreden (Bern 1973) 223-48.

21:29-33 DERRETT, J. D. M, "Figtrees in the New Testament" HeyJ 14 (1973) 249-65. CARLSTON, C. E., The Parables of the Triple

Tradition (Philadelphia 1975) 45-46, 81-84, 190-97. SCHNEI-
DER, G., Das Evangelium nach Lukas (Gütersloh/Würzburg 1977)
428 (lit!).

21:29-31 JÜLICHER, D. A. Die Gleichnisreden Jesu (1910) 3-11. PATSCH,
H. Abendmahl und historischer Jesus (1972) 116f. MANEK, J., . . .
und brachte Frucht. Die Gleichnisse Jesu (Berlin 1977) 33-34.
KLAUCK, H.-J., Allegorie und Allegorese in Synoptischen
Gleichnistexten (Münster 1978) 316-25.

21:29 GOULDER, M. D. Midrash and Lection in Matthew (1974) 60,
370, 425.

21:30 NESTLE, E. Einführung in das Griechische Neue Testament (1909)
230f.

21:31 STONEHOUSE, N. B. The Witness of Matthew and Mark to Christ
(1944) 229. STAEHELIN, E. Die Verkündigung des Reiches Gottes
in der Kirche Jesu Christi I (1951) 162. JEREMIAS, J. Neutestamentliche Theologie I (1971) 40f., 254. HIERS, R. H., The Historical Jesus and the Kingdom of God (Gainesville 1973) 13-14, 29.
CLARK, K. W., "Realized Eschatology" in: The Gentile Bias and
other Essays (Leiden 1980) 53. McDONALD, J. I. H., Kerygma
and Didache (Cambridge 1980) 18-19.

21:32 BLASS, F. Philosophy of the Gospels (1898) 49ff. KNOX, W. L.
The Sources of the Synoptic Gospels II (1957) 19. ROBINSON,
W. C. Der Weg des Herrn (1964) 65f. HASLER, V. Amen (1969)
47. WILSON, S. G., The Gentiles and the Gentile Mission in Luke-
Acts (Cambridge 1973) 70, 74, 76, 77, 82. KÜNZI, M., Das Nah-
erwartungslogion Markus 9,1 par. (Tübingen 1977) 213-14. MAT-
TILL, A. J., Luke and the Last Things (Dillsboro 1979) 96-104.
SCHILDENBERGER, J., "Die Vertauschung der Aussagen über
Zeichen und Bezeichnetes, eine hermeneutisch bedeutsame Rede-
weise" in: Kirche und Bibel, FS. E. Schick (Paderborn 1979) 405-
06. HARRINGTON, D. J., God's People in Christ (Philadelphia
1980) 25.

21:34-38 SCHRAMM, T. Der Markus-Stoff bei Lukas (1971) 181f.

21:34-36 LOEVESTAM, E. Spiritual Wakefulness in the New Testament
(1963) 122-32. ROBINSON, W. C. Der Weg des Herrn (1964) 66.
OTT, W. Gebet und Heil (1965) 73-75, 102, 109, 139, 140.
KRAENKL, E. Jesus der Knecht Gottes (1972) 204f. RAHNER,
K., Was sollen wir jetzt tun? Vier Meditationen (Freiburg 1974).
SCHNEIDER, G., Das Evangelium nach Lukas (Gütersloh 1977)
431. FRIEDRICH, G., "I Thessalonicher 5,11, der apologetische
Einschub eines Späteren" in: Auf das Wort kommt es an (Göttin-
gen 1978) 265. MATTILL, A. J., Luke and the Last Things (Dills-
boro 1979) 104-09.

21:34 REICKE, B. Diakonie, Festfreude und Zelos (1951) 339f. STAE-
HELIN, F. Die Verkündigung des Reiches Gottes in der Kirche Jesu
Christi I (1951) 395. JEREMIAS, J., Die Sprache des Lukas-
evangeliums (Göttingen 1980) 283.

21:36 OTT, W. Gebet und Heil (1965) 137f. JÜNGEL, E. Paulus und Jesus (1966) 230. JEREMIAS, J. Neutestamentliche Theologie I
(1971) 196, 248, 251, 259, 262. SCHNEIDER, G., " 'Der Menschensohn' in der lukanischen Christologie" in: R. Pesch/R.
Schnackenburg (eds.) Jesus und der Menschensohn (Freiburg 1975)
268-71. JEREMIAS, J., Die Sprache des Lukasevangeliums (Göttingen 1980) 283-84.

21:37-38 SCHNEIDER, G., Das Evangelium nach Lukas (Gütersloh 1977)
434. SWIDLER, L., Biblical Affirmations of Woman (Philadelphia 1979) 220, 250, 275.

21:37 JEREMIAS, J. Die Abendmahlsworte Jesu (1960) 36f., 49,
PETZKE, G. Die Traditionen über Apollonius von Tyana und das
Neue Testament (1970) 78, 170. JEREMIAS, J., Die Sprache des
Lukasevangeliums (Göttingen 1980) 284.

21:38 JEREMIAS, J., Die Sprache des Lukasevangeliums (Göttingen
1980) 284-85.

22ff. SCHÜTZ, F. Der leidende Christus (1969).

22-24 TAYLOR, V. Behind the Third Gospel (1926) 34-75. LEIVES-
TAD, R. Christ the Conqueror (1954) 71-76. GRUNDMANN, W.
Das Evangelium nach Lukas (1961) 454-57. GOLLWITZER, H.
Jesu Tod und Auferstehung nach dem Bericht des Lukas (^{5}1963).
VÖÖBUS, A. The Prelude to the Lukan Narrative (1968). BLINZ-
LER, J. ''Passionsgeschehen und Passionsbericht des Lukas-
evangeliums,'' BuK 24 (1, 1969) 1-4. STÖGER, A. "Eigenart und
Botschaft der lukanischen Passionsgeschichte,'' BuK 24 (1, 1969)
4-8. TAYLOR, V. The Passion Narrative of St. Luke (1972) NEI-
RYNCK, F., "La Matière dans Luc'' in: F. Neirynck (ed.) L'E-
vangile de Luc (Gembloux 1973) 195-99. CRIBBS, F. L.., "The
Agreements that Exist Between John and the Acts'' in: C. H. Tal-
bert (ed.) Perspectives on Luke-Acts (Danville 1978) 41, 43.

22-23 TAYLOR, V. The Gospel According to St. Mark (1953) 526.
TAYLOR, V. "Sources of the Lucan Passion Narrative,'' ET 68
(1956-1957) 95. TYSON, J. B. "The Lucan Version of the Trial

of Jesus,'' NovTest 3 (1959) 249-58. STOLLE, V., Der Zeuge als Angeklagter (Stuttgart 1973) 215-20. TALBERT, C. H., Literary Patterns, Theological Themes, and the Genre of Luke-Acts (Missoula 1974) 26, 27, 111, 120, 142, 143. KLEIN, H., ''Die lukanisch-johanneische Passionstradition'' ZNW 67 (1976) 155-86. GERSTENBERGER, G. and SCHRAGE, W., Leiden (Stuttgart 1977) 123-25, 147; ET: J. E. Steeley, Suffering (Nashville 1980) 143-46, 170-71. SCHNEIDER, G., Das Evangelium nach Lukas (Gütersloh 1977) 435. TOWNSEND, J. T., A Liturgical Interpretation of Our Lord's Passion in Narrative Form (New York 1977). TRITES, A. A., The New Testament Concept of Witness (Cambridge 1977) 185-90.

22:1-23:49 PERRIN, N., The New Testament (New York 1974) 210-12.

22 GREENLEE, J. H. Nine Uncial Palimpsests of the Greek New Testament (1968) 78-81. VÖÖBUS, A. The Prelude to the Lukan Passion Narrative (1968) 22-28. SCHNEIDER, G. Verleugnung, Verspottung und Verhör Jesu nach Lukas 22,54-71 (1969) 151, 152, 156, 160, 162. LEHMANN, M. Synoptische Quellenanalyse und die Frage nach dem historischen Jesus (1970) 103-12.

22:1-38 ROLOFF, J. Apostolat-Verkündigung-Kirche (1965) 228f. CHARBEL, A., ''Prelúdio da Paixáo e o Ciclo da Ceia à Luz do Terceiro Evangelho'' RCB 11 (1974) 43-57.

22:1-23 FRANSEN, I. ''Le Baptmê de Sang (Luc 22,1-23),'' BVieC 25 (1959) 20-28. DÖMER, M., Das Heil Gottes (Köln-Bonn 1978) 89-90.

22:1-13 SCHRAMM, T. Der Markus-Stoff bei Lukas (1971) 182-84. WANKE, J., Die Emmauserzählung (Leipzig 1973) 105.

22:1-6 SCHNEIDER, G., Das Evangelium nach Lukas (Gütersloh 1977) 439.

22:1-2 TEMPLE, S. NTS 7 (1960-1961) 77f. VÖÖBUS, A. The Prelude to the Lukan Passion Narrative (1968) 57-60. KRAFT,H., Die Entstehung des Christentums (Darmstadt 1981) 191-93.

22:2 BOUSSET, W. Die Religion des Judentums im Späthellenistischen Zeitalter (1966 = 1926) 167. SCHNEIDER, G. Verleugnung, Verspottung und Verhör Jesu nach Lukas 22,54-71 (1969) 56, 106, 109, 159, 193, 196.

22:3-6 CRIBBS, F. L. in: SBL Seminar Papers 2 (1973) 48-49. BÖHLIG, A., Die Gnosis III: Der Manichäismus (Zürich 1980) 344 n.66.

22:3-4 PESCH, R., ''Die Salbung Jesu in Bethanien (Mk 14,3-9)'' in: P. Hoffmann (ed.) Orientierung an Jesus. FS. J. Schmid (Freiburg 1973) 269-70.

22:3 BETZ, H. D. Lukian von Samosata und das Neue Testament (1961) 155f. BAILEY, J. A. The Traditions Common to the Gospels of

Luke and John (1963) 29-31. BAUMBACH, G. Das Verständnis des Bösen in den synoptischen Evangelien (1963) 187ff. HAHN, F. Christologische Hoheitstitel (1963) 167. BROWN, S. Apostasy and Perseverance in the Theology of Luke (1969) 1, 5f., 8f., 12, 64, 68, 82, 84f., 98, 106, 112f., 123. SCHNEIDER, G. Verleugnung, Verspottung und Verhör Jesu nach Lukas 22,54-71 (1969) 153, 170, 182, 183, 201, 204, 205. CRIBBS, F. L. in: SBL Seminar Papers 2 (1973) 4. NEIRYNCK, F., "La Matière Marcienne dans Luc" in: F. Neirynck (ed.) L'Evangile de Luc (Gembloux 1973) 168-70. DAVIES, W. D., The Gospel and the Land (London 1974) 246, 246 n.9, 247, 250. METZGER, B. M., The Early Versions of the New Testament (Oxford 1977) 172.

22:4 BROWN, S. Apostasy and Perseverance in the Theology of Luke (1969) 82-84, 86, 92, 112.

22:6 PALLIS, A., Notes on St. Luke and the Acts (London 1928) 41. SCHNEIDER, G. Verleugnung, Verspottung und Verhör Jesu nach Lukas 22,54-71 (1969) 106, 146, 148, 153, 193.

22:7-23:16 TALBERT, C. H., Literary Patterns, Theological Themes, and the Genre of Luke-Acts (Missoula 1974) 26-34.

22:7-38 GOODSPEED, E. J. A Life of Jesus (1950) 195-202. SCHÜRMANN, H. Quellenkritische Untersuchung des lukanischen Abendmahlsberichtes Lk 22,7-38, I (1953); II (1955); III (1957). SCHÜRMANN, H. Der Abendmahlsbericht Lukas 22,7-38 als Gottesdienstordnung, Gemeindeordnung, Lebensordnung I (1957). WINTER, P. "Dritter Teil einer quellenkritischen Untersuchung des Lukanischen Abendmahlsberichtes, Lk. 22:7-38," NTS 4 (1957-1958) 223ff. ZERWICK, M. "Praehistoria textus sacricue bona?" VerbDom 36 (3, 1958) 154-60. LEON-DUFOUR, X. RechSR 48 (3, 1960) 498-502. SCHÜRMANN, H. Der Abendmalsbericht. Lukas 22,7-38 als Gottesdienstordnung, Gemeindeordnung, Lebensordnung II (1960). HAHN, F. Christologische Hoheitstitel (1963) 60, 84. SCHÜRMANN, H. Le récit de las dernière Céne. Luc 22,7-38 (1966). SCHÜRMANN, H. Der Paschamahlbericht. Lk 22, (7-14.) 15-18. I. Teil Einer quellenkritischen Untersuchung des lukanischen Abendmahlsberichtes Lk 22,7-38 (1968). SCHÜRMANN, H. Ursprung und Gestalt (1970) 79, 91, 108-50, 205, 208.

22:7-23 BLASS, F. Philosophy of the Gospels (1898) 179ff. KRAFT, H., Die Entstehung des Christentums (Darmstadt 1981) 197-200.

22:7-20 TALBERT, C. H., Literary Patterns, Theological Themes, and the Genre of Luke-Acts (Missoula 1974) 26, 27.

22:7-16 "Abendmahl" in: TRE I (1977) 48.

22:7-13 RENGSTORF, K. H. Das Evangelium nach Lukas (1949) 232f.

SCHÜRMANN, H. Der Paschamahlbericht (1953) 76-103. VÖÖBUS, A. The Prelude to the Lukan Passion Narrative (1968) 17-21, 62-63. SCHNEIDER, G. Verleugnung, Verspottung und Verhör Jesu nach Lukas 22,54-71 (1969) 152, 154, 180, 182. SCHNEIDER, G., Das Evangelium nach Lukas (Gütersloh 1977) 441. RIST, J. M., On the Independence of Matthew and Mark (Cambridge 1978) 84-85.

22:7 BRAUN, H. Qumran und NT II (1966) 49.

22:8 MIYOSHI, M., Der Anfang des Reiseberichts Lk 9,51-10,24 (Rome 1974) 28-29. STANTON, G. N., Jesus of Nazareth in New Testament Preaching (Cambridge 1974) 40, 41, 42, 58. MUSS- NER, F., Petrus und Paulus (Freiburg 1976) 24.

22:14-24:11 TAYLOR, V. The Formation of the Gospel Tradition (1949) 51f., 55-57. 194-97. SCHRAMM, T. Der Markus-Stoff bei Lukas (1971) 50f.

22:14-38 HIRSCH, E. Frühgeschichte des Evangeliums (1941) 153ff., 252- 61. ROUSTANG, F. "La conversion eucharistique," Christus 8 (32, 1961) 438-53. BAILEY, J. A. The Traditions Common to the Gospels of Luke and John (1963) 32-46. CONZELMANN, H. Die Mitte der Zeit (1964) 73ff. ROLOFF, J. Apostolat-Verkündigung- Kirche (1965) 184-88. VÖÖBUS, A. "A New Approach to the Problem of the Shorter and Longer Text in Luke," NTS 15 (4, 1969) 457-63. ELTESTER, W. "Israel im Lukanischen Werk" in: Jesus in Nazareth (1972) eds. Grässer, E. et al., 132-34. MICHEL, H.- J. Die Abschiedsrede des Paulus an die Kirche Apg 20:17-38 (München 1973) 63. LaVERDIERE, E. A. "A Discourse at the Last Supper," BibleToday 71 (1974) 1540-48. PRAST, F., Presbyter und Evangelium in nachapostolischer Zeit (Stuttgart 1979) 24, 102, 315-16. MCDONALD, J. I. H., Kerygma and Didache (Cam- bridge 1980) 86.

22:14-27 GLÖCKNER, R., Die Verkündigung des Heils beim Evangelisten Lukas (Mainz 1975) 178ff. JEWETT, R., Jesus against the Rap- ture (Philadelphia 1979) 122-42.

22:14-24.53 JEREMIAS, J. Neutestamentliche Theologie I (1971) 48f., 260.

22:14-23 VÖÖBUS, A. The Prelude to the Lukan Passion Narrative (1968) 64-107. CRIBBS, F. L. in: SBL Seminar Papers 2 (1973) 49-53. SCHNEIDER, G., Das Evangelium nach Lukas (Gütersloh 1977) 444, 447-48.

22:14-20 TAYLOR, V. Jesus and His Sacrifice (1948) 175-79. TAYLOR, V. "Theologians of our Time: Heinz Schürmann," ET 74 (3, 1962) 77-81. IWAND, H.-J. in: Herr, tue meine Lippen auf Bd. 3 (1964) G. Eichholz, ed., 173ff. BAHR, G. J. "The Seder of Passover and

the Eucharistic Words," NovTest 12 (2, 1970) 181-202. TAY-
LOR, V. New Testament Essays (1968) 56-59.

22:14-19 FLUSSER, D.. "The Last Supper and the Essenes," Immanuel 2
(1973) 23-27.

22:14 SCHÜRMANN, H. Der Paschamahlbericht (1953) 104ff. JE-
REMIAS, J. Die Abendmahlsworte Jesu (1960) 42f. HAHN, F.
Christologische Hoheitstitel (1963) 384. LEHMANN, M. Synoptische Quellenanalyse und die Frage nach dem historischen Jesus
(1970) 149f. WANKE, J., Die Emmauserzählung (Leipzig 1973)
105. JEREMIAS, J., Die Sprache des Lukasevangeliums (Göttingen 1980) 286.

22:15ff. ANDERSEN, A., "Zu Lk 22:15ff" ZNW 7 (1906). STAE-
HELIN, E. Die Verkündigung des Reiches Gottes in der Kirche Jesu
Christ I (1951) 68.

22:15-50 RIST, J. M., On the Independence of Matthew and Mark (Cambridge 1978) 85.

22:15-38 VERHOEVEN, R. P., "Von der Erzählung zur Formel" Schrift 1
(1969) 174-85.

22:15-20 FEINE, P. Der Apostel Paulus (1927) 336ff. GAUGLER, E. Das
Abendmahl im Neuen Testament(1943) 17f. MANSON, W. Jesus
the Messiah (1948) 134-35, 140-43. CHADWICK, H. "The Shorter
Text of Luke XXII,15-20," HThR 50 (4, 1957) 249-58. BOSCH,
D. Die Heidenmission in der Zukunftsschau Jesu (1959) 175-83.
DU TOIT, A. B. Der Aspekt der Freude im urchristlichen Abend-
mahl (1965) 76-102. KÜNG, H. Die Kirche (Freiburg 1967) 254-
59; ET: The Church (London 1967) 212-15. SCHÜRMANN, H.
Ursprung und Gestalt (1970) 87, 117, 118, 124, 125, 126, 127, 128,
129, 191, 204. TALBERT, C. H., Literary Patterns, Theological
Themes, and the Genre of Luke-Acts (Missoula 1974) 21, 28, 33.
GOPPELT, L., Theologie des Neuen Testaments. I (Göttingen
1975) 261-70 WILLIAMS, S. K., Jesus' Death as Saving Event
(Missoula 1975) 204-11. SCHELKLE, K. M., "Das Herrenmahl"
in: J. Friedrich/W. Pöhlmann/P. Stuhlmacher (eds.) Rechtfertigung. FS. E. Käsemann (Tübingen/Göttingen 1976) 388-90.
"Abendmahlsfeier" in: TRE 1 (1977) 230. PESCH, R., Wie Jesus
das Abendmahl hielt (Freiburg 1977). VERHEUL, A., "La prière
eucharistique dans la Didachè" Questions Liturgiques 60 (1979)
197-207. KRAFT, H., Die Entstehung des Christentums (Darmstadt 1981) 174-80.

22:15-18 SCHÜRMANN, H. Der Paschamahlbericht (1953) 110ff.
SPARKS, H. F. D. "St. Luke's Transpositions," NTS 3 (1956-
1957) 219ff. DERREIT, J. D. M. Law in the New Testament (1970)
439-42. SCHENKE, L., Studien zur Passionsgeschichte des Mar-

kus (Würzburg 1971) 303ff. DORMEYER, D., Die Passion Jesu als Verhaltensmodell (Münster 1974) 106ff.

22:15-16 LIGHTFOOT, R. H. History and Interpretation in the Gospels (1934) 167f. TAYLOR, V. Jesus and His Sacrifice (1948) 180-83.

22:15 SCHÜRMANN, H. Der Paschamahlbericht (1953) 3-14. BARRETT, C. K. "Luke XXII.15: To Eat the Passover," JThS 9 (2, 1958) 305-07. NICKELS, P. Targum and New Testament (1967) 46. RUPPERT, L., Jesus als der leidende Gerechte? (Stuttgart 1972) 47a16. WANKE, J., Die Emmauserzählung (Leipzig 1973) 90. "Abendmahl" in TRE 1 (1977) 62. JEREMIAS, J., Die Sprache des Lukasevangliums (Göttingen 1980) 286.

22:16-18 MOORE, G. F. Judaism II (1946) 365.

22:16, 37, 43 HASLER, V. Amen (1969) 112.

22:16 DALMAN, G. Jesus-Jeschua (1922) 118ff., 165. PALLIS, A., Notes on St. Luke and the Acts (London 1928) 41. SCHÜRMANN, H. Der Paschamahlbericht (1953) 14-23. ROBINSON, J. M. Kerygma und historischer Jesus (1960) 157, 162. BLACK, M. An Aramaic Approach to the Gospels and Acts (1967) 229f., 234f. NICKELS, P. Targum and New Testament (1967) 46. JEREMIAS, J. Neutestamentliche Theologie I (1971) 22, 40, 138, 185, 238, 275, 282f. BANKS, R., Jesus and the Law in the Synoptic Tradition (London 1975) 211-12. JEREMIAS, J., Die Sprache des Lukasevangeliums (Göttingen 1980) 286-87.

22:17-20 RESE, M., "Zur Problematik von Kurz- und Langtext in Luk. xxii. 17ff." NTS 22 (1975) 15-31.

22:17-19 FRIEDRICH, G., "Ursprung, Urform und Urbedeutung des Abendmahls" in: Auf das Wort kommt es an (Göttingen 1978) 309-14.

22:17-18 METZGER, B. M., The Early Versions of the New Testament (Oxford 1977) 40, 48-55.

22:17 PALLIS, A., Notes on St. Luke and the Acts (London 1928) 41-42. NICKELS, P. Targum and New Testament (1967) 47. "Abendmahl" in: TRE 1 (1977) 226. "Abendmahlsfeier" in: TRE 1 (1977) 233. METZGER, B. M., The Early Versions of the New Testament (Oxford 1977) 212. WESTERMANN, C., Blessing (Philadelphia 1978) 86, 98-101. JEREMIAS, J., Die Sprache des Lukasevangeliums (Göttingen 1980) 287.

22:18 GRILL, J., Untersuchungen über die Entstehung des vierten Evangeliums. II (Leipzig 1923) 201, 267, 274, 287. ROBINSON, J. M. Kerygma und historischer Jesus (1960) 157, 162. BRAUN, H. Qumran und NT II (1966) 39. HASLER, V. Amen (1969) 49. SCHNEIDER, G. Verleugnung, Verspottung und Verhör Jesu nach Lukas 22,54-71 (1969) 58, 146, 149, 179. HIERS, R. H., The Historical Jesus and the Kingdom of God (Gainesville 1973) 13-14. "Abendmahl" in: TRE 1 (1977) 49, 52. MATTILL, A. J., Luke and the Last Things (Dillsboro 1979) 109-11. JEREMIAS, J., Die Sprache des Lukasevangeliums (Göttingen 1980) 287.

22:19-20 GRILL, J., Untersuchungen über die Entstehung. II (Leipzig 1923) 285-86.STONEHOUSE, N. B. The Witness of Luke to Christ (1951) 131ff. SCHÜRMANN, H. Der Einsetzungsbericht Lk. 22,19-20. II. Teil (1955). DENNEY, J. The Death of Christ (1956) 35f. COOPER, J. C. "The Problem of the Text in Luke 22:19-20," LQ 14 (1, 1962) 39-48. HAHN, F. Christologische Hoheitstitel (1963) 60. ALAND, K. NTS 12 (1965-1966) 198f. VÖÖBUS, A. The Prelude to the Lukan Passion Narrative (1968) 77-107. SCHMID, J. Gnomon 41 (1, 1969) 90-92. SCHÜRMANN, H. Ursprung und Gestalt (1970) 117-24. WANKE, J., Die Emmausrezählung (Leipzig 1973) 2. WILSON, S. G., The Gentiles and the Gentile Mission in Luke-Acts (Cambridge (1973) 49-50. DOR-MEYER, D., Die Passion Jesu als Verhaltensmodell (Münster 1974) 104, 106ff. MAHONEY, R., Two Disciples at the Tomb (Bern/ Frankfurt 1974) 46-49. TALBERT, C. H., Literary Patterns, Theological Themes, and the Genre of Luke-Acts (Missoula 1974) 33. "Abendmahl" in: TRE 1 (1977) 47, 50. METZGER, B. M., The Early Versions of the New Testament (Oxford 1977) 134. PESCH, R., Das Markusevangelium. II (Freiburg 1977) 364-77. JEREMIAS, J., Die Sprache des Lukasevangeliums (Göttingen 1980) 287-88.

22:19b-20 SCHÜRMANN, H. "Lk 22,19b-20 als ursprüngliche Textüberlieferungen", Biblica 32 (1951) 364-92, 522-41. SCHAEFER, K. TH. "Zur Textgeschichte von Lk 22,19b-20", Biblica 33 (1952) 390-93. TAYLOR, V. The Text of the New Testament (1961) 19f., 91. PARKER, P. "Three Variant Readings in Luke-Acts," JBL 83 (2, 1964) 165-70.

22:19 CLEMEN, C. Primitive Christianity and Its Non-Jewish Sources (1912) 238f. PALLIS, A., Notes on St. Luke and the Acts (London 1928) 42. HANSON, S. The Unity of the Church in the New Testament (1946) 32f. BONSIRVEN, J. "Hoc est corpus meum. Recherches sur l'original araméen", Biblica 29 1948) 205-19. HAHN, F. Christologische Hoheitstitel (1963) 60. BLIGH, J. "Scripture Enquiry: 'Do this in commemoration of me'," The Way 5 (2, 1965) 154-59. NICKELS, P. Targum and New Testament (1967) 47. POPKES, W. Christus Traditus (1967) 205, 213ff., 235, 256, 282. JEREMIAS, J. Neutestamentliche Theologie I (1971) 40f., 138, 185, 238, 275, 282f. TALBERT, C. H., Literary Patterns, Theological Themes, and the Genre of Luke-Acts (Missoula 1974) 17, 21. LÉON-DUFOUR, X., " 'Faites ceci en mémoire de moi.' Luc

22,19-I Corinthiens 11,25'' Christus 24 (1977) 200-08. GREGG, D. W. A., ''Hebraic Antecedents to the Eucharistic *Anamnēsis* Formula'' TB 20 (1979) 165-68.

22:20 HOLTZMANN, O. ZNW 3 (1902) 359. NESTLE, E. ZNW 3 (1902) 252. NESTLE, E., ''Zu Lk 22:20'' ZNW 7 (1906). GRILL, J., Untersuchungen über die Entstehung des vierten Evangeliums. II (Leipzig 1923) 286-87. MASSAUX, E. Influence de l'Evangile de saint Matthieu sur la littérature chrétienne avant saint Irénée (1950) 18-21. HOOKER, M. D. Jesus and the Servant (1959) 80-83. HAHN, F. Christologische Hoheitstitel (1963) 60, 216. NICKELS, P. Targum and New Testament (1967) 47. GESE, H. ''Psalm 22 und das Neue Testament. Der älteste Bericht vom Tode Jesu und die Entstehung des Herrenmahles,'' ZThK 65 (1968) 1-22. WILLIAMS, J. A., A Conceptual History of Deuteronomism in the Old Testament, Judaism, and the New Testament (Ph.D. Diss., Louisville 1976) 310-18. ''Abendmahl'' in: TRE 1 (1977) 50, 51, 56. ''Agapen'' in: TRE 1 (1977) 748.

22:21-38 SCHÜRMANN, H. Jesu Abschiedsrede Lk. 22,21-38 (1957). HAHN, F. Christologische Hoheitstitel (1963) 84, 169.

22:21-30 BRAUN, H. Qumran und NT II (1966) 19, 31, 35, 39f., 102, 335.

22:21-23, TAYLOR, V. ''Theologians of Our Time: VII Friedrich Reh-
47-53 kopf,'' ET 74 (9, 1963) 262-66.

22:21-23 SCHNEIDER, G. Verleugnung, Verspottung und Verhör Jesu nach Lukas 22,54-71 (1969) 15, 71, 145, 146, 149, 152, 179. SCHÜRMANN, H. Ursprung und Gestalt (1970) 125, 127, 140-43. WANKE, J., Die Emmauserzählung (Leipzig 1973) 30. TALBERT, C. H., Literary Patterns, Theological Themes, and the Genre of Luke-Acts (Missoula 1974) 27, 29.

22:21 REHKOPF, F. Die lukanische Sonderquelle (1959) 8ff. JEREMIAS, J., Die Sprache des Lukasevangeliums (Göttingen 1980) 288.

22:22 HOOKER, M. D. Jesus and the Servant (1959) 74-79, 98f. REHKOPF, F. Die lukanische Sonderquelle (1959) 13ff. NICKELS, P. Targum and New Testament (1967) 47. SANFORD, J. A., The Kingdom Within (New York 1970) 134-36. WANKE, J., Die Emmauserzählung (Leipzig 1973) 94, 118. SAND, A., Das Gesetz und die Propheten (Regensburg (1974) 86. GLÖCKNER, R., Die Verkündigung des Heils beim Evangelisten Lukas (Mainz 1975) 161-62.

22:23 REHKOPF, F. Die lukanische Sonderquelle (1959) 22ff. CLARK, K. W., ''The Meaning of APA'' in: The Gentile Bias and other Essays (Leiden 1980) 197-98. JEREMIAS, J., Die Sprache des Lukasevangeliums (Göttingen 1980) 288-90.

22:24ff. RICHTER, G. Die Fusswaschung im Johannesevangelium (1967) 161, 172, 173, 176, 178, 179, 192, 205, 206, 210, 214, 215, 219, 220, 221f., 238, 239, 240, 241, 249, 270, 274, 314. WANKE, J., Die Emmauserzählung (Leipzig 1973) A.651, 653.

22:24-30 TANNEHILL, R. A Study in the Theology of Luke-Acts,'' AThR 43 (2, 1961) 195-203. MINEAR, P., To Heal and to Reveal (New York 1976) 19-22. SCHNEIDER, G., Das Evangelium nach Lukas (Gütersloh 1977) 449. ''Apostel'' in: TRE 3 (1978) 442. BUCK, E., ''The Function of the Pericope 'Jesus Before Herod' in the Passion Narrative of Luke'' in: W. Haubeck/M. Bachmann (eds.) Wort in der Zeit. FS. K. H. Rengstorf (Leiden 1980) 171.

22:24-27 REICKE, B. Diakonie, Festfreude und Zelos (1951) 22ff. FLEW, R. N. Jesus and His Church (1956) 137n. SCHULZ, A. Nachfolge und Nachahmen (1962) 252-56, 261f., 264f. BAUMBACH, G. Das Verständnis der Bösen in den synoptischen Evangelien (1963) 192ff. JEREMIAS, J. Abba; Studien zur neutestamentlichen Theologie und Zeitgeschichte (1966) 224-27. VÖÖBUS, A. The Prelude to the Lukan Passion Narrative (1968) 30-33, 109-16, EISINGER, W. ''Soziale Strukturen der Gerechtigkeit,'' in: Zuwendung und Gerechtigkeit (1969) 49-54. SCHÜRMANN, H. Ursprung und Gestalt (1970) 125, 136-40, 276. JEREMIAS, J. New Testament Theology I (1971) 213, 217, 293. PATSCH, H. Abendmahl und historischer Jesus (1972) 172f. TALBERT, C. H., Literary Patterns, Theological Themes, and the Genre of Luke-Acts (Missoula 1974) 27, 29. GLÖCKNER, R., Die Verkündigung des Heils beim Evangelisten Lukas (Mainz 1975) 177ff., 183. HOFFMANN, P. und EID, V., Jesus von Nazareth und eine christliche Moral (Freiburg 1975) 189-90, 190-200. KLAPPERT, B., ''Arbeit Gottes und Mitarbeit des Menschen (Phil 2:6-11)'' in: J. Moltmann (ed.) Recht auf Arbeit - Sinn der Arbeit (München 1979) 101-02. PRAST, F., Presbyter und Evangelium in nachapostolischer Zeit (Stuttgart 1979) 64, 101-03, 227, 259-62, 349-50, 435.

22:24 JEREMIAS, J., Die Sprache des Lukasevangeliums (Göttingen 1980) 290.

22:25ff. RICHTER, G. Die Fusswaschung im Johannesevangelium (1967) 163, 197, 223, 244.

22:25-28 BOUHOURS, J. F. ''Une étude de l'ordonnance de la triple tradition,'' RechSR 60 (4, 1972) 595-614.

22:25-27 ARENS, E., The HAΘON-Sayings in the Synoptic Tradition (Fribourg 1976) 117-61.

22:25.27 TAYLOR, V. "The Origin of the Markan Passion Sayings," NTS 1 (1954-1955) 163ff.

22:25 BOUSSET, W. Die Religion des Judentums im Späthellenistischen Zeitalter (1966 = 1926) 375. RICKARDS, R. R., "Luke 22.25 - They are called 'Friends of the People' " BTr 28 (1977) 445-46. FRIEDRICH, G., "Das Problem der Autorität im Neuen Testament" in: Auf das Wort kommt es an (Göttingen 1978) 405. SHERWIN-WHITE, A. N., Roman Society and Roman Law in the New Testament (Grand Rapids 1978) 137, 143. SCHILLE-BEECKX, E., Die Auferstehung Jesu als Grund der Erlösung" in: K. Rahner/H. Schlier (eds.) Quaestiones Disputatae (Basel 1979) 71. CLARK, K. W., "The Meaning of (KATA) KYRIEYEIN" in: The Gentile Bias and other Essays (Leiden 1980) 207-12.

22:26ff. DALMANN, G. Jesus-Jeschua (1922) 109f.

22:26-27 PRAST, F., Presbyter und Evangelium in nachapostolischer Zeit (Stuttgart 1979) 197.

22:26 TALBERT, C. H., Literary Patterns, Theological Themes, and the Genre of Luke-Acts (Missoula 1974) 17, 22.

22:27 HOOKER, M. D. Jesus and the Servant (1959) 74-79. HAHN, F. Christologische Hoheitstitel (1963) 45. TÖDT, H. E. Der Menschensohn in der synoptischen Ueberlieferung (1963) 192-94. SHIMADA, K., The Formulary Material in First Peter (Th.D. Diss., Ann Arbor 1966) 248-52. NICKELS, P. Targum and New Testament (1967) 47. RICHTER, G. Die Fusswaschung im Johannesevangelium (1967) 91, 96, 215, 219, 223, 225, 226, 229, 284. SCHÜRMANN, H. Ursprung und Gestalt (1970) 48, 57, 137-38, 165, 171, 276, 289. JEREMIAS, J. Neutestamentliche Theologie I (1971) 210, 278f. PATSCH, H. Abendmahl und historischer Jesus (1972) 170ff. HOWARD, V. P., Das Ego in den Synoptischen Evangelien (Marburg 1975) 230-34. "Amt" in: TRE 2 (1978) 512. PRAST, F., Presbyter und Evangelium in nachapostolischer Zeit (Stuttgart 1979) 210. BERGMEIER, R., Glaube als Gabe nach Johannes (Stuttgart 1980) 208.

22:28ff. JÜNGEL, E. Paulus und Jesus (1966) 239.

22:28-32 LEIVESTAD, R. Christ the Conqueror (1954) 59ff.

22:28-30 TAYLOR, V. Jesus and His Sacrifice (1948) 176f., 187-90. BORNKAMM-BARTH-HELD, Ueberlieferung und Auslegung im Matthäus-Evangelium (1961) 262. SCHULZ, A. Nachfolge und Nachahmen (1962) 119-24. DUPONT, J. "Le logion des douze (Mt 19,28; Lc 22,29-30)," Biblica 45 (3, 1964) 355-92. VÖÖBUS, A. The Prelude to the Lukan Passion Narrative (1968) 33-40, 116-26. BROWN, S. Apostasy and Perseverance in the Theology of Luke (1969) 8f., 11f., 62-66. BORSCH, F. H. The Christian & Gnostic

Son of Man (1970) 26-27. OTOMO, Y. Nachfolge Jesu and Anfänge der Kirche im Neuen Testament (1970) 57-60. SCHÜR-
MANN, H. Ursprung und Gestalt (1970) 50, 83, 124-28, 129, 177.
HOFFMANN, P. Studien zur Theologie der Logienquelle (1972)
5, 42, 150, 304. SCHULZ, S. Q Die Spruchquelle der Evangelisten (1972) 330-36. SCHMAHL, G., Die Zwölf im Markusevangelium (Trier 1974) 29-36. TALBERT, C. H., Literary
Patterns, Theological Themes, and the Genre of Luke-Acts (Mis-
soula 1974) 26, 28. LOHFINK, G., Die Sammlung Israels
(München 1975) 80-83. THEISOHN, J., Der auserwählte Richter
(Göttingen 1975) 157, 168ff., 173-74, 181ff., 253. POLAG, A.,
Die Christologie der Logienquelle (Neukirchen-Vluyn 1977) 46, 49,
97. TRILLING, W., "Die Entstehung des Zwölferkreises. Eine
geschichtskritische Ueberlegung" in: H. Schürmann (ed.) Die
Kirche des Anfangs (Freiburg 1978) 213-20. KUHN, H.-W.,
"Nachfolge nach Ostern" in: D. Lührmann/G. Strecker (eds.)
Kirche. FS. G. Bornkamm (Tübingen 1980) 117.

22:28-29 MANEK, J. "Vier Bibelstudien zur Problematik der sozialen Umwandlung", CommViat 10 (1, 1967) 61-70; (2-3, 1967) 179-82.

22:28 BAUMBACH, G. Das Verständnis des Bösen in den synoptischen
Evangelien (1963) 191ff. HENNECKE, E./SCHNEEMELCHER,
W. Neutestamentliche Apokryphen (1964) II 15. JEREMIAS, J.
Neutestamentliche Theologie I (1971) 78, 223, 253, 261. LOH-
FINK, G., Die Sammlung Israels (München 1975) 66, 80-82.
PRAST, F., Presbyter und Evangelium in nachapostolischer Zeit
(Stuttgart 1979) 67-68.

22:29-30 STONEHOUSE, N. B. The Witness of Luke to Christ (1951) 154,
159f., 161. FLEW, R. N. Jesus and His Church (1956) 29, 53, 76-
77. SCHWEIZER, E. Erniedrigung und Erhöhung bei Jesus und
seinen Nachfolgern (1962) § 3g. JEREMIAS, J. Neutestamentliche Theologie I (1971) 223, 225, 239, 261. DUNN, J. D. G., Jesus and the Spirit (London 1975) 36, 41.

22:29 HAHN, F. Christologische Hoheitstitel (1963) 321. KAESE-
MANN, E. Exegetische Versuch und Besinnungen (1964) I 28.
VÖGTLE, A. Das Neue Testament und die Zukunft des Kosmos
(1970) 160f., 163. HOWARD, V. P., Das Ego in den Synop-
tischen Evangelien (Marburg 1975) 176-83. LOHFINK, G., Die
Sammlung Israels (München 1975) 80-83, 94. THEISOHN, J., Der
auserwählte Richter (Göttingen 1975) 165ff., 256. DUNN, J. D.
G., Unity and Diversity in the New Testament (London 1977) 214.

22:30 FLEW, R. N. Jesus and His Church (1956) 86. SCHWEIZER, E.
Gemeinde und Gemeinde-Ordnung im Neuen Testament (1959) §
2k. NICKELS, P. Targum and New Testament (1967) 47.
VÖGTLE, A. Das Neue Testament und die Zukunft des Kosmos

(1970) 148, 160f. JEREMIAS, J. Neutestamentliche Theologie I (1971) 238, 253, 259, 261. ORBE, A., "El Diácono del Jordán en el sistema de Basílides" Augustinianum 13 (1973) 165-83. CAV-ALLIN, H. C. C., Life After Death. I (Lund 1974) 4, 4n8. DAV-IES, W. D., The Gospel and the Land (London 1974) 363, 364 n.79. LOHFINK, G., Die Sammlung Israels (München 1975) 81-82. SWIDLER, L., Biblical Affirmations of Woman (Philadelphia 1979) 289. JEREMIAS, J., Die Sprache des Lukasevangeliums (Göttingen 1980) 291.

22:31ff. VÖÖBUS, A. The Prelude to the Lukan Passion Narrative (1968) 127-36.

22:31-38 CONZELMANN, H. Die Mitte der Zeit (1964) 74ff. FLENDER, H. Heil und Geschichte in der Theologie des Lukas (1965) 78-79. VÖÖBUS, A. The Prelude to the Lukan Passion Narrative (1968) 41-47. WANKE, J., Die Emmauserzählung (Leipzig 1973) 121.

22:31-34, BROWN, S. Apostasy and Perseverance in the Theology of Luke
54-62 (1969) 69-71. DIETRICH, W. Das Petrusbild der lukanischen Schriften (1972) 116-39.

22:31-34 SCHNIEWIND, J., Die Parallelperikopen bei Lukas und Johannes (Darmstadt 1958 = 1914) 28-32. STRECKER, G. Der Weg der Gerechtigkeit (1962) 202$_4$. BAUMBACH, G. Das Verständnis des Bösen in den synoptischen Evangelien (1963) 193ff. OTT, W. Gebet und Heil (1965) 75, 79-81, 86, 98, 137. BROWN, S. Apostasy and Perseverance in the Theology of Luke (1969) 69f. LEH-MANN, M. Synoptische Quellenanalyse und die Frage nach dem historischen Jesus (1970) 103-06. CRIBBS, F. L. in: SBL Seminar Papers 2 (1973) 4, 53-54. TALBERT, C. H., Literary Patterns, Theological Themes, and the Genre of Luke-Acts (Missoula 1974) 26, 27, 28. SCHNEIDER, G., Das Evangelium nach Lukas (Gütersloh 1977) 452. BUCK, E., "The Function of the Pericope 'Jesus before Herod' in the Passion Narrative of Luke" in: W. Haubeck/M. Bachmann (eds.) Wort in der Zeit. FS. K. H. Rengstorf (Leiden 1980) 171.

22:31-33 BOMAN, T. Die Jesus-Ueberlieferung im Lichte der Neueren Volkskunde (1967) 208-21. DRURY, J., Tradition and Design in Luke's Gospel (Atlanta 1976) 68-69.

22:31-32 SCHELKLE, K. H. Die Passion Jesu in der Verkündigung des Neuen Testament (1949) 17ff. FEINE, D. P. & BEHM, D. J. Einleitung in das Neue Testament (1950) 72f. FOERSTER, W. "Lukas 22,31f.," ZNW 46 (1955) 129-33. HAHN, F. Christologische Hoheitstitel (1963) 84. BOMAN, T. NTS 10 (1963-1964) 269f. SCHNEIDER, B. "The Faith of Peter," KatorShin 7 (1, 1968) 93-

107. /In Japanese./ KLEIN, G. "Die Verleugnung des Petrus", Rekonstruktion und Interpretation (1969) 49-98. LINNEMANN, E. Studien zur Passionsgeschichte (1970) 72-77. SANFORD, J. A. The Kingdom Within (New York 1970) 136. SCHÜRMANN, H. Ursprung und Gestalt (1970) 50, 125, 128-31, 143-45, 268, 271, 273. JEREMIAS, J. Neutestamentliche Theologie I (1971) 17, 26, 78, 140, 180, 182, 184, 232. BROWN, R. E. et al. (eds.) Peter in the New Testament (Minneapolis 1973) 119-25. WANKE, J., Die Emmauserzählung (Leipzig 1973) 90. TALBERT, C. H., Literary Patterns, Theological Themes, and the Genre of Luke-Acts (Missoula 1974) 33. LOHFINK, G., Die Sammlung Israels (München 1975) 80-83. MUSSNER, F., Petrus und Paulus (Freiburg 1976) 24-26. GERSTENBERGER, G. und SCHRAGE, W., Leiden (Stuttgart 1977) 234-35; ET: J. E. Steeley, Suffering (Nashville 1980) 270.

22:31 PALLIS, A. Notes on St. Luke and the Acts (London 1928) 42-43. STAEHELIN, E. Die Verkündigung des Reiches Gottes in der Kirche Jesu Christi I (1951) 166. ARGYLE, A. W./BOTHA, F. J. "Luke XXII,31" ET 64 (4, 1953) 125; (7, 1953) 222. FARRER, A. St Matthew and St Mark (1954) 166n. STRECKER, G. Der Weg der Gerechtigkeit (1962) 206$_4$. HAHN, F. Christologische Hoheitstitel (1963) 168. OTT, W. Gebet und Heil (1965) 75-79, 85. JEREMIAS, J., Die Sprache des Lukasevangeliums (Göttingen 1980) 291. KRAFT, H., Die Entstehung des Christentums (Darmstadt 1981) 154.

22:32 BROWN, S. Apostasy and Perseverance in the Theology of Luke (1969) 71-74. PRETE, B. "Confirma fratres tuos," SaDo 15 (58, 1970) 181-218. JEREMIAS, J. Neutestamentliche Theologie I (1971) 26, 163, 242. HOWARD, V. P., Das Ego in den Synoptischen Evangelien (Marburg 1975) 238-44. GOPPELT, L., Theologie des Neuen Testaments. II (Göttingen 1976) 244. SCHNEIDER, G., " 'Stärke deine Brüder!' (Lk 22,32). Die Aufgabe des Petrus nach Lukas" Catholica 30 (1976) 200-06. "Ablass" in: TRE 1 (1977) 349. FRIEDRICH, G., "Die Fürbitte im Neuen Testament" in: Auf das Wort kommt es an (Göttingen 1978) 437-38. MEDIAVILLA, R., "La Oraciòn de Jesus en el tercer evangelio" Mayeutica (1978) 5-34. JEREMIAS, J., Die Sprache des Lukasevangeliums (Göttingen 1980) 291-92. KRAFT, H., Die Entstehung des Christentums (Darmstadt 1981) 209.

22:33-34 JEREMIAS, J. Die Abendmahlsworte Jesu (1960) 93f. HAHN, F. Christologische Hoheitstitel (1963) 84. SCHNEIDER, G. Verleugnung, Verspottung und Verhör Jesu nach Lukas 22,54-71 (1969) 137, 141, 145, 146, 150, 153, 179. LINNEMANN, E. Studien zur Passionsgeschichte (1970) 93-95. SCHÜRMANN, H. Ursprung und

Gestalt (1970) 131, 143-45, 271. TALBERT, C. H., Literary Patterns, Theological Themes, and the Genre of Luke-Acts (Missoula 1974) 33.

22:33 HAHN, F. Christologische Hoheitstitel (1963) 84, 85.

22:34-38 JEREMIAS, J. Die Abendmahlsworte Jesu (1960) 94f.

22:34 STREETER, B. H. The Four Gospels (1951) 404f. HASLER, V. Amen (1969) 49. LEHMANN, M. Synoptische Quellenanalyse und die Frage nach dem historischen Jesus (1970) 109f. WILCOX, M. "The Denial-Sequence in Mark 14:26-31, 66-72," NTS 17 (1970-1971) 431f.

22:25ff. WANKE, J., Die Emmauserzählung (Leipzig 1973) 90.

22:35-38 TAYLOR, V. Jesus and His Sacrifice (1948) 191-94. HAHN, F. Christologische Hoheitstitel (1963) 168. DEGENHARDT, H.-J. Lukas, Evangelist der Armen (1964) 66-68. LEHMANN, M. Synoptische Quellenanalyse und die Frage nach dem historischen Jesus (1970) 146-52. SCHÜRMANN, H. Ursprung und Gestalt (1970) 53, 56, 58, 131-36. HENGEL, M., Was Jesus a Revolutionist? (Philadelphia 1971) 21-22. JEREMIAS, J. Neutestamentliche Theologie I (1971) 231, 233, 269f., 279f. JEREMIAS, J. New Testament Theology I (1971) 241, 243, 283, 284, 294. BARTSCH, H.-W. "Jesu Schwertwort, Lukas xxii. 35-38: Ueberlieferungsgeschichtliche Studie," NTS 20 (2, 1974) 190-203. TALBERT, C. H., Literary Patterns, Theological Themes, and the Genre of Luke-Acts (Missoula 1974) 26,27. DRURY, J., Tradition and Design in Luke's Gospel (Atlanta 1976) 69. SCHNEIDER, G., Das Evangelium nach Lukas (Gütersloh 1977) 454. SCHWARZ, G., "κυριε, ιδου μαχαιραι ωδε δυο" in: M. Görg (ed.) Biblische Notizen 8 (Bamberg 1979) 22.

22:35-36 KARRIS, R. J., "Poor and Rich: The Lukan Sitz im Leben" in: C. H. Talbert (ed.) Perspectives on Luke-Acts (Danville 1978) 114, 118-19.

22:35 FLEW, R. N. Jesus and His Church (1956) 78. LEHMANN, M. Synoptische Quellenanalyse und die Frage nach dem historischen Jesus (1970) 149f. TALBERT, C. H., Literary Patterns, Theological Themes, and the Genre of Luke-Acts (Missoula 1974) 27. JEREMIAS, J., Die Sprache des Lukasevangeliums (Göttingen 1980) 292. KRAFT,H., Die Entstehung des Christentums (Darmstadt 1981) 155.

22:36ff. HENGEL, M., Was Jesus a Revolutionist? (Philadelphia 1971) 8.

22:36-46 MIYOSHI, M., Der Anfang des Reiseberichts Lk 9,51-10,24 (Rome 1974) 29-30.

22:36-38 HAHN, F. Christologische Hoheitstitel (1963) 167-70. CROSSAN, J. D. in: SBL Seminar Papers 2 (1973) 95-96. HIERS, R.

H., The Historical Jesus and the Kingdom of God (Gainesville 1973) 104-05.

22:36 PALLIS, A., Notes on St. Luke and the Acts (London 1928) 43-44. HAHN, F. Christologische Hoheitstitel (1963) 166. GOULDER, M. D. Type and History in Acts (1964) 142f. MINEAR, P. S. "A Note on Luke xxii 36," NovTest 7 (2, 1964) 128-34. BROWN, S. Apostasy and Perseverance in the Theology of Luke (1969) 6, 11f. SCHÜTZ, F. Der leidende Christus (1969) 14-20. WILSON, S. G., The Gentiles and the Gentile Mission in Luke-Acts (Cambridge 1973) 65, 66.

22:37 DENNEY, J. The Death of Christ (1956) 29, 50. WILCKENS, U. Die Missionsreden der Apostelgeschichte (1961) 124, 134, 140, 158. HAHN, F. Christologische Hoheitstitel (1963) 54, 202. HOLTZ, T. Untersuchungen über die Alttestamentlichen Zitate bei Lukas (1968) 41-43. STROBEL, A. Erkenntnis und Bekenntnis der Sünde in neutestamentlicher Zeit (1968) 41. RESE, M. Alttestamentliche Motive in der Christologie des Lukas (1969) 154-64. JEREMIAS, J. Neutestamentliche Theologie I (1971) 231, 272f., 279f., SCHRAMM, T. Der Markus-Stoff bei Lukas (1971) 133f. RUPPERT, L., Jesus als der leidende Gerechte? (Stuttgart 1972) 49a24. WANKE, J., Die Emmauserzählung (Leipzig 1973) 92. TALBERT, C. H., Literary Patterns, Theological Themes, and the Genre of Luke-Acts (Missoula 1974) 97. DUNN, J. D. G., Unity and Diversity in the New Testament (London 1977) 211. LARKIN, W. J., Jr., "Luke's Use of the Old Testament as a Key to His Soteriology" JEThS 20 (1977) 325-35. JEREMIAS, J., Die Sprache des Lukasevangeliums (Göttingen 1980) 292-93.

22:38 HAHN, F. Christologische Hoheitstitel (1963) 84, 85, 169. ELLIS, E. E. NTS 10 (1963-1964) 275f. BRAUN, H. Qumran und NT II (1966) 107. NICKELS, P. Targum and New Testament (1967) 47. SCHNEIDER, G. Verleugnung, Verspottung und Verhör Jesu nach Lukas 22,54-71 (1969) 128, 142, 185, 190, 191. CLARK, K. W., "The Making of the Twentieth Century New Testament" in: The Gentile Bias and other Essays (Leiden 1980) 152.

22:39-53 HIRSCH, E. Frühgeschichte des Evangeliums (1941) 261-64. BROWN, S. Apostasy and Perseverance in the Theology of Luke (1969) 66-69. TALBERT, C. H., Literary Patterns, Theological Themes, and the Genre of Luke-Acts (Missoula 1974) 29, 33.

22:39-53a BAILEY, J. A. The Traditions Common to the Gospels of Luke and John (1963) 47-54.

22:39-46 SCHELKLE, K. H. Die Passion Jesu in der Verkündigung des Neuen Testament (1949) 42f. DENNEY, J. The Death of Christ (1956) 41ff. OTT, W. Gebet und Heil (1965) 73, 82-85, 94, 124.

CRIBBS, F. L. in: SBL Seminar Papers 2 (1973) 54-56. HOL-
LERAN, J. W., The Synoptic Gethsemane (Rome 1973). TAL-
BERT, C. H., Literary Patterns, Theological Themes, and the Genre
of Luke-Acts (Missoula 1974) 26, 28, 33. GLÖCKNER, R., Die
Verkündigung des Heils beim Evangelisten Lukas (Mainz 1975)
174ff. HOWARD, V. P., Das Ego in den Synoptischen Evangelien
(Marburg 1975) 123-32. RADL, W., Paulus und Jesus im lukanischen Doppelwerk (Bern 1975) 166-68. FEUILLET, A., "Le récit lucanien de l'agonie de Gethsémani (Lc xxii. 39-46)" NTS 22
(1976) 397-417. FEUILLET, A., L'agonie de Gethsémani (Paris
1977). SCHNEIDER, G., Das Evangelium nach Lukas (Gütersloh
1977) 457. MEDIAVILLA, R., "La Oraciòn de Jesus en el tercer
evangelio" Mayeutica (1978) 5-34. NEYREY, J. H., "The Ab-
sence of Jesus' Emotions—the Lucan Redaction of Lk 22,39-46"
Biblica 61 (1980) 153-71.

22:39-40 PATSCH, H. Abendmahl und historischer Jesus (1972) 255f.

22:39 SCHNIEWIND, J., Die Parallelperiokopen bei Lukas und Johan-
nes (Darmstadt 1958-1914) 32f. SCHNEIDER, G. Verleugnung,
Verspottung und Vehör Jesu nach Lukas 22,54-71 (1969) 96, 144,
150, 177, 185, 190, 204. DAUER, A. Die Passionsgeschichte im
Johannesevangelium (1972) 22, 24, 26, 53f., 55f. STANTON, G.
N., Jesus of Nazareth in New Testament Preaching (Cambridge
1974) 39, 41ff. TALBERT, C. H., Literary Patterns, Theological
Themes, and the Genre of Luke-Acts (Missoula 1974) 28. BUCK,
E., "The Function of the Pericope 'Jesus before Herod' in the Pas-
sion Narrative of Luke" in: W. Haubeck/M. Bachmann (eds.) Wort
in der Zeit. FS. K. H. Rengstorf (Leiden 1980) 171. JEREMIAS,
J., Die Sprache des Lukasevangeliums (Göttingen 1980) 293.

22:40-46 BOMAN, T. NTS 10 (1963-1964) 261f. BENOIT, P. Passion et
Résurrection du Seigneur (1966) 24-27. BOMAN, T. Die Jesus-
Ueberlieferung im Lichte der neueren Volkskunde (1967) 208-21.
LESCOW, T. "Jesus in Gethsemane bei Lukas und im Hebräer-
brief," ZNW 58 (3-4, 1967) 215-39. KRAFT, H., Die Entstehung
des Christentums (Darmstadt 1981) 200-02. LÉON-DUFOUR, X.,
"Jésus à Gethsémani. Essai de lecture synchronique" SciE 31
(1979) 151-68.

22:40 FARRER, A. St Matthew and St Mark (1954) 166n. SCHNEI-
DER, G. Verleugnung, Verspottung und Verhör Jesu nach Lukas
22,54-71 (1969) 158, 171, 184, 185, 190. SANFORD, J. A., The
Kingdom Within (New York 1970) 136-37. DAUER, A. Die
Passionsgeschichte im Johannesevangelium (1972) 54f. THEI-
SOHN, J., Der auserwählte Richter (Göttingen 1975) 163-64.
PRAST, F., Presbyter und Evangelium in nachapostolischer Zeit

(Stuttgart 1979) 67-68. JEREMIAS, J., Die Sprache des Lukas-evangeliums (Göttingen 1980) 293.

22:41 JEREMIAS, J., Die Sprache des Lukasevangeliums (Göttingen 1980) 294.

22:42-43 RENGSTORF, K. H. Das Evangelium nach Lukas (1949) 243.

22:42.44 O'NEILL, J. C. The Theology of Acts in Its Historical Setting (1970) 42-43, XII.

22:42 HENNECKE, E./SCHNEEMELCHER, W. Neutestamentliche Apokryphen (1964) II 310. NICKELS, P. Targum and New Testament (1967) 48.WILLIAMS, J. A., A Conceptual History of Deuteronomism in the Old Testament, Judaism, and the New Testament (Ph.D. Diss., Louisville 1976) 317. BLAISING, C. A., "Gethsemane: A Prayer of Faith" JEThS (1979) 333-43.

22:43-44 HARNACK, A. von, Studien zur Geschichte des Neuen Testaments und der Alten Kirche (1931) 86ff. BRUN, L., "Engel und Blutschweiss" ZNW 32 (1933) 265. ASCHERMANN, H. "Zum Agoniegebet Jesu, Luk 22,43-44," Theologia Viatorum V (1953-1954) 143-49. FEDERKIEWICZ, P. "Agonia Chrystusa Pana w Ogrojcu. (Uwagi egzegetyczne do Lk. 22,43n.)" RBL 13 (2, 1960) 119-26. TAYLOR, V. The Text of the New Testament (1961) 35f., 93f.ALAND, K. NTS 12 (1965-1966) 199f. SCHNEIDER, G., "Engel und Blutschweiss (Lk 22,43-44). 'Redaktionsgeschichte' im Dienste der Textkritik" BZ 20 (1976) 112-16. METZGER, B. M., The Early Versions of the New Testament (Oxford 1977) 41. LARKIN, W. J., "The Old Testament Background of Luke xxii. 43-44" NTS 25 (1979) 250-54. METZGER, B. M., "St. Jerome's explicit references to variant readings in manuscripts of the New Testament" in: E. Best/R. McL. Wilson (eds.) Text and Interpretation. FS. M. Black (Cambridge 1979) 183. KRAFT, H., Die Entstehung des Christentums (Darmstadt 1981) 153.

22:43 FARRER, A. St Matthew and St. Mark (1954) 166n. RIEDL, J. BuL 41 (1968) 99-100. TALBERT, C. H., Literary Patterns, Theological Themes, and the Genre of Luke-Acts (Missoula 1974) 33.

22:44 OTT, W. Gebet und Heil (1965) 69, 96-98, 99. GAMBA, G. G. "Agonia di Gesu," RivB 16 (2, 1968) 159-66. KLAPPERT, B., "Arbeit Gottes und Mitarbeit des Menschen (Phil 2:6-11)" in: J. Moltmann (ed.) Recht auf Arbeit - Sinn der Arbeit (München 1979) 105. JEREMIAS, J., Die Sprache des Lukasevangeliums (Göttingen 1980) 294.

22:45 PALLIS, A., Notes on St. Luke and the Acts (London 1928) 44. INDEMANS, J. H. H. A. Das Lukasevangelium XXII,45. Symbolae Osloenses (1956) 81-83. WANKE, J., Die Emmauserzählung (Leipzig 1973) 36, 89, A.409. METZGER, B. M., The Early Versions of the New Testament (Oxford 1977) 209.

22:46 FARRER, A. St Matthew and St Mark (1954) 166n. THEISOHN, J., Der auserwählte Richter (Göttingen 1975) 163-64. PRAST, F., Presbyter und Evangelium in nachapostolischer Zeit (Stuttgart 1979) 67-68. JEREMIAS, J., Die Sprache des Lukasevangeliums (Göttingen 1980) 294-95.

22:47-24:12 SCHNEIDER, G., Die Passion Jesu nach den älteren Evangelien (München 1973).

22:47-23:25 RADL, W., Paulus und Jesus im lukanischen Doppelwerk (Bern 1975) 211-21. SCHNIEWIND, J., Die Parallelperikopen bei Lukas und Johannes (Darmstadt (1958 = 1914) 32-37. TALBERT, C. H., Literary Patterns, Theological Themes, and the Genre of Luke-Acts (Missoula 1974) 26, 28, 29. SCHNEIDER, G., Das Evangelium nach Lukas (Gütersloh 1977) 460. BÖHLIG, A., Die Gnosis III: Der Manichäismus (Zürich 1980) 344 n.67.

22:47ff. VÖÖBUS, A. The Prelude to the Lukan Passion Narrative (1968) 60-62.

22:47-53 GOODSPEED, E. J. A Life of Jesus (1950) 205-07. BENOIT, P. Passion et Résurrection du Seigneur (1966) 53-56.

22:47-52 RENGSTORF, K. H. Das Evangelium nach Lukas (1949) 243f.

22:47-48 CRIBBS, F. L. in: SBL Seminar Papers 2 (1973) 55-56. SUGGIT, J. N., "Poetry's Next-door Neighbour" Journal of Theology for Southern Africa (1978) 3-17.

22:47 PALLIS, A. Notes on St. Luke and the Acts (London 1928) 44. DAUER, A. Die Passionsgeschichte im Johannesevangelium (1972) 26, 56f. JEREMIAS, J., Die Sprache des Lukasevangeliums (Göttingen 1980) 295.

22:47a REHKOPF, F. Die lukanische Sonderquelle (1959) 31ff.

22:47b.48 REHKOPF, F. Die lukanische Sonderquelle (1959) 40ff.

22:48 MANSON, T. W. The Teaching of Jesus (1945) 224ff. HAHN, F. Christologische Hoheitstitel (1963) 46. NICKELS, P. Targum and New Testament (1967) 48. GOULDER, M. D. Midrash and Lection in Matthew (1974) 350f. RUPPERT, L., Jesus als der leidende Gerechte? (Stuttgart 1972) 63. SCHNEIDER, G., " 'Der Menschensohn' in der lukanischen Christologie" in: R. Pesch/R. Schnackenburg (eds.) Jesus und der Menschensohn (Freiburg 1975) 271-72.

22:49-54 CRIBBS, F. L. in: SBL Seminar Papers 2 (1973) 57-58.

22:49-51 REHKOPF, F. Die lukanische Sonderquelle (1959) 56ff. HAHN, F. Christologische Hoheitstitel (1963) 168f.

22:49 HAHN, F. Christologische Hoheitstitel (1963) 84, 85, 168. NICK-

ELS, P. Targum and New Testament (1967) 48. JEREMIAS, J., Die Sprache des Lukasevangeliums (Göttingen 1980) 295.

22:50 ROSTOVTZEFF, M. "Οὓς δεξιὸν ἀποτέμνειν," ZNW 33 (1934) 196. NICKELS, P. Targum and New Testament (1967) 48. DAUER, A. Die Passionsgeschichte im Johannesevangelium (1972) 46, 57ff. CRIBBS, F. L. in: SBL Seminar Papers 2 (1973) 4.

22:51 FARRER, A. St Matthew and St Mark (1954) 53, 56, 130n. HAHN, F. Christologische Hoheitstitel (1963) 168. SCHNEIDER, G. Verleugnung, Verspottung und Verhör Jesu nach Lukas 22,54-71 (1969) 22, 74, 118, 192. TALBERT, C. H., Literary Patterns, Theological Themes, and the Genre of Luke-Acts (Missoula 1974) 29. DUNN, J. D. G., Jesus and the Spirit (London 1975) 379. JEREMIAS, J., Die Sprache des Lukasevangeliums (Göttingen 1980) 295.

22:52-53 REHKOPF, F. Die lukanische Sonderquelle (1959) 71ff. DORMEYER, D., Die Passion Jesu als Verhaltensmodell (Münster 1974) 142A, 483.

22:52 NICKELS, P. Targum and New Testament (1967) 48. SCHALIT, A. König Herodes (1969) 721. JEREMIAS, J., Die Sprache des Lukasevangeliums (Göttingen 1980) 296.

22:53b-71 BAILEY, J. A. The Traditions Common to the Gospels of Luke and John (1963) 55-36.

22:53 BORNKAMM-BARTH-HELD, Ueberlieferung und Auslegung im Matthäus-Evangelium (²1961) 112. BRAUN, H. Qumran und NT II (1966) 96f. DAUER, A. Die Passionsgeschichte im Johannesevangelium (1972) 60, 80f. DRURY, J., Tradition and Design in Luke's Gospel (Atlanta 1976) 69.

22:53b TAYLOR, V. Jesus and His Sacrifice (1948) 195-97, 242, 245, 260, 280.

22:54-23:49 WALASKAY, P. W., "The Trial and Death of Jesus in the Gospel of Luke" JBL 94 (1975) 81-93.

22:54-23:25 TYSON, J. B. "The Lukan Version of the Trial of Jesus," NovTest 3, (4, 1959) 249-58.

22:54-23:1 DRURY, J., Tradition and Design in Luke's Gospel (Atlanta 1976) 109-13.

22:54-71 RENGSTORF, K. H. Das Evangelium nach Lukas (1949) 245f. GOODSPEED, E. J. A Life of Jesus (1950) 207-12. SCHNIEWIND, J., Die Parallelperikopen bei Lukas und Johannes (Darmstadt 1958 = 1914) 37-62. SCHNEIDER, G. Verleugnung, Verspottung und Verhör Jesu nach Lukas 22,54-71 (1969). CATCHPOLE, D. R. The Trial of Jesus (1971) 153-220. MOULE, C. F. D. JThS 22 (1, 1971) 194-97. LOHSE, E., Die Einheit des Neuen Testaments (Göttingen 1973) 89-91. HOWARD, V. P., Das

Ego in den Synoptischen Evangelien (Marburg 1975) 132-48. BUCK, E., ''The Function of the Pericope 'Jesus before Herod' in the Passion Narrative of Luke'' in: W. Haubeck/M. Bachmann (eds.) Wort in der Zeit. FS. K. H. Rengstorf (Leiden 1980) 172-73. STROBEL, A., Die Stunde der Wahrheit (Tübingen 1980) 14-21.

22:54-65 HIRSCH, E. Frühgeschichte des Evangeliums (1941) 264-66. SCHNEIDER, G., Das Evangelium nach Lukas (Gütersloh 1977) 464.

22:54-62 BENOIT, P. Passion et Résurrection du Seigneur (1966) 77-80. BROWN, S. Apostasy and Perseverance in the Theology of Luke (1969) 70f. KLEIN, G. ''Die Verleugnung des Petrus'', Rekonstruktion und Interpretation (1969) 49-98. DIETRICH, W. Das Petrusbild der lukanischen Schriften (1972) 139-63. CRIBBS, F. L. in: SBL Seminar Papers 2 (1973) 58-61. DORMEYER, D., Die Passion Jesu als Verhaltensmodell (Münster 1974) 150A, 520.

22:54b-62 LEHMANN, M. Synoptische Quellenanalyse und die Frage nach dem historischen Jesus (1970) 106-12.

22:54b-61 TAYLOR, V. The Formation of the Gospel Tradition (1949) 194f., 197.

22:54 NICKELS, P. Targum and New Testament (1967) 48. DAUER, A. Die Passionsgeschichte im Johannesevangelium (1972) 59, 67, 68, 73, 97, 98. TALBERT, C. H., Literary Patterns, Theological Themes, and the Genre of Luke-Acts (Missoula 1974) 17, 21.

22:55 JEREMIAS, J., Die Sprache des Lukasevangeliums (Göttingen 1980) 296.

22:56 PALLIS, A., Notes on St. Luke and the Acts (London 1928) 45. DÖMER, M., Das Heil Gottes (Köln-Bonn 1978) 89-90.JEREMIAS, J., Die Sprache des Lukasevangeliums (Göttingen 1980) 296.

22:57 METZGER, B. M., The Early Versions of the New Testament (Oxford 1977) 243.

22:58 DAUER, A. Die Passiongeschichte im Johannesevangelium (1972) 77, 88, 97f.

22:59 JEREMIAS, J., Die Sprache des Lukasevangeliums (Göttingen 1980) 297.

22:61 KNOX, W. L. The Sources of the Synoptic Gospels II (1957) 87. HAHN, F. Christologische Hoheitstitel (1963) 88. NICKELS, P. Targum and New Testament (1967) 48. LEHMANN, M. Synoptische Quellenanalyse und die Frage nach dem historischen Jesus (1970) 107, 109f. ZINGG, P., Das Wachsen der Kirche (Freiburg 1974) 70. DRURY, J., Tradition and Design in Luke's Gospel (Atlanta 1976) 70-71. JEREMIAS, J., Die Sprache des Lukasevangeliums (Göttingen 1980) 297-98.

22:62-23:23 CLARK, K. W., "The Theological Relevance of Textual Variation in Current Criticism of the Greek New Testament" in: The Gentile Bias and other Essays (Leiden 1980) 118.

. 22:62 ALAND, K. NTS 12 (1965-1966) 199f.

22:63-71 BLINZLER, J. Der Prozess Jesu (⁴1969) 137-62, 170-73.

22:63-65 BENOIT, P. Passion et Résurrecion du Seigneur (1966) 95-98. CRIBBS, F. L. in: SBL Seminar Papers 2 (1973)61-62.

22:63-64 HOOKER, M. D. Jesus and the Servant (1959) 89-91. MILLER, D. L. "Empaizein: Playing the Mock Game (Luke 22:63-64)," JBL 90 (3,1971) 309-13. TALBERT, C. H., Literary Patterns, Theological Themes, and the Genre of Luke-Acts (Missoula 1974) 27, 22.

22:64 BLACK, M. An Aramaic Approach to the Gospels and Acts (1967) 103f. METZGER, B. M., The Early Versions of the New Testament (Oxford 1977) 421. JEREMIAS, J., Die Sprache des Lukasevangeliums (Göttingen 1980) 298.

22:66-23:25 CONZELMANN, H. Die Mitte der Zeit (1964) 76ff.

22:66-23:1 FLENDER, H. Heil und Geschichte in der Theologie des Lukas (1965) 44-46, 60. FLENDER,H. St. Luke Theologian of Redemptive History (1967) 44ff., 57, 61ff., 98.

22:66ff. BAMMEL, E. The Trial of Jesus (1970) 37, 64f.

22:66-71 HIRSCH, E. Frühgeschichte des Evangeliums (1941) 266-68. BENOIT, P. Passion et Résurrection du Seigneur (1966) 127f. CRIBBS, F. L. in: SBL Seminar Papers 2 (1973) 62-65. TALBERT, C. H., Literary Patterns, Theological Themes, and the Genre of Luke-Acts (Missoula 1974) 97. SCHNEIDER, G., Das Evangelium nach Lukas (Gütersloh 1977) 467. BÖHLIG, A., Die Gnosis III: Der Manichäismus (Zürich 1980) 344 n.68.

22:66b-71 WINTER, P. "Luke xxii 66b-71," StTh 9 (2, 1955) 112-15.

22:66 BOUSSET, W. Die Religion des Judentums im Späthellenistischen Zeitalter (1966 = 1926) 167. JEREMIAS, J., Die Sprache des Lukasevangeliums (Göttingen 1980) 299.

22:67-71 SCHÜTZ, F. Der leidende Christus (1969) 37-39. CRIBBS, F. L. in: SBL Seminar Papers 2 (1973) 66f.

22:67-70 MASSAUX, E. Influence de l'Evangile de saint Matthieu sur la littérature chrétienne avant saint Irénée (1950) 71-73. HAY, D. H. Glory at the Right Hand: Psalm 110 in Early Christianity (1973) 69-70, 115. BUSSE, U., Das Nazareth-Manifest Jesu (Stuttgart 1978) 70. SWIDLER, L., Biblical Affirmations of Woman (Philadelphia 1979) 287.

22:67-68 MOORE, G. F. Judaism II (1946) 335. DERRETT, J. D. M., "Midrash in the New Testament: The Origin of Luke XXII 67-68" StTh 29 (1975) 147-56.

22:67 THEYSSEN, G. W. "Unbelief" in the New Testament (1965) 34ff. JÜNGEL, E. Paulus und Jesus (1966) 223. FLENDER, H. St. Luke Theologian of Redemptive History (1967) 42, 44, 45, 62. NICK-ELS, P. Targum and New Testament (1967) 48.

22:68 PALLIS, A. Notes on St. Luke and the Acts (London 1928) 45. DUPLACY, J. "Une variante méconnue de texte recu: H ΑΠΟ-ΛΥΣΗΤΕ (Lc 22,68)", in: Neutestamentliche Aufsätze (1963), J. Blinzler/O. Kuss/F. Mussner, eds., 42-52. SCHNEIDER, G. Verleugnung, Verspottung und Verhör Jesu nach Lukas 22,54-71 (1969) 116-18.

22:69 STONEHOUSE, N. B. The Witness of Matthew and Mark to Christ (1944) 239, 241. MANSON, T. W. The Teaching of Jesus (1945) 224ff., 266ff. GLASSON, T. F. NTS 7 (1960-1961) 89f. HAHN, F. Christologische Hoheitstitel (1963) 181, 291. HAHN, F. Das Verständnis der Mission im Neuen Testament (²1965) 55. JÜN-GEL, E. Paulus und Jesus (1966) 243. PESCH, R. Die Vision des Stephanus (1966) 14, 15, 18, 20, 22, 23, 31, 33, 34, 45, 53, 56, 62, 66. FLENDER, H. St Luke Theologian of Redemptive History (1967) 45 & n, 62, 98ff., 102. SCHNEIDER, G. Verleugnung, Verspottung und Verhör Jeus nach Lukas 22,54-71 (1969) 118-22. RESE, M. Alttestamentliche Motive in der Christologie des Lukas (1969) 199. JEREMIAS, J. Neutestamentliche Theologie I (1971) 21, 36, 253, 259-63, 272. KRÄNKL, E., Jesus der Knecht Gottes (Regensburg 1972) 149, 155-56, 204, 207. RUPPERT, L., Jesus als der leidende Gerechte? (Stuttgart 1972) 55. ZMIJEWSKI, J., Die Eschatologiereden des Lukas-Evangeliums (Bonn 1972) 238, 245, 248, 249, 255-57, 284, 318, 320, 323, 560. WILSON, S. G., The Gentiles and the Gentile Mission in Luke-Acts (Cambridge 1973) 67, 68, 69, 70, 78, 82, 84, 130. TALBERT, C. H., Literary Patterns, Theological Themes, and the Genre of Luke-Acts (Missoula 1974) 97. MATTILL, A. J., Luke and the Last Things (Dillsboro 1979) 145-50. BÖHLIG, A., Die Gnosis III: Der Manichäismus (Zürich 1980) 344 n.78.

22:70-71 LIGHTFOOT, R. H. History and Interpretation in the Gospels (1934) 169ff. NICKELS, P. Targum and New Testament (1967) 49. SCHNEIDER, G. Verleugnung, Verspottung und Verhör Jesu nach Lukas 22,54-71 (1969) 112-26, 127-32.

22:71 NELLESSEN, E., Zeugnis für Jesus und das Wort (Köln 1976) 58-59. TRITES, A. A., The New Testament Concept of Witness (Cambridge 1977) 128-29.

23 GREENLEE, J. H. Nine Uncial Palimpsests of the Greek New Testament (1968) 82-83.

23:1ff. KNOX, W. L. The Sources of the Synoptic Gospels I (1953) 135ff.

23:1-25 GOODSPEED, E. J. A Life of Jesus (1950) 213-15. SCHNIE-WIND, J., Die Parallelperikopen bei Lukas und Johannes (Darmstadt 1958 = 1914) 62-77. BAILEY, J. A. The Traditions Common to the Gospels of Luke and John (1963) 64-77. BUCK, E., "The Function of the Pericope 'Jesus before Herod' in the Passion Narrative of Luke" in: W. Haubeck/M. Bachmann (eds.) Wort in der Zeit. FS. K. H. Rengstorf (Leiden 1980) 165-78.

23:1-15 HOEHNER, H. W. Herod Antipas (1972) 224-25, 249-50.

23:1-7 RENGSTORF, K. H. Das Evangelium nach Lukas (1949) 251f.

23:1-5 BENOIT, P. Passion et Résurrection du Seigneur (1966) 163f. CRIBBS, F. L. in: SBL Seminar Papers 2 (1973) 66-68. SCHNEIDER, G., Das Evangelium nach Lukas (Gütersloh 1977) 471.

23:1 HIRSCH, E. Frühgeschichte des Evangeliums (1941) 266-68. BLINZLER, J. Der Prozess Jesu (⁴1969) 243-55. SCHNEIDER, G. Verleugnung, Verspottung und Verhör Jesu nach Lukas 22,54-71 (1969) 31, 32, 38, 64, 71, 74, 105, 157, 192. TALBERT, C. H., Literary Patterns, Theological Themes, and the Genre of Luke-Acts (Missoula 1974) 17, 22.

23:2-25 HIRSCH, E. Frühgeschichte des Evangeliums (1941) 268-70. CONZELMANN, H. Die Mitte der Zeit (1964) 78ff.

23:2-7 NICKELS, P. Targum and New Testament (1967) 49.

23:2-5 BAKSIC, A. "Pilatus, Jesus und Barabbas", Biblica 48 (1967) 12-13. BLINZLER, J. Der Prozess Jesu (⁴1969) 284-93. SWIDLER, L., Biblical Affirmations of Woman (Philadelphia 1979) 277. STROBEL, A., Die Stunde der Wahrheit (Tübingen 1980) 95-99.

23:2-3 SANDMEL, S., We Jews and Jesus (New York 1977) 35.

23:2 FARRER, A. St Matthew and St Mark (1954) 141n. DOEVE, J. W. "Jodendom en koningschap bij het begin van onze jaartellig", VoxTheol 32 (3, 1961) 69-83. HAHN, F. Christologische Hoheitstitel (1963) 178, 224. BLINZLER,J. Der Prozess Jesu (⁴1969) 42, 49, 86, 187, 278, 280, 342, 364. DERRETT, J. D. M. Law in the New Testament (1970) 337-38, 337 n.2. HENGEL, M., Was Jesus a Revolutionist? (Philadelphia 1971) 8. JEREMIAS, J. Neutestamentliche Theologie I (1971) 218-20. DAUER, A. Die Passionsgeschichte im Johannesevangelium (1972) 129, 162f. LEISTNER, R., Antijudaismus im Johannesevangelium? (Bern

1974) 120. METZGER, B. M., The Early Versions of the New Testament (Oxford 1977) 329. JEREMIAS, J., Die Sprache des Lukasevangeliums (Göttingen 1980) 300. STROBEL, A. Die Stunde der Wahrheit (Tübingen 1980) 114-15 (cf.86ff).

23:3 RIEDL, J. BuL 41 (1968) 102-04. CRIBBS, F. L. in: SBL Seminar Papers 2 (1973) 4.

23:4 DAUER, A. Die Passionsgeschichte im Johannesevangelium (1972) 105, 115, 122, 123, 156f., 233. TALBERT, C. H., Literary Patterns, Theological Themes, and the Genre of Luke-Acts (Missoula 1974) 17, 22. BÖHLIG, A., Die Gnosis III: Der Manichäismus (Zürich 1980) 344 n.69.JEREMIAS, J., Die Sprache des Lukasevangeliums (Göttingen 1980) 300-01.

23:5 ROBINSON, J. M. Kerygma und historischer Jesus (1960) 146. ROBINSON, W. C., Jr., The Way of the Lord (Diss. Basel 1960) 43-56. ROBINSON, W. C. Der Weg des Herrn (1964) 30ff. NICKELS, P. Targum and New Testament (1967) 49. DAUER, A. Die Passionsgeschichte im Johannesevangelium (1972) 158f. SAMAIN, E., "La Notion de APXH" in: F. Neirynck (ed.) L'Evangile de Luc (Gembloux 1973) 304-05, 307. LEISTNER, R., Antijudaismus im Johannesevangelium? (Bern 1974) 120. ZINGG, P., Das Wachsen der Kirche (Freiburg 1974) 13-14. METZGER, B. M., The Early Versions of the New Testament (Oxford 1977) 326, 329. JEREMIAS, J., Die Sprache des Lukasevangeliums (Göttingen 1980) 301.

23:6-16 STUCKRATH, W. "Die Verschwörung der Macht," in: Die Passiontexte (1967), F. Frey, ed., 219-24. SCHÜTZ, F. Der leidende Christus (1969) 128ff. DORMEYER, D., Die Passion Jesu als Verhaltensmodell (Münster 1974) 178. TALBERT, C. H., Literary Patterns, Theological Themes, and the Genre of Luke-Acts (Missoula 1974) 26, 27.

23:6-12 BENOIT, P. Passion et Résurrection de Seigneur (1966) 163f. BLINZLER, J. Der Prozess Jesu (⁴1969) 125, 284-93. CRIBBS, F. L. in: SBL Seminar Papers 2 (1973) 68-69. TALBERT, C. H., Literary Patterns, Theological Themes, and the Genre of Luke-Acts (Missoula 1974) 17, 22. SCHNEIDER, G., Das Evangelium nach Lukas (Gütersloh 1977) 473. CORBIN, M., "Jesus devant Hérode. Lecture de Luk 23,6-12" Christus 25 (1978) 190-97.

23:6 METZGER, B. M., The Early Versions of the New Testament (Oxford 1977) 243.

23:7 METZGER, B. M., The Early Versions of the New Testament (Oxford 1977) 92. JEREMIAS, J., Die Sprache des Lukasevangeliums (Göttingen 1980) 301.

23:8-12 RENGSTORF, K. H. Das Evangelium nach Lukas (1949) 254. STONEHOUSE, N. B. The Witness of Luke to Christ (1951) 119f.

23:8 GOULDER, M. D. Type and History in Acts (1964) 40f. TALBERT, C. H., Literary Patterns, Theological Themes, and the Genre of Luke-Acts (Missoula 1974) 17, 22, 27. BUCK, E., "The Function of the Pericope 'Jesus before Herod' in the Passion Narrative of Luke" in: W. Haubeck/M. Bachmann (eds.) Wort in der Zeit. FS. K. H. Rengstorf (Leiden 1980) 167-68. JEREMIAS, J., Die Sprache des Lukasevangeliums (Göttingen 1980) 301-02.

23:9 HOOKER, M. D. Jesus and the Servant (1959) 87-89.

23:10-16 CRIBBS, F. L. in: SBL Seminar Papers 2 (1973) 4.

23:10 BOUSSET, W. Die Religion des Judentums im Späthellenistischen Zeitalter (1966 = 1926) 167.

23:11 KNOX, W. L. The Sources of the Synoptic Gospels II (1957) 115. BLINZLER, J. Der Prozess Jesu (⁴1969) 163, 289, 290, 296, 299, 354. METZGER, B. M., The Early Versions of the New Testament (Oxford 1977) 212. BUCK, E., "The Function of the Pericope 'Jesus before Herod' in the Passion Narrative of Luke" in: W. Haubeck/M. Bachmann (eds.) Wort in der Zeit. FS. K. H. Rengstorf (Leiden 1980) 168-69. JEREMIAS, J., Die Sprache des Lukasevangeliums (Göttingen 1980) 302.

23:12 BUCK, E., "The Function of the Pericope 'Jesus before Herod' in the Passion Narrative of Luke" in: W. Haubeck/M. Bachmann (eds.) Wort in der Zeit. FS. K. H. Rengstorf (Leiden 1980) 166-67. JEREMIAS, J., Die Sprache des Lukasevangeliums (Göttingen 1980) 302-03.

23:13-25 RENGSTORF, K. H. Das Evangelium nach Lukas (1949) 256f. BENOIT, P. Passion et Résurrection du Seigneur (1966) 163f. BLINZLER, J. Der Prozess Jesu (⁴1969) 301-17. CRIBBS, F. L. in: SBL Seminar Papers 2, (1973) 69-71. SCHNEIDER, G., Das Evangelium nach Lukas (Gütersloh 1977) 476, 478.

23:13-14 BÖHLIG, A., Die Gnosis III: Der Manichäismus (Zürich 1980) 344 n.69.

23:13 RAU, G. "Das Volk in der lukanischen Passionsgeschichte, eine Konjektur zu Lk 23:13," ZNW 56 (1-2, 1965) 41-51. TALBERT, C. H., Literary Patterns, Theological Themes, and the Genre of Luke-Acts (Missoula 1974) 17, 22.

23:14-22 SHERWIN-WHITE, A. N., Roman Society and Roman Law in the New Testament (Grand Rapids 1978) 27.

23:14-15 DAUER, A. Die Passionsgeschichte im Johannesevangelium (1972) 115, 159f.

23:14 TALBERT, C. H., Literary Patterns, Theological Themes, and the

Genre of Luke-Acts (Missoula 1974) 17, 22. JEREMIAS, J., Die Sprache des Lukasevangeliums (Göttingen 1980) 303.

23:15-16 DORMEYER, D., Die Passion Jesu als Verhaltensmodell (Münster 1974) 98A, 234.

23:15 BAMMEL, E. The Trial of Jesus (1970) 86, 89f. METZGER, B. M., The Early Versions of the New Testament (Oxford 1977) 178.

23:16 BAJSIC, A. "Pilatus, Jesus und Barabbas", Biblica 48 (1967) 13-14. DAUER, A. Die Passionsgeschichte im Johannesevangelium (1972) 124, 126, 160, 233.TALBERT, C. H., Literary Patterns, Theological Themes, and the Genre of Luke-Acts (Missoula 1974) 17, 22.

23:17-23 STROBEL, A., Die Stunde der Wahrheit (Tübingen 1980) 118-31.

23:17 BÖHLIG, A., Die Gnosis III: Der Manichäismus (Zürich 1980) 344 n.69.

23:18-19 DAUER, A. Die Passionsgeschichte im Johannesevangelium (1972) 157f. CRIBBS, F. L. in: SBL Seminar Papers 2 (1973) 71-72.

23:18 TALBERT, C. H., Literary Patterns, Theological Themes, and the Genre of Luke-Acts (Missoula 1974) 18, 22. METZGER, B. M., The Early Versions of the New Testament (Oxford 1977) 202. JEREMIAS, J., Die Sprache des Lukasevangeliums (Göttingen 1980) 303.

23:19-26 WILCKENS,U. Die Missionsreden der Apostelgeschichte (1961) 115, 127-28, 130, 134.

23:20-22 CRIBBS, F. L. in: SBL Seminar Papers 2 (1973) 73.

23:22 EPP, E. J. The Theological Tendency of Codex Bezae Cantabrigiensis in Acts (1966) 126 n. 1f. DAUER, A. Die Passionsgeschichte im Johannesevangelium (1972) 115, 125, 158-60, 233. TALBERT, C. H., Literary Patterns, Theological Themes, and the Genre of Luke-Acts (Missoula 1974) 17, 22.

23:23-25 CRIBBS, F. L. in: SBL Seminar Papers 2 (1973) 74.

23:23 JEREMIAS, J., Die Sprache des Lukasevangeliums (Göttingen 1980) 304.

23:24-25 DAUER, A. Die Passionsgeschichte im Johannesevangelium (1972) 233.STROBEL, A., Die Stunde der Wahrheit (Tübingen 1980) 132-37.

23:24 STROBEL, A., Die Stunde der Wahrheit (Tübingen 1980) 105-06.

23:25-26 BAILEY, J. A. The Traditions Common to the Gospels of Luke and John (1963) 78-84.

23:25 BROER, I. Die Urgemeinde und das Grab Jesu (1972) 55f. WILCKENS, U., Die Missionsreden der Apostelgeschichte (Neukirchen 1974 *(3)*) 128, 129, 131, 135. SHERWIN-WHITE, A. Roman Society and Roman Law in the New Testament (Grand Rapids 1978) 26.

23:26-56 SCHNIEWIND, J., Die Parallelperikopen bei Lukas und Johannes (Darmstadt 1958 = 1914) 77-85.

23:26-49 HIRSCH, E. Frühgeschichte des Evangeliums (1941) 270-73. GOODSPEED, E. J. A Life of Jesus (1950) 216-22. GRUND-MANN, W. Die Geschichte Jesu Christi (1957) 348-50. TAY-LOR, V. "The Narrative of the Crucifixion," NTS 8 (4, 1962) 333-34. CRIBBS, F. L. in: SBL Seminar Papers 2 (1973) 74-75. SCHENK, W., Der Passionsbericht nach Markus (Gütersloh 1974) 86ff. COUSIN, H., Le prophète assassiné (Paris 1976). FLUS-SER, D., "The Crucified One and the Jews" Immanuel 7 (1977) 25-37.

23:26-46 DAUER, A. Die Passionsgeschichte im Johannesevangelium (1972) 165f.

23:26-34 BORNKAMM, G. GPM 6/2 (1951-52) 99-102.

23:26-32 CRIBBS, F. L. in: SBL Seminar Papers 2 (1973) 75. SCHNEI-DER, G., Das Evangelium nach Lukas (Gütersloh 1977) 480. SWIDLER, L., Biblical Affirmations of Woman (Philadelpia 1979) 198, 278.

23:26-24:1 BÖHLIG, A., Die Gnosis III: Der Manichäismus (Zürich 1980) 344 n.72.

23:26 RUPPERT, L., "Das Skandalon eines gekreuzigten Messias und seine Ueberwindung mit Hilfe der geprägten Vorstellung vom leidenden Gerechten" in: Kirche und Bibel. FS. E. Schick (Paderborn 1979) 322-27. JEREMIAS, J., Die Sprache des Lukasevangeliums (Göttingen 1980) 304-05.

23:27ff. KÜMMEL, W. G. Einleitung in das Neue Testament (1973) 108f.

23:27-34a HAMEL, J. GPM 12/2 (1957-58) 102-05.

23:27-32 BUCK. E., "The Function of the Pericope 'Jesus before Herod' in the Passion Narrative of Luke" in: W. Haubeck/M. Bachmann (eds.) Wort in der Zeit. FS. K. H. Rengstorf (Leiden 1980) 173.

23:27-31 ROBINSON, W. C., Jr., The Way of the Lord (Diss. Basel (1960) 91-92. ROBINSON, W. C. Der Weg des Herrn (1964) 56. GAS-TON, L. No Stone on Another (1970) 364-65. KUDASIEWICZ, J., " 'Córki Jerozolimskie, nie placzcie nade mna . . . ' (Lk 23,27-31)" RTK 22 (1975) 39-47. DRURY, J., Tradition and Design in Luke's Gospel (Atlanta 1976) 69. MATTILL, A. J., Luke and the Last Things (Dillsboro 1979) 8.

23:27 BETZ, H. D. Lukian von Samosata und das Neue Testament (1961) 85, 125.

23:28-31 JEWETT, R., Jesus against the Rapture (Philadelphia 1979) 105-21.

23:28 KNOX, W. L. The Sources of the Synoptic Gospels II (1957) 87. NICKELS, P. Targum and New Testament (1967) 49. JEREMIAS, J., Die Sprache des Lukasevangeliums (Göttingen 1980) 305.

23:29 SCHRAGE, W. Das Verhältnis des Thomas-Evangeliums zur Synoptischen Tradition und zu den Koptischen Evangelienübersetzungen (1964) 164. RINALDI, B. "Beate le sterile (Lc. 23,29), Riflessioni sull'ottava stazione della Via Crucis," BiOr 15 (2, 1973) 61-64. KLIJN, A. F. J., "Die syrische Baruch-Apokalypse" in: W. G. Kümmel (ed.) Jüdische Schriften aus hellenistisch-römischer Zeit. V. (Gütersloh 1976) 129 n.14a. JEREMIAS, J., Die Sprache des Lukasevangeliums (Göttingen 1980) 305.

23:29b KAESER, W. "Exegetische und theologische Erwägungen zur Seligpreisung der Kinderlosen Lc 23:29b," ZNW 54 (3-4, 1963) 240-54.

23:30 HOLTZ, T. Untersuchungen über die Alttestamentlichen Zitate bei Lukas (1968) 27-29.

23:31 FARRER, A. St Matthew and St Mark (1954) 140n. SMITH, M. Tannaitic Parallels to the Gospels (1968) 4 b n 1. DELLING, G. Studien zum Neuen Testament und zum hellenistischen Judentum (1970) 251-54. JEREMIAS, J. Neutestamentliche Theologie I (1971) 20f., 35, 270. MATTILL, A. J., Luke and the Last Things (Dillsboro 1979) 220-22.

23:32-56 SMALLEY, W. A., "Translating Luke's Passion Story from the TEV" BTr 28 (1977) 231-35.

23:32 METZGER, B. M., The Early Versions of the New Testament (Oxford 1977) 326. JEREMIAS, J., Die Sprache des Lukasevangeliums (Göttingen 1980) 305.

23:33ff. GERSTENBERGER, G. und SCHRAGE, W., Leiden (Stuttgart 1977) 161; ET: J. E. Steeley, Suffering (Nasvhille 1980) 187.

23:33-49 CONZELMANN, H. Die Mitte der Zeit (1964) 81ff. KARABIDOPOULOS, I. D. "To pathos tou doulou tou Theou epi tou staurou kata tēn diēgēsin tou euangelistou Louka (23,33-49)" DBM 1 (3,1972) 189-211. DRURY, J., Tradition and Design in Luke's Gospel (Atlanta 1976) 113-19. WOLF, B. und KÖPPEN, W., in: P. Krusche et al. (eds.) Predigtstudien für das Kirchenjahr 1980-1981. I (Stuttgart 1980) 186-97. HINZ, C., in: GPM 35 (1981) 194-204.

23:33-48 DOERNE, M. Er kommt auch noch heute (1961) 69-73. Glaubet an den Gottgesandten, Predigtgedanken aus Vergangenheit und Gegenwart, Reihe C, Bd. 2 (1962) 120-48. DINKLER, E. GPM 17

(1, 1963) 161-67. SEITZ, M. GPM 23 (1968-1969) 156-63. GROO, G., in: GPM 29 (1975) 190-96.

23:33-43 SCHNEIDER, G., Das Evangelium nach Lukas (Gütersloh 1977) 482.

23:33-39 RUPPERT, L., "Das Skandalon eines gekreuzigten Messias und seine Ueberwindung mit Hilfe der geprägten Vorstellung vom leidenden Gerechten" in: Kirche und Bible, FS. E. Schick (Paderborn 1979) 322-27.

23:33-34 HARNACK, A. von. Studien zur Geschichte des Neuen Testaments und der Alten Kirche (1931) 91ff. SWIDLER, L., Biblical Affirmations of Woman (Philadelphia 1979) 286.

23:33 RENGSTORF, K. H. Das Evangelium nach Lukas (1949) 260. NICKELS, P. Targum and New Testament (1967) 49. DAUER, A. Die Passionsgeschichte im Johannesevangelium (1972) 165, 204, 296. CRIBBS, F. L. in: SBL Seminar Papers 2 (1973) 76-77.

23:34f., 39 HENNECKE, E./SCHNEEMELCHER, W. Neutestamentliche Apokryphen (1964) I 88, 340.

23:34 TAYLOR, V. Jesus and His Sacrifice (1948) 114, 194, 197-99. DAUBE, D. "For they know not what they do": Luke 23,34, in: Studia Patristica IV (1961), F. L. Cross ed., 58-69. TAYLOR, V. The Text of the New Testament (1961) 94f. HAHN, F. Christologische Hoheitstitel (1963) 322. BEYSCHLAG, K. Clemens Romanus und der Frühkatholizismus (1966) 318. STROBEL, A. Erkenntnis und Bekenntnis der Sünde in neutestamentlicher Zeit (1968) 60. SCHNEIDER, G. Verleugnung, Verspottung und Verhör Jesu nach Lukas 22,54-71 (1969) 53, 74, 92, 186, 190. JEREMIAS, J. Neutestamentliche Theologie I (1971) 68, 70, 161, 182, 185, 272f., 283. RUPPERT, L., Jesus als der leidende Gerechte? (Stuttgart 1972) 50a31. TALBERT, C. H., Literary Patterns, Theological Themes, and the Genre of Luke-Acts (Missoula 1974) 97. METZGER, B. M., The Early Versions of the New Testament (Oxford 1977) 41. "Agrapha" in: TRE 2 (1978) 104. MEDIAVILLA, R., "La Oraciòn de Jesus en el tercer evangelio" Mayeutica (1978) 5-34. SABOURIN, L., "As Sete Palavras de Jesus na Cruz" RCB 74 (1978) 299-303. JEREMIAS, J., Die Sprache des Lukasevangeliums (Göttingen 1980) 306.

23:34a DAMMERS, A. H. "Studies in Texts, Luke xxiii, 34a," Theology LII (346, 1949) 138f.

23:35-43 CRIBBS, F. L. in: SBL Seminar Papers 2 (1973) 77-78. TRILLING, W., "Le Christ, roi crucifié. Lc 23,35-43" AssS 65 (1973) 56-65.

23:35-39 DAUER, A. Die Passionsgeschichte im Johannesevangelium (1972) 200, 224.

23:35 VOLZ, P. Die Eschatologie der jüdischen Gemeinde (1934) 187.
MASSAUX, E. Influence de l'Evangile de saint Matthieu sur la littérature chrétienne avant saint Irénée (1950) 71-73. KNOX, W. L.
The Sources of the Synoptic Gospels II (1957) 96. WILCKENS,
U. Die Missionsreden der Apostelgeschichte (1961) 132f. HAHN,
F. Christologische Hoheitstitel (1963) 224. SMITH, M. Tannaitic
Parallels to the Gospels (1968) 6 b n 5. SCHNEIDER, G. Verleugnung, Verspottung und Verhör Jesu nach Lukas 22,54-71 (1969)
99, 112, 146, 161, 185, 186, 190, 193, 195, 196. DAUER, A. Die
Passionsgeschichte im Johannesevangelium (1972) 177, 204, 296.
SANDMEL, S., We Jews and Jesus (New York 1977) 49. DÖMER,
M., Das Heil Gottes (Köln-Bonn 1978) 44. JEREMIAS, J., Die
Sprache des Lukasevangeliums (Göttingen 1980) 306.

23:36 DAUER, A. Die Passionsgeschichte im Johannesevangelium (1972)
204, 208, 224f., 296, 298. RUPPERT, L., Jesus als der leidende
Gerechte? (Stuttgart 1972) 51. MÜLLER, U. B., "Die griechische
Esra-Apokalypse" in: W. G. Kümmel (ed.) Jüdische Schriften aus
hellenistisch-römischer Zeit. V (Gütersloh 1976) 93 n.25a.

23:37 SCHNEIDER, G. Verleugnung, Verspottung und Verhör Jesu nach
Lukas 22,54-71 (1969) 113, 186, 190, 196. GLÖCKNER, R., Die
Verkündigung des Heils beim Evangelisten Lukas (Mainz 1975)
147, 171ff., 193.

23:38 METZGER, B. M., The Early Versions of the New Testament
(Oxford 1977) 40. SANDMEL, S., We Jews and Jesus (New York
1977) 35.

23:39ff. STAEHELIN, E. Die Verkündigung des Reiches Gottes in der
Kirche Jesus Christi I (1951) 69. STROBEL, A. Erkenntnis und Bekenntnis der Sünde in neutestamentlicher Zeit (1968) 42. GERSTENBERGER, G. und SCHRAGE, W., Leiden (Stuttgart 1977)
180; ET: J. E. Steeley, Suffering (Nashville 1980) 208.

23:39-48 MOHN, W. "Stellungnahmen zum Kreuz!," in: Die Passionstexte
(1967), F. Frey, ed., 232-37.

23:39-46 IWAND, H.-J. in: Herr, tue meine Lippen auf Bd. 3 (1964) G.
Eichholz, ed., 185ff.

23:39-43 OTTO, G. Denken-um zu glauben (1970) 30-34. TALBERT, C.
H., Literary Patterns, Theological Themes, and the Genre of Luke-Acts (Missoula 1974) 97. SMITH, R. H., "Paradise Today: Luke's
Passion Narrative" CuThM 3 (1976) 323-36.

23:39-41 MASSAUX, E. Influence de l'Evangile de saint Matthieu sur la littérature chrétienne avant saint Irénée (1950) 377-79.

23:39 SCHNEIDER, G. Verleugnung, Verspottung und Verhör Jesu nach
Lukas 22,54-71 (1969) 185, 186, 190, 192, 196. JEREMIAS, J.,
Die Sprache des Lukasevangeliums (Göttingen 1980) 306-07.

23:40ff. STAEHELIN, E. Die Verkündigung des Reiches Gottes in der Kirche Jesu Christi I (1951) 310.

23:40-43 DAUER, A. Die Passionsgeschichte im Johannesevangelium (1972) 224.

23:40 PALLIS, A., Notes on St. Luke and the Acts (London 1928) 45-46. STONEHOUSE, N. B. The Witness of Matthew and Mark to Christ (1944) 107.

23:41 EPP, E. J. The Theological Tendency of Codex Bezae Cantabrigiensis in Acts (1966) 44f. STROBEL, A. Erkenntnis und Bekenntnis der Sünde in neutestamentlicher Zeit (1968) 41. TALBERT, C. H., Literary Patterns, Theological Themes, and the Genre of Luke-Acts (Missoula 1974) 97. RICE, G. E., ''The anti-Judaic Bias of the Western Text in the Gospel of Luke'' AUSS 18 (1980) 52-53.

23:42-43 BIEDER, W. Die Vorstellung von der Höllenfahrt Jesu Christ (1949) 57f. STAEHELIN, E. Die Verkündigung des Reiches Gottes in der Kirche Jesu Christi I (1951) 283. HANHART, K. The Intermediate State in the New Testament (1966) 199-215.

23:42 WULF, F. '' 'Jesus, gedenke meiner, wenn du in dein Königtum kommst' (Lk 23,42),'' GuL 37 (1, 1964) 1-3. STROBEL, A. Erkenntnis und Bekenntnis der Sünde in neutestamentlicher Zeit (1968) 42.

23:43-53 HENNECKE, E./SCHNEEMELCHER, W. Neutestamentliche Apokryphen (1964) I 88, 341, 352.

23:43 VOLZ, P. Die Eschatologie der jüdischen Gemeinde (1934) 265, 269, 271, 408, 416. MOORE, G. F. Judaism II (1946) 391n. RENGSTORF, K. H. Das Evangelium nach Lukas (1949) 262f. STAEHELIN, E. Die Verkündigung des Reiches Gottes in der Kirche Jesu Christi I (1951) 24, 187, 298. MacRAE, G. W. ''With Me in Paradise,'' Worship 35 (4, 1961) 235-40. HAHN, F. Christologische Hoheitstitel (1963) 130. ELLIS, E. E. NTS 12 (1965-1966) 35f. BOUSSET, W. Die Religion des Judentums im Späthellenistischen Zeitalter (1966 = 1926) 294. HOFFMANN, P. Die Toten in Christus (1966) 318. GRELOT, P., '' 'Aujourd' hui tu seras avec moi dans le Paradis' (Luc, XXIII, 43),'' RevBi 74 (2, 1967) 194-214. HAUBST, R. ''Eschatologie. 'Der Wetterwinkel' - 'Theologie der Hoffnung','' TThZ 77 (1968) 35-65.; RIEDL, J. BuL 41 (1968) 104-06. STROBEL, A. Erkenntnis und Bekenntnis der Sünde in neutestamentlicher Zeit (1968) 60. BERGER, K. Die Amen-Worte Jesus (1970) 88-89. NÖTSCHER, F., Altorientalischer und alttestamentlicher Auferstehungsglaube (Darmstadt 1970 = 1926) 313. DUPONT, J., ''Die individuelle Eschatologie im Lukas-Evangelium und in der Apostelgeschichte'' in: P. Hoffmann (ed.) Orientierung an Jesus. FS. J. Schmid (Freiburg 1973) 44-46, 50. ELLIS, E. E., "La Fonction de L'Eschatologie dans Luc" in: F. Neirynck (ed.) L'Evangile de Luc (Gembloux 1973) 149-51. DRURY, J., Tradition and Design in Luke's Gospel (Atlanta 1976) 70-71. DE LA CALLE, F., " 'Hoy estarás conmigo en el Paraíso.' Visión inmediata de Dios o purificación en el 'más allá'?" Biblia y Fe (1977) 276-89. FISCHER, U., Eschatologie und Jenseitserwartung im hellenistischen Diasporajudentum (Berlin 1978) 260. SABOURIN, L., "As Sete Palavras de Jesu na Cruz" RCB 14 (1978) 299-303. MATTILL, A. J., Luke and the Last Things (Dillsboro 1979) 33-34, 40. JEREMIAS, J., Die Sprache des Lukasevangeliums (Göttingen 1980) 307.

23:44ff. STAEHELIN, E. Die Verkündigung des Reiches Gottes in der Kirche Jesu Christi I (1951) 309.

23:44-49 SCHNEIDER, G., Das Evangelium nach Lukas (Gütersloh 1977) 486.

23:44-48 SCHNEIDER, G., "Die theologische Sicht des Todes Jesu in den Kreuzigungsberichten der Evangelien" TPQ 126 (1978) 14-22.

23:44-45 SAWYER, J. F. A. "Why is a Solar Eclipse Mentioned in the Passion Narrative (Luke xxiii. 44-5)?" JThS 23 (1, 1972) 124-28.

23:44 BÖHLIG, A., Die Gnosis III: Der Manichäismus (Zürich 1980) 344 n.71.

23:45 METZGER, B. M. "Explicit references in the works of Origen to variant readings in New Testament manuscripts", in: Historical and Literary Studies (1968) 95f. BÖHLIG, A., Die Gnosis III: Der Manichäismus (Zürich 1980) 344 n.75, 76. SCHRECKENBERG, H., "Flavius Josephus und die lukanischen Schriften" in: W. Haubeck/M. Bachmann (eds.) Wort in der Zeit. FS. K. H. Rengstorf (Leiden 1980) 192-93.

23:46.48 BETZ, H. D. Lukian von Samosata und das Neue Testament (1961) 71f., 122. GESE, H., Vom Sinai zum Zion (München 1974) 194-95.

23:46 BLIGH, J. "Christ's Death Cry," HeyJ 1 (2, 1960) 142-46. BARDA, Tj. "A Syriac Fragment of Mar Ephraem's Commentary on the Diatessaron," NTS 8 (1961-1962) 290f. KOEBERT, R. "Neues aus Vat. Borg. Syr. 82," Biblica 44 (1963) 124-25. HAHN, F. Christologische Hoheitstitel (1963) 130, 322. DALTON, W. J., Christ's Proclamation to the Spirits (Rome 1965) 146-47. ABRAMOWSKI, L./GOODMAN, A. E. "Luke xxiii. 46 paratithemai in a Rare Syriac Rendering," NTS 13 (3, 1967) 290-91. BOMAN, T. Die Jesus-Ueberlieferung im Lichte der neueren Volkskunde (1967) 221-36. HOLTZ, T. Untersuchungen über die Alttestamentlichen Zitate bei Lukas (1968) 58f. RESE, M. Alttestamentliche Motive in der Christologie des Lukas (1969) 200-02. JEREMIAS, J. Neutestamentliche Theologie I (1971) 68, 70, 182, 199. DAUER, A. Die Passionsgeschichte im Johannesevangelium (1972) 210, 215, 296. DELLING, G. Der Kreuzestod Jesu in der urchristlichen Verkündigung (1972) 80-82. RUPPERT, L., Jesus als der leidende Gerechte? (Stuttgart 1972) 46a15., 51, 58. TALBERT, C. H., Literary Patterns, Theological Themes, and the Genre of Luke-Acts (Missoula 1974) 97. GERSTENBERGER, G. und SCHRAGE, W., Leiden (Stuttgart 1977) 150-51; ET: J. E. Steeley, Suffering (Nashville 1980) 174-75. MEDIAVILLA, R., "La Oraciòn de Jesus en el tercer evangelio" Mayeutica (1978) 5-34. RUDOLPH, K., Die Gnosis (Göttingen 1978) 160. SABOURIN, L., "As Sete Palavras de Jesus na Cruz" RCB 14 (1978) 299-303. FARICY, R., Praying for Inner Healing (London 1979) 37. JEREMIAS, J., Die Sprache des Lukasevangeliums (Göttingen 1980) 307.

23:47 SCHELKLE, K. H. Die Passion Jesu in der Verkündigung des Neuen Testaments (1949) 115f. HAHN, F. Christologische Hoheitstitel (1963) 384. RIEDL, J. BuL 41 (1968) 106-07. SCHNEIDER, G. Verleugnung, Verspottung und Verhör Jesu nach Lukas 22,54-71 (1969) 88, 112, 171, 181, 195. RUPPERT, L., Jesus als der leidende Gerechte? (Stuttgart 1972) 13, 48, 57, 58. TALBERT, C. H., Literary Patterns, Theological Themes, and the Genre of Luke-Acts (Missoula 1974) 18, 22. GLÖCKNER, R., Die Verkündigung des Heils beim Evangelisten Lukas (Mainz 1975) 187-88, 190, 194. SWIDLER, L., Biblical Affirmations of Woman (Philadelphia 1979) 285. JEREMIAS, J., Die Sprache des Lukasevangeliums (Göttingen 1980) 308.

23:48 STROBEL, A. Erkenntnis und Bekenntnis der Sünde in neutestamentlicher Zeit (1968) 42. RUPPERT, L., Jesus als der leidende Gerechte? (Stuttgart 1972) 58. METZGER, B. M., The Early Versions of the New Testament (Oxford 1977) 326. JEREMIAS, J., Die Sprache des Lukasevangeliums (Göttingen 1980) 308-09.

23:49-24:53 PERRIN, N., The Resurrection According to Matthew, Mark and Luke (Philadelphia 1977).

23:49 SCHNEIDER, G. Verleugnung, Verspottung und Verhör Jesu nach Lukas 22,54-71 (1969) 71, 76, 95, 122, 192, 204. DAUER, A. Die Passionsgeschichte im Johannesevangelium (1972) 54, 192, 198, 199, 234, 296, 316. RUPPERT, L., Jesus als der leidende Gerechte? (Stuttgart 1972) 58. WANKE, J. Die Emmauserzählung (Leipzig 1973) 115. TALBERT, C. H., Literary Patterns, Theological Themes, and the Genre of Luke-Acts (Missoula 1974) 114. METZGER, B. M., The Early Versions of the New Testament (Oxford 1977) 11, 12. SWIDLER, L., Biblical Affirmations of

Woman (Philadelphia 1979) 199, 221, 234, 279. JEREMIAS, J., Die Sprache des Lukasevangeliums (Göttingen 1980) 309.

23:50-24:53 MARSHALL, I. H., "The Resurrection of Jesus in Luke" Tyndale Bulletin 24 (1973) 55-98.

23:50-24:11 HIRSCH, E. Frühgeschichte des Evangeliums (1941) 274-78.

23:50ff. HARTMAN, L. Testimonium Linguae (1963) 15ff., 27.

23:50-56 BENOIT, P. Passion et Résurrection du Seigneur (1966) 247f. BLINZLER, J. Der Prozess Jesu (⁴1969) 385-404. BROER, I. Die Urgemeinde und das Grab Jesu (1972) 44-59. CRIBBS, F. L. in: SBL Seminar Papers 2 (1973) 79-81. MAHONEY, R., Two Disciples at the Tomb (Bern 1974) 118-21. SCHNEIDER, G. Das Evangelium nach Lukas (Gütersloh 1977) 488. SWIDLER, L., Biblical Affirmations of Woman (Philadelphia 1979) 200.

23:50 ZIESLER, J. A. The Meaning of Righteousness in Paul (1972) 138f., 145. ADINOLFI, M., "La giustizia nel terzo vangelo" RivB 27 (1979) 233-60. JEREMIAS, J., Die Sprache des Lukasevangeliums (Göttingen 1980) 309.

23:51 STONEHOUSE, N. B. The Witness of Matthew and Mark to Christ (1944) 229. McNAMARA, M. The New Testament and the Palestinian Targum to the Pentateuch (1966) 241. NICKELS, P. Targum and New Testament (1967) 49. SCHNEIDER, G. Verleugnung, Verspottung und Verhör Jesu nach Lukas 22,54-71 (1969) 69, 195, 214, 220. METZGER, B. M., The Early Versions of the New Testament (Oxford 1977) 11.

23:53 BLASS, F. Philosophy of the Gospels (1898) 185ff. DALMAN, G. Orte und Wege Jesu (1967) 395f. CRIBBS, F. L. in: SBL Seminar Papers 2 (1973) 4. CHARBEL, A., "A Sepultura de Jesus como Resulta dos Evangelhos" RCB 14 (1978) 351-62.

23:54 BLACK, M. An Aramaic Approach to the Gospels and Acts (1967) 136f. METZGER, B. M., The Early Versions of the New Testament (Oxford 1977) 11.

23:55-56 SWIDLER, L. Biblical Affirmations of Woman (Philadelphia 1979) 234, 261.

23:55 NICKELS, P. Targum and New Testament (1967) 50. SMITH, M. Clement of Alexandria and a Secret Gospel of Mark (1973) 120, 189f. WANKE, J., Die Emmauserzählung (Leipzig 1973) 74. TALBERT, C. H., Literary Patterns, Theological Themes, and the Genre of Luke-Acts (Missoula 1974) 113, 114. JEREMIAS, J., Die Sprache des Lukasevangeliums (Göttingen 1980) 310.

23:56-24:53 BARTSCH, H. W., Wachet aber zu jeder Zeit! (Hamburg-Bergstedt 1963) 16-28.

23:56 WANKE, J., Die Emmauserzählung (Leipzig 1973) 73.

24 LUCE, H. K. The Gospel According to S. Luke (1949) 365-67. RENGSTORF, K. H. Das Evangelium nach Lukas (1949) 276. STONEHOUSE, N. B. The Witness of Luke to Christ (1951) 142ff. CREED, J. M. The Gospel According to St. Luke (1953) 314-18. SCHUBERT, P. "The Structure and Significance of Luke 24", in: Neutestamentliche Studien für Rudolf Bultmann (1954) 165-86. BRAENDLE, M. "Auferstehung Jesu nach Lukas," Orientierung 24 (1, 1960) 85-89. LOHSE, E. Die Auferstehung Jesu Christi im Zeugnis des Lukasevangeliums (1961). BAILEY, J. A. The Traditions Common to the Gospels of Luke and John (1963) 85-102. HAHN, F. Christologische Hoheitstitel (1963) 123. GOULDER, M. D. Type and History in Acts (1964) 10, 16, 61, 72, 74. HEB-BLETHWAITE, P. "Theological Themes in the Lucan Post-Resurrection Narratives," ClR 50, (5, 1965) 360-69. GREENLEE, J. H. Nine Uncial Palimpsests of the Greek New Testament (1968) 84-85. NEIRYNCK, F. "Les Femmes au Tomneau: Etude de la Rédactions Matthéene (Matt. XXVIII. 1-10)," NTS 15 (1968-1969) 168ff. CURTIS, K. P. G. "Linguistic Support for Three Western Readings in Luke 24," ET 83 (11, 1972) 344-45. KÜMMEL, W. G. Einleitung in das Neue Testament (1973) 126f. SCHNIEWIND, J., Die Parallelperikopen bei Lukas und Johannes (Darmstadt 1958 = 1914) 85-95. FENS, K., "Lesen in Luk 24" Heiligland 19 (1966) 130-32. DAVIES, W. D., The Gospel and the Land (London 1974) 255 n.40, 265 n.64, 429, 430. LEON-DUFOUR, X., The Resurrection and the Message of Easter (London 1974) 150-68. TALBERT, C. H., Literary Patterns, Theological Themes, and the Genre of Luke-Acts (Missoula 1974) 18, 22, 58-61, 120, 142, 143. DRURY, J., Tradition and Design in Luke's Gospel (Atlanta 1976) 127-28. MINEAR, P., To Heal and to Reveal (New York 1976) 131ff. KREMER, J., Die Osterevangelien (Stuttgart 1977). SCHNEIDER, G., Das Evangelium nach Lukas (Gütersloh 1977) 492. DILLON, R. J., From Eye-Witness to Ministers of the Word (Rome 1978). DÖMER, M., Das Heil Gottes (Köln-Bonn 1978) 90-92. FRIEDRICH, G., "Lukas 9,51 und die Entrückungschristologie des Lukas" in: Auf das Wort kommt es an (Göttingen 1978) 33-34. MEYNET, R., "Comment établir un chiasme. À propos des 'pèlerins d'Emmaüs' " NRTh 100 (1978) 233-49.

24:1ff. RENGSTORF, K. H. Die Auferstehung Jesu (1960) Passim. GRASS, H. Ostergeschehen und Osterberichte (1970) 32ff., 145.

24:1-53 ROLOFF, J. Apostolat-Verkündigung-Kirche (1965) 188-93. CRIBBS, F. L. in: SBL Seminar Papers 2 (1973) 81-82.

24:1-52 KUDASIEWICZ, J., "Jeruzalem-miejscem ukazywań sie zmartwychwstalego Chrystusa (Lk 24,1-52)" RoczTeolKan 21 (1974) 51-60.

24:1-49 GLÖCKNER, R., Die Verkündigung des Heils beim Evangelisten Lukas (Mainz 1975) 57ff., 205ff., 219. MATTILL, A. J., Luke and the Last Things (Dillsboro 1979) 59-60.

24:1-12 LOHSE, E. Die Auferstehung Jesu Christi im Zeugnis des Lukas-Evangeliums (1961) 16-22. FISCHER, M. GPM 19 (1, 1965) 157-68. SCHMIEDEHAUSEN, H. "Sein Opfer hat Sinn", in: Kleine Predigt-Typologie III (1965), L. Schmidt, ed., 286-91. STENDAHL, K., The Bible and the Role of Women (Philadelphia 1966) 25. FALKENROTH, A. in: Hören und Fragen Bd. 5,3 (1967) G. Eichholz/A. Falkenroth, eds. 247ff. KAMPHAUS, F. Von der Exegese zur Predigt (^{2}1968) 35-36. KREMER, J. Die Osterbotschaft der vier Evangelien (1968) 54-60, 143. BODE, E. L. The First Easter Morning (1970) 7-10, 59-71. KLEIN, G. GPM 25 (1971) 181-97. LANGE, E. ed., Predigtstudien für das Kirchenjahr 1970-1971 (1970) 36-44. ALSUP, J. E., The Post-Resurrection Appearance Stories of the Gospel-Tradition (Stuttgart 1975) 114ff. LUZ, U. and WINTZER, F., in: P. Krusche et al. (eds.) Predigtstudien für das Kirchenjahr 1976-1977. II (Stuttgart 1977) 9-17. SCHNEIDER, G., Das Evangelium nach Lukas (Gütersloh 1977) 492. WALTER, N., in: GPM (1976-1977) 179-85. DÖMER, M., Das Heil Gottes (Köln-Bonn 1978) 95. Stagg, E. and F., Woman in the World of Jesus (Philadelphia 1978) 144-60, 222. "Auferstehung" in: TRE 4 (1979) 503. SCHILLEBEECKX, E., Jesus: An Experiment in Christology (London 1979) 340-44. SWIDLER, L., Biblical Affirmations of Woman (Philadelphia 1979) 202.

24:1-11 HIRSCH, E. Frühgeschichte des Evangeliums (1941) 274-78. IWAND, H.-J. Predigt-Meditationen (1964) 67-71. SEIDENSTICKER, Ph. Die Auferstehung Jesu in der Botschaft der Evangelisten (1968) 92ff. BROWN, S. Apostasy and Perseverance in the Theology of Luke (1969) 74f. GUTBROD, K. Die Auferstehung Jesu im Neuen Testament (1969) 61f. SCHNIDER, F./ STENGER, W. Die Ostergeschichten der Evangelien (1969) 55-67. MARXSEN, W. The Resurrection of Jesus of Nazareth (1970) 49-51. CRIBBS, F. L. in: SBL Seminar Papers 2 (1973) 82-85. WANKE, J., Die Emmauserzählung (Leipzig 1973) 13-14, 69, 73-76, A.158. MAHONEY, R., Two Disciples at the Tomb (Bern 1974) 165-70, 194-202, 225-26, 303-06. TALBERT, C. H., Literary Patterns, Theological Themes, and the Genre of Luke-Acts (Missoula 1974) 22, 139. BARTLETT, D. L., Fact and Faith (Valley Forge 1975) 112-13. COUSIN, H., Le prophète assassiné (Paris 1976). GOULDER, M. D., "Mark xvi. 1-8 and Parallels" NTS 24

(1977-1978) 235-40. SWIDLER, L., Biblical Affirmations of Woman (Philadelphia 1979) 279.

24:1-9 HUBBARD, B. J., "The Role of Commissioning Accounts in Acts" in: C. H. Talbert (ed.) Perspectives on Luke-Acts (Danville 1978) 190.

24:1-8 SWIDLER, L., Biblical Affirmations of Woman (Philadelphia 1979) 221, 234.

24:1-6 BOHREN, R., Predigtlehre (München 1971) 246.

24:1-2 MAHONEY, R., Two Disciples at the Tomb (Bern 1974) 202-12.

24:1 NICKELS, P. Targum and New Testament (1967) 50. MOULE, C. F. D. ed., The Significance of the Message of the Resurrection for Faith in Jesus Christ (1968) 80, 83. BODE, E. L. The First Easter Morning (1970) 14-16.

24:2 HAHN, F. Christologische Hoheitstitel (1963) 123.

24:3 ALAND, K. NTS 12 (1965-1966) 199f. TALBERT, C. H. NTS 14 (1967-1968) 262f. SCHNEIDER, G. Verleugnung, Verspottung und Verhör Jesu nach Lukas 22,54-71 (1969) 74, 92, 155, 191. BODE, E. L. The First Easter Morning (1970) 68-69. DESCAMPS, A./DE HALLEUX, A. Mélanges Bibliques en hommage au R. P. Béda Rigaux (1970) 121-23, 146. FRIEDRICH, G., "Lk 9,51 und die Entrückungschristologie des Lukas" in: P. Hoffmann (ed.) Orientierung an Jesus. FS. J. Schmid (Freiburg 1973) 55-56, 57. MAHONEY, R., Two Disciples at the Tomb (Bern 1974) 46-49, 67-69. TALBERT, C. H., Literary Patterns, Theological Themes, and the Genre of Luke-Acts (Missoula 1974) 113, 114.

24:4-9 LOHFINK, G. Die Himmelfahrt Jesu (1971) 196-98.

24:4 HAHN, F. Christologische Hoheitstitel (1963) 88, 403. NICKELS, P. Targum and New Testament (1967) 50. BODE, E. L. The First Easter Morning (1970) 59-61, 165-71. CRIBBS, F. L. in: SBL Seminar Papers 2 (1973) 4. NEIRYNCK, R., "La Matière Marcienne dans Luc" in: F. Neirynck (ed.) L'Evangile de Luc (Gembloux 1973) 184-93. WANKE, J., Die Emmasuerzählung (Leipzig 1973) 83-84. JEREMIAS, J., Die Sprache des Lukasevangeliums (Göttingen 1980) 310-11.

24:5ff. WANKE, J., Die Emmauserzählung (Leipzig 1973) 12.

24:5-7 PRETE, B. "L'annunzio dell'evento pasquale nella formulazione di Luca 24,5-7," SaDo 16 (63-64, 1971) 485-523.

24:5-6 JÜNGEL, E. Paulus und Jesus (1966) 282.

24:5 NICKELS, P. Targum and New Testament (1967) 50. BODE, E. L. The First Easter Morning (1970) 61-62, 166-67. JEREMIAS, J., Die Sprache des Lukasevangeliums (Göttingen 1980) 311.

24:6-7 LIGHTFOOT, R. H. Locality and Doctrine in the Gospels (1938)

80ff.WANKE,J., Die Emmauserzählung (Leipzig 1973) 47, 73, 90. DRURY, J., Tradition and Design in Luke's Gospel (Atlanta 1976) 69.

24:6 ALAND, K. NTS 12 (1965-1966) 196f. ODENKIRCHEN, P. C. " 'Pracedam vos in Galilaeam' (Mt 26,32 cf. 28,7,10; Mc 14,28; 16,7 cf. Lc 24,6)", VerbDom 46 (1968) 193-223. BODE, E. L. The First Easter Morning (1970) 62-63, 68-69, 166-67. MAHO- NEY, R., Two Disciples at the Tomb (Bern 1974) 46-49, 67-69, 167-69. ZINGG, P., Das Wachsen der Kirche (Freiburg 1974) 140. METZGER, B. M., The Early Versions of the New Testament (Oxford 1977) 134.

24:7 SCHELKLE, K. H. Die Passion Jesu in der Verkündigung des Neuen Testaments (1949) 33f. WILCKENS, U. Die Missionsre- den der Apostelgeschichte (1961) 115, 117, 124, 131, 138, 143, 180. SCHWEIZER, E. Erniedrigung und Erhöhung bei Jesus und seinen Nachfolgern 1962) § 3k. HAHN, F., Christologische Ho- heitstitel (1963) 46, 205. NICKELS, P. Targum and New Testa- ment (1967) 50. POPKES, W. Christus Traditus (1967) 153ff., 163, 165, 180, 184. SCHNEIDER, G. Verleugnung, Verspottung und Verhör Jesu nach Lukas 22,54-71 (1969) 38, 171, 175, 181, 202. BODE, E. L. The First Easter Morning (1970) 63-67, 166-67. LOHSE, E. et al., eds., Der Ruf Jesu und die Antwort der Ge- meinde (1970) 204-12. JEREMIAS, J., Neutestamentliche Theo- logie I (1971) 22, 248, 250, 267f., 272, 280. PATSCH, H. Abendmahl und historischer Jesus (1972) 194f. WANKE, J., Die Emmauserzählung (Leipzig 1973) 66, 73-74, 92, A.528a. TAL- BERT, C. H., Literary Patterns, Theological Themes, and the Genre of Luke-Acts (Missoula 1974) 97. WILCKENS, U., Die Missions- reden der Apostelgeschichte (Neukirchen 1974*(3)*) 115, 118, 125, 132, 139, 143, 181. WILLIAMS, J. A., A Conceptual History of Deuteronomism in the Old Testament, Judaism and the New Tes- tament (Ph.D. Diss., Louisville 1976) 303-04. JEREMIAS, J., Die Sprache des Lukasevangeliums (Göttingen 1980) 311.

24:8 SCHRAMM, T. Der Markus-Stoff bei Lukas (1971) 134f. WANKE, J., Die Emmauserzählung (Leipzig 1973) 73, 118.

24:9-11 SWIDLER, L., Biblical Affirmations of Woman (Philadelphia 1979) 209, 222, 234, 262.

24:9-10 PRAST, F., Presbyter und Evangelium in nachapostolischer Zeit (Stuttgart 1979) 316.

24:9 WANKE, J., Die Emmauserzählung (Leipzig 1973) 113. PLEV- NIK, J., " 'The Eleven and Those with Them' According to Luke" CBQ 40 (1978) 205-11. JEREMIAS, J., Die Sprache des Lukas- evangeliums (Göttingen 1980) 311-12.

24:10 NICKELS, P. Targum and New Testament (1967) 50. WANKE,

J., Die Emmauserzählung (Leipzig 1973) 12, 75-76, 116. MA-
HONEY, R., Two Disciples at the Tomb (Bern 1974) 202-12.

24:11-35 D'ARC, J., "Un grand jeu d'inclusions dans 'les pèlerins d'Emmaüs' " NRTh 99 (1977) 62-76.

24:11 THEYSSEN, G. W. "Unbelief" in the New Testament (1965) 64ff.
GRASS, H. Ostergeschehen und Osterberichte (1970) 15, 22, 29,
34, 57, 65, 86, 109, 116, 118 n.2, 120. WANKE, J., Die
Emmauserzählung (Leipzig 1973) 35, 52, 76, 84. JEREMIAS, J.,
Die Sprache des Lukasevangeliums (Göttingen 1980) 312.

24:12-35 LEANEY, A. R. C. The Resurrection Narratives in Luke
(XXIV.12-53), NTS 2 (1955) 110-14.

24:12 JEREMIAS, J. Die Abendmahlsworte Jesu (1960) 143f. TAY-
LOR, V. The Text of the New Testament (1961) 19f. ALAND, K.
NTS 12 (1965-1966) 196f. MOULE, C. F. D. ed., The Signifi-
cance of the Resurrection for Faith in Jesus Christ (1968) 71. BODE,
E. L. The First Easter Morning (1970) 68-70, 171-72. CURTIS, K.
P. G. "Luke xxiv. 12 and John xx. 3-10," JThS 22 (2, 1971) 512-
15. JEREMIAS, J. Neutestamentliche Theologie I (1971) 289f.
MUDDIMAN, J. "A Note on Reading Luke XXIV.12," EphT 48
(3-4, 1972) 542-48. NEIRYNCK, F. "The Uncorrected Historic
Present in Lk. XXIV.12," EphT 48 (3-4, 1972) 548-53. WANKE,
J., Die Emmauserzählung (Leipzig 1973) 48, 69, 75, 76-82, 116,
A.119, 393. MAHONEY, R., Two Disciples at the Tomb (Bern
1974) 41-69, 218-19. ALSUP, J. E., The Post-Resurrection Ap-
pearance Stories of the Gospel-Tradition (Stuttgart 1975) 102ff.
METZGER, B. M., The Early Versions of the New Testament
(Oxford 1977) 134. NEIRYNCK, F., "*PARAKYPSAS BLEPEI*. Lc
24,12, et Jn 20,5" EphT 53 (1977) 113-52. NEIRYNCK, F.,
"Apelthen pros heauton" EphT 54 (1978) 104-18. SCHILLE-
BEECKX, E., Die Auferstehung Jesu als Grund der Erlösung (Basel
1979) 104-05. JEREMIAS, J., Die Sprache des Lukasevangeliums
(Göttingen 1980) 312-13.

24:13ff. DUPONT, J. "Le repas d'Emmaus," LuVie 31 (1957) 77-92.
MOULE, C. F. D. ed., The Significance of the Message of the
Resurrection for Faith in Jesus Christ (1968) 80, 83. CRIBBS, F.
L. in: SBL Seminar Papers 2 (1973) 4.

24:13-52 BOHREN, R., Predigtlehre (München 1971). HENDRIKX, H.,
The Resurrection Narratives of the Synoptic Gospels (Manila 1978).

24:13-43 SEIDENSTICKER, Ph. Die Auferstehung Jesu in der Botschaft der
Evangelisten (1968) 96f.

24:13-36 ORLETT, R. "An Influence of the Early Liturgies upon the Emmaus Account," CBQ 21 (2, 1959) 212-19.

24:13-35 SURKAU, GPM 4 (1949-1950) 127ff. DUPONT, J. "Les pèlerins

d'Emmaus (Luc XXIV,13-35)," Misc.Bibl.B.Ubach. Montserrat
(1953) 349-74. WEBER, O. GPM 9 (1954-1955) 111ff. DEHN,
G. in: Herr, tue meine Lippen auf Bd. 1 (1957), G. Eichholz, ed.,
139-44. DINKLER, GPM 15 (1960-1961) 124ff. BRUNOT, A.
"Emmaüs, cité pascale de la Fraction du Pain," BibTerreSainte 36
(1961) 4-11. BUZY, D. "Emmaüs dans l'Evangile et la tradi-
tion," BibTerreSainte 36 (1961) 4-5. DOERNE, M., Er kommt
auch noch heute (1961) 75-77. LOHSE, E. Die Auferstehung Jesu
Christi im Zeugnis des Lukasevangeliums (1961) 23-33. BULT-
MANN, R. The History of the Synoptic Tradition (1963) 288-90.
HAHN, F., Christologische Hoheitstitel (1963) 387-90. EHR-
HARDT, A. A. T. "The Disciples of Emmaus," NTS 10 (2, 1964)
182-201. GRASSI, J. A. "Emmaus Revisited (Luke 24,13-35 and
Acts 8,26-40)," CBQ 26 (1964) 463-467. SWANSTON, H., "The
Road to Emmaus," C1R 50 (7, 1965) 506-23. Es Freu' sich alle
Christenheit, Predigtgedanken aus Vergangenheit und Gegenwart,
Reihe A, Bd. 4 (1966) 31-51. WEBER, O. Predigtmeditationen
(1967) 221-24. KAMPHAUS, F. Von der Exegese zur Predigt
(^{2}1968) 45-57, 86-92. KREMER, J. Die Osterbotschaft der vier
Evangelien (1968) 60-72. SEIDENSTICKER, Ph. Die Auferste-
hung Jeus in der Botschaft der Evangelien (1968) 97f. BROWN,
S. Apostasy and Perseverance in the Theology of Luke (1969) 75-
77. DEMBOWSKI, H. "Jesus Christus-Herr der Götter dargestellt
am Verhältnis Jesus Christus zu Athene." EvTh 29 (11, 1969) 572-
88. LOHSE, E. Das Ägernis des Kreuzes (1969) 24-29. PESCH,
W. Den Menschen helfen (1969) 30-38. SCHNIDER, F./STEN-
GER, W. Die Ostergeschichten der Evangelien (1969) 67-82. EV-
ANS, C. F. Resurrection and the New Testament (1970) 92ff.
GRASS, H. Ostergeschehen und Osterberichte (1970) 35ff., 283f.
MARXSEN, W. The Resurrection of Jesus of Nazareth (1970) 50-
54. ROGGE, J./SCHILLE, G. eds., Theologische Versuche II
(1970) 77-81. ROLOFF, J. Das Kerygma und der irdische Jesus
(1970) 256-58. WILCKENS, U. Auferstehung (1970) 76-85.
STOEGER, A. "L'esprit synodal," Christus 18 (71, 1971) 406-
19. FEUILLET, A. "Les pèlerins d'Emmaüs (Lc 24,13-35)," NV
47 (2, 1972) 89-98. GROENEWALD, E. P. "Jeremia 14:8-9 en
Emmaüs" NGTT 13 (2, 1972) 77-82. SCHNIDER, F./STEN-
GER, W. "Beobachtungen zur Struktur der Emmausperikope (Lk
24,13-35)," BZ 16 (1, 1972) 94-114. HAAR, J. GPM 27 (2,1973)
209-14. HAMMEL, J. GPM 27 (2, 1973) 215-20. LOSADA, D.
A. "El Episodo de Emaus. Lc 24,13-35," RevBi 35 (1, 1973) 3-
13. SCHNIDER, F., Jesus der Prophet (Freiburg 1973) 124ff.
WANKE, J., Die Emmauserzählung (Leipzig 1973). WANKE, J.,
" ' . . . wie sie ihn beim Brotbrechen erkannten.' Zur Auslegung

der Emmauserzählung Lk 24,13-35" BZ 18 (1974) 180-92. AL-SUP, J. E., The Post-Resurrection Appearance Stories of the Gospel-Tradition (Stuttgart 1975) 190ff. BARTLETT, D. L., Fact and Faith (Valley Forge 1975) 113-14. D'ARC, J., Les pèlerins d'Emmaüs (Paris 1977). SCHNEIDER, G., Das Evangelium nach Lukas (Gütersloh 1977) 496. STRAVINSKAS, P. M. J., "The Eammaus Pericope: Its Sources, Theology and Meaning for Today" Biblebhashyam 3 (1977) 97-115. VELOSO, M., "Una lectura viviente de la Biblia según san Lucas" RevBi 39 (1977) 197-209. DÖMER, M., Das Heil Gottes (Köln-Bonn 1978) 96. FEUILLET, A., "L'apparition du Christ à Marie-Madeleine Jean 20,11-18. Comparaison avec l'apparition aux disciples d'Emmaüs Luc 24,13-35" EsVie 88 (1978) 193-204, 209-23. IERSEL, B. van, "Terug van Emmaüs. Bijdragen tot een structurele tekstanalyse van Lc. 24,13-35" TvTh 18 (1978) 294-323. "Auferstehung" in: TRE 4 (1979) 504. SCHUNACK, G., in: GPM 33 (1979) 190-95. GILL, J. H., "Jesus, Irony, and the 'New Quest' " Encounter (1980) 139-51. SCHINELLER, J. P., "The Church—from Emmaus to the New Jerusalem" ChSt 19 (1980) 63-75. THEVENOT, X., "Emmaüs, une nouvelle Genèse? Une lecture psychanalytique de Genèse 2-3 et Luc 24,13-35" MSR 37 (1980) 3-18.

24:13-33 HIRSCH, E. Frühgeschichte des Evangeliums (1941) 278-80. GIBBS, J. M., "Luke 24:13-33 and Acts 8:26-39: The Emmaus Incident and The Eunuch's Baptism as Parallel Stories" Bangalore Theological Forum 7 (1975) 17-30. GIBBS, J. M., "Canon Cuming's 'Service-Endings in the Epistles': A Rejoinder" NTS 24 (1978) 545-47. KUDASIEWICZ, J., "Jerusalem—miejscem zbawczej śmierci Jezusa (Lk 24,13-33) (Jérusalem-lieu de la mort salvatrice de Jésus [Luc 24,13-33])" RTK 25 (1978) 69-74.

24:13-32 DESREUMAUX, J. "Les disciples d'Emmaüs. Luc 24,13-32," BVieC 56 (1964) 45-56. LEE, G. M. "The Walk to Emmaus," ET 77 (12, 1966) 380-81. BETZ, H. D. "The Origin and Nature of Christian Faith According to the Eammaus Legend (Luke 24,13-32)," Interpretation 23 (1, 1969) 32-46. BETZ, H. D. "Ursprung und Wesen christlichen Glaubens nach der Emmauslegende (Lk 24,13-32)," ZThK 66 (1, 1969) 7-21. MAGNE, J. "L'épisode des disciples d'Emmaüs et le récit du paradis terrestre," CahCER 18 (71, 1971) 29-32. FRIEDRICH, G., "Lk 9,51 und die Entrückungschristologie des Lukas" in: P. Hoffmann (ed.) Orientierung an Jesus. FS. J. Schmid (Freiburg 1973) 56-59. TALBERT, C. H., Literary Patterns, Theological Themes, and the Genre of Luke-Acts (Missoula 1974) 22.

24:13-31 LIGHTFOOT, R. H. Locality and Doctrine in the Gospels (1938) 87ff.

24:13-29 D'ARC, J., "Catechesis on the Road to Eammaus" LuVit 32 (1977) 143-56.

24:13-25 EHRHARDT, A. NTS 10 (1963-1964) 182f.

24:13-16 WANKE, J., Die Emmauserzählung (Leipzig 1973) 23-42.

24:13-14 WANKE, J., Die Emmauserzählung (Leipzig 1973) 23-28, 33-34.

24:13 ARCE, P. A. "Eammaus y algunos textos desconocidos," EstBi XIII/1 (1954) 53-90. BATAINI, G. " + 'Emmaus die S. Luca: punti sugli i?", PaC1 XXXIV/6 (1955) 241-49. BARRETT, C. K. The New Testament Background: Selected Documents (1956) 133. WANKE, J., Die Emmauserzählung (Leipzig 1973) 8, 10, 12, 16, 18, 38-42, 47. METZGER, B. M., The Early Versions of the New Testament (Oxford 1977) 201. JEREMIAS, J., Die Sprache des Lukasevangeliums (Göttingen 1980) 313. MACKOWSKI, R. M., "Where is Biblical Emmaus?" SciE 32 (1980) 93-103.

24:14 NICKELS, P. Targum and New Testament (1967) 50. WANKE, J., Die Emmauserzählung (Leipzig 1973) 10, 14. JEREMIAS, J., Die Sprache des Lukasevangeliums (Göttingen 1980) 313.

24:15-16 WANKE, J., Die Emmauserzählung (Leipzig 1973) 29-31, 34-37.

24:15 NEIRYNCK, F., "La Matière Marcienne dans Luc" in: F. Neirynck (ed.) L'Evangile de Luc (Gemboux 1973) 184-93. WANKE, J., Die Emmauserzählung (Leipzig 1973) 7-8, 12, 14,16. JEREMIAS, J., Die Sprache des Lukasevangeliums (Göttingen 1980) 313-14.

24:16 MOULE, C. F. D. ed., The Significance of the Message of the Resurrection for Faith in Jesus Christ (1968) 84. WANKE, J., Die Emmauserzählung (Leipzig 1973) 7, 12, 14ff., 18. JEREMIAS, J., Die Sprache des Lukasevangeliums (Göttingen 1980) 314.

24:17-27 WANKE, J., Die Emmauserzählung (Leipzig 1973) 14, 19, 115.

24:17-21 WANKE, J., Die Emmauserzählung (Leipzig 1973) 55-68.

24:17-19 WANKE, J., Die Emmauserzählung (Leipzig 1973) 55-58.

24:18 WANKE, J., Die Emmauserzählung (Leipzig 1973) 10, 23. METZGER, B. M., The Early Versions of the New Testament (Oxford 1977) 92, 313. JEREMIAS, J., Die Sprache des Lukasevangeliums (Göttingen 1980) 314.

24:19-21 WANKE, J., Die Emmauserzählung (Leipzig 1973) 11, 14.

24:19-20 WILCKENS, U. Die Missionsreden der Apostelgeschichte (1961) 116, 123, 131.

24:19 GILS, F. Jésus Prophète D'Apres Les Evangiles Synoptiques (1957) 28-30. RENGSTORF, K. H. Die Auferstehung Jesu (1960) 27, 36, 86, 157. RUPPERT, L., Jesus als der leidende Gerechte? (Stuttgart 1972) 57. WANKE, J., Die Emmauserzählung (Leipzig 1973) 60-

64, 123. JEREMIAS, J., Die Sprache des Lukasevangeliums (Göttingen 1980) 315.

24:19b HAHN, F. Christologische Hoheitstitel (1963) 392.

24:20-21 WANKE, J., Die Emmauserzählung (Leipzig 1973) 58-60, 64-68.

24:20 SCHNEIDER, G. Verleugnung, Verspottung und Verhör Jesu nach Lukas 22,54-71 (1969) 36, 38, 193, 214, 220. WANKE, J., Die Emmauserzählung (Leipzig 1973) 65-66, 73, 93, A.448. METZGER, B. M., The Early Versions of the New Testament (Oxford 1977) 246. JEREMIAS, J., Die Sprache des Lukasevangeliums (Göttingen 1980) 315-16.

24:21ff. RENGSTORF, K. H. Die Auferstehung Jesu (1960) 138, passim.

24:21-24 TALBERT, C. H., Literary Patterns, Theological Themes, and the Genre of Luke-Acts (Missoula 1974) 60.

24:21 PALLIS, A. Notes on St. Luke and the Acts (London 1928) 46. HAHN, F. Christologische Hoheitstitel (1963) 220. SHIMADA, K., The Formulary Material in First Peter (Th.D. Diss., Ann Arbor 1966) 240. NICKELS, P. Targum and New Testament (1967) 50. WANKE, J., Die Emmauserzählung (Leipzig 1973) 4, 67-68, 118. DRURY, J., Tradition and Design in Luke's Gospel (Atlanta 1976) 70-71. JEREMIAS, J., Die Sprache des Lukasevangeliums (Göttingen 1980) 316.

24:21a HAHN, F. Christologische Hoheitstitel (1963) 392, 396.

24:22-24 WANKE, J., Die Emmauserzählung (Leipzig 1973) 5, 7, 11, 13ff., 19, 41, 69-84, 113-14, 116. ALSUP, J. E., The Post-Resurrection Appearance Stories of the Gospel-Tradition (Stuttgart 1975) 102ff., 114ff.

24:22-23 TALBERT, C. H., Literary Patterns, Theological Themes, and the Genre of Luke-Acts (Missoula 1974) 113.

24:22 STONEHOUSE, N. B. The Witness of Matthew and Mark to Christ (1944) 106.

24:23.24 NICKELS, P. Targum and New Testament (1967) 50.

24:24 JEREMIAS, J. Die Abendmahlsworte Jesu (1960) 143f. WANKE, J., Die Emmauserzählung (Leipzig 1973) 12, 79-82. JEREMIAS, J., Die Sprache des Lukasevangeliums (Göttingen 1980) 316.

24:25-27 DENNEY, J. The Death of Christ (1956) 44f. BRAUN, H. Qumran und NT II (1966) 78, 267, 315. SUMMERS, R. The Secret Sayings of the Living Jesus (1968) 67. WANKE, J., Die Emmauserzählung (Leipzig 1973) 6, 11ff., 66, 85-95. TALBERT, C. H., Literary Patterns, Theological Themes, and the Genre of Luke-Acts (Missoula 1974) 22, 97, 98. SCHNEIDER, G., Das Evangelium nach Lukas (Gütersloh 1977) 503.

24:25-26 WILCKENS, U. Die Missionsreden der Apostelgeschichte (1961)

97, 102, 115, 117-18, 140, 158. FRIEDRICH, G., "Die Bedeutung der Auferweckung Jesu nach Aussagen des Neuen Testaments" in: Auf das Wort kommt es an (Göttingen 1978) 359.

24:25 BLACK, M. An Aramaic Approach to the Gospels and Acts (1967)
254f. MOULE, C. F. D. ed., The Significance of the Message of
the Resurrection for Faith in Jesus Christ (1968) 93. WANKE, J.,
Die Emmauserzählung (Leipzig 1973) 16. DRURY, J., Tradition
and Design in Luke's Gospel (Atlanta 1976) 69. JEREMIAS, J.,
Die Sprache des Lukasevangeliums (Göttingen 1980) 317.

24:26-27 VAN UNNIK, W. C. "Jesus the Christ," NTS 8 (1961-1962) 110f.
KURZ, W. S., "Hellenistic Rhetoric in the Christological Proof of
Luke-Acts" CBQ 42 (1980) 171-95.

24:26 BLAIR, E. P. Jesus in the Gospel of Matthew (1960) 54. ROB-
INSON, Kerygma und historischer Jesus (1960) 175, 179. HAHN,
F. Christologische Hoheitstitel (1963) 51, 217. NICKELS, P. Targum and New Testament (1967) 50. MOULE, C. F. D. The Significance of the Message of the Resurrection for Faith in Jesus Christ
(1968) 89. LOHFINK, G. Die Himmelfahrt Jesu (1971) 236-39.
RUPPERT, L., Jesus als der leidende Gerechte? (Stuttgart 1972)
47a16., 59. WANKE, J., Die Emmauserzählung (Leipzig 1973) 15-
16, 87-88, 93, 119. TALBERT, C. H., Literary Patterns, Theological Themes, and the Genre of Luke-Acts (Missoula 1974) 115,
122, 124. WILCKENS, U., Die Missionsreden der Apostelgeschichte (Neukirchen 1974*(3)*) 97, 116, 117, 118, 140, 159.
GLÖCKNER, R., Die Verkündigung des Heils beim Evangelisten
Lukas (Mainz 1975) 162, 201ff., 211. DUNN, J. D. G., Unity and
Diversity in the New Testament (London 1977) 43. BUSSE, U.,
Das Nazareth-Manifest Jesu (Stuttgart 1978) 71, 73-74. DÖMER.
M., Das Heil Gottes (Köln-Bonn 1978) 70-79.

24:27.32 WOLFF, H. W. Wegweisung (1965) 141f.

24:27 BOUSSET, W. Die Religion des Judentums im Späthellenisti-
schen Zeitalter (1966 = 1926) 144. NICKELS, P. Targum and New
Testament (1967) 51. HARMAN, A. M., Paul's Use of the Psalms
(Ann Arbor 1968) 276-77. WANKE, J., Die Emmauserzählung
(Leipzig 1973) 14. JEREMIAS, J., Die Sprache des Lukasevangel-
iums (Göttingen 1980) 317.

24:28ff. HAHN, F., "Thesen zur Frage einheitsstiftender Elemente in Lehre
und Praxis des urchristlichen Herrenmahls" in: D. Lührman/G.
Strecker (eds.) Kirche. FS. G. Bornkamm (Tügingen 1980) 417.

24:28-31 WANKE, J., Die Emmauserzählung (Leipzig 1973) 6ff., 10, 12,
16, 96-102, 105-08, 115-16, 124-25.

24:29-43 LANDUCCI, P. C. "Gesù veramente taumaturgo, risorto, sacra-
mentato," PaCl 52 (5, 1973) 260-74.

24:29 SCHNEIDER, G. Verleugnung, Verspottung und Verhör Jesu nach Lukas 22,54-71 (1969) 81, 113, 177, 204. WANKE, J., Die Emmauserzählung (Leipzig 1973) 41-42, 101-02. JANSSEN, E., "Testament Abrahams" in: W. G. Kümmel (ed.) Jüdische Schriften aus hellenistisch-römischer Zeit. III (Gütersloh 1975) 208 n.57. JEREMIAS, J., Die Sprache des Lukasevangeliums (Göttingen 1980) 318.

24:30-36 WILCKENS, U. Die Missionsreden der Apostelgeschichte (1961) 79, 137-38, 144, 147, 168.

24:30.31 BEST, E. One Body in Christ (1955) 90n.

24:30 JEREMIAS, J. Die Abendmahlsworte Jesu (1960) 166-68, 196. DUPONT, J. "The Meal at Emmaus", in: The Eucharist in the New Testament (1964) 105-21. NICKELS, P. Targum and New Testament (1967) 51. NEIRYNCK, F., "La Matière Marcienne dans Luc" in: F. Neirynck (ed.) L'Evangile de Luc (Gembloux 1973) 184-93. WANKE, J., Die Emmauserzählung (Leipzig 1973) 2, 98. "Abendmahlsfeier" in: TRE 1 (1977) 230. WESTERMANN, C., Blessing (Philadelphia 1978) 86, 98-101. JEREMIAS, J., Die Sprache des Lukasevangeliums (Göttingen 1980) 318.

24:31 BETZ, H. D. Lukian von Samosata und das Neue Testament (1961) 169f. MOULE, C. F. D. ed., The Significance of the Message of the Resurrection for Faith in Jesus Christ (1968) 84, 86. WANKE, J., Die Emmauserzählung (Leipzig 1973) 7, 12-13, 16, 18, 35, 84, 91, 98. JEREMIAS, J., Die Sprache des Lukasevangeliums (Göttingen 1980) 318-19.

24:32 PALLIS, A. Notes on St. Luke and the Acts (London 1928) 46-47. KNOX, W. L. The Sources of the Synoptic Gospels II (1957) 59. ALAND, K. NTS 12 (1965-1966) 196f. NICKELS, P. Targum and New Testament (1967) 51. WANKE, J., Die Emmauserzählung (Leipzig 1973) 8, 12, 14, 18, 91, 99. TALBERT, C. H., Literary Patterns, Theological Themes, and the Genre of Luke-Acts (Missoula 1974) 22, 97. JEREMIAS, J., Die Sprache des Lukasevangeliums (Göttingen 1980) 319.

24:33-53 TALBERT, C. H., Literary Patterns, Theological Themes, and the Genre of Luke-Acts (Missoula 1974) 114.

24:33b-53 HIRSCH, E. Frühgeschichte des Evangeliums (1941) 280-83.

24:33-51 LIGHTFOOT, R. H. Locality and Doctrine in the Gospels (1938) 87ff.

24:33-49 FLEW, R. N. Jesus and His Church (1956) 136, 128, 175. TALBERT, C. H., Literary Patterns, Theological Themes, and the Genre of Luke-Acts (Missoula 1974) 22.

24:33-35 ANNAND, R. " 'He Was Seen of Cephas', a suggestion about the first resurrection appearance to Peter," SJTh 11 (2, 1958) 180-87.

WANKE, J., Die Emmauserzählung (Leipzig 1973) 7, 13ff., 19, 41, 114.

24:33-34 TALBERT, C. H., Literary Patterns, Theological Themes, and the Genre of Luke-Acts (Missoula 1974) 59, 60. MUSSNER, F., Petrus und Paulus (Freiburg 1976) 26-27. PRAST, F., Presbyter und Evangelium in nachapostolischer Zeit (Stuttgart 1979) 316.

24:33 BLACK, M. An Aramaic Approach to the Gospels and Acts (1967) 111f. WANKE, J., Die Emmauserzählung (Leipzig 1973) 8, 12, 43-44, 47-49. WILSON, S. G., The Gentiles and the Gentile Mission in Luke-Acts (Cambridge 1973) 88, 89, 98. PLEVNIK, J., " 'The Eleven and Those with Them' According to Luke" CBQ 40 (1978) 205-11. PFITZNER, V. C., " 'Pneumatic' Apostleship? Apostle and Spirit in the Acts of the Apostles" in: W. Haubeck/M. Bachmann (eds.) Wort in der Zeit. FS. K. H. Rengstorf (Leiden 1980) 215-16.

24:34-53 LEON-DUFOUR, X., The Resurrection and the Message of Easter (London 1974) 82-94.

24:34 STONEHOUSE, N. B. The Witness of Matthew and Mark to Christ (1944) 114, 255. FARRER, A. St Matthew and St Mark (1954) 154. STRECKER, G. Der Weg der Gerechtigkeit (1962) 94_2, 206_4. HAHN, F. Christologische Hoheitstitel (1963) 88, 123, 204. STREEFKERK, N. "De verschijning van de opgestane Christus aan Simon Petrus" HomBib 22 (2, 1963) 57-61. HAHN, F. Das Verständnis der Mission im Neuen Testament (^{2}1965) 37. ROLOFF, J. Apostolat-Verkündigung-Kirche (1965) 48f. MOULE, C. F. D. ed., The Significance of the Message of the Resurrection for Faith in Jesus Christ (1968) 26, 33, 34, 73, 83, 87, 122. DESCAMPS, A./DE HALLEUX, A. Mélanges Bibliques en hommage au R. P. Béda Rigaux (1970) 123-24, 146. GRASS, H. Ostergeschehen und Osterberichte (1970) 18, 34, 36, n.3, 81, 90, 98, 107, 119, 122, n.1, 186, 255. DIETRICH, W. Das Petrusbild der lukanischen Schriften (1972) 158-63. BROWN, R. E. et al. (eds.) Peter in the New Testament (Minneapolis 1973) 125-28. LANE, J., Das Erscheinen des Auferstandenen im Evangelium nach Mattäus (Würzburg 1973) WANKE, J., Die Emmauserzählung (Leipzig 1973) 3ff., 8, 13, 35, 44ff., 49-53, 115ff., A.395, 403, 753. TALBERT, C. H., Literary Patterns, Theological Themes, and the Genre of Luke-Acts (Missoula 1974) 60. 114. ALSUP, J. E., The Post-Resurrection Appearance Stories of the Gospel-Tradition (Stuttgart 1975) 61ff. GOPPELT, L., Theologie des Neuen Testaments. I (Göttingen 1975) 280-81, 283. "Auferstehung" in: TRE 4 (1979) 485. SWIDLER, L., Biblical Affirmations of Woman (Philadelphia 1979) 217, 233. "Benediktionen" in: TRE 5 (1980) 566.

24:35 KNOX, W. L. The Sources of the Synoptic Gospels II (1957) 59.

WULF, F. "Sie erkannten ihn beim Brechen des Brotes (Lk 24,35)," GuL 37 (2, 1964) 81-83. WANKE, J., Die Emmauserzählung (Leipzig 1973) 8, 16, 46, 53-54, 84, 102, 117, 121, 126. "Abendmahl" in: TRE 1 (1977) 56. JEREMIAS, J., Die Sprache des Lukasevangeliums (Göttingen 1980) 319-20.

24:36ff. MOULE, C. F. D. ed., The Significance of the Message of the Resurrection for Faith in Jesus Christ (1968) 75, 83. GRASS, H. Ostergeschehen und Osterberichte (1970) 40ff. PETZKE, G. Die Traditionen über Apollonius von Tyana und das Neue Testament (1970) 141, 186f.

24:36-53 KREMER, J. Die Osterbotschaft der vier Evangelien (1968) 72-86, 143. GEORGE, A., "Les récits d'apparitions aux Onze à partir" Lectio divina 50 (1969) 75-104. LOHFINK, G. Die Himmelfahrt Jesu (1971) 147-51. ZEHNLE, R. F. Peter's Pentecost Discourse (1971) 95-194. WANKE, J., Die Emmauserzählung (Leipzig 1973) 11-12, 15, 52, 113, 115, A.42, 119, 189, 409. HUBBARD, B. J., The Matthean Redaction of a Primitive Apostolic Commissioning (Missoula 1974) 101-28. ALSUP, J. E., The Post-Resurrection Appearance Stories of the Gospel-Tradition (Stuttgart 1975) 148ff. HUBBARD, B. J., "Commissioning Stories in Luke-Acts" Semeia 8 (1977) 103-26. HUBBARD, B. J., "The Role of Commissioning Accounts in Acts" in: C. H. Talbert (ed.) Perspectives on Luke-Acts (Danville 1978) 190. "Auferstehung" in: TRE 4 (1979) 491, 504. MCDONALD, J. I. H., Kerygma and Didache (Cambridge 1980) 87.

24:36-49 LOHSE, E. Die Auferstehung Jesu Christi im Zeugnis des Lukasevangeliums (1961) 34-38. Glaubet an den Gottgesandten, Predigtgedanken aus Vergangenheit und Gegenwart, Reihe C, Bd. 2 (1962) 163-71. FROER, K. GPM 17 (1963) 174-78. KAMPHAUS, F. Von der Exegese zur Predigt (²1968) 47, 48. MOULE, C. F. D. ed., The Significance of the Message of the Resurrection for Faith in Jesus Christ (1968) 92. SMOLIK, J. GPM 23 (1968-1969) 168-73. BURCHARD, C. Der dreizehnte Zeuge (1970) 130-33. MARXSEN, W. The Resurrection of Jesus of Nazareth (1970) 52-54. WILCKENS, U. Auferstehung (1970) 71-75. PETERS, G. W. A Biblical Theology of Missions (1972) 9, 118, 176, 178, 248, 310-11. SIMPFENDÖRFER, G. and SIMPFENDÖRFER, W., in: P. Krusche et al. (eds.) Predigtstudien für das Kirchenjahr 1974-1975. III/2 (1975) 19-26. STECK, K. G., in: GPM 29 (203-10. SCHNEIDER, G., Das Evangelium nach Lukas (Gütersloh 1977) 500-01.

24:36-45 HINZ, C., in: GPM 35 (1981) 213-18.

24:36-43 TALBERT, C. H. NTS 14 (1967-1968) 262f. SEIDENSTICKER, Ph. Die Auferstehung Jesu in der Botschaft der Evangelisten (1968)

67f. BROWN, S. Apostasy and Perseverance in the Theology of Luke (1969) 77-79. SCHNIDER, F./STENGER, W. Die Osterge-schichten der Evangelien (1969) 82-88. BOISMARD, M.-E. "Le réalisme des récits évangéliques," LuVie 21 (197, 1972) 31-41. WANKE, J., Die Emmauserzählung (Leipzig 1973) 12, 15, 117. TALBERT, C. H., Literary Patterns, Theological Themes, and the Genre of Luke-Acts (Missoula 1974) 59, 60, 113, 114. DÖMER, M., Das Heil Gottes (Köln-Bonn 1978) 96-98. PRAST, F., Presbyter und Evangelium in nachapostolischer Zeit (Stuttgart 1979) 316.

24:36-41 HENNECKE, E./SCHNEEMELCHER, W. Neutestamentliche Apokryphen (1964) I 83.

24:36-40 CRIBBS, F. L. in: SBL Seminar Papers 2 (1973) 85-86.

24:36-39 BULTMANN, R. The History of the Synoptic Tradition (1963) 288-90.

24:36 JEREMIAS, J. Die Abendmahlsworte Jesu (1960) 143-45. BETZ, H. D. Lukian von Samosata und das Neue Testament (1961) 162, 170. TAYLOR, V. The Text of the New Testament (1961) 19f. ALAND, K. NTS 12 (1965-1966) 196f., 206f. MOULE, C. F. D. ed., The Significance of the Message of the Resurrection for Faith in Jesus Christ (1968) 86. CRIBBS, F. L. in: SBL Seminar Papers 2 (1973) 4. MAHONEY, R., Two Disciples at the Tomb (Bern 1974) 46-49, 61-64. TALBERT, C. H., Literary Patterns, Theological Themes, and the Genre of Luke-Acts (Missoula 1974) 59-60. METZGER, B. M., The Early Versions of the New Testament (Oxford 1977) 134.

24:37-39 DALTON, W. J., Christ's Proclamation to the Spirits (Rome 1965) 147. SCHWEIZER, E., Heiliger Geist (Stuttgart 1978) 153.

24;37 JEREMIAS, J., Die Sprache des Lukasevangeliums (Göttingen 1980) 320.

24:38 JEREMIAS, J., Die Sprache des Lukasevangeliums (Göttingen 1980) 320-21.

24:39-43 DUNN, J. D. G., Jesus and the Spirit (London 1975) 121-22.

24:39 STONEHOUSE, N. B. The Witness of Matthew and Mark to Christ (1944) 114. MESSINA, G. "Lezioni apocrife nel diatessaron Persiano," Biblica 30 (1959) 10-14. BORNKAMM-BARTH-HELD, Ueberlieferung und Auslegung im Matthäus-Evangelium (²1961) 124. ALAND, K. NTS 12 (1965-1966) 206f. MOULE, C. F. D. ed., The Significance of the Message of the Resurrection for Faith in Jesus Christ (1968) 79, 86. BROER, I. Die Urgemeinde und das Grab Jesu (1972) 205f., 225. TALBERT, C. H., Literary Patterns, Theological Themes, and the Genre of Luke-Acts (Missoula 1974) 113. SCHEP, J. A., The Nature of the Resurrection Body (Grand

Rapids 1976) 131-33. METZGER, B. M., The Early Versions of the New Testament (Oxford 1977) 214. "Bibel" in: TRE 6 (1980) 30. BÖHLIG, A., Die Gnosis III: Der Manichäismus (Zürich 1980) 348 n.4.

24:40 JEREMIAS, J. Die Abendmahlsworte Jesu (1960) 143-45. TAYLOR, V. The Text of the New Testament (1961) 19f. ALAND, K. NTS 12 (1965-1966) 196f., 206f. CRIBBS, F. L., in: SBL Seminar Papers 2 (1973) 4. MAHONEY, R., Two Disciples at the Tomb (Bern 1974) 46-49, 61-64. METZGER, B. M., The Early Versions of the New Testament (Oxford 1977) 134.

24:41-43 MOULE, C. F. D. ed., The Significance of the Message of the Resurrection for Faith in Jesus Christ (1968) 86. JEREMIAS, J. Neutestamentliche Theologie I (1971) 287f.

24:41-42 "Abendmahlsfeier" in: TRE 1 (1977) 230.

24:41 PALLIS, A. Notes on St. Luke and the Acts (London 1928) 47. BORNKAMM-BARTH-HELD, Ueberlieferung und Auslegung im Matthäus-Evangelium ([2]1961) 123f. THEYSSEN, G. W. "Unbelief" in the New Testament (1965) 34ff. WANKE, J., Die Emmauserzählung (Leipzig 1973) 36, 52, A.409, 424. JEREMIAS, J., Die Sprache des Lukasevangeliums (Göttingen 1980) 321.

24:42 BETZ, H. D. Lukian von Samosata und das Neue Testament (1961) 35, 42, 176. WANKE, J., Die Emmauserzählung (Leipzig 1973) 98. CAVALLIN, H. C. C., Life After Death. I (Lund 1974) 4, 9n16. METZGER, B. M., The Early Versions of the New Testament (Oxford 1977) 42.

24:43 TALBERT, C. H., Literary Patterns, Theological Themes, and the Genre of Luke-Acts (Missoula 1974) 113. "Abendmahl" in: TRE 1 (1977) 50.

24:44ff. BEYSCHLAG, K. Clemens Romanus und der Frühkatholizismus (1966) 276, 336.

24:44-53 GEORGE, A. "L'intelligence des Ecritures (Luc 24,44-53)," BVieC 18 (1957) 65-71. SCHNIDER, F./STENGER, W. Die Ostergeschichten der Evangelien (1969) 88-91. WANKE, J., Die Emmauserzählung (Leipzig 1973) 11-12, 91, 118, 121. DAVIES, W. D., The Gospel and the Land (London 1974) 255. ZINGG, P., Das Wachsen der Kirche (Freiburg 1974) 140-42. PRAST, F., Presbyter und Evangelium in nachapostolischer Zeit (Stuttgart 1979) 302-08.

24:44-52 MICHEL, H-J., Die Abschiedsrede des Paulus an die Kirche Apg. 20:17-38 (München 1973) 57, 59ff.

24:44-49 WILCKENS, U. Die Missionsreden der Apostelgeschichte (1961) Passim. HAHN, F. Das Verständnis der Mission im Neuen Testament (²1965) 113f. SEIDENSTICKER, Ph. Die Auferstehung Jesu in der Botschaft der Evangelisten (1968) 67f., 99f. BROWN, S. Apostasy and Perseverance in the Theology of Luke (1969) 80-81. KASTING,H. Die Anfänge der Urchristlichen Mission (1969) 41-43. WANKE, J., Die Emmauserzählung (Leipzig 1973) 12, 117, 121. TALBERT, C. H., Literary Patterns, Theological Themes, and the Genre of Luke-Acts (Missoula 1974) 22, 60, 97, 98. WILCK-ENS, U., Die Missionsreden der Apostelgeschichte (Neukirchen 1974(3)) 56, 97, 102, 144, 148, 159. DÖMER, M., Das Heil Gottes (Köln-Bonn 1978) 99-106, 134, 203, 205-06.

24:44-48 KURZ, W. S., "Hellenistic Rhetoric in the Christological Proof of Luke-Acts" CBQ 42 (1980) 171-95.

24:44-47 SEEBERG, A. Der Katechismus der Urchristenheit (1966) 129-32. O'NEILL, J. C. The Theology of Acts in Its Historical Setting (1970) 76n, 151-52. SCHNEIDER, G., Das Evangelium nach Lukas (Gütersloh 1977) 503. "Apostelgeschichte" in: TRE 3 (1978) 516.

24:44-46 MOULE, C. F. D. ed., The Significance of the Message of the Resurrection for Faith in Jesus Christ (1968) 91. RUPPERT, L., Jesus als der leidende Gerechte? (Stuttgart 1972) 59.

24:44-45 VAN UNNIK, W. C. Jesus the Christ. NTS 8 (1961-1962) 110f. BRAUN, H. Qumran und NT II (1966) 78, 267, 315.

24:44 STRECKER, G. Der Weg der Gerechtigketi (1962) 84₁. BOUS-SET, W. Die Religion des Judentums im Späthellenistischen Zeitalter (1966 = 1926) 146. NICKELS, P. Targum and New Testament (1967) 51. SCHNEIDER, G. Verleugnung, Verspottung und Verhör Jesu nach Lukas 22,54-71 (1969) 81, 175,177, 180, 204. BERGER, K. Die Gesetzesauslegung Jesu (1972) 209-27. TALBERT, C. H., Literary Patterns, Theological Themes, and the Genre of Luke-Acts (Missoula 1974) 22. LAMPARTER, H., "Das Christuszeugnis in den Psalmen" in: G. Müller (ed.) Rechtfertigung Realismus. FS. A. Köberle (Darmstadt 1978) 22-23. PRAST, F., Presbyter und Evangelium in nachapostolischer Zeit (Stuttgart 1979) 316. "Bibel" in: TRE 6 (1980) 10. JEREMIAS, J., Die Sprache des Lukasevangeliums (Göttingen 1980) 321.

24:45-48 RENGSTORF, K. H. Die Auferstehung Jesu (1960) 33, 35f., 44, 51, 70, 73, 137-40, 146.

24:45 WANKE, J., Die Emmauserzählung (Leipzig 1973) 9, 91. DRURY, J., Tradition and Design in Luke's Gospel (Atlanta 1976) 69.

24:46ff. LJUNGMAN, H. Pistis; A Study of its Presuppositions and its Meaning in Pauline Use (1964) 98f.

24:46-49 DELLING, G. NTS 13 (1966-1967) 298ff.

24:46-48 LEROY, H., Zur Vergebung der Sünden (Stuttgart 1974) 63, 71.
TREVIJANO ETCHEVERRIA, R., "La misión de la Iglesia primitiva y los mandatos del Señor en los Evangelios" Salmanticensis
25 (1978) 5-36.

24:46-41 DENNEY, J. The Death of Christ (1956) 45f. DUPONT, J. Etudes
sur le Actes des Apôtres (1967) 246, 251, 278, 280, 402, 454.
WREGE, H.-T. Die Ueberlieferungsgeschichte der Bergpredigt
(1968) 179f. WILSON, S. G., The Gentiles and the Gentile Mission in Luke-Acts (Cambridge 1973) 47, 48, 53, 54, 94. GLÖCK-
NER, R., Die Verkündigung des Heils beim Evangelisten Lukas
(Mainz 1975) 210ff. RAYAN, S., The Holy Spirit (New York 1978)
101. PRAST, F., Presbyter und Evangelium in nachapostolischer
Zeit (Stuttgart 1979) 281-84, 351.

24:46 HAHN, F. Christologische Hoheitstitel (1963) 205, 216f. DU-
PONT, J. Etudes sur les Acts des Apôtres (1967) 256, 322, 327,
328. RUPPERT, L., Jesus als der leidende Gerechte? (Stuttgart
1972) 47a16. WANKE, J., Die Emmauserzählung (Leipzig 1973)
92, 118, A.424. CAVALLIN, H. C. C., Life After Death. I (Lund
1974) 5, 8nI7. TALBERT, C. H., Literary Patterns, Theological
Themes, and the Genre of Luke-Acts (Missoula 1974) 124.
WILCKENS, U., Die Missionsreden der Apostelgeschichte (Neukirchen 1974(3)) 116, 117, 118, 139, 140, 143. DUNN, J. D. G.,
Unity and Diversity in the New Testament (London 1977) 43.
DÖMER, M., Das Heil Gottes (Köln-Bonn 1978) 70-79.

24:47-49 HAHN, F. Das Verständnis der Mission im Neuen Testament
(²1965) 114. KREMER, J., Pfingstbericht und Pfingstgeschehen
(Stuttgart 1973) 180-90. PFITZNER, V. C., " 'Pneumatic' Apostleship? Apostle and Spirit in the Acts of the Apostles" in: W. Hau-
beck/M. Bachmann (eds.) Wort in der Zeit. FS. K. H. Rengstorf
(Leiden 1980) 215-16.

24:47-48 MOULE, C. F. D. ed., The Significance of the Message of the
Resurrection for Faith in Jesus Christ (1968) 92. KASTING, H. Die
Anfänge der Urchristlichen Mission (1969) 41-44.TALBERT, C.
H., Literary Patterns, Theological Themes, and the Genre of Luke-
Acts (Missoula 1974) 59-60. PRAST, F., Presbyter und Evangel-
ium in nachapostolischer Zeit (Stuttgart 1979) 323.

24:47 MOORE, G. F. Judaism (1946) I 516n. FARRER, A. St Matthew
and St Mark (1954) 54. DUPONT, J. "La Salut des Gentils et la
Signification Théologique du Livre des Actes," NTS 6 (1959-1960)
150f. DELLING, G. Die Zueignung des Heils in der Taufe (1961)
43, 47, 48, 50, 51, 52. KAESEMANN, E. Exegetische Versuche
und Besinnungen (1964) I 45. HAHN, F. Das Verständnis der Mission im Neuen Tesament (²1965) 111-14, 119. DUPONT, J., Etudes
sur les Actes des Apôtres (1967) 259, 261, 265, 329, 403, 404, 418,

438, 500. NICKELS, P. Targum and New Testament (1967) 51. STROBEL, A. Erkenntnis und Bekenntnis der Sünde in neutestamentlicher Zeit (1968) 42, 57, ZEHNLE, R. F. Peter's Pentecost Discourse (1971) 61, 98, 99. KRÄNKL, E., Jesus der Knecht Gottes (Regensburg 1972) 80, 89, 118, 120, 181, 208. SA-MAIN, E., "La Notion de APXH" in: F. Neirynck (ed.) L'Evangile de Luc (Gembloux 1973) 300-02. WANKE, J., Die Emmauserzählung (Leipzig 1973) 47, 118. WILSON, S. G., The Gentiles and the Gentile Mission in Luke-Acts (Cambridge 1973) 36, 47, 51-55, 57, 91, 124, 240, 241, 243. DUPONT, J., "La portée christologique de l'evangélisation des nations d'après Luc 24,47" in: J. Gnilka (ed.) Neues Testament und Kirche. FS. R. Schnackenburg (Freiburg 1974) 125-43. TALBERT, C. H., Literary Patterns, Theological Themes, and the Genre of Luke-Acts (Missoula 1974) 98. WILCKENS, U., Die Missionsreden der Apostelgeschichte (Neukirchen 1974*(3)*) 97, 107, 181, 182, 227, 228. "Agricola" in: TRE 2 (1978) 112. "Apostel" in: TRE 3 (1978) 442, 443. PRAST, F., Presbyter und Evangelium in nachapostolischer Zeit (Stuttgart 1979) 321, 331. JEREMIAS, J., Die Sprache des Lukasevangeliums (Göttingen 1980) 322.

24:48 BROX, N. Zeuge und Märtyrer (1961) 43ff. BURCHARD, C. Der dreizehnte Zeuge (1970) 130-35, 139, 175. BEUTLER, J. Martyria (1972) 192, 194f., 303. KRÄNKL, E. Jesus der Knecht Gottes (1972) 167f. WANKE, J., Die Emmauserzählung (Leipzig 1973) 117. GLÖCKNER, R., Die Verkündigugng des Heils beim Evangelisten Lukas (Mainz 1975) 45ff. NELLESSEN, E., Zeugnis für Jesus und das Wort (Köln 1976) 107-18. TRITES, A. A., The New Testament Concept of Witness (Cambridge 1977) 128-29. PRAST, F., Presbyter und Evangelium in nachapostolischer Zeit (Stuttgart 1979) 316.

24:49 STONEHOUSE, N. B. The Witness of Matthew and Mark to Christ (1944) 171. MOULE, C. F. D. "The Post-Resurrection Appearances in the Light of Festival Pilgrimages," NTS 4 (1957-1958) 60ff. MUNCK, J. Paul and the Salvation of Mankind (1959) 210f. DELLLING, G. Die Taufe im Neuen Testament (1963) 121. HAHN, F. Christologische Hoheitstitel (1963) 321. SEEBERG, A. Der Katechismus der Urchristenheit (1966) 205, 217, 222f., 227. MOULE, C. F. D. ed., The Significance of the Message of the Resurrection for Faith in Jesus Christ (1968) 5. KRÄNKL, E., Jesus der Knecht Gottes (Regensburg 1972) 150, 165, 168, 180, 208. KREMER, J., Pfingstbericht und Pfingstgeschehen (Stuttgart 1973) 100, 175, 218, 229, 236. KÜMMEL, W. G. Einleitung in das Neue Testament (1973) 125f. STOLLE, V., Der Zeuge als Angeklagter (Stuttgart 1973) 149-51. WANKE, J., Die Emmauserzählung

(Leipzig 1973) 5, 47. WILSON, S. G., The Gentiles and the Gentile Mission in Luke-Acts (Cambridge 1973) 55, 56. TALBERT, C. H., Literary Patterns, Theological Themes, and the Genre of Luke-Acts (Missoula 1974) 59, 60, 97. WILCKENS, U., Die Missionsreden der Apostelgeschichte (Neukirchen ³1974) 56, 57, 58, 59, 94, 150, 233. KUDASIEWICZ, J., ''Jeruzalem—miejscem zeslania Ducha Swietego (Lk 24,49; Dz 1,4)'' RTK 23 (1976) 85-96. RAYAN, S., The Holy Spirit: Heart of the Gospel and Christian Hope (New York 1978) 2,10-11. PRAST, F., Presbyter und Evangelium in nachapostolischer Zeit (Stuttgart 1979) 321. JEREMIAS, J., Die Sprache des Lukasevangeliums (Göttingen 1980) 322.

24:50-53 SAHLIN, H. Der Messias und das Gottesvolk (1945) 11-17. MENOUD, P. ''Remarques sur les textes de l'ascension dans Luc-Actes,'' in: Neutestamentliche Studien für Rudolf Bultmann (1954) 148-56. VAN STEMPVOORT, P. A. ''The Interpretation of the Ascension in Luke and Acts,'' NTS 5 (1, 1959) 30-42. DOEVE, J. W. ''De Hemelvaart in het Evangelie naar Lucas'' HomBib 20 (3, 1961) 75-79. LOHSE, E. Die Auferstehung Jesu Christi im Zeugnis des Lukasevangeliums (1961) 39f. SCHLIER, H. ''Jesu Himmelfahrt nach den Lukanischen Schriften,'' GuL 34 (2, 1961) 91-99. JOHNSTON, E. D. ''The Johannine Version of the Feeding of the Five Thousand—an Independent Tradition?'' NTS 8 (1961-1962) 155f. BUECKMANN, O. in: Herr, tue meine Lippen auf Bd. 3 (1964) G. Eichholz ed., 252ff. DUPONT, J. The Sources of Acts (1964) 24, 25, 28, 32. KAMPHAUS, F. Von der Exegese zur Predigt (²1968) 53-57. GRASS, H. Ostergeschehen und Osterberichte (1970) 43ff. LOHFINK, G. Die Himmelfahr Jesu (1971) 112-15. KÜMMEL, W. G. Einleitung in das Neue Testament (1973) 125f. FRIEDRICH, G., ''Lk 9,51 und die Entrückungschristologie des Lukas'' in: P. Hoffmann (ed.) Orientierung an Jesus. FS. J. Schmid (Freiburg 1973) 59-61. WANKE, J., Die Emmauserzählung (Leipzig 1973) 117. TALBERT, C. H., Literary Patterns, Theological Themes, and the Genre of Luke-Acts (Missoula 1974) 60, 112, 122. BARTLETT, D. L., Fact and Faith (Valley Forge 1975) 114-16. MENOUD, P. H., ''Remarques sur les textes de l'ascension dans Luc-Acts'' in: Jésus-Christ et la foi (Neuchátel-Paris 1975) 76-84. SCHNEIDER, G., Das Evangelium nach Lukas (Gütersloh 1977) 504, 506. DÖMER, M., Das Heil Gottes (Köln-Bonn 1978) 106-108. LaVERDIERE, E. A., ''The Ascension of the Risen Lord'' Bible Today 95 (1978) 153-59. ENGELHARDT, K., in: GPM 33 (1979) 230-35.

24:50-52 SCHRECKENBERG, H., ''Flavius Josephus und die lukanischen

Schriften" in: W. Haubeck/M. Bachmann (eds.) Wort in der Zeit. FS. K. H. Rengstorf (Leiden 1980) 193-94.

24:50-51 SCHENK, W. Der Segen im Neuen Testament (1967) 54-58. LOHFINK, G. Die Himmelfahrt Jesu (1971) 160-62.WILSON, S. G., The Gentiles and the Gentile Mission in Luke-Acts (Cambridge 1973) 96, 97, 98, 100, 104, 105. WESTERMANN, C., Blessing (Philadelphia 1978) 70, 86-91, 98-101.

24:50 JEREMIAS, J. Die Abendmahlsworte Jesu (1960) 144f. DAL-MAN, G. Orte und Wege Jesu (1967) 284f. LOHFINK, G. Die Himmelfahrt Jesu (1971) 163-69. JEREMIAS, J., Die Sprache des Lukasevangeliums (Göttingen 1980) 323.

24:51ff. BLASS, F. Philosophy of the Gospels (1898) 138ff., 213f.

24:51-53 NESTLE, E. Einführung in das Griechische Neue Testament (1909) 249ff.

24:51-52 ALAND, K. NTS 12 (1965-1966) 197f., 208f. TALBERT, C. H., Literary Patterns, Theological Themes, and the Genre of Luke-Acts (Missoula 1974) 59, 60.

24:51 STONEHOUSE, N. B. The Witness of Matthew and Mark to Christ (1944) 118. STREETER, B. H. The Four Gospels (1951) 142f. JE-REMIAS, J. Die Abendmahlsworte Jesu (1960) 144f. TAYLOR, V. The Text of the New Testament (1961) 19f. SCHLIER, H. "Jesu Himmelfahrt nach den Lukanischen Schriften", Besinnung auf das Neue Testament (1964) 227-41. DUPONT, J. Etudes sur les Actes des Apôtres (1967) 478-80. MOULE, C. F. D. ed., The Significance of the Message of the Resurrection for Faith in Jesus Christ (1968) 5. NEIRYNCK, F., "La Matière Marcienne dans Luc" in: F. Neirynck (ed.) L'Evangile de Luc (Gembloux 1973) 184-93. TALBERT, C. H., Literary Patterns, Theological Themes, and the Genre of Luke-Acts (Missoula 1974) 122. METZGER, B. M., The Early Versions of the New Testament (Oxford 1977) 41. JE-REMIAS, J., Die Sprache des Lukasevangeliums (Göttingen 1980) 323.

24:52-53 HENNECKE, A./SCHNEEMELCHER, W. Neutestamentliche Apokryphen (1964) II 483.

24:52 TAYLOR, V. The Text of the New Testament (1961) 19f. LOH-FINK, G. Die Himmelfahrt Jesu (1971) 171-76. WANKE, J., Die Emmauserzählung (Leipzig 1973) 47. JEREMIAS, J., Die Sprache des Lukasevangeliums (Göttingen 1980) 323.

24:53 TAYLOR, V. The Text of the New Testament (1961) 52f. SCHENK, W. Der Segen im Neuen Testament (1967) 118. WANKE, J., Die Emmauserzählung (Leipzig 1973) A.409. JE-REMIAS, J., Die Sprache des Lukasevangeliums (Göttingen 1980) 323.

Acts

ΠΡΑΞΕΙΣ
ΑΠΟΣΤΟΛΩΝ

1-28 EHRHARDT, A. The Acts of the Apostles (1969) 1f., 42.SCHNEIDER, G., Die Apostelgeschichte I (Freiburg/Basel/ Wien 1980) 26-52 (lit!).

1-15 ROBERTSON, A. T. Luke the Historian in the Light of Research (1920) 18, 37, 77, 84, 86ff. FEINE, D. P./BEHM, D. J. Einleitung in das Neue Testament (1950) 88f. DUPONT, J. The Sources of Acts (1964) 29, 32, 59, 60. MARTIN, R. A. "Syntactical Evidence of Aramaic Sources in Acts i-xv," NTS 11 (1, 1964) 38-59. BRAUN, H. Qumran und NT II (1966) 240, 242. BLACK, M. An Aramaic Approach to the Gospels and Acts (1967) 62f. TALBERT, C. H., Literary Patterns, Theological Themes, and the Genre of Luke-Acts (Missoula 1974) 25, 32, 36, 37. GASQUE, W., A History of the Criticism of the Acts of the Apostles (Tübingen 1975) 166, 172, 270. KILGALLEN, J. J., "Acts: Literary and Theological Turning Points" BThB 7 (1977) 177-80.

1-13 VAN IERSEL, B. M. F. "Der Quellenwert von Apg. 1-13" in: 'Der Sohn' in den Synoptischen Jesusworten (1961) 31. VAN IERSEL, B. M. F. "Saint Paul et la prédication de l'Eglise primitive," Studiorum Paulinorum Congressus Internationalis Catholicus 1961 Vol. I (1963) 433-41.

1-12 DIBELIUS, M. Aufsätze zur Apostelgeschichte (1951) 110f. ET. Studies in the Acts of the Apostles (1956) 126f. DUPONT, J. The Sources of Acts (1964) 20, 29, 31, 34. KAESEMANN, E. Exegetische Versuche und Besinnungen I (1964) 162. HAHN, F. Das Verständnis der Mission im Neuen Testament (^{2}1965) 38, 43. TALBERT, C. H., Literary Patterns, Theological Themes, and the Genre of Luke-Acts (Missoula 1974) 23-25. GASQUE, W., A History of the Criticism of the Acts of the Apostles (Tübingen 1975) 25, 33, 36, 79, 88, 111, 133.

1-10 DENNEY, J. The Death of Christ (^{3}1956) 47ff.

1-8 JOHNSON, L. T., The Literary Function of Possessions in Luke-Acts (Missoula 1977) 36-38.

1-7 "Amt" in: TRE 2 (1978) 512.

1-5 DIBELIUS, M. Aufsätze zur Apostelgeschichte (1951) 15f. ET. Studies in the Acts of the Apostles (1956) 9f. HAHN, Christologische Hoheitstitel (1963) 179. DUPONT, J. The Sources of Acts (1964) 36, 38, 53, 54, 58, 112. BLEVINS, W. L., "The Early Church: Acts 1 - 5" RevEx 71 (1974) 463-74. TALBERT, C. H., Literary Patterns, Theological Themes, and the Genre of Luke-Acts (Missoula 1974) 1, 2, 13, 35-39, 43. MARTIN, R. P., New Testament Foundations II: Acts - Revelation (Exeter 1978) 70-82.

1-4 HAMEL, E., "La legge nuova per una comunità nuova," CiCa 124

(2957, 1973) 351-60. MEALAND, D. L., "Community of Goods and Utopian Allusions in Acts I-IV" JThS 28 (1977) 96-99.

1-2 WILCOX, M. The Semitisms of Acts (1965) 59ff. LAURENTIN, R., "Les charismes de Marie. Ecriture, Tradition et Sitz im Leben" EphM 28 (1978) 309-21. HARRINGTON, D. J., God's People in Christ (Philadelphia 1980) 38-43. KESICH, V., "Resurrection, Ascension, and the Giving of the Spirit" GOThR 25 (1980) 249-60. STRAVINSKAS, P. M. J., "The Role of the Spirit in Acts 1 and 2" BiTod 18 (1980) 263-68.

1 DUPONT, J. The Sources of Acts (1964) 28, 37, 39, 40, 60. TALBERT, C. H. NTS 14 (1967-1968) 261f. GNILKA, J. "Der Missionsauftrag des Herrn nach Mt 28 und Apg 1," BuL 9 (1968) 1-9. SELBY, D. J., Introduction to the New Testament (New York 1971) 291-92. TALBERT, C. H., Literary Patterns, Theological Themes, and the Genre of Luke-Acts (Missoula 1974) 58-60, 61-66. "Auferstehung" in: TRE 4 (1979) 503.

1:1ff. STAEHELIN, E. Die Verkündigung des Reiches Gottes in der Kirche Jesu Christi I (1951) 69.

1:1-26 REICKE, B. Glaube und Leben der Urgemeinde (1957) 9-26.

1:1-14 GOULDER, M. D. Type and History in Acts (1964) 16, 54, 146-49, 183. ROLOFF, J. Apostolat-Verkündigung-Kirche (1965) 192-94. DUPONT, J. Etudes sur les Actes des Apôtres (1967) 81-83. ZEHNLE, R. F. Peter's Pentecost Discourse (1971) 95-104, 105. HARDER, G. GPM 28 (2, 1974) 254-62. HUBBARD, B. J., "The Role of Commissioning Accounts in Acts" in: C. H. Talbert (ed.) Perspectives on Luke-Acts (Danville 1978) 190, 193, 195-96. WEISER, A., Die Apostelgeschichte I (Gütersloh/Würzburg 1981) 46, 60 (lit!).

1:1-12 FRANKLIN, E. "The ascension and the eschatology of Luke-Acts," SJTh 23 (1970) 191-200. GRASS, H., Ostergeschehen und Osterberichte (1970) 43ff. TALBERT, C. H., Literary Patterns, Theological Themes, and the Genre of Luke-Acts (Missoula 1974) 61. MENOUD, P. H., "Remarques sur les textes de l'ascension dans Luc-Acts" in: Jésus Christ et la foi (Neuchâtel/Paris 1975) 76-84; [orig. in: Neutestamentliche Studien für Rudolf Bultmann (Berlin 1954) 148-56]. BOVON, F., Luc le Théologien (Neuchâtel/Paris 1978) 181-88.

1:1-11 SALIN, H. Der Messias und das Gottesvolk (1945) 11-13. IWAND, H.-J. Predigt-Meditationen (1964) 492-501. WALVOORD, J. F. "The Ascension of Christ," BiblSa 121 (481, 1964) 2-12. RAMSEY, A. M. "What was the Ascension?" in: Historicity and Chronology in the New Testament (1965) D. Nineham ed., 135-44. STECK, K. G., in: Herr, tue meine Lippen auf Bd. II (1966⁵) G.

Eicholz ed., 296-308. DOERNE, M. Die alten Episteln (1967) 134-38. EISLINGER, W. GPM 22 (2, 1967-1968) 238-47. RISTOW, H. "Himmelfahrt," in: Wandelt in der Liebe (1968) 189-201. PESCH, R. "Der Anfang der Apostelgeschichte," in: Evangelisch-Katholischer Kommentar zum Neuen Testament Vorarbeiten Heft 3 (1971) 7-35. LOHFINK, G. Die Himmelfahrt Jesu (1971). FRANCIS, F. O. JBL 91 (3, 1972) 424-25. DEVOR, R. C. "The Ascension of Christ and the Dissension of the Church," Encounter 33 (4, 1972) 340-58. BARTLETT, D. L., Fact and Faith (Valley Forge 1975) 114-16. FRIEDRICH, G., "Lk 9,51 und die Entrückungschristologie des Lukas" in: Auf das Wort kommt es an (Göttingen 1978) 39-44; [orig. in: P. Hoffman (ed.) Orientierung an Jesus. FS. J. Schmid (Freiburg 1973) 61-66.]

1:1-8 DUPONT, D. J., The Salvation of the Gentiles (New York 1979) 17-19.

1:1-5 SAHLIN, H, Der Messias und das Gottesvolk (1945) 14-16. KUEMMEL, W. G. Einleitung in das Neue Testament (1973) 125f. TALBERT, C. H., Literary Patterns, Theological Themes, and the Genre of Luke-Acts (Missoula 1974) 16, 18, 65, 122. ALSUP, J. E., The Post-Resurrection Stories of the Gospel-Tradition (Stuttgart 1975) 69ff.

1:1-4 WILSON, S. G. The Gentiles and the Gentile Mission in Luke-Acts (1973) 48, 55, 89, 92, 100. ROBBINS, V. K., "Prefaces in Greco-Roman Biography and Luke-Acts" in: P. J. Achtemeier (ed.) SBL Papers 1978/II (Missoula 1978) 193-207.

1:1-3 DELEBECQUE, É., "Les deux prologues des Actes des Apôtres" RThom 80 (1980) 628-34. SCHNEIDER, G., Die Apostelgeschichte I (Freiburg/Basel/Wien 1980) 188-89 (lit!).

1:1-2 LOHFINK, G. Die Himmelfahrt Jesu (1971) 218-23. SAMAIN, E. "La notion de APXH dans l'æuvre lucanienne," in: L'Evangile de Luc (1973) F. Neirynck ed., 313-16.TALBERT, C. H., Literary Patterns, Theological Themes, and the Genre of Luke-Acts (Missoula 1974) 59. "Apostelgeschichte" in: TRE 3 (1978) 502. DÖMER, M., Das Heil Gottes: Studien zur Theologie des lukanischen Doppelwerkes (Köln/Bonn 1978) 5-14, 109-11. FEUILLET, A., "Le 'Commencement' de l'economie Chrétienne d'apres He ii.3-4, Mc i.1 et Ac i.1-2" NTS 24 (1978) 163-74.

1:1 STONEHOUSE, N. B. The Witness of Matthew and Mark to Christ (1944) 8. FEINE, D. P./BEHM, D. J. Einleitung in das Neue Testament (1950) 65f. STONEHOUSE, N. B. The Witness of Luke to Christ (1951) 26f., 116. NORDEN, E. Agnostos Theos (1956 = 1912) 311ff. TALBERT, C. H., Literary Patterns, Theological Themes, and the Genre of Luke-Acts (Missoula 1974) 18,

98. GASQUE, W., A History of the Criticism of the Acts of the Apostles (Tübingen 1975) 29, 144, 145, 186. GLÖCKNER, R., Die Verkündigung des Heils beim Evangelisten Lukas (Mainz 1975) 12, 23-24. METZGER, B. M., The Early Versions of the New Testament (Oxford 1977) 140. QUINN, J. D., "The Last Volume of Luke: The Relation of Luke - Acts to the Pastoral Epistles" in: C. H. Talbert (ed.) Perspectives on Luke-Acts (Danville 1978) 70. ROBBINS, V. K., "Prefaces in Greco-Roman Biography and Luke-Acts" in: P. J. Achtemeier (ed.) SBL Seminar Papers 1978/II (Missoula 1978) 195-98. HENGEL, M., Zur urchristlichen Geschichtsschreibung (Stuttgart 1979) 15: ET: J. Bowden (trans.) Acts and the History of Earliest Christianity (London 1979) 9. MARX, W. G., "A New Theophilus" EQ 52 (1980) 17-26.

1:2ff. BLASS, F. Philosophy of the Gospels (1898) 132ff. BEY-SCHLAG, K. Clemens Romaus und der Frühkatholizismus (1966) 326f., 336.

1:2-3 WILCKENS, U. Die Missionsreden der Apostelgeschichte (1961) 57, 107, 116-17, 143-44, 150-51, 162.

1:2 PALLIS, A. Notes on St. Luke and the Acts (London 1928) 49. CLARK, A. C. The Acts of the Apostles (1933) xlix, 189, 202, 227, 256, 258, 293, 331, 336. ARVEDSON, T. Das Mysterium Christi (1937) 136f. MASSAUX, E. Influence de l'Evangile de Saint Matthieu sur la littérature chrétienne avant Saint Irénée (1950) 69-83. DIBELIUS, M. Aufsätze zur Apostelgeschichte (1951) 81f. ET: Studies in the Acts of the Apostels (1956) 90f. STREETER, B. H. The Four Gospels (1951) 142f. FLEW, R. N. Jesus and His Church (1956) 85. VAN STEMPVOORT, P. A., NTS 5 (1958-1959) 32ff. DUPONT, J. "'Anelēmphthē (Act. i.2)," NTS 8 (2, 1962) 154-57. EPP, E. J. The theological tendency of Codex Bezae Cantabrigiensis in Acts (1966) 65f., 116f. DUPONT, J. Etudes sur les Actes des Apôtres (1967) 477-80. DUNN, J. D. G. Baptism in the Holy Spirit (1970) 45, 46. WILSON, S. G. The Gentiles and the Gentile Mission in Luke-Acts (1973) 88, 97-98, 109. TAL-BERT, C. H., Literary Patterns, Theological Themes, and the Genre of Luke-Acts (Missoula 1974) 122. WILCKENS, U. Die Missionsreden der Apostelgeschichte (^{3}1974) 57, 107, 143, 151, 163. PRAST, F. Presbyter und Evangelium in nachapostolischer Zeit (Stuttgart 1979) 309, 316. PFITZNER, V. C., " 'Pneumatic' Apostleship? Apostle and Spirit in the Acts of the Apostles" in: W. Haubeck/M. Bachmann (eds.) Wort in der Zeit. FS. K. H. Rengstorf (Leiden 1980) 215-16.

1:3-14 SHEPARD, J. W., The Life and Letters of St. Paul (Grand Rapids 1950) 26-68. KUEMMEL, W. G. Einleitung in das Neue Testament (1973) 125f.

1:3-11 DAVIES, W. D., The Gospel and the Land (London 1974) 264. BOEHMIG, W. und SIMPFENDÖRFER, G., in: P. Krusche et al. (eds.) Predigtstudien für das Kirchenjahr 1979-1980. II/2 (Stuttgart 1980) 72-80. HOFIUS, O., in: GPM 34 (1980) 229-37.

1:3-8 DÖMER, M., Das Heil Gottes: Studien zur Theologie des luka-nischen Doppelwerkes (Köln/Bonn 1978) 111-17, 134.

1:3-4 TALBERT, C. H., Literary Patterns, Theological Themes, and the Genre of Luke-Acts (Missoula 1974) 61, 62.

1:3 WIKENHAUSER, A. "Die Belehrung der Apostel durch den Auf-erstandenen nach Apg. 1,3," in: Vom Wort des Lebens (1951) M. Meinertz ed., 105-13. STEMPVOORT, P. A. van, "De betekenis van λέγων τὰ περὶ τῆς βασιλείας τοῦ θεοῦ in Apg. 1,3" NedThT 9/6 (1954-1955) 349-55. DELLING Die Zueignung des Heils in der Taufe (1961) 90. MENOUD, Ph. H. " 'Pendant quar-ante jours' (Actes i 3)," in: Neotestamentica et Patristica (1962) 148-56. DELLING, G. Die Taufe im Neuen Testament (1963) 135. HAHN, F. Christologische Hoheitstitel (1963) 217. NIBLEY, H. "Evangelium Quadraginta Dierum," VigChr 20 (1, 1966) 1-24. LOHFINK, G. Die Himmelfahrt Jesu (1971) 25-27, 152f., 176-86. KRAENKL, E. Jesus der Knecht Gottes (1972) 144-46, 176. WIL-SON, S. G. The Gentiles and the Gentile Mission in Luke-Acts (1973) 89, 98, 100-01, 127. WILCKENS, U. Die Missionsreden der Apostelgeschichte (³1974) 57, 116, 117, 145, 150. LEANEY, A. R. C., "Why there were Forty Days between the Resurrection and the Ascension" StEv 4 (1968) 417-19. RUPPERT, L., Jesus als der leidende Gerechte? (Stuttgart 1972) 47n.16. BAUMERT, N., Täglich sterben und auferstehen. Der Literalsinn von 2 Kor 4,12 - 5,10 (München 1973) 298-99. WANKE, J., Die Emmaus-erzählung. Eine redaktionsgeschichtliche Untersuchung zu Lk 24,13-35 (Leipzig 1973) 24, 90. TALBERT, C. H., Literary Pat-terns, Theological Themes, and the Genre of Luke-Acts (Missoula 1974) 59, 60, 122. MENOUD, P. H., "Pendant quarante jours" in: Jésus Christ et la foi (Neuchâtel/Paris 1975) 110-18; [orig. in: Neotestamentica et Patristica. FS. O. Cullmann (Leiden 1962) 148-56]. "Auferstehung" in: TRE 4 (1979) 519. PRAST, F. Prebyter und Evangelium in nachapostolischer Zeit (Stuttgart 1979) 280-81, 316-17, 333. KRAUSE, M., "Christlich-gnostische Texte als Quellen für die Auseinandersetzung von Gnosis und Christentum" in: M. Krause (ed.) Gnosis and Gnosticism (Leiden 1981) 53-54, 56.

1:4ff. STAEHELIN, E. Die Verkündigung des Reiches Gottes in der Kirche Jesu Christi I (1951) 69. "Agrapha" in: TRE 2 (1978) 104.

1:4-14 SCHNEIDER, G., Die Apostelgeschichte I (Freiburg/Basel/Wien 1980) 195 (lit!).

1:4-11 BENOIT, P. "The ascension of Christ," TheolDig 8 (2, 1960) 105-10. LOHFINK, G. "Der historische Ansatz der Himmelfahrt Christi," Catholica 17 (1, 1963) 44-84. BLENKINSOPP, J. "The Bible and the People: The Ascension as Mystery of Salvation," ClR 50 (5, 1965) 369-74. GUTBROD, K. Die Apostelgeschichte (1968) 15ff.

1:4-9 MICHEL, H-J., Die Abschiedsrede des Paulus an die Kirche, Apg 20:17-38. Motivgeschichte und theologische Bedeutung (München 1973) 57, 62-63.

1:4-8 WILSON, S. G. The Gentiles and the Gentile Mission in Luke-Acts (1973) 78, 102, 121, 124, 241.

1:4-5.8 KREMER, J. "Die Voraussagen des Pfingstgeschehen in Apg 1, 4-5 und 8," in: Die Zeit Jesu (1970) B. Bornkamm/K. Rahner eds., 145-168.

1:4-5 ROBINSON, J. A. T. "The One Baptism" in: Twelve New Testament Studies (1962) 158-75. KREMER, J., Pfingstbericht und Pfingstgeschehen. Eine exegetische Untersuchung zu Apg 2,1-13 (Stuttgart 1973) 197-90. PRAST, F. Presbyter und Evangelium in nachapostolischer Zeit (Stuttgart 1979) 321.

1:4 RUDOLPH, K. Die Mandäer I (1960) 241. WILCOX, M. The Semitisms of Acts (1965) 106-09, 110, 171. NICKELS, P. Targum and New Testament (1967) 59. LOHFINK, G. Die Himmelfahrt Jesu (1971) 264f., 266f. ZEHNLE, R. F. Peter's Pentecost Discourse (1971) 96-97. BOWEN, C. R., "The Meaning of συναλιζόμενος in Act 1:4" ZNW 13 (1912) 247-59. WANKE, J., Die Emmauserzählung. Eine redaktionsgeschichtliche Untersuchung zu Lk 24,13-35 (Leipzig 1973) 104. TALBERT, C. H., Literary Patterns, Theological Themes, and the Genre of Luke-Acts (Missoula 1974) 22, 59, 60, 97. ALSUP, J. E., The Post-Resurrection Appearance Stories of the Gospel-Tradition (Stuttgart 1975) 78ff, 183-84. KUDASIEWICZ, J., "Jeruzalem - miejscem zeslania Ducha Swietego (Lk 24,49. Dz 1,4)" RTK 23 (1976) 85-96. "Abendmahl" in: TRE 1 (1977) 50. DUPONT, D. J., The Salvation of the Gentiles (New York 1979) 45-52. PFITZNER, V. C., " 'Pneumatic' Apostleship? Apostle and Spirit in the Acts of the Apostles" in: W. Haubeck/M. Bachmann (eds.) Wort in der Zeit. FS. K. H. Rengstorf (Leiden 1980) 215-16.

1:5-11 DUPONT, D. J., The Salvation of the Gentiles (New York 1979) 53-58.

1:5-8 MOULE, C. F. D. "The Post-Resurrection Appearances in the light of Festival Pilgrimages," NTS 4 (1957-1958) 60ff.

1:5 CLARK, A. C. The Acts of the Apostles (1933) 256, 293, 331, 337. ADLER, N. Das erste christliche Pfingstfest (1938) 69, 80f., 91,

133f., 154, 157, 159. DELLING, G. Die Zueignung des Heils in der Taufe (1961) 92. DELLING, G. Die Taufe im Neuen Testament (1963) 46, 59, 62, 63. YATES, J. E. The Spirit and the Kingdom (1963) 26f., 168ff., 175ff. HENNECKE, E./ SCHNEEMELCHER, W. Neutestamentliche Apokryphen (1964) II 267. BIEDER, W., Die Verheissung der Taufe im Neuen Testament (Zürich 1966) 45-46. BRAUN, H. Qumran und NT (1966) 253ff. SEEBERG, A. Der Katechismus der Urchristenheit (1966) 217, 220, 221, 222. DUNN, J. D. G. Baptism in the Holy Spirit (1970) 2, 18n, 43, 44, 45, 46, 68, 69, 70, 71, 90, 100, 128, 129, 207, 227. LOHFINK, G. Die Himmelfahrt Jesu (1971) 256-57. DUNN, J. D. G., Jesus and the Spirit (London 1975) 148, 190, 398. METZGER, B. M., The Early Versions of the New Testament (Oxford 1977) 245. MCDONALD, J. I. H., Kerygma and Didache (Cambridge 1980) 17. BARTH, G., Die Taufe in frühchristlicher Zeit Neukirchen-Vluyn 1981) 23, 25, 37, 44, 60-63, 68.

1:6ff. KUEMMEL, W. G. Einleitung in das Neue Testament (1973) 125f.

1:6-14 TALBERT, C. H., Literary Patterns, Theological Themes, and the Genre of Luke-Acts (Missoula 1974) 37.

1:6-12 WILCKENS, U. GPM 18 (1, 1964) 195-200. ZINGG, P., Das Wachsen der Kirche (Freiburg 1974) 141-42.

1:6-11 WILCKENS, U. Die Missionsreden der Apostelgeschichte (³1974) 200f. METZGER, B. M. "The Meaning of Christ's Ascension," ChrTo 10 (May 27, 1966) 863-64. GLÖCKNER, R., Die Verkündigung des Heils beim Evangelisten Lukas (Mainz 1975) 45ff. SCHEP, J. A., The Nature of the Resurrection Body (Grand Rapids 1976) 158-61. LaVERDIERE, E. A., "The Ascension of the Risen Lord" BiTod 95 (1978) 1553-59. GOODING, D. W., "Demythologizing Old and New, and Luke's Description of the Ascension: a Layman's Appraisal" IBS 2 (1980) 95-119. DUNN, J. D. G., "Demythologizing the Ascension - A Reply to Professor Gooding" IBS 3 (1, 1981) 15-27.

1:6-8 PALLIS, A., Notes on St. Luke and the Acts (London 1928) 49. KLEIN, G. Die Zwölf Apostel (1961) 209f. MUSSNER, F. "Die Idee der Apokatastasis in der Apostelgeschichte," Praesentia Salutis (1967) 223. LOHFINK, G. Die Himmelfahrt Jesu (1971) 153-58. WILSON, S. G. The Gentiles and the Gentile Mission in Luke-Acts (1973) 68, 78-79, 82, 84, 86, 88-96, 125. LADD, G. E., A Theology of the New Testament (Grand Rapids 1974) 315, 332, 333, 339, 343. GOPPELT, L., Theologie des Neuen Testaments II (Göttingen 1976) 608. SANDMEL, S., We Jews and Jesus (New York 1977) 35. TREVIJANO ETCHEVERRÍA, R., "La misión de la Iglesia primitiva y los mandatos del Señor en los Evangelios" Salmanticensis 25 (1978) 5-36. DUPONT, D. J., The Salvation of the Gentiles (New York 1979) 51-52. MATTILL, A. J., Luke and the Last Things (Dillsboro 1979) 150-55. POUPON, G., "L'accusation de magie dans les Actes aprocryphes" in: F. Bovon et al. (eds.) Les Actes Apocryphes des Apôtres (Geneva 1981) 88. TIEDE, D. L., "Acts 1:6-8 and the Theo-Political Claims of Christian Witness" Word World 1 (1, 1981) 41-51.

1:6f. DELLING, G. Die Zueignung des Heils in der Taufe (1961) 90.

1:6 KNOX, W. L. The Sources of the Synoptic Gospels II (1957) 44, 108. HAHN, F. Christologische Hoheitstitel (1963) 220. KAESEMANN, E. Exegetische Versuche und Besinnungen (1964) I 28. McNAMARA, M. The New Testament and the Palestinian Targum to the Pentateuch (1966) 250 n.33. NICKELS, P. Targum and New Testament (1967) 59. EHRHARDT, A. The Acts of the Apostels (1969) 14f. HENGEL, M. Judentum und Hellenismus (1969) 569. ET: Judaism and Hellenism (1974) I 313. KRAENKL, E. Jesus der Knecht Gottes (1972) 194f., 204. WILSON, S. G. The Gentiles and the Gentile Mission in Luke-Acts (1973) 88-89, 102-03, 106, 168. WILCKENS, U. Die Missionsreden der Apostelgeschichte (³1974) 57, 155, 235, 236.

1:7-9 BETZ, H. D. Lukian von Samosata und das Neue Testament (1961) 98, 103, 143, 156, 158, 168, 191.

1:7-8 KRAENKL, E. Jesus der Knecht Gottes (1972) 188f., 204.

1:7 STAEHELIN, E. Die Verkündigung des Reiches Gottes in der Kirche Jesu Christi I (1951) 357. HARNISCH, W. Eschatologische Existenz (1973) 9f., 13, 55A. LUCCHESI, E., "Précédents non bibliques à l'expression néo-testamentaire: 'Les temps et les moments' " JThS 28 (1977) 537-40.

1:8 ADLER, N. Das erste christliche Pfingstfest (1938) 66, 71, 80, 135, 141-44, 154, 156f., 159. ADLER, N., Taufe und Handauflegung (Münster 1951) 22, 33, 43, 48, 109. FARRER, A. St Matthew and St Mark (1954) 53, 54. BEST, E. One Body in Christ (1955) 164. FLEW, R. N. Jesus and His Church (1956) 105, 106. RENGSTORF, K. H. Die Auferstehung Jesu (1960) 44, 46, 137, 139-40. BROX, N. Zeuge und Märtyrer (1961) 44f. LOHFINK, G. " 'Aufgefahren in den Himmel', GuL 35 (2, 1962) 84-85. DELLING, G. Die Taufe im Neuen Testament (1963) 61. GOULDER, M. D. Type and History in Acts (1964) 16, 55, 62f., 98n. HAHN, F. Das Verständnis der Mission im Neuen Testament (²1965) 115. BEYSCHLAG, K. Clemens Romanus und der Frühkatholizismus (1966) 276f., 336. HAGEMEYER, O. " 'Ihr seid meine Zeugen'," EuA 42 (5, 1966) 375-84. PESCH, R. Die Vision des Stephanus (1966) 38, 39, 40, 48, 60. van UNNIK, W. C., "Luke-Acts, a Storm Center in Contemporary Scholarship" in: L. E. Keck/J. L. Martyn (eds.)

Studies in Luke-Acts. FS. P. Schubert (Nashville 1966) 29. DU-
PONT, J. Etudes sur les Actes des Apôtres (1967) 402-04. KUENG,
H. Die Kirche (1967) 360, 417, 419, 443. ET: The Church (1967)
303, 352, 354, 375. BROWN, S. Apostasy and Perseverance in the
Theology of Luke (1969) 76, 80, 117, 127, 135, 138, 141. KAST-
ING, H. Die Anfänge der Urchristlichen Mission (1969) 41-43, 90,
96, 109. SCHNEIDER, G. Verleugnung, Verspottung und Verhör
Jesu nach Lukas 22,54-71 (1969) 196, 203, 205, 206, 208. BUR-
CHARD, C. Der dreizehnte Zeuge (1970) 130-36, 139, 142, 161,
166, 174f., 177. KUENZI, M. Das Naherwartungslogion Matthäus 10,23 (1970) 47, 62f. O'NEILL, J. C. The Theology of Acts
in its historical setting 1970) 15, 65f., 74. JERVELL, J., "The Lost
Sheep of the House of Israel" in: Luke and the People of God (Minneapolis 1972) 113-32. KRAENKL, E. Jesus der Knecht Gottes
(1972) 167f. ZMIJEWSKI, J. Die Eschatologiereden des Lukas-
Evangeliums (1972) 3, 18, 156, 161, 174, 204, 205, 209, 228, 315,
329, 383. KECK, L. E. "Listening To and Listening For. From
Text to Sermon (Acts 1:8)," Interpretation 27 (2, 1973) 184-202.
KREMER, J., Pfingstbericht und Pfingstgeschehen. (Stuttgart;
1973) 179-90. KUEMMEL, W. G. Einleitung in das Neue Testament (1973) 114f. SAMAIN, E. "La notion de ARXH dans l'æuvre
lucanienne," in: L'Evangile de Luc (1973) F. Neirynck ed., 302-
03, 326. STAEHLIN, G. "τὸ πνεῦμα 'Ιησοῦ (Apostelgeschichte 16:7)," in: Christ and the Spirit in the New Testament
(1973) Lindars, B./Smalley, S. S. eds., 238, 242f., 246f., 250.
WILSON, S. G. The Gentiles and the Gentile Mision in Luke-Acts
(1973) 90-96, 123-25, 228-29, 237-38, 240-41, 257-59. BEY-
SCHLAG, K., Simon Magus und die christliche Gnosis (Tübingen
1974) 165, 167, n.75, 178n.96, 188. DAVIES, W. D. The Gospel
and the Land (1974) 251, 265, 279, 280, 364, 412, 421, 422. DU-
PONT, J. "La portée christoloique de l'evangelisation des nations
d'après Luc 24,47," in: Neues Testament und Kirche (1974) J.
Gnilka ed., 126, 128, 136, 138, 141. TALBERT, C. H., Literary
Patterns, Theological Themes, and the Genre of Luke-Acts (Missoula 1974) 22, 59, 60, 61, 62, 96. WILCKENS, U. Die Missionsreden der Apostelgeschichte (³1974) 57, 58, 146, 147, 150, 227,
228, 233, 236. ZINGG, P., Das Wachsen der Kiche (Freiburg 1974)
143-44. DINKLER, E., "Phillippus und der ANHP ΑΙΘΙΟΨ
(Apg 8, 26-40). Historische und geographische Bemerkungen zum
Missionsablauf nach Lukas" in: E. E. Ellis (ed.) Jesus und Paulus.
FS. W. G. Kümmel (Göttingen 1975) 85-95. GLÖCKNER, R., Die
Verkündigung des Heils beim Evangelisten Lukas (Mainz 1975)
45ff. NELLESSEN, E., Zeugnis für Jesus und das Wort (Köln 1976)
118-28. RUSSELL, E. A., "Some Aspects of Change in the New

Testament'' BTh 27 (1, 1977) 9-19. "Apokalyptik" in: TRE 3
(1978) 254. "Apostel" in: TRE 3 (1978) 442, 443. JEWETT, P.
K. Infant Baptism and the Covenant of Grace (Grand Rapids 1978)
120. THORNTON, T. C. G., "To the end of the earth: Acts 1:8"
ET 89 (1978) 374-75. PRAST, F. Presbyter und Evangelium in
nachapostolischer Zeit (Stuttgart 1979) 17, 306, 307, 316, 321-23,
328, 331. PFITZNER, V. C., " 'Pneumatic' Apostleship? Apostle
and Spirit in the Acts of the Apostles" in: W. Haubeck/M. Bachmann (eds.) Wort in der Zeit. FS. K.H. Rengstorf (Leiden 1980)
215-16.

1:9-11:18 LOCKYER, H. All the Parables of the Bible (1963) 341ff.

1:9ff. STRECKER, G. Der Weg der Gerechtigkeit (1962) 211$_2$. HAHN,
F. Christologische Hoheitstitel (1963) 107, 126f. FLENDER, H.
Heil und Geschichte in der Theologie des Lukas (1965) 87.

1:9-12 MICHIELS, R. "Eenheid van Pasen, Hemelvaart en Pinksteren"
Collationes 20 (1, 1974) 3-35. FREY, C., "Der Himmelfahrtsber-
icht des Lukas nach Apg 1:1-12. Exegetische und didaktische
Problematik" KatBl 95 (1970) 10-21. DÖMER, M., Das Heil
Gottes: Studien zur Theologie des lukanischen Doppelwerkes (Köln/
Bonn 1978) 117-22.

1:9-11 WIKENHAUSER, A. Die Apostelgeschichte (1951) 26-29. JAN-
SEN, J. F. "The Ascension, the Church and Theology," ThT 16
(1, 1959) 17-29. MIQUEL, P. "Le mystère de l'Ascension,"
QuestLitPar 40 (2, 1959) 105-26. VAN STEMPVOORT, P. A.
"The Interpretation of the Ascension in Luke and Acts," NTS 5 (1,
1959) 30-42. SCHLIER, H. "Jesu Himmelfahrt nach den lukanischen Schriften," GuL 34 (2, 1961) 91-99. DALTON, W. J.,
Christ's Proclamation to the Spirits (Rome 1965) 185. SCHILLE,
G. "Die Himmelfahrt," ZNW 57 (3-4, 1966) 183-99. WILSON,
S. G. "The Ascension: A Critique and an Interpretation," ZNW 59
(3-4, 1968) 269-81. LOHFINK, G. Die Himmelfahrt Jesu (1971)
160-62, 269f. ZEHNLE, R. F. Peter's Pentecost Discourse (1971)
100-02. KRAENKL, E. Jesus der Knecht Gottes (1972) 163-66.
ZMIJEWSKI, J. Die Eschatologiereden des Lukas-Evangeliums
(1972) 230, 232, 247, 248, 249, 255, 289. WILSON, S. G. The
Gentiles and the Gentile Mission in Luke-Acts (1973) 96-107.
HAHN, F., "Die Himmelfahrt Jesu. Ein Gespräch mit Gerhard
Lohfink" Biblica 55 (1974) 418-26. TALBERT, C. H., Literary
Patterns, Theological Themes, and the Genre of Luke-Acts (Mis-
soula 1974) 60, 61, 62, 112. KURZ, W. S., "Acts 3:19-26 as a
Test of the Role of Eschatology in Lukan Christology" in: P. J.
Achtemeier (ed.) SBL Seminar Papers 1977 (Missoula 1977) 314-
15.

1:9-10 SCHRECKENBERG, H., "Flavius Josephus und die lukanischen

Schriften'' in: W. Haubeck/M. Bachmann (eds.) Wort in der Zeit. FS. K. H. Rengstorf (Leiden 1980) 193-94

1:9 MOORE, G. F. Judaism II (1946) 336. MOULE, C. F. D. "The Ascension-Acts i.9," ET 68 (7, 1957) 205-09. HENNECKE, E./ SCHNEEMELCHER, W. Neutestamentliche Apokryphen (1964) I 155, 248. PERRIN, N. NTS 12 (1965-1966) 151f. LOHFINK, G. Die Himmelfahrt Jesus (1971) 186-93. WANKE, J., Die Emmauserzählung (Leipzig 1973) 36, n.304. TALBERT, C. H., Literary Patterns, Theological Themes, and the Genre of Luke-Acts (Missoula 1974) 59, 61, 113. "Apostelgeschichte" in: TRE 3 (1978) 509. DUPONT, D. J., The Salvation of the Gentiles (New York 1979) 70.

1:10-14 VOIGT, G. Der zerrissene Vorhang I (1969) 234-39. FRICK, R. GPM 24 (1970-1971) 243-49. ENGELHARDT, K., in: GPM 30 (1976) 240-45. LÖWE, H. and ZIPPERT, C., in: P. Krusche et al. (eds.) Predigtstudien für das Kirchenjahr (1975-1976). IV/2 (Stuttgart 1976) 76-83.

1:10-12 LOHFINK, G. Die Himmelfahrt Jesus (1971) 193-200, 200-02.

1:10-11 DALTON, W. J. Christ's Proclamation to the Spirits (Rome 1965) 160.

1:10 WANKE, J., Die Emmauserzählung (Leipzig 1973) 74, 118, n.234. TALBERT, C. H., Literary Patterns, Theological Themes, and the Genre of Luke-Acts (Missoula 1974) 61, 62, 113, 115. BERGER, K., "Das Buch der Jubiläen" in: JüdSchr II/3 (1981) 484n.20a.

1:11 RUDOLPH, K. Die Mandäer I (1960) 115. WILCKENS, U. Die Missionsreden der Apostelgeschichte (1961) 151, 214f. ROBINSON, J. A. T. "Ascendancy," ANQ 5 (2, 1964) 5-9. LOHFINK, G., " 'Was steht ihr da und schauet' (Apg 1,11). Die 'Himmelfahrt Jesu' im lukanischen Geschichtswerk" BuK 20 (1965) 43-48. TALBERT, C. H., Literary Patterns, Theological Themes, and the Genre of Luke-Acts (Missoula 1974) 61, 113, 114, 115, 116. KÜMMEL, W. G. (ed.), Jüdische Schriften aus hellenistisch-römischer Zeit III (Gütersloh 1975) 220.

1:12-4:23 TALBERT, C. H., Literary Patterns, Theological Themes, and the Genre of Luke-Acts (Missoula 1974) 35-38.

1:12-2:1 VAN STEMPVOORT, P. A. "The Interpretation of the Ascension in Luke and Acts," NTS 5 (1, 1959) 30-42. TYSON, J. B., "The Problem of Food in Acts: A Study of Literary Patterns with Particular Reference to Acts 6:1-7" in: P. J. Achtemeier (ed.) SBL Seminar Papers 1979/I (Missoula 1979) 71.

1:12ff. SCHWEIZER, E. Gemeinde und Gemeinde-Ordnung im Neuen Testament (1959) § 24a.

1:12-26 RASCO, E. "Dans l'attente de l'esprit, le choix d'un nouvel apôtre.

Ac 1,12-14.15-17.20a.20c-17," AssS 29 (1973) 6-18.TALBERT, C. H., Literary Patterns, Theological Themes, and the Genre of Luke-Acts (Missoula 1974) 35. JOHNSON, L. T., The Literary Function of Possessions in Luke-Acts (Missoula 1977) 174-83.

1:12-14 JOHNSON, L. T., The Literary Function of Possessions in Luke-Acts (Missoula 1977) 176-77.

1:12 NESTLE, E. ZNW 3 (1902) 247-49. BORNKAMM-BARTH-HELD, Ueberlieferung und Auslegung im Matthäus-Evangelium (^{2}1961) 123. HENNECKE, E./SCHNEEMELCHER, W. Neutestamentliche Apokryphen (1964) I 248. STROBEL, A. "Der Berg der Offenbarung (Mt 28,16; Apg 1,12)," in: Verborum Veritas (1970) O. Böcher/K. Haacker eds., 133-46. LOHFINK, G. Die Himmelfahrt Jesus (1971) 164-67, 202-08. KUEMMEL, W. G. Einleitung in das Neue Testament (1973) 125f. WANKE, J., Die Emmauserzählung (Leipzig 1973) 26, 33. TALBERT, C. H., Literary Patterns, Theological Themes, and the Genre of Luke-Acts (Missoula 1974) 59, 60, 61, 65. METZGER, B. M., The Early Versions of the New Testament (Oxford 1977) 81. KRAUSE, M., "Christlich-gnostische Texte als Quellen für die Auseinandersetzung von Gnosis und Christentum" in: M. Krause (ed.) Gnosis and Gnosticism (Leiden 1981) 53-54.

1:13-26 DÖMER, M., Das Heil Gottes (Köln/Bonn 1976) 122-28.

1:13-14 GUTBROD, K. Die Apostelgeschichte (1968) 19f. PRETE, B. "Il sommario di Atti 1,13-14 e suo aporto per la conoscenza della Chiesa delle origini," SaDo 18 (69-70, 1973) 65-124. DUPONT, D. J., The Salvation of the Gentiles (New York 1979) 37-39. SWIDLER, L., Biblical Affirmations of Woman (Philadelphia 1979) 301. GERSTENBERGER, E. S. und SCHRAGE, W., Frau und Mann (Stuttgart 1980) 132-33.

1:13 ADLER, N. Das erste christliche Pfingstfest (1938) 19, 127f. STAEHELIN, E. Die Verkündigung des Reiches Gottes in der Kirche Jesu Christi I (1951) 55. ROBINSON, J. M. Kerygma und historischer Jesus (1960) 124. HAHN, F. Christologische Hoheitstitel (1963) 164. BRAUN, H, Qumran und NT II (1966) 152, 335. THURSTON, B. B. "to hyperōon in Acts i.13," ET 80 (1, 1968) 21-22. ITTEL, G. W. Jesus und die Jünger (1970) 28-41. LADD, G. E., A Theology of the New Testament (Grand Rapids 1974) 349, 351f. TALBERT, C. H., Literary Patterns, Theological Themes, and the Genre of Luke-Acts (Missoula 1974) 113, 116. "Apostel" in: TRE 3 (1978) 434. SCHMITHALS, W., "Zur Herkunft der gnostischen Elemente in der Sprache des Paulus" in: B. Aland et al. (eds.) Gnosis. FS. H. Jonas (Göttingen 1978) 412. STAGG, E. and F., Woman in the World of Jesus (Philadelphia 1970) 123-35. BÖHLIG, A., Die Gnosis III: Der Manichäismus

(Zürich/München 1980) 344 n.50, 344 n.51. KAESTLI, J.-D.,
"Les scènes d'attribution des champs de mission et de départ de
l'apôtres dans les Actes aprocryphes" in: F. Bovon et al. (eds.) Les
Actes Apocryphes des Apôtres (Geneva 1981) 252.

1:14-26 BRAUN, H. Qumran und NT II (1966) 147, 151ff., 155, 197, 200,
328, 333-36.

1:14 THIELE, W. "Eine Bemerkung zu Act 1:14," ZNW 53 (1-2, 1962)
110-11. GOULDER, M. D. Type and History in Acts (1964) 17,
25, 194, 217n, 222. HENNECKE, E./SCHNEEMELCHER, W.
Neutestamentliche Apokryphen (1964) I 312. OTT, W. Gebet Und
Heil (1965) 124f., 126, 128, 131. THORNTON, T. C. G. " 'Con-
tinuing steadfast in prayer'—New Light on a New Testament
Phrase," ET 83 (1, 1971) 23-24. BLINZLER, J., Die Brüder und
Schwestern Jesu (Stuttgart 1967) 89, 123. TALBERT, C. H., Literary Patterns, Theological Themes, and the Genre of Luke-Acts
(Missoula 1974) 16, 18. "Apostelgeschichte" in: TRE 3 (1978)
513. SWIDLER, L., Biblical Affirmations of Woman (Philadel-
phia 1979) 291. GERSTENBERGER, E. S. und SCHRAGE, W.,
Frau und Mann (Stuttgart 1980) 120.

1:15ff. RENGSTORF, K. H. "Die Zuwahl des Matthias, (Apg 1, 15ff.),"
StTh 15 (1, 1961) 35-67. Also in: Current Issues in New Testament
Interpretation (1962) 178-92 "The Election of Matthias". BEY-
SCHLAG, K. Clemens Romanus und der Frühkatholizismus (1966)
326f. GUTBROD, K. Die Apostelgeschichte (1968) 49ff.

1:15-26 WAGENMANN, J. Die Stellung des Apostels Paulus neben den
Zwölf (1926) 66f. SHEPARD, J. W., The Life and Letters of St.
Paul (Grand Rapids 1950) 28-30. BEARDSLEE, W. A. "The
Casting of Lots at Qumran and in the Book of Acts," NovTest 4,
(4, 1960) 245-52. MASSON, C. Vers les Sources D'eau Vive
(1961) 178ff. FLENDER, H. Heil und Geschichte in der Theologie
des Lukas (1965) 107-09. ROLOFF, J. Apostolat-Verkündigung-
Kirche (1965) 172-78, 196-99. DUPONT, J. Etudes sur les Actes
des Apôtres (1967) 83-85. DUNN, J. D. G. Baptism in the Holy
Spirit (1970) 45f. ZEHNLE, R. F. Peter's Pentecost Discourse
(1971) 104-11. JERVELL, J., "The Twelve on Israel's Thrones"
in: Luke and the People of God (Minneapolis 1972) 83-89. DIE-
TRICH, W. Das Petrusbild der lukanischen Schriften (1972) 166-
194. WILCOX, M. "The Judas-Tradition in Acts i.15-26," NTS
19 (4, 1973) 438-52. WILSON, S. G. The Gentiles and the Gentile
Mission in Luke-Acts (1973) 107-113. FULLER, R. J., "The
Choice of Matthias" StEv 6 (1973) 140-46. JAUREGUI, J. A.,
Testimonio apostolado-misión. Teológia Deusto 3 (Bilbao 1973).
WANKE, J., Die Emmauserzählung (Leipzig 1973) 12. TAL-
BERT, C. H., Literary Patterns, Theological Themes, and the Genre

of Luke-Acts (Missoula 1974) 37. NELLESSEN, E. "Tradition und Schrift in der Perikope von der Erwählung des Mattias (Apg 1,15-26)" BZ 19 (1975) 205-18. NELLESSEN, E., Zeugnis für Jesus und das Wort (Köln 1976) 128-78. GRÄSSER, E., "Acta-Forschung seit 1960" ThR 42 (1977) 1-68. "Amt" in: TRE 2 (1978) 512. "Apostel" in: TRE 3 (1978) 430, 434. "Apostelgeschichte" in: TRE 3 (1978) 492, 497. DÖMER, M., Das Heil Gottes (Köln/Bonn 1978) 130-34. McDONALD, J. I. H., Kerygma and Didache (Cambridge 1980) 109. PFITZNER, V. C., " 'Pneumatic' Apostelship? Apostle and Spirit in the Acts of the Apostles" in: W. Haubeck/M. Bachmann (eds.) Wort in der Zeit. FS. K. H. Rengstorf (Leiden 1980) 216-19. SCHNEIDER, G., Die Apostelgeschichte I (Freiburg/Basel/Wein 1980) 211-12 (lit!). WEISER, A., Die Apostelgeschichte I (Gütersloh/Würzburg 1981) 63 (lit!).

1:15-22 BLOCH, R., "Midrash" in: W. S. Green (ed.) Approaches to Ancient Judaism: Theory and Practice (Missoula 1978) 48.

1:15-20 JOHNSON, L. T., The Literary Function of Possessions in Luke-Acts (Missoula 1977) 177-78.

1:15 DELLING, G. Die Taufe im Neuen Testament (1963) 62. NICKELS, P. Targum and New Testament (1967) 59. WANKE, J., Die Emmauserzählung (Leipzig 1973) 115. ZINGG, P., Das Wachsen der Kirche (Freiburg, Schweiz 1974) 161-62, 165. LOHFINK, G., Die Sammlung Israels (München 1975) 67, 69, 70-72. NELLESSEN, E., Zeugnis für Jesus und das Wort (Köln 1976) 136-40. METZGER, B. M., The Early Versions of the New Testament (Oxford 1977) 92. "Apostelgeschichte" in: TRE 3 (1978) 492.

1:16-22 SCHWEIZER, E. "Zu Apg. 1,16-22," ThZ 14 (1, 1958) 46. DUPONT, J. "Les discourse de Pierre dans les Actes et le chapitre XXIV de l'evangile de Luc," in: L'Evangile de Luc (1973) F. Neirynck ed., 362-65.

1:16-20 BENOIT, P. "La Mort de Judas," in: Synoptische Studien (1953) Wikenhauser ed., 1-19. DUPONT, J. "La Destinée de Judas prophétisée par David (Actes 1,16-20)," CBQ 23 (2, 1961) 41-51. MANNS, F., "Un midrash chrétien: le récit de la mort de Judas" RevSR 54 (1980) 197-203.

1:16 STRECKER, G. Der Weg der Gerechtigkeit (1962) 85. BISHOP, E. F. F. " 'Guide to Those who Arrested Jesus,' " EQ 40 (1, 1968) 41-42. NELLESSEN, E., Zeugnis für Jesus und das Wort (Köln 1976) 140-42. SWETNAM, J., "Jesus as Λόγος in Hebrews 4:12-13" in: Biblica 62 (1981) 218-19.

1:17 WILCOX, M. The Semitisms of Acts (1965) 36, 115-16, 121. NICKELS, P. Targum and New Testament (1967) 59. NELLESSEN, E., Zeugnis für Jesus und das Wort (Köln 1976) 142-45.

1:18ff. JOHNSON, L. T., The Literary Function of Possessions in Luke-Acts (Missoula 1977) 178-81.

1:18-19 STRECKER, G. Der Weg der Gerechtigkeit (1962) 77$_2$, 80, 82. NELLESSEN, E., Zeugnis für Jesus und das Wort (Köln 1976) 145-48. DERRETT, J. D., "Miscellanea: a Pauline Pun and Judas' Punishment" ZNW 72 (1981) 132-33.

1:18 PALLIS, A., Notes on St. Luke and the Acts (London 1928) 50. CLARK, A. C. The Acts of the Apostles (1933) 256, 258, 296, 338. SMITH, M. Tannaitic Parallels to the Gospels (1968) 3 b n 62. GORDON, A. B. "The Fate of Judas According to Acts 1:18," EQ 44 (2, 1971) 97-100. "Apostelgeschichte" in: TRE 3 (1978) 509.

1:19 WILCOX, M. The Semitisms of Acts (1965) 13, 87-89, 171. NICKELS, P. Targum and New Testament (1967) 59. "Aramäisch" in: TRE 3 (1978) 603.

1:20-22 CLARK, S. B., Man and Woman in Christ (Ann Arbor 1980) 129.

1:20 LINDARS, B. New Testament Apologetic (1961) 102, 199f. HOLTZ, T. Untersuchungen über die Alttestamentlichen Zitate bei Lukas (1968) 43-48. NELLESSEN, E., Zeugnis für Jesus und das Wort (Köln 1976) 148-51. KRAFT, H., Die Entstehung des Christentums (Darmstadt 1981) 221.

1:21ff. SCHOEPS, H.-J. Paulus (1959) 66f.

1:21f. STONEHOUSE, N. B. The Witness of Matthew and Mark to Christ (1944) 8. KLEIN, G. Die Zwölf Apostel (1961) 204. DELLING, G. Die Taufe im Neuen Testament (1963) 42. FLENDER, H. Heil und Geschichte in der Theologie des Lukas (1965) 109-11. KASTING, H. Die Anfänge der Urchristlichen Mission (1969) 42ff. BURCHARD, C. Der dreizehnte Zeuge (1970) 130-35. JEREMIAS, J. Neutestamentliche Theologie I (1971) 52, 164, 285f. LOHFINK, G. Die Himmelfahrt Jesu (1971) 218-23. KRAENKL, E. Jesus der Knecht Gottes (1972) 54, 80, 145, 167-75, 210.

1:21-22 FLEW, R. N. Jesus and His Church (1956) 131n. WILCKENS, U. Die Missionsreden der Apostelgeschichte (1961) 58, 101, 107, 139, 145, 191, 208. NICKELS, P. Targum and New Testament (1967) 59. BROWN, S. Apostasy and Perseverance in the Theology of Luke (1969) 53-57, 86, 94, 125. SAMAIN, E. "La notion de APXH dans l'æuvre lucanienne," in: L'Evangile de Luc (1973) F. Neirynck ed., 303-04, 319. WILSON, S. G. The Gentiles and the Gentile Mission in Luke-Acts (1973) 88-90. WILCKENS, U. Die Missionsreden der Apostelgeschichte (^{3}1974) 58, 102, 107, 140, 146, 148, 152. TALBERT, C. H., Literary Patterns, Theological Themes, and the Genre of Luke-Acts (Missoula 1974) 24, 116, 122. NELLESSEN, E., Zeugnis für Jesus und das Wort (Köln 1976)

77ff., 151-53, 173-78. DUNN, J. D. G., Unity and Diversity in the New Testament (London 1977) 238, 355, 362. CRIBBS, F. L. "The Agreements that Exist between John and Acts" in: C. H. Talbert (ed.) Perspectives on Luke-Acts (Danville 1978) 49. PRAST, Presbyter und Evangelium in nachapostolischer Zeit (Stuttgart 1979) 161-62, 304-07.

1:21 KAESEMANN, E. Exegetische Versuche und Besinnungen (1964) I 130. EPP, E. J. The theological tendency of Codex Bezae Cantabrigiensis in Acts (1966) 54, 62f., 154. "Apostel" in: TRE 3 (1978) 442. BERGER, K., "Das Buch der Jubiläen" JüdSchr II/3 (1981) 497n.7a.

1:22 BEST, E. One Body in Christ (1955) 164. ROBINSON, J. M. Kerygma und historischer Jesus (1960) 145f. BROX, N. Zeuge und Märtyrer (1961) 50f. KAESEMANN, E. Exegetische Versuche und Besinnungen (1964) I 130. HAHN, F. Das Verständnis der Mission im Neuen Testament (²1965) 117. ROLOFF, J. Apostolat-Verkündigung-Kirche (1965) 191f. DUPONT, J. Etudes sur les Actes des Apôtres (1967) 268, 277, 399, 478, 479. NICKELS, P. Targum and New Testament (1967) 60. KRAENKL, E. Jesus der Knecht Gottes (1972) 88f., 90, 96, 130, 164f. SMITH, M. Clement of Alexandria and a secret Gospel of Mark (1973) 206f. TALBERT, C. H., Literary Patterns, Theological Themes, and the Genre of Luke-Acts (Missoula 1974) 114. GLÖCKNER, R., Die Verkündigung des Heils beim Evangelisten Lukas (Mainz 1975) 45ff. NELLESSEN, E., Zeugnis für Jesus und das Wort (Köln 1976) 128-78. "Apostel" in: TRE 3 (1978) 442. CRIBBS, F. L., "The Agreements that Exist Between John and Acts" in: C. H. Talbert (ed.) Perspectives on Luke-Acts (Danville 1978) 49-50.

1:23.26 BETZ, H. D. Lukian von Samosata und das Neue Testament (1961) 58f., 143. "Apostelgeschichte" in: TRE 3 (1978) 498. RUDOLPH, K., Die Gnosis (Göttingen 1978) 331.

1:23 FLEW, R. N. Jesus and His Church (1956) 106. EPP, E. J. The theological tendency of Codex Bezae Cantabrigiensis in Acts (1966) 157f., 167 n.7. JEREMIAS, J. Neutestamentliche Theologie I (1971) 163, 224, 285f. BEYSCHLAG, K., Simon Magus und die christliche Gnosis (Tübingen 1974) 97. NELLESSEN, E., Zeugnis für Jesus und das Wort (Köln 1976) 153-54. "Aramäisch" in: TRE 3 (1978) 604. KRAFT, H., Die Entstehung des Christentums (Darmstadt 1981) 221.

1:24-26 JUNOD, E., "Origène, Eusèbe et la tradition sur la répartition des champs de mission des apôtres" in: F. Bovon et al. (eds.) Les Actes Apocryphes des Apôtres (Geneva 1981) 243.

1:24-25 NELLESSEN, E., Zeugnis für Jesus und das Wort (Köln 1976) 154-56.

1:24 SAHLIN, H. Der Messias und das Gottesvolk (1945) 178-80.
BROWN, S. Apostasy and Perseverance in the Theology of Luke
(1969) 54, 89, 95, 115. STAEHLIN, G. "Τὸ πνεῦμα 'Ιησοῦ,"
in: Christ and the Spirit in the New Testament(1973), B. Lindars/
S. S. Smalley eds., 238f. TALBERT, C. H., Literary Patterns,
Theological Themes, and the Genre of Luke-Acts (Missoula 1974)
16, 18. CRIBBS, F. L., "The Agreements that Exist Between John
and Acts" in: C. H. Talbert (ed.) Perspectives on Luke-Acts (Danville 1978) 50.

1:25-26 DUPONT, J. Le Discours de Milet (1962) 369-72. BEYSCHLAG,
K. Clemens Romanus und der Frühkatholizismus (1966) 326ff.,
338ff. BROWN, S. Apostasy and Perseverance in the Theology of
Luke (1969) 82-84, 86, 89, 96f. CONZELMANN, H. Die
Apostelgeschichte (1963) 24.

1:25 JOHNSON, L. T., The Literary Function of Possessions in Luke-
Acts (Missoula 1977) 181-82. FRIEDRICH, G., "Das Amt im
Neuen Testament" in: Auf das Wort kommt es an (Göttingen 1978)
420-21.

1:26 LOHFINK, G., "Der Losvorgang in Apg 1,26" BZ 19 (1975) 247-
49. NELLESSEN, E., Zeugnis für Jesus und das Wort (Köln 1976)
156-58. METZGER, B. M., The Early Versions of the New Tes-
tament(Oxford 1977) 196.

———————————

2-13 SCHMITT, J., "Les discours missionnaires des Actes et l'histoire
des traditions prépauliniennes" RechSR 69 (1981) 165-80.

2:1-8:2 GUTBROD, K. Die Apostelgeschichte (1968) 21ff.

2-8 SELBY, D. J., Introduction to the New Testament (New York 1971)
292-95.

2-5 DUPONT, J. The Sources of Acts (1964) 36, 37, 45, 46, 49, 51,
56, 64, 65. JEREMIAS, J. Abba; Studien zur neutestamentlichen
Theologie und Zeitgeschichte (1966) 238-47. COPPENS, J. "La
koinōnia dans l'Eglise primitive," EphT 46 (1, 1970) 116-21.
GOPPELT, L., Theologie des Neuen Testaments II (Göttingen
1976) 329.

2-3 ZEHNLE, R. F. Peter's Pentecost Discourse (1971). PETERSEN,
N. R., JBL 90 (4, 1971) 499-500.

2:1-3:6 MUSSNER, F. "Die Idee der Apokatastasis in der Apostelgeschichte," in: Praesentia Salutis (1967) 223.

2 BUECHSEL, D. F. Der Geist Gottes im Neuen Testament (1926) 234-42. SHEPHARD, J. W., The Life and Letters of Paul (Grand Rapids 1950) 31-35. BARRETT, C. K. The New Testament Background (1956) 157. MUNCK, J. Paul and the Salvation of Mankind (1959) 213f. GILMOUR, S. MacL. "Easter and Pentecost," JBL 81 (1, 1962) 62-66. MENOUD, Ph. H. "La Pentecôte lucanienne et l'histoire," RHPhR 42 (1962) 141-47. NOACK, B. "The Day of Pentecost in Jubilees, Qumran, and Acts," in: ASThI Vol. I (1962) 73-95. DUPONT, J. The Sources of Acts (1964) 29, 36, 38, 39, 40, 43. HENNECKE, E./SCHNEEMELCHER, W. Neutestamentliche Apokryphen (1964) I 100. SLEEPER, C. F. "Pentecost and Resurrection," JBL 84 (4, 1965) 389-99. BRAUN, H. Qumran und NT II (1966) 26. SWAIN, L. "Pentecost and the New Covenant," ClR 51 (5, 1966) 369-77. DOERNE, M. Die alten Episteln (1967) 142-46. HENRY, A., "La Pentecôte. Gedanken zum Verständnis von Apg 2" Terre Sainte 5 (Jerusalem 1967) 97-99. NICKELS, P. Targum and New Testament (1967) 60. WAGNER, S. ed., Bible und Qumran (1968) 29-32. WANSBROUGH, H. W. "The Coming of the Spirit," ClR 54 (5, 1969) 357-61. DUNN, J. D. G. Baptism in the Holy Spirit (1970) 38ff., 45, 49, 92, 173. LEDEAUT, R. "Pentecost and Jewish tradition," DoLi (5, 1970) 250-67. ZEHNLE, R. F. Peter's Pentecost Discourse (1971) 19ff., 61ff., 95ff. BROWN, S. "Easter and Pentecost: A Biblical Reflection on Their Relationship," Worship 46 (5, 1972) 277-86. POTIM, J. La fête juive de la Pentecôte. HARRINGTON, D. J. CBQ 34 (3, 1972) 381-83. TALBERT, C. H., Literary Patterns, Theological Themes, and the Genre of Luke-Acts (Missoula 1974) 37, 38. CONZELMANN, H. und Lindemann, A., Arbeitsbuch zum Neuen Testament (Tübingen 1975) 102. DUNN, J. D. G., Jesus and the Spirit (London 1975) 130, 135-56. GASQUE, W., A History of the Cricitism of the Acts of the Apostles (Tübingen 1975) 58, 133, 220, 231. GOURGUES, M., "Lecture christologique du Psaume CX et fête de la Pentecôte" RB 83 (1976) 5-24. MINGUEZ, D., Pentecostés. Ensayo de Semiótica narrativa en Hch. 2. Analecta Biblica 75 (Rome 1976). COCCHINI, F., "L'evoluzione storico-religiosa della festa de Pentecoste" RivB 25 (1977) 297-326. DUNN, J. D.. G., Unity and Diversity in the New Testament (London 1977) 177. MARSHALL, I. H., "The Significance of Pentecost" SJTh 30 (1977) 347-69. MATTA-EL-MESKÏN, P., "La Pentecôte" Irénikon 50 (1977) 5-45. STENDAHL, K., "Glossolalia and the Charismatic Movement" in: J. Jervell/W. A. Meeks (eds.) God's Christ and His People. FS. N. A. Dahl (Minneapolis 1977) 125-26. BETZ, O., "Rechtfertigung und Heiligung" in: G. Müller (ed.) Rechtfertigung, Realismus,

Universalimus in Biblischer Sicht. FS. A. Köberle (Darmstadt 1978) 38-39. BOVON, F., Luc le Théologien (Neuchâtel/Paris 1978) 235-44. MOULE, C. F. D., The Holy Spirit (London 1978) 35-36. RAYAN, S., The Holy Spirit: Heart of the Gospel and Christian Hope (New York 1978) 8-9, 10-17. SCHWEIZER, E., Heiliger Geist (Stuttgart 1978) 85-88. VIA, E. J., "An Interpretation of Acts 7:35-37 from the Perspective of Major Themes in Luke-Acts" in: P. J. Achtemeier (ed.) SBL Seminar Papers 1978/II (Missoula 1978) 218-19. WEINFELD, M., "Pentecost as a Festival of the Giving of the Law" Immanuel 8 (1978) 7-18. Le DÉAUT, R., "Šāvū'ōt och den kristna pingsten i NT" SEA 44 (1979) 148-70. MCDON-ALD, J. I. H., Kerygma and Didache (Cambridge 1980) 31. PFITZNER, V. C., " 'Pneumatic' Apostleship? Apostle and Spirit in the Acts of the Apostles" in: W. Haubeck/M. Bachmann (eds.) Wort in der Zeit. FS. K. H. Rengstorf (Leiden 1980) 219-21. JUEL, D., "Social Dimensions of Exegesis: The Use of Psalm 16 in Acts 2" CBQ 43 (1981) 543-56.

2:1ff. SABBE, M. "Het Pinksterverhaal," CooBrugGand 3 (2, 1957) 161-78. HAHN, F. Christologische Hoheitstitel (1963) 107. GRUNDMANN, W. "Der Pfingstbericht der Apostelgeschichte in seinem theologischen Sinn," in: Studia Evangelica II (1964) F. L. Cross eds., 584-94. SCHILLE, G. Anfänge der Kiche (1966) 156ff. RICHTER, H.-F. Auferstehung und Wirklichkeit (1969) 45f. WILCKENS, U. Die Missionsreden der Apostelgeschichte (³1974) 32, 59, 74, 94,151.

2:1-47 ABRI, J. "The Theological Meaning of Pentecost," Kator Shin 4 (1, 1965) 133-51. /In Japanese./

2:1-42 PONTET, M. "Pentecôte et charité fraternelle," Christus 9 (35, 1962) 340-54. DOWNES, J. A. "The Feast of Pentecost. Some meanings of the festival in the Bible and the liturgy," RVO 34 (2, 1964) 62-69. UNGER, M. F. "The Significance of Pentecost," BiblSa 122 (486, 1965) 169-77. BRAUN, H. Qumran und NT II (1966) 10, 26, 28, 145-47, 152ff., 159, 169, 176, 200f., 253f., 258, 266, 271, 308f., 312, 355. VAN HALSEMA, J. H. "De historischen betrouwbaarheid van het Pinksterverhaal," NedThT 20 (2, 1966) 218. GUTBROD, K. Die Apostelgeschichte (1968) 43f.

2:1-41 MEYER, B. F. "The Meaning of Pentecost," Worship 40 (5, 1966) 281-87. COLLINS, J. D. "Discovering the Meaning of Pentecost," Scripture 20 (51, 1968) 73-79.

2:1-40 FRANKLIN, E., Christ and Lord: A Study in the Purpose and Theology of Luke-Acts (London 1975) 97-99. MENOUD, H., "La Pentecôte lucanienne et l'histoire" in: Jésus-Christ et la foi. (Neuchatel/Paris 1975) 118-24. ETIENNE, A., "Etude du récit de l'évément de Pentecôte dans Actes 2" FV 80 (1981) 47-67.

2:1-36 SATAKE, A. Die Gemeindeordnung in der Johannesapokalypse (1966) 163f.

2:1-21 KUNTZ, M. und RIESS, H., in: P. Krusche et al. (eds.) Predigtstudien für das Kirchenjahr 1979-1980. II/2 (Stuttgart 1980) 84-92.

2:1-18 RISTOW, H. "Pfingstsonntag," in: Wandelt in der Liebe (1968) 216-33. KOCH, E., in: GPM 34 (1980) 245-50.

2:1-14 GOULDER, M. D. Type and History in Acts (1964) 149-59, 184-88. BERGEN, P. van, "L'Epître de la Pentecôte" ParLi 4 (1961) 253-62. CASALIS, G. GPM 22/3 (1967-1968) 264-70. SOMMERAUER, A. "Heute ist Pfingsten," in: Kleine Predigt-Typologie III (1965) Schmidt, L. ed., 367-72. ZEHNLE, R. F. Peter's Pentecost Discourse (1971) 111-23.

2:1-13 ADLER, N. Das erste christliche Pfingstfest (1938). BEYER, H. W. Die Apostelgeschichte (1947) 13f. HEUTHORST, G. "The Apologetic Aspect of Acts 2:1-13," Scripture 9 (6, 1957) 33-43. REICKE, G. Glaube und Leben der Urgemeinde (1957) 27-37. MENOUD, P.-H. "La Pentecôte lucanienne et l'histoire," RHPhR 42 (2-3, 1962) 141-47. CONZELMANN, H. Die Apostelgeschichte (1963) 27. BEEK, A. van der, The Giving of the Spirit at the Day of Pentecost (1964). MISKOTTE, H. in: Herr, tue meine Lippen auf Bd. II (1965₅) G. Eichholz ed., 319-31. WEBER, O. Predigtmeditationen (1967) 165-68. BAUMHAUER, O. ed., Entmythologisierung des Evangeliums (1968) 23-51. GRASS, H. Ostergeschehen und Osterberichte (1970) 99f., 199f. HAACKER, K. "Das Pfingstwunder als exegetisches Problem," in: Verborum Veritas (1970) O. Böcher/K. Haacker eds., 125-31. WEGENAST, K. Glaube-Schule-Wirklichkeit (1970) 163-71. BROER, I. "Der Geist und die Gemeinde. Zur Auslegung der lukanischen Pfingstgeschichte (Apg 2, 1-13)" BuL 13 (4, 1972) 261-83. KREMER, J. Pfingstbericht und Pfingstgeschehen (1973). KREMER, J. "Was geschah Pfingsten? Zur Historizität des Apg 2, 1-13 berichteten Pfingstereignisses," WortWahr 28 (2, 1973) 195-207. LOHSE, E. Die Einheit des Neuen Testaments (1973) 178-92. WILSON, S. G. The Gentiles and the Gentile Mission in Luke-Acts (1973) 121-28. O'HAGAN, A. P., "The first Christian Pentecost (Acts 2:1-13)" SBFLA 23 (1973) 50-66. TALBERT, C. H., Literary Patterns, Theological Themes, and the Genre of Luke-Acts (Missoula 1974) 16, 18, 35. GOPPELT, L., Theologie des Neuen Testaments. I (Göttingen 1975) 297ff. SAMAIN, E., "A Igreja, uma Communidade Libertadora e Criadora? Uma exegese de Atos 2,1-3" REB 35 (1975) 326-62. TSCHIEDEL, H. J., "Ein Pfingstwunder im Apollonhymnos (*Hymn. Hom. Ap.* 156-64 and Apg. 2,1-13)" ZRGG 27 (1975) 22-39. WILLIAMS, C. G., "Glossolalia as a religious phenomenon: 'Tongues' at Corinth and Pentecost" Religion 5 (1975) 16-32. MANGATT, G., "The Pentecostal Gift of the Spirit" Biblehashyam 2 (1976) 227-39, 300-14. MEIS, W., "Problematica de la Carismatica Neotestamentaria" TyV 17 (1976) 193-208. THEOHARIS, A., "Hē emphanisis tou anastantos Kyriou kata Iō.20,19-23 en schesei pros to Prax. Keph. II (The Appearance of the Risen Lord according to Jn 20:19-23 as Compared with Acts chap. 2) DBM 4 (1976) 68-85. TACHAU, P., "Die Pfingstgeschichte nach Lukas. Exegetische Ueberlegungen zu Apg. 2,1-13" EvErz 29 (1977) 86-102. DÖMER, M., Das Heil Gottes: Studien zur Theologie des lukanischen Doppelwerkes (Köln/Bonn 1978) 139-59. SCHNEIDER, G., Die Apostelgeschichte. I (Freiburg/Basel/Wien 1980) 239-41 (lit!.). KRAFT, H., Die Entstehung des Christentums (Darmstadt 1981) 242-47. WEISER, A., Apostelgeschichte. I (Gütersloh/Würzburg 1981) 76 (lit!).

2:1-11 LOHSE, E. "Die Bedeutung des Pfingstberichtes im Rahmen des lukanischen Geschichtswerkes," EvTh 13 (1953) 422-36. DUPONT, J. Etudes sur les Actes des Apôtres (1967) 481-502.

2.1ff.9-11 HAHN, F. Das Verständnis der Mission im Neuen Testament (²1965) 115.

2:1-4 ADLER, N. Das erste christliche Pfingstfest (1938) 28f. GOETTMANN, J. "La Pentecôte, prémices de la nouvelle création," BVieC 27 (1959) 59-69. DELLING, G. Die Taufe in Neuen Testament (1963) 62. TALBERT, C. H., Literary Patterns, Theological Themes, and the Genre of Luke-Acts (Missoula 1974) 23, 37. DUPONT, D. J., The Salvation of the Gentiles (New York 1979) 36-45. MATTILL, A. J., Luke and the Last Things (Dillsboro 1979) 292, 301. SCHRECKENBERG, H., "Flavius Jospehus und die lukanischen Schriften" in: W. Haubeck/M. Bachmann (eds.) Wort in der Zeit. FS. K. H. Rengstorf (Leiden 1980) 194-95.

2:1 ADLER, N. Das erste christliche Pfingstfest (1928) 28, 32-34, 44f., 118-32. VAN STEMPVOORT, P. A. "Het liep tegen de vijtigste dag. De beteknis van Hand. 2:1,"HomBib 21 (5, 1962) 97-103. DUPONT, J. Etudes sur les Actes des Apôtres (1967) 482-84. NICKELS, P. Targum and New Testament (1967) 60. LOHSE, E. Die Einheit des Neuen Testaments (1973) 152, 178f., 186f. CHARNOV, B. H., "Shavuot, 'Matan Torah,' and the Triennial Cycle" Judaism 23 (1974) 332-36. "Apostelgeschichte" in: TRE III (1978) 492, 509.

2:2ff. ADLER, N. Das erste christliche Pfingstfest (1938) 28f., 34f., 77-85, 109f., 112-14, 160f.

2:2-16 KREMER, J., Pfingstbericht und Pfingstgeschehen (Stuttgart 1973) 191-92.

2:2-3 DUNN, J. D. G., Jesus and the Spirit (London 1975) 147-48.

2:2 DUPONT, J. Etudes sur les Actes des Apôtres (1967) 485-86. ZEHNLE, R. F. Peter's Pentecost Discourse (1971) 115-16.

2:3-4 SCHMITHALS, W., "Zur Herkunft der gnostichen Elemente in der Sprache des Paulus" in: B. Aland et al. (eds.) Gnosis. FS. H. Jonas (Göttingen 1978) 412.

2:3 WILCOX, M. The Semitisms of Acts (1965) 101-02, 110, 171. McNAMARA, M. The New Testament and the Palestinian Targum to the Pentateuch (1966) 235 n.129. DUPONT, J. Etudes sur les Actes des Apôtres (1967) 486-88. NICKELS, P. Targum and New Testament (1967) 60. ZEHNLE, R. F. Peter's Pentecost Discourse (1971) 117-18. ROBINSON, J. A., Pelagius's Expositions of Thirteen Epistles of St. Paul. I (Cambridge 1922) 169-70.

2:4ff. GUY, H. A. New Testament Prophecy (1947) 91f.

2:4 FLEW, R. N. Jesus and His Church (1956) 105, 106. STAEHLIN, G. "Τὸ πνεῦμα 'Ιησοῦ." in: Christ and the Spirit in the New Testament (1973) B. Lindars/S. S. Smalley eds., 236-38, 256. DUNN, J. D. G., Jesus and the Spirit (London 1975) 122, 137, 148-52, 171, 176.

2:5-13 ADLER, N. Das erste christliche Pfingstfest (1938) 29f., 33f., 45f., 75f., 113f., 144f.

2:5-11 DUPONT, J. Etudes sur les Actes des Apôtres (1967). PRAST, F., Presbyter und Evangelium in nachapostolischer Zeit (Stuttgart 1979) 324. "Diaspora" in: TRE 8 (1981) 711.

2:6 METZGER, B. M., The Early Versions of the New Testament (Oxford 1977) 148.

2:7-11 STENGER, W., "Beobachtungen zur sogenannten Völkerliste des Pfingstwunders (Apg 2,7-11)" Kairos 21 (1979) 206-14.

2:7 STONEHOUSE, N. B. The Witness of Matthew and Mark to Christ (1944) 106. RUDOLPH, K. Die Mandäer I (1960) 115. WILCOX, M. The Semitisms of Acts (1965) 150-51. NICKELS, P. Targum and New Testament (1967) 60.

2:9ff. MOHRMANN, C. "Linguistic Problems in the Early Christian Church," VigChr 11 (1, 1957) 11-36. BEYSCHLAG, K. Clemens Romanus und der Frühkatholizismus (1966) 288f.

2:9-11 BRINKMAN, J. A. "The Literary Background of the 'Catalogue of the Nations' (Acts 2,9-11)," CBQ 25 (3, 1963) 418-27. CONZELMANN, H. Die Apostelgeschichte (1963) 26. BOUSSET, W. Die Religion des Judentums im Späthellenistischen Zeitalter (1966 = 1926) 68. NICKELS, P., Targum and New Testament (1967) 60. THOMAS, J. "Formgesetze des Begriffs-Katalogs im N.T.," ThZ 24 (1, 1968) 15-28. METZGER, B. M. "Ancient Astrological Geography and Acts 2:9-11," in: Apostolic History and the Gospel (1970) W. W. Gasque/R. P. Martin eds., 123-33.

ZEHNLE, R. F. Peter's Pentecost Discourse (1971) 120-22. WIL-SON, S. G. The Gentiles and the Gentile Mission in Luke-Acts (1973) 121-23. GÜTING, E., "Der geographische Horizont der sogenannten Völkerliste des Lukas (Acta 2,9-11)," ZNW 66 (1975) 149-69. KILPATRICK, G. D., "A Jewish Background to Acts 2,9-11" JJS 26 (1975) 48-49. GEORG, M., "Apg 2,9-11 in ausser-biblischer Sicht" in: Biblische Notizen 1 (Bamberg 1976) 15-18. METZGER, B. M., The Early Versions of the New Testament (Oxford 1977) 148. "Apostelgeschichte" in: TRE 3 (1978) 484, 509. SHERWIN-WHITE, A. N., Roman Society and Roman Law in the New Testament (Grand Rapids 1978) 181.

2:9 EISSFELDT, O. Kleine Schriften IV (1968) 99-120. HATCH, W. H, "Zur Apostelgeschichte 2,9" ZNW 9 (1908) 255-56. NE-STLE, E., "Ein eilfter Einfall zu Apostelgeschichte 2,9" ZNW 9 (1908) 253-54. METZGER, B. M., The Early Versions of the New Testament (Oxford 1977) 87, 274. "Armenien" in: TRE 4 (1979) 42.

2:10 BARRETT, C. K. The New Testament Background (1956) 164. VOLLMER, H., "Zu Luthers 'Enden der Libyen' Acta 2,10" ZNW 35 (1936) 96-97.

2:11 WIKENHAUSER, A, Die Apostelgeschichte (1951) 34-36. DELLING, G. Die Taufe im Neuen Testament (1963) 63. DU-PONT, J. Etudes sur les Actes des Apôtres (1967) 407, 492, 493, 495, 497, 498. CAVALLIN, H. C. C., Life After Death. I (Lund 1974) 4,2n4. QUINN, J. D., "The Last Volumne of Luke: The Re-lations of Luke-Acts to the Pastoral Epistles" in: C. H. Talbert (ed.) Perspectives on Luke-Acts (Danville 1978) 65.

2:12 CLARK, A. C. The Acts of the Apostles (1933) 227, 257, 258, 296. STONEHOUSE, N. B. The Witness of Matthew and Mark to Christ (1944) 106. NICKELS, P. Targum and New Testament (1967) 60. SWETNAM, J., "Jesus as Λόγος in Hebrews 4:12-13" Biblica 62 (1981) 218-19.

2:13 SCHMITHALS, W., "Zur Herkunft der gnostischen Elemente in der Sprache des Paulus" in: B. Aland et al. (eds.) Gnosis. FS. H. Jonas (Göttingen 1978) 412.

2:14-42 ZEHNLE, R. F. Peter's Pentecost Discourse (1971) 19-23, 26-27, 61-70, 123-25.

2:14-41 REICKE, B. Glaube und Leben der Urgemeinde (1957) 38-54. DIETRICH, W. Das Petrusbild der lukanischen Schriften (1972) 195-216. WEISER, A., Die Apostelgeschichte. I (Gütersloh/Würzburg 1981) 90 (lit!). KREMER, J., Pfingstbericht und Pfing-stgeschehen (Stuttgart 1973) 167-79. TALBERT, C. H., Literary Patterns, Theological Themes, and the Genre of Luke-Acts (Missoula 1974) 16, 18, 19, 23, 25, 35, 38. GLÖCKNER, R., Die Verkündigung des Heils beim Evangelisten Lukas (Mainz 1975) 227ff. BARCLAY, W. Great Themes of the New Testament (Philadelphia 1979). DUPONT, D. J., The Salvation of the Gentiles (New York 1979) 22. SCHNEIDER, G., Die Apostelgeschichte. I (Freiburg/Basel/Wien 1980) 260-61 (lit!). WEISER, A., Die Apostelgeschichte. I (Gütersloh/Würzburg 1981) 90 (lit!).

2:14-40 BARCLAY, W. "Great Themes of the New Testament-IV Acts ii. 14-40, ET 70 (7, 1959) 196-99; (8, 1959) 243-46. DUPONT, J. "Le Salut der Gentils et la Signification Theologique de Livre des Actes," NTS 6 (1959-1960) 144f. NICKELS, P. Targum and New Testament (1967) 60. GASTON, L. No Stone on Another (1970) 100, 301-02.

2:14-39 WILCKENS,U. Die Missionsreden der Apostelgeschichte (1961) Passim. BURCHARD, C. Der dreizehnte Zeuge (1970) 138-42. PLUEMACHER, E. Lukas als hellenistischer Schriftsteller (1972) 41-43.

2:14-36.38 DIEBELIUS, M. Aufsätze zur Apostelgeschichte (1951) 104f., 142f., 152f.

2:14-36 LAMPE, G. W. H. "The Lucan Portrait of Christ," NTS 1 (1955-1956) 161ff. DALTON, W. J. "The Preaching of the Gospel: St. Peter's First Sermon," Our Apostolate 6 (3, 1958) 5-12. WEISER, A. "Die Pfingstpredigt der Lukas," BuL 14 (1, 1973) 1-12. GRYGLEWICZ, F., "Teologiczne aspekty Piotrowych przemowien (Dz 2,14-36; 3,12-26). ZNKUL 12 (1969) 23-34. KLIESCH, K., Das heilsgeschichtliche Credo in den Reden der Apostelgeschichte (Köln/Bonn 1975) 75ff., 144-48. MEYER, B. F., The Aims of Jesus (London 1979) 66-69. MCDONALD, J. I. H., Kerygma and Didache (Cambridge 1980) 51-53.

2:14-21 ROBECK, C., "The Gift of Prophecy in Acts and Paul, Part I" SBT 5 (1975) 15-38.

2:14-18 SWIDLER, L., Biblical Affirmations of Woman (Philadelphia 1979) 301.

2:14 GOULDER, M. D. Type and History in Acts (1964) 18, 22, 26, 28f., 74, 79-83, 84. WILCOX, M. The Semitisms in Acts (1965) 90-91, 110, 161, 171. DUPONT, J. Etudes sur les Actes der Apôtres (1967) 179, 407, 484, 495, 498. NICKELS, P. Targum and New Testament (1967) 60. FITZMYER, J. A. Essays on the Semitic Background of the New Testament (1971) 276-91.

2:15-39 BEYER, H. W. Die Apostelgeschichte (1947) 26f.

2:15 KLIESCH, K., Das heilsgeschichtliche Credo in den Reden der Apostelgeschichte (Köln/Bonn 1975) 137, 138.

2:16ff. REICKE, B. Diakonie, Festfreude und Zelos (1951) 194f.

2:16-39 QUESNELL, Q. This Good News (1964) 16f.

2:16-21 FLEW, R. N. Jesus and His Church (1956) 100, 103, 125-26n. TALBERT, C. H., Literary Patterns, Theological Themes, and the Genre of Luke-Acts (Missoula 1974) 97. KLIESCH, K., Das heilsgeschichtliche Credo in den Reden der Apostelgeschichte (Köln/ Bonn 1975) 127. MINEAR, P. S., "Some Archetypal Origins of Apocalyptic Predictions" Horizons in Biblical Theology (Pittsburg 1979) 105-35.

2:16.17-21 ELLIS, E. E. "Midrashic Features in the Speeches of Acts," in: Mélanges Bibliques en hommage au R. P. Béda Regaux (1970) A. Descamps/A. de Halleux eds., 306-07, 307-09.

2:16 STONEHOUSE, N. B. The Witness of Matthew and Mark to Christ.

2:16.17 ROELS, E. D. God's Mission (1962) 264f. "Apokalyptik" in: TRE 3 (1978) 154.

2:17ff. HAHN, F. Christologische Hoheitstitel (1963) 116. KAESEMANN, E. Exegetische Versuche und Besinnungen (1964) I 118. HAHN, F. Das Verständnis der Mission im Neuen Testament (²1965) 112, 115.

2:17-36 SEEBERG, A. Der Katechismus der Urchristenheit (1966) 126f.

2:17-21 DUPONT, J. Etudes sur les Actes des Apôtres (1967) 255, 270, 281, 352, 481. HOLTZ, T. Untersuchungen über die Alttestamentlichen Zitate bei Lukas (1968) 5-14. RESE, M. Alttestamentliche Motive in der Christologie des Lukas (1969) 46-55. ZEHNLE, R. F. Peter's Pentecost Discourse (1971) 28-34. KRAENKL, E. Jesus der Knecht Gottes (1972) 187, 190-93, 207. HUBBARD, B. J., "The Role of Commissioning Accounts in Acts" in: C. H. Talbert (ed.) Perspectives on Luke-Acts (Danville 1978) 194-95. DUPONT, D. J., The Salvation of the Gentiles (New York 1979) 151. KRAFT, H., Die Entstehung des Christentums (Darmstadt 1981) 217.

2:17-18 GAERTNER, B. The Areopagus speech and natural revelation (1955) 30f. DELLING, G. Die Taufe im Neuen Testament (1963) 98, 144. DUNN, J. D. G., Jesus and the Spirit (London 1975) 152, 160, 170, 190. GERSTENBERGER, E. S. und SCHRAGE, W., Frau und Mann (Stuttgart 1980) 134-35. CLARK, S. B., Man and Woman in Christ (Ann Arbor 1980) 104. JONES, P., 'Y a-t-il deux types de prophéties dans le Nouveau Testament?" RevR 31 (1980) 303-17.

2:17 FLEW, R. N., Jesus and His Church (1956) 103, 143. STRECKER, G. Der Weg der Gerechtigkeit (1962) 47₄. DELLING, G. Die Taufe im Neuen Testament (1963) 60. EPP, E. J. The theological tendency of Codex Bezae Cantabrigiensis in Acts (1966) 66-72, 164, 167f., 170. DUNN, J. D. G. Baptism in the Holy Spirit (1970) 46f.,

71, 165n. WILSON, S. G. The Gentiles and the Gentile Mission in Luke-Acts (1973) 123-25. LADD, G. E., A Theology of the New Testament (Grand Rapids 1974) 344, 350, 596. "Amt" in: TRE 2 (1978) 514. JEWETT, P. K., Infant Baptism and the Covenant of Grace (Grand Rapids 1978) 120. RAYAN, S., The Holy Spirit (New York 1978) 38, 127.

2:17a MUSSNER, F. " 'In den letzten Tagen' (Apg 2,17a)," BZ 5 (2, 1961) 263-65.

2:20-21 HAHN, F. Christologische Hoheitstitel (1963) 72.

2:20 BRANDENBURGER, E., "Himmelfahrt Moses" in: JüdSchr V/ 2 (1976) 77n.5b.

2:21-22 BOWKER, J. W. NTS 14 (1967-1968) 105f.

2:21.39 HAHN, F. Das Verständnis der Mission im Neuen Testament (^{2}1965) 115.

2:21 WAINWRIGHT, A. W. The Trinity in the New Testament (1962) 82-84. DELLING, G. Die Taufe im Neuen Testament (1963) 78. HAHN, F. Christologische Hoheitstitel (1963) 118. OTT, W., Gebet und Heil (1965) 132-36. WILSON, S. G., The Gentiles and the Gentile Mission in Luke-Acts (1973) 123-24, 241. WILCKENS, U. Die Missionsreden der Apostelgeschichte (^{3}1974) 33ff., 226, 229. GLÖCKNER, R., Die Verkündigung des Heils beim Evangelisten Lukas (Mainz 1975) 228ff., 237-38. "Apostelgeschichte" in: TRE 3 (1978) 492.

2:22ff. STAEHELIN, E. Die Verkündigung des Reiches Gottes in der Kirche Jesus Christi I (1951) 2.

2:22-39 HOOKER, M. D. Jesus and the Servant (1959) 118-20.

2:22-38 DUPONT, D. J., The Salvation of the Gentiles (New York 1979) 67.

2:22-36 LEIVESTAD, R. Christ the Conqueror (1954) 82ff. SCHNEIDER, G. Der Herr unser Gott (1965) 162-66. FRANTZEN, P. "Das 'Zeichen des Jonas'," ThG 57 (1, 1967) 61-66. BOERS, H. W. "Psalm 116 and the historical origin of the Christian faith," ZNW 60 (1-2, 1969) 105-10.

2:22-24 HAHN, F. Christologische Hoheitstitel (1963) 215. KASSING, A. Auferstanden für uns (1969) 35-37.

2:22-23 WANKE, J., Die Emmauserzählung Leipzig 1973) 11. TALBERT, C. H., Literary Patterns, Theological Themes, and the Genre of Luke-Acts (Missoula 1974) 32. WILCKENS, U. Die Missionsreden der Apostelgeschichte (^{3}1974) 12, 16, 33, 34, 38, 109, 123, 134, 186, 221, 230, 238.

2:22 ROBINSON, J. M. Kerygma und historischer Jesus (1960) 66, 71, 73. RUDOLPH, K. Die Mandäer I (1960) 115. BORNKAMM-

BARTH-HELD, Ueberlieferung und Auslegung im Matthäus-Evangelium (^{2}1961) 264. DELLING, G. Die Zueignung des Heils in der Taufe (1961) 88. STRECKER, G. Der Weg der Gerechtigkeit (1962) 62$_1$. HAHN, F. Christologische Hoheitstitel (1963) 388f., 392. QUESNELL, Q. This Good News (1964) 56f. ZEHNLE, R. F. Peter's Pentecost Discourse (1971) 52-53. KRAENKL, E. Jesus der Knecht Gottes (1972) 33, 51, 80, 98-100, 101, 119, 208, 210. ZMIJEWSKI, J. Die Eschatologiereden des Lukas-Evangeliums (1972) 14, 158, 230, 282, 374, 477. STANTON, G. N.Jesus of Nazareth in New Testament Preaching (1974) 16, 21, 22, 72, 82, 181. ZINGG, P., Das Wachsen der Kirche (Freiburg 1974) 147. DUNN, J. D. G., Jesus and the Spirit (London 1975) 70, 164. TRITES, A. A., The New Testament Concept of Witness (Cambridge 1977) 136, 142, 143, 149, 150. CRIBBS, F. L., "The Agreements that Exist Between John and Acts" in: C. H. Talbert (ed.) Perspectives on Luke-Acts (Danville 1978) 52. GERHARDSON, B., "Jesus maktgärningar. Om de urkristna berättarnas val av termer" SEA (1979) 122-33. MOULTON, H. K., "Acts 2.22—'Jesus . . . a man approved by God'?" BTr 30 (1979) 344-45. JUEL, D., "Social Dimensions of Exegesis: The Use of Psalm 16 in Acts 2" CBQ 43 (1981) 544, 547.

2:23-24 FLEW, R. N. Jesus and His Church (1956) 122

2:23 BLAIR, E. P. Jesus in the Gospel of Matthew (1960) 141. EPP, E. J. The theological tendency of Codex Bezae Cantabrigiensis in Acts (1966) 59-61. SHIMADA, K., The Formulary Material in First Peter (Th.D. Diss., Ann Arbor, Michigan 1966) 282-84, 291-92. POPKES, W. Christus Traditus (1967) 149, 184ff., 245, 280. KRAENKL, E. Jesus der Knecht Gottes (1972) 31, 68, 102f., 119, 208-10. SMALLEY, S. S. "The Christology of Acts Again," in: Christ and the Spirit in the New Testament (1973), B. Lindars/S. S. Smalley eds., 80f., 89, 92. WILCKENS, U. Die Missionsreden der Apostelgeschichte (^{3}1974) 34, 36, 42, 45, 51, 110, 124, 125, 132, 133, 147, 171, 181, 186.JEWETT, P. K., Infant Baptism and the Covenant of Grace (Grand Rapids 1978) 119. HUBBARD, B. J., "Luke, Josephus and Rome: A Comparative Approach to the Lukan Sitz im Leben," in: P. J. Achtemeier (ed.) SBL Seminar Papers 1979/I (Missoula 1979) 65. BERGMEIER, R., Glaube als Gabe nach Johannes (Stuttgart 1980) 102 n.246. WILCH, J. R., "Jüdische Schuld am Tode Jesu - Antijudaismus in der Apostelgeschichte?" in: W. Haubeck/M. Backmann (eds.) Wort in der Zeit. FS. K. H. Rengstorf (Leiden 1980) 238-40.

2:24-32 KRAENKL, E. Jesus der Knecht Gottes (1972) 131-36, 207.

2:24-31 BIEDER, W. Die Vorstellung von der Höllenfahrt Jesu Christi

(1949) 63ff. MIGUENS, M. ''Appunti sull'esegesi dell' epoca apostolica,'' BiblOr 3 (6, 1961) 201-06.

2:24 BRATCHER, R. G. '' 'Having Loosed the Pangs of Death,' '' BTr 10 (1, 1959) 18-20. HAHN, F. Christologische Hoheitstitel (1963) 204. WILCOX, M. The Semitisms of Acts (1965) 46-48. DU-PONT, J. Etudes sur les Actes des Apôtres (1967) 267, 280, 281, 284, 287, 288. RESE, M. Alttestamentliche Motive in der Christologie der Lukas (1969) 105-107. WILCKENS, U. Die Missionsreden der Apostelgeschichte (³1974) 10, 34, 35, 40, 45, 122, 125, 137. KRAENKL, E. Jesus der Knecht Gottes (1972) 38, 80, 130, 140, 144, 206, 210. TALBERT, C. H., Literary Patterns, Theological Themes, and the Genre of Luke-Acts (Missoula 1974) 32. HANSON, A., The New Testament Interpretation of Scripture (London 1980) 150-53. POKORNY, P., ''Christologie et Baptême à l'Epoque du Christianisme Primitif'' NTS 27 (1980-1981) 370.

2:25-4:2 WILCOX, M. The Semitisms of Acts (1965) 59ff., 164, 167ff.

2:25-36 BURGER, C. Jesus als Davidssohn (1970) 137-41. FRIEDRICH, G., ''Lukas 9,51 und die Entrückungschristologie des Lukas'' in: Auf das Wort kommt es an (Göttingen 1978) 44-46; [orig. in: P. Hoffmann (ed.) Orientierung an Jesus. FS. J. Schmid (Freiburg 1973) 66-68.]

2:25-33 KAISER, W. C., ''The Promise to David in Psalm 16 and its Application in Acts 2:25-33 and 13:32-37'' JEThS 23 (1980) 219-29.

2:25-31 HAHN, F. Christologische Hoheitstitel (1963) 278. DUPONT, J. Etudes sur les Acts des Apôtres (1967) 265, 266, 286-90.

2:25-28 NÖTSCHER, F., Altorientalischer und alttestamentlicher Auferstehungsglaube (Darmstadt 1970 = 1926) 231. HOLTZ, T. Untersuchungen über die Alttestamentlichen Zitate bei Lukas (1968) 48-51. RESE, M. Alttestamentliche Motive in der Christologie des Lukas (1969) 55-58. SCHMITT, A. ''Ps 16,8-11 als Zeugnis der Auferstehung in der Apg,'' BZ (2, 1973) 229-48. KLIESCH, K., Das heilsgeschichtliche Credo in der Reden der Apostelgeschichte (Köln/Bonn 1975) 128. DUPONT, D. J., The Salvation of the Gentiles (New York 1979) 107-08, 147. HANSON, A. T., The New Testament Interpretation of Scripture (London 1980) 153-55.

2:25 HAHN, F. Christologische Hoheitstitel (1963) 72. METZGER, B. M., The Early Versions of the New Testament (Oxford 1977) 141.

2:26-41 SMEND, R. GPM 26 (2, 1972) 241-55.

2:26-27 DUNN, J. D. G., Jesus and the Spirit (London 1975) 118, 119.

2:26 JEWETT, P. K., Infant Baptism and the Covenant of Grace (Grand Rapids 1978) 119.

2:29ff. LOEVESTAM, E. Son and Saviour (1961) 41f.

2:29-37 DUPONT, D. J., The Salvation of the Gentiles (New York 1979) 108-11.

2:29-31 HOLTZ, T. Untersuchungen über die Alttestamentlichen Zitate bei Lukas (1968) 145-53. WILCKENS, U. Die Missionsreden der Apostelgeschichte (³1974) 10, 35, 51, 141. KLIESCH, K., Das heilsgeschichtliche Credo in den Reden der Apostelgeschichte (Köln/Bonn 1975) 132-36.

2:29 DELLING, G. Die Taufe im Neuen Testament (1963) 141. TAL-BERT, C. H., Literary Patterns, Theological Themes, and the Genre of Luke-Acts (Missoula 1974) 32. MUSSNER, F., ''Zur stilistischen und semantischen Struktur der Formel von I Kor 15:3-5'' in: R. Schnackenburg et al. (eds.) Die Kirche des Anfangs. FS. H. Schürmann (Freiburg/Basel/Wein 1978) 411-12. DUPONT, D. J., The Salvation of the Gentiles (New York 1979) 155. ''Bruderschaften'' in: TRE 7 (1981) 195. JUEL, D., ''Social Dimensions of Exegesis: The Use of Psalm 16 in Acts 2'' CBQ 43 (1981) 544-46.

2:30-32 TALBERT, C. H., Literary Patterns, Theological Themes, and the Genre of Luke-Acts (Missoula 1974) 32.

2:30 LOHFINK, G. Die Himmelfahrt Jesu (1971) 234-35. DUPONT, J. Etudes sur les Actes des Apôtres (1967) 254, 265, 268, 281, 282, 284, 285, 293, 303. RESE, M. Alttestamentliche Motive in der Christologie des Lukas (1969) 107-09. FITZMYER, J. A. ''David, 'Being Therefore a Prophet . . . '(Acts 2:30),'' CBQ 34 (1972) 332-339. KRAENKL, E. Jesus der Knecht Gottes (1972) 86, 156f., 158, 207. THEISOHN, J., Der auserwählte Richter (Göttingen 1975) 156-57. DUPONT, D. J., The Salvation of the Gentiles (New York 1979) 149.

2:31 DELLING, G. Die Zueignung des Heils in der Taufe (1961) 88. DELLING, G. Die Taufe im Neuen Testament (1963) 90. HAHN, F. Christologische Hoheitstitel (1963) 216. RESE, M. Alttestamentliche Motive in der Christologie des Lukas (1969) 109-10. WILCKENS, U. Die Missionsreden der Apostelgeschichte (³1974) 35, 140, 142, 158, 174, 237, 238. WANKE, J., Die Emmauserzählung Leipzig 1973) 15. DUNN, J. D. G., Jesus and the Spirit (London 1975) 115, 119, 390.

2:32-39 PETERS, G. W. A Biblical Theology of Missions (1972) 135, 137, 139-41, 143, 180, 254, 270.

2:32-36 TALBERT, C. H., Literary Patterns, Theological Themes, and the Genre of Luke-Acts (Missoula 1974) 115. DUPONT, D. J., The Salvation of the Gentiles (New York 1979) 112, 148, 151.

2:32-35 LOHFINK, G. Die Himmelfahrt Jesu (1971) 226-29,

2:32-33 BARTH, M., Die Taufe - ein Sakrament? (Zürich 1951) 28ff.

TALBERT, C. H., Literary Patterns, Theological Themes, and the Genre of Luke-Acts (Missoula 1974) 122. DUPONT, D. J., The Salvation of the Gentiles (New York 1979) 73.

2:32 FLEW, R. N. Jesus and His Church (1956) 106. HAHN, F. Christologische Hoheitstitel (1963) 204. DUPONT, J. Etudes sur les Actes des Apôtres (1967) 269, 289, 292, 443. BURCHARD, C. Der dreizehnte Zeuge (1970) 130-35. KRAENKL, E. Jesus der Knecht Gottes (1972) 33, 80, 130, 167f., 206, 210. WILCKENS, U. Die Missionsreden der Apostelgeschichte (³1974) 10, 35, 45, 95, 137, 145, 146, 147, 150, 234. ALSUP, J. E., The Post-Resurrection Appearance Stories of the Gospel-Tradition (Stuttgart 1975) 81. NELLESSEN, E., Zeugnis für Jesus und das Wort (Köln 1976) 178-80. TRITES, A. A., The New Testament Concept of Witness (Cambridge 1977) 136, 137, 144. "Auferstehung" in: TRE 4 (1979) 480. PRAST, F., Presbyter und Evangelium in nachapostolischer Zeit (Stuttgart 1979) 306-07, 319.

2:33-36 FLENDER, H. Heil und Geschichte in der Theologie des Lukas (1965) 96.

2:33-34 STONEHOUSE, N. B. The Witness of Matthew and Mark to Christ (1944) 242. DUPONT, J. Etudes sur les Actes des Apôtres (1967) 143, 144, 284, 292, 300, 479. DUPONT, J. "Ascension du Christ et don de l'Esprit d'après Actes 2:33," in: Christ and the Spirit in the New Testament (1973) B. Lindars/S. S. Smalley eds., 226f.

2:33.36 SCHWEIZER, E. Erniedrigung und Erhöhung bei Jesus und seinen Nachfolgern (1962) § 4g.

2:33 MUNCK, J. Paul and the Salvation of Mankind (1959) 210f. DELLING, G. Die Taufe im Neuen Testament (1963) 98. HAHN, F. Christologische Hoheitstitel (1963) 107, 130. HIGGINS, A. J. B. Menschensohn-Studien (1965) 30-32. SHIMADA, K., The Formulary Material in First Peter (Th.D. Diss., Ann Arbor, Michigan 1966) 391-93. VOSS, G., "Durch die Rechte Gottes erhöht, hat er den Geist ausgegossen (Apg 2,33). Pfingstgeschehen und Pfingstbotschaft nach Apostelgeschichte Kap. 2" BuK 21 (1966) 45-47. DUPONT, J. Etudes sur les Actes des Apôtres (1967) 302-04. FLENDER, H., St Luke Theologian of Redemptive History (1967) 45n, 104n, 105, 118, 138 & n, 140, 141. RESE, M. Alttestamentliche Motive in der Christologie des Lukas (1969) 110. KRAENKL, E. Jesus der Knecht Gottes (1972) 33, 38, 80, 149f., 168, 176, 180, 206, 208, 211. RUPPERT, L., Jesus als der leidende Gerichte? (Stuttgart 1972) 11. DUPONT, J. "Ascension du Christ et don l'Esprit d'apres Actes 2;33," in: Christ and the Spirit in the New Testament (1973) B. Lindars/S. S. Smalley eds., 219-28. STAEHLIN, G. "Tò πνεῦμα 'Ιησοῦ (Apostelgeschichte 16:7)," in: Christ and the Spirit in the New Testament (1973) B.

Lindars/S. S. Smalley eds., 232, 234ff., 241, 245, 252. WILCK-
ENS, U. Die Missionsreden der Apostelgeschichte (^{3}1974) 16, 32,
35, 39, 43, 45, 59, 60, 62, 94, 143, 150, 151, 152, 233. CAV-
ALLIN, H. C. C., Life After Death. I (Lund 1974) 7, 2n18.
GOURGUES, M., "Exalté à la droite de Dieu (Ac 2,33; 5,31)"
SciE 27 (1975) 303-27. GOURGUES, M. A la droite de Dieu. Rés-
urrection de Jésus et actualisation du Psaume 110:1 dans le Nou-
veau Testament (Paris 1978). BARRETT, C. K., "Is there a
Theological Tendency in Codex Bezae?" in: E. Best/R. McL. Wil-
son (eds.) Text and Interpretation. FS. M. Black (Cambridge 1979)
25. DUPONT, D. J., The Salvation of the Gentiles (New York
1979) 124-26. BÖHLIG, A., Die Gnosis III: Der Manichäismus
(Zürich/Münich 1980) 344 n.78. DUNN, J. D., Christology in the
Making (London 1980) 142, 148.

2:34-36 HAHN, F. Christologische Hoheitstitel (1963) 115-17, 191. DU-
PONT, J. Etudes sur les Actes des Apôtres (1967) 267, 270, 282,
450, 467.

2:34-35 DUPONT, J. Etudes sur les Actes des Apôtres (1967) 255, 270,
291-93. RESE, M. Alttestamentliche Motive in der Christologie des
Lukas (1969) 58-66. KRAENKL, E. Jesus der Knecht Gottes (1972)
35, 86, 150-52, 207. WILCKENS, U. Die Missionsreden der
Apostelgeschichte (^{3}1974) 10, 42, 162, 237. KLIESCH, K., Das
heilsgeschichtliche Credo in den Reden der Apostelgeschichte
(Köln/Bonn 1975) 136-37.

2:34 HAHN, F. Christologische Hoheitstitel (1963) 72, 131. PERRIN,
N. NTS 12 (1965-1966) 151f. PESCH, R. Die Vision des Stephanus (1966) 20, 34, 52, 56. TALBERT, C. H., Literary Patterns, Theological Themes, and the Genre of Luke-Acts (Missoula
1974) 122. HORTON, F. L., The Melchizedek Tradition (London
1976) 23-24.

2:35 BÖHLIG, A., Die Gnosis III: Der Manichäismus (Zürich/München
1980) 339n.101.

2:36-42 BACH, U., in: GPM 32 (1978-1979) 222-39.

2:36-41 MUELLER-SCHWEFE, H. R. GPM 20 (1965-1966) 242-48.
BERGNER, H. M./MENSCHING, J./SEYDEL, O./v. STUCK-
RAD-BARRE, J./UBBELOHDE, J. H./DANNOWSKI, H. W.
"Pfingstsonntag", in: Predigtstudien (1971-1972) E. Lange ed.,
83-88.

2:36-40 GLOMBITZA, O. "Der Schluss der Petrusrede Acta 2:36-40. Ein
Beitrag zum Problem der Predigten in Acta," ZNW 52 (1-2, 1961)
115-18.

2:36 ADLER, N. Das erste christliche Pfingstfest (1938) 134, 150-52,
155. STAEHELIN, E. Die Verkündigung des Reiches Gottes in der

Kirche Jesu Christi I (1951) 234. WIKENHAUSER, A. Die Apostelgeschichte (1951) 40f. GAERTNER, B. The Areopagus speech and natural revelation (1955) 30f. FLEW, R. N., Jesus and His Church (1956) 116. BLAIR, E. P. Jesus in the Gospel of Matthew (1960) 53. ROBINSON, J. M. Kerygma und historischer Jesus (1960) 139. DELLING, G. Die Zueignung des Heils in der Taufe (1961) 86, 88. ROBINSON, J. A. T. "The Most Primitive Christology of All?" in: Twelve New Testament Studies (1962) 139-53. WAINWRIGHT, A. W. The Trinity in the New Testament (1962) 183-84. DELLING, G. Die Taufe im Neuen Testament (1963) 141. HAHN, F. Christologische Hoheitstitel (1963) 98, 106, 116, 117, 191, 192, 207, 291, 389. KAESEMANN, E. Exegetische Versuche und Besinnungen (1964) I 215. SEEBERG, A. Der Katechismus der Urchristenheit (1966) 185f. DUPONT, J. Etudes sur les Acts des Apôtres (1967) 147, 149, 269-71, 367-90. VOSS, G. " 'Zum Herrn und Messias gemacht hat Gott diesen Jesus' (Apg 2,36). Zur Christologie der lukanischen Schriften," BuL 8 (4, 1967) 236-48. SCHNEIDER, G. Verleugnung, Verspottung und Verhör Jesu nach Lukas 22,54-71 (1969) 36, 185, 206, 214. SCHUETZ, F. Der leidende Christus (1969) 31, 36, 81f., 83, 134f., 136. ZEHNLE, R. F. Peter's Pentecost Discourse (1971) 66-70. KRAENKL, E. Jesus der Knecht Gottes (1972) 31, 33f., 44, 47, 58, 99, 102, 108, 159-63, 185f, 197, 208, 211. SCHUESSLER-FIORENZA, E. Priester für Gott (1972) 224f. WILCKENS, U. Die Missionsreden der Apostelgeschichte ([3]1974) 12, 35, 36, 37, 38, 39, 45, 55, 109, 132, 152, 156, 170-74, 179, 180, 221, 237, 238, 239. LADD, G. E., A Theology of the New Testament (Grand Rapids 1974) 171, 316, 331, 334, 336, 338, 339, 341. TALBERT, C. H., Literary Patterns, Theological Themes, and the Genre of Luke-Acts (Missoula 1974) 111, 122. ZINGG, P., Das Wachsen der Kirche (Freiburg 1974) 147. GLÖCKNER, R., Die Verkündigung des Heils beim Evangelisten Lukas (Mainz 1975) 9, 36, 120, 231-32. KLIESCH, K., Das heilsgeschichtliche Credo in den Reden der Apostelgeschichte (Köln/Bonn 1975) 142. GOPPELT, L., Theologie des Neuen Testaments. II (Göttingen 1976) 347-48. METZGER, B. M., The Early Versions of the New Testament (Oxford 1977) 253. SANDMEL, S., We Jews and Jesus (New York 1977) 37. TRITES, A. A., The New Testament Concept of Witness (Cambridge 1977) 130, 133, 144, 152. DUPONT, D. J., The Salvation of the Gentiles (New York 1979) 117. HENGEL, M., Zur urchristlichen Geschichtsschreibung (Stuttgart 1979) 88; ET: J. Bowden (trans.) Acts and the History of Earliest Christianity (London 1979) 104. PRAST, E., Presbyter und Evangelium in nachapostolischer Zeit (Stuttgart 1979) 318-19, 323. WILCH, J.

R., "Jüdische Schuld am Tode Jesu - Antijudaismus in der Apostelgeschichte?" in: W. Haubeck/M. Bachmann (eds.) Wort in der Zeit. FS. K. H. Rengstorf (Leiden 1980) 238-40.

2:37-42 GIBLET, J., "Baptism in the Spirit in the Acts of the Apostles" One Christ 10 (1974) 162-71.

2:37-41 BIEDER, W., Die Verheissung der Taufe im Neuen Testament (Zürich 1966) 134-37. SAUVAGNAT, B., "Se repentir, être baptisé, recevoir L'Esprit, Actes 2,37ss." FV 80 (1981) 77-89.

2:37-38 DUNN, J. D. G., Unity and Diversity in the New Testament (London 1977) 144.

2:37 CLARK, A. C. The Acts of the Apostles (1933) xxvi, 227, 243, 294. DELLING, G. Die Taufe im Neuen Testament (1963) 73. EPP, E. J. The theological tendency of Codex Bezae Cantabrigiensis in Acts (1966) 73f., 86, 154, 159, 164. BARTH, M., Die Taufe - ein Sakrament? (Zürich 1951) 134-45. METZGER, B. M., The Early Versions of the New Testament (Oxford 1977) 40. "Apostelgeschichte" in: TRE 3 (1978) 506. "Bruderschaften" in: TRE 7 (1981) 195.

2:38-40 MEYER, B. F., The Aims of Jesus (London 1979) 66-69. "Busse" in: TRE 7 (1981) 449.

2:38-39 FLEW, R. N. Jesus and His Church (1956) 100-01, 105, 119-20. JEWETT, P. K., Infant Baptism and the Covenant of Grace (Grand Rapids 1978) 235. MINGUEZ, D., "Estructura dinámica de la conversión. Reflexión sobre Hch 2,38-39" EstEc 54 (1979) 383-94. BARTH, G., Die Taufe in frühchristlicher Zeit (Neukirchen-Vluyn 1981) 11, 38-40, 44, 53, 60, 64, 71, 141-42.

2:38 FEINE, P. Der Apostel Paulus (1927) 344f. BEYER, H. W. Die Apostelgeschichte (1947) 27f. ADLER, N., Taufe und Handauflegung (Münster 1951) 26-28, 57, 74-75, 96. BARTH, M. Die Taufe—ein Sakrament? (Zürich 1951) 134-45. WIKENHAUSER, A. Die Apostelgeschichte (1951) 42-44. GILMORE, A. Christian Baptism (1959) 116-18. DELLING, G. Die Zueignung des Heils in der Taufe (1961) 13, 85f., 88, 89, 91, 92. DELLING, Die Taufe im Neuen Testament (1963) 59f., 62, 64, 66, 67, 68, 76, 118, 140, 141. KAESEMANN, E. Exegetische Versuche und Besinnungen (1964) I 45. ROMANIUK, K. NTS 12 (1965-1966) 268f. EPP, E. J. The theological tendency of Codex Bezae Cantabrigiensis in Acts (1966) 54, 62f., 68, 72. SEEBERG, A. Der Katechismus der Urchristenheit (1966) 184, 213-219, 236, 258. DUPONT, J. Etudes sur les Actes des Apôtres (1967) 380, 423, 434, 452, 463. STROBEL, A. Erkenntnis und Bekenntnis der Sünde in neutestamentlicher Zeit (1968) 48. BURCHARD, C. Der dreizehnte Zeuge (1970) 116-18. DUNN, J. D. G. Baptism in the Holy Spirit (1970)

90ff. THYEN, H. Studien zur Sündenvergebung (1970) 147, 149f. PARRATT, J. K. "The Holy Spirit and Baptism. Part I. The Gospels and the Acts of the Apostles," ET 82 (8, 1971) 231-35. ZEHNLE, R. F. Peter's Pentecost Discourse (1971) 61-63. KRAENKL, E. Jesus der Knecht Gottes (1972) 120, 180f., 184f., 208. ZMIJEWSKI, J. Die Eschatologiereden des Lukas-Evangeliums (1972) 18, 159, 161, 442. WILCKENS, U. Die Missionsreden der Apostelgeschichte (³1974) 37, 45, 157, 180, 181, 182, 183, 185. LADD, G. E., A Theology of the New Testament (Grand Rapids 1974) 317, 331, 345, 350, 542. GOPPELT, L., Theologie der Neuen Testaments. II (Göttingen 1976) 380ff. "Abendmahl" in: TRE 1 (1977) 52. BEST, E., From Text to Sermon (Atlanta 1978) 24. JEWETT, P. K., Infant Baptism and the Covenant of Grace (Grand Rapids 1978) 119-20, 199. BARRETT, C. K., "Is there a Theological Tendency in Codex Bezae?" in: E. Best/R. McL. Wilson (eds.) Text and Interpretation. FS. M. Black (Cambridge 1979) 25. DAVIS, J. C., "Another Look at the Relationship Between Baptism and Forgiveness of Sins in Acts 2:38," RestQ 24 (1981) 80-88.

2:39 DELLING, G. Die Taufe im Neuen Testament (1963) 144. EPP, E. J. The theological tendency of the Codex Bezae Cantabrigiensis in Acts (1966) 69 n.4, 70f., 167. DUPONT, J. Etudes sur les Actes des Apôtres (1967) 255, 262, 270 277, 281, 351, 352, 408, 415, 418, 455, 481. KRAENKL, E. Jesus der Knecht Gottes (1972) 34f., 80, 192. WILSON, S. G. The Gentiles and the Gentile Mission in Luke-Acts (1973) 132, 219, 228, 243. WILCKENS, U. Die Missionsreden der Apostelgeschichte (³1974) 34, 37, 51f, 185. JEWETT, P. K., Infant Baptism and the Covenant of Grace (Grand Rapids 1978) 119-20. BARTH, G., Die Taufe in frühchristlicher Zeit (Neukirchen-Vluyn 1981) 64, 68, 141-42.

2:40-42 MATTILL, A. J., Luke and the Last Things (Dillsboro 1979) 61-62.

2:40 DELLING, G. Die Taufe im Neuen Testament (1963) 60. NICKELS, P. Targum and New Testament (1967) 60. KRAENKL, E. Jesus der Knecht Gottes (1972) 34f., 182, 192. WILCKENS, U. Die Missionsreden der Apostelgeschichte (³1974) 34, 146, 179, 184, 185, 206. NELLESSEN, E., Zeugnis für Jesus und das Wort (Köln 1976) 95-99. "Apostelgeschichte" in: TRE 3 (1978) 505.

2:41-12:17 TALBERT, C. H., Literary Patterns, Theological Themes, and the Genre of Luke-Acts (Missoula 1974) 16, 19.

2:41-5:52 DUPONT, J. Etudes sur les Actes des Apôtres (1967) 34-37.

2:41-5:40 TALBERT, C. H., Literary Patterns, Theological Themes, and the Genre of Luke-Acts (Missoula 1974) 49.

2:41-47 DEGENHARDT, H.-J., Lukas, Evangelist der Armen (1964) 163-
68. HAAR, J. GPM 18 (3, 1964) 343-48. ROLOFF, J. Apostolat-
Verkündigung-Kirche (1965) 221-23. ZIMMERMAN, H. Neutestamentliche Methodenlehre (1967) 243-45. DUNN, J. D. G. Baptism in the Holy Spirit (1970) 50f., 57. RUHBACH, G., in: GPM
30 (1975-1976) 417-23. JOHNSON, L. T., The Literary Function
of Possessions in Luke-Acts (Missoula 1977) 183-90. KARRIS, R.
J., "Poor and Rich: The Lukan Sitz im Leben" in: C. H. Talbert
(ed.) Perspectives on Luke-Acts (Danville 1978) 114, 116-17.
PANIKULAM, G., Koinōnia in the New Testament (Rome 1979)
113, 117-20. TYSON, J. B., "The Problem of Food in Acts: A
Study of Literary Patterns with Particular Reference to Acts 6:1-7"
in: P. J. Achtemeier (Ed.) SBL Seminar Papers 1979/I (Missoula
1979) 74-75. GÁBRIŠ, K., in: GPM 34 (1980) 298-306. ON-
NASH, K. und LEMBKE, I., in: P. Krusche et al. (eds.) Predigtstudien für das Kirchenjahr 1979-1980 II/2 (Stuttgart 1980) 150-56

2:41-42 OTT, W. Gebet und Heil (1965) 125-29. ARRINGTON, F. L., New
Testament Exegesis: Examples (Washington 1977) 21-46.

2:41 ADLER, N. Das erste christliche Pfingstfest (1938) 132, 140f.
FLEW, R. N. Jesus and His Church (1956) 154n. DELLING, G.
Die Taufe im Neuen Testament (1963) 41, 69, 70, 75, 141. DU-
PONT, J. The Sources of Acts (1964) 24, 40, 43, 47, 57. BRUN,
L., "Etwa 3000 Seelen, Act 2,41" ZNW 14 (1913) 94-96. ZINGG,
P., Das Wachsen der Kirche (Freiburg 1974) 162-65, 165-67, 170.
ARRINGTON, F. L., New Testament Exegesis: Examples (Wash-
ington 1977) 29-32, 42. JOHNSON, L. T., The Literary Functions
of Possessions in Luke-Acts (Missoula 1977) 184-85. JEWETT, P.
K., Infant Baptism and the Covenant of Grace (Grand Rapids 1978)
198. BARTH, G., Die Taufe in frühchristlicher Zeit (Neukirchen-
Vluyn 1981) 11, 38-39. KRAFT, H., Die Entstehung des Chris-
tentums (Darmstadt 1981) 214-19.

2:42-4:31 REICKE, B. Glaube und Leben der Urgemeinde (1957) 55-84.
TALBERT, C. H., Literary Patterns, Theological Themes, and the
Genre of Luke-Acts (Missoula 1974) 38.

2:42-47 REICKE, B. Diakonie, Festfreude und Zelos (1951) 25ff. WI-
KENHAUSER, A. Die Apostelgeschichte (1951) 58. BEST, E. One
Body in Christ (1955) 198. ZIMMERMANN, H. "Die Sammel-
berichte der Apostelgeschichte," BZ 5 (1, 1961) 71-82. DU-
PONT, J. The Sources of Acts (1964) 23, 36, 41, 43, 47, 48.
IWAND, H.-J. Predigt-Meditationen (1964) 365-70. Du TOIT, A.
B. Der Aspekt der Freude im urchristlichen Abendmahl (1965) 103-
12. HERTZSCH, K.-P. GPM 24 (4, 1969-1970) 400-05. BORI, P.
C., Chiesa primitiva. Testi e ricerche de Scienze religiose 10 (Bres-
cia 1974). TALBERT, C. H., Literary Patterns, Theological

Themes, and the Genre of Luke-Acts (Missoula 1974) 35, 38, 101. DOWNEY, J. "The Early Jerusalem Christians" BiTod 91 (1977) 1295-1303. "Apostelgeschichte" in: TRE 3 (1978) 513. GÓMEZ de MORALES, M. V., "La comunidad primitiva modelo de consagración a Dios" (Biblia y Fe 4 (Madrid 1978) 271-92. BOERMA, C., Rich Man, Poor Man - and the Bible (London 1979) 57-58. PFITZNER, V. C., " 'Pneumatic' Apostleship? Apostle and Spirit in the Acts of the Apostles" in: W. Haubeck/M. Bachmann (eds.) FS. K. H. Rengstorf. Wort in der Zeit (Leiden 1980) 221-22. SCHNEIDER, G., Die Apostelgeschichte. I (Freiburg/Basel/Wien 1980) 283 (lit!). HAULOTTE, E., "La vie en communion, phase ultime de al Pentecôte, Actes 2,42-47" FV 80 (1981) 69-75. WEISER, A., Die Apostelgeschichte. I (Gütersloh/Würzburg 1981) 100-01 (lit!).

2:42-46 SQUILLACI, D. "La frazione del pane," PaC1 39 (17, 1960) 913-17. WANKE, J., Die Emmauserzählung (Leipzig 1973) 54, 102, 105ff., 120. JEWETT, P. K., Infant Baptism and the Covenant of Grace (Grand Rapids 1978) 53.

2:42-45 BENOIT, P. "Remarques sur les 'sommaires' de Actes 2.42 à 45," in: Aux Sources dela Tradition Chrétienne (1950) M. M. Goguel ed., 1-10.

2:42 BONHOEFFER, D. Nachfolge (1950) 176f. REICKE, B. Diakonie, Fetsfreude und Zelos (1951) 25ff. WIKENHAUSER, A. Die Apostelgeschichte (1951) 44f. BEST, E. One Body in Christ (1955) 89. FLEW, R. N. Jesus and His Church (1956) 109-13, 131, 355n. JEREMIAS, J. Die Abendmahlsworte Jesu (1960) 111-14. GOULDER, M. D. Type and History in Acts (1964) 18f., 22, 26. DUPONT, J. Etudes sur les Actes der Apôtres (1967) 430, 475, 503-19. KUENG, H. Die Kirche (1967) 134, 135, 261, 324, 361. ET: The Church (1967) 110, 218, 272, 304. MUSSNER, F. "Die UNA SANCTA nach Apg 2:42," in: Praesentia Salutis (1967) 212. BROWN, S. Apostasy and Perseverance in the Theology of Luke (1969) 99f., 106, 115, 117, 125f., 128, 144. SCHUERMANN, H. Ursprung und Gestalt (1970) 64, 65, 79, 82, 85, 86, 87, 88, 91, 93, 101, 131, 134, 188, 190. FITZMEYER, J. A. Essays on the Semitic Background of the New Testament (1971) 275-77, 283. LADD, G. E., A Theology of the New Testament (Grand Rapids 1974) 350, 353, 543. ZINGG, P., Das Wachsen der Kirche (Freiburg 1974) 146-47. MENOUD, P. H., "Les Actes des Apôtres et l'eucharistie" in: Jésus Christ et la foi (Neuchâtel/Paris (1975) 64-67; [Orig. in: RHPR 33 (1953) 21-36.] "Abendmahl" in: TRE 1 (1977) 56. ARRINGTON, F. L., New Testament Exegesis: Examples (Washingon 1977) 32-35, 42-44. MANZANERA, M., "Koinonía en Hch 2,42. Notas sobre su interpretación y orígen histórico-doctrinal'' EstEc 52 (1977) 307-29. ''Armenfürsorge'' in: TRE 4 (1979) 16. DUPONT, D. J., The Salvation of the Gentiles (New York 1979) 85-87. PANIKULAM, G., Koinōnia in the New Testament (Rome 1979) 109-29. MCDONALD, J. I. H., Kerygma and Didache (Cambridge 1980) 107.

2:43-47 FLEW, R. N. Jesus and His Church (1956) 198. OTT, W. Gebet und Heil (1965) 125-29. MANEK, J. ''Vier Bibelstudien zur Problematik der sozialen Umwandlung,'' CommViat 10, (1, 1967) 61-70; (2-3, 1967) 179-82.

2:43 FLEW, R. N. Jesus and His Church (1956) 132. CONZELMANN, H. Die Apostelgeschichte (1963) 31. TALBERT, C. H., Literary Patterns, Theological Themes, and the Genre of Luke-Acts (Missoula 1974) 35. JOHNSON, L. T., The Literary Function of Possessions in Luke-Acts (Missoula 1977) 186.

2:44-47 DUNN, J. D. G., Jesus and the Spirit (London 1975) 161.

2:44-46 BRAUN, H. Qumran und NT II (1966) 148, 155-57, 162, 209, 213, 224, 271, 288, 292, 327, 334f.

2:44.46.47 NICKELS, P. Targum and New Testament (1967) 61.

2:44-45 REICKE, B. Diakonie, Festfreude und Zelos (1951) 26f. DUPONT, J. Etudes sur les Actes des Apôtres (1967) 503-19. JOHNSON, L. T., The Literary Function of Possessions in Luke-Acts (Missoula 1977) 186-87.

2:44.46.47 NICKELS, P. Targum and New Testament (1967) 61.

2:44 RIECKE, B. Diakonie, Festfreude und Zelos (1951) 27f. BETZ, H. D. Lukian von Samosata und das Neue Testament (1961) 19, 97. WILCOX, M. The Semitisms of Acts (1965) 93-95, 97-99. JOHNSON, L. T., The Literary Function of Possessions in Luke-Acts (Missoula 1977) 186-87. ''Apostelgeschichte'' in: TRE 3 (1978) 492, 517. DUPONT, D. J., The Salvation of the Gentiles (New York 1979) 87, 101.

2:45-47 REICKE, B. Diakonie, Festfreude und Zelos (1951) 26f.

2:45 CONZELMANN, H. Die Apostelgeschichte (1963) 31. DUPONT, J. L'union entre les premiers chrétiens dans les Actes des Apôtres,'' NRTh 91 (9, 1969) 897-915. JOHNSON, L. T., The Literary Function of Possessions in Luke-Acts (Missoula 1977) 187.

2:46-47 Du TOIT, A. B. Der Aspekt der Freude im urchristlichen Abendmahl (1965) 103-39. JOHNSON, L. T., The Literary Function of Possessions in Luke-Acts (Missoula 1977) 188-89.

2:46 PALLIS, A., Notes on St. Luke and the Acts (London 1928) 51. CULLMANN, O. Urchristentum und Gottesdienst (1950) 11, 13, 14, 16, 18, 30. REICKE, B. Diakonie, Fetsfreude und Zelos (1951) 75f., 202ff. JEREMIAS, J. Die Abendmalsworte Jesu (1960) 112-

14. ORLETT, R. "The Breaking of Bread in Acts," Bible Today 1 (2, 1962) 108-12. HAHN, F. Christlogische Hoheitstitel (1963) 105. GAERTNER, B. The Temple and the Community in Qumran and the New Testament (1965) 100. PETZKE, G. Die Traditionen über Apollonius von Tyana und das Neue Testament (1970) 209, 211. ROGGE, J./SCHILLE, G. eds., Theologische Versuche II (1970) 71-73. SCHUERMANN, H. Ursprung und Gestalt (1970) 62, 70, 79, 82, 85, 90, 92, 102, 188, 190, 304. MENOUD, P. H., "Les Actes des Apôtres et l'eucharistie" in: Jésus Christ et la foi (Neuchâtel/Paris 1975) 64-67; [orig. in RHPR 33 (1953) 21-36.] LADD, G. E., A Theology of the New Testament (Grand Rapids 1974) 348, 349, 540. DUNN, J. D. G., Jesus and the Spirit (London 1975) 160, 184-85, 188, 405-06. GOPPELT, L., Theologie des Neuen Testaments. II (Göttingen 1976) 336. FRIEDRICH, G., "Ursprung, Urform und Urbedeutung des Abendmahls" in: Auf das Wort kommt es an (Göttingen 1978) 315. HAHN, F., "Thesen zur Frage einheitsstiftender Elemente in Lehre und Praxis des urchristlichen Herrenmahls" in: D. Lührmann/G. Strecker (eds.) Kirche. FS. G. Bornkamm (Tübingen 1980) 419. KRAFT, H., Die Entstehung des Christentums (Darmstadt 1981) 222.

2:47 CHEETHAM, F. P. "Acts ii. 47: echontes charin pros holon ton laon," ET 75 (7, 1963) 214-15. DELLING, G. Die Taufe im Neuen Testament (1963) 60, 70. WILCOX, M. The Semitisms of Acts (1965) 93-100. EPP, E. J. The theological tendency of the Codex Bezae Cantabrigiensis in Acts (1966) 25, 68, 76-79, 118, 166f. WILCKENS, U. Die Missionsreden der Apostelgeschichte (³1974) 95, 179, 184, 185. ZINGG, P., Das Wachsen der Kirche (Freiburg 1974) 30-32, 38, 160. "Apostelgeschichte" in: TRE 3 (1978) 492. HORTON, F. L., "Reflections on the Semitisms of Luke-Acts" in: C. H. Talbert (ed.) Perspectives on Luke-Acts (Danville 1978) 19-20. BERGMEIER, R., Glaube als Gabe nach Johannes (Stuttgart 1980) 60. DELEBECQUE, É., "Trois simples mots, chargés d'une lumière neuve (*Actes des Apôtres*, II,47b)" RThom 80 (1980) 75-85. GAMBA, G. G., "Significato letterale e portata dottrinale dell'inciso participiale di Atti 2,47b: *echontes charin pros holon ton laon*" Salesianum 43 (1981) 45-70.

3-5 TALBERT, C. H., Literary Patterns, Theological Themes, and the Genre of Luke-Acts (Missoula 1974) 37, 38.

3:1-5:16 DUPONT, J. The Sources of Acts (1964) 36, 37, 51.

   3-4 DUPONT, J. Les Problèmes du Livre des Actes (1950) 85ff. LOH-MEYER, E. Gottesknecht und Davidsohn (1954) 15-25. DU-PONT, J. The Sources of Acts (1964) 18, 37, 38, 40. SCHILLE, G. Anfänge der Kirche (1966) 146ff. EHRHARDT, A. The Acts of the Apostles (1969) 18f. JOHNSON, L. T., The Literary Function of Possessions in Luke-Acts (Missoula 1977) 60-69. BOVON, F., "La vie des Apôtres: traditions bibliques et narrations apocryphes" in: F. Bovon et al. (eds.) Les Actes Apocryphes des Apôtres (Geneva 1981) 153.

3:1-4:31 SHEPARD, J. W., The Life and Letters of St. Paul (Grand Rapids 1950) 35-40.

3:1-4:22 DIETRICH, W. Das Petrusbild der lukanischen Schriften (1972) 216-32.

   3 WILCOX, M. The Semitisms of Acts (1965) 160-61. HOLTZ, T. Untersuchungen über die Alttestamentlichen Zitate bei Lukas (1968) 71-81. LENTZEN-DEIS, F. Die Taufe Jesu nach den Synoptikern (1970) 274. ZEHNLE, R. F. Peter's Pentecost Discourse (1971) 19ff., 44ff., 71ff., 131ff. FRANKLIN, E., Christ the Lord (London 1975) 100-02. MINEAR, P. S., To Die and to Live (New York 1977) 49-50. CRIBBS, F. L., "The Agreements That Exist Between John and Acts" in: C. H. Talbert (ed.) Perspectives on Luke-Acts (Danville 1978) 45. VIA, E. J., "An Interpretation of Acts 7:35-37 from the Perspective of Major Themes in Luke-Acts" in: P. J. Achtemeier (ed.) SBL Seminar Papers 1978/II (Missoula 1978) 217-19. SCOBIE, C. H. H., "The Use of Source Material in the Speeches of Acts III and VII" NTS 25 (1979) 399-41. BOVON, F., "La vie des apôtres: traditions bibliques et narrations apocryphes" in: F. Bovon et al. (eds.) Les Actes Apocryphes des Apôtres (Geneva 1981) 147.

3:1-21 SMOLIK, J. GPM 18 (1, 1964) 160-66. VOIGT, G. Der zerrissene Vorhang I (1969) 195-201. MERKEL, F. GPM 24 (2, 1970-1971) 203-08. BOHREN, R., Predigtlehre (München 1971) 180-81. GEBHARDT, R., und JUNG, H.-G., in: P. Krusche et al. (eds.) Predigtstudien für das Kirchenjahr 1975-1976. IV/2 (Stuttgart 1976) 33-39. HAAR, J., in: GPM 30 (1976) 202-07. FISCHER, K. M., Das Ostergeschehen (Göttingen 1980[2]).

3:1-16 IWAND, H.-J. Predigtmeditationen (1964) 158-62. NIESEL, W. in: Herr, tue meine Lippen auf Bd. 4 (1965) G. Eichholz ed., 364ff.

3:1-13 BEYER, H. W. Die Apostelgeschichte (1947) 15-19.

3:1-11 SEIDENSTICKER, Ph. Die Auferstehung Jesu in der Botschaft der Evangelisten (1968) 102f. SCHNEIDER, G., Die Apostelgeschichte. I (Freiburg/Basel/Wien 1980) 296 (lit!).

3:1-10 DIBELIUS, M. Aufsätze zur Apostelgeschichte (1951) 19f. ET: Studies in the Acts of the Apostles (1956) 14f. BORNKAMM-BARTH-HELD, Ueberlieferung und Auslegung im Matthäus-Evangelium (²1961) 258. TALBERT, C. H., Literary Patterns, Theological Themes, and the Genre of Luke-Acts (Missoula 1974) 16, 19, 23, 35. SIMON, L., "La prière non religieuse chez Luc" FV 74 (1975) 8-22. JOHNSON, L. T., The Literary Function of Possessions in Luke-Acts (Missoula 1977) 190-91. "Apostelgeschichte" in: TRE 3 (1978) 492, 496, 498. CRIBBS, F. L., "The Agreements that Exist Between John and Acts," in: C. H. Talbert (ed.) Perspectives on Luke-Acts (Danville 1978) 52. BOERMA, C., Rich Man, Poor Man - and the Bible (London 1979) 84-85. FILIPPINI, R., "Atti 3,1-10: Proposta di analisi del racconto" RivB 28 (1980) 305-17. WEISER, A., Die Apostelgeschichte. I (Gütersloh/Würzburg 1981) 106-07 (lit!). SCHULZ, R., und TILMANN, R., in: P. Krusche et al. (eds.) Predigtstudien für das Kirchenjahr 1981-1982 IV/2 (Stuttgart 1982) 189-96.

3:1-7 SEYBOLD, K. und MÜLLER, U., Krankheit und Heilung (Stuttgart 1978) 125.

3:1 BLAIR, E. P. Jesus in the Gospel of Matthew (1960) 144. GOULDER, M. D. Type and History in Acts (1964) 17f., 22, 25, 74. GAERTNER, B. The Temple and the Community in Qumran and the New Testament (1965) 100. BRAUN, H. Qumran und NT II (1966) 200f. JEREMIAS, J. Neutestamentliche Theologie I (1971) 180, 182f.

3:2 CONZELMANN, H. Die Apostelgeschichte (1963) 32f. WILCOX, M. The Semitisms of Acts (1965) 61-62, 127, 128, 133, 153, 171, 172. NICKELS, P. Targum and New Testament (1967) 61. SCHALIT, A. König Herodes (1969) 389. SCHÜRER, E., Die θύρα oder πύλη ὡραία in Act 3:2 u.10" ZNW 7 (1906) 51-68. BEYSCHLAG, K., Simon Magus und die christliche Gnosis (Tübingen 1974) 104, n.14, 106 n.18. HAGE, W., "Die griechische Baruch-Apokalypse" in: JüdSchr V/1 (1974) 22 n.2c.

3:3-5 EPP, E. J. The theological tendency of the Codex Bezae Cantabrigiensis in Acts (1966) 155f.

3:6 MOORE, G. F. Judaism I (1946) 379. BEYER, H. W. Die Apostelgeschichte (1947) 32. FLEW, R. N. Jesus and His Church (1956) 147n. RUDOLPH, K. Die Mandäer I (1960) 115. DELLING, G. Die Zueignung des Heils in der Taufe (1961) 48, 49f., 88. STRECKER, G. Der Weg der Gerechtigkeit (1962) 62₁. WILCKENS, U. Die Missionsreden der Apostelgeschichte (³1974)41, 60, 123, 166.

3:7 BETZ, H. D. Lukian von Samosata und das Neue Testament (1961)

150, 157. MATTILL, A. J., Luke and the Last Things (Dillsboro 1979) 56-58.

3:8 PALLIS, A., Notes on St. Luke and the Acts (London 1928) 51-52.

3:9 WILCOX, The Semitisms of Acts (1965) 113-14. NICKELS, P. Targum and New Testament (1967) 61. MATTILL, A. J., Luke and the Last Things (Dillsboro 1979) 56-58.

3:10-16 DUPONT, D. J., The Salvation of the Gentiles (New York 1979) 73.

3:10.11.12 DELLING, G. Die Zueignung des Heils in der Taufe (1961) 91.

3:10 STONEHOUSE, N. B. The Witness of Matthew and Mark to Christ (1944) 106. SCHÜRER, E., "Die θύρα oder πύλη ὡραία in Act 3.2 u.10" ZNW 7 (1906) 51-68.

3:11-26 JERVELL, J., "The Divided People of God" in: Luke and the People of God (Minneapolis 1972) 58-60. MÜLLER, P.-G., ΧΡΙΣΤΟΣ ΑΡΧΗΓΟΣ. Der religionsgeschichtliche und theologische Hintergrund einer neutestamentlichen Christusprädikation. (Frankfurt 1973) 249ff. WEISER, A., Die Apostelgeschichte. I (Gütersloh/Würzburg 1981) 111-12 (lit!).

3:11-21 BRAUN, H., GPM 7/2 (1952-53) 111-14.

3:11 DIBELIUS, M. Aufsätze zur Apostelgeschichte (1951) 20, 77, 164 n.1. DUPLACY, J. "A propos d'une variante 'occidentale' des Actes des Apôtres (III,11)," REA 2 (1956) 231-42. BEYSCHLAG, K., Simon Magus und die christliche Gnosis (Tübingen 1974) 104 n.14. "Apostelgeschichte" in: TRE 3 (1978) 487. BARRETT, C. K., "Is there a Theological Tendency in Codex Bezae?" in: E. Best/R. McL. Wilson (eds.) Text and Interpretation. FS. M. Black (Cambridge 1979) 25.

3:12ff. NORDEN, E. Agnostos Theos (1956 = 1912) 8 f.

3:12-36 EVANS, C. F. " 'Speeches' in Acts," in: Mélanges Bibliques en hommage au R. P. Béda Rigaux (1970) A. Descamps/A. de Halleux eds., 299-301.

3:12-26 DIBELIUS, M. Aufsätze zur Apostelgeschichte (1951) 104f., 142f., 152f. STAEHELIN, E. Die Verkündigung des Reiches Gottes in der Kirche Jesu Christi I (1951) 3. DIBELIUS, M. Studies in the Acts of the Apostles (1956) 119f., 165f., 178f. ROBINSON, J. A. T. "The Most Primitive Christology of all?", JThS n.s. VII (1956) 177-89. ROBINSON, J. A. T. "Elijah, John and Jesus. An Essay in Detection," NTS IV (1958) 276f. WILCKENS, U. Die Missionsreden der Apostelgeschichte (³1974) Passim. HAHN, F. Christologische Hoheitstitel (1963) 219, 385f., 390, 397, 403. SEEBERG, A. Der Katechismus der Urchristenheit (1966) 127. GRYGLEWICZ, F., "Teologiczne aspekty Piotrowych przemowien (Dz 2,14-36; 3,12-26). Les aspects theologique des discours de Pierre'' ZNKUL 12 (1969) 23-34. KASSING, A. Auferstanden für uns (1969) 37-39. BURCHARD, C. Der dreizehnte Zeuge (1970) 138-42. GASTON, L. No Stone on Another (1970) 100, 264, 266-68, 278-80. ZEHNLE, R. F. Peter's Pentecost Discourse (1971) 19-22, 41-60, 71-94. PLUEMACHER, E. Lukas als hellenistischer Schriftsteller (1972) 43-46. SCHNIDER, F. Jesus der Prophet (1973) 89ff., 97, 237. BEYSCHLAG, K., Simon Magus und die christliche Gnosis (Tübingen 1974) 89 n.26, 101 n.6. TALBERT, C. H., Literary Patterns, Theological Themes, and the Genre of Luke-Acts (Missoula 1974) 19, 23, 35, 38. KLIESCH, K., Das heilsgeschichtliche Credo in den Reden der Apostelgeschichte (Köln/Bonn 1975) 75ff., 148-52. WILLIAMS, J. A., A Conceptual History of Deuteronomism in the Old Testament, Judaism and the New Testament (Ph. D. Diss., Louisville 1976) 257-62, 290. JOHNSON, L. T., The Literary Function of Possessions in Luke-Acts (Missoula 1977) 63-65, 191-92. MEYER, B. F., The Aims of Jesus (London 1979) 66-69. SCHNEIDER, G., Die Apostelgeschichte. I (Freiburg/Basel/Wien (1980) 310-11 (lit!).

3:12-21 HOOKER, M. D. Jesus and the Servant (1959) 118-20.

3:12-13 BOWKER, J. W. NTS 14 (1967-1968) 106f.

3:12 GOULDER, M. D. Type and History in Acts (1964) 79-82, 84. DUPONT, J. ''Les discours de Pierre dans les Actes et le chapitre XXIV de l'evangile de Luc,'' in: L'Evangile de Luc (1973) F. Neirynck ed., 333-34. LADD, G. E., A Theology of the New Testament (Grand Rapids 1974) 372, 373, 480. KLIESCH, K., Das heilsgeschichtliche Credo in den Reden der Apostelgeschichte (Köln/Bonn 1975) 138-39.

3:13ff. HAHN, F. Christologische Hoheitstitel (1963) 116.

3:13-26 VAWTER, B. This Man Jesus (1973) 91ff. WANKE, J., Die Emmauserzählung (Leipzig 1973) 11, n.492. DUPONT, D. J., The Salvation of the Gentiles (New York 1979) 132.

3:13-21 GLÖCKNER, R., Die Verkündigung des Heils beim Evangelisten Lukas (Mainz 1975) 203-04, 221.

3:13-19 DUPONT, D. J., The Salvation of the Gentiles (New York 1979) 67.

3:13-18 BARRETT, C. K., ''Is There a Theological Tendency in Codex Bezae?'' in: E. Best/R. McL. Wilson (eds.) Text and Interpretation. FS. M. Black (Cambridge 1979) 23-24.

3:13-16 KURZ, W. S., ''Acts 3:19-26 as a Test of the Role of Eschatology in Lukan Christology'' in: P. J. Achtemeier (ed.) SBL Seminar Papers 1977 (Missoula 1977) 312.

3:13-15 SCHELKLE, K. H. Die Passion Jesu in der Verkündigung des

Neuen Testaments (1949) 116f. HAHN, F. Christologische Hoheitstitel (1963) 215. KRAENKL, E. Jesus der Knecht Gottes (1972)
31, 103-05. WILCKENS, U. Die Missionsreden der Apostelgeschichte (^{3}1974) 39f., 42, 44, 45, 109, 110, 115, 127, 131, 132,
133, 134, 166, 170, 175, 212, 220. WILCH, J. R., ''Jüdische
Schuld am Tode Jesu - Antijudaismus in der Apostelgeschichte?''
in: W. Haubeck/M. Bachmann (eds.) Wort in der Zeit. FS. K. H.
Rengstorf (Leiden 1980) 240.

3:13-14 GREEN, E. M. B., 2. Peter Reconsidered (London 1961) 13-14.
SCHWEIZER, E. Erniedrigung und Erhöhung bei Jesus und seinen
Nachfolgern (1962) § 6a. DALTON, W. J., Christ's Proclamation
to the Spirits (Rome 1965) 122.

3:13, TAYLOR, V. The Origin of the Markan Passion Sayings. NTS 1
26-27, 30 (1954-1955) 162ff.

3:13 BEYER, H. W. Die Apostelgeschichte (1947) 32f. HOOKER, M.
D. Jesus and the Servant (1959) 107-10. BLAIR, E. P. Jesus in the
Gospel of Matthew (1960) 78. HAHN, F. Christologische Ho-
heitstitel (1963) 55. KAESEMANN, E. Exegetische Vesuche und
Besinnungen (1964) I 102. WILCOX, M. The Semitisms of Acts
(1965) 29-30, 32, 34, 37, 52n, 53n, 56n, 67, 145n, 158, 159, 160,
161, 164. EPP, E. J. The theological tendency of the Codex Bezae
Cantabrigiensis in Acts (1966) 52, 54-56, 63, 71, 95. DUPONT,
J. Etudes sur les Actes des Apôtres (1967) 146-48, 252, 260, 281,
329, 446, 468, 528, 534, 535. NICKELS, P. Targum and New
Testament (1967) 61. POPKES, W. Christus Traditus (1967) 149,
174, 188, 217, 220f., 242, 244, 247. RESE, M. Alttestamentliche
Motive in der Christologie des Lukas (1969) 111-13. LOHSE, E.
et al., eds., Der Ruf Jesu und die Antwort der Gemeinde (1970)
204-12. MIKALSEN, T. ''The Traditio-Historical Place of the
Christology of 1 Peter in Light of 1:18-21,'' (Rüschlikon 1971) 89f.
ZEHNLE, R. F. Peter's Pentecost Discourse (1971) 44-47, 48-49.
DELLING, G. Der Kreuzestod Jesu in der urchristlichen Verkün-
digung (1972) 84-86. KRAENKL, E. Jesus der Knecht Gottes
(1972) 19, 35, 51, 105, 108, 116, 118, 120, 125-29, 211. KLIJN,
A. F. J./REININK, G. J. Patristic Evidence for Jewish-Christian
Sects (1973) 46. DE KRUIJF, T., Der Sohn des Lebendigen Gottes
(Rome 1962) 26, 28, 30, 31. REIM, G., Studien zum Alttesta-
mentlichen Hintergrund des Johannesevangeliums (Cambridge
1974) 173-74. KLIESCH, K., Das heilsgeschichtliche Credo in den
Reden der Apostelgeschichte (Köln/Bonn 1975) 128-29. KLIJN,
A. F. J., ''Die syrische Baruch-Apokalypse'' in: JüdSchr V/2 (1976)
170n.9a. CLARK, K. W., ''The Israel of God'' in: The Gentile Bias
and other Essays (Leiden 1980) 23.

3:14-15 FLEW, R. N. Jesus and His Church (1956) 122. BOWKER, J. W. NTS 14 (1967-1968) 96f. HUBBARD, B. J., "Luke, Josephus and Rome: A Comparative Approach to the Lukan Sitz im Leben" in: P. J. Achtemeier (ed.) SBL Seminar Papers 1979/I (Missoula 1979) 65.

3:14 WILCKENS, U. Die Missionsreden der Apostelgeschichte (^{3}1974) 123, 134, 167f., 169-74. SCHWEIZER, E. Erniedrigung und Erhöhung bei Jesus und seinen Nachfolgern (1962) § 4b. HAHN, F. Christologische Hoheitstitel (1963) 384. WILCOX, M. The Semitisms of Acts (1965) 139-41. EPP, E. J. The theological tendency of the Codex Bezae Cantabrigiensis in Acts (1966) 51-53, 55. DUPONT, J. Etudes sur les Actes des Apôtres (1967) 110, 147, 531, 532. ZEHNLE, R. F. Peter's Pentecost Discourse (1971) 49-52. RUPPERT, L., Jesus als der leidende Gerechte? (Stuttgart 1972) 13, 47. ZIESLER, J. A. The Meaning of Righteousness in Paul (1972) 136f., 146. WILCKENS, U. Die Missionsreden der Apostelgeschichte (^{3}1974) 123, 135, 168f. CRIBBS, F. L., "The Agreements that Exist Between John and Acts" in: C. H. Talbert (ed.) Perspectives on Luke-Acts (Danville 1978) 55. HORTON, F. L., "Reflections on the Semitisms of Luke-Acts" in: C. H. Talbert (ed.) Perspectives on Luke-Acts (Danville 1978) 22.

3:15-21 TALBERT, C. H., Literary Patterns, Theological Themes, and the Genre of Luke-Acts (Missoula 1974) 115.

3:15 DUPONT, J. Essais sur la Christologie de Saint Jean (1951) 138-40. GAERTNER, B. The Areopagus speech and natural revelation (1955) 31f. WAINWRIGHT, A. W. The Trinity in the New Testament (1962) 141-42. DELLING, G. Die Taufe im Neuen Testament (1963) 64. HAHN, F. Christologische Hoheitstitel (1963) 204. KRAMER, W. Christos Kyrios Gottessohn (1963) § 3f. ROLOFF, J. Apostolat-Verkündigung-Kirche (1965) 191f. DUPONT, J. Etudes sur les Actes des Apôtres (1967) 107, 114, 141, 148, 149, 443. FLENDER, H. St Luke Theologian of Redemptive History (1967) 19 & n, 74, 121, 157n, 159n, 170. BURCHARD, C. Der dreizehnte Zeuge (1970) 130-35. BALLARINI, T. "ARCHEGOS (Atti 3,15; 5,31; Ebr. 2,10; 12,2): autore o condottiero?" SaDo 16 (63-64, 1971) 535-51. ZEHNLE, R. F. Peter's Pentecost Discourse (1971) 47-48. KRAENKL, E. Jesus der Knecht Gottes (1972) 58, 80, 130, 167f., 206, 210. MÜLLER, P.-G., ΧΡΙΣΤΟΣ ΑΡΧΗΓΟΣ. Der religionsgeschichtliche und theologische Hintergrund einer neutestamentlichen Christusprädikation (Frankfurt 1973) 15, 105ff. WILCKENS, U. Die Missionsreden der Apostelgeschichte (^{3}1974) 175f. ALSUP, J. E., The Post-Resurrection Appearance Stories of the Gospel-Tradition (Stuttgart 1975) 81. NELLESSEN, E., Zeugnis für Jesus und das Wort (Köln 1976)

91-93. MINEAR, P. S., To Die and to Live (New York 1977) 39-65. TRITES, A. A., The New Testament Concept of Witness (Cambridge 1977) 136, 137, 143, 144. "Auferstehung" in: TRE 4 (1979) 480, 484. PRAST, F., Presbyter und Evangelium in nachapostolischer Zeit (Stuttgart 1979) 306-07, 319. "Autorität" in: TRE 5 (1980) 20.

3:16-26 SCHELKLE, K. H. Die Passion Jesu in der Verkündigung des Neuen Testaments (1949) 93f., 97f.

3:16 PALLIS, A., Notes on St. Luke and the Acts (London 1928) 52-53. DELLING, G. Die Zueignung des Heils in der Taufe (1961) 49, 52. WILCOX, M. The Semitisms of Acts (1965) 144-46. NICKELS, P. Targum and New Testament (1967) 61. ZEHNLE, R. F. Peter's Pentecost Discourse (1971) 90-91. KRAENKL, E. Jesus der Knecht Gottes (1972) 178f., 208. WILCKENS, U. Die Missionsreden der Apostelgeschichte (³1974) 40-42. KLIESCH, K., Das heilsgeschichtliche Credo in den Reden der Apostelgeschichte (Köln/Bonn 1975) 138-39. METZGER, B. M., The Early Versions of the New Testament (Oxford 1977) 149.

3:17-26 TALBERT, C. H., Literary Patterns, Theological Themes, and the Genre of Luke-Acts (Missoula 1974) 122.

3:17-21 HAHN, F. Christologische Hoheitstitel (1963) 184.

3:17-18 WANKE, J., Die Emmauserzählung (Leipzig 1973) 119. TALBERT, C. H., Literary Patterns, Theological Themes, and the Genre of Luke-Acts (Missoula 1974) 97.

3:17 BLAIR, E. P. Jesus in the Gospel of Matthew (1960) 151. HAHN, F. Das Verständnis der Mission im Neuen Testament (²1965) 113, 118. EPP, E. J. The theological tendency of the Codex Bezae Cantabrigiensis in Acts (1966) 38, 42-51, 53, 55, 167, 169f. KRAENKL, E. Jesus der Knecht Gottes (1972) 105-07, 113, 116, 118. ESCUDERO FREIRE C., " 'Kata Agnoian' (Hch 3,17). ¿Disculpa o acusación?" Communio 9 (1976) 221-31. RICE, G. E., "The Anti-Judaic Bias of the Western Text in the Gospel of Luke" AUSS 18 (1980) 51-52, 54. BERGER, K., "Das Buch der Jubiläen" in: JüdSchr II/3 (1981) 524n. 25a.

3:18-26 WANKE, J., Die Emmauserzählung (Leipzig 1973) 11, 93.

3:18-23 MINEAR, P., To Heal and to Reveal (New York 1976) 105ff.

3:18-21 ARRINGTON, F. L., New Testament Exegesis: Examples (Washington 1977) 21-46.

3:18.20 DELLING, G. Die Zueignung des Heils in der Taufe (1961) 88.

3:18 BLAIR, E. P. Jesus in the Gospel of Matthew (1960) 119. DELLING, G. Die Taufe im Neuen Testament (1963) 60. HAHN, F. Christologische Hoheitstitel (1963) 51, 216f. DUPONT, J. Etudes sur les Actes des Apôtres (1967) 146, 248, 328, 369. KRAENKL,

E. Jesus der Knecht Gottes (1972) 35, 68, 103, 107f., 119, 209f.
RUPPERT, L., Jesus als der leidende Gerechte? (Stuttgart 1972)
47n16. SMALLEY, S. S. "The Christology of Acts Again," in:
Christ and the Spirit in the New Testament (1973) B. Lindars/S. S.
Smalley eds., 80, 85, 89f. LADD, G. E., A Theology of the New
Testament (Grand Rapids 1974) 329, 330, 331, 336. TALBERT,
C. H., Literary Patterns, Theological Themes, and the Genre of
Luke-Acts (Missoula 1974) 22. WILCKENS, U. Die Missionsre-
den der Apostelgeschichte (^{3}1974) 102, 117, 134, 159, 160, 186.
ARRINGTON, F. L., New Testament Exegesis: Examples (Wash-
ington 1977) 35-37, 44. GERSTENBERGER, G. und SCHRAGE,
W., Leiden (Stuttgart 1977) 152-53; ET: J. E. Steely (trans.) Suf-
fering (Nashville 1980) 177.

3:19-26 KRAENKL, E. Jesus der Knecht Gottes (1972) 187-193-202.
DUNN, J. D. G., Jesus and the Spirit (London 1975) 160, 194.
KURZ, W. S., "Acts 3:19-26 as a Test of the Role of Eschatology
in Lukan Christology" in: P. J. Achtemeier (ed.) SBL Seminar Papers 1977 (Missoula 1977) 309-23.

3:19-25 FLEW, R. N. Jesus and His Church (1956) 101, 103, 121. HAHN,
F. Christologische Hoheitstitel (1963) 184.

3:19-22 BOUSSET, W. Die Religion des Judentums im Späthellenistischen Zeitalter (1966= 1926) 232f., 248, 390. WILSON, S. G.
The Gentiles and the Gentile Mission in Luke-Acts (1973) 79-80,
125, 251.

3:19-21 KNOX, W. L. The Sources of the Synoptic Gospels II (1957) 44.
GREEN, E. M. B., 2. Peter Reconsidered (London 1961) 13.
KASTING, H. Die Anfänge der urchristlichen Mission (1969) 130f.
LOHFINK, G. "Christologie und Geschichtsbild in Apg 3,19-21,"
BZ 13 (2, 1969) 223-41. LOHFINK, G. Die Himmelfahrt Jesu
(1971) 224f. ZEHNLE, R. F. Peter's Pentecost Discourse (1971)
71-75. KRAENKL, E. Jesus der Knecht Gottes (1972) 193-98.
DUNN, J. D. G., Unity and Diversity in the New Testament (Lon-
don 1977) 217. KURZ, W. S., "Acts 3:19-26 as a Test of the Role
of Eschatology in Lukan Christology" in: P. J. Achtemeier (ed.)
SBL Seminar Papers 1977 (Missoula 1977) 317-18. FRIEDRICH,
G., "Lukas 9,51 und die Entrückungschristologie des Lukas" in:
Auf das Wort kommt es an (Göttingen 1978) 46-48; [orig. in: P.
Hoffmann (ed.) Orientierung an Jesus. FS. J. Schmid (Freiburg
1973) 68-79.] BARBI, A., Il Cristo celeste presente nella Chiesa.
Analecta Biblica 64 (Rome 1979). DUPONT, D. J., The Salvation
of the Gentiles (New York 1979) 78.

3:19 DELLING, G. Die Taufe im Neuen Testament (1963) 140. TER-
NANT, P., "Repentez-vous et convertissez-vous" AssS 21 (1963)
50-79. DUPONT, J. Etudes sur les Actes des Apôtres (1967) 423,

424, 428, 430, 434, 439, 446, 456, 464, 473. STROBEL, A. Erkenntnis und Bekenntnis der Sünde in neutestamentlicher Zeit (1968) 48. DELLING, G. Der Kreuzestod Jesu in der urchristlichen Verkündigung (1972) 89-91. WILCKENS, U. Die Missionsreden der Apostelgeschichte (³1974) 42, 45, 179, 180, 181. ARRINGTON, F. L., New Testament Exegesis: Examples (Washington 1977) 37-38, 44-45.

3:20-21 BAUERNFEIND, O. "Tradition und Komposition in dem Apokatastasisspruch Apostelgeschichte 3,20f.," in: Abraham unser Vater (1963) 13-23. ZEHNLE, R. F. Peter's Pentecost Discourse (1971) 57-59, 92-93. WILCKENS, U. Die Missionsreden der Apostelgeschichte (³1974) 43, 44, 49, 85, 153-56, 158, 235. DUNN, J. D. G., Unity and Diversity in the New Testament (London 1977) 43. KURZ, W. S., "Acts 3:19-26 as a Test of the Role of Eschatology in Lukan Christology" in: P. J. Achtemeier (ed.) SBL Seminar Papers 1977 (Missoula 1977) 309-11, 313-14, 317. BAUERNFEIND, O., "Tradition und Komposition in dem Apokatastasisspruch Apostelgeschichte 3,20f." in: Kommentar und Studien zur Apostelgeschichte (Tübingen 1980) 464-72; [orig. in: Abraham unser Vater. FS. O. Michel (Leiden 1963) 13-23.]

3:20.21a HAHN, F. Christologische Hoheitstitel (1963) 184-86, 189, 389.

3:20 SAHLIN, H. "Till förståelse av två ställen i Apostlagärningarna," SEA 22-23 (1957-1958) 127-36. HAHN, F. Christlogische Hoheitstitel (1963) 106, 126, 193. KAESEMANN, E. Exegetische Versuche und Besinnungen (1964) I 106. BURCHARD, C. Der dreizehnte Zeuge (1970) 107, 143f., 182. LADD, G. E. A Theology of the New Testament (Grand Rapids 1974) 331, 333, 336. WILCKENS, U. Die Missionsreden der Apostelgeschichte (³1974) 43, 147, 150, 154, 157, 158. FERRARO, G., "*Kairoi anapsyxeōs*. Annotazioni zu Atti 3, 20" RivB 23 (1975) 67-78. ARRINGTON, F. L., New Testament Exegesis: Examples (Washington 1977) 38-40, 45. KURZ, W. S., "Acts 2:19-26 as a Test of the Role of Eschatology in Lukan Christology" in: P. J. Achtemeier (ed.) SBL Seminar Papers 1977 (Missoula 1977) 310, 312, 313, 317.

3:21 STAEHELIN, E. Die Verkündigung des Reiches Gottes in der Kirche Jesu Christi I (1951) 266. SCHNEIDER, G. Neuschöpfung oder Wiederkehr (Düsseldorf 1961) 70-71. HAHN, F. Christologische Hoheitstitel (1963) 106, 126, 247. FLENDER, Heil und Geschichte in der Theologie des Lukas (1965) 97-98. FLENDER, H. St Luke Theologian of Redemptive History (1967) 49n, 61n, 97, 105, 106, 160, 167. MUSSNER, F. "Die Idee der Apokatastasis in der Apostelgeschichte," in: Praesentia Salutis (1967) 223. RAHNER, K./THUESING, W. Christologie-systematisch und exegetisch (1972) 218-20, 222. ZMIJEWSKI, J. Die Eschatologiereden des Lukas-Evangeliums (1972) 189, 282, 402, 406, 422, 434, 442, 505, 517, 536. STAEHLIN, G. "Tò πνεῦμα 'Ιησοῦ (Apostelgeschichte 16:7)," in: Christ and the Spirit in the New Testament (1973) B. Lindars/S. S. Smalley eds., 235f. LADD, G. E. A Theology of the New Testament (Grand Rapids (1974) 316, 329, 333. WILCKENS, U. Die Missionsreden der Apostelgeschichte (³1974) 10, 43, 102, 153, 154. ARRINGTON, F. L., New Testament Exegesis: Examples (Washington 1977) 40-42, 45. KURZ, W. S., "Acts 3:19-26 as a Test of the Role of Eschatology in Lukan Christology" in: P. J. Achtemeier (ed.) SBL Seminar Papers 1977 (Missoula 1977) 320n.11. "Apostelgeschichte" in: TRE 3 (1978) 516.

3:22ff. HAHN, F. Christologische Hoheitstitel (1963) 184, 384, 386.

3:22-26 WANKE, J., Die Emmauserzählung (Leipzig 1973) 62-63. TALBERT, C. H., Literary Patterns, Theological Themes, and the Genre of Luke-Acts (Missoula 1974) 97. KURZ, W. S., "Acts 3:19-26 as a Test of the Role of Eschatology in Lukan Christology" in: P. J. Achtemeier (ed.) SBL Seminar Papers 1977 (Missoula 1977) 310. DUPONT, D. J., The Salvation of the Gentiles (New York 1979) 155.

3:22-25 KLIESCH, K., Das heilsgeschichtliche Credo in den Reden der Apostelgeschichte (Köln/Bonn 1975) 129-30.

3:22-24 BRAUN, H. Qumran und NT II (1966) 62, 68, 81, 83f., 159, 266, 272, 306, 309, 311.

3:22-23 GILS, F. Jésus Prophète D'Après Les Evangiles Synoptiques (1957) 30-35. LINDARS, B. New Testament Apologetic (1961) 207. RESE, M. Alttestamentliche Motive in der Christologie des Lukas (1969) 66-71. DE WAARD, J. "The Quotation from Deuteronomy in Acts 3,22, 23, and the Palestinian Text: Additional Arguments," Biblica 52 (4, 1971) 537-40. KRAENKL, E. Jesus der Knecht Gottes (1972) 198-201, 207.

3:22 DAVIES, W. D. Torah in the Messianic Age and/or the Age to come (1952) 44. BLAIR, E. P. Jesus in the Gospel of Matthew (1960) 146. DE KRUIJF, T., Der Sohn des Lebendigen Gottes (Rome 1962) 26, 28, 29, 30. HAHN, F. Christologische Hoheitstitel (1963) 72. DUPONT, J. Etudes sur les Actes des Apôtres (1967) 249, 253, 281, 443. WILCKENS, U. Die Missionsreden der Apostelgeschichte (³1974) 43, 138, 143, 157, 164. LOHFINK, G., Die Sammlung Israels (München 1975) 60-61. KURZ, W. S., "Acts 3:19-26 as a Test of the Role of Eschatology in Lukan Christology" in: P. J. Achtemeier (ed.) SBL Seminar Papers 1977 (Missoula 1977) 314. SAITO, T., Die Mosevorstellungen im Neuen Testa-

ment (Bern 1977) 77-79. BARRETT, C. K., "Is there a Theolog-
ical Tendency in Codex Bezae?" in: E. Best/R. McL. Wilson (eds.)
Text and Interpretation FS. M. Black (Cambridge 1979) 25. O'-
TOOLE, R. F., "Some Observations on *anistēmi*, 'I raise', in Acts
3:22, 26" SciE 31 (1979) 85-92. DUNN, J. D., Christology in the
Making (London 1980) 44, 138, 158.

3:23 FLEW, R. N. Jesus and His Church (1956) 151. MARTINI, C. M.
"L'esclusione dalla communità del popolo di Dio e il nuovo Israele
secondo Atti 3,23," Biblica 50 (1, 1969) 1-14.

3:24-26 KRAENKL, E. Jesus der Knecht Gottes (1972) 201f.

3:24-25 TALBERT, C. H., Literary Patterns, Theological Themes, and the
Genre of Luke-Acts (Missoula 1974) 97.

3:24 WILCKENS, U. Die Missionsreden der Apostelgeschichte (^{3}1974)
43, 102, 158, 226, 235.

3:25-26 FLEW, R. N. Jesus and His Church (1956) 101. NICKELS, P.
Targum and New Testament (1967) 61. SCHENK, W. Der Segen
im Neuen Testament (1967) 46-48. WOOD, J. E. "Isaac Typology
in the New Testament," NTS 14 (1968) 583-89. WILSON, S. G.
The Gentiles and the Gentile Mission in Luke-Acts (1973) 219-22,
224, 228-31. WESTERMANN, C., Blessing (Philadelphia 1978)
70, 76-78, 98-101.

3:25 DUPONT, J. Etudes sur les Actes des Apôtres (1967) 251, 281,
351, 357, 455. RESE, M. Alttestamentliche Motive in der Christologie des Lukas (1969) 71-77. ZEHNLE, R. F. Peter's Pentecost Discourse (1971) 53-56. BERGER, K., "Das Buch der
Jubiläen" in: JüdSchr II/3 (1981) 405n. 4a.

3:26 GILS, F. Jésus Prophète D'Après Les Evangiles Synoptiques (1957)
33-35. HOOKER, M. D. Jesus and the Servant (1959) 107-10.
BLAIR, E. P. Jesus in the Gospel of Matthew (1960) 78. HAHN,
F. Christologische Hoheitstitel (1963) 55. HAHN, F. Das Ver-
ständnis der Mission im Neuen Testament (^{2}1965) 117. SHI-
MADA, K., The Formulary Material in First Peter (Th. D. Diss.,
Ann Arbor, Michigan 1966) 216-17. DUPONT, J. Etudes sur les
Actes des Apôtres (1967) 109, 141, 146, 251, 260, 263, 281, 295,
357, 423, 430, 443, 446, 447, 473, 486. ZEHNLE, R. F. Peter's
Pentecost Discourse (1971) 48-49. KRAENKL, E. Jesus der Knecht
Gottes (1972) 19, 34f., 80, 118, 120, 125-29, 130, 184, 208, 210f.
KLIJN, A. F. J./REININK, G. J. Patristic Evidence for Jewish-
Christian Sects (1973) 46. SMALLEY, S. S. "The Christology of
Acts Again," in: Christ and the Spirit in the New Testament (1973)
B. Lindars/S. S. Smalley eds., 80f., 85f., 89, 91. WILCKENS, U.
Die Missionsreden der Apostelgeschichte (^{3}1974) 36, 43, 45, 60,
137, 153, 157, 148, 164, 166, 180, 181, 184, 227, 231, 235, 237.

ZINGG, P., Das Wachsen der Kirche (Freiburg 1974) 255-57. KURZ, W. S., "Acts 3:19-26 as a Test of the Role of Eschatology in Lukan Christology" in: P. J. Achtemeier (ed.) SBL Seminar Papers 1977 (Missoula 1977) 311-12. DUPONT, D. J., The Salvation of the Gentiles (New York 1979) 80, 144. O'TOOLE, R. F., "Some Observations on *anistēmi*, 'I raise' in Acts 3,22, 26" SciE 31 (1979) 85-92. PRAST, F., Presbyter und Evangelium in nachapostolischer Zeit (Stuttgart 1979) 323.

4:1-8:3 TALBERT, C. H., Literary Patterns, Theological Themes, and the Genre of Luke-Acts (Missoula 1974) 16, 19.

4-5 DELLING, G. Die Zueignung des Heils in der Taufe (1961) 48, 52. GUTBROD, K. Die Apostelgeschichte (1968) 45ff.

4 MINEAR, P. S. Images of the Church in the New Testament (1960) 140f. DUPONT, J. The Sources of Acts (1964) 41, 42, 44, 46, 48, 49. TALBERT, C. H., Literary Patterns, Theological Themes, and the Genre of Luke-Acts (Missoula 1974) 39. MARTYN, J. L., The Gospel of John in Christian History (New York 1978) 70-74.

4:1-31 ADINOLFI, M., " 'Obbedire a Dio piuttosto che agli uomini.' La Comunità cristiana et il Sinedrio in Atti 4,1-31; 5;17-42" RivB 27 (1979) 69-93.

4:1-22 JEREMIAS, J. Abba: Studien zur neutestamentlichen Theologie und Zeitgeschichte (1966) 238-47. STOLLE, V. Der Zeuge als Angeklagter (1973) 220-26. JOHNSON, L. T., The Literary Function of Possessions in Luke-Acts (Missoula 1977) 192-93. SCHNEIDER, G., Die Apostelgeschichte. I (Freiburg/Basel/Wien 1980) 339 (lit!). WEISER, A., Die Apostelgeschichte. I (Gütersloh/Würzburg 1981) 120-21 (lit!).

4:1-12 NIESEL, W. in: Herr, tue meine Lippen auf Bd. 4 (1965) 369ff. METZGER, M. GPM 21 (3, 1966-1967) 251-56.

4:1-7 TALBERT, C. H., Literary Patterns, Theological Themes, and the Genre of Luke-Acts (Missoula 1974) 36.

4:1-2 BOUSSET, W. Die Religion des Judentums im Späthellenistischen Zeitalter (1966 = 1926) 198. GOPPELT, L. Christologie und Ethik (1968) 96f. NÖTSCHER, F., Altorientalischer und alttestamentlicher Auferstehungsglaube (Darmstadt 1970 = 1926) 271.

4:1 ELLIS, E. E./WILCOX, M. eds., Neotestamentica et Semitica

(1969) 206ff. HENGEL, M. Judentum und Hellenismus (1969) 47. ET: Judaism and Hellenism (1974) I 25. "Apostelgeschichte" in: TRE 3 (1978) 506.

4:2 CAVALLIN, H. C. C., Life After Death. I (Lund 1974) 6, 2, 2. WILCKENS, U. Die Missionsreden der Apostelgeschichte (^{3}1974) 61, 140, 147, 175, 231.

4:3-5:18 WILCOX, M.. The Semitisms of Acts (1965) 59ff.

4:4 FLEW, R. N. Jesus and His Church (1956) 154n. DELLING, G. Die Taufe im Neuen Testament (1963) 70. GOULDER, M. D. Type and History in Acts (1964) 22, 26, 215, 225f. NICKELS, P. Targum and New Testament (1967) 61. ZINGG, P., Das Wachsen der Kirche (Freiburg 1974) 164-67, 170.

4:5-20 FOULKES, I. W., "Two Semantic Problems in the Translations of Acts 4,5-20" BTr 29 (1978) 121-25.

4:5-12 TALBERT, C. H., Literary Patterns, Theological Themes, and the Genre of Luke-Acts (Missoula 1974) 37.

4:5-6 WIKENHAUSER, A. Die Apostelgeschichte (1951) 51-53.

4:5 CONZELMANN, H. und LINDEMANN, A., Arbeitsbuch zum Neuen Testament (Tübingen 1975) 102-03.

4:6 METZGER, B. M., The Early Versions of the New Testament (Oxford 1977) 172.

4:7 DELLING, G. Die Zueignung des Heils in der Taufe (1961) 48, 49. HENNECKE, E./SCHNEEMELCHER, W. Neutestamentliche Apokryphen (1964) II 349, 362. BLOCH, R., "Midrash" in: W. S. Green (ed.) Approaches to Ancient Judaism (Missoula 1978) 49.

4:8ff. GAERTNER, B. "The Habakkuk Commentary (DSH) and the Gospel of Matthew," StTh 8 (1954) 23f.

4:8-20 BURCHARD, C. Der dreizehnte Zeuge (1970) 138-42.

4:8-13 WILCOX, M. The Semitism of Acts (1965) 172-73.

4:8-12 FRANSEN, I. "Par le nom de Jésus Christ le Nazaréen. Actes 4,8-12," BVieC 59 (1964) 38-44. DIETRICH, W. Das Petrusbild der lukanischen Schriften (1972) 230-32. TALBERT, C. H., Literary Patterns, Theological Themes, and the Genre of Luke-Acts (Missoula 1974) 36, 38. KLIESCH, K., Das heilsgeschichtliche Credo in den Reden der Apostelgeschichte (Köln/Bonn 1975) 75ff., 152-53. DUPONT, D. J., The Salvation of the Gentiles (New York 1979) 122-24.

4:8 REILING, J. Hermas and Christian Prophecy (1973) 113f., 146, 156. METZGER, B. M., The Early Versions of the New Testament (Oxford 1977) 345.

4:9-12 WILCKENS, U. Die Missionsreden der Apostelgeschichte (^{3}1974) Passim. MEYER, B. F., The Aims of Jesus (London 1979) 66-69.

4:9 DELLING, G. Die Zueignung des Heils in der Taufe (1961) 49, 91, 93.

4:10-12 DUPONT, D. J., The Salvation of the Gentiles (New York 1979) 68.

4:10 MOORE, G. F. Judaism I (1946) 379. FLEW, R. N. Jesus and His Church (1956) 122. RUDOLPH, K. Die Mandäer I (1960) 115. DELLING, G. Die Zueignung des Heils in der Taufe (1961) 48, 49, 88, 93. HAHN, F. Christologische Hoheitstitel (1963) 116, 204. KRAMER, W. Christos Kyrios Gottessohn (1963) § 3f. WILCOX, M. The Semitisms of Acts (1965) 90-91, 110, 161, 165, 171, 175. DUPONT, J. Etudes sur les Actes des Apôtres (1967) 141, 148, 252, 443, 446, 468, 522. NICKELS, P. Targum and New Testament (1967) 61. SMALLEY, S. S. "The Christology of Acts Again," in: Christ and the Spirit in the New Testament (1973) B. Lindars/S. S. Smalley eds., 85, 87, 89. WILCKENS, U. Die Missionsreden der Apostelgeschichte (^{3}1974) 41, 45, 62, 109, 110, 123, 131, 137, 156, 171, 184. LADD, G. E., A Theology of the New Testament (Grand Rapids 1974) 317, 331, 339. TRITES, A. A., The New Testament Concept of Witness (Cambridge 1977) 138, 144, 152. "Auferstehung" in: TRE 4 (1979) 480, 485. WILCH, J. R., "Jüdische Schuld am Tode Jesu - Antijudaismus in der Apostelgeschichte?" in: W. Haubeck/M. Bachmann (eds.) Wort in der Zeit. FS. K. H. Rengstorf (Leiden 1980) 140-41.

4:11-12 GLÖCKNER, R., Die Verkündigung des Heils beim Evangelisten Lukas (Mainz 1975) 232ff. DALY, R. J., Christian Sacrifice (Washington D. C. 1978) 228.

4:11 KNOX, W. L. The Sources of the Synoptic Gospels II (1957) 115. HAHN, F. Christologische Hoheitstitel (1963) 52. DUPONT, J. Etudes sur les Actes des Apôtres (1967) 260, 261, 268, 281, 284, 300-02, 330. RESE, M. Alttestamentliche Motive in der christologie des Lukas (1969) 113-15. KRAENKL, E. Jesus der Knecht Gottes (1972) 157f., 162, 207. ELLIS, E. E. "Midrashic Features in the Speeches of Acts," in: Mélanges Bibliques en hommage au R. P. Béda Rigaux (1970) A. Descamps/A. de Halleux,eds., 310-12. DORMEYER, D., Die Passion Jesu als Verhaltensmodell (Münster 1974) 162. TALBERT, C. H., Literary Patterns, Theological Themes, and the Genre of Luke-Acts (Missoula 1974) 97. KLIESCH, K., Das heilsgeschichtliche Credo in den Reden der Apostelgeschichte (Köln/Bonn 1975) 130-31. DUPONT, D. J., The Salvation of the Gentiles (New York 1979) 142, 148-49. VIELHAUER, P., "Oikodome. Das Bild vom Bau in der christlichen Literatur vom Neuen Testament bis Clemens Alexandrinus" in: G.

Klein (ed.) Oikodome (München 1979) 58. LEA, T. D., "How Peter Learned the Old Testament" SouJTh 22 (1980) 99.

4:12 FLEW, R. N. Jesus and His Church (1956) 113. DELLING, G. Die Zueignung des Heils in der Taufe (1961) 42, 48f., 93. WILCOX, M. The Semitisms of Acts (1965) 91-92, 101, 110, 171. DUPONT, J. Etudes sur les Actes des Apôtres (1967) 120, 248, 302, 353, 380, 435, 450, 452, 464, 471, 522. GOLLWITZER, H. "Ausser Christus kein Heil? (Johannes 14,6)," in: Antijudaismus im Neuen Testament? (1967) W. P. Eckert/N. P. Levinson/M. Stöhr eds., 171-94. NICKELS, P. Targum and New Testament (1967) 71. WILCKENS, U. Die Missionsreden der Apostelgeschichte (³1974) 41, 44, 62, 176, 179, 184, 186. BAUMERT, N., Täglich Sterben und Auferstehen (München 1973) 405. KLIESCH, K., Das heilsgeschichtliche Credo in den Reden der Apostelgeschichte (Köln/Bonn 1975) 139-40. NEGRI, G., " 'Non est in alio aliquo salus' (Act 4,12): Come presentare il Salvatore ad un mondo in lotta per salvarsi" Presbyteri 8 (Trento 1975) 26-38.

4:13-17 TALBERT, C. H., Literary Patterns, Theological Themes, and the Genre of Luke-Acts (Missoula 1974) 35.

4:13 BRAUN, H. Qumran und NT II (1966) 339. EPP, E. J. The theological tendency of Codex Bezae Cantabrigiensis in Acts (1966) 121-24. NICKELS, P. Targum and New Testament (1967) 61. MARTYN, J. L., The Gospel of John in Christian History (New York 1978) 72-74. PFITZNER, V. C., " 'Pneumatic' Apostleship? Apostle and Spirit in the Acts of the Apostles" in: W. Haubeck/M. Bachmann (eds.) Wort in der Zeit. FS. K. H. Rengstorf (Leiden 1980) 221-22.

4:14 DELLING, G. Die Zueignung des Heils in der Taufe (1961) 49. EPP, E. J. The theological tendency of Codex Bezae Cantabrigiensis in Acts (1966) 121-24, 147, 154, 167.

4:16 PALLIS, A., Notes on St. Luke and the Acts (London 1928) 53. CRIBBS, F. L., "The Agreements that Exist Between John and Acts" in: C. H. Talbert (ed.) Perspectives on Luke-Acts (Danville 1978) 52-53.

4:17ff. DELLING, G. Die Zueignung des Heils in der Taufe (1961) 43, 48, 88, 91.

4:18 TALBERT, C. H., Literary Patterns, Theological Themes, and the Genre of Luke-Acts (Missoula 1974) 36, 102.

4:19-20 MEYER, B. F., The Aims of Jesus (London 1979) 66-69.

4:20 GERSTENBERGER, G. und SCHRAGE, W., Leiden (Stuttgart 1977) 216-17; ET: Steely, J. E. (trans.) Suffering (Nashville 1980) 249. PRAST, F., Presbyter und Evangelium in nachapostolischer Zeit (Stuttgart 1979) 316.

4:23-33 WILCKENS, U. Die Missionsreden der Apostelgeschichte ([3]1974) Passim.

4:24-5:42 TALBERT, C. H., Literary Patterns, Theological Themes, and the Genre of Luke-Acts (Missoula 1974) 34, 38, 89.

4:24-31 FLEW, R. N. Jesus and His Church (1956) 117. RIMAUD, D. "La première prière liturgique dans le livre des Actes (Actes, 4,23-31; cf. Ps. 2 et 145)," Maison Dieu 51 (1957) 99-115. TALBERT, C. H., Literary Patterns, Theological Themes, and the Genre of Luke-Acts (Missoula 1974) 35, 37, 38. JOHNSON, L. T., The Literary Function of Possessions in Luke-Acts (Missoula 1977) 193-94. DÖMER, M., Das Heil Gottes (Köln/Bonn 1978) 63-66. HAMM, D., "You are precious in my sight" Way 18 (1978) 193-203. SCHNEIDER, G., Die Apostelgeschichte. I (Freiburg/Basel/Wien 1980) 352-53. WEISER, A., Die Apostelgeschichte. I (Gütersloh/ Würzburg 1981) 130 (lit!).

4:24-30 DELLING, G. Die Zueignung des Heils in der Taufe (1961) 88. LOVESTAM, E. Son and Saviour (1961) 23ff. HAMMAN, A. "La nouvelle Pentecôte (Actes 4:24-30)," BVie C 14 (1956) 82-90. DUPONT, J. Le Discours de Milet (1962) 369-72. WILCOX, M. The Semitisms of Acts (1965) 69-72, 74.

4:24-26 DUPONT, D. J., The Salvation of the Gentiles (New York 1979) 117, 146.

4:24 HOLTZ, T. Untersuchungen über die Alttestamentlichen Zitate bei Lukas (1968) 84.

4:25-30 GLÖCKNER, K., Die Verkündigung des Heils beim Evangelisten Lukas (Mainz 1975) 191ff. CONZELMANN, H. und LINDE-MANN, A., Arbeitsbuch zum Neuen Testament (Tübingen 1975) 28. HORTON, F. L., "Reflections on the Semitisms of Luke-Acts" in: C. H. Talbert (ed.) Perspectives on Luke-Acts (Danville 1978) 10.

4:25-28 BLINZLER, J. Der Prozess Jesu (1969) 292, 297, 432f. KRAENKL, E. Jesus der Knecht Gottes (1972) 109-11, 119, 207.

4:25-26 HOLTZ, T. Untersuchungen über die Alttestamentlichen Zitate bei Lukas (1968) 53-56. RESE, M. Alttestamentliche Motive in der Christologie des Lukas (1969) 94-97. ALLEN, L. G., NTS 17 (1970-1971) 105-07.

4:25 CLARK, A. C. The Acts of the Apostles (1933) li,340f. HAHN, F. Christologische Hoheitstitel (1963) 265. WILSON, M. The Semitisms of Acts (1965) 144, 146-47. DUPONT, J. Etudes sur les Actes des Apôtres (1967) 88, 136, 239, 317, 537. NICKELS, P. Targum and New Testament (1967) 62.

4:26-27 HAHN, F. Christologische Hoheitstitel (1963) 220, 224. WIL-COX, M. The Semitisms of Acts (1965) 65-66.

4:26 DELLING, G. Die Zueignung des Heils in der Taufe (1961) 88. "Apostelgeschichte" in: TRE 3 (1978) 492. DÖMER, M., Das Heil Gottes (Köln/Bonn 1978) 44.

4:27-30 HOOKER, M. D. Jesus and the Servant (1959) 107-10. ´

4:27-28 WREGE, H.-T. Die Ueberlieferungsgeschichte der Bergpredigt (1968) 167f., 180. WILCKENS, U. Die Missionsreden der Apostelgeschichte (³1974) 109, 110, 132, 230.

4:27.30 BLAIR, E. P. Jesus in the Gospel of Matthew (1960) 78. SCHWEIZER, E. Erniedrigung und Erhöhung bei Jesus und seinen Nachfolgern (1962) § 6a.

4:27 HAHN, F. Christologische Hoheitstitel (1963) 55, 116, 386f., 392, 395. KAESEMANN, E. Exegetische Versuche und Besinnungen (1964) I 102. JEREMIAS, J. Abba: Studien zur neutestamentlichen Theologie und Zeitgeschichte (1966) 196-98. DUPONT, J. Etudes sur les Actes des Apôtres (1967) 109, 146, 260, 281, 297-99, 528. RESE, M. Alttestamentliche Motive in der Christologie des Lukas (1969) 119-20. ZEHNLE, R. F. Peter's Pentecost Discourse (1971) 48-49. KRAENKL, E. Jesus der Knecht Gottes (1972) 19, 31, 35, 90, 120, 125-29, 211. KLIJN, A. F. J./REININK, G. J. Patristic Evidence for Jewish-Christian Sects (1973) 46. WILCKENS, U. Die Missionsreden der Apostelgeschichte (³1974) 108, 110, 133, 159, 160, 164, 166, 169, 173, 236.

4:27 DE KRUIJF, T., Der Sohn des Lebendigen Gottes (Rome 1962) 29, 30, 31, 32. TALBERT, C. H., Literary Patterns, Theological Themes, and the Genre of Luke-Acts (Missoula 1974) 123. KLIJN, A. F. J., "Die syrische Baruch-Apokalypse" in: JüdSchr V/2 (1976) 170n. 9a. DÖMER, M., Das Heil Gottes (Köln/Bonn 1978) 63, 68. QUINN, J. D., "The Last Volume of Luke: The Relations of Luke-Acts to the Pastoral Epistles" in: C. H. Talbert (ed.) Perspectives on Luke-Acts (Danville 1978) 65. WILCH, J. R., "Jüdische Schuld am Tode Jesu - Antijudaismus in der Apostelgeschichte?" in: W. Haubeck/M. Bachmann (eds.) Wort in der Zeit. FS. K. H. Rengstorf (Leiden 1980) 242-43.

4:29-32 BETZ, H. D. Lukian von Samosata und das Neue Testament (1961) 10, 97, 155, 165, 210.

4:29-31 FLEW, R. N. Jesus and His Church (1956) 154n. KREMER, J. Pfingstbericht und Pfingstgeschehen (Stuttgart 1973) 201-04. MÄRZ, C.-P., Das Wort Gottes bei Lukas (Leipzig 1973) 24-28. DUNN, J. D. G., Jesus and the Spirit (London 1975) 188. PFITZNER, V. C., " 'Pneumatic' Apostleship? Apostle and Spirit in the Acts of the Apostles" in: W. Haubeck/M. Bachmann (eds.) Wort in der Zeit. FS. K. H. Rengstorf (Leiden 1980) 221-22.

4:29 PRAST, F., Presbyter und Evangelium in nachapostolischer Zeit (Stuttgart 1979) 59.

4:30 DELLING, G. Die Zueignung des Heils in der Taufe (1961) 50, 88. HAHN, F. Christologische Hoheitstitel (1963) 55, 386, 387, 392. WILCOX, M. The Semitisms of Acts (1965) 69-71. JE-REMIAS, J. Abba: Studien zur neutestamentlichen Theologie und Zeitgeschichte (1966) 195-98. DUPONT, J. Etudes sur les Actes des Apôtres (1967) 109, 146, 147, 260, 281. KRAENKL, E. Jesus der Knecht Gottes (1972) 19, 35, 120, 125-29, 179, 211. KLIJN, A. F. J./REININK, G. J. Patristic Evidence for Jewish-Christian Sects (1973) 46. WILCKENS, U. Die Missionsreden der Apostelgeschichte (^{3}1974) 41, 124, 165, 166, 169, 172. KLIJN, A. F. J., "Die syrische Baruch-Apokalypse" in: JüdSchr V/2 (1976) 179n.9a.

4:31-5:11 METTAYER, A., "Ambiguïté et terrorisme de sacré: Analyse d'un texte des Actes des Apôtres (4,31-5,11)" StR/SciR 7 (1978) 415-24.

4:31c-35 DEGENHARDT, H.-J. Lukas, Evangelist der Armen (1964) 168-72. KARRIS, R. J., "Poor and Rich: The Lukan Sitz im Leben" in: C. H. Talbert (ed.) Perspectives on Luke-Acts (Danville 1978) 114, 116-17.

4:31.33 PETERS, G. W. A Biblical Theology of Missions (1972) 135, 143-44.

4:31 YATES, J. E. The Spirit and the Kingdom (1963) 207ff. GOULDER, M. D. Type and History in Acts (1964) 20, 22f., 26, 62, 77, 79, 87, 91. FLENDER, H. St Luke Theologian of Redemptive History (1967) 137n, 139, 140, 141. ZMIJEWSKI, J. Die Eschatologiereden des Lukas-Evangeliums (1972) 18, 137, 289, 429. REILING, J. Hermas and Christian Prophecy (1973) 112f., 146, 156. HAGE, W., "Die griechische Baruch-Apokalypse" in: JüdSchr V/1 (1974) 28n.13b. TALBERT, C. H., Literary Patterns, Theological Themes, and the Genre of Luke-Acts (Missoula 1974) 35, 38.

4:32-5:42 REICKE, B. Glaube und Leben der Urgemeinde (1957) 85-114.

4:32-5:11 SHEPARD, J. W., The Life and Letters of St. Paul (Grand Rapids 1950) 40-42. COMBET-GALLAND, A.-E., "Actes 4,32 - 5,11" EThR 52 (1977) 548-53. JOHNSON, L. T., The Literary Functions of Possessions in Luke-Acts (Missoula 1977) 191-92, 198-211. TYSON, J. B., "The Problem of Food in Acts: A Study of Literary Patterns with Particular Reference to Acts 6:1-7" in: P. J. Achtemeier (ed.) SBL Seminar Papers 1979/I (Missoula 1979) 71.

4:32-37 REICKE, B. Diakonie, Festfreude und Zelos (1951) 26f. DU-PONT, J. The Sources of Acts (1964) 36, 38, 41, 47. BORI, P. C.,

Chiesa primitiva. L'immagine della communità delle origin - Atti 2,42-47; 4,32-37 - nella storia della chiesa antica (Brescia 1974). TALBERT, C. H., Literary Patterns, Theological Themes, and the Genre of Luke-Acts (Missoula 1974) 101. DUNN, J. D. G., Jesus and the Spirit (London 1975) 161. GERSTENBERGER, G., und SCHRAGE, W., Leiden (Stuttgart 1977) 227-28; ET: J. E. Steely (trans.) Suffering (Nashville 1980) 262. JOHNSON, L. T., The Literary Function of Possessions in Luke-Acts (Missoula 1977) 1-28. BOERMA, C., Rich Man, Poor Man - and the Bible (London 1979) 57-58. SCHNEIDER, G., Die Apostelgeschichte. I (Freiburg/Basel/Wien 1980) 362 (lit!). WEISER, A., Die Apostelgeschichte. I (Gütersloh/Würzburg 1981) 135 (lit!).

4:32-36 GÓMEZ de MORALES, M. V., "La Comunidad Primitiva Modelo de Consagración a Dios" Biblia y Fe 4 (Madrid 1978) 271-82. RAYAN, S., The Holy Spirit: Heart of the Gospel and Christian Hope (New York 1978) 60-61.

4:32-35 WIKENHAUSER, A. Die Apostelgeschichte (1951) 58. ZIMMERMAN, H. "Die Sammelberichte der Apostelgeschichte," BZ 5 (1, 1961) 71-82. DUPONT, J. The Sources of Acts (1964) 23, 43, 48, 63. DU TOIT, A. B. Der Aspekt der Freude im urchristlischen Abendmahl (1965) 108-12. FISCHER, M. in: Herr, tue meine Lippen auf, Bd 4 (1965) 352ff. ZIMMERMANN, H. Neutestamentliche Methodenlehre (1967) 245-46. TALBERT, C. H., Literary Patterns, Theological Themes, and the Genre of Luke-Acts (Missoula 1974) 35, 38. CRUMBACH, K.-H., "Auferstehungszeugnis" GuL 48 (1975) 81-84. "Apostelgeschichte" in: TRE 3 (1978) 513.

4:32 BEST, E. One Body in Christ (1955) 198. SUDBRACK, J. " 'Die Schar der Gläubigen war ein Herz und eine Seele' (Apg 4,32)," GuL 38 (3, 1965) 161-68. BRAUN, H. Qumran und NT II (1966) 210. DUPONT, J. Etudes sur les Actes des Apôtres (1967) 475, 484, 503-19. BROWN, S. Apostasy and Perseverance in the Theology of Luke (1969) 40f., 99f., 106f., 125. GERHARDSSON, B. "Några anmärkninger till Apg 4:32," SEA 35 (1970) 96-103. GERHARDSSON, B. "Einige Bermerkungen zu Apg 4,32," StTh 24 (2, 1970) 142-49. BERGER, K. Die Gesetzesauslegung Jesu (1972) 248f. JOHNSON, L. T., The Literary Function of Possessions in Luke-Acts (Missoula 1977) 199. MEALAND, D. L., "Community of Goods and Utopian Allusions in Acts II-IV" JThS 28 (1977) 96-99. "Apostelgeschichte" in: TRE 3 (1978) 517. DUPONT, D. J., The Salvation of the Gentiles (New York 1979) 87-91, 95-102. BERGER, K., "Das Buch der Jubiläen" in: JüdSchr II/3 (1981) 530n. 14a.

4:33 PALLIS, A., Notes on St. Luke and the Acts (London 1928) 54.

EPP, E. J. The theological tendency of Codex Bezae Cantabrigiensis in Acts (1966) 54, 62f. DUPONT, J. Etudes sur les Acts des Apôtres (1967) 238, 446, 468, 522. WILCKENS, U. Die Missionsreden der Apostelgeschichte (³1974) 96, 140, 146, 147, 171, 175, 240. NELLESSEN, E., Zeugnis für Jesus und das Wort (Köln 1976) 81-85. JOHNSON, L. T., The Literary Function of Possessions in Luke-Acts (Missoula 1977) 199-200. TRITES, A. A., The New Testament Concept of Witness (Cambridge 1977) 138, 144, 152. PRAST, F., Presbyter und Evangelium in nachapostolischer Zeit (Stuttgart 1979) 306-07.

4:34-42 NIESEL, W. in: Herr, tue meine Lippen auf Bd. 4 (1965) 374ff.

4:34-36 DUPONT, D. J., The Salvation of the Gentiles (New York 1979) 91-92, 94.

4:34-35 FLEW, R. N. Jesus and His Church (1956) 132n. DUPONT, J. Etudes sur les Actes des Apôtres (1967) 503-19. BROWN, S. Apostasy and Perseverance in the Theology of Luke (1969) 99, 101f., 125. DUPONT, J. " 'L'union entre les premièrs chrétiens dans les Actes des Apôtres," NRTh 91 (1969) 897-915. JOHNSON, L. T., The Literary Function of Possessions in Luke-Acts (Missoula 1977) 200-04.

4:34 JOHNSON, L. T., The Literary Function of Possessions in Luke-Acts (Missoula 1977) 200.

4:35 SWIDLER, L., Biblical Affirmations of Woman (Philadelphia 1979) 305.

4:36-37 CLARK, A. C. The Acts of the Apostles (1933) liv,342f. STAEHELIN, E. Die Verkündigung des Reiches Gottes in der Kirche Jesu Christi I (1951) 6, 96. SCHMITHALS, W. Paulus und Jakobus (1963) 23 n.6. DEGENHARDT, H.-J. Lukas, Evangelist der Armen (1964) 172. HAHN, F. Das Verständnis der Mission im Neuen Testament (1965²) 49, 117. BURCHARD, C. Der dreizehnte Zeuge (1970) 26, 37, 146f., 160. COMBET-GALLAND, A.-E., "Actes 4,32 - 5,11" EThR 52 (1977) 548-53. JOHNSON, L. T., The Literary Function of Possessions in Luke-Acts (Missoula 1977) 203-04. THEISSEN, G., Soziologie der Jesusbewegung (München 1977) 18. "Apostelgeschichte" in: TRE 3 (1978) 496. "Armut" in: TRE 4 (1979) 76.

4:36 STAEHELIN, E. Die Verkündigung des Reiches Gottes in der Kirche Jesu Christi I (1951) 81. DELLING, G. Die Taufe im Neuen Testament (1963) 65. GLOVER, R. NTS 11 (1964-1965) 103f. BROCK, S. P. "BARNABAS: HUIOS PARAKLĒSĒOS," JThS 25 (1, 1974) 93-98. CAVALLIN, H. C. C., Life After Death. I (Lund 1974) 4, 2n4. HENGEL, M. Judentum und Hellenismus (1969) 194. ET: Judaism and Hellenism (1974) I 105. "Apostelgeschichte" in: TRE 3 (1978) 498. "Aramäisch" in: TRE 3 (1978) 604. FRANCE, R. T., "Barnabas - Son of encouragement" Themelios 4 (1978) 3-6. HENGEL, M., Zur urchristlichen Geschichtsschreibung (Stuttgart 1979) 86; ET: J. Bowden (trans.) Acts and the History of Earliest Christianity (London 1979) 101.

4:37 "Armenfürsorge" in: TRE 4 (1979) 16.

---

5 DUPONT, J. The Sources of Acts (1964) 42, 44, 46, 48. BRAUN, H. Qumran und NT II (1966) 148, 156f. BEYSCHLAG, K., Simon Magus und die christliche Gnosis (Tübingen 1974) 61n.122, 188. TALBERT, C. H., Literary Patterns, Theological Themes, and the Genre of Luke-Acts (Missoula 1974) 39. CONZELMANN, H. und LINDEMANN, A., Arbeitsbuch zum Neuen Testament (Tübingen 1975) 392-93. JOHNSON, L. T., The Literary Function of Possessions in Luke-Acts (Missoula 1977) 69. MOULE, C. F. D., The Holy Spirit (London 1978) 31-32.

5:1ff. PETZKE, G. Die Traditionen über Apollonius von Tyana und das Neue Testament (1970) 175, 180.

5:1-11 BEYER, H. W. Die Apostelgeschichte (1947) 38f. MENOUD, P. H. "La mort d'Ananias el de Saphira (Actes 5,1-11)," in: Aux Sources de la Tradition Chrétienne (1950) M. M. Goguel ed., 146-54. DUPONT, J. The Sources of Acts (1964) 18, 28, 36, 41, 47, 60. BRANDENBURGER/MERKEL, GPM 21 (2, 1966-1967) 228-33. BROWN, S. Apostasy and Perseverance in the Theology of Luke (1969) 98-109. DERRETT, J. D. M. "Ananias, Sapphira, and the Right of Property," DRev 89 (296, 1971) 225-32. DIETRICH, W. Das Petrusbild der lukanischen Schriften (1972) 232-37. MEURER, S. Das Recht im Dienst der Versöhnung und des Friedens (1972) 83-92. TALBERT, C. H., Literary Patterns, Theological Themes, and the Genre of Luke-Acts (Missoula 1974) 101. DUNN, J. D. G., Jesus and the Spirit (London 1975) 161, 163, 166. COMBET-GALLAND, A.-E., "Actes 4,32 - 5,11" EThR 52 (1977) 548-53. JOHNSON, L. T., The Literary Function of Possessions in Luke-Acts (Missoula 1977) 204-11. "Apostelgeschichte" in: TRE 3 (1978) 498. "Armut" in: TRE 4 (1979) 76. BOERMA, C., Rich Man, Poor Man - and the Bible (London 1979) 58-59. DUPONT, D. J., The Salvation of the Gentiles (New York 1979) 93. WEISER, A., "Das Gottesurteil über Hananias und Saphira-Apg

5,1-11'' ThG 69 (1979) 148-58. SCHNEIDER, G., Die Apostelgeschichte. I (Freiburg/Basel/Wien 1980) 368 (lit!). KRAFT, H., Die Entstehung des Christentums (Darmstadt 1981) 223-24. WEISER, A., Die Apostelgeschichte. I (Gütersloh/Würzburg 1981) 139 (lit!).

5:1-10 DEGENHARDT, H.-J. Lukas, Evangelist der Armen (1964) 172.

5:1 "Aramäisch" in: TRE 3 (1978) 608.

5:2 JOHNSON, L. T., The Literary Function of Possessions in Luke-Acts (Missoula 1977) 205-07.

5:3-4 JOHNSON, L. T., The Literary Function of Possessions in Luke-Acts (Missoula 1977) 207-08.

5:3 HAHN, F. Christologische Hoheitstitel (1963) 107.

5:4-39 TALBERT, C. H., Literary Patterns, Theological Themes, and the Genre of Luke-Acts (Missoula 1974) 24, 36, 38.

5:4 SCHEIDWEILER, F. "Zu Act 5:4," ZNW 49 (1-2, 1958) 136-37. WILCOX, M. The Semitisms of Acts (1965) 62-63. EPP, E. J. The theological tendency of Codex Bezae Cantabrigiensis in Acts (1966) 44f.

5:5 PALLIS, A., Notes on St. Luke and the Acts (London 1928) 54. TALBERT, C. H., Literary Patterns, Theological Themes, and the Genre of Luke-Acts (Missoula 1974) 35, 38.

5:6 FLEW, R. N. Jesus and His Church (1956) 141.

5:7ff. HAHN, F. Christologische Hoheitstitel (1963) 107.

5:9 DELLING, G. Die Zueignung des Heils in der Taufe (1961) 91. SCHNEIDER, G., "Gott und Christus als κύριος nach der Apostelgeschichte" in: J. Zmijewski/E. Nellessen (eds.) Begegnung mit dem Wort. FS. A. Zimmermann (Bonn 1980) 163, 168, 171-72.

5:10 BETZ, H. D. Lukian von Samosata und das Neue Testament (1961) 157, 178.

5:11-42 SHEPARD, J. W., The Life and Letters of St. Paul (Grand Rapids 1950) 42-47.

5:11-16 ZIMMERMANN, H. "Die Sammelberichte der Apostelgeschichte," BZ 5 (1, 1961) 71-82. DU TOIT, A. B. Der Aspekt der Freude im urchristlichen Abendmahl (1965) 108-12. ZIMMERMANN, H. Neutestamentliche Methodenlehre (1967) 245-46.

5:11 TALBERT, C. H., Literary Patterns, Theological Themes, and the Genre of Luke-Acts (Missoula 1974) 35, 38. "Altar" in: TRE 2 (1978) 317.

5:12-42 TYSON, J. B., "The Problem of Food in Acts: A Study of Literary Patterns with Particular Reference to Acts 6:1-7" in: P. J. Achtemeier (ed.) SBL Seminar Papers 1979/I (Missoula 1979) 71-72.

5:12-16 PETZKE, G. Die Traditionen über Apollonius von Tyana und das Neue Testament (1970) 78, 180. EGGER, W., Frohbotschaft und Lehre (Frankfurt 1976) 37. JOHNSON, L. T., The Literary Function of Possessions in Luke-Acts (Missoula 1977) 194-96. "Apostelgeschichte" in: TRE 3 (1978) 513. SCHNEIDER, G., Die Apostelgeschichte. I (Freiburg/Basel/Wien (1980) 378 (lit!). WEISER, A., Die Apostelgeschichte. I (Gütersloh/Würzburg 1981) 149 (lit!).

5:12-15 GOMEZ de MORALES, M. V., "La Comunidad Primitiva Modelo de Consagración a Dios" Biblia y Fe 4 (Madrid 1978) 271-82.

5:12 CLARK, A. C. The Acts of the Apostles (1933) 242, 245, 301, 331, NICKELS, P. Targum and New Testament (1967) 62. TALBERT, C. H., Literary Patterns, Theological Themes, and the Genre of Luke-Acts (Missoula 1974) 35, 38. METZGER, B. M., The Early Versions of the New Testament (Oxford 1977) 136.

5:13-16 TALBERT, C. H., Literary Patterns, Theological Themes, and the Genre of Luke-Acts (Missoula 1974) 35.

5:13 PALLIS, A., Notes on St. Luke and the Acts (London 1928) 54-55. BEYSCHLAG, K., Simon Magus und die christliche Gnosis (Tübingen 1974) 104n.14.

5:14-15 "Apostelgeschichte" in: TRE 3 (1978) 498.

5:14 DELLING, G. Die Taufe im Neuen Testament (1963) 70. TALBERT, C. H., Literary Patterns, Theological Themes, and the Genre of Luke-Acts (Missoula 1974) 38. ZINGG, P., Das Wachsen der Kirche (Freiburg 1974) 30-32, 38-39, 160, 170. SCHNEIDER, G., "Gott und Christus als χύριος nach der Apostelgeschichte" in: J. Zmijewski/E. Nellessen (eds.) Begegnung mit dem Wort. FS. H. Zimmerman (Bonn 1980) 163, 168,171-72.

5:15-16.19 BETZ, H. D. Lukian von Samosata und das Neuen Testament (1961) 9, 146, 151, 157, 170.

5:15-16 TALBERT, C. H., Literary Patterns, Theological Themes, and the Genre of Luke-Acts (Missoula 1974) 38. DUNN, J. D. G., Jesus and the Spirit (London 1975) 163, 165-66. EGGER, W., Frohbotschaft und Lehre (Frankfurt a.M. 1976) 136-37. SCHWEIZER, E., Heiliger Geist (Stuttgart 1978) 83-85.

5:15 BIEDER, W. "Der Petrusschatten, Apg 5,15," ThZ 16 (5, 1960) 407-09. DELLING, G. Die Zueignung des Heils in der Taufe (1961) 51. KAESEMANN, E. Exegetische Versuche und Besinnungen (1964) I 215. EPP, E. J. The theological tendency of Codex Bezae Cantabrigiensis in Acts (1966) 156f, 163. DIETRICH, W. Das Petrusbild der lukanischen Schriften (1972) 238-39. VAN DER HORST, P. W., "Peter's Shadow: The Religio-Historical Background of Acts v. 15" NTS 23 (1977) 204-12. "Apostelgeschichte" in: TRE 3 (1978) 498. BARRETT, C. K., "Is there a Theological Tendency in Codex Bezae?" in: E. Best/R. McL. Wilson (eds.) Text and Interpretation. FS. M. Black (Cambridge 1979) 25-26.

5:17ff. DIETRICH, W. Das Petrusbild der lukanischen Schriften (1972) 239-45.

5:17-42 PALLIS, A., Notes on St. Luke and the Acts (London 1928) 55-56. DUPONT, J. The Sources of Acts (1964) 35, 36, 38, 39, 40. JEREMIAS, J. Abba: Studien zur neutestamentlichen Theologie und Zeitgeschichte (1966) 238-47. STOLLE, V. Der Zeuge als Angeklagter (1973) 220-26. JOHNSON, L. T., The Literary Function of Possessions in Luke-Acts (Missoula 1977) 196-98. ADINOLFI, M., " 'Obbedire a Dio piuttosto che agli uomini.' La comunità cristiana et il Sinedrio in Atti 4,1-31; 5,17-42" RivB 27 (1979) 69-93. SCHNEIDER, G., Die Apostelgeschichte. I (Freiburg/Basel/Wien 1980) 383 (lit!). WEISER, A., Die Apostelgeschichte. I (Gütersloh/Würzburg 1981) 153 (lit!).

5:17-25 KRATZ, R., Auferweckung als Befreiung (Stuttgart 1973) 26-27, 33.

5:17-21 HUBBARD, B. J., "Commissioning Stories in Luke-Acts: A Study of their Antecedents, Form and Content" Semeia 8 (1977) 103-26. HUBBARD, B. J., "The Role of Commissioning Accounts in Acts" in: C. H. Talbert (ed.) Perspectives on Luke-Acts (Danville 1978) 190, 193, 196.

5:17-18 EHRHARDT, A. The Acts of the Apostles (1969) 25ff.

5:17 GOULDER, M. D. Type and History in Acts (1964) 22, 25f., 28, 44f., 74, 91, 93, 115, 202.

5:18ff. O'NEILL, J. C. The Theology of Acts in its historical setting (1970) 145-46.

5:18 EPP, E. J. The theological tendency of Codex Bezae Cantabrigiensis in Acts (1966) 11, 129f.

5:19-24 DUNN, J. D. G., Jesus and the Spirit (London 1975) 163, 166-67.

5:19-7:9 WILCOX, M. The Semitisms of Acts (1965) 59ff.

5:19 KNOX, W. L. The Sources of the Synoptic Gospels II (1957) 40. HAHN, F. Christologische Hoheitstitel (1963) 313. GOULDER, M. D. Type and History in Acts (1964) 22, 25f., 91, 219. EPP, E. J. The theological tendency of Codex Bezae Cantabrigiensis in Acts (1966) 129f.

5:20 DELLING, G. Die Taufe im Neuen Testament (1963) 64.

5:24 HENNECKE, E./SCHNEEMELCHER, W. Neutestamentliche Apokryphen 1964) I 376. HENGEL, M. Judentum umd Hellenismus (1969) 47. ET: Judaism and Hellenism (1974) I 25. CLARK,

K. W., "The Making of the Twentieth Century New Testament" in: The Gentile Bias and other Essays (Leiden 1980) 152.

5:26 HENGEL, M. Judentum und Hellenismus (1969) 47. ET: Judaism and Hellenism (1974) I 25.

5:28-32 DIBELIUS, M. Aufsätze zur Apostelgeschichte (1951) 142f. FLEW, R. N. Jesus and His Church (1956) 117. BURCHARD, C. Der dreizehnte Zeuge (1970) 138-42. ZEHNLE, R. F. Peter's Pentecost Discourse (1971) 39-40. PETERS, G. W. A Biblical Theology of Missions (1972) 135, 137, 141, 142-44, 254.

5:28 DELLING, G. Die Zueignung des Heils in der Taufe (1961) 43, 48. NICKELS, P. Targum and New Testament (1967) 62. TALBERT, C. H., Literary Patterns, Theological Themes, and the Genre of Luke-Acts (Missoula 1974) 102.

5:29ff. GUTBROD, K. Die Apostelgeschichte (1968) 59ff.

5:29-33 DIETRICH, W. Das Petrusbild der lukanischen Schriften (1972) 237-38.

5:29-32 KLIESCH, K., Das heilsgeschichtliche Credo in den Reden der Apostelgeschichte (Köln/Bonn 1975) 75ff., 153-55. MEYER, B. F., The Aims of Jesus (London 1979) 66-69.

5:29-31 MÜLLER, P.-G., ΧΡΙΣΤΟΣ ΑΡΧΗΓΟΣ. Die religionsgeschichtliche und theologische Hintergrund einer neutestamentlichen Christusprädikation (Frankfurt 1973) 271ff.

5:29 KLIESCH, K., Das heilsgeschichtliche Credo in den Reden der Apostelgeschichte (Köln/Bonn 1975) 142-43. "Autorität" in: TRE 5 (1980) 33.

5:30ff. SEEBERG, A. Der Katechismus der Urchristenheit (1966) 127f., 205.

5:30-32 TALBERT, C. H., Literary Patterns, Theological Themes, and the Genre of Luke-Acts (Missoula 1974) 36, 38, 122.

5:30-31 DELLING, G. Die Zueignung des Heils in der Taufe (1961) 89. DUPONT, J. Etudes sur les Actes des Apôtres (1967) 179, 252, 435, 456, 464. WILCKENS, U. Die Missionsreden der Apostelgeschichte (³1974) 45, 142f., 147. "Auferstehung" in: TRE 4 (1979) 485. DUPONT, D. J., The Salvation of the Gentiles (New York 1979) 68.

5:30 FARRER, A. St Matthew and St Mark (1954) 186n. HAHN, F. Christologische Hoheitstitel (1963) 116, 204. WILCOX, M. The Semitisms of Acts (1965) 32, 34-35, 43, 52n, 56n, 163, 164, 166. DUPONT, J. Etudes sur les Actes des Apôtres (1967) 141, 179, 281, 303, 331, 443. RESE, M. Alttestamentliche Motive in der Christologie des Lukas (1969) 115-16. KRAENKL, E. Jesus der Knecht Gottes (1972) 33, 80, 108, 111f., 118-120, 130, 150, 207.

ALSUP, J. E., The Post-Resurrection Appearance Stories of the Gospel Tradition (Stuttgart 1975) 81. TRITES, A. A., The New Testament Concept of Witness (Cambridge 1977) 131, 138, 143, 144. WILCOX, M.,'' 'Upon the Tree' - Deut 21:22-23 in the New Testament'' JBL 96 (1977) 85-99. HUBBARD, B. J., "Luke, Josephus and Rome: A Comparative Approach to the Lukan Sitz im Leben" in: P. Achtemeier (ed.) SBL Seminar Papers 1979/I (Missoula 1979) 65. WILCH, J. R., "Jüdische Schuld am Tode Jesu - Antijudaismus in der Apostelgeschichte?'' in: W. Haubeck/M. Bachmann (eds.) Wort in der Zeit. FS. K. H. Rengstorf (Leiden 1980) 240-41.

5:31 MOORE, G. F. Judaism I (1946) 516n. GAERTNER, B. The Areopagus speech and natural revelation (1955) 31f. SCHWEIZER, E. Erniedrigung und Erhöhung bei Jesus und seinen Nachfolgern (1962) § 4g. DELLING, G. Die Taufe in Neuen Testament (1963) 64, 140. HAHN, F. Christologische Hoheitstitel (1963) 107, 130, 386. KAESEMANN, E. Exegetische Versuche und Besinnungen (1964) I 45. FLENDER, H. Heil und Geschichte in der Theologie des Lukas (1965) 97. SEEBERG, A. Der Katechismus der Urchristenheit (1966) 77, 126, 131, 134, 137, 185, 214, 215, 217. DUPONT, J. Etudes sur les Actes des Apôtres (1967) 300, 303-04. FLENDER, H. St Luke Theologian of Redemptive History (1967) 9n, 18, 19n, 74, 104, 105, 158n. STROBEL, A. Erkenntnis und Bekenntnis der Sünde in neutestamentlicher Zeit (1968) 48, 57. DELLING, G. Der Kreuzestod Jesu in der urchristlichen Verkündigung (1972) 88-92. KRAENKL, E. Jesus der Knecht Gottes (1972) 149f., 161f., 184-86, 206-08, 211. STAEHLIN, G. ''Tὸ πνεῦμα 'Iησοῦ (Apostelgeschichte 16:7),'' in: Christ and the Spirit in the New Testament (1973) B. Lindars/S. S. Smalley eds., 235f., 241. RUPPERT, L., Jesus als der leidende Gerechte? (Stuttgart 1972) 11. MÜLLER, P.-G., ΧΡΙΣΤΟΣ ΑΡΧΗΓΟΣ. Der religionsgeschichtliche und theologische Hintergrund einer neutestamentlichen Christusprädikation (Frankfurt 1973) 15, 105ff. CAVALLIN, H. C. C., Life After Death. I (Lund 1974) 7, 2nI8. WILCKENS, U. Die Missionsreden der Apostelgeschichte (³1974) 142, 143, 150, 151, 152, 175, 176f., 179, 182, 186, 212, 217, 220, 240, 241. GASQUE, W., A History of the Criticism of the Acts of the Apostles (Tübingen 1975) 220, 286, 298. GOURGUES, M., ''Exalté à la droite de Dieu (Ac 2,33; 5,31)'' SciE 27 (1975) 303-27. FRIEDRICH, G., "Die Bedeutung der Auferweckung Jesu nach Aussagen des Neuen Testaments" in: Auf das Wort kommt es an (Göttingen 1978) 364. GOURGUES, M., A la droite de Dieu (Paris 1978). DUPONT, D. J., The Salvation of the Gentiles (New York 1979) 75. "Autorität" in: TRE 5 (1980) 20.

5:32 BROX, N. Zeuge und Märtyrer (1961) 45f. LOHFINK, G., " 'Wir sind Zeugen dieser Ereignisse' (Apg 5,32). Die Einheit der neutestamentlichen Botschaft von Erhöhung und Himmelfahrt Jesu" BuK 20 (1965) 49-52. ROLOFF, J. Apostolat-Verkündigung-Kirche (1965) 191f. BURCHARD, C. Der dreizehnte Zeuge (1970) 130-35. BEUTLER, J. Martyria (1972) 195, 300, 304. KRAENKL, E. Jesus der Knecht Gottes (1972) 167f., 180. STAEHLIN, G. "Tò πνεῦμα 'Ιησοῦ (Apostelgeschichte 16:7)," in: Christ and the Spirit in the New Testament (1973) B. Lindars/S. S. Smalley eds., 236, 242, 246, 250f. ALSUP, J. E., The Post-Resurrection Appearance Stories of the Gospel-Tradition (Stuttgart 1975) 81. NELLESSEN, E., Zeugnis für Jesus und das Wort (Köln 1976) 85-89, 254-55. TRITES, A. A., The New Testament Concept of Witness (Cambridge 1977) 135, 138, 148, 149, 150, 152, 153, 167. CRIBBS, F. L., "The Agreements that Exist Between John and Acts" in: C. H. Talbert (ed.) Perspectives on Luke-Acts (Danville 1978) 50. PRAST, F., Presbyter und Evangelium in nachapostolischer Zeit (Stuttgart 1979) 306-07, 319.

5:33-39 HUBBARD, B. J., "Luke, Josephus and Rome: A Comparative Approach to the Lukan Sitz im Leben" in: P. J. Achtemeier (ed.) SBL Seminar Papers (1979/II (Missoula 1979) 65.

5:33-34 RIVKIN, E., A Hidden Revolution (Nashville 1978) 120.

5:34 BARRETT, C. K., "Is there a theological tendency in Codex Bezae?" in: E. Best/R. McL. Wilson (eds.) Text and Interpretation. FS. M. Black (Cambridge 1979) 25-26.

5:35ff. EHRHARDT, A. The Acts of the Apostles (1969) 2f., 26.

5:35-39 DIBELIUS, M. Die Reden der Apostelgeschichte und die Antike Geschichtsschreibung (1949) 54-55. DIBELIUS, M. Aufsätze zur Apostelgeschichte (1951) 159f. ZINGG, P., Das Wachsen der Kirche (Freiburg 1974) 118-34, 168. LOHFINK, G., Die Sammlung Israels (München 1975) 85-87, 91.

5:35 ZINGG, P., Das Wachsen der Kirche (Freiburg 1974) 121-22.

5:36ff. BEYSCHLAG, K. Clemens Romanus und der Frühkatholizismus (1966) 332.

5:36-37 CLARK, A. C. The Acts of the Apostles (1933) liv,342f., 389. CAMPEAU, L. "Theudas le Faux Prophète et Judas le Galiléen," Sciences Ecclésiastiques V (1954) 235-45. GASQUE, W., A History of the Criticism of the Acts of the Apostles (Tübingen 1975) 10n, 11, 89n, 104. "Apostelgeschichte" in: TRE 3 (1978) 506. SCHRECKENBERG, H., "Flavius Josephus und die lukanischen Schriften" in: W. Haubeck/M. Bachmann (eds.) Wort in der Zeit. FS. K. H. Rengstorf (Leiden 1980) 195-98.

5:36 KNOX, W. L. The Sources of the Synoptic Gospels II (1957) 143.

HAHN, F. Christologische Hoheitstitel (1963) 361. BOUSSET, W. Die Religion des Judentums im Späthellenistischen Zeitalter (1966 = 1926) 224. BEYSCHLAG, K., Simon Magus und die christliche Gnosis (Tübingen 1974) 102, n.9. ZINGG, P., Das Wachsen der Kirche (Freiburg 1974) 122-23, 130. ARRINGTON, F. L., New Testament Exegesis: Examples (Washington 1977) 26. METZGER, B. M., The Early Versions of the New Testament (Oxford 1977) 140, 151-52.

5:37 VOLZ, P. Die Eschatologie der jüdischen Gemeinde (1934) 184. MOORE, G. F. Judaism II (1946) 375n. ZEITLIN, S., "Who Were the Galileans? New Light on Josephus' Activities in Galilee" JQR 64 (1974) 189-203. ZINGG, P., Das Wachsen der Kirche (Freiburg 1974) 128-29, 130. DRURY, J., Tradition and Design in Luke's Gospel (Atlanta 1976) 189-90.

5:38-39 FLENDER, H. Heil und Geschichte in der Theolgie des Lukas (1965) 106-07. BRAUN, H. Qumran und NT II (1966) 161. EPP, E. J. The theological tendency of Codex Bezae Cantabrigiensis in Acts (1966) 130f., 132n,1, 154, 167, 170. ZINGG, P., Das Wachsen der Kirche (Freiburg 1974) 124-27. BERGMEIER, R., Glaube als Gabe nach Johannes (Stuttgart 1980) 214.

5:38 LOHFINK, G., "Gibt es noch Taten Gottes?" Orientierung 31 (1978) 124-26. BARRETT, C. K., "Is there a Theological Tendency in Codex Bezae?" in: E. Best/R. McL. Wilson (eds.) Text and Interpretation. FS. M. Black (Cambridge 1979) 26.

5:39 PETZKE, G. Die Traditionen über Apollonius von Tyana und das Neue Testament (1970) 190f., 222. LOHFINK, G., Die Sammlung Israels (München 1975) 86-87. DUPONT, D. J., The Salvation of the Gentiles (New York 1979) 134.

5:40-42 TALBERT, C. H., Literary Patterns, Theological Themes, and the Genre of Luke-Acts (Missoula 1974) 36.

5:40 PALLIS, A. Notes on St. Luke and the Acts (London 1928) 56. DELLING, G. Die Zueignung des Heils in der Taufe (1961) 48, 88. FLENDER, H. St Luke Theologian of Redemptive History (1967) 27n, 131, 139, 157.

5:41 QUESNELL, Q. This Good News (1964) 69f., 95f. KLIJN, A. F. J., "Die syrische Baruch-Apokalypse" in: JüdSchr V/2 (1976) 147n6a. DALY, R. J., Christian Sacrifice (Washington D. C. 1978) 226.

5:42 CULLMANN, O. Urchristentum und Gottesdienst (1950) 11, 13, 14, 30. DELLING, G. Die Zueignung des Heils in der Taufe (1961) 88. CONZELMANN, H. Die Mitte der Zeit (1964) 206ff. EPP, E. J. The theological tendency of Codex Bezae Cantabrigiensis in Acts (1966) 54, 62f. KRAENKL, E. Jesus der Knecht Gottes (1972) 57f.

PRAST, F., Presbyter und Evangelium in nachapostolischer Zeit (Stuttgart 1979) 323.

———————

6:1-11:26 BORSE, U. "Der Rahmentext im Umkreis der Stephanusgeschichte (Apg 6,1-11, 26)," BuL 14 (3, 1973) 187-204.

6:1-8:4 DUPONT, J. The Sources of Acts (1964) 36, 51, 53, 54, 62, 63, 64, 68. RICHARD, E., Acts 6:1 - 8:4. The Author's Method of Composition, SBL Dissertation Series 41 (Missoula 1978).

6:1-8:3 SCHMITHALS, W. Paulus und Jakobus (1963) 9-29. RINALDI, G. "Stefano," BiOr 6 (4-5, 1964) 153-62. GRÄSSER, E., "Acta-Forschung seit 1960" ThR 42 (1977) 1-68. SCHNEIDER, G. Die Apostelgeschichte. I (Freiburg/Basel/Wien 1980) 417-18 (lit!).

6:1-8:2 KASTING, H. Die Anfänge der Urchristlichen Mission (1969) 54, 100-03.

6 HENGEL, M. Judentum und Hellenismus (1969) 194. ET: Judaism and Hellenism (1974) I 105. KAESEMANN, E. Exegetische Versuche und Besinnungen (1964) I 218. QUESNELL, Q. This Good News (1964) 113f.

6:1ff. SCHWEIZER, E. Gemeinde und Gemeinde-Ordnung im Neuen Testament (1959) §§ 51, m, 241, 25c. BLAIR, E. P. Jesus in the Gospel of Matthew (1960) 143. HAHN, F. Das Verständnis der Mission im Neuen Testament (²1965) 48, 50. GOULDER, M. D. Midrash and Lection in Matthew (1974) 138, 140.

6:1-15 REICKE, B. Glaube und Leben der Urgemeinde (1957) 115-28. CONZELMANN, H. und LINDEMANN, A., Arbeitsbuch zum Neuen Testament (Tübingen 1975) 102, 397. HENGEL, M., "Zwischen Jesus und Paulus. Die 'Hellenisten', die 'Sieben' und Stephanus (Apg 6,1-15; 7,54 - 8,3)" ZThK 72 (1975) 151-206. DUPONT, D. J., The Salvation of the Gentiles (New York 1979) 94. "Diakonie" in: TRE 8 (1981) 621, 622.

6:1-7 BEYER, H. W. Die Apostelgeschichte (1947) 44f. WIKENHAUSER, A. Die Apostelgeschichte (1951) 64. SCHMITHALS, W. Paulus und Jakobus (1963) 9-11, 18f., 27. FUERST, W. GPM 20 (1965-1966) 346-51. WEBER, O. Predigtmeditationen (1967) 284-88. HUEBNER, E. GPM 26 (4, 1972) 349-56. JOHNSON, L. T., The Literary Function of Possessions in Luke-Acts (Missoula (1977) 211-13. OSTEN-SACKEN, P. v. d., in: GPM 32 (1978) 336-44. RICHARD, E., Acts 6:1 - 8:4. The Au-

thor's Method of Composition (Missoula 1978) 215-19, 267-74.
TYSON, J. B., "The Problem of Food in Acts: A Study of Literary
Patterns with Particular Reference to Acts 6:1-7" in: P. J. Achte-
meier (ed.) SBL Seminar Papers 1979/I (Missoula 1979) 69-85.
SCHNEIDER, G., Die Apostelgeschichte. I (Freiburg/Basel/Wein
1980) 418-19 (lit!). KRAFT, H., Die Entstehung des Christentums
(Darmstadt 1981) 226-40. WEISER, A., Die Apostelgeschichte. I
(Gütersloh/Würzburg 1981) 163-64 (lit!).

6:1-6 SHEPARD, J. W. The Life and Letters of St. Paul (Grand Rapids
1950) 48-53. LOHSE, E. Die Ordination im Spätjudentum und im
Neuen Testament (1951) 74-79. REICKE, B. Diakonie, Festfreude
und Zelos (1951) 28ff., 37f.. FLEW, R. N. Jesus and His Church
(1956) 138-41. ROSLON, J. " 'Impositio manuum' w Dziejach
Apostolskich," RBL 10 (2, 1957) 102-14. McCAUGHEY, J. D.
"The Intention of the Author. Some questions about the exegesis
of Acts vi. 1-6," AusBR 7 (1-4, 1958) 27-36. BIHLER, J. Die
Stephanusgeschichte (1963) 192-95. ROLOFF, J. Apostolat-Verkündigung-Kirche (1965) 210f., 217-27. STROBEL, A. "Ar-
menpfleger 'um des Friedens willen' (Zum Verständnis von Act 6:1-
6)," ZNW 63 (3-4, 1972) 271-76. MARTINI, C. M. "Ministères
et entraide fraternelle dans la communauté primitive. Ac 6,1-6,"
AssS 26 (1973) 4-11. MÄRZ, C.-P., Das Wort Gottes bei Lukas
(Leipzig 1973) 16-52. TALBERT, C. H., Literary Patterns, Theological Themes, and the Genre of Luke-Acts (Missoula 1974) 24,
38, 101, 102. LIENHARD, J. T., "Acts 6:1-6: A Redactional
View" CBQ 37 (1975) 228-36. "Amt" in: TRE 2 (1978) 514.
DÖMER, M., Das Heil Gottes (Köln/Bonn 1978) 161-62. PRAST,
F., Presbyter und Evangelium in nachapostolischer Zeit (Stuttgart
1979) 225, 319-320. SWIDLER, L. Biblical Affirmations of
Woman (Philadelphia 1979) 305-11. "Diakonie" in: TRE 8 (1981)
621.

6:1-4 "Armensfürsorge" in: TRE 4 (1979) 16.

6:1-2 "Armensfürsorge" in: TRE 4 (1979) 17.

6:1 CLARK, A. C. The Acts of the Apostles (1933) 236, 237, 250, 253.
FLEW, R. N. Jesus and His Church (1956) 138. MOULE, C. F.
D. "Once More, Who Were the Hellenists?" ET 70 (4, 1959) 100-
02. DELORME, J. "Note sur les Hellénistes des Actes des
Apôtres," AmiCler 71 (July 13, 1961) 445-47. CONZELMANN,
H. Die Apostelgeschichte (1963) 43. GOULDER, M. D. Type and
History in Acts (1964) 22f., 26, 66, 73, 85. HENGEL, M. Juden-
tum und Hellenismus (1969) 3. ET: Judaism and Hellenism (1974)
I 2. WILSON, S. G. The Gentiles and the Gentile Mission in Luke-
Acts (1973) 129-30, 139-40. ZINGG, P., Das Wachsen der Kirche
(Freiburg 1974) 168, 171. METZGER, B. M. The Early Versions

of the New Testament (Oxford 1977) 92, 141. SCHMITHALS, W.,
"Zur Herkunft der gnostischen Elemente in der Sprache des Paulus" in: B. Aland et al. (eds.) Gnosis. FS. H. Jonas (Göttingen 1978)
412. PESCH, R., GERHARD, F. und SCHILLING, F., " 'Hellenisten' und 'Hebräer.' Zu Apg 9,29 und 6,1" BZ 23 (1979) 87-
92. TYSON, J. B., "The Problem of Food in Acts: A Study of Literary Patterns with Particular Reference to Acts 6:1-7" in: P. J.
Achtemeier (ed.) SBL Seminar Papers 1979/I (Missoula 1979) 79-
81. GERSTENBERGER, E. S. und SCHRAGE, W., Frau und Man
(Stuttgart 1980) 126-27.

6:2 CLARK, A. C. The Acts of the Apostles (1933) 285, 299, 303, 331.
FLEW, R. N. Jesus and His Church (1956) 132, 140. BRAUN, H.
Qumran und NT II (1966) 146, 334. WANKE, J., Die Emmaus-
erzählung (Leipzig 1973) 102.

6:3-6 CONZELMANN, H. Die Apostelgeschichte (1963) 43.

6:3 CLARK, A. C. The Acts of the Apostles (1933) 215, 236, 251, 303.
FLEW, R. N. Jesus and His Church (1956) 139. NELLESSEN, E.,
Zeugnis für Jesus und das Wort (Köln 1976) 60-61.

6:4 PRAST, F., Presbyter und Evangelium in nachapostolischer Zeit
(Stuttgart 1979) 319-20.

6:5ff. SCHARLEMANN, M. H. Stephen, a reappraisal (1964).

6:5.6.9 BOUSSET, W. Die Religion des Judentums im Späthellenistischen Zeitalter (1966 = 1926) 84, 169, 173.

6:5 BARRETT, C. K. The New Testament Background (1956) 164.
KNOX, W. L. The Sources of the Synoptic Gospels II (1957) 114.
MUNCK, J. Paul and the Salvation of Mankind (1959) 226f.
BROX, N. "Nikolaos und Nikolaiten," Vig Chr 19 (1, 1965) 23-
30. HAHN, F. Das Verständnis der Mission im Neuen Testament
(²1965) 49. SCHILLE, G. Die urchristliche Kollegialmission (1967)
38ff. BEYSCHLAG, K., Simon Magus und die christliche Gnosis
(Tübingen 1974) 4n.6, 97. CONZELMANN, H. und LINDE-
MANN, A., Arbeitsbuch zum Neuen Testament (Tübingen 1975)
397. RUDOLPH, K., Die Gnosis (Göttingen 1978) 323. SCHMI-
THALS, W., "Zur Herkunft der gnostischen Elemente in der
Sprache des Paulus" in: B. Aland et al. (eds.) Gnosis. FS. H. Jonas
(Göttingen 1978) 412. HENGEL, M., Zur urchristlichen
Geschichtsschreibung (Stuttgart 1979) 63, 65, 68; ET: J. Bowden
(trans.) Acts and the History of Earliest Christianity (London 1979)
71, 74, 78. SCHUNCK, K.-D., "1. Makkabäerbuch" in: JüdSchr
I/4 (1980) 311n.37a.

6:6 FLEW, R. N. Jesus and His Church (1956) 132n, 146. DELLING,
G. Die Taufe im Neuen Testament (1963) 66. KAESEMANN, E.
Exegetische Versuche und Besinnungen (1964) I 131.

6:7 PALLIS, A., Notes on St. Luke and the Acts (London 1928) 56. FLEW, R. N. Jesus and His Church (1956) 122, 154n. GOULDER, M. D. Type and History in Acts (1964) 20f., 226, 235. WILCOX, M. The Semitisms of Acts (1965) 79, 94, 128-29, 130, 154. BRAUN, H. Qumran und NT II (1966) 24, 140, 145, 158f., 180, 332f. NICKELS, P. Targum and New Testament (1967) 62. MÄRZ, C.-P., Das Wort Gottes bei Lukas (Leipzig 1973) 17-19. KODELL, J., " 'The Word of God grew'. The Ecclesial Tendency of *Logos* in Acts 6,7; 12,24; 19,20" Biblica 55 (1974) 505-19. ZINGG, P., Das Wachsen der Kirche (Freiburg 1974) 23-29, 38, 61-62, 160, 172-74. GASQUE, W., A History of the Criticism of the Acts of the Apostles (Tübingen 1975) 126, 127. "Apostelgeschichte" in: TRE 3 (1978) 513. HORTON, F. L., "Reflections on the Semitism of Luke-Acts" in C. H. Talbert (ed.) Perspectives on Luke-Acts (Danville 1978) 21.

6:8-8:8 TYSON, J. B., "The Problem of Food in Acts: A Study of Literary Patterns with Particular Reference to Acts 6:1-7" in: P. J. Achtemeier (ed.) SBL Seminar Papers 1979/I (Missoula 1979) 72.

6:8-8:3 DIBELIUS, M. Aufsätze zur Apostelgeschichte (1951) 16, 28, 94, 109. DOCKX, S. "Date de la mort d'Etienne le Protomartyr," Biblica 55 (1, 1974) 65-73. HUNTER, A. M., Gospel and Apostle (London 1975) 109-14. COMBRINK, H. J. B., Structural Analysis of Acts 6:8 - 8:3 (Cape Town 1979).

6:8-8:2 BURCHARD, C. Der dreizehnte Zeuge (1970) 26-31. MUSSNER, F., "Wohnung Gottes und Menschensohn nach der Stephanusperikope (Apg 6,8 - 8,2)" in: R. Pesch/R. Schnackenburg (eds.) Jesus und der Menschensohn. FS. A. Vögtle (Freiburg/Basel/Wien 1975) 283-99. BOISMARD, M.-E., "Le martyre d'Etienne. Actes 6,8 - 8,2" RechSR 69 (1981) 181-94.

6:8-7:60 FRANKLIN, E., Christ the Lord (London 1975) 99-108. DÖMER, M., Das Heil Gottes (Köln/Bonn 1978) 162-66.

6:8-7:59 GRASS, H. Ostergeschehen und Osterberichte (1970) 203ff.

6:8-7:2 RICHARD, E., Acts 6:1 - 8:4 (Missoula 1978) 19-22, 219-24, 274-304.

6:8-7:1 "Apostelgeschichte" in: TRE 3 (1978) 497, 498. SCHNEIDER, G., Die Apostelgeschichte. I (Freiburg/Basel/Wien 1980) 431 (Lit!).

6:8ff. SIMON, M. "Saint Stephen and the Jerusalem Temple," JEH 3 (1951) 127-42. HAHN, F. Das Verständnis der Mission im Neuen Testament (²1965) 48, 50, 51, 115.

6:8-15 SHEPARD, J. W., The Life and Letters of St. Paul (Grand Rapids 1950) 54-56. BIHLER, J. "Der Stephanusbericht (Apg 6,8-15 and 7,54-8,2)," BZ 3 (2, 1959) 252-70. BIHLER, J. Die Stephanusgeschichte (1963) 7-29. SAITO, T., Die Mosevorstellungen im

Neuen Testament (Bern 1977) 92-94, 147. PRAST, F., Presbyter und Evangelium in nachapostolischer Zeit (Stuttgart 1979) 224n.5. WEISER, A., Die Apostelgeschichte. I (Gütersloh/Würzburg 1981) 170 (lit!).

6:8-12 RICHARD, E., Acts 6:1 - 8:4 (Missoula 1978) 220.

6:8 CLARK, A. C. The Acts of the Apostles (1933) 236, 242, 243, 303, 311, 331. EPP, E. J. The theological tendency of Codex Bezae Cantabrigiensis in Acts (1966) 54, 62f. NICKELS, P. Targum and New Testament (1967) 62. STOLLE, V. Der Zeuge als Angeklagter (1973) 226-33. METZGER, B. M., "The Practice of New Testament Textual Criticism" in: V. L. Tollers/J. R. Maier (eds.) The Bible in its Literary Milieu (Grand Rapids 1979) 245-47.

6:9 BARRETT, C. K. The New Testament Background (1956) 51. BIHLER, J. Die Stephanusgeschichte (1963) 26-28.CAVALLIN, H. C. C., Life After Death. I (Lund 1974) 4, 2n4. BERGMEIER, R., Glaube als Gabe nach Johannes (Stuttgart 1980) 222. DRANE, J. W., "Why did Paul Write Romans?" in: D. A. Hagner/M. J. Harris (eds.) Pauline Studies. FS. F. F. Bruce (Exeter 1980) 214.

6:10 EPP, E. J. The theological tendency of Codex Bezae Cantabrigiensis in Acts (1966) 116f., 123, 132f., 155.

6:11-14 HAHN, F. Das Verständnis der Mission im Neuen Testament (²1965) 64.

6:11.13 NICKELS, P. Targum and New Testament (1967) 62.

6:11 SCHMITHALS, W. Paulus und Jakobus (1963) 13. WILCOX, M. The Semitisms of Acts (1965) 134-36, 153, 171, 173n. EPP, E. J. The theological tendency of Codex Bezae Cantabrigiensis in Acts (1966) 132f., 167. MÜLLER, U. B., "Zur Rezeption Gesetzeskritischer Jesusüberlieferung im frühen Christentum" NTS 27 (1981) 164.

6:12-15 RICHARD, E., Acts 6:1 - 8:4. The Author's Method of Composition (Missoula 1978) 220-21.

6:13-14 BLAIR, E. P. Jesus in the Gospel of Matthew (1960) 145. SCHMITHALS, W. Paulus und Jakobus (1963) 13, 19. DALY, R. J., Christian Sacrifice (Washington D. C. 1978) 228. MÜLLER, U. B., "Zur Rezeption Gesetzeskritischer Jesusüberlieferung im frühen Christentum" NTS 27 (1981) 163-64, 167.

6:13 HAHN, F. Das Verständnis der Mission im Neuen Testament (²1965) 51. WILCOX, M. The Semitisms of Acts (1965) 134-36, 153, 173, 173n. NELLESSEN, E., Zeugnis für Jesus und das Wort (Köln 1976) 54-58.

6:14 FLEW, R. N. Jesus and His Church (1956) 40. RUDOLPH, K. Die Mandäer I (1960) 115. DELLING, G. Die Zueignung des Heils in der Taufe (1961) 88. HAHN, F. Christologische Hoheitstitel (1963)

176. GAERTNER, B. The Temple and the Community in Qumran and the New Testament (1965) 113. HAHN, F. Das Verständnis der Mission im Neuen Testament (²1965) 29f. BRAUN, H. Qumran und NT II (1966) 271. SCHNEIDER, G. Verleugnung, Verspottung, und Verhör Jesu nach Lukas 22,54-71 (1969) 68, 80, 130, 131, 173, 201. O'NEILL, J. C. The Theology of Acts in its historical setting (1970) 89-91. WILSON, S. G. The Gentiles and the Gentile Mission in Luke-Acts (1973) 131-32, 145-46. DORMEYER, D., Die Passion Jesu als Verhaltensmodell (Münster 1974) 159. DUNN, J. D. G., Jesus and the Spirit (London 1975) 186, 237-38. KILGALLEN, J., The Stephen Speech (Rome 1976) 32, 34, 116-18, 132. VIELHAUER, P., "Oikodome. Das Bild vom Bau in der christlichen Literatur vom Neuen Testament bis Clemens Alexandrinus" in: G. Klein (ed.) Oikodome (München 1979) 59, 63-64, 64-66. WILSON, S. G., "Law and Judaism in Acts" in: P. J. Achtemeier (ed.) SBL Seminar Papers 1980) Chico, Cal. 1980) 255-56.

6:15 PESCH, R. Die Vision des Stephanus (1966) 27, 28, 29, 30, 49, 50, 60, 62. EHRHARDT, A. The Acts of the Apostles (1969) 33f. METZGER, B. M., The Early Versions of the New Testament (Oxford 1977) 140.

7-15 SAHLIN, H. Der Messias und das Gottesvolk (1945) 364-69.

7:1-8:3 REICKE, B. Glaube und Leben der Urgemeinde (1957) 129-76.

7 MUNDLE, W., "Die Stephanusrede Apg 7: eine Märtyrerapologie" ZNW 20 (1921) 133-47. STONEHOUSE, N. B. The Areopagus Address (1949). GRANT, F. C. The Gospels (1957) 126f. SOFFRITTI, O. "Stefano, testimone del Signore," RivB 10 (2, 1962) 182-88. BIHLER, J. Die Stephanusgeschichte (1963) 127-34. HAHN, F. Christlogische Hoheitstitel (1963) 219. GEORGI, D. Die Gegner des Paulus im 2. Korinther-Brief (1964) 216f. GAERTNER, B. The Temple and the Community in Qumran and the New Testament (1965) 112. BRAUN, H. Qumran und NT II (1966) 158, 183, 303, 319. PESCH, R. Die Vision des Stephanus (1966) 18, 20, 35, 44, 57. GUTBROD, K. Die Apostelgeschichte (1968) 45ff., 66ff. HOLTZ, T. Untersuchungen über die Alttestamentlichen Zitate bei Lukas (1968) 85-109. BERTRAM, G. ThLZ 94 (11, 1969) 826-28. BETZ, H. D. Interpretation 23 (2, 1969) 252.

MAY, E. CBQ 31 (3, 1969) 455-57. BIHLER, J. Biblica 51 (1, 1970) 149-52. PESCH, R. "Der Christ als Nachnahmer Christi. Der Tod des Stephanus (Apg 7) im Vergleich mit dem Tod Christi," BuK 24 (1, 1969) 10-11. GASTON, L. No Stone on Another (1970) 154, 156-60, 280-81. MARE, W. H. "Acts 7: Jewish or Samaritan in Character?" WThJ 34 (1, 1971) 1-21. KRAENKL, E. Jesus der Knecht Gottes (1972) 14f., 118. RUPPERT, L., Jesus als der leidende Gerechte? (Stuttgart 1972) 46. DAVIES, W. D. The Gospel and the Land (1974) 267, 271-77, 286, 366. HANSON, A. T. Studies in Paul's Technique and Theology (1974) 78-79, 185. SCOTT, J. J. "Stephen's Speech: A Possible Model for Luke's Historical Method?" JETh 17 (2, 1974) 91-97. CULLMANN, O., Der johanneische Kreis (Tübingen 1975) 45, 46, 48, 53, 54, 56. GASQUE, W., A History of the Criticism of the Acts of the Apostles (Tübingen 1975) 11, 172, 196. STEMBERGER, G., "Die Stephanusrede (Apg 7) und die jüdische Tradition" in: A. Fuchs (ed.) Jesus in der Verkündigung der Kirche (Freistadt 1976) 154-74. BRUCE, F. F., First Century Faith (Leicester 1977) 23-28. DUNN, J. D. G., Unity and Diversity in the New Testament (London 1977) 128-29. KOIVISTO, R. A., "Stephen's Speech: A Case Study in Rhetoric and Biblical Inerrancy" JEThS (1977) 353-64. RICHARD, E., "Acts 7: An Investigation of the Samaritan Evidence" CBQ 39 (1977) 190-208. "Amt" in: TRE 2 (1978) 565. BLOCH, R., "Methodological Note for the Study of Rabbinic Literature" in: W. S. Green (ed.) Approaches to Ancient Judaism: Theory and Practice (Missoula 1978) 59. RICHARD, E., Acts 6:1 - 8:4. The Author's Method of Composition (Missoula 1978) 254-59. HENGEL, M., Zur urchristlichen Geschichtsschreibung (Stuttgart 1979) 41; ET: J. Bowden (trans.) Acts and the History of Earliest Christianity (London 1979) 42. SCOBIE, C. H. H., "The Use of Source Material in the Speeches of Acts III and VII" NTS 25 (1979) 399-421. KURZ, W. S., "Luke-Acts and Historiography in the Greek Bible" in: P. J. Achtemeier (ed.) SBL Seminar Papers 1980 (Chico, Cal. 1980) 284. DONALDSON, T. "Moses Typology and the Sectarian Nature of Early Christian Anti-Judaism: A Study in Acts 7" JSNT 12 (1981) 27-52.

7:1-60 SCHNIDER, F. Jesus der Prophet (1973) 94ff.

7:1-53 SAHLIN, H. Der Messias und das Gottesvolk (1945) 351-54. SHEPARD, J. W., The Life and Letters of St. Paul (Grand Rapids 1950) 56-59. SCHMITHALS, W. Paulus und Jacobus (1963) 13, 14 n.2. RAVANELLI, V., "Las testimonianza di Stefano su Gesù Cristo" SBFLA 24 (1974) 121-41. GLÖCKNER, R., Die Verkündigung des Heils beim Evangelisten Lukas (Mainz 1975) 165ff.

WEISER, A., Die Apostelgeschichte (Gütersloh/Würzburg 1981) 177 (lit!).

7:1-2 RICHARD, E., Acts 6:1 - 8:4. The Author's Method of Composition (Missoula 1978) 221.

7:2-53 BEYER, H. W. Die Apostelgeschichte (1947) 51. DIBELIUS, M. Die Reden der Apostelgeschichte und die antike Geschichtsschreibung (1949) 35-39. DIBELIUS, M. Aufsätze zur Apostelgeschichte (1951) 143-46. ET: Studies in the Acts of the Apostles (1956) 167-70. FLEW, R. N. Jesus and His Church (1956) 126-28. KLIJN, A. F. J. "Stephen's Speech-Acts vii.2-53," NTS 4 (1, 1957) 25-31. BARNARD, L. W. "Saint Stephen and Early Alexandrian Christianity," NTS 7 (1, 1960) 31-45. CONZELMANN, H. Die Apostelgeschichte (1963) 50f. HAHN, F. Christologische Hoheitstitel (1963) 382-85, 390, 403. NICKELS, P. Targum and New Testament (1967) 62. ZEHNLE, R. F. Peter's Pentecost Discourse (1971) 76-82, 86-88. RAVANELLI, P. V., "Las testimonianza di Stefano su Gesù Cristo" SBFLA 24 (1974) 121-41. KLIESCH, K., Das heilsgeschichtliche Credo in den Reden der Apostelgeschichte (Köln/Bonn 1975) 5-38, 45-47, 110, 155-59. KILGALLEN, J., The Stephen Speech (Rome 1976). Williams, J. A., A Conceptual History of Deuteronomism in the Old Testament, Judaism, and the New Testament (Ph. D. Diss., Louisville 1976) 248-56, 286, 290. JOHNSON, L. T., The Literary Function of Possessions in Luke-Acts (Missoula 1977) 70-76. "Apostelgeschichte" in: TRE 3 (1978) 492, 497, 503. MARTIN, R. P., New Testament Foundations. II (Exeter 1978) 86-89. RICHARD, E., Acts 6:1 - 8:4. The Author's Method of Composition (Missoula 1978) 33-155, 249-53. SCHARLEMANN, M. H., "Acts 7:2-53. Stephen's Speech: A Lucan Creation?" CJ 4 (1978) 52-57. VIA, E. J., "An Interpretation of Acts 7:35-37 from the Perspective of Major Themes in Luke-Acts" in: P. J. Achtemeier (ed.) SBL Seminar Papers 1978/II (Missoula 1978) 211n.7. MEYER, B. F., The Aims of Jesus (London 1979) 66-69. MCDONALD, J. I. H., Kerygma and Didache (Cambridge 1980) 53. SCHNEIDER, G., Die Apostelgeschichte. I (Freiburg/Basel/Wien 1980) 441-42. (lit!).

7:2-50 SCOBIE, C. H. H. "The Origins and Development of Samaritan Christianity," NTS 19 (4, 1973) 390-414.

7:2-37 BIHLER, J. Die Stephanusgeschichte (1963) 38.

7:2-16 RICHARD, E., Acts 6:1 - 8:4. The Author's Method of Composition (Missoula 1978) 39-76, 260-61.

7:2-8 BIHLER, J. Die Stephanusgeschichte (1963) 38-46. RICHARD, E., Acts 6:1 - 8:4. The Author's Method of Composition (Missoula 1978) 39-59, 182-85. DUPONT, D. J., The Salvation of the Gentiles (New York 1979) 135-36.

7:2-4 CLARK, A. C. The Acts of the Apostles (1933) 343f. STEMBER-
GER, G., ''Die Stephanusrede (Apg 7) und die jüdische Tradition'' in: A. Fuchs (ed.) Jesus in der Verkündigung der Kirche
(Freistadt 1976) 155-59. RICHARD, E., Acts 6:1 - 8:4. The Author's Method of Composition (Missoula 1978) 183.

7:2 DUPONT, J. Etudes sur les Actes des Apôtres (1967) 253, 269.,
284, 286, NICKELS, P. Targum and New Testament (1967) 62.
RICHARD, E., Acts 6:1 - 8:4. The Author's Method of Composition (Missoula 1978) 39-40. SCHRAGE, W., ''Die Elia-Apokalypse'' in: JüdSchr V/3 (1980) 231 n.19g.

7:3ff. STRECKER, G. Der Weg der Gerechtigkeit (1962) 64.

7:3 WILCOX, M. The Semitisms of Acts (1965) 26-27, 32, 52n, 56n,
159. NICKELS, P. Targum and New Testament (1967) 62.
WANKE, J., Die Emmauserzählung (Leipzig 1973) 92, 119.
RICHARD, E., Acts 6:1 - 8:4. The Author's Method of Composition (Missoula 1978) 41-43.

7:3b, 10b McNAMARA, M. The New Testament and the Palestinian Targum to the Pentateuch (1966) 259 n.37.

7:4 WILCOX, M. The Semitisms of Acts (1965) 28-29, 52, 56n, 159.
NICKELS, P. Targum and New Testament (1967) 62. METZ-
GER, B. M., The Early Versions of the New Testament (Oxford
1977) 147. RICHARD, E., Acts 6:1 - 8:4. The Author's Method
of Composition (Missoula 1978) 43-45.

7:5 PALLIS, A., Notes on St. Luke and the Acts (London 1928) 56-
57. NICKELS, P. Targum and New Testament (1967) 63. RICH-
ARD, E., Acts 6:1 - 8:4. The Author's Method of Composition
(Missoula 1978) 45-48, 183-84.

7:6-13 STEMBERGER, G., ''Die Stephanusrede (Apg 7) und die jüdische Tradition'' in: A. Fuchs (ed.) Jesus in der Verkündigung der
Kirche (Freistadt 1976) 159-60.

7:6-7 RICHARD, E., Acts 6:1 - 8:4. The Author's Method of Composition (Missoula 1978) 184.

7:6 RICHARD, E., Acts 6:1 - 8:4. The Author's Method of Composition (Missoula 1978) 49-51.

7:7 RICHARD, E., Acts 6:1 - 8:4. The Author's Method of Composition (Missoula 1978) 51-54.

7:8 RICHARD, E., Acts 6:1 - 8:4. The Author's Method of Composition (Missoula 1978) 54-56. ''Beschneidung'' in: TRE 5 (1980)
721.

7:9-16 BIHLER, J. Die Stephanusgeschichte (1963) 46-51. CONZEL-
MANN, H. Die Apostelgeschichte (1963) 47. RICHARD, E., Acts
6:1 - 8:4. The Author's Method of Composition (Missoula 1978)

60-76, 185-88. RICHARD, E., "The Polemical Character of the Joseph Episode in Acts 7" JBL 98 (1979) 255-67.

7:9-14 DIETZFELBINGER, C., "Pseudo-Philo: Antiquitates Biblicae" in: JüdSchr II/2 (1975) 121n.10d.

7:9-11 RICHARD, E., Acts 6:1 - 8:4. The Author's Method of Composition (Missoula 1978) 186-87.

7:9-10 RICHARD, E., Acts 6:1 - 8:4. The Author's Method of Composition (Missoula 1978) 60-62.

7:9 GOULDER, M. D. Type and History in Acts (1964) 161f. RICHARD, E., Acts 6:1 - 8:4. The Author's Method of Composition (Missoula 1978) 60.

7:10-8:1a WILCOX, M. The Semitisms of Acts (1965) 59ff.

7:10 DELLING, G. Die Taufe im Neuen Testament (1963) 136. WILCOX, M. The Semitisms of Acts (1965) 27-28, 67, 159. DUPONT, J. Etudes sur les Actes des Apôtres (1967) 269, 281, 282, 284, 537. NICKELS, P. Targum and New Testament (1967) 63. RICHARD, E., Acts 6:1 - 8:4. The Author's Method of Composition (Missoula 1978) 62-64. DUPONT, D. J. The Salvation of the Gentiles (New York 1979) 150.

7:11.36 KILPATRICK, G. D. "The Land of Egypt in the New Testament," JThS 17 (1, 1966) 70.

7:11 RICHARD, E., Acts 6:1 - 8:4. The Author's Method of Composition (Missoula 1978) 64-68.

7:12-13 RICHARD, E., Acts 6:1 - 8:4. The Author's Method of Composition (Missoula 1978) 187-88.

7:12 RICHARD, E., Acts 6:1 - 8:4. The Author's Method of Composition (Missoula 1978) 68-69.

7:13 RICHARD, E., Acts 6:1 - 8:4. The Author's Method of Composition (Missoula 1978) 69-70.

7:14 BRAUN, H. Qumran und NT II (1966) 303. STEMBERGER, G., "Die Stephanusrede (Apg 7) und die jüdische Tradition" in: A. Fuchs (ed.) Jesus in der Verkündigung der Kirche (Freistadt 1976) 160-62. RICHARD, E., Acts 6:1 - 8:4. The Author's Method of Composition (Missoula 1978) 70-72, 188. BERGER, K., "Das Buch der Jubiläen" in: JüdSchr II/3 (1981) 533n. 33c.

7:15-16 RICHARD, E., Acts 6:1 - 8:4. The Author's Method of Composition (Missoula 1978) 188.

7:15 RICHARD, E., Acts 6:1 - 8:4. The Author's Method of Composition (Missoula 1978) 72-73.

7:16 STEMBERGER, G., "Die Stephanusrede (Apg 7) und die jüdische Tradition" in: A. Fuchs (ed.) Jesus in der Verkündigung der

Kirche (Freistadt 1976) 162-65. RICHARD, E., Acts 6:1 - 8:4. The Author's Method of Composition (Missoula 1978) 73.

7:17-44 JELONEK, T., "Typologia mojžesz—Chrystus w dzieach św. lukasza" Analecta Cracoviensia 8 (Cracow 1976) 111-24.

7:17-43 ATIENZA, J. C., "Hechos 7,17-43 y las corrientes cristologicas dentro de la primitiva comunidad cristiana" EstBi 33 (1974) 31-62. SAITO, T., Die Mosevorstellungen im Neuen Testament (Bern 1977) 80-92, 142-43, 147, 165ff.

7:17-42 DUPONT, D. J., The Salvation of the Gentiles (New York 1979) 133-34.

7:17-41 RICHARD, E., Acts 6:1 - 8:4. The Author's Method of Composition (Missoula 1978) 334-38.

7:17-34 RICHARD, E., Acts 6:1 - 8:4. The Author's Method of Composition (Missoula 1978) 76-102, 188-92, 261-62.

7:17-29 JOHNSON, L. T., The Literary Function of Possessions in Luke-Acts (Missoula 1977) 72-73.

7:17-22 RICHARD, E., Acts 6:1 - 8:4. The Author's Method of Composition (Missoula 1978) 189.

7:17-19 RICHARD, E., Acts 6:1 - 8:4. The Author's Method of Composition (Missoula 1978) 76-80.

7:17 RICHARD, E., Acts 6:1 - 8:4. The Author's Method of Composition (Missoula 1978) 77-78.

7:18-37 KURZ, W. S., "Luke-Acts and Historiography in the Greek Bible" in: P. J. Achtemeier (ed.) SBL Seminar Papers 1980 (Chico, Cal. 1980) 288-89.

7:18 RICHARD, E., Acts 6:1 - 8:4. The Author's Method of Composition (Missoula 1978) 78-79.

7:19 RICHARD, E., Acts 6:1 - 8:4. The Author's Method of Composition (Missoula 1978) 79-80.

7:20-43 STEMBERGER, G., "Die Stephanusrede (Apg 7) und die jüdische Tradition" in: A. Fuchs (ed.) Jesus in der Verkündigung der Kirche (Freistadt 1976) 165-70.

7:20-41 NICKELS, P. Targum and New Testament (1967) 63.

7:20-37 BIHLER, J. Die Stephanusgeschichte (1963) 51-63.

7:20-29 RICHARD, E., Acts 6:1 - 8:4. The Author's Method of Composition (Missoula 1978) 80-87.

7:20.22 BLAIR, E. P. Jesus in the Gospel of Matthew (1960) 146.

7:21 METZGER, B. M., The Early Versions of the New Testament (Oxford 1977) 235.

7:22-53 SCHILLEBEECKX, E., Christ: the Christian Experience in the

Modern World (London 1980) 315, 317-18; GT: Christus und die Christen (Freiburg/Basel/Wien 1977) 302-03, 305.

7:22-32 BLOCH, R., "Midrash" in: W. S. Green (ed.) Approaches to Ancient Judaism: Theory and Practice (Missoula 1978) 49.

7:22 WANKE, J., Die Emmauserzählung (Leipzig 1973) 62. BERGER, K., "Das Buch der Jubiläen" in: JüdSchr II/3 (1981) 540n.a.

7:22b HAHN, F. Christologische Hoheitstitel (1963) 388.

7:23-29 RICHARD, E., Acts 6:1 - 8:4. The Author's Method of Composition (Missoula 1978) 190-91.

7:23.35 SCHUESSLER-FIORENZA, E. Priester für Gott (1972) 257f.

7:23 RICHARD, E., Acts 6:1 - 8:4. The Author's Method of Composition (Missoula 1978) 82.

7:24 RICHARD, E., Acts 6:1 - 8:4. The Author's Method of Composition (Missoula 1978) 82-83.

7:25 BLAIR, E. P. Jesus in the Gospel of Matthew (1960) 151.

7:26 WILCOX, M. The Semitisms of Acts (1965) 42-43, 56n, 160. RICHARD, E., Acts 6:1 - 8:4. The Author's Method of Composition (Missoula 1978) 83-85.

7:27-28 RICHARD, E., Acts 6:1 - 8:4. The Author's Method of Composition (Missoula 1978) 85-86.

7:27 BLAIR, E. P. Jesus in the Gospel of Matthew (1960) 145.

7:29 RICHARD, E., Acts 6:1 - 8:4. The Author's Method of Composition (Missoula 1978) 86-87.

7:30-43 JOHNSON, L. T., The Literary Function of Possessions in Luke-Acts (Missoula 1977) 73-75.

7:30-39 BRAUN, H. Qumran und NT II (1966) 158, 311.

7:30-34 JOHNSON, L. T., The Literary Function of Possessions in Luke-Acts (Missoula 1977) 73. RICHARD, E., Acts 6:1 - 8:4. The Author's Method of Composition (Missoula 1978) 87-100, 191-92.

7:30 BOUSSET, W. Die Religion des Judentums im Späthellenistischen Zeitalter (1966 = 1926) 120. RICHARD, E., Acts 6:1 - 8:4. The Author's Method of Composition (Missoula 1978) 88.

7:31-34 METZGER, B. M., The Early Versions of the New Testament (Oxford 1977) 141.

7:31 RICHARD, E., Acts 6:1 - 8:4. The Author's Method of Composition (Missoula 1978) 89.

7:32-33 RICHARD, E., Acts 6:1 - 8:4. The Author's Method of Composition (Missoula 1978) 91-98.

7:32 WILCOX, M. The Semitisms of Acts (1965) 29-30, 32, 34, 37, 52n, 53n, 56n, 159. NICKELS, P. Targum and New Testament

(1967) 63. ZEHNLE, R. F. Peter's Pentecost Discourse (1971) 45-47.

7:33 DELLING, G. Die Zueignung des Heils in der Taufe (1961) 91. WILCOX, M. The Semitisms of Acts (1965) 39, 41-42, 52n, 56n.

7:34 RICHARD, E., Acts 6:1 - 8:4. The Author's Method of Composition (Missoula 1978) 98-100.

7:35-53 HENGEL, M. Judentum und Hellenismus (1969) 564. ET: Judaism and Hellenism (1974) I 309. WILLIAMS, J. A., A Conceptual History of Deuteronomism in the Old Testament, Judaism, and the New Testament (Ph. D. Diss., Louisville 1976) 250-56.

7:35-50 RICHARD, E., Acts 6:1 - 8:4. The Author's Method of Composition (Missoula 1978) 102-37, 262-64.

7:35-41 RICHARD, E., Acts 6:1 - 8:4. The Author's Method of Composition (Missoula 1978) 102-21, 192-96.

7:35-39 JOHNSON, L. T. The Literary Function of Possessions in Luke-Acts (Missoula 1977) 73-74.

7:35-37 VIA, E. J., "An Interpretation of Acts 7:35-37 from the Perspective of Major Themes in Luke-Acts" in: P. J. Achtemeier (ed.) SBL Seminar Papers 1978/II (Missoula 1978) 209-22. VIA, J., "An Interpretation of Acts 7.35-37 from the Perspectives of Major Themes in Luke-Acts" PRSt 6 (1979) 190-207.

7:35.39.51f. BIHLER, J. Die Stephanusgeschichte (1963) 118-27.

7:35.37 LUZ, U. Das Geschichtsverständnis des Paulus (1968) 58f.

7:35 DE LORENZI, L. "Gesù lytrōtēs: Atti 7,35," RivB 7 (4, 1959) 294-321; 8 (1, 1960) 10-41. BLAIR, E. P. Jesus in the Gospel of Matthew (1960) 145, 146. DUPONT, J. Etudes sur les Actes des Apôtres (1967) 148, 263, 281, 303, 304, 486. NICKELS, P. Targum and New Testament (1967) 63. WILCKENS, U. Die Missionsreden der Apostelgeschichte (^{3}1974) 130, 175, 177, 211, 217, 220, 223, 234, 238, 240. RICHARD, E., Acts 6:1 - 8:4. The Author's Method of Composition (Missoula 1978) 102-04, 194-96.

7:36 HAHN, F. Christologische Hoheitstitel (1963) 388. BRANDENBURGER, E., "Himmelfahrt Moses" in: JüdSchr V/2 (1976) 71n.11b. JOHNSON, L. T., The Literary Function of Possessions in Luke-Acts (Missoula 1977) 74. RICHARD, E., Acts 6:1 - 8:4. The Author's Method of Composition (Missoula 1978) 104-08.

7:37 BLAIR, E. P. Jesus in the Gospel of Matthew (1960) 145, 146. LINDARS, B. New Testament Apologetic (1961) 207, 209f. LOEVESTAM, E. Son and Saviour (1961) 9f. HAHN, F. Christologische Hoheitstitel (1963) 389. BOUSSET, W. Die Religion des Judentums im Späthellenistischen Zeitalter (1966 = 1926) 233. RESE, M. Alttestamentliche Motive in der Christologie des Lukas

(1969) 78-80. ZEHNLE, R. F. Peter's Pentecost Discourse (1971) 76-77. WANKE, J., Die Emmauserzählung (Leipzig 1973) 11, 63. WILCKENS, U. Die Missionsreden der Apostelgeschichte (³1974) 137, 143, 164, 211, 216. JOHNSON, L. T., The Literary Function of Possessions in Luke-Acts (Missoula 1977) 74. RICHARD, E., Acts 6:1 - 8:4. The Author's Method of Composition (Missoula 1978) 108-10. DUPONT, D. J., The Salvation of the Gentiles (New York 1979) 132-33. DUNN, J. D., Christology in the Making (London 1980) 94, 138.

7:38-50 BIHLER, J. Die Stephanusgeschichte (1963) 63-77.

7:38.53 BOUSSET, W. Die Religion des Judentums im Späthellenistischen Zeitalter (1966 = 1926) 120.

7:38 PALLIS, A. Notes on St. Luke and the Acts (London 1928) 57. BLAIR, E. P. Jesus in the Gospel of Matthew (1960) 146, 147. HAHN, F. Christologische Hoheitstitel (1963) 388. JOHNSON, L. T., The Literary Function of Possessions in Luke-Acts (Missoula 1977) 74-75. RICHARD, E., Acts 6:1 - 8:4. The Author's Method of Composition (Missoula 1978) 110-14. CALLAN, T., ''Pauline Midrash: The Exegetical Background of Gal. 3:19b'' JBL (1980) 553.

7:39 BLAIR, E. P. Jesus in the Gospel of Matthew (1960) 145. NICKELS, P. Targum and New Testament (1967) 63. JOHNSON, L. T., The Literary Function of Possessions in Luke-Acts (Missoula 1977) 75. RICHARD, E., Acts 6:1 - 8:4. The Author's Method of Composition (Missoula 1978) 114-16.

7:40 RICHARD, E., Acts 6:1 - 8:4. The Author's Method of Composition (Missoula 1978) 117.

7:41-50 DUNN, J. D. G., Unity and Diversity in the New Testament (London 1977) 98. DALY, R. J., Christian Sacrifice (Washington D. C. 1978) 229-30.

7:41 CULLMANN, O. NTS 5 (1958-1959) 166ff. BRAUN, H. Qumran und NT II (1966) 24, 133, 158f., 163, 306, 309f., 319. PELLETIER, A. ''Une création de l'apologétique chrétienne: moschopoiein,'' RechSR 54 (3, 1966) 411-16. PELLETIER, A. ''Valeur évocatrice d'un démarquage chrétien de la Septante,'' Biblica 48 (3, 1967) 388-94. RICHARD, E., Acts 6:1 - 8:4. The Author's Method of Composition (Missoula 1978) 117-19.

7:42-50 RICHARD, E., Acts 6:1 - 8:4. The Author's Method of Composition (Missoula 1978) 121-37, 196-99, 329-30.

7:42-43 FITZMYER, J. A. NTS 7 (1960-1961) 321f. HOLTZ, T. Untersuchungen über die Alttestamentlichen Zitate bei Lukas (1968) 14-19. JOHNSON, L. T., The Literary Function of Possessions in Luke-Acts (Missoula 1977) 75. ''Amos'' in: TRE 2 (1978) 484.

RICHARD, E., Acts 6:1 - 8:4. The Author's Method of Composition (Missoula 1978) 198-99. "Astrologie" in: TRE 4 (1979) 308. DUPONT, D. J., The Salvation of the Gentiles (New York 1979) 139. SOMERVILLE, E. R., "The Divine Purpose: The Jews and the Gentile Mission (Acts 15)" in: P. J. Achtemeier (ed.) SBL Seminar Papers 1980 (Chico, Cal. 1980) 272. RICHARD, E., "The Creative Use of Amos by the Author of Acts" NovT 24 (1982) 38-44.

7:42 PALLIS, A., Notes on St. Luke and the Acts (London 1928) 57-58. METZGER, B. M., The Early Versions of the New Testament (Oxford 1977) 141. BLOCH, R., "Midrash" in: W. S. Green (ed.) Approaches to Ancient Judaism: Theory and Practice (Missoula 1978) 49. RICHARD, E., Acts 6:1 - 8:4. The Author's Method of Composition (Missoula 1978) 121-26. BERGER, K., "Das Buch der Jubiläen" in: JüdSchr II/3 (1981) 433n. 22d.

7:44ff. WILCKENS, U. Die Missionsreden der Apostelgeschichte (³1974) 208, 213, 214, 217.

7:44-50 BIHLER, J. Die Stephanusgeschichte (1963) 71-77. MÜLLER, U. B., "Zur Rezeption Gesetzeskritischer Jesusüberlieferung im frühen Christentum" NTS 27 (1981) 164.

7:44-46 BLAIR, E. P. Jesus in the Gospel of Matthew (1960) 147.

7:44 DALTON, W. J., Christ's Proclamation to the Spirits (Rome 1965) 211. NELLESSEN, E., Zeugnis für Jesus und das Wort (Köln 1976) 276. RICHARD, E., Acts 6:1 - 8:4. The Author's Method of Composition (Missoula 1978) 126-28. GEORGI, D., "Weisheit Salomos" in: JüdSchr III/4 (1980) 9n.8b.

7:45 DELLING, G. Die Zueignung des Heils in der Taufe (1961) 87. METZGER, B. M., The Early Versions of the New Testament (Oxford 1977) 253. RICHARD, E., Acts 6:1 - 8:4. The Author's Method of Composition (Missoula 1978) 128-30.

7:46.47 BRAUN, H. Qumran und NT II (1966) 158, 183, 221, 288, 293.

7:46 DUPONT, J. Etudes sur les Actes des Apôtres (1967) 25, 269, 282, 284, 285. RICHARD, E., Acts 6:1 - 8:4. The Author's Method of Composition (Missoula 1978) 130-32.

7:47-48 FLEW, R. N. Jesus and His Church (1956) 40.

7:47 RICHARD, E., Acts 6:1 - 8:4. The Author's Method of Composition (Missoula 1978) 132. VIELHAUER, P., "Oikodome. Das Bild vom Bau in der christlichen Literatur vom Neuen Testament bis Clemens Alexandrinus" in: G. Klein (ed.) Oikodome. FS. P. Vielhauer (München 1979) 54.

7:48-52 THORNTON, T. C. G., "Stephen's Use of Isaiah LXVI. 1" JThS 25 (1974) 432-34.

7:48-50 CONZELMANN, H. Die Apostelgeschichte (1963) 50.

   7:48 GAERTNER, B. The Areopagus speech and natural revelation (1955) 208f. KNOX, W. L. The Sources of the Synoptic Gospels II (1957) 41. LE DEAUT, R. "Actes 7,48 et Matthieu 17,4 (par.) à la lumière du targum palestinien," RechSR (1, 1964) 85-90. McNAMARA, M. The New Testament and the Palestinian Targum to the Pentateuch (1966) 32 n.158. NICKELS, P. Targum and New Testament (1967) 63. HENGEL, M. Judentum und Hellenismus (1969) 540. ET: Judaism and Hellenism (1974) I 296. KILGALLEN, J., The Stephen Speech (Rome 1976) 91-95, 115-19. METZGER, B. M., The Early Versions of the New Testament (Oxford 1977) 141. RICHARD, E., Acts 6:1 - 8:4. The Author's Method of Composition (Missoula 1978) 132-34. "Benediktionen" in: TRE 5 (1980) 571.

7:49-50 DAVIES, W. D., The Gospel and the Land (London 1974) 271. RICHARD, E., Acts 6:1 - 8:4. The Author's Method of Composition (Missoula 1978) 134-35. HOLTZ, T. Untersuchungen über die Alttestamentlichen Zitate bei Lukas (1968) 29-31.

  7:51ff. SCHUETZ, F. Der leidende Christus (1969) 34ff.

7:51-58 GIRARD, R., "Les malédiction contre les Pharisien et la révélation évangélique" Bulletin du Centre Protestant d'Etudes 27 (Geneva 1975) 5-29.

7:51-53 GNILKA, J. Die Verstockung Isarels (1961) 144f. BIHLER, J. Die Stephanusgeschichte (1963) 77-81. HOLTZ, T. Untersuchungen über die Alttestamentlichen Zitate bei Lukas (1968) 109-27. WILCKENS, U. Die Missionsreden der Apostelgeschichte (³1974) 200, 201, 214, 215, 216. WILLIAMS, J. A., A Conceptual History of Deuteronomism in the Old Testament, Judaism, and the New Testament (Ph. D. Diss., Louisville 1976) 256. RICHARD, E., Acts 6:1 - 8:4. The Author's Method of Composition (Missoula 1978) 137-41, 199-203. VIA, E. J., "An Interpretation of Acts 7:35-37 from the Perspective of Major Themes in Luke-Acts" in: P. J. Achtemeier (ed.) SBL Seminar Papers 1978/II (Missoula 1978) 213, 213n.11.

7:51-52 SCHELKLE, K. H. Die Passion Jesu in der Verkündigung des Neuen Testament (1949) 28f. WILCKENS, U. Die Missionsreden der Apostelgeschichte (1961) 31, 102, 109-10, 119, 125, 167. BRAUN, H. Qumran und NT II (1966) 158. BUSSE, U., Das Nazareth-Manifest Jesu (Stuttgart 1978) 100-01. HUBBARD, B. J., "Luke, Josephus and Rome: A Comparative Approach to the Lukan Sitz im Leben" in: P. J. Achtemeier (ed.) SBL Seminar Papers 1979/I (Missoula 1979) 65. "Beschneidung" in: TRE 5 (1980) 721.

   7:51 HESSE, F. Das Verstockungsproblem im Alten Testament (1955)

3, 4, 5, 16, 23. BLAIR, E. P. Jesus in the Gospel of Matthew (1960) 145. CONZELMANN, H. Die Mitte der Zeit (1964) 82ff. RICHARD, E., Acts 6:1 - 8:4. The Author's Method of Composition (Missoula 1978) 137-38.

7:52 VOLZ, P. Die Eschatologie der jüdischen Gemeinde (1934) 187. KNOX, W. L. The Sources of the Synoptic Gospels II (1957) 13. SCHWEIZER, E. Erniedrigung und Erhöhung bei Jesus und seinen Nachfolgern (1962) § 4b. EPP, E. J. The theological tendency of Codex Bezae Cantabrigiensis in Acts (1966) 51n, 2, 95f., 170. DUPONT, J. Etudes sur les Actes des Apôtres (1967) 110, 147, 252, 260, 281, 350. NICKELS, P. Targum and New Testament (1967) 63. POPKES, W. Christus Traditus (1967) 143, 174, 184ff., 228. SCHUETZ, F. Der leidende Christus (1969) 33f., 83f., 102, 134f. KRAENKL, E. Jesus der Knecht Gottes (1972) 68, 108, 112f., 146, 207f. PATSCH, H. Abendmahl und historischer Jesus (1972) 204f. RUPPERT, L., Jesus als der leidende Gerechte? (Stuttgart 1972) 13, 47, 70. ZIESLER, J. A. The Meaning of Righteousness in Paul (1972) 136f., 146. SCHNIDER, F. Jesus der Prophet (1973) 125, 130, 237f. WILSON, S. G. The Gentiles and the Gentile Mission in Luke-Acts (1973) 133-34. WILCKENS, U. Die Missionsreden der Apostelgeschichte (³1974) 102, 110, 120, 168, 201, 206, 220. BEYSCHLAG, K., Simon Magus und die christliche Gnosis (Tübingen 1974) 70n.145. ''Apostelgeschichte'' in: TRE 3 (1978) 488. HORTON, F. L., ''Reflections on the Semitisms of Luke-Acts'' in: C. H. Talbert (ed.) Perspectives on Luke-Acts (Danville 1978) 21. RICHARD, E., Acts 6:1 - 8:4. The Author's Method of Composition (Missoula 1978) 138-40. WILCH, J. R., ''Jüdische Schuld am Tode Jesu—Antijudaismus in der Apostelgeschichte?'' in: W. Haubeck/M. Bachmann (eds.) Wort in der Zeit. FS. K. H. Rengstorf (Leiden 1980) 240-41.

7:53 BLAIR, E. P. Jesus in the Gospel of Matthew (1960) 147. DELLING, G. Die Zueignung des Heils in der Taufe (1961) 84f. WILCKENS, U. Die Missionsreden der Apostelgeschichte (³1974) 201, 208, 215, 216, 217. METZGER, B. M., The Early Versions of the New Testament (Oxford 1977) 145. RICHARD, E., Acts 6:1 - 8:4. The Author's Method of Composition (Missoula 1978) 140. BERGER, K. ''Das Buch der Jubiläen'' in: JüdSchr II/3 (1981) 319n. 27b.

7:54 - 8:4 RICHARD, E., Acts 6:1 - 8:4. The Author's Method of Composition (Missoula 1978) 19-22, 224-29, 274-304.

7:54 - 8:3 HENGEl, M., ''Zwischen Jesus und Paulus. Die 'Hellenisten', die 'Sieben' und Stephanus (Apg 6,1-15; 7,54 - 8,3)'' ZThK 72 (1975) 151-206. SCHNEIDER, G. Die Apostelgeschichte. I (Freiburg/

Basel/Wien 1980) 469-70 (lit!). WEISER, A., Die Apostelge-schichte. I (Gütersloh/Würzburg 1981) 189 (lit!).

7:54-8:2 BIHLER, J. Die Stephanusgeschichte (1963) 7-29.

7:54 - 8:1 SHEPARD, J. W., The Life and Letters of St. Paul (Grand Rapids 1950) 59-60.

7:54-60 "Apostelgeschichte" in: TRE 3 (1978) 497, 498. RICHARD, E., Acts 6:1 - 8:4. The Author's Method of Composition (Missoula 1978) 20-21. PRAST, F., Presbyter und Evangelium in nachapostolischer Zeit (Stuttgart 1979) 224n.5.

7:54-58 CONZELMANN, H. und LINDEMANN, A., Arbeitsbuch zum Neuen Testament (Tübingen 1975) 102. DUPONT, D. J., The Salvation of the Gentiles (New York 1979) 114.

7:54-55 DÖMER, M., Das Heil Gottes (Köln/Bonn 1978) 164.

7:54 GOULDER, M. D. Type and History in Acts (1964) 23, 25f., 46, 74. "Apostelgeschichte" in: TRE 3 (1978) 490.

7:55-60 LANGEVIN, P.-E. "Etienne, témoin du Seigneur Jésus. Ac 7,55-60," AsS 29 (1973) 19-24.

7:55-56 OWEN, H. P. "Stephen's Vision in Acts VII,55f.," NTS 1 (3, 1955) 224-26. HAHN, F. Christologische Hoheitstitel (1963) 128. PESCH, R. "Die Vision des Stephanus Apg 7,55f. im Rahmen der Apostelgeschichte," BuL 6 (2, 1965) 92-107; (3, 1965) 170-83. PERRIN, N. NTS 12 (1965-1966) 151f. PESCH, R. Die Vision des Stephanus (1966). MARTIN, R. P. Carmen Christi (1967) 312f. DUPONT, J. Etudes sur les Actes des Apôtres (1967) 267, 282, 284, 293, 381. LENTZEN-DEIS, F. Die Taufe Jesu nach den Synoptikern (1970) 114. KRAENKL, E. Jesus der Knecht Gottes (1972) 152-56, 169f., 172, 207. ZMIJEWSKI, J. Die Eschatolo-giereden des Lukas-Evangeliums (1972) 166-68, 171, 246, 318. ALSUP, J. E., The Post-Resurrection Appearance Stories of the Gospel-Tradition (Stuttgart 1975) 83-84. GOURGUES, M., A la droite de Dieu. Résurrection de Jésus et actualisation du Psaume 110:1 dans le Nouveau Testament (Paris 1978).

7:55 STONEHOUSE, N. B. The Witness of Matthew and Mark to Christ (1944) 242. BLAIR, E. P. Jesus in the Gospel of Matthew (1960) 154. O'NEILL, J. C. The Theology of Acts in its historical setting (1970) 89, 91-92. SCHMITHALS, W., "Zur Herkunft der gnos-tischen Elemente in der Sprache des Paulus" in: B. Aland et al. (eds.) Gnosis, FS. H. Jonas (Göttingen 1978) 412. BÖHLIG, A., Die Gnosis III: Der Manichäismus (Zürich/München 1980) 344 n.78.

7:56 MOORE, G. F. Judaism I (1946) 335n. BLAIR, E. P. Jesus in the Gospel of Matthew (1960) 68, 75, 154. ROBINSON, J. M. Kerygma und historischer Jesus (1960) 123. HAHN, F. Christologi-

sche Hoheitstitel (1963) 26, 38, 291. HAHN, F. Das Verständnis
der Mission im Neuen Testament (²1965) 55. HIGGINS, A. J. B.
Menschensohn-Studien (1965) 11-16. KILPATRICK, G. D. "Acts
vii. 56: Son of Man?" ThZ 21 (3, 1965) 209. BOUSSET, W. Die
Religion des Judentums im Späthellenistischen Zeitalter
(1966 = 1926) 268. JUENGEL, E. Paulus und Jesus (1966) 234.
O'NEILL, J. C. The Theology of Acts in its historical setting (1970)
91-92. JEREMIAS, J. Neutestamentliche Theologie I (1971) 252f.,
260, 286. RUPPERT, L., Jesus als der leidende Gerechte? (Stuttgart 1972) 70. WILSON, S. G. The Gentiles and the Gentile Mission in Luke-Acts (1973) 77-78. BEYSCHLAG, K., Simon Magus
und die christliche Gnosis (Tübingen 1974) 42, 43n.74. LADD, G.
E., A Theology of the New Testament (Grand Rapids 1974) 146,
304, 337. GOPPELT, L., Theologie des Neuen Testaments. I
(Göttingen 1975) 227-28. KLIJN, A. F. J., "Die syrische Baruch-
Apokalypse" in: JüdSchr V/2 (1976) 138n.1a. FISCHER, U., Eschatologie und Jenseitserwartung im hellenistischen Diasporajudentum (Berlin 1978) 260. FRIEDRICH, G., "Die Auferweckung
Jesu, eine Tat Gottes oder ein Interpretament der Jünger" in: Auf
das Wort kommt es an (Göttingen 1978) 332. KILPATRICK, G.
D., "Again Acts vii.56: Son of Man?" ThZ 34 (1978) 232. HEN-
GEL, M., Zur urchristlichen Geschichtsschreibung (Stuttgart 1979)
88: ET: J. Bowden (trans.) Acts and the History of Earliest Christianity (London 1979) 104.

7:57-60 CONZELMANN, H. Die Apostelgeschichte (1963) 52f.

7:58-8:5 SAHLIN, H. Der Messias und das Gottesvolk (1945) 354-57.

7:58-8:3 KLEIN, G. Die Zwölf Apostel (1961) 115f.

7:58-60 KOPP, C. "Steinigung und Grab des Stephanus," ThG 55 (4, 1965)
260-70.

7:58 DIBELIUS, M. Aufsätze zur Apostelgeschichte (1951) 175f.
BURCHARD, C. Der dreizehnte Zeuge (1970) 26ff. BARDTKE,
H., "Zusätze zu Ester" in: JüdSchr I/1 (1973) 52n. 18a. BA-
GATTI, B., "Nuove testimonianze sul luogo della lapidazione di
S. Stefano" Antonianum 49 (1974) 527-32. NELLESSEN, E.
Zeugnis für Jesus und das Wort (Köln 1976) 54-58.

7:58a Jüdische Schriften aus hellenistisch-römischer Zeit I (1, 1973) W.
G. Kümmel ed., 52.

7:59 DALTON, W. J., Christ's Proclamation to the Spirits (Rome 1965)
146-47. O'NEILL, J. C. The Theology of Acts in its historical setting (1970) 89, 92-93. FISCHER, U., Eschatologie und Jenseitserwartung im hellenistischen Diasporajudentum (Berlin 1978)
260).

7:60 HARNACK, A. von, Studien zur Geschichte des Neuen Testaments und der Alten Kirche (1931) 92ff. HAUBST, R. "Eschatologie. 'Der Wetterwinkel'—'Theologie der Hoffnung', TThZ 77 (1968) 35-65.

8-15 SELBY, D. J., Introduction to the New Testament (New York 1971) 295-300.

8:1-12:25 GUTBROD, K. Die Apostelgeschichte (1968) 25ff.

8-10 KAESEMANN, E. Exegetische Versuche und Besinnungen (1964) I 131.

8 VOLZ, P. Die Eschatologie der jüdischen Gemeinde (1934) 55. RUDOLPH, K. Die Mandäer I (1960) 101. GOULDER, M. D. Type and History in Acts (1964) 67, 73, 175f. DAVIES, W. D., The Sermon on the Mount (Cambridge 1966) 67-68. KUENZI, M. Das Naherwartungslogion Matthäus 10,23 (1970) 40, 45, 113, 151. CULLMANN, O., Der johanneische Kreis (Tübingen 1975) 45, 51, 52, 62. PFITZNER, V. C. " 'Pneumatic' Apostleship? Apostle and Spirit in the Acts of the Apostles" in: W. Haubeck/M. Bachmann (eds.) Wort in der Zeit. FS. K. H. Rengstorf (Leiden 1980) 222-26. SCHILLEBEECKX, E., Christ: the Christian Experience in the Modern World (London 1980) 319-20; GT: Christus und die Christen (Freiburg/Basel/Wien 1977) 306-08.

8:1ff. ORLINSKY, H. M./SNAITH, N. H. Studies on the Second Part of the Book of Isaiah (1967) 93f. HENGEL, M. Judentum und Hellenismus (1969) 492. ET: Judaism and Hellenism (1974) II 180. LAUB, F., Eschatologische Verkündigung und Lebensgestaltung nach Paulus (1973) 47f.

8:1-25 SHEPHARD, J. W., The Life and Letters of St. Paul (Grand Rapids 1950) 81-83.

8:1-4 WILSON, S. G. The Gentiles and the Gentile Mission in Luke-Acts (1973) 143, 152, 169, 258.

8:1.4f. DELLING, G. Die Taufe im Neuen Testament (1963) 64.

8:1.4 VAN UNNIK, W. C. "Kruising van eenzaamheid en gemeenschap in het Nieuwe Testament," Vox Theol 28 (1957-1958) 81-86.

8:1 ADLER, N., Taufe und Handauflegung. Eine exegetisch-theologische Untersuchung von Apg 8,14-17 (Münster 1951) 33, 40-41, 45, 48. FARRER, A. St Matthew and St Mark (1954) 53, 54.

CULLMANN, O. NTS 5 (1958-1959) 161ff. BLAIR, E. P. Jesus in the Gospel of Matthew (1960) 144. SCHMITHALS, W. Paulus und Jakobus (1963) 11f. EPP, E. J. The theological tendency of Codex Bezae Cantabrigiensis in Acts (1966) 128f., 134, 137, 168. BURCHARD, C. Der dreizehnte Zeuge (1970) 26ff. O'NEILL, J. C. The Theology of Acts in its historical setting (1970) 88-89. JER-VELL, J. "The Lost Sheep of the House of Israel" in: Luke and the People of God (Minneapolis 1972) 113-32. WILSON, S. G. The Gentiles and the Gentile Mission in Luke-Acts (1973) 137-38, 142, 157, 168. DUNN, J. D. G., Unity and Diversity in the New Testament (London 1977) 355. METZGER, B. M., The Early Versions of the New Testament (Oxford 1977) 179. THEISSEN, G., Soziologie der Jesusbewegung (München 1977) 17. "Amt" in: TRE 2 (1978) 514. HENGEL, M., Zur urchristlichen Geschichtsschreibung (Stuttgart 1979) 66; ET: J. Bowden (trans.) Acts and the History of Earliest Christianity (London 1979) 74. PRAST, F., Presbyter und Evangelium in nachapostolischer Zeit (Stuttgart 1979) 323.

8:2 DELLING, G. Die Zueignung des Heils in der Taufe (1961) 91. WILCOX, M. The Semitisms of Acts (1965) 136-37, 153, 171. NICKELS, P. Targum and New Testament (1967) 63. O'NEILL, J. C. The Theology of Acts in its historical setting (1970) 88-89.

8:3 DIBELIUS, M. Aufsätze zur Apostelgeschichte (1951) 207f. ET: Studies in the Acts of the Apostles (1956) 207f. WIKENHAUSER, A. Die Apostelgeschichte (1951) 75. BURCHARD, C. Der dreizehnte Zeuge (1970) 40-42. ZINGG, P. Das Wachsen der Kirche (Freiburg 1974) 150. SWIDLER, L., Biblical Affirmations of Woman (Philadelphia 1979) 275, 292.

8:4ff. HENGEL, M. Judentum und Hellenismus (1969) 569. ET: Judaism and Hellenism (1974) I 313.

8:4-25 SCHILLE, G. Anfänge der Kirche (1966) 73ff. BIEDER, W., Die Verheissung der Taufe im Neuen Testament (Zürich 1966) 124-30. SCHNEIDER, G., Die Apostelgeschichte I (Freiburg/Basel/Wien 1980) 481 (lit!). POUPON, G., "L'accusation de magie dans les Actes Apocryphes" in: F. Bovon et al (eds.) Les Actes Apocryphes des Apôtres (Geneva 1981) 79n.51. WEISER, A., Die Apostelgeschichte I (Gütersloh/Würzburg 1981) 197-98 (lit!).

8:4-24 GARCÍA BAZÁN, F., "En torno a Hechos 8,4-24. Milagro y magia entre los gnósticos" RevBi 40 (1978) 27-38. MÜLLER, U. B., "Zur Rezeption Gesetzeskritischer Jesusüberlieferung im Frühen Christentum" NTS 27 (1981) 166.

8:4-13 DRANE, J. W., "Simon the Samaritan and the Lucan Concept of Salvation History" EQ 57 (1975) 131-37.

8:4-8 EGGER, W., Frohbotschaft und Lehre (Frankfurt 1976) 37.

8:4 ADLER, N., Taufe und Handauflegung. Eine exgetisch-theologische Untersuchung von Apg 8.14-17 (Münster 1951) 32, 41, 45, 52-53. FLEW, R. N. Jesus and His Church (1956) 129, 154n. SCHMITHALS, W. Paulus und Jakobus (1963) 22f. GOULDER, M. D. Type and History in Acts (1964) 69, 159, 216, 235. WILSON, S. G. The Gentiles and the Gentile Mission in Luke-Acts (1973) 61, 129, 138, 143-44, 151, 260. "Amt" in: TRE 2 (1978) 514. SWIDLER, L., Biblical Affirmations of Woman (Philadelphia 1979) 275.

8:5-40 DUPONT, J. The Sources of Acts (1964) 18, 36, 37, 51, 53, 64. BEYSCHLAG, K., Simon Magus und die christliche Gnosis (Tübingen 1974) 7ff, 8n.4, 10n.10, 78, 99ff, 212. "Apostelgeschichte" in: TRE 3 (1978) 498.

8:5-25 ADLER, N., Taufe und Handauflegung. Eine exegetisch-theologische Untersuchung von Apg 8,14-17 (Münster 1951) 21, 25-31. FARRER, A. St Matthew and St Mark (1954) 53. HAHN, F. Das Verständnis der Mission im Neuen Testament (1965²) 38f., 49, 50, 115. SCHREINER, J. Gestalt und Anspruch des Neuen Testaments (1969) 205-09. DUNN, J. D. G. Baptism in the Holy Spirit (1970) 55ff.

8:5-24 KRAFT, H., Die Entstehung des Christentums (Darmstadt 1981) 256-60.

8:5-8 BEYSCHLAG, K., Simon Magus und die christliche Gnosis (Tübingen 1974) 7ff, 8n.4, 10n.10, 78, 99ff, 212.

8:5 ADLER, N., Taufe und Handauflegung. Eine exegetisch-theologische Untersuchung von Apg 8,14-17 (Münster 1951) 25, 33, 35, 36, 38, 44. DELLING, G. Die Zueignung des Heils in der Taufe (1961) 88. DELLING, G. Die Taufe im Neuen Testament (1963) 61. BEYSCHLAG, K., Simon Magus und die christliche Gnosis (Tübingen 1974) 101. RUDOLPH, K., "Simon Magus oder Gnosticus? Zum Stand der Debatte" ThR 42 (1977) 279-359. DÖMER, M., Das Heil Gottes: Studien zur Theologie des lukanischen Doppelwerkes (Köln/Bonn 1978) 166-67.

8:6ff. GEORGI, D. Die Gegner des Paulus im 2. Korinther-Brief (1964) 210f.

8:6-13 TYSON, J. B., "The Problem of Food in Acts: A Study of Literary Patterns with Particular Reference to Acts 6:1-7" in: P. J. Achtemeier (ed.) SBL Seminar Papers 1979/I (Missoula 1979) 73.

8:6-7 BEYSCHLAG, K., Simon Magus und die christliche Gnosis (Tübingen 1974) 101.

8:6 STEINMETZ, F.-J. " 'Sie sahen die Wunder, die er tat' (Apg 8,6). Ereignis und Bedeutung religiöser Krafttaten in unserer Zeit," GuL

46 (2, 1973) 99-114. CRIBBS, F. L., "The Agreements that Exist between John and Acts" in: C. H. Talbert (ed.) Perspectives on Luke-Acts (Danville 1978) 53, 60.

8:7-8 BEYSCHLAG, K., Simon Magus und die christliche Gnosis (Tübingen 1974) 122n.48.

8:8 WILCOX, M. The Semitisms of Acts (1965) 139, 142-43, 154n. NICKELS, P. Targum and New Testament (1967) 63, BEY-SCHLAG, K., Simon Magus und die christliche Gnosis (Tübingen 1974) 101.

8:9ff. VAN UNNIK, W. C. "Die Apostelgeschichte und die Häresien," ZNW 58 (3-4, 1967) 240-46. BEYSCHLAG, K. Simon Magus und die christliche Gnosis (Tübingen 1974) 101n.6. SCHMITHALS, W., "Zur Herkunft der gnostische Elemente in der Sprache des Paulus" in: B. Aland et al. (eds.) Gnosis. FS. H. Jonas (Göttingen 1978) 412.

8:9-25 CONZELMANN, H. Die Apostelgeschichte (1963) 53f. RU-DOLPH, K., Die Gnosis (Göttingen 1978) 292, 312-16.

8:9-24 BEYER, H. W. Die Apostelgeschichte (1947) 55-57. BROWN, S. Apostasy and Perseverance in the Theology of Luke (1969) 110-14. JOHNSON, L. T., The Literary Function in Luke-Acts (Missoula 1977) 137-42. MEEKS, W. A., "Simon Magus in Recent Research" RStR 3 (1977) 137-42. "Apostelgeschichte" in: TRE 3 (1978) 497, 519. PRAST, F., Presbyter und Evangelium in nachapostolischer Zeit (Stuttgart 1979) 168-69. SCHRECKEN-BERG, H., "Flavius Josephus und die lukanischen Schriften" in: W. Haubeck/M. Bachmann (eds.) Wort in der Zeit. FS. K. H. Rengstorf (Leiden 1980) 198-99.

8:9-13 "Antichrist" in: TRE 3 (1978) 22.

8:9-10 BOUSSET, W. Die Religion des Judentums im Späthellenistischen Zeitalter (1966 = 1926) 316, 340. BERGMEIER, R. "Quellen vorchristlicher Gnosis," in: Tradition und Glaube (1971) G. Jeremias ed., 203-08. BEYSCHLAG, K., Simon Magus und die christliche Gnosis (Tübingen 1974) 80n.26, 121.

8:9 STONEHOUSE, N. B. The Witness of Matthew and Mark to Christ (1944) 106. ADLER, N., Taufe und Handauflegung. Eine exegetisch-theologische Untersuchung von Apg 8,14-17 (Münster 1951) 25, 33, 38, 47, 92. BETZ, H. D. Lukian vom Samosata und das Neue Testament (1961) 108, 112. HENGEL, M. Judentum und Hellenismus (1969) 442. ET: Judaism und Hellenism (1974) II 163. BEYSCHLAG, K., Simon Magus und die christliche Gnosis (Tübingen 1974) 8, 101, n.7, 102, n.9, 105.

8:10 BLAIR, E. P. Jesus in the Gospel of Matthew (1960) 163. WIL-COX, M. The Semitisms of Acts (1965) 6, 144, 155-56, 171, 174.

NICKELS, P. Targum and New Testament (1967) 64. KIPPEN-BERG, H. G. Garizim und Synagoge (1971) 122f., 328ff. BEY-SCHLAG, K., Simon Magus und die christliche Gnosis (Tübingen 1974) 8-10, 43-44, 88-89, 93-95, 99-126. DUNN, J. D. Christology in the Making (London 1980) 21, 328n.59.

8:11 STONEHOUSE, N. B. The Witness of Matthew and Mark to Christ (1944) 106. HENGEL, M. Judentum und Hellenismus (1969) 442. ET: Judaism and Hellenism (1974) II 163. BEYSCHLAG, K., Simon Magus und die christliche Gnosis (Tübingen 1974) 89n.26, 101.

8:12-24 BARTH, M. Die Taufe—ein Sakrament? (Zürich 1951) 145-54.

8:12-17 DELLING, G. Die Taufe im Neuen Testament (1963) 64-67.

8:12-13 ADLER, N., Taufe und Handauflegung. Eine exegetisch-theologische Untersuchung von Apg 8,14-17 (Münster 1951) 24-25, 46, 47, 92, 100. FLEW, R. N. Jesus and His Church (1956) 120. DUNN, J. D. G. Baptism in the Holy Spirit (1970) 55, 63, 65f., 96. BARTH, G. Die Taufe in frühchristlicher Zeit (Neukirchen-Vluyn 1981) 11, 38-40, 65, 135.

8:12 DELLING, G. Die Zueignung des Heils in der Taufe (1961) 88, 89f. DELLING, G. Die Taufe im Neuen Testament (1963) 61, 79. HAHN, F. Das Verständnis der Mission im Neuen Testament (²1965) 51. WILSON, S. G. The Gentiles and the Gentile Mission in Luke-Acts (1973) 61, 65, 78-79. WILCKENS, U. Die Missionsreden der Apostelgeschichte (³1974) 183, 206, 207, 236. BEYSCHLAG, K., Simon Magus und die christliche Gnosis (Tübingen 1974) 101, n.5, 6. LADD, G. E., A Theology of the New Testament (Grand Rapids 1974) 111, 331, 333, 345, 350. MERK, O., "Das Reich Gottes in den lukanischen Schriften" in: E. E. Ellis/E. Grässer (eds.) Jesus und Paulus, FS. W. G. Kümmel (Göttingen 1975) 204, 205ff. JEWETT, P. K., Infant Baptism and the Covenant of Grace (Grand Rapids 1978) 53. PRAST, F., Presbyter und Evangelium in nachapostolischer Zeit (Stuttgart 1979) 280-81, 333. RUSSELL, E. A., " 'They believed Philip preaching' (Acts 8.12)" IBS 1 (1979) 169-76.

8:13 STONEHOUSE, N. B. The Witness of Matthew and Mark to Christ (1944) 106. BROWN, S. Apostasy and Perseverance in the Theology of Luke (1969) 40, 46, 110, 112, 121. BEYSCHLAG, K., Simon Magus und die christliche Gnosis (Tübingen 1974) 13n.15, 100, 101n.6, 122. FULLER, D. P., Gospel and Law: Contrast or Continuum? (Grand Rapids 1980) 152. "Apostelgeschichte" in: TRE 3 (1978) 498.

8:14-24:15 ERHARDT, A. The Acts of the Apostles (1969) 45f.

8:14ff. WIKENHAUSER, A. Die Apostelgeschichte (1951) 79f. RU-

DOLPH, K. Die Mandäer I (1960) 77. KAESEMANN, E. Exegetische Versuche und Besinnungen (1963) I 131, 165ff. BEYSCHLAG, K., Simon Magus und die christliche Gnosis (Tübingen 1974) 8n.5. DUNN, J. D. G., Jesus and the Spirit (London 1975) 137, 153, 154-55, 176.

8:14-25 BRAUN, F. M. "Avoir soif et boire (Jn 4,10-14; 7,37-39)," in: Mélanges Bibliques en hommage au R. P. Béda Rigaux (1970) A. Descamps/A. de Halleux eds., 249-51. DIETRICH, W. Das Petrusbild der lukanischen Schriften (1972) 245-46. "Apostelgeschichte" in: TRE 3 (1978) 498. HENGEL, M., Zur urchristlichen Geschichtsschreibung (Stuttgart 1979) 80; ET: J. Bowden (trans.) Acts and the History of Earliest Christianity (London 1979) 93-94. PRAST, F., Presbyter und Evangelium in nachapostolischer Zeit (Stuttgart 1979) 320, 324. TYSON, J. B., "The Problem of Food in Acts: A Study of Literary Patterns with Particular Reference to Acts 6:1-7" in: P. J. Achtemeier (ed.) SBL Seminar Papers 1979/I (Missoula 1979) 73. BARTH, G., Die Taufe in frühchristlicher Zeit (Neukirchen-Vluyn 1981) 60, 65-67, 71.

8:14-18 KREMER, J., Pfingstbericht und Pfingstgeschehen. Eine exegetische Untersuchung zu Apg 2,1-13 (Stuttgart 1973) 198-201.

8:14-17 ADLER, N., Taufe und Handauflegung. Eine exegetisch-theologische Untersuchung von Apg 8,14-17 (Münster 1951) passim. FLEW, R. N. Jesus and His Church (1956) 132n., 154n. JEWETT, P. K., Infant Baptism and the Covenant of Grace (Grand Rapids 1978) 188.

8:14 DELLING, G. Die Taufe im Neuen Testament (1963) 69. GOULDER, M. D. Type and History in Acts (1964) 26, 74, 76, 87. BROWN, R. E. et al (eds.) Peter in the New Testament (Minneapolis 1973) 45-49. BEYSCHLAG, K., Simon Magus und die christliche Gnosis (Tübingen 1974) 8, 101n.5.

8:15-16 DELLING, G. Die Taufe im Neuen Testament (1963) 68, 69, 76, 118. MOULE, C. F. D., The Holy Spirit (London 1978) 85.

8:16-17 POUPON, G., "L'accusation de magie dans les Actes apocryphes" in: F. Bovon et al (eds.) Les Actes Apocryphes des Apôtres (Geneva 1981) 91.

8:16 DELLING, G. Die Zueignung des Heils in der Taufe (1961) 85f., 89f., 91, 94. EPP, E. J. The theological tendency of Codex Bezae Cantabrigiensis in Acts (1966) 54, 62f. LADD, G. E., A Theology of the New Testament (Grand Rapids 1974) 272, 339, 345. BARTH, G., Die Taufe in frühchristlicher Zeit (Neukirchen-Vluyn 1981) 44, 66, 135.

8:18ff. BEYSCHLAG, K., Simon Magus und die christliche Gnosis (Tübingen 1974) 74.

8:18-24 DELLING, G. Die Taufe im Neuen Testament (1963) 64, 65. DUNN, J. D. G., Jesus and the Spirit (London 1975) 166, 168-69, 181. "Antichrist" in: TRE 3 (1978) 22.

8:18-19 BEYSCHLAG, K., Simon Magus und die christliche Gnosis (Tübingen 1974) 24.

8:18 BEYSCHLAG, K., Simon Magus und die christliche Gnosis (Tübingen 1974) 8, 69n.143, 79n.1, 187-88.

8:20-23 FULLER, D. P., Gospel and Law: Contrast or Continuum? (Grand Rapids 1980) 152.

8:20-22 DUPONT, D. J., The Salvation of the Gentiles (New York 1979) 65-66.

8:20.22 DELLING, G. Die Zueignung des Heils in der Taufe (1961) 85, 87.

8:20 BEYSCHLAG, K., Simon Magus und die christliche Gnosis (Tübingen 1974) 10n.10, 74n.160, 78, 96, 187. METZGER, B. M., The Early Versions of the New Testament (Oxford 1977) 245.

8:21 CAVALLIN, H. C. C., Life After Death I (Lund 1975) 7, 2n.16. WILCOX, M. The Semitisms of Acts (1965) 102-05, 110, 171.

8:22 NICKELS, P. Targum and New Testament (1967) 64. SCHNEIDER, G., "Gott und Christus als κύριος nach der Apostelgeschichte" in: J. Zmijewski/E. Nellessen (eds.) Begegnung mit dem Wort. FS. H. Zimmermann (Bonn 1980) 163, 168-69, 171-72.

8:23 PALLIS, A., Notes on St. Luke and the Acts (London 1928) 59. DELLING, G. Die Zueignung des Heils in der Taufe (1961) 84f. DUPONT, J. Etudes sur les Actes des Apôtres (1967) 222, 233, 234, 521, 524.

8:24 CLARK, A. C. The Acts of the Apostles (1933) 227, 242, 312, 317. DELLING, G. Die Zueignung des Heils in der Taufe (1961) 87. BEYSCHLAG, K., Simon Magus und die christliche Gnosis (Tübingen 1974) 13n.14, 69n.143. SCHNEIDER, G., "Gott und Christus als κύριος nach der Apostelgeschichte" in: J. Zmijewski/E. Nellessen (eds.) Begegnung mit dem Wort. FS. H. Zimmermann (Bonn 1980) 168-69, 171-72.

8:25-40 MÍNGUEZ, D., "Hechos 8,25-40. Análisis estructural del relato" Biblica 57 (1976) 168-91.

8:25 FLEW, R. N. Jesus and His Church (1956) 154n. HAENCHEN, E. MTS 7 (1960-1961) 190f. NELLESSEN, E., Zeugnis für Jesus und das Wort (Köln 1976) 93-95.

8:26-40 SHEPARD, J. W., The Life and Letters of St. Paul (Grand Rapids 1950) 83-85. BARTH, M., Die Taufe - ein Sakrament? (Zürich 1951) 159-60. SQUILLACI, D. "La conversione dell'Etiope. Att. 8,26-40," PaC1 39 (22, 1960) 1197-1201. GRASSI, J. S. "Emmaus Revisited (Luke 24,13-35 and Acts 8,26-40)," CBQ 26 (4, 1964) 463-67. SURKAU, H. W. GPM 18 (2, 1964) 250-57. HAHN, F. Das Verständnis der Mission im Neuen Testament (²1965) 49, 50, 51f., 116. EHRHARDT, A. The Acts of the Apostels (1969) 46f. RESE, M. Alttestamentliche Motive in der Christologie der Lukas (1969) 97-104. HAHN, F. GPM 24/3 (1970-1971) 309-16. WILSON, S. G. The Gentiles and the Gentile Mission in Luke-Acts (1973) 171-72. WANKE, J., Die Emmauserzählung. Eine redaktionsgeschichtliche Untersuchung zu Lk 24,13-35 (Leipzig 1973) 7, 11, 53, 57, 68, 119, 121-22, n. 315. ALSUP, J. E., The Post-Resurrection Appearance Stories of the Gospel-Tradition (Stuttgart 1975) 84. DINKLER, E., "Philippus und der ANHP AIΘΙΟΨ (Apg 8,26-40). Historische und geographische Bemerkungen zum Missionsablauf nach Lukas" in: E. E. Ellis/E. Grässer (eds.) Jesus und Paulus. FS. W. G. Kümmel (Göttingen 1975) 85-95. GEENSE, A., in: GPM 30 (1976) 310-17. TER-NEDDEN-AMSLER, B. und SKRIVER, J., in: P. Krusche et al (eds.) Predigtstudien für das Kirchenjahr (1975-1976). IV/2 (Stuttgart 1976) 140-46. CORBIN, M., "Connais-tu ce que tu lis? Une lecture d'Actes 8,v.26 à 40" Christus 24 (1977) 73-85. GRÄSSER, E., "Acta-Forschung seit 1960," ThR 42 (1977) 1-68. DALY, R. J., Christian Sacrifice (Washington 1978) 226. DÖMER, M., Das Heil Gottes: Studien zur Theologie des lukanischen Doppelwerkes (Köln/Bonn 1978) 167. SCHMITHALS, W., "Zur Herkunft der gnostischen Elemente in der Sprache des Paulus" in: B. Aland et al (eds.) Gnosis. FS. H. Jonas (Göttingen 1978) 411. de MEESTER, P., "Le pèlerin d'Ethiopie. Essai d'une interprétation 'africaine' des Actes 8,26-40" Telema 18 (1979) 5-18. SCHNEIDER, G., Die Apostelgeschichte I (Freiburg/Basel/Wien 1980) 496 (lit!). KRAFT, H., Die Entstehung des Christentums (Darmstadt 1981) 260-62. de MEESTER, P., "Phillipe et l'eunuque éthiopien' ou 'Le baptême d'un pélerin de Nubie'?" NRTh 103 (1981) 360-74. MÜLLER, U. B., "Zur Rezeption Gesetzeskritischer Jesusüberlieferung im frühen Christentum" NTS 27 (1981) 166-67. WEISER, A., Die Apostelgeschichte I (Gütersloh/Würzburg 1981) 207 (lit!).

8:26-39 ADLER, N., Taufe und Handauflegung. Eine exegetisch-theologische Untersuchung von Apg 8,14-17 (Münster 1951) 12, 24, 41, 47, 54, 102. DIBELIUS, M. Aufsätze zur Apostelgeschichte (1951) 20f. ET: Studies in the Acts of the Apostles (1956) 15f. KRAUS, H.-J. in: Herr, tue meine Lippen auf Bd. 4 (1965) G. Eichholz ed., 378ff. GIBBS, J. M., "Luke 24:13-33 and Acts 8:26-39: The Emmaus Incident and the Eunuch's Baptism as Parallel Stories" Bangalore Theological Forum 7 (1975) 17-30. "Apostelgeschichte" in:

TRE 3 (1978) 496. GIBBS, J. M., "Canon Cuming's 'Service-Endings in the Epistles'-A Rejoinder" NTS 24 (1978) 545-47. KRAUSS, M. und WIEDMANN, H.-G., in: P. Krusche et al (eds.) Predigtstudien für das Kirchenjahr 1981-1982. IV/2 (Stuttgart 1982) 139-47. TRAUB, H., in: GPM 36 (1981-1982) 202-09.

8:26-30 HUBBARD, B. J., "The Role of Commissioning Accounts in Acts" in: C. H. Talbert (ed.) Perspectives on Luke-Acts (Danville 1978) 190, 193, 196.

8:26-27 VAN UNNIK, W. C. "Der Befehl an Philippus," ZNW 47 (1956) 181-91.

8:26 KNOX, W. L. The Sources of the Synoptic Gospels II (1957) 40. GOULDER, M. D. Type and History in Acts (1964) 70, 74, 79, 156. TRIGGER, B. G., "La Candace, personnage mystérieux" Archéologia 77 (1974) 10-17. DINKLER, E., "Phillippus und der ANHP AIΘIOΨ (Apg 8,26-40)" in: E. E. Ellis/E. Grässer (eds.) Jesus und Paulus. FS. W. G. Kümmel (Göttingen 1975) 86, 88-89. GASQUE, W., A History of the Criticism of the Acts of the Apostles (Tübingen 1975) 39, 70, 121.

8:27-39 "Bekehrung" in: TRE 5 (1980) 443.

8:27 ULLENDORFF, E. "Candace (Acts VIII, 27) and the Queen of Sheba," NTS 2 (1955-1956) 53ff. DELLING, G. Die Taufe im Neuen Testament (1963) 70. BARDTKE, H., "Zusätze zu Esther" in: JüdSchr I/1 (1973) 36n.1d. METZGER, B. M., The Early Versions of the New Testament (Oxford 1977) 147, 196. "Apostelgeschichte" in: TRE 3 (1978) 502.

8:28-30 HARNISCH, W. Eschatologische Existenz (1973) 123, 123A, 124, 124A, 125.

8:28 RAHNER, E./THUESIN, W. Christologie-systematisch und exegetisch (1972) 225f.

8:29 CONZELMANN, H. und LINDEMANN, A., Arbeitsbuch zum Neuen Testament (Tübingen 1975) 399.

8:30 WANKE, J., Die Emmauserzählung. Eine redaktionsgeschichtliche Untersuchung zu Lk 24,13-35 (Leipzig 1973) 60. TRUMMER, P., " 'Verstehst du auch, was du liest?' (Apg 8,30)" Kairos 22 (1980) 103-13.

8:30-35 FLEW, R. N. Jesus and His Church (1956) 122.

8:32-35 HAHN, F. Christologische Hoheitstitel (1963) 202. KRAENKL, E. Jesus der Knecht Gottes (1972) 113-16, 119f., 126, 128, 207.

8:32-33 HAHN, F. Christologische Hoheitstitel (1963) 54. ORLINKSY, H. M./SNAITH, N. H. Studies in the second part of the Book of Isaiah (1967) 69, 72, 73f. DUPONT, J. Etudes sur les Actes des Apôtres (1967) 109, 260, 272, 281, 334. HOLTZ, T. Untersuchungen über die Alttestamentlichen Zitate bei Lukas (1968) 31-32. SCHUETZ, F. Der leidende Christus (1969) 93, 102ff. DUPONT, D. J., The Salvation of the Gentiles (New York 1979) 141.

8:32 SCHWEIZER, E. Erniedrigung und Erhöhung bei Jesus und seinen Nachfolgern (1962) § 6b. MIKALSEN, T. "The Traditio-Historical Place of the Christology of 1 Peter in the Light of 1:18-21," (Rüschlikon 1971) 51f. GLÖCKNER, R., Die Verkündigung des Heils beim Evangelisten Lukas (Mainz 1975) 100, 171ff, 193, 211-12.

8:35-36 DELLING, G. Die Taufe im Neuen Testament (1963) 60.

8:35 EPP, E. J. The theological tendency of Codex Bezae Cantabrigiensis in Acts (1966) 54, 62f., 117f., 155. METZGER, B. M., The Early Versions of the New Testament (Oxford 1977) 141.

8:36-38 DELLING, G. Die Taufe im Neuen Testament (1963) 68-70. BIEDER, W., Die Verheissung der Taufe im Neuen Testament (Zürich 1966) 179-85. METZGER, B. M., Manuscripts of the Greek Bible (Oxford 1981) 96.

8:36-37 DELLING, G. Die Zueignung des Heils in der Taufe (1961) 10.

8:36 KNOX, W. L. The Sources of the Synoptic Gospels II (1957) 59. RUDOLPH, K. Die Mandäer I (1960) 232; II (1961) 394,4. BARTH, G., Die Taufe in frühchristlicher Zeit (Neukirchen-Vluyn 1981) 40, 134, 143.

8:37 CLARK, A. C. The Acts of the Apostles (1933) 244, 265, 276, 280, 317. WAINWRIGHT, A. W. The Trinity in the New Testament (1962) 179-80. DELLING, G. Die Taufe im Neuen Testament (1963) 78. HAHN, F. Christologische Hoheitstitel (1963) 318. WENGST, K. Christologische Formeln und Lieder des Urchristentums (1972) 105-07. DUNN, J. D. G., Unity and Diversity in the New Testament (London 1977) 55, 144.

8:38-39 HARNISCH, W. Eschatologische Existenz (1973) 124f.

8:38 DELLING, G. Die Taufe im Neuen Testament (1963) 74. KLIJN, A. F. J., "Die syrische Baruch-Apokalypse" in: JüdSchr V/2 (1976) 126n.3b. BARTH, G., Die Taufe in frühchristlicher Zeit (Neukirchen-Vluyn 1981) 11, 38, 45, 47, 128.

8:39 CLARK, A. C. The Acts of the Apostles (1933) 264, 265, 295, 312, 345. BETZ, H. D. Lukian von Samosata und das Neue Testament (1961) 169. DELLING, G. Die Taufe im Neuen Testament (1963) 69. WILCOX, M. The Semitisms of Acts (1965) 137-38, 153, 171. EPP, E. J. The theological tendency of Codex Bezae Cantabrigiensis in Acts (1966) 116-198. NICKELS, P. Targum and New Testament (1967) 64. CREHAN, J. H., "The Confirmation of the Ethiopian Eunuch (Acts 8:39)" OCP 195 (1974) 187-95. DUNN, J. D. G., Jesus and the Spirit (London 1975) 153, 171, 176, 188,

401. METZGER, B. M., The Early Versions of the New Testament (Oxford 1977) 141. STAGG, F., "Establishing a Text for Luke-Acts" in: P. J. Achtemeier (ed.) SBL Seminar Papers 1979/ I (Missoula 1979) 55.

8:40 NICKELS, P. Targum and New Testament (1967) 64. "Apostelgeschichte" in: TRE 3 (1978) 498.

9-28 DOCKX, S. "Chronologie de le vie de Saint Paul, depuis conversion jusqu'à son séjour à Rome," NovTest 13 (4, 1971) 261-304.

9-15 SAHLIN, H. Der Messias und das Gottesvolk (1945) 48-50, 366-68.

9-11 SANDERS, J. N. "Peter and Paul in Acts," NTS 2 (1955-1956) 133ff. DIETRICH, W. Das Petrusbild der lukanischen Schriften (1972) 291ff.

9 MUNCK, J. Paul and the Salvation of Mankind (1959) 14f., 17f. GOULDER, M. D. Type and History in Acts (1964) 67, 75, 78, 86, 97. LOHFINK, G. "Eine alttestamentliche Darstellungsform für Gotteserscheinungen in den Damaskusberichten (Apg 9; 22; 26)," BZ 9 (2, 1965) 246-57. BEYSCHLAG, K. Clemens Romanus und der Frühkatholizismus (1966) 223. GUTBROD, K. Die Apostelgeschichte (1968) 48f. KUENZI, M. Das Naherwartungslogion Matthäus 10,23 (1970) 41, 44f., 59. KUEMMEL, W. G. Römer 7 und das Bild des Menschen im Neuen Testament (1974) 149f. BEYSCHLAG, K., Simon Magus und die christliche Gnosis (Tübingen 1974) 79. GILL, D., "The Structure of Acts 9" Biblica 55 (1974) 546-48.

9:1ff. SCHMITHALS, W., "Zur Herkunft der gnostischen Elemente in der Sprache des Paulus" in: B. Aland et al (eds.) Gnosis. FS. H. Jonas (Göttingen 1978) 297.

9:1ff., 15 HAHN, F. Das Verständnis der Mission im Neuen Testament (²1965) 81, 116.

9:1-31 SHEPARD, J. W., The Life and Letters of St. Paul (Grand Rapids 1950) 61-72. TYSON, J. B., "The Problem of Food in Acts: A Study of Literary Patterns with Particular Reference to Acts 6:1-7" in: P. J. Achtemeier (ed.) SBL Seminar Papers 1979/I (Missoula 1979) 73-74.

9:1-30 ROBERTSON, A. T. Luke the Historian in the Light of Research

(1920) 81-84. DUPONT, J. The Sources of Acts (1964) 26, 28, 40, 53, 55, 56, 57, 60, 61, 62, 64, 65, 68, 70, 71, 112. MATTILL, A. J., "The Value of Acts as a Source for the Study of Paul" in: C. H. Talbert (ed.) Perspectives on Luke-Acts (Danville 1978) 84.

9:1-29 GIRLANDA, A. "De Conversione Pauli in Actibus Apostolorum tripliciter narrata," VerbDom 39 (2, 1961) 66-81; (3, 1961) 129-40; (4, 1961) 173-84.

9:1-22 GRASS, H. Ostergeschehen und Osterberichte (1970) 207ff. PANNENBERG, W., in: New Testament Issues (1970) R. Batey ed., 110-22. LOENING, K. Die Saulustradition in der Apostelgeschichte (1973) 48ff. DÖMER, M., Das Heil Gottes: Studien zur Theologie des lukanischen Doppelwerkes (Köln/Bonn 1978) 167-68.

9:1-20 FRICK, R. GPM 18 (2, 1964) 244-50. KRUSE, M. GPM 24/3 (1970-1971) 305-09. FÜRST, W., in: GPM 39 (1976) 304-09. KÜCHLER, E.-A. und RÜCKE, H., in: P. Krusche et al (eds.) Predigtstudien für das Kirchenjahr 1975-1976. IV/2 (Stuttgart 1976) 131-49. BRILL, S. und RAISS, H., in: P. Krusche et al (eds.) Predigtstudien für das Kirchenjahr 1979-1980. II/2 (Stuttgart 1980) 184-91. KRAUS, H. J., in: GPM 34 (1980) 341-46.

9:1-19 SQUILLACI, D. "La conversione di San Paolo (Att. 9,1-19)," PaCl 40 (5, 1961) 233-39. LOHFINK, G. Paulus von Damaskus (1966). SEIDENSTICKER, Ph. Die Auferstehung Jesu in der Botschaft der Evangelisten (1968) 36f. BURCHARD, C. Der dreizehnte Zeuge (1970) 52-88, 121ff., 125ff. DUNN, J. D. G. Baptism in the Holy Spirit (1970) 61, 73ff., 92. LUNDGREN, S. "Ananias and the Calling of Paul in Acts," StTh 25 (2, 1971) 117-22. STOLLE, V. Der Zeuge als Angeklagter (1973) 157, 161. WILSON, S. G. The Gentiles and the Gentile Mission in Luke-Acts (1973) 143, 151, 161-66, 242-43. SABUGAL, S., "La conversion der S. Pablo en Damasco: ciudad de Siria o region de Qumran?" Augustinianum 15 (1975) 213-24. LOHFINK, G., The Conversion of St. Paul: Narrative and History in Acts (Chicago 1976) passim. STECK, O. H., "Formgeschichtliche Bemerkungen zur Darstellung des Damaskusgeschehens in der Apostelgeschichte" ZNW 67 (1976) 20-28. "Apostelgeschichte" in: TRE 3 (1978) 496, 499. GEIGER, G., Kirche Unterwegs. Ein Arbeitsheft zum zweiten Teil der Apostelgeschichte (Klosterneuburg 1981). HEDRICK, C., "Paul's Conversion/Call: A Comparative Analysis of the Three Reports in Acts" JBL 100 (1981) 415-32. MEINARDUS, O. F., "The Site of the Apostle Paul's Conversion at Kaukab" BA 44 (1981) 57-59. WEISER, A., Die Apostelgeschichte I (Gütersloh/Würzburg 1981) 215-16 (lit!).

9:1-9 DAVIES, W. D. Invitation to the New Testament (1966) 254-65.

HUBBARD, B. J., "Commissioning Stories in Luke-Acts: A Study of their Antecedents, Form and Content" in: Semeia 8 (1977) 117-18. HUBBARD, B. J., "The Role of Commissioning Accounts in Acts" in: C. H. Talbert (ed.) Perspectives on Luke-Acts (Danville 1978) 190, 193, 196. MATTILL, A. J., "The Value of Acts as a Source for the Study of Paul" in: C. H. Talbert (ed.) Perspectives on Luke-Acts (Danville 1978) 91. MICHEL, O., "Das Licht des Messias" in: E. Bammel et al (eds.) Donum Gentilicium. FS. D. Daube (Oxford 1978) 40-50.

9:1f.13f.21 KLEIN, G. Die Zwölf Apostel (1961) 120ff., 145ff.

9:1-2 BURCHARD, C. Der dreizehnte Zeuge (1970) 43ff. STOLLE, V. Der Zeuge als Angeklagter (1973) 167-70. SWIDLER, L., Biblical Affirmations of Woman (Philadelphia 1979) 275, 292.

9:1 MUNCK, J. Paul and the Salvation of Mankind (1959) 13f. VAN DER HORST, P. W. "Drohung und Mord schnaubend (Acta IX 1)," NovTest 12 (3, 1970) 257-69.

9:2.5 MINEAR, P. S. Images of the Church in the New Testament (1960) 148f.

9:2 FLEW, R. N. Jesus and His Church (1956) 113. ZON, A. "Ekleziologiczny sens terminu 'Droga' w Dz 9,2,"RBL 17 (4, 1964) 207-15. WILCOX, M. The Semitisms of Acts (1965) 105-06, 110. BRAUN, H. Qumran und NT II (1966) 18, 148, 299. NICKELS, P. Targum and New Testament (1967) 64. STOLLE, V. Der Zeuge als Angeklagter (1973) 118f. HENGEL, M., Zur urchristlichen Geschichtsschreibung (Stuttgart 1979) 68; ET: J. Bowden (trans.) Acts and the History of Earliest Christianity (London 1979) 77.

9:3ff. CONZELMANN, H. Die Apostelgeschichte (1963) 59. BURCHARD, C. Der dreizehnte Zeuge (1970) 88ff.

9:3-22 HENGEL, M., Zur urchristlichen Geschichtsschreibung (Stuttgart 1979) 70-78; ET: J. Bowden (trans.) Acts and the History of Earliest Christianity (London 1979) 81-91.

9:3-19 LEON-DUFOUR, X., The Resurrection and the Message of Easter (London 1974) 62-79.THRALL, M. E. Biblica 53 (3, 1972) 459-60.

9:3-9 RICHTER, H.-F. Auferstehung und Wirklichkeit (1969) 89f.

9:3-7 PAGELS, E. H., "Visions, Appearances and Apostolic Authority: Gnostic and Orthodox Traditions" in: B. Aland et al (eds.) Gnosis. FS. H. Jonas (Göttingen 1978) 415, 418.

9:3-4 STOLLE, V. Der Zeuge als Angeklagter (1973) 171-74.

9:3 MATTILL, A. J., "The Value of Acts as a Source for the Study of Paul" in: C. H. Talbert (ed.) Perspectives on Luke-Acts (Danville 1978) 91.

9:4ff. "Agrapha" in: TRE 2 (1978) 104.

9:4-6 STOLLE, V. Der Zeuge als Angeklagter (1973) 175-77.

9:4-5 BEST, E. One Body in Christ (1955) 133. SCHWEIZER, E. Erniedrigung und Erhöhung bei Jesus und seinen Nachfolgern (1962) § 14e.

9:4 CLARK, A. C. The Acts of the Apostles (1933) 226, 244, 295, 317. TURNER, N. Grammatical Insights into the New Testament (1965) 84ff.

9:5 DELLING, G. Die Zueignung des Heils in der Taufe (1961) 86.

9:6.17.27 KAESEMANN, E. Exegetische Versuche und Besinnungen (1964) I 131.

9:6 MUNCK, J. Paul and the Salvation of Mankind (1959) 15f.

9:7-9 "Bekehrung" in: TRE 5 (1980) 443.

9:7-8 STOLLE, V. Der Zeuge als Angeklagter (1973) 178f.

9:7 MOEHRING, H. R. "The Verb akouein in Acts IX,7 and XXII,9," NovTest 3 (1-2, 1959) 80-99. BRATCHER, R. G. "akouō in Acts ix.7 and xxii.9," ET 71 (8, 1960) 243-45. HEDRICK, C., "Paul's Conversion/Call: A Comparative Analysis of the Three Reports in Acts" JBL 100 (1981) 428-32.

9:9 DELLING, G. Die Taufe im Neuen Testament (1963) 74.

9:10-19 "Apostelgeschichte" in: TRE 3 (1978) 519. HUBBARD, B. J., "The Role of the Commissioning Accounts in Acts" in: C. H. Talbert (ed.) Perspectives on Luke-Acts (Danville 1978) 190, 193, 196.

9:10-17 HUBBARD, B. J., "Commissioning Stories in Luke-Acts: A Study of their Antecedents, Form and Content" in: Semeia 8 (1977) 117-18.

9:10-16 WICKENHAUSER, A. Biblica 28 (1948) 100-11. STAEHLIN, G. "τὸ πνεῦμα 'Iησοῦ (Apostelgeschichte 16:7)," in: Christ and the Spirit in the New Testament (1975) B. Lindars/S. S. Smalley eds., 237ff. STOLLE, V. Der Zeuge als Angeklagter (1973) 166f., 180.

9:10 BEYSCHLAG, K., Simon Magus und die christliche Gnosis (Tübingen 1974) 212.

9:11 METZGER, B. M., The Early Versions of the New Testament (1977) 196.

9:12-18 DELLING, G. Die Taufe im Neuen Testament (1963) 66.

9:12 HEDRICK, C., "Paul's Conversion/Call: A Comparative Analysis of the Three Reports in Acts" JBL 100 (1981) 419, 420, 422.

9:13-16 LOENING, K. Die Saulustradition in der Apostelgeschichte (1973) 26ff.

9:13 STRECKER, G. Der Weg der Gerechtigkeit (1962) 217$_7$.

9:14 DELLING, G. Die Taufe im Neuen Testament (1963) 78. HAHN, F. Christologische Hoheitstitel (1963) 118. GLÖCKNER, R., Die Verkündigung des Heils beim Evangelisten Lukas (Mainz 1975) 237-38.

9:15-16 MUNCK, J. Paul and the Salvation of Mankind (1959) 28f. LOENING, K. Die Saulustradition in der Apostelgeschichte (1973) 32ff. RADL, W., Paulus und Jesus im lukanischen Doppelwerk (Bern/Frankfurt 1975) 69-81. ''Apostelgeschichte'' in: TRE 3 (1978) 499.

9:15 LONGENECKER, R. N. Paul Apostle of Liberty (1964) 252f. LOHFINK, G. '' 'Meinen Namen zu tragen . . . ' (Apg 9, 15),'' BZ 10 (1, 1966) 108-15. SMITH, M. Tannaitic Parallels to the Gospels (1968) 3 b n 58. HEDRICK, C., ''Paul's Conversion/Call: A Comparative Analysis of the Three Reports in Acts'' JBL 100 (1981) 419-22.

9:16 PALLIS, A., Notes on St. Luke and the Acts (London 1928) 60. FLENDER, H. St. Luke Theologian of Redemptive History (1967) 131, 139, 144, 158. WANKE, J., Die Emmauserzählung. Eine redaktionsgeschichtliche Untersuchung zu Lk 24, 13-35 (Leipzig 1973) 169n, 676. DALY, R. J., Christian Sacrifice (Washington D. C. 1978) 226. HEDRICK, C., ''Paul's Conversion/Call: A Comparative Analysis of the Three Reports in Acts'' JBL 100 (1981) 419-22.

9:17-10:25 WILCOX, M. The Semitisms of Acts (1965) 59ff.

9:17-18 DELLING, G. Die Taufe im Neuen Testament (1963) 60, 68, 69, 70, 101. ADLER, N., Taufe und Handauflegung. Eine exegetisch-theologische Untersuchung von Apg 8,14-17 (Münster 1971) 29, 115-16. BARTH, G. Die Taufe in frühchristlicher Zeit (Neukirchen-Vluyn 1981) 11, 38, 40, 60, 67, 126, 136.

9:17 JEWETT, P. K., Infant Baptism and the Covenant of Grace (Grand Rapids 1978) 188. HEDRICK, C., ''Paul's Conversion/Call: A Comparative Analysis of the Three Reports in Acts'' JBL 100 (1981) 419-20, 422.

9:18 HEDRICK, C., ''Paul's Conversion/Call: A Comparative Analysis of the Three Reports in Acts'' JBL 100 (1981) 419, 422, 428, 431.

9:19-31 WEISER, A., Die Apostelgeschichte I (Gütersloh/Würzburg 1981) 229-30 (lit!).

9:19-30 BURCHARD, C. Der dreizehnte Zeuge (1970) 136-61. WAINWRIGHT, A. W., ''The Historical Value of Acts 9:10b-30'' TU 6 (1973) 589-94.

9:19-25 MASSON, C. ''A propos de Act. 9.19b-25. Note sur l'utilisation de Gal. et de 2 Cor. par l'auteur des Actes,'' ThZ 18 (3, 1962) 161-66. STOLLE, V. Der Zeuge als Angeklagter (1973) 162.

9:19 DELLING, G. Die Taufe im Neuen Testament (1963) 74.

9:20 CLARK, A. C. The Acts of the Apostles (1933) 252, 253, 303, 333. BLAIR, E. P. Jesus in the Gospel of Matthew (1960) 64. DELLING, G., Die Zueignung des Heils in der Taufe (1961) 47. de KRUIJF, T., Der Sohn des lebendigen Gottes (Rome 1962) 34, 35, 38, 96, 99. HAHN, F. Christologische Hoheitstitel (1963) 219. CONZELMANN, H. Die Mitte der Zeit (1964) 206ff. EPP, E. J. The theological tendency of Codex Bezae Cantabrigiensis in Acts (1966) 63, 123, 134f. CRIBBS, F. L., ''The Agreements that Exist between John and Acts'' in: C. H. Talbert (ed.) Perspectives in Luke-Acts (Danville 1978) 69.

9:21 DELLING, G. Die Taufe im Neuen Testament (1963) 78. HAHN, F. Christologische Hoheitstitel (1963) 118. BRAUN, H. Qumran und NT II (1966) 162, 213. GLÖCKNER, R., Die Verkündigung des Heils beim Evangelisten Lukas (Mainz 1975) 237-38. MENOUD, P. H., ''Le sens du verbe ΠΟΡΘΕΙΝ'' in: Jésus-Christ et la foi (Neuchâtel-Paris 1975) 40-47.

9:22 WINDISCH, H., ''Die Christusepiphanie vor Damaskus und ihre religionsgeschichtlichen Parallelen'' ZNW 31 (1932) 1-23. DELLING, G. Die Zueignung des Heils in der Taufe (1961) 88. de-KRUIJF, T., Der Sohn des lebendigen Gottes (Rome 1962) 34, 35, 38, 96, 99. HAHN, F. Christologische Hoheitstitel (1963) 219, 224. LOHFINK, J., ''Eine alttestamentliche Darstellungform für Gotteserscheinungen in den Damaskusberichten (Apg 9:22,26)'' BZ 8 (1965) 246-57. EPP, E. J. The theological tendency of Codex Bezae Cantabrigiensis in Acts (1966) 64, 134f. SCHILLE, G. Anfänge der Kirche (1966) 79ff. SMALLEY, S. S. ''The Christology of Acts Again,'' in: Christ and the Spirit in the New Testament (1973) B. Lindars/S. S. Smalley eds., 85f. STECK, O. H., ''Formgeschichtliche Bemerkungen zur Darstellung des Damaskusgeschehens in der Apostelgeschichte'' ZNW 67 (1976) 20-28. CRIBBS, F. L., ''The Agreements that Exist between John and Acts'' in: C. H. Talbert (ed.) Perspectives on Luke-Acts (Danville 1978) 60.

9:23-30 ''Apostelgeschichte'' in: TRE 3 (1978) 519.

9:23-25 JEWETT, R., A Chronology of Paul's Life (Philadelphia 1979) 30-33.

9:23 ''Apostelgeschichte'' in: TRE 3 (1978) 499.

9:24 ''Apostelgeschichte'' in: TRE 3 (1978) 499.

9:25 FARRER, A. St Matthew and St Mark (1954) 68. KUENZI, M.

Das Naherwartungslogion Matthäus 10,23 (1970) 16, 61, 69, 81, 108, 112f. "Apostelgeschichte" in : TRE 3 (1978) 498, 499.

9:26ff. FEINE, P. Der Apostel Paulus (1927) 422ff. CAMBIER, J. "Le Voyage de S. Paul à Jérusalem en Act. ix.26ss. et le Schéma Missionnaire Théologique de S. Luc," NTS 8 (3, 1962) 249-57.

9:26-31 LANGEVIN, P.-E. "Les débuts d'un apôtre. Ac 9,26-31," AssS 26 (1973) 32-38.

9:26-30 MUNCK, J. Paul and the Salvation of Mankind (1959) 80f., 286. KLEIN, G. Die Zwölf Apostel (1961) 162ff. ROLOFF, J. Apostolat-Verkündigung-Kirche (1965) 296f. ECKERT, J. Die Urchristliche Verkündigung im Streit zwischen Paulus und seinen Gegnern nach dem Galaterbrief (1971) 177, 180, 181, 182, 214, 218. DE LACEY, D. R. "Paul in Jerusalem," NTS 20 (1, 1973) 82-86. STOLLE, V. Der Zeuge als Angeklagter (1973) 162f., 164f., 254f. "Apostelgeschichte" in: TRE 3 (1978) 499.

9:26 WINDISCH, H., "Die Christusepiphanie vor Damaskus und ihre religionsgeschichtlichen Parallelen" ZNW 31 (1932) 1-23. LOHFINK, J., "Eine alttestamentliche Darstellungsform für Gotteserscheinungen in den Damaskusberichten (Apg 9:22,26)" BZ 9 (1965) 246-57. KUEMMEL, W. G. Einleitung in das Neue Testament (1973) 263f. STECK, O. H., "Formgeschichtliche Bemerkungen zur Darstellung des Damaskusgeschehens in der Apostelgeschichte" ZNW 67 (1976) 20-28.

9:27ff. HAHN, F. Das Verständnis der Mission im Neuen Testament (²1965) 73f., 116.

9:27-29 PFITZNER, V. C., " 'Pneumatic' Apostleship? Apostle and Spirit in the Acts of the Apostles" in: W. Haubeck/M. Bachmann (eds.) Wort in der Zeit. FS. K. H. Rengstorf (Leiden 1980) 221-22.

9:27-28 DELLING, G. Die Zueignung des Heils in der Taufe (1961) 43, 47, 52, 86, 88, 91.

9:27 DELLING, G. Die Taufe im Neuen Testament (1963) 65. SCHMITHALS, W. Paulus und Jakobus (1963) 23. HAHN, F. Das Verständnis der Mission im Neuen Testament (²1965) 49, 117. "Aramäisch" in: TRE 3 (1978) 604. ELLIGER, W., Paulus in Griechenland (Stuttgart 1978) 175n.58. PRAST, F., Presbyter und Evangelium in nachapostolischer Zeit (Stuttgart 1979) 320. SCHILLEBEECKX, E., Jesus. An Experiment in Christology (London 1979) 360.

9:28-29 SCHILLE, G. Anfänge der Kirche (1966) 79ff.

9:29 MUNCK, J. Paul and the Salvation of Mankind (1959) 218-20, 326. SCHMITHALS, W. Paulus und Jakobus (1963) 19. KASTING, H. Die Anfänge der Urchristlichen Mission (1969) 101f. WILSON, S. G. The Gentiles and the Gentile Mission in Luke-Acts (1973) 140-

41, 149-50. PESCH, R., GERHART, E. und SCHILLING, F., " 'Hellenisten' und 'Hebräer'. Zu Apg 9,29 und 6,1'' BZ 23 (1979) 87-92. TYSON, J. B., "The Problem of Food in Acts: A Study of Literary Patterns with Particular Reference to Acts 6:1-7'' in: P. J. Achtemeier (ed.) SBL Seminar Papers 1979/I (Missoula 1979) 79.

9:31-11:18 DUPONT, J. The Sources of Acts (1964) 28, 29, 31, 38, 40, 51, 54, 55, 60, 61, 64.

9:31ff. KNOX, W. L. The Sources of the Synoptic Gospels II (1957) 136. EHRHARDT, A. The Acts of the Apostles (1969) 47, 65f., 90, 104.

9:31 FARRER, A. St Matthew and St Mark (1954) 53. FLEW, R. N. Jesus and His Church (1956) 128. DELLING, G. Die Zueignung des Heils in der Taufe (1961) 87. SCHMITHALS, W. Paulus und Jakobus (1963) 25. GOULDER, M. D. Type and History in Acts (1964) 106n, 23f., 66-69. HAHN, F. Das Verständnis der Mission im Neuen Testament (^{2}1965) 115f. FLENDER, H. St. Luke Theologian of Redemptive History (1967) 83n, 97, 133, 139. JERVELL, J., "The Lost Sheep of the House of Israel'' in: Luke and the People of God (Minneapolis 1972) 113, 143. ENSLIN, M. S. Reapproaching Paul (1972) 41f. STOLLE, V. Der Zeuge als Angeklagter (1973) 163. DAVIES, W. D. The Gospel and the Land (1974) 412, 421, 422, 425. ZINGG, P., Das Wachsen der Kirche (Freiburg 1974) 30, 32-34. BEYSCHLAG, K., Simon Magus und die christliche Gnosis (Tübingen 1974) 167n.75. "Apostelgeschichte'' in: TRE 3 (1978) 513. RAYAN, S., The Holy Spirit: Heart of the Gospel and Christian Hope (New York 1978) 129. PRAST, F., Presbyter und Evangelium in nachapostolischer Zeit (Stuttgart 1979) 144-45. VIELHAUER, P., "Oikodome. Das Bild vom Bau in der christlichen Literatur vom Neuen Testament bis Clemens Alexandrinus'' in: G. Klein (ed.) Oikodome. FS. P. Vielhauer (München 1979) 105-06. SCHNEIDER, G., "Gott und Christus als κυριος nach der Apostelgeschichte'' in: J. Zmijewski/E. Nellessen (eds.) Begegnung mit dem Wort. FS. H. Zimmermann (Bonn 1980) 163, 169, 171-72. KRAFT, H., Die Entstehung des Christentums (Darmstadt 1981) 280.

9:32-11:18 SHEPARD, J. W., The Life and Letters of St. Paul (Grand Rapids 1950) 85-92. HAENCHEN, E. NTS 7 (1960-1961) 190f. DIETRICH, W. Das Petrusbild der lukanischen Schriften (1972) 256-95. MUSSNER, F., Petrus und Paulus—Pole der Einheit (Freiburg/Basel/Wien 1976) 28-36.

9:32ff.36ff. HAHN, F. Das Verständnis der Mission im Neuen Testament (^{2}1965) 38f.

9:32-43 DÖMER, M., Das Heil Gottes: Studien zur Theologie des lukanischen Doppelwerkes (Köln/Bonn 1978) 168. HENGEL, M., Zur urchristlichen Geschichtsschreibung (Stuttgart 1979) 79-80; ET: J. Bowden (trans.) Acts and the History of Earliest Christianity (London 1979) 93. WEISER, A., Die Apostelgeschichte I (Gütersloh/ Würzburg 1981) 236 (lit!.).

9:32-35 "Apostelgeschichte" in: TRE 3 (1978) 498.

9:32 STRECKER, G. Der Weg der Gerechtigkeit (1962) 217₇. GOULDER, M. D. Type and History in Acts (1964) 24, 26, 66f., 69f., 74, 93, 96, 107. BROWN, R. E. et al (eds.) Peter in the New Testament (Minneapolis 1973) 45-49.

9:33-35 "Apostelgeschichte" in: TRE 3 (1978) 497.

9:34-35 DUPONT, D. J., The Salvation of the Gentiles (New York 1979) 71.

9:34 PALLIS, A., Notes on St. Luke and the Acts (London 1928) 60-61. DELLING, G. Die Zueignung des Heils in der Taufe (1961) 49, 88. DUPONT, J. Etudes sur les Actes des Apôtres (1967) 91, 179, 427, 466.

9:35 DELLING, G. Die Taufe im Neuen Testament (1963) 70. GOULDER, M. D. Type and History in Acts (1964) 69f. Mc-NAMARA, M. The New Testament and the Palestinian Targum to the Pentateuch (1966) 179. DUPONT, J. Etudes sur les Actes des Apôtres (1967) 423, 427, 446, 466.

9:36-43 KRUSE, O., in: GPM 30 (1976) 359-66. STADTLAND, T. und JÖRNS, K-P., in: P. Krusche et al (eds.) Predigtstudien für das Kirchenjahr 1975-1976. IV/2 (Stuttgart 1976) 183-87. CRIBBS, F. L., "The Agreements that Exist between John and Acts" in: C. H. Talbert (ed.) Perspectives on Luke-Acts (Danville 1978) 45, 53-54. KRAFT, H., Die Entstehung des Christentums (Darmstadt 1981) 270-72.

9:36-42 TRAUB, H. GPM 18 (2, 1964) 288-94. HAAR, J. GPM 24/3 (1970-1971) 341-47. "Apostelgeschichte" in: TRE 3 (1978) 498. SWIDLER, L., Biblical Affirmations of Woman (Philadelphia 1979) 214, 299, 305.

9:36-41 DUNN, J. D. G., Jesus and the Spirit (London 1975) 163, 165.

9:36-39 CLARK, S. B., Man and Woman in Christ (Ann Arbor/Mich. 1980) 110, 246.

9:36.40 NICKELS, P. Targum and New Testament (1967) 64.

9:36 WILCOX, M. The Semitisms of Acts (1965) 13n, 109-10, 152, 171, 174. "Aramäisch" in: TRE 3 (1978) 609. SCHRAGE, W., "Die Elia-Apokalypse" in: JüdSchr V/3 (1980) 255n.34h.

9:37 RUDOLPH, K. Die Mandäer II (1961) 416, 5.

9:39 PALLIS, A., Notes on St. Luke and the Acts (London 1928) 61.

9:40 DELLING, G. Die Zueignung des Heils in der Taufe (1961) 50.

HENNECKE, E./SCHNEEMELCHER, W. Neutestamentliche Apokryphen (1964) II 146. WILCOX, M. The Semitisms of Acts (1965) 13n, 109-10, 152, 171, 174, 175. EPP, E. J. The theological tendency of Codex Bezae Cantabrigiensis in Acts (1966) 54, 62f., 157. "Aramäisch" in: TRE 3 (1978) 609. SCHWEIZER, E., Heiliger Geist (Stuttgart 1978) 153.

9:41 BAUMERT, N., Täglich Sterben und Auferstehen. Der Literalsinn von 2 Kor 4,12 - 5,10 (München 1973) 95, 298-99.

9:42 CRIBBS, F. L, ''The Agreements that Exist between John and Acts'' in: C. H. Talbert (ed.) Perspectives on Luke-Acts (Danville 1978) 58.

9:43 EHRHARDT, A. The Acts of the Apostles (1969) 60ff.

─────────────────────

10-11 FEINE, D. P./BEHM, D. J. Einleitung in das Neue Testament (1950) 83f. DELLING, G. Die Taufe im Neuen Testament (1963) 64. SCHILLE, G. Die urchristliche Kollegialmission (1967) 40ff. BARTHES, R. "L'Analyse Structurale du Récit. A propos d'Actes X-XI," RechSR 58 (1, 1970) 17-37. WILSON, S. G. The Gentiles and the Gentile Mission in Luke-Acts (1973) 31-32, 151-52, 172-73, 192-93, 221-23. "Apostelgeschichte" in: TRE 3 (1978) 496. PFITZNER, V. C., " 'Pneumatic' Apostleship? Apostle and Spirit in the Acts of the Apostles" in: W. Haubeck/M. Bachmann (eds.) Wort in der Zeit. FS. K. H. Rengstorf (Leiden 1980) 222-26. DILLON, R. J., "Previewing Luke's Project from His Prologue (Luke 1:1-4)" CBQ 43 (1981) 220.

10:1-11:18 DIBELIUS, M. Aufsätze zur Apostelgeschichte (1951) 96-107, 139-41. ET: Studies in the Acts of the Apostles (1956) 109-22, 161-64. WICKENHAUSER, A. Die Apostelgeschichte (1951) 102. MUNCK, J. Paul and the Salvation of Mankind (1959) 228-31. BOVON, F. De Vocatione Gentium (1967). DUPONT, J. Etudes sur les Actes des Apôtres (1967) 75-81. GRIBOMONT, J. Biblica 50 (1, 1969) 102-05. DE LUBAC, H. "De vocatione gentium," RThPh 19 (5, 1969) 331-32. BURCHARD, C. Der dreizehnte Zeuge (1970) 53-55, 166-68. FENASSE, J. M., "Pièrre et Corneille, le centurion. Une recontre très importante pur le dévelopement futur de l'Église" BTS 41 (1961) 4-5. BOVON, F., "Tradition et rédaction en Acts 10:1 - 11:18" ThZ 36 (1970) 22-45. GRASS, H. Ostergeschehen und Osterberichte (1970) 199ff., 231. HAU-

LOTTE, E. ''Fondation d'une communautée de type universel: Actes 10, 1-11, 18. Etude critique sur la rédaction, la 'structure' et la 'tradition' du récit,'' RechSR 58 (1970) 63-100. MARIN, L., ''Essai structurale d'Actes 10,1-11, 18,'' RechSR 58 (1, 1970) 39-61. COURTES, J. ''Apg 10,1-11, 18 als System mystischer Vorstellungen,'' in: Exegese im Methodenkonflikt (1971) X. Léon-Dufour ed., 142ff. ECKERT,J. Die Urchristliche Verkündigung im Streit zwischen Paulus und seinen Gegnern nach dem Galaterbrief (1971) 62f. HAULOTTE, E. ''Die Gründung einer universalistischen Gemeinde,'' in: Exegese im Methodenkonflikt (1971) X. Léon-Dufour ed., 221-64. WILCKENS, U. Die Missionsreden der Apostelgeschichte (³1974) 46, 58, 63, 192, 226, 228. BROWN, R. E. et al (eds.) Peter in the New Testament (Minneapolis 1973) 43-45. LOHSE, E., Grundriss der neutestamentlichen Theologie (Stuttgart 1974) 71-72. MÜLLER, P-G., ''Die 'Bekehrung' des Petrus. Zur Interpretation von Apg 10,1 - 11,18'' HerKor 28 (1974) 372-75. NELLESSEN, E., Zeugnis für Jesus und das Wort (Köln 1976) 180-84. ''Apostelgeschichte'' in: TRE 3 (1978) 512. DÖMER, M., Das Heil Gottes: Studien zur Theologie des lukanischen Doppelwerkes (Köln/Bonn 1978) 169-71. MARTIN, R. P., New Testament Foundations II: Acts - Revelation (Exeter 1978) 101-03. SCHMITHALS, W., ''Zur Herkunft der gnostischen Elemente in der Sprache des Paulus'' in: B. Aland et al (eds.) Gnosis. FS. H. Jonas (Göttingen 1978) 411. PRAST, F., Presbyter und Evangelium in nachapostolischer Zeit (Stuttgart 1979) 320. HAACKER, K., ''Dibelius und Cornelius: Ein Beispiel formgeschichtlicher Überlieferungskritik'' BZ 24 (1980) 234-51. WEISER, A., Die Apostelgeschichte I (Gütersloh/Würzburg 1981) 249 (lit!).

10 KRUMMACHER, F. A., Der Hauptmann Cornelius: Betrachtung über das zehnte Kapitel der Apostelgeschichte (Bremen 1829) passim. DIBELIUS, M. ''Die Bekehrung des Cornelius,'' in: Coniectanea Neotestamentica (1947) 50-65. SQUILLACI, D. ''La conversione del centurione Cornelio (Atti cap. 10),'' PaCl 39 (23, 1960) 1265-69. GOULDER, M. D. Type and History in Acts (1964) 60, 69ff., 97, 168. HENNECKE, E./SCHNEEMELCHER, W. Neutestamentliche Apokryphen (1964) I 100. SCHOONHEIM, P. L. ''De centurio Cornelius'' NedThT 18 (6, 1964) 453-75. EHRHARDT, A. The Acts of the Apostles (1969) 59f., 67. KASTING, H. Die Anfänge der Urchristlichen Mission (1969) 42, 96, 104f., 117f. DUPONT, J. ''Les discours de Pierre dans les Actes et le chapitre XXIV de l'evangile de Luc,'' in: L'Evangile de Luc (1973) F. Neirynck ed., 365-70. LÖNING, K., ''Die Korneliustradition'' BZ 18 (1974) 1-19. ''Apostelgeschichte'' in: TRE 3 (1978) 498, 509. JEWETT, P. K., Infant Baptism and the Covenant of Grace

(Grand Rapids 1978) 48, 120, 157. PRAST, F., Presbyter und Evangelium in nachapostolischer Zeit (Stuttgart 1979) 324. "Bekehrung" in: TRE 5 (1980) 443.

10:1ff. HAHN, F. Das Verständnis der Mission im Neuen Testament (²1965) 39, 41f., 115, 116.

10:1-48 BIEDER, W. "Zum Problem Religion-christlicher Glaube," ThZ 15 (6, 1959) 431-45. STOLLE, V. Der Zeuge als Angeklagter (1973) 194-200.

10:1-43 DUPONT, D. J., The Salvation of the Gentiles (New York 1979) 24-27.

10:1-11 BOVON, F. De Vocatione Gentium (1967). BOVON, F., "La vie des apôtres: traditions bibliques et narrations apocryphes" in: F. Bovon et al (eds.) Les Actes Apocryphes des Apôtres (Geneva 1981) 157.

10:1-8 van der MEER, W., "Informatieve kanttekeningen bij een methode van exegese" GThT 75 (1975) 193-206.

10:1 KRAFT, H., Die Entstehung des Christentums (Darmstadt 1981) 272-73.

10:2ff. CONZELMANN, H. Die Apostelgeschichte (1963) 61f.

10:2, LOHSE, E. et al., (eds.), Der Ruf Jesu und die Antwort der Ge-
34f., 42f. meinde (1970) 58f.

10:2 STRECKER, G. Der Weg der Gerechtigkeit (1962) 99$_2$. DELLING, G. Die Taufe im Neuen Testament (1963) 136. EHRHARDT, A. The Acts of the Apostles (1969) 54f., 60. JEWETT, P. K., Infant Baptism and the Covenant of Grace (Grand Rapids 1978) 51. MILCOX, M., "The 'God-Fearers' in Acts—A Reconsideration" JSNT 13 (1981) 104-105, 107.

10:3-5 BURCHARD, C. Der dreizehnte Zeuge (1970) 88-91, 122.

10:4 van UNNIK, W. C., Sparsa Collecta I (Leiden 1973) 213-58.

10:5 FITZMEYER, J. A., "Aramaic Kepha and Peter's Name in the New Testament" in: E. Best/R. McL. Wilson (eds.) Text and Interpretation. FS. M. Black (Cambridge 1979) 122-24.

10:9-48 CATRICE, P. "Réflexions missionnaires sur la vision de Saint Pierre à Joppé. Du judéo-christianisme à l'Eglise de tous les peuples," BVieC 79 (1968) 20-39.

10:9-23 HUBBARD, B. J., "The Role of Commissioning Accounts in Acts" in: C. H.Talbert (ed.) Perspectives on Luke-Acts (Danville 1978) 188-91, 193, 196.

10:9-16 DIBELIUS, M. Aufsätze zur Apostelgeschichte (1951) 98f. ET: Studies in the Acts of the Apostles (1956) 111f. BEST, E. One Body in Christ (1955) 164. PAGELS, E. H., "Visions, Appearances and

Apostolic Authority: Gnostic and Orthodox Traditions'' in: B. Aland et al (eds.) Gnosis. FS. H. Jonas (Göttingen 1978) 423.

10:9 GOULDER, M. D. Type and History in Acts (1964) 73f. BRAUN, H. Qumran und NT II (1966) 200f.

10:10-16 MUNCK, J. Paul and the Salvation of Mankind (1959) 228f. "Apostelgeschichte" in: TRE 3 (1978) 510.

10:10 STONEHOUSE, N. B. The Witness of Matthew and Mark to Christ (1944) 106.

10:11-16 LINDSEY, R. L. A Hebrew Translation of the Gospel of Mark (1970) 59f.

10:11-15 DELLING, G. Die Taufe im Neuen Testament (1963) 61.

10:13-15 WILCOX, M. The Semitisms of Acts (1965) 72-73, 74.

10:13 SINT, J. "Schlachten und Opfern. Zu Apg. 10,13; 11,7,'' ZKTh 78 (1956) 194-205.

10:14ff. KAESEMANN, E. Exegetische Versuche und Besinnungen (1964) I 166.

10:14-15 EHRHARDT, A. The Acts of the Apostles (1969) 56f.

10:15 BERGER, K. Die Gesetzesauslegung Jesu (1940) 472f. KNOX, W. L. The Sources of the Synoptic Gospels II (1957) 26. "Apostelgeschichte" in: TRE 3 (1978) 490.

10:19-33 MÜLLER, U. B., "Zur Rezeption gesetzeskritischer Jesusüberlieferung im frühen Christentum" NTS 27 (1981) 167.

10:19-25 BIEDER, W., Die Verheissung der Taufe im Neuen Testament (Zürich 1966) 146-52.

10:19 WILCOX, M. The Semitisms of Acts (1965) 121-22, 153, 171. NICKELS, P. Targum and New Testament (1967) 64. STAEHLIN, G. "τὸ πνεῦμα Ἰησοῦ (Apostelgeschichte 16:7)," in: Christ and the Spirit in the New Testament (1973) B. Lindars/S. S. Smalley eds., 231, 244, 246, 249. GUNKEL, H., The Influence of the Holy Spirit (Philadelphia 1979) 22-23.

10:20 KNOX, W. L. The Sources of the Synoptic Gospels II (1957) 104.

10:22 WILSON, S. G. The Gentiles and the Gentile Mission in Luke-Acts (1973) 176-77. NELLESSEN, E., Zeugnis für Jesus und das Wort (Köln 1976) 61-62. BERGMEIER, R., Glaube als Gabe (Stuttgart 1980) 238n.40. MILCOX, M., "The 'God-Fearers' in Acts - A Reconsideration" JSNT 13 (1981) 105-07.

10:24-25 EPP, E. J. The theological tendency of Codex Bezae Cantabrigiensis in Acts (1965) 160f.

10:24 DELLING, G. Die Taufe im Neuen Testament (1963) 136.

10:25-26 SCHÜRMANN, H., "Christliche Weltverantwortung im Lichte des Neuen Testaments" Catholica 34 (1980) 99, 100.

10:25 BLASS, F. Philosophy of the Gospels (1898) 116ff. BARDTKE, H., "Zusätze zu Esther" in: JüdSchr I/1 (1973) 40n.6a. BARRETT, C. K., "Is there a Theological Tendency in Codex Bezae?" in: E. Best/R. McL. Wilson (eds.) Text and Interpretation. FS. M. Black (Cambridge 1979) 22.

10:26-11:30 WILCOX, M. The Semitisms of Acts (1965) 59ff.

10:27ff. HAHN, F. Christologische Hoheitstitel (1963) 336.

10:27-29 DIBELIUS, M. Aufsätze zur Apostelgeschichte (1951) 99f. ET: Studies in the Acts of the Apostles (1956) 113f.

10:28-29, PERROT, C. "Un fragment christo-palestinien découvert à Khir-
32-41 bet Mird (Act., X, 28-29; 32-41)," RevBi 70 (4, 1963) 506-55.

10:28.30 BOUSSET, W. Die Religion des Judentums im Späthellenisti-schen Zeitalter (1966 = 1926) 94, 180.

10:28 JEWETT, P. K., Infant Baptism and the Covenant of Grace (Grand Rapids 1978) 126. PRAST, F., Presbyter und Evangelium in nachapostolischer Zeit (Stuttgart 1979) 54. WILSON, S. G., "Law and Judaism in Acts" in: P. J. Achtemeier (ed.) SBL Seminar Papers 1980 (Chico, Cal. 1980) 257-58.

10:30-33 HUBBARD, B. J., "The Role of Commissioning Accounts in Acts" in: C. H. Talbert (ed.) Perspectives on Luke-Acts (Danville 1978) 190, 193, 197.

10:30 PALLIS, A. Notes on St. Luke and the Acts (London 1928) 62. BRAUN, H. Qumran und NT II (1966) 200f. WILSON, S. G. The Gentiles and the Gentile Mission in Luke-Acts (1973) 176-77. WANKE, J., Die Emmauserzählung. Eine redaktionsge-schichtliche Untersuchung zu Lk 24,13-35 (Leipzig 1973) 83.

10:33 PALLIS, A., Notes on St. Luke and the Acts (London 1928) 62. CLARK, A. C. The Acts of the Apostles (1933) xl, 264, 312, 330. DELLING, G. Die Zueignung des Heils in der Taufe (1961) 87. EPP, E. J. The theological tendency of Codex Bezae Cantabrigien-sis in Acts (1966) 157, 160-62, 164. METZGER, B. M., The Early Versions of the New Testament (Oxford 1977) 178.

10:34-43 DIBELIUS, M. Die Reden der Apostelgeschichte und die antike Geschichtsschreibung (1949) 34-35. DIBELIUS, M. Aufsätze zur Apostelgeschichte (1951) 10, 72, 93, 97f., 100, 104f., 116, 130, 138, 152f. ET.; Studies in the Acts of the Apostles (1956) 13, 79, 105, 110, 119, 132, 133, 165f., 178, 213. WILCKENS, U. "Ke-rygma und Evangelium bei Lukas (Beobachtungen zu Acts 19:34-43)," ZNW 49 (3-4, 1958) 223-37. MUNCK, J. Paul and the Sal-vation of Mankind (1959) 228-30. WILCKENS, U. Die Missions-reden der Apostelgeschichte (1961) passim. DELLING, M. Die Taufe im Neuen Testament (1963) 61. DOERNE, M. Die alten Episteln (1967) 111-15. KOCH, G. GPM 22/2 (1967-1968) 198-205. MARXSEN, W. Predigten (1968) 141-50. RESE, M. Alttesta-mentliche Motive in der Christologie des Lukas (1969) 117. BUR-CHARD, C. Der dreizehnte Zeuge (1970) 135, 138-42. STANTON, G. N. Jesus of Nazareth in New Testament Preaching (1974) 13, 15, 18, 19, 20, 24, 25, 26, 27, 28, 64, 67, 70. JERVELL, J., "The Divided People of God" in: Luke and the People of God (Minne-apolis 1972) 57. GASQUE, W., A History of the Criticism of the Acts of the Apostles (Tübingen 1975) 208, 221. KLIESCH, K., Das heilsgeschichtliche Credo in den Reden der Apostelgeschichte (Köln/Bonn 1975) 75ff, 160-63. NELLESSEN, E., Zeugnis für Je-sus und das Wort (Köln 1976) 180-97. "Apostelgeschichte" in: TRE 3 (1978) 504. MEYER, B. F., The Aims of Jesus (London 1979) 66-69.

10:34-41 STECK, K. G. in: Herr, tue meine Lippen auf Bd II (⁵1966) G. Ei-cholz ed., 259-68.

10:34-36, DOBIAS, F. GPM 22/3 (1967-1968) 270-77. RISTOW, H.
42-48 "Pfingstmontag," in: Wandelt in der Liebe (1968) 233-46.

10:34a.36-43 RISTOW, H. "Ostermontag," in: Wandelt in der Liebe (1968) 118-28.

10:34-36 KLIESCH, K., Das heilsgeschichtliche Credo in den Reden der Apostelgeschichte (Köln/Bonn 1975) 140-42.

10:34 GOULDER, M. D. Type and History in Acts (1964) 74, 79, 81f., 84. SHIMADA, K., The Formulary Material in First Peter: A Study According to the Method of Traditionsgeschichte (ThD. Diss, Ann Arbor, Mich. 1966) 212, 219-29.

10:35 van UNNIK, W. C., Sparsa Collecta I (Leiden 1973) 213-58. WILSON, S. G., Law and Judaism in Acts" in: P. J. Achtemeier (ed.) SBL Seminar Papers 1980 (Chico, Cal. 1980) 258. WIL-COX, M., "The 'God-Fearers' in Acts - A Reconsideration" JSNT 13 (1981) 106-07.

10:36-43 BERGER, K. Exegese des Neuen Testaments (Heidelberg 1977) 70-71.

10:36-40 HENGEL, M., Zur urchristlichen Geschichtsschreibung (Stuttgart 1979) 27; ET: J. Bowden (trans.) Acts and the History of Earliest Christianity (London 1979) 24.

10:36-38 CLARK, A. C. The Acts of the Apostles (1933) 236f. DE JONGE, M./VAN DER WOUDE, A. S. NTS 12 (1965-1966) 311f. DU-PONT, D. J., The Salvation of the Gentiles (New York 1979) 152.

10:36-37 DIBELIUS, M. Aufsätze zur Apostelgeschichte (1951) 82. ET: Studies in the Acts of the Apostles (1956) 91f.

10:36 DELLING, G. Die Zueignung des Heils in der Taufe (1961) 86,

88. HAHN, F. Christologische Hoheitstitel (1963) 116, 385. WIL-
COX, M. The Semitisms of Acts (1965) 151-53, 163. DUPONT,
J. Etudes sur les Actes des Apôtres (1967) 146, 147, 256, 262, 277,
279-81, 396, 412, 441, 455. NICKELS, P. Targum and New Tes-
tament (1967) 64. STANTON, G. N. Jesus of Nazareth in New
Testament Preaching (1974) 25, 28, 69-72, 78, 80, 83, 84, 85, 111.
STAEHLIN, G. "τὸ πνεῦμα 'Ιησοῦ (Apostelgeschichte 16:7),"
in: Christ and the Spirit in the New Testament (1973) B. Lindars/
S. S. Smalley, eds. 240f. MÄRZ, C-P., Das Wort Gottes bei Lukas
(Leipzig 1973) 21-24. WILCKENS, U. Die Missionsreden der
Apostelgeschichte (³1974) 46-48, 51, 99, 143, 157, 170, 329.
CORELL, J., "Actos 10,36" EstFr 76 (1975) 101-13. PRAST, F.,
Presbyter und Evangelium in nachapostolischer Zeit (Stuttgart 1979)
286-89, 323, 351. RIESENFELD, H., "The Text of Acts 10:36"
in: E. Best/R. McL. Wilson (eds.) Text and Interpretation. FS. M.
Black (Cambridge 1979) 191-94.

10:37-43 NELLESSEN, E., Zeugnis für Jesus und das Wort (Köln 1976) 186-
97.

10:37-42 HAHN, F. Christologische Hoheitstitel (1963) 215.

10:37-41 SAMAIN, E. "La notion de APXH dans l'æuvre lucanienne," in:
L'Evangile de Luc (1973) F. Neirynck ed., 305-13. EGGER, W.,
Frohbotschaft und Lehre (Frankfurt 1976) 14, 24-25. LAMBIASI,
F., L'autenticità storica dei vangeli. Studio di criteriologia (Bo-
logna 1976).

10:37-40 LOHSE, E. Die Einheit des Neuen Testaments (1973) 35f.

10:37-38 STONEHOUSE, N. B. The Witness of Matthew and Mark to Christ
(1944) 8. ROBINSON, J. M. Kerygma und historischer Jesus
(1960) 72, 146. LENTZEN-DEIS, F. Die Taufe Jesu nach den
Synoptikern (1970) 147. KRAENKL, E. Jesus der Knecht Gottes
(1972) 31, 80, 89-91, 95f. KNOCH, O. "Jesus, der 'Wohltäter'
und 'Befreier' des Menschen. Das Christuszeugnis der Predigt des
Petrus von Kornelius (Apg 10, 37f)," GuL 46 (1, 1973) 1-7.
FRIEDRICH, G., "Beobachtungen zur messianischen Hohepriestererwartung in den Synoptikern" in: Auf das Wort kommt es an
(Göttingen 1978) 76-77.

10:37 PALLIS, A., Notes on St. Luke and the Acts (London 1928) 63.
FARRER, A. St Matthew and St. Mark (1954) 53. KAESE-
MANN, E. Exegetische Versuche und Besinnungen (1964) II 135.
WILCOX, M. The Semitisms of Acts (1965) 39, 148-49, 150. DU-
PONT, J. Etudes sur les Actes des Apôtres (1967) 277, 399, 426,
441. NICKELS, P. Targum and New Testament (1967) 64. WIL-
SON, S. G. NTS 16 (1969-1970) 331f. SMITH, M. Clement of Al-
exandria and a secret Gospel of Mark (1973) 206f., 209.

STANTON, G. N. Jesus of Nazareth in New Testament Preaching (1974) 19, 20, 21, 46, 62, 78, 79, 80. WILCKENS, U. Die Missionsreden der Apostelgeschichte (³1974) 16, 46, 47, 48, 49, 65, 69, 70. NELLESSEN, E., Zeugnis für Jesus und das Wort (Köln 1976) 186-87. PRAST, F., Presbyter und Evangelium in nachapostolischer Zeit (Stuttgart 1979) 323.

10:38-39 WANKE, J., Die Emmauserzählung. Eine redaktionsgeschichtliche Untersuchung zu Lk 24,13-35 (Leipzig 1973) 11.

10:38 ROBINSON, J. M. Kerygma und historischer Jesus (1960) 71, 73. BAUMBACH, G. Das Verständnis des Bösen in den synoptischen Evangelien (1963) 185ff. DELLING, G. Die Taufe im Neuen Testament (1963) 107. HAHN, F. Christologische Hoheitstitel (1963) 220, 224, 238, 388, 392, 395. WILCOX, M. The Semitisms of Acts (1965) 116-18, 121, 132, 152, 153, 171. DUPONT, J. Etudes sur les Actes des Apôtres (1967) 262-64, 269, 277, 441, 522. MUSSNER, F. Die Wunder Jesu (1967) 31f. NICKELS, P. Targum and New Testament (1967) 64. ZMIJEWSKI, J. Die Eschatologiereden des Lukas-Evangeliums (1972) 10, 158, 282, 330. SCHNIDER, F. Jesus der Prophet (1973) 125, 165, 188f., 238. WILCKENS, U. Die Missionsreden der Apostelgeschichte (³1974) 16, 47, 48-101, 108, 120, 123, 132, 174, 186, 236, 238. STANTON, G. N. Jesus of Nazareth in New Testament Preaching (1974) 69, 72, 75, 78, 89, 181. GLÖCKNER, R., Die Verkündigung des Heils beim Evangelisten Lukas (Mainz 1975) 134-35, 184, 191, 193, 201, 237. EGGER, W., Frohbotschaft und Lehre (Frankfurt 1976) 37. NELLESSEN, E., Zeugnis für Jesus und das Wort (Köln 1976) 187. METZGER, B. M., The Early Versions of the New Testament (Oxford 1977) 89. BUSSL, U., Das Nazareth-Manifest Jesu (Stuttgart 1978) 71. CRIBBS, F. L., ''The Agreements that Exist between John and Acts'' in: C. H. Talbert (ed.) Perspectives on Luke-Acts (Danville 1978) 60. DÖMER, M., Das Heil Gottes: Studien zur Theologie des lukanischen Doppelwerkes (Köln/Bonn 1978) 63-68. DUPONT, D. J., The Salvation of the Gentiles (New York 1979) 143, 156. PRAST, F., Presbyter und Evangelium in nachapostolischer Zeit (Stuttgart 1979) 287-88. DUNN, J. D. G., Christology in the Making (London 1980) 138, 142, 343. KRAFT, H., Die Entstehung des Christentums (Darmstadt 1981) 78.

10:39-42 MINEAR, P., To Heal and to Reveal (New York 1976) 131ff. NELLESSEN, E., Zeugnis für Jesus und das Wort (Köln 1976) 191-97.

10:39-40 DUPONT, J. Etudes sur les Actes des Apôtres (1967) 148, 252, 331.

10:39 KLEIN, G. Die Zwölf Apostel (1961) 204f. KAESEMANN, E. Exegetische Versuche und Besinnungen (1964) I 130. WILCOX,

M. The Semitisms of Acts (1965) 32, 34-35, 43, 52n, 56n, 67, 80n, 162, 163, 164, 166. DUPONT, J. Etudes sur les Actes des Apôtres (1967) 251, 252, 281, 426, 435, 440, 441, 464. BURCHARD, C. Der dreizehnte Zuege (1970) 130-35. KRAENKL, E. Jesus der Knecht Gottes (1972) 91, 111f., 118-20, 145, 167f., 207. WILCKENS, U. Die Missionsreden der Apostelgeschichte (³1974) 45, 68, 107, 108, 148. ZINGG, P., Das Wachsen der Kirche (Freiburg 1974) 143. NELLESSEN, E., Zeugnis für Jesus und das Wort (Köln 1976) 187-88. TRITES, A. A., The New Testament Concept of Witness (Cambridge 1977) 138, 143, 144. WILCOX, M., " 'Upon the Tree' - Deut 21:22-23 in the New Testament" JBL 96 (1977) 85-99. DUPONT, D. J., The Salvation of the Gentiles (New York 1979) 68, 134-35. PRAST, F., Presbyter und Evangelium in nachapostolischer Zeit (Stuttgart 1979) 307, 319, 323. WILCH, J. R., "Jüdische Schuld am Tode Jesu - Antijudaismus in der Apostelgeschichte?" in: W. Haubeck/M. Bachmann (eds.) Wort in der Zeit. FS. K. H. Rengstorf (Leiden 1980) 241-42.

10:40-41 MAIWORM, J. "Fremde Gestalten des Verklärten," BuK 4 (1955) 120-22. KRAENKL, E. Jesus der Knecht Gottes (1972) 80, 130, 143-45, 171, 210f. ALSUP, J. E., The Post-Resurrection Appearance Stories of the Gospel Tradition (Stuttgart 1975) 81-83.

10:40 HAHN, F. Christologische Hoheitstitel (1963) 116, 204f. KRAMER, W. Christos Kyrios Gottessohn (1963) § 3f. WILCOX, M. The Semitisms of Acts (1965) 64-65, 80n, 167. DUPONT, J. Etudes sur les Actes des Apôtres (1967) 151, 321-36. 443. WANKE, J., Die Emmauserzählung. Eine redaktionsgeschichtliche Untersuchung zu Lk 24,13-35. (Leipzig 1973) 169n.696. WILCKENS, U. Die Missionsreden der Apostelgeschichte (³1974) 48, 50, 79, 108, 110, 122, 126, 133, 137, 139, 144f., 174, 186. NELLESSEN, E., Zeugnis für Jesus und das Wort (Köln 1976) 188. "Auferstehung" in: TRE 4 (1979) 485.

10:41 CLARK, A. C. The Acts of the Apostles (1933) 237, 266, 294, 295, 312. VOLZ, P. Die Eschatologie der jüdischen Gemeinde (1934) 368. BROX, N. Zeuge und Märtyrer (1961) 44f. HAHN, F. Christologische Hoheitstitel (1963) 185. ROLOFF, J. Apostolat-Verkündigung-Kirche (1965) 191f. 205. FLENDER, H. St. Luke Theologian of Redemptive History (1967) 121, 143, 159, 160. BURCHARD, C. Der dreizehnte Zeuge (1970) 107, 112, 129, 130-35. KRAENKL, E. Jesus der Knecht Gottes (1972) 145f., 167f., 210f. HARNISCH, W. Eschatologische Existenz (1973) 32f. WANKE, J., Die Emmauserzählung. Eine redaktionsgeschichtliche Untersuchung zu Lk 24,13-35. (Leipzig 1973) 104, 117, 126. WILCKENS, U. Die Missionsreden der Apostelgeschichte (³1974) 48, 80, 139, 144f., 150, 186. NELLESSEN, E.,

Zeugnis für Jesus und das Wort (Köln 1976) 189. PRAST, F., Presbyter und Evangelium in nachapostolischer Zeit (Stuttgart 1979) 306-07, 316, 319. BOVON, E., "La vie des apôtres: traditions bibliques et narrations apocryphes" in: F. Boyon et al (eds.) Les Actes Apocryphes des Apôtres (Geneva 1981) 153.

10:42ff. STROBEL, A. Erkenntnis und Bekenntnis der Sünde in neutestamentlicher Zeit (1968) 57.

10:42-48 MISKOTTE, K. H. in: Herr, tue meine Lippen auf Bd. II (1966⁵) G. Eichholz ed., 332-41.

10:42-43 DUPONT, J. Etudes sur les Actes des Apôtres (1967) 386, 451, 455, 470. DUPONT, D. J., The Salvation of the Gentiles (New York 1979) 77, 152.

10:42 DELLING, G. Die Taufe im Neuen Testament (1963) 64. HAHN, F. Christologische Hoheitstitel (1963) 185, 254. HENNECKE, E./ SCHNEEMELCHER, W. Neutestamentliche Apokryphen (1964) II 320f. DALTON, W. J., Christ's Proclamation to the Spirits. A Study of 1 Peter 3:18 - 4:6 (Rome 1965) 266. BEYSCHLAG, K. Clemens Romanus und der Frühkatholizismus (1966) 269. SEE-BERG, A. Der Katechismus der Urchristenheit (1966) 62, 135, 193, 205. ALLEN, L. C., "Old Testament Background." NTS 17 (1970-1971) 104f. WILCKENS, U. Die Missionsreden der Apostelgeschichte (³1974) 48, 63f., 85, 108, 124. NELLESSEN, E.,Zeugnis für Jesus und das Wort (Köln 1976) 189-91. TRITES, A. A., The New Testament Concept of Witness (Cambridge 1977) 133, 136, 145. MATTILL, A. J., Luke and the Last Things: a Perspective for the Understanding of Lukan Thought (Dillsboro 1979) 41-43. PRAST, F., Presbyter und Evangelium in nachapostolischer Zeit (Stuttgart 1979) 307-08, 316.

10:43-48 DUNN, J. D. G. Baptism in the Holy Spirit (1970) 79ff., 92.

10:43 MUNCK, J. Paul and the Salvation of Mankind (1959) 228f. DELLING, G. Die Zueignung des Heils in der Taufe (1961) 50, 89. DELLING, G. Die Taufe im Neuen Testament (1963) 64. HAHN, F. Christologische Hoheitstitel (1963) 216. KAESE-MANN, E. Exegetische Versuche und Besinnungen (1964) I 45. SEEBERG, A. Der Katechismus der Urchristenheit (1966) 130, 131, 215, 216, 217. DUPONT, J. Etudes sur les Actes des Apôtres (1967) 248, 263, 271, 281, 353, 356, 358, 412, 440, 441, 450, 455, 456, 460. BURCHARD, C. Der dreizehnte Zeuge (1970) 116f., 139. BEUTLER, J. Martyria (1972) 180, 204, 221, 287, 354. DELLING, G. Der Kreuzestod Jesu in der urchristlichen Verkün-digung (1972) 88-91. KRAENKL, E. Jesus der Knecht Gottes (1972) 33, 80, 181, 184f., 208. WILCKENS, U. Die Missionsre-den der Apostelgeschichte (³1974) 49, 67, 102, 146, 148, 154, 170,

179, 183, 186, 240. GASQUE, W., A History of the Criticism of the Acts of the Apostles (Tübingen 1975) 220, 286, 298. NEL-LESSEN, E., Zeugnis für Jesus und das Wort (Köln 1976) 191, 257-58. "Agende" in: TRE 2 (1978) 3. DUPONT, D. J., The Salvation of the Gentiles (New York 1979) 62.

10:44ff. RUDOLPH, K. Die Mandäer I (1960) 77. KAESEMANN, E. Exegetische Versuche und Besinnungen (1964) I 165.

10:44-48 ADLER, N., Taufe und Handauflegung. Eine exegetisch-theologische Untersuchung von Apg 8,14-17 (Münster 1951) 17, 26, 28-29, 31, 33, 59, 73-74, 85, 88, 96-98, 101, 103-04. BARTH, M., Die Taufe - ein Sakrament? (Zürich 1951) 154-59. DELLING, G. Die Taufe im Neuen Testament (1963) 61f. McNAMARA, M. The New Testament and the Palestinian Targum to the Pentateuch (1966) 187 n.99. BIEDER, W., Die Verheissung der Taufe im Neuen Testament (Zürich 1966) 230-34. KREMER, J., Pfingstbericht und Pfingstgeschehen. Eine exegetische Untersuchung zu Apg 2, 1-13 (Stuttgart 1973) 191-97. DUNN, J. D. G., Jesus and the Spirit (London 1975) 122, 153, 154-55, 176, 193. SCHMITHALS, W., "Zur Herkunft der gnostischen Elemente in der Sprache des Paulus" in: B. Aland et al (eds.) Gnosis. FS. H. Jonas (Göttingen 1978) 412. BARTH, G., Die Taufe in frühchristlicher Zeit (Neukirchen-Vluyn 1981) 60, 63, 67, 71.

10:44-47 ADLER, N. Das erste christliche Pfingstfest (1938) 108, 110, 136, 161f. DUPONT, D. J., The Salvation of the Gentiles (New York 1979) 46.

10:44 DELLING, G. Die Taufe im Neuen Testament (1963) 63, 69, 136. HAHN, F. Christologische Hoheitstitel (1963) 107. GOULDER, M. D. Type and History in Acts (1964) 26, 62, 74, 76f. STAN-TON, B. N. Jesus of Nazareth in New Testament Preaching (1974) 20, 23, 24, 25, 28. "Apostelgeschichte" in: TRE 3 (1978) 509.

10:45-46 DELLING, G. Die Taufe im Neuen Testament (1963) 63, 98.

10:45 STONEHOUSE, N. B. The Witness of Matthew and Mark to Christ (1944) 106. STRECKER, G. Der Weg der Gerechtigkeit (1962) 217₇.

10:46 ADLER, N. Das erste christliche Pfingstfest (1938) 95f., 161f. HAHN, F. Christologische Hoheitstitel (1963) 107. DUPONT, D. J., The Salvation of the Gentiles (New York 1979) 46-50.

10:47-48 DELLING, G. Die Taufe im Neuen Testament (1963) 57, 61, 63, 64, 70, 76, 118, 136.

10:47 JEWETT, P. K., Infant Baptism and the Covenant of Grace (Grand Rapids 1978) 57.

10:48 DELLING, G. Die Zueignung des Heils in der Taufe (1961) 13, 85f., 88, 91, 92f. EPP, E. J. The theological tendency of Codex

Bezae Cantabrigiensis in Acts (1966) 54, 62f. BARTH, G., Die Taufe in frühchristlicher Zeit (Neukirchen-Vluyn 1981) 11, 38, 42, 44, 53, 126, 128.

---

11 DUPONT, J. D. Les Problèmes du Livre des Actes (1950) 53, 61. KAESEMANN, E. Exegetische Versuche und Besinnungen (1964) I 131. GASQUE, W., A History of the Criticism of the Acts of the Apostles (Tübingen 1975) 23, 25, 46n.58, 178. JEWETT, R., A Chronology of Paul's Life (Philadelphia 1979) 69-75, 89-91.

11:1ff. NICKLE, K. F. The Collection (1966) 27f., 36f., 65f.

11:1-18 DUPONT, J. Etudes sur les Actes des Apôtres (1967) 70, 71, 74, 154, 176, 177. PRAST, F., Presbyter und Evangelium in nachapostolischer Zeit (Stuttgart 1979) 324.

11:1-2 BOUSSET, W. Die Religion des Judentums im Späthellenistischen Zeitalter (1966 = 1926) 113.

11:1 DELLING, G. Die Taufe im Neuen Testament (1963) 69. EPP, E. J. The theological tendency of Codex Bezae Cantabrigiensis in Acts (1966) 104-06, 107.

11:2-18 FLEW, R. N. Jesus and His Church (1956) 133n.

11:2 CLARK, A. C. The Acts of the Apostles (1933) xxxiv, xliii, 164, 192, 309, 347. EPP, E. J. The theological tendency of Codex Bezae Cantabrigiensis in Acts (1966) 11, 104-07, 163, 168. KLIJN, A. F. J./REININK, G. J. Patristic Evidence for Jewish-Christian Sects (1973) 9. "Aramäisch" in: TRE 3 (1978) 604.

11:3 FLEW, R. N. Jesus and His Church (1956) 94n.

11:4, PETERS, G. W. A Biblical Theology of Missions (1972) 140-41.
17-18, 21, 24

11:4-17 DUPONT, J. "Les discours de Pierre dans les Acts et le chapitre XXIV de l'évangile de Luc," in: L'Evangile de Luc (1973) F. Neirynck ed., 365-67.

11:4-12 HUBBARD, B. J., "The Role of Commissioning Accounts in Acts" in: C. H. Talbert (ed.) Perspectives on Luke-Acts (Danville 1978) 190, 193, 197.

11:4 NICKELS, P. Targum and New Testament (1967) 65.

11:5ff. EHRHARDT, A. The Acts of the Apostles (1969) 59f.

11:5-17 DIBELIUS, M. Die Reden der Apostelgeschichte und die antike Geschichtsschreibung (1949) 17, 30.

11:5-10 DIBELIUS, M. Aufsätze zur Apostelgeschichte (1951) 98f. ET: Studies in the Acts of the Apostles (1956) 112f.

11:5-9 DELLING, G. Die Taufe im Neuen Testament (1963) 61. DELEBECQUE, E., "L'hellenisme de la 'relative complexe' dans le Nouveau Testament et principalement chez saint Luc" Biblica 62 (1981) 235.

11:8 METZGER, B. M., The Early Versions of the New Testament (Oxford 1977) 147, 235.

11:9 METZGER, B. M., The Early Versions of the New Testament (Oxford 1977) 147.

11:12 STAEHLIN, G. "τὸ πνεῦμα 'Ιησοῦ (Apostelgeschichte 16:7)." in: Christ and the Spirit in the New Testament (1973) B. Lindars/ S. S. Smalley eds., 231, 244, 246, 249.

11:14-18 DUNN, J. D. G. Baptism in the Holy Spirit (1970) 79ff., 92, 100.

11:14 DELLING, G. Die Taufe im Neuen Testament (1963) 136.

11:15ff. SMITH, M. Clement of Alexandria and a secret Gospel of Mark (1973) 210, 253f.

11:15-18 McNAMARA, M. The New Testament and the Palestinian Targum to the Pentateuch (1966) 187 n.99. KREMER, J., Pfingstbericht und Pfingstgeschehen. Eine exegetische Untersuchung zu Apg 2,1-13 (Stuttgart 1973) 191-97.

11:15-17 DELLING, G. Die Taufe im Neuen Testament (1963) 46, 59, 61, 62f., 69. DUPONT, D. J., The Salvation of the Gentiles (New York 1979) 46.

11:15 ADLER, N. Das erste christliche Pfingstfest (1938) 10, 19, 67, 91, 108, 161f. STONEHOUSE, N. B. The Witness of Matthew and Mark to Christ (1944) 106. KAESEMANN, E. Exegetische Versuche und Besinnungen (1964) II 122. WILCKENS, U. Die Missionsreden der Apostelgeschichte (³1974) 66, 67, 107, 183. SCHMITHALS, W., "Zur Herkunft der gnostischen Elemente in der Sprache des Paulus" in: B. Aland et al (eds.) Gnosis. FS. H. Jonas (Göttingen 1978) 412.

1:16-17 DELLING, G. Die Zueignung des Heils in der Taufe (1961) 87, 92.

11:16 YATES, J. E. The Spirit and the Kingdom (1963) 167ff., 175ff. McDONALD, J. I. H., Kerygma and Didache (Cambridge 1980) 17. BARTH, G., Die Taufe in frühchristlicher Zeit (Neukirchen-Vluyn 1981) 23, 25, 37, 44, 63, 68.

11:17-18 EGGER, W., Frohbotschaft und Lehre (Frankfurt 1976) 50-51.

11:17 EPP, E. J. The theological tendency of Codex Bezae Cantabrigiensis in Acts (1966) 89 n.1,3; 116-18, 162. JEWETT, P. K., Infant Baptism and the Covenant of Grace (Grand Rapids 1977) 57.

11:18-19 BEYSCHLAG, K., Simon Magus und die christliche Gnosis (Tübingen 1974) 167n.75.

11:18 DELLING, G. Die Taufe im Neuen Testament (1963) 61, 62, 63f., 140. QUESNELL, Q. This Good News (1964) 46f. DUPONT, J. Etudes sur les Actes des Apôtres (1967) 200, 201, 412, 423, 438, 447, 452, 455, 462, 469. NICKELS, P. Targum and New Testament (1967) 65. STROBEL, A. Erkenntnis und Bekenntnis der Sünde in neutestamentlicher Zeit (1968) 48. CLARK, K. W., "The Meaning of ARA" in: The Gentile Bias and Other Essays (Leiden 1980) 198.

11:19ff. HAHN, F. Das Verständnis der Mission im Neuen Testament (²1965) 49, 50, 116, 117. HENGEL, M. Judentum und Hellenismus (1969) 194f., 569. ET: Judaism and Hellenism (1974) I 105, 313. MERKLEIN, H. Das Kirchliche Amt nach dem Epheserbrief (1973) 240, 250, 276, 333.

11:19-15:35 O'NEILL, J. C. The Theology of Acts in its historical setting (1970) 65-72, 78, 86.

11:19-30 SHEPARD, J. W., The Life and Letters of St. Paul (Grand Rapids 1950) 92-94. SCHMITHALS, W. Paulus und Jakobus (1963) 22-27. DUPONT, J. The Sources of Acts (1964) 20, 26, 28, 36, 39, 40, 51, 53, 54, 55, 56, 57, 58, 60, 61, 62, 64, 68, 72. EHRHARDT, A. The Acts of the Apostels (1969) 67ff. MARTIN, R. P., New Testament Foundations II: Acts - Revelation (Exeter 1978) 103-04. WEISER, A., Die Apostelgeschichte I (Gütersloh/Würzburg 1981) 272-73 (lit!).

11:19-29 "Amt" in TRE 2 (1978) 515.

11:19-26 ZINGG, P., Das Wachsen der Kirche (Freiburg 1974) 197. MONSENGWO PASINYA, "Antioche, berceau de l'Eglise des Gentils? Act 11, 19-26" Revue Africaine de Théologie 1 (Kinshasa 1977) 31-66. DÖMER, M., Das Heil Gottes: Studien zur Theologie des lukanischen Doppelwerkes (Köln/Bonn 1978) 171.

11:19-21 MÜLLER, U. B., "Zur Rezeption gesetzeskritischer Jesusüberlieferung im frühen Christentum" NTS 27 (1981) 161, 166.

11:19-20 BLAIR, E. P. Jesus in the Gospel of Matthew (1960) 158. DELLING, G. Die Zueignung des Heils in der Taufe (1961) 91. DELLING, G. Die Taufe im Neuen Testament (1963) 64. GOULDER, M. D. Type and History in Acts (1964) 25, 67, 71, 216. HAHN, F. Das Verständnis der Mission im Neuen Testament (²1965) 63. SCHILLE, G. Anfänge der Kirche (1966) 78ff. KASTING, H. Die Anfänge der Urchristlichen Mission (1969) 102, 103-05, 106. WILSON, S. G. The Gentiles and the Gentile Mission in Luke-Acts (1973) 139-42, 144-45, 147, 151, 172, 260, 263. "Apostelgeschichte" in: TRE 3 (1978) 498. TYSON, J. B., "The Problem of

Food in Acts: A Study of Literary Patterns with Particular Reference to Acts 6:1-7'' in: P. J. Achtemeier (ed.) SBL Seminar Papers 1979/I (Missoula 1979) 79.

11:20-25 NICKLE, K. F. The Collection (1966) Passim.

11:20-21 HAHN, F. Das Verständnis der Mission im Neuen Testament (²1965) 49, 52. EGGER, W., Frohbotschaft und Lehre (Frankfurt 1976) 49. DUPONT, D. J., The Salvation of the Gentiles (New York 1979) 71.

11:20 FLEW, R. N. Jesus and His Church (1956) 118-19. BLAIR, E. P. Jesus in the Gospel of Matthew (1960) 157. SCHMITHALS, W. Paulus und Jakobus (1963) 9, 19, 23. PARKER, P., ''Three Variant Readings in Luke-Acts'' JBL 83 (1964) 167-68. EPP, R. J. The theological tendency of Codex Bezae Cantabrigiensis in Acts (1966) 54, 62f. MERKLEIN, H. Das Kirchliche Amt nach dem Epheserbrief (1973) 251, 255, 275, 276. WILSON, S. G. The Gentiles and the Gentile Mission in Luke-Acts (1973) 139-42. CAVALLIN, H. C. C., Life After Death I (Lund 1974) 4, 2n.4. DUNN, J. D. G., Unity and Diversity in the New Testament (London 1977) 52. ''Apostelgeschichte'' in: TRE 3 (1978) 496, 498. HENGEL, M., Zur urchristlichen Geschichtsschreibung (Stuttgart 1979) 63, 84; ET: J. Bowden (trans.) Acts and the History of Earliest Christianity (London 1979) 71, 99.

11:21 KNOX, W. L. The Sources of the Synoptic Gospels II (1957) 40. DELLING, G. Die Taufe im Neuen Testament (1963) 70. Mc-NAMARA, M. The New Testament and the Palestinian Targum to the Pentateuch (1966) 179. DUPONT, J. Etudes Sur les Actes des Apôtres (1967) 423, 427, 431, 466, 474. ZINGG, P., Das Wachsen der Kirche (Freiburg 1974) 30-35. FISCHER, U., Eschatologie und Jenseitserwartung im hellenistischen Diasporajudentum (Berlin 1978) 94.

11:22-26 PRAST, F., Presbyter und Evangelium in nachapostolischer Zeit (Stuttgart 1979) 324.

11:22-23 HAHN, F. Das Verständnis der Mission im Neuen Testament (²1965) 49.

11:22 DELLING, G. Die Taufe im Neuen Testament (1963) 65. ''Apostelgeschichte'' in: TRE 3 (1978) 490.

11:23 KNOX, W. L. The Sources of the Synoptic Gospels II (1957) 90. DUPONT, J. Etudes sur les Actes des Apôtres (1967) 431, 453, 457, 474. SCHNEIDER, G., ''Gott und Christus als κυριος nach der Apostelgeschichte'' in: J. Zmijewski/E. Nellessen (eds.) Begegnung mit dem Wort. FS. H. Zimmermann (Bonn 1980) 163, 168, 170ff.

11:24 KNOX, W. L. The Sources of the Synoptic Gospels II (1957) 114.

DELLING, G. Die Taufe im Neuen Testament (1963) 70. ZINGG, P., Das Wachsen der Kirche (Freiburg 1974) 63. SCHNEIDER, G., "Gott und Christus als κυριος" in: J. Zmijewski/E. Nellessen (eds.) Begegnung mit dem Wort. FS. H. Zimmerman (Bonn 1980) 163, 168, 171-72.

11:25-12:25 SAHLIN, H. Der Messias und das Gottesvolk (1945) 359-63.

11:25f.30 KLEIN, G. Die Zwölf Apostel (1961) 166ff.

11:25-26 HAHN, F. Das Verständnis der Mission im Neuen Testament (²1965) 49, 50, 74, 77. ENSLIN, M. S. Reapproaching Paul (1972) 41f. HOLMBERG, B., Paul and Power (Lund 1978) 17.

11:26 CLARK, A. C. The Acts of the Apostles (1933) xxxiii, 182, 217, 264, 265. SPICO, C. "Ce que signifie le titre de chrétien," StTh 15 (1, 1961) 68-78. LIFSHITZ, B. "L'origine du nom des Chrétiens," Vig Chr 16 (2, 1962) 65-70. CONZELMANN, H. Die Apostelgeschichte (1963) 68. HAHN, F. Christologische Hoheitstitel (1963) 222. QUESNELL, Q. This Good News (1964) 35f. HAHN, F. Das Verständnis der Mission im Neuen Testament (²1965) 65. LADD, G. E., A Theology of the New Testament (Grand Rapids 1974) 135, 340, 353, 409. "Antiochien" in: TRE 3 (1978) 102. "Apostelgeschichte" in: TRE 3 (1978) 498. KRAFT, H., Die Entstehung des Christentums (Darmstadt 1981) 266-68. MÜLLER, U. B., "Zur Rezeption gesetzeskritischer Jesusüberlieferung im frühen Christentum" NTS 27 (1981) 160.

11:27ff. EHRHARDT, A. The Acts of the Apostles (1969) 36f., 74.

11:27-30 WIKENHAUSER, A. Die Apostelgeschichte (1951) 110-12. STRECKER, G. "Die sogenannte zweite Jerusalemreise des Paulus," ZNW 53 (1-2, 1962) 67-77. STRECKER, G. "Die sogenannte Zweite Jerusalemreise des Paulus (Act. 11,27-30)" in: Eschaton und Historie (Göttingen 1979) 132-41. DUPONT, J. The Sources of Acts (1964) 34, 40, 51, 64, 68, 71. HURD, J. C. The Origin of 1 Corinthians (1965) 16-18, 21³, 24, 34, 34³, 35, 37³. ROLOFF, J. Apostolat-Verkündigung-Kirche (1965) 208f. JEREMIAS, J. Abba: Studien zur neutestamentlichen Theologie und Zeitgeschichte (1966) 234-37, 250-52. NICKLE, K. F. The Collection (1966) Passim. DUPONT, J. Etudes sur les Actes des Apôtres (1967) 56-72, 178, 197, 225, 229, 231, 233. WILSON, S. G. The Gentiles and the Gentile Mission in Luke-Acts (1973) 178-82. SCHNIDER, F. Jesus der Prophet (1973) 58f. LÜDEMANN, G., Paulus der Heidenapostel I (Göttingen 1980) 165-69. ROBECK, C., "The Gift of Prophecy in Acts and Paul, Part I" SBT 5 (1975) 15-38. CATCHPOLE, D. R., "Paul, James and the Apostolic Decree" NTS 28 (1977) 428-44. JOHNSON, L. T., The Literary Function of Possessions in Luke-Acts (Missoula 1977) 217-

20. MATTILL, A. J., "The Value of Acts as a Source for the Study of Paul" in: C. H. Talbert (ed.) Perspectives on Luke-Acts (Danville 1978) 91. JEWETT, R., A Chronology of Paul's Life (Philadelphia 1979) 34.

11:27-28 HARNACK, A. von, Studien zur Geschichte des Neuen Testaments und der Alten Kirche (1931) 33ff. HAHN, F. Das Verständnis der Mission im Neuen Testament (²1965) 70, 77, 78. SATAKE, A. Die Gemeindeordnung in der Johannesapokalypse (1966) 166-68. WILCOX, M. The Semitisms of Acts (1965) 144, 147-48, 154. NICKELS, P. Targum and New Testament (1967) 65. MÜLLER, U. B., "Zur Rezeption gesetzeskritischer Jesusüberlieferung im frühen Christentum" NTS 27 (1981) 160.

11:27 BAUMGARTEN, J., Paulus und die Apokalyptik (Neukirchen-Vluyn 1975) 51-52. METZGER, B. M., The Early Versions of the New Testament (Oxford 1977) 92. HORTON, F. L., "Reflections on the Semitisms of Luke-Acts" in: C. H. Talbert (ed.) Perspectives on Luke-Acts (Danville 1978) 21.

11:28-30 TORNOS, A. M. "La fecha del hambre de Jerusalém, aludida por Act 11,28-30," EstEc 33 (130, 1959) 303-16.

11:28 FLEW, R. N. Jesus and His Church (1956) 143n. STROBEL, A. "Lukas der Antiocher (Bemerkungen zu Act 11, 28d)," ZNW 49 (1-2, 1958) 131-34. DUPONT, J. Etudes sur les Actes des Apôtres (1967) 163, 165, 229, 230. HENGEL, M. Judentum und Hellenismus (1969) 439. ET: Judaism and Hellenism (1974) I 240. CONZELMANN, H. und LINDEMANN, A., Arbeitsbuch zum Neuen Testament (Tübingen 1975) 142, 386. METZGER, B. M., The Early Versions of the New Testament (Oxford 1977) 87. "Amt" in: TRE 2 (1978) 514. "Apostelgeschichte" in: TRE 3 (1978) 492-93. HORTON, F. L., "Reflections on the Semitisms of Luke-Acts" in: C. H. Talbert (ed.) Perspectives on Luke-Acts (Danville 1978) 22. HENGEL, M. Zur urchristlichen Geschichtsschreibung (Stuttgart 1979) 64; ET: J. Bowden (trans.) Acts and the History of Earliest Christianity (London 1979) 72. SCHRECKENBERG, H., "Flavius Josephus und die lukanischen Schriften" in: W. Haubeck/M. Bachmann (eds.) Wort in der Zeit. FS. K. H. Rengstorf (Leiden 1980) 199-201.

11:29-12:25 STOLLE, V. Der Zeuge als Angeklagter (1973) 255.

11:29-30 ROBERTSON, A. T. Luke the Historian in the Light of Research (1920) 171f. HAHN, F. Das Verständnis der Mission im Neuen Testament (²1965) 73f. DUPONT, J. Etudes sur les Actes des Apôtres (1967) 230-32, 236, 511. "Apostelgeschichte" in: TRE 3 (1978) 498.

11:30 BENOIT, P. "La deuxième visite de Saint Paul à Jérusalem," Bib-

lica 40 (3, 1959) 778-92. GOULDER, M. D. Type and History in
Acts (1964) 30, 162, 197, 203. HAHN, F. Das Verständnis der
Mission im Neuen Testament (²1965) 49. ROLOFF, J. Apostolat-
Verkündigung-Kirche (1965) 219f. EHRHARDT, A. The Acts of
the Apostles(1969) 71ff., 87. KUEMMEL, W. G. Einleitung in das
Neue Testament (1973) 263f. GASQUE, W., A History of the
Criticism of the Acts of the Apostles (Tübingen 1975) 101, 141,
254, 265. METZGER, B. M., The Early Versions of the New Tes-
tament (Oxford 1977) 141. "Amt" in: TRE 2 (1978) 514. "Ara-
mäisch" in: TRE 3 (1978) 604. PRAST, F. Presbyter und
Evangelium in nachapostolischer Zeit (Stuttgart 1979) 225, 356-57.

12:1-13:22a WILCOX, M. The Semitisms of Acts (1965) 59ff.

12:1ff. WIKENHAUSER, A. Die Apostelgeschichte (1951) 117-19.

12:1-23 DUPONT, J. Etudes sur les Actes des Apôtres (1967) 223-26, 232,
233. KUEMMEL, W. G. Einleitung in das Neue Testament (1973)
142f.

12:1-17 SURKAU, H. W. GPM 20 (1965-1966) 360-66. DIETRICH, W.
Das Petrusbild der lukanischen Schriften (1972) 298-306.
FISCHER, K. M. GPM 26 (4, 1972) 271-78.

12:1-12 EULENSTEIN, R., "Die wundersame Befreiung des Petrus aus
Todesgefahr, Acta 12,1-12. Ein Beispiel für die philologische Analyse einer neutestamentlichen Texteinheit" WuD 12 (1973) 43-69.

12:1-11 KRATZ, R., Auferweckung als Befreiung. Eine Studie zur Pas-
sions- und Auferstehungstheologie des Matthäus (Stuttgart 1973)
26, 27-28, 33. KUHLI, H. und CASPARY, H-N., in: P. Krusche
et al (eds.) Predigtstudien für das Kirchenjahr 1981-1982. IV/2
(Stuttgart 1982) 216-25.

12:1-2 BEYER, H. W. Die Apostelgeschichte (1947) 75f. FLEW, R. N.
Jesus and His Church (1956) 141. DUPONT, J. The Sources of Acts
(1964) 36, 37, 51, 55, 56, 64. GOULDER, M. D. Type and His-
tory in Acts (1964) 45, 59, 61, 69, 97, 150, 188, 194, 201.
SCHILLE, G. Anfänge der Kirche (1966) 141ff. GUTBROD, K.
Die Apostelgeschichte (1968) 45ff. PESCH, R. Die Vision des
Stephanus (1968) 40-43. EHRHARDT, A. The Acts of the Apos-
tles (1969) 73f. DÖMER, M., Das Heil Gottes: Studien zur Theo-
logie des lukanischen Doppelwerkes (Köln/Bonn 1978) 171.
BOVON, F., "La vie des apôtres: traditions bibliques et narrations

apocryphes'' in: F. Bovon et al (eds.) Les Actes Apocryphes des Apôtres (Geneva 1981) 147. WEISER, A., Die Apostelgeschichte 1 (Gütersloh/Würzburg 1981) 282 (lit!).

12:1 TORNOA, A. M. "Kat' ekeinon de ton kairon en Act 12,1 y simultaneidad de Act 12 con Act 11,27-30," EstEc 33 (131, 1959) 411-28. CONZELMANN, H., Die Apostelgeschichte (1963) 69. GOULDER, M. D. Type and History in Acts (1964) 26, 74, 86, 115, 193. ZMIJEWSKI, J. Die Eschatologiereden des Lukas-Evangeliums (1972) 101, 116, 130, 132, 152, 155, 173. "Apostelgeschichte" in: TRE 3 (1978) 490.

12:2.3ff.17 HAHN, F. Das Verständnis der Mission im Neuen Testament (²1965) 77.

12:2 GRILL, J. Untersuchungen über die Entstehung des vierten Evangeliums II (1923) 311, 313f., 316f., 319. ANON, "New Testament Studies: 3. The brother of the Lord," Hib Journ 61 (1, 1962) 44-45. BLINZLER, J. "Rechtgeschichtliches zur Hinrichtung des Zebedäiden Jakobus (Apg xii 2)," (1962) 191-206. NovTest 5 (2-3, 1962) 191-206. BOEHLING, A. "Zum Martyrium des Jakobus," NovTest 5 (2-3, 1962) 207-13. EPP, E. J. The theological tendency of Codex Bezae Cantabrigiensis in Acts (1966) 144f. RICHTER, H.-F. Auferstehung und Wirklichkeit (1969) 49f. JEREMIAS, J. Neutestamentliche Theologie I (1971) 233f. PALLIS, A., Notes on St. Luke and the Acts (London 1928) 63-64. "Apostelgeschichte" in: TRE 3 (1978) 498.

12:3ff. STROBEL, A. "Passa-Symbolik und Passa-Wunder in Act. xii. 3ff.," NTS 4 (3, 1958) 210-15. BEYSCHLAG, K. Clemens Romanus und der Frühkatholizismus (1966) 328f. SCHILLE, G. Anfänge der Kirche (1966) 151ff.

12:3-17 "Apostelgeschichte" in: TRE 3 (1978) 496, 498.

12:3-6 "Apostelgeschichte" in: TRE 3 (1978) 496.

12:3 RUDOLPH, K. Die Mandäer II (1961) 133, 4. "Apostelgeschichte" in: TRE 3 (1978) 490. KRAFT, H., Die Entstehung des Christentums (Darmstadt 1981) 282-84, 286-88.

12:4 DELEBECQUE, E., "L'hellenisme de la 'relative complexe' dans le Nouveau Testament et principalement chez saint Luc" Biblica 62 (1981) 232.

12:5-7 DIBELIUS, M. Aufsätze zur Apostelgeschichte (1951) 25f. ET: Studies in the Acts of the Apostles (1956) 21f.

12:5 CLARK, A. C. The Acts of the Apostles (1933) xxxv, 183, 264, 300, 312.

12:6-12 HUBBARD, B. J., "The Role of Commissioning Accounts in Acts" in: C. H. Talbert (ed.) Perspectives on Luke-Acts (Danville 1978) 190, 193, 197.

12:6-11 DUNN, J. D. G., Jesus and the Spirit (London 1975) 163, 166-67.

12:7-11 BEST, E. One Body in Christ (1955) 126n.

12:7 KNOX, W. L. The Sources of the Synoptic Gospels II (1957) 40.

12:8-9 METZGER, B. M., The Early Versions of the New Testament (Oxford 1977) 141.

12:10 CLARK, A. C. The Acts of the Apostles (1933) xlv, 190, 263, 299, 348f. KAESEMANN, E. Exegetische Versuche und Besinnungen (1964) II 122. POUPON, G., "L'accusation de magie dans les Actes apocryphes" in: F. Bovon et al (eds.) Les Actes Apocryphes des Apôtres (Geneva 1982) 75n.28, 90.

12:11 NICKELS, P. Targum and New Testament (1967) 65.

12:12-17 ELLIOTT, J. H., "Peter, Sylvanus and Mark in 1 Peter and Acts: Sociological-Exegetical Perspectives on a Petrinic Group in Rome" in: W. Haubeck/M. Bachmann (eds.) Wort in der Zeit. FS. K. H. Rengstorf (Leiden 1980) 260-62.

12:12 PALLIS, A., Notes on St. Luke and the Acts (London (1928) 64. BRUNS, J. E. "John Mark: A Riddle within the Johannine Enigma," Scripture 15 (31, 1963) 88-92. HENGEL, M. Judentum und Hellenismus (1969) 194. ET: Judaism and Hellenism (1974) I 105. SWIDLER, L., Biblical Affirmations of Woman (Philadelphia 1979) 296.

12:13-14 BOUSSET, W. Die Religion des Judentums im Späthellenistischen Zeitalter (1966 = 1926) 324.

12:14-15 MOORE, G. F. Judaism I (1936) 404.

12:14 WANKE, J., Die Emmauserzählung. Eine redaktionsgeschichtliche Untersuchung zu Lk 24,13-35 (Leipzig 1973) 36n.409.

12:15 "Dämonen" in: TRE 8 (1981) 280.

12:16 STONEHOUSE, N. B. The Witness of Matthew and Mark to Christ (1944) 106.

12:17 GRILL, J. Untersuchungen über die Entstehung des vierten Evangeliums II (1923) 316f., 320. FLEW, R. N. Jesus and His Church (1956) 133n. JOYCE, E. "James, the Just," Bible Today 1 (4, 1963) 256-64. BEYSCHLAG, K. Clemens Romanus und der Frühkatholizismus (1966) 327f., 339. OSBORNE, R. E. "Where Did Peter Go?" CanJournTheol 14 (4, 1968) 274-77. WENHAM, J. "Did Peter Go to Rome in AD 42?" TB 23 (1972) 94-102. HAHN, F. Das Verständnis der Mission im Neuen Testament (²1965) 43. "Amt" in: TRE 2 (1978) 513.

12:18 CADBURY, H. J. "Litotes in Acts," in: Festschrift to Honor F. Wilbur Gingrich (1972) E. H. Barth/R. E. Cocraft eds., 62. CLARK, K. W., "The Meaning of APA" in: The Gentile Bias and Other Essays (Leiden 1980) 198.

12:20-23 "Apostelgeschichte" in: TRE 3 (1978) 497.

12:20 NICKELS, P. Targum and New Testament (1967) 65.

12:21-23 SCHRECKENBERG, H., "Flavius Josephus und die lukanischen Schriften" in: W. Haubeck/M. Bachmann (eds.) Wort in der Zeit. FS. K. H. Rengstorf (Leiden 1980) 201.

12:21 METZGER, B. M., The Early Versions of the New Testament (Oxford 1977) 141.

12:22 BETZ, H. D. Lukian von Samosata und das Neue Testament (1961) 102, 157, 178f. SCHALIT, A. König Herodes (1969) 666.

12:22-23 HABICHT, C., "2 Makkabäerbuch" in: JüdSchr I/3 (1976) 245n.9a.

12:23 PALLIS, A., Notes on St. Luke and the Acts (London 1928) 64-65. KNOX, W. L. The Sources of the Synoptic Gospels II (1957) 40. CONZELMANN, H. Die Apostelgeschichte (1963) 71. EPP, E. J. The theological tendency of Codex Bezae Cantabrigiensis in Acts (1966) 145f.

12:24 GOULDER, M. D. Type and History in Acts (1964) 24, 66f., 164. MÄRZ, C-P., Das Wort Gottes bei Lukas (Leipzig 1973) 17-19. HAMBLIN, R. L., "Miracles in the Book of Acts" SouJTh 17 (1974) 19-34. KODELL, J., "The Word of God Grew. The Ecclesial Tendency of λόγος in Acts 6,7; 12,24; 19,20" Biblica 55 (1974) 505-19. ZINGG, P., Das Wachsen der Kirche (Freiburg 1974) 23-29. GASQUE, W., A History of the Criticism of the Acts of the Apostles (Tübingen 1975) 125, 127.

12:25 - 15:35 MATTILL, A. J., " The Value of Acts as a Source for the Study of Paul" in: C. H. Talbert (ed.) Perspectives on Luke-Acts (Danville 1978) 84.

12:25 - 13:14 MIESNER, D. R., "The Missionary Journeys Narrative: Patterns and Implications" in: C. H. Talbert (ed.) Perspectives on Luke-Acts (Danville 1978) 203-05.

12:25 CLARK, A. C. The Acts of the Apostles (1933) xxxvi, 264, 313, 349f. DUPONT, J. "La Mission de Paul 'A Jérusalem' (Act XII,25)," NovTest 1 (4, 1956) 275-303. MUNCK, J. Paul and the Salvation of Mankind (1959) 286f. KLEIN, G. Die Zwölf Apostel (1961) 166f. DUPONT, J. The Sources of Acts (1964) 26, 28, 34, 36, 40, 65, 68, 71, 123. PARKER, P., "Three Variant Readings in Luke-Acts" JBL 83 (1964) 168-70. HAHN, F. Das Verständnis der Mission im Neuen Testament (²1965) 49, 50, 70, 73, 77. HURD, J. C. The Origin of 1 Corinthians (1965) 29, 34-35, 36². JEREMIAS, J. Abba: Studien zur neutestamentlichen Theologie und Zeitgeschichte (1966) 234-37. DUPONT, J. Etudes sur les Actes des Apôtres (1967) 57, 59, 61, 165, 176, 190, 197, 199, 210, 217-41. HENGEL, M. Judentum und Hellenismus (1969) 194. ET: Judaism and Hellenism (1974) I 105. KUEMMEL, W. G. Einleitung in das Neue Testament (1973) 263f. JOHNSON, L. T., The Literary Function of Possessions in Luke-Acts (Missoula 1977) 217-20. "Apostel" in: TRE 3 (1978) 435, 436. "Apostelgeschichte" in: TRE 3 (1978) 498.

13-28 DIBELIUS, M. Aufsätze zur Apostelgeschichte (1951) 163f. ET: Studies in the Acts of the Apostles (1956) 193f. GUTBROD, K. Die Apostelgeschichte (1958) 30ff. KUEMMEL, W. G. Einleitung in das Neue Testament (1973) 151f. TALBERT, C. H., Literary Patterns, Theological Themes, and the Genre of Luke-Acts (Missoula 1974) 23-25. GASQUE, W., A History of the Criticism of the Acts of the Apostles (Tübingen 1975) 25, 33, 36, 79, 88, 103, 111, 133, 195n.101.

13-21 DUPONT, J. The Sources of Acts (1964) 116, 118, 147, 150, 151, 157.

13-19 CULPEPPER, R. A., "Paul's Mission to the Gentile World: Acts 13-19" RevEx 71 (1974) 487-97. SOMMERVILLE, E. R., "The Divine Purpose: The Jews and the Gentile Mission (Acts 15)" in: P. J. Achtemeier (ed.) SBL Seminar Papers 1980 (Chico, Cal. 1980) 273-74.

13 - 15 MARTIN, R. A. NTS 11 (1964-1965) 41f. GUTBROD, K. Die Apostelgeschichte (1968) 31ff.

13 - 14 DIBELIUS, M. Aufsätze zur Apostelgeschichte (1951) 12f. ET: Studies in the Acts of the Apostles (1956) 5f. SCHMITHALS, W. Paulus und Jakobus (1963) 41f. DUPONT, J. The Sources of Acts (1964) 17, 28, 39, 53, 54, 55, 62, 63, 67, 70, 83, 127, 135, 145, 153, 154. HAHN, F. Das Verständnis der Mission im Neuen Testament (^{2}1965) 50, 63, 71, 74. SCHILLE, G. Die urchristliche Kollegialmission (1967) 21f., 97ff. KUEMMEL, W. G. Einleitung in das Neue Testament (1973) 263f. DÖMER, M., Das Heil Gottes: Studien zur Theologie des lukanischen Doppelwerkes (Köln/Bonn 1978) 172-73. HOLMBERG, B., Paul and Power (Lund 1978) 64. MARTIN, R. P., New Testament Foundations. II (Exeter 1978) 104-08. MATTILL, A. J., "The Value of Acts as a Source for the Study of Paul" in: C. H. Talbert (ed.) Perspectives on Luke-Acts (Danville 1978) 84, 91. JEWETT, R., A Chronology of Paul's Life (Philadelphia 1979) 11-14, 56. PRAST, F.,

Presbyter und Evangelium in nachapostolischer Zeit (Stuttgart 1979) 213, 224n.5.

13 FEINE, D. P./BEHM, D. J. Einleitung in das Neue Testament (1950) 141f. LOEVESTAM, E. Son and Saviour (1961) 7, 15, 38ff., 49f., 73, 79, 81ff., 85ff. GOULDER, M. D. Type and History in Acts (1964) 97, 106, 150, 202. BOUSSET, W. Die Religion des Judentums im Späthellenistischen Zeitalter (1966 = 1926) 218. SCHILLE, G. Anfänge der Kirche (1966) 53ff. VIELHAUER, P., "On the 'Paulism' of Acts" in: L. E. Keck/J. L. Martyn (eds.) Studies in Luke-Acts. FS. P. Schubert (Nashville 1966) 44-45. HOLTZ, T. Untersuchungen über die Alttestamentlichen Zitate bei Lukas (1968) 131-36. SCHREINER, J. Gestalt und Anspruch des Neuen Testaments (1969) 74f. GASQUE, W., A History of the Criticism of the Acts of the Apostles (Tübingen 1975) 119, 196, 220, 231. VIA, E. J., "An Interpretation of Acts 7:35-37 from the Perspective of Major Themes in Luke-Acts" in: P. J. Achtemeier (ed.) SBL Seminar Papers 1978/II (Missoula 1978) 214-16. KURZ, W. S., "Luke-Acts and Historiography in the Greek Bible" in: P. J. Achtemeier (ed.) SBL Seminar Papers 1980 (Chico, Cal. 1980) 285. GEIGER, G., Kirche unterwegs (Klosterneuburg 1981).

13:1ff. BORNKAMM-BARTH-HELD, Ueberlieferung und Auslegung im Matthäus-Evangelium ([2]1961) 16. HAHN, F. Das Verständnis der Mission im Neuen Testament ([2]1965) 49, 66, 116f. MERKLEIN, H. Das Kirchliche Amt nach dem Epheserbrief (1973) 240, 241, 232, 247, 249, 250, 253, 254, 255, 276, 277, 279.

13:1-13 HUBBARD, B. J., "The Role of Commissioning Accounts in Acts" in: C. H. Talbert (ed.) Perspectives on Luke-Acts (Danville 1978) 190, 193, 197.

13:1-7 SWIDLER, L., Biblical Affirmations of Woman (Philadelphia 1979) 333.

13:1-5 BAUMGARTEN, J., Paulus und die Apokalyptik (Neukirchen-Vluyn 1975) 51-52.

13:1-4 SHEPARD, J. W., The Life and Letters of St. Paul (Grand Rapids 1950) 95-98. SCHNIDER, F. Jesus der Prophet (1973) 58f., 98.

13:1-3 LOHSE, E. Die Ordination im Spätjudentum und im Neuen Testament (1951) 71-74. SEVENSTER, G. Studia Paulina (1953) 188-201. FLEW, R. N. Jesus and His Church (1956) 143n, 148n. SCHWEIZER, E. Gemeinde und Gemeinde-Ordnung im Neuen Testament (1959) §§ 51m, 22c, 241, 25c. BEST, E. "Acts xiii. 1-3," JThS 11 (2, 1960) 344-48. KLEIN, G. Die Zwölf Apostel (1961) 168ff. STRECKER, G., Der Weg der Gerechtigkeit (1962) 40. ROLOFF, J. Apostolat-Verkündigung-Kirche (1965) 207-10.

SATAKE, A. Die Gemeindeordnung in der Johannesapokalypse (1966) 169ff. KERTELGE, K. Gemeinde und Amt im Neuen Testament (1972) 97f. BROCKHAUS, U., Charisma und Amt (Wuppertal 1975²) 120ff. ROBECK, C., "The Gift of Prophecy in Acts and Paul, Part I" Studies in Biblical Theology 5 (1975) 15-38. DOCKX, S., "L'ordination de Barnabé et de Saul d'après Actes 13,1-3" NRTh 98 (1976) 238-50. LOHSE, E., "Das Amt 'das die Versöhnung predigt' " in: J. Friedrich et al. (eds.) Rechtfertigung. FS. E. Käsemann (Tübingen/Göttingen 1976) 343-44. "Amt" in: TRE 2 (1978) 515. PRAST, F., Presbyter und Evangelium in nachapostolischer Zeit (Stuttgart 1979) 225.

13:1-2 WILSON, S. G. The Gentiles and the Gentile Mission in Luke-Acts (1973) 181-82.

13:1 ROBERTSON, A. T. Luke the Historian in the Light of Research (1920) 17, 18, 22, 75, 80, 83. CLARK, A. C. The Acts of the Apostles (1933) 201, 238, 266, 350. FLEW, R. N. Jesus and His Church (1956) 144n. SCHMITHALS, W. Paulus und Jakobus (1963) 23. GOULDER, M. D. Type and History in Acts (1964) 69, 71, 73f., 101, 103, 171, 233. HAHN, F. Das Verständnis der Mission im Neuen Testament (²1965) 49. DUPONT, J. Etudes sur les Actes des Apôtres (1967) 210, 221, 222, 227, 362. SCHILLE, G. Die urchristliche Kollegialmission (1967) 23f., 42ff., 69. HENGEL, M. Judentum und Hellenismus (1969) 194. ET: Judaism and Hellenism (1974) I 105. CAVALLIN, H. C. C., Life After Death. I (Lund 1974) 4, 2n4. ZINGG, P., Das Wachsen der Kirche (Freiburg 1974) 191-92. METZGER, B. M., The Early Versions of the New Testament (Oxford 1977) 86. HOLMBERG, B., Paul and Power (Lund 1978) 17. HENGEL, M., Zur urchristlichen Geschichtsschreibung (Stuttgart 1979) 63; ET: J. Bowden (trans.) Acts and the History of Earliest Christianity (London 1979) 72. MÜLLER, U. B., "Zur Rezeption gesetzeskritischer Jesusüberlieferung im frühen Christentum" NTS 27 (1981) 160.

13:2.3.6 BOUSSET, W. Die Religion des Judentums im Späthellenistischen Zeitalter (1966 = 1926) 169, 180, 340.

13:2-3 EHRHARDT, A. The Acts of the Apostles (1969) 78ff., 104.

13:2 DELLING, G. Die Zueignung des Heils in der Taufe (1961) 87. GOULDER, M. D. Type and History in Acts (1964) 28, 76, 78f., 101, 105. KAESEMANN, E. Exegetische Versuche und Besinnungen (1964) II 88. KAESEMANN, E. New Testament Questions of Today (1969) 88. STAEHLIN, G. "τὸ πνεῦμα 'Ιησου (Apostelgeschichte 16:7)," in: Christ and the Spirit in the New Testament (1973) B. Lindars/S. S. Smalley, eds., 231, 239, 244, 249f. TRITES, A. A., The New Testament Concept of Witness (Cambridge 1977) 134, 135, 149, 152. "Apostelgeschichte" in:

TRE 3 (1978) 493. SCHNEIDER, G., "Gott und Christus als κυριος nach der Apostelgeschichte" in: J. Zmijewski/E. Nellessen
(eds.) Begegnung mit dem Wort. FS. H. Zimmermann (Bonn 1980)
163, 169, 171-72. MÜLLER, U. B., "Zur Rezeption gesetzeskritischer Jesusüberlieferung im frühen Christentum" NTS 27 (1981)
160, 167.

13:3 ADLER, N., Taufe und Handauflegung. Eine exegetisch-theologische Untersuchung von Apg 8,14-17 (Münster 1951) 60-61, 64-
65. FLEW, R. N. Jesus and His Church (1956) 146, 146n. DELL-
ING, G. Die Taufe im Neuen Testament (1963) 66. HENGEL, M.
Judentum und Hellenismus (1969) 194. ET: Judaism and Hellenism (1974) I 105.

13:4-15.39 KLEIN, G. Die Zwölf Apostel (1961) 168ff.

13:4-14.28 SHEPARD, J. W., The Life and Letters of St. Paul (Grand Rapids
1950) 95-98.

13:4-12 BEYER, H. W. Die Apostelgeschichte (1947) 79.

13:4 DUPONT, J. The Sources of Acts (1964) 60, 62, 100, 126, 135.

13:5.7.12 FLEW, R. N. Jesus and His Church (1956) 112.

13:5 BEYER, H. W. Die Apostelgeschichte (1947) 79f. STONE-
HOUSE, N. B. The Witness of Luke to Christ (1951) 37f. BLAIR,
E. P. Jesus in the Gospel of Matthew (1960) 39. DUPONT, J.
Etudes sur les Actes des Apôtres (1967) 93, 210, 226, 521, 524.

13:6ff. HAHN, F. Das Verständnis der Mission im Neuen Testament
(²1965) 52.

13:6-12 RICHARDSON, A. The Miracle-Stories of the Gospels (1948) 17f.
DANIEL, C. "Un Essénien mentionné dans les Actes des Apôtres:
Barjésu," Muséon 84 (3-4, 1971) 455-76. "Apostelgeschichte" in:
TRE 3 (1978) 497. JEWETT, R., A Chronology of Paul's Life
(Philadelphia 1979) 36. PRAST, F., Presbyter und Evangelium in
nachapostolischer Zeit (Stuttgart 1979) 168-69.

13:6-8 CLARK, A. C. The Acts of the Apostles (1933) 350-54.

13:6.8.10f. BETZ, H. D. Lukian von Samosata und das Neue Testament (1961)
107f., 110, 112, 147, 185.

13:6 NICKELS, P. Targum and New Testament (1967) 65. HENGEL,
M. Judentum und Hellenismus (1969) 442. ET: Judaism and Hellenism (1974) II 163. PETZKE, G. Die Traditionen über Apollonius von Tyana und das Neue Testament (1970) 91, 192.
"Aramäisch" in: TRE 3 (1978) 603.

13:7-12 BEYER, J. W. Die Apostelgeschichte (1947) 80f. VAN ELD-
EREN, B. "Some Archaeological Observations on Paul's First
Missionary Journey," in: Apostolic History and the Gospel (1970)
W. W. Gasque/R. P. Martin eds., 151-61.

13:8-12 "Apostelgeschichte" in: TRE 3 (1978) 499.

13:8-11 DUNN, J. D. G., Jesus and the Spirit (London 1975) 163, 166, 168-69.

13:8 YAURE, L. "Elymas-Nehelamite-Pethor," JBL 79 (4, 1960) 297-314. EHRHARDT, A. The Acts of the Apostles (1969) 80f. HENGEL, M. Judentum und Hellenismus (1969) 442. ET: Judaism and Hellenism (1974) II 163. KRAFT, H., Die Entstehung des Christentums (Darmstadt 1981) 265-66.

13:9 BEYER, H. W. Die Apostelgeschichte (1947) 81. BURCHARD, C. Der dreizehnte Zeuge (1970) 36f.

13:10-41 BETHGE, F. Die paulinischen Reden der Apostelgeschichte (1887) 12-64.

13:10 BAUMBACH, G. Das Verständnis des Bösen in den synoptischen Evangelien (1963) 168ff. HAHN, F. Christologische Hoheitstitel (1963) 72. BROWN, S. Apostasy and Perseverance in the Theology of Luke (1969) 125, 135f. METZGER, B. M., The Early Versions of the New Testament (Oxford 1977) 88. BERGMEIER, R., Glaube als Gabe nach Johannes (Stuttgart 1980) 223. SCHNEIDER, G., "Gott und Christus als κυριος nach der Apostelgeschichte" in: J. Zmijewski/E. Nellessen (eds.) Begegnung mit dem Wort. FS. H. Zimmermann (Bonn 1980) 163, 169, 171-72.

13:11 PALLIS, A., Notes on St. Luke and the Acts (London 1928) 65-66. KNOX, W. L. The Sources of the Synoptic Gospels II (1957) 40, 115. NICKELS, P. Targum and New Testament (1967) 65.

13:12 DELLING, G. Die Zueignung des Heils in der Taufe (1961) 87, 91.

13:13-52 WIKENHAUSER, A. Die Apostelgeschichte (1951) 128-31. O'-TOOLE, R. F., "Christ's Resurrection in Acts 13,13-52" Biblica 60 (1979) 361-72.

13:13 PARKER, P. The Gospel Before Mark (1953) 150-51. HENGEL, M. Judentum und Hellenismus (1969) 194. ET: Judaism and Hellenism (1974) I 105. NORTH, J. L., "Μάρκος ὁ κολοβοδάκτυλος: Hippolytus, Elenchus, VII.30" JThS 28 (1977) 498-507. ELLIOTT, J. H., "Peter, Sylvanus and Mark in 1 Peter and Acts: Sociological-Exegetical Perspectives on a Petrine Group in Rome" in: W. Haubeck/M. Bachmann (eds.) Wort in der Zeit. FS. K. H. Rengstorf (Leiden 1980) 260-61

13:14ff. HAHN, F. Das Verständnis der Mission im Neuen Testament (²1965) 52.

13:14-16, FUCHS, E. GPM 21/1 (1966-1967) 182-84. LANGE, E. (ed.),
26-33, 37-39 Predigtstudien für das Kirchenjahr (1970-1971) 45-53.

13:14-52 RADL, W., Paulus und Jesus im lukanischen Doppelwerk ((Bern/ Frankfurt 1975) 82-94. MIESNER, D. R., ''The Missionary Journeys Narrative: Patterns and Implications'' in: C. H. Talbert (ed.) Perspectives on Luke-Acts (Danville 1978) 205.

13:14 CONZELMANN, H. Die Apostelgeschichte (1963) 75. CONZELMANN, H. und LINDEMANN, A., Arbeitsbuch zum Neuen Testament (Tübingen 1974) 118.

13:15-41 GLOMBITZA, O. ''Akta xiii. 15-41. Analyse einer Lukanischen Predigt vor Juden,'' NTS 5 (4, 1959) 306-17. McDONALD, J. I. H., Kerygma and Didache (Cambridge 1980) 50-52.

13:15f. BOUSSET, W. Die Religion des Judentum im Späthellenistischen Zeitalter (1966 = 1926) 80f., 144, 161, 173.

13:15 BERGER, K. Die Gesetzesauslegung Jesu (1972) 109-27.

13:16ff. BAUERNFEIND, O. ''Der Schluss der antiochenischen Paulusrede,'' in: Theologie als Glaubenswagnis (1954) K. Heim ed., 74-78. LOEVESTAM, E. Son and Saviour (1961) 6, 10, 37f., 71f., 83ff. HAHN, F. Christologische Hoheitstitel (1963) 384.

13:16-41 DIBELIUS, M. Aufsätze zur Apostelgeschichte (1951) 104f., 142f. ET: Studies in the Acts of the Apostles (1956) 119f., 165f. HARTMAN, L. ''David's son. Apropå Acta 13, 16-41,'' SEA 28-29 (1963-1964) 117-34. HAHN, F. Das Verständnis der Mission im Neuen Testament (²1965) 117. WILCOX, M. The Semitisms of Acts (1965) 158, 161ff. NICKELS, P. Targum and New Testament (1967) 65. BLANK, J. Paulus und Jesus (1968) 34-42. JERVELL, J. ''Midt i Israels historie,'' NTT 69 (3, 1968) 130-38. BURCHARD, C. Der dreizehnte Zeuge (1970) 116, 138-42. EVANS, C. F. '' 'Speeches' in Acts,'' in: Mélanges Bibliques en hommage au R. P. Béda Rigaux (1970) A. Descamps/A. de Halleux eds., 294-95. GASTON, L. No Stone on Another (1970) 254, 256, 307-08. DELLING, G. ''Israels Geschichte und Jesusgeschehen nach Acta,'' in: Neues Testament und Geschichte (1972) H. Baltensweiler/B. Reicke eds., 187-97. KRAENKL, W. Jesus der Knecht Gottes (1972) 8, 14-17, 53, 57, 60, 71, 78, 175. KLIESCH, K., Das heilsgeschichtliche Credo in den Reden der Apostelgeschichte (Köln/Bonn 1975) 75ff., 163-69. DUMAIS, M., Le langage de l'evangélisation. L'annonce missionnaire en milieu juif (Acts 13,16-41) (Montreal 1976) passim. NELLESSEN, E., Zeugnis für Jesus und das Wort (Köln 1976) 198-202. ''Apostelgeschichte'' in: TRE 3 (1978) 492, 497. BAUERNFEIND, O., ''Der Schluss der Antiochenischen Paulusrede'' in: Kommentar und Studien zur Apostelgeschichte (Tübingen 1980) 449-63; [orig. in: Theologie als Glaubenswagnis. FS. K. Heim (Hamburg 1954) 64-78]. PILLAI, C. A. J., Apostolic Interpretation of History. A

Commentary on Acts 13:16-41 (Hicksville 1980) passim. DOWN-ING, F. G., "Ethical Pagan Theism and the Speeches in Acts" NTS 27 (1980-1981) 554-561.

13:16 WILCOX, M., "The 'God-Fearers' in Acts—A Reconsideration" JSNT 13 (1981) 107.

13:17-41 MEYER, B. M., The Aims of Jesus (London 1979) 66-69.

13:17-23 WILCKENS, U. Die Missionsreden der Apostelgeschichte (³1974) 38, 50, 53, 54, 102, 104, 143, 163, 221, 231.

13:17-22 KLIESCH, K., Das heilsgeschichtliche Credo in den Reden der Apostelgeschichte (Köln/Bonn 1975) 38-44, 45-47, 110.

13:17 DUPONT, D. J., The Salvation of the Gentiles (New York 1979) 125.

13:18 GORDON, R. P., "Targumic Parallels to Acts XIII 18 and Didache XIV 3" NovT 16 (1974) 285-89.

13:19-21 CLARK, A. C. The Acts of the Apostles (1933) xlix, 354ff.

13:20 MERRILL, E. H., "Paul's use of 'About 450 Years' in Acts 13:20" BiblSa 138 (1981) 246-57.

13:21-23 DUPONT, D. J., The Salvation of the Gentiles (New York 1979) 136-37, 144.

13:21 STONEHOUSE, N. B. The Witness of Matthew and Mark to Christ (1944) 114.

13:22-14:23 WILCOX, M. The Semitisms of Acts (1965) 59ff.

13:22-23 HAHN, F. Christologische Hoheitstitel (1963) 278. KRAENKL, E. Jesus der Knecht Gottes (1972) 85-87.

13:22 WILCOX, M. The Semitisms of Acts (1965) 21-24, 52, 54n, 56n, 128n, 161, 162, 164, 181, 182. DUPONT, J. Etudes sur les Actes des Apôtres (1967) 263, 269, 281, 282, 284, 285, 346, 347. NICKELS, P. Targum and New Testament (1967) 65. HARMAN, A. M., Paul's Use of Psalms (Ann Arbor, Mich. 1968) 26-29. BEUTLER, J. Martyria (1972) 180, 184, 205, 213, 221, 290, 293. WILCKENS, U. Die Missionsreden der Apostelgeschichte (³1975) 123, 143, 146, 148, 162, 164, 222. GORDON, R. P., "Targumic Parallels to Acts XIII 18 and Didache XIV 3" NovT 16 (1974) 286-87. NELLESSEN, E., Zeugnis für Jesus und das Wort (Köln 1976) 259-60.

13:23-41 QUESNELL, Q. This Good News (1963) 123f.

13:23.32-37 BURGER, C. Jesus als Davidssohn (1970) 137-52.

13:23 PALLIS, A., Notes on St. Luke and the Acts (London 1928) 66. LOEVESTAM, E. Son and Saviour (1961) 6f., 10f., 38f., 56, 71, 79ff., 84f. HAHN, F. Christologische Hoheitstitel (1963) 253. SEEBERG, A. Der Katechismus der Urchristenheit (1966) 136f. DUPONT, J. Etudes sur les Actes des Apôtres (1967) 107, 114,

149, 263, 268, 278, 291, 358, 359. WILCKENS, U. Die Missionsreden der Apostelgeschichte ([3]1974) 10, 45, 51, 102, 103, 143, 171, 176, 177, 184, 186, 217, 222, 227, 232. KLIESCH, K., Das heilsgeschichtliche Credo in den Reden der Apostelgeschichte (Köln/Bonn 1975) 72-74, 110. PRAST, F. Presbyter und Evangelium in nachapostolischer Zeit (Stuttgart 1979) 290-91, 323.

13:24-25 STONEHOUSE, N. B. The Witness of Matthew and Mark to Christ (1944) 8. ROBINSON, J. M. Kerygma und historischer Jesus (1960) 72, 146. KRAENKL, E. Jesus der Knecht Gottes (1972) 35, 54, 59, 68, 80, 91-93, 94f., 96. WILCKENS, U. Die Missionsreden der Apostelgeschichte ([3]1974) 16, 51, 54, 101, 102, 103-05, 229, 241.

13:24 DELLING, G. Die Taufe im Neuen Testament (1963) 43. HAHN, F. Das Verständnis der Mission im Neuen Testament ([2]1965) 114. SMITH, M. Clement of Alexandria and a secret Gospel of Mark (1973) 206f.

13:25 HAHN, F. Christologische Hoheitstitel (1963) 374, 393. NICKELS, P. Targum and New Testament (1967) 65. NEUSNER, J. (ed.) Christianity, Judaism and Other Greco-Roman Cults I FS. M. Smith (Leiden 1975) 187-91. CRIBBS, F. L., "The Agreements that Exist between John and Acts" in: C. H. Talbert (ed.) Perspectives on Luke-Acts (Danville 1978) 47-48, 60.

13:26-41 HOOKER, M. D. Jesus and the Servant (1959) 118-20.

13:26 DUPONT, J. Etudes sur les Actes des Apôtres (1967) 269, 284, 359, 441. HARMAN, A. M., Paul's use of the Psalms (Ann Arbor, Mich 1968) 170-71. MÄRZ, C-P., Das Wort Gottes bei Lukas (Leipzig 1973) 19-21. STANTON, G. N. Jesus of Nazareth in New Testament Preaching (1974) 26, 65, 72, 74, 83, 111. WILCKENS, U. Die Missionsreden der Apostelgeschichte ([3]1974) 51, 102, 104, 176, 179, 185, 186. PRAST, F. Presbyter und Evangelium in nachapostolischer Zeit (Stuttgart 1979) 289-92, 351. CLARK, K. W., "The Israel of God" in: The Gentile Bias and Other Essays (Leiden 1980) 25. WILCOX, M., "The 'God-Fearers' in Acts—A Reconsideration" JSNT 13 (1981) 107.

13:27ff. BARRETT, C. K., "Is There a Theological Tendency in Codex Bezae?" in: E. Best/R. McL. Wilson (eds.) Text and Interpretation. FS. M. Black (Cambridge 1979) 24-25.

13:27-31 HAHN, F. Christologische Hoheitstitel (1963) 215.

13:27-30 SCHELKLE, K. H. Die Passion Jesu in der Verkündigung des Neuen Testaments (1949) 248f.

13:27-29 BROER, I. Die Urgemeinde und das Grab Jesu (1972) 258, 261ff. KRAENKL, E. Jesus der Knecht Gottes (1972) 116f. NELLESSEN, E., Zeugnis für Jesus und das Wort (Köln 1976) 202-03.

WILCOX, M., " 'Upon the Tree' - Deut 21:22-23 in the New Testament" JBL 96 (1977) 85-99.

13:27-28 WILCKENS, U., Die Missionsreden der Apostelgeschichte (³1974) 51, 53, 110, 134f. DUPONT, D. J., The Salvation of the Gentiles (New York 1979) 68-69/ WILCH, J. R., "Jüdische Schuld am Tode Jesu - Antijudaismus in der Apostelgeschichte?" in: W. Haubeck/ M. Bachmann (eds.) Wort in der Zeit. FS. K. H. Rengstorf (Leiden 1980) 241.

13:27 PALLIS, A., Notes on St. Luke and the Acts (London 1928) 66. LOEVESTAM, E. Son and Saviour (1961) 39f. DELLING, G. Die Taufe im Neuen Testament (1963) 60. PROUBCAN, S. "The Pauline Message and the Prophets," in: Studiorum Paulinorum Congressus Internationalis Catholicus (1961) Vol. I (1963) 253f. HAHN, F. Das Verständnis der Mission im Neuen Testament (²1965) 113, 118. EPP, E. J. The theological tendency of Codex Bezae Cantabrigiensis in Acts (1966) 38, 45n.1, 46-48, 59n.2, 50, 55-57, 58n.1, 168, 170. SCHNEIDER, G. Verleugnung, Verspottung und Verhör Jesu nach Lukas 22,54-71 (1969) 36, 157, 214, 215. WILSON, S. G. NTS 16 (1969-1970) 331f. BROER, I., Die Urgemeinde und das Grab Jesu (1972) 30, 260f. KRAENKL, E. Jesus der Knecht Gottes (1972) 35, 103, 106f., 209. WANKE, J., Die Emmauserzählung. Eine redaktionsgeschichtliche Untersuchung zu Lk 24,13-25 (Leipzig 1973) 119.

13:28-31 WILCOX, M. The Semitisms of Acts (1965) 163ff.

13:28 PALLIS, A., Notes on St. Luke and the Acts (London 1928) 66-67. KAESEMANN, E. Exegetische Versuche und Besinnungen (1964) I 102. WILCOX, M. The Semitisms of Acts (1965) 67, 118-20, 121, 127-28, 130n, 154, 162, 163, 166, 171. EPP, E. J. The theological tendency of Codex Bezae Cantabrigiensis in Acts (1966) 47, 56-58, 126, 152, 169. DUPONT, J. Etudes sur les Actes des Apôtres (1967) 252, 281, 434, 528, 540. NICKELS, P. Targum and New Testament (1967) 65f. BROER, I. Die Urgemeinde und das Grab Jesu (1972) 256f. WILCKENS, U. Die Missionsreden der Apostelgeschichte (³1974) 102, 132, 133, 134, 135, 170. HUBBARD, B. J., "Luke, Josephus and Rome: A Comparative Approach to the Lukan Sitz im Leben" in: P. J. Achtemeier (ed.) SBL Seminar Papers 1979/I (Missoula 1979) 65.

13:29-31 MUSSNER, F., "Zur stilistischen und semantischen Struktur der Formel von 1 Kor 15:3-5" in: R. Schnackenburg et al (eds.) Die Kirche des Anfangs. FS. H. Schürmann (Freiburg/Basel/Wien 1978) 411-12.

13:29 FARRER, A. St Matthew and St Mark (1954) 187. EPP, E. J. The theological tendency of Codex Bezae Cantabrigiensis in Acts (1966)

11, 47, 48, 56-58, 152, 169. BLINZER, J. Der Prozess Jesu (⁴1969) 33, 359, 389, 436f. BROER, I. Die Urgemeinde und das Grab Jesu (1972) 250-63. WILCKENS, U. Die Missionsreden der Apostelgeschichte (³1974) 135f.

13:30-31 ALSUP, J. E., The Post-Resurrection Appearance Stories of the Gospel-Tradition (Stuttgart 1975) 81-83. "Auferstehung" in: TRE 4 (1979) 485.

13:30 LOEVESTAM, E. Son and Saviour (1961) 8f. HAHN, F. Christologische Hoheitstitel (1963) 205. KRAMER, W. Christos Kyrios Gottessohn (1963) § 3f. WILCKENS, U. Die Missionsreden der Apostelgeschichte (³1974) 51, 122, 135, 137, 139.

13:31-33 MÄRZ, C-P., Das Wort Gottes bei Lukas (Leipzig 1973) 52-55. PRAST, F. Presbyter und Evangelium in nachapostolischer Zeit (Stuttgart 1979) 320.

13:31-32 ZINGG, P., Das Wachsen der Kirche (Freiburg 1974) 143-44.

13:31 KLEIN, G. Die Zwölf Apostel (1961) 204f. ROLOFF, J. Apostolat-Verkündigung-Kirche (1965) 191f. BURCHARD, C. Der dreizehnte Zeuge (1970) 130-35. KRAENKL, E. Jesus der Knecht Gottes (1972) 59, 80, 100, 145, 167, 168, 171. WILCKENS, U. Die Missionsreden der Apostelgeschichte (³1974) 10, 51, 80, 144f., 145, 147, 150, 192. NELLESSEN, E., Zeugnis für Jesus und das Wort (Köln 1976) 198-211. PRAST, F., Presbyter und Evangelium in nachapostolischer Zeit (Stuttgart 1979) 306-07, 314, 310, 324.

13:32ff. HAHN, F. Christologische Hoheitstitel (1963) 384.

13:32-37 LOEVESTAM, E. Son and Saviour (1961). FITZMYER, J. A. ThS 23 (3, 1962) 467-69. HOLTZ, T. ThLZ 88 (3, 1963) 202-03. LINDARS, B. JThS 14 81, 1963, 146-49. GNILKA, J. ThR 60 (1, 1963) 21-23. HAHN, F. Christologische Hoheitstitel (1963) 291. KRAENKL, E. Jesus der Knecht Gottes (1972) 54, 136-43. KAISER, W. C., "The Promise to David in Psalm 16 and its Application in Acts 2:25-33 and 13:32-37" JEThS 23 (1980) 219-29.

13:32-36 HAHN, F. Christologische Hoheitstitel (1963) 278. BERGER, K., Exegese des Neuen Testaments (Heidelberg 1977) 24-25.

13:32-33 DUPONT, J. Etudes sur les Actes des Apôtres (1967) 290, 295, 351, 358, 359. MOULE, C. F. D. NTS 14 (1967-1968) 312f. KRAENKL, E. Jesus der Knecht Gottes (1972) 33f. KLIESCH, K., Das heilsgeschichtliche Credo in den Reden der Apostelgeschichte (Köln/Bonn 1975) 72-74, 110. NELLESSEN, E., Zeugnis für Jesus und das Wort (Köln 1976) 204-05. DUPONT, D. J., The Salvation of the Gentiles (New York 1979) 115.

13:32 KAESEMANN, E. Exegetische Versuche und Besinnungen (1964)

I 131. PRAST, F., Presbyter und Evangelium in nachapostolischer Zeit (Stuttgart 1979) 291.

13:33-37 GOLDSMITH, D. "Acts 13:33-37: A Pesher on II Samuel 7," JBL 87 (3, 1968) 321-24.

13:33-35 HOLTZ, T. Untersuchungen über die Alttestamentlichen Zitate bei Lukas (1968) 137-45. LONGENECKER, R. N., Biblical Exegesis in the Apostolic Period (Grand Rapids 1975) 87, 96-98, 102-03.

13:33-34 HAHN, F. Christologische Hoheitstitel (1963) 204. WILCKENS, U. Die Missionsreden der Apostelgeschichte (³1974) 137, 139, 177, 178, 185, 227. FRIEDRICH, G., "Die Bedeutung der Auferweckung Jesu nach Aussagen des Neuen Testaments" in: Auf das Wort kommt es an (Göttingen 1978) 360.

13:33 BLAIR, E. P. Jesus in the Gospel of Matthew (1960) 64. KILPATRICK, G. D. "Acts XIII. 33 and Tertullian, Adv. Marc. IV. xxii.8," JThS 11 (1, 1960) 53. LOEVESTAM, E. Son and Saviour (1961) 5, 8ff., 15, 37ff., 42, 47ff., 79, 84, 97, 109. SCHWEIZER, E. Erniedrigung und Erhöhung bei Jesus und seinen Nachfolgern (1962) § 4g, 5c. WAINWRIGHT, A. W. The Trinity in the New Testament (1962) 183-84. HAHN, F. Christologische Hoheitstitel (1963) 291. EPP, E. J. The theological tendency of Codex Bezae Cantabrigiensis in Acts (1966) 48, 54, 62f., 79f. DUPONT, J. Etudes sur les Actes des Apôtres (1967) 118, 149, 265, 268, 281, 284, 294-97, 301, 320, 337, 350. HARMAN, A. M., Paul's Use of the Psalms (Ann Arbor, Michigan 1968) 30-40. RESE, M. Alttestamentliche Motive in der Christologie des Lukas (1969) 81-86. KRAENKL, E. Jesus der Knecht Gottes (1972) 80, 130, 136-38, 162, 207, 210. KLIESCH, K., Das heilsgeschichtliche Credo in den Reden der Apostelgeschichte (Köln/Bonn 1975) 131-32. GOPPELT, L., Theologie des Neuen Testaments. II (Göttingen 1976) 347-48. GAFFIN, R. B., The Centrality of the Resurrection (Grand Rapids 1978) 113-14, 118-19. "Auferstehung" in: TRE 4 (1979) 479. DUPONT, D. J., The Salvation of the Gentiles (New York 1979) 117, 147. DUNN, J. D., Christology in the Making (London 1980) 35-36, 50-51.

13:34-37 DUPONT, J. Etudes sur les Actes des Apôtres (1967) 266, 281, 290, 291, 338, 358. KRAENKL, E. Jesus der Knecht Gottes (1972) 34f., 146.

13:34 DUPONT, J. "TA OSIA DAVID TA PISTA (Ac xiii 34 = Is lv 3)," Rev Bi 58 (1, 1961) 91-114. DUPONT, J. Etudes sur les Actes des Apôtres (1967) 337-59. MUSSNER, F. "Die Idee der Apokatastasis in der Apostelgeschichte," in: Praesentia Salutis (1967) 223. RESE, M. Alttestamentliche Motive in der Christologie des Lukas (1959) 69-89. KRAENKL, E. Jesus der Knecht Gottes (1972)

80, 130, 139f., 194, 207, 210. WILCKENS, U. Die Missionsreden der Apostelgeschichte (³1974) 142, 162, 178, 227, 232. FRIEDRICH, G., "Die Bedeutung der Auferweckung Jesu nach Aussagen des Neuen Testaments" in: Auf das Wort kommt es an (Göttingen 1978) 370-71. "Auferstehung" in: TRE 4 (1979) 490. DUPONT, D. J., The Salvation of the Gentiles (New York 1979) 145-46, 155.

13:35ff. DUNN, J. D. G., Jesus and the Spirit (London 1975) 118, 119.

13:35-37 KRAENKL, E. Jesus der Knecht Gottes (1972) 61, 140f., 207.

13:35 HARMAN, A. M., Paul's Use of the Psalms (Ann Arbor, Michigan 1968) 40-45. RESE, M. Alttestamentliche Motive in der Christologie des Lukas (1969) 89-93. NÖTSCHER, F., Altorientalischer und alttestamentlicher Auferstehungsglaube (Darmstadt 1970 = 1926) 231.

13:36-37 DELLING, G. Die Taufe im Neuen Testament (1963) 90. KLIESCH, K., Das heilsgeschichtliche Credo in den Reden der Apostelgeschichte (Köln/Bonn 1975) 132-36.

13:36 DUPONT, J. Etudes sur les Actes des Apôtres (1967) 339-41. FISCHER, U., Eschatologie und Jenseitserwartung im hellenistischen Diasporajudentum (Berlin 1978) 219.

13:37-38 STROBEL, A. Erkenntnis und Bekenntnis der Sünde in neutestamentlicher Zeit (1968) 57.

13:37 HAHN, F. Christologische Hoheitstitel (1963) 204. KRAMER, W. Christos Kyrios Gottessohn (1963) § 3f. "Auferstehung" in: TRE 4 (1979) 480.

13:38-41 QUESNELL, Q. This Good News (1964) 45f.

13:38-39 STUHLMACHER, P. Gerechtigkeit Gottes bei Paulus (1965) 194f. KRAENKL, E. Jesus der Knecht Gottes (1972) 15, 18, 34, 54, 66, 139, 181-83, 186, 208. WILCKENS, U. Die Missionsreden der Apostelgeschichte (³1974) 52, 54, 179, 183, 184, 186. MENOUD, P. H., "Le salut par la foi selon le livre des Actes - Actes 13:38-39" in: Jésus-Christ et la foi (Neuchâtel/Paris 1975) 136-42. MUSSNER, F., Petrus und Paulus - Pole der Einheit (Freiburg/Basel/Wien 1976) 106-07. WILSON, S. G., "Law and Judaism in Acts" in: P. J. Achtemeier (ed.) SBL Seminar Papers 1980 (Chico, Cal. 1980) 254.

13:38 DELLING, G. Die Zueignung des Heils in der Taufe (1961) 89. KAESEMANN, E. Exegetische Versuche und Besinnungen (1964) I 45. DELLING, G. Die Taufe im Neuen Testament (1963) 64. WILCOX, M. The Semitisms of Acts (1965) 90-91, 110, 161, 171. EPP, E. J. The theological tendency of Codex Bezae Cantabrigiensis in Acts (1966) 73 n.2, 81f., 168. DUPONT, J. Etudes sur les Actes des Apôtres (1967) 352, 358, 359, 439, 441, 456. NICK-

ELS, P. Targum and New Testament (1967) 66. DUPONT, D. J.,
The Salvation of the Gentiles (New York 1979) 63. PRAST, F.,
Presbyter und Evangelium in nachapostolischer Zeit (Stuttgart 1979)
291.

13:39 KNOX, W. L. The Sources of the Synoptic Gospels II (1957) 115.
DELLING, G. Die Zueignung des Heils in der Taufe (1961) 93.
Epp, E. J. The theological tendency of Codex Bezae Cantabrigien-
sis in Acts (1966) 81f., 118. ZIESLER, J. A. The Meaning of
Righteousness in Paul (1972) 129f., 144f.

13:40-46 DUPONT, D. J., The Salvation of the Gentiles (New York 1979)
140.

13:40-41 STROBEL, A. Untersuchungen zum Eschatologischen Verzöge-
rungsproblem (1961) 281f. WILCKENS, U. Die Missionsreden der
Apostelgeschichte (^{3}1974) 53, 54, 102, 184. LOHFINK, G., Die
Sammlung Israels (München 1975) 85, 87-88, 91.

13:41 BRAUN, H. Qumran und NT II (1966) 306, 310, 320f. EPP, E. J.
The theological tendency of Codex Bezae Cantabrigiensis in Acts
(1966) 82f., 155, 164. DUPONT, J. Etudes sur les Actes des
Apôtres (1967) 258, 281, 356, 403. HOLTZ, T. Untersuchungen
über die Alttestamentlichen Zitate bei Lukas (1968) 19-21.

13:42-52 IWAND, H.-J. Predigt-Meditationen (1964) 690-96. SMOLIK, J.
GPM 20 (1965-1966) 317-22. BRESSAU, J./LOEWE, H. "Sonntag nach Trinitatis," in: Predigtstudien 1971-1972 (1971) E. Lange
ed., 154-59. HAAR, J. GPM 26 (3, 1972) 327-33.

13:42-43 PALLIS, A., Notes on St. Luke and the Acts (London 1928) 67.
ZINGG, P., Das Wachsen der Kirche (Freiburg 1974) 231-33.

13:42 DELLING, G. Die Zueignung des Heils in der Taufe (1961) 85.

13:43.50 BARRETT, C. K. The New Testament Background (1956) 164.

13:43 CLARK, A. C. The Acts of the Apostles (1933) xxxvi, 189, 227,
243, 313. EPP, E. J. The theological tendency of Codex Bezae
Cantabrigiensis in Acts (1966) 83f., 119, 136, 155, 168. WIL-
SON, S. G. The Gentiles and the Gentile Mission in Luke-Acts
(1973) 227-28. METZGER, B. M., The Early Versions of the New
Testament (Oxford 1977) 141. CLARK, K. W., "The Israel of
God" in: The Gentile Bias and Other Essays (Leiden 1980) 25.
WILCOX, M., "The 'God-Fearers' in Acts - a Reconsideration"
JSNT 13 (1981) 108.

13:44-52 IWAND, H.-J. Predigt-Meditationen (1964) 392-401. WILCOX,
M. The Semitisms of Acts (1965) 176-77. "Antisemitismus" in:
TRE 3 (1978) 125, 126. HUBBARD, B. J., "Luke, Josephus and
Rome: A Comparative Approach to the Lukan Sitz im Leben" in:
P. J. Achtemeier (ed.) SBL Seminar Papers 1979/I (Missoula 1979)
65.

13:44-47 ZINGG, P., Das Wachsen der Kirche (Freiburg 1974) 233-34.

13:45ff. WREGE, H.-T. Die Ueberlieferungsgeschichte der Bergpredigt (1968) 164, 174, 178f.

13:45-48 "Apostelgeschichte" in: TRE 3 (1978) 520.

13:45 WILCOX, M. The Semitisms of Acts (1965) 135-36, 154, 171, 176. NICKELS, P. Targum and New Testament (1967) 66.

13:46ff. WILCKENS, U. Die Missionsreden der Apostelgeschichte ([3]1974) 52f.

13:46-48 HAHN, F. Das Verständnis der Mission im Neuen Testament ([2]1965) 64, 117. WILSON, S. G. The Gentiles and the Gentile Mission in Luke-Acts (1973) 222-24, 226-30, 232-33.

13:46-47 HOOKER, M. D. Jesus and the Servant (1959) 114-16. DUPONT, D. J. "Le Salut des Gentils et la Signification Théologique du Livre des Actes," NTS 6 (1959-1960) 140f. DUPONT, D. J., The Salvation of the Gentiles (New York 1979) MEYER, B. F., The Aims of Jesus (London 1979) 66-69.

13:46 STRECKER, G. Der Weg der Gerechtigkeit (1962) 108. DELLING, G. Die Taufe im Neuen Testament (1963) 64. SHIMADA, K., The Formulary Material in First Peter (Th.D. Diss., Ann Arbor, Mich. 1966) 217-18. DUPONT, J. Etudes sur les Actes des Apôtres (1967) 402, 438, 452, 471, 521, 523, 524. KUENZI, M. Das Naherwartungslogion Matthäus 10,23 (1970) 16, 29, 76. ZINGG, P., Das Wachsen der Kirche (Freiburg 1974) 255-57, 257-63.

13:47 HAHN, F. Das Verständnis der Mission im Neuen Testament ([2]1965) 115. WILCOX, M. The Semitisms of Acts (1965) 49-51, 52n, 56n, 62, 171, 176. DUPONT, J. Etudes sur les Actes des Apôtres (1967) 261, 281, 414, 418, 455, 500, 524. HOLTZ, T. Untersuchungen über die Alttestamentlichen Zitate bei Lukas (1968) 32f. DUPONT, J. "La portée christologique de l'évangélisation des nations d'après Luc, 24,47," in: Neues Testament und Kirche (1974) J. Gnilka ed., 126, 136, 138, 140, 142. WESTERMANN, C., "Prophetenzitate im Neuen Testament" in: Forschung am Alten Testament. II (München 1974) 288-89; [orig. in: EvTh 27 (1967)]. PRAST, F., Presbyter und Evangelium in nachapostolischer Zeit (Stuttgart 1979) 274, 323, 326-28.

13:48-49 ZINGG, P., Das Wachsen der Kirche (Freiburg 1974) 234-36.

13:48 DELLING, G. Die Taufe im Neuen Testament (1963) 64, 70. DUPONT, J. Etudes sur les Actes des Apôtres (1967) 201, 356, 438, 448, 452, 453, 469, 472, 524. MÄRZ, C.-P., Das Wort Gottes bei Lukas (Leipzig 1973) 11-14.

13:49 MÄRZ, C.-P., Das Wort Gottes bei Lukas (Leipzig 1973) 14-17. ZINGG, P., Das Wachsen der Kirche (Freiburg 1974) 23-29.

13:50-52 ZINGG, P., Das Wachsen der Kirche (Freiburg 1974) 236-37.

13:50 EPP, E. J. The theological tendency of Codex Bezae Cantabrigiensis in Acts (1966) 134, 136f., 167, 169. EHRHARDT, A. The Acts of the Apostels (1969) 82f. ELLIGER, W., Paulus in Griechenland (Stuttgart 1978) 116n.54. SWIDLER, L., Biblical Affirmations of Woman (Philadelphia 1979) 293. WILCOX, M., "The 'God-Fearers' in Acts - A Reconsideration" JSNT 13 (1981) 109-11.

13:51-14:21 UNGER, M. F. "Archaeology and Paul's Visit to Iconium, Lystra, and Derbe," BiblSa 118 (470, 1961) 107-12.

13:52 LOHFINK, G. Die Himmelfahrt Jesu (1971) 232-36.

---

14 FEINE, D. P./BEHM, D. J. Einleitung in das Neue Testament (1950) 141f. SCHREINER, J. Gestalt und Anspruch des Neuen Testaments (1969) 74f. MIESNER, D. R., "The Missionary Journeys Narrative: Patterns and Implications" in: C. H. Talbert (ed.) Perspectives on Luke-Acts (Danville 1978) 205-06.

14:1ff. BLASS, F. Philosophy of the Gospels (1898) 121ff. HAHN, F. Das Verständnis der Mission im Neuen Testament (²1965) 52.

14:1-20 BEUTLER, J. "Die paulinische Heidenmission am Vorabend des Apostelkonzils. Zur Redaktionsgeschichte von Apg 14,1-20," ThPh 43 (3, 1968) 360-83.

14:1-2 BEYSCHLAG, K., Simon Magus und die christliche Gnosis (Tübingen 1974) 122n.49.

14:1 DELLING, G. Die Taufe im Neuen Testament (1963) 70. PALLIS. A., Notes on St. Luke and the Acts (London 1928) 67.

14:2 CLARK, A. C. The Acts of the Apostles (1933) 227, 243, 294, 357. THEYSSEN, G. W. "Unbelief" in the New Testament (Rüschlikon 1965) 58f. EPP, E. J. The theological tendency of Codex Bezae Cantabrigiensis in Acts (1966) 51 n.2, 137f., 167, 169. NICKELS, P. Targum and New Testament (1967) 66. "Apostelgeschichte" in: TRE 3 (1978) 488, 490. HORTON, F. L., "Reflections on the Semitisms of Luke-Acts" in: C. H. Talbert (ed.) Perspectives on Luke-Acts (Danville 1978) 21.

14:3 DELLING, G. Die Zueignung des Heils in der Taufe (1961) 91. WILCOX, M. The Semitisms of Acts (1965) 64, 122-23, 154n. NICKELS, P. Targum and New Testament (1967) 66. BEUTLER, J. Martyria (1972) 171, 178, 181, 205, 221, 295, 357. WILCK-

ENS, U. Die Missionsreden der Apostelgeschichte (^{3}1974) 124, 125, 144, 146, 148, 184. MÄRZ, C.-P., Das Wort Gottes bei Lukas (Leipzig 1973) 8-11. NELLESSEN, E., Zeugnis für Jesus und das Wort (Köln 1976) 260-63. PRAST, F., Presbyter und Evangelium in nachapostolischer Zeit (Stuttgart 1979) 270-71. SCHNEIDER, G., "Gott und Christus als κυριος nach der Apostelgeschichte" in: J. Zmijewski/E. Nellessen (eds.) Begegnung mit dem Wort. FS. H. Zimmermann (Bonn 1980) 163, 170, 171-72.

14:4.14 FLEW, R. N. Jesus and His Church (1956) 85. KAESEMANN, E. Exegetische Versuche und Besinnungen (1964) I 131. HAHN, F. Das Verständnis der Mission im Neuen Testament (^{2}1965) 117.

14:4 KUENG, H. Die Kirche (1967) 410, 412, 414, 416. ET: The Church (1967) 346-47, 349, 351. MERKLEIN, H. Das Kirchliche Amt nach dem Epheserbrief (1973) 74, 240, 241, 242, 247, 249, 250, 252, 255, 259, 277, 291, 333. WILSON, S. G. The Gentiles and the Gentile Mission in Luke-Acts (1973) 111-12, 116-18, 120. ZINGG, P., Das Wachsen der Kirche (Freiburg 1974) 193-95. DOCKX, S., "L'ordination de Barnabé et de Saul d'après Actes 13,1-3" NRTh 98 (1976) 238-50. "Amt" in: TRE 2 (1978) 515. "Apostel" in: TRE 3 (1978) 435, 443. "Apostelgeschichte" in: TRE 3 (1978) 519. QUINN, J. D., "The Last Volume of Luke: The Relations of Luke-Acts to the Pastoral Epistles" in: C. H. Talbert (ed.) Perspectives on Luke-Acts (Danville 1978) 67. PFITZNER, V. C., " 'Pneumatic' Apostleship? Apostle and Spirit in the Acts of the Apostles" in: W. Haubeck/M. Bachmann (eds.) Wort in der Zeit. FS. K. H. Rengstorf (Leiden 1980) 230-33.

14:5-6 EPP, E. J. The theological tendency of Codex Bezae Cantabrigiensis in Acts (1966) 138-40, 166f.

14:6ff. BEYSCHLAG, K., Simon Magus und die christliche Gnosis (Tübingen 1974) 110, 122.

14:6-20 "Apostelgeschichte" in: TRE 3 (1978) 496.

14:6 OGG, G. "Derbe," NTS (4, 1963) 367-70. BRAUN, H. Qumran und NT II (1966) 161. STULMACHER, P. Das paulinische Evangelium (1968) 210.

14:7-20 SHEPARD, J. W., The Life and Letters of St. Paul (Grand Rapids 1950) 109-12.

14:7.15 KAESEMANN, E. Exegetische Versuche und Besinnungen (1964) I 131.

14:8ff. BEYSCHLAG, K., Simon Magus und die christliche Gnosis (Tübingen 1974) 102,n.8.

14:8-18 BETHGE, F. Die paulinischen Reden der Apostelgeschichte (1887) 65-116. SEITZ, M. GPM 20 (1965-1966) 373-80. NIEBER-

GALL, A. GPM 26 (4, 1972) 385-95. PLUEMACHER, E. Lukas als hellenistischer Schriftsteller (1972) 92-97. SIMON, L., "La prière non religieuse chez Luc" FV 75 (1975) 8-22. "Apostelgeschichte" in: TRE 3 (1978) 499, 509, 512. STECK, K. G., in: GPM 32 (1977-1978) 379-84.

14:8-17 "Apologetik" in: TRE 3 (1978) 372.

14:8-15 GAERTNER, B. "Paulus und Barnabas in Lystra. Zu Apg. 14,8-15," SEA 27 (1962) 83-88.

14:8.10f.13f. BETZ, H. D. Lukian von Samosata und das Neue Testament (1961) 54, 68, 72, 78, 102, 116, 140, 155.

14:8 GOULDER, M. D. Type and History in Acts (1964) 74, 85, 101, 104, 106. WILCOX, M. The Semitisms of Acts (1965) 61-62, 133. "Apostelgeschichte" in: TRE 3 (1978) 509.

14:9 CLARK, A. C. The Acts of the Apostels (1933) 203, 250, 300, 334, 357. DELLING, G. Die Zueignung des Heils in der Taufe (1961) 50.

14:10 CLARK, A. C. The Acts of the Apostles (1933) 184, 227, 229, 332. DELLING, G. Die Zueignung des Heils in der Taufe (1961) 49f. WILCOX, M. The Semitisms of Acts (1965) 133-34, 154, 171. EPP, E. J. The theological tendency of Codex Bezae Cantabrigiensis in Acts (1966) 54, 62f., 163. NICKELS, P. Targum and New Testament (1967) 66. BARRETT, C. K., "Is there a theological tendency in Codex Bezae?" in: E. Best/R. McL. Wilson (eds.) Text and Interpretation, FS. M. Black (Cambridge 1979) 22.

14:11-18 O'NEILL, J. C. The Theology of Acts in its historical setting (1970) 143-45, 150.

14:11 "Apostelgeschichte" in: TRE 3 (1978) 509.

14:12-13 METZGER, B. M. The Early Versions of the New Testament (Oxford 1977) 87.

14:12 EITREM, S. "De Paulo Et Barnabe Deorum Numero Habitis," in: Coniectanea Neotestamentica (1938) A. Fridrichsen ed., 9. BEYSCHLAG, K., Simon Magus und die christliche Gnosis (Tübingen 1974) 102n.8. METZGER, B. M., The Early Versions of the New Testament (Oxford 1977) 173.

14:14 BEST, E. One Body in Christ (1955) 164. FLEW, R. N. Jesus and His Church (1956) 85. GREEN, W. M., " 'Apostles' - Acts 14:14" RestQ 4 (1960) 245-47. KAESEMANN, E. Exegetische Versuche und Besinnungen (1964) I 131. MERKLEIN, H. Das Kirchliche Amt nach dem Epheserbrief (1973) 240, 241, 242, 247, 249, 250, 252, 255, 259, 277, 291, 333. WILSON, S. G. The Gentiles and the Gentile Mission in Luke-Acts (1973) 111-12, 116-18, 120. BEYSCHLAG, K. Simon Magus und die christliche Gnosis (Tübingen 1974) 102. ZINGG, P., Das Wachsen der Kirche (Freiburg

1974) 193-95. GOPPELT, L., Theologie des Neuen Testaments. I (Göttingen 1975) 227-28, 230. DOCKX, S., "L'ordination de Barnabé et de Saul d'après Actes 13,1-3" NRTh 98 (1976) 238-50. "Amt" in: TRE 2 (1978) 515. "Apostel" in: TRE 3 (1978) 435, 443. "Apostelgeschichte" in: TRE (1978) 519. QUINN, J. D., "The Last Volume of Luke: The Relations of Luke-Acts to the Pastoral Epistles" in: C. H. Talbert (ed.) Perspectives on Luke-Acts (Danville 1978) 67. PFITZNER, V. C., " 'Pneumatic' Apostleship? Apostle and Spirit in the Acts of the Apostles" in: W. Haubeck/M. Bachmann (eds.) Wort in der Zeit. FS. K. H. Rengstorf (Leiden 1980) 230-33.

14:15ff. HANSON, S. The Unity of the Church in the New Testament (1946) 103f.

14:15-18 LERLE, E. "Die Predigt in Lystra (Acta xiv. 15-18)," NTS 7 (2, 1960) 46-55.

14:15-17 DIBELIUS, M. Die Reden der Apostelgeschichte und die antike Geschichtsschreibung (1949) 17, 22. STRECKER, G. Der Weg der Gerechtigkeit (1962) 474. HAHN, F. Das Verständnis der Mission im Neuen Testament ([2]1965) 52, 65, 118. DUPONT, J. Etudes sur les Actes des Apôtres (1967) 93, 99, 138, 139, 416. GUTBROD, K. Die Apostelgeschichte (1968) 62f. BURCHARD, C. Der dreizehnte Zeuge (1970) 138-42. WILSON, S. G. The Gentiles and the Gentile Mission in Luke-Acts (1973) 194, 210, 215, 243, 245, 267. WILCKENS, U. Die Missionsreden der Apostelgeschichte ([3]1974) 86-91, 228. GLÖCKNER, R., Die Verkündigung des Heils beim Evangelisten Lukas (Mainz 1975) 214-15. KLIESCH, K., Das heilsgeschichtliche Credo in den Reden der Apostelgeschichte (Köln/Bonn 1975) 62-65, 110, 169-70. HOLTZ, T., " 'Euer Glaube an Gott' Zu Form und Inhalt von 1 Thess. 1:9f" in: R. Schnackenburg et al. (eds.) Die Kirche des Anfangs. FS. H. Schürmann (Freiburg/Basel/Wien 1978) 461-63. WILSON, S. G., "Law and Judaism in Acts" in: P. J. Achtemeier (ed.) SBL Seminar Papers 1980 (Chico, Cal. 1980) 261.

14:15 KAESEMANN, E. Exegetische Versuche und Besinnungen (1964) I 131. SHIMADA, K., The Formulary Material in First Peter (Th.D. Diss., Ann Arbor, Mich. 1966) 260-61. DUPONT, J. Etudes sur les Actes des Apôtres (1967) 423, 425, 428, 431, 466, 473. HARMAN, A. M., Paul's Use of the Psalms (Ann Arbor, Mich. 1968) 171-72. BEYSCHLAG, K., Simon Magus und die christliche Gnosis (Tübingen 1974) 89n.26, 101n.6, 102. NELLESSEN, E., Zeugnis für Jesus und das Wort (Köln 1976) 266-67. DUPONT, D. J., The Salvation of the Gentiles (New York 1979) 70. PRIEUR, J.-M., "La figure de l'apôtre dans les Actes apocryphes d'André" in: F. Bovon et al. (eds.) Les Actes Apocryphes des Apôtres (Geneva 1981) 126n.15.

14:16 DUPONT, J. Etudes sur les Actes des Apôtres (1967) 353, 431, 437, 457, 473. NELLESSEN, E., Zeugnis für Jesus and das Wort (Köln 1976) 257-68.

14:17 LAGERCRANTZ, O., "Act 14:17" ZNW 31 (1932) 86-87. BIEDER, W. "Zum Problem Religion-christlicher Glaube," ThZ 15 (5, 1959) 431-45. NELLESSEN, E., Zeugnis für Jesus und das Wort (Köln 1976) 264-74. BERGER, K., "Das Buch der Jubiläen" in: JüdSchr II/3 (1981) 391n.4a.

14:18ff. CLARK, A. C. The Acts of the Apostles (1933) xxvi, xxxvi, 215, 228, 229, 250, 251, 252, 253, 254, 294, 295, 324, 358.

14:19-20 EPP, E. J. The theological tendency of Codex Bezae Cantabrigiensis in Acts (1966) 123, 140ff., 151 n.2, 155, 166. "Apostelgeschichte" in: TRE 3 (1978) 297, 499.

14:20-21 SHEPARD, J. W., The Life and Letters of St. Paul (Grand Rapids 1950) 112.

14:21-28 SHEPARD, J. W., The Life and Letters of St. Paul (Grand Rapids 1950) 112-14.

14:21-27 DUPONT, J. "La première organisation des Eglises. Ac 14,21-27," AssS 26 (1973) 60-66.

14:21-23 PRAST, F., Presbyter und Evangelium in nachapostolischer Zeit (Stuttgart 1979) 212-22.

14:21 HAHN, F. Das Verständnis der Mission im Neuen Testament (²1965) 105. NICKELS, P. Targum and New Testament (1967) 66.

14:22-23 PRAST, F., Presbyter und Evangelium in nachapostolischer Zeit (Stuttgart 1979) 435. NELLESSEN, E., "Die Einsetzung von Presbytern durch Barnabas und Paulus (Apg 14,23)" in: J. Zmijewski/E. Nellessen (eds.) Begegnung mit dem Wort. FS. H. Zimmermann (Bonn 1980) 179-80, 182, 190.

14:22 MOORE, G. F. Judaism II (1946) 255n. DELLING, G. Die Zueignung des Heils in der Taufe (1961) 90. DELLING, G., Die Taufe im Neuen Testament (1963) 135. BROWN, S. Apostasy and Perseverance in the Theology of Luke (1969) 13f., 17, 21, 31, 45, 50, 73, 114f., 119, 122f., 128, 139f. ZMIJEWSKI, J. Die Eschatologiereden des Lukas-Evangeliums (1972) 139, 184, 214, 406, 529. WANKE, J., Die Emmauserzählung (Leipzig 1973) 95, 118. "Agrapha" in: TRE 2 (1978) 107. QUINN, J. D., "The Last Volume of Luke: The Relations of Luke-Acts to the Pastoral Epistles" in: C. H. Talbert (ed.) Perspectives on Luke-Acts (Danville 1978) 67. SATAKE, A., "Inklusio als ein beliebtes Ausdrucksmittel in der Johannesapokalypse" AJBI 6 (1980) 79.

14:23-16:8 WILCOX, M. The Semitisms of Acts (1965) 59ff.

14:23 ROSS, J. M. "The Appointment of Presbyters in Acts XIV, 23," ET 632 (9, 1952) 288-89. FLEW, R. N. Jesus and His Church (1956) 151n, 146n. SCHWEIZER, E. Gemeinde und Gemeinde-Ordnung im Neuen Testament (1959) §§ 5i, 23c, 26e. KLEIN, G. Die Zwölf Apostel (1961) 175f. DUPONT, J. Le Discours de Milet (1962) 235-37. BOUSSET, W. Die Religion des Judentums im Späthellenistischen Zeitalter (1966 = 1926) 180. SATAKE, A., Die Gemeindeordnung in der Johannesapokalypse (Neukirchen-Vluyn 1966) 2. MICHEL, H.-J., Die Abschiedsrede des Paulus an die Kirche Apg. 20:17-38 (München 1973) 25, 32, 86, 93, 95-97. LADD, G. E., A Theology of the New Testament (Grand Rapids 1974) 271, 352, 353, 543. DOCKX, S., "L'ordination de Barnabé et de Saul d'après Acts 13,1-3" NRTh 98 (1976) 238-50. "Amt" in: TRE 2 (1978) 521. PRAST, F., Presbyter und Evangelium in nachapostolischer Zeit (Stuttgart 1979) 141, 177, 356-61. CLARK, K. W., "The Israel of God" in: The Gentile Bias and other Essays (Leiden 1980) 26. NELLESSEN, E., "Die Einsetzung von Presbytern durch Barnabas und Paulus (Apg 14,23)" in: J. Zmijewski/ E. NELLESSEN (eds.) Begegnung mit dem Wort. FS. H. Zimmermann (Bonn 1980) 175-93.

14:24 KLIJN, A. F. J./REININK, G. J. Patristic Evidence for Jewish-Christian Sects (1973) 9.

14:25 METZGER, B. M., The Early Versions of the New Testament (Oxford 1977) 141.

14:26 FLEW, R. N. Jesus and His Church (1956) 147. METZGER, B. M., The Early Versions of the New Testament (Oxford 1977) 235. PRAST, F., Presbyter und Evangelium in nachapostolischer Zeit (Stuttgart 1979) 141-42.

14:27 - 15:35 BORSE, U., "Kompositionsgeschichtliche Beobachtungen zum Apostelkonzil" in: J. Zmijewski/E. Nellessen (eds.) Begegnung mit dem Wort. FS. H. Zimmermann (Bonn 1980) 195-212.

14:27 WILCOX, M. The Semitisms of Acts (1965) 84n, 131, 132, 133, 154-55. NICKELS, P. Targum and New Testament (1967) 66. PRAST, F., Presbyter und Evangelium in nachapostolischer Zeit (Stuttgart 1979) 72.

14:28 "Apokalyptik" in: TRE 3 (1978) 253.

———————————

15-18 KAYE, V. N., "Acts' Portrait of Silas" NovT 21 (1979) 13-26.

15 BRUN, D. L./FRIDRICHSEN, A. Paulus und die Urgemeinde (1921). SAHLIN, H. Der Messias und das Gottesvolk (1945) 347-51. DIBELIUS, M. Die Reden der Apostelgeschichte und die antike Geschichtsschreibung (1949) 30-33. DUPONT, J. D. Les Problèmes du Livre des Actes (1950) 57. FEINE, D. P./BEHM, D. J. Einleitung in das Neue Testament (1950) 82f. DIBELIUS, M. Aufsätze zur Apostelgeschichte (1951) 93-101. ET: Studies in the Acts of the Apostles (1956) 102-08. WIKENHAUSER, A. Die Apostelgeschichte (1951) 143-46. SANDERS, J. N. "Peter and Paul in Acts," NTS 3 (1955-1956) 133ff. GRANT, F. C. The Gospels (1957) 124ff. SANDMEL, S. The Genius of Paul (1958) 143ff. MUNCK, J. Paul and the Salvation of Mankind (1959) 81f., 94-97, 231-39. HAENCHEN, E. "Quellenanalyse und Kompositionsanalyse in Act 15," Judentum, Urchristentum, Kirche (1960) 153-64. RUDOLPH, K. Die Mandäer I (1960) 232. KESICH, V. "The Apostolic Council at Jerusalem," SVThQ 6 (3, 1962) 108-17. RAVAROTTO, E., "De Hierosolymitano Concilio (Act. Cap. 15)," Antonianum 37 (2, 1962) 185-218. DUPONT, J. The Sources of Acts (1964) 34, 40, 54, 55, 57, 69, 70, 71, 78, 79. GOULDER, M. D. Type and History in Acts (1964) 27, 108, 161, 168ff., 173, 194, 197, 200f. KAESEMANN, E. Exegetische Versuche und Besinnungen (1964) I 131. HURD, J. C. The Origin of 1 Corinthians (1965) 35-41. BRAUN, H. Qumran und NT II (1966) 320. FLUSSER, D. "Die Christenheit nach dem Apostelkonzil," in: Antijudaismus im Neuen Testament? (1967) W. P. Eckert/N. P. Levinson/ M. Stöhr eds., 60-81. PARKER, P. "Once More, Acts and Galatians," JBL 86 (2, 1967) 175-82. GUTBROD, K. Die Apostelgeschichte (1968) 49f. BLINZLER, J. "Petrus und Paulus—Ueber eine angebliche Folge des Tages von Antiochien (Gal 2)," in: Aus der Welt und Umwelt des Neuen Testaments (1969) 147-57. FENSHAM, F. C. "Die Konvensie van Jerusalem—'n Keerpunt in die Geskiedenis van die Kerk," NGTT 10 (1, 1969) 32-38. DIETRICH, W. Das Petrusbild der lukanischen Schriften (1972) 306-21. KERTELGE, K. Gemeinde und Amt im Neuen Testament (1972) 99f. ECKERT, J. Die Urchristliche Verkündigung im Streit zwischen Paulus und seinen Gegnern nach dem Galaterbrief (1971) 219-24. BROWN, R. E. et al. (eds.) Peter in the New Testament (Minneapolis 1973) 49-56. CONZELMANN, H. und LINDEMANN, A., Arbeitsbuch zum Neuen Testament (Tübingen 1975) 6, 384, 409-13. DRANE, J. W., Paul: Libertine or Legalist? (London 1975) 115-20. GASQUE, W., A History of the Criticism of the Acts of the Apostles (Tübingen 1975) 46, 59, 63-64, 141-42, 178-79, 209n.24, 281-82. SIEBEN, H.-J., "Zur Entwicklung der Konzilsidee X: Die Konzilsidee des Lukas" ThPh 50 (1975) 481-503.

STEMBERGER, G., "Stammt das synodale Element der Kirche aus der Synagoge?" Annuarium Historiae Conciliorum 8 (Paderborn 1976) 1-14. "Amt" in: TRE 2 (1978) 513. MARTIN, R. P., New Testament Foundations. II (Exeter 1978) 109-15. BRUCE, F. F., Men and Movements in the Primitive Church (Exeter 1979) 97-101. HENGEL, M., Zur urchristlichen Geschichtsschreibung (Stuttgart 1979) 93-105; ET. J. Bowden (trans.) Acts and the History of Earliest Christianity (London 1979) 111-26. JEWETT, R., A Chronology of Paul's Life (Philadelphia 1979) 64-69. PRAST, F., Presbyter und Evangelium in nachapostolischer Zeit (Stuttgart 1979) 225, 320, 324. ELLIOTT, J. H., "Peter, Sylvanus and Mark in 1 Peter and Acts: Sociological-Exegetical Perspectives on a Petrine Group in Rome" in: W. Haubeck/M. Bachmann (eds.) Wort in der Zeit. FS. K. H. Rengstorf (Leiden 1980) 261-64. ELLIS, I. M., "Codex Bezae at Acts 15" IBS 2 (1980) 134-40. LÜDE-MANN, G., Paulus, der Heidenapostel. I (Göttingen 1980) 165-69. PIERCE, J. A., "The Twelve as Apostolic Overseers" BiTod 18 (1980) 72-76. SOMERVILLE, E. R., "The Divine Purpose: The Jews and the Gentile Mission (Acts 15)" in: P. J. Achtemeier (ed.) SBL Seminar Papers 1980 (Chico, Cal. 1980) 267-82. WILSON, S. G., "Law and Judaism in Acts" in: P. J. Achtemeier (ed.) SBL Seminar Papers 1980 (Chico, Cal. 1980) 258-61. "Cassianus" in: TRE 7 (1981) 656.

15:1ff. ENSLIN, M. S. The Literature of the Christian Movement (1956) 227f. EHRHARDT, A. The Acts of the Apostles (1969) 72f., 86, 107. KUEMMEL, W. G. Einleitung in das Neue Testament (1973) 263f.

15:1-35 ROLOFF, J. Apostolat-Verkündigung-Kirche (1965) 210f. KUEMMEL, W. G. Einleitung in das Neue Testament (1973) 142f. STEIN, R. H., "The Relationship of Galatians 2:1-10 and Acts 15:1-35: Two Neglected Arguments" JEThS 17 239-42. PANI-MOLLE, S. A., Il discorso di Pietro all'assemblea apostolica (Bologna 1976). DÖMER, M., Das Heil Gottes (Köln/Bonn 1978) 173-87. MATTILL, A. J., "The Value of Acts as a Source for the Study of Paul" in: C. H. Talbert (ed.) Perspectives on Luke-Acts (Danville 1978) 91. "Armut" in: TRE 4 (1979) 80. SOMERVILLE, E. R., "The Divine Purpose: The Jews and the Gentile Mission (Acts 15)" in: P. J. Achtemeier (Ed.) SBL Seminar Papers 1980 (Chico, Cal. 1980) 267-69.

15:1-34 SQUILLACI, D. "Nel XIX Centenario Paolino-II primo Concilio e San Paolo," PaCl 40 (Aug. 1-15, 1961) 829-34.

15:1-33 HAHN, F. Das Verständnis der Mission im Neuen Testament (²1965) 48, 50, 66-68, 72f., 77, 78, 116. "Apostelgeschichte" in:

TRE 3 (1978) 486. ROLOFF, J., Neues Testament (Neukirchen-Vluyn 1979) 58-62.

15:1-32 CATCHPOLE, D. R., "Paul, James and the Apostolic Decree" NTS 23 (1977) 428-44. GEIGER, G., Kirche unterwegs (Klosterneuburg 1981).

15:1-30 WILSON, S. G. The Gentiles and the Gentile Mission in Luke-Acts (1973) 111, 174, 177-96, 240-41, 260-61.

15:1-29 DIBELIUS, M. Aufsätze zur Apostelgeschichte (1951) 84-90, 140f., 155, 156. ET: Studies in the Acts of the Apostles (1956) 93-101, 162f., 181, 182. CONZELMANN, E. Die Apostelgeschichte (1963) 87. MIESNER, D. R., "The Missionary Journeys Narrative: Patterns and Implications" in: C. H. Talbert (ed.) Perspectives on Luke-Acts (Danville 1978) 206-07. NIXON, R., "Fulfilling the Law: The Gospels and Acts" in: B. Kaye/G. Wenham (eds.) Law, Morality and the Bible (Downers Grove, Ill. 1978) 68-69. FERRARESE, G. Il concilio di Gerusalemme in Ireneo di Lione (Brescia 1979). ROLOFF, J., Neues Testament (Neukirchen-Vluyn 1979) 47-62.

15:1-26 GUTBROD, K. Die Apostelgeschichte (1968) 19ff.

15:1-21 NICKLE, K. F. The Collection (1966) Passim. ROBBINS, V. K., "By Land and by Sea: The We-Passages and Ancient Sea Voyages" in: C. H. Talbert (ed.) Perspectives on Luke-Acts (Danville 1978) 235.

15:1-5 SHEPARD, J. W., The Life and Letters of St. Paul (Grand Rapids 1950) 118-20.

15:1-4, 12, O'NEILL, J. C. The Theology of Acts in its historical setting (1970)
22, 23 125-31.

15:1-2 KLEIN, G. Die Zwölf Apostel (1961) 173ff.

15:1 MUNCK, J. Paul and the Salvation of Mankind (1959) 96f. DUPONT, J. Etudes sur les Actes des Apôtres (1967) 200, 210, 412, 431, 474, 531.

15:2-30 STOLLE, V. Der Zeuge als Angeklagter (1973) 255-57.

15:2-29 ROBERTSON, A. T. Luke the Historian in the Light of Research (1920) 171f.

15:2 WILCOX, M. The Semitisms of Acts (1965) 131-32, 154n, 171. EPP, E. J. The theological tendency of Codex Bezae Cantabrigiensis in Acts (1966) 97, 101-03, 129. NICKELS, P. Targum and New Testament (1967) 66. HORTON, F. L., "Reflections on the Semitisms of Luke-Acts" in: C. H. Talbert (ed.) Perspectives on Luke-Acts (Danville 1978) 21. PRAST, F., Presbyter und Evangelium in nachapostolischer Zeit (Stuttgart 1979) 356-57. "Bekehrung" in: TRE 5 (1980) 443.

15:3ff. EPP, E. J. The theological tendency of Codex Bezae Cantabrigiensis in Acts (1966) 29f., 96f., 97, 100, 102, 168.

15:3.5 MUNCK, J. Paul and the Salvation of Mankind (1959) 96f., 122f., 232f., 243f. DUPONT, J. Etudes sur les Actes des Apôtres (1967) 200, 201, 412, 423, 425, 428, 431, 453, 474.

15:3 JERVELL, J., "The Lost Sheep of the House of Israel" in: Luke and the People of God (Minneapolis 1972) 113-32.

15:4-29 HOLMBERG, B., Paul and Power (Lund 1978) 18-32.

15:4 PRAST, F., Presbyter und Evangelium in nachapostolischer Zeit (Stuttgart 1979) 72, 356-57.

15:5ff. WANKE, J., Die Emmauserzählung (Leipzig 1973) 12.

15:5-11, 13-21 O'NEILL, J. C. The Theology of Acts in its historical setting (1970) 125-31.

15:5-11 DELLING, G. Die Taufe im Neuen Testament (1963) 61, 72.

15:5 PARKER, P. The Gospel Before Mark (1953) 102-03. SCHMITHALS, W. Paulus und Jakobus (1964) 91. WILSON, S. G. The Gentiles and the Gentile Mission in Luke-Acts (1973) 183-84, 192, 254. WANKE, J., Die Emmauserzählung (Leipzig 1973) 8. HENGEL, M., Zur urchristlichen Geschichtsschreibung (Stuttgart 1979) 82; ET: J. Bowden (trans.) Acts and the History of Earliest Christianity (London 1979) 96. SOMERVILLE, E. R., "The Divine Purpose: The Jews and the Gentile Mission (Acts 15)" in: P. J. Achtemeier (ed.) SBL Seminar Papers 1980 (Chico, Cal. 1980) 270. WANKE, J., "Kommentarworte" BZ 24 (1980) 214.

15:6-30 SCHOEPS, H.-J. Paulus (1959) 57ff.

15:6-29 SHEPARD, J. W., The Life and Letters of St. Paul (Grand Rapids 1950) 120-24. MIGUENS, M. "Pietro nel concilio apostolico," RivB 10 (3, 1962) 240-51. FAHY, T. "The Council of Jerusalem," IThQ 30 (3, 1963) 232-61. GAECHTER, P. "Geschichtliches zum Apostelkonzil," ZKTh 85 (3, 1963) 339-54. BALLARINI, T. "Collegialità della Chiesa in Atti e ein Galati," BiOr 6 (6, 1964) 255-62.

15:6-21 BEYER, H. W. Die Apostelgeschichte (1947) 92-94.

15:6-7 BROWN, R. E. et al. (eds.) Peter in the New Testament (Minneapolis 1973) 45-49.

15:6 PRAST, F., Presbyter und Evangelium in nachapostolischer Zeit (Stuttgart 1979) 356-57.

15:7-12 STECK, K. G. GPM 12 (1957-1958) 177-82.

15:7-11 DUPONT, D. J. "Le Salut des Gentils et la Signification Théologique du Livre des Actes," NTS 6 (1959-1960) 146f. DUPONT,

J. "Les Discours de Pierre dans les Actes et le chapitre XXIV de l'évangile de Luc," in: L'Evangile de Luc (1973) F. Neirynck ed., 367-69. MUSSNER, F., Petrus und Paulus—Pole der Einheit (Freiburg/Basel/Wien 1976) 36-39. "Apostelgeschichte" in: TRE 3 (1978) 505. DÖMER, M., Das Heil Gottes (Köln/Bonn 1978) 182-84. DUPONT, D. J., The Salvation of the Gentiles (New York 1979) 24-25.

15:7-9 DUNN, J. D. G. Baptism in the Holy Spirit (1970) 79ff.

15:7 HENNECKE, E./SCHNEEMELCHER, W. Neutestamentliche Apokryphen (1964) I 127. WILCOX, M. The Semitisms of Acts (1965) 6, 76n, 92-93, 110, 171. EPP, E. J. The theological tendency of Codex Bezae Cantabrigiensis in Acts (1966) 43 n.4, 71, 103f., 116, 118. DUPONT, J. Etudes sur les Actes des Apôtres (1967) 179, 197, 410, 412. NICKELS, P. Targum and New Testament (1967) 66. WILSON, S. G. The Gentiles and the Gentile Mission in Luke-Acts (1973) 192-93. WANKE, J., Die Emmauserzählung (Leipzig 1973) 7, 9. PRAST, F., Presbyter und Evangelium in nachapostolischer Zeit (Stuttgart 1979) 54.

15:8-9 YATES, E. J. The Spirit and the Kingdom (1963) 168ff. DUNN, J. D. G. Baptism in the Holy Spirit (1970) 71, 80n, 81f.

15:8 DUPONT, J. Etudes sur les Actes des Apôtres (1967) 200, 410, 415, 445, 491. BEUTLER, J. Martyria (1972) 181, 205, 221, 290, 295, 300, 357. WILSON, S. G. The Gentiles and the Gentile Mission in Luke-Acts (1973) 193-94. NELLESSEN, E., Zeugnis für Jesus und das Wort (Köln 1976) 274-76. DUPONT, D. J., The Salvation of the Gentiles (New York 1979) 46.

15:9-11 MUSSNER, F., Petrus und Paulus - Pole der Einheit (Freiburg/Basel/Wien 1976) 107-08.

15:9 KNOX, W. L. The Sources of the Synoptic Gospels II (1957) 26. EPP, E. J. The theological tendency in Codex Bezae Cantabrigiensis in Acts (1966) 98f. DUPONT, J. Etudes sur les Actes des Apôtres (1967) 410-12, 415, 440, 445, 448, 455, 460. BROWN, S. Apostasy and Perseverance in the Theology of Luke (1969) 42, 44, 121.

15:10-11 HAHN, F. Das Verständnis der Mission im Neuen Testament (²1965) 118. MENOUD, P. H., "Le salut par la foi selon le livre des Actes - Actes 15:10-11" in: Jésus-Christ et la foi (Neuchâtel/Paris 1975) 131-35. WILSON, S. G., "Law and Judaism in Acts" in: P. J. Achtemeier (ed.) SBL Seminar Papers 1980 (Chico, Cal. 1980) 254.

15:10 DUPONT, D. J., The Salvation of the Gentiles (New York 1979) 81. HENGEL, M., Zur urchristlichen Geschichtsschreibung (Stuttgart 1979) 41; ET: J. Bowden (trans.) Acts and the History of

Earliest Christianity (London 1979) 42. NOLLAND, J. L., ''A Fresh Look at Acts 15:10'' NTS 27 (1980) 105-15.

15:11-12 EPP, E. J. The theological tendency of Codex Bezae Cantabrigiensis in Acts (1955) 54, 62f., 83, 97f., 103, 125.

   15:11 MICHEL, H.-J., Die Abschiedsrede des Paulus an die Kirche Apg 20:17-38 (München 1973) 16, 86ff.

   15:12 MUNCK, J. Paul and the Salvation of Mankind (1959) 232f.

  15:13ff. JERVELL, J., ''James: The Defender of Paul'' in: Luke and the People of God (Minneapolis 1972) 195-207.

15:13-21 GASTON, L. No Stone on Another (1970) 308-10. FRANKLIN, E., Christ the Lord (London 1975) 124-28. DÖMER, M., Das Heil Gottes (Köln/Bonn 1978) 184-86. SOMERVILLE, E. R., ''The Divine Purpose: The Jews and the Gentile Mission (Acts 15)'' in: P. J. Achtemeier (ed.) SBL Seminar Papers 1980) Chico, Cal. 1980) 269.

15:13-20 PETERS, G. W. A Biblical Theology of Missions (1972) 140-41, 156.

15:13-18 LOHFINK, G., Die Sammlung Israels (München 1975) 58-60, 51. KAISER, W. C., Jr., ''The Davidic Promise and the Inclusion of the Gentiles (Amos 9:9-15 and Acts 15:13-18): A Test Passage for Theological Systems'' JEThS 20 (1977) 97-111. ''Amos'' in: TRE 3 (1978) 484. FULLER, D. P., Gospel and Law: Contrast or Continuum? (Grand Rapids 1980) 179-81.

  15:14ff. JERVELL, J., ''The Law in Luke-Acts'' in: Luke and the People of God (Minneapolis 1972) 143-44.

15:14-21 BOWKER, J. W. NTS 14 (1967-1968) 107f.

15:14-18 HAHN, F. Christologische Hoheitstitel (1963) 278. VIELHAUER, P., ''Oikodome. Das Bild vom Bau in der christlichen Literatur vom Neuen Testament bis Clemens Alexandrinus'' in: G. Klein (ed.) Oikodome. FS. P. Vielhauer (München 1979) 106-08.

15:14-17 WILSON, S. G. The Gentiles and the Gentile Mission in Luke-Acts (1973) 219, 224-25.

   15:14 DAHL, N. A. '' 'A People for his Name' (Acts xv. 14),'' NTS 5 (4, 1958) 319-27. DUPONT, J. Etudes sur les Actes des Apôtres (1967) 197, 361-65, 396, 411, 412, 448, 469. FLENDER, H. St Luke Theologian of Redemptive History (1967) 16, 132 & n, 133 & n. NICKELS, P. Targum and New Testament (1967) 66. FITZMYER, J. A., ''Aramaic 'Kepha' and Peter's Name in the New Testament'' in: E. Best/R. McL. Wilson (eds.) Text and Interpretation. FS. M. Black (Cambridge 1979) 121. SOMERVILLE, E. R., ''The Divine Purpose: The Jews and the Gentile Mission (Acts

15)'' in: P. J. Achtemeier (ed.) SBL Seminar Papers 1980 (Chico, Cal. 1980) 271.

15:15-18 BRUCE, F. F., Men and Women in the Primitive Church (Exeter 1979) 93-97.

15:16ff. BARRETT, C. K. The New Testament Background (1956) 208. ELLIS, E. E. Paul's Use of the Old Testament (1957) 91, 107f., 112.

15:16-18 DUPONT, J. "Laos ex Ethnon," NTS 3 (1, 1956) 47-50. BURGER, C. Jesus als Davissohn (1970) 141-52. GASTON, L. No Stone on Another (1970) 200-05. KRAENKL, E. Jesus der Knecht Gottes (1972) 86, 158, 207. WILSON, S. G. The Gentiles and the Gentile Mission in Luke-Acts (1973) 224-25, 228-31. LOHFINK, G., Die Sammlung Israels (München 1975) 59, 85, 88-89. DÖMER, M., Das Heil Gottes (Köln/Bonn 1978) 178-79. FULLER, D. P., Gospel and Law: Contrast or Continuum? (Grand Rapids 1980) 177-80.

15:16-17 BRAUN, H. Qumran und NT II (1966) 309, 319. DUPONT, J. Etudes sur les Actes des Apôtres (1967) 257, 264, 281, 411, 412. MUSSNER, F. "Die Idee der Apokatastasis in der Apostelge-schichte," in: Praesentia Salutis (1967) 223. HOLTZ, T. Unter-suchungen über die Alttestamentlichen Zitate bei Lukas (1968) 21-27. JERVELL, J., "The Divided People of God" in: Luke and the People of God (Minneapolis 1972) 51-53. BRAUN, M. A., "James' Use of Amos at the Jerusalem Council: Steps Toward a Possible Solution of the Textual and Theological Problems" JEThS 20 (1977) 113-21. DUPONT, D. J., The Salvation of the Gentiles (New York 1979) 139, 145. SOMERVILLE, E. R., "The Divine Purpose: The Jews and the Gentile Mission (Acts 15)" in: P. J.Achtemeier (ed.) SBL Seminar Papers 1980 (Chico, Cal. 1980) 275-76. RICHARD, E., "The Creative Use of Amos by the Author of Acts" NovT 24 (1982) 45-52.

15:16 PALLIS, A. Notes on St. Luke and the Acts (London 1928) 68. FITZMYER, J. A. NTS 7 (1960-1961) 328f. GAERTNER, B. The Temple and the Community in Qumran and the New Testament (1965) 42. O'NEILL, J. C. The Theology of Acts in its historical setting (1970) 122-23. SOMERVILLE, E. R., "The Divine Pur-pose: The Jews and the Gentile Mission (Acts 15)" in: P. J. Ach-temeier (ed.) SBL Seminar Papers 1980 (Chico, Cal. 1980) 272.

15:17 HAHN, F. Christologische Hoheitstitel (1963) 72. HAHN, F. Das Verständnis der Mission im Neuen Testament (²1965) 60. SOM-ERVILLE, E. R., "The Divine Purpose: The Jews and the Gentile Mission (Acts 15)" in: P. J. Achtemeier (ed.) SBL Seminar Papers 1980 (Chico, Cal. 1980) 272.

15:18 DUPONT, J. Etudes sur les Actes des Apôtres (1967) 264, 271, 281, 411. FERRÉ, N. F. S., The Extreme Center (Waco, Texas 1973) 173-78. DUPONT, D. J., The Salvation of the Gentiles (New York 1979) 152.

15:19-21 SOMERVILLE, E. R., "The Divine Purpose: The Jews and the Gentile Mission (Acts 15)" in: P. J. Achtemeier (ed.) SBL Seminar Papers 1980 (Chico, Cal. 1980) 272-73.

15:19-20 MOORE, G. F. Judaism II (1946) 74. FAHY, T. "A Phenomenon of Literary Style in Acts of Apostles," IThQ (4, 1962) 314-18. METZGER, B. M., The Early Versions of the New Testament (Oxford 1977) 136. PERROT, C., "Les décisions de l'Assemblée de Jerusalem" RechSR 69 (1981) 195-208.

15:19 FLEW, R. N. Jesus and His Church (1956) 133n. DUPONT, J. Etudes sur les Actes des Apôtres (1967) 180, 423, 425, 428, 431, 466, 474. DUPONT, D. J., The Salvation of the Gentiles (New York 1979) 81. SOMERVILLE, E. R., "The Divine Purpose: The Jews and the Gentile Mission (Acts 15)" in: P. J. Achtemeier (ed.) SBL Seminar Papers 1980 (Chico, Cal. 1980) 273.

15:20ff. PHILONENK O, M. "Le Décret apostolique et les interdits alimentaires du Coran," RHPhR (2, 1967) 165-72.

15:20-21 WIKENHAUSER, A. Die Apostelgeschichte (1951) 140f.

15:20.29 NESTLE, E. Einführung in das Griechische Neue Testament (1909) 252ff. TAYLOR, V. The Text of the New Testament (1961) 99f. HAHN, F. Das Verständnis der Mission im Neuen Testament (²1965) 72, 118. KLIJN, A. F. J. "The Pseudo-Clementines and the Apostolic Decree," NovTest 10 (4, 1968) 305-12.

15:20 HARNACK, A. von, Studien zur Geschichte des Neuen Testaments und der Alten Kirche (1931) 4ff. CLARK, A. C. The Acts of the Apostles (1933) xlix, 282, 285, 294, 332, 360f. MOORE, G. F. Judaism II (1946) 87n. RUDOLPH, K. Die Mandäer II (1961) 299, 5. SCHRAGE, W. Die konkreten Einzelgebote in der paulinischen Paränese (1961) 191. CONZELMANN, H. Die Apostelgeschichte (1963) 84f. HENNECKE, E./SCHNEEMELCHER, W. Neutestamentliche Apokryphen (1964) I 135. HURD, J. C. The Origin of 1 Corinthians (1965) 16, 246-50, 267. BOUSSET, W. Die Religion des Judentums im Späthellenistischen Zeitalter (1966 = 1926) 72, 138, 172. EPP, E. J. The theological tendency of Codex Bezae Cantabrigiensis in Acts (1966) 22, 38, 50 n.1, 107-11, 167-70. PETZKE, G. Die Traditionen über Apollonius von Tyana und das Neue Testament (1970) 201, 225. MANEK, J. "Das Aposteldekret im Kontext der Lukastheologie," CommViat 15 (2-3, 1972) 151-60. HEIN, K., Eucharist and Excommunication (Bern/Frankfurt 1975) 83-85. CATCHPOLE, D. R., "Paul, James and the Apostolic Decree" NTS 23 (1977) 428-44. METZGER, B. M., The Early Versions of the New Testament (Oxford 1977) 196. MANNS, F., "Remarques sur Actes 15,20.29" Antonianum 53 (1978) 443-51. "Apostelgeschichte" in: TRE 3 (1978) 487, 509. "Blut" in: TRE 6 (1980) 733.

15:21 O'NEILL, J. C. The Theology of Acts in its historical setting (1970) 82-83, 127, 128. SOMERVILLE, E. R., "The Divine Purpose: The Jews and the Gentile Mission (Acts 15)" in: P. J. Achtemeier (ed.) SBL Seminar Papers 1980 (Chico, Cal. 1980) 272-73. WILSON, S. G., "Law and Judaism in Acts" in: P. J. Achtemeier (ed.) SBL Seminar Papers 1980 (Chico, Cal. 1980) 259, 261.

15:22ff. KUEMMEL, W. G. Einleitung in das Neue Testament (1973) 147-49. CONZELMANN, H. und LINDEMANN, A., Arbeitsbuch zum Neuen Testament (Tübingen 1975) 102.

15:22-35 PRAST, F., Presbyter und Evangelium in nachapostolischer Zeit (Stuttgart 1979) 225.

15:22-30 SCHWEIZER, E. Gemeinde und Gemeinde-Ordnung im Neuen Testament (1959) § 23c.

15:22-29 HOLMBERG, B., Paul and Power (Lund 1978) 65-66.

15:22-23 BROWN, R. E. et al. (eds.) Peter in the New Testament (Minneapolis 1973) 45-49. ROBBINS, V. K., "Prefaces in Greco-Roman Biography and Luke-Acts" in: P. J. Achtemeier (ed.) SBL Seminar Papers 1978/II (Missoula 1978) 199.

15:22 FLEW, R. N. Jesus and His Church (1956) 142. KLEIN, G. Die Zwölf Apostel (1961) 173ff. DELLING, G. Die Taufe im Neuen Testament (1963) 65. BRAUN, H. Qumran und NT II (1966) 328. HENGEL, M. Judentum und Hellenismus (1969) 194. ET: Judaism and Hellenism (1974) I 105. SCHNIDER, F., Jesus der Prophet (1973) 58f. "Aramäisch" in: TRE 3 (1978) 604, 609. PRAST, F., Presbyter und Evangelium in nachapostolischer Zeit (Stuttgart 1979) 356-57.

15:23ff. PETZKE, G. Die Traditionen über Apollonius von Tyana und das Neue Testament (1970) 123f.

15:23-29 BARRETT, C. K. The New Testament Background (1956) 27-28. LIETZMANN, H. "Der Sinn des Aposteldekrets und seine Textwandlung," in: Kleine Schriften II (1958) 292-98. DUPONT, J. Etudes sur les Actes des Apôtres (1967) 72-75, 177, 182, 184. SIMON, M. "The Apostolic Decree and its Setting in the Ancient Church," BJRL 52 (2, 1970) 437-60. DÖMER, M., Das Heil Gottes (Köln/Bonn 1978) 186. MATTILL, A. J., "The Value of Acts as a Source for the Study of Paul" in: C. H. Talbert (ed.) Perspectives on Luke-Acts (Danville 1978) 84. SIMON, M., "De

l'observance rituelle à l'ascèse: recherches sur le Décret Apostolique'' RHR 193 (1978) 27-104.

15:23 GREEN, E. M. B. ''Syria and Cilicia-A Note,'' ET 71 (2, 1959)
52-53. HAHN, F. Das Verständnis der Mission im Neuen Testament (²1965) 77. ''Apostelgeschichte'' in: TRE 3 (1978) 502.
PRAST, F., Presbyter und Evangelium in nachapostolischer Zeit
(Stuttgart 1979) 356-57.

15:24-29 ROBBINS, V. K., ''Prefaces in Greco-Roman Biography and Luke-
Acts'' in: P. J. Achtemeier (ed.) SBL Seminar Papers 1978/II
(Missoula 1978) 199-200, 204.

15:24-27 O'NEILL, J. C. The Theology of Acts in its historical setting (1970)
125-31.

15:24 SCHMITHALS, W. Paulus und Jakobus (1963) 92. EPP, E. J. The
theological tendency of Codex Bezae Cantabrigiensis in Acts (1966)
100f.

15:26 DELLING, G. Die Zueignung des Heils in der Taufe (1961) 87.
POPKES, W. Christus Traditus (1967) 128f., 149, 235, 282.

15:27 HENGEL, M. Judentum und Hellenismus (1969) 19f. ET: Judaism
and Hellenism (1974) I 105. ''Aramäisch'' in: TRE 3 (1978) 604,
609.

15:28-29 MOORE, G. F. Judaism II (1946) 74, 87n. MÜLLER, U. B., Zur
frühchristlichen Theologiegeschichte (Gütersloh 1976) 17-21.
METZGER, B. M., The Early Versions of the New Testament
(Oxford 1977) 136. SAGI, J., Textus decreti Concilii Hierosolym-
itani Lucano Opere et antiquioris Ecclesiae disciplina illustratus
(Rome 1977). CLARK, K. W., ''The Israel of God'' in: The Gentile Bias and other Essays (Leiden 1980) 24.

15:28 KAESEMANN, E. Exegetische Versuche und Besinnungen (1964)
II 76. BROWN, S. Apostasy and Perseverance in the Theology of
Luke (1969) 12f. KAESEMANN, E. New Testament Questions of
Today (1969) 74. WILSON, S. G. The Gentiles and the Gentile
Mission in Luke-Acts (1973) 187, 194, 241, 254. RAYAN, S., The
Holy Spirit (New York 1978) 129-30. WILSON, S. G., ''Law and
Judaism in Acts'' in: P. J. Achtemeier (ed.) SBL Seminar Papers
1980 (Chico, Cal. 1980) 259. MÜLLER, U. B., ''Zur Rezeption
gesetzeskritischer Jesusüberlieferung im frühen Christentum'' NTS
27 (1981) 160.

15:29 HARNACK, A. von, Studien zur Geschichte des Neuen Testaments und der Alten Kirche (1931) 1ff. CLARK, A. C. The Acts
of the Apostles (1933) xlix, 280, 294, 313, 360f. RUDOLPH, K.
Die Mandäer II (1961) 299, 5. SCHMITHALS, W. Paulus und Jakobus (1963) 81-85. BOMAN, T. ''Das textkritische Problem des
sogenannten Aposteldekrets,'' NovTest 7 (1, 1964) 26-36.

GOULDER, M. D. Type and History in Acts (1964) 169f. HENNECKE, E./SCHNEEMELCHER, W. Neutestamentliche Apokryphen (1963) I 135. HURD, J. C. The Origin of 1 Corinthians (1965) 246-50, 258⁵. BOUSSET, W. Die Religion des Judentums im Späthellenistischen Zeitalter (1966, ¹1926) 138. EPP, E. J. The theological tendency of Codex Bezae Cantabrigiensis in Acts (1966) 38, 50 n.1, 107-11, 116-18, 167. PETZKE, G. Die Traditionen über Apollonius von Tyana und das Neue Testament (1970) 123, 225. HEIN, K., Eucharist and Excommunication (Bern/Frankfurt 1975) 83-85. "Apostelgeschichte" in: TRE 3 (1978) 487. DÖMER, M., Das Heil Gottes (Köln/Bonn 1978) 177-78. MANNS, F., "Remarques sur Actes 15,20.29" Antonianum 53 (1978) 443-51. METZGER, B. M., "St. Jerome's explicit references to variant readings in manuscripts of the New Testament" in: F. Best/R. McL. Wilson (eds.) Text and Interpretation. FS. M. Black (Cambridge 1979) 183-84. "Blut" in: TRE 6 (1980) 733. WILSON, S. G., "Law and Judaism in Acts" in: P. J. Achtemeier (ed.) SBL Seminar Papers 1980 (Chico, Cal. 1980) 259-60. DELEBECQUE, E., "L'hellenisme de la 'relative complexe' dans le Nouveau Testament et principalement chez saint Luc" Biblica 62 (1981) 235. "Didache" in: TRE 8 (1981) 732.

15:30 - 16:19 MIESNER, D. R., "The Missionary Journeys Narrative: Patterns and Implications" in: C. H. Talbert (ed.) Perspectives on Luke-Acts (Danville 1978) 207.

15:30ff. LÜDEMANN, G., Paulus, der Heidenapostel. I (Göttingen 1980) 170.

15:30-34 O'NEILL, J. C. The Theology of Acts in its historical setting (1970) 125-31.

15:31 DELLING, G. Die Zueignung des Heils in der Taufe (1961) 91.

15:32-35 ROBECK, C., "The Gift of Prophecy in Acts and Paul, Part I" SBT 5 (1975) 15-38.

15:32 FLEW, R. N. Jesus and His Church (1956) 143n. EPP, E. J. The theological tendency of Codex Bezae Cantabrigiensis in Acts (1966) 111, 116-18. SATAKE, A., Die Gemeindeordnung in der Johannesapokalypse (Neukirchen-Vluyn 1966) 164-66. HENGEL, M. Judentum und Hellenismus (1969) 194. ET: Judaism and Hellenism (1974) I 105. "Aramäisch" in: TRE 3 (1978) 609.

15:33-34 CLARK, A. C. The Acts of the Apostles (1933) xlvii, 183, 269, 280, 294, 318, 332, 361f.

15:33 BEYER, H. W. Die Apostelgeschichte (1947) 96f. "Apostelgeschichte" in: TRE 3 (1978) 486.

15:35-21:16 DIBELIUS, M. Aufsätze zur Apostelgeschichte (1951) 12f., 64. ET: Studies in the Acts of the Apostles (1956) 5f., 69.

15:35-36 DUPONT, J. Etudes sur les Acts des Apôtres (1967) 191, 199, 203-05, 222, 524.

15:35 O'NEILL, J. C. The Theology of Acts in its historical setting (1970) 66-68, 126. "Apostelgeschichte" in: TRE 3 (1978) 486, 487.

15:36 - 28:31 SELBY, D. J., Introduction to the New Testament (New York 1971) 300-07.

15:36-19:20 O'NEILL, J. C. The Theology of Acts in its historical setting (1970) 65-72.

15:36-18:22 KASTING, H. Die Anfänge der Urchristlichen Mission (1969) 106f.

15:36-18:17 GUTBROD, K. Die Apostelgeschichte (1968) 34ff.

15:36ff. HAHN, F. Das Verständnis der Mission im Neuen Testament (^{2}1965) 71.

15:36-41 SCHMITHALS, W. Paulus und Jakobus (1963) 58. BRUZZONE, G. B. Il dissenso tra Paolo e Barnaba in atti 15,39 (1973).

15:36-39 SHEPARD, J. W., The Life and Letters of St. Paul (Grand Rapids 1950) 129-31.

15:37-40 PACKER, J., "Conscience, Choice and Character" in: B. Kaye/ G. Wenham (eds.) Law, Morality and the Bible (Downers Grove, Ill. 1978) 183.

15:37-39 ELLIOTT, J. H., "Peter, Sylvanus and Mark in 1 Peter and Acts: Sociological-Exegetical Perspectives on a Petrine Group in Rome" in: W. Haubeck/M. Bachmann (eds.) Wort in der Zeit. FS. K. H. Rengstorf (Leiden 1980) 260-61.

15:37 HENGEL, M. Judentum und Hellenismus (1969) 194. ET: Judaism and Hellenism (1974) I 105.

15:38-39 "Apostelgeschichte" in: TRE 3 (1978) 497, 500.

15:40-18:17 HAHN, F. Das Verständnis der Mission im Neuen Testament (^{2}1965) 82.

15:40-16:5 SHEPARD, J. W., The Life and Letters of St. Paul (Grand Rapids 1950) 131-35.

15:40 CLARK, A. C. The Acts of the Apostles (1933) 361f. GOULDER, M. D. Type and History in Acts (1964) 28, 101-04. "Aramäisch" in: TRE 3 (1978) 609. PRAST, F., Presbyter und Evangelium in nachapostolischer Zeit (Stuttgart 1979) 141-42.

15:41 GREEN, E. M. B. "Syria and Cilicia - A Note," ET 71 (2, 1959) 52-53. EHRHARDT, A. The Acts of the Apostles (1969) 91f. TISSOT, Y. "Les prescriptions des presbytres (Actes, XV,41,D). Exégèse et origine du décret dans le texte syrooccidental des Actes," RevBi 77 (3, 1970) 321-46. "Antiochien" in: TRE 3 (1978) 102.

16-28 MARTIN, A. A. NTS 11 (1964-1965) 41f. GASQUE, W., A History of the Criticism of the Acts of the Apostles (Tübingen 1975) 171-72, 370, 376-77. MATTILL, A. J., "The Value of Acts as a Source for the Study of Paul" in: C. H. Talbert (Ed.) Perspectives on Luke-Acts (Danville 1978) 76-98.

16-21 DUPONT, J. The Sources of Acts (1964) 69, 115, 128, 133, 147.

16:1-10 DIBELIUS, M. Aufsätze zur Apostelgeschichte (1951) 169f. ET: Studies in the Acts of the Apostles (1956) 200f.

16:1-5 LÜDEMANN, G., Paulus, der Heidenapostel I (Göttingen 1980) 170-71.

16:1-3 SCHMITHALS, W. Paulus und Jakobus (1963) 78-80. "Apostelgeschichte" in: TRE 3 (1978) 497, 499. WALKER, W. O., "The Timothy-Titus Problem Reconsidered" ET 92 (1981) 231-35.

16:1 BEYER, H. W. Die Apostelgeschichte (1947) 98f.

16:2 NELLESSEN, E., Zeugnis für Jesus und das Wort (Köln 1976) 62-63. BERGMEIER, R., Glaube als Gabe nach Johannes (Stuttgart 1980) 238n.40.

16:3 LADD, G. E., A Theology of the New Testament (Grand Rapids 1974) 355, 400, 503. HENGEL, M., Zur urchristlichen Geschichtsschreibung (Stuttgart 1979) 58; ET: J. Bowden (trans.) Acts and the History of Earliest Christianity (London 1979) 64.

16:4 HARNACK, A. von, Studien zur Geschichte des Neuen Testaments und der Alten Kirche (1931) 19ff. EPP, E. J. The theological tendency of Codex Bezae Cantabrigiensis in Acts (1966) 54, 62, 113f., 119, 123. "Amt" in: TRE 3 (1978) 513. PRAST, F., Presbyter und Evangelium in nachapostolischer Zeit (Stuttgart 1979) 225, 356-57. WILSON, S. G., "Law and Judaism in Acts" in: P. J. Achtemeier (ed.) SBL Seminar Papers 1980 (Chico, Cal. 1980) 259-60.

16:5 BROWN, S. Apostasy and Perseverance in the Theology of Luke (1969) 44, 73, 128, 141, 146. ZINGG, P., Das Wachsen der Kirche (Freiburg 1974) 20-34.

16:6-18:5 BRUCE, F. F., "St. Paul in Macedonia" BJRL 61 (1979) 337-54.

16:6ff. LENTZEN-DEIS, F. Die Taufe Jesu nach den Synoptikern (1970) 274-85.

16:6-11 "Apostelgeschichte" in: TRE 3 (1978) 500.

16:6-10 SHEPARD, J. W., The Life and Letters of St. Paul (Grand Rapids

1950) 187-38. HAHN, F. Das Verständnis der Mission im Neuen Testament (²1965) 80.

16:6-9 "Apostelgeschichte" in: TRE 3 (1978) 494.

16:6-8 LÜDEMANN, G., Paulus, der Heidenapostel I (Göttingen 1980) 171-72.

16:6-7 SCHRAGE, W. Die konkreten Einzelgebote in der paulinischen Paränese (1961) 87. STAEHLIN, G. "τὸ πνεῦμα 'Ιησοῦ,'' (Apostelgeschichte 16:7),'' in: Christ and the Spirit in the New Testament (1973) B. Lindars/S. S. Smalley eds., 231f., 239f., 242, 243f, 247f., 249ff. DUNN, J. D. G., Jesus and the Spirit (London 1975) 153, 172, 176, 180, 217.

16:6 DUPONT, J. Etudes sur les Actes des Apôtres (1967) 93, 168, 521, 524. LEE, G. M. "New Testament Gleanings," Biblica 51 (2, 1970) 235-40. BORSE, U. Der Standort des Galaterbriefes (1972) 1-3, 45f., 58f., A 211. CONZELMANN, H. und LINDEMANN, A., Arbeitsbuch zum Neuen Testament (Tübingen 1975) 193-94. HEMER, C. J., "The Adjective 'Phrygia' " JThS 27 (1976) 122-126. HEMER, C. J., "Phrygia: A Further Note" JThS 28 (1977) 99-101. METZGER, B. M., The Early Versions of the New Testament (Oxford 1977) 179. GUNKEL, H., The Influence of the Holy Spirit (Philadelphia 1979) 23-24.

16:7 PENNA, R. "Lo 'Spirito di Gesù' in Atti 16,7. Analisi letteraria e teologica," RivB 20 (3, 1972) 241-61. STAEHLIN, G. "τὸ πνεῦμα 'Ιησοῦ (Apostelgeschichte 16:7),'' in: Christ and the Spirit in the New Testament (1973) B. Lindars/S. S. Smalley eds., 229-52. MOULE, C. F. D., The Holy Spirit (London 1978) 34.

16:8-10 HUBBARD, B. J., "The Role of the Commissioning Accounts in Acts" in: C. H. Talbert (ed.) Perspectives on Luke-Acts (Danville 1978) 190, 193, 197.

16:8 BOWERS, W. P., "Paul's Route Through Mysia: A Note on Acts XVI.8" JThS 30 (1979) 507-11.

16:9-17:15 SCHWANK, B. " 'Setze über nach Mazedonien und hilf uns!' Reisenotizen zu Apg 16,9-17,15," EuA 39 (5, 1963) 399-416.

16:9-17:14 WILCOX, M. The Semitisms of Acts (1965) 59ff.

16:9-15 GLOMBITZA, O. "Der Schritt nach Europa: Erwägungen zu Act 16, 9-15," ZNW 53 (1-2, 1962) 77-82. DEHN, G. in: Herr, tue meine Lippen auf Bd. 4 (1965) G. Eichholz ed., 422ff. STECK, K. G. GPM 20 (1965-1966) 380-87. SCHMIDT, H., in: GPM 32 (1977-1978) 372-79.

16:9-10 BURCHARD, C. Der dreizehnte Zeuge (1970) 111f. HUBBARD, B. J., "Commissioning Stories in Luke-Acts: A Study of their Antecedents, Form and Content" in: Semeia 8 (1977) 103-26.

16:9 BOHREN, R., Predigtlehre (München 1971) 490-91. SOARES PRABHU, G. M., The Formula Quotations in the Infancy Narratives of Matthew (Rome 1976) 224-25. MATTILL, A. J., "The Value of Acts as a Source for the Study of Paul" in: C. H. Talbert (ed.) Perspectives on Luke-Acts (Danville 1978) 91.

16:10ff. "Apostelgeschichte" in: TRE 3 (1978) 494.

16:10-17 STONEHOUSE, N. B. The Witness of Luke to Christ (1951) 15ff. "Apostelgeschichte" in: TRE 3 (1978) 514. ROBBINS, V. K., "By Land and By Sea: The We-Passages and Ancient Sea Voyages" in: C. H. Talbert (ed.) Perspectives on Luke-Acts (Danville 1978) 215-42.

16:10-11 "Apostelgeschichte" in: TRE 3 (1978) 487, 488.

16:10 HAENCHEN, E. "Das 'Wir' in der Apostelgeschichte und das Itinerar," ZThK 58 (3, 1961) 329-66. KAESEMANN, E. Exegetische Versuche und Besinnungen (1964) I 131."Apostelgeschichte" in: TRE 3 (1978) 494.

16:11-40 SHEPARD, J. W., The Life and Letters of St. Paul (Grand Rapids 1950) 138-44. SCHILLE, G. Anfänge der Kirche (1966) 43ff. REDALIÉ, Y., "Conversion ou libération? Notes sur Actes 16,11-40" Bulletin du Centre Protestant d'Etudes 26 (Geneva 1974) 7-17.

16:11-15 FURNISH, V. P., The Moral Teachings of Paul (Nashville 1979) 104.

16:11 JEWETT, R., A Chronology of Paul's Life (Philadelphia 1979) 47-48.

16:12 BLASS, F. Philosophy of the Gospels (1898) 67ff. CLARK, A. C. The Acts of the Apostles (1933) li, 300, 362-65. CONZELMANN, H. Die Apostelgeschichte (1963) 90f. SHERWIN-WHITE, A. N., Roman Society and Roman Law in the New Testament (Grand Rapids 1978) 93.

16:13-15 "Apostelgeschichte" in: TRE 3 (1978) 497, 500.

16:13 RUDOLPH, K. Die Mandäer II (1961) 369. ELLIGER, W., Paulus in Griechenland (Stuttgart 1978) 47-50. SWIDLER, L., Biblical Affirmations of Woman (Philadelphia 1979) 293.

16:14-40 GORSKI, R. und SCHRAGE, W. in: GPM 36 (1982) 217-25.

16:14-15 KNOX, W. L. The Sources of the Synoptic Gospels II (1957) 90. DELLING, G. Die Taufe im Neuen Testament (1963) 70-72. CHERRY, R. S. "Acts xvi. 14f.," ET 75 (4, 1964) 114. BIEDER, W., Die Verheissung der Taufe im Neuen Testament (Zürich 1966) 73-76. SWIDLER, L., Biblical Affirmations of Woman (Philadelphia 1979) 293, 296. BARTH, G., Die Taufe in frühchristlicher Zeit (Neukirchen-Vluyn 1981) 11, 38, 40, 126, 138, 140.

16:14 BARRETT, C. K. The New Testament Background (1956) 164.

DELLING, G. Die Taufe im Neuen Testament (1963) 73. BOUS-
SET, W. Die Religion des Judentums im Späthellenistischen Zei-
talter (1966 = 1926) 80. HORTON, F. L., ''Reflections on the
Semitisms of Luke-Acts'' in: C. H. Talbert (ed.), Perspectives on
Luke-Acts (Danville 1978) 21. WILCOX, M., ''The 'God-Fear-
ers' in Acts - A Reconsideration'' JSNT 13 (1981) 110-11, 113.

16:15 DELLING, G. Die Zueignung des Heils in der Taufe (1961) 87.
CONZELMANN, H. Die Apostelgeschichte (1963) 96. DELL-
ING, G. Die Taufe im Neuen Testament (1963) 60, 69, 135. EPP,
E. J. The theological tendency of Codex Bezae Cantabrigiensis in
Acts (1966) 89f., 167. WANKE, J., Die Emmauserzählung. Eine
redaktionsgeschichtliche Untersuchung zu Lk 24,13-35 (Leipzig
1973) 100-01. JEWETT, P. K., Infant Baptism and the Covenant
of Grace (Grand Rapids 1978) 49. SCHNEIDER, G., ''Gott und
Christus als κυριος nach der Apostelgeschichte'' in: J. Zmi-
jewski/E. Nellessen (eds.) Begegnung mit dem Wort. FS. H. Zimmermann (Bonn 1980) 163, 171, 172.

16:16-40 PLUEMACHER, E. Lukas als hellenistischer Schriftsteller (1972)
95-97. BEYSCHLAG, K., Simon Magus und die christliche Gnosis
(Tübingen 1974) 188. GROÓ, G., in: GPM 30 (1975-1976) 220-
24. SCHMIDT, E. und SIMPFENDÖRFER, G., in: P. Krusche et
al (eds.) Predigtstudien für das Kirchenjahr 1975-1976. IV/2
(Stuttgart 1976) 55-61. GERSTENBERGER, G. und SCHRAGE,
W., Leiden (Stuttgart 1977) 173; ET: J. E. Steely (trans.) Suffering
(Nashville 1980) 200-01. ''Apostelgeschichte'' in: TRE 3 (1978)
496, 509, 512, 519.

16:16-34 HELD, J. GPM 18 (1, 1964) 177-81. VOIGT, G. Der zerrissene
Vorhang I (1969) 215-20. KRAUSE, O. GPM 24/2 (1970-1971)
223-29.

16:16-32 DEHN, G. in: Herr, tue meine Lippen auf Bd. 4 (1965) G. Eichholz ed., 397ff.

16:16-20 CLARK, A. C. The Acts of the Apostles (1933) 271f.

16:16-19 ''Apostelgeschichte'' in: TRE 3 (1978) 497.

16:16-18 TRITES, A. A., The New Testament Concept of Witness (Cambridge 1977) 177-78. ''Apostelgeschichte'' in: TRE 3 (1978) 499.

16:16-17 ''Apostelgeschichte'' in: TRE 3 (1978) 494.

16:16 GOULDER, M. D. Type and History in Acts (1964) 101, 106f.
''Apostelgeschichte'' in: TRE 3 (1978) 509.

16:17-18 ''Apostelgeschichte'' in: TRE 3 (1978) 494.

16:17 KNOX, W. L. The Sources of the Synoptic Gospels II (1957) 41.
BROWN, S. Apostasy and Perseverance in the Theology of Luke
(1969) 140f. HENGEL, M. Judentum und Hellenismus (1969) 546.
ET: Judaism and Hellenism (1974) II 101. KAESEMANN, E. New

Testament Questions of Today (1969) 85. ELLIGER, W., Paulus in Griechenland (Stuttgart 1978) 67-68, 92n.19. PRAST, F., Presbyter und Evangelium in nachapostolischer Zeit (Stuttgart 1979) 59.

16:18-24 EHRHARDT, A. The Acts of the Apostles (1969) 94f.

16:18 DELLING, G. Die Zueignung des Heils in der Taufe (1961) 51, 88. "Apostelgeschichte" in: TRE 3 (1978) 490.

16:19-40 MATTILL, A. J., "The Value of Acts as a Source for the Study of Paul" in: C. H. Talbert (ed.) Perspectives on Luke-Acts (Danville 1978) 91. SHERWIN-WHITE, A. N., Roman Society and Roman Law in the New Testament (Grand Rapids 1978) 78-79.

16:19-24 "Apostelgeschichte" in: TRE 3 (1978) 499.

16:20-40 MIESNER, D. R., "The Missionary Journeys Narrative: Patterns and Implications" in: C. H. Talbert (ed.) Perspectives on Luke-Acts (Danville 1978) 208.

16:20-21 van UNNIK, W. C., Sparsa Collecta I (Leiden 1973) 374-85.

16:20 DALTON, W. J., Christ's Proclamation to the Spirits. A Study of 1 Peter 3:18 - 4:6 (Rome 1965) 123.

16:22-35 KRATZ, R., Auferweckung als Befreiung (Stuttgart 1973) 15, 26, 28, 34.

16:22-28 O'NEILL, J. C. The Theology of Acts in its historical setting (1970) 145-46.

16:22-23 SCHRAGE, W. Die konkreten Einzelgebote in der paulinischen Paränese (1961) 225.

16:23-34 HIRSCHLER, H. und STIERLE, B., in: P. Krusche et al (eds.) Predigtstudien für das Kirchenjahr 1981-1982. IV/2 (Stuttgart 1982) 48-55.

16:23.25-27 BETZ, H. D. Lukian von Samosata und das Neue Testament (1961) 9, 157, 165, 170f.

16:23-24 "Apostelgeschichte" in: TRE 3 (1978) 509.

16:23 POUPON, G., "L'accusation de magie dans les Actes apocryphes" in: F. Bovon et al (eds.) Les Actes Apocryphes des Apôtres (Geneva 1981) 90n.9.

16:25-34 DIBELIUS, M. Aufsätze zur Apostelgeschichte (1951) 26-28. ET: Studies in the Acts of the Apostles (1956) 23-24. DUPONT, J. The Sources of Acts (1964) 27, 83, 118, 133, 148, 153. BIEDER, W., Die Verheissung der Taufe im Neuen Testament (Zürich 1966) 76-79. "Apostelgeschichte" in: TRE 3 (1978) 496, 499. JEWETT, P. K., Infant Baptism and the Covenant of Grace (Grand Rapids 1978) 49. BOVON, F., "La vie des apôtres: traditions bibliques et narrations apocryphes" in: F. Bovon et al (eds.) Les Actes Apocryphes des Apôtres (Geneva 1981) 150n 35.

16:25 BRAUN, H. Qumran und NT II (1966) 202. POUPON, G., "L'accusation de magie dans les Actes apocryphes'' in: F. Bovon et al (eds.) Les Actes Apocryphes des Apôtres (Geneva 1981) 88.

16:26-30 DELLING, G. Die Taufe im Neuen Testament (1963) 73.

16:26 KRATZ, R., Auferweckung als Befreiung (Stuttgart 1973) 14, 15, 28, 38. DUNN, J. G. D., Jesus and the Spirit (London 1975) 163, 166-67. "Apostelgeschichte" in: TRE 3 (1978) 509. POUPON, G., "L'accusation de magie dans les Actes apocryphes" in: F. Bovon et al (eds.) Les Actes Apocryphes des Apôtres (Geneva 1981) 74n.28.

16:27-28 "Apostelgeschichte" in: TRE 3 (1978) 509.

16:27 CLARK, K. W., "The Meaning of APA" in: The Gentile Bias and Other Essays (Leiden 1980) 198.

16:30-34 DELLING, G. Die Taufe im Neuen Testament (1963) 60, 71-73, 135, 136.

16:30-31 BURCHARD, C. Der dreizehnte Zeuge (1970) 95f.

16:30 "Apostelgeschichte" in: TRE 3 (1978) 488.

16:31 EPP, E. J. The theological tendency of Codec Bezae Cantabrigiensis in Acts (1966) 54, 62f., 89 n.3.

16:33-34 REICKE, B. Diakonie, Festfreude und Zelos (1951) 216f.

16:33 BARTH, G., Die Taufe in frühchristlicher Zeit (Neukirchen-Vluyn 1981) 11, 38, 40, 126, 138.

16:34 WANKE, J., Die Emmauserzählung. Eine redaktionsgeschichtliche Untersuchung zu Lk 24, 13-35 (Leipzig 1973) 100-01. MENOUD, P. H., "Actes 16:34" in: Jésus-Christ et la foi (Neuchâtel-Paris 1976) 67-68.

16:35ff. "Apostelgeschichte" in: TRE 3 (1978) 499.

16:35 "Apostelgeschichte" in: TRE 3 (1978) 488.

16:36 HENNECKE, E./SCHNEEMELCHER, W. Neutestamentliche Apokryphen (1963) I 155.

16:37-40 STOLLE, V. Der Zeuge als Angeklagter (1973) 99.

16:37-39 BURCHARD, C. Der dreizehnte Zeuge (1970) 37-39.

16:37 SCHNEIDER, G. Verleugnung, Verspottung und Verhör Jesu nach Lukas 22, 54-71 (1969) 67, 85, 100, 125. BAUMERT, N., Täglich Sterben und Auferstehen. Der Literalsinn von 2 Kor 4,12 - 5,10 (München 1973) 361.

16:38 "Apostelgeschichte" in: TRE 3 (1978) 488.

16:39 EPP, E. J. The theological tendency of Codec Bezae Cantabrigiensis in Acts (1966) 49, 50f., 51 n.1, 147-50.

16:40 FURNISH, V. P., The Moral Teaching of Paul (Nashville 1979) 104. SWIDLER, L., Biblical Affirmations of Woman (Philadelphia 1979) 104.

17-18 BOUSSET, W. Die Religion des Judentums im Späthellenistischen Zeitalter (1966 = 1926) 218.

  17 GAERTNER, B. The Areopagus Speech and Natural Revelation (1955). OWEN, H. P. NTS 5 (1958-1959) 135ff. LEBRAM, J. C. "Der Aufbau der Areopagrede," ZNW 55 (1964) 221-43. LEBRAM, J.-C. "Zwei Bemerkungen zu katechetischen Traditionen in der Apostelgeschichte," ZNW 56 (3-4, 1965) 202-13. CONZELMANN, H. Theologie als Schriftauslegung (1974) 91. CONZELMANN, H. und LINDEMANN, A., Arbeitsbuch zum Neuen Testament (Tübingen 1975) 183. GASQUE, W., A History of the Criticism of the Acts of the Apostles (Tübingen 1975) 211-13, 232.

17:1-31 DUPONT, D. J., The Salvation of the Gentiles (New York 1979) 31-32.

17:1-15 MIESNER, D. R., "The Missionary Journeys Narrative: Patterns and Implications" in: C. H. Talbert (ed.) Perspectives on Luke-Acts (Danville 1978) 208.

17:1-9 SHEPARD, J. W., The Life and Letters of St. Paul (Grand Rapids 1950) 145, 146-49.

17:2ff. GUTBROD, K. Die Apostelgeschichte (1968) 59ff.

17:2-4 KEMMLER, D. W., Faith and Human Reason (Leiden 1975) 11-142.

17:2-3 KRAENKL, E. Jesus der Knecht Gottes (1972) 48, 57f., 78f., 209.

17:3-4 HAHN, F. Christologische Hoheitstitel (1963) 205, 215f., 217, 224. SCHILLE, G. Anfänge der Kirche (1966) 79ff.

  17:3 DELLING, G. Die Zueignung des Heils in der Taufe (1961) 88. HARNISCH, W. Eschatologische Existenz (1973) 32f. WILCKENS, U. Die Missionsreden der Apostelgeschichte (^{3}1973) 115, 117, 118, 139, 159, 238, 239.

  17:4 BARRETT, C. K. The New Testament Background (1956) 164. BOUSSET, W. Die Religion des Judentums im Späthellenistischen Zeitalter (1966 = 1926) 80f. SWIDLER, L., Biblical Affirmations of Woman (Philadelphia 1979) 293. WILCOX, M., "The 'God-Fearers' in Acts - A Reconsideration" JSNT 13 (1981) 111.

17:5-9 SCHILLE, G. Anfänge der Kirche (1966) 95ff. STOLLE, V. Der Zeuge als Angeklagter (1973) 99-100. ELLIGER, W., Paulus in Griechenland (Stuttgart 1978) 91.

17:5-7 JUDGE, E. A. "The Decrees of Caesar at Thessalonica," RThR 30 (1, 1971) 1-7.

17:6 GASQUE, W., A History of the Criticism of the Acts of the Apostles (Tübingen 1975) 122.

17:7 HAHN, Christologische Hoheitstitel (1963) 224. CRIBBS, F. L., "The Agreements that Exist between John and Acts" in: C. H. Talbert (ed.) Perspectives on Luke-Acts (Danville 1978) 45. SHERWIN-WHITE, A. N., Roman Society and Roman Law in the New Testament (Grand Rapids 1978) 103-04.

17:10ff. EHRHARDT, A. The Acts of the Apostles (1969) 96f.

17:10-15 SHEPARD, J. W., The Life and Letters of St. Paul (Grand Rapids 1950) 149-50.

17:10-13 GEIGER, G., Kirche Unterwegs. Ein Arbeitsheft zum zweiten Teil der Apostelgeschichte (Klosterneuburg 1981).

17:10f.14 SCHILLE, G. Anfänge der Kirche (1966) 79ff.

17:11-12 "Bibel" in: TRE 6 (1980) 19.

17:11 BONHOEFFER, A. Epiktet und das Neue Testament (1911) 206, 220, NESTLE, E., "Act 17,11" ZNW 15 (1914) 91-92. CLARK, A. C. The Acts of the Apostles (1933) 211, 237, 295, 314. KNOX, W. L. The Sources of the Synoptic Gospels II (1957) 115. DANKER, F. W. NTS 10 (1963-1964) 366f.

17:12 DELLING, G. Die Taufe in Neuen Testament (1963) 70. EPP, E. J. The theological tendency of Codex Bezae Cantabrigiensis in Acts (1966) 74f., 86, 118, 166, 167 n. 7. CRIBBS, F. L., "The Agreements that Exist between John and Acts" in: C. H. Talbert (ed.) Perspectives on Luke-Acts (Danville 1978) 58. SWIDLER, L., Biblical Affirmations of Woman (Philadelphia 1979) 293. WILCOX, M., "The 'God-Fearers' in Acts - A Reconsideration" JSNT 13 (1981) 111.

17:13 RUPPERT, L., Jesus als der leidende Gerechte? (Stuttgart 1972) 27n.16.

17:14-15 CLARK, A. C. The Acts of the Apostles (1933) 366f.

17:15-34 SHEPARD, J. W., The Life and Letters of St. Paul (Grand Rapids 1950) 150-59. van der WALT, B. J., "Handelinge 17:15-34 en Romeine 1:18-25: bewyse vir aansluitingspunte in de sending of vir 'n natuurlike teologie?" In die Skriflig 10 (1976) 47-51.

17:15-19:1 WILCOX, M. The Semitisms of Acts (1965) 59ff.

17:15 BRONEER, O. "Athens, City of Idol Worship," BA 21 (1, 1958) 2-28. EPP, E. J. The theological tendency of Codex Bezae Cantabrigiensis in Acts (1966) 117-19, 142-44, 147. KILPATRICK, G. D., "Eclecticism and Atticism" EphT 53 (1977) 107-12.

17:16ff. STONEHOUSE, N. B. Paul Before the Areopagus; and Other New Testament Studies (1957). CONZELMANN, H. Theologie als Schriftauslegung (1973) 91-105, 152.

17:16-34 BETHGE, F. Die paulinischen Reden der Apostelgeschichte (1887) 65-116. BEYER, H. W. Die Apostelgeschichte (1947) 106f. DIBELIUS, M. Aufsätze zur Apostelgeschichte (1951) 114f. ET: Studies in the Acts of the Apostles (1956) 130f. SOUCEK, J. B. GPM 18 (1, 1964) 173-77. FLENDER, H. Heil und Geschichte in der Theologie des Lukas (1965) 64-69. JENTSCH, W. "Der deutliche Gott," in: Kleine Predigt-Typologie Bd. III (1965) L. Schmidt ed., 192-205. LANG, F. in: Herr, tue meine Lippen auf Bd. 4 (1965) G. Eichholz ed., 403ff. MARE, W. H. "Pauline Appeals to Historical Evidence," BullEvangTheolSoc 11 (3, 1968) 121-30. BARNES, T. D. "An Apostle on Trial," JThS 20 (2, 1969) 407-19. VOIGT, G. Der zerrissene Vorhang I (1969) 208-14. HAAR, J. GPM 24/2 (1970-1971) 214-23. HEMER, C. J. "Paul at Athens: A Topographical Note," NTS 20 (3, 1974) 341-50. PRIOR, K. F. W., The Gospel in a Pagan Society. The Relevance for Today of Paul's Ministry in Athens (London/Sydney/Auckland 1975) passim. HERR, T., Naturrecht aus der kritischen Sicht des Neuen Testaments (München 1976) 148-55. PANNENBERG, W. und MÜLLER, H. M., in: P. Krusche et al (eds.) Predigtstudien für das Kirchenjahr 1975-1976. IV/2 (Stuttgart 1976) 48-54. STECK, K. G., in: GPM 30 (1975-1976) 213-20. MARTIN, R. P., New Testament Foundations II: Acts - Revelation (Exeter 1978) 119-21. MIESNER, D. R., "The Missionary Journeys Narrative: Patterns and Implications" in: C. H. Talbert (ed.) Perspectives on Luke-Acts (Danville 1978) 209. CALLOUD, J., "Paul devant l'Aréopage d'Athènes. Actes 17,16-34" RechSR 69 (1981) 209-48. GEIGER, G., Kirche Unterwegs. Ein Arbeitsheft zum zweiten Teil der Apostelgeschichte (Klosterneuburg 1981).

17:16, 17, O'NEILL, J. C. The Theology of Acts in its historical setting (1970)
24-31, 34 116-71.

17:16-31 GAERTNER, B. "The Areopagus Speech and Natural Revelation," Acta Seminarii Neotestamentici Upsaliensis XXI (1955) 7-289. WILKINSON, T. L., "Acts 17: The Gospel Related to Paganism. Contemporary Relevance" VR 35 (1980) 1-14.

17:16-21 DIBELIUS, M. Aufsätze zur Apostelgeschichte (1951) 60-64. ET: Studies in the Acts of the Apostles (1956) 64-69.

17:16.23 WYCHERLEY, R. E. "St. Paul at Athens," JThS 19 (2, 1968) 619-21.

17:16 BEYER, H. W. Die Apostelgeschichte (1947) 105. O'NEILL, J. C. The Theology of Acts in its historical setting (1970) 162-63, 165. CONZELMANN, H. Theologie als Schriftauslegung (1974) 92-94. "Apostelgeschichte" in: TRE 3 (1978) 503.

17:17-18 CONZELMANN, H. Theologie als Schriftauslegung (1974) 92f.

17:17 BARRETT, C. K. New Testament Background (1956) 164. BOUSSET, W. Die Religion des Judentums im Späthellenistischen Zeitalter (1966 = 1926) 80. O'NEILL, J. C. The Theology of Acts in its historical setting (1970) 166-67. ''Apostelgeschichte'' in: TRE 3 (1978) 517. WILCOX, M., ''The 'God-Fearers' in Acts - A Reconsideration'' JSNT 13 (1981) 112-13.

17:18– O'NEILL, J. C. The Theology of Acts in its historical setting (1970)
23:32f. 166-71.

17:18f., BETZ, H. D. Lukian von Samosata und das Neue Testament (1961)
22-25 26, 48, 61, 68, 111, 116, 129, 164, 208.

17:18-19 DUPONT, D. J. ''Le Salut des Gentils et la Signification Théologique du Livre des Actes,'' NTS 6 (1959-1960) 152f.

17:18 KAESEMANN, E. Exegetische Versuche und Besinnungen (1964) I 131. PETZKE, G. Die Traditionen über Apollonius von Tyana und das Neue Testament (1970) 166, 200, 217. FERRE, N. F. S., The Extreme Centre (Waco, Texas 1973) 142-49. ROBINSON, M. A. ''ΣΠΕΡΜΟΛΟΓΟΣ: Did Paul Preach from Jesus' Parables?'' Biblica 56 (1975) 231-40. METZGER, B. M., The Early Versions of the New Testament (Oxford 1977) 245. ''Apostelgeschichte'' in: TRE 3 (1978) 517.

17:19-23 CONZELMANN, H. ''The Address of Paul on the Areopagus,'' in: Studies in Luke-Acts (1966) L. E. Keck/J. L. Martyn (eds.), 217-20. VELTMAN, F., ''The Defense Speeches of Paul in Acts'' in: C. H. Talbert (ed.) Perspectives on Luke-Acts (Danville 1978) 243-56.

17:19 ELLIS, E. E./WILCOX, M. (eds.), Neotestamentica (1969) 198-202. MORRICE, W. G. ''Where did Paul speak in Athens-on Mars' Hill or before the Court of the Areopagus? (Acts 17:19),'' ET 83 (1, 2 1972) 377-78.

17:20 ''Apostelgeschichte'' in: TRE 3 (1978) 517.

17:21 NORDEN, E. Agnostos Theos (1956) 333ff. O'NEILL, J. C. The Theology of Acts in its historical setting (1970) 168-69. ''Apostelgeschichte'' in: TRE 3 (1978) 502.

17:22-34 van UNNIK, W. C., ''Luke-Acts, a Storm Center in Contemporary Scholarship'' in: L. E. Keck/J. L. Martyn (eds.) Studies in Luke-Acts. FS. P. Schubert (Nashville 1966) 26. VIELHAUER, P., ''On the 'Paulism' of Acts'' in: J. E. Keck/J. L. Martyn (eds.) Studies in Luke-Acts. FS. P. Schubert (Nashville 1966) 34-37.

17:22-32 WILCKENS,U. Die Missionsreden der Apostelgeschichte ([3]1974) 87-91, 192.

17:22-31 HANSON, S. The Unity of the Church in the New Testament (1946) 101-05. DIBELIUS, M. Aufsätze zur Apostelgeschichte (1951) 72f., 131-33. ET: Studies in the Acts of the Apostles (1956) 79f., 119f. MUSSNER, F. "Einige Parallelen aus den Qumrântexten zur Areopagrede (Apg 17,22-31)," BZ 1, (1, 1957) 125-30. MUSSNER, F. "Anknüpfung und Kerygma in der Areopagrede (Apg 17,22b-31)," TThZ 67 (6, 1958) 344-54. CONZELMANN, H. Die Apostelgeschichte (1963) 102-04. LEBRAM, J.-C. "Der Aufbau der Areopagrede," ZNW 55 (2-4, 1964) 221-43. SCHNEIDER, G. Der Herr unser Gott (1965) 167-72. DUPONT, J. Etudes sur les Actes des Apôtres (1967) 50-54, 138-39, 157-60, 416-18, 436, 437, 461. GUTBROD, K. Die Apostelgeschichte (1967) 63ff. BURCHARD, C. Der dreizehnte Zeuge (1970) 138-42. EVANS, C. F. " 'Speeches' in Acts," in: Mélanges Bibliques en hommage au R. P. Béda Rigaux (1970) A. Descamps/A. de Halleux (eds.), 293-94. FUDGE, E. "Paul's Apostolic Self-Consciousness at Athens," JEThS 14 (3, 1971) 193-98. DUBARLE, A.-M. "Le discours à l'Aréopage (Actes 17,22-31 et son arrièreplan biblique," RSPhTh 57 (4, 1973) 576-610. LAUB, F. Eschatologische Verkündigung und Lebensgestaltung nach Paulus (1973) 36-40, 45. WILSON, S. G. The Gentiles and Gentile Mission in Luke-Acts (1973) 194-218, 243, 245, 252, 262. CONZELMANN, H. Theologie als Schriftauslegung (1974) 63 n.11, 94-105. GLÖCKNER, R., Die Verkündigung des Heils beim Evangelisten Lukas (Mainz 1975) 214-15. HUNTER, A. M., Gospel and Apostle (London 1975) 123-27. KLIESCH, K., Das heilsgeschichtliche Credo in den Reden der Apostelgeschichte (Köln/Bonn 1975) 170-74. BRUCE, F. F., "Paul and the Athenians" ET 88 (1976) 8-12. DUBARLE, A.-M., La manifestation naturelle d'Dieu d'après l'Écriture (Paris 1976). BRUCE, F. F., First Century Faith (Leicester 1977) 39-49. BRUCE, F. F., Paul: Apostle of the Free Spirit (Exeter 1977) 238-47. ELLIGER, W., Paulus in Griechenland (Stuttgart 1978) 135-43. HOLTZ, T., " 'Euer Glaube an Gott'. Zu Form and Inhalt von 1 Thess 1:9f" in: R. Schnackenburg et al (eds.) Die Kirche des Anfangs. FS. H. Schürmann (Freiburg/Basel/Wien 1978) 461-63. NIXON, R., "The Universality of the Concept of Law" in: B. Kaye/ G. Wenham (eds.) Law, Morality and the Bible (Downers Grove, Ill. 1970) 117. DUPONT, J., "Le discours à l'Aréopage (Ac 17,22-31) lieu de recontre entre christianisme et hellénisme" Biblica 60 (1979) 530-46. MEYER, B. F., The Aims of Jesus (London 1979) 66-69. McDONALD, J. I. H., Kerygma and Didache (Cambridge 1980) 53-54.

17:22-29 KLIESCH, K., Das heilsgeschichtliche Credo in den Reden der Apostelgeschichte (Köln/Bonn 1975) 65-72, 110.

17:22-23 DIBELIUS, M. Aufsätze zur Apostelgeschichte (1951) 29f., 38-41. ET: Studies in the Acts of the Apostles (1956) 27f., 37-41. WILSON, S. G., "Law and Judaism in Acts" in: P. J. Achtemeier (ed.) SBL Seminar Papers 1980 Chico, Cal. 1980) 261.

17:22 BONHOEFFER, A. Epiktet und das Neue Testament (1911) 180ff. PALLIS, A., Notes on St. Luke and the Acts (London 1928) 69. GAERTNER, B. "The Areopagus Speech and Natural Revelation," SvTK 32 (1956) 59-62. NAUCK, W. "Die Tradition und Komposition in der Areopagrede," ZThK 53 (1956) 11-52. NORDEN, E. Agnostos Theos (1956, ¹1912) 1ff. MOELLERING, H. A. "Deisidaimonia, a Footnote to Acts 17:22," CThM 34 (8, 1963) 466-71. DES PLACES, E. "Quasi Superstitiosiores," in: Studiorum Paulinorum Congressus Internationalis Catholicus 1961 Vol. II (1963) 183-91. HAHN, F. Das Verständnis der Mission im Neuen Testament (²1965) 65, 118. CONZELMANN, H. Theologie als Schriftauslegung (1974) 93f. CONZELMANN, H. und LINDEMANN, A., Arbeitsbuch zum Neuen Testament (Tübingen 1975) 40-41. "Apostelgeschichte" in: TRE 3 (1978) 503.

17:23ff. SMITH, M. Tannaitic Parallels to the Gospels (1968) 4 b n 22.

17:23-31 AUFFRET, P. "Essai sur la structure littéraire du discours d'Athènes (Ac xvii 23-32)" NovT 20 (1978) 185-202.

17:23 GAERTNER, B. The Areopagus Speech and Natural Revelation (1955) 236ff. DES PLACES, E. " 'Au dieu inconnu' (Act 17,23)," Biblica 40 (3, 1959) 793-99. EPP, E. J. The theological tendency of Codex Bezae Cantabrigiensis in Acts (1966) 48f. O'NEILL, J. C. The Theology of Acts in its historical setting (1970) 14-15. CONZELMANN, H. Theologie als Schriftauslegung (1974) 93f., 123 A9. DELEBECQUE, E., "L'hellenisme de la 'relative complexe' dans le Nouveau Testament et principalement chez saint Luc" Biblica 62 (1981) 232.

17:24ff. CLEMEN, C. Primitive Christianity and Its Non-Jewish Sources (1912) 58ff.

17:24-30 SHIELDS, B. E., "The Areopagus Sermon and Romans 1:18ff: A Study in Creation Theology" RestQ 20 (1977) 3-40. DUPONT, D. J., The Salvation of the Gentiles (New York 1979) 64.

17:24-29 O'NEILL, J. C. The Theology of Acts in its historical setting (1970) 163-64. GATTI, V., Il discorso di Paolo ad Atene. Storia dell'interpretazione-esegesi-teologia della Missione e delle Religioni (Parma 1979) passim.

17:24-27 STRECKER, G. Der Weg der Gerechtigkeit (1962) 47₄. LAUB, F. Eschatologische Verkündigung und Lebensgestaltung nach Paulus (1973) 37f.

17:24-26 CONZELMANN, H. Theologie als Schriftauslegung (1974) 95-98.

17:24-25 DIBELIUS, M. Aufsätze zur Apostelgeschichte (1951) 41-45. ET: Studies in the Acts of the Apostels (1956) 41-46. GAERTNER, B. The Areopagus Speech and Natural Revelation (1955) 211f. WILSON, S. G. The Gentiles and the Gentile Mission in Luke-Acts (1973) 198-200, 209, 216.

17:24 DES PLACES, E., " 'Des temples faits de main d'homme' (Actes des Apôtres, 17,24)," Biblica 42 (2, 1961) 217-23.

17:25 DES PLACES, E., "Actes 17,25," Biblica 46 (2, 1965) 219-22. ZEHNLE, R. F. Peter's Pentecost Discourse (1971) 115-16.

17:26-27 DIBELIUS, M. Aufsätze zur Apostelgeschichte (1951) 30-38. ET: Studies in the Acts of the Apostles (1956) 27-37. GAERTNER, B. The Areopagus Speech and Natural Revelation (1955) 146ff., 151ff., WILSON, S. G. The Gentiles and the Gentile Mission in Luke-Acts (1973) 200-06.

17:26 PALLIS, A., Notes on St. Luke and the Acts (London 1928) 70. MOORE, G. F. Judaism I (1946) 445. ELTESTER, W. "Gott und die Natur in der Areopagrede," in: Neutestamentliche Studien für Rudolf Bultmann (1954) 207-27. LAPOINTE, R. "Que sont les kairoi d'Act 17,26? Etude sémantique et stylistique," ETh 3 (3, 1972) 323-38. ZMIJEWSKI, J. Die Eschatologiereden des Lukas-Evangeliums (1972) 101, 242, 282, 289, 293. WILSON, S. G. The Gentiles and the Gentile Mission in Luke-Acts (1973) 216-17. CONZELMANN, H. Theologie als Schriftauslegung (1974) 96-98.

17:27-28 HENGEL, M. Judentum und Hellenismus (1969) 299. ET: Judaism and Hellenism (1974) II 107.

17:27 GAERTNER, B. The Areopagus Speech and Natural Revelation (1955) 155f., 158ff., 184f. WIKENHAUSER, A. Die Christusmystik des Apostels Paulus (^{2}1956) 34. TURBESSI, G. "Quaerere Deum. Il tema della 'ricera di Dio' nella S. Scittura," RivB 10 (3, 1962) 282-96. Also in: Studiorum Paulinorum Congressus Internationalis Catholicus II (1963) 383-98. DES PLACES, E. "Actes 17,27," Biblica 48 (1, 1967) 1-6. CONZELMANN, H. Theologie als Schriftauslegung (1974) 98f. GEORGI, D., "Weisheit Salomos" in: JüdSchr III/4 (1980) 13n.6b.

17:28-29 DIBELIUS, M. Aufsätze zur Apostelgeschichte (1951) 45-53. ET: Studies in the Acts of the Apostles (1956) 47-55. GAERTNER, B. The Areopagus Speech and Natural Revelation (1955) 165f., 179f., 183f., 193f., 222f. SWIDLER, L., Biblical Affirmations of Woman (Philadelphia 1979) 328. KURZ, W. S., "Luke-Acts and Historiography in the Greek Bible" in: P. J. Achtemeier (ed.) SBL Seminar Papers 1980 (Chico, Cal. 1980) 299-03.

17:28 DIBELIUS, M. Die Reden der Apostelgeschichte und die antike Geschichtsschreibung (1949) 55-56. BEST, E. One Body in Christ

(1955) 21n. BARRETT, C. K. The New Testament Background (1956) 63. STACEY, W. D. The Pauline View of Man (1956) 36f. HOMMEL, H. "Platonisches bei Lukas. Zu Act 17,28a (Leben-Bewegung-Sein)," ZNW 48 (3-4, 1957) 193-200. DES PLACES, E. " 'Ipsius enim et genus sumus' (Act 17,28)," Biblica 43 (3, 1962) 388-95. FOLLIET, G. "Les citations de Actes 17,28 et Tite 1,12 chez Augustin," REA 11 (3-4, 1965) 293-94. COLA-CLIDES, P. "Acts 17, 28a and Bacchae 506," VigChr 27 (3, 1973) 161-64. KUEMMEL, W. G. Römer 7 und das Bild des Menschen im Neuen Testament (1974) 209-14, 22. RENEHAN, R., "Acts 17,28" GRBS 20 (1979) 347-53. van de BUNT-van den HOEK, A., "Aristobulos, Acts, Theophilus, Clement. Making use of Aratus' Phainomena: a peregrination" Bijdragen 41 (1980) 290-99. DOIGNON, J., " 'Ipsius enim genus sumus' (Actes 17,28b) chez Hilaire de Poitiers" JAC 23 (1980) 58-64.

17:29-30 WILSON, S. G. The Gentiles and the Gentile Mission in Luke-Acts (1973) 206-12, 214.

17:29 BETZ, H. D. Lukian von Samosata und das Neue Testament (1961) 40, 43. PETZKE, G. Die Traditionen über Apollonius von Tyana und das Neue Testament (1970) 193, 199, 202. CONZELMANN, H. Theologie als Schriftauslegung (1974) 91, 99f. GEORGI, D., "Weisheit Salomos" in: JüdSchr III/4 (1980) 13n.10b, 15n16b.

17:30ff. BERKHOF, H. Der Sinn der Geschichte: Christus (1959) 95f.

17:30-31 DIBELIUS, M. Aufsätze zur Apostelgeschichte (1951) 38f., 53f.. ET: Studies in the Acts of the Apostles (1956) 27f., 38. HAHN, F. Das Verständnis der Mission im Neuen Testament (²1965) 65, 118. SMITH, M. Tannaitic Parallels to the Gospels (1968) 4 b n 23. DES PLACES, E. "Actes 17,30-31," Biblica 52 (4, 1971) 526-34. WILSON, S. G. The Gentiles and the Gentile Mission in Luke-Acts (1973) 48, 125, 298-99. DUPONT, D. J., The Salvation of the Gentiles (New York 1979) 76.

17:30 DELLING, G. Die Taufe im Neuen Testament (1963) 140. EPP, E. J. The theological tendency of Codex Bezae Cantabrigiensis in Acts (1966) 38, 48-50, 55. STROBEL, A. Erkenntnis und Bekenntnis der Sünde in neutestamentlicher Zeit (1968) 48. O'-NEILL, J. C. The Theology of Acts in its historical setting (1970) 152, 163-64. KRAENKL, E. Jesus der Knecht Gottes (1972) 106f. WANKE, J., Die Emmauserzählung. Eine redaktionsgeschichtliche Untersuchung zu Lk 24,13-35 (Leipzig 1973) 119. BARRETT, C. K., "Is There a Theological Tendency in Codex Bezae?" in: E. Best/R. McL. Wilson (eds.) Text and Interpretation. FS. M. Black (Cambridge 1979) 25. GEORGI, D., "Weisheit Salomos" in: JüdSchr III/4 (1980) 11n.23a. BERGER, K., "Das Buch der Jubiläen" in: JüdSchr II/3 (1981) 524n.25a.

17:31 DELLING, G. Die Taufe im Neuen Testament (1963) 64. HAHN, F. Christologische Hoheitstitel (1963) 185, 204, 254, 290. SEE-BERG, A. Der Katechismus der Urchristenheit (1966) 62, 97, 135, 139. DUPONT, J. Etudes sur les Actes des Apôtres (1967) 141, 284, 353, 386, 443, 450, 453. HARMAN, A. M., Paul's Use of the Psalms (Ann Arbor, Mich 1968) 172-73. RESE, M. Alttestamentliche Motive in der Christologie des Lukas (1969) 119. NÖTSCHER, F., Altorientalischer und alttestamentlicher Auferstehungsglaube (Darmstadt 1970 = 1926) 192. BERKOUWER, G. C. The Return of Christ (1972) 155, 156, 164, 184. KRAENKL, E. Jesus der Knecht Gottes (1972) 80, 103, 130, 147, 205, 209-11. WILCKENS, U. Die Missionsreden der Apostelgeschichte (³1974) 98, 123, 124, 137, 139, 147, 175, 182, 190. FRIEDRICHS, G., "Ein Tauflied hellenistischer Judenchristen. I Thess 1,9f" in: Auf das Wort kommt es an (Göttingen 1978) 240-41. "Auferstehung" in: TRE 4 (1979) 479. MATTILL, A. J., Luke and the Last Things (Dillsboro 1979) 41-54.

17:32-33 O'NEILL, J. C. The Theology of Acts in its historical setting (1970) 165-66.

17:34 DIBELIUS, M. Aufsätze zur Apostelgeschichte (1951) 66f., 68, 69, ET: Studies in the Acts of the Apostles (1956) 72f., 74, 75. DELLING, G. Die Taufe im Neuen Testament (1963) 70. DU-PONT, J. The Sources of Acts (1964) 117, 135, 149. GRIFFITHS, J. G. "Was Damaris an Egyptian? (Acts 17,34)," BZ 8 (2, 1964) 293-95. O'NEILL, J. C. The Theology of Acts in its historical setting (1970) 162-63. "Apostelgeschichte" in: TRE 3 (1979) 497. SWIDLER, L., Biblical Affirmations of Woman (Philadelphia 1979) 293.

---

18 VAN UNNIK, W. C., Sparsa Collecta. I (Leiden 1973) 386-401.

18:1-27 HARNACK, A. von, Studien zur Geschichte des Neuen Testaments und der Alten Kirche (1931) 48ff.

18:1-26 FURNISH, V. P., The Moral Teaching of Paul (Nashville 1979) 105-08).

18:1-21 SHEPARD, J. W., The Life and Letters of St. Paul (Grand Rapids 1950) 159-63.

18:1-18 HAHN, F. Das Verständnis der Mission im Neuen Testament (²1965) 78f. O'NEILL, J. C. The Theology of Acts in its historical setting (1970) 118-20.

18:1-17 MARTIN, R. P., New Testament Foundations: II Exeter 1978) 121-22. LÜDEMANN, G., Paulus, der Heidenapostel. I (Göttingen 1980) 174-203.

18:1-8 SCHMITHALS, W. Paulus und Jakobus (1963) 49.

18:1-7 MIESNER, D. R., "The Missionary Journeys Narrative: Patterns and Implications" in: C. H. Talbert (ed.) Perspectives on Luke-Acts (Danville 1978) 208.

18:1-3 SWIDLER, L., Biblical Affirmations of Woman (Philadelphia 1979) 16, 297.

18:1 BEYER, H. W. Die Apostelgeschichte (1947) 110f.

18:2-11 "Apostelgeschichte" in: TRE 3 (1978) 497, 500.

18:2-3 CLARK, A. C. The Acts of the Apostels (1933) xxxvi, 228, 230, 251, 303, 367f.

18:2 FEINE, D. P./BEHM, D. J. Einleitung in das Neue Testament (1950) 125f. BARRETT, C. K. The New Testament Background (1956) 15. HOERBER, R. O. "The Decree of Claudius in Acts 18:2," CThM 31 (11, 1960) 690-94. CONZELMANN, H. Die Apostelgeschichte (1963) 105. HAHN, F. Das Verständnis der Mission im Neuen Testament (²1965) 50. EHRHARDT, A. The Acts of the Apostles (1969) 96, 98f. CONZELMANN, H. und LINDEMANN, A., Arbeitsbuch zum Neuen Testament (Tübingen 1975) 142. HENGEL, M., Zur urchristlichen Geschichtsschreibung (Stuttgart 1979) 39; ET: J. Bowden (trans.) Acts and the History of Earliest Christianity (London 1979) 39. JEWETT, R., A Chronology of Paul's Life (Philadelphia 1979) 36-38. DRANE, J. W., "Why did Paul Write Romans?" in: D. A. Hagner/M. J. Harris (eds.) Pauline Studies. FS. F. F. Bruce (Exeter 1980) 216-17.

18:3 SILVA, R., " 'Eran, pues, de oficio, fabricantes de tiendas (skenopoioi)' (Act. 18,3)" EstBi 24 (1965) 123-24. BURCHARD, C. Der dreizehnte Zeuge (1970) 39. HOCK, R. F., The Social Context of Paul's Ministry (Philadelphia 1980) 20-49.

18:4ff. EHRHARDT, A. The Acts of the Apostles (1969) 77f. "Antisemitismus" in: TRE 3 (1978) 126.

18:4-6 EPP, E. J. The Theological Tendency of Codex Bezae Cantabrigiensis in Acts (1966) 84-87, 90., 166f.

18:4 CLARK, A. C. The Acts of the Apostles (1933) 228, 250, 280, 281. TRITES, A. A., The New Testament Concept of Witness (Cambridge 1977) 134, 141, 145, 146. CLARK, K. W., "The Israel of God" in: The Gentile Bias and other Essays (Leiden 1980) 25, 26.

18:5ff. SCHILLE, G. Anfänge der Kirche (1966) 79ff.

18:5-9 SHERWIN-WHITE, A. N. Roman Society and Roman Law in the
New Testament (Grand Rapids 1978) 95.

18:5-8 CLARK, A. C. The Acts of the Apostles (1933) 192, 250, 295, 314,
368f.

18:5-7 "Apostelgeschichte" in: TRE 3 (1978) 520.

18:5-6 HUBBARD, B. J., "Luke, Josephus and Rome: A Comparative
Approach to the Lukan Sitz im Leben" in: P. J. Achtemeier (ed.)
SBL Seminar Papers 1979/I (Missoula 1979) 65.

18:5 MICHAELIS, W. Paulusstudien (1925) 28f., 33ff. PALLIS, A.,
Notes on St. Luke and the Acts (London 1928) 8f., 33ff. 70-71.
FEINE, D. P./BEHM, D. J. Einleitung in das Neue Testament
(1950) 129f. DELLING, G. Die Zueignung des Heils in der Taufe
(1961) 88. HAHN, F. Christologische Hoheitstitel (1963) 224.
KRAENKL, E. Jesus der Knecht Gottes (1972) 57f. KUEMMEL,
W. G. Einleitung in das Neue Testament (1973) 220-22. NELLES-
SEN, E., Zeugnis für Jesus und das Wort (Köln 1976) 238-39.

18:6 MUNCK, J. Paul and the Salvation of Mankind (1959) 203f.
HAHN, F. Das Verständnis der Mission im Neuen Testament
(²1965) 64, 117. WILCOX, M. The Semitism of Acts (1965) 65-
66. WREGE, H.-T. Die Ueberlieferungsgeschichte der Bergpredigt (1968) 48, 108, 164, 168, 174f. O'NEILL, J. C. The Theology of Acts in its historical setting (1970) 75, 86-87, 133.
WILSON, S. G. The Gentiles and the Gentile Mission in Luke-Acts
(1973) 225-30, 232-33. PRAST, F., Presbyter und Evangelium in
nachapostolischer Zeit (Stuttgart 1979) 117.

18:7-11 HUBBARD, B. J., "The Role of Commissioning Accounts in
Acts" in: C. H. Talbert (ed.) Perspectives on Luke-Acts (Danville
1978) 190, 193, 197.

18:7-8 CLARK, K. W., "The Israel of God" in: The Gentile Bias and other
Essays (Leiden 1980) 25, 26.

18:7 SHERWIN-WHITE, A. N., Roman Society and Roman Law in the
New Testament (Grand Rapids 1978) 158. WILCOX, M., "The
'God-Fearers' in Acts—A Reconsideration" JSNT 13 (1981) 113-
14. BARRETT, C. K. The New Testament Background (1956) 163,
BOUSSET, W. Die Religion des Judentums im Späthellenistischen Zeitalter (1966 = 1926) 80. EPP, E. J. The Theological Tendency of Codex Bezae Cantabrigiensis in Acts (1966) 91-93, 167
n.7.

18:8-18 MIESNER, D. R., "The Missionary Journeys Narrative: Patterns
and Implications" in: C. H. Talbert (ed.) Perspectives on Luke-Acts
(Danville 1978) 208.

18:8 DELLING, G. Die Taufe im Neuen Testament (1963) 60, 69, 70,
73, 118. SCHMITHALS, W. Paulus und Jakobus (1963) 45. EPP,

E. J. The Theological Tendency of Codex Bezae Cantabrigiensis in Acts (1966) 54, 62f., 87f., 89, 90, 118, 146. "Apostelgeschichte" in: TRE 3 (1978) 500. CRIBBS, F. L., "The Agreements that Exist Between John and Acts" in: C. H. Talbert (ed.) Perspectives on Luke-Acts (Danville 1978) 58. BARTH, G., Die Taufe in früchristlicher Zeit (Neukirchen-Vluyn 1981) 11, 38, 40, 138.

18:9-11 HUBBARD, B. J., "Commissioning Stories in Luke-Acts: A Study of their Antecedents, Form and Content" in: Semeia 8 (1977) 103-26.

18:9-10 BURCHARD, C. Der dreizehnte Zeuge (1970) 111f. BOHREN, R., Predigtlehre (München 1971) 490-91. SOARES PRABHU, G. M., The Formula Quotations in the Infancy Narrative of Matthew (Rome 1976) 224-25.

18:9 DELLING, G. Die Zueignung des Heils in der Taufe (1961) 87.

18:10 KAESTLI, J.-D., "Les scènes d'attribution des champs de mission et de départ de l'apôtre dans les Actes apocryphes" in: F. Bovon et al. (eds.) Les Actes Apocryphes des Apôtres (Geneva 1981) 261.

18:11 HENNECKE, E./SCHNEEMELCHER, W. Neutestamentliche Apokryphen (1964) II 236. HAHN, F. Das Verständnis der Mission im Neuen Testament (²1965) 81.

18:12-17 DINKLER, E. "Das Bema zu Korinth - Archäologische, lexikographische, rechtsgeschichtliche und ikonographische Bemerkungen zu Apostelgeschichte 18,12-17," in: Signum Crucis (1967) 118-33. STOLLE, V. Der Zeuge als Angeklagter (1973) 100f., 252. SUHL, A., Paulus und seine Briefe (Gütersloh 1975) 119-29. "Apostelgeschichte" in: TRE 3 (1978) 509, 512, 518. ELLIGER, W., Paulus in Griechenland (Stuttgart 1978) 231-27. HEMER, C. J., "Observations on Pauline Chronology" in: D. A. Hagner/M. J. Harris (eds.) Pauline Studies. FS. F. F. Bruce (Exeter 1980) 6-9. GEIGER, G., Kirche unterwegs (Klosterneuburg 1981).

18:12 FEINE, D. P./BEHM, D. J. Einleitung in das Neue Testament (1950) 125f. WIKENHAUSER, A. Die Apostelgeschichte (1951) 170. BARRETT, C. K. The New Testament Background (1956) 48. EPP, E. J. The Theological Tendency of Codex Bezae Cantabrigiensis in Acts (1966) 144f., 167f. BAUMERT, N., Täglich Sterben und Auferstehen (München 1973) 246. "Apostelgeschichte" in: TRE 3 (1978) 509. ELLIGER, W., Paulus in Griechenland (Stuttgart 1978) 226. JEWETT, R. A., A Chronology of Paul's Life (Philadelphia 1979) 38-40.

18:13 CONZELMANN, H. und LINDEMANN, A., Arbeitsbuch zum Neuen Testament (Tübingen 1975) 41. SHERWIN-WHITE, A. N.,

Roman Society and Roman Law in the New Testament (Grand Rapids 1978) 101-02.

18:14 - 19:20 MARTIN, R. P., New Testament Foundations. II (Exeter 1978) 123-24.

18:16-17 BAUMERT, N., Täglich Sterben und Auferstehen (Münster 1973) 246.

18:17 CLARK, A. C. The Acts of the Apostles (1933) 220, 250, 295, 332, 369. BEYER, H. W. Die Apostelgeschichte (1947) 112. CONZELMANN, H. Die Apostelgeschichte (1963) 106f. EPP, E. J. The Theological Tendency of Codex Bezae Cantabrigiensis in Acts (1966) 146f. "Apostelgeschichte" in: TRE 3 (1978) 497.

18:18-20:38 GUTBROD, K. Die Apostelgeschichte (1968) 38f.

18:18-19:40 HAHN, F. Das Verständnis der Mission im Neuen Testament (²1965) 82.

18:18 - 19:20 MIESNER, D. R., "The Missionary Journeys Narrative: Patterns and Implications" in: C. H. Talbert (ed.) Perspectives on Luke-Acts (Danville 1978) 207.

18:18-23 LÜDEMANN, G., Paulus, der Heidenapostel. I (Göttingen 1980) 155-74.

18:18-19 "Apostelgeschichte" in: TRE 3 (1978) 497, 500. SWIDLER, L., Biblical Affirmations of Woman (Philadelphia 1979) 297.

18:18 SCHMITHALS, W. Paulus und Jakobus (1963) 80.

18:19 CONZELMANN, H. Die Apostelgeschichte (1963) 109. WILSON, S. G. The Gentiles and the Gentile Mission in Luke-Acts (1973) 237, 240, 249, 262. MATTILL, A. J., "The Value of Acts as a Source for the Study of Paul" in: C. H. Talbert (ed.) Perspectives on Luke-Acts (Danville 1978) 91.

18:21 "Apostelgeschichte" in: TRE 3 (1978) 497, 500. BARRETT, C. K., "Is there a theological tendency in Codex Bezae?" in: E. Best/ R. McL. Wilson (eds.) Text and Interpretation. FS. M. Black (Cambridge 1979) 15-27.

18:22-21:16 SHEPARD, J. W., The Life and Letters of St. Paul (Grand Rapids 1950) 191ff.

18:22-19:7 KRAFT, H., Die Entstehung des Christentums (Darmstadt 1981) 40-43.

18:22-23 DUPONT, J. Etudes sur les Actes des Apôtres (1967) 48, 62, 66, 167, 178, 191, 198, 203. "Apostelgeschichte" in: TRE 3 (1978) 500.

18:22 GOULDER, M. D. Type and History in Acts (1964) 28, 99, 103, 197f. NICKLE, K. F. The Collection (1966) 21f., 60f. WILSON, S. G. The Gentiles and the Gentile Mission in Luke-Acts (1973) 178-79. JEWETT, R., A Chronology of Paul's Life (Philadelphia

1979) 78-85. LÜDEMANN, G., Paulus, der Heidenapostel. I (Göttingen 1980) 163-73.

18:23 BORSE, U. Der Standort des Galaterbriefes (1972) 1-3, 12, 16, 33, 46-49, 57, 147, 175.

18:24ff. RUDOLPH, K. Die Mandäer I (1960) 66, 77. KAESEMANN, E. Exegetische Versuche und Besinnungen (1964) I 131, 163f., 167. HAHN, F. Das Verständnis der Mission im Neuen Testament (²1965) 49, 81. DUNN, J. D. G. Baptism in the Holy Spirit (1970) 88f.

18:24-19:7 FLENDER, H. Heil und Geschichte in der Theologie des Lukas (1965) 114-16. BRAUN, H. Qumran und das Neue Testament II (1966) 24, 139, 180. BEUTLER, J. Martyria (1972) 246, 342f.

18:24-19:6 PREISKER, H., ''Apollos und die Johannesjünger in Acts 18:24-19:6.'' ZNW 30 (1931) 301-04.

18:24 - 19:1 BRUCE, F. F., ''Apollos in the New Testament'' Ekklesiastikos Pharos 57 (Addis Abeba 1975) 354-66. BRUCE, F. F., Men and Movements in the Primitive Church (Exeter 1979) 66-70.

18:24-28 SHEPARD, J. W., The Life and Letters of St. Paul (Grand Rapids 1950) 192-93. PARKER, P. The Gospel Before Mark (1953) 97-98. SCHWEIZER, E. ''Die Bekehrung des Apollos,'' EvTh 15 (6, 1955) 247-54. HUNTER, A. M., Gospel and Apostle (London 1975) 115-22. ''Alexandrien'' in: TRE 2 (1978) 251. ''Apostelgeschichte'' in: TRE 3 (1978) 496. ROBBINS, V. K., ''Prefaces in Greco-Roman Biography and Luke-Acts'' in: P. J. Achtemeier (ed.) SBL Seminar Papers 1978/II (Missoula 1978) 200-05. CLARK, S. B., Man and Woman in Christ (Ann Arbor, Mich. 1980) 107, 115.

18:24-26 SCHWEIZER, E. Beiträge zur Theologie des Neuen Testaments (1970) 71-79. SWIDLER, L., Biblical Affirmations of Woman (Philadelphia 1979) 298.

18:24-25 BLASS, F. Philosophy of the Gospels (1898) 30ff. BOUSSET, W. Die Religion des Judentums im Späthellenistischen Zeitalter (1966 = 1926) 161. HENGEL, M., Zur urchristlichen Geschichtsschreibung (Stuttgart 1979) 90-91; ET: J. Bowden (trans.) Acts and the History of Earliest Christianity (London 1979) 107.

18:24 GOULDER, M. D. Type and History in Acts (1964) 29, 99, 101, 103f. KILPATRICK, G. D. ''Apollos-Apelles,'' JBL 89 (1, 1970) 77.

18:25-26 FLEW, R. N. Jesus and His Church (1956) 113. DELLING, G. Die Taufe im Neuen Testament (1963) 62, 68.

18:25 BEYER, H. W. Die Apostelgeschichte (1947) 114. DELLING, G. Die Zueignung des Heils in der Taufe (1961) 87. DELLING, G. Die Taufe im Neuen Testament (1963) 42. METZGER, B. M., The Early Versions of the New Testament (Oxford 1977) 99. PO-

KORNỲ, P., "Christologie et Baptême à l'Epoque du Christianisme Primitif" NTS 27 (1980-1981) 373.

18:26-27 VAN UNNIK, W. C., Sparsa Collecta. I (Leiden 1973) 328-39.

18:26 BRAUN, H. Qumran und das Neue Testament II (1966) 162, 213. SWIDLER, L., Biblical Affirmations of Woman (Philadelphia 1979) 304.

18:27-19:1 DELLING, G. Die Zueignung des Heils in der Taufe (1961) 68.

18:27 CLARK, A. C. The Acts of the Apostles (1933) 369ff. DELLING, G. Die Taufe im Neuen Testament (1963) 72. BARRETT, C. K., "Is there a theological tendency in Codex Bezae?" in: E. Best/R. McL. Wilson (eds.) Text and Interpretation. FS. M. Black (Cambridge 1979) 22.

18:28 DELLING, G. Die Zueignung des Heils in der Taufe (1961) 88. HAHN, F. Christologische Hoheitstitel (1963) 224.

---

19 SHEPARD, J. W., The Life and Letters of St. Paul (Grand Rapids 1950) 193-203. RUDOLPH, K. Die Mandäer I (1960) 66, 78. SQUILLACI, D. "San Paolo in Efeso (Atti c. 19)," PaCl 40 (Nov. 1, 1961) 1137-44. JOHNSON, W. E., "The Apostle Paul and the Riot in Ephesus" LThQ 15 (1979) 79-88.

19:1ff. YATES, J. E. The Spirit and the Kingdom (1963) 167ff. HAHN, F. Das Verständnis der Mission im Neuen Testament (²1965) 81. THYEN, H. Studien zur Sündenvergebung (1970) 143, 146ff., 215.

19:1-9 KAESEMANN, E. "The Disciples of John the Baptist in Ephesus," in: Essays on New Testament Themes (1964) 136-48.

19:1-8 POKORNỲ, P., "Christologie et Baptême à l'Epoque du Christianisme Primitif" NTS 27 (1980-1981) 373.

19:1-7 RUDOLPH, K. Die Mandäer I (1960) 77. KLEIN, G. Die Zwölf Apostel (1961) 176ff. DELLING, G. Die Taufe im Neuen Testament (1963) 62, 67f. KAESEMANN, E. Exegetische Versuche und Besinnungen (1964) I 158-68. BIEDER, W., Die Verheissung der Taufe im Neuen Testament (Zürich 1966) 46-50. SCHREINER, J., "Sonntag nach Christi Himmelfahrt. Homilie zu Apg. 19:1-7" BiLe 8 (1967) 68-70. PARRATT, J. K. "The Rebaptism of the Ephesian Disciples," ET 79 (6, 1968) 182-83. WINK, W. John the Baptist in the Gospel Tradition (1968). EHRHARDT, A. The Acts of the Apostles (1969) 101f., 107. DUNN, J. D. G. Baptism in the Holy

Spirit (1970) 83ff. KREMER, J. Pfingstbericht und Pfingstgeschehen (Stuttgart 1973) 197-201. KAISER, C. B., "The 'Rebaptism' of the Ephesian Twelve: Exegetical Study on Acts 19:1-7"
The Reformed Review 31 (1977) 57-61.

19:1-6 BARTH, G., Die Taufe in frühchristlicher Zeit (Neukirchen-Vluyn
1981) 23, 37, 54, 60, 65, 67, 71, 135.

19:1 MICHAELIS, W. Paulusstudien (1925) 39f. BARRETT, C. K.,
"Is there a theological tendency in Codex Bezae?" in: E. Best/R.
McL. Wilson (eds.) Text and Interpretation. FS. M. Black (Cam-
bridge 1979) 22.

19:2-20:9 WILCOX, M. The Semitism of Acts (1965) 59ff.

19:2-3 DUNN, J. D. G. Baptism in the Holy Spirit (1970) 96, 102.

19:2 BURCHARD, C. " 'Ei' nach einem Ausdruck des Wissens oder
Nichtwissens Joh 9:25, Act 19:2, I Cor 1:16, 7:16," ZNW 52 (1-
2, 1961) 73-82. DUNN, J. D. G. Baptism in the Holy Spirit (1970)
46, 60, 69, 70, 83, 86f., 96.

19:3-4 BRAUMANN, G. Vorpaulinische christliche Taufverkündigung bei
Paulus (1962) 30f., 45.

19:3 DELLING, G. Die Zueignung des Heils in der Taufe (1961) 91,
93f. DELLING, G. Die Taufe im Neuen Testament (1963) 42.

19:4ff. DELLING, G. Die Taufe im Neuen Testament (1963) 43. 61, 66,
76, 118.

19:4-5 DELLING, G. Die Zueignung des Heils in der Taufe (1961) 85f.,
90, 93f. CRIBBS, F. L., "The Agreements that Exist Between John
and Acts" in: C. H. Talbert (ed.) Perspectives on Luke-Acts (Danville 1978) 48.

19:5-6 DUNN, J. D. G. Baptism in the Holy Spirit (1970) 87f., 90, 93.
MOULE, C. F. D., The Holy Spirit (London 1978) 85.

19:5 BARTH, G., Die Taufe in frühchristlicher Zeit (Neukirchen-Vluyn
1981) 38, 40, 44.

19:6 CLARK, A. C. The Acts of the Apostles (1933) 225, 230, 231, 264,
376. ADLER, N. Das erste christliche Pfingstfest (1938) 10, 67,
95f., 108, 110, 163. ADLER, N., Taufe und Handauflegung
(Münster 1951) 69, 77, 85, 89, 92, 98-99, 110, 116-17. ELLIS, E.
E. Paul's Use of the Old Testament (1957) 36f., 109. KAESE-
MANN, E. Exegetische Versuche und Besinnungen (1964) II 122.
KREMER, J., Pfingstbericht und Pfingstgeschehen (Stuttgart 1973)
34-37, 48, 121. ROBECK, C., "The Gift of Prophecy in Acts and
Paul, Part I" SBT 5 (1975) 15-38. JEWETT, P. K., Infant Baptism
and the Covenant of Grace (Grand Rapids 1978) 188. DUPONT,
D. J., The Salvation of the Gentiles (New York 1979) 48-50.

19:8ff. SCHILLE, G. Anfänge der Kirche (1966) 79ff.

19:8-10.22 HAHN, F. Das Verständnis der Mission im Neuen Testament (²1965) 79, 81.

19:8-10 "Apostelgeschichte" in: TRE 3 (1978) 497, 500. JEWETT, R. , A Chronology of Paul's Life (Philadelphia 1979) 19. CLARK, K. W., "The Israel of God" in: The Gentile Bias and Other Essays (Leiden 1980) 26.

19:8-9 O'NEILL, J. C. The Theology of Acts in its historical setting (1970) 74-75, 133.

19:8 BEYER, H. W. Die Apostelgeschichte (1947) 117. DELLING, G. Die Taufe in Neuen Testament (1963) 135. WILSON, S. G. The Gentiles and the Gentile Mission in Luke-Acts (1973) 78-79, 89, 222. 249. PRAST, F., Presbyter und Evangelium in nachapostolischer Zeit (Stuttgart 1979) 280-81, 333.

19:9.23 NICKELS, P. Targum and New Testament (1967) 67.

19:9 CLARK, A. C. The Acts of the Apostels (1933) xlv, 285, 300, 314, 318. FLEW, R. N. Jesus and His Church (1956) 113n. THEYSSEN, G. W. "Unbelief" in the New Testament (Rüschlikon 1965) 58f. WILCOX, M. The Semitism of Acts (1965) 105-06. EPP, E. J. The theological tendency of Codex Bezae Cantabrigiensis in Acts (1966) 94f., 166. BARRETT, C. K., "Is there a theological tendency in Codex Bezae?" in: E. Best/R. McL. Wilson (eds.) Text and Interpretation. FS. M. Black (Cambridge 179) 22-23.

19:11-20 PRAST, F., Presbyter und Evangelium in nachapostolischer Zeit (Stuttgart 1979) 168-69.

19:11-12 DUNN, J. D. G., Jesus and the Spirit (London 1975) 163, 165-66. HOCK, R. F., The Social Context of Paul's Ministry (Philadelpia 1980) 26-49.

19:11 EGGER, W., Frohbotschaft und Lehre (Frankfurt 1976) 37, 136-37. PREISIGKE, F., "Die Gotteskraft der frühchristlichen Zeit" in: A. Suhl (ed.) Der Wunderbegriff im Neuen Testament (Darmstadt 1980) 222-23.

19:12ff. SMITH, M. Clement of Alexandria and a secret Gospel of Mark (1973) 230f.

19:12-16 CLARK, A. C. The Acts of the Apostles (1933) 220ff.

19:12 DELLING, G. Die Zueignung des Heils in der Taufe (1961) 51. HAHN, F. Christologische Hoheitstitel (1963) 313. KAESEMANN, E. Exegetische Versuche und Besinnungen (1964) I 215. "Apostelgeschichte" in: TRE 3 (1978) 499. SCHWEIZER, E., Heiliger Geist (Stuttgart 1978) 83-85.

19:13ff. BOUSSET, W. Die Religion des Judentums im Späthellinistischen Zeitalter (1966 = 1926) 340. HENGEL, M. Judentum und Hellenismus (1969) 442, 562. ET: Judaism and Hellenism (1974) I 308; II 163.

19:13-16 DELLING, G. Die Zueignung des Heils in der Taufe (1961) 51. "Apostelgeschichte" in: TRE 3 (1978) 497. DUNN, J. D. G., Jesus and the Spirit (London 1975) 165, 168-69, 170.

19:13 CLARK, A. C. The Acts of the Apostels (1933) 195, 370ff. BARRETT, C. K. The New Testament Background (1956) 31, 34. DELLING, G. Die Zueignung des Heils in der Taufe (1961) 46, 51. POUPON, G., "L'accusation de magie dans les Actes apocryphes" in: F. Bovon et al. (eds.) Les Actes Apocryphes des Apôtres (Geneva 1981) 74.

19:14 PALLIS, A., Notes on St. Luke and the Acts (London 1928) 71-72. MASTIN, B. A., "Scaeva the Chief Priest" JThS 27 (1976) 405-12. MASTIN, B. A., "A Note on Acts 19,14" Biblica 59 (1978) 97-99.

19:16 CLARK, K. W., "The Meaning of (KATA) KYRIEYEIN" in: The Gentile Bias and Other Essays (Leiden 1980) 207-12.

19:17ff. BOUSSET, W. Die Religion des Judentums im Späthellenistischen Zeitalter (1966 = 1926) 218, 340.

19:18 DELLING, G. Die Taufe im Neuen Testament (1963) 70, 72. STROBEL, A. Erkenntnis und Bekenntnis der Sünde in neutestamentlicher Zeit (1968) 48. PRAST, F., Presbyter und Evangelium in nachapostolischer Zeit (Stuttgart 1979) 72.

19:19 NICKELS, P. Targum and New Testament (1967) 67.

19:20 DELLING, G. Die Zueignung des Heils in der Taufe (1961) 87. ARGYLE, A. W. "Acts xix. 20," ET 75 (5, 1963) 151. MÄRZ, C.-P., Das Wort Gottes bei Lukas (Leipzig 1973) 17-19. ZINGG, P., Das Wachsen der Kirche (Freiburg 1974) 23-29. KODELL, J., " 'The Word of God grew.' The Ecclesial Tendency of λόγος in Acts 6,7; 12,24; 19,20" Biblica 55 (1974) 505-19.

19:21-28:31 O'NEILL, J. C. The Theology of Acts in its historical setting (1970) 65-72.

19:21-21:17 PRAST, F., Presbyter und Evangelium in nachapostolischer Zeit (Stuttgart 1979) 23-25, 83-93, 197, 232.

19:21-20:1 DUNCAN, G. S. "Paul's Ministry in Asia—the Last Phase," NTS 3 1956-1957) 211ff.

19:21ff. RICHARDS, J. R. NTS 13 (1966-1967) 25ff.

19:21-41 MEISNER, D. R., "The Missionary Journeys Narrative: Patterns and Implications" in: C. H. Talbert (ed.) Perspectives on Luke-Acts (Danville 1978) 206-07. RUETHER, R. R., Mary—The Feminine Face of the Church (London 1979) 9-14.

19:21-22 ROBERTSON, A. T., Epochs in the Life of Paul (New York 1920)

178, 183, 184, 209, 213. DOCKX, S., "Chronologie paulinienne de l'année de la grande collecte" RB 81 (1974) 183-95. "Apostelgeschichte" in: TRE 3 (1978) 500.

19:21 MICHAELIS, W. Paulusstudien (1925) 43ff., 56f. NICKLE, K. F. The Collection (1966) 14f. STAEHLIN, G. "τὸ πνεῦμα Ἰησοῦ (Apostelgeschichte 16:7)," in: Christ and the Spirit in the New Testament (1973) B. Lindars/S. S. Smalley eds., 231f., 238, 240, 244. RADL, W., Paulus und Jesus im lukanischen Doppelwerk (Frankfurt 1975) 103-17. ELLIGER, W., Paulus in Griechenland (Stuttgart 1978) 230. "Armut" in: TRE 4 (1979) 79. HAUSER, J., Strukturen der Abschlusserzählung der Apostelgeschichte (Apg. 28:16-31) (Rome 1979) 211-14. PRAST, F., Presbyter und Evangelium in nachapostolischer Zeit (Stuttgart 1979) 21, 83-84, 85, 87. RIUS-CAMPS, J., "Questions sobre la doble obra lucana. I. La darrera pujada de Pau a Jerusalem: 'Desviació' del camí cap a Roma" Revista Catalana de Teologia 5 (Barcelona 1980) 1-94.

19:22-40 SOKOLOWSKI, F. "A New Testimony on the Cult of Artemis of Ephesus," HThR 58 (4, 1965) 427-31.

19:22 MICHAELIS, W. Paulusstudien (1925) 43f., 66ff., 109f., 112ff. DUNCAN, G. S. "Paul's Ministry in Asia—the Last Phase," NTS 3 (1956-1957) 211ff. HARRISON, P. N., Paulines and Pastorals (London 1964) 100-05. ELLIGER, W., Paulus in Griechenland (Stuttgart 1978) 228.

19:23ff. HENNECKE,E./SCHNEEMELCHER, W. Neutestamentliche Apokryphen (1964) II 233. PETZKE, G. Die Traditionen über Apollonius von Tyana und das Neue Testament (1970) 202, 209. OSTER, R., "The Ephesian Artemis as an opponent of Early Christianity" JAC 19 (1976) 30-44. GERSTENBERGER, G. und SCHRAGE, W., Leiden (Stuttgart 1977) 173-74. ET: J. E. Steely (trans.) Suffering (Nashville 1980) 201.

19:23 - 20:1 GEIGER, G., Kirche unterwegs (Klosterneuburg 1981).

19:23-40 SCHILLLE, G. Anfänge der Kirche (1966) 91ff. HAAR, J. GPM 21/4 (1966-1967) 335-40. PLUEMACHER, E. Lukas als hellenistischer Schriftsteller (1972) 98-100, 101, 104. "Apostelgeschichte" in: TRE 3 (1978) 497, 509, 512.

19:23 WILCOX, M. The Semitisms of Acts (1965) 105-06. "Apostelgeschichte" in: TRE 3 (1978) 509.

19:24-27 GEORGI, D., "Weisheit Salomos" in: JüdSchr III/4 (1980) 15n.12a.

19:24.26 BETZ, H. D. Lukian von Samosata und das Neue Testament (1961) 40f., 43, 113.

19:24 SHERWIN-WHITE, A. N., Roman Society and Roman Law in the New Testament (Grand Rapids 1978) 90.

19:25 CLARK, A. C. The Acts of the Apostles (1933) 298, 300, 314, 332. DELEBECQUE, E., "L'hellenisme de la 'relative complexe' dans le Nouveau Testament et principalement chez saint Luc" Biblica 62 (1981) 234.

19:26-27 "Apostelgeschichte" in: TRE 3 (1978) 512.

19:26 RUCKSTUHL, E. Die literarische Einheit des Johannesevangeliums (1951) 194f. ZINGG, P., Das Wachsen der Kirche (Freiburg 1974) 63.

19:27ff. BEYSCHLAG, K., Simon Magus und die christliche Gnosis (Tübingen 1974) 111. CLARK, A. C. The Acts of the Apostles (1933) xxxiii, xl, li, 182, 183, 298. KILPATRICK, G. D. "Acts XIX.27 apelegmon," JThS 10 (2, 1959) 327.

19:28 WIKENHAUSER, A. Die Apostelgeschichte (1951) 179-81. BARRETT, C. K., "Is there a theological tendency in Codex Bezae?" in: E. Best/R. McL. Wilson (eds.) Text and Interpretation. FS. M. Black (Cambridge 1979) 23.

19:32.39.41 SCHWEIZER, E. Gemeinde und Gemeinde-Ordnung im Neuen Testament (1959) § 23a.

19:35-40 ZINGG, P., Das Wachsen der Kirche (Freiburg 1974) 133.

19:35 CLARK, A. C. The Acts of the Apostles (1933) 211, 235, 282, 295, 310.

19:38-39 SHERWIN-WHITE, A. N., Roman Society and Roman Law in the New Testament (Grand Rapids 1978) 83.

———————————

20-28 SONGER, H. S., "Paul's Mission to Jerusalem: Acts 20-28" RevEx 71 (1974) 499-510.

20-21 SAHLIN, H. Der Messias und das Gottesvolk (1945) 20-22.

20:1-21:17 HAHN, F. Das Verständnis der Mission im Neuen Testament (^{2}1965) 82, 93.

20 CONZELMANN, H. und LINDEMANN, A., Arbeitsbuch zum Neuen Testament (Tübingen 1975) 239.

20:1-17 MIESNER, D. R., "The Missionary Journeys Narrative: Patterns and Implications" in: C. H. Talbert (ed.) Perspectives on Luke-Acts (Danville 1978) 205-06.

20:1-6 "Apostelgeschichte" in: TRE 3 (1978) 500.

20:1-3 SHEPARD, J. W., The Life and Letters of St. Paul (Grand Rapids 1950) 321-26. DIBELIUS, M. Aufsätze zur Apostelgeschichte (1951) 177f. ET: Studies in the Acts of the Apostles (1956) 209f. HAHN, F. Das Verständnis der Mission im Neuen Testament (²1965) 79.

20:2-3 MUNCK, J. Paul and the Salvation of Mankind (1959) 169f.

20:2 HENNECKE, E./SCHNEEMELCHER, W. Neutestamentliche Apokryphen (1964) II 236. ELLLIGER, W., Paulus in Griechenland (Stuttgart 1978) 69.

20:3 MICHAELIS, W. Paulusstudien (1925) 81f. EPP, E. J. The Theological Tendency of Codex Bezae Cantabrigiensis in Acts (1966) 117f., 125, 143f., 168. JEWETT, R., A Chronology of Paul's Life (Philadelphia 1979) 55-56.

20:4-5 CONZELMANN, H., "Miszelle zu Act 20,4f.," ZNW 45 (1954) 266. MUNCK, J. Paul and the Salvation of Mankind (1959) 293f.

20:4 MICHAELIS, W. Paulusstudien (1925) 84f. CLARK, A. C. The Acts of the Apostles (1933) xxxvii, xlix, 216, 269, 374ff. GOULDER, M. D. Type and History in Acts (1964) 30, 10, 103f., 227n. SCHILLE, G. Die urchristliche Kollegialmission (1967) 44ff., 49, 53f., 57f., 64, 102ff. KUEMMEL, W. G. Einleitung in das Neue Testament (1973) 258f., 325f. CONZELMANN, H. und LINDEMANN, A., Arbeitsbuch zum Neuen Testament (Tübingen 1975) 193. "Apostelgeschichte" in: TRE 3 (1978) 487. PRAST, F., Presbyter und Evangelium in nachapostolischer Zeit (Stuttgart 1979) 84.

20:5-15 GASQUE, W., A History of the Criticism of the Acts of the Apostles (Tübingen 1975) 68. ROBBINS, V. K., "By Land and By Sea: The We-Passages and Ancient Sea Voyages" in: C. H. Talbert (ed.) Perspectives on Luke-Acts (Danville 1978) 215-42.

20:5-11 JEWETT, R., A Chronology of Paul's Life (Philadelphia 1979) 49-50.

20:5-8 "Apostelgeschichte" in: TRE 3 (1978) 514.

20:5-6 NICKLE, K. F. The Collection (1966) 68f.

20:5 MUNCK, J. Paul and the Salvation of Mankind (1959) 294f. "Apostelgeschichte" in: TRE 3 (1978) 494.

20:7ff. REICKE, B. Diakonie, Festfreude und Zelos (1951) 75f.

20:7-12 DIBELIUS, M. Aufsätze zur Apostelgeschichte (1951) 22f., 78, 116, 168, 4. ET: Studies in the Acts of the Apostles (1956) 17f., 87, 132. MOREL, B. "Eutychus et les fondements bibliques du culte," EThR 37 (1, 1962) 41-47. ROGGE, J./SCHILLE, G. (eds.), Theologische Versuche II (1970) 76f. WANKE, J., Die Emmaus-

erzählung (Leipzig 1973) 54, 102, 105ff., 120. "Apostelgeschichte" in: TRE 3 (1978) 496, 497. TRÉMEL, B., "A propos
d'Actes 20, 7-12: puissance du thaumaturge ou du témoin?" RThPh
30 (1980) 359-69. BOVON, F., "La vie des apôtres: traditions
bibliques et narrations apocryphes" in: F. Bovon et al. (eds.) Les
Actes Apocryphes des Apôtres (Geneva 1981) 150n.34.

20:7-11 SQUILLACI, D. "La frazione del pane," PaCl 39 (17, 1960) 913-
17. MENOUD, P. H., "Actes 20:7-11" in: Jésus Christ et la foi
(Neuchâtel/Paris 1975) 68-73.

20:7-10 BRAUN, H. Qumran und das Neue Testament II (1966) 152, 157.

20:7 JEREMIAS, J. Die Abendmahlsworte Jesu (1960) 112-14. BAIRD,
W. The Corinthian Church (1964) 130, 156, 200. SCHUER-
MANN, H. Ursprung und Gestalt (1970) 82, 88, 90, 91, 116, 189,
190, 316. POKORNÝ, P., "Christologie et Baptême à l'Epoque
du christianisme Primitif" NTS 27 (1980-1981) 356.

20:8-35 SHEPARD, J. W., The Life and Letters of St. Paul (Grand Rapids
1950) 454-56.

20:8-9 "Apostelgeschichte" in: TRE 3 (1978) 494.

20:8 ADLER, N. Das erste christliche Pfingstfest (1938) 127-29.

20:9ff. NÖTSCHER, F., Altorientalischer und alttestamentlicher Auferstehungsglaube (Darmstadt 1970 = 1926) 303.

20:9-12 DUNN, J. D. G., Jesus and the Spirit (London 1975) 163, 165.

20:9 PALLIS, A., Notes on St. Luke and the Acts (London 1928) 72-
73.

20:10 SCHWEIZER, E., Heiliger Geist (Stuttgart 1978) 153.

20:11 BEYSCHLAG, K. Clemens Romanus und der Frühkatholizismus
(1966) 310f.

20:12 CADBURY, H. J. "Litotes in Acts," in: Festschrift to Honor F.
Wilbur Gingrich (1972) Barth, E. H./Cocraft, R. E. (eds.), 61-62.

20:13ff. HAHN, F. Das Verständnis der Mission im Neuen Testament
(²1965) 79.

20:13-17 "Apostelgeschichte" in: TRE 3 (1978) 500.

20:13-15 "Apostelgeschichte" in: TRE 3 (1978) 514.

20:13-14 "Apostelgeschichte" in: TRE 3 (1978) 497.

20:13 "Apostelgeschichte" in: TRE 3 (1978) 494.

20:15-16 "Apostelgeschichte" in: TRE 3 (1978) 494.

20:16 PRAST, F., Presbyter und Evangelium in nachapostolischer Zeit
(Stuttgart 1979) 30. CLARK, K. W., "The Israel of God" in: The
Gentile Bias and other Essays (Leiden 1980) 26.

20:17ff. KAESEMANN, E. Exegetische Versuche und Besinnungen (1964)
I 130, 165.

20:17-38 BETHGE, F. Die paulinischen Reden der Apostelgeschichte (1887) 117-67. MITTON, C. L. The Epistle to the Ephesians (1951) 210ff. HENNECKE, E./SCHNEEMELCHER, W. Neutestamentliche Apokryphen (1964) I 54, II 237. QUERVAIN, A. de, in: Herr, tue meine Lippen auf Bd. 4 (1965) G. Eichholz ed., 412ff. ROLOFF, J., Apostolat-Verkündigung-Kirche (1965) 227-31. AUSTGEN, R. J., Natural Motivation in the Pauline Epistles (1966) 58-63. SEITZ, M., GPM 21/2 (1966-1967) 189-95. DUPPONT, J. Etudes sur les Actes des Apôtres (1967) 54-56. O'NEILL, J. C. The Theology of Acts in its historical setting (1970) 182-83. BORNKAMM, G. Geschichte und Glaube II (1971) 183f. STOLLE, V. Der Zeuge als Angeklagter (1973) 68-72. MICHEL, H.-J., Die Abschiedsrede des Paulus an die Kirche Apg 20:17-38 (München 1973) 26-27, 28-33, 68ff. CONZELMANN, H. und LINDEMANN, A., Arbeitsbuch zum Neuen Testament (Tübingen 1975) 416. GLÖCKNER, R., Die Verkündigung des Heils beim Evangelisten Lukas (Mainz 1975) 181ff. BUDESHEIM, T. L., "Paul's Abschiedsrede in the Acts of the Apostles" HThR 69 (1976) 9-30. CASALEGNO, A., "Il discorso di Mileto (Atti 20, 17-38)" RivB 25 (1977) 29-58. "Apostelgeschichte" in: TRE 3 (1978) 517. DÖMER, M., Das Heil Gottes (Köln/Bonn 1978) 189-202. PRAST, F., Presbyter und Evangelium in nachapostolischer Zeit (Stuttgart 1979). KURZ, W. S., "Luke-Acts and Historiography in the Greek Bible" in: P. J. Achtemeier (ed.) SBL Seminar Papers 1980 (Chico, Cal. 1980) 286. McDONALD, J. I. H., Kerygma and Didache (Cambridge 1980) 98-99. GEIGER, G., Kirche unterwegs (Klosterneuburg 1981).

20:17-34 VÖGTLE, A., "Exegetische Reflexionen zur Apostolizität des Amtes und zur Amtssukzession" in: R. Schnackenburg et al. (eds.) Die Kirche des Anfangs. FS. H. Schürmann (Freiburg/Basel/Wien 1978) 570-77.

20:17-33 KLEIN, G. Die Zwölf Apostel (1961) 178ff.

20:17-18 PRAST, F., Presbyter und Evangelium in nachapostolischer Zeit (Stuttgart 1979) 39-40.

20:17 SATAKE, A., Die Gemeindeordnung in der Johannesapokalypse (Neukirchen-Vluyn 1966) 2. "Amt" in: TRE 2 (1978) 523. PRAST, F., Presbyter und Evangelium in nachapostolischer Zeit (Stuttgart 1979) 177. 183, 356-61, 413, 435.

20:18-38 MIESNER, D. R., "The Missionary Journeys Narrative: Patterns and Implications" in: C. H. Talbert (ed.) Perspectives on Luke-Acts (Danville 1978) 205.

20:18-36 DUPONT, J. Le Discours de Milet (1962) GT.: Paulus an die Seelsorger (1966).

20:18-35 DIBELIUS, M. Die Reden der Apostelgeschichte und die antike

Geschichtsschreibung (1949) 17, 22-26. DIBELIUS, M. Aufsätze zur Apostelgeschichte (1951) 133-36. ET: Studies in the Acts of the Apostles (1956) 155-58. DUPONT, J. Le Discours de Milet (1962) 22-26. HAHN, F. Das Verständnis der Mission im Neuen Testament (^{2}1965) 118, 122. DUPONT, J., Paulus und die Seelsorger (1966) 17-20. EXUM, C./TALBERT, C. "The Structure of Paul's Speech to the Ephesian Elders (Acts 20,18-35)," CBQ 29 (2, 1967) 233-36. PLUEMACHER, E. Lukas als hellenistischer Schriftseller (1972) 48-50. KNOCH, O., Die "Testamente" des Petrus und Paulus (Stuttgart 1972) 32-43. RADL, W., Paulus und Jesus im lukanischen Doppelwerk (Bern/Frankfurt 1975) 127-32. BARRETT, C. K., "Paul's Address to the Ephesian Elders" in: J. Jervel/W. A. Meeks (eds.) God's Christ and His People. FS. N. A. Dahl (New York 1977) 107-21. "Apostelgeschichte" in: TRE 3 (1978) 503, 506. KURICHIANIL, J., "The Speeches in Acts and the Old Testament" IndTheolStud 17 (1980) 181-86. PRIEUR, J.-M., "La figure de l'apôtre dans les Actes apocryphes d'André" in: F. Bovon et al. (eds.) Les Actes Apocryphes des Apôtres (Geneva 1981) 130n.30.

20:18-24 PRAST, F., Presbyter und Evangelium in nachapostolischer Zeit (Stuttgart 1979) 52-110.

20:18-21 DÖMER, M., Das Heil Gottes (Köln/Bonn 1978) 192-94. PRAST, F., Presbyter und Evangelium in nachapostolischer Zeit (Stuttgart 1979) 52-81.

20:18-19 PRAST, F., Presbyter und Evangelium in nachapostolischer Zeit (Stuttgart 1979) 52-68.

20:18 CLARK, A. C. The Acts of the Apostles (1933) 211, 241, 243, 332. PRAST, F., Presbyter und Evangelium in nachapostolischer Zeit (Stuttgart 1979) 52-55, 178.

20:19 DELLING, G. Die Zueignung des Heils in der Taufe (1961) 87. PRAST, F., Presbyter und Evangelium in nachapostolischer Zeit (Stuttgart 1979) 194-95, 195-96, 261-62.

20:20-21 PRAST, F., Presbyter und Evangelium in nachapostolischer Zeit (Stuttgart 1979) 68-81, 177-80, 186, 188, 351.

20:21 DELLING, G. Die Taufe im Neuen Testament (1963) 140. DUPONT, J. Etudes sur les Actes des Apôtres (1967) 248, 423, 426, 438, 456, 462. STROBEL, A. Erkenntnis und Bekenntnis der Sünde in neutestamentlicher Zeit (1968) 48. WILCKENS, U., Die Missionsreden der Apostelgeschichte (^{3}1974) 146, 171, 181, 182, 241. EGGER, W., Frohbotschaft und Lehre (Frankfurt 1976) 51. NELLESSEN, E., Zeugnis für Jesus und das Wort (Köln 1976) 239. METZGER, B. M., The Early Versions of the New Testament (Oxford 1977) 235. TRITES, A. A., The New Testament Concept of Witness (Cambridge 1977) 130, 141, 145. JEWETT, P. K., Infant Baptism and the Covenant of Grace (Grand Rapids 1978) 172. PRAST, F., Presbyter und Evangelium in nachapostolischer Zeit (Stuttgart 1979) 319.

20:22-25 RADL, W., Paulus und Jesus im lukanischen Doppelwerk (Bern/ Frankfurt 1975) 133-49.

20:22-24 DÖMER, M., Das Heil Gottes (Köln/Bonn 1978) 194. PRAST, F., Presbyter und Evangelium in nachapostolischer Zeit (Stuttgart 1979) 82-110, 196-97, 261-62.

20:22-23 PRAST, F., Presbyter und Evangelium in nachapostolischer Zeit (Stuttgart 1979) 83-93.

20:22 STAEHLIN, G., "τὸ πνεῦμα Ἰησοῦ (Apostelgeschichte 16:7)," in: Christ and the Spirit in the New Testament (1973) B. Lindars/ S. S. Smalley eds., 231, 240, 244, 249. STOLLE, V. Der Zeuge als Angeklagter (1973) 33f. DUNN, J. D. G., Jesus and the Spirit (London 1975) 176, 177, 180.

20:23 NELLESSEN, E., Zeugnis für Jesus und das Wort (Köln 1976) 255-57.

20:24 STOLLE, V. Der Zeuge als Angeklagter (1973) 146f.A. MICHEL, H.-J., Die Abschiedsrede des Paulus an die Kirche: Apg. 20:17-38 (München 1973) 24, 79, 85ff. PRAST, F., Presbyter und Evangelium in nachapostolischer Zeit (Stuttgart 1979) 94-110, 177-80, 186, 188, 193-94, 263-64, 265, 270-71, 351.

20:25-32 PRAST, F., Presbyter und Evangelium in nachapostolischer Zeit (Stuttgart 1979) 119-48.

20:25-27 DUPONT, J. Le Discours de Milet (1962) 113-34. GT.: Paulus an die Seelsorger (1966) 81-96. DÖMER, M., Das Heil Gottes (Köln/ Bonn 1978) 194-95. PRAST, F., Presbyter und Evangelium in nachapostolischer Zeit (Stuttgart 1979) 111-19.

20:25.38 O'NEILL, J. C. The Theology of Acts in its historical setting (1970) 60-61, 68.

20:25 WILSON, S. G. The Gentiles and the Gentile Mission in Luke-Acts (1973) 78-79, 89, 101, 233, 235. PRAST, F., Presbyter und Evangelium in nachapostolischer Zeit (Stuttgart 1979) 111-16, 177-80, 188, 263-64, 265, 275, 278, 280-81, 312, 317, 333, 340, 351-52.

20:26-28 ROBINSON, J. A., Pelagius's Expositions of Thirteen Epistles of St. Paul. I (Cambridge 1922) 170-71.

20:26-27 PRAST, F., Presbyter und Evangelium in nachapostolischer Zeit (Stuttgart 1979) 116-19, 178, 197.

20:26 PALLIS, A., Notes on St. Luke and the Acts (London 1928) 73.

20:27-28 FLEW, R. N. Jesus and His Church (1956) 141n, 142.

20:27 WANKE, J., Die Emmauserzählung (Leipzig 1973) 94. BUDES-

HEIM, T. L., "Paul's Abschiedsrede in the Acts of the Apostles" HThR 69 (1976) 9-30. PRAST, F., Presbyter und Evangelium in nachapostolischer Zeit (Stuttgart 1979) 177-80, 186, 188, 351.

20:28-31 SCHWEIZER, E. Gemeinde und Gemeinde-Ordnung im Neuen Testament (1959) §§ 5i, 1, 24a. DÖMER, M., Das Heil Gottes (Köln/Bonn 1978) 195-200. PRAST, F., Presbyter und Evangelium in nachapostolischer Zeit (Stuttgart 1979) 120-37, 185-86, 190-91.

20:28 CLARREBOETS, C. Biblica 24 (1943) 370-87. DUPONT, J. Le Discours de Milet (1962) 23-25, 135-98. WAINWIGHT, A. W. The Trinity in the New Testament (1962) 73-74. HAHN, F. Christologische Hoheitstitel (1963) 216. METZGER, B. M. The Text of the New Testament (1964) 234-36. BRAUN, H. Qumran und das Neue Testament II (1966) 330f. DUPONT, J. Paulus an die Seelsorger (1966) 97-141. KUENG, H. Die Kirche (1967) 103, 199, 472, 476, 481, 504. ET: The Church (1967) 83, 165, 400, 404, 408, 428. BEST, K. NTS 16 (1969-1970) 97f. DELLING, G. Der Kreuzestod Jesu in der urchristlichen Verkündigung (1972) 93-95. KRAENKL, E. Jesus der Knecht Gottes (1972) 122f. MERKLEIN, H. Das Kirchliche Amt nach dem Epheserbrief (1973) 362, 364, 368, 369, 370, 373, 374. MICHEL, H.-J., Die Abschiedsrede des Paulus an die Kirche Apg 20:17-38 (München 1973) 16, 24-25, 81, 88-89, 92-93, 95, 97. LADD, G. E., A Theology of the New Testament (Grand Rapids 1974) 352, 353, 532, 533. LOHFINK, G., Die Sammlung Israels (München 1975) 58, 85, 89-92. SCHNACKENBURG, R., "Episkopos und Hirtenamt. Zu Apg 20,28" in: K. Kertelge (ed.) Das Kirchliche Amt im Neuen Testament (Darmstadt 1977) 418-41. "Agende" in: TRE 2 (1978) 10. "Amt" in: TRE 2 (1978) 523. DALY, R. J., Christian Sacrifice (Washington D. C. 1978) 226. KERTELGE, K., "Offene Fragen zum Thema 'Geistliches Amt' und das neutestamentliche Verständnis von der 'repraesentatio Christi' " in: R. Schnackenburg et al. (eds.) Die Kirche des Anfangs. FS. H. Schürmann (Freiburg/Basel/Wien 1978) 595-96. PRAST, F., Presbyter und Evangelium in nachapostolischer Zeit (Stuttgart 1979) 120-30, 183-85, 194-95, 199-202, 356-61, 385, 395n.114, 413, 435. "Bischof" in: TRE 6 (1980) 653. MÜLLER, U. B., "Zur Rezeption gesetzeskritischer Jesusüberlieferung im frühen Christentum" NTS 27 (1981) 160.

20:29ff. SMITH, M. Clement of Alexandria and a secret Gospel of Mark (1973) 257-52.

20:29-31 DUPONT, J. Le Discours de Milet (1962) 199-233. GT.: Paulus an die Seelsorger (1966) 142-67. PRAST, F., Presbyter und Evangelium in nachapostolischer Zeit (Stuttgart 1979) 131-37.

20:29-30 "Apostelgeschichte" in: TRE 3 (1978) 518. MENESTRINA, G.,

"*Aphixis*" BiOr 20 (1978) 50. RUDOLPH, K., Die Gnosis (Göttingen 1978) 318. PRAST, F., Presbyter und Evangelium in nachapostolischer Zeit (Stuttgart 1979) 183.

20:29 LAMPE, G. W. H. " 'Grievous Wolves' (Acts 29:29)," in: Christ and the Spirit in the New Testament (1973) B. Lindars/S. S. Smalley eds., 253-68. DANIEL, C., "O importantá mentionare a Esenienilor făctută de Sfîntul Apostol Pavel" Studii Teologice Seria 29 (Bucharest 1977) 148-59.

20:30-31 STOLLE, V. Der Zeuge als Angeklagter (1973) 253f.

20:31 HAHN, F. Das Verständnis der Mission im Neuen Testament (²1965) 79, 81. Agende" in: TRE 2 (1978) 10. PRAST, F., Presbyter und Evangelium in nachapostolischer Zeit (Stuttgart 1979) 178, 195-96, 197, 261-62.

20:32 DUPONT, J., Le Discours de Milet (1962) 235-84. GT.: Paulus an die Seelsorger (1966) 168-201. WILCOX, M. The Semitism of Acts (1965) 32, 35-37, 56n, 158n, 159, 164. DUPONT, J. Etudes sur les Actes des Apôtres (1967) 251, 415, 448, 472, 525. BURCHARD, C. Der dreizehnte Zeuge (1970) 117f., 179. MÄRZ, C.-P., Das Wort Gottes bei Lukas (Leipzig 1973) 61-64. MICHEL, H.-J., Die Abschiedsrede des Paulus an die Kirche Apg. 20:17-38 (München 1973) 85ff., 89-90, 93, 95. DÖMER, M., Das Heil Gottes (Köln/Bonn 1978) 200. PRAST, F., Presbyter und Evangelium in nachapostolischer Zeit (Stuttgart 1979) 138-48, 177-80, 186-87, 188-89, 194-95, 199-202, 263-64, 265, 270-71, 351-52. VIELHAUER, P., "Oikodome. Das Bild vom Bau in der christlichen Literatur vom Neuen Testament bis Clemens Alexandrinus" in: G. Klein (ed.) Oikodome. (München 1979) 104-05.

20:33-35 DUPONT, J. Le Discours de Milet (1962) 235-84, 285, 304. GT.: Paulus an die Seelsorger (1966) 202-15, 216-40. AGRELL, G., Work, Toil and Sustenance (Hägersten, Sweden 1976). DÖMER, M., Das Heil Gottes (Köln/Bonn 1978) 200-01. PRAST, F., Presbyter und Evangelium in nachapostolischer Zeit (Stuttgart 1979) 149-56, 191-92, 195-96, 261-62.

20:33-34 PRAST, F., Presbyter und Evangelium in nachapostolischer Zeit (Stuttgart 1979) 150-52.

20:33 PRAST, F., Presbyter und Evangelium in nachapostolischer Zeit (Stuttgart 1979) 197.

20:34 HOCK, R. F., The Social Context of Paul's Ministry (Philadelphia 1980) 26-49.

20:35 PALLIS, A., Notes on St. Luke and the Acts (London 1928) 73-74. d'ARAGON, J. L. "Il faut soutenir les faibles" (Actes 20,35), Sciences Ecclesiastiques VII (1955) 5-22, 173-205. GLOVER, R. NTS 5 (1958-1959) 15ff. SCHRAGE, W. Die konkreten Einzelgebote in der paulinischen Paränese (1961) 262. SUMMERS, R. The Secret Sayings of the Living Jesus (1968) 15. RESCH, A. Agrapha, Ausserkanonische Schrift-Fragmente (1967) ''Agrapha'' in: TRE 3 (1978) 104. ''Antike und Christentum'' in: TRE 3 (1978) 57. ''Apokryphen'' in: TRE 3 (1978) 322. PRAST, F., Presbyter und Evangelium in nachapostolischer Zeit (Stuttgart 1979) 152-56, 197, 226, 232-33, 349.

20:36-38 RADL, W., Paulus und Jesus im lukanischen Doppelwerk (Bern/ Frankfurt 1975) 159-66.

20:36 DUPONT, J. Le Discours de Milet (1962) 341-75. GT.: Paulus an die Seelsorger (1966) 241-62.

20:38 DELLING, G. Die Zueignung des Heils in der Taufe (1961) 91.

21-28 GUTBROD, K. Die Apostelgeschichte (1968) 39ff. JERVELL, J. ''Paulus- der Lehrer Israels. Zu den apologetischen Paulusreden in der Apostelgeschichte,'' NovTest 10 (1968) 164-90. JERVELL, J., ''Paul: The Teacher of Israel'' in: Luke and the People of God (Minneapolis 1972) 153-83. KEPPLE, R. J., ''The Hope of Israel, the Resurrection of the Dead and Jesus: A Study of their Relationship in Acts with Particular Regard to the Understanding of Paul's Trial Defense'' JEThS 20 (1977) 231-41.

21 DUNN, J. D. G., Unity and Diversity in the New Testament (London 1977) 256-57.

21:1-18 ''Apostelgeschichte'' in: TRE 3 (1978) 514. ROBBINS, V. K., ''By Land and Sea: The We-Passages and Ancient Sea Voyages'' in: C. H. Talbert (ed.) Perspectives on Luke- Acts (Danville 1978) 215-42.

21:1-17 STOLLE, V. Der Zeuge als Angeklagter (1973) 72-74.

21:1-16 MIESNER, D. R., ''The Missionary Journeys Narrative: Patterns and Implications'' in: C. H. Talbert (ed.) Perspectives on Luke-Acts (Danville 1978) 203-05.

21:1-9 ''Apostelgeschichte'' in: TRE 3 (1978) 500.

21:1-8 SCHNEIDER, G. Der Herr unser Gott (1965) 189-92.

21:1 CLARK, A. C. The Acts of the Apostles (1933) 269, 301, 333, 377. ''Apostelgeschichte'' in: TRE 3 (1978) 494.

21:2 LADD, G. E., A Theology of the New Testament (Grand Rapids 1974) 236, 372, 480.

21:3 KNOX, W. L. The Sources of the Synoptic Gospels II (1957) 115.

21:4 DUNN, J. D. G., Jesus and the Spirit (London 1975) 172, 175-77. RADL, W., Paulus und Jesus im lukanischen Doppelwerk (Bern/ Frankfurt 1975) 133-49. PRAST, F., Presbyter und Evangelium in nachapostolischer Zeit (Stuttgart 1979) 89-90.

21:5-6 RADL, W., Paulus und Jesus im lukanischen Doppelwerk (Bern/ Frankfurt 1975) 159-66.

21:5 JEWETT, P. K., Infant Baptism and the Covenant of Grace (Grand Rapids 1978) 53.

21:6-21 LEON-DUFOUR, X., The Resurrection and the Message of Easter (London 1974) 62-79.

21:7-9 SWIDLER, L., Biblical Affirmations of Woman (Philadelphia 1979) 301, 302.

21:8ff. SCHMITHALS, W., "Zur Herkunft der gnostische Elemente in der Sprache des Paulus" in: B. Aland et al. (eds.) Gnosis. FS. H. Jonas (Göttingen 1978) 412.

21:8-14 ROBECK, C., "The Gift of Prophecy in Acts and Paul, Part I" SBT 5 (1975) 15-38.

21:8-9 HAHN, F. Das Verständnis der Mission im Neuen Testament (²1965) 49. SATAKE, A. Die Gemeindeordnung in der Johannes- apokalypse (1966) 166. SCHILLE, G. Die urchristliche Kollegial- mission (1967) 39ff. EHRHARDT, A. The Acts of the Apostles (1969) 36f., 40, 105. SATAKE, A. Die Gemeindeordnung in der Johannesapokalypse (Neukirchen-Vluyn 1966) 166. "Apostelge- schichte" in: TRE 3 (1978) 497.

21:8 FLEW, R. N. Jesus and His Church (1956) 144n. BROX, N. Zeuge und Märtyrer (1961) 64f. "Amt" in: TRE 2 (1978) 523. "Askese" in: TRE 4 (1979) 205.

21:9-11 GERSTENBERGER, E. S. und SCHRAGE, W., Frau und Mann (Stuttgart 1980) 135.

21:9-10 FLEW, R. N. Jesus and His Church (1956) 143n.

21:9 CLARK, S. B., Man and Woman in Christ (Ann Arbor, Mich 1980) 103.

21:10-14 "Apostelgeschichte" in: TRE 3 (1978) 494.

21:10-12 RADL, W., Paulus und Jesus im lukanischen Doppelwerk (Bern/ Frankfurt 1975) 133-49.

21:10-11 PATSCH, H. "Die Prophetie des Agabus," ThZ 28 (3, 1972) 228- 32. PRAST, F., Presbyter und Evangelium in nachapostolischer Zeit (Stuttgart 1979) 89-91.

21:10 KNOX, W. L. The Sources of the Synoptic Gospels II (1957) 34. SATAKE, A. Die Gemeindeordnung in der Johannesapokalypse

(Neukirchen-Vluyn 1966) 168. HENGEL, M. Judentum und Hellenismus (1969) 439. ET: Judaism and Hellenism (1974) I 240.

21:11ff. DAVIES, W. D. The Gospel and the Land (1974) 195, 277, 277n.78.

21:11-14 SHEPARD, J. W., The Life and Letters of St. Paul (Grand Rapids 1950) 458-59.

21:11 ELLIS, E. E. Paul's Use of the Old Testament (1957) 109ff. STAEHLIN, G., "τὸ πνεῦμα Ἰησοῦ (Apostelgeschichte 16:7)," in: Christ and the Spirit in the New Testament (1973) B. Lindars/ S. S. Smalley eds., 232, 238, 244, 250f.

21:13-14 RADL, W., Paulus und Jesus im lukanischen Doppelwerk (Bern/ Frankfurt 1975) 159-66.

21:13 PRAST, F., Presbyter und Evangelium in nachapostolischer Zeit (Stuttgart 1979) 94-95.

21:14 DELLING, G. Die Zueignung des Heils in der Taufe (1961) 87. HAHN, F. Das Verständnis der Mission im Neuen Testament (²1965) 69. GERSTENBERGER, G. und SCHRAGE, W., Leiden (Stuttgart 1977) 206-07; ET: J. E. Steely (trans.) Suffering (Nashville 1980) 238-39.

21:15ff. BLASS, F. Philosophy of the Gospels (1898) 128ff.

21:15-26 SCHMITHALS, W. Paulus und Jakobus (1964) 70-80.

21:15 RUDOLPH, K. Die Mandäer II (1961) 299.5. LÜDEMANN, G., Paulus, der Heidenapostel I (Göttingen 1980) 163-65.

21:16-17 "Apostelgeschichte" in: TRE 3 (1978) 500.

21:16 CLARK, A. C. The Acts of the Apostles (1933) xxxiii, xlv, 182, 189, 228. DUPONT, J. The Sources of Acts (1963) 118, 217, 134, 161. CAVALLIN, H. C. C., Life After Death I (Lund 1973) 4, 2n4. "Apostelgeschichte" in: TRE 3 (1978) 497.

21:17-28:31 DIBELIUS, M. Aufsätze zur Apostelgeschichte (1951) 14f. ET: Studies in the Acts of the Apostles (1956) 7f.

21:17-26 RINALDI, G. "Giacomo, Paolo e i Giudei (Atti 21,17-26)," RivB 14 (4, 1966) 407-23. HOLMBERG, B., Paul and Power (Lund 1978) 42-43.

21:17-25 PRAST, F., Presbyter und Evangelium in nachapostolischer Zeit (Stuttgart 1979) 324.

21:17-23 SHEPARD, J. W., The Life and Letters of St. Paul (Grand Rapids 1950) 460-67.

21:17-21 JEWETT, P. K., Infant Baptism and the Covenant of Grace (Grand Rapids 1976) 229.

21:17 MUNCK, J. Paul and the Salvation of Mankind (1959) 239f. SCHMITHALS, W. Paulus und Jakobus (1963) 72. GOULDER, M. D. Type and History in Acts (1964) 29, 197f.

21:18-28:31 HAHN, F. Das Verständnis der Mission im Neuen Testament (²1965) 82.

21:18ff. KLEIN, G. Die Zwölf Apostel (1961) 173ff.

21:18-28 VIELHAUER, P., "On the 'Paulinism' of Acts" in: L. E. Keck/ J. L. Martyn (eds.) Studies in Luke-Acts. FS. P. Schubert (Nashville 1966) 39-40.

21:18-26 STOLLE, V. Der Zeuge als Angeklagter (1973) 74-80, 216f. WILSON, S. G., "Law and Judaism in Acts" in: P. J. Achtemeier (ed.) SBL Seminar Papers 1980 (Chico, Cal. 1980) 256-57.

21:18-19 "Apostelgeschichte" in: TRE 3 (1978) 494.

21:18 KERTELGE, K. Gemeinde und Amt im Neuen Testament (1972) 98f. "Amt" in: TRE 2 (1978) 514. "Apostelgeschichte" in: TRE 3 (1978) 494. PRAST, F., Presbyter und Evangelium in nachapostolischer Zeit (Stuttgart 1979) 225, 356.

21:20ff. SMITH, M. Clement of Alexandria and a secret Gospel of Mark (1973) 255f.

21:20-26 HARNACK, A. von, Studien zur Geschichte des Neuen Testaments und der Alten Kirche (1931) 23ff.

21:20-25 ROBBINS, V. K., "Prefaces in Greco-Roman Biography and Luke-Acts" in: P. J. Achtemeier (ed.) SBL Seminar Papers 1978/II (Missoula 1978) 200-04.

21:20-21 MUNCK, J. Paul and the Salvation of Mankind (1959) 241f.

21:20 PARKER, P. The Gospel Before Mark (1953) 101ff. DELLING, G. Die Taufe im Neuen Testament (1963) 72. SCHMITHALS, W. Paulus und Jakobus (1963) 73. BURCHARD, C. Der dreizehnte Zeuge (1970) 21f. ZINGG, P., Das Wachsen der Kirche (Freiburg 1974) 167.

21:21 WINDISCH, H. Paulus und das Judentum (1935) 27ff. MOORE, G. F. Judaism II (1946) 21. DELLING, G. Die Taufe im Neuen Testament (1963) 140f. SCHMITHALS, W. Paulus und Jakobus (1963) 28, 73f.

21:23ff. O'NEILL, J. C. The Theology of Acts in its historical setting (1970) 80-81.

21:23 PALLIS, A., Notes on St. Luke and the Acts (London 1928) 75.

21:24-22:30 WILCOX, M. The Semitisms of Acts (1965) 59ff.

21:25 HARNACK, A. von, Studien zur Geschichte des Neuen Testaments und der Alten Kirche (1931) 4ff., 23ff. MOORE, G. F. Judaism II (1946) 74. DELLING, G. Die Taufe im Neuen Testament (1963) 72. SCHMITHALS, W. Paulus und Jakobus (1963) 81-85. HAHN, F. Das Verständnis der Mission im Neuen Testament (²1965) 72, 73, 118. HURD, J. C. The Origin of 1 Corinthians (1965) 40, 246-50, 255[4]. EPP, E. J. The Theological Tendency of

Codex Bezae Cantabrigiensis in Acts (1966) 38, 50 n.1, 107-12, 114, 170, WILSON, S. G. The Gentiles and the Gentile Mission in Luke-Acts (1974) 188-91. HEIN, K., Eucharist and Excommunication. A Study in Early Christian Doctrine and Discipline (Bern/Frankfurt 1975) 83-85. DÖMER, M., Das Heil Gottes: Studien zur Theologie des lukanischen Doppelwerkes (Köln/Bonn 1978) 177-78. "Blut" in: TRE 6 (1980) 733. CLARK, K. W., "The Israel of God" in: The Gentile Bias and Other Essays (Leiden 1980) 24.

21:26-30 BARRETT, C. K. The New Testament Background (1956) 50.

21:26 PALLIS, A., Notes on St. Luke and the Acts (London 1928) 75-76. CLARK, K. W., "The Israel of God" in: The Gentile Bias and Other Essays (Leiden 1980) 26.

21:27 - 26:32 RADL, W., Paulus und Jesus im lukanischen Doppelwerk (Bern/Frankfurt 1975) 169-221. LÉGASSE, S., "L'apologétique à l'égard de Rome dans le procès de Paul. Actes 21,27 - 26,32" RechSR 69 (1981) 249-55.

21:27 - 22:29 RADL, W., Paulus und Jesus im lukanischen Doppelwerk (Bern/Frankfurt 1975) 170-77, 203. VELTMAN, F., "The Defense Speeches of Paul in Acts" in: P. J. Achtemeier (ed.) SBL Seminar Papers 1977 (Missoula 1977) 333-34. VELTMAN, F., "The Defense Speeches of Paul in Acts" in: C. H. Talbert (ed.) Perspectives on Luke-Acts (Danville 1978) 243-56.

21:27-28 STOLLE, V. Der Zeuge als Angeklagter (1973) 91f., 234f.

21:27 GOULDER, M. D. Type and History in Acts (1964) 93, 98, 101, 109, 115, 230.

21:28 MUNCK, J. Paul and the Salvation of Mankind (1959) 242f. SCHMITHALS, W. Paulus und Jakobus (1963) 19f., 28. BRAUN, H. Qumran und das NT II (1966) 162, 178, 213. KLIJN, A. F. J./ REININK, G. J. Patristic Evidence for Jewish-Christian Sects (1973) 9.

21:29 SHERWIN-WHITE, A. N., Roman Society and Roman Law in the New Testament (Grand Rapids 1978) 52.

21:34 - 22:22 PALLIS, A., Notes on St. Luke and the Acts (London 1928) 76-77.

21:36 WILCOX, M. The Semitism of Acts (1965) 67-68.

21:37-39 SHERWIN-WHITE, A. N., Roman Society and Roman Law in the New Testament (Grand Rapids 1978) 179.

21:37 STOLLE, V. Der Zeuge als Angeklagter (1973) 262.

21:38 VOLZ, P. Die Eschatologie der jüdischen Gemeinde (1934) 194. CULLMANN, O. The State in the New Testament (1956) 13f. HAHN, F. Christologische Hoheitstitel (1963) 361. BOUSSET, W.

Die Religion des Judentums im Späthellenistischen Zeitalter (1966 = 1926) 224. JEWETT, R., A Chronology of Paul's Life (Philadelphia 1979) 40. SCHRECKENBERG, H., "Flavius Josephus und die lukanischen Schriften" in: W. Haubeck/M. Bachmann (eds.) Wort in der Zeit. FS. K. H. Rengstorf (Leiden 1980) 202-03.

21:39 SCHWARTZ, J. "A Propos du statut personnel de l'apôtre Paul," RHPhR 37 (1, 1957) 91-96. BURCHARD, C. Der dreizehnte Zeuge (1970) 37-39. CADBURY, H. J. "Litotes in Acts," in: Festschrift to Honor F. Wilbur Gingrich (1972) E. H. Barth/R. E. Cocraft eds., 59-61.

22-26 SCHUBERT, P. "The Final Cycle of Speeches in the Book of Acts," JBL 87 (1, 1968) 1-16.

22 MUNCK, J. Paul and the Salvation of Mankind (1959) 19f. BLANK, J. Paulus und Jesus (1968) 242-48. KUEMMEL, W. G. Römer 7 und das Bild des Menschen im Neuen Testament (1974) 149f.

22:1-21 BETHGE, F. Die paulinischen Reden der Apostelgeschichte (1887) 168-205. DIBELIUS, M. Die Reden der Apostelgeschichte und die antike Geschichtsschreibung (1949) 17, 26-29. DIBELIUS, M. Aufsätze zur Apostelgeschichte (1951) 136-39. ET: Studies in the Acts of the Apostles (1956) 158-61. HAHN, F. Das Verständnis der Mission in Neuen Testament (²1965) 82. STOLLE, V. Der Zeuge als Angeklagter (1973) 57f, 103-15. WILSON, S. G. The Gentiles and the Gentile Mission in Luke-Acts (1973) 161-66, 252. BUDESHEIM, T. L., "Paul's *Abschiedsrede* in the Acts of the Apostles" HThR 69 (1976) 9-30. "Apostelgeschichte" in: TRE 3 (1978) 503.

22:3ff.19 KLEIN, G. Die Zwölf Apostel (1961) 122ff.

22:3ff. GRASS, H. Ostergeschehen und Osterberichte (1970) 194f., 209f., cf. 108, 113.

22:3-21 LOHFINK, G. Paulus vor Damaskus (1966). PANNENBERG, W. in: New Testament Issues (1970) R. Batey ed., 110-11. GLÖCKNER, R., Die Verkündigung des Heils beim Evangelisten Lukas (Mainz 1975) 49-50. LOHFINK, G., The Conversion of St. Paul: Narrative and History in Acts (Chicago 1976). SCHMITHALS, W., "Zur Herkunft der gnostischen Elemente in der Sprache des Paulus'' in: B. Aland et al. (eds.) Gnosis. FS. H. Jonas (Göttingen 1978) 397.

22:3-16 SABUGAL, S., "La conversion de S. Pablo en Damasco: ciudad de Siria o region de Qumran?'' Augustinianum 15 (1975) 213-24.

22:3 MUNCK, J. Paul and the Salvation of Mankind (1959) 14f., 219, 243, 285. HENNECKE, E./SCHNEEMELCHER, W. Neutesta-mentliche Apokryphen (1964) I 376. LONGENECKER, R. N. Paul Apostle of Liberty (1964) 22f., 25f. TURNER, W. Grammatical Insights into the New Testament (1965) 83ff. McNAMARA, M. The New Testament and the Palestinian Targum to the Pentateuch (196) 254. BURCHARD, C. Der dreizehnte Zeuge (1970) 31ff. CAVALLIN, H. C. C., Life After Death I (Lund 1974) 5n5. CON-ZELMANN, H. und LINDEMANN, A., Arbeitsbuch zum Neuen Testament (Tübingen 1975) 406. "Apostelgeschichte'' in: TRE 3 (1978) 500, 517. SHERWIN-WHITE, A. N., Roman Society and Roman Law in the New Testament (Grand Rapids 1978) 179. HENGEL, M., Zur urchristlichen Geschichtsschreibung (Stuttgart 1979) 71; ET: J. Bowden (trans.) Acts and the History of Earliest Christianity (London 1979) 81. KIM, S., The Origin of Paul's Gospel (Tübingen 1981) 32-33, 36-37.

22:4-21 HEDRICK, C., "Paul's Conversion/Call: A Comparative Analy-sis of the Three Reports in Acts'' JBL 100 (1981) 415-32.

22:4-5 BEYSCHLAG, K. Clemens Romanus und der Frühkatholizismus (1966) 223. BURCHARD, C. Der dreizehnte Zeuge (1970) 45. STOLLE, V. Der Zeuge als Angeklagter (1973) 118f., 168-70. SWIDLER, L.., Biblical Affirmations of Woman (Philadelphia 1979) 292.

22:4 FLEW, R. N. Jesus and His Church (1956) 113n. KNOX, W. L. The Sources of the Synoptic Gospels II (1957) 13. WILCOX, M. The Semitisms of Acts (1965) 105-06. NICKELS, P. Targum and New Testament (1967) 67. LYONNET, S., " 'La voie' dans les Actes des Apôtres'' RechSR 69 (1981) 149-64.

22:5-16 MATTILL, A. J., "The Value of Acts as a Source for the Study of Paul'' in: C. H. Talbert (ed.) Perspectives on Luke-Acts (Danville 1978) 91.

22:5 MUNCK, J. Paul and the Salvation of Mankind (1959) 13f. NEL-LESSEN, E., Zeugnis für Jesus und das Wort (Köln 1976) 50-52. DELEBECQUE, E., "L'hellenisme de la 'relative complexe' dans le Nouveau Testament et principalement chez saint Luc'' Biblica 62 (1981) 235.

22:6ff. KLEIN, G. Die Zwölf Apostel (1961) 152ff.

22:6-16 SEIDENSTICKER, P. Die Auferstehung Jesu in der Botschaft der Evangelisten (1968) 36f. BURCHARD, C. Der dreizehnte Zeuge

(1970) 105-08. DUNN, J. D. G. Baptism in the Holy Spirit (1970) 73ff.

22:6-11 HUBBARD, B. J., "Commissioning Stories in Luke-Acts: A Study of their Antecedents, Form and Content" in: Semeia 8 (1977) 103-26. HUBBARD, B. J., "The Role of Commissioning Accounts in Acts" in: C. H. Talbert (ed.) Perspectives on Luke-Acts (Danville 1978) 190. 193, 197.

22:6.9.11 STOLLE, V. Der Zeuge als Angeklagter (1973) 172-74, 178f.

22:6 MATTILL, A. J., "The Value of Acts as a Source for the Study of Paul" in: C. H. Talbert (ed.) Perspectives on Luke-Acts (Danville 1978) 91. MICHEL, O., "Das Licht des Messias" in: E. Bammel et al. (eds.) Donum Gentilicium. FS. D. Daube (Oxford 1978) 40-50.

22:7f.10 STOLLE, V. Der Zeuge als Angeklagter (1973) 176f., 184f.

22:7-8 SCHWEIZER, E. Erniedrigung und Erhöhung bei Jesus und seinen Nachfolgern (1962) § 14e.

22:8 RUDOLPH, K. Die Mandäer I (1960) 115. DELLING, G. Die Zueignung des Heils in der Taufe (1961) 86, 88. RUPPERT, L., Jesus als der leidende Gerechte? (Stuttgart 1972) 48n.17. LYON-NET, S., " 'La voie' dans les Acts des Apôtres" RechSR 69 (1981) 149-64.

22:9 MOEHRING, H. R. "The Verb akouein in Acts IX,7 and XXII,9," NovTest 3 (1-2, 1959) 80-99. BRATCHER, R. G. "akouo in Acts ix.7 and xxii.9," ET 71 (1960) 243-45. HEDRICK, C., "Paul's Conversion/Call: A Comparative Analysis of the Three Reports in Acts" JBL 100 (1981) 423-25, 428-30.

22:10.21 FLEW, R. N. Jesus and His Church (1956) 146n.

22:10 DELLING, G. Die Taufe im Neuen Testament (1963) 73. HED-RICK, C., "Paul's Conversion/Call: A Comparative Analysis of the Three Reports in Acts" JBL 100 (1981) 424-26.

22:11 WANKE, J., Die Emmauserzählung. Eine redaktionsge-schichtliche Untersuchung zu Lk 24,13-35 (Leipzig 1973) 36. DIETZFELBINGER, C., "Pseudo-Philo: Antiquitates Biblicae" in: JüdSchr II/2 (1975) 133n.1a. METZGER, B. M., The Early Versions of the New Testament (Oxford 1977) 235.

22:12-21 HAHN, F. Das Verständnis der Mission im Neuen Testament (²1965) 118.

22:12-16 STOLLE, V. Der Zeuge als Angeklagter (1973) 166f. WILSON, S. G. The Gentiles and the Gentile Mission in Luke-Acts (1973) 165-66. HUBBARD, B. J., "The Role of Commissioning Accounts in Acts" in: C. H. Talbert (ed.) Perspectives on Luke-Acts (Danville 1978) 190, 193, 197.

22:12 NELLESSEN, E., Zeugnis für Jesus und das Wort (Köln 1976) 64. BERGMEIER, R., Glaube als Gabe nach Johannes (Stuttgart 1980) 238n.40.

22:14-21 LOENING, K. Die Saulustradition in der Apostelgeschichte (1973) 163.

22:14-15 STOLLE, V. Der Zeuge als Angeklagter (1973) 141-44. HEDRICK, C., "Paul's Conversion/Call: A Comparative Analysis of the Three Reports in Acts" JBL 100 (1981) 424-26, 431.

22:14 VOLZ, P. Die Eschatologie der jüdischen Gemeinde (1934) 187. SCHWEIZER, E. Erniedrigung und Erhöhung bei Jesus und seinen Nachfolgern (1962) §4b. HAHN, F., Christologische Hoheitstitel (1963) 185. ZIESLER, J. A. The Meaning of Righteousness in Paul (1972) 136f., 146. RUPPERT, L., Jesus als der leidende Gerechte? (Stuttgart 1972) 13, 47.

22:15-21 KIM, A., The Origin of Paul's Gospel (Tübingen 1981) 64-66.

22:15 BEUTLER, J. Martyria (1972) 188, 195f., 330f. 337. KRAENKL, E. Jesus der Knecht Gottes (1972) 169, 171f., 210. WILCKENS, U. Die Missionsreden der Apostelgeschichte (³1974) 146-48, 233. GLÖCKNER, R., Die Verkündigung des Heils beim Evangelisten Lukas (Mainz 1975) 48ff. NELLESSEN, E., Zeugnis für Jesus und das Wort (Köln 1976) 212-15. "Apostel" in: TRE 3 (1978) 443. CRIBBS, F. L., "The Agreements that exist between John and Acts" in: C. H. Talbert (ed.) Perspectives on Luke-Acts (Danville 1978) 50.

22:16-18 NELLESSEN, E., Zeugnis für Jesus und das Wort (Köln 1976) 222-31.

22:16 DELLING, G. Die Taufe im Neuen Testament (1963) 64, 78, 88, 97, 101f., 139. HAHN, F. Christologische Hoheitstitel (1963) 118. BIEDER, W., Die Verheissung der Taufe im Neuen Testament (Zürich 1966) 235-39. SEEBERG, A. Der Katechismus der Urchristenheit (1966) 187, 188, 213, 220. DUPONT, J. Etudes sur les Actes des Apôtres (1967) 255, 281, 442, 456, 461. DUNN, J. D. G. Baptism in the Holy Spirit (1970) 33n74, 78n, 96, 97, 98. KRAENKL, E. Jesus der Knecht Gottes (1972) 68, 169, 171f., 197, 210.DUPONT, D. J., The Salvation of the Gentiles (New York 1979) 64. BARTH, G., Die Taufe in frühchristlicher Zeit (Neukirchen-Vluyn 1981) 40-41, 74.

22:17ff. FEINE, P. Der Apostel Paulus (1927) 422f. GRASS, H. Ostergeschehen und Osterberichte (1970) 194f., 250ff.

22:17-21 BLAIR, E. P. "Paul's Call to the Gentile Mission," BR 10 (1965) 19-33. BETZ, O. "Die Vision des Paulus im Tempel von Jerusalem - Apg 22,17-21 als Beitrag zur Deutung des Damaskuserlebnisses," in: Verborum Veritas (1970) O. Böcher/K. Haacker eds.,

113-23. BURCHARD, C. Der dreizehnte Zeuge (1970) 161-68. STAEHLIN, G. "τὸ πνεῦμα 'Ιησοῦ (Apostelgeschichte 16:7)," in: Christ and the Spirit in the New Testament (1973) B. Lindars/ S. S. Smalley eds., 238f. STOLLE, V. Der Zeuge als Angeklagter (1973) 163-66. WILSON, S. G. The Gentiles and the Gentile Mission (1973) 161, 163, 165-67, 169, 242-43. HUBBARD, B.-J., "Commissioning Stories in Luke-Acts: A Study of their Antecedents, Form and Content" in: Semeia 8 (1977) 103-26. "Apostelgeschichte" in: TRE 3 (1978) 500, 512. HUBBARD, B. J., "The Role of Commissioning Accounts in Acts" in: C. H. Talbert (ed.) Perspectives on Luke-Acts (Danville 1978) 190, 193, 197-98.

22:17 STONEHOUSE, N. B. The Witness of Matthew and Mark to Christ (1944) 106. NELLESSEN, E., Zeugnis für Jesus und das Wort (Köln 1976) 217.

22:18-19 KAESEMANN, E. Exegetische Versuche und Besinnungen (1964) II 77.

22:18 BEUTLER, J. Martyria (1972) 172, 188, 205, 228f., 304, 337, 365. NELLESSEN, E., Zeugnis für Jesus und das Wort (Köln 1976) 217-18.

22:19-20 BURCHARD, C. Der dreizehnte Zeuge (1970) 45f. STOLLE, V. Der Zeuge als Angeklagter (1973) 245f. NELLESSEN, E., Zeugnis für Jesus und das Wort (Köln 1976) 218-19. "Apostelgeschichte" in: TRE 3 (1978) 510.

22:19 KNOX, W. L. The Sources of the Synoptic Gospels II (1957) 78.

22:20 BROX, N. Zeuge und Märtyrer (1961) 61-66. NELLESSEN, E., Zeugnis für Jesus und das Wort (Köln 1976) 215-22, 246-52.

22:21 FLEW, R. N. Jesus and His Church (1956) 146n. DUPONT, J. Etudes sur les Actes des Apôtres (1967) 154, 262, 381, 408, 415, 418, 455. STOLLE, V. Der Zeuge als Angeklagter (1973) 245-48. NELLESSEN, E., Zeugnis für Jesus und das Wort (Köln 1976) 219-29. HAUSER, J., Strukturen der Abschlusserzählung der Apostelgeschichte (Apg. 28:16-31) (Rome 1979) 105-07.

22:22 WILCOX, M. The Semitisms of Acts (1965) 56n, 67-68. STOLLE, V. Der Zeuge als Angeklagter (1973) 234f. "Apostelgeschichte" in: TRE 3 (1978) 506. JEWETT, P. K., Infant Baptism and the Covenant of Grace (Grand Rapids 1978) 60. CLARK, K. W., "The Making of the Twentieth Century New Testament" in: The Gentile Bias and other Essays (Leiden 1980) 152.

22:23 BETZ, H. D. Lukian von Samosata und das Neue Testament (1961) 72, 78, 140.

22:24-29 STOLLE, V. Der Zeuge als Angeklagter (1973) 112f.

22:25-29 BURCHARD, C. Der dreizehnte Zeuge (1970) 37-39. KAYE, B.,

"The New Testament and Social Order" in: B. Kaye/G. Wenham (eds.) Law, Morality and the Bible (Downers Grove, Ill. 1978) 102.

22:25 SHERWIN-WHITE, A. N., Roman Society and Roman Law in the New Testament (Grand Rapids 1978) 71.

22:28 SHERWIN-WHITE, A. N., Roman Society and Roman Law in the New Testament (Grand Rapids 1978) 151-52.

22:29 EPP, E. J. The Theological Tendency of Codex Bezae Cantabrigiensis in Acts (1966) 30, 150f.

22:30-23:11 COX, D. "Paul Before the Sanhedrin: Acts. 22,30-23,11," SBFLA 21 (1971) 54-75. RADL, W., Paulus und Jesus im lukanischen Doppelwerk (Bern/Frankfurt 1975) 177-85, 203-04.

22:30-23:10 STOLLE, V. Der Zeuge als Angeklagter (1973) 262f. PALLIS, A., Notes on St. Luke and the Acts (London 1928) 78-79. TRITES, A. A., "The Importance of Legal Scenes and Language in the Book of Acts" NovT 16 (1974) 278-84.

22:30 GLÖCKNER, R., Die Verkündigung des Heils beim Evangelisten Lukas (Mainz 1975) 7-8. RIVKIN, E., A Hidden Revolution (Nashville 1978) 96-97.

———————

23ff. FEINE, D. P./BEHM, D. J. Einleitung in das Neue Testament (1950) 182f. KUEMMEL, W. G. Einleitung in das Neue Testament (1973) 288f.

23-25 BRUCE, F. F., "The Full Name of the Procurator Felix" JSNT 1 (1978) 33-36.

23:1-24:14 WILCOX, M. The Semitisms of Acts (1965) 59ff.

23:1-11 BETHGE, F. Die paulinischen Reden der Apostelgeschichte (1887) 206-25.

23:1-5 JEWETT, R., A Chronology of Paul's Life (Philadelphia 1979) 44.

23:1.6 STOLLE, V. Der Zeuge als Angeklagter (1973) 58, 118.

23:1 REICKE, B. The Disobedient Spirits and Christian Baptism (1946) 178f. MUNCK, J. Paul and the Salvation of Mankind (1959) 313f. GOULDER, M. D. Type and History in Acts (1964) 74, 88, 101, 108.

23:5 HOLTZ, T. Untersuchungen über die Alttestamentlichen Zitate bei Lukas (1968) 127-30.

23:6-10 RIVKIN, E., A Hidden Revolution (Nashville 1978) 96-97.

23:6-9 "Amt" in: TRE 2 (1978) 504.

23:6-8 BOUSSET, W. Die Religion des Judentums im Späthellenistischen Zeitalter (1966 = 1926) 193, 331.

23:6.10 NICKELS, P. Targum and New Testament (1967) 67.

23:6 ROBERTSON, A. T., Epochs in the Life of Paul (New York 1920) 7, 68, 233, 234. NÖTSCHER, F., Altorientalischer und alttestamentlicher Auferstehungsglaube (Darmstadt 1970 = 1926) 298. BURCHARD, C. Der dreizehnte Zeuge (1970) 39f. O'NEILL, J. C. The Theology of Acts in its historical setting (1970) 75-76. STOLLE, V. Der Zeuge als Angeklagter (1973) 123-26. "Apostelgeschichte" in: TRE 3 (1978) 497.

23:8 BAMBERGER, B. J. "The Sadducees and the Belief in Angels," JBL 82 (4, 1963) 433-35. NÖTSCHER, F., Altorientalischer und alttestamentlicher Auferstehungsglaube (Darmstadt 1970 = 1926) 189, 271. CAVALLIN, H. C. C., Life After Death I (Lund 1974) 6,2,2. LACHS, S. T., "The Pharisees and Sadducees on Angels: A Reexamination of Acts XXIII.8" Graz College Annual of Jewish Studies 6 (Philadelphia 1977) 35-42. FISCHER, U., Eschatologie und Jenseitserwartung im hellenistischen Diasporajudentum (Berlin 1978) 154.

23:11 - 28:11 MARTIN, R. P., New Testament Foundations II (Exeter 1978) 129-41.

23:11 BEYSCHLAG, K. Clemens Romanus und der Frühkatholizismus (1966) 269. BEUTLER, J. Martyria (1972) 171, 180, 188, 203, 205, 213, 219, 331. STOLLE, V. Der Zeuge als Angeklagter (1973) 43f., 63-65, 146f.,A, 252f., 263. NELLESSEN, E., Zeugnis für Jesus und das Wort (Köln 1976) 237-38. SOARES PRABHU, G. M., The Formula Quotations in the Infancy Narrative of Matthew (Rome 1976) 224-25. HUBBARD, B. J., "Commissioning Stories in Luke-Acts: A Study of their Antecedents, Form and Content" in: Semeia 8 (1977) 103-26. HUBBARD, B. J., "The Role of Commissioning Accounts in Acts" in: C. H. Talbert (ed.) Perspectives on Luke-Acts (Danville 1978) 190, 193, 198. HAUSER, J., Strukturen der Abschlusserzählung der Apostelgeschichte (Apg. 28:16-31) (Rome 1979) 214-25. PRAST, F., Presbyter und Evangelium in nachapostolischer Zeit (Stuttgart 1979) 84.

23:12 - 25:12 RADL, W., Paulus und Jesus im lukanischen Doppelwerk (Bern/Frankfurt 1975) 185-96, 204-09.

23:12-21 "Apostelgeschichte" in: TRE 3 (1978) 497.

23:12 STOLLE, V. Der Zeuge als Angeklagter (1973) 43-45.

23:15 CLARK, A. C. The Acts of the Apostles (1933) 230, 238, 249, 303, 333, 379.

23:16-35 STOLLE, V. Der Zeuge als Angeklagter (1973) 49-52.

23:16 "Apostelgeschichte" in: TRE 3 (1978) 500. FURNISH, V. P., The Moral Teaching of Paul (Nashville 1979) 102.

23:23-30 BEYER, H. W. Die Apostelgeschichte (1947) 140.

23:23-24 CLARK, A. C. The Acts of the Apostles (1933) 252, 279f.

23:23 KILPATRICK, G. D. "Acts XXIII. 23 DEXIOLABOI," JThS 14 (2, 1963) 393-94. METZGER, B. M., The Early Versions of the New Testament (Oxford 1977) 243.

23:24 BAUMERT, N., Täglich Sterben und Auferstehen (München 1973) 296.

23:25ff. PETZKE, G. Die Traditionen über Apollonius von Tyana und das Neue Testament (1970) 123f.

23:26-30 BARRETT, C. K. The New Testament Background (1956) 27, 28. ROBBINS, V. K., "Prefaces in Greco-Roman Biography and Luke-Acts" in: P. J. Achtemeier (ed.) SBL Seminar Papers 1978/II (Missoula 1978) 201.

23:26 CONZELMANN, H. Die Apostelgeschichte (1963) 129f. "Apostelgeschichte" in: TRE 3 (1978) 502.

23:27 BURCHARD, C. Der dreizehnte Zeuge (1970) 37-39.

23:29 EPP, E. J. The Theological Tendency of Codex Bezae Cantabrigiensis in Acts (1966) 151f.

23:33 BAUMERT, N., Täglich Sterben und Auferstehen (München 1973) 292.

23:33-35 SCHALIT, A. König Herodes (1969) 403.

———————

24-28 GILCHRIST, J. M. "On what charge was St. Paul brought to Rome?" ET 78 (9, 1967) 264-66.

24-26 SHEPARD, J. W., The Life and Letters of St. Paul (Grand Rapids 1950) 467-75.

24 VIA, E. J., "An Interpretation of Acts7:35-37 from the Perspective of Major Themes in Luke-Acts" in: P. J. Achtemeier (ed.) SBL Seminar Papers 1978/II (Missoula 1978) 221-22.

24:1-23 TRITES, A. A., "The Importance of Legal Scenes and Language in the Book of Acts" NovT 16 (1974) 278-84. VELTMAN, F., "The Defense Speeches of Paul in Acts" in : P. J. Achtemeier (ed.), SBL Seminar Papers 1977 (Missoula 1977) 334. VELTMAN, F., "The Defense Speeches of Paul in Acts" in: C. H. Talbert (ed.) Perspectives on Luke-Acts (Danville 1978) 243-56.

24:1-9 STOLLE, V. Der Zeuge als Angeklagter (1973) 92-94.

24:1 JEWETT, R., A Chronology of Paul's Life (Philadelphia 1979) 44.

24:2-8 DIBELIUS, M. Aufsätze zur Apostelgeschichte (1951) 146f., ET: Studies in the Acts of the Apostles (1956) 170f. EPP, E. J. The Theological Tendency of Codex Bezae Cantabrigiensis in Acts (1966) 151f. STOLLE, V. Der Zeuge als Angeklagter (1966) 56f., 234f. "Apostelgeschichte" in: TRE 3 (1978) 505.

24:3 ROBBINS, V. K. "Prefaces in Greco-Roman Biography and Luke-Acts" in: P. J.Achtemeier (ed.) SBL Seminar Papers 1978/II (Missoula 1978) 201.

24:4 BETZ, H. D. Lukian von Samosata und das Neue Testament (1961) 118, 298.

24:5.14 FLEW, R. N. Jesus and His Church (1956) 101n, 113n.

24:5 RUDOLPH, K. Die Mandäer I (1960) 115, 116. HAHN, F. Christologische Hoheitstitel (1963) 237. GAERTNER, B. The Temple and the Community in Qumran and the New Testament (1965) 133. EPP, E. J. The Theological Tendency of Codex Bezae Cantabrigiensis in Acts (1966) 166f. KLIJN, A. F. J./REININK, G. J. Patristic Evidence for Jewish-Christian Sects (1973) 44. SHERWIN-WHITE, A. N., Roman Society and Roman Law in the New Testament (Grand Rapids 1978) 51. KRAFT, H., Die Entstehung des Christentums (Darmstadt 1981) 80.

24:8 ROBBINS, V. K., "Prefaces in Greco-Roman Biography and Luke-Acts" in: P. J. Achtemeier (ed.) SBL Seminar Papers 1978/II (Missoula 1978) 201.

24:10-21 BETHGE, F. Die paulinischen Reden der Apostelgeschichte (1887) 226-44. DIBELIUS, M. Die Reden der Apostelgeschichte und die antike Geschichtsschreibung (1949) 39-40. DIBELIUS, M. Aufsätze zur Apostelgeschichte (1951) 146-48. ET: Studies in the Acts of the Apostles (1956) 170-72. EVANS, C. F. " 'Speeches' in Acts," in: Mélanges Bibliques en hommage au R. P. Béda Rigaux (1970) A. Descamps/A. deHalleux eds., 292-93. STOLLE, V. Der Zeuge als Angeklagter (1973) 58f., 115-24. SELBY, D. J., Introduction to the New Testament (New York 1971) 287-88. "Apostelgeschichte" in: TRE 3 (1978) 505. ROBBINS, V. K., "Prefaces in Greco-Roman Biography and Luke-Acts" in: P. J. Achtemeier (ed.) SBL Seminar Papers 1978/II (Missoula 1978) 201-02.

24:11-18 CLARK, K. W., "The Israel of God" in: The Gentile Bias and other Essays (Leiden 1980) 27.

24:12 BOUSSET, W. Die Religion des Judentums im Späthellenistischen Zeitalter (1966 = 1926) 173.

24:14-15 PORUBCAN, S. "The Pauline Message and the Prophets," Studiorum Paulinorum Congressus Internationalis Catholicus I (1963) 254.

24:14.22 NICKELS, P. Targum and New Testament (1967) 67.

24:14 BERGER, K. Die Gesetzesauslegung Jesu (1940) 209-27. FLEW, R. N. Jesus and His Church (1956) 101n, 113n. STACEY, W. D. The Pauline View of Man (1956) 14-16. MINEAR, P. S. Images of the Church in the New Testament (1960) 148f. LONGE-NECKER, R. N. Paul Apostle of Liberty (1964) 262f. WILCOX, M. The Semitisms of Acts (1965) 105-06. BOUSSET, W. Die Religion des Judentums im Späthellenistischen Zeitalter (1966 = 1926) 144. BRAUN, H. Qumran und das Neue Testament II (1966) 148, 299. DUPONT, D. J., The Salvation of the Gentiles (New York 1979) 82.

24:15-26:9 WILCOX, M. The Semitisms of Acts (1965) 59ff.

24:15-16 NÖTSCHER, F., Altorientalischer und alttestamentlicher Auferstehungsglaube (Darmstadt 1970 = 1926) 298, 306, 309.

24:15 NICKELS, P. Targum and New Testament (1967) 67. CAVALLIN, H. C. C., Life After Death I (Lund 1974) 2, 2n10, 3n14. MATTILL, A. J., Luke and the Last Things (Dillsboro 1979) 47-48.

24:16 DALTON, W. J., Christ's Proclamation to the Spirits (Rome 1965) 233.

24:17ff. "Armut" in: TRE 4 (1979) 80.

24:17 DIBELIUS, M. Aufsätze zur Apostelgeschichte (1951) 151f. ET: Studies in the Acts of the Apostles (1956) 176f.

24:20-21 STOLLE, V. Der Zeuge als Angeklagter (1973) 263.

24:22 FLEW, R. N. Jesus and His Church (1956) 113n. WILCOX, M., The Semitisms of Acts (1965) 105-06. STOLLE, V. Der Zeuge als Angeklagter (1973) 46-48, 123f.

24:23 STOLLE, V. Der Zeuge als Angeklagter (1973) 48-50.

24:24-27 CLARK, A. C. The Acts of the Apostles (1933) 380f. STOLLE, V. Der Zeuge als Angeklagter (1973) 45-49, 264.

24:24-25 TRITES, A. A., "The Importance of Legal Scenes and Language in the Book of Acts" NovT 16 (1974) 278-84. VELTMAN, F., "The Defense Speeches of Paul in Acts" in: C. H. Talbert (ed.) Perspectives on Luke-Acts (Danville 1978) 243-56.

24:24 BEYER, H. W. Die Apostelgeschichte (1947) 142f. DELLING, G. Die Zueignung des Heils in der Taufe (1961) 88. EPP, E. J. The Theological Tendency of Codex Bezae Cantabrigiensis in Acts (1966) 89 n.3, 152f. LEE, G. M. "Two linguistic parallels from Babrius," NovTest 9 (1, 1967) 41-42. BEYSCHLAG, K., Simon Magus und die christliche Gnosis (Tübingen 1974) 8n.4.

24:25-26 CONZELMANN, H. und LINDEMANN, A., Arbeitsbuch zum Neuen Testament (Tübingen 1975) 146.

24:25 DELLING, G. Die Taufe im Neuen Testament (1963) 64. O'-NEILL, J. C. The Theology of Acts in its historical setting (1970) 78, 157-58. METZGER, B. M., The Early Versions of the New Testament (Oxford 1977) 366. MATTILL, A. J., Luke and the Last Things (Dillsboro 1979) 48-49.

24:26 BEYSCHLAG, K., Simon Magus und die christliche Gnosis (Tübingen 1974) 188.

24:27 HAHN, F. Das Verständnis der Mission im Neuen Testament (²1965) 79.

25-26 O'TOOLE, R. F., "Luke's Notion of 'Be Imitators of Me as I Am of Christ' in Acts 25-26" BThB (1978) 155-61.

25 GOULDER, M. D. Type and History in Acts (1964) 31f., 40.

25:1-22 KAYE, B., "The New Testament and Social Order" in: B. Kaye/ G. Wenham (eds.) Law, Morality and the Bible (Downers Grove, Ill. 1978) 102-03.

25:1-12 BETHGE, F. Die paulinischen Reden der Apostelgeschichte (1887) 245-53.

25:1 JEWETT, R., A Chronology of Paul's Life (Philadelphia 1979) 40-44.

25:3 KNOX, W. L. The Sources of the Synoptic Gospels II (1957) 59.

25:6-12 TRITES, A. A., "The Importance of Legal Scenes and Language in the Book of the Acts" NovT 16 (1974) 278-84. VELTMAN, F., "The Defense Speeches of Paul in Acts" in: C. H. Talbert (ed.) Perspectives on Luke-Acts (Danville 1978) 243-56.

25:8 MUNCK, J. Paul and the Salvation of Mankind (1959) 316f. O'-NEILL, J. C. The Theology of Acts in its historical setting (1970) 75-76, 81, 116.

25:9-11 STOLLE, V. Der Zeuge als Angeklagter (1973) 264.

25:9 SCHALIT, A. "Zu AG 25,9," ASThI 6 (1968) 106-13.

25:10-11 SCHRAGE, W. Die konkreten Einzelgebote in der paulinischen Paränese (1961) 267. ROBBINS, V. K., "Prefaces in Greco-Roman Biography and Luke-Acts" in: P. J. Achtemeier (ed.) SBL Seminar Papers 1978/II (Missoula 1978) 202.

25:11 DUPONT, J. Etudes sur les Actes des Apôtres (1967) 96, 529-31, 534, 540.

25:12 CONZELMANN, H. Die Apostelgeschichte (1963) 135. COLIN, J. "Une affaire de tapage nocturne devant l'empereur Auguste," Revue belge de philologie et d'histoire 44 (1, 1966) 21-24. SHER-WIN-WHITE, A. N., Roman Society and Roman Law in the New Testament (Grand Rapids 1978) 64.

25:13 - 26:32 RADL, W., Paulus und Jesus im lukanischen Doppelwerk (Bern/ Frankfurt 1975) 196-202, 209-10. "Apostelgeschichte" in: TRE 3 (1978) 512.

25:13 BEYER, H. W. Die Apostelgeschichte (1947) 145f. CONZEL-MANN, H. Die Apostelgeschichte (1963) 135. STOLLE, V. Der Zeuge als Angeklagter (1973) 264.

25:14 - 26:32 MATTILL, A. J.,"The Value of Acts as a Source for the Study of Paul" in: C. H. Talbert (ed.) Perspectives on Luke-Acts (Danville 1978) 92.

25:14-21 EHRHARDT, A. The Acts of the Apostles (1969) 119f.

25:16 DUPONT, J. "Aequitas romana. Notes sur Actes, 25,16," RechSR 49 (3, 1961) 354-85. DUPONT, J. Etudes sur les Actes des Apôtres (1967) 527-52.

25:18-19 SHERWIN-WHITE, A. N., Roman Society and Roman Law in the New Testament (Grand Rapids 1978) 50.

25:18 DELEBECQUE, E., "L'hellenisme de la 'relative complexe' dans le Nouveau Testament et principalement chez saint Luc" Biblica 62 (1981) 235.

25:19 KNOX, W. L. The Sources of the Synoptic Gospels II (1957) 155. "Apostelgeschichte" in: TRE 3 (1978) 510.

25:21 SHERWIN-WHITE, A. N., Roman Society and Roman Law in the New Testament (Grand Rapids 1978) 65.

25:23-26:32 PLUEMACHER, E. Lukas als hellenistischer Schriftsteller (1972) 82-85, 103. VELTMAN, F., "The Defense Speeches of Paul in Acts" in: P. J. Achtemeier (ed.) SBL Seminar Papers 1977 (Missoula 1977) 335.

25:23 EHRHARDT, A. The Acts of the Apostles (1969) 120f.

25:24-27 STOLLE, V. Der Zeuge als Angeklagter (1973) 56f. ROBBINS, V. K., "Prefaces in Greco-Roman Biography and Luke-Acts" in: P. J. Achtemeier (ed.) SBL Seminar Papers 1978/II (Missoula 1978) 202.

25:24-25 CLARK, A. C. The Acts of the Apostles (1933) 231, 285, 381f.

25:26-27 GLÖCKNER, R., Die Verkündigung des Heils beim Evangelisten Lukas (Mainz 1975) 7-8.

25:26 HAHN, F. Christologische Hoheitstitel (1963) 70. FURNISH, V. P. NTS 10 (1963-1964) 84f.

_____

26-28 DAUVILLIER, J. "A propos de la venue de saint Paul à Rome. Notes sur son procès et son voyage maritime," BLE 61 (1, 1960) 3-26. WILSON, S. G. The Gentiles and the Gentile Mission in Luke-Acts (1973) 225-27.

26 BETHGE, F. Die paulinischen Reden der Apostelgeschichte (1887) 254-304. MUNCK, J. Paul and the Salvation of Mankind (1959) 14f., 17, 19, 23f. GOULDER, M. D. Type and History in Acts (1964) 31f., 40, 94n. BLANK, J. Paulus und Jesus (1968) 242-48. KUEMMEL, W. G. Römer 7 und das Bild des Menschen im Neuen Testament (1974) 149f., 151, 155. TRITES, A. A., "The Importance of Legal Scenes and Language in the Book of the Acts" NovT 16 (1974) 278-84. VELTMAN, F., "The Defense Speeches of Paul in Acts" in: C. H. Talbert (ed.) Perspectives on Luke-Acts (Danville 1978) 243-56.

26:1-23 EVANS, C. F. " 'Speeches' in Acts," in: Mélanges Bibliques en hommage au R. P. Béda Rigaux (1970) A. Descamps/A. de Halleux eds., 292-93. GRASS, H. Ostergeschehen und Osterberichte (1970) 211ff. PANNENBERG, W. in: New Testament Issues (1970) R. Batey ed., 110-11.

26:1-18 SABUGAL, S., "La conversion de S. Pablo en Damasco: cuidad de Siria o region e Qumran?" Augustinianum 15 (1975) 213-24.

26:1 EPP, E. J. The Theological Tendency of Codex Bezae Cantabrigiensis in Acts (1966) 117f., 153.

26:2-29 "Apostelgeschichte" in: TRE 3 (1978) 517.

26:2-23, 25-27 DIBELIUS, M. Aufsätze zur Apostelgeschichte (1951) 148f. ET: Studies in the Acts of the Apostles (1956) 172f.

26:2-23 DUPONT, J. "Le Salut des Gentils et la Signification Theologique du Livre des Actes," NTS 6 (1959-1960) 150f. HAHN, F. Das Verständnis der Mission im Neuen Testament (²1965) 82. STOLLE, V. Der Zeuge als Angeklagter (1973) 59, 124-36. DUPONT, D. J., The Salvation of the Gentiles (New York 1979) 28-29.

26:4ff. KLEIN, G. Die Zwölf Apostel (1961) 122ff.

26:4-5 BURCHARD, C. Der dreizehnte Zeuge (1970) 36.

26:5-8 MUNCK, J. Paul and the Salvation of Mankind (1959) 14f.

26:5 NELLESSEN, E., Zeugnis für Jesus und das Wort (Köln 1976) 50-51, 52-54.

26:6 DELLING, G, Die Zueignung des Heils in der Taufe (1961) 91. "Apostel" in: TRE 3 (1978) 442.

26:7 VOLZ, P. Die Eschatologie der jüdischen Gemeinde (1934) 347. DELEBECQUE, E., "L'hellenisme de la 'relative complexe' dans le Nouveau Testament et principalement chez saint Luc" Biblica 62 (1981) 236.

26:9ff. SCHMITHALS, W., "Zur Herkunft der gnostischen Elemente in der Sprache des Paulus" in: B. Aland et al. (eds.) Gnosis. FS. H. Jonas (Göttingen 1978) 397.

26:9-18 LOHFINK, G. Paulus vor Damaskus (1966). LOHFINK, G., The Conversion of St. Paul: Narrative and History in Acts (Chicago 1976).

26:9-11 BURCHARD, C. Der dreizehnte Zeuge (1970) 46f.

26:9 RUDOLPH, K. Die Mandäer I (1960) 115. DELLING, G. Die Zueignung des Heils in der Taufe (1961) 88.

26:10-27:27 WILCOX, M. The Semitisms of Acts (1965) 59ff.

26:10-12 STOLLE, V. Der Zeuge als Angeklagter (1973) 168-70.

26:10-11 BEYSCHLAG, K. Clemens Romanus und der Frühkatholizismus (1966) 223.

26:10 ZMIJEWSKI, J. Die Eschatologiereden des Lukas-Evangeliums (1972) 131, 132, 155, 161.

26:11 KNOX, W. L. The Sources of the Synoptic Gospels II (1957) 13. WILSON, S. G. The Gentiles and the Gentile Mission in Luke-Acts (1973) 157-58.

26:12ff. KLEIN, G. Die Zwölf Apostel (1961) 155ff.

26:12-23 LEON-DUFOUR, X., The Resurrection and the Message of Easter (London 1974) 62-79.

26:12-20 HUBBARD, B. J., "Commissioning Stories in Luke-Acts: A Study of their Antecedents, Form and Content" in: Semeia 8 (1977) 103-26. HUBBARD, B. J., "The Role of Commissioning Accounts in Acts" in: C. H. Talbert (ed.) Perspectives on Luke-Acts (Danville 1978) 190, 193, 198.

26:12-18 BEYER, H. W. Die Apostelgeschichte (1947) 149-51. SEIDEN-STICKER, P. Die Auferstehung Jesu in der Botschaft der Evangelisten (1968) 36f. RICHTER, H.-F. Auferstehung und Wirklichkeit (1969) 89f. BURCHARD, C. Der dreizehnte Zeuge (1970) 109-18, 124f., 128f. DUNN, J. D. G. Baptism in the Holy Spirit (1970) 73ff. WILSON, S. G. The Gentiles and the Gentile Mission in Luke-Acts (1973) 161-67, 243. MATTILL, A. J., "The Value of Acts as a Source for the Study of Paul" in: C. H. Talbert (ed.) Perspectives on Luke-Acts (Danville 1978) 91. HEDRICK, C., "Paul's Conversion/Call: A Comparative Analysis of the Three Reports in Acts" JBL 100 (1981) 415-32.

26:12-13 DELEBECQUE, E., "L'hellenisme de la 'relative complexe' dans le Nouveau Testament et principalement chez saint Luc" Biblica 62 (1981) 232-33.

26:12 MUNCK, J. Paul and the Salvation of Mankind (1959) 13f.

26:13-18 KRATZ, R., Auferweckung als Befreiung (Stuttgart 1973) 17, 20-21.

26:13-14 STOLLE, V. Der Zeuge als Angeklagter (1973) 172-74, 178f. MATTILL, A. J., "The Value of Acts as a Source for the Study of Paul" in: C. H. Talbert (ed.) Perspectives on Luke-Acts (Danville 1978) 91. MICHEL, O., "Das Licht des Messias" in: E. Bammel et al. (eds.) Donum Gentilicium. FS. D. Daube (Oxford 1978) 40-50.

26:14-20 HAHN, F. Das Verständnis der Mission im Neuen Testament (²1965) 118.

26:14-18 WILCOX, M. The Semitisms of Acts (1965) 73-74. STOLLE, V. Der Zeuge als Angeklagter (1973) 176f., 184f.

26:14-15 SCHWEIZER, E. Erniedrigung und Erhöhung bei Jesus und seinen Nachfolgern (1962) § 14e.

26:14 DIBELIUS, M. Die Reden der Apostelgeschichte und die antike Geschichtsschreibung (1949) 56-59. DIBELIUS, M. Aufsätze zur Apostelgeschichte (1951) 153f., 160-62. ET: Studies in the Acts of the Apostles (1956) 179f., 188-91. MUNCK, J. Paul and the Salvation of Mankind (1959) 20f. BRAUN, H. Qumran und das Neue Testament II (1966) 162, 213. KUEMMEL, W. G. Römer 7 und das Bild des Menschen im Neuen Testament (1974) 151, 154f., 156. "Apostelgeschichte" in: TRE 3 (1978) 517. HEDRICK, C., "Paul's Conversion/Call: A Comparative Analysis of the Three Reports in Acts" JBL 100 (1981) 426-27, 430-43.

26:15 DELLING, G. Die Zueignung des Heils in der Taufe (1961) 86.

26:16ff. GLÖCKNER, R., Die Verkündigung des Heils beim Evangelisten Lukas (Mainz 1975) 48ff.

26:16-18 FLEW, R. N. Jesus and His Church (1956) 146n. HOOKER, M. D. Jesus and the Servant (1959) 114-16. STOLLE, V. Der Zeuge als Angeklagter (1973) 142-44. MÄRZ, C.-P., Das Wort Gottes bei Lukas (Leipzig 1973) 55-57.

26:16 PALLIS, A., Notes on St. Luke and the Acts (London 1928) 81. STONEHOUSE, N. B. The Witness of Matthew and Mark to Christ (1944) 114. MUNCK, J. Paul and the Salvation of Mankind (1959) 27f. HAHN, F. Christologische Hoheitstitel (1963) 185. RO-

LOFF, J. Apostolat-Verkündigung-Kirche (1965) 202-05. WILSON, S. G. The Gentiles and the Gentile Mission in Luke-Acts (1973) 167-68. WILCKENS, U. Die Missionsreden der Apostelgeschichte (³1974) 144, 146-48.

26:17-18 DUPONT, J. Etudes sur les Actes des Apôtres (1967) 415, 456, 461. MINEAR, P., To Heal and to Reveal (New York 1976) 143ff. DUPONT, D. J., The Salvation of the Gentiles (New York 1979) 63.

26:18 DELLING, G. Die Taufe im Neuen Testament (1963) 64, 105. KAESEMANN, E. Exegetische Versuche und Besinnungen (1964) I 45. WILCOX, M. The Semitism of Acts (1965) 32, 35-37, 56n, 158n, 159, 164. BRAUN, H. Qumran und das Neue Testament II (1966) 160. SEEBERG, A. Der Katechismus der Urchristenheit (1966) 215, 216, 228, 229. DEICHGRÄBER, R. "Weitere Texte mit ähnlicher Terminologie," in: Gotteshymnus und Christushymnus in der frühen Christenheit (1967) 82-87. DUPONT, J. Etudes sur les Actes des Apôtres (1967) 251, 264, 281, 414, 418, 423, 425, 431, 441, 466. CAVALLIN, H. C. C., Life After Death I (Lund 1974) 7, 2n16. FISCHER, U., Eschatologie und Jenseitserwartung im hellenistischen Diasporajudentum (Berlin 1978) 113. DUPONT, D. J., The Salvation of the Gentiles (New York 1979) 71, 146.

26:19-20 CLARK, A. C. The Acts of the Apostles (1933) 382f.

26:20 GAERTNER, B. The Areopagus Speech and Natural Revelation (1955) 31f. HAHN, F. Christologische Hoheitstitel (1963) 184. DUPONT, J. Etudes sur les Actes des Apôtres (1967) 238, 423, 424, 426, 430, 438, 456, 457, 462, 473. BURCHARD, C. Der dreizehnte Zeuge (1970) 117, 148, 163f., 166, 177. WILCKENS, U. Die Missionsreden der Apostelgeschichte (³1974) 89, 180, 181, 241. DUPONT, D. J., The Salvation of the Gentiles (New York 1979) 65, 80.

26:22f.27 PORCUBAN, S. "The Pauline Message and the Prophets," Studiorum Paulinorum Congressus Internationalis Catholicus I (1963) 255f.

26:22-23 SCHELKLE, K. H. Die Passion Jesu in der Verkündigung des Neuen Testaments (1949) 97f. MUNCK, J. Paul and the Salvation of Mankind (1959) 316f. HAHN, F. Christologische Hoheitstitel (1963) 215f. KRAENKL, E. Jesus der Knecht Gottes (1972) 57f., 78f., 175, 209. DUPONT, J. "La portée christologique de L'evangélisation des nations d'après Luc 24,47," in: Neues Testament und Kirche (1974) J. Gnilka ed., 126, 128, 138, 141, 142. DÖMER, M., Das Heil Gottes (Köln/Bonn 1978) 204-06. PRAST, F., Presbyter und Evangelium in nachapostolischer Zeit (Stuttgart 1979) 284-85, 251.

26:22 STOLLE, V. Der Zeuge als Angeklagter (1973) 143-45. WANKE, J., Die Emmauserzählung (Leipzig 1973) 11. NELLESSEN, E., Zeugnis für Jesus und das Wort (Köln 1976) 235-36.

26:23 GAERTNER, B. The Aeropagus Speech and Natural Revelation (1955) 30f. DELLING, G. Die Zueignung des Heils in der Taufe (1961) 88. HAHN, F. Christologische Hoheitstitel (1963) 88. DUPONT, J. Etudes sur les Actes des Apôtres (1967) 149, 261, 265, 281, 402, 414, 454. NOACK, B. "Si passibilis Christus," SEA 37-38 (1972-1973) 211-21. SMALLEY, S. S. "The Christology of Acts Again," in: Christ and the Spirit in the New Testament (1973) B. Lindars/S. S. Smalley eds., 85f., 89. WANKE, J., Die Emmauserzählung (Leipzig 1973) 92. WILCKENS, U. Die Missionsreden der Apostelgeschichte (³1974) 116, 117, 118, 138, 140, 158, 175, 238. PRAST, F., Presbyter und Evangelium in nachapostolischer Zeit (Stuttgart 1979) 274, 327-28.

26:24 "Apostelgeschichte" in: TRE 3 (1978) 517.

26:25 "Apostelgeschichte" in: TRE 3 (1978) 517.

26:26 "Apostelgeschichte" in: TRE 3 (1978) 517. PRAST, F., Presbyter und Evangelium in nachapostolischer Zeit (Stuttgart 1979) 337.

26:28-29 HARLÉ, P., "Un 'private-joke' de Paul dans le livre des Actes (xxvi.28-29)" NTS 24 (1978) 527-33.

26:28 FRIDRICHSEN, A. "Acts 26,28," in: Coniectanea Neotestamentica (1938) A. Fridrichsen ed., 13. CLARK, K. W., "The Making of the Twentieth Century New Testament" in: The Gentile Bias and Other Essays (Leiden 1980) 153.

26:31 "Apostelgeschichte" in: TRE 3 (1978) 512.

26:32 SHERWIN-WHITE, A. N., Roman Society and Roman Law in the New Testament (Grand Rapids 1978) 65.

27-28 SHEPARD, J. W., The Life and Letters of St. Paul (Grand Rapids 1950) 476-88. DUPONT, J. The Sources of Acts (1963) 126, 127, 130, 146, 157. ACWORTH, A. "Where was St. Paul Shipwrecked? A Re-examination of the Evidence," JThS 24 (1, 1973) 190-93. POKORNY, P. "Die Romfahrt des Paulus und der antike Roman," ZNW 64 (3-4, 1973) 233-44. STOLLE, V. Der Zeuge als Angeklagter (1973) 28f., 66f. MEINARDUS, O. F. A. "Melita Illyrica or Africana: An Examination of the Site of St. Paul's

Shipwreck," OKS 23 (1, 1974) 21-36. HEMER, C. J., "Euraquilo und Melita" JThS 26 (1975) 100-11. RADL, W., Paulus und Jesus im lukanischen Doppelwerk (Bern/Frankfurt 1975) 237-51. MEINARDUS, O. F. A., "St. Paul Shipwrecked in Dalmatia" BA 39 (1976) 145-47. MILES, G. B. and TROMPF, G., "Luke and Antiphon: The Theology of Acts 27-28 in the Light of Pagan Beliefs about Divine Retribution, Pollution, and Shipwreck" HThR 69 (1976) 259-67. LADOUCEUR, D., "Hellenistic Preconceptions of Shipwreck and Pollution as a Context for Acts 27-28" HThR 73 (1980) 435-49.

27 ROBERTSON, A. T. Luke the Historian in the Light of Research (1920) 58, 206ff. BETZ, H. D. Lukian von Samosata und das Neue Testament (1961) 172, 174. CONZELMANN, H. Die Apostelgeschichte (1963) 146f. DUPONT, J. The Sources of Acts (1964) 88, 96, 135, 142, 147. HAENCHEN, E. "Acts 27," in: Zeit und Geschichte (1964) E. Dinkler ed., 235-54. "Apostelgeschichte" in: TRE 3 (1978) 500. HAUSER, J., Strukturen der Abschlusserzählung der Apostelgeschichte (Apg. 28:16-31) (Rome 1979) 216-17. GEIGER, G., Kirche unterwegs (Klosterneuburg 1981).

27:1-28:18 ORR, R. W. "Paul's Voyage and Shipwreck," EQ 35 (2, 1963) 103-04.

27:1-28:16 STONEHOUSE, N. B. The Witness of Luke to Christ (1951) 15ff. "Apostelgeschichte" in: TRE 3 (1978) 514. ROBBINS, V. K., "By Land and By Sea: The We-Passages and Ancient Sea Voyages" in: C. H. Talbert (ed.) Perspectives on Luke-Acts (Danville 1978) 215-42. PRAST, F., Presbyter und Evangelium in nachapostolischer Zeit (Stuttgart 1979) 330.

27:1-28:13 LEONARD, W. "From Caesarea to Malta: St. Paul's Voyage and Shipwreck," ACR 37 (4, 1960) 274-84.

27:1-10 ROUGE, J. "Actes 27,1-10," VigChr 14 (4, 1960) 193-203.

27:1-2 "Apostelgeschichte" in: TRE 3 (1978) 494.

27:1 "Apostelgeschichte" in: TRE 3 (1978) 494.

27:2 METZGER, B. M., The Early Versions of the New Testament (Oxford 1977) 367.

27:3.5f. HENNECKE, E./SCHNEEMELCHER, W. Neutestamentliche Apokryphen (1964) II 230f.

27:4-13 KRAFT, R. A., "A Sahidic Parchment Fragment of Acts 27:4-13 at University Museum, Philadelphia (E 16690 Coptic l)" JBL 94 (1974) 256-65.

27:7-12 SCHWANK, B. " 'Wir umsegelten Kreta bei Salome.' Reisebericht zu Apg 27, 7-12," EuA 48 (1, 1972) 16-25, plates 1-7.

27:7 METZGER, B. M., The Early Versions of the New Testament

(Oxford 1977) 370. QUINN, J. D., "The Last Volume of Luke: The Relations of Luke-Acts to the Pastoral Epistles" in: C. H. Talbert (ed.) Perspectives on Luke-Acts (Danville 1978) 65.

27:8 NICKELS, P. Targum and New Testament (1967) 67. METZGER, B. M., The Early Versions of the New Testament (Oxford 1977) 171.

27:9-11 "Apostelgeschichte" in: TRE 3 (1979) 500.

27:9 JEWETT, R., A Chronology of Paul's Life (Philadelphia 1979) 50-52.

27:12 OGILVIE, R. M. "Phoenix," JThS 9 (2, 1958) 308-14. METZGER, B. M., The Early Versions of the New Testament (Oxford 1977) 370. QUINN, J. D., "The Last Volume of Luke: The Relation of Luke-Acts to the Pastoral Epistles" in: C. H. Talbert (ed.) Perspectives on Luke-Acts (Danville 1978) 65.

27:13 QUINN, J. D., "The Last Volume of Luke: The Relation of Luke-Acts to the Pastoral Epistles" in: C. H. Talbert (ed.) Perspectives on Luke-Acts (Danville 1978) 65.

27:17 DELEBECQUE, E., "L'hellenisme de la 'relative complexe' dans le Nouveau Testament et principalement chez saint Luc" Biblica 62 (1981) 236.

27:18-19 CLARK, D. J., "What Went Overboard First?" BTr 26 (1975) 144-46.

27:21-26 BETHGE, F. Die paulinischen Reden der Apostelgeschichte (1887) 305-36. HUBBARD, B. J., "Commissioning Stories in Luke-Acts: A Study of their Antecedents, Form and Content" in: Semeia 8 (1977) 103-26. "Apostelgeschichte" in: TRE 3 (1979) 500. HUBBARD, B. J., "The Role of Commissioning Accounts in Acts" in: C. H. Talbert (ed.) Perspectives on Luke-Acts (Danville 1978) 190, 193, 198.

27:21 PALLIS, A., Notes on St. Luke and the Acts (London 1928) 82. GAERTNER, B. The Areopagus Speech and Natural Revelation (1955) 55f. QUINN, J. D., "The Last Volume of Luke: The Relation of Luke-Acts to the Pastoral Epistles" in: C. H. Talbert (ed.) Perspectives on Luke-Acts (Danville 1978) 65.

27:22 METZGER, B. M., The Early Versions of the New Testament (Oxford 1977) 370.

27:23 RUCKSTUHL, E. Die literarische Einheit des Johannesevangeliums (1951) 194f. SOARES PRABHU, G. M., The Formula Quotations in the Infancy Narrative of Matthew (Rome 1976) 224-25.

27:24 O'NEILL, J. C. The Theology of Acts in its historical setting (1970) 68, 149-50. STOLLE, V. Der Zeuge als Angeklagter (1970) 252f. BAUMERT, N., Täglich Sterben und Auferstehen (München 1973)

246, 287. HAUSER, J., Strukturen der Abschlusserzählung der Apostelgeschichte (Apg. 28:16-31) (Rome 1979) 215-16.

27:27 PALLIS, A., Notes on St. Luke and the Acts (London 1928) 82.

27:28-28:31 WILCOX, M. The Semitisms of Acts (1965) 59ff.

27:31 "Apostelgeschichte" in: TRE 3 (1979) 500.

27:33-36 MENOUD, P. H., "Actes 27:33-36" in: Jésus-Christ et la foi (Neuchatel/Paris 1975) 73-76. "Apostelgeschichte" in: TRE 3 (1978) 500.

27:34 PETZKE, G. Die Traditionen über Apollonius von Tyana und das Neue Testament (1970) 174, 178.

27:35 WANKE, J., Die Emmauserzählung (Leipzig 1973) 98, 105-06.

27:37 METZGER, B. M., The Early Versions of the New Testament (Oxford 1977) 235. FISCHER, U., Eschatologie und Jenseitserwartung im hellenistischen Diasporajudentum (Berlin 1978) 68.

27:40 PALLIS, A., Notes on St. Luke and the Acts (London 1928) 83.

27:43 "Apostelgeschichte" in: TRE 3 (1978) 500.

27:44 DELLING, G. Die Zueignung des Heils in der Taufe (1961) 91.

---

28 GOULDER, M. D. Type and History in Acts (1964) 61,74, 80, 101, 111, 165, 203. QUINN, J. D., "The Last Volume of Luke: The Relations of Luke-Acts to the Pastoral Epistles" in: C. H. Talbert (ed.), Perspectives on Luke-Acts (Danville 1978) 72. BOVON, F., "La vie des apôtres: traditions bibliques et narrations apocryphes" in: F. Bovon et al. (eds.) Les Actes Apocryphes des Apôtres (Geneva 1981) 150.

28:1-2 WIKENHAUSER, A. Die Apostelgeschichte (1951) 227.

28:1 SAYDON, P. P. "The Site of St. Paul's Shipwreck," MTh 14 (1-2, 1962) 58-61. MEINARDUS, O. F., "St. Paul Shipwrecked in Dalmatia" BA 38 (1976) 145-47.

28:2ff.6.8 BETZ, H. D. Lukian von Samosata und das Neue Testament (1961) 37, 52, 94, 102, 116, 147, 150, 175, 178.

28:2 ARRINGTON, F. L., New Testament Exegesis: Examples (Washington 1977) 24-25.

28:3-6 DUNN, J. D. G., Jesus and the Spirit (London 1975) 163, 166-67, 246. "Apostelgeschichte" in: TRE 3 (1978) 497.

28:6 KNOX, W. L. The Sources of the Synoptic Gospels II (1957) 115.

BEYSCHLAG, K., Simon Magus und die christliche Gnosis (Tübingen 1974) 122n.49. METZGER, B. M., The Early Versions of the New Testament (Oxford 1977) 367.

28:8 ADLER, N., Taufe und Handauflegung (Münster 1951) 62-63, 68. DELLING, G. Die Taufe im Neuen Testament (1963) 66. "Apostelgeschichte" in: TRE 3 (1978) 499. DELEBECQUE, E., "L'hellenisme de la 'relative complexe' dans le Nouveau Testament et principalement chez saint Luc" Biblica 62 (1981) 236.

28:11 BETZ, H. D. Lukian von Samosata und das Neue Testament (1961) 173f.

28:12-14 GLASSON, T. F. "St Paul, Virgil and the Sybil," LondQuart HolRev 37 (1, 1968) 70-76.

28:13-14 ADINOLFI, M. "San Paolo a Pozzuoli (Atti 28,13b-14a)," RivB 8 (3, 1960) 206-24. CALVINO, R., "Cristiani a Puteoli nell'anno 61. Riflessioni sull'importanza della notizia concisa degli 'Atti' (28,13b-14a) e risposta all interrogativo sulle testimonianze monumentali coeve" RivAC 56 (1980) 323-30.

28:14 SCHWANK, B. "Und so kamen wir nach Rom (Apg 28,14). Reisenotizen zu den letzten beiden Kapiteln der Apostelgeschichte," EuA 36 (3, 1960) 169-92. MECHAM, F. A. "And So We Came to Rome," ACR 50 (2, 1973) 170-73.

28:15 DAVIES, W. D. The Gospel and the Land (1973) 281, 283, 283 n.87. DELEBECQUE, E., "L'hellenisme de la 'relative complexe' dans le Nouveau Testament et principalement chez saint Luc" Biblica 62 (1981) 234.

28:16-31 HAUSER, H. J., Strukturen der Abschlusserzählung der Apostelgeschichte (Apg. 28,16-31) (Rome 1979).

28:16-17 STRECKER, G. Der Weg der Gerechtigkeit (1962) 70_3. "Apostelgeschichte" in: TRE 3 (1978) 494.

28:16 CLARK, A. C. The Acts of the Apostles (1933) xlvi, 264, 315, 386-88. HANSON, R. P. C. NTS 12 (1965-1966) 222f. KUEMMEL, W. G. Einleitung in das Neue Testament (1973) 284f. SHERWIN-WHITE, A. N., Roman Society and Roman Law in the New Testament (Grand Rapids 1978) 108-09. HAUSER, J., Strukturen der Abschlusserzählung der Apostelgeschichte (Apg. 28:16-31) (Rome 1979) 17-18, 191-94. JEWETT, R., A Chronology of Paul's Life (Philadelphia 1979) 44.

28:17ff. GOULDER, M. D. Type and History in Acts (1964) 31, 79, 82, 101, 106. WREGE, H.-T. Die Ueberlieferungsgeschichte der Bergpredigt (1968) 178f.

28:17-31 STOLLE, V. Der Zeuge als Angeklagter (1973) 80-89. MIESNER, D. R., "The Circumferential Speeches of Luke-Acts: Patterns and Purpose'' in: P. J. Achtemeier (ed.) SBL Seminar Papers 1978/II (Missoula 1978) 229-32, 234-35.

28:17-28 BETHGE, F. Die paulinischen Reden der Apostelgeschichte (1887) 305-36. SURKAU, H. GPM 21/3 (1966-1967) 299-303. ''Apostelgeschichte'' in: TRE 3 (1978) 520.

28:17-27 PRAST, F., Presbyter und Evangelium in nachapostolischer Zeit (Stuttgart 1979) 328-39.

28:17-22 HAUSER, J., Strukturen der Abschlusserzählung der Apostelgeschichte (Apg. 28:16-31) (Rome 1979) 18, 194-98.

28:17-20 MIESNER, D. R., ''The Circumferential Speeches of Luke-Acts: Patterns and Purpose'' in: P. J. Achtemeier (ed.) SBL Seminar Papers 1978/II (Missoula 1978) 231. HAUSER, J., Strukturen der Abschlusserzählung der Apostelgeschichte (Apg. 28:16-31) (Rome 1979) 19-25, 27-29, 218-19.

28:17-19 RADL, W., Paulus und Jesus im lukanischen Doppelwerk (Bern/Frankfurt 1975) 252-58. HAUSER, J., Strukturen der Abschlusserzählung der Apostelgeschichte (Apg. 28:16-31) (Rome 1979) 21-24.

28:17 PRAST, F., Presbyter und Evangelium in nachapostolischer Zeit (Stuttgart 1979) 91.

28:18-19 SHERWIN-WHITE, A. N., Roman Society and Roman Law in the New Testament (Grand Rapids 1978) 65.

28:19 HAUSER, J., Strukturen der Abschlusserzählung der Apostelgeschichte (Apg. 28:16-31) (Rome 1979) 98-99.

28:20-31 DUPONT, D. J., The Salvation of the Gentiles (New York 1979) 14-16, 18.

28:20-21 BOUSSET, W. Die Religion des Judentums im Späthellenistischen Zeitalter (1966 = 1926) 72.

28:20 GNILKA, J. Die Verstockung Isarels (1961) 152-54. WANKE, J., Die Emmauserzählung (Leipzig 1973) 68. HAUSER, J., Strukturen der Abschlusserzählung der Apostelgeschichte (Apg. 28:16-31) (Rome 1979) 20, 24-25, 110-11, 125-26.

28:21-22 ROBBINS, V. K., ''Prefaces in Greco-Roman Biography and Luke-Acts'' in: P. J. Achtemeier (ed.) SBL Seminar Papers 1978/II (Missoula 1978) 205-06. HAUSER, J., Strukturen der Abschlusserzählung der Apostelgeschichte (Apg. 28:16-31) (Rome 1979) 25-29, 60-61, 98-99, 111-12. PRAST, F., Presbyter und Evangelium in nachapostolischer Zeit (Stuttgart 1979) 171.

28:23-31 GEIGER, G., Kirche unterwegs (Klosterneuburg 1981).

28:23-28 HAUSER, J., Strukturen der Abschlusserzählung der Apostelgeschichte (Apg. 28:16-31) (Rome 1979) 29-43. HUBBARD, B. J., ''Luke, Josephus and Rome: A Comparative Approach to the Lukan Sitz im Leben'' in: P. J. Achtemeier (ed.) SBL Seminar Papers 1979/I (Missoula; 1979) 65.

28:23-24 HAUSER, J., Strukturen der Abschlusserzählung der Apostelgeschichte (Apg. 28:16-31) (Rome 1979) 198-99.

28:23 BERGER, K. Die Gesetzesauslegung Jesu (1940) 209-27. DELLING, G. Die Zueignung des Heils in der Taufe (1961) 90. DELLING, G. Die Taufe im Neuen Testament (1963) 135. WILSON, S. G. The Gentiles and the Gentile Mission in Luke-Acts (1973) 65, 78, 89, 254. WANKE, J., Die Emmauserzählung (Leipzig 1973) 11. MERK, O., ''Das Reich Gottes in den lukanischen Schriften'' in: E. E. Ellis/E. Grässer (eds.) Jesus und Paulus. FS. W. G. Kümmel (Göttingen 1975) 204ff. NELLESSEN, E. , Zeugnis für Jesus und das Wort (Köln 1976) 242. MIESNER, D. R., ''The Circumferential Speeches of Luke-Acts: Patterns and Purpose'' in: P. J. Achtemeier (ed.) SBL Seminar Papers 1978/II (Missoula 1978) 232. HAUSER, J., Strukturen der Abschlusserzählung der Apostelgeschichte (Apg. 28:16-31) (Rome 1979) 30-31, 112-18, 126-36. PRAST, F., Presbyter und Evangelium in nachapostolischer Zeit (Stuttgart 1979) 280-81, 332-33.

28:24 THEYSSEN, G. W. ''Unbelief'' in the New Testament (Rüschlikon 1965) 58f. MIESNER, D. R., ''The Circumferential Speeches of Luke-Acts: Patterns and Purpose'' in: P. J. Achtemeier (ed.) SBL Seminar Papers 1978/II (Missoula 1978) 232. HAUSER, J., Strukturen der Abschlusserzählung der Apostelgeschichte (Apg. 28:16-31) (Rome 1979) 32, 62-66.

28:25-31 DUPONT, J. ''Le Salut des Gentils et la Signification Theologique du Livre des Actes,'' NTS 6 (1959-1960) 136f. MIESNER, D. R., ''The Circumferential Speeches of Luke-Acts: Patterns and Purpose'' in: P. J. Achtemeier (ed.) SBL Seminar Papers 1978/II (Missoula 1978) 231-32.

28:25-29 MIESNER, D. R., ''The Circumferential Speeches of Luke-Acts: Patterns and Purpose'' in: P. J. Achtemeier (ed.) SBL Seminar Papers 1978/II (Missoula 1978) 233-34.

28:25-28 HAHN, F. Das Verständnis der Mission im Neuen Testament (^{2}1965) 64, 117. O'NEILL, J. C. The Theology of Acts in its historical setting (1970) 86-87, 133. HAUSER, J., Strukturen der Abschlusserzählung der Apostelgeschichte (Apg. 28-16-31) (Rome 1979) 200-02.

28:25-27 LINDARS, B. New Testament Apologetic (1961) 160-66. BLOCH, R., ''Midrash'' in: W. S. Green (ed.) Approaches to Ancient Judaism: Theory and Practice (Missoula 1978) 49. HAUSER, J., Strukturen der Abschlusserzählung der Apostelgeschichte (Apg. 28:16-31) (Rome 1979) 99-102.

28:25 HAUSER, J., Strukturen der Abschlusserzählung der Apostelgeschichte (Apg. 28:16-31) (Rome 1979) 32-36, 66-69.

28:26-28 SOMERVILLE, E. R., "The Divine Purpose: The Jews and the
Gentile Mission (Acts 15)" in: P. J. Achtemeier (ed.) SBL Seminar Papers 1980 (Chico, Cal. 1980) 274-75.

28:26-27 MOORE, G. F. Judaism I (1946) 526n. HESSE, F. Das Verstockungsproblem im Alten Testament (1955) 4, 64, 66. HOLTZ, T.
Untersuchungen über die Alttestamentlichen Zitate bei Lukas (1968)
33-37. "Apostelgeschichte" in: TRE 3 (1978) 520. DUPONT, D.
J., The Salvation of the Gentiles (New York 1979) 141. HAUSER,
J., Strukturen der Abschlusserzählung der Apostelgeschichte (Apg.
28:16-31) (Rome 1979) 36-39. BERGMEIER, R.,Glaube als Gabe
nach Johannes (Stuttgart 1980) 266n.492.

28:26 WANKE, J., Die Emmauserzählung (Leipzig 1973) 118. HAU-
SER, J., Strukturen der Abschlusserzählung der Apostelgeschichte
(Apg. 28:16-31) (Rome 1979) 69-71.

28:27 HAUSER, J., Strukturen der Abschlusserzählung der Apostelgeschichte (Apg. 28:16-31) (Rome 1979) 71-75.

28:28-31 PRAST, F., Presbyter und Evangelium in nachapostolischer Zeit
(Stuttgart 1979) 328-34.

28:28 HAHN, F. Das Verständnis der Mission im Neuen Testament
([2]1965) 112, 119. WILCOX, M. The Semitisms of Acts (1965) 90-
91, 162, 173n. DUPONT, J. Etudes sur les Actes des Apôtres (1967)
259, 262, 281, 284, 400, 402, 403, 418, 439, 455, 500. NICK-
ELS, P. Targum and New Testament (1967) 67. HARMAN, A. M.,
Paul's Use of the Psalms (Ann Arbor, Mich. 1968) 173-74. WIL-
SON, S. G. The Gentiles and the Gentile Mission in Luke-Acts
(1973) 227-30, 232-33. "Apokalyptik" in: TRE 3 (1978) 254.
HAUSER, J., Strukturen der Abschlusserzählung der Apostelgeschichte (Apg. 28:16-31) (Rome 1979) 39-42, 75-79, 103-04, 107,
110-24. PRAST, F. Presbyter und Evangelium in nachapostolischer Zeit (Stuttgart 1979) 274.

28:29 "Apostelgeschichte" in: TRE 3 (1978) 487. MIESNER, D. R.,
"The Circumferential Speeches of Luke-Acts: Patterns and Purpose" in: P. J. Achtemeier (ed.) SBL Seminar Papers 1978/II
(Missoula 1978) 234. HAUSER, J., Strukturen der Abschlusserzählung der Apostelgeschichte (Apg. 28:16-31) (Rome 1979) 42-
43.

28:30-31 SALIN, H. Der Messias und das Gottesvolk (1945) 51-56. WI-
KENHAUSER, A. Die Apostelgeschichte (1951) 233. HEN-
NECKE, E./SCHNEEMELCHER, W. Neutestamentliche
Apokryphen (1964) II 238. GASQUE, W., A History of the Crit-
icism of the Acts of the Apostles (Tübingen 1975) 84, 127-28,

144n.34. METZGER, W., Die letzte Reise des Apostels Paulus (Stuttgart 1976) 17. "Apostelgeschichte" in: TRE 3 (1978) 484. HAUSER, J., Strukturen der Abschlusserzählung der Apostelgeschichte (Apg. 28:16-31) (Rome 1979) 43-46, 202-03. PRAST, F., Presbyter und Evangelium in nachapostolischer Zeit (Stuttgart 1979) 22,25.

28:30 EPP, E. J. The Theological Tendency of Codex Bezae Cantabrigiensis in Acts (1966) 114f. HANSACK, E., " 'Er lebte . . . von seinem eigenen Einkommen' (Apg. 28,30)" BZ 19 (1975) 249-53. SAUM, F., " 'Er lebte . . . von seinem eigenen Einkommen' (Apg 28,30)" BZ 20 (1976) 226-29. HANSACK, E., "Nochmals zu Apostelgeschichte 28,30. Erwiderung auf F. Saums kritische Anmerkungen" BZ 21 (1977) 118-21. SHERWIN-WHITE, A. N., Roman Society and Roman Law in the New Testament (Grand Rapids 1978) 108. HAUSER, J., Strukturen der Abschlusserzählung der Apostelgeschichte (Apg. 28:16-31) (Rome 1979) 136-58. JEWETT, R., A Chronology of Paul's Life (Philadelphia 1979) 45-46.

28:31 FLEW, R. N. Jesus and His Church (1956) 111. DELLING, G. Die Zueignung des Heils in der Taufe (1961) 87. CONZELMANN, H. Die Apostelgeschichte (1963) 150. HANSON, R. P. C. NTS 12 (1965-1966) 225f. DELLING, G. "Das Letzte Wort der Apostelgeschichte," NovTest 15 (3, 1973) 193-204. MERK, O., "Das Reich Gottes in den lukanischen Schriften" in: E. E. Ellis/E. Grässer (eds.) Jesus und Paulus. FS. W. G. Kümmel (Göttingen 1974) 204ff. "Apokalyptik" in: TRE 3 (1978) 254. HAUSER, J., Strukturen der Abschlusserzählung der Apostelgeschichte (Apg. 28:16-31) (Rome 1979) 112-18. PRAST, F., Presbyter und Evangelium in nachapostolischer Zeit (Stuttgart 1979) 280-81, 312, 337, 340.